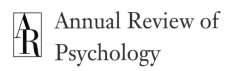

Annual Review of
Psychology

Production Editor: Lisa Dean
Bibliographic Quality Control: Mary A. Glass
Electronic Content Coordinator: Suzanne Moses

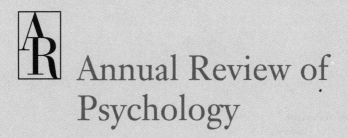

Annual Review of Psychology

Volume 63, 2012

Susan T. Fiske, *Editor*

Princeton University

Daniel L. Schacter, *Associate Editor*

Harvard University

Shelley E. Taylor, *Associate Editor*

University of California, Los Angeles

www.annualreviews.org • science@annualreviews.org • 650-493-4400

Annual Reviews

4139 El Camino Way • P.O. Box 10139 • Palo Alto, California 94303-0139

Annual Reviews
Palo Alto, California, USA

International Standard Serial Number: 0066-4308
International Standard Book Number: 978-0-8243-0263-4
Library of Congress Catalog Card Number: 50-13143

TYPESET BY APTARA
PRINTED AND BOUND BY MALLOY INCORPORATED, ANN ARBOR, MICHIGAN

Preface

Okay, I admit it: I use Google Scholar as much as anyone, alongside the Annual Reviews Web page and the psychology-specific search engine provided by the American Psychological Association. Each has its strong suits. Yet I come not to praise search engines but rather to bear a note of caution. Inevitably and understandably, students often present outlines or drafts of literature reviews that lack the Big Picture, but now for a specific, fixable reason: They started with the search engine. If they start with most search engines, using their best guess regarding key words, students often go astray. A random walk, even organized by highly cited articles using uncertain keywords, does not make a good argument.

Of course, the student is ultimately responsible for Making an Argument for something, and no search engine can provide that. A mentor's job is teaching people to discover, develop, and defend their arguments. But first they have to obtain the evidence in a systematic, principled way.

Without an orienting guide to the literature, the students—or any of us researching a new topic—literally don't know where to begin. Annual Reviews editorial committees can help: We select expert authors to tell us where to look among the scores of relevant articles. Automated search engines, although they are our friends, cannot be our guides. Annual Reviews authors, vetted as expert, reliable, skilled communicators, provide leadership through the thickets of the sprawling literature. They take an informed perspective on the literature, selecting relevant papers, providing structure, interpreting patterns, and defending conclusions. Readers may agree or disagree, but at least the material on offer is not arbitrary or ordered by only one metric, such as citations.

Aided by the Annual Reviews authors and our Web site, a seeker can find live links within each article to the rest of the literature. These articles first appear within a context for understanding their relevance. Given some review papers' contexts, the reader can then engage a search engine on a more focused quest for additional leads. And the search will be more successful, thanks to our distinguished editorial committee and our expert authors.

Susan T. Fiske, Princeton, New Jersey

Daniel L. Schacter, Cambridge, Massachusetts

Shelley E. Taylor, Los Angeles, California

**Annual Review of
Psychology**

Volume 63, 2012

Contents

Neuroscience Methods

Indexes

Errata

An online log of corrections to *Annual Review of Psychology* articles may be found at
http://psych.AnnualReviews.org/errata.shtml

Related Articles

From the *Annual Review of Clinical Psychology*, Volume 8 (2012)

Alan Baddeley

Working Memory: Theories, Models, and Controversies

Alan Baddeley

Department of Psychology, University of York, York YO10 5DD, United Kingdom;
email: ab50@york.ac.uk

Annu. Rev. Psychol. 2012. 63:1–29

First published online as a Review in Advance on
September 27, 2011

The *Annual Review of Psychology* is online at
psych.annualreviews.org

This article's doi:
10.1146/annurev-psych-120710-100422

Keywords

attention, central executive, phonological loop, episodic buffer,
visuo-spatial sketchpad, short-term memory

Abstract

I present an account of the origins and development of the multicomponent approach to working memory, making a distinction between the overall theoretical framework, which has remained relatively stable, and the attempts to build more specific models within this framework. I follow this with a brief discussion of alternative models and their relationship to the framework. I conclude with speculations on further developments and a comment on the value of attempting to apply models and theories beyond the laboratory studies on which they are typically based.

Contents

WORKING MEMORY: THEORIES, MODELS, AND CONTROVERSIES

I was honored, pleased, and challenged by the invitation to write this prefatory chapter, pleased because it offered the chance to take a broad and somewhat autobiographical view of my principal area of interest, working memory (WM), but challenged by the potential magnitude of the task. The topic of working memory has increased dramatically in citation counts since the early years, not all of course related to or supportive of my own work, but a recent attempt to review it (Baddeley 2007) ended with more than 50 pages of references. What follows is a partial, as opposed to impartial, account of the origins of the concept of multicomponent working memory (M-WM) and of my own views on its subsequent development. My first draft would have filled the chapter page allowance with references; I apologize to

WM: working memory

M-WM: multicomponent working memory

all of those whose work should have been cited and is not.

I entered psychology as a student at University College London in 1953, a very exciting time for the field of psychology, which had benefited greatly from developments during the Second World War, where theory was enriched by the need to tackle practical problems. As a result, prewar issues such as the conflict between Gestalt psychology and neobehaviorism began to be challenged by new data and new ideas, some based on cybernetics, the study of control systems, with others influenced by the newly developed digital computers. This in turn led to a renewed interest in the philosophy of science as applied to psychology. Typical questions included, is psychology a science?; if so, is it cumulative or are we doomed to keep on asking the same questions, as appeared to be the case in philosophy? What would a good psychological theory look like?

As students we were offered two answers to this question. The first, championed by Cambridge philosopher Richard Braithwaite (1953), regarded Newton's Principia as the model to which scientific theories should aspire, involving as it does postulates, laws, equations, and predictions. Within psychology, the Newtonian model was explicitly copied by Clark Hull in his attempt to produce a general theory of learning, principally based on the study of maze learning in the albino rat.

An alternative model of theorizing came from Oxford, where Stephen Toulmin (1953) argued that theories were like maps, ways of organizing our existing knowledge of the world, providing tools both for interacting with the world and for further exploration. Edward Tolman in Stanford had a view of learning in rats that fitted this model, using it to challenge Hull's neo-behaviorist approach. This raised the crucial question as to how you might decide between the two apparently opposing views. The dominant answer to that question, in the United Kingdom at least, was provided by Karl Popper (1959), a Viennese-trained philosopher who argued strongly that a valid theory should make clear, testable predictions, allowing the rival theories to confront each other in the all-important "crucial experiment" that settles the issue. This approach was closer in spirit to Hull than to Tolman.

My own first published study (Baddeley 1960) attempted just such a crucial experiment, predicting that rats would be smarter than they should be according to Hullian theory, and demonstrating, to my own satisfaction at least, that this was the case. Alas, by the time it was published, the whole field of learning theory seemed to have collapsed. Neither side was able to deliver a knockout blow, and people simply abandoned the research area. I resolved at that point that if I myself were to develop a theory, it would be based very closely on the evidence, which would survive even if the theory proved totally wrong. It is an approach I have followed ever since.

But what is the answer to our original question, should theorists be architects, building elegant structures such as Newton did, or should they be explorers, gradually extending the theory on the basis of more and more evidence, as in the case of Darwin? Clearly both Newton and Darwin got it right, but for fields at a different stage of development. Newton claimed that his success resulted from "standing on the shoulders of giants," who no doubt stood on the shoulders of lesser mortals like ourselves. Darwin had few such giants available. I suggest that any complete theory is likely to require explorers in its initial stages and architects to turn the broad concepts into detailed models. I myself am very much at the explorer end of the continuum, but I fully accept the importance of the skills of the architect if theory is to develop.

My research career really began with my arrival at the Medical Research Council Applied Psychology Unit (APU) in Cambridge. Its role was to form a bridge between psychological theory and practical problems, and the year I arrived, Donald Broadbent, its director, had just published his seminal book, *Perception and Communication*, which provided one of the sparks that ignited what subsequently became known as the cognitive revolution. I was assigned to work on optimizing the design of postal codes,

STM: short-term
memory

LTM: long-term
memory

which led me to combine the classic tradition of nonsense syllable learning with new ideas from information theory, resulting in my generating memorable postal codes for each town in the United Kingdom. The Post Office thanked me and went on their way regardless; the code they adopted could, however, have been much worse, as is indeed the case in some countries, but that is another story.

By this time my approach to theory was evolving away from Popper's idea of the need for crucial experiments, largely on the grounds that clear predictions only appeared to be possible in situations that were far narrower than the ones I found interesting. I subsequently discovered that within the philosophy of science, Lakatos (1976), and allegedly Popper himself, had subsequently abandoned the reliance on falsification, arguing instead that the mark of a good theory is that it should be productive, not only giving an account of existing knowledge, but also generating fruitful questions that will increase our knowledge. This more map-like view of theory is the one that I continue to take.

Short-Term Memory

The term "working memory" evolved from the earlier concept of short-term memory (STM), and the two are still on occasion used interchangeably. I will use STM to refer to the simple temporary storage of information, in contrast to WM, which implies a combination of storage and manipulation.

My interest in STM began during my time at the APU in Cambridge and was prompted by an applied problem, that of finding a way of evaluating the quality of telephone lines that might be more effective than a simple listening test. My PhD supervisor Conrad had recently discovered the acoustic similarity effect. He was studying memory for proposed telephone dialing codes when he noted that even with visual presentation, memory errors resembled acoustic mis-hearing errors (e.g., *v* for *b*), and that memory for similar sequences (*b g t p c*) was poorer than for dissimilar (*k r l q y*), concluding that STM depends on an acoustic code (Conrad & Hull 1964).

I decided to see if the acoustic similarity effect could be used to provide sensitive indirect measure of telephone line quality. It did not; the effects of noise and similarity were simply additive, but I was intrigued by the sheer magnitude of the similarity effect. Similarity was a central variable within the dominant stimulus-response interference theory of verbal learning (see Osgood 1949), but the type of similarity seemed not to be regarded as important. So, would Conrad's effect generalize to other types of similarity in STM?

I tested this, comparing recall of sequences with five phonologically similar words (*man, mat, can, map, cat*), five dissimilar words (e.g., *pit, day, cow, pen, sup*), and five semantically similar sequences (*huge, big, wide, large, tall*) with five dissimilar (*wet, soft, old, late, good*). I found (Baddeley 1966a) a huge effect of phonological similarity[1] (80% sequences correct for dissimilar, 10% for similar) and a small but significant effect for semantic similarity (71% versus 65%). I went on to demonstrate that this pattern reversed when long-term memory (LTM) was required by using ten-word lists and several learning trials; semantic similarity then proved critical (Baddeley 1966b). I concluded that there were two storage systems, a short-term phonological and a long-term semantically based system. My telephony project was passed on to a newly arrived colleague and I was left free to explore this line of basic research.

I saw my work as fitting into a pattern of evidence for separate STM and LTM stores. Other evidence came from amnesic patients who had preserved STM and impaired LTM, while other patients showed the reverse pattern (Shallice & Warrington 1970). A third source of evidence came from two-component memory tasks, which comprised a durable LTM component together with a temporary component. A typical example of this was the recency effect

---

[1] I subsequently abandoned the term "acoustic similarity" because it suggested an input modality-based system, which is not the case; I mistakenly assumed that phonological was a more neutral term. It was not intended as a statement of the linguistic basis of the memory system, which remains an open question.

in free recall (Glanzer 1972); the last few words of a list are well recalled on immediate test but not after a brief filled delay, unlike earlier items.

At this point, my simple assumption of two stores, with STM phonologically based and LTM semantically based, led to some clear predictions. Amnesic patients should have semantic coding problems, and recency should be acoustically based. Studies based on amnesic patients suffering from Korsakoff's syndrome did suggest a semantic encoding deficit (Cermak et al. 1974), but our own work showed no evidence of such a deficit (Baddeley & Warrington 1970), and later work (Cermak & Reale 1978) attributed their previously observed deficit to additional executive problems, often found in Korsakoff's syndrome.

In the case of two-component tasks, it became clear that recency did not depend on verbal STM (Baddeley & Hitch 1977) and that the use of semantic or phonological coding was strategy dependent. Phonological coding of verbal material is rapid, attentionally undemanding, and very effective for storing serial order. Semantic coding can be rapid for meaningful sequences such as sentences, but it is much harder to use for storing the order of unrelated words (Baddeley & Levy 1971). We also showed that word sequences can simultaneously be encoded both phonologically and semantically (Baddeley & Ecob 1970) and that standard tasks such as immediate serial recall can reflect both long-term and short-term components, each of which may be influenced by either phonological or semantic factors. In short, STM, retention of material over a brief period, may be based on either phonological or semantic coding. The former is easy to set up but readily forgotten; the latter may take longer to set up but tends to be more durable. Both can operate over brief delays, and the fact that we can learn new words indicates that long-term phonological learning also occurs.

It is worth emphasizing the need to distinguish between STM as a label for a paradigm in which small amounts of information are stored over brief delays and STM as a theoretical storage system. This point was made by Waugh & Norman (1965) and by Atkinson & Shiffrin (1968), but it has often been neglected in subsequent years. Material tested after a brief delay (i.e., an STM task) is likely to reflect both LTM and some form of temporary storage.

Evolution of a Multicomponent Theory

After nine years at the APU, I moved to Sussex into a new department of experimental psychology, where, in 1972, I was joined by Graham Hitch as a post-doctoral fellow on my first research grant. After a first degree in physics, he had done a psychology MSc in Sussex and a PhD with Broadbent at the APU. We had proposed (perhaps unwisely) to investigate the link between STM and LTM, beginning our grant just when the previously popular field of STM was downsizing itself following criticism of the dominant Atkinson & Shiffrin (1968) model for three reasons. First, the model assumed that merely holding information in STM would guarantee transfer to LTM, whereas Craik & Lockhart (1972) showed that the nature of processing is crucial, with deeper, more elaborate processing leading to better learning. Second, its assumption that the short-term store was essential for access to LTM proved to be inconsistent with neuropsychological evidence. Patients with a digit span of only two items and an absence of recency in free recall should, according to Atkinson and Shiffrin, have a defective short-term store that should lead to impaired LTM. This was not the case. Third, given that Atkinson and Shiffrin assumed their short-term store to be a working memory, playing an important general role in cognition, such patients should have major intellectual deficits. They did not. One patient, for instance, was an efficient secretary, and another ran a shop and a family. Interest in the field began to move from STM to LTM, to semantic memory and levels of processing.

Graham Hitch and I did not have access to these rare but theoretically important STM-deficit patients and instead decided that we would try to manufacture our own "patients" using student volunteers. We did so, not by removing the relevant part of their brain, but by functionally disabling it by requiring participants to do a concurrent task that was likely to occupy the limited-capacity short-term storage system to varying degrees. The concurrent task we chose was serial verbal recall of sequences of spoken digits. As sequence length increased, the digits should occupy more and more of available capacity, with the result that performance on any task relying on WM should be progressively impaired. In one study, participants performed a visually presented grammatical reasoning task while hearing and attempting to recall digit sequences of varying length. Response time increased linearly with concurrent digit load. However, the disruption was far from catastrophic: around 50% for the heaviest load, and perhaps more strikingly, the error rate remained constant at around 5%. Our results therefore suggested a clear involvement of whatever system underpins digit span, but not a crucial one. Performance slows systematically but does not break down. We found broadly similar results in studies investigating both verbal LTM and language comprehension, and on the basis of these, abandoned the assumption that WM comprised a single unitary store, proposing instead the three-component system shown in **Figure 1** (Baddeley & Hitch 1974).

We aimed to keep our proposed system as simple as possible, but at the same time, potentially capable of being applied across a wide range of cognitive activities. We decided to split attentional control from temporary storage, which earlier research suggested might rely on separate verbal and visuo-spatial short-term systems, all of which were limited in capacity. We labeled the central controller as a "central executive" (CE), initially referring to the verbal system as the "articulatory loop," after the subvocal rehearsal assumed to be necessary to maintain information, and later adopting the term "phonological loop" to emphasize storage rather than rehearsal. We termed the third component the "visuo-spatial sketchpad," leaving open the issue of whether it was basically visual, spatial, or both.

We began by focusing on the phonological loop on the grounds that it seemed the most tractable system to investigate, given the very extensive earlier research on verbal STM. At this point, I unexpectedly received an invitation from Gordon Bower to contribute a chapter to an influential annual publication presenting recent advances in the area of learning and memory. We hesitated; our model was far from complete, should we perhaps wait? We went ahead anyhow (Baddeley & Hitch 1974), presenting a model that is still not complete nearly 40 years and many publications later.

Over the next decade we continued to explore the model and its potential for application beyond the cognitive laboratory. At this point I agreed to summarize our progress in a monograph (Baddeley 1986). This was approaching completion when I realized that I had said nothing about the CE, very much a case of Hamlet without the prince. My reluctance to tackle the executive stemmed from two sources: first, its probable complexity, and second, because of the crucial importance of its attentional capacity. Although there were a number of highly developed and sophisticated theories of attention, most were concerned with the role of attention in perception, whereas the principal role of the CE was the attentional control of action. The one directly relevant article I could find (Norman & Shallice 1986) appeared as a chapter because of the difficulty of persuading a journal to accept it (Shallice 2010, personal communication), alas, all too common with papers presenting new ideas.

Norman and Shallice proposed that action is controlled in two rather separate ways. One is

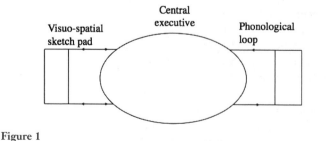

Figure 1

The original Baddeley & Hitch (1974) working memory model.

based on well-learned habits or schemata, demanding little in the way of attentional control. An example of this might be the activity of driving a well-learned route to your office. This source of control can be overridden by a second process, the supervisory attentional system (SAS), which responds to situations that are not capable of being handled by habit-based processes, for example, coping with the closure of a road on your normal route.

With some relief, I incorporated the Norman and Shallice model into my own concept of a CE, producing a book (Baddeley 1986) that attempted to pull together developments in WM that had occurred in the previous decade and then apply them to data from the literature in three areas: fluent reading, the development of WM in children, and the effects of aging. Although I tended to refer to our proposals as a model, using the criteria proposed earlier, it might better be regarded as a simple theory, in the sense of Toulmin's idea of theories as maps, linking together existing knowledge and encouraging further investigation. If so, it was a map with many blank areas that I hoped would be filled by myself and others, leading in due course to more detailed modeling.

What then are the essentials of the broad theory? The basis is the assumption that it is useful to postulate a hypothetical limited-capacity system that provides the temporary storage and manipulation of information that is necessary for performing a wide range of cognitive activities. A second assumption is that this system is not unitary but can be split into an executive component and at least two temporary storage systems, one concerning speech and sound while the other is visuo-spatial. These three components could be regarded as modules in the sense that they comprise processes and storage systems that are tightly interlinked within the module and more loosely linked across modules, with somewhat more remote connections to other systems such as perception and LTM. I regard the very rigid definition of modularity by Fodor (1983) as unhelpful and neuropsychologically implausible. A consequence of my rejection of Fodorian simplicity

is the assumption that each of these systems can be fractionated into subsystems and that these will be linked to perceptual and LTM processes in ways that require further investigation.

My overall view of WM therefore comprised, and still comprises, a relatively loose theoretical framework rather than a precise model that allows specific predictions. The success of such a framework should be based, as suggested by Lakatos (1976), not only on its capacity to explain existing data but also on its productivity in generating good, tractable questions linked to empirical methods that can be widely applied. The proposed components of WM are discussed in turn, beginning with the phonological loop.

CHARACTERISTICS OF THE PHONOLOGICAL LOOP

We saw the phonological loop as a relatively modular system comprising a brief store together with a means of maintaining information by vocal or subvocal rehearsal. In the 1960s, a number of studies attempted to decide whether forgetting in the STM system was based on trace decay or interference (see Baddeley 1976). None of these studies proved to be conclusive, a state of affairs that remains true, in my own opinion. We opted to assume a process of trace decay, partly on the basis of our results and partly because it avoided the need to become involved in the many controversies surrounding traditional approaches to interference theory at the time (see Baddeley 1976, chapter 5), although we did assume a limited-capacity store, which in turn implies some unspecified form of interference, either by displacement or by overwriting. We used existing results, together with our own subsequent studies, to create a simple model that is based on the method of converging operations. This involves combining evidence from a range of different phenomena, each consistent with the model, but each individually explicable in other ways. If none of the competing interpretations are able to explain the whole pattern, whereas the phonological loop model can, then this provides valuable support. This approach has the advantage of potentially producing a robust model, but it has the disadvantage of being required to confront a range of different possible alternative explanations for each individual phenomenon.

The Phonological Similarity Effect

As described above, this is regarded as an indication that phonological storage is involved. Its effect is principally on the storage of order information. Indeed, item information may be helped by similarity since it places constraints on possible responses. For this reason, studies that specifically attempt to investigate the loop tend to minimize the need to retain item information by repeatedly using the same limited set, for example, consonants. Studies using open sets, for instance, different words for each sequence, are more likely to reflect loss of item information and to show semantic and other LTM-based effects.

The Word Length Effect

We assumed that vocal or subvocal rehearsal was likely to occur in real time, with longer words taking longer and hence allowing more time for trace decay, thus leading to poorer performance. We studied the immediate recall of sequences of five words ranging in length from one syllable (e.g., *pen day hot cow tub*) to five syllables (e.g., *university, tuberculosis, opportunity, hippopotamus, refrigerator*) and found that performance declined systematically with word length. As expected, when participants were required to read out words of different lengths as rapidly as possible, there was a close correspondence between word length and articulation time. The simple way of expressing our results was to note that people are able to remember as many words as they can articulate in two seconds (Baddeley et al. 1975b).

We interpreted our data by assuming that longer words take longer to rehearse, resulting in more trace decay and poorer recall. Such decay is also likely to continue during the slower spoken recall of longer words. We presented evidence for time-based decay, which has

since faced challenge and counter-challenge (see Baddeley 2007, pp. 43–49). Fortunately, however, the general hypothesis of a phonological loop will function equally well with either a decay or interference interpretation of short-term forgetting, illustrating the value of combining a broad theoretical map while leaving more detailed modeling to be decided by further experimentation.

Articulatory Suppression

If the word length effect is dependent on subvocalization, then preventing it should eliminate the effect. This is indeed the case (Baddeley et al. 1975b). When participants are required to continuously utter a single word such as "the," performance drops and is equivalent for long and short words. Suppression also removes the phonological similarity effect for visually presented materials but not when presentation is auditory (Baddeley et al. 1984). We interpret this as suggesting that spoken material gains obligatory access to the phonological store, whereas written material needs to be subvocalized if it is to register.

The claim that auditory presentation allows a phonological trace to be laid down despite suppression has recently been challenged. Jones et al. (2006) have suggested that the effect is limited to the recency component of immediate serial recall, suggesting that it is better regarded as a perceptual effect. However, although this may be true for long lists, shorter lists show an effect that operates throughout the serial position curve (Baddeley & Larsen 2007).

Irrelevant Sound Effects

Colle & Welsh (1976) required their participants to recall sequences of visually presented digits presented either in silence or accompanied by white noise or by speech in an unfamiliar language that they were told to ignore. Only the spoken material disrupted performance on the visually presented digits, an effect that was independent of the loudness of the irrelevant sound sources. Pierre Salame, a French visitor to Cambridge, and I followed up and extended

Colle's work, demonstrating that visual STM was disrupted to the same extent by irrelevant words and nonsense syllables; indeed, irrelevant digits had no more effect on digit recall than did nondigit words containing the same phonemes (e.g., *one two* replaced by *tun woo*), suggesting that interference was operating at a prelexical level. We did, however, find slightly less disruption of our monosyllabic digits from bisyllabic words than from monosyllabic words, concluding rather too hastily that this suggested that interference was dependent on phonological similarity (Salame & Baddeley 1986). Like Colle and Welsh, we suggested an interpretation in terms of some form of mnemonic masking. This proved to be something of an embarrassment when it was clearly demonstrated that irrelevant items that were phonemically similar to the remembered sequence were no more disruptive than dissimilar items (Jones & Macken 1995, Larsen et al. 2000). Unfortunately, our initial hypothesis came to be regarded as central to WM, despite our subsequent withdrawal, a salutary lesson in premature theorizing.

Meanwhile Dylan Jones and colleagues in Wales were developing a very extended program of research on irrelevant sound. They showed that STM was disrupted not only by irrelevant speech, but also by a range of other sounds, including, for example, fluctuating tones (Jones & Macken 1993). In order to account for their results they proposed the "changing state" hypothesis, whereby the crucial feature was that the irrelevant sound needed to fluctuate. Jones (1993) coupled this with the object-orientated episodic record (OOE-R) hypothesis, which assumes that both digits and irrelevant sounds are represented as potentially competing paths on a multidimensional surface. The OOE-R hypothesis is not spelled out in detail but would appear to assume that serial order is based on chaining, whereby each item acts as a stimulus for the response that follows, which in turn acts as a further stimulus.

Retaining Serial Order

A typical memory span is around six or seven digits, not because the digits themselves are forgotten, but rather because their order is lost. Retaining serial order is a crucial demand for a wide range of activities, notably including language, in which sequences of sounds within words and words within sentences must be maintained, and skilled motor performance such as striking a ball with a bat or playing the piano. However, as Lashley (1951) points out, it is far from easy to explain how this is achieved. The most obvious hypothesis is through the previously described mechanism of chaining through sequential associations. However, this has some major potential problems; if one item is lost, then the chain is broken and subsequent recall should fail, and yet it is often the case that despite errors in the middle of a sequence, the latter part is reproduced correctly. Similarly, if an item is repeated within the chain (e.g., *7 5 3 5 9 6*), then the chain should be disrupted, but this disruption, when it occurs, is typically far from dramatic.

A third phenomenon appears to be even more problematic. This again is an effect that was discovered when trying to solve a practical problem, that of trying to reduce the negative impact of phonological similarity on the recall of postal codes. It seemed plausible to me to assume that the principal effect of similarity would come from having two or more similar items bunched together, in which case it might prove possible to greatly minimize the effect by alternating similar and dissimilar items (e.g., *dfvkpl*). The results were disappointing; the similar items appeared to be just as liable to be forgotten when sandwiched between dissimilar items as when they were adjacent, so we put the experiment to one side. It was only later, when I was attempting to pin down the nature of the phonological loop effect, that I realized that our result had clear implications for theories of serial order retrieval in general (Baddeley 1968) and were in particular inconsistent with hypotheses that depended upon chaining. The argument goes as follows: If one considers a sequence of six letters as a series of pairs, then we know that the principal source of interference comes from similarity at the stimulus level, which then gives rise to errors on the subsequent response (Osgood 1949). We would therefore expect errors to follow the similar items, whereas in fact the similar items themselves were the main source of error (Baddeley 1968). This result has continued to present a challenge to models of serial order.

The past decade has seen considerable activity in the attempt to produce clearly specified computational or mathematical models of serial order retention, with a number located within the phonological loop tradition. Very briefly, approaches fall into two categories. One class of models assumes that items are associated with a series of internal markers, which may be temporal oscillators as in Brown et al.'s (2000) OSCAR hypothesis, or other forms of ordinal marking, as in the case of the model and its subsequent refinement by Burgess & Hitch (1999, 2006). A second approach is typified by the primacy hypothesis of Page & Norris (1998), which assumes a limited capacity of excitation that is shared among the sequence of items. The first item is the most strongly activated, the second slightly less, and so forth. At recall, the strongest item is retrieved first and then inhibited to avoid further repetition before going on to the next strongest. Both of these approaches can handle the similarity sandwich effect, as they do not depend upon chaining. Furthermore, they require two stages, a store and a serial order link, offering an interpretation of the irrelevant sound effect in terms of adding noise to this additional stage (Page & Norris 2003), an explanation as to why similarity between irrelevant and remembered items is not important.

Modeling serial order continues to be a very lively field with considerable interaction between proponents of the different models, which are now starting to become more ambitious. Burgess and Hitch are now attempting to model the link between the phonological loop and long-term phonological learning (Burgess & Hitch 2006, Hitch et al. 2009), while a further challenge being addressed lies in the interpretation of chunking, the effect that makes sentences so much more readily recalled than scrambled words (Baddeley et al. 2009). Can models of serial order in verbal STM be generalized to visual STM? The answer seems to be that they can (Hurlstone 2010). If so, do they reflect a single common system? I myself think it more likely that evolution has applied the same solution to a problem, maintaining serial order, that crops up in a range of different domains.

The Phonological Loop and LTM

What function might the phonological loop (PL) serve, other than making telephoning easier (an unlikely target for Mother Nature)? The opportunity to investigate this question cropped up when an Italian colleague, Giuseppe Vallar, invited me to help him to investigate a patient, PV, with a very pure and specific deficit in phonological STM. Her intellect was preserved, but her auditory digit span was only two items. She had fluent language production and comprehension, except for long, highly artificial sentences in which ambiguity could only be resolved by retaining the initial part of a long sentence until the end, again not a great evolutionary gain. We then came up with the idea that her phonological loop might be necessary for new long-term phonological learning. We tested this by requiring her to learn Russian vocabulary (e.g., *flower-svieti*), comparing this with her capacity for learning to pair unrelated Italian words, for example (*castle-table*). When compared to a group of matched controls, her capacity to learn native language pairs was normal, whereas she failed to learn a single Russian word after ten successive trials, a point at which all the normal participants had perfect performance (Baddeley et al. 1988). We had found a function for the phonological loop.

Although the work with PV had a major influence on my theoretical views, of much greater practical importance was my collaboration with Susan Gathercole, in which we explored the role of the phonological loop in vocabulary learning, both in children with specific language impairment and in normal children. A series of studies showed that WM plays a significant role in the initial stages of vocabulary acquisition and is also linked to reading skills (see

Baddeley et al. 1998 for a review). It formed the basis of an extensive and successful application of the M-WM theory to the identification and treatment of WM deficits in school-age children (Gathercole & Alloway 2008; Gathercole et al. 2004a,b).

At a theoretical level, work with PV led to a major development. I had previously tended to treat WM and LTM as separate though interrelated systems. The fact that the loop specifically facilitates new phonological learning implies a direct link from the loop to LTM. Gathercole (1995) showed that existing language habits influence immediate nonword recall, making the nonwords that have a similar letter structure to English, such as *contramponist*, easier than less familiar sounding nonwords such as *loddenapish* (Gathercole 1995). This suggests that information flows from LTM to the loop, as well as the reverse. Furthermore, it seemed reasonable to assume that a similar state of affairs would occur for the visuo-spatial sketchpad, leading to a revision of the original model along the lines indicated in **Figure 2**. Here, a crucial distinction is made between WM, represented by a series of fluid systems that require only temporary activation, and LTM, representing more permanent crystallized skills and knowledge.

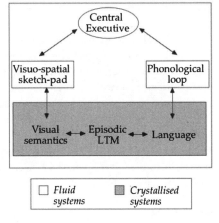

Figure 2

A modification of the original model to take account of the evidence of links between working memory and long-term memory (LTM).

The Phonological Loop: Master or Slave?

In formulating our model, we referred to the loop and sketchpad as slave systems, borrowing the term from control engineering. It is, however, becoming increasingly clear that the loop can also provide a means of action control. In my own case, this first became obvious during a series of studies of the CE, in this case concentrating on its capacity for task switching. We used a very simple task in which participants were given a column of single digits and required in one condition to add 1 and write down a total, and in another condition, to subtract 1, or in the switching condition, to alternate addition and subtraction. Switching leads to a substantial slowing, and we wanted to know why. We used dual task methods, disrupting the CE with an attentionally demanding verbal task and a task involving simple verbal repetition. To our surprise, switching was disrupted almost as much by articulatory suppression as by the much more demanding executive task. It became clear that people were using a simple subvocal code of "plus-minus-plus," etc., to cue their responses. When the relevant plus and minus signs were provided on the response sheet, the suppression effect disappeared (Baddeley et al. 2001). Similar results have been obtained and further developed by Emerson & Miyake (2003).

The importance of self-instruction had of course already been beautifully demonstrated by the great Russian psychologist Alexander Luria, who showed that children gradually learn to control their actions using overt self-instruction, a process that later becomes subvocal. He went on to demonstrate the value of self-instructions in neuropsychological rehabilitation (Luria 1959).

The Phonological Loop: Critique

The loop is probably the best-developed and most widely investigated component of WM, possibly because of the availability of a few simple tools such as the phonological similarity, word length, and suppression effects. It is, however, only one very limited component of WM. When its use in digit span is prevented by combining visual presentation with articulatory suppression, the cost is something in the region of two digits (Larsen & Baddeley 2003). Its strength is that it can provide temporary sequential storage, using a process that is rapid, and requires minimal attention. It is a system that is extremely useful, widespread, and one that, as experimenters, we ignore at our peril. The analogy that comes to mind is that of the role of the thumb in our motor behavior: small, not essential, but very useful. There is, however, a danger of exaggerating its importance. It appears to be this that Nairne criticized under the label "the standard hypothesis" (Nairne 2002), by which he appears to refer to attempts to account for a range of time-specified STM effects purely in terms of the loop. This hypothesis seemed to be attributed to myself, although as discussed elsewhere (Baddeley 2007, pp. 35–38), Nairne's criticisms do not apply to WM more generally. I agree that what Nairne describes as the standard hypothesis is far from adequate as a theory of WM or even as a general account of STM.

I have discussed the phonological loop thus far as if it were limited to the storage of heard and spoken speech. It is important to note, however, that the same system, operating under broadly similar constraints, appears to underpin memory for both lip-read and signed material (see Rönnberg et al. 2004 for a review). All of these are language related, which raises the question of whether the same system is used for nonlinguistic auditory information such as environmental sounds and music. Neither of these topics is well explored, although there is growing interest in comparing language and music and some indication of overlap (Williamson et al. 2010).

VISUO-SPATIAL SKETCHPAD

Interest in visuo-spatial memory developed during the 1960s, when Posner & Konick (1966) showed that memory for a point on a line was well retained over a period ranging up to 30 seconds, but it was disrupted by an interpo-

lated information-processing task, suggesting some form of active rehearsal. Dale (1973) obtained a similar result for remembering a point located in an open field. In contrast to these spatial memory tasks, Posner & Keele (1967) produced evidence suggesting a visual store lasting for only two seconds. However, their method was based on speed of processing letters, in which a visual letter code appeared to be superseded by a phonological code after two seconds. Although this could reflect the duration of the visual trace, it could equally well reflect a more slowly developing phonological code that then overrides the visual.

Visual STM

A colleague, Bill Phillips, and I decided to test this using material that would not be readily nameable. We chose 5 × 5 matrices in which approximately half the cells would be filled at random on any given trial. We tested retention over intervals ranging from 0.3 to 9 seconds, by presenting either an identical stimulus or one in which a single cell was changed, with participants making a same/different judgment. We found a steady decline over time, regardless of whether we measured performance in terms of accuracy or reaction time (Phillips & Baddeley 1971). A range of studies by Kroll et al. (1970), using articulatory suppression to disrupt the use of a name code in letter judgments, came to a similar conclusion, that the Posner and Keele result was based on switching from a visual to a phonological code, perhaps because of easier maintenance by subvocal rehearsal. Meanwhile, Phillips went on to investigate the visual memory store using matrix stimuli, demonstrating that accuracy declines systematically with number of cells to be remembered (Phillips 1974), suggesting limited visual STM capacity. It was this work that influenced our initial concept of the visuo-spatial sketchpad.

Spatial STM

The most frequently used clinical test of visuo-spatial memory is the Corsi block-tapping test (Milner 1971), which is spatially based and involves sequential presentation and recall.

The participant views an array of nine blocks scattered across a test board. The tester taps a sequence of blocks, and the participant attempts to imitate this. The number of blocks tapped is increased until performance breaks down, with Corsi span typically being around five, about two less than digit span. Della Sala et al. (1999), using a modified version of the Phillips matrix task, showed that visual pattern span is dissociable from spatial Corsi span, with some patients being impaired on one while the other is preserved, and vice versa. Furthermore, pattern span can be disrupted by concurrent visual processing, whereas Corsi span is more susceptible to spatial disruption (Della Sala et al. 1999). I return to the visual-spatial distinction at a later point.

Visuo-Spatial WM

During the 1970s, research moved from visual STM to its role in visual imagery. Our own studies used a technique developed by Brooks (1968), in which participants are required to remember and repeat back a sequence of spoken sentences. In half of the cases the sentences can be encoded as a path through a visually presented matrix. The other half of the instructions were not readily encodable spatially. We found that recall of the visuo-spatially codable sentences was differentially disrupted by pursuit tracking (Baddeley et al. 1975a). We interpreted this result in terms of the sketchpad, leading to the question of whether the underlying store was visual or spatial. This we tested using a task in which blindfolded participants tracked a sound source (spatial but not visual) or detected the brightening of their visual field (visual but not spatial), again while performing the Brooks task. We found that the tracking still disrupted the spatial but did not interfere with the verbal task, whereas the brightness judgment showed a slight tendency in the opposite direction, leading us to conclude that the system was spatial rather than visual (Baddeley & Lieberman 1980).

Although these results convinced me that the system was essentially spatial, Robert Logie, who was working with me at the time,

disagreed and set out to show that I was wrong. He succeeded, demonstrating that some imagery tasks were visual rather than spatial. He used a visual imagery mnemonic whereby two unrelated items are associated by forming an image of them interacting; for example, *cow* and *chair* could be remembered as a cow sitting on a chair. Logie (1986) showed that this process can be disrupted by visual stimuli such as irrelevant line drawings or indeed by simple patches of color. There are now multiple demonstrations of the dissociation of visual and spatial WM. Klauer & Zhao (2004) critically review this literature before performing a very thorough series of investigations controlling for potential artifacts; their results support the distinction between visual and spatial STM, a distinction that is also supported by neuroimaging evidence (Smith & Jonides 1997).

Yet further fractionation of the sketchpad seems likely. Research by Smyth and colleagues has suggested a kinesthetic or movement-based system used in gesture and dance (Smyth & Pendleton 1990). Another possible channel of information into the sketchpad comes from haptic coding as used in grasping and holding objects, which in turn is likely to involve a tactile component. Touch itself depends on a number of different receptor cells capable of detecting pressure, vibration, heat, cold, and pain. We currently know very little about these aspects of STM, and my assumption that information from all of these sources converges on the sketchpad is far from clearly established.

The nature of rehearsal in the sketchpad is also uncertain. Logie (1995, 2011) suggests a distinction between a "visual cache," a temporary visual store, and a spatial manipulation and rehearsal system, the "inner scribe," although the precise nature of visuo-spatial rehearsal remains unclear.

THE CENTRAL EXECUTIVE

The Executive as Homunculus

The CE is the most complex component of WM. Within the original model it was assumed to be capable of attentional focus, storage, and decision making, virtually a homunculus, a little man in the head, capable of doing all the clever things that were outside the competence of the two subsystems. Although our model tended to be criticized for taking this approach, like Attneave (1960) I regard homunculi as potentially useful if used appropriately. It is important that they are not seen as providing an explanation, but rather as a marker of issues requiring explanation. Provided the various jobs performed by the homunculus are identified, they can be tackled one at a time, hopefully in due course allowing the homunculus to be pensioned off.

Much of our work has used concurrent tasks to disrupt the various components of WM, with the assumption typically being that attentionally demanding tasks will place specific demands on the CE, in contrast to tasks that require simple maintenance. For example, counting backward in threes from a number such as 271 is assumed to load the executive, whereas simply repeating 271 would not. This and related tasks have proved to be a successful strategy for separating out contributions of the three initially proposed WM subcomponents (e.g., Baddeley et al. 2011).

Fractionating the Executive

In an attempt to specify the functions of the CE, I speculated as to what these might be; what would any adequate executive need to be able to do? I came up with four suggestions (Baddeley 1996). First it would need to be able to focus attention; evidence of this came from the impact of reducing attention on complex tasks such as chess (Robbins et al. 1996). A second desirable characteristic would be the capacity to divide attention between two important targets or stimulus streams. I had been studying this in collaboration with Italian colleagues for a number of years, focusing on Alzheimer's disease. We selected two tasks involving separate modalities: one verbal, involving recall of digit sequences, and the other requiring visuospatial tracking. We titrated the level of difficulty for each of these to a point at which our patients were performing at the same level as both

young and elderly controls. We then required tracking and digit recall to operate simultaneously. There was a marked deficit in the performance of the patients when compared to either of the two control groups. Perhaps surprisingly, age did not disrupt this specific executive capacity, provided the level of difficulty is equated in the first place (Logie et al. 2004). In the absence of titration of level of difficulty, however, performance tends to decline with age on the tasks when performed singly, with the deficit even greater when the two tasks are performed at the same time (Riby et al. 2004).

The third executive capacity we investigated involved switching between tasks, for which we felt there might be a specific control system. As mentioned earlier, we chose to study a task involving alternating between simple addition and subtraction, using a demanding concurrent verbal executive task and articulatory suppression as its nondemanding equivalent. We found a large effect of articulatory suppression coupled with a rather small additional effect when an executive load accompanied suppression. The study of task switching has expanded very substantially in recent years (Monsell 2005), becoming theoretically rather complex, and in my view at least, arguing against a unitary executive capacity for task switching. I should point out that there are many other suggestions as to the basic set of executive capacities that are too numerous to discuss in this context (see, for example, Engle & Kane 2004, Miyake et al. 2000, Shallice 2002).

Interfacing with LTM

The fourth executive task that I assigned to our homunculus was the capacity to interface with LTM. In an attempt to constrain our WM model, we had made the assumption that the CE was a purely attentional system with no storage capacity (Baddeley & Logie 1999). However, this created a number of problems. One concerned the question of how subsystems using different codes could be integrated without some form of common storage. Participants do not simply use either one code or another, but rather combine them, with both visual and phonological codes being usable simultaneously (Logie et al. 2000). This capacity is particularly marked in the case of language processing, where a single phrase can show the influence of phonological coding at short delays and semantic coding at longer intervals (Baddeley & Ecob 1970). Memory span for unrelated words is around 5, increasing to 15 when the words make up a sentence. This enhanced span for sentence-based sequences seems to reflect an interaction between phonological and semantic systems rather than a simple additive effect (Baddeley et al. 1987), a conclusion that is consistent with later dual-task studies (Baddeley et al. 2009). But how might this interaction occur?

A further challenge to the concept of a purely attentional executive came from the very extensive work on individual differences in WM stemming from the initial demonstration by Daneman & Carpenter (1980) of a correlation between a measure they termed "WM span" and capacity for prose comprehension. Their measure required participants to read out a sequence of sentences and then recall the final word of each. This and similar tests that require the combination of temporary storage and processing have proved enormously successful in predicting performance on cognitive tasks ranging from comprehension to complex reasoning and from learning a programming language to resisting distraction (see Daneman & Merikle 1996 and Engle et al. 1999 for reviews). Such results were gratifying in demonstrating the practical significance of WM, but embarrassing for a model that had no potential for storage other than the limited capacities of the visuo-spatial and phonological subsystems. In response to these and related issues, I decided to add a fourth component, the episodic buffer (Baddeley 2000). Although I was reluctant to add further systems to the multicomponent theory, I felt that one in 25 years was perhaps acceptable.

THE EPISODIC BUFFER

The characteristics of the new system are indicated by its name; it is episodic in that it is assumed to hold integrated episodes or chunks in a multidimensional code. In doing so, it acts as a buffer store, not only between the components of WM, but also linking WM to perception and LTM. It is able to do this because it can hold multidimensional representations, but like most buffer stores it has a limited capacity. On this point we agree with Cowan (2005) in assuming a capacity in the region of four chunks. I made the further assumption that retrieval from the buffer occurred through conscious awareness, providing a link with our earlier research on the vividness of visual and auditory imagery (Baddeley & Andrade 2000). This results in a theory of consciousness that resembles that proposed by Baars (1988), which assumes that consciousness serves as a mechanism for binding stimulus features into perceived objects. He uses the metaphor of a stage on which the products of preconscious processes, the actors, become available to conscious awareness, the audience.

Our new component could be regarded as a fractionation of our initial 1974 version of the CE into separate attentional and storage systems. It had a number of advantages in addition to providing a possible answer to the question of the interaction between LTM and WM. At a theoretical level it formed a bridge between our own bottom-up approach based on attempting to understand the peripheral systems first, and the more top-down approaches predominant in North America, which were more concerned with analyzing the executive and attentional aspects of WM (e.g., Cowan 2005, Engle et al. 1999). Perhaps for this reason, the concept appears to have been welcomed and is frequently cited. However, although that suggests that people find it useful, if it is to be theoretically productive, there is a need to use it to ask interesting and tractable questions, a challenge that has kept Graham Hitch, Richard Allen, and myself busy over recent years.

WM and Binding

Like Baars (1988), we assume that a central role of the buffer is to provide a multidimensional

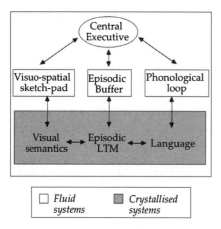

Figure 3

The model following the introduction of a fourth component, the episodic buffer, a system for integrating information from a range of sources into a multidimensional code (Baddeley 2000).

medium that allows features from different sources to be bound into chunks or episodes, not only perceptually but also creatively, allowing us to imagine something new, for example, an ice-hockey-playing elephant. We could then reflect on this new concept and decide, for example, whether our elephant would be better doing a mean defensive body check or keeping goal. This all seemed likely to be an attention-demanding process, so we speculated that the buffer would depend heavily on the CE. In the initial (Baddeley 2000) model (see **Figure 3**), I intentionally required all access to go through the executive, arguing that we could then investigate empirically whether other links were needed.

We studied the role in binding played by each of the three initial components of WM, using our well-tried concurrent task strategy to disrupt each in turn. If, as our initial hypothesis proposed, the CE controls access to and from the buffer, then an attentionally demanding concurrent task should have a very substantial effect on the capacity to bind information, in contrast to minor effects from disrupting the other subsystems. We decided to examine binding in two very different modalities, namely the binding of visual features into perceived objects

on one hand, and the binding of words into sentences on the other.

Visual Binding and WM

Our work on visual binding was strongly influenced by some new developments that were beginning to extend the methods applied to the study of visual attention to the subsequent short-term storage of perceived items. A central question of this approach concerned the factors that determine the conditions under which features such as color and shape are integrated and bound into perceived and remembered objects. The basic experimental paradigm was developed by Luck & Vogel (1997, Vogel et al. 2001). As in the work of Phillips (1974), it involved presenting an array of visual stimuli, followed (after a brief delay) by a probe stimulus, with participants deciding whether or not the probe had been in the array. A number of important results emerged, notably including the observation that capacity was limited to about four objects and was approximately the same, regardless of whether participants were remembering only a single feature, for example, color or shape, or were required to bind the two features and remember not only that a red stimulus had been presented, or a square, but also that the two had been bound together as a red square (Vogel et al. 2001). A subsequent study by Wheeler & Treisman (2002) obtained the same result when testing involved a single probe item. However, they found a binding impairment when the memory test required searching through an array of stimuli in order to find a target match, a result they interpreted as suggesting that maintaining the binding of features was attentionally demanding.

We ourselves tested the attentional hypothesis using our concurrent task procedure. Presentation of the stimulus array was accompanied by a demanding task such as counting backward by threes. If the CE is heavily involved in binding, then the concurrent task should prove more detrimental to the binding condition (e.g., remembering a red square) than to either of the single-feature probe tasks (e.g., red or square). We compared the backward counting condition to one involving articulatory suppression. As expected, we found an overall impairment in performance when accompanied by backward counting. However, this was just as great for the single features as for the binding condition.

A series of further studies explored this finding, using other concurrent tasks and more demanding binding conditions. In one case, for example, shapes and the color patches to which each shape should be bound were presented in separate locations. In another study, the features to be bound were separated in time, while a third experiment presented one feature visually (e.g., a patch of red) and the associated shape verbally. Although some of these activities led to a lower overall level of performance, in no case did we obtain a differential disruption of binding (see Baddeley et al. 2011 for a review).

The final experiment of the Allen et al. (2006) paper did, however, obtain a differential effect. In this study, colored shapes were presented sequentially, followed by a probe. When the final item was probed, the results were as before: no additional binding deficit. However, earlier items did show poorer retention of bound stimuli. We interpreted this as suggesting that binding did not demand extra attention but that maintaining it against distraction did. We explored this disruption effect further, again using simultaneous presentation, but this time inserting a single additional item that participants were instructed to ignore between presentation and test. Binding was differentially impaired even though participants were told to ignore the suffix, which suggests that although visual binding per se is not attention demanding, maintaining bindings against distraction is (see Baddeley et al. 2011 for an overview).

Binding in Verbal WM

Although it appears that attention may be useful for maintaining visual bindings, our data indicate that the simple binding of color and shape is not itself attention demanding. It could, of course, be argued that perceptual binding is atypical in not requiring central resources. Fortunately, however, as part of our converging operations approach to theory, we had pursued a parallel series of experiments investigating the role of executive processes in the binding of words into chunks during retention of spoken sentences.

We carried out a series of experiments, the results of which can be summarized quite simply (Baddeley et al. 2009). Concurrent tasks involving the visuo-spatial sketchpad had a small but significant effect on recall that increased when they also had a visually based executive component. Simple articulatory suppression had a greater effect that was further amplified when both suppression and attentional load were required. Most importantly, however, none of these tasks differentially disrupted the binding of words into chunks as reflected in magnitude of the advantage in recalling sentences over unrelated word sequences. Hence, just as with visual binding, although concurrent tasks impair overall performance, they do not appear to interfere with the binding process itself, which in the case of sentences, we assume operates relatively automatically in LTM.

The evidence from both visual and verbal binding is thus inconsistent with the original proposal that the process of binding involves the active manipulation of information within the episodic buffer, which we now regard as being an important but essentially passive structure on which bindings achieved elsewhere can be displayed. It remains important in that it allows executive processes to carry out further manipulation. This may in turn lead to further bindings involving, for example, the binding of phrases into integrated sentences or objects into complex scenes.

In conclusion, although binding is sometimes discussed as if it were a unitary function, we suggest that it differs depending on the specific type of binding involved. For example, binding may be perceptual or linguistic, and it may be temporary, as required to perform WM tasks, or durable, as in the binding of new information to its context in LTM, a capacity that is disrupted in amnesic patients, who may nonetheless show normal binding in WM (Baddeley et al. 2010). All of these types of binding may, however, result in bound representations accessible through the episodic buffer.

LINKING LONG-TERM AND WORKING MEMORY

Is WM Just Activated LTM?

A number of approaches describe WM as activated LTM (e.g., Cowan 2005, Ruchkin et al. 2003). My view on this issue is that working memory involves the activation of many areas of the brain that involve LTM. This is also true of language, for which activated LTM is not taken as an explanation. I assume that in the case of Cowan's (2005) model, it is a way of referring to those aspects of WM that are not his current principal concern and not a denial of a need for further explanation. He and I would, I think, agree that the phonological loop, the simplest component of WM, is likely to depend on phonological and lexical representations within LTM as well as procedurally based language habits for rehearsal.

Long-Term WM

Ericsson & Kintsch (1995) proposed this concept in explaining the superior performance of expert mnemonists, going on to extend it to the use of semantic and linguistic knowledge to boost memory performance. They argue that these and other situations utilize previously developed structures in LTM as a means of boosting WM performance. I agree, but I cannot see any advantage in treating this as a different kind of WM rather than a particularly clear example of the way in which WM and LTM interact.

LTM and the Multicomponent Model

It seems likely that some of the misunderstandings confronting M-WM stem from the rather limited links with LTM shown in **Figures 2** and **3**. This was also reflected in a disagreement between myself and Robert Logie, who insisted that all information entered the sketchpad via LTM. It was only when I tried to represent my views in the simple model shown in **Figure 4** that we found we agreed. Incoming information is processed by systems that themselves are influenced by LTM. I see WM as a complex interactive system that is able to provide an interface between cognition and action, an interface that is capable of handling information in a range of modalities and stages of processing.

NEUROBIOLOGICAL APPROACHES TO WORKING MEMORY

The development of my own views on WM has been strongly influenced by the study of patients with neuropsychological deficits, and particularly by patients with specific impairment in the absence of general cognitive deficits. Brain damage can be seen scientifically as producing a series of unfortunate experiments of nature. Nature is not usually a good experimenter: Patients typically have a range of different deficits, but just occasionally "pure" deficits occur that potentially, given careful and thorough investigation, allow clear theoretical conclusions to be drawn. These can then be extended to help diagnose and treat patients with related but more complex disabilities.

There are two aspects of such research: the behavioral, linking the performance of

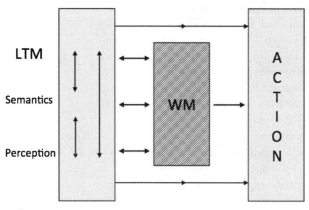

Figure 4

My current view of the complex and multiple links between working memory (WM) and long-term memory (LTM).

the patient to cognitive psychology, and the neurobiological, linking it to its anatomical and neurophysiological basis. Both are important and will ultimately be combined. However, my own expertise and current concern is for the behavioral and the extent to which neurobiological research has so far contributed to the cognitive understanding of M-WM.

There is no doubt that the popularity of the concept of WM owes a great deal to neurobiological studies that appear to suggest that WM may depend on one or more specific anatomical locations. Single-unit recording of the brains of awake monkeys performing a visual STM task found that continued activation of cells in the frontal cortex was associated with successful recall, and disrupted activation was associated with failure (Goldman-Rakic 1988). This led some to conclude that it reflected a specific frontal location of WM. My own view was that it probably formed part of a complex circuit underpinning the visuo-spatial sketchpad. Subsequent discovery of similar cells elsewhere in the brain is consistent with this view.

A second source of apparent support for the concept of WM came from neuroimaging when the various subsystems of M-WM appeared to be relatively closely localizable (for reviews, see Henson 2001, Smith & Jonides 1997). This led to a large number of further neuroimaging investigations from many different laboratories, producing a range of different results, which when fed into a meta-analysis often failed to show a consistent pattern (see Baddeley 2007, chapter 7). My own view is that this simply reflects the unreliability of such results and the complexity of WM, as well as the need to modify paradigms to fit the constraints of neuroimaging, for example, avoiding overt speech.

A different interpretation is offered by Jonides et al. (2008), who comment on the "near-revolutionary changes in psychological theories about STM, with similarly great advances in the neurosciences" that have occurred in the past decade. Their very ambitious interpretation of the "mind and brain of STM" is discussed below. More generally, although I think it is very important to understand the

neurobiological basis of WM, I am not yet convinced that it has made a major contribution to psychological theories of WM. This does not reflect a general rejection of neuroimaging, which offers an essential and potentially powerful tool for understanding cognition and its neural basis. There are some important areas, such as those investigating conscious awareness, in which neuroimaging provides a crucial component in testing and potentially validating distinctions such as that between "remembering" and "knowing" (Düzel et al. 2001). In the case of WM, however, I have two major sources of doubt. The first concerns the lack of apparent replicability in the field. The second more basic concern is the validity of the assumption that anatomical localization will provide a firm theoretical basis for a system as complex as WM in the absence of a much better understanding of the temporal structure of activation than is typically available at present.

SOME ALTERNATIVE APPROACHES

Theories of STM

A good deal of the controversy surrounding M-WM concerns those aspects associated with STM rather than WM, and in particular with the phonological loop model. Whereas some are concerned with the specifics of the model, such as trace decay, for example, other concerns stem from a difference in purpose. Much of our own work has focused on analyzing one source of short-term storage, that based on phonological coding. That means using tasks that minimize semantic and other longer-term factors. Other theorists focus on the whole range of codes that may be contributing, as in the case of Nairne's (1990) feature model. These will inevitably include long-term factors such as semantic coding and will emphasize the similarities between STM and LTM. I regard these two approaches as complementary.

Theories of WM

There are a number of ambitious models of WM that I regard as broadly consistent with the multicomponent framework, although each has a different emphasis and terminology.

Cowan's Embedded Processes Theory

Cowan defines WM as "cognitive processes that are maintained in an unusually accessible state" (Cowan 1999, p. 62). His theory involves a limited-capacity attentional focus that operates across areas of activated LTM. A central issue for Cowan over recent years has been to specify the capacity of this attentional focus and hence the capacity of WM. He produces extensive evidence to suggest that, unlike an earlier suggestion of seven items, the capacity is much closer to four. Importantly, however, this is four chunks or episodes, each of which may contain more than a single item (Cowan 2005).

At a superficial level, Cowan's theories might seem to be totally different from my own. In practice, however, we agree on most issues but differ in our terminology and areas of current focus. I see Cowan's model as principally concerned, in my terminology, with the link between the CE and the episodic buffer. Cowan refers to the material on which his system works as "activated LTM" but does not treat this as providing an adequate explanation, accepting the need for a more detailed analysis of the processes operating beyond attentional focus as reflected in his extensive and influential work on verbal STM, research that interacts with and is complementary to the phonological loop hypothesis of verbal STM (e.g., Cowan et al. 1992). I regard our differences as principally ones of emphasis and terminology.

Individual Difference–Based Theories

The demonstration by Daneman & Carpenter (1980) that WM-span measures can predict comprehension has provided a major focus of research on WM over the past 30 years, involving multiple replications and extensions (Daneman & Merikle 1996). At a theoretical level, there has been considerable interest in identifying the feature of such complex span measures that allows them to predict cognitive performance so effectively. Purely correlational approaches to this issue have a number of limitations, and in my view, the most promising work in this area comes from combining experimental and correlational methods to tackle the question of why some people are better able to sustain material under these complex conditions. Some explanations focus on the capacity to utilize gaps between the processing operations of the span task in order to maintain a fading memory trace (Barrouillet et al. 2004). Others also assume the need to resist time-based decay but emphasize efficiency at switching between the various tasks involved in span (Towse et al. 2000) or they emphasize the role of interference rather than decay (Saito & Miyake 2004).

However, the most extensively developed theoretical account of the mechanisms underpinning WM capacity is that proposed by Engle and colleagues (Engle et al. 1999, Engle & Kane 2004). They emphasize the importance of inhibitory processes, which they argue are crucial to shielding the memory content from potential disruption. Much of their work involves a combination of individual difference and experimental approaches, typically initially testing a large group of participants and then selecting two subgroups, those with very high and those with very low WM span. They have demonstrated that such groups differ not only in WM performance but also in susceptibility to interference across tasks ranging from recall from episodic LTM, through the capacity to generate items from a semantic category, to performance on an antisaccade task of eye movement control (for a review, see Engle & Kane 2004). Although this is an impressive program of work, I suspect that a theory of executive processing based entirely on inhibitory control may be a little narrow. Control is clearly important, but I suspect people also differ in more positive aspects of attentional capacity.

In general, I would see most of the models of WM based on individual differences as consistent with the broad M-WM framework typically focusing on executive control but accepting the contribution of separate visual and verbal STM components (see Alloway et al. 2006 for an example of such a model). Once again, overall similarities may be obscured by terminological differences. Engle and colleagues (Unsworth & Engle 2007) have recently reverted to an earlier distinction between primary and secondary memory, which I would interpret in terms of the distinction between the fluid and crystallized systems that reflect temporary structural representations in the M-WM model (see **Figure 2**).

Jonides and the Mind and Brain of STM

This approach (Jonides et al. 2008) is strongly influenced by neuroimaging in assuming, for each of a range of modalities, that perception, STM, and LTM are all performed in the same anatomical locations. They also cite evidence from neuropsychology, suggesting that amnesic patients have a general difficulty in binding features together (Hannula et al. 2006, Olson et al. 2006). However, this evidence has been criticized on two grounds: first, that the measures used comprise both long- and short-term components (Shrager et al. 2008), and second, that the conclusions are based on spatial binding. There is strong evidence that both spatial processing and episodic LTM depend on the hippocampus. Nonspatial binding such as that of color to shape was not found to be impaired in a hippocampally compromised amnesic patient (Baddeley et al. 2010), whereas classic amnesic patients do not appear to show evidence of a WM deficit (Baddeley & Warrington 1970, Squire 2004). Furthermore, developmental amnesic patient Jon, who has greatly reduced hippocampal volume, performs well on a range of complex WM tasks (Baddeley et al. 2011).

The major source of evidence cited by Jonides et al. comes from neuroimaging, where STM tasks often activate areas of the brain that also are involved in LTM (e.g., Ruchkin et al. 2003). However, as Jonides et al. note in their discussion of the single-unit studies, the fact that an area becomes active during a given task does not mean that it is essential for performance on that task. Presenting a word is likely to activate regions responsible for its phonological, articulatory, lexical, and semantic dimensions, but that does not mean that all these are necessary in order to repeat that word. Potentially more powerful evidence exists based on lesions in neuropsychological patients (Olson et al. 2006), but the interpretation of this has been questioned (Baddeley et al. 2010); the classic neuropsychological literature typically reports a dissociation between perceptual and memory deficits (Shallice 1988).

The "mind and brain" model proposed by Jonides et al. is somewhat complex, involving five psychological assumptions and six assumptions about neurobiological processing levels. They go on to illustrate their model, using the case of remembering three visual items over a two-second delay, resulting in a figure that involves 13 psychological processes operating across 10 neural levels. I remain somewhat skeptical as to how productive such a model will prove to be. This reflects a difference between us in theoretical style, with my own preference for the gradual development of detailed modes within a broad theoretical framework, whereas Jonides et al. are rather more ambitious.

Computational Models of WM

The WM theorists discussed so far have all taken a broad-based approach to theory. There are, however, theorists who attempt a much more detailed account of WM, typically accompanied by computer simulation. This is a very flexible approach, giving rise to a range of different models of WM, which can on occasion result in subcomponents resembling aspects of M-WM including the sketch pad (Anderson et al. 2004, p. 1037) and the loop (Anderson et al. 1996).

Barnard's (1985) ambitious computationally based "interacting cognitive subsystems" model can also be mapped directly onto M-WM. It was initially developed to account for language processing but was subsequently used extensively by Barnard to analyze situations involving human–computer interaction (Barnard 1987). The model can simulate most aspects of WM while linking it to motor control, emotion, and levels of awareness as part of a broad, ambitious, and insightful model, which in Barnard's hands has been applied with success to an impressive range of situations from choreography to theories of depression (Teasdale & Barnard 1993). However, the sheer complexity of the model makes it difficult for others to use. It is also unclear how important the computational detail really is, and indeed whether it gives an adequate account of what is happening within the more peripheral subcomponents. In discussing his attempt to produce a full simulation of the model, Howard Bowman (2011), a computer scientist who had worked with Barnard in a simulation, now advocates a hierarchical decomposition of the model using components that can be built in isolation, avoiding unnecessary detail such as premature attempts to specify at a neural level.

I suspect that undue complexity may in due course also prove to be a problem for an ambitious new model proposed by Oberauer (2010), who attempts to provide a blueprint for the whole WM system. He sees the main focus of WM as being "to serve as a blackboard for information processing on which we can construct new representations with little interference from old memories." He proposes six requirements for a WM system, namely, (*a*) maintaining structural representations by dynamic bindings, (*b*) manipulating them, (*c*) flexibly reconfiguring them, (*d*) partially decoupling these from LTM, (*e*) controlling LTM retrieval, and (*f*) encoding new structures into LTM. He postulates mechanisms for achieving each of these, hence attempting to put flesh on the previously vague concept of "activated LTM."

A crucial feature of Oberauer's model is the distinction he makes between declarative and procedural WM. Declarative WM is the aspect of WM of which we are aware, comprising most of the current work in the area, whereas procedural WM is concerned with the nondeclarative processes that underpin such operations: I assume that an example would be the process controlling subvocal rehearsal. However, he also considers a higher level of procedural control through what he refers to as the "bridge," as in the bridge of a ship, and what I myself would call the central executive. Consider the following: A participant in my experiment is instructed to press the red button when the number 1 appears, press the green for number 2, and neither for 3. We would expect this simple instruction to be followed throughout the experiment. It is as if some mini-program is set up and then runs, but we currently know very little about how this is achieved. I think the investigation of this aspect of procedural working memory, sometimes referred to as "task set," will become increasingly influential.

This is certainly a very ambitious program, and as Oberauer points out, the evidence at present is rather sparse, but it could be an exciting development. However, the sheer complexity of the model may make it difficult to evaluate experimentally. But then, I am a theoretical mapmaker and temperamentally skeptical of complex theoretical architectures. Time will tell.

WHAT NEXT?

A Speculative Model and Some Questions

I have described my attempts to turn a broad theoretical framework into a more detailed model by a process of speculation followed by empirical exploration. It is therefore perhaps appropriate to end on my own current speculations and some of the many questions they raise.

As **Figure 5** shows, my current views are not dramatically different from our original speculation, apart from the episodic buffer, and the attempt to provide considerably more speculative detail. In each case this suggests questions that will not be easily answered but that potentially offer a way forward. I consider the various components in turn.

Central executive. This is an attentional system; how does it differ from the limited-capacity component of Cowan's (2005) model?

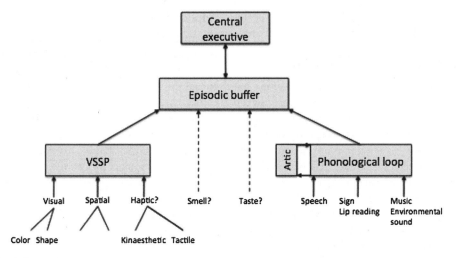

Figure 5

A speculative view of the flow of information from perception to working memory. VSSP, visuo-spatial sketchpad.

I assume that it comprises a number of executive functions, but how many, and how are they organized and interrelated? Just how far can one take attempts to explain executive control in terms of a single factor such as that of inhibition? Do we need to worry about precisely what is being inhibited and whether this differs between individuals? Do we need a concept of cognitive energy?

Episodic buffer. How should we measure its capacity? To what extent is this limited by number of chunks and to what extent by similarity between chunks? If similarity is important, can other modalities such as smell and taste be added without impacting visual or verbal capacity? Are there separate subsystems for smell and taste? How is rehearsal maintained? My current speculation is that it operates according to the principle of attentionally based refreshing, as discussed by Johnson et al. (2002). What about emotion? Elsewhere (Baddeley 2007) I have suggested that it impacts WM via a hedonic detector system; where within the M-WM system is this located?

I assume that the buffer provides access to conscious awareness; does this mean that we are not directly aware of the other subsystems but only of their products when registered in the buffer?

Phonological loop. Can we reach a conclusion on the ancient trace decay/interference controversy? Is subvocal rehearsal atypical of other types of rehearsal, as I suspect? To what extent is the loop used for remembering nonverbal material such as music or environmental sounds?

Visuo-spatial sketchpad. The visual and spatial aspects appear to be clearly separable but linked within the sketchpad; is this true of haptic, tactile, and kinesthetic memory? What is the mechanism of visuo-spatial rehearsal? Is it a spatial analogue to the phonological loop, as Logie (1995) suggests, or is it more like attentionally based refreshing? Finally, given that our attempt to link the loop with LTM through language acquisition proved very fruitful, would pursuing the link between the sketchpad and LTM prove equally useful?

Integration

Finally, how do these increasingly detailed accounts fit together to provide an interactive unitary system that mediates between perception, LTM, and action?

In Praise of Negative Results

It is of course very easy to raise questions, but much more difficult to answer them. This can lead to a program that cautiously seeks easy confirmation of what we are pretty sure we already know, resulting in confirmation bias, and an avoidance of too much risk of negative results. Negative results are a pain for a number of reasons. First of all, they are hard to interpret. They could result from a poor design or sloppy experimentation. They also raise the question of whether the experiment has sufficient power and indeed whether the question is worth asking in the first place, with all these factors making negative results harder to publish. If we are to understand WM, however, it is important to know what it does not do, and this is likely to involve negative results, as has often proved to be the case in the various stages of developing the current M-WM model. Publication is justifiably more difficult, and there needs to be a good justification for the question. Negative results can, however, be very important and publishable, provided the problem of sensitivity is addressed through inclusion of other conditions showing positive effects together with clear evidence of replication. This was the case with our original 1974 studies, where the effect of concurrent tasks was much less than anticipated, and even more so in our recent exploration of the episodic buffer (Baddeley et al. 2009, 2011).

So what does WM not do? My own conclusion after surveying the experimental literature and its implications for clinical and social psychology (Baddeley 2007) is that we have evolved an overall cognitive system that attempts to minimize the demands made on WM while allowing it to intervene where necessary. A very basic example is that of breathing, far too important to be left to working memory. However, as any diver or singer will know, we clearly do have considerable, though limited, control. Suicide by breath holding is not an option.

Applications

A central requirement of our original framework was that it should be applicable outside the laboratory. Although I have not discussed this aspect of M-WM, it does appear to have had success in achieving this, at two levels. First, through direct application of the M-WM framework to specific practical problems, Gathercole's extensive development of a WM measure applied to school-aged children has been successful in identifying children at risk and providing methods of helping teachers identify and help children with WM problems (Gathercole & Alloway 2008). Another instance is the development and validation of a dual-task performance measure for the early detection of Alzheimer's disease (Kaschel et al. 2009, Logie et al. 2004).

A second aspect of theoretical application is the use of the M-WM theory as a tool for investigating and understanding other research areas. Here the applications are very extensive, ranging from human factors to psychiatry, neuropharmacology to language therapy, and even to paleoanthropology, where the development of working memory is proposed as an explanation of the differences between Neanderthal man and homo sapiens, suggested by a study of surviving artifacts (Wynn & Coolidge 2010).

My own view is that this breadth of application has reflected the simplicity of the theoretical framework together with the availability of a few basic methodologies, such as the use of similarity effects as an indication of coding dimension and of dual-task performance as a way of controlling processing. Such techniques are easily learned, and while not guaranteeing fruitful answers, do at least provide conceptual and practical tools for investigating a wide range of problems. From a theoretical viewpoint, such practical applications can be extremely valuable both in helping explore the boundaries of the laboratory-based effects and in highlighting theoretical anomalies that have the potential to become future growing points.

CONCLUSION

So where does this leave our early question of what makes a good theory? Clearly, my own preference has been for Toulmin's view of theories as maps, coupled with the Lakatos criterion of judging success by productiveness rather than predictive accuracy. However, as we begin to fill in the empty spaces on the theoretical map, it hopefully will be increasingly possible to develop interlinked and more detailed models of the components of WM and their mode of interaction.

ACKNOWLEDGMENTS

I am grateful to Graham Hitch, Richard Allen, Robert Logie, Susan Gathercole, and Christopher Jarrold for many stimulating discussions and for commenting on an earlier draft.

LITERATURE CITED

Allen R, Baddeley AD, Hitch GJ. 2006. Is the binding of visual features in working memory resource-demanding? *J. Exp. Psychol.: Gen.* 135:298–313

Alloway TP, Gathercole SE, Pickering SJ. 2006. Verbal and visuospatial short-term and working memory in children: Are they separable? *Child Dev.* 77:1698–716

Anderson JR, Bothell D, Byrne MD, Douglass S, Lebiere C, Qin Y. 2004. An integrated theory of the mind. *Psychol. Rev.* 111:1036–60

Anderson JR, Reder LM, Lebiere C. 1996. Working memory: activation limitations on retrieval. *Cogn. Psychol.* 30:221–56

Atkinson RC, Shiffrin RM. 1968. Human memory: a proposed system and its control processes. In *The Psychology of Learning and Motivation: Advances in Research and Theory*, ed. KW Spence, JT Spence, pp. 89–195. New York: Academic

Attneave F. 1960. In defense of homunculi. In *Sensory Communication*, ed. W Rosenblith, pp. 777–82. Cambridge, MA: MIT Press

Baars BJ. 1988. *A Cognitive Theory of Consciousness.* Cambridge, UK: Cambridge Univ. Press

Baddeley AD. 1960. Enhanced learning of a position habit with secondary reinforcement for the wrong response. *Am. J. Psychol.* 73:454–57

Baddeley AD. 1966a. Short-term memory for word sequences as a function of acoustic, semantic and formal similarity. *Q. J. Exp. Psychol.* 18:362–65

Baddeley AD. 1966b. The influence of acoustic and semantic similarity on long-term memory for word sequences. *Q. J. Exp. Psychol.* 18:302–9

Baddeley AD. 1968. How does acoustic similarity influence short-term memory? *Q. J. Exp. Psychol.* 20:249–64

Baddeley AD. 1976. *The Psychology of Memory.* New York: Basic Books

Baddeley AD. 1986. *Working Memory.* Oxford, UK: Oxford Univ. Press

Baddeley AD. 1996. Exploring the central executive. *Q. J. Exp. Psychol. A* 49:5–28

Baddeley AD. 2000. The episodic buffer: a new component of working memory? *Trends. Cogn. Sci.* 4:417–23

Baddeley AD. 2007. *Working Memory, Thought and Action.* Oxford, UK: Oxford Univ. Press

Baddeley AD, Allen RJ, Hitch GJ. 2011. Binding in visual working memory: the role of the episodic buffer. *Neuropsychologia* 49:1393–400

Baddeley AD, Allen RJ, Vargha-Khadem F. 2010. Is the hippocampus necessary for visual and verbal binding in working memory? *Neuropsychologia* 48:1089–95

Baddeley AD, Andrade J. 2000. Working memory and the vividness of imagery. *J. Exp. Psychol.: Gen.* 129:126–45

Baddeley AD, Ecob JR. 1970. Simultaneous acoustic and semantic coding in short-term memory. *Nature* 277:288–89

Baddeley AD, Gathercole SE, Papagno C. 1998. The phonological loop as a language learning device. *Psychol. Rev.* 105:158–73

Baddeley AD, Grant W, Wight E, Thomson N. 1975a. Imagery and visual working memory. In *Attention and Performance V*, ed. PMA Rabbitt, S Dornic, pp. 205–17. London: Academic

Baddeley AD, Hitch GJ. 1974. Working memory. In *The Psychology of Learning and Motivation: Advances in Research and Theory*, ed. GA Bower, pp. 47–89. New York: Academic

Baddeley AD, Hitch GJ. 1977. Recency re-examined. In *Attention and Performance VI*, ed. S Dornic, pp. 647–67. Hillsdale, NJ: Erlbaum

Baddeley AD, Hitch GJ, Allen RJ. 2009. Working memory and binding in sentence recall. *J. Mem. Lang.* 61:438–56

Baddeley AD, Larsen JD. 2007. The phonological loop unmasked? A comment on the evidence for a "perceptual-gestural" alternative. *Q. J. Exp. Psychol.* 60:497–504

Baddeley AD, Levy BA. 1971. Semantic coding and short-term memory. *J. Exp. Psychol.* 89:132–36

Baddeley AD, Lewis V, Vallar G. 1984. Exploring the articulatory loop. *Q. J. Exp. Psychol. A* 36:233–52

Baddeley AD, Lieberman K. 1980. Spatial working memory. In *Attention and Performance VIII*, ed. R Nickerson, pp. 521–39. Hillsdale, NJ: Erlbaum

Baddeley AD, Logie RH. 1999. Working memory: the multiple component model. In *Models of Working Memory: Mechanisms of Active Maintenance and Executive Control*, ed. A Miyake, P Shah, pp. 28–61. Cambridge, UK: Cambridge Univ. Press

Baddeley AD, Papagno C, Vallar G. 1988. When long-term learning depends on short-term storage. *J. Mem. Lang.* 27:586–95

Baddeley AD, Thomson N, Buchanan M. 1975b. Word length and the structure of short-term memory. *J. Verbal Learn. Verbal Behav.* 14:575–89

Baddeley AD, Vallar G, Wilson BA. 1987. Sentence comprehension and phonological memory: some neuropsychological evidence. In *Attention and Performance XII: The Psychology of Reading*, ed. M Coltheart, pp. 509–29. London: Erlbaum

Baddeley AD, Vargha-Khadem F, Mishkin M. 2001. Preserved recognition in a case of developmental amnesia: implications for the acquisition of semantic memory. *J. Cogn. Neurosci.* 13:357–69

Baddeley AD, Warrington EK. 1970. Amnesia and the distinction between long- and short-term memory. *J. Verbal Learn. Verbal Behav.* 9:176–89

Barnard PJ. 1985. Interactive cognitive subsystems: a psycholinguistic approach to short-term memory. In *Progress in the Psychology of Language*, ed. A Ellis, pp. 197–258. London: Erlbaum

Barnard PJ. 1987. Cognitive resources and the learning of human-computer dialogs. In *Interfacing Thought: Cognitive Aspects of Human-Computer Interaction*, ed. JM Carroll, pp. 112–58. Cambridge, MA: MIT Press

Barrouillet P, Bernardin S, Camos V. 2004. Time constraints and resource sharing in adults' working memory spans. *J. Exp. Psychol.: Gen.* 133:83–100

Bowman H. 2011. *Is there a future in architectural modeling of mind?* Paper presented at Philip Barnard retirement symp., MRC Appl. Psychol. Unit, Cambridge, UK

Braithwaite RB. 1953. *Scientific Explanation*. Cambridge, UK: Cambridge Univ. Press

Brooks LR. 1968. Spatial and verbal components in the act of recall. *Can. J. Psychol.* 22:349–68

Brown GDA, Preece T, Hulme C. 2000. Oscillator-based memory for serial order. *Psychol. Rev.* 107:127–81

Burgess N, Hitch GJ. 1999. Memory for serial order: a network model of the phonological loop and its timing. *Psychol. Rev.* 106:551–81

Burgess N, Hitch GJ. 2006. A revised model of short-term memory and long-term learning of verbal sequences. *J. Mem. Lang.* 55:627–52

Cermak LS, Butters N, Moreines J. 1974. Some analyses of the verbal encoding deficit of alcoholic Korsakoff patients. *Brain Lang.* 1:141–50

Cermak LS, Reale L. 1978. Depth of processing and retention of words by alcoholic Korsakoff patients. *J. Exp. Psychol. Hum. Learn.* 4:165–74

Colle HA, Welsh A. 1976. Acoustic masking in primary memory. *J. Verbal Learn. Verbal Behav.* 15:17–32

Conrad R, Hull AJ. 1964. Information, acoustic confusion and memory span. *Br. J. Psychol.* 55:429–32

Cowan N. 1999. An embedded-processes model of working memory. In *Models of Working Memory*, ed. A Miyake, P Shah, pp. 62–101. Cambridge, UK: Cambridge Univ. Press

Cowan N. 2005. *Working Memory Capacity*. Hove, UK: Psychol. Press

Cowan N, Day L, Saults JS, Keller TA, Johnson T, Flores L. 1992. The role of verbal output time and the effects of word-length on immediate memory. *J. Mem. Lang.* 31:1–17

Craik FIM, Lockhart RS. 1972. Levels of processing: a framework for memory research. *J. Verbal Learn. Verbal Behav.* 11:671–84

Dale HCA. 1973. Short-term memory for visual information. *Br. J. Psychol.* 64:1–8

Daneman M, Carpenter PA. 1980. Individual differences in working memory and reading. *J. Verbal Learn. Verbal Behav.* 19:450–66

Daneman M, Merikle PM. 1996. Working memory and language comprehension: a meta-analysis. *Psychonom. Bull. Rev.* 3:422–33

Della Sala S, Gray C, Baddeley A, Allamano N, Wilson L. 1999. Pattern span: a tool for unwelding visuo-spatial memory. *Neuropsychologia* 37:1189–99

Düzel E, Vargha-Khadem F, Heinze HJ, Mishkin M. 2001. Brain activity evidence for recognition without recollection after early hippocampal damage. *Proc. Natl. Acad. Sci. USA* 98:8101–6

Emerson MJ, Miyake A. 2003. The role of inner speech in task switching: a dual-task investigation. *J. Mem. Lang.* 48:148–68

Engle RW, Kane MJ. 2004. Executive attention, working memory capacity and two-factor theory of cognitive control. In *The Psychology of Learning and Motivation*, ed. B Ross, pp. 145–99. New York: Elsevier

Engle RW, Kane MJ, Tuholski SW. 1999. Individual differences in working memory capacity and what they tell us about controlled attention, general fluid intelligence, and functions of the prefrontal cortex. In *Models of Working Memory: Mechanisms of Active Maintenance and Executive Control*, ed. A Miyake, P Shah, pp. 102–34. New York: Cambridge Univ. Press

Ericsson KA, Kintsch W. 1995. Long-term working memory. *Psychol. Rev.* 102:211–45

Fodor JA. 1983. *The Modularity of Mind*. Cambridge, MA: MIT Press

Gathercole SE. 1995. Is nonword repetition a test of phonological memory or long-term knowledge? It all depends on the nonwords. *Mem. Cognit.* 23:83–94

Gathercole SE, Alloway TP. 2008. *Working Memory and Learning: A Practical Guide*. London: Sage

Gathercole SE, Pickering SJ, Ambridge B, Wearing H. 2004a. The structure of working memory from 4 to 15 years of age. *Dev. Psychol.* 40:177–90

Gathercole SE, Pickering SJ, Knight C, Stegmann Z. 2004b. Working memory skills and educational attainment: evidence from National Curriculum assessments at 7 and 14 years of age. *Appl. Cogn. Psychol.* 40:1–16

Glanzer M. 1972. Storage mechanisms in recall. In *The Psychology of Learning and Motivation: Advances in Research and Theory*, ed. GH Bower, pp. 129–93. New York: Academic

Goldman-Rakic PW. 1988. Topography of cognition: parallel distributed networks in primate association cortex. *Annu. Rev. Neurosci.* 11:137–56

Hannula DE, Tranel D, Cohen NJ. 2006. The long and the short of it: relational memory impairments in amnesia, even at short lags. *J. Neurosci.* 26:8352–59

Henson R. 2001. Neural working memory. In *Working Memory in Perspective*, ed. J Andrade, pp. 151–74. Hove, UK: Psychol. Press

Hitch GJ, Flude B, Burgess N. 2009. Slave to the rhythm: experimental tests of a model for verbal short-term memory and long-term sequence learning. *J. Mem. Lang.* 61:97–111

Hurlstone MJ. 2010. *The problem of serial order in visuospatial short-term memory*. Unpubl. PhD dissert., Univ. York, UK

Johnson MK, Reeder JA, Raye CL, Mitchell KJ. 2002. Second thoughts versus second looks: an age-related deficit in reflectively refreshing just-activated information. *Psychol. Sci.* 13:64–67

Jones D, Hughes RW, Macken WJ. 2006. Perceptual organization masquerading as phonological storage: further support for a perceptual-gestural view of short-term memory. *J. Mem. Lang.* 54:265–81

Jones DM. 1993. Objects, streams and threads of auditory attention. In *Attention: Selection, Awareness and Control*, ed. AD Baddeley, L Weiskrantz, pp. 87–104. Oxford, UK: Clarendon

Jones DM, Macken WJ. 1993. Irrelevant tones produce an irrelevant speech effect: implications for phonological coding in working memory. *J. Exp. Psychol.: Learn. Mem. Cogn.* 19:369–81

Jones DM, Macken WJ. 1995. Phonological similarity in the irrelevant speech effect: within- or between-stream similarity? *J. Exp. Psychol.: Learn. Mem. Cogn.* 21:103–15

Jonides J, Lewis RL, Nee DE, Lustig CA, Berman MG, Moore KS. 2008. The mind and brain of short-term memory. *Annu. Rev. Psychol.* 59:193–224

Kaschel R, Logie RH, Kazén M, Della Sala S. 2009. Alzheimer's disease, but not ageing or depression, affects dual-tasking. *J. Neurol.* 256:1860–68

Klauer KC, Zhao Z. 2004. Double dissociations in visual and spatial short-term memory. *J. Exp. Psychol.: Gen.* 133:355–81

Kroll NE, Parks T, Parkinson SR, Bieber SL, Johnson AL. 1970. Short-term memory while shadowing: recall of visually and aurally presented letters. *J. Exp. Psychol.* 85:220–24

Lakatos I. 1976. *Proofs and Reputations*. Cambridge, UK: Cambridge Univ. Press

Larsen J, Baddeley AD. 2003. Disruption of verbal STM by irrelevant speech, articulatory suppression and manual tapping: Do they have a common source? *Q. J. Exp. Psychol. A* 56:1249–68

Larsen JD, Baddeley AD, Andrade J. 2000. Phonological similarity and the irrelevant speech effect: implications for models of short-term verbal memory. *Memory* 8:145–57

Lashley KS. 1951. The problem of serial order in behavior. In *Cerebral Mechanisms in Behavior: The Hixon Symposium*, ed. LA Jeffress, pp. 112–36. New York: John Wiley

Logie RH. 1986. Visuo-spatial processing in working memory. *Q. J. Exp. Psychol.* 38A:229–47

Logie RH. 1995. *Visuo-Spatial Working Memory*. Hove, UK: Erlbaum

Logie RH. 2011. The functional organisation and the capacity limits of working memory. *Curr. Dir. Psychol. Sci.* 20:240–45

Logie RH, Cocchini G, Della Sala S, Baddeley A. 2004. Is there a specific capacity for dual task co-ordination? Evidence from Alzheimer's disease. *Neuropsychology* 18:504–13

Logie RH, Della Sala S, Wynn V, Baddeley AD. 2000. Visual similarity effects in immediate serial recall. *Q. J. Exp. Psychol.* 53A:626–46

Luck SJ, Vogel EK. 1997. The capacity of visual working memory for features and conjunctions. *Nature* 390:279–81

Luria AR. 1959. The directive function of speech in development and dissolution, part I. *Word* 15:341–52

Milner B. 1971. Interhemispheric differences in the localization of psychological processes in man. *Br. Med. Bull.* 27:272–77

Miyake A, Friedman NP, Emerson MJ, Witzki AH, Howenter A, Wager TD. 2000. The unity and diversity of executive functions and their contributions to complex "frontal lobe" tasks: a latent variable analysis. *Cogn. Psychol.* 41:49–100

Monsell S. 2005. The chronometrics of task-set control. In *Measuring the Mind: Speed, Control, and Age*, ed. J Duncan, L Phillips, P McLeod, pp. 161–90. Oxford, UK: Oxford Univ. Press

Nairne JS. 1990. A feature model of immediate memory. *Mem. Cognit.* 18:251–69

Nairne JS. 2002. Remembering over the short-term: the case against the standard model. *Annu. Rev. Psychol.* 53:53–81

Norman DA, Shallice T. 1986. Attention to action: willed and automatic control of behaviour. In *Consciousness and Self-Regulation. Advances in Research and Theory*, ed. RJ Davidson, GE Schwartz, D Shapiro, pp. 1–18. New York: Plenum

Oberauer K. 2010. Design for a working memory. *Psychol. Learn. Motiv.* 51:45–100

Olson IR, Moore KS, Stark M, Chatterjee A. 2006. Visual working memory is impaired when the medial temporal lobe is damaged. *J. Cogn. Neurosci.* 18:1087–97

Osgood CE. 1949. The similarity paradox in human learning: a resolution. *Psychol. Rev.* 56:132–43

Page MPA, Norris D. 1998. The primacy model: a new model of immediate serial recall. *Psychol. Rev.* 105:761–81

Page MPA, Norris DG. 2003. The irrelevant sound effect: what needs modeling, and a tentative model. *Q. J. Exp. Psychol.* 56A:1289–300

Phillips WA. 1974. On the distinction between sensory storage and short-term visual memory. *Percept. Psychophys.* 16:283–90

Phillips WA, Baddeley AD. 1971. Reaction time and short-term visual memory. *Psychon. Sci.* 22:73–4

Popper K. 1959. *The Logic of Scientific Discovery*. London: Hutchison

Posner MI, Keele SW. 1967. Decay of visual information from a single letter. *Science* 158:137–39

Posner MI, Konick AF. 1966. Short-term retention of visual and kinesthetic information. *Organ. Behav. Hum. Perform.* 1:71–86

Riby LM, Perfect TJ, Stollery B. 2004. The effects of age and task domain on dual task performance: a meta-analysis. *Eur. J. Cogn. Psychol.* 16:863–91

Robbins T, Henderson E, Barker D, Bradley A, Fearneyhough C, et al. 1996. Working memory in chess. *Mem. Cognit.* 24:83–93

Rönnberg J, Rudner M, Ingvar M. 2004. Neural correlates of working memory for sign language. *Cogn. Brain Res.* 20:165–82

Ruchkin DS, Grafman J, Cameron K, Berndt RS. 2003. Working memory retention systems: a state of activated long-term memory. *Behav. Brain Sci.* 26:709–77

Saito S, Miyake A. 2004. On the nature of forgetting and the processing-storage relationship in reading span performance. *J. Mem. Lang.* 50:425–43

Salame P, Baddeley AD. 1986. Phonological factors in STM: similarity and the unattended speech effect. *Bull. Psychonom. Soc.* 24:263–65

Shallice T. 1988. *From Neuropsychology to Mental Structure*. Cambridge, UK: Cambridge Univ. Press

Shallice T. 2002. Fractionation of the supervisory system. In *Principles of Frontal Lobe Function*, ed. DT Stuss, RT Knight, pp. 261–77. New York: Oxford Univ. Press

Shallice T, Warrington EK. 1970. Independent functioning of verbal memory stores: a neuropsychological study. *Q. J. Exp. Psychol.* 22:261–73

Shrager Y, Levy DA, Hopkins RO, Squire LR. 2008. Working memory and the organization of brain systems. *J. Neurosci.* 28:4818–22

Smith EE, Jonides J. 1997. Working memory: a view from neuroimaging. *Cognit. Psychol.* 33:5–42

Smyth MM, Pendleton LR. 1990. Space and movement in working memory. *Q. J. Exp. Psychol.* 42A:291–304

Squire LR. 2004. Memory systems of the brain: a brief history and current perspective. *Neurobiol. Learn. Mem.* 82:171–77

Teasdale JD, Barnard PJ. 1993. *Affect, Cognition and Change: Remodeling Depressive Thought*. Hove, UK: Erlbaum

Toulmin S. 1953. *The Philosophy of Science*. London: Hutchison

Towse JN, Hitch GJ, Hutton U. 2000. On the interpretation of working memory span in adults. *Mem. Cognit.* 28:341–48

Unsworth N, Engle RW. 2007. The nature of individual differences in working memory capacity: active maintenance in primary memory and controlled search from secondary memory. *Psychol. Rev.* 114:104–32

Vogel EK, Woodman GF, Luck SJ. 2001. Storage of features, conjunctions, and objects in visual working memory. *J. Exp. Psychol.: Hum. Percept. Perform.* 27:92–114

Waugh NC, Norman DA. 1965. Primary memory. *Psychol. Rev.* 72:89–104

Wheeler ME, Treisman AM. 2002. Binding in short-term visual memory. *J. Exp. Psychol.: Gen.* 131:48–64

Williamson V, Baddeley A, Hitch G. 2010. Musicians' and nonmusicians' short-term memory for verbal and musical sequences: comparing phonological similarity and pitch proximity. *Mem. Cognit.* 38:163–75

Wynn T, Coolidge FL. 2010. Beyond symbolism and language: an introduction to Supplement 1, *Working Memory*. *Curr. Anthropol.* 51:5–16

Learning to See Words

Brian A. Wandell,[1] Andreas M. Rauschecker,[1,2]
and Jason D. Yeatman[1]

[1]Psychology Department, [2]Medical Scientist Training Program and Neurosciences
Program, Stanford University, Stanford, California 94305; email: wandell@stanford.edu,
andreasr@stanford.edu, jdyeatman@stanford.edu

Annu. Rev. Psychol. 2012. 63:31–53

First published online as a Review in Advance on
July 29, 2011

The *Annual Review of Psychology* is online at
psych.annualreviews.org

This article's doi:
10.1146/annurev-psych-120710-100434

Keywords

reading, visual word form area, dyslexia, visual field maps, diffusion
tensor imaging (DTI), fMRI

Abstract

Skilled reading requires recognizing written words rapidly; functional
neuroimaging research has clarified how the written word initiates a series of responses in visual cortex. These responses are communicated to
circuits in ventral occipitotemporal (VOT) cortex that learn to identify
words rapidly. Structural neuroimaging has further clarified aspects of
the white matter pathways that communicate reading signals between
VOT and language systems. We review this circuitry, its development,
and its deficiencies in poor readers. This review emphasizes data that
measure the cortical responses and white matter pathways in individual
subjects rather than group differences. Such methods have the potential
to clarify why a child has difficulty learning to read and to offer guidance
about the interventions that may be useful for that child.

Contents

INTRODUCTION

Although most children learn to read well, there are many who fail to learn or learn only with great difficulty. There are many reasons why a child may have difficulty learning to read. These reasons range from social impediments that limit training to biological impediments within specific brain structures. The research we review here is aimed at clarifying the neural circuits essential for reading and at understanding specific failure modes that may arise in the brain systems of a child learning to read in a supportive environment.

Many modern neuroimaging methods can trace signals and structures of specific neural pathways in a single subject. Using these methods, the signals and structures in a child who is having difficulty reading can be compared to the corresponding measurements obtained from a cohort of good readers. This analysis is not a group comparison (poor readers versus good readers). Rather, it is an engineering approach to understanding disability in individuals. We begin with the assumption that all good readers operate within a compliance range ["Happy families are all alike; every unhappy family is unhappy in its own way" (Tolstoy 1911)]. We aim to find the specific signals and structures that are outside of this compliance range in an individual who has difficulty reading. Problems may arise for many reasons. Some may be due to developmental failures of the systems dedicated to reading per se, whereas others may be due to inadequate signals from related but essential systems, such as the visual or auditory systems. With enough experience we may hope to learn which neural systems commonly limit reading and ultimately to understand the underlying genetic or environmental biological factors that cause these deviations.

Given that widespread literacy is a relatively recent development, it is likely that many components of the reading circuitry are used for purposes in addition to reading. For example, to read a child must develop adequate visual acuity and learn to understand speech. Competence at these tasks is predictive of future reading: Children who are efficient at hearing and manipulating the sounds of speech are usually good at learning to read (Shaywitz et al. 2008, Torgesen et al. 1999, Wagner & Torgesen 1987). The development of reading relies on the proper developmental progression of all of these systems. Once the preconditions for reading are met, the next step is to learn the association between orthography (i.e., the written or printed symbols) and language sounds. A child who does not learn this skill, as measured by single-word reading, will not reach an efficient level of reading. A deficit in learning single-word reading in a child of normal intelligence is called developmental dyslexia.

We can now preview our main points. First, skilled single-word reading depends on the correct processing in a series of cortical circuits. Some of these circuits are in classic visual cortex; others are in regions identified by investigators working on reading and language. It is important to consider the development of all reading circuits jointly. In preparing this review, we have learned that there is room to improve how investigators localize and coordinate these measurements. Second, reading circuitry includes local cortical circuits and their connecting white matter tracts; this hierarchy of processing stages must develop in a temporal sequence. Certain brain systems must develop and provide signals to other systems, or else the entire circuit specialization for reading will not develop properly. Understanding the system should include measuring the sequence of development in individual subjects.

To take a practical approach to understanding reading failures, we need to know both the parts list and the sequence-of-assembly instructions for the reading circuitry. There has been good progress on all fronts, and there remains much to be done.

BACKGROUND

The past 30 years have transformed our ability to measure signals and structures in the human brain. The earliest human neuroimaging measurements included experiments to understand reading and language. The rich neurological history of reading and language formed an excellent basis for these early investigations (Binder et al. 1992; Damasio & Damasio 1983; Dejerine 1891, 1895; Wernicke 1874). The earliest experiments used positron emission tomography (PET); subsequent advances in magnetic resonance imaging

(MRI), magnetoencephalography (MEG), and electroencephalography (EEG) built on this history and provided a great deal of new and more precise information about neural signals and structures (Wandell 2011).

An important part of that history was an effort to classify neural structures into sensory (visual) and language. Indeed, the nineteenth-century neurological literature opens with a dispute between Dejerine and Wernicke as to whether the neural basis of reading was intimately connected with visual cortex or alternatively whether reading is embedded within a language system and relies only on generic visual information (Bub et al. 1993). This debate continues in the modern era (McCandliss et al. 2003, Price & Devlin 2003, Wandell 2011). As we have learned more about the visual system using modern neuroimaging, it appears that the focus on this question is not helpful in several ways. For example, modern imaging methods show that even activity in primary sensory areas of the brain, such as the lateral geniculate nucleus (LGN) and primary visual cortex (V1), are modulated by task-dependent manipulations such as shifts in attention (Brefczynski & DeYoe 1999, Gandhi et al. 1999, O'Craven et al. 1997). Moreover, allowing for separations of only two or three synapses, anatomical studies show that cortex is massively interconnected (Braitenberg & Schüz 1991). An alternative approach is to study how reading signals are communicated in the brain and the operational compliance range for these signals and structures. We point out three advances here, and we spend most of this review describing the experimental basis of these advances.

Critical Neural Circuitry for Seeing Words Is Located in Ventral Occipitotemporal Cortex

Since the French neurologist Dejerine described a patient with pure alexia (word blindness) caused by brain damage (Dejerine 1892), the idea of a neural structure critical for seeing words has been influential in theories of reading (Bub et al. 1993). Many such patients

Orthography: the written or printed symbols of language

Developmental dyslexia: failure or difficulty learning to read in a child whose cognitive skills are otherwise unimpaired

MEG: magnetoencephalography

EEG: electroencephalography

V1: primary visual cortex

Pure alexia: the inability to read even when visual and language functions are intact; also known as word blindness and alexia without agraphia

VOT: ventral occipitotemporal cortex

VWFA: visual word form area

have since been described, and neurological lesions tend to overlap in ventral occipitotemporal (VOT) cortex and the splenium of the corpus callosum (Damasio & Damasio 1983). In the 1990s, modern imaging methods allowed investigators to search for the likely position of cortical circuits essential for reading in healthy subjects. Measurements using MEG, PET, and MRI of neurological lesions, and intracranial recordings initially emphasized somewhat different parts of cortex (Allison et al. 1994; Howard et al. 1992; Nobre et al. 1994; Paulesu et al. 1995; Petersen et al. 1988; Petersen & Fiez 1993; Price et al. 1994, 1998; Salmelin et al. 1996; Wandell 2011). By the year 2000, however, Cohen and colleagues summarized the findings by asserting the existence of "a standard model of word reading" that includes "a left inferior temporal region that is specifically devoted to the processing of letter strings" (Cohen et al. 2000). In a confident and controversial move, Cohen and Dehaene labeled the particular VOT region they studied as the visual word form area (VWFA), which added cortical specificity to the classic notion that there is a visual word form system (Warrington & Shallice 1980). This term has endured[1] despite the reluctance of some authors to make such a specific and strong functional assignment (Price & Devlin 2003, 2004). At present, there is consensus that a role for VOT signals in reading does not deny a significant role for other VOT circuit functions or that nonvisual factors influence responses in VOT cortex (Xue et al. 2006, Yoncheva et al. 2010).

Over this same period, a great deal also has been learned about the organization of human visual cortex (Wandell et al. 2007, Wandell & Winawer 2010). We learned that responses to many types of visual stimuli extend into VOT cortex, and regions within VOT are particularly responsive to specific types of visual signals, including color and specific classes of images (Epstein & Kanwisher 1998, Kanwisher

2001, Kanwisher et al. 1997, Zeki 2005, Zeki et al. 1991). These circuits develop over time (Rossion et al. 2002, Tarr & Gauthier 2000), and during the years when we teach children to read, the VOT circuits change their responses (Ben-Shachar et al. 2011, Booth et al. 2001, Brem et al. 2010, Maurer et al. 2010).

Critical White Matter Pathways for Reading Can Be Identified Using Diffusion Imaging, and the Tissue Properties of These Pathways Correlate with Reading Performance

As recently as 15 years ago, there were no noninvasive methods for identifying the major white matter fiber tracts in the living human brain and measuring the tract properties. The development of diffusion imaging methods has changed this situation entirely, so that measurements of the large axon bundles carrying information between cortical regions are now straightforward and performed widely (Conturo et al. 1999, Mori 2007, Mori et al. 1999). Properties of such tracts can be compared across groups (e.g., good versus poor readers), monitored over time (e.g., as children learn to read), and measured in individual subjects (e.g., dyslexic individuals). Although current technology reliably identifies the large fiber tracts located near the middle of the brain, it is not yet possible to confidently identify tracts located at the edges of the white matter, such as where the tracts enter the gray matter folds.

There has been good progress in identifying which large tracts carry signals important for reading (Ben-Shachar et al. 2007c). Many of these studies further identify correlations between the tissue properties of these tracts and specific aspects of skilled reading (Beaulieu et al. 2005, Deutsch et al. 2005, Klingberg et al. 2000, Niogi & McCandliss 2006). The reliably identified fiber tracts are mainly located in regions that carry signals between auditory and language regions, or perhaps between visual and language cortex. The tissue properties of the fiber tracts, for example their degree of myelination, develop significantly

---

[1]A PubMed search of the period 2000 to 2011 identified more than 150 published papers that included the phrase "visual word form area."

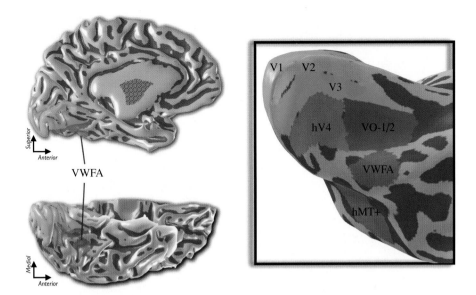

Figure 1

The location of the VWFA in relation to visual field maps. The left images are medial (*top*) and ventral (*bottom*) views of the left hemisphere of a single subject. The surface was defined by segmenting the gray and white matter. The gray shading codes surface curvature: sulci (*dark*) and gyri (*light*). The colored overlays denote the locations of visual field maps and the VWFA that were measured in this subject using fMRI. The image on the right is an expanded view of the VOT cortex, computationally inflated in order to visualize the depths of the sulci. The individual maps are labeled. The VWFA position is shown as a 10-mm radius disk, centered at standard MNI coordinates for the VWFA [−44 −58 −15] (Jobard et al. 2003). fMRI, functional magnetic resonance imaging; MNI, Montreal Neurological Institute; VOT, ventral occipitotemporal; VWFA, visual word form area.

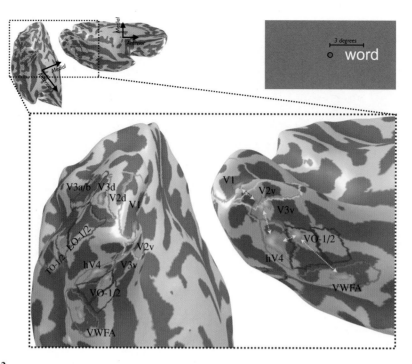

Figure 2

Measuring responses to words within the human visual field maps. A word presented just to the right of fixation (inset, *upper right*) produces predictably localized responses in the hierarchy of the outlined visual field maps (matching **Figure 1**). Two views of the left hemisphere of a subject (inset, *upper left*) are shown expanded in the two main images. The orange overlays represent the amplitudes of functional magnetic resonance imaging responses in a single subject. The posterior view (*left*) is positioned to show visualization of the dorsal (V2d, V3d, V3a/b, LO-1, LO-2, TO-1, and TO-2) and ventral (V2v, V3v, hV4, VO-1, and VO-2) visual field maps and the visual word form area. The ventral view (*right*) emphasizes visualization of activity along the ventral visual field maps. The dotted arrows on the ventral view indicate the proposed information flow between the maps, possibly via U-fibers.

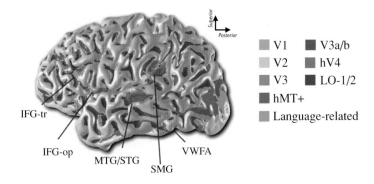

Figure 3

Left hemisphere reading-related areas. The red color overlays on this lateral view of a left hemisphere are relatively anterior cortical locations that are active during reading tasks. The color overlays in the posterior region are the locations of visual field maps in this individual subject. Language-related regions are placed at the MNI coordinates in Jobard et al. (2003). IFG-tr, inferior frontal gyrus, pars triangularis; IFG-op, inferior frontal gyrus, pars opercularis; MTG/STG, middle/superior temporal gyrus, including superior temporal sulcus; SMG, supramarginal gyrus; VWFA, visual word form area.

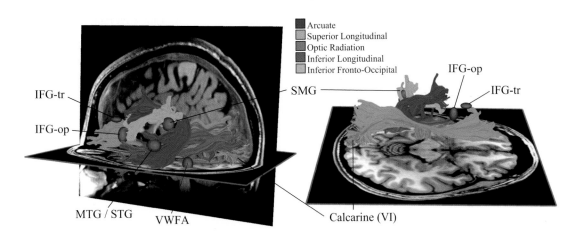

Figure 4

White matter pathways that carry essential reading signals. The two images show several major white matter fascicles in the left hemisphere from different points of view. Three of these fascicles communicate information to and from the occipital lobe. The red ellipsoids are located near cortical regions that respond (fMRI) during reading tasks (Jobard et al. 2003); these are the same locations as shown in **Figure 3**. The ellipsoids are scaled to reflect the uncertainty (standard deviation) of the center positions, measured across studies. The arcuate and superior longitudinal fasciculi include axons that terminate near these cortical regions.

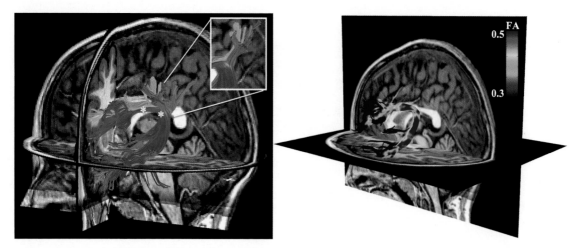

Figure 5

The arcuate fasciculus contains axons that communicate between phonological processing regions. The image on the left shows the arcuate fasciculus (*blue*) and two adjacent fascicles (*orange* and *green*) that pass through the same voxels that contain arcuate axons. The inset shows an expanded view of the region containing these three pathways and their divergent directions. In the image on the right, the arcuate is colored to indicate the fractional anisotropy (FA) along its trajectory. Some of the FA variation is due to tract curvature and partial voluming with neighboring anatomical structures. For example, FA is low at the arcing location where several distinct groups of fibers converge (left image). The effect of such geometric properties and partial voluming can be reduced by measuring the FA in the anterior portion of the tract, which is relatively straight, and the arcuate can be distinguished from nearby tracts.

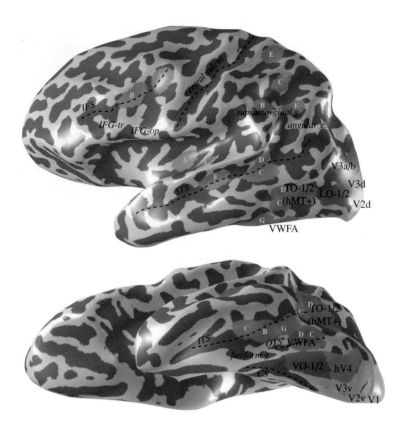

Figure 6

Cortical regions where fMRI responses differ between good and poor readers. Lateral (*top*) and ventral (*bottom*) view of a computationally inflated left hemisphere. The visual field maps were measured using fMRI. Other labeled regions (*purple with yellow letters*) were identified as showing greater responses to visual word stimuli in controls than dyslexics. The positions are reported by (*A*) Paulesu et al. (1996), (*B*) Rumsey et al. (1997), (*C*) Brunswick et al. (1999), (*D*) Paulesu et al. (2001), (*E*) Eden et al. (2004), (*F*) Grünling et al. (2004), (*G*) McCrory et al. (2005). Several of these regions are in VOT, either overlapping or near the VWFA location, which is centered at standard MNI coordinates [−44 −58 −15] (Jobard et al. 2003). CS, calcarine sulcus; OTS, occipitotemporal sulcus; ITS, inferotemporal sulcus.

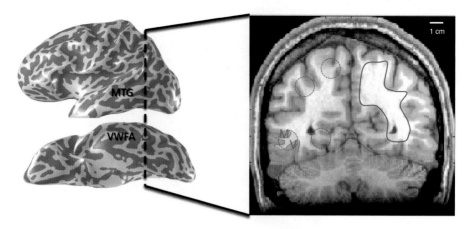

Figure 7

Spatial resolution considerations when analyzing functional responses and white matter pathways using magnetic resonance imaging.

through the first 20 years of life (Bourgeois & Rakic 1993, Lebel et al. 2008, Sowell et al. 2004). The current measurements reveal significant correlations between reading or reading-related behaviors and tissue properties in these tracts. So far, the most consistently observed correlations between white matter tract tissue properties and reading performance are related to the phonological aspects of reading performance, but this field is nascent and further discoveries will follow.

Structures and Signals in Reading Circuits Change During Development and Are Influenced by Training

Both cross-sectional and longitudinal studies have measured the typical development of signals and structures in the reading circuitry (Ben-Shachar et al. 2011, Booth et al. 2001, Brem et al. 2010, Helenius et al. 1999, Maurer et al. 2010, Turkeltaub et al. 2008). There is good agreement across methods and studies that VOT responses and specific white matter structures change with development and that there are correlations between these changes and reading performance. Investigators have also tested whether specific reading interventions change group responses in locations that are part of the neural circuitry of reading (Shaywitz et al. 2004, Simos et al. 2002, Temple et al. 2003).

In summary, instrument sensitivity and signal-processing methods have advanced enormously over the past 30 years. We can assess functional signals and white matter tracts in single subjects during the ages they are learning to read. Data from individuals can be compared with corresponding signals and structures in other subjects from the same age cohort, and in this way neuroimaging tools can help to identify the neural basis for reading difficulties in a particular child. As we accumulate more data, it should be possible to classify individuals according to particular individual differences. We may then be able to devise behavioral tests and individualized training paradigms to identify specific deficits and improve corresponding systems.

FUNCTIONAL NEUROIMAGING OF VISION AND READING

In addition to advances in neuroimaging instrumentation, the past 30 years has seen great progress in the associated signal-processing and visualization methods. The processing and visualization of the measurements is particularly helpful in coordinating findings from different laboratories or subdisciplines. In this section, we offer an overview of the spatial organization in the posterior regions of the brain, from the occipital pole to VOT. The goal of this overview is to summarize the findings and to explain limitations in current measurements. Our understanding of the spatial layout of these responses is mainly obtained using functional magnetic resonance imaging (fMRI). Our knowledge about the stimulus specificity and response development comes from a range of different techniques.

Visual Field Maps

A century ago, neurologists discovered that human posterior cortex contains at least one map of the retina: nearby neurons respond principally to stimuli in nearby retinal locations (Henschen 1893, Inouye 1909). Over the next 50 years, multiple maps were discovered in a variety of animal species (Van Essen et al. 2001, Wandell et al. 2007), but as recently as 25 years ago, the number and spatial organization of the human maps were uncertain (Horton & Hoyt 1991a,b). During the past 25 years, we learned that visual field maps tile virtually all of occipital cortex and that maps are also present in parietal and temporal cortex (Wandell & Winawer 2010).

The general organization of the human retinotopic maps is the same in different individuals (**Figure 1**, see color insert), although the absolute size of the maps varies by severalfold (Andrews et al. 1997, Dougherty et al. 2003, Stensaas et al. 1974). V1 is located in

fMRI: functional magnetic resonance imaging

Retinotopic maps: mapping of visual space onto the brain surface such that neighboring neurons respond to neighboring parts of the visual field

Magnetic susceptibility: the degree of magnetization of the material or tissue in response to a magnetic field applied by the MR scanner

the calcarine sulcus. V1 receives input from the retina via the LGN, and it also receives substantial feedback connections from other parts of cortex. Neurons in V1 respond to visual stimuli in the contralateral hemifield.

In primates, V1 is surrounded by two additional maps, V2 and V3, that also respond to stimuli in the contralateral visual field. A series of maps extend anterior from V2/V3 on both the dorsal and ventral surfaces. Together, these maps cover the occipital lobe and much of the posterior temporal and parietal lobes. A strip within the VOT has not been identified as retinotopic. This region is surrounded by retinotopic cortex laterally (LO-1, LO-1, TO-1, and TO-2) and medially (hV4, VO-1, VO-2, PHC-1, and PHC-2). As techniques for measuring maps improve, new maps continue to be reported. Regions on the lateral surface of occipital and temporal cortex that were thought to be nonretinotopic (Tootell et al. 1996) have now been mapped; visually responsive regions not yet identified as retinotopic may be revealed as retinotopic as measurements improve.

Currently, two significant methodological problems limit fMRI measurements in VOT. First, the anterior portion of the VOT is on the ventral portion of the temporal lobe, near the auditory canal. There is a significant difference in magnetic susceptibility between the brain and the auditory canal. Special methods are needed to obtain reliable fMRI signals in regions near large susceptibility changes, and these methods are not performed in most fMRI experiments. Second, a large vein—the transverse dural sinus—passes near the surface of VOT. This vein often passes near the hV4 map and travels forward toward the anterior temporal lobe over the nonretinotopic region of VOT. The magnetic field near this vein is inhomogeneous, and this interferes with fMRI measurements (Winawer et al. 2010). The artifact from this venous sinus is quite large when measuring with 3-mm voxels, and somewhat smaller for 1.5-mm voxels (K. Weiner, personal communication). The precise relationship of the artifacts, caused by anatomical structures, in relation to functional tissue such as the visual

field maps can vary across individuals. However, neither of these artifacts—the auditory canal susceptibility or the transverse dural sinus—is removed by averaging. It is possible that new methods will develop that enable reliable measurements of the responses in these VOT regions. For now, the reader should understand that even though important signals can be identified, investigators do not have a clear view of responses in the entire VOT cortex.

Early Visual Cortex

A written word stimulus evokes a response pattern in the cone photoreceptors and retinal neurons. These signals are communicated to the LGN and ultimately to V1 and other cortical maps for further processing. The cortical activity evoked by printed words in successive stages of the visual hierarchy (V1, V2, V3, and hV4) can be measured in individual subjects (**Figure 2**, see color insert). The response to a small word is confined to discrete locations within each of the visual field maps at a position determined by the location of the word form in the visual field.

These measurements confirm that the signal is passing through visual cortex, and the amplitude and spatial distribution of the activity can be tested against the expected distribution. But important diagnostic information is missing from these blood oxygen–level dependent (BOLD) measurements. The circuitry communicates in both directions between most of the connections: say, from the LGN to V1 and then from V1 back to the LGN, or from V1 to V2 and vice versa. The timing of the BOLD signal used in most fMRI applications is too slow to separate these interacting signals. It is entirely possible that one side of this signaling system is deficient, but not the other. In theory, a deficit in either the feedforward or feedback signal could lead to an unexpected fMRI signal in, say, primary visual cortex (Wandell & Smirnakis 2009). To distinguish these signals requires the use of technologies with better temporal resolution. Significant advances have been made in the methods for coordinating EEG measures with structural MRI measures and for localizing these signals to cortical structures (Appelbaum et al. 2006, Dale & Sereno 1993, Hagler et al. 2009).

Motion-Selective Cortex

There is a series of retinotopic maps on the lateral surface at the occipital-temporal border (Amano et al. 2009, Huk et al. 2002, Kolster et al. 2010) (**Figure 2**). Several of these maps appear to be homologous to middle temporal visual area (MT) and its surrounding maps in animal models. The maps in this region are called the human motion complex, or hMT+. In animal models, MT was identified first by its retinotopic map; subsequently, it was found to have a large population of motion-direction-selective neurons (Zeki 1980, 2005) and dense myelination. The homologous region was identified in human because of its strong response to moving stimuli (Tootell et al. 1995, Zeki et al. 1991) and comparable myelination (Tootell & Taylor 1995).

One prominent theory of reading disability is that magnocellular neurons in the LGN, which are the main source of stimulus-driven excitation for MT (Maunsell et al. 1990), are dysfunctional in poor readers (Cornelissen et al. 1998; Livingstone et al. 1991; Lovegrove et al. 1980, 1982; Stein 2001). Three groups have confirmed that hMT+ responses are weaker in poor readers compared with controls (Demb et al. 1997, Eden et al. 1996). HMT+ is responsive during reading, and there is a relationship between performance on phonological awareness tasks and contrast sensitivity of motion-selective cortex in controls (Ben-Shachar et al. 2007a). The relationship between hMT+ responses and other parts of the reading circuitry is not yet understood. But if one believes that visual cortex learns to recognize specific patterns associated with word forms, it is plausible that hMT+ regions learn the specific pattern of eye movements and control of attention that are used in skilled reading. Perhaps hMT+ circuitry learns these elements of reading behavior (Wandell 2011).

Ventral Occipitotemporal Cortex

Several visual specializations are located within VOT cortex (**Figure 1**), a region nestled between the ventral occipital maps (VO-1, VO-2) and the hMT+ maps (TO-1, TO-2). Both the VWFA and a face-selective region (the fusiform face area, FFA) are located within VOT. These regions are in close proximity to one another and both are near the foveal representation of the VO retinotopic visual field maps. It is not common for investigators to measure both visual field maps and these object-selective responses; consequently, we have much less information than we should about the spatial arrangement of these regions.

Several VWFA response sensitivity properties support the hypothesis that the VWFA is a reading specialization. These are: (*a*) VWFA responses are insensitive to retinotopic position (Cohen et al. 2002) and leTTeR CaSe (Dehaene et al. 2001, 2004), (*b*) lesions near the VWFA can produce pure alexia (Cohen et al. 2003, Gaillard et al. 2006, Leff et al. 2001, Warrington & Shallice 1980), (*c*) VOT responses are sensitive to bigram frequency (Binder et al. 2006, Vinckier et al. 2007), (*d*) there is a word-specific pattern of orthographic priming in VWFA (Dehaene et al. 2001), and (*e*) VWFA responses differ between words and their mirror images (Dehaene et al. 2010a, Pegado et al. 2010). But the data supporting these claims are not complete. For example, the assertion of position invariance or case insensitivity is supported by coarse measurements, but this observation may be overturned as measurement resolution and sensitivity increase.

There are two general hypotheses as to why the VWFA responds more powerfully than other cortical locations while subjects view words (Ben-Shachar et al. 2007c). One hypothesis is that the VWFA circuits learn to respond to the specific line contours in word forms (Szwed et al. 2009). The relatively large responses to words, then, are present because VOT circuits become specialized from exposure to hundreds of thousands of words. A

hMT+: human motion complex

Phonological awareness: ability to manipulate the sounds of speech ("What is bat minus /b/ ?"); used as a predictor of reading difficulties

VWFA response sensitivity: a stimulus-referred approach where the responses to a stimulus embedded in multiple levels of noise are measured

second hypothesis is that the VWFA is simply the location in visual cortex that is most densely interconnected with language regions (Devlin et al. 2006, Powell et al. 2006, Twomey et al. 2011). On this view, word-specific responses arise because there is an interaction between language systems and visual cortex during reading. This hypothesis is supported by the evoked potential data showing that lateralization of the putative VWFA response appears to follow the lateralization of language (Cai et al. 2008) and that auditory signals can modulate the response of VOT (Dehaene et al. 2010b, Yoncheva et al. 2010). These two hypotheses are not mutually exclusive and may both turn out to be true.

Analyses of the VWFA are advancing, and two issues should be resolved in the next few years. First, the spatial relationship between the retinotopic maps and the VWFA and FFA regions should clarify. Until quite recently, very few groups measured visual field maps, the VWFA, the FFA, and other specializations simultaneously (Ben-Shachar et al. 2007b, Brewer et al. 2005, Szwed et al. 2011). Understanding the spatial relationship of these regions requires measurements in individual subjects at relatively high spatial resolution. For example, one recent high-resolution (1.4 mm) method separates the FFA and VWFA peaks by only 9 mm (Song et al. 2010). Given this small separation, understanding the pattern of activity requires single-subject analyses and voxel resolutions below the typical 3 mm.

Second, we should learn more about VWFA stimulus selectivity. Many regions of cortex respond to written text (**Figure 2**), and the VWFA responds to many stimulus classes. One would like a model that predicts the VWFA response to any arbitrary stimulus. Modeling these responses has not been a focus of neuroimaging. Rather, studies typically rely on the subtraction methodology and response comparisons (contrasts) between stimuli of interest (e.g., text) with a series of control stimuli. It is clear that the size of the text versus control mismatch will depend on the precise nature of the text stimulus and comparison (Szwed et al. 2011). Rather than contrast the response to a few types of patterns, it is preferable to build a model of the responses. This approach is being developed in visual cortex (Dumoulin & Wandell 2008, Kay et al. 2008, Thirion et al. 2006), and it is desirable to extend these models to VOT regions—including both the VWFA and FFA. This will be a challenging task because the VWFA response can be influenced by many experimental conditions, including language tasks.

There has been some quantification of VWFA sensitivity to different stimulus classes. For example, Ben-Shachar et al. (2007b) measured the size of the VWFA sensitivity to words, false fonts, and line drawings. Because the BOLD response has no units and it is not closely tied to a specific neural signal, Ben-Shachar and colleagues used a stimulus-referred approach to quantify sensitivity (Salmelin et al. 1996, 2000; Sperling et al. 2005). Specifically, they introduced noise into these stimuli and measured the noise power when the VWFA responses were equated. The VWFA is about 15% more sensitive to words than line drawings (0.82–0.72/0.82); the VWFA is 60% more sensitive to words than false fonts (0.82–0.3/0.82). The VWFA responds to these patterns during a variety of tasks including passive fixation even though the subject is not reading actively or involved in a language task. Sensitivity to words in the presence of noise has also been measured behaviorally; good readers are more resistant to noise than are poor readers (Sperling et al. 2005, 2006).

Based on current findings, it appears likely that the VWFA is part of the typical reading pathway; hence, assessments of reading difficulties should include tests of the responses in the VOT generally and the VWFA specifically.

Development and the VOT

Typically, children start formal reading training at age 5–6 years, toward the end of the critical period for early visual cortex (Murphy et al. 2005). One hypothesis is that instructional training should be coordinated with the process of neural development. On this view, a child's instruction should be delivered when the systems needed to learn the material are adequately developed but still have a potential for further plasticity that enables them to respond to instruction. In this case, the critical period for linking language and sensory systems should extend beyond the critical period of early visual cortex.

Decoding the visual pattern quickly is important for skilled reading. Hence, there is value in training cortex to automatize the recognition of common word forms. In engineering practice such efficiency is obtained by using memory to store information in pre-existing look-up tables. Because there will be novel patterns that may not be stored, there must also be a fallback algorithmic mechanism to decode visual patterns into phonological representations (e.g., letter-by-letter reading). Computational algorithms are typically much slower and require more energy than look-up tables, but they guarantee a reasonable decoding in most cases. These two systems are at the heart of the dual-route theory of reading (Coltheart et al. 2001, 2010). Using this theory as a framework, one would interpret learning as the process of developing the algorithm and then developing a means to store common results in the look-up table mechanism.

The neural development of word recognition is being examined by many groups. Using cross-sectional designs, many groups find a developmental change in VOT responses to single-word reading tasks (Booth et al. 2001; Brem et al. 2006, 2010; Church et al. 2008; Maurer et al. 2007; Turkeltaub et al. 2008). A theory of VOT development is that the increased response amplitude reflects the fact that children learn the automatic mapping from orthography to phonology. In a longitudinal design, Ben-Shachar et al. (2011) measured children's (age 7–15 years) VWFA responses to words presented in different levels of noise. Sensitivity increases over this age range, and the size of the increase correlates with the size of improvement in sight-word efficiency (rapidly recognizing a word from a nonword). The cortical surface area of the VWFA follows

an interesting and perhaps surprising pattern. The size increases until the age of 12 years and then decreases.

Reading training transforms EEG responses in posterior cortex. When adults see a word, the occipital electrodes produce a small positive response followed by a larger negative response at 170 ms (Bentin et al. 1999, Nobre et al. 1994). The negative response amplitude is larger for words than control stimuli (word tuning). In children prior to reading instruction, the initial positive response is larger than in adults, and the negative response is 210 ms later (Spironelli & Angrilli 2009). There is no word tuning. After children learn letter–speech sound correspondences, word tuning develops. The timing remains sluggish compared to adult (Brem et al. 2010, Maurer et al. 2007).

It has been proposed that learning to recognize words colonizes neighboring cortical territory that would be devoted to processing other forms, such as faces (Cantlon et al. 2011, Dehaene et al. 2010b). This hypothesis implies that learning to recognize words stretches the learning capacity of VOT cortex.

Anterior Systems for Reading and Language

Cortical circuits specialized for seeing words must communicate with circuits specialized in phonology and language, and understanding the reading circuitry requires us to specify the connections and role of these parts. For investigators comfortable with the compact orderly representation of the visual field maps, the complex array of phonological and linguistic tasks and the characterization of the cortical responses are daunting. In visual neuroscience, investigators generally agree on the parts list (V1, V2, V3, etc.). Measurements are now typically made on a single-subject level aimed at understanding and modeling the precise computations that these regions perform.

Although neuroimaging of language has not yet mapped cortical regions with similar precision, there has been progress in identifying cortical circuitry that is critical for reading and

Phonology: the study of how sounds are organized and used in natural languages

language (Jobard et al. 2003, Shaywitz et al. 2008, Vigneau et al. 2011) (**Figure 3**, see color insert). In a meta-analysis aimed at understanding the neural bases for the dual-route theory of reading, Jobard et al. (2003) found a set of repeatable functional activities that cluster in several distinct regions (**Figure 3**). This meta-analysis offers several likely target regions for projections from VOT cortex. By knowing the parts, finding connections between the circuits for seeing words and those extracting linguistic information should now be possible.

WHITE MATTER PATHWAYS AND READING

The human brain has an enormous number of neural connections. If the axons within a single cubic millimeter of cortex are laid out end to end, they extend about 3 kilometers (Braitenberg & Schüz 1991); this shows that even at the finest scale the cortex is massively interconnected. At a coarser scale the cortical gray matter and cerebral white matter have very similar volumes. Human cortical gray matter, which contains both neurons and local connections, has a volume of roughly 460 cm³. The cerebral white matter volume, which contains exclusively connections, is nearly as large at 380 cm³ (Walhovd et al. 2005).

During development the white matter axons are guided between cortical destinations by molecular signaling mechanisms (Goodman & Shatz 1993). Damage to certain groups of axons (fascicles) has specific neurological consequences, and a prominent view in neurology is that many of the defining characteristics of human thought can be explained by understanding these connections (Geschwind 1965a). For example, Wernicke proposed that cortex is a mosaic of sensory and motor representations with functions arising from cortical interactions determined by connections (Wernicke 1874).

It was not possible to identify specific fascicles in the living human brain until recently, when diffusion-weighted imaging and computational procedures enabled such measurements (Basser 1995, Conturo et al.

1999, Le Bihan et al. 2001, Mori et al. 1999). About a dozen major fascicles that carry intrahemispheric signals can be reliably identified using diffusion-weighted imaging; in addition, the corpus callosum contains major fascicles that carry interhemispheric information (Mori 2007, Wakana et al. 2004). Many smaller fascicles (U-fibers) make short-range connections (1–3 cm) between nearby cortical regions. These travel parallel to the cortical surface rather than diving deep into the white matter.

There are several limitations in the ability to measure human fascicles. First, fascicles are located in close proximity to one another; at certain locations it is difficult to distinguish whether a measured voxel contains axons from just one fascicle or several. Methods are just developing that appropriately estimate the core and periphery of major fascicles (Yeatman et al. 2011). Second, axons do not necessarily travel the full length of a fascicle. Some axons enter and exit along the fascicle trajectory, so that the fascicle is akin to a highway with entrances and exits (Catani et al. 2003). Hence, the axons may differ when locations along the length of a fascicle are compared. Third, the ability to find fascicles and estimate the tissue properties of these fascicles depends on a number of factors, including curvature, thickness, proximity to the cortex, and crossing fascicles. Consequently, diffusion differences between fascicles may be caused by any of these factors.

Although there are limitations, it is also true that great progress has been made. In the past 15 years we have advanced from no measurements of white matter fascicles in the living human brain to routine measurements of many fascicles. During this time we also learned about significant relationships between the fascicle properties and reading.

Intra-Hemispheric Reading Pathways

At least five large white matter fascicles are candidates for carrying signals essential for reading (**Figure 4**, see color insert); improper functioning of any of these may interfere with skilled reading. The optic radiation (green) connects the lateral geniculate nucleus of the thalamus and primary visual cortex. Both the inferior longitudinal fasciculus (ILF, purple) and inferior fronto-occipital fasciculus (orange) connect with visual cortex and may carry critical feedforward and feedback information. The arcuate fasciculus (AF, dark blue) comprises axons that connect with phonological regions in the temporal lobe and language areas in prefrontal cortex. Some authors prefer to describe the arcuate as part of the superior longitudinal fasciculus (light blue), though in our view the two can be distinguished at several places.

Signals traversing the relatively short distance between V1 and VOT cortex are probably carried by U-fibers, not major fascicles. But it is likely that at some point orthographic signals in VOT are communicated to more frontal areas along a major fascicle (Catani et al. 2003). It has been suggested based on neurosurgical observations that VWFA and language regions are connected by axons that enter the ILF (Epelbaum et al. 2008). The ability to securely identify the white matter carrying orthographic signals in healthy humans will be a valuable advance.

The Arcuate Fasciculus

The AF has long been considered a candidate pathway for carrying phonological and language information (Geschwind 1965a,b). Some authors have speculated about specific functionality of AF signals. One hypothesis is that AF axons carry signals used for the manipulation and articulation of phonological information (Hickok & Poeppel 2004, 2007). Another is that AF signals reactivate phonological material in verbal working memory (Friedmann & Gvion 2003) and short-term storage and verbal repetition of speech (Catani & Ffytche 2005, Glasser & Rilling 2008, Rilling et al. 2008, Saur et al. 2008). The AF is a large bundle, and all of these hypotheses may be true (Bernal & Ardila 2009).

Most of our knowledge about reading and the AF are based on neurological cases, and these models are based on interpreting the correspondence between lesion sites and behavioral deficits. For example, using methods to compare diffusion data from a single individual to a group of healthy controls, Rauschecker et al. (2009) report the case of a child without an arcuate who was unable to develop skilled reading. Studies are now underway to more fully elucidate the role of the AF in normal reading. In a recent study with healthy children, Yeatman et al. (2011) measured reading and AF properties in healthy children aged 7–11. Measuring a portion of the white matter where the AF could be isolated, Yeatman et al. found that radial diffusivity is higher for children with better phonological awareness. This correlation is present in the left AF but not in adjacent fascicles or the right AF. These measurements support the hypothesis that the left AF carries signals essential for phonological awareness, an important component of skilled reading.

Temporo-Parietal White Matter

Klingberg et al. (2000) were the first to report a white matter difference between good and poor adult readers. This difference was confirmed in studies with children (Beaulieu et al. 2005, Deutsch et al. 2005, Nagy et al. 2004, Niogi & McCandliss 2006), but the precise location of the difference with respect to the major fascicles has been difficult to isolate. The largest difference between good and poor readers is in the corona radiata, a fascicle between the AF and the large band of callosal fibers. It has not been possible, however, to be confident that the difference is caused by tissue properties confined to the fascicle; alternative hypotheses are described in Ben-Shachar et al. (2007c).

Two problems limit the ability to locate diffusion differences between good and poor readers to a specific fascicle. First, the white matter difference is in a region where several fascicles are in close proximity (**Figure 5**, see color insert). Second, in most studies the differences were measured by comparing groups of good and poor readers rather than individual subjects, and the location is specified in atlas coordinates. Even when restricted to control groups, any coordinate will have mixtures of fiber

AF: arcuate fasciculus

Radial diffusivity: the apparent diffusivity measured in the direction perpendicular to the length of a fascicle; to be differentiated from the apparent diffusivity measured along the length (axial diffusivity)

groups at a particular coordinate. Hua et al. (2008) document the limits in analyzing specific fascicles in group studies where all the subjects are transformed into a common atlas system. These authors coregistered 28 brains and created a fiber tract template. No voxel in the AF template contained AF data from more than 20 of the 28 subjects; the majority of voxels in the AF template included AF data from less than half of the subjects (10–14). When comparing between two distinct groups (e.g., good and poor readers), the problem may be even worse. Thus, it is difficult to confidently identify a fascicle on the basis of group-averaged differences.

Callosal Pathways

A postmortem analysis of Dejerine's alexic patient revealed a large set of lesions including damage to the posterior corpus callosum (Dejerine 1891). Dejerine was uncertain of the significance of the callosal lesion, but subsequent neurological studies provided compelling reasons to believe that this pathway carries information that is used in reading (Damasio & Damasio 1983, Wandell 2011).

Three modern reports in healthy subjects show a correlation between the tissue properties of a posterior callosal region and reading. Specifically, in a small region of the posterior callosum, radial diffusivity is correlated with certain behaviors (e.g., phonological awareness) that are essential for skilled reading (Dougherty et al. 2007, Frye et al. 2008, Odegard et al. 2009). Where these fibers project to cortex is unsettled; preliminary analyses in our laboratory suggest that they project to the angular or superior temporal gyrus (Kevan et al. 2012).

DYSLEXIA

In the Introduction we identified a long-term goal of identifying the computations of all the neural circuits used in reading. It is important to look for ways to use our current understanding even as we work toward the larger goal. One application is to use neuroimaging measurements to predict the likelihood of success of specific interventions. For example, EEG potentials (Maurer et al. 2009, Molfese 2000) and MR measures (Davis et al. 2010; Hoeft et al. 2007, 2011) have been used to predict reading outcomes. Such measures can be used to select the best intervention for an individual (Gabrieli 2009).

Many neuroimaging measurements compare responses in good and poor readers, but there are critical limitations in our ability to explain these findings (Shaywitz et al. 2008). One limitation is the diversity of findings themselves. For example, some investigators report that the principal difference is in temporoparietal cortex, and others report that principal differences are in inferior temporo-occipital cortex. A second limitation concerns how to integrate measurements from different modalities [EEG, MEG, fMRI, and diffusion tensor imaging (DTI)]. The fMRI responses are not driven by the same neural signals that give rise to scalp measurements (Logothetis & Wandell 2004), and EEG and MEG signals arise from different sources (Sharon et al. 2007). Hence, the N170 measured by an occipital electrode in EEG may not measure the same neural signal as the VWFA response measured by fMRI. To combine the data across the variety of imaging technologies requires models that can integrate the data from different measurements into a coherent understanding of the underlying neural circuitry; such modeling is a hope, not yet a reality.

Good and Poor Readers

Despite some limitations, neuroimaging has provided useful guidance concerning dyslexia and potential interventions. Using both temporally and spatially resolved methods, many investigators have shown that responses to single-word identification are smaller in left VOT cortex of poor readers compared to good readers.

Salemelin and colleagues reported that MEG responses to words localized to left inferior occipitotemporal cortex differ significantly between good and poor adult readers

(Helenius et al. 1999, Salmelin et al. 1996). These responses arise within 200 ms of stimulus presentation, and the amplitude of these responses is significantly lower in poor readers than in good readers. Using MEG in children, Simos et al. (2000, 2002, 2007) report differences between poor and good readers in the same left occipitotemporal regions, but at slightly delayed times (220 ms). They further report differences in left temporo-parietal cortex near the superior temporal gyrus.

The earliest PET and fMRI studies included measurements of responses of good and poor readers. The visualization tools and instrumental sensitivity did not produce a clear picture of the differences. For example, Paulesu et al. (1996) reported differences between controls and compensated adult dyslexics in Broca's area and Wernicke's area, but not in VOT cortex. They concluded that dyslexic subjects "activated the same brain areas as controls, but unlike controls, they did not activate them in concert." Rumsey and colleagues (Rumsey et al. 1997, Horwitz et al. 1998) used a range of behavioral tests to understand the relationship between specific brain regions and different components of reading and found many differences between good and poor readers, including a significant VOT response difference on orthographic decision-making (e.g., which is a word: hoal or hole?). Subsequently, Brunswick et al. (1999) and Paulesu et al. (2001) found that good and poor reader responses differed in a region they labeled the left inferior/middle temporal region that falls in VOT cortex at the VWFA location (Wandell 2011).

Pugh et al. (2001) offered a neurobiological account based on a dorsal and ventral stream for reading. They suggested that the dorsal stream, which includes the left angular gyrus, dominates early reading and interpretation of the relationship between orthography and phonology. Over time, the ventral stream, which includes the VOT circuitry, develops into a fast word-recognition system that is needed for fluent reading. Their neurobiological account matches the dual-route theory (Coltheart et al. 2001).

Maisog et al. (2008) performed a quantitative meta-analysis of the literature and found that the most reliable difference between good and poor readers was in left extrastriate cortex, including the region of the VWFA. The reduced responses are not restricted to reading: The region responds less during picture naming, which suggests VOT is involved in integrating phonology and visual information broadly (McCrory et al. 2005).

Although there is general agreement on the importance of VOT cortex, the precision of the measurements could be improved. To visualize the locations identified in several of these reports, we draw the positions as 1-cm-radius disks on segmented cortical gray matter of an individual subject. The gray matter surface is inflated to visualize the sulci (**Figure 6**, see color insert). In the sidebar titled Responses in the Medial Temporal Gyrus and the VWFA, we describe the challenges in localizing responses in group studies. Additional factors that may contribute to differences between studies are the age of subjects and the fMRI task.

Interventions

Many recent reading interventions were guided by the hypothesis that dyslexia arises from an inability to perceive and manipulate the sounds of speech (phonological awareness and decoding) (Snow et al. 1998). This hypothesis is based on two key findings. First, a powerful correlation exists between the ability to perceive the sounds of speech and the ability to read (Bradley & Bryant 1978, Stanovich et al. 1984). Second, explicit training in speech sounds can improve reading (Bradley & Bryant 1983, Torgesen et al. 1999, Wagner & Torgesen 1987). Reading interventions based on the phonological awareness theory use a variety of training paradigms. In some interventions children are trained to hear phonemes, in others they are trained to hear the association between sounds and text, and in some cases children are trained to hear nonlanguage sounds such as tones. Modern treatments based on phonological awareness have not ended dyslexia, and there are open questions about the interpretation of phonemic awareness interventions. For example, some authors challenge the hypothesis that learning to hear phonemes, without teaching the sound-text connection, improves reading (Castles & Coltheart 2004).

Several groups have studied changes in the functional response of poor readers following phonological interventions. For example, in an fMRI study with children, Shaywitz et al. (2004) found that a phonologically based intervention transformed the left occipitotemporal system. In a recent review, they write, "the failure of the word form area to function properly in dyslexic children and young adults is responsible for their characteristic inefficient, slow reading" (Shaywitz & Shaywitz 2008). Similar increases in left VOT responses after reading interventions have been reported using MEG (Simos et al. 2007). In contrast, Meyler and colleagues (Meyler et al. 2007, 2008) used fMRI to measure the effect of phonological training using a sentence comprehension task. They found that training increases responses in the left angular gyrus region. They write, "Conspicuously absent in the present data is any hint of an effect of either reading ability or intensive remediation on activation in left occipito-temporal areas" (Meyler et al. 2008, p. 2588). Eden et al. (2004) measured fMRI responses during phonological tasks in adults who underwent reading remediation. They found an increased response in the left angular gyrus as well as in the fusiform/parahippocampal gyrus anterior to the VWFA. The pattern of outcomes does not simplify by incorporating results from the other investigations (Aylward et al. 2003, Odegard et al. 2008, Temple et al. 2003).

In addition to measurements of functional responses, there are reports that reading interventions change both white matter (Keller & Just 2009) and gray matter (Krafnick et al. 2011). So far, these measures have failed to find changes in the same reading networks found by fMRI. Many factors could account for these differences, and as measurement technologies improve, we may hope to find converging results across different methodologies.

RESPONSES IN THE MEDIAL TEMPORAL GYRUS AND THE VWFA

Acquiring MRI data involves many experimental and processing choices, each of which may have important consequences for scientific conclusions. The MRI acquisition and processing choices can be opaque to casual readers of the MRI literature. This sidebar illustrates the impact that certain methodological choices can have on scientific conclusions.

When measuring the whole brain, investigators use a range of voxel sizes and smoothing. It is not uncommon to see measurements with 5-mm isotropic voxels followed by 9-mm FWHM (full width at half maximum) spatial averaging. In this case, functional signals from a single point in the brain are pooled over a region roughly the size of the overlaid disks (**Figure 7**, see color insert). Data in many studies are further combined across brains, each with its own unique gyral and sulcal patterns.

An anatomical region in the VOT is shown in a single coronal slice in **Figure 7**. The point labeled on the lateral aspect of the brain is near the middle temporal gyrus; the point labeled on the ventral surface is in the occipitotemporal sulcus. These regions are separated by centimeters when measured along the cortical surface. However, they are separated by only ~4–5 mm in the brain volume. If one pools fMRI signals over 5- to 10-mm regions, there is no realistic chance of reliably distinguishing responses originating near the middle temporal gyrus from those in the occipitotemporal sulcus. This confusion is very problematic because a long history of neuroscientific exploration has established that the organization and computation of neurons is best understood by proximity on the cortical sheet. Neurons that are nearby in the volume only due to the cortical folding pattern may perform very different functions, and their responses should not be averaged.

This problem is not unique to the study of reading or VOT. As a second example, consider the pre- and postcentral gyri, which perform motor and somatosensory functions, respectively. These gyri are in close proximity within the volume, but one would not want to average their responses. Throughout the brain, regions at the bottom of sulci are in close proximity when described in

(Continued)

One hypothesis concerning the effects of remediation is based on the lateralization of reading signals (Pugh et al. 2001). A number of groups have observed that in poor readers responses to words are relatively right lateralized, and that after reading interventions, MEG and fMRI responses in ventral occipital cortex become left lateralized (Maisog et al. 2008, Shaywitz et al. 2008, Simos et al. 2002, Spironelli et al. 2010).

CONCLUSION

A picture of the functional responses and anatomical structures essential for skilled reading is coming into focus. In the early years of neuroimaging, it might have been hoped that the list would be small and that differences between good and poor readers could be summarized by a spot in cortex or a single lesion in white matter. Just as genomics has taught us that human performance is rarely dependent on a single gene, neuroimaging has taught us that human performance is rarely dependent on a single brain structure or a single class of neurons.

By emphasizing measurements that can be made in individual subjects, we hope to develop methods so that dysfunction can be understood from the differences in an individual who is struggling to read compared to the typical set of responses in good readers. We should anticipate that each individual may deviate in his or her own way, and there may be individualized interventions to address the dysfunction of particular cortical circuits.

As instrumentation and methods improve, we will be able to follow signals and measure structures with increasing precision. Consequently, we will find many more statistically reliable differences between groups or between individuals. Anticipating these advances, we can expect that experimental designs will change from an effort to identify reliable statistical differences to designs that evaluate quantitative models of signals and structures. Individuals may be reliably different from one another, but only some differences will

the volume; these regions are separated by less than 1 cm when measured through the white matter. One indication of imprecise spatial positioning is the localization of principal activation to the white matter rather than the gray matter.

Modern MRI scanners can perform functional measurements at 2-mm or better resolution within individual subjects. Because the cortical sheet thickness is 2 to 3 mm, and the opposite sides of sulci are separated by about 2 mm, smaller voxels reduce the scope of the problem. Better spatial localization of the signals can be achieved by segmenting white and gray matter and averaging along the gray matter surface. Tools for achieving good segmentations are now freely distributed and are commonly used in certain subfields of neuroimaging (Fischl et al. 2004, Yushkevich et al. 2006).

Issues of spatial resolution are also important to consider in diffusion imaging and tractography (**Figure 7**, right side). Notice that the white matter separating various sulci on the lateral and ventral surface is about 3- to 5-mm thick. The standard size of a diffusion voxel is 2 mm isotropic, so that for tractography one would obtain no more than two measurements between the opposite sides of a typical gyrus. Given these measurement limitations, we do not obtain precise information about the location on a gyrus where a fascicular projection terminates. A fair heuristic of the measurement precision is to imagine a surface connecting the base of the sulci (**Figure 7**, red outline). Projections of the white matter up to this surface, before the white matter becomes thin in the gyri, are relatively secure. The figure illustrates that we can obtain better estimates of fascicles projecting to some cortical regions than others. Given diffusion measurements with sufficiently high signal to noise, the shape and gross trajectory of major white matter fascicles and their diffusion characteristics can be reliably measured in individuals (Danielian et al. 2010).

interfere with performance. Hence, we anticipate a future in which the current emphasis on hypothesis testing for differences is replaced by measurements that characterize system performance.

An enormous amount has been learned about the reading circuitry over the past 25 years. In the 1980s, the neural basis of reading was informed mainly by lesion-induced alexias, but reading difficulties in otherwise healthy children were opaque (Wandell 2011). Since those days, we have developed tools that can explore the signals and structures with much better resolution. We have learned how to trace the reading signal as it passes from early visual cortex to VOT, and a compelling case has been made that the VOT contains responses that are essential for reading; these responses can be measured using both spatially and temporally resolved signals. The development of these responses has been measured in healthy children and in children and adults undergoing reading interventions. The white matter pathways that carry signals between VOT and anterior cortical regions, such as the angular gyrus and temporo-parietal cortex, may well clarify in the next few years. There is reason to hope that basic investigations into reading circuits will pay off in the form of practical advice about the intervention that is best suited for an individual child.

FUTURE ISSUES

1. Understand the spatio-temporal reading circuitry transformations from input (retina/V1), through visual, auditory, and language circuitry, to output (semantic access).

2. Quantify the developmental trajectory of gray and white matter structures used for reading.

3. Identify specific structural or functional deficiencies in individual subjects with reading difficulties.

4. Associate specific behavioral traits with specific neural differences.

5. Predict reading difficulties and the likely success of individualized interventions from neuroimaging or behavioral measurements.

DISCLOSURE STATEMENT

The authors are unaware of any affiliation, funding, or financial holdings that might be perceived as affecting the objectivity of this review.

LITERATURE CITED

Allison T, McCarthy G, Nobre A, Puce A, Belger A. 1994. Human extrastriate visual cortex and the perception of faces, words, numbers, and colors. *Cereb. Cortex* 4:544–54

Amano K, Wandell BA, Dumoulin SO. 2009. Visual field maps, population receptive field sizes, and visual field coverage in the human MT+ complex. *J. Neurophysiol.* 102:2704–18

Andrews TJ, Halpern SD, Purves D. 1997. Correlated size variations in human visual cortex, lateral geniculate nucleus, and optic tract. *J. Neurosci.* 17:2859–68

Appelbaum LG, Wade AR, Vildavski VY, Pettet MW, Norcia AM. 2006. Cue-invariant networks for figure and background processing in human visual cortex. *J. Neurosci.* 26:11695–708

Aylward EH, Richards TL, Berninger VW, Nagy WE, Field KM, et al. 2003. Instructional treatment associated with changes in brain activation in children with dyslexia. *Neurology* 61:212–19

Basser P. 1995. Inferring microstructural features and the physiological state of tissues from diffusion-weighted images. *NMR Biomed.* 8:333–44

Beaulieu C, Plewes C, Paulson LA, Roy D, Snook L, et al. 2005. Imaging brain connectivity in children with diverse reading ability. *NeuroImage* 25:1266–71

Ben-Shachar M, Dougherty RF, Deutsch GK, Wandell BA. 2007a. Contrast responsivity in MT+ correlates with phonological awareness and reading measures in children. *NeuroImage* 37:1396–406

Ben-Shachar M, Dougherty RF, Deutsch GK, Wandell BA. 2007b. Differential sensitivity to words and shapes in ventral occipito-temporal cortex. *Cereb. Cortex* 17:1604–11

Ben-Shachar M, Dougherty RF, Deutsch GK, Wandell BA. 2011. The development of cortical sensitivity to visual word forms. *J. Cogn. Neurosci.* 23:2387–99

Ben-Shachar M, Dougherty RF, Wandell BA. 2007c. White matter pathways in reading. *Curr. Opin. Neurobiol.* 17:258–70

Bentin S, Mouchetant-Rostaing Y, Giard MH, Echallier JF, Pernier J. 1999. ERP manifestations of processing printed words at different psycholinguistic levels: time course and scalp distribution. *J. Cogn. Neurosci.* 11:235–60

Bernal B, Ardila A. 2009. The role of the arcuate fasciculus in conduction aphasia. *Brain* 132:2309–16

Binder JR, Lazar RM, Tatemichi TK, Mohr JP, Desmond DW, Ciecierski KA. 1992. Left hemiparalexia. *Neurology* 42:562–69

Binder JR, Medler DA, Westbury CF, Liebenthal E, Buchanan L. 2006. Tuning of the human left fusiform gyrus to sublexical orthographic structure. *NeuroImage* 33:739–48

Booth JR, Burman DD, Van Santen FW, Harasaki Y, Gitelman DR, et al. 2001. The development of specialized brain systems in reading and oral-language. *Child Neuropsychol.* 7:119–41

Bourgeois J, Rakic P. 1993. Changes of synaptic density in the primary visual cortex of the macaque monkey from fetal to adult stage. *J. Neurosci.* 13:2801–20

Bradley L, Bryant PE. 1978. Difficulties in auditory organisation as a possible cause of reading backwardness. *Nature* 271:746–47

Bradley L, Bryant PE. 1983. Categorizing sounds and learning to read—a causal connection. *Nature* 301:419–21

Braitenberg V, Schüz A. 1991. *Anatomy of the Cortex: Statistics and Geometry*. Berlin: Springer-Verlag

Brefczynski JA, DeYoe EA. 1999. A physiological correlate of the "spotlight" of visual attention. *Nat. Neurosci.* 2:370–74

Brem S, Bach S, Kucian K, Guttorm TK, Martin E, et al. 2010. Brain sensitivity to print emerges when children learn letter-speech sound correspondences. *Proc. Natl. Acad. Sci. USA* 107:7939–44

Brem S, Bucher K, Halder P, Summers P, Dietrich T, et al. 2006. Evidence for developmental changes in the visual word processing network beyond adolescence. *NeuroImage* 29:822–37

Brewer AA, Liu J, Wade AR, Wandell BA. 2005. Visual field maps and stimulus selectivity in human ventral occipital cortex. *Nat. Neurosci.* 8:1102–9

Brunswick N, McCrory E, Price CJ, Frith CD, Frith U. 1999. Explicit and implicit processing of words and pseudowords by adult developmental dyslexics: a search for Wernicke's Wortschatz? *Brain* 122(Pt. 10):1901–17

Bub DN, Arguin M, Lecours AR. 1993. Jules Dejerine and his interpretation of pure alexia. *Brain Lang.* 45:531–59

Cai Q, Lavidor M, Brysbaert M, Paulignan Y, Nazir TA. 2008. Cerebral lateralization of frontal lobe language processes and lateralization of the posterior visual word processing system. *J. Cogn. Neurosci.* 20:672–81

Cantlon JF, Pinel P, Dehaene S, Pelphrey KA. 2011. Cortical representations of symbols, objects, and faces are pruned back during early childhood. *Cereb. Cortex* 21:191–99

Castles A, Coltheart M. 2004. Is there a causal link from phonological awareness to success in learning to read? *Cognition* 91:77–111

Catani M, Ffytche DH. 2005. The rises and falls of disconnection syndromes. *Brain* 128:2224–39

Catani M, Jones DK, Donato R, Ffytche DH. 2003. Occipito-temporal connections in the human brain. *Brain* 126:2093–107

Church JA, Coalson RS, Lugar HM, Petersen SE, Schlaggar BL. 2008. A developmental fMRI study of reading and repetition reveals changes in phonological and visual mechanisms over age. *Cereb. Cortex* 18:2054–65

Cohen L, Dehaene S, Naccache L, Lehericy S, Dehaene-Lambertz G, et al. 2000. The visual word form area: spatial and temporal characterization of an initial stage of reading in normal subjects and posterior split-brain patients. *Brain* 123(Pt. 2):291–307

Cohen L, Lehericy S, Chochon F, Lemer C, Rivaud S, Dehaene S. 2002. Language-specific tuning of visual cortex? Functional properties of the visual word form area. *Brain* 125:1054–69

Cohen L, Martinaud O, Lemer C, Lehericy S, Samson Y, et al. 2003. Visual word recognition in the left and right hemispheres: anatomical and functional correlates of peripheral alexias. *Cereb. Cortex* 13:1313–33

Coltheart M, Rastle K, Perry C, Langdon R, Ziegler J. 2001. DRC: a dual route cascaded model of visual word recognition and reading aloud. *Psychol. Rev.* 108:204–56

Coltheart M, Tree JJ, Saunders SJ. 2010. Computational modeling of reading in semantic dementia: comment on Woollams, Lambon Ralph, Plaut, and Patterson (2007). *Psychol. Rev.* 117:256–71; discussion 271–72

Conturo TE, Lori NF, Cull TS, Akbudak E, Snyder AZ, et al. 1999. Tracking neuronal fiber pathways in the living human brain. *Proc. Natl. Acad. Sci. USA* 96:10422–27

Cornelissen PL, Hansen PC, Gilchrist I, Cormack F, Essex J, Frankish C. 1998. Coherent motion detection and letter position encoding. *Vision Res.* 38:2181–91

Dale AM, Sereno MI. 1993. Improved localization of cortical activity by combining EEG and MEG with MRI cortical surface reconstruction: a linear approach. *J. Cogn. Neurosci.* 5:162–76

Damasio AR, Damasio H. 1983. The anatomic basis of pure alexia. *Neurology* 33:1573–83

Danielian LE, Iwata NK, Thomasson DM, Floeter MK. 2010. Reliability of fiber tracking measurements in diffusion tensor imaging for longitudinal study. *NeuroImage* 49:1572–80

Davis N, Fan Q, Compton DL, Fuchs D, Fuchs LS, et al. 2010. Influences of neural pathway integrity on children's response to reading instruction. *Front. Syst. Neurosci.* 4:150

Dehaene S, Jobert A, Naccache L, Ciuciu P, Poline JB, et al. 2004. Letter binding and invariant recognition of masked words: behavioral and neuroimaging evidence. *Psychol. Sci.* 15:307–13

Dehaene S, Naccache L, Cohen L, Bihan DL, Mangin JF, et al. 2001. Cerebral mechanisms of word masking and unconscious repetition priming. *Nat. Neurosci.* 4:752–58

Dehaene S, Nakamura K, Jobert A, Kuroki C, Ogawa S, Cohen L. 2010a. Why do children make mirror errors in reading? Neural correlates of mirror invariance in the visual word form area. *NeuroImage* 49:1837–48

Dehaene S, Pegado F, Braga LW, Ventura P, Nunes Filho G, et al. 2010b. How learning to read changes the cortical networks for vision and language. *Science* 330:1359–64

Dejerine J. 1891. Sur un cas de cecite verbale avec agraphie, suivi d'autopsie. *Mém. Soc. Biol.* 3:197–201

Dejerine J. 1892. Contribution a l'étude anatomoclinique etclinique des differentes varietes de cecite verbal. *C. R. Hebd. Séances Mém. Soc. Biol.* 4:61–90

Dejerine J. 1895. *Anatomie des Centres Nerveux.* Paris: Rueff

Demb JB, Boynton GM, Heeger DH. 1997. Brain activity in visual cortex predicts individual differences in reading performance. *Proc. Natl. Acad. Sci. USA* 94:13363–66

Deutsch GK, Dougherty RF, Bammer R, Siok WT, Gabrieli JD, Wandell B. 2005. Children's reading performance is correlated with white matter structure measured by diffusion tensor imaging. *Cortex* 41:354–63

Devlin JT, Jamison HL, Gonnerman LM, Matthews PM. 2006. The role of the posterior fusiform gyrus in reading. *J. Cogn. Neurosci.* 18:911–22

Dougherty RF, Ben-Shachar M, Deutsch GK, Hernandez A, Fox GR, Wandell BA. 2007. Temporal-callosal pathway diffusivity predicts phonological skills in children. *Proc. Natl. Acad. Sci. USA* 104:8556–61

Dougherty RF, Koch VM, Brewer AA, Fischer B, Modersitzki J, Wandell BA. 2003. Visual field representations and locations of visual areas V1/2/3 in human visual cortex. *J. Vis.* 3:586–98

Dumoulin SO, Wandell BA. 2008. Population receptive field estimates in human visual cortex. *NeuroImage* 39:647–60

Eden GF, Jones KM, Cappell K, Gareau L, Wood FB, et al. 2004. Neural changes following remediation in adult developmental dyslexia. *Neuron* 44:411–22

Eden GF, VanMeter JW, Rumsey JM, Maisog JM, Woods RP, Zeffiro TA. 1996. Abnormal processing of visual motion in dyslexia revealed by functional brain imaging. *Nature* 382:66–69

Epelbaum S, Pinel P, Gaillard R, Delmaire C, Perrin M, et al. 2008. Pure alexia as a disconnection syndrome: new diffusion imaging evidence for an old concept. *Cortex* 44:962–74

Epstein R, Kanwisher N. 1998. A cortical representation of the local visual environment. *Nature* 392:598–601

Fischl B, van der Kouwe A, Destrieux C, Halgren E, Segonne F, et al. 2004. Automatically parcellating the human cerebral cortex. *Cereb. Cortex* 14:11–22

Friedmann N, Gvion A. 2003. Sentence comprehension and working memory limitation in aphasia: a dissociation between semantic-syntactic and phonological reactivation. *Brain Lang.* 86:23–39

Frye RE, Hasan K, Xue L, Strickland D, Malmberg B, et al. 2008. Splenium microstructure is related to two dimensions of reading skill. *Neuroreport* 19:1627–31

Gabrieli JD. 2009. Dyslexia: a new synergy between education and cognitive neuroscience. *Science* 325:280–83

Gaillard R, Naccache L, Pinel P, Clemenceau S, Volle E, et al. 2006. Direct intracranial, FMRI, and lesion evidence for the causal role of left inferotemporal cortex in reading. *Neuron* 50:191–204

Gandhi SP, Heeger DJ, Boynton GM. 1999. Spatial attention affects brain activity in human primary visual cortex. *Proc. Natl. Acad. Sci. USA* 96:3314–19

Geschwind N. 1965a. Disconnexion syndromes in animals and man. I. *Brain* 88:237–94

Geschwind N. 1965b. Disconnexion syndromes in animals and man. II. *Brain* 88:585–644

Glasser MF, Rilling JK. 2008. DTI tractography of the human brain's language pathways. *Cereb. Cortex* 18:2471–82

Goodman CS, Shatz CJ. 1993. Developmental mechanisms that generate precise patterns of neuronal connectivity. *Cell* 72(Suppl.):77–98

Grünling C, Ligges M, Huonker, R, Klingert M, Mentzel, H-J, et al. 2004. Dyslexia: the possible benefit of multimodal integration of fMRI- and EEG-data. *J. Neural Transm.* 111:951–69

Hagler DJ Jr, Halgren E, Martinez A, Huang M, Hillyard SA, Dale AM. 2009. Source estimates for MEG/EEG visual evoked responses constrained by multiple, retinotopically-mapped stimulus locations. *Hum. Brain Mapp.* 30:1290–309

Helenius P, Tarkiainen A, Cornelissen P, Hansen PC, Salmelin R. 1999. Dissociation of normal feature analysis and deficient processing of letter-strings in dyslexic adults. *Cereb. Cortex* 9:476–83

Henschen SE. 1893. On the visual path and centre. *Brain* 16:170–80

Hickok G, Poeppel D. 2004. Dorsal and ventral streams: a framework for understanding aspects of the functional anatomy of language. *Cognition* 92:67–99

Hickok G, Poeppel D. 2007. The cortical organization of speech processing. *Nat. Rev. Neurosci.* 8:393–402

Hoeft F, McCandliss BD, Black JM, Gantman A, Zakerani N, et al. 2011. Neural systems predicting long-term outcome in dyslexia. *Proc. Natl. Acad. Sci. USA* 108:361–66

Hoeft F, Ueno T, Reiss AL, Meyler A, Whitfield-Gabrieli S, et al. 2007. Prediction of children's reading skills using behavioral, functional, and structural neuroimaging measures. *Behav. Neurosci.* 121:602–13

Holmes G. 1918. Disturbances of vision by cerebral lesions. *Br. J. Ophthalmol.* 2:353–84

Horton JC, Hoyt WF. 1991a. Quadrantic visual field defects: a hallmark of lesions in extrastriate (V2/V3) cortex. *Brain* 114:1703–18

Horton JC, Hoyt WF. 1991b. The representation of the visual field in human striate cortex. A revision of the classic Holmes map. *Arch. Ophthalmol.* 109:816–24

Horwitz B, Rumsey JM, Donohue BC. 1998. Functional connectivity of the angular gyrus in normal reading and dyslexia. *Proc. Natl. Acad. Sci. USA* 95:8939–44

Howard D, Patterson K, Wise R, Brown WD, Friston K, et al. 1992. The cortical localization of the lexicons. Positron emission tomography evidence. *Brain* 115(Pt. 6):1769–82

Hua K, Zhang J, Wakana S, Jiang H, Li X, et al. 2008. Tract probability maps in stereotaxic spaces: analyses of white matter anatomy and tract-specific quantification. *NeuroImage* 39:336–47

Huk AC, Dougherty RF, Heeger DJ. 2002. Retinotopy and functional subdivision of human areas MT and MST. *J. Neurosci.* 22:7195–205

Inouye T. 1909. *Die Sehstörungen bei Schussverletzungen der kortikalen Sehsphäre.* Leipzig, Germany: Engelmann

Jobard G, Crivello F, Tzourio-Mazoyer N. 2003. Evaluation of the dual route theory of reading: a meta-analysis of 35 neuroimaging studies. *NeuroImage* 20:693–712

Kanwisher N. 2001. Faces and places: of central (and peripheral) interest. *Nat. Neurosci.* 4:455–56

Kanwisher N, McDermott J, Chun MM. 1997. The fusiform face area: a module in human extrastriate cortex specialized for face perception. *J. Neurosci.* 17:4302–11

Kay KN, Naselaris T, Prenger RJ, Gallant JL. 2008. Identifying natural images from human brain activity. *Nature* 452:352–55

Keller TA, Just MA. 2009. Altering cortical connectivity: remediation-induced changes in the white matter of poor readers. *Neuron* 64:624–31

Kevan A, Perry LM, Rykhlevskaia E, Ben-Shachar M, Sherbondy A, et al. 2011. White matter pathways between callosum and posterior superior temporal cortex predict phonological skills in children. Manuscript submitted

Klingberg T, Hedehus M, Temple E, Salz T, Gabrieli JD, et al. 2000. Microstructure of temporo-parietal white matter as a basis for reading ability: evidence from diffusion tensor magnetic resonance imaging. *Neuron* 25:493–500

Kolster H, Peeters R, Orban GA. 2010. The retinotopic organization of the human middle temporal area MT/V5 and its cortical neighbors. *J. Neurosci.* 30:9801–20

Krafnick AJ, Flowers DL, Napoliello EM, Eden GF. 2011. Gray matter volume changes following reading intervention in dyslexic children. *NeuroImage.* In press

Lebel C, Walker L, Leemans A, Phillips L, Beaulieu C. 2008. Microstructural maturation of the human brain from childhood to adulthood. *NeuroImage* 40:1044–55

Le Bihan D, Mangin JF, Poupon C, Clark CA, Pappata S, et al. 2001. Diffusion tensor imaging: concepts and applications. *J. Magn. Reson. Imaging* 13:534–46

Leff AP, Crewes H, Plant GT, Scott SK, Kennard C, Wise RJ. 2001. The functional anatomy of single-word reading in patients with hemianopic and pure alexia. *Brain* 124:510–21

Livingstone MS, Rosen GD, Drislane FW, Galaburda AM. 1991. Physiological and anatomical evidence for a magnocellular defect in developmental dyslexia. *Proc. Natl. Acad. Sci USA* 88:7943–47

Logothetis NK, Wandell BA. 2004. Interpreting the BOLD signal. *Annu. Rev. Physiol.* 66:735–69

Lovegrove W, Martin F, Bowling A, Blackwood M, Badcock D, Paxton S. 1982. Contrast sensitivity functions and specific reading disability. *Neuropsychologia* 20:309–15

Lovegrove WJ, Bowling A, Badcock D, Blackwood M. 1980. Specific reading-disability: differences in contrast sensitivity as a function of spatial-frequency. *Science* 210:439–40

Maisog JM, Einbinder ER, Flowers DL, Turkeltaub PE, Eden GF. 2008. A meta-analysis of functional neuroimaging studies of dyslexia. *Ann. N. Y. Acad. Sci.* 1145:237–59

Maunsell JH, Nealey TA, DePriest DD. 1990. Magnocellular and parvocellular contributions to responses in the middle temporal visual area (MT) of the macaque monkey. *J. Neurosci.* 10:3323–34

Maurer U, Blau VC, Yoncheva YN, McCandliss BD. 2010. Development of visual expertise for reading: rapid emergence of visual familiarity for an artificial script. *Dev. Neuropsychol.* 35:404–22

Maurer U, Brem S, Bucher K, Kranz F, Benz R, et al. 2007. Impaired tuning of a fast occipito-temporal response for print in dyslexic children learning to read. *Brain* 130:3200–10

Maurer U, Bucher K, Brem S, Benz R, Kranz F, et al. 2009. Neurophysiology in preschool improves behavioral prediction of reading ability throughout primary school. *Biol. Psychiatry* 66:341–48

McCandliss BD, Cohen L, Dehaene S. 2003. The visual word form area: expertise for reading in the fusiform gyrus. *Trends Cogn. Sci.* 7:293–99

McCrory EJ, Mechelli A, Frith U, Price CJ. 2005. More than words: a common neural basis for reading and naming deficits in developmental dyslexia? *Brain* 128:261–67

Meyler A, Keller TA, Cherkassky VL, Gabrieli JD, Just MA. 2008. Modifying the brain activation of poor readers during sentence comprehension with extended remedial instruction: a longitudinal study of neuroplasticity. *Neuropsychologia* 46:2580–92

Meyler A, Keller TA, Cherkassky VL, Lee D, Hoeft F, et al. 2007. Brain activation during sentence comprehension among good and poor readers. *Cereb. Cortex* 17:2780–87

Molfese DL. 2000. Predicting dyslexia at 8 years of age using neonatal brain responses. *Brain Lang.* 72:238–45

Mori S. 2007. *Introduction to Diffusion Tensor Imaging*. Amsterdam: Elsevier

Mori S, Crain BJ, Chacko VP, van Zijl PC. 1999. Three-dimensional tracking of axonal projections in the brain by magnetic resonance imaging. *Ann. Neurol.* 45:265–69

Murphy KM, Beston BR, Boley PM, Jones DG. 2005. Development of human visual cortex: a balance between excitatory and inhibitory plasticity mechanisms. *Dev. Psychobiol.* 46:209–21

Nagy Z, Westerberg H, Klingberg T. 2004. Maturation of white matter is associated with the development of cognitive functions during childhood. *J. Cogn. Neurosci.* 16:1227–33

Niogi SN, McCandliss BD. 2006. Left lateralized white matter microstructure accounts for individual differences in reading ability and disability. *Neuropsychologia* 44:2178–88

Nobre AC, Allison T, McCarthy G. 1994. Word recognition in the human inferior temporal lobe. *Nature* 372:260–63

O'Craven KM, Rosen BR, Kwong KK, Treisman A, Savoy RL. 1997. Voluntary attention modulates fMRI activity in human MT-MST. *Neuron* 18:591–98

Odegard TN, Farris EA, Ring J, McColl R, Black J. 2009. Brain connectivity in non-reading impaired children and children diagnosed with developmental dyslexia. *Neuropsychologia* 47:1972–77

Odegard TN, Ring J, Smith S, Biggan J, Black J. 2008. Differentiating the neural response to intervention in children with developmental dyslexia. *Ann. Dyslexia* 58:1–14

Paulesu E, Connelly A, Frith CD, Friston KJ, Heather J, et al. 1995. Functional MR imaging correlations with positron emission tomography. Initial experience using a cognitive activation paradigm on verbal working memory. *Neuroimaging Clin. N. Am.* 5:207–25

Paulesu E, Demonet JF, Fazio F, McCrory E, Chanoine V, et al. 2001. Dyslexia: cultural diversity and biological unity. *Science* 291:2165–67

Paulesu E, Frith U, Snowling M, Gallagher A, Morton J, et al. 1996. Is developmental dyslexia a disconnection syndrome? Evidence from PET scanning. *Brain* 119:143–57

Pegado F, Nakamura K, Cohen L, Dehaene S. 2010. Breaking the symmetry: mirror discrimination for single letters but not for pictures in the visual word form area. *NeuroImage* 55:742–49

Petersen S, Fox P, Posner M, Mintun M, Rachle M. 1988. Positron emission tomographic studies of the cortical anatomy of single-word processing. *Nature* 331:585–89

Petersen SE, Fiez JA. 1993. The processing of single words studied with positron emission tomography. *Annu. Rev. Neurosci.* 16:509–30

Powell HW, Parker GJ, Alexander DC, Symms MR, Boulby PA, et al. 2006. Hemispheric asymmetries in language-related pathways: a combined functional MRI and tractography study. *NeuroImage* 32:388–99

Price CJ, Devlin JT. 2003. The myth of the visual word form area. *NeuroImage* 19:473–81

Price CJ, Devlin JT. 2004. The pro and cons of labelling a left occipitotemporal region: "the visual word form area." *NeuroImage* 22:477–79

Price CJ, Howard D, Patterson K, Warburton EA, Friston KJ, Frackowiak SJ. 1998. A functional neuroimaging description of two deep dyslexic patients. *J. Cogn. Neurosci.* 10:303–15

Price CJ, Wise RJ, Watson JD, Patterson K, Howard D, Frackowiak RS. 1994. Brain activity during reading. The effects of exposure duration and task. *Brain* 117(Pt. 6):1255–69

Pugh KR, Mencl WE, Jenner AR, Katz L, Frost SJ, et al. 2001. Neurobiological studies of reading and reading disability. *J. Commun. Disord.* 34:479–92

Rauschecker AM, Deutsch GK, Ben-Shachar M, Schwartzman A, Perry LM, Dougherty RF. 2009. Reading impairment in a patient with missing arcuate fasciculus. *Neuropsychologia* 47:180–94

Rilling JK, Glasser MF, Preuss TM, Ma X, Zhao T, et al. 2008. The evolution of the arcuate fasciculus revealed with comparative DTI. *Nat. Neurosci.* 11:426–28

Rossion B, Gauthier I, Goffaux V, Tarr MJ, Crommelinck M. 2002. Expertise training with novel objects leads to left-lateralized facelike electrophysiological responses. *Psychol. Sci.* 13:250–57

Rumsey JM, Nace K, Donohue B, Wise D, Maisog JM, Andreason P. 1997. A positron emission tomographic study of impaired word recognition and phonological processing in dyslexic men. *Arch. Neurol.* 54:562–73

Salmelin R, Helenius P, Service E. 2000. Neurophysiology of fluent and impaired reading: a magnetoencephalographic approach. *J. Clin. Neurophysiol.* 17:163–74

Salmelin R, Service E, Kiesila P, Uutela K, Salonen O. 1996. Impaired visual word processing in dyslexia revealed with magnetoencephalography. *Ann. Neurol.* 40:157–62

Saur D, Kreher BW, Schnell S, Kummerer D, Kellmeyer P, et al. 2008. Ventral and dorsal pathways for language. *Proc. Natl. Acad. Sci. USA* 105:18035–40

Sharon D, Hamalainen MS, Tootell RB, Halgren E, Belliveau JW. 2007. The advantage of combining MEG and EEG: comparison to fMRI in focally stimulated visual cortex. *NeuroImage* 36:1225–35

Shaywitz BA, Shaywitz SE, Blachman BA, Pugh KR, Fulbright RK, et al. 2004. Development of left occipitotemporal systems for skilled reading in children after a phonologically based intervention. *Biol. Psychiatry* 55:926–33

Shaywitz SE, Morris R, Shaywitz BA. 2008. The education of dyslexic children from childhood to young adulthood. *Annu. Rev. Psychol.* 59:451–75

Shaywitz SE, Shaywitz BA. 2008. Paying attention to reading: the neurobiology of reading and dyslexia. *Dev. Psychopathol.* 20:1329–49

Simos PG, Breier JI, Fletcher JM, Foorman BR, Bergman E, et al. 2000. Brain activation profiles in dyslexic children during non-word reading: a magnetic source imaging study. *Neurosci. Lett.* 290:61–65

Simos PG, Fletcher JM, Bergman E, Breier JI, Foorman BR, et al. 2002. Dyslexia-specific brain activation profile becomes normal following successful remedial training. *Neurology* 58:1203–13

Simos PG, Fletcher JM, Sarkari S, Billingsley RL, Denton C, Papanicolaou AC. 2007. Altering the brain circuits for reading through intervention: a magnetic source imaging study. *Neuropsychology* 21:485–96

Snow CE, Burns MS, Griffin P. 1998. *Preventing Reading Difficulties in Young Children*. Washington, DC: Natl. Acad. Press

Song Y, Bu Y, Hu S, Luo Y, Liu J. 2010. Short-term language experience shapes the plasticity of the visual word form area. *Brain Res.* 1316:83–91

Sowell ER, Thompson PM, Toga AW. 2004. Mapping changes in the human cortex throughout the span of life. *Neuroscientist* 10:372–92

Sperling AJ, Lu ZL, Manis FR, Seidenberg MS. 2005. Deficits in perceptual noise exclusion in developmental dyslexia. *Nat. Neurosci.* 8:862–63

Sperling AJ, Lu ZL, Manis FR, Seidenberg MS. 2006. Motion-perception deficits and reading impairment: it's the noise, not the motion. *Psychol. Sci.* 17:1047–53

Spironelli C, Angrilli A. 2009. Developmental aspects of automatic word processing: language lateralization of early ERP components in children, young adults and middle-aged subjects. *Biol. Psychol.* 80:35–45

Spironelli C, Penolazzi B, Vio C, Angrilli A. 2010. Cortical reorganization in dyslexic children after phonological training: evidence from early evoked potentials. *Brain* 133:3385–95

Stanovich KE, Cunningham AE, Cramer BB. 1984. Assessing phonological awareness in kindergarten children: issues of task comparability. *J. Exp. Child Psychol.* 38:175–90

Stein J. 2001. The magnocellular theory of developmental dyslexia. *Dyslexia* 7:12–36

Stensaas SS, Eddington DK, Dobelle WH. 1974. The topography and variability of the primary visual cortex in man. *J. Neurosurg.* 40:747–55

Szwed M, Cohen L, Qiao E, Dehaene S. 2009. The role of invariant line junctions in object and visual word recognition. *Vision Res.* 49:718–25

Szwed M, Dehaene S, Kleinschmidt A, Eger E, Valabregue R, et al. 2011. Specialization for written words over objects in the visual cortex. *NeuroImage* 56:330–44

Tarr MJ, Gauthier I. 2000. FFA: a flexible fusiform area for subordinate-level visual processing automatized by expertise. *Nat. Neurosci.* 3:764–69

Temple E, Deutsch GK, Poldrack RA, Miller SL, Tallal P, et al. 2003. Neural deficits in children with dyslexia ameliorated by behavioral remediation: evidence from functional MRI. *Proc. Natl. Acad. Sci. USA* 100:2860–65

Thirion B, Duchesnay E, Hubbard E, Dubois J, Poline JB, et al. 2006. Inverse retinotopy: inferring the visual content of images from brain activation patterns. *NeuroImage* 33:1104–16

Tolstoy L. 1911. *Anna Karenina*. New York: John Lane. 919 pp.

Tootell RB, Dale AM, Sereno MI, Malach R. 1996. New images from human visual cortex. *Trends Neurosci.* 19:481–89

Tootell RB, Reppas JB, Kwong KK, Malach R, Born RT, et al. 1995. Functional analysis of human MT and related visual cortical areas using magnetic resonance imaging. *J. Neurosci.* 15:3215–30

Tootell RB, Taylor JB. 1995. Anatomical evidence for MT and additional cortical visual areas in humans. *Cereb. Cortex* 5:39–55

Torgesen JK, Wagner RK, Rashotte CA, Rose E, Lindamood P, et al. 1999. Preventing reading failure in children with phonological processing difficulties: group and individual responses to instruction. *J. Educ. Psychol.* 81:579–93

Turkeltaub PE, Flowers DL, Lyon LG, Eden GF. 2008. Development of ventral stream representations for single letters. *Ann. N. Y. Acad. Sci.* 1145:13–29

Twomey T, Kawabata Duncan KJ, Price CJ, Devlin JT. 2011. Top-down modulation of ventral occipito-temporal responses during visual word recognition. *NeuroImage* 55:1242–51

Van Essen DC, Lewis JW, Drury HA, Hadjikhani N, Tootell RB, et al. 2001. Mapping visual cortex in monkeys and humans using surface-based atlases. *Vision Res.* 41:1359–78

Vigneau M, Beaucousin V, Herve PY, Jobard G, Petit L, et al. 2011. What is right-hemisphere contribution to phonological, lexico-semantic, and sentence processing? Insights from a meta-analysis. *NeuroImage* 54:577–93

Vinckier F, Dehaene S, Jobert A, Dubus JP, Sigman M, Cohen L. 2007. Hierarchical coding of letter strings in the ventral stream: dissecting the inner organization of the visual word-form system. *Neuron* 55:143–56

Wagner RK, Torgesen JK. 1987. The nature of phonological processing and its causal role in the acquisition of reading skills. *Psychol. Bull.* 101:192–212

Wakana S, Jiang H, Nagae-Poetscher LM, van Zijl PC, Mori S. 2004. Fiber tract-based atlas of human white matter anatomy. *Radiology* 230:77–87

Walhovd KB, Fjell AM, Reinvang I, Lundervold A, Dale AM, et al. 2005. Effects of age on volumes of cortex, white matter and subcortical structures. *Neurobiol. Aging* 26:1261–70; discussion 75–78

Wandell BA. 2011. The neurobiological basis of seeing words. *Ann. N. Y. Acad. Sci.* 1224:63–80

Wandell BA, Dumoulin SO, Brewer AA. 2007. Visual field maps in human cortex. *Neuron* 56:366–83

Wandell BA, Smirnakis SM. 2009. Plasticity and stability of visual field maps in adult primary visual cortex. *Nat. Rev. Neurosci.* 10:873–84

Wandell BA, Winawer J. 2010. Imaging retinotopic maps in the human brain. *Vision Res.* 51:718–37

Warrington EK, Shallice T. 1980. Word-form dyslexia. *Brain* 103:99–112

Wernicke C. 1874. Der aphasischer Symptomenkomplex: eine psychologische Studie auf anatomischer Basis. In *Wernicke's Works on Aphasia: A Sourcebook and Review*, transl. GH Eggert, pp. 91–145. The Hague: Mouton

Winawer J, Horiguchi H, Sayres RA, Amano K, Wandell BA. 2010. Mapping hV4 and ventral occipital cortex: the venous eclipse. *J. Vis.* 10:1

Xue G, Chen C, Jin Z, Dong Q. 2006. Language experience shapes fusiform activation when processing a logographic artificial language: an fMRI training study. *NeuroImage* 31:1315–26

Yeatman JD, Dougherty R, Rykhlevskaia E, Sherbondy A, Deutsch G, et al. 2011. Anatomical properties of the arcuate fasciculus predict phonological and reading skills in children. *J. Cogn. Neurosci.* In press

Yoncheva YN, Zevin JD, Maurer U, McCandliss BD. 2010. Auditory selective attention to speech modulates activity in the visual word form area. *Cereb. Cortex* 20:622–32

Yushkevich PA, Piven J, Hazlett HC, Smith RG, Ho S, et al. 2006. User-guided 3D active contour segmentation of anatomical structures: significantly improved efficiency and reliability. *NeuroImage* 31:1116–28

Zeki S. 1980. The response properties of cells in the middle temporal area (area MT) of owl monkey visual cortex. *Proc. R. Soc. Lond. B Biol. Sci.* 207:239–48

Zeki S. 2005. The Ferrier Lecture 1995 behind the seen: the functional specialization of the brain in space and time. *Philos. Trans. R. Soc. Lond. B Biol. Sci.* 360:1145–83

Zeki S, Watson JD, Lueck CJ, Friston KJ, Kennard C, Frackowiak RS. 1991. A direct demonstration of functional specialization in human visual cortex. *J. Neurosci.* 11:641–49

Remembering in Conversations: The Social Sharing and Reshaping of Memories

William Hirst[1] and Gerald Echterhoff[2]

[1]Cognitive Science Lab, Department of Psychology, New School for Social Research, New York, New York 10011; email: hirst@newschool.edu

[2]Social Psychology Lab, Department of Psychology, University of Münster, 48149 Münster, Germany; email: g.echterhoff@uni-muenster.de

Annu. Rev. Psychol. 2012. 63:55–79

First published online as a Review in Advance on September 27, 2011

The *Annual Review of Psychology* is online at psych.annualreviews.org

This article's doi: 10.1146/annurev-psych-120710-100340

0066-4308/12/0110-0055$20.00

Keywords

communication, collaborative facilitation/inhibition, social contagion, retrieval effects, retrieval-induced forgetting, shared reality, social network

Abstract

People constantly talk about past experiences. Burgeoning psychological research has examined the role of communication in remembering by placing rememberers in conversational settings. In reviewing this work, we first discuss the benefits of collaborative remembering (transactive memory and collaborative facilitation) and its costs (collaborative inhibition, information sampling biases, and audience tuning). We next examine how conversational remembering affects subsequent memory. Here, we address influences on listeners' memory through social contagion, resistance to such influences, and then retrieval/reexposure effects on either speaker or listener, with a focus on retrieval-induced forgetting. Extending the perspective beyond single interactions, we consider work that has explored how the above effects can spread across networks of several individuals. We also explore how a speaker's motive to form a shared reality with listeners can moderate conversational effects on memory. Finally, we discuss how these various conversational effects may promote the formation of collective memories.

Contents

INTRODUCTION

Human memory can serve a variety of functions (see, for instance, Bluck 2003), but what might be unique to humans is that their remembering has a communicative function (Pillemer 1992). One diary study revealed that 62% of the events recorded by participants had already been told to others by the evening of the day that they occurred (Pasupathi et al. 2009). Another study tracked conversational exchanges about a class field trip to a morgue. Although the original class contained only 33 students, after three exchanges, 881 people knew of the visit to the morgue, a propagation rate of 26.7 (Harber & Cohen 2005). And in a survey conducted by Skagerberg & Wright (2008b), 58% of the interviewed eyewitnesses reported having discussed the witnessed incident with at least one cowitness. This pervasive exchange of memories may be becoming both broader and quicker as social media supplies yet other means of communicating about the past. Whatever the format, the constant chatter can be about jointly experienced events, individually experienced events, or facts. That is, people share with each other both their episodic and semantic memories.

We are interested here in exploring acts of remembering when they serve a communicative function. We focus here exclusively on communicative remembering in nonelderly adults. An examination of the developmental literature and work on the elderly is beyond the scope of this review. We are particularly interested in remembering within a conversation. People converse with others about the past or about previously learned information for a variety of reasons: to inform others, to seek desired information, to create a sense of intimacy, or to influence others (for a taxonomy of communication goals, see McCann & Higgins 1988). Even when remembering alone, there may still be a virtual audience, consistent with the notion of the looking-glass self (Mead 1934).

Our interest here is not in the reasons for conversing about the past, but rather in the consequences of conversational remembering for memory. To study these consequences, experimenters need to place rememberers in conversational settings. The past few years have seen a break from traditional approaches to the experimental study of memory, which rarely investigate conversational remembering per se. We review this recently burgeoning experimental psychological literature here. We consider two sets of questions (cf. Pasupathi 2001). The first focuses on the memories emerging within a conversation. How does individual remembering differ from conversational remembering? Is remembering in a conversation more effective than remembering in isolation? And do answers to these questions depend on the circumstances of the conversation and the participants in the conversation?

The second set of questions focuses on memories held after the conversation. This set of questions is further subdivided by distinguishing the person doing the remembering in the preceding conversation—the speaker—from the person listening to the remembering—the listener. Conversational participants will probably adopt both roles within a conversation, but at any point in the conversation, one can usually identify a single speaker and one or more listeners. Researchers have summed instances in a conversation in which a participant assumes the role of speaker, and summed instances in which the same participant assumes the role of listener. In this way, they have studied the effects of conversational remembering on speakers and listeners. The second set of questions, then, is divided into concerns about (*a*) the effect of what a participant says while in the role of a speaker on her own memory and (*b*) the effect of what she says on listeners' subsequent memory. Before addressing these two sets of questions, we situate the study of conversation and memory within a larger theoretical framework.

Conversational Remembering and the Extended Mind

Research that focuses on not just what happens in the head while remembering, but also what occurs within and after a conversation, could be viewed as treating the mind as extended. A number of scholars have observed that cognition is often scaffolded by external resources, such as media, cultural institutions, or social networks (Clark 2010, Hutchins 1995, Sutton et al. 2011, Wilson 2005). In the case of conversational remembering, the conversation could be treated as a scaffold. One person in the conversation, for instance, might remind another of an initially forgotten memory. In this way, the performance of any individual conversational participant depends critically on others (see Hirst & Echterhoff 2008, Wegner 1987). Those espousing an extended mind aver that external influences, in our case, conversations, and internal processing can become so intertwined as to make it difficult, if not impossible, to separate the two. For proponents of an extended mind,

scaffolds are as much a part of the mind as what happens inside the head.

Bateson (1979) illustrates this point with his example of a blind man navigating through the world with a cane. To explain the blind man's navigation, researchers might investigate the cortical activity accompanying the navigation and treat any input from the outside world in terms of cortical input. Many researchers might also want to go beyond an exclusive focus on cortical activity and include in their explanations the origins of cortical inputs, for instance, the activation occurring on the nerve endings of the fingers holding the cane. The configuration of these nerve endings might be important, inasmuch as different configurations might be the source of different patterns of cortical input. A proponent of an extended mind would ask: Why not go beyond the surface of the skin and include the cane? Unquestionably, the nature of the cane—for instance, its rigidity—is as much a factor in the blind man's ease of navigation as the configuration of nerve endings or the processing in the cortex. There is no a priori reason to exclude the cane from explanations. For proponents of an extended mind, the most principled approach would include the cortex, the fingertips, and the cane.

In a similar way, those postulating an extended mind would want to include in their explanation of remembering the external resources scaffolding the remembering, including the conversations in which the remembering takes place (Wilson & Clark 2009). Although one can, in some instances, distinguish between the retrieval of a memory and its conversion into an expression of this memory, often in the form of some type of verbal communication (Tulving 1983), proponents of an extended mind would insist that, in many cases, it is impossible to separate the memory from its expression (Barnier et al. 2008, Echterhoff & Hirst 2002). As we will see in this review, what is remembered often depends on both the audience and conversational dynamics. For example, a conversation of Jane with her mother about her date last night might differ in content from her conversation with her girlfriend about the same date. In a conversation with her mother, Jane may sometimes intentionally censor what she says, but in many instances, she may simply talk to her mother in a free-flowing manner, without any sense of censoring herself. The nuances of the ending of the date may simply not come to mind in her conversation with her mother because that is not what her mother is interested in or asks her about. On the other hand, details about the end of the date may figure centrally in Jane's conversation with her girlfriend. These details may be what the girlfriend is interested in, what she asks Jane about, and what Jane remembers. In her conversational remembering, Jane is simply tuning her remembering to her audience.

How do we separate the communicative demands of the situation from what is—or is not—remembered? One does not have to accept that the mind is extended to find it difficult to make this separation. Remembering often occurs within a conversation, and one can be interested in the psychology underlying this phenomenon whether or not one embraces the notion of an extended mind. The extended mind approach, however, places the study of conversational remembering front and center in a way more traditional approaches to the study of memory do not.

REMEMBERING IN A CONVERSATION: HOW DOES THE ACT OF CONVERSING SHAPE REMEMBERING?

In many instances, people may experience the same event and then come together to talk about it, as college alumni do at a college reunion or as couples do after returning home from a dinner party. In both instances, the remembering is often collaborative. The group or couple views their task as helping each other to remember the past. Does this collaborative effort at remembering differ from individual acts of remembering? Does the group remember more or less than individuals? How does the way individuals remember in a group differ from how they might remember in isolation?

There is now a burgeoning literature addressing such questions. In some cases, the experiments focus on quantity of recall; in others, quality or accuracy (Koriat et al. 2000). What we want to stress here is that, in any event, researchers have identified both benefits and costs to collaborative remembering.

Benefits of Collaborative Remembering

Transactive memory. When several people come together as a team or group to work on a task, they can, under the right circumstances, perform better than they could as individuals (Kerr & Tindale 2004). Research on transactive memory suggests that this general finding also holds true for memory tasks (for a review, see Hollingshead & Brandon 2003). According to the theory of transactive memory, people can divide a memory task among themselves so as to make it easy for them to fill in gaps in each other's recall. In this way, they distribute the burden of remembering, using one another as external memory aids. Wegner (1987) referred to this division of responsibilities as a transactive memory system.

In transactive memory studies, participants complete a memory task, typically the recall of information in specific knowledge domains (e.g., history or science). Participants first estimate the other person's and their own expertise. Subsequently, both members of a dyad study relevant material and then recall the learned information jointly with each other. The benefit of transactive memory has been demonstrated for close relationships, work teams, and professional relationships (see Hollingshead & Brandon 2003).

To achieve effective transactive memory, group members need a sufficient amount of knowledge, or correct intuitions, about what each other can remember. For instance, dating couples, who presumably have exquisite knowledge about each other, exhibit better memory than do pairs of unacquainted individuals (Hollingshead 1998a). However, even unacquainted dyads can benefit from collaborative efforts. When unacquainted pairs and dating couples were given the opportunity to communicate during the study phase of an experiment, the unacquainted couples subsequently jointly recalled the studied material better than the dating couples (Hollingshead 1998b). The poor performance of the dating couples may have arisen because their conversations during encoding might have interfered with the operation of an evolved transactive memory system.

Collaborative facilitation. Even when unrelated individuals collaboratively remember previously individually studied material, benefits can be observed. In a typical experiment on collaborative remembering, participants study material (the study phase) and then recall the material as a group or individually (respectively, the experimental or control phase). In some instances, a memory test is inserted between the study phase and the experimental/control phase. In yet other instances, a final memory test follows the experimental/control phase. Distracter tasks are usually placed between the different phases of the study. In most studies, during the experimental phase, participants are asked to remember, as a group, what they had previously studied.

Using this paradigm, experimenters have repeatedly shown that the group, as a unit, recalls more than at least some of the individual members of the group might recall alone (Weldon 2001). This collaborative facilitation arises in part because not all the original material is equally memorable across participants, and hence, some of the participants may contribute to the group recounting something that would not appear in other members' individual recall. Interestingly, one might also expect the facilitation to occur because a recollection offered by one participant in the group recounting cues new memories from another person, memories that might not otherwise be remembered. Surprisingly, such cross-cueing is rarely observed (e.g., Meudell et al. 1995). Experimenters, however, may have failed to uncover evidence for cross-cueing because it is masked by disruptions occurring while participants

collaboratively remember rather than because it does not occur (Congleton & Rajaram 2010). Whatever the extent of cross-cueing, it is clearly the case that groups, as a unit, remember more than individuals might when recalling alone.

Costs of Collaborative Remembering

Just because a group may remember more than an individual would remember in isolation, the group does not necessarily remember all that individual recalls would suggest the group is capable of remembering. That is, group recounting is not the sum of the individual capacities of the group members. We discuss below several ways collaborative remembering comes with a cost, specifically collaborative inhibition, information sampling biases, and audience tuning.

Collaborative inhibition. These experiments contrast group recall scores with nominal recall scores. A nominal recall score is calculated by examining individual recall performance, for instance, in the control phase. An experimenter might test two individuals, one of whom remembers in isolation items A, B, D, and F from the original study material and the second of whom remembers in isolation items B, C, and F. The nominal recall score would be 5, inasmuch as five distinct items are recalled across these two individuals. This nominal score is contrasted with performance when two individuals remember collaboratively. For instance, they might jointly remember items B, D, and F in a group recounting. The group recall score, then, would be 3. In this example, as is the case in much of the experimental literature, the group recall score is less than the nominal recall score (for a review, see Rajaram & Pereira-Pasarin 2010). The collaboration seemingly inhibits some memories from emerging into the group recounting, thereby leading the group to recount less than one would expect by summing the unique memories recalled by individual group members when remembering in isolation.

Collaborative inhibition could be attributed to social loafing or "free-riding" (see Rajaram

Collaborative inhibition: reduced recall performance of groups compared to the sum of individual performances (group recall score < nominal recall score)

Audience tuning: goal-dependent adaptation of a message to the audience's assumed characteristics (typically inner states such as knowledge, expectations, attitudes)

& Pereira-Pasarin 2010). However, when personal accountability and motivation are manipulated to control for social loafing, collaborative inhibition still remains robust (Weldon et al. 2000). According to the retrieval disruption hypothesis, collaborative inhibition occurs, at least in part, because one group member's pursuit of an effective retrieval strategy disrupts the use of retrieval strategies that may be more effective for other group members (Basden et al. 1997). As a result, some group members may not be able to undertake their most effective retrieval strategy. In such an instance, they may recall less during the group recounting than they would if recalling by themselves. The group recall score will fall below the nominal recall score.

Tests of retrieval disruption often contrast conditions in which the organizational representation of the to-be-remembered material is more or less likely to be shared across group members. The more organizational representations differ across participants, the more likely it is that different retrieval strategies will be effective for different participants. With different organizational representations across group members, then, collaborative inhibition should appear. On the other hand, with similar organizational representations across group members, collaborative inhibition should be diminished or disappear. Thus, Findlay and colleagues (2000) found that when they ensured that the organizational structure was similar across group members, collaborative inhibition disappeared. As to the presence of different organizational representations, one experiment examined groups recounting 90 previously studied items (Basden et al. 1997). In the large-sized categories condition, the 90 items consisted of 15 exemplars from six categories; in the small-sized category condition, the list contained six exemplars from 15 categories. Participants were more likely to have variable organizational representations with large-sized categories (here, defined as the extent to which the exemplars are neatly organized into categories). That is, different participants may have assigned an exemplar to different categories when the categories are large. As organizational variability increased, so did collaborative inhibition.

Following the same logic, Basden et al. (1997) predicted and found that, again for lists of categorizable words, collaborative inhibition disappeared when the experimenter forced participants to recall one category at a time during the group recounting rather than allowed the participants to follow their own devices. The latter procedure is likely to produce more variable organization and hence greater collaborative inhibition. Together, these studies provide strong support for the retrieval disruption hypothesis.

The findings of inhibition with collaborative remembering are similar to those found in part-list cueing studies, which focus entirely on individual recall (Basden & Basden 1995). Generally, cueing aids memory. In part-list cueing studies, participants study a list of words and then receive as a cue a subset of the studied items. Rather than enhancing memory performance, the part-list cue significantly lowers it. The most widely accepted explanation for the part-list cueing effect involves retrieval disruption. The partial list may not contain optimal cues, inasmuch as they may not link effectively with the organizational representation participants formed of the list as they studied it. As a result, the partial list may elicit from participants ineffective rather than effective retrieval strategies. The similarity of explanations for collaborative inhibition and the part-list cueing effect is not coincidental. The material that one member of a group recalls while collaboratively remembering may be viewed as a partial list, suggesting that the inhibition in the collaborative remembering experiments and in the part-list cueing experiments arises for similar reasons.

Collaborative inhibition can be found for a wide range of material: related and unrelated words, word pairs, stories, semantic and episodic memory tasks, pictures, short film clips, and emotionally charged events (see Rajaram & Pereira-Pasarin 2010). Moreover, it varies with group size (Basden et al. 2000). Members of large groups are more likely to have diverse mnemonic representations than are members of small groups. Consequently, according to the retrieval disruption account, large groups should, and do, exhibit greater levels of collaborative inhibition than do small groups. Similar reasoning would also suggest that collaborative inhibition should be greater in groups of unrelated individuals than in groups of familiars, in that familiars should be more likely to form similar representations of the past than would strangers. Studies of dyads of friends and married couples have routinely failed to find collaborative inhibition (e.g., Andersson 2001). However, collaborative inhibition is not inevitable when strangers collaboratively remember. Meade and colleagues (2009) contrasted collaborative remembering of scenarios involving the navigation of planes. Nonexpert pilots exhibit the standard collaborative inhibition, whereas expert pilots recalling with other expert pilots produce a group recall score greater than the nominal score. Presumably, the expert pilots shared the same organization and knowledge about flying. The similarity led to a cross-participant efficient use of retrieval strategies.

These findings would suggest that the way people study the to-be-remembered material, what Congleton & Rajaram (2011) called the study history, should affect the size of the collaborative inhibition, in that study history should affect the similarity and strength of mnemonic organization across participants. For instance, Pereira-Pasarin & Rajaram (2011) exposed participants to lists of target words either once or repeatedly in a spaced format. They then asked groups of three to recall the words jointly, thereby presumably inducing them to achieve a solidified organized representation. Repeated presentation during study not only improved overall recall, but also substantially attenuated the level of collaborative inhibition. In a related study, Congleton & Rajaram (2011) contrasted the effects of different learning histories, e.g., study-study-study or study-recall-recall, either of which occurred prior to collaborative remembering. Employing these two "histories" allowed Congleton & Rajaram

to contrast the contribution of study and test to the final recounting. As they predicted, the repeated testing was more likely to solidify a retrieval strategy than was repeated study and, as a result, repeated testing, but not repeated study, decreased collaborative inhibition.

Other support for the retrieval disruption hypothesis can be found by imposing a secondary task on participants as they study. Divided attention tasks during study have been shown to diminish the level of mnemonic organization, as evidenced in a subsequent individual recall test. As the retrieval disruption hypothesis would predict, the same divided attention study task produces greater collaborative inhibition in a group recall task (Rajaram & Pereira-Pasarin 2010). In a similar vein, Takahashi & Saito (2004) showed that the less idiosyncratic the retrieval strategies employed by members of a group, the smaller the collaborative inhibition.

Taken together, the retrieval disruption account has strong predictive value and can explain the presence and absence of collaborative inhibition in a wide range of settings.

Information sampling biases. Retrieval disruption may not be the only reason why participants in a group recounting fail to remember all they are capable of remembering. In a series of experiments, Stasser, Wittenbaum, and their colleagues taught participants about a political candidate and then assembled small groups to discuss with each other what they knew about the candidate. The original material was constructed in such a way that, whereas all participants in the group knew certain facts about the candidate, each participant also knew several unique facts, that is, facts that only he or she knew. Stasser, Wittenbaum, and colleagues repeatedly found that participants in the group recounting were more likely to recall their shared information than their uniquely held information (for a review, see Wittenbaum & Park 2001). The failure to mention the unshared information was attributed to a fairly straightforward sampling bias (Stasser & Titus 1987). Specifically, a group will fail to discuss an item only if all members fail to mention it. As a result, when memories are shared, there is a greater probability that they will be mentioned by at least one group member than when they are uniquely held (see Wittenbaum et al. 2004 for a review of alternative explanations).

A number of studies have examined the condition under which unshared memories are more likely to emerge in a group recounting. Although we cannot offer here a complete review of this substantial literature (again, see Wittenbaum et al. 2004), we can offer a general observation: Early work tended to examine what might be viewed as structural features of the conversational interactions, e.g., finding that information is more likely to be discussed as the number of group members who know it increases (Cruz et al. 1997). More recent work has focused on motivational factors (see Wittenbaum et al. 2004).

Audience tuning. Another way to understand why less is remembered in a group recounting than might be remembered by each participant alone is to focus on the way each member of the group takes into account her audience. Marsh (2007) has distinguished recalling from retelling. In a standard, laboratory-based recall experiment, participants are explicitly told to remember all that they can remember as accurately as possible. Marsh reserved the term "recall" for just such an activity. In everyday life, however, people may simply wish to retell a story about the past without trying to be either accurate or complete. This retelling can be shaped by the goals of the retelling. For instance, what will be recounted will differ substantially if the goal of the conversation is to explain the facts than if the goal is simply to entertain. Dudukovic and colleagues (2004) found that entertaining retellings contained fewer story events, less sensory references, and more intrusions than did factual retellings. Moreover, in comparison with factual retellings, the entertaining stories were less accurate, were more likely to be told in the present tense, and contained more emotion words and fewer disfluencies (e.g., uh's).

While retelling, speakers will also tune their recollections to what they believe the audience expects to hear. For instance, Pasupathi et al. (1998) found that speakers conveyed more, particularly more novel and more elaborated, information to an attentive as opposed to a distracted listener. Another experiment uncovered that people will recount more details, such as everything involved in a trip to the doctors, when talking to a hypothetical Martian, who presumably knows little about how things work on Earth, than when talking to a peer, who presumably knows a lot more (Vandierendonck & Van Damme 1988). Yet another experiment showed that a story told to peers contains more interpretations about the content of the story than if told to an experimenter, when participants largely stuck to the "facts" (Hyman 1994). There is also experimental work establishing that when helping a listener identify a specific person among a group of individuals, speakers will emphasize the target's positive qualities if they know the listener likes the target, and the target's negative qualities if they know the listener dislikes the target (Echterhoff et al. 2009a). In general, retellings conform to conversational maxims, such as "say no more than is necessary" (Grice 1975) or "be relevant" (Sperber & Wilson 1986). Considered together, the extant research establishes that a retelling almost always contains less than might emerge in a test of recall, with audience tuning, conversational goals, retrieval disruption, and sampling biases contributing in their own ways to a less-than-optimal performance.

THE EFFECT OF CONVERSATIONAL REMEMBERING ON SUBSEQUENT MEMORY

The thrust of the extant work on collaborative remembering is that remembering is selective. The research specifies what kinds of social interactional factors shape what people will or will not remember, but repeatedly it establishes that, in ordinary conversations, people do not remember all that they are capable of remembering. We are interested in this section on the consequences of this selectivity on subsequent memory. What people remember is almost always a product not just of the original encoding of an event, but also the conversations occurring between the initial encoding and an act of remembering. As a consequence, any act of recall must be viewed as having a social history.

This basic social-historical character of remembering is widely acknowledged, even by the founding fathers of the psychological study of memory. Bartlett (1932) averred that remembering could not be divorced from current attitudes and environmental and social influences, emphasizing more the social nature of remembering over its historical character. Along similar lines, Vygotsky (1978) emphasized that one could not understand why people remember what they do without placing their acts of remembering into a larger socio-historical context. For him, acts of remembering reflected previous acts of remembering. Even Ebbinghaus (1964) acknowledged that memory was inevitably socially encrusted and historically based. Unlike Bartlett and Vygotsky, his solution was to strip away social and historical influences, and in doing so, reveal the raw material of memory. Our approach here is clearly closer to that of Bartlett and Vygotsky than to that of Ebbinghaus.

In what follows, we focus on two ways that remembering in a social, communicative setting can influence subsequent memory, through social contagion and through retrieval/reexposure effects. One person in a conversation can influence another by virtue of what they say or do not say. When they offer new or misleading information, they may implant this information into the memory of their audience. This is known as social contagion. On the other hand, they can selectively remember information known both to themselves and to their audience. This selectivity sets the stage for the study of retrieval/reexposure effects.

Social Contagion

In a general sense, social contagion means the spread of information, ideas, or practices via interpersonal contact, interaction, and communication. Within the domain of memory psychology, social contagion refers to the spread of a memory from one person to another by means of social interaction, including conversational interactions (Roediger et al. 2001; see Hirst & Echterhoff 2008). In some instances, the speaker can impose a new memory onto the listener, that is, a memory of something that the listener did not experience. In other instances, a speaker imposes on the listener an alternative rendering of something that the listener experienced.

Although Elizabeth Loftus did not initially frame her work this way, experimental work on social contagion can be traced back to her influential demonstration of the postevent misinformation effect (for a review, see Loftus 2005). In typical experiments, participants first watch visual material (e.g., slides, video) depicting an event, often an eyewitness incident like a theft or an accident. They then receive postevent misinformation about the event, for instance, a written narrative about the event that contains several incorrect details (e.g., a stop sign at an intersection). In a final memory test, participants receiving postevent misinformation often falsely report postevent misinformation (e.g., the stop sign) more frequently than do control participants, who do not receive the misinformation.

As to implanting entirely new information, people can come to remember incorrectly that they were lost in a shopping mall as a child simply by listening to a relative's story about the incident (see Loftus 2005). They can also be induced to remember putting slime, a gelatinous toy substance, into a teacher's desk in elementary school (Lindsay et al. 2004). None of these events occurred, yet people reported that their memories of them were extremely vivid and compelling. It is estimated that false information can successfully be implanted in about 30% of study participants through made-up stories told by relatives (Lindsay et al. 2004).

In many of pioneering postevent misinformation studies, the source of the biasing information was a narrative, a slide show, or

Social contagion (of memory): the spread of a memory from one person to others by means of verbal interaction

a film. The person behind these presentations was never mentioned; he or she was implicit. In some recent experiments, however, a physically present person (in our terminology, a speaker) serves as the source of the biasing information. In these experiments, participants first study target material (e.g., slides of household scenes; Roediger et al. 2001), often together with one or more co-respondents (speakers). During the second phase, the participants remember the material collaboratively with the co-respondent(s), who provides some incorrect information. In a final, third phase, participants remember the material again individually. In these studies, the to-be-influenced participant interacts face-to-face with the sources of biasing information. In memory conformity studies, during the collaborative phase, one participant conveys biasing information to another participant (e.g., Wright et al. 2000). The biasing information is usually a different version of a critical detail of the studied material. In confederate studies, again during the collaborative phase, a confederate recalls as naturally as possible to a naive participant several correct but also a few incorrect items (e.g., Meade & Roediger 2002). In conversational remembering studies, during the collaborative phase, naive members of mostly four-person groups converse about a past event or original material. The influence of the group conversation is assessed by comparing individual memories that the group members report before the conversation with individual memories they report after the conversation (e.g., Cuc et al. 2006; for distinctions of experimental paradigms, see Barnier et al. 2008, Wright et al. 2009).

Studies employing these paradigms have consistently revealed the susceptibility of listeners' memory to information communicated by speakers (e.g., Cuc et al. 2006; Gabbert et al. 2003, 2004, 2006; Meade & Roediger 2002; Paterson & Kemp 2006; Roediger et al. 2001; Wright et al. 2000). Such contagion is not a rare occurrence. In one of the first memory conformity studies (Gabbert et al. 2003), more than 70% of the participants incorporated incorrect items mentioned by a cowitness during collaborative recall into their individual memory of the witnessed event.

Results from social contagion studies harken back to classical work on conformity, such as that of Asch (1956) and Sherif (1936), in which participants' judgments about visual stimuli were influenced by judgments of other co-present respondents. A prominent, more recent account attributes social contagion to the confusion people have about sources of information (Mitchell & Johnson 2009). According to this approach, recognition errors arise because listeners have trouble deciding whether a remembered event was mentioned in the original material or in the subsequent narrative, slideshow, or conversation. Because of these source-monitoring problems, participants may falsely claim, for instance, that information contained in the postevent narrative occurred in the original material. The source-monitoring account could be viewed as an informational influence, in that the judgment is based on the belief that information provided by a speaker is true and/or trustworthy.

In addition to informational influences, normative influence may also produce social contagion (Deutsch & Gerard 1955). An influence is normative when one accepts a speaker's position as a norm to avoid social costs of dissent without necessarily believing the speaker. Although most evidence from social contagion studies can be more easily explained by informational influence, Baron et al. (1996) found that normative influence can take precedence when the memory task is relatively easy and when incentives enhance participants' motivation for accuracy.

Moderators of social contagion: How can the effect be altered? Effective moderators can be classified as either primarily cognitive or primarily social-interpersonal. The evidence we review is occasionally based on single studies. Additional research is needed to replicate and to allow a precise meta-analytical examination of moderating factors.

Regarding cognitive moderators, studies indicate that social contagion is greater when the "contagious" items are consistent with expectations and cognitive schemas (Roediger et al. 2001, Meade & Roediger 2002), when the time for encoding the original material is short rather than long (Baron et al. 1996, Roediger et al. 2001), and when the communicated memory refers to peripheral (versus central) details (Dalton & Daneman 2006, Echterhoff et al. 2007). Furthermore, researchers (Gabbert et al. 2006, Wright et al. 2005) compared memory conformity effects for old information (items presented in the first study phase) versus new information (items not presented in the first phase). The results indicated that it is easier to create new memories than to undo old memories through means of social influence, in that conformity was greater for new than for old items.

Regarding social and interpersonal moderators, it has been consistently found that perceived experts are more successful at imposing their memories onto others than are perceived nonexperts (e.g., Brown et al. 2009). In most of the relevant studies, it is not that the "expert" actually knows more than the participant, but rather the experimenter manipulates the situation so that participants believe that she knows more and hence perceive her as an expert (for an elaborate technique for inducing expertise judgments, see French et al. 2011). Expertise effects are consistent with source monitoring accounts of social contagion. Source monitoring is often effortful, and in many circumstances, error prone. Consequently, as listeners believe in the truth of the speaker's utterances—as they might if they view the speaker as an expert—they may decrease their efforts at source monitoring. In such instances, more social contagion should be present.

Social contagion effects are also stronger when (*a*) the speaker has more (rather than less) power than the listener (Skagerberg & Wright 2008a); (*b*) when the speaker is the listener's friend or romantic partner (versus a stranger) (French et al. 2008, Peker & Tekcan 2009); (*c*) when a listener is more (versus less) anxious about a negative evaluation or when she has a low (versus high) tendency to avoid social contact (Wright et al. 2010); (*d*) when there are more (versus fewer) speakers suggesting the same memory (Meade & Roediger 2002); (*e*) when a group of several speakers agrees unanimously on a memory (versus does not agree unanimously due to one or more dissenters) (Walther et al. 2002); (*f*) when the biasing information is delivered face-to-face by physically co-present speakers (versus delivered in a less immediate way such as in writing) (Gabbert et al. 2004, Meade & Roediger 2002, Paterson & Kemp 2006); and (*g*) when the biasing information in a multiperson group conversation is produced by the narrator, i.e., the person who dominates the recounting of a past event (Brown et al. 2009, Cuc et al. 2006).

Warnings and resistance. In the studies we have discussed so far, participants had little reason to suspect that the source of postevent information provided erroneous information. As a result, the situation was rife with possibilities for social contagion. But people may realize that their memories may be influenced by what others say, and, accordingly, try to resist any possible influence. To study this resistance, psychologists have warned participants that the postevent narrative or what a speaker says may mislead them (see Echterhoff et al. 2005). Warnings can reduce the extent to which a speaker can influence a listener's memory. Although warnings provided before the misinformation (prewarnings) have been consistently effective (e.g., Boon & Baxter 2000), warnings after the misinformation (postwarnings) also reduce social contagion, but under more limited conditions. For instance, postwarnings are more effective the higher the participants' motive is to be accurate (Blank 1998) and the higher the perceived threat of appearing gullible and being unduly influenced (Echterhoff et al. 2005). Note, however, that even when social contagion effects are reduced by postwarnings, they frequently remain significant (e.g., Echterhoff et al. 2005, Meade & Roediger 2002), testifying to the robustness of the effect.

Interestingly, both prewarnings and postwarnings can come at a cost. Prewarnings, for instance, can have the paradoxical result of increasing social contagion. When listeners have a fragile memory and are uncertain of the veracity of their recollections, they may pay careful attention to what a speaker says. This increased attention may lead listeners to form a more robust memory of what the speaker says, increasing the chance of false memories for the original material. Consistent with this prediction, Muller & Hirst (2010) found that, with a prewarning, memory-challenged listeners will not only find it difficult to discriminate what was in a conversation from what was in the original material, but will also be more likely to falsely recognize new items introduced by a dominant speaker in the conversation. This effect represents the opposite of what a warning is intended to accomplish.

Postwarnings can not only reduce social contagion with a conversation, but they can also increase the incorrect rejection of old material (Echterhoff et al. 2007). Presumably, with a postwarning, people will try to monitor more carefully the source of their memory. As a result of this increased effort, rememberers may correctly reject material that they recollect as originating in the postevent conversation, thereby reducing the effect of the conversation on subsequent remembering. However, they may also incorrectly reject old items that appeared in both the original material and the postevent information. Thus, with a postwarning, rememberers may find themselves falsely rejecting valid event information.

Retrieval/Reexposure Effects

What is remembered in a conversation can affect the subsequent memories of conversational participants not only by implanting new and misleading memories, but also by reinforcing some memory and inducing forgetting for others. We consider the two separately.

Reinforcing existing memories. When a speaker in a conversation repeats something already known to the speaker and/or listeners, by virtue of the repetition, the preexisting memory is reinforced and subsequently remembered better than it would if it had not been repeated (Blumen & Rajaram 2008, Rajaram & Pereira-Pasarin 2007, Weldon & Bellinger 1997). The effect is generally stronger for the speaker (the person doing the remembering) than for listeners (Cuc et al. 2006). The advantage of the speaker could also be viewed as consistent with the generation effect, which established that items generated by a person are remembered better than those supplied by an outside source, such as an experimenter (Slamecka & Graf 1978; for a review, see Mulligan & Lozito 2004).

Retrieval-induced forgetting. When people selectively remember in a conversation, they are not only reinforcing existing memories, but, by not mentioning other memories, they are setting up conditions conducive for forgetting. Stone et al. (2011b) have referred to these unmentioned memories as mnemonic silences and argued that it is important to understand how the silences in conversational remembering shape subsequent memory. The most obvious explanation for why mnemonic silences might promote forgetting is that they allow the memory to decay (Wixted 2004).

Recently, it has been highlighted that more may be occurring than simple decay. Selective remembering may lead to retrieval-induced forgetting (RIF). There are some circumstances in which selective retrieval can facilitate subsequent recollection of the unmentioned material, e.g., when participants are encouraged to think about everything they previously studied (Chan et al. 2006). However, as Hirst & Echterhoff (2008) contended, the rapid give-and-take of a conversation sets up conditions conducive to retrieval-induced forgetting.

The effect on the speaker. RIF was originally studied without any concern about the social context in which selective retrieval takes place (see Anderson et al. 1994). Participants study material, such as category-exemplar word pairs, and then receive additional practice on some of this material. Some of the unpracticed material is related to the original material, some unrelated. Thus, if participants originally studied *fruit-apple*, *fruit-orange*, *vegetable-broccoli*, *vegetable-pea*, they might receive additional practice only on *fruit-apple*. The experimenter controls for what is or is not practiced by asking participants to complete the stem *fruit-ap___* and only that stem. According Anderson et al.'s nomenclature, the practice item (*apple*) is Rp+ (retrieval practiced), the related, unpracticed item (*orange*) is Rp- (unpracticed but related to a retrieval practiced item), and the unrelated, unpracticed items (*broccoli*, *pea*) are Nrp (not retrieval practiced). A final recall test followed the practice phase. Researchers have repeatedly found not only a practice effect (Rp+ > Nrp), but also evidence of retrieval-induced forgetting (Nrp > Rp-; for a review, see Anderson & Levy 2007). The most widely accepted explanation for RIF involves inhibition (Anderson & Levy 2007, but see, e.g., Perfect et al. 2004). That is, in order to retrieve successfully *apple*, participants must inhibit competing responses. This inhibition lingers, leading to RIF.

RIF is relevant to any discussion of the mnemonic consequences of conversational remembering because selective remembering in a conversational setting also elicits RIF. For example, when speaking about a trip to Coney Island, a speaker might remember the event *Rode on a roller coaster* but leave unmentioned the event *Ate a hot dog*. In this case, the selective retrieval of the roller coaster event will induce forgetting of the unmentioned, but related, hot dog event (Cuc et al. 2007). Selective conversational remembering, then, can not only reinforce the memories offered by a speaker, but can also induce forgetting in the speaker for unmentioned, related memories.

The effect on listeners. RIF is found not only when participants adopt the role of speaker in a conversation, but also when they serve the role of listener (Cuc et al. 2007). When discussing the induced forgetting associated with the speaker, Cuc et al. used the term "within-individual retrieval-induced

forgetting" (WI-RIF); when discussing the induced forgetting associated with the listener, they used the term "socially shared retrieval-induced forgetting" (SS-RIF). Cuc et al. (2007) argued that SS-RIF should emerge when listeners concurrently, albeit covertly, retrieve with the speaker. With this concurrent, covert retrieval, which can be as effective as overt retrieval in eliciting RIF (Anderson & Bell 2001), the listener will be in a situation similar to that of the speaker. As a result, similar retrieval-induced forgetting should be found for listeners and speakers.

As with WI-RIF, SS-RIF can be found for a wide variety of materials and situations: in a stem-completion task and when it is embedded in a free-flowing conversation (Cuc et al. 2007); for paired-associates and stories, but also for scientific material (Koppel et al. 2011), autobiographical memories (Stone et al. 2011a), and central elements as well as the details of a story (Stone et al. 2010). It also can be found for emotionally charged material, although here the results are not consistent (for work on either WI-RIF or SS-RIF and emotional material, see Barnier et al. 2004, Coman et al. 2009, Stone et al. 2011a).

Recently, Coman et al. (2009) showed that speakers and listeners do not have to study the same material or experience the same event for SS-RIF to occur. Rather, as long as what the speaker says evokes a related memory in the listener, SS-RIF can be found for the listener. Coman et al. examined conversations in which two people talk to each other about how they spent their day on September 11, 2001. Clearly, their autobiographical memories will be different. They did not spend the day in exactly the same way. Nevertheless, there will be similarities: Both would have awakened in the morning, both would have interacted with others after learning about the terrorist attacks in the United States, and so on. That is, the details differ, even if the overall script is similar. John awoke at 9; Mary at 7. John learned of the attacks at 10:15; Mary at 9:10, and so on. The assertion is that one participant's recollection of when she woke up will elicit similar, albeit

Socially shared retrieval-induced forgetting (SS-RIF): retrieval-induced forgetting found for listeners' memory of information selectively omitted (unmentioned) by a speaker

covert, recollections on the part of the other participant. As a result, Coman et al. found that the selective remembering in the conversation induced selective forgetting, both in speaker and listener. If one participant in the conversation mentioned that he learned of the attacks while home, but failed to mention that it was his mother who informed him, both members of the pair, on a subsequent memory test, found it hard to remember who informed them of the attacks. What the speaker and listener mutually forgot was not the same—after all, they had different memories. Nevertheless, they experienced trouble remembering similar classes of information.

Boundary conditions for RIF for both speakers and listeners. WI-RIF and SS-RIF do not occur in all circumstances. For instance, WI-RIF, and presumably SS-RIF, is diminished or eliminated when participants integrate the to-be-remembered material (Anderson & McCulloch 1999). This result may arise because, as Smith et al. (1978) have shown, integration diminishes response competition. Also, a negative mood appears to protect the rememberer from WI-RIF (Bäuml & Kuhbandner 2007). It is not at present known whether these findings also apply to SS-RIF.

Furthermore, and critically, SS-RIF depends on how listeners are monitoring the speaker's utterances. People often listen to speakers with different goals in mind. Jury members presumably monitor for the accuracy of what is recalled during jury deliberations as they try to remember a witness's testimony. On the other hand, a husband might only monitor for something superficial like entertainment value when he listens to his wife recount a funny story at a dinner party. Cuc et al. (2007) asked listeners to monitor either for the accuracy of what a speaker recollected or the fluency of their recollections. They reasoned that listeners should be more likely to concurrently retrieve, and hence exhibit SS-RIF, when monitoring for accuracy than when monitoring for fluency. They found that monitoring instructions mattered. RIF was present for both speaker and listener when the listener monitored for accuracy, but RIF was present only for the speaker when the listener monitored for fluency.

More recently, Koppel et al. (2011) went beyond explicit monitoring instructions and examined how the social relationship between speaker and listener might moderate concurrent retrieval and hence SS-RIF. The listener was told that the speaker, in this case, a lecturer, was or was not an expert on the presented material. There is little reason on the part of the listener to monitor for accuracy if the lecturer is perceived as an expert. Such monitoring is more likely if the lecturer is perceived as a nonexpert. Consequently, and as Koppel et al. found, SS-RIF should be significantly less when participants perceived the lecturer as an expert than when he is perceived as a poorly prepared nonexpert. Clearly, the presence of SS-RIF depends upon the social relation between speaker and listener, in this case, the status of expertise that exists between them. Interestingly, Koppel and colleagues (2011) included in their experiment an assessment of social contagion. As noted above, social contagion increases if the source of the contagion is viewed as an expert. Koppel et al. replicated this result. Hence, expertise apparently has divergent effects on the listener: increasing social contagion and decreasing induced forgetting.

MOVING BEYOND A SINGLE SOCIAL INTERACTION

The previous sections outlined ways in which joint conversational remembering can reshape the memories of speakers and listeners— through social contagion, reinforcement, and retrieval-induced forgetting. It mainly focuses on a single social interaction between two (or sometimes three or four) individuals. But social interactions usually involve a sequence of exchanges. Consider a news event. A group of people might read a newspaper article, listen to a politician speak, and talk to friends about the speech and the newspaper coverage. The friends in turn talk to others with similar experiences. In this way, the memory can be established, altered, and spread in some form or another across a social network. How do mnemonic influences propagate through a network of individuals? Can we extrapolate from what is known about social interactions between two people to more complex sequences of social interactions?

Bartlett's (1932) work on the serial reproduction task is the classic starting point for studying mnemonic propagation. One person tells another, uninformed person about a story; this second person then tells an uninformed third, and so on. As anyone who has experimented with this task at a party knows, the original story can be radically altered as it passes from one person to the next. Bartlett stressed that the changes are schema consistent. The story is simplified, modified, and rationalized according to the schema held by participants along the chain. Earlier work on the spread of rumors also stressed the role of schema (Allport & Postman 1965).

Kashima and colleagues (for a review, see Kashima 2008) used the serial reproduction task to study the formation of stereotypes. In a representative study, participants received stereotypic information on the characteristics of a fictitious group, the "Jamayans" (Lyons & Kashima 2003). They then studied a story about a member of the group, which contained information about the members that was both stereotype consistent and stereotype inconsistent. The authors examine the conditions under which the stereotype is transmitted in a four-person serial reproduction chain. It was found that stereotype-consistent information about the group member was transmitted along the chain to a greater extent than stereotype-inconsistent information. This finding demonstrated the enhanced transmission of stereotype-consistent information through chains of communication. Notably, the effect was larger when participants believed that the stereotypical view of the Jamayans was shared by their audience. In discussing their findings, Kashima and colleagues focus more on the principles governing transmission than on the effect of the transmission on memory.

One limit of the work on serial reproduction is that it largely examines situations in which new information is spread across a network, with each individual in the network learning the information for the first time. But, as our illustration about learning and talking about a current event makes clear, there are many examples of people already having a memory when they listen, for instance, to a politician speak about a current event or when they talk to each other about the event. The work on single social interactions suggests that these exchanges might reshape participants' memory, but does this influence propagate through more than one social interaction? After listening to the politician's speech, will the politician's influence, in turn, affect subsequent conversations and propagate through these conversations to produce a lasting impact on memory? If mnemonic influences are limited to a single exchange, they may have little relevance in the real world. However, if they propagate through a sequence of exchanges, they may have a great bearing on what people finally remember about the past.

Recently, in an effort to move beyond the effects that follow a single conversation, Coman & Hirst (2012) traced how RIF can propagate through a series of social interactions. They focused on two types of social interactions that occur in everyday life: (*a*) one-way listening, as when one listens to a lecture or a political speech, and (*b*) conversational interaction. They looked at how listening to a lecture reshapes memories of learned material and whether the influence of the lecture propagates into a conversation and then through the conversation to a final recall test. Such sequences are common in everyday life, as, per our previous example, when someone reads an account of an event in a newspaper, then listens to a presidential address, and then talks to friends and relatives about the event. Coman & Hirst (2012) assessed practice effects and RIF in such sequences. They found, not surprising given their previous work, that the lecturer influenced participants' memories, as measured by practice effects and RIF. Moreover, in reaching beyond a single social interaction, they found that, when

Serial reproduction task: method to study (often schema-consistent) changes of information passed from one person to another in a series of dyadic interactions

conversations were between like-minded individuals, these influences shaped what was remembered in the conversation. In the end, when examining individuals with similar attitudes, the lecturer's influence on participants' memories propagated into a final recall test, suggesting a lasting influence. The results indicate that mnemonic influences exhibit a principle of transitivity as they propagate through a sequence of social interactions. Moreover, and importantly, as they propagate through the exchange, their effect increases rather than decreases. Politicians can have a profound influence on what people remember, even when their listeners turn to each other to discuss the issue in an effort to remember the original material as best as they can.

Coman & Hirst's (2012) study is only a first step, in that they examined propagation in a small sequence of social interactions. Their results, however, suggest that researchers could understand propagation in larger networks by (*a*) considering the effects of a single social interaction on memory and then (*b*) extending what is observed at this local level to the larger network. In other words, researchers might observe macrolevel principles of a network of individuals emerge in predictable ways out of microlevel processing. This assertion is a central assumption in the growing field of agent-based modeling and related work on network theory (e.g., Epstein 2006). Coman & Hirst (2012) explored how microlevel processing in a single social interaction shapes the emergent memories in a small network. The next step might be to use agent-based modeling techniques and network theory to extend the approach to larger networks.

MOTIVES IN CONVERSATIONAL REMEMBERING AND THE CREATION OF A SHARED REALITY

Our focus is on the impact of conversational remembering on memory, not the motives that shape what is said in a conversation (for discussions of communication goals, see McCann

& Higgins 1988; for discussions of motives for social sharing and autobiographical recounting, see Pasupathi 2001, Rimé 2007). But motives are important not only in shaping what is said, but also for the impact of conversations on subsequent memory. In discussing SS-RIF, for instance, we noted that the way in which the listener monitors the speaker matters. SS-RIF emerged, for instance, when listeners monitored for accuracy, not fluency (Cuc et al. 2007).

One intensely studied area pertinent to the study of motives and conversational remembering is the effect audience tuning has on the subsequent memory of the speaker. As we noted, speakers tune what they say to an audience, often taking into account the attitude of the audience. The effect of this tuning on subsequent memory has been studied extensively in the context of the saying-is-believing paradigm (Higgins & Rholes 1978; for a review, see Echterhoff et al. 2009a). In these studies, participants are given several passages presenting a target character in ambiguous terms (e.g., the passage, "Donald uses coupons, buys things on sale, avoids donating money or lending money to friends") that can be labeled as either "thrifty" or "stingy". They are then told to describe Donald to an audience that either likes or dislikes him. Participants tune their message to their audience, describing the character as "thrifty" to the favorable audience and as "stingy" to the unfavorable audience. Importantly, in a final recall test, where participants are told to recall the initial story, they remember the character in a manner consistent with the tuned message. The participants will come to believe and remember what they said to their audience rather than what they originally learned about the character. Speakers' expectations about the beliefs or attitudes of an audience often shape not only their message, but under certain conditions, also shape their memory (Echterhoff et al. 2009a).

The presence of this memory bias appears to depend on the motives of the speakers, in particular, whether they are motivated to create a shared reality with the audience. Shared reality is conceptualized as the motivated and experienced commonality between one's own and others' representations and evaluations of the world (Echterhoff et al. 2009a). In order to demonstrate the role of shared reality in the saying-is-believing effect, Echterhoff et al. (2008) asked German participants to describe the target person to a Turkish audience (a minority outgroup in Germany) or to a German audience. Both the Turkish audience and the German audience either liked the target or disliked him. Interestingly, participants made greater efforts to tune their message to their Turkish audience than to their German audience, so they seemed motivated to tune to their audience. However, the tuning to the Turkish audience had no effect in terms of memory restructuring. That is, although they described the target consistent with the Turkish audience's attitudes, the tuning did not translate in memory restructuring, as it did in the German audience condition. According to Echterhoff et al. (2008), the key difference was in the motive underlying audience tuning: creating a shared reality with a German ingroup audience versus complying with (politeness, egalitarian) norms with the Turkish outgroup audience.

The creation of a shared reality can satisfy two core human motives—epistemic and relational (Echterhoff et al. 2009a). Epistemic motives refer to the need to achieve a valid and reliable understanding of the world and to establish what is real (Higgins 2012). Humans are motivated by what Bartlett (1932) called effort after meaning, a fundamental need to understand the events and circumstances of their lives. The urgency of such epistemic needs increases with the uncertainty or ambiguity that individuals experience about a target entity. Relational motives refer to the need to affiliate and feel connected with others.

In the saying-is-believing studies, the ambiguity of the original information about the target supplied in the experiments should elicit epistemic motives to reduce the uncertainty. Speakers achieve this reduction, at least to some extent, by incorporating into their view of the target the audience-tuned message and thus

create a shared reality with the audience (see Echterhoff et al. 2009a). Evidence from several experiments is consistent with the prediction that speakers' motivation to create a shared reality varies with (*a*) their need to reduce uncertainty about a target (Kopietz et al. 2010), (*b*) the extent to which their audience tuning serves epistemic goals (Echterhoff et al. 2008), and (*c*) the appropriateness (trustworthiness) of the audience for creating a shared reality (Echterhoff et al. 2005a, 2009b; Kopietz et al. 2009). Critically, under these motivational conditions, the result is a "shared reality" between speaker and audience about the target person.

COLLECTIVE MEMORY

Conversational remembering can be viewed as a social practice that promotes the formation of a collective memory (for a discussion of collective memories formed through communication, see Assmann 1995). By collective memory, we mean memories shared across a community that bear on the identity of that community (see Manier & Hirst 2008 for further elaboration). The study of collective memory has a long history, dating back to the original work of Durkheim's student Maurice Halbwachs (1950/1980). Social scientists studying collective memory often focus more on less-ephemeral means of promoting the formation of collective memories than on conversations, e.g., memorials and commemorations. Still, there is agreement that when it comes to vernacular or informal collective memories, especially those formed by the populace in a repressive society, conversations are a main means through which collective memories are established and maintained. For instance, only through conversational interactions could Lithuanians of Lithuanian descent construct a collective memory around national historical events not found in the Russian textbooks they studied in school (Schuman et al. 1994).

Recent attempts to build a naturalistic account of culture nicely divide the study of collective memory into two distinct subtopics: social practices and psychological mechanisms. Scholars interested in a naturalistic approach

Collective memory: representations of the past held by members of a community that contribute to the community's sense of identity

often likened the study of culture to an epidemiology of beliefs (e.g., Hirst & Manier 2008, Sperber 1996; see also the work on memes, e.g., Dawkins 1976). Just as epidemiologists study why some, and not other, viruses spread quickly across a community and survive over time, so can students of culture (read here, collective memory) study why some, and not other, beliefs and memories spread quickly across a community and survive. The spread of a virus—or a memory—will depend on at least two factors, that is, the social practice of a community and the mechanisms specific to the virus or memory that ensure survival. When trying to understand the spread of HIV among the gay community in the 1980s, epidemiologists discuss possible social practices that might foster its spread, such as frequent visits to bathhouses. They also underscore various characteristics of the virus itself that make the social practices effective, e.g., the fact that it takes months after infection for any health consequences to appear. In a similar way, when it comes to the study of collective memories, an examination of both mnemonic/social practices and underlying psychological processes is essential to understanding the formation of a collective memory. Clearly, mnemonic/social practices, including the practice of conversing, matter. For instance, the accuracy of memories for public traumatic events, such as those of 9/11, depends on the extent to which people talk about the event (Hirst et al. 2009). But psychological mechanisms also play a role (for a more extensive discussion of this point, see Hirst & Manier 2008; for a psychological approach to collective memory that does not involve communication, see Shteynberg 2010; see also Brown et al. 2009, Curci et al. 2001, Sahdra & Ross 2007, Schuman & Scott 1989).

Our review of the literature on conversational remembering articulates some of the psychological mechanisms that might be involved in the formation of collective memories. Indeed, the review suggests that the human memory system seems designed, in part, to promote the formation of collective memories through conversations. Social contagion, reinforcement, and retrieval-induced forgetting are all means by which speakers and listeners can come to share a similar rendering of the past. As a speaker implants a memory into listeners, the speaker and listeners come to share the same implanted memory. As a speaker restates a past event, both speaker and listeners rehearse the memory and subsequently find it more accessible. And as a speaker leaves some memories unmentioned, the unmentioned related memories are more likely forgotten in subsequent acts of remembering than the unmentioned, unrelated memories, again, for both speaker and listeners.

This convergence is well documented. Work on memory conformity and conversational remembering studies establishes that memories of participants in a conversation overlap more after the conversation than before the conversation, in part because of reinforcement and in part because of social contagion (Cuc et al. 2006, Wright et al. 2000). Stone et al. (2010) have similarly shown that there is more evidence of collective remembering and collective forgetting after a conversation than before a conversation. Critically, they established that the pattern of collective remembering and collective forgetting is just what one would expect from practice effects and retrieval-induced forgetting. Coman & Hirst's (2012) study of mnemonic propagation revealed that collective memories solidify as mnemonic influence transfers through a sequence of social exchanges.

Of course, psychological mechanisms other than social contagion, reinforcement, and retrieval-induced forgetting also govern the formation of collective memories through conversation. Bartlett (1932) underscored the role of schema. Of particular relevance in this regard is Wertsch's (2002, 2008) work on schematic narrative templates. According to Wertsch, a community's schematic narrative template shapes what people remember about their national historical past and how they remember it. In contrast to specific narratives, these are generalized structures used to generate multiple specific narratives with the same basic plots. Russians, for instance, often render historical episodes employing the following template:

(*a*) Russia is peaceful and does not interfere with others. (*b*) A foreign enemy treacherously attacks Russia without provocation. (*c*) Russia is almost fully defeated as it suffers from the enemy's attempts to destroy it as a civilization. (*d*) Through heroism, and against all odds, Russia and its people triumph and succeed in expelling the foreign enemy, thus justifying its status as a great nation. The Russian rendering of the Napoleonic invasion and defeat, for instance, nicely reflects this template.

Not every nation has a close-to-defeat-then-triumph template. As we said, they are often community specific. The United States has several quite different templates, for instance, "the mystique of Manifest Destiny" and the "reluctant hegemon." These guide Americans' rendering of their historical past just as the triumphal template guides that of Russians.

Although schematic narrative templates are often established through formal means, in many instances, they can be established only through conversation. The conversationally derived templates, in turn, shape subsequent conversations and, through these conversations, promote the formation of a collective memory. It is through conversational interactions that Estonians reject the Russian-derived narrative template of "liberation of the proletariat" and develop an independent narrative of their continued subjugation by Russia (Wertsch 2002). Similarly, the Camisards of the south of France adopt a distinctive template of separatism and religious antagonism to account for, among other things, the revolt of 1702–1704 (Fentress & Wickham 1992).

It appears, then, that conversations repeatedly contribute to the formation of collective memory. They do so by reshaping memory in similar ways across a group, through psychological phenomena such as social contagion, rehearsal, or retrieval-induced forgetting. And they do so by fostering or altering schema. Government and other sources of power have formal means for providing social practices that engage each of these psychological phenomena. Conversations can also occur outside of this institutional, or authoritarian, framework and promote the development of alternative collective representations of the past.

CONCLUSION

Memory researchers have always known that social influences shape what is remembered. Traditionally, following the Ebbinghausian program, they have reacted to this knowledge by carefully controlling for social influence, thereby revealing the "raw material" of memory. One cannot, however, predict what people remember in daily life from what one learns from studying this raw material. Remembering is always embedded within a social context.

This review has focused on understanding how one type of social context, conversation, shapes memory. People are constantly talking to each other about the past. This continuous communication profoundly alters what people remember as they converse and what they remember subsequent to the conversation. In particular, acts of remembering within a conversation supply a context in which conversing individuals can influence each other's memory. This mutual influence can lead to a convergence among participants on a shared representation of the past. This possibility suggests that the usual characterization of memory implantation or forgetting as flaws or "sins" of memory may not be entirely accurate. They may also be treated as assets in that they promote the formation of a collective memory (Hirst 2010). Given the sociality of humans—and the possible critical role collective memories might play in undergirding this sociality—one can see why the malleability and unreliability of memory—and in particular, social contagion and induced forgetting—might have been preserved through evolution.

This latter point underscores the benefits of opening up the study of memory to the social settings in which remembering takes place. One might not have realized how well tuned the memory system is for promoting the formation of collective memories if one had not examined conversational remembering. Twenty years ago, social, and, in particular, conversational aspects of remembering would not have figured in most psychological discussions of memory. As this review makes clear, not only is there a substantial and ever-growing literature, but the extant research allows psychologists to reassess how memory functions in daily life.

SUMMARY POINTS

1. Remembering in a conversation is always selective. People remember more than they might when remembering alone (collaborative facilitation), but less than the sum of the potential of all conversational participants (collaborative inhibition).

2. One participant in a conversation can influence the memory of other participants in various ways, including through social contagion, rehearsal/reexposure effects, and retrieval-induced forgetting.

3. The effect of one member of a conversation on her own or others' memory must be understood in social terms since the effect is moderated by social factors.

4. It is difficult to eliminate social influences on memory in conversations. The presence of others in the conversation typically leads conversational participants to influence the memory of the others.

5. The social influences present in a conversation produce, in many instances, similar effects on both speaker and listeners. As a result, a conversation may serve as a social practice promoting the formation of a collective memory.

6. Although the social influences in a conversation often affect speaker and listeners in similar ways, at least one difference is worth noting. For speakers to reshape their own memories, they often need to be motivated to create a shared reality with the listener. For the speaker to reshape the memories of the listener, the motivation of the listener is often critical, but not the motivation of the speaker. Regarding the speaker, then, the influences of communication on listeners' memory can be unintended and hence can be understood as emergent side effects of conducting conversations.

DISCLOSURE STATEMENT

The authors are not aware of any affiliations, funding, or financial holdings that might be perceived as affecting the objectivity of this review.

ACKNOWLEDGMENTS

The authors wish to thank Jens Hellmann and Robert Meksin for comments on an early version of the review and Evelyn Alex for assistance with the reference management. The support of National Science Foundation grant #BCS-0819067 is gratefully acknowledged.

LITERATURE CITED

Allport GW, Postman LJ. 1965. *The Psychology of Rumor*. New York: Russell & Russell

Anderson MC, Bell TA. 2001. Forgetting our facts: the role of inhibitory processes in the loss of propositional knowledge. *J. Exp. Psychol.: Gen.* 130:544–70

Anderson MC, Bjork RA, Bjork EL. 1994. Remembering can cause forgetting: retrieval dynamics in long-term memory. *J. Exp. Psychol.: Learn. Mem. Cogn.* 20L 1063–87

Anderson MC, Levy BJ. 2007. Theoretical issues in inhibition: insights from research on human memory. In *Inhibition in Cognition*, ed. MC Anderson, BJ Levy, pp. 81–102. Washington, DC: Am. Psychol. Assoc.

Anderson MC, McCulloch KC. 1999. Integration as a general boundary condition on retrieval-induced forgetting. *J. Exp. Psychol.: Learn. Mem. Cogn.* 25:608–29

Andersson J. 2001. Net effect of memory collaboration: How is collaboration affected by factors such as friendship, gender, and age? *Scand. J. Psychol.* 42:367–75

Asch SE. 1956. Studies of independence and conformity: a minority of one against a unanimous majority. *Psychol. Monogr.* 70:Whole No. 416

Assmann J. 1995. Collective memory and cultural identity. *New German Crit.* 65:125–33

Barnier AJ, Hung L, Conway MA. 2004. Retrieval-induced forgetting of emotional and unemotional autobiographical memories. *Cogn. Emot.* 18:457–77

Barnier AJ, Sutton J, Harris CB, Wilson RA. 2008. A conceptual and empirical framework for the social distribution of cognition: the case of memory. *Cogn. Syst. Res.* 9:33–51

Baron RS, Vandello JA, Brunsman B. 1996. The forgotten variable in conformity research: impact of task importance on social influence. *J. Personal. Soc. Psychol.* 71:915–27

Bartlett F. 1932. *Remembering: A Study in Experimental and Social Psychology*. New York: Cambridge Univ. Press

Basden BH, Basden DR, Bryner S, Thomas RL III. 1997. A comparison of group and individual remembering: Does collaboration disrupt retrieval strategies? *J. Exp. Psychol.: Learn. Mem. Cogn.* 23:1176–89

Basden BH, Basden DR, Henry S. 2000. Cost and benefits of collaborative remembering. *Appl. Cogn. Psychol.* 14:497–507

Basden DR, Basden BH. 1995. Some tests of the strategy disruption interpretation of part-list cuing inhibition. *J. Exp. Psychol.: Learn. Mem. Cogn.* 21:1656–69

Bateson G. 1979. *Mind and Nature: A Necessary Unity (Advances in Systems Theory, Complexity, and the Human Sciences)*. New York: Hampton

Bäuml K-H, Kuhbandner C. 2007. Remembering can cause forgetting—but not in negative moods. *Psychol. Sci.* 18:111–15

Blank H. 1998. Memory states and memory tasks: an integrative framework for eyewitness memory and suggestibility. *Memory* 6:481–529

Bluck S. 2003. Autobiographical memory: exploring its functions in everyday life. *Memory* 11:113–23

Blumen S, Rajaram S. 2008. Effects of group collaboration and repeated retrieval on individual recall. *Memory* 16:231–44

Boon JCW, Baxter JS. 2000. Minimizing interrogative suggestibility. *Legal Criminol. Psychol.* 5:273–84

Brown AD, Coman A, Hirst W. 2009. The role of narratorship and expertise in social remembering. *Soc. Psychol.* 40:113–29

Brown NR, Lee PJ, Krsiak M, Conrad FG, Havelka J, Reddon JR. 2009. Living in history: how war, terrorism, and natural disaster affect the organization of autobiographical memory. *Psychol. Sci.* 20:399–405

Chan JCK, McDermott KB, Roediger HL III. 2006. Retrieval-induced facilitation: Initially nontested material can benefit from prior testing of related material. *J. Exp. Psychol.* 135:553–71

Clark A. 2010. *Supersizing the Mind: Embodiment, Action, and Cognitive Extension*. New York: Oxford Univ. Press

Coman A, Hirst W. 2012. The propagation of socially shared retrieval induced forgetting in social networks. *J. Exp. Psychol.: Gen.* In press

Coman A, Manier D, Hirst W. 2009. Forgetting the unforgettable through conversation: Socially shared retrieval-induced forgetting of September 11 memories. *Psychol. Sci.* 20:627–33

Congleton A, Rajaram S. 2011. The influence of learning history on collaborative and individual retrieval. *J. Exp. Psych: Gen.* doi: 10.1037/a0024308. In press

Cruz MG, Boster FJ, Rodriguez JI. 1997. The impact of group size and proportion of shared information on the exchange and integration of information in groups. *Commun. Res.* 24:291–313

Cuc A, Koppel J, Hirst W. 2007. Silence is not golden: a case for socially shared retrieval-induced forgetting. *Psychol. Sci.* 18:727–37

Cuc A, Ozuru Y, Manier D, Hirst W. 2006. The transformation of collective memories: studies of family recounting. *Mem. Cogn.* 34:752–62

Curci A, Luminet O, Finkenauer C, Gisle L. 2001. Flashbulb memories in social groups: a comparative test-retest study of the memory of French President Mitterand's death in a French and Belgian group. *Memory* 9:81–101

Dalton AL, Daneman M. 2006. Social suggestibility to central and peripheral misinformation. *Memory* 14:486–501

Dawkins R. 1976. *The Selfish Gene*. New York: Oxford Univ. Press

Deutsch M, Gerard HB. 1955. A study of normative and informational social influences upon individual judgment. *J. Abnorm. Soc. Psychol.* 51:629–36

Dudukovic NM, Marsh EJ, Tversky B. 2004. Telling a story or telling it straight: the effects of entertaining versus accurate retellings on memory. *Appl. Cogn. Psychol.* 18:125–43

Ebbinghaus H. 1964. *Memory*. New York: Dover

Echterhoff G, Groll S, Hirst W. 2007. Tainted truth: overcorrection for misinformation influence on eyewitness memory. *Soc. Cogn.* 25:367–409

Echterhoff G, Higgins ET, Kopietz R, Groll S. 2008. How communication goals determine when audience tuning biases memory. *J. Exp. Psychol.: Gen.* 137:3–21

Echterhoff G, Higgins ET, Levine JM. 2009a. Shared reality: experiencing commonality with others' inner states about the world. *Perspect. Psychol. Sci.* 4:496–521

Echterhoff G, Hirst W. 2002. Remembering in a social context: a conversational view of the study of memory. In *Kontexte und Kulturen des Erinnerns: Maurice Halbwachs und das Paradigma des Kollektiven Gedächtnisses* [*Contexts and Cultures of Remembering: Maurice Halbwachs and the Paradigm of Collective Memory*], ed. G Echterhoff, M Saar, pp. 75–101. Konstanz, Germany: Univ. Konstanz

Echterhoff G, Hirst W, Hussy W. 2005. How eyewitnesses resist misinformation: social postwarnings and the monitoring of memory characteristics. *Mem. Cogn.* 30:770–82

Echterhoff G, Lang S, Krämer N, Higgins ET. 2009b. Audience-tuning effects on memory: the role of audience status in sharing reality. *Soc. Psychol.* 40:150–63

Epstein J. 2006. *Generative Social Science: Studies in Agent-Based Computational Modeling*. Princeton, NJ: Princeton Univ. Press

Fentress J, Wickham C. 1992. *Social Memory*. Cambridge, MA: Blackwell

Findlay F, Hitch ET, Meudell PR. 2000. Mutual inhibition in collaborative recall: evidence for a retrieval-based account. *J. Exp. Psychol.: Learn. Mem. Cogn.* 26:1556–67

French L, Garry M, Mori K. 2008. You say tomato? Collaborative remembering leads to more false memories for intimate couples than for strangers. *Memory* 16:262–73

French L, Garry M, Mori K. 2011. Relative—not absolute—judgments of credibility affect susceptibility to misinformation conveyed during discussion. *Acta Psychol.* 136:119–28

Gabbert F, Memon A, Allan K. 2003. Memory conformity: Can eyewitnesses influence each other's memories for an event? *Appl. Cogn. Psychol.* 17:533–44

Gabbert F, Memon A, Allan K, Wright DB. 2004. Say it to my face: examining the effects of socially encountered misinformation. *Legal Criminol. Psychol.* 9:215–27

Gabbert F, Memon A, Allan K, Wright DB. 2006. Memory conformity: disentangling the steps towards influence during a discussion. *Psychon. Bull. Rev.* 13:480–85

Grice HP. 1975. Logic and conversation. In *Syntax and Semantics 3: Speech Acts*, ed. P Cole, JL Morgan, pp. 41–58. San Diego, CA: Academic

Halbwachs M. 1950. *Collective Memory*. Transl. FJ Ditter, VY Ditter, 1980. New York: Harper & Row

Harber KD, Cohen DJ. 2005. The emotional broadcaster theory of social sharing. *J. Lang. Soc. Psychol.* 24:382–400

Higgins ET. 2012. *Beyond Pleasure and Pain: How Motivation Works*. New York: Oxford Univ. Press

Higgins ET, Rholes WS. 1978. Saying is believing: effects of message modification on memory and liking for the person described. *J. Exp. Soc. Psychol.* 14:363–78

Hirst W. 2010. A virtue of memory: the contribution of mnemonic malleability to collective memory. In *The Cognitive Neuroscience of the Mind: A Tribute to Michael S. Gazzaniga*, ed. PA Reuter-Lorenz, K Baynes, GR Mangun, EA Phelps, pp. 139–54. Cambridge, MA: MIT Press

Hirst W, Echterhoff G. 2008. Creating shared memories in conversation: toward a psychology of collective memory. *Soc. Res.* 75:78–91

Hirst W, Manier D. 2008. Towards a psychology of collective memory. *Memory* 16:183–200

Hirst W, Phelps EA, Buckner RL, Budson AE, Cuc A, et al. 2009. Long-term retention of the terrorist attack of September 11: flashbulb memories, event memories, and the factors that influence their retention. *J. Exp. Psychol.: Gen.* 138:161–76

Hollingshead AB. 1998a. Retrieval processes in transactive memory systems. *J. Personal. Soc. Psychol.* 74:659–71

Hollingshead AB. 1998b. Communication, learning, and retrieval in transactive memory systems. *J. Personal. Soc. Psychol.* 34:423–42

Hollingshead AB, Brandon DP. 2003. Potential benefits of communication in transactive memory systems. *Hum. Commun. Res.* 29:607–15

Hutchins E. 1995. *Cognition in the Wild*. Cambridge, MA: MIT Press

Hyman IE. 1994. Conversational remembering: story recall with a peer versus for an experimenter. *Appl. Cogn. Psychol.* 8:49–66

Kashima Y. 2008. A social psychology of cultural dynamics: examining how cultures are formed, maintained, and transformed. *Soc. Personal. Psychol. Compass* 2:107–20

Kerr NL, Tindale RS. 2004. Group performance and decision making. *Annu. Rev. Psychol.* 55:623–55

Kopietz R, Echterhoff G, Niemeier S, Hellmann JH, Memon A. 2009. Audience-congruent biases in eyewitness memory and judgment: influences of a co-witness' liking for a suspect. *Soc. Psychol.* 40:138–49

Kopietz R, Hellmann JH, Higgins ET, Echterhoff G. 2010. Shared-reality effects on memory: communicating to fulfill epistemic needs. *Soc. Cogn.* 28:353–78

Koppel J, Wohl D, Meksin R, Hirst W. 2011. The role of expertise and resistance in moderating socially shared retrieval-induced forgetting. Manuscript in preparation

Koriat A, Goldsmith M, Pansky A. 2000. Towards a psychology of memory accuracy. *Annu. Rev. Psychol.* 51:481–537

Lindsay DS, Hagen L, Read JD, Wade KA, Garry M. 2004. True photographs and false memories. *Psychol. Sci.* 15:149–54

Loftus EF. 2005. Planting misinformation in the human mind: a 30-year investigation of the malleability of memory. *Learn. Mem.* 12:361–66

Lyons A, Kashima Y. 2003. How are stereotypes maintained through communication? The influence of stereotype sharedness. *J. Personal. Soc. Psychol.* 85:989–1005

Manier D, Hirst W. 2008. A cognitive taxonomy of collective memories. In *Cultural Memory Studies*, ed. A Erll, A Nünning, pp. 253–62. New York: Walter de Gruyter

Marsh EJ. 2007. Retelling is not the same as recalling: implications for memory. *Curr. Dir. Psychol. Sci.* 16:16–20

McCann CD, Higgins ET. 1988. Motivation and affect in interpersonal relations: the role of personal orientations and discrepancies. In *Communication, Social Cognition, and Affect*, ed. L Donohew, HE Sypher, ET Higgins, pp. 53–79. Hillsdale, NJ: Erlbaum

Mead GH. 1934. *Mind, Self, and Society*. Chicago, IL: Univ. Chicago Press

Meade ML, Nokes TJ, Morrow DG. 2009. Expertise promotes facilitation on a collaborative memory task. *Memory* 17:39–48

Meade ML, Roediger HL. 2002. Explorations in the social cognition of memory. *Mem. Cogn.* 30:995–1009

Meudell PR, Hitch GJ, Boyle MM. 1995. Collaboration in recall: Do pairs of people cross-cue each other to produce new memories? *Q. J. Exp. Psychol. A* 48:141–52

Mitchell KJ, Johnson MK. 2009. Source monitoring 15 years later: What have we learned from fMRI about the neural mechanisms of source memory? *Psychol. Bull.* 135:638–77

Muller F, Hirst W. 2010. Resisting the influence of others: limits to the formation of a collective memory through conversational remembering. *Appl. Cogn. Psychol.* 24:608–25

Mulligan NW, Lozito JP. 2004. Self-generation and memory. *Psychol. Learn. Motiv.* 45:175–214

Pasupathi M. 2001. The social construction of the personal past and its implications for adult development. *Psychol. Bull.* 127:651–72

Pasupathi M, McLean KC, Weeks T. 2009. To tell or not to tell: disclosure and the narrative self. *J. Personal.* 77:1–35

Pasupathi M, Stallworth LM, Murdoch K. 1998. How what we tell becomes what we know: listener effects on speakers' long-term memory for events. *Discourse Process.* 26:1–25

Paterson HM, Kemp RI. 2006. Comparing methods of encountering postevent information: the power of co-witness suggestion. *Appl. Cogn. Psychol.* 20:1083–99

Peker M, Tekcan AI. 2009. The role of familiarity among group members in collaborative inhibition and social contagion. *Soc. Psychol.* 40:111–18

Pennebaker JW, Paez D, Rime B. 1997. *Collective Memory of Political Events: Social Psychological Perspectives.* Hillsdale, NJ: Erlbaum

Pereira-Pasarin LP, Rajaram S. 2011. Study repetition and divided attention: effects of encoding manipulations on collaborative inhibition in group recall. *Mem. Cogn.* doi: 10.3758/s13421-011-0087-y. In press

Perfect TJ, Stark L, Tree J, Moulin C, Ahmed L, Hutter R. 2004. Transfer appropriate forgetting: the cue-dependent nature of retrieval-induced forgetting. *J. Mem. Lang.* 51:399–417

Pillemer DB. 1992. Remembering personal circumstances: a functional analysis. In *Affect and Accuracy in Recall: Studies of Flashbulb Memories*, ed. U Neisser, E Winograd, pp. 121–37. New York: Cambridge Univ. Press

Rajaram S, Pereira-Pasarin LP. 2007. Collaboration can improve individual recognition memory: evidence from immediate and delay tests. *Psychon. Bull. Rev.* 14:95–100

Rajaram S, Pereira-Pasarin LP. 2010. Collaborative memory: cognitive research and theory. *Perspect. Psychol. Sci.* 5:649–63

Rimé B. 2007. Interpersonal emotion regulation. In *Handbook of Emotion Regulation*, ed. JJ Gross, pp. 466–85. New York: Guilford

Roediger HL, Meade ML, Bergman E. 2001. Social contagion of memory. *Psychon. Bull. Rev.* 8:365–71

Sahdra B, Ross M. 2007. Group identification and historical memory. *Personal. Soc. Psychol. Bull.* 33:384–95

Schuman HS, Rieger C, Gaidys V. 1994. Collective memories in the United States and Lithuania. In *Autobiographical Memory and the Validity of Retrospective Reports*, ed. N Schwarz, S Sudman, pp. 313–33. New York: Springer-Verlag

Schuman HS, Scott J. 1989. Generations and collective memories. *Am. Sociol. Rev.* 54:359–81

Sherif M. 1936. *The Psychology of Social Norms*. New York: Harper & Brothers

Shteynberg G. 2010. A silent emergence of culture: the social tuning effect. *J. Personal. Soc. Psychol.* 99:683–89

Skagerberg EM, Wright DB. 2008a. Manipulating power can affect memory conformity. *Appl. Cogn. Psychol.* 22:207–16

Skagerberg EM, Wright DB. 2008b. The prevalence of co-witnesses and co-witness discussions in real eyewitnesses. *Psychol. Crime Law* 14:513–21

Slamecka NJ, Graf P. 1978. The generation effect: delineation of a phenomenon. *J. Exp. Psychol.: Hum. Learn. Mem.* 4:592–604

Smith EE, Adams NE, Schorr D. 1978. Fact retrieval and the paradox of interference. *Cogn. Psychol.* 10:438–64

Sperber D. 1996. *Explaining Culture: A Naturalistic Approach*. Cambridge, MA: Blackwell

Sperber D, Wilson D. 1986. *Relevance: Communication and Cognition*. Oxford, UK: Blackwell

Stasser G, Titus W. 1987. Effects of information load and percentage of shared information on the dissemination of unshared information during group discussion. *J. Personal. Soc. Psychol.* 53:81–93

Stone CB, Barnier AJ, Sutton J, Hirst W. 2010. Building consensus about the past: schema consistency and convergence in socially shared retrieval-induced forgetting. *Memory* 18:170–84

Stone CB, Barnier AJ, Sutton J, Hirst W. 2011a. Forgetting our personal past: socially shared retrieval-induced forgetting for autobiographical memories. Manuscript under review

Stone CB, Coman A, Brown AD, Koppel J, Hirst W. 2011b. Toward a science of silence: the consequences of leaving a memory unsaid. *Perspect. Psychol. Sci.* In press

Sutton J, Harris CB, Keil PG, Barnier AJ. 2011. The psychology of memory, extended cognition, and socially distributed remembering. *Phenomenol. Cogn. Sci.* 9:521–60

Takahashi M, Saito S. 2004. Does test delay eliminate collaborative inhibition? *Memory* 38:722–31

Tulving E. 1983. *Elements of Episodic Memory*. New York: Oxford Univ. Press

Vandierendonck A, Damme R. 1988. Schema anticipation in recall: memory process or report strategy? *Psychol. Res.* 50:116–22

Vygotsky LS. 1978. *Mind in Society: The Development of Higher Psychological Processes*. Cambridge, MA: Harvard Univ. Press

Walther E, Bless H, Strack F, Rackstraw P, Wagner D, Werth L. 2002. Conformity effects in memory as a function of group size, dissenters and uncertainty. *Appl. Cogn. Psychol.* 16:793–810

Wegner DM. 1987. Transactive memory: a contemporary analysis of group mind. In *Theories of Group Behavior* (*Springer Series of Social Psychology*), ed. B Mullen, GR Goethals, pp. 185–208. New York: Springer-Verlag

Weldon MS. 2001. Remembering as a social process. In *The Psychology of Learning and Motivation: Advances in Research and Theory*, ed. DL Medin, pp. 67–120. San Diego, CA: Academic

Weldon MS, Bellinger KD. 1997. Collective memory: collaborative and individual processes in remembering. *J. Exp. Psychol.: Learn. Mem. Cogn.* 23:1160–75

Weldon MS, Blair C, Huebsch D. 2000. Group remembering: Does social loafing underlie collaborative inhibition? *J. Exp. Psychol.: Learn. Mem. Cogn.* 26:1568–77

Wertsch JV. 2002. *Voices of Collective Remembering*. New York: Cambridge Univ. Press

Wertsch JV. 2008. Collective memory and narrative templates. *Soc. Res.* 75:133–56

Wilson RA. 2005. Collective memory, group minds, and the extended mind thesis. *Cogn. Process.* 6:227–36

Wilson RA, Clark A. 2009. How to situate cognition: letting nature take its course. In *The Cambridge Handbook of Situated Cognition*, ed. P Robbins, M Aydede, pp. 55–77. New York: Cambridge Univ. Press

Wittenbaum GM, Hollingshead AB, Botero IC. 2004. From cooperative to motivated information sharing in groups: moving beyond the hidden profile paradigm. *Commun. Monogr.* 71:286–310

Wittenbaum GM, Park ES. 2001. The collective preference for shared information. *Curr. Dir. Psychol. Sci.* 10:70–73

Wixted JT. 2004. The psychology and neuroscience of forgetting. *Annu. Rev. Psychol.* 55:235–69

Wright DB, London K, Waechter M. 2010. Social anxiety moderates memory conformity in adolescents. *Appl. Cogn. Psychol.* 24:1034–45

Wright DB, Mathews SA, Skagerberg EM. 2005. Social recognition memory: the effect of other people's responses for previously seen and unseen items. *J. Exp. Psychol.: Appl.* 11:200–9

Wright DB, Memon A, Skagerberg EM, Gabbert F. 2009. When eyewitnesses talk. *Curr. Dir. Psychol. Sci.* 18:174–78

Wright DB, Self G, Justice C. 2000. Memory conformity: exploring misinformation effects when presented by another person. *Br. J. Psychol.* 91:189–202

Experimental Philosophy

Joshua Knobe,[1,2] Wesley Buckwalter,[3]
Shaun Nichols,[4] Philip Robbins,[5] Hagop Sarkissian,[6]
and Tamler Sommers[7]

[1]Program in Cognitive Science, Yale University, New Haven, Connecticut 06520-8306;
email: joshua.knobe@yale.edu

[2]Department of Philosophy, Yale University, New Haven, Connecticut 06520-8306

[3]Department of Philosophy, City University of New York, Graduate Center, New York,
New York 10016

[4]Department of Philosophy, University of Arizona, Tucson, Arizona 85721

[5]Department of Philosophy, University of Missouri, Columbia, Missouri 65211

[6]Department of Philosophy, City University of New York, Baruch College, New York,
New York 10010

[7]Department of Philosophy, University of Houston, Houston, Texas 77004

Annu. Rev. Psychol. 2012. 63:81–99

First published online as a Review in Advance on
July 29, 2011

The *Annual Review of Psychology* is online at
psych.annualreviews.org

This article's doi:
10.1146/annurev-psych-120710-100350

Keywords

moral psychology, moral relativism, free will, consciousness, causation

Abstract

Experimental philosophy is a new interdisciplinary field that uses methods normally associated with psychology to investigate questions normally associated with philosophy. The present review focuses on research in experimental philosophy on four central questions. First, why is it that people's moral judgments appear to influence their intuitions about seemingly nonmoral questions? Second, do people think that moral questions have objective answers, or do they see morality as fundamentally relative? Third, do people believe in free will, and do they see free will as compatible with determinism? Fourth, how do people determine whether an entity is conscious?

Contents

INTRODUCTION

Contemporary work in philosophy is shot through with appeals to intuition. When a philosopher wants to understand the nature of knowledge or causation or free will, the usual approach is to begin by constructing a series of imaginary cases designed to elicit prereflective judgments about the nature of these phenomena. These prereflective judgments are then treated as important sources of evidence. This basic approach has been applied with great sophistication across a wide variety of different domains.

Although this approach remains influential within the discipline of philosophy, it has inspired a growing ambivalence within the broader field of cognitive science. On the one hand, work using this approach has helped to shape a number of successful scientific research programs (Keil 1989, Rips et al. 2006, Xu 1997). On the other, there is a persistent worry that the key claims made about intuition are not be-

ing subjected to empirical testing and that the approach as a whole is insufficiently attentive to psychological theories about how people's minds actually work (Stich 2001).

Experimental philosophy arose in part as a reaction to these worries. Experimental philosophers pursue the traditional questions of philosophy (free will, the mind-body problem, moral relativism), but they examine people's intuitions about these questions using the tools of contemporary psychology. Claims about intuition are tested in controlled experiments, and results are subjected to the usual statistical analyses. Most importantly, the patterns observed in people's intuitions are explained in terms of psychological processes, which are then explored using all of the usual methods: mediation analysis, developmental research, reaction time studies, patient studies, and so on.

At this point, it may seem natural to ask: "How exactly is the project of experimental philosophy, thus defined, distinct from that of social psychology?" The best answer is that this is precisely the sort of question that experimental philosophers want to reject. A guiding theme of the experimental philosophy movement is that it is not helpful to maintain a rigid separation between the disciplines of philosophy and psychology. Experimental philosophers explore issues that are central to traditional philosophical concerns, but in practice many papers in experimental philosophy are coauthored with psychologists, and many have been published in psychology journals. Much as in psycholinguistics or experimental economics, what we see emerging is an interdisciplinary research program in which philosophers and psychologists work closely together by combining the tools once thought native to each field in the pursuit of questions of renewed interest to both disciplines. (For contrasting perspectives on the more general nature of experimental philosophy, see Alexander et al. 2009, Knobe & Nichols 2008, Nadelhoffer & Nahmias 2007, Sosa 2007.)

Perhaps the best way to become acquainted with the field of experimental philosophy is to look in detail at the actual research findings.

To illustrate the substantive contributions of experimental philosophy, this review focuses on research programs in four specific domains. Within each domain, recent work has involved a complex collaboration among philosophers and psychologists, and the resulting research draws on insights from both disciplines. Though research in each of the domains is concerned with a distinct substantive question, our hope is that, together, they will serve to illustrate the general approach that has been characteristic of the experimental philosophy movement as a whole.

MORALITY AND CONCEPT APPLICATION

Moral deliberations about agents and actions often begin with a series of questions. Did the agent act intentionally or accidentally? Did the agent know what would happen when choosing a particular course of action? Was the agent causally responsible for the relevant outcome? People's answers to these questions frequently influence their moral judgments (Cushman 2008, Guglielmo et al. 2009).

However, one of the major findings in experimental philosophy is that this influence can also go in the opposite direction. Evaluative judgments, and in particular moral judgments, can themselves influence judgments about what was done intentionally, what agents know, and what agents cause.

Asymmetry in Folk Concepts

Perhaps the best-documented instance of the impact of moral judgment on concept application concerns the concept of intentional action. This body of research shows that people's moral evaluations about a particular action influence their judgments about whether that action was performed intentionally. To see this, consider the contrast between the following two vignettes (Knobe 2003):

(a) The vice president of a company went to the chairman of the board and said, "We are thinking of starting a new program. It will help us increase profits, and it will also help

the environment." The chairman of the board answered, "I don't care at all about helping the environment. I just want to make as much profit as I can. Let's start the new program." They started the new program. Sure enough, the environment was helped.

Did the chairman intentionally help the environment?

(b) The vice president of a company went to the chairman of the board and said, "We are thinking of starting a new program. It will help us increase profits, and it will also harm the environment." The chairman of the board answered, "I don't care at all about harming the environment. I just want to make as much profit as I can. Let's start the new program." They started the new program. Sure enough, the environment was harmed.

Did the chairman intentionally harm the environment?

Participants presented with these cases make asymmetric intentionality judgments. Those who are given the help case typically say that the chairman helped unintentionally, whereas those who are given the harm case typically say that the chairman harmed intentionally. Yet it seems that the only major difference between the two cases lies in the moral status of the chairman's action. A broad array of researchers have therefore concluded that the moral status of the chairman's action is somehow affecting intuitions regarding whether or not that action was performed intentionally (Malle 2006, Nadelhoffer 2005, Nado 2008).

This effect has been replicated and extended in a number of subsequent studies (Cushman & Mele 2008, Feltz & Cokely 2007, Mallon 2008, Nadelhoffer 2005, Nichols & Ulatowski 2007, Phelan & Sarkissian 2008). Such studies show that the effect arises with different vignettes (Cushman & Mele 2008, Mallon 2008, Nadelhoffer 2005, Phelan & Sarkissian 2008), in different cultures (Knobe & Burra 2006), and in children as young as 3 years old (Leslie et al. 2006, Pellizzoni et al. 2009). It has also been shown that individual differences in moral judgment lead to corresponding differences in intuitions about whether an action was performed intentionally (Ditto et al. 2009).

It was originally thought that this asymmetry might be due entirely to certain aspects of the concept of intentional action. However, subsequent work indicates that the same basic effect arises for other concepts as well. Take the concept of knowledge. One can investigate the impact of moral judgments on ascriptions of this concept by simply giving participants the very same vignettes quoted above, but this time asking a different question:

Did the chairman know that the new program would help [harm] the environment?

Faced with this latter question, participants show the same asymmetry, indicating greater agreement with the knowledge ascription in the harm case than in the help case (Beebe & Buckwalter 2010). Just as for the concept of intentional action, this effect of moral judgment on knowledge attribution has also been found in a wide variety of other scenarios (Beebe & Jensen 2011; Buckwalter 2011a,b).

Continuing research in this vein has shown impacts of moral judgment on people's use of numerous other folk-psychological concepts: desiring (Tannenbaum et al. 2009), valuing (Knobe & Roedder 2009), deciding (Pettit & Knobe 2009), weakness of will (May & Holton 2011), and happiness (Phillips et al. 2011). At this point, it is beginning to seem that the effect found for intentional action is really just one symptom of a far more pervasive effect of moral judgment on the way that people understand each other's minds.

But the impact of moral judgment does not seem to be confined to the domain of folk psychology. Several studies indicate that moral considerations can also influence ordinary intuitions about causation (Alicke 2000, Buckwalter 2011b, Cushman et al. 2008, Hitchcock & Knobe 2011, Roxborough & Cumby 2009, Solan & Darley 2001). These studies show that an agent is more likely to be considered a cause of an event when that agent's action was first judged to be morally bad. For a simple example of this phenomenon (Knobe & Fraser 2008), consider the following vignette:

The receptionist in the philosophy department keeps her desk stocked with pens. The administrative assistants are allowed to take the pens, but faculty members are supposed to buy their own. The administrative assistants typically take the pens. Unfortunately, so do the faculty members. The receptionist has repeatedly emailed them reminders that only administrative assistants are allowed to take the pens. On Monday morning, one of the administrative assistants encounters Professor Smith walking past the receptionist's desk. Both take pens. Later that day, the receptionist needs to take an important message . . . but she has a problem. There are no pens left on her desk.

In this case of the missing pens, people typically agree with the statement that the professor caused the problem and disagree that the administrative assistant caused the problem. Yet the only thing that is different about the actions of both characters is their moral status, suggesting that moral judgments of the actions of the professor and the administrative assistant affect participants' judgments about the cause of the pen shortage.

In short, moral considerations appear to have a powerful and robust impact on the application of a wide variety of folk judgments that one might have expected to be quite independent of moral judgment.

Explanatory Theories

At this point, then, there is a considerable body of evidence indicating that moral judgments can in some way influence intuitions about what appear to be purely descriptive questions. The principal aim of continuing research on this topic is therefore to go beyond simply showing that the effect arises and provide a broader theory that can explain why it is arising.

Answers to this question fall into two broad groups. Distortion theories say that although people have an entirely nonmoral understanding of concepts such as intention, knowledge, and causation, there is some additional cognitive process that distorts people's intuitions and allows moral judgments to impact them (Adams & Steadman 2004, Alicke 2000, Ditto et al. 2009, Nadelhoffer 2006). By contrast, competence theories say that the impact of moral judgment revealed in these studies reflects people's fundamental way of making sense of the world (Cushman & Mele 2008, Halpern & Hitchcock 2011, Knobe 2010, Phelan & Sarkissian 2009). According to this latter group of views, there is no hidden nonmoral capacity that is distorted by moral factors. Instead, asymmetric application arises because morality informs a fundamental part of what it means to correctly apply these folk psychological and causal concepts. Much of the recent experimental work on these topics is devoted to testing hypotheses derived from specific views within either the distortion or competence theoretical framework. Although this has led to the development and profusion of theoretical proposals that invoke a wide variety of different cognitive processes, no single view has emerged unchallenged.

Beginning with the former group, some have suggested that the impact of morality arises because certain emotional or affective processes distort the normal application of these concepts (Malle 2006, Malle & Nelson 2003, Nadelhoffer 2006). The proposal is that, in the above chairman vignettes for instance, when the agent's action leads to harmful effects on the environment, this generates a negative emotional reaction that leads people to say that the agent intentionally harmed the environment. To put this hypothesis to the test, Young and colleagues (2006) conducted a study on patients with severe emotional deficits resulting from damage to the ventromedial prefrontal cortex (VMPC). Although such patients show highly unusual patterns of judgment when presented with moral decisions that are thought to rely on emotion (Koenigs et al. 2007), they showed no unusual behavior

on the questions under discussion here. Just like normal participants, they tended to say that the chairman harmed the environment intentionally but helped unintentionally (Young et al. 2006). Such results cast doubt on the view that asymmetric judgments can indeed be explained by appeal to emotional response.

To address the challenge of these neuropsychological data, defenders of distortion theories have suggested that people's judgments are being distorted, not by emotion, but by a desire to blame (Alicke 2008). This view holds that an immediate desire to blame the chairman for the bad outcome induces posthoc attributions of intentionality (for instance) in an attempt to justify prior assessments of blameworthiness. However, this kind of explanation also does not go unchallenged. A number of researchers have argued that although the effects observed in these cases seem to have some relation to morality, they do not have any special connection to blame in particular. First, reaction time studies demonstrate that people generally make judgments of blame after they make judgments regarding intentionality (Guglielmo & Malle 2010), suggesting that people actually make the intentionality judgments before they have even engaged in an assessment of blame. Second, studies involving the application of other folk psychological concepts such as knowledge have shown that the crucial asymmetry persists when the desire to blame is diminished (Buckwalter 2011a, Schaffer & Knobe 2011). Finally, the effects seem to emerge even when one looks at cases in which there is no opportunity for moral blame per se but only a tendency to conclude that the agent violated some other sort of norm or incurred some other sort of cost (Machery 2008, Uttich & Lombrozo 2010).

Accordingly, some researchers have concluded that it might be a mistake to understand these effects as arising from any kind of distortion. Instead, such theorists offer competence theories, according to which moral judgment actually figures in people's basic capacity for applying the relevant concepts (Cushman & Mele 2008, Halpern & Hitchcock 2011, Knobe 2010, Phelan & Sarkissian 2009). A variety of such theories have been proposed, but all of them seek to explain the relevant effects without appealing to a distorting influence of blame. Indeed, many of them assign no role to judgments of blame at all; they focus rather on some other sort of judgment (a judgment that the agent has violated a norm, or incurred a cost, or simply done something wrong; Knobe 2010, Machery 2008, Uttich & Lombrozo 2010). For example, one hypothesis is that, independent of anything about blame, people's judgments about norm violations can impact their counterfactual reasoning and that counterfactual reasoning plays an important role in the competence underlying causal intuitions (Halpern & Hitchcock 2011).

Yet this approach, too, has been met with criticism. Researchers have used structural equation modeling to show that the impact of condition on people's causal judgments can sometimes be mediated by blame attribution (Alicke et al. 2011). Although such an effect could in principle be compatible with a competence theory, it is not predicted by any of the specific competence theories that have been developed thus far.

Summary

Work in experimental philosophy has provided strong evidence for the claim that moral considerations can impact the application of a number of important folk concepts. However, although a great deal of evidence has been amassed for and against theories attempting to understand this general phenomenon, no consensus has emerged.

Despite the theoretical progress in providing explanations for the observed moral asymmetry in concept application, the questions that originally framed the debate continue to occupy experimental philosophers: Could morality really be at the core of how people make sense of their world? Alternatively, could additional factors in association with moral considerations distort the normal application of concepts such as intentionality, knowledge, or causation, and if so, which factors? With the aid of more advanced techniques in the social
sciences, research in experimental philosophy will undoubtedly lead to the further development of distortion and competence theories in an attempt to explain the observed impact of evaluative judgment on the application of these different folk psychological and causal concepts.

MORAL OBJECTIVISM AND MORAL RELATIVISM

Imagine two people having an argument. One claims that billiards is an exciting game to play, and the other claims that, quite the contrary, it is not. During the course of their argument each invokes many good reasons, each argues passionately and with conviction, yet at the end of it all they remain in stalemate. In such a case, we might conclude that there is no single fact of the matter—billiards is just exciting for some and dull for others. The whole question, one might say, is fundamentally relative.

Now suppose the two people move on to another topic—Venus's orbit. One claims that Venus orbits the sun faster than the Earth, while the other claims that it does not. Again, they argue to stalemate, with no resolution. This case seems different. Here, it seems correct to say that there is a single right answer, and so one of them must, in fact, be wrong. This second question might be said to be objective.

Now that we have at least a rough sense for these two categories, a question arises about the status of moral questions. Are moral questions entirely relative, like the question as to whether billiards is exciting? Or do moral questions have objective answers, like the question about the orbit of Venus? This issue has generated tremendous controversy in the philosophical literature, with some philosophers saying that moral questions are fundamentally relative (Dreier 1990; Harman 1975; Prinz 2007; Wong 1984, 2006) and others saying that moral questions are just as objective as the questions of science (Shafer-Landau 2003, Smith 1994).

Despite this continuing controversy about whether morality actually is relative or objective, researchers have shown a striking degree of consensus about how ordinary people see the issue. Both philosophers and psychologists have suggested that ordinary folks take moral claims to be objectively true (e.g., Brink 1989, Goodwin & Darley 2008, Mackie 1977, Nichols 2004a, Shafer-Landau 2003, Smith 1994). We refer to this as the thesis of folk moral objectivism.

The thesis of folk moral objectivism has played an important role in theoretical arguments both in philosophy and in cognitive science. But is the thesis correct? Experimental philosophers have conducted a range of studies to put it to the test. In one early experiment (Nichols 2004a), all participants were given a vignette about two people who held opposite views on a moral question:

> John and Fred are members of different cultures, and they are in an argument. John says, "It's okay to hit people just because you feel like it," and Fred says, "No, it is not okay to hit people just because you feel like it."

Participants were then asked to choose between three options: (*a*) It is okay to hit people just because you feel like it, so John is right and Fred is wrong. (*b*) It is not okay to hit people just because you feel like it, so Fred is right and John is wrong. (*c*) There is no fact of the matter about unqualified claims such as, "It's okay to hit people just because you feel like it." Different cultures believe different things, and it is not absolutely true or false that it's okay to hit people just because you feel like it.

The first two options seem to accord with objectivism, whereas the third fits more with relativism. Just as one might predict, the majority of participants chose one of the first two options. So the results of this first study seemed to support the thesis.

However, more recent work suggests an unexpected and more complicated picture of folk morality. It simply does not seem to be the case that people in general show a strong and robust tendency to endorse objectivist claims about morality. Instead, the experimental results suggest that people's responses depend on a complex array of different variables, including the subjects' age and personality traits, the way they are asked about morality, and even the specific moral question at stake.

Age

Studies suggest that young children are objectivists about morality (Nichols & Folds-Bennett 2003, Wainryb et al. 2004). As early as the age of 5, children display greater intolerance of dissenting judgments or opinions when they concern moral matters as opposed to other matters, such as matters of taste and fact; indeed, children can be as objectivist about moral disagreements as they are about purely factual disagreements (e.g., disagreement about whether pencils fall down or shoot up when you drop them) (Wainryb et al. 2004). Other work shows a striking difference between children's judgments about matters of taste and their judgments about morality. When children are asked whether watermelon is "yummy for real" or just "yummy for some people," they respond that watermelon is only yummy for some people; but when children are asked a corresponding question about morality, they tend to reject the claim that certain actions are "simply good for some people"; they say that these actions are "good for real" (Nichols & Folds-Bennett 2003).

Although young children seem to consistently endorse objectivism, there appears to be a strong tendency for people's views to change over the course of development. As individuals enter adulthood, their commitment to moral objectivism sometimes falls away, and they come to respond more as relativists. Studies on college-aged adults show sizable minorities of relativists (Nichols 2004a). Individuals tend to embrace moral relativism in their late teens to early thirties, only to revert back to objectivism as they grow older; indeed, it seems the older one gets, the more objectivist one becomes (Beebe & Sackris 2010). It seems as though a person's commitment to moral objectivism is not fixed but instead ebbs and flows across the lifespan.

Personality

Recent work has also shown that one's meta-ethical commitments might be related to other facets of one's psychology—specifically, to one's personality traits. Some studies have suggested a correlation between being high on the personality trait of being open to new experience and embracing a form of moral relativism (Feltz & Cokely 2008). Relatedly, relativists score high on disjunctive thinking, which measures one's ability to unpack alternative possibilities when problem solving (Goodwin & Darley 2010). Relativists also tend to be tolerant of alternative points of view, as opposed to objectivists (Wright et al. 2008), and they were better able to explain these alternative points of view (Goodwin & Darley 2010). Taken together, these studies suggest that whether one is a moral objectivist will hinge upon a cluster of related personality traits, such as one's levels of tolerance and one's ability to imaginatively engage with differing perspectives; the higher one scores on these traits, the less likely one is to be an objectivist about morality.

Framing of the Issue

A common feature of many of these studies is that they use a disagreement task to probe people's meta-ethical commitments. The method presents subjects with individuals who have differing judgments on some moral matter and then ask whether these individuals can both be correct. Recent work has suggested that an important variable in these studies is whether the individuals who have differing judgments belong to the same culture. If so, then subjects seem to think that one of them must be wrong—that two individuals of the same culture can't disagree about a moral issue without one of them being mistaken. However, people's intuitions undergo a systematic shift as they begin considering individuals of radically different cultural backgrounds. As they come to think about individuals who are deeply dissimilar—individuals with radically different cultures, values, or ways of life—people shift

away from objectivism and tend to think that the disagreeing individuals can both be correct (Sarkissian et al. 2011). Thus, how moral disagreement is framed can be an important variable in gauging folk views about morality.

Specific Moral Issue

Finally, even though previous studies have found overall high mean levels of objectivism about moral issues, a closer inspection of the pattern of results reveals a great deal of variation according to the moral issue being considered. For example, even while Goodwin & Darley (2008) found high mean levels of objectivism about moral issues, a number of particular issues garnered extremely low scores of objectivism; some moral transgressions (such as cheating on an exam or opening gunfire in a crowd) seemed to be deemed objectively wrong, whereas other transgressions garnered far lower scores of objectivism. In fact, some of the most highly charged and divisive moral issues of recent times (such as abortion, assisted suicide, and stem cell research) yielded very relativistic responses. For these latter issues, individuals tended to allow that individuals with differing moral judgments might both be correct. Further work is needed to understand what makes certain moral issues seem more objective than others.

Discussion

At least at first glance, these experimental results seem to spell trouble for the thesis of folk moral objectivism. After all, if participants had been asked a simple question about, say, whether a certain English sentence was grammatically correct, we would have expected to find a strong and robust consensus, with almost no variance in responses and very little impact of subtle experimental manipulations. But that is not what one finds in the case of questions about moral objectivism. Instead, the experimental results show powerful effects of both individual differences and experimental manipulation, with certain people under certain circumstances giving seemingly objectivist answers and other people under other circumstances giving seemingly relativistic answers. How can we explain these results?

One hypothesis is that, despite what we see in people's explicit responses, the traditional view in philosophy and psychology was actually right all along (see, e.g., Nichols 2004b). Perhaps people have a core capacity for understanding morality—a capacity whose workings we see coming out clearly in developmental studies—and this core capacity yields an understanding of morality as objective. Later on, people can develop explicit theories according to which morality is relative. Nonetheless, it might be that these explicit theories override a more immediate understanding of morality that retains its objectivist core.

Alternatively, it might be thought that the experimental data correctly reveal the actual nature of people's moral understanding. If so, perhaps the best way to make sense of the results is to deny that there is a fact of the matter as to whether people are moral objectivists or moral relativists. On some occasions, and with regard to some issues, people may give objectivist responses, and on other occasions, and with regard to other issues, they may give relativist responses. There might then be no straightforward answer to the question, "Are people moral objectivists?" The real question would be about which factors can draw people to one view or another.

For example, looking across the studies above, those responding as relativists seem to share certain features in common: They tend to be in their late teens to early thirties, are open to new experiences, are willing to engage with diverse ways of life, and are tolerant of people with opposite opinions. One possible hypothesis would be that all of these different findings are explained by a single underlying process. Specifically, it might be that there is a general effect whereby people become more inclined to endorse relativism to the extent that they are more inclined to open their minds to alternative perspectives (Sarkissian et al. 2011).

To decide between these opposing explanations, it may be necessary to adopt new methodologies that allow us to look not only at people's final conclusions but also at the psychological processes that lead up to those conclusions. Such work could further illuminate the patterns of intuition observed in studies thus far.

FREE WILL

In 1924, Clarence Darrow defended Nathan Leopold and Richard Loeb for the kidnapping and murder of their 14-year-old schoolmate Bobby Franks. Because the defendants had pled guilty to the crime, Darrow's task was to save them from the death penalty. The challenge was finding a basis for mitigation. Leopold and Loeb were rich, healthy, and well educated; they seemed to have every advantage young men could have. So Darrow appealed to the only mitigating factor that was available: the deterministic nature of the universe itself. "Your Honor," Darrow said during his famous 12-hour closing statement, "Why did they kill little Bobby Franks? Not for money, not for spite; not for hate . . . They killed him because they were *made* that way. Because somewhere in the infinite processes that go to the making up of the boy or the man something slipped, and those unfortunate lads sit here hated, despised, outcasts, with the community shouting for their blood" (Darrow 1988).

Darrow's defense here touches on one of the oldest and most controversial questions of philosophy. If a person's actions are completely determined, can that person still be morally responsible for what he or she is doing? This question, in various guises, has obsessed philosophers since at least the time of the Ancient Greeks, and settling on an answer is just as difficult today as it was in fifth century B.C. The absence of a satisfactory resolution after all this time suggests that people's intuitions about free will are deeply conflicted. It seems that one set of intuitions leads us to attribute free will and moral responsibility to agents who meet appropriate conditions even if their actions are the result of deterministic processes, whereas another pulls us toward withdrawing these attributions once we recognize that the causes of behavior do not originate ultimately within the agent. Experimental philosophers have sought to get at the psychological roots of the free will debate by examining the underlying causes of this conflict. The aim is to arrive at a better understanding of the factors that can draw people's intuitions toward one side or the other.

One such factor is emotional salience. Even in cases where an agent's behavior is entirely determined, people appear to be inclined to ascribe moral responsibility as long as the behavior elicits a strong emotional response. Thus, in one study (Nichols & Knobe 2007, p. 669), all participants were asked to imagine a deterministic universe:

> Imagine a universe (Universe A) in which everything that happens is completely caused by whatever happened before it. This is true from the very beginning of the universe, so what happened in the beginning of the universe caused what happened next, and so on right up until the present. For example one day John decided to have French Fries at lunch. Like everything else, this decision was completely caused by what happened before it. So, if everything in this universe was exactly the same up until John made his decision, then it had to happen that John would decide to have French Fries.

Participants were then assigned to either a concrete high-affect condition or to an abstract low-affect condition. In the low-affect condition, participants were simply asked if people in Universe A could be fully morally responsible for their actions in this deterministic universe. Here, a large majority (86%) of the subjects answered "no." In the high-affect condition, participants read about a specific man named Bill in Universe A who burns down his house, killing his wife and three children, so that he can be with his secretary. Participants were then asked whether this specific man was fully morally responsible for his behavior. In this condition, 72% of the subjects answered "yes."

These results suggest one possible explanation for the intractability of this age-old problem. When we consider the problem abstractly, one set of cognitive processes leads us to the conclusion that determinism is incompatible with free and responsible action. But cases like the story about Bill trigger a different set of processes that dispose us to assign blame and responsibility for terrible crimes and worry less about how they were caused.

A related factor influencing free will judgments is psychological distance, the distance (either in space or time) between subjects and the event or object and events they are considering. Weigel (2011) asked participants to imagine hearing a lecture about a deterministic universe; participants were then asked if a murderer in this universe acted freely. Some participants were assigned to a condition in which the lecture on determinism was taking place in a few days; others were assigned to a condition in which the lecture was taking place in a few years. This seemingly small manipulation had a significant effect. The results showed that subjects were less inclined to say that this man freely decided to kill when they imagined hearing about it at a more distant time. Research on psychological distance suggests that greater distance triggers cognitive processes that deal with questions more abstractly, so these results lend support to the view that our conflicting intuitions on free will are the product of different cognitive processes (see also Roskies & Nichols 2011).

Feltz & Cokely (2009) adopt the same basic framework in their studies, but with the following twist: The authors investigate whether personality differences can affect intuitions on free will. Specifically, Feltz & Cokely (2009) predicted that subjects who were high in personal trait extroversion would be more likely to assign free will and moral responsibility to a murderer in the deterministic scenario. The results showed a significant correlation between extroversion and a willingness to attribute free will and responsibility for determined behavior. These results may also support the emotional salience model because extroverted people, due to their increased sensitivity to the social features of a scenario, may consider concrete cases less abstractly (and so have a greater affective response) than their introverted counterparts. Certainly, the results shed light on why philosophical reflection and debate alone have not led to more universal agreement about the free will problem.

In the above studies, participants are asked to imagine a world where human behavior is caused deterministically, but no detail is given about the nature of causes. Several studies have shown, however, that the type of causal explanation can influence free will and responsibility judgments. Nahmias and colleagues (2007) and Nahmias & Murray (2010) separated participants into two conditions: In one condition, the agents' decision-making is described "in terms of neuroscientific, mechanistic processes"; in the other, decision-making is described "in terms of psychological, intentional processes." They found that in both abstract and concrete cases, subjects found neuroscientific descriptions of decision-making to be more of a threat to freedom and responsibility than psychological ones. Nahmias and colleagues offer their results as evidence that participants are prone to confuse determinism with fatalism, the view that our conscious desires and deliberations do not causally influence our behavior and destiny. Because this is a mistake—determinism does not entail that our conscious deliberations are causally impotent—the authors conclude that folk intuitions might be more unified in favor of the view that we can be free and responsible as long as our actions are determined in the right way.

The common ingredient in all of the above studies is this: The more real and personal the case, the more prone we are to attribute free will and moral responsibility to agents even when their behavior is determined. At one end of the spectrum, we might imagine someone deliberately harming a family member or loved one. Few of us would withhold blame due to theoretical considerations about the deterministic nature of the universe. But when the case is more abstract, involving strangers in another time or universe, we find it less plausible to hold agents free and responsible when the causes of their actions trace back beyond their control. A few important questions remain, however. First, how should we regard the intuitions generated in high-affect cases? Should we view them as distortions of the folk concept of free will, or as reliable indicators of what we really believe? Second, what, if anything, can experiments like these tell us about the accuracy of our intuitions? In other words, can experimental philosophy shed light on the correct understanding of the relationship between free will and determinism? Following Nichols (2008), we may call these the descriptive and substantive questions, respectively.

The verdict on the descriptive question is mixed. Nichols and Knobe offer evidence suggesting that our judgments in the high-affect cases are the result of a performance error due to the distorting influence of our emotions. They tentatively conclude that the folk concept of responsibility is incompatible with the truth of determinism. Nahmias and colleagues take the opposite view: The performance error, they argue, occurs when people mistakenly assume that determinism rules out effective deliberation. Weigel argues for a middle position, holding that neither set of intuitions should be regarded as a distortion; both reveal competencies with our concepts in different contexts. More philosophical analysis and experimental work are needed if we are to arrive at a confident resolution.

Thus far, we have been discussing empirical questions about the psychological roots of people's intuitions about free will. Some researchers, in addition, employ the results of these studies to address the substantive philosophical question of whether our beliefs in free will and moral responsibility are justified. The key suggestion here is that a proper understanding of the nature and origins of our intuitions will enable us to explain away or debunk the widespread belief that people can be free and responsible. It will show us that people's belief in free will arises from a psychological source that carries no warrant or justification and should therefore be dismissed as misleading. Sommers (2007), for example, argues that our beliefs in free will and moral responsibility are the product of adaptations formed in hunter-gatherer environments, and so there is no reason to think they reflect any kind of moral truth. Greene & Cohen (2004) argue that our responsibility judgments reflect a false but evolutionarily useful presupposition of a dualist agent-self. And Ross & Shestowski (2003) present evidence that our responsibility attributions are contaminated by a "dispositional bias" that overrates the influence of stable character traits and underestimates the power of situational factors to govern. All of the authors acknowledge the difficulty of overcoming these biases and beliefs given how deeply rooted they are in our psychologies. But like Darrow, they believe that when the stakes are high—in theories of criminal justice, for example—we are obligated to acknowledge the truth.

The first thing to note about such debunking strategies is that they assume a particular answer to the descriptive question: namely, that most people regard free will and moral responsibility as incompatible with an accurate naturalistic understanding of human behavior. Otherwise, there is no basis for claiming that our current attributions of free will would (or should) change once we reject our false beliefs. Second, even granting these assumptions, we cannot yet infer that the rational response is to reject our assignments of free will and moral responsibility. Further argument is needed to show that rejecting the belief in free will and moral responsibility is preferable to revising our criteria for their application (Nichols 2007, Vargas 2007). For this, we need to take into account a wide range of factors, among them the practical implications of retaining or rejecting these concepts.

Several recent studies have been developed to explore these implications. Vohs & Schooler (2008) offer some evidence that denying free will may lead people to behave immorally, by providing "the ultimate excuse to behave as one likes." Baumeister et al. (2009) expand on these results with a study that suggests that inducing disbelief in free will leads to an increase in aggression and a reduction in willingness to help. If the authors are correct, this may undermine the rationality of rejecting free will and moral responsibility, since the belief in the concepts would have important social functions (but see Nadelhoffer & Feltz 2007, Sommers 2010). However, because the studies are designed to test for short-term rather than long-term effects, it is not clear how worried free will skeptics should be about these results.

PHENOMENAL CONSCIOUSNESS

One of the oldest and thorniest questions in philosophy is the "problem of other minds." How can we know that another entity has a mind? It seems clear that the person down the hall is capable of beliefs, intentions, and emotions, whereas the toaster in the kitchen is not capable of thinking or feeling anything at all, but what sorts of evidence can we use to tell the difference?

Just in the past few years, a number of researchers in both psychology and experimental philosophy have argued that this traditional question needs to be reformulated (Gray et al. 2007, Knobe & Prinz 2008, Robbins & Jack 2006). These researchers have suggested that it might be a mistake to suppose that there is one unified process involved in attributing a mind. Instead, they have suggested that there might be fundamentally different processes involved in attributing distinct psychological capacities.

In philosophy, it is common to distinguish between mental states that involve phenomenal consciousness and those that do not (Block 1995). Take the difference between the mental state "feeling upset" and the mental state "knowing that $2 + 2 = 4$." The former state involves a certain kind of feeling or experience—there is something that it is like to feel upset at a particular time—whereas the latter does not directly involve any feeling or experience. Philosophers mark this distinction by saying that the former state involves phenomenal consciousness whereas the latter does not.

Recent work suggests that ordinary people also appreciate this distinction. Moreover, the work suggests that the judgment that an entity is capable of having states that involve phenomenal consciousness (e.g., feeling upset) is driven by different cues than the judgment that an entity is capable of having states that do not involve phenomenal consciousness (e.g., knowing that $2 + 2 = 4$). There might also be different mechanisms that are activated by these different sets of cues. In short, this research has proposed the hypothesis that phenomenal consciousness is special.

Two Dimensions of Mind

Initial evidence for the complexity of the folk conception of mind comes from an investigation of mental-state attribution by Gray et al. (2007). In a large-scale, online-survey-based study, participants provided ratings for a cast of characters (e.g., a normal adult, a child, a dog, a robot). Participants were presented with pairs of the characters and asked to rank them across a wide range of capacities: memory, planning, fear, pain, pleasure, and so forth.

Interestingly, the results did not show a single continuum whereby certain characters scored high on all capacities while others scored low on all capacities. Instead, a factor analysis revealed two distinct dimensions of mind—capacities for cognition, such as self-control and planning, and then, separately, capacities for phenomenal consciousness, such as pain and fear. Some characters (e.g., a baby) were rated relatively high on consciousness and low on cognition; others (e.g., God) showed the opposite pattern.

These results do not directly show that people think that there are two different kinds of minds—cognitive minds and conscious minds. But they do suggest that there are separate cognitive capacities for attributing states that have phenomenal consciousness and those that do not. This is precisely the suggestion of Robbins & Jack (2006), who also maintain that judg-

ments of moral considerability depend preferentially upon judgments of the capacity for conscious experience (see also Robbins 2008), whereas judgments of moral responsibility have more to do with perception of a target's capacity for sophisticated cognition.

The studies by Gray and colleagues provide some evidence for this (Gray et al. 2007; see also Waytz et al. 2010). In addition to ranking characters on a range of mental capacities, participants in that study also ranked characters on two dimensions of moral status: (a) moral agency, or the capacity to perform right or wrong actions and to be held accountable as such, and (b) moral patiency, or the capacity to receive such actions and to be given due consideration on that basis. Correlational analysis of the data revealed that these dimensions of morality were strongly positively correlated with different dimensions of mind—capacities for cognition and capacities for phenomenal consciousness, respectively. For example, entities judged to be high on cognition and low on consciousness (like God) tend to be categorized more or less exclusively as moral agents, whereas experientially rich but cognitively impoverished entities (like infants) tend to be categorized almost exclusively as moral patients (Gray & Wegner 2009, 2010). These studies of the relation between different dimensions of mentality and morality provide further support for the idea that there is a deep rift between attributions of states that have phenomenal consciousness and those that do not.

The Role of Embodiment

If attributions of phenomenally conscious mental states actually are deeply distinct from attributions of nonphenomenal states, it seems that these different sorts of attributions should rely on different cues. A considerable body of research suggests that one main cue people use to determine whether an entity has nonphenomenal mental states is its behavior (Johnson 2003). (Indeed, people will even attribute beliefs and goals to pictures of little triangles on a screen when these triangles are exhibiting the right sorts of behaviors; see Heider & Simmel

1944.) But what cues do people use to determine whether an entity has states with phenomenal consciousness? One possible answer is that the main cue here is not a matter of exhibiting certain behaviors—that it is instead a matter of having a biological body (Knobe 2011).

A natural way to test this hypothesis is to look at people's intuitions about entities that do exhibit complex rational patterns of behavior but that do not have the right sorts of bodies. For example, suppose that we look at attributions of mental states to corporations. A corporation might show all the right patterns of behavior (gathering information, reacting flexibly to achieve certain goals), but instead of having a biological body composed of flesh and blood, it is composed of far-flung committees and departments communicating with each other through emails and memoranda. The key question now is what mental states people will attribute to an entity like this one.

In one recent study (Knobe & Prinz 2008), participants were given a list of sentences ascribing mental states to corporations. Some of these sentences ascribed nonphenomenal mental states:

Acme Corporation believes that its profit margin will soon increase.

Acme Corporation wants to change its corporate image.

Other sentences ascribed states that involved phenomenal consciousness:

Acme Corporation is experiencing a sudden urge to pursue Internet advertising.

Acme Corporation is now experiencing great joy.

Participants tended to regard the ascription of conscious states as linguistically anomalous, whereas they had no qualms about ascriptions of nonphenomenal states. This asymmetry might be taken as evidence for the claim that

the body plays a special role in attributions of phenomenal consciousness.

This first argument has been a controversial one. Subsequent work has shown that participants are willing to attribute certain kinds of apparently phenomenal states to corporations (e.g., "McDonald's is feeling upset about the court's recent ruling") (Arico 2010). Cross-cultural studies show that the effect is significantly weaker in participants in Hong Kong than in participants in the United States (Huebner et al. 2010). Finally, on a more theoretical level, it has been suggested that the difference between corporations and individuals might have more to do with their differing patterns of behavior than with any difference in their embodiment (Sytsma & Machery 2009a).

However, additional evidence for the same hypothesis has been found in studies of mental-state attributions to artifacts, such as robots (Huebner 2010, Sytsma & Machery 2009b). Like corporations, robots lack a biological body, so by hypothesis they should elicit a similar pattern of attribution. And this does indeed appear to be the case. In one study (Huebner 2010), participants were given a brief vignette about a robot that behaves exactly like a human being in every way and asked whether they agreed with the statements:

He believes that triangles have three sides.

He feels happy when he gets what he wants.

As predicted, participants were willing to attribute the nonphenomenal state (belief) but unwilling to attribute the state involving phenomenal consciousness (feeling happy).

Finally, the embodiment hypothesis appears to find support in the results of the factor analysis described above (Gray et al. 2007). Participants saw newborn babies as having ample capacity for phenomenal consciousness but little capacity for nonphenomenal states, whereas they saw God as having the maximum possible capacity for nonphenomenal states but little capacity for phenomenal consciousness. This is exactly the result one would expect if one assumes that complex behavior is the main cue for attributions of nonphenomenal states whereas embodiment is the main cue for attributions of phenomenal consciousness.

Models and Mechanisms

Thus, a diverse range of data suggests that the attribution of phenomenal states is driven by different cues from the attribution of nonphenomenal states. What kinds of explanations are available for this striking pattern of results?

One proposal is that the findings reflect a deep difference in the mechanisms underlying the attribution of mental states. In this view, the capacity to attribute feelings to something rests on a functionally specialized mechanism, at least partially distinct from the mechanism responsible for the attribution of thoughts (Robbins & Jack 2006).

An alternative view is that there is really just one core mechanism that is responsible for the attribution of both nonphenomenal and phenomenal mental states. In this view, if an entity is identified as an agent with goals and thoughts, that will be sufficient to generate an inclination also to attribute feelings (Arico et al. 2011, Fiala et al. 2011). If that view is right, then when people deny conscious states to something they regard as an agent, it should be the case that at some deeper level, they really are inclined to attribute conscious states to the entity. A recent reaction time study provides some support for this—participants were significantly slower to deny conscious states to agents than to nonagents (Arico et al. 2011). If, however, there are entities—such as groups— for which people really have no inclination to attribute conscious states, then the single mechanism view must explain why people are willing to attribute ordinary nonphenomenal states such as goals and thoughts. One possibility is that attributions of goals and thoughts to groups are better interpreted as somehow figurative rather than literal ascriptions of goals and thoughts to groups (Phelan et al. 2011).

It remains quite unclear which of these approaches is correct, but the advent of experimental philosophy of consciousness has initiated a new way to investigate some fundamental philosophical questions about how people ordinarily attribute psychological capacities.

CONCLUSION

This review has focused on four specific areas of research in experimental philosophy. Within each of these areas, one finds the emergence of an interdisciplinary conversation in which philosophers and psychologists work closely together to address a set of questions that lie at the intersection of the two fields.

Although we discuss work in four major areas, this is far from an exhaustive review. Experimental philosophers have also investigated cross-cultural differences in philosophical intuitions (e.g., Machery et al. 2004, Weinberg et al. 2001), judgments about whether a person truly knows something as opposed to merely believing it (for a review, see Pinillos 2011), and people's ordinary conceptions of race (Glasgow et al. 2009). The possibilities for productive work in experimental philosophy are broad, and many of the topics explored by psychologists make contact with closely related philosophical issues. Future work in experimental philosophy could take the same interdisciplinary approach found in the four areas reviewed here and apply it to questions about causation, the self, religion, aesthetics, and elsewhere.

This interdisciplinary approach of the experimental philosophy movement has sometimes been characterized as a revolutionary new attack on the longstanding division between the disciplines of philosophy and psychology (e.g., Appiah 2007, Lackman 2006). It seems to us that this characterization is not quite right. After all, philosophers have been concerned with psychological questions for thousands of years (think of the work of Plato and Aristotle), and this fluid boundary between philosophy and psychology persisted up through the twentieth century (think of William James). Perhaps then, the kind of interdisciplinary collaboration one sees in experimental philosophy is best understood not as a radical break with the past, but rather as a return to a more traditional conception of how philosophy and psychology should relate and develop.

DISCLOSURE STATEMENT

The authors are unaware of any affiliation, funding, or financial holdings that might be perceived as affecting the objectivity of this review.

LITERATURE CITED

Adams F, Steadman A. 2004. Intentional action in ordinary language: core concept or pragmatic understanding? *Analysis* 64:173–81

Alexander J, Mallon R, Weinberg J. 2009. Accentuate the negative. *Rev. Philos. Psychol.* 1:297–314

Alicke MD. 2000. Culpable control and the psychology of blame. *Psychol. Bull.* 126:556–74

Alicke MD. 2008. Blaming badly. *J. Cogn. Cult.* 8:179–86

Alicke MD, Rose D, Bloom D. 2011. Causation, norm violation and culpable control. *J. Philosophy.* In press

Appiah KA. 2007. The new new philosophy. *N.Y. Times.* Dec. 9

Arico A. 2010. Folk psychology, consciousness, and context effects. *Rev. Philos. Psychol.* 1:371–93

Arico A, Fiala B, Goldberg RF, Nichols S. 2011. The folk psychology of consciousness. *Mind Lang.* 18:327–52

Baumeister RF, Masicampo EJ, DeWall CN. 2009. Prosocial benefits of feeling free: Disbelief in free will increases aggression and reduces helpfulness. *Personal. Soc. Psychol. Bull.* 35:260–62

Beebe JR, Buckwalter W. 2010. The epistemic side-effect effect. *Mind Lang.* 25:474–98

Beebe JR, Jensen R. 2011. Surprising connections between knowledge and action: the robustness of the epistemic side-effect effect. *Philos. Psychol.* In press

Beebe JR, Sackris D. 2010. Moral objectivism across the lifespan. *Exp. Philos. Soc. Meet. East. Div. Meet. Am. Philos. Assoc., Boston, MA, Dec. 28*

Block N. 1995. On a confusion about the function of consciousness. *Behav. Brain Sci.* 18:227–47

Brink DO. 1989. *Moral Realism and the Foundations of Ethics.* New York: Cambridge Univ. Press

Buckwalter W. 2011a. Gettier made ESEE. New York: City Univ. N. Y. Grad. Cent. Unpublished manuscript

Buckwalter W. 2011b. Experiments in metaphysics, solving the puzzle of causation by absence. New York: City Univ. N. Y. Grad. Cent. Unpublished manuscript

Cushman F. 2008. Crime and punishment: distinguishing the roles of causal and intentional analyses in moral judgment. *Cognition* 108:353–80

Cushman F, Knobe J, Sinnott-Armstrong W. 2008. Moral appraisals affect doing/allowing judgments. *Cognition* 108:353–80

Cushman F, Mele A. 2008. Intentional action: two-and-a-half folk concepts? In *Experimental Philosophy*, ed. J Knobe, S Nichols, pp. 171–88. New York: Oxford Univ. Press

Darrow C. 1988. *Clarence Darrow's Sentencing Speech in State of Illinois v. Leopold and Loeb.* Classics of the Courtroom Series. Minnetonka, MN: Prof. Educ.

Ditto PH, Pizarro DA, Tannenbaum D. 2009. Motivated moral reasoning. In *Psychology of Learning and Motivation, Vol. 50: Moral Judgment and Decision Making*, ser. ed. BH Ross, ed. DM Bartels, CW Bauman, LJ Skitka, DL Medin, pp. 307–38. San Diego, CA: Academic

Dreier J. 1990. Internalism and speaker relativism. *Ethics* 101:6–26

Feltz A, Cokely ET. 2008. The fragmented folk: more evidence of stable individual differences in moral judgments and folk intuitions. In *Proc. 30th Annu. Conf. Cogn. Sci. Soc.*, ed. BC Love, K McRae, VM Sloutsky, pp. 1771–76 Austin, TX: Cogn. Sci. Soc.

Feltz A, Cokely ET. 2007. An anomaly in intentional action ascription: more evidence of folk diversity. In *Proc. 29th Annu. Meet. Cogn. Sci. Soc.*, ed. DS McNamara, G Trafton, p. 1748. Mahwah, NJ: Erlbaum

Feltz A, Cokely ET. 2009. Do judgments about freedom and responsibility depend on who you are? Personality differences in intuitions about compatibilism and incompatibilism. *Conscious. Cogn.* 18:342–50

Fiala B, Arico A, Nichols S. 2011. On the psychological origins of dualism: dual-process cognition and the explanatory gap. *Mind Lang.* In press

Glasgow J, Shulman J, Covarrubias E. 2009. The ordinary conception of race in the United States and its relation to racial attitudes: a new approach. *J. Cogn. Cult.* 9:15–38

Goodwin GP, Darley JM. 2008. The psychology of meta-ethics: exploring objectivism. *Cognition* 106:1339–66

Goodwin GP, Darley JM. 2010. The perceived objectivity of ethical beliefs: psychological findings and implications for public policy. *Rev. Philos. Psychol.* 1:1–28

Gray H, Gray K, Wegner D. 2007. Dimensions of mind perception. *Science* 315:619

Gray K, Wegner D. 2009. Moral typecasting: divergent perceptions of moral agents and moral patients. *J. Personal. Soc. Psychol.* 96:505–20

Gray K, Wegner D. 2010. Blaming God for our pain: human suffering and the divine mind. *Personal. Soc. Psychol. Rev.* 14:7–16

Greene J, Cohen J. 2004. For the law, neuroscience changes nothing and everything. *Philos. Trans. R. Soc. Lond. B Biol. Sci.* 359:1775–85

Guglielmo S, Malle BF. 2010. The timing of blame and intentionality: testing the moral bias hypothesis. *Personal. Soc. Psychol. Bull.* 36:1635–47

Guglielmo S, Monroe AE, Malle BF. 2009. At the heart of morality lies folk psychology. *Inquiry* 52:449–66

Halpern J, Hitchcock C. 2011. Actual causation and the art of modeling. In *Heuristics, Probability, and Causality: A Tribute to Judea Pearl*, ed. R Dechter, H Geffner, J Halpern, pp. 383–406. London: College Publ.

Harman G. 1975. Moral relativism defended. *Philos. Rev.* 84:3–22

Heider F, Simmel G. 1944. An experimental study of apparent behavior. *Am. J. Psychol.* 57:243–59

Hitchcock C, Knobe J. 2011. Cause and norm. *J. Philos.* 106:587–612

Huebner B. 2010. Commonsense concepts of phenomenal consciousness: Does anyone *care* about functional zombies? *Phenomenol. Cogn. Sci.* 9:133–55

Huebner B, Bruno M, Sarkissian H. 2010. What does the nation of China think about phenomenal states? *Rev. Philos. Psychol.* 1:225–43

Johnson SC. 2003. Detecting agents. *Philos. Trans. R. Soc. Lond. B Biol. Sci.* 358:549–59

Keil FC. 1989. *Concepts, Kinds, and Conceptual Development*. Cambridge, MA: MIT Press

Knobe J. 2003. Intentional action and side effects in ordinary language. *Analysis* 63:190–94

Knobe J. 2010. Person as scientist, person as moralist. *Behav. Brain Sci.* 33:315–29

Knobe J. 2011. Finding the mind in the body. In *What's Next 2*, ed. M Brockman. New York: Vintage. In press

Knobe J, Burra A. 2006. Intention and intentional action: a cross-cultural study. *J. Cult. Cogn.* 6:113–32

Knobe J, Fraser B. 2008. Causal judgment and moral judgment: two experiments. In *Moral Psychology, Vol. 2: The Cognitive Science of Morality: Intuition and Diversity*, ed. W Sinnott-Armstrong, pp. 441–48. Cambridge, MA: MIT Press

Knobe J, Nichols S. 2008. An experimental philosophy manifesto. In *Experimental Philosophy*, ed. J Knobe, S Nichols, pp. 3–14. London: Oxford Univ. Press

Knobe J, Prinz J. 2008. Intuitions about consciousness: experimental studies. *Phenomenol. Cogn. Sci.* 7:67–83

Knobe J, Roedder E. 2009. The ordinary concept of valuing. *Philos. Issues* 19:131–47

Koenigs M, Young L, Adolphs R, Tranel D Cushman F, et al. 2007. Damage to the prefrontal cortex increases utilitarian moral judgments. *Nature* 446:908–11

Lackman J. 2006. March 2. The X-Philes: Philosophy meets the real world. **http://www.slate.com/id/2137223/**

Leslie A, Knobe J, Cohen A. 2006. Acting intentionally and the side-effect effect: "theory of mind" and moral judgment. *Psychol. Sci.* 17:421–27

Machery E. 2008. Understanding the folk concept of intentional action: philosophical and experimental issues. *Mind Lang.* 23:165–89

Machery E, Mallon R, Nichols S, Stich S. 2004. Semantics, cross-cultural style. *Cognition* 92:B1–12

Mackie JL. 1977. *Ethics: Inventing Right and Wrong*. New York: Penguin

Malle BF. 2006. Intentionality, morality, and their relationship in human judgment. *J. Cogn. Cult.* 6:61–86

Malle BF, Nelson SE. 2003. Judging mens rea: the tension between folk concepts and legal concepts of intentionality. *Behav. Sci. Law* 21:563–80

Mallon R. 2008. Knobe versus Machery: testing the trade-off hypothesis. *Mind Lang.* 23:247–55

May J, Holton R. 2011. What in the world is weakness of will? *Philos. Stud.* In press

Nadelhoffer T. 2005. Skill, luck, control, and folk ascriptions of intentional action. *Philos. Psychol.* 18:343–54

Nadelhoffer T. 2006. Bad acts, blameworthy agents, and intentional actions: some problems for jury impartiality. *Philos. Explorations* 9:203–20

Nadelhoffer T, Feltz A. 2007. Folk intuitions, slippery slopes, and necessary fictions: an essay on Saul Smilansky's free will illusionism. *Midwest Stud. Philos.* 31:202–13

Nadelhoffer T, Nahmias E. 2007. The past and future of experimental philosophy. *Philos. Explorations* 10:123–49

Nado J. 2008. Effects of moral cognition on judgments of intentionality. *Br. J. Philos. Sci.* 59:709–31

Nahmias E, Coates D, Kvaran T. 2007. Free will, moral responsibility, and mechanism: experiments on folk intuitions. *Midwest Stud. Philos.* 31:214–42

Nahmias E, Murray D. 2010. Experimental philosophy on free will: an error theory for incompatibilist intuitions. In *New Waves in Philosophy of Action*, ed. J Aguilar, A Buckareff, K Frankish. Hampshire, UK: Palgrave-Macmillan

Nichols S. 2004a. After objectivity: an empirical study of moral judgment. *Philos. Psychol.* 17:3–26

Nichols S. 2004b. *Sentimental Rules*. New York: Oxford Univ. Press

Nichols S. 2007. After incompatibilism. *Philos. Perspect.* 21:405–28

Nichols S. 2008. How can psychology contribute to the free will debate? In *Psychology and Free Will*, ed. J Baer, J Kaufman, R Baumeister. London: Oxford Univ. Press

Nichols S, Folds-Bennett T. 2003. Are children moral objectivists? Children's judgments about moral and response-dependent properties. *Cognition* 90:B23–32

Nichols S, Knobe J. 2007. Moral responsibility and determinism: the cognitive science of folk intuitions. *Nous* 43:663–85

Nichols S, Ulatowski J. 2007. Intuitions and individual differences: the Knobe effect revisited. *Mind Lang.* 22:346–65

Pellizzoni S, Siegal M, Surian L. 2009. Foreknowledge, caring, and the side-effect effect in young children. *Dev. Psychol.* 45:289–95

Pettit D, Knobe J. 2009. The pervasive impact of moral judgment. *Mind Lang.* 24(5):586–604

Phelan M, Sarkissian H. 2008. The folk strike back; or, why you didn't do it intentionally, though it was bad and you knew it. *Philos. Stud.* 138:291–98

Phelan M, Sarkissian H. 2009. Is the trade-off hypothesis worth trading for? *Mind Lang.* 24:164–80

Phelan M, Arico A, Nichols S. 2011. Thinking things and feeling things: on an alleged discontinuity in folk metaphysics of mind. In press

Phillips J, Nyholm S, Liao S. 2011. The ordinary concept of happiness. New Haven, CT: Yale Univ. Unpublished manuscript

Pinillos N. 2011. Some recent work in experimental epistemology. *Philos. Compass.* In press

Prinz J. 2007. *The Emotional Construction of Morals*. New York: Oxford Univ. Press

Rips LJ, Blok S, Newman G. 2006. Tracing the identity of objects. *Psychol. Rev.* 113:1–30

Robbins P. 2008. Consciousness and the social mind. *Cogn. Syst. Res.* 9:15–23

Robbins P, Jack A. 2006. The phenomenal stance. *Philos. Stud.* 127:59–85

Roskies AL, Nichols S. 2011. Bringing moral responsibility down to earth. *J. Philos.* In press

Ross L, Shestowsky D. 2003. Contemporary psychology's challenges to legal theory and practice. *Northwestern Univ. Law Rev.* 97:1081

Roxborough C, Cumby J. 2009. Folk psychological concepts: causation. *Philos. Psychol.* 22:205–13

Sarkissian H, Park JJ, Tien D, Wright JC, Knobe J. 2011. Folk moral relativism. *Mind Lang.* In press

Schaffer J, Knobe J. 2011. Contrastivism surveyed. *Nous.* In press

Shafer-Landau R. 2003. *Moral Realism: A Defence*. New York: Oxford Univ. Press

Smith M. 1994. *The Moral Problem*. Oxford: Blackwell

Solan L, Darley J. 2001. Causation, contribution, and legal liability: an empirical study. *Law Contemp. Probl.* 64:265–98

Sommers T. 2007. The illusion of freedom evolves. In *Distributed Cognition and the Will*, ed. D Spurrett, H Kincaid, D Ross, L Stephens. Cambridge, MA: MIT Press

Sommers T. 2010. Experimental philosophy and free will. *Philos. Compass* 5:199–212

Sosa E. 2007. Experimental philosophy and philosophical intuition. *Philos. Stud.* 132:99–107

Stich S. 2001. Plato's method meets cognitive science. *Free Inquiry* 21:36–38

Sytsma J, Machery E. 2009a. How to study folk intuitions about phenomenal consciousness. *Philos. Psychol.* 22:21–35

Sytsma J, Machery E. 2009b. Two conceptions of subjective experience. *Philos. Stud.* 151:299–327

Uttich K, Lombrozo T. 2010. Norms inform mental state ascriptions: a rational explanation for the side-effect effect. *Cognition* 116:87–100

Vargas M. 2007. Revisionism. In *Four Views on Free Will*, ed. J Fischer, R Kane, D Pereboom, M Vargas. New York: Wiley Blackwell

Vohs KD, Schooler JW. 2008. The value of believing in free will: Encouraging a belief in determinism increases cheating. *Psychol. Sci.* 19:49–54

Wainryb C, Shaw LA, Langley M, Cottam K, Lewis R. 2004. Children's thinking about diversity of belief in the early school years: judgments of relativism, tolerance, and disagreeing persons. *Child Dev.* 75:687–703

Waytz A, Gray K, Epley N, Wegner DM. 2010. Causes and consequences of mind perception. *Trends Cogn. Sci.* 14:383–88

Weigel C. 2011. Distance, anger, freedom: an account of the role of abstraction in compatibilist and incompatibilist intuition. *Philos. Psychol.* In press

Weinberg J, Nichols S, Stich S. 2001. Normativity and epistemic intuitions. *Philos. Topics* 29:429–60

Wong DB. 1984. *Moral Relativity*. Berkeley: Univ. Calif. Press

Wong DB. 2006. *Natural Moralities: A Defence of Pluralistic Relativism*. New York: Oxford Univ. Press

Wright JC, Cullum J, Schwab N. 2008. The cognitive and affective dimensions of moral conviction: implications for attitudinal and behavioral measures of interpersonal tolerance. *Personal. Soc. Psychol. Bull.* 34:1461–76

Xu F. 1997. From Lot's wife to a pillar of salt: evidence that physical object is a sortal concept. *Mind Lang.* 12:365–92

Young L, Cushman F, Adolphs R, Tranel D, Hauser M. 2006. Does emotion mediate the effect of an action's moral status on its intentional status? Neuropsychological evidence. *J. Cogn. Cult.* 6:291–304

Distributed Representations in Memory: Insights from Functional Brain Imaging

Jesse Rissman[1,3] and Anthony D. Wagner[1,2]

[1]Department of Psychology and [2]Neurosciences Program, Stanford University, Stanford, California, 94305; [3]Department of Psychology, University of California, Los Angeles, California 90095; email: rissman@psych.ucla.edu, awagner@stanford.edu

Annu. Rev. Psychol. 2012. 63:101–28

First published online as a Review in Advance on September 13, 2011

The *Annual Review of Psychology* is online at psych.annualreviews.org

This article's doi:
10.1146/annurev-psych-120710-100344

Keywords

episodic memory, working memory, encoding, retrieval, MVPA, multivariate

Abstract

Forging new memories for facts and events, holding critical details in mind on a moment-to-moment basis, and retrieving knowledge in the service of current goals all depend on a complex interplay between neural ensembles throughout the brain. Over the past decade, researchers have increasingly utilized powerful analytical tools (e.g., multivoxel pattern analysis) to decode the information represented within distributed functional magnetic resonance imaging activity patterns. In this review, we discuss how these methods can sensitively index neural representations of perceptual and semantic content and how leverage on the engagement of distributed representations provides unique insights into distinct aspects of memory-guided behavior. We emphasize that, in addition to characterizing the contents of memories, analyses of distributed patterns shed light on the processes that influence how information is encoded, maintained, or retrieved, and thus inform memory theory. We conclude by highlighting open questions about memory that can be addressed through distributed pattern analyses.

Contents

INTRODUCTION

There is broad consensus that the represented contents of a person's memories, as well as the cognitive processes that facilitate the formation, storage, and retrieval of these memories, depend on the coordinated activity of neural ensembles that are distributed across numerous cortical and subcortical brain regions (e.g., Eichenbaum & Cohen 2001, Fuster 2009, Jonides et al. 2008, Martin & Chao 2001, McClelland et al. 1995, McClelland & Rogers 2003, Schacter et al. 2007, Simons & Spiers 2003). Functional neuroimaging techniques, with their privileged capability of simultaneously measuring correlates of neural activity throughout the brain, have been productively applied to the study of learning and memory, supplementing and often extending the insights derived from lesion studies and neurophysiological recordings. The vast majority of this work has focused on localizing and functionally characterizing brain areas that support distinct aspects of our multifaceted mnemonic abilities (e.g., Badre & Wagner 2007, Binder et al. 2009, Carr et al. 2010, Davachi 2006, Ranganath 2006, Rugg & Yonelinas 2003, Wagner et al. 2005). While this research approach has shed considerable light on the differential contributions of distinct neural structures and networks to specific mnemonic operations, the past decade has witnessed the emergence of a powerful new approach for interrogating human brain function with functional neuroimaging. In particular, researchers have increasingly gained appreciation for the insights that can be gleaned by characterizing distributed activation patterns, rather than concentrating exclusively on peak regional effects. By leveraging novel statistical analysis techniques to extract the representational content of information-rich brain patterns (Haynes & Rees 2006, Norman et al. 2006, Tong & Pratte 2012), this approach has already advanced understanding of the neural and psychological mechanisms supporting memory, and it sets the stage for future discoveries.

This review aims to highlight ways in which pattern-based analyses of functional magnetic resonance imaging (fMRI) data have been utilized to capture and characterize the distributed neural representations that support human memory, as well as how leverage on these distributed representations has supported progress in addressing mechanistic questions about the workings of memory. We begin by reviewing key neuroimaging findings that suggest that while particular categories and concepts often preferentially engage specific cortical regions over others, their neural representations are likely distributed and overlapping. We discuss how the ability to characterize elements of these distributed neural codes with fMRI has paved the way for a richer understanding of the cortical organization of perceptual and conceptual knowledge. Critically, these representations form the foundation of semantic memory—our database of accumulated factual knowledge about the world—and provide the building blocks for episodic memories—the contextually detailed records we store of specific life events. The ability to track the moment-to-moment activation state of such representations has proven a vital new tool with which to test theories of memory.

Given that theoretical accounts of memory generally posit an essential role for attentional control in the regulation of memory encoding, maintenance, and retrieval (e.g., Awh & Jonides 2001, Badre & Wagner 2007, Chun & Turk-Browne 2007, Mecklinger 2010, Race et al. 2009), we next review empirical demonstrations that an individual's goal state can serve to modulate the activation of distributed cortical representations associated with task-relevant and -irrelevant perceptual features or object categories. Many of the same general mechanisms that facilitate the top-down modulatory control of perception are likely central to the flexible goal-directed engagement of mnemonic processes (e.g., Rissman et al. 2009). We discuss recent experimental findings demonstrating that distributed neural populations in early visual processing areas are recruited in a targeted fashion to support the transient maintenance of relevant visual features, consistent with the hypothesis that short-term maintenance of perceptual content relies on the persistent activation of the same neural ensembles that support the perception of that content (e.g., Cowan 1993, Postle 2006, Ruchkin et al. 2003).

An analogous theoretical framework holds that long-term storage of episodic memories ultimately involves plastic changes in many of the same neural ensembles that were engaged during the initial processing of a given episode, with subsequent retrieval of episodic memories involving the reinstatement of these distributed neural codes, aided by the pattern competition mechanisms of the medial temporal lobe (for review, see Danker & Anderson 2010, Rugg et al. 2008). We consider how distributed pattern analyses have been exploited to (*a*) measure the activation of specific representational elements of an event memory, (*b*) track the cortical reinstatement of these representations during retrieval, (*c*) examine the intricate interplay between reactivation and subjective mnemonic experience, remembering and forgetting, and memory-based decision-making, and (*d*) test how the similarity of cortical patterns during encoding relates to later memory performance. This emerging line of research has helped elucidate the cascade of neural events that allow past experiences to influence present and future behavior. We conclude by highlighting open questions about the nature of memory that may be profitably examined through distributed pattern analyses.

DISTRIBUTED CORTICAL REPRESENTATIONS OF CATEGORIES AND CONCEPTS

Because our memories for events are partially built upon pre-existing cortical representations of perceptual and semantic features, we begin by selectively reviewing what functional neuroimaging has revealed about how such information is represented in the brain, emphasizing advances stemming from the application of analytical techniques for capturing the rich information represented within distributed blood oxygenation level–dependent (BOLD) fMRI activity patterns.

Characterizing the Cortical Activation Topography of Visual Object Categories

The field's efforts to use fMRI to examine putative distributed cortical representations began with a series of innovative studies by James

BOLD: blood oxygenation level–dependent signal

VTC: ventral
temporal cortex

MVPA: multivoxel
pattern analysis

Haxby and colleagues that provided evidence suggesting that the neural representations of stimuli from discrete visual object categories are more distributed and overlapping than previously thought (Haxby et al. 2001; Ishai et al. 1999, 2000). Haxby and colleagues hypothesized that, while certain patches of ventral temporal cortex (VTC) respond preferentially to individual visual categories, such as faces, houses, and chairs (see also Aguirre et al. 1998, Epstein & Kanwisher 1998, Kanwisher et al. 1997, Malach et al. 1995, Puce et al. 1995), the magnitude of the BOLD response observed in any given VTC voxel likely carries information about the degree to which the features represented by neurons within that voxel are present in the stimulus (for related data, see Martin & Chao 2001, Tanaka 1993). Accordingly, so long as exemplars within a category share more features with each other than they do with exemplars from different categories, then each visual category should have

its own "neural signature"—a distributed VTC activation pattern that reflects the mean feature weightings for stimuli from the category. This framework allows for the existence of a virtually infinite number of category-specific cortical representations without the need to posit modularized cortical representations of individual categories.

Consistent with the distributed coding hypothesis, Haxby and colleagues (2001) demonstrated that by comparing the spatial correlation between VTC activity patterns measured during the perception of eight individual visual object categories, the category being viewed by an observer could be decoded with considerable accuracy. Importantly, decoding could succeed even when voxels with strong category preferences were excluded from analysis, indicating that information diagnostic of visual category is present in VTC well beyond focal category-selective regions. In addition, analyses restricted to voxels that responded maximally to a single category or a select group of categories also supported robust classification of the nonpreferred categories, suggesting that even focal regions that appear to show functional specialization for a given stimulus class may in fact contribute to the representation of other classes of visual stimuli (although see Spiridon & Kanwisher 2002 for an alternative perspective). Together, these results not only provided fMRI evidence for the distributed nature of visual object representations, but also served to foster appreciation for the rich, complementary information that can be garnered by characterizing activation "landscapes," relative to assessing the peaks and valleys of an activity map.

It did not take long before researchers began to apply more sophisticated multivariate pattern classification algorithms to the analysis of fMRI data—an approach that has become known as multivoxel pattern analysis or MVPA (see sidebar Multivoxel Pattern Analysis; Carlson et al. 2003, Cox & Savoy 2003, Haynes & Rees 2006, Mitchell et al. 2004, Norman et al. 2006). For example, Cox & Savoy (2003) used a support vector machine classifier to

MULTIVOXEL PATTERN ANALYSIS

Multivoxel pattern analysis (MVPA) typically begins with the division of each participant's fMRI data into training and test patterns, where "patterns" refer to brain activity measures extracted from those segments of fMRI data that one wishes to classify (e.g., individual time points or trial/block-specific activity estimates). Each training pattern is labeled as an example of a particular class. From the training patterns, the classifier formulates a model that can then be used to predict whether a new pattern (i.e., a test pattern) is likely to be an example of one class or another. In the model, some voxels are weighted more strongly than others, owing to their differential value in informing the classifier's predictions. To achieve stable results, the process of training and testing the classifier is typically repeated with different subsets of the total data set in an iterative fashion, known as cross-validation. The accuracy of the classifier's predictions provides an index of how robustly examples from different classes can be distinguished. Classification accuracy is often improved by limiting the number of voxels fed into the classifier (i.e., feature selection) since the inclusion of noisy or uninformative features can disrupt the classifier's ability to capture diagnostic patterns in the data.

achieve robust classification of the visual category of individual object stimuli, and they further demonstrated that the neural signatures of distinct categories are stable across scans collected more than a week apart. As with Haxby et al. (2001), Cox & Savoy also observed that the distributed activity patterns associated with certain visual object categories are more similar and hence more readily confusable with those of certain other categories; O'Toole et al. (2005) demonstrated that shared image-based attributes are a factor driving such neural similarity. Beyond distinguishing visual object categories, more recent studies have shown that activity patterns in the lateral occipital complex (LOC), an object-selective visual area just posterior to VTC, can facilitate classification of within-category exemplars, with these exemplar-level LOC representations generalizing across changes in stimulus size, location, and viewpoint (Cichy et al. 2011a, Eger et al. 2008). Other work has related distributed activation patterns in LOC to participants' judgments about the identity (Hsieh et al. 2010), category membership (Walther et al. 2009, Williams et al. 2007), or perceptual similarity (Haushofer et al. 2008, Weber et al. 2009) of viewed stimuli. Collectively, these studies illustrate how distributed pattern analyses provide a means to uncover neural representational structure and to relate neural representations to perception (see also Kriegeskorte et al. 2008).

Predicting Neural Representations of Perceptual and Semantic Content

Although decoding-based MVPA classification approaches have offered insight into the types of stimulus attributes that might be represented in distributed activity patterns (e.g., Kriegeskorte et al. 2008, O'Toole et al. 2005), they are inherently limited in their ability to characterize the underlying feature space. Moreover, despite their ability to infer aspects of a person's current experience from observed activity, decoding models typically lack the capacity to predict the activity patterns that should be associated with perceptual or cognitive experiences on which

the classifier was not trained. Fortunately, the canonical MVPA-based decoding framework can be flipped around to allow for construction of theoretically guided forward prediction models (for review, see Naselaris et al. 2011). Generative classification approaches capture the relevant representational variables that mediate the mapping between stimuli and evoked activity patterns. Rather than simply decoding a finite set of states from a finite set of observed activity patterns, neural encoding models seek to learn the specific features represented within each voxel, and, in so doing, allow for the generative prediction of future activity patterns that should be associated with a potentially infinite number of stimuli.

Two recent studies of visual processing illustrate the power and potential of neural encoding models. In the first, Kay and colleagues (2008) developed a predictive model of early visual encoding based on extant evidence that early visual areas represent at least three low-level visual dimensions—spatial position, spatial frequency, and orientation. Given that any visual stimulus, however complex, can be compactly represented as a set of Gabor wavelets that together reflect the stimulus' attributes along these three dimensions (Daugman 1985), Kay et al. trained a classifier to learn the mapping between this Gabor wavelet feature space and fMRI activity levels, estimating the Gabor feature weightings for each voxel in early visual cortex as participants viewed over 1,000 randomly selected natural images. The resulting model's predictive power was evidenced by its remarkably accurate ability to forecast patterns of fMRI activity associated with viewing individual natural image stimuli that were not part of the training set. In the second study, Naselaris and colleagues (2009) went a step further, demonstrating that they could reconstruct the image being viewed from the brain activity pattern it elicits. Again, their generative model operated on an intermediate, or latent, feature space rather than on the manifest Cartesian space of the two-dimensional images themselves (see also Brouwer & Heeger 2009; cf. Miyawaki et al. 2008, Thirion et al. 2006).

LOC: lateral occipital complex

Importantly, it characterized the responses of (*a*) early visual cortex according to a structural encoding model (i.e., Gabor wavelets) and (*b*) higher-level visual regions according to a semantic encoding model, thus incorporating explicit priors regarding the structure and semantic content of natural images. The semantic model, based on a category-level designation of each image, explained over half the variance in the voxel activity levels observed in anterior occipital cortex, and its inclusion dramatically improved the likeness of the reconstructed images to the observed images.

Generative classifier models have also been applied to characterize more abstract conceptual representations. For instance, the neuroscientific study of lexical semantics has centered on understanding the brain's scheme for interpreting what the words of a language denote. In a pioneering study, Mitchell and colleagues (2008) trained an encoding classifier to learn the mapping between whole-brain fMRI activity patterns associated with a set of concrete nouns and a latent feature space derived from the semantic properties of the nouns. In particular, guided by empirical and theoretical work suggesting that semantic representations of concrete entities are heavily linked to their sensorimotor attributes (Barsalou 2008, Farah & McClelland 1991, Martin & Chao 2001), Mitchell and colleagues constructed their model's semantic feature space around 25 verbs of perception and action. Each noun was then assigned a set of semantic feature weights based on the frequency of its textual co-occurrence with each verb. Impressively, by learning the neural correlates of these intermediate semantic features, the model could predict the future activation patterns elicited by test nouns. Moreover, the large-scale brain activity patterns that characterized each of the semantic features illustrated the highly distributed nature of conceptual representations while also revealing a number of focal regions that appeared to play a differential role in the representation of specific features (e.g., an area of right superior temporal sulcus often associated with the processing of biological motion was strongly linked to the semantic features for the verb "run," whereas a putative gustatory cortex area was associated with "eat"). In a subsequent study, Just and colleagues (2010) used a bottom-up factor analysis approach to reveal the semantic feature space (rather than relying on a preselected set of verb-based features), parsimoniously accounting for the multidimensional structure of noun-related activity patterns. Furthermore, they found that a classifier model trained on fMRI activity patterns from one group of participants could predict the activity patterns elicited by novel nouns read by another group of participants, suggesting that the neural organization of coarse-level semantic representations is partially shared across individuals (see also Chang et al. 2011; Pulvermüller et al. 2009; Shinkareva et al. 2008, 2011).

Taken together, the studies reviewed thus far illustrate how aspects of a person's perceptual experience and semantic cognition can be reliably decoded, or even reconstructed, from distributed fMRI activity patterns. We next consider how distributed pattern analyses have been used to test theories of attention and working memory.

ATTENTION, WORKING MEMORY, AND DISTRIBUTED CORTICAL REPRESENTATIONS

During everyday experiences, we frequently find ourselves bombarded with many more stimuli than we can simultaneously process. To be effective, we often must selectively attend to the subset of stimuli or stimulus features that are most relevant to our goals, using top-down control to regulate the processing of environmental stimuli based on current attentional priorities. At the neural level, considerable evidence indicates that the cortical representations of goal-relevant stimuli or stimulus features are up-regulated and/or sharpened, whereas representations of irrelevant stimuli/features are suppressed (e.g., Desimone & Duncan 1995, Gazzaley et al. 2005, Kastner & Pinsk 2004). In addition to regulating stimulus processing, top-down attentional processes also support the

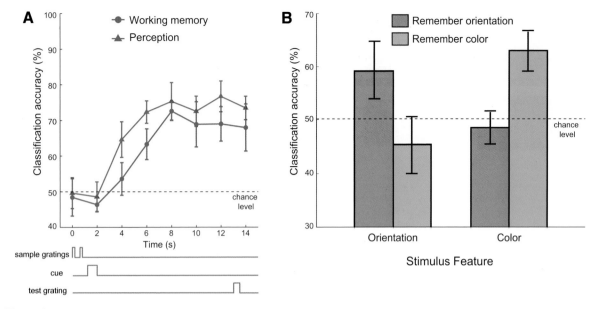

Figure 1

Recruitment of feature-specific visual representations during working memory maintenance. (*A*) Data illustrating that the orientation of a to-be-remembered line grating can be decoded from multivoxel activity patterns measured from visual areas V1–V4 throughout the entire duration of the working memory delay period. The diagram below the graph depicts the presentation times of the two sample gratings, the ensuing cue (indicating which of the two gratings should be maintained), and the final test grating (upon which participants make their memory-based judgment). The classifier's ability to decode which orientation was maintained in working memory (*green circles*) was statistically indistinguishable from its ability to decode the orientation of a perceived grating that was presented throughout the entire trial (*red triangles*). Adapted with permission from Harrison & Tong (2009). (*B*) Delay period activity patterns from V1 contain sufficient information to decode which of two orientations a participant was maintaining in working memory (on trials in which participants were cued to remember orientation) as well as to decode which of two colors participants were maintaining (on trials in which participants were cued to remember color). In both cases, decoding performance was at chance for the irrelevant stimulus dimension. Adapted with permission from Serences et al. (2009).

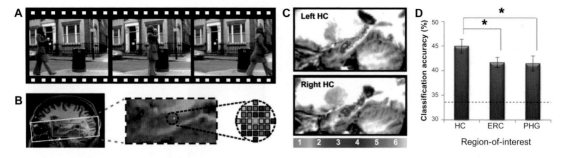

Figure 2

Decoding the content of episodic retrieval from medial temporal lobe activity patterns. (*A*) Selected frames from one of three movie clips viewed by participants prior to scanning. During each trial of the scanning session, participants closed their eyes and attempted to recall one of the three clips as vividly as possible. (*B*) Illustration of the spherical searchlight analysis approach. High-resolution fMRI data were collected from the medial temporal lobe, and classification analyses were run on the data from small spherical cliques of voxels to evaluate the accuracy with which local activity patterns could be used to decode which episode was recalled on each trial. (*C*) Frequency heat maps for the left and right hippocampi illustrating the number of participants (out of 10) for whom searchlights centered at each voxel showed above-chance mnemonic decoding performance. High across-participant consistency was observed in bilateral anterior and right posterior hippocampus (HC). (*D*) Comparison of classification performance within the HC, entorhinal cortex (ERC), and parahippocampal gyrus (PHG) revealed above-chance (dashed line: 33%) classification in all three ROIs, with decoding accuracy being significantly higher within the HC. Adapted with permission from Chadwick et al. (2010) and Hassabis et al. (2009).

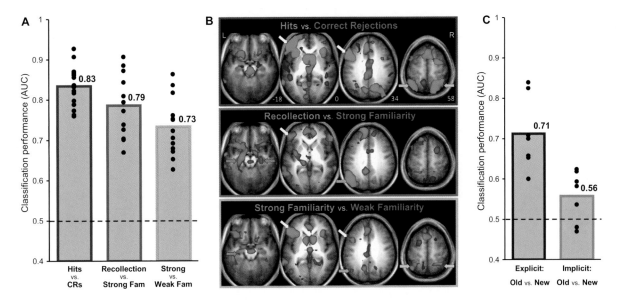

Figure 3

Decoding the mnemonic status of individual stimuli. (*A*) Classifier performance, as indexed by the mean area under the receiver operating characteristic curve [area under the curve (AUC)], is plotted for whole-brain classifier models trained to differentiate recognized studied faces (hits) from unrecognized novel faces [correct rejections (CRs)], hits associated with subjective reports of contextual recollection from those for which participants only indicated a strong feeling of familiarity, and hits associated with strong versus weak familiarity. Neural discriminability was well above chance (*dashed line*) for each classification; individual participant classification results are indicated by the black dots. (*B*) Group mean importance maps highlight lateral frontoparietal and medial temporal lobe voxels wherein greater activity drove the classifier toward a class A prediction (*green*) or class B prediction (*violet*). Comparisons across the importance maps suggest that bilateral hippocampus (*orange arrows*) and left angular gyrus (*blue arrow*) were associated with the classifier's prediction of Recollection, whereas these regions were less important for the classification of Strong versus Weak Familiarity. Rather, classification of item recognition strength appeared to depend on dorsal posterior parietal cortex (*yellow arrows*) and left lateral prefrontal cortex regions (*white arrows*) that were also observed for the Hits versus Correct Rejections classification. (*C*) Results from a second functional magnetic resonance imaging experiment reveal that a classifier's ability to discriminate old faces from new faces was dramatically diminished when recognition was probed implicitly (participants made male/female judgments rather than memory judgments) relative to old/new decoding performance during explicit retrieval conditions. Adapted with permission from Rissman et al. (2010).

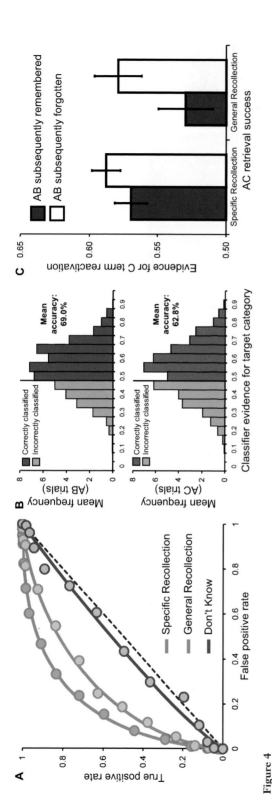

Figure 4

Selective cortical reinstatement of content-specific activity patterns scales with the specificity of episodic retrieval, diminishes with interference from competing memories, and predicts subsequent memory outcomes. (A) Receiver operating characteristic curves depict the ability of a multivoxel pattern analysis classifier, trained to discriminate face- versus scene-related activity patterns measured from ventral occipitotemporal cortex during event encoding, to index the reinstatement of these patterns during cued associative retrieval. The degree of neural reinstatement tracked participants' phenomenological retrieval experience such that decoding performance was most robust when participants reported recalling the specific face or scene associated with a given cue word (Specific Recollection; AUC = 0.83), significantly lower when they only were able to recall the generic category (General Recollection; AUC = 0.75), and no better than chance when participants reported that they could not recall whether the associate was a face or scene (Don't Know; AUC = 0.54). (B) Neural evidence for selective reactivation of the target category was diminished during competitive retrieval (AC trials) relative to noncompetitive retrieval (AB trials). Histograms depict the mean distribution of trial-specific estimates of target category reinstatement and illustrate that the classifier's predictions were less heavily skewed toward the target category when interference was present from an overlapping association. (C) Weaker reactivation of the C term (i.e., the target associate) during AC retrieval was linked to an increased likelihood that the competing AB associate would later be remembered in a postscan memory test. This subsequent memory effect, which was observed regardless of whether AC retrieval yielded Specific or General Recollection, suggests that lower fidelity (i.e., less selective) reactivation during AC retrieval may in fact reflect the coactivation of both the target (C term) and competing (B term) associations. Adapted with permission from Kuhl et al. (2011).

generation and maintenance of mental images, with mental imagery serving to activate many of the same cortical regions that are involved in bottom-up stimulus processing (e.g., Kosslyn 2005, O'Craven & Kanwisher 2000). Likewise, the ability to maintain recently encountered stimuli in working memory (WM) is thought to depend on cortical regulation by top-down attentional control. In this section, we review some of the methodological strategies and key results that have emerged from research on the goal-directed attentional modulation of distributed fMRI activity patterns, beginning with the effects of attention during online stimulus processing and mental imagery, and then turning to studies of WM. Because the encoding and retrieval of representations in episodic memory are also modulated by top-down control (e.g., Race et al. 2009), many of the findings reviewed here are directly relevant to our later discussion of distributed representations in episodic memory.

Attentional Influences on Distributed Cortical Patterns

In the first fMRI study to apply MVPA techniques to examine the influence of goal-directed attention on distributed sensory representations, Kamitani & Tong (2005) examined whether the focus of attention—directed toward one of two superimposed oriented line gratings—could be decoded from distributed brain activity patterns measured from early visual areas (see also Haynes & Rees 2005). They reasoned that if different line orientations are associated with distinct neural signatures, then it should be possible to track the activation state of neural ensembles associated with a given line orientation and use this information to infer the degree to which an observer is allocating attention to that particular orientation. Indeed, Kamitani & Tong (2005) demonstrated that when subjects viewed a single oriented line grating, the elicited activity patterns in individual visual areas, including areas V1–V4, contained sufficient information to facilitate orientation decoding. Subse-

quently, to evaluate the influence of attention on these distributed neural representations, participants were scanned while viewing a "plaid" stimulus composed of two overlapping orthogonally oriented line gratings, one of which was cued to be task relevant. Critically, an MVPA classifier initially trained to differentiate the neural signatures of the two line orientations when each was presented alone was also able to decode which of the two line orientations was being attended when the stimuli were concurrently displayed. Distributed information about the attended orientation was present even at the earliest cortical level of visual processing (V1). Thus, despite equivalent bottom-up input, attentional signals served to bias neural patterns in favor of the task-relevant stimulus/feature (see sidebar Decoding Cortical Columns or Larger-Scale Maps?).

WM: working memory

DECODING CORTICAL COLUMNS OR LARGER-SCALE MAPS?

Kamitani & Tong (2005) hypothesized that fMRI-based orientation decoding capitalizes on slight biases in the distribution of orientation-tuned cortical columns within each voxel. The seemingly random spatial variance in fine-scale columnar architecture and its supporting microvasculature was posited to lead individual voxels in visual cortex to exhibit weak but consistent orientation tuning, which could be exploited by a pattern classifier supplied with activation states from many such voxels. This conjecture has been challenged by data indicating that V1 contains a topographic map of orientation at a much coarser spatial scale than previously realized (Freeman et al. 2011). This may explain why modest spatial smoothing of V1 activity patterns has little detrimental effect on orientation decoding (Freeman et al. 2011, Op de Beeck 2010; but see Kriegeskorte et al. 2010, Swisher et al. 2010). Moreover, the close correspondence between cortical maps of orientation and radial position could imply that previous demonstrations of orientation decoding were in fact capturing neural correlates of observers' preferential attention to positions along the long-axis of oriented gratings. Although the role of radial bias in orientation decoding remains a point of contention, the fact that reliable orientation information can be extracted from BOLD activity patterns in early visual cortex nevertheless provides a valuable means to investigate the neural substrates of visual attention and WM.

Subsequent studies have documented the attentional modulation of distributed cortical patterns across a variety of low-level and high-level stimulus materials, ranging from simultaneously presented motion fields (Kamitani & Tong 2006, Liu et al. 2011) to simultaneously presented visual objects (Macevoy & Epstein 2009, Reddy & Kanwisher 2006). Moreover, it is not only possible to decode which of multiple stimuli is currently being attended, but also what aspect of a given stimulus is being attended. For instance, distributed fMRI patterns across face-selective voxels in the fusiform and occipital cortices can be used to decode whether participants are preferentially attending to the race or the gender of a face (Chiu et al. 2011). Taken together, these studies provide powerful evidence that attentional priorities and expectations sculpt the distributed neural representations of visual stimuli, even at very early stages of cortical processing.

Researchers have also leveraged MVPA methods to decode the subjective contents of visual imagery, with initial results largely supporting prior univariate fMRI studies that demonstrate that self-generated mental images depend on the recruitment of the same neural populations that support stimulus perception (Kosslyn 2005). For instance, after training an MVPA classifier to differentiate the distributed cortical patterns associated with perception of the letters "X" and "O", Stokes and colleagues (2009, 2011) showed that the classifier could also succeed at decoding participants' imagery of these particular letters. Likewise, the category of imagined objects can be decoded from the same VTC voxel patterns that are engaged during the perception of stimuli from these categories (Cichy et al. 2011b, Reddy et al. 2010), and MVPA techniques can even reconstruct a coarse visual representation of what a participant is currently imagining based on fMRI activity patterns in retinotopic cortex (Thirion et al. 2006). Collectively, these studies of attention and mental imagery shed light on the specificity with which distributed cortical representations that support stimulus perception can be modulated by top-down

attentional signals in a goal-directed fashion. This insight has provided powerful leverage on the nature of mnemonic representations and a means to exploit these representations to test mechanistic models of working memory.

Distributed Representations in Working Memory

One critical way in which memory serves as a bridge between our past and present is through the transient maintenance of just-experienced or just-retrieved stimuli. By allowing behaviorally relevant representations to remain active across brief intervals of time, WM facilitates a host of complex cognitive abilities (Baddeley 1992). From one theoretical perspective, recently dubbed the "sensory recruitment model" of WM (Serences et al. 2009), WM does not depend on neural systems specialized for transient memory maintenance; rather WM is an emergent product of sustained interactions between top-down control signals and neural representations of perceptual, conceptual, linguistic, affective, or other stimuli (e.g., Cowan 1993, D'Esposito 2007, Postle 2006, Ruchkin et al. 2003). In this model, the sustained allocation of attention to the neural ensembles (or a subset thereof) that are engaged during the neural encoding of encountered or retrieved stimuli serves to actively maintain these representations. The sensory recruitment model contrasts with the influential theoretical proposal that short-term maintenance involves the transfer of relevant stimulus representations to one or more dedicated storage buffers, putatively in prefrontal and/or parietal cortices (e.g., Baddeley 1992). From this WM systems perspective, the actively maintained neural representations of stimuli are distinct from those encoded during initial stimulus processing.

Some empirical support for the sensory recruitment model derives from demonstrations that during WM delay periods there is persistent firing of stimulus-selective VTC neurons (e.g., Fuster & Jervey 1981, Miyashita & Chang 1988) and sustained fMRI activation in sensory cortical areas thought to differentially represent the maintained stimuli (e.g., Postle et al. 2003). Other data also suggest that the transient maintenance of neural representations in sensory regions involves top-down support from prefrontal and/or parietal cortices, presumably in the form of active neural communication between these regions (e.g., Fuster 2009, Gazzaley et al. 2004). That said, many fMRI studies that have reported sustained BOLD activity in sensory cortex during the delay period of WM tasks have documented relatively weak signal levels in these regions compared to the strong signals evoked during the stimulus encoding and decision stages of the tasks. Although low-amplitude BOLD activity during WM delays does not necessarily rule out a role for sensory areas in short-term maintenance of visual representations (see Rissman et al. 2004), traditional univariate fMRI analyses have been limited in their ability to relate delay period BOLD activity in sensory areas to the maintenance of specific stimuli or features.

The ability of MVPA techniques to sensitively index the activation state of distributed neural representations of specific stimuli in sensory cortex has caught the attention of researchers interested in delineating the structure and neural substrates of WM. For example, two contemporaneous fMRI studies exploited MVPA methods to directly test the sensory recruitment model of WM (Harrison & Tong 2009, Serences et al. 2009; **Figure 1**, see color insert). In Harrison & Tong's (2009) study, each WM trial began with the sequential presentation of two distinct orientation gratings, followed by a cue indicating whether the task was to maintain the first or the second grating across a subsequent 11-second delay. Following the delay, participants were presented a third unique grating and judged which direction it was rotated relative to the maintained grating. Strikingly, although BOLD signal levels in visual cortex fell dramatically after stimulus encoding, analyses of the activity patterns in V1–V4 during the delay period revealed that there was sufficient information, within each visual region and temporally extended across the entire delay period, to accurately decode

the content of WM. Importantly, since participants were cued as to which grating they should maintain only after both gratings had offset, the diagnostic brain activity patterns measured during the delay period were not attributable to residual hemodynamic responses evoked during stimulus encoding. That is, top-down influences of attention must have acted upon a stimulus-specific neural representation, maintaining the representation over the delay. Moreover, a classifier trained on fMRI data that captured purely stimulus-driven neural responses to each grating was subsequently able to successfully generalize its orientation predictions when applied to the delay period data from the WM task, providing further support for the sensory recruitment model.

Serences and colleagues (2009) also demonstrated that the orientation of a maintained line grating could be reliably decoded from delay period activity patterns in early visual cortex. In their experiment, the orientation gratings were presented on colored backgrounds, with task cues indicating whether the grating or the color hue should be maintained. MVPA revealed that delay period activity patterns only contained diagnostic information about the relevant stimulus dimension—when orientation was relevant, the classifier achieved above-chance decoding of orientation but not of color, with the converse being true when color was relevant. Moreover, delay period decoding was more robust when based on voxel patterns from V1, relative to those from later visual areas, suggesting that maintenance-related delay period activity can manifest itself at the earliest cortical stage of visual processing (though the experimental design left open the possibility that classification was partially based on the residual hemodynamic effects of attentional modulation that took place during stimulus encoding).

Harrison & Tong's (2009) and Serences and colleagues' (2009) data provide powerful demonstrations that, despite low signal amplitudes, sustained BOLD activity patterns associated with WM maintenance resemble the activity patterns associated with the bottom-up perception of the same stimuli, suggesting

PFC: prefrontal cortex

that the neural representations that support online sensory processing are also actively maintained in WM over delays (rather than being transferred to a separate WM buffer). Further extending this conclusion, Ester and colleagues (2009) showed that the orientation of lateralized gratings can be decoded not only from delay period activity in contralateral visual areas involved in the initial perception of the gratings, but also from ipsilateral visual areas. This suggests that sensory recruitment during visual WM maintenance may extend well beyond the retinotopic representation of the stimulus, with involvement of ipsilateral cortices potentially serving to bolster the fidelity of the maintained representation by incorporating additional feature-selective neural ensembles into the total pool of neurons operating in support of stimulus retention.

MVPA has also been used to investigate the active maintenance of distributed representations of content retrieved from long-term memory (Lewis-Peacock & Postle 2008). In this study, participants initially learned arbitrary cue-associate pairings of stimuli from three visual categories (faces, locations, and common objects) and were then scanned while recalling the learned associate of a given cue and maintaining this representation over an 11-s delay period. Critical associative pairs consisted of stimuli from two distinct classes (e.g., a face-location association), and MVPA examined BOLD activity patterns relating to neural representations of the presented cue and the retrieved associate. Importantly, when a classifier trained (on independent data) to differentiate between the neural patterns associated with the three stimulus categories was subsequently tested on the delay period data, it revealed relatively sustained activation of cortical patterns tied to the visual classes of both the cue and the retrieved associate, as compared with patterns tied to the third (irrelevant) stimulus class. The presence of sustained associate-related neural patterns documents the maintenance of internally generated (i.e., retrieved) representations that prospectively anticipate future events (Bar 2009, Schacter et al. 2007).

Moreover, this study revealed that stimulus category-selective cortical patterns were widely distributed, extending from sensory cortical areas to prefrontal cortex (PFC). However, despite the presence of diagnostic voxels in PFC, the classifier achieved similar success when PFC voxels were excluded, but failed to yield above-chance decoding when exclusively trained on PFC voxels. These data further suggest that WM representations are not exclusively maintained within a PFC-mediated storage buffer. Rather, WM appears to depend on the targeted and sustained activation of cortical representations tied to the distinguishing features of the relevant memoranda.

It is important to note that no study to date has established a direct link between the sustained engagement of stimulus-selective cortical activity patterns and WM behavioral performance. To the extent that distributed cortical representations of stimuli are actively maintained to support goal-directed behavior that bridges short delays between perception and action (e.g., Fuster 2009), then one would expect the fidelity of these cortical representations to be closely related to participants' accuracy and/or response times on the WM tasks. Future studies, perhaps using challenging WM tasks that are structured to provide sensitive behavioral assays of performance (e.g., Curtis et al. 2004), may ultimately provide compelling evidence that delay period activity patterns support behavior, ruling out the possibility that they are an epiphenomenal consequence of back-propagating neural feedback from higher-level areas.

Decoding Putative Top-Down Control Signals in Frontoparietal Cortex

The studies of attention and WM discussed thus far have primarily been concerned with documenting the consequences of top-down control processes on the activation state of neural ensembles within posterior perceptual cortices. MVPA techniques can also be leveraged to gain insights into the putative frontoparietal sources of these regulatory control signals. For instance, information about an individual's current attentional priorities can be extracted from fMRI activity patterns within dorsal regions of the frontal and parietal lobes. Whereas these regions have been commonly associated with the control of spatial attention and action intention (e.g., Bisley & Goldberg 2010, Corbetta & Shulman 2002), recent MVPA results have suggested that these areas may also support nonspatial feature-based attention, such as specifying which color or which motion direction happens to be relevant on a given trial (Liu et al. 2011) or specifying whether the processing of a face's gender should be prioritized over its race (Chiu et al. 2011). The role of these frontoparietal structures may also extend to the specification and maintenance of more abstract task sets, such as representing which stimulus-response mapping scheme (Bode & Haynes 2009, Woolgar et al. 2011), perceptual categorization rule (Li et al. 2007), or mathematical operation (Haynes et al. 2007) should be applied at a given moment in time.

Beyond examining the degree to which frontoparietal activity patterns reflect the neural coding of specific attentional priorities and/or task set configurations, researchers have used MVPA to identify activity patterns associated with the act of shifting one's attention between aspects of environmental stimuli or between representations held in WM (Esterman et al. 2009, Greenberg et al. 2010, Tamber-Rosenau et al. 2011). Although several frontal and parietal lobe structures exhibited activity patterns that could decode select types of attentional shifts, these studies converged in implicating the medial superior parietal cortex as playing a domain-general role in the transient reconfiguration of one's attentional set. We anticipate that further applications of MVPA to the study of attentional control and WM will serve to strengthen mechanistic understanding of how frontal and parietal cortical regions interact to specify current attentional priorities, to update these priorities as needed, and ultimately to modulate the activation state of neuronal ensembles that represent goal-relevant (or irrelevant) features.

INFORMATION CODING WITHIN THE HUMAN MEDIAL TEMPORAL LOBE

As the preceding sections illustrate, MVPA techniques have provided unique leverage on the cortical representations of sensory features, perceptual categories, semantic content, and other higher-level cognitive states. With respect to memory theory, application of distributed pattern analyses has yielded compelling evidence in favor of the sensory recruitment model of WM. Given the demonstrated power of these techniques for revealing characteristics of neural representations, recent work has extended MVPA to test hypotheses regarding information coding in the human medial temporal lobe (MTL). By acquiring fMRI data with a higher spatial resolution than that afforded by standard whole-brain imaging parameters (see Carr et al. 2010), extant studies have attempted to characterize fine-grained voxel activity patterns within the specific anatomical subregions that comprise the MTL, including the hippocampus (dentate gyrus, CA1, CA3, and subiculum) and surrounding MTL cortical areas [parahippocampal cortex (PHC), perirhinal cortex (PRC), and entorhinal cortex (ERC)]. Much as researchers have investigated the representational structure of specific visual areas by determining the types of features that can be decoded from each area's distributed fMRI activity patterns, the application of MVPA methods to high-resolution MTL data has begun to yield insights into how event content is coded in distinct MTL subregions.

Illustrative of the approach, Diana and colleagues (2008) used MVPA to evaluate the hypothesis that certain MTL regions—specifically, the hippocampus and PHC—are selectively tuned to the representation of spatial information (Burgess et al. 2002, Epstein & Kanwisher 1998, O'Keefe & Nadel 1978), whereas other MTL regions—specifically,

MTL: medial temporal lobe

PHC: parahippocampal cortex

PRC: perirhinal cortex

ERC: entorhinal cortex

PRC—are selectively tuned to the representation of complex visual objects (Bussey & Saksida 2007). In their high-resolution (hr-fMRI) study, pattern classification analyses were applied to hippocampal, PHC, and PRC data acquired while participants viewed stimuli from five categories (scenes, faces, toys, other common objects, and abstract shapes). Given that visual scenes inherently contain more spatial features than stimuli from the other four categories, neural structures that are highly specialized for topographical representation of space should differentiate scene from nonscene stimuli, while showing minimal sensitivity to the distinctions between the nonscene categories. In contrast to this prediction, however, Diana et al. (2008) observed that PHC activity patterns reliably distinguished between all five stimulus categories and that, even when scenes were excluded from analysis, above-chance decoding of the four nonscene visual categories was achieved. Beyond PHC, above-chance decoding was not observed when analyzing activity patterns in the hippocampus or PRC. Although these latter null results should be cautiously interpreted (see Preston et al. 2010 for hr-fMRI data demonstrating face and scene novelty and subsequent memory effects in PRC), the successful decoding of visual categories based on PHC activity patterns suggests that distributed neural representations within PHC carry information that distinguishes between multiple visual categories. At the same time, it should be emphasized that the features coded by PHC neural ensembles remain a subject of debate (Bar et al. 2008, Epstein 2008).

Although Diana et al. were unable to decode the viewing of complex scenes relative to other visual categories from hr-fMRI activity patterns in human hippocampus, recent hr-fMRI data indicate that it is possible to decode which of two complex scenes is being viewed based on distributed BOLD signals in the hippocampus (as well as in ERC and PHC) (Bonnici et al. 2011). Moreover, extensive neurophysiological data in rodents (Moser et al. 2008) and recent intracranial electrocorticography data in humans (Ekstrom et al. 2003)

have revealed and characterized hippocampal "place cells" that are selectively tuned to specific environmental locations. Whereas the prevailing view from nonhuman animal work is that place cells are uniformly distributed throughout the hippocampus, without local anatomical asymmetries in location-selective tuning (e.g., Redish et al. 2001), Hassabis and colleagues (2009) examined whether it is possible to predict an individual's location within a virtual-reality environment based on distributed hr-fMRI activity patterns from human MTL. In this study, participants navigated two unique rooms, each consisting of four target positions. Decoding analyses were conducted using a "searchlight analysis" approach (Kriegeskorte et al. 2006), whereby a series of MVPA classifiers were serially trained and tested on the activation patterns within small spherical clusters of voxels, allowing evaluation of the representational content of relatively focal brain regions. The analyses revealed activation clusters within the posterior hippocampus that supported above-chance classification of an individual's location within a room and activation clusters within PHC that supported differentiation between the two rooms. Univariate analyses, on the other hand, failed to reveal activity differences associated with specific locations or rooms. From these results, the authors suggested that the ability of the hippocampus to discriminate individual locations within a room may reflect its role in the representation of an allocentric cognitive map of the room's layout, whereas PHC may extract contextual information from each room. Moreover, it was argued that the ability to decode spatial location from hr-fMRI data challenge the proposal that place cells are uniformly distributed, raising the possibility that location-selective hippocampal neurons in the human have sufficient consistency in their anatomical distribution to permit reliable location preferences to emerge at the voxel level.

It should be noted, however, that Hassabis et al. (2009) did not directly evaluate whether hr-fMRI was critically necessary to successfully decode location from MTL activity patterns, and thus it is unclear whether their analyses exploited fine-scale irregularities in the distribution of location-selective neurons or whether information about a person's location was coded at a coarser scale. Bearing on this issue, a recent fMRI study by Rodriguez (2010), which also used a virtual navigation task, revealed that standard-resolution fMRI activity patterns in the hippocampus could be used to predict in which of four locations a participant was currently located. Given the increased coarseness with which hippocampal BOLD activity was sampled in the Rodriguez study, it is possible that location decoding in both studies relied not on hippocampal maps of allocentric space, but rather on more abstract hippocampal representations of the visuo-semantic qualities and/or internally generated verbal labels associated with each goal location in the virtual environments. Future work will be needed to critically examine whether hr-fMRI affords advantages for location-based decoding, and if so, what this indicates about the nature of the underlying MTL representations.

Taken together, the preceding studies highlight ways in which MVPA techniques provide leverage on the nature of information coding in specific MTL subregions. At the same time, these studies do not address whether distributed MTL patterns can be used to differentiate between complex individual events. Promising new data from Chadwick and colleagues (2010) suggest that distributed analyses of hr-fMRI data from the MTL may ultimately enable decoding of rich episodic memories. In this experiment, participants recalled one of three brief movie clips on each retrieval trial (each clip had been viewed prior to scanning); the resulting fMRI data were submitted to searchlight classification analysis. Impressively, activity patterns within the hippocampus, ERC, and parahippocampal gyrus each independently supported above-chance decoding of the retrieved episode, demonstrating that, with sufficient variance in the perceptual and/or semantic content of events, MTL voxel patterns contain information that differentiates between complex episodes (**Figure 2**, see color insert). Although

it remains to be seen whether the decoding of rich, multiattribute event memories is further facilitated by simultaneously considering MTL activation patterns along with distributed patterns in cortical and subcortical structures beyond the MTL, Chadwick et al.'s (2010) findings suggest content-based biases in the distributed coding of event memories in the MTL.

Given these initial successes in information decoding from human MTL, it is important to emphasize that future work is needed to determine whether and how distributed MTL activity patterns are linked to behavioral performance on tasks requiring category discrimination and spatial navigation, as well as those assaying memory encoding, consolidation, and retrieval. We also anticipate that MVPA techniques will ultimately provide leverage on the role of hippocampal subregions in pattern separation (i.e., creating distinctive neural codes for highly similar events) and pattern completion (i.e., retrieving multiple event details associated with a partial cue). For instance, using MVPA to quantify the representational similarity of neural patterns elicited by pairs of events (e.g., Kriegeskorte et al. 2008) could provide a measure of how the two events are represented within distinct components of the hippocampal circuit, such as the CA3 and CA1 subfields (for initial MVPA findings bearing on pattern separation within MTL, see Bonnici et al. 2011).

DISTRIBUTED REPRESENTATIONS IN EPISODIC MEMORY

Beyond providing leverage on information coding within the MTL, distributed pattern analyses have yielded new insights into the psychological and neural processes supporting the encoding and retrieval of episodic memories. In this section we review how distributed pattern analyses have been used to (*a*) measure the activation of specific representational elements of an event memory, (*b*) track the cortical reinstatement of these representations during retrieval, and (*c*) examine the intricate interplay between reactivation and subjective mnemonic experience, remembering and forgetting, and memory-based decision-making. MVPA methods have also shed light on how the similarity of across-event encoding patterns relate to later memory performance. As we emphasize, the ability of distributed analyses to quantify the strength of cortical representations, as well as the similarity between representations, has provided novel purchase on central theoretical questions.

Cortical Reinstatement and Event Recollection

In the first MVPA study of episodic memory, Polyn and colleagues (2005) tested two critical predictions of the contextual reinstatement hypothesis of memory retrieval (Tulving & Thompson 1973)—namely that the act of recalling an event from memory involves the targeted reactivation of stored representations of the properties (attributes) of the event, which, in turn, serve as additional cues that guide and constrain subsequent mnemonic searches. Some support for the first prediction has come from fMRI studies, implementing univariate analyses, demonstrating that the cortical regions active during episodic retrieval tend to mimic those active during event encoding, suggesting that retrieval is associated with the reinstatement of cortical representations that were present during event encoding (e.g., Danker & Anderson 2010, Kahn et al. 2004). For instance, regions of auditory and visual sensory cortex are respectively reactivated during the cued retrieval of auditory and visual memories (Nyberg et al. 2000, Wheeler et al. 2000). Polyn and colleagues (2005) expanded upon this earlier work, using MVPA to index the engagement of content-sensitive cortical activation patterns during encoding and then examining the reemergence of these cortical patterns during recall. Importantly, to the extent that the reactivation of encoding-related activity patterns constitutes neural evidence for the psychological construct of contextual reinstatement, Polyn and colleagues further predicted that cortical reactivation would

temporally precede the recall of items from memory. In their experiment, participants were scanned while encoding famous faces, famous locations, and common objects, and subsequently freely recalling the names of as many items as possible. Based on the fMRI encoding data, a classifier was trained to characterize the activity patterns that distinguished the three stimulus categories; subsequently, the classifier quantified the re-engagement of these category-sensitive activity patterns during recall. Strikingly, the results indicated that the cortical activity pattern associated with the encoding of a particular stimulus category was reactivated prior to participants' behavioral expressions that they had successfully retrieved an exemplar from the category (for related single-unit neurophysiology data, see Gelbard-Sagiv et al. 2008). Although these results do not specify what attributes were reinstated, nor whether reinstatement depended on strategic processes, the temporal dynamics of the observed cortical reactivation is consistent with the hypothesis that subsequent retrieval depends upon the internal generation of effective retrieval cues.

Given the demonstration that cortical reinstatement accompanies event recall, Johnson and colleagues (2009) sought to determine whether reinstatement is a specific marker of event recollection or whether reinstatement also occurs during familiarity-based recognition decisions. To do so, participants were scanned as they encoded visual words under one of three orienting task contexts. During a subsequent recognition test, participants indicated whether they "remembered" details surrounding each word's encoding presentation or, absent the experience of "remembering," participants indicated their confidence that the item was old or new; the latter responses were argued to reflect recognition decisions based on gradations in item familiarity (e.g., Yonelinas et al. 2005). During analysis, a classifier was trained to distinguish the activity patterns associated with each of the three encoding contexts and then applied to the retrieval data. Consistent with Polyn et al., Johnson and colleagues observed robust cortical reinstatement during "remembered" items, as revealed by the classifier's ability to decode the item's encoding context from the retrieval data. Importantly, the classifier also demonstrated above-chance context decoding for test items recognized as old but for which participants were unwilling to respond "remembered."

Based on this latter finding, Johnson et al. (2009) argued that the cortical reinstatement of contextual details is not sufficient to produce the subjective experience of recollection, which could have important implications for psychological and neural theories of recognition memory (Eichenbaum et al. 2007, Mayes et al. 2007, Wixted & Mickes 2010, Wixted & Squire 2011, Yonelinas et al. 2010). For example, it has been argued that recollection-based recognition depends on pattern completion processes, whereas familiarity-based recognition depends on pattern matching between retrieval cues and stored representations (e.g., Gonsalves et al. 2005, Norman & O'Reilly 2003). However, to the extent that cortical reinstatement subserves familiarity-based recognition, this would suggest that familiarity also depends, at least in part, on pattern completion. It should be noted, though, that subjective reports of the bases for recognition decisions likely depend on a signal-detection decision process, whereby the amount of recollected event details is weighed relative to an internally calibrated decision threshold (Dunn 2008, Rotello et al. 2004, Wixted & Mickes 2010). Although Johnson et al. encouraged participants to adopt a lenient threshold for warranting a "remembered" response, it is possible that participants subjectively experienced some amount of recollection even on those trials for which they ultimately reported recognition in the absence of "remembering." Although future work is needed to determine whether cortical reinstatement contributes to pure familiarity-based recognition decisions, Johnson et al. illustrate how MVPA methods, by providing an index of cortical reinstatement, can provide unique leverage on pressing, and long-debated, theoretical issues. Their approach also sets the stage for investigating the ways in which frontoparietal circuits

"read out" retrieved mnemonic evidence, integrating this evidence to guide memory-based decisions (e.g., Dobbins et al. 2002, Donaldson et al. 2010, Wagner et al. 2005).

Decoding Mnemonic States

Although the preceding studies focused on measuring cortical reinstatement during retrieval, other studies have used MVPA techniques to characterize the neural signatures of distinct cognitive states associated with memory retrieval. For instance, Quamme and colleagues (2010) examined the neural processes that support the psychological construct of "listening for recollection"—an internally directed attentional state posited to promote recollection of event details and bias mnemonic decision-making toward the reliance on recollected details over perceived familiarity. To this end, a classifier was trained to distinguish between neural signatures of familiarity-oriented versus recollection-oriented retrieval and was then used to index the relative engagement of the two retrieval orientations during individual trials from an independent retrieval task. The latter task required participants to differentiate old items from highly similar lures (e.g., a plural version of a word that had initially been studied in the singular form; Hintzman et al. 1992) and thus emphasized the recollection of event details, since targets and similar lures would both elicit familiarity. Strikingly, a searchlight MVPA approach revealed a region of right inferior parietal cortex that exhibited a prestimulus activity profile consistent with a putative role in "listening for recollection." Moreover, increased engagement of this recollection-related activity pattern was associated with reduced false recognition of the similar lures, suggesting that this region plays a role in promoting detailed episodic retrieval or in biasing attention toward recollected content during decision-making. Although right-lateralized parietal activation is not commonly reported in univariate fMRI studies of episodic retrieval (e.g., Wagner et al. 2005), Quamme et al.'s innovative methodological approach highlights a promising avenue for investigating how goal-specific attentional states gate retrieval and influence the weighing of evidence during memory-based decisions.

Quamme et al.'s (2010) study is grounded by a rich behavioral literature documenting the active nature of episodic retrieval. Indeed, extensive evidence indicates that retrieval goals can render certain features of a past experience more relevant than others, with attentional processes serving to enhance the processing of prioritized content (e.g., Jacoby et al. 2005). For example, during source memory retrieval, people can adopt single-agenda or multiagenda source monitoring strategies (Johnson et al. 1993)—the former emphasize monitoring of a single source detail (e.g., deciding whether a stimulus was studied in a particular source context), whereas the latter emphasize monitoring of multiple potential sources. Recently, McDuff et al. (2009) had participants perform a source retrieval task that emphasized either single- or multiagenda monitoring; in both conditions, a particular source was defined as the "target" source to which participants were to respond "yes." When a classifier that had been trained to differentiate between three distinct encoding contexts was applied to the retrieval data, cortical reinstatement of the target source context was revealed to be more robust during single- relative to multiagenda source monitoring. This outcome suggests that retrieval processes were focused on recovering information related to the target source. In contrast, cortical reinstatement of the actual source context (i.e., when it diverged from the target source), although robust in both conditions, was selectively associated with participants' behavioral performance during multiagenda monitoring. Along with Quamme et al.'s data, these findings indicate that a person's retrieval goals influence the probability that cortical representations of encoded details will be reinstated, as well as the manner in which reinstated details are weighed during mnemonic decision-making.

In related work, Rissman and colleagues (2010) used MVPA to examine whether the mnemonic states of recollection, graded item familiarity, and perceived novelty are associated with distinguishable activity patterns, and whether the emergence of these patterns depends on retrieval orientation (explicit versus implicit). Using fMRI data from a face memory task, separate MVPA classifiers were trained to identify activity patterns associated with subjective recognition states (irrespective of memory accuracy), as well as activity patterns that might reveal an item's true old/new status (irrespective of subjective recognition). Analyses revealed a remarkably accurate ability to classify whether a given face was subjectively experienced as old or new, as well as whether recognition was associated with vivid recollection, or a strong versus weak sense of familiarity (**Figure 3**, see color insert). Perhaps most strikingly, a participant's subjective memory state could be decoded from her/his brain patterns even when using a classifier that had been trained on brain patterns from other participants, suggesting a high degree of neuroanatomical consistency across individuals and a relatively coarse coding of the cortical patterns associated with perceived oldness and novelty. In contrast to this robust classification of subjective memory states, the ability to decode whether or not a particular face had actually been previously experienced was rather limited (when controlling for subjective memory state or when participants adopted an implicit retrieval orientation); for example, discrimination between true and false recognition was only modestly above chance. Moreover, whereas distributed activity patterns in frontal, parietal, and MTL areas provided highly diagnostic information about subjective memory states, the ability to distinguish true from false recognition was limited to perceptual cortical regions (e.g., fusiform cortex), consistent with univariate data suggesting that true and false memories often differ most in their perceptual qualities (Schacter & Slotnick 2004).

Rissman et al.'s (2010) results have implications for memory theory and for possible forensic extensions of fMRI-based MVPA memory decoding. First, from a neuroscientific perspective, classifier-derived "importance maps" revealed that widely distributed and coarsely coded neural patterns in frontal, parietal, occipitotemporal, and MTL regions putatively underlie the subjective experiences of novelty, familiarity, and recollection. Second, the finding that mnemonic classification performance was substantially diminished when test probes were processed under an implicit retrieval orientation (i.e., when participants were not instructed to reflect on their memories for the faces) further emphasizes the profound influence that goal states exert on mnemonic retrieval processes. Third, from a forensic perspective, these data highlight the potential power of distributed fMRI analyses for decoding a person's recognition of specific stimuli while raising concerns about whether these methods are adequate to uncover a person's true experiential history.

Beyond Single-Event Memory

Memory for the past is often reinstated during the encoding and retrieval of subsequent events that share attributes (i.e., overlap) with the past event (O'Reilly & McClelland 1994). Recently, such reinstatement has been argued to foster the building of integrative multievent representations that support across-event generalization (Shohamy & Wagner 2008) and protect memories from interference-driven forgetting (Kuhl et al. 2010). Exploiting the ability of MVPA techniques to measure content-specific cortical reactivation, Kuhl and colleagues (2011) examined the behavioral consequences of reinstating neural representations of competing (past) memories during the attempted retrieval of subsequently acquired target memories. In this experiment, participants initially encoded and recalled a set of arbitrary associations between words and pictures of either famous faces or scenes (A-B associations). Subsequently, for a subset of the words, participants encoded a new (C) associate, drawn from the opposite category as the old (B) associate. Thus, when participants were later challenged to recall the most recent (C) associate of each word, the relative degree of face- or scene-related reactivation in VTC served as a quantitative index of the selectivity with which participants

were able to bring the target associate back to mind. This classifier-derived measure of reactivation fidelity was found to predict overall retrieval success as well as the phenomenological experience of remembering specific event details, with the fidelity of reactivation substantially diminished during competitive retrieval trials (**Figure 4**, see color insert). Moreover, lower-fidelity reactivation of target (C) memories was associated with a greater likelihood of later remembering the competing (B) events, raising the possibility that the failure to selectively reactivate VTC representations associated with the target memory reflected the retrieval of both the target and its competitor (activation in frontoparietal cortical regions independently supported this conclusion). As such, Kuhl et al.'s data indicate that one consequence of reinstating older memories when attempting to remember newer memories is reduced forgetting of the past (i.e., reduced retroactive interference). Future research, exploiting MVPA approaches, promises to further reveal whether failures of selective retrieval result in the encoding of integrated multievent representations that confer additional benefits (e.g., fostering mnemonic consolidation) as well as costs (e.g., fostering across-event memory blending that gives rise to memory errors and distortion).

Distributed Activity During Event Encoding

In addition to providing leverage on the psychological and neural mechanisms subserving episodic retrieval, MVPA methods also have utility for testing hypotheses about event encoding. For example, following in the tradition of numerous fMRI studies that have used univariate analyses to examine the relationship between encoding activity in frontoparietal and MTL regions and later memory behavior (for recent meta-analyses of such studies, see Kim 2011, Uncapher & Wagner 2009), Watanabe and colleagues (2011) demonstrated that multivoxel patterns within MTL are predictive of whether visually presented pseudowords will be subsequently recognized or forgotten.

From these data alone, it is unclear whether the predictive value of the classifier was driven by diagnostic information contained within distributed activity patterns per se or whether it capitalized on the fact that many MTL voxels tended to show greater BOLD signal on trials associated with later recognition. Indeed, a voxel-wise univariate analysis of the data (liberally thresholded) revealed greater parahippocampal activity during the encoding of subsequently remembered items. Future studies are needed to assess whether MVPA analyses offer increased sensitivity for documenting neural signatures of memory formation within the MTL and beyond. If so, then distributed pattern analyses may provide novel leverage on pressing issues, such as how to characterize the differential computations subserved by the hippocampus and MTL cortical regions during encoding (e.g., Brown & Aggleton 2001, Davachi et al. 2003, Eichenbaum et al. 2007, Mayes et al. 2007, Wixted & Squire 2011).

Approaching episodic encoding from a theory-driven perspective, Jenkins & Ranganath (2010) examined whether MVPA methods can predict subsequent recall of the temporal context of a given event memory. The ability to remember when an event occurred is thought to depend, at least in part, on the fact that contextual cues inevitably drift from one moment to the next, a phenomenon that allows successively encoded events to each be associated with a partially unique temporal context (see Polyn et al. 2009). In Jenkins & Ranganath's (2010) experiment, participants were scanned while encoding visual objects and later were asked to estimate the approximate time at which each stimulus had been presented. Univariate analyses revealed that regions of the PFC and hippocampus exhibited greater activity immediately following the encoding of stimuli for which participants subsequently provided the most accurate estimates of the time of encounter. MVPA was then used to test the hypothesis that memory for temporal context would be most accurate when neural activity patterns associated with temporally adjacent stimuli were maximally distinctive. This prediction was motivated by theory suggesting that increased trial-to-trial drift in temporal context would result in individual events being associated with a greater number of trial-unique temporal context cues, thus allowing participants to more accurately estimate the time of encounter. In support of this hypothesis, activity patterns within rostrolateral PFC (RLPFC) showed a greater degree of trial-to-trial distinctiveness for items that later received an accurate estimate of temporal occurrence than those that received an inaccurate estimate. In other words, when the RLPFC activity pattern observed during a given trial was compared with the activity patterns observed during the trials that preceded or followed it, the multivariate distance between these patterns was found to progressively increase with temporal lag, with the overall magnitude of pattern dissimilarity predicting subsequent temporal memory. Importantly, this finding held even when activity patterns from RLPFC were mean centered, indicating that this putative neural correlate of temporal context indexed the pattern itself and not temporal drift in the overall BOLD signal. Jenkins and Ranganath speculated that the RLPFC's representation of temporal context might be tied to its proposed role in continuously updating high-level rule representations that specify which items and relationships are relevant in a given behavioral context; this in turn might serve to segment ongoing experience into discrete episodes. Regardless of whether this interpretation turns out to be correct, this study highlights how MVPA approaches can assess mechanistic theories of episodic memory. Future studies should examine whether temporally drifting multivoxel patterns can also account for serial position effects in free recall behavior, given that the development of the temporal context model has been heavily influenced by free recall output patterns (Howard & Kahana 2002).

The effects of representational similarity during encoding on later memory were also examined by Xue and colleagues (2010). Rather than focus on context, this study evaluated whether the degree of neural pattern similarity across multiple encounters with a given item is predictive of later memory for the item. These authors sought to test the encoding variability hypothesis (e.g., Bower 1972), which posits that repeated exposures to a given stimulus will benefit subsequent memory to the extent that the features encoded during each exposure are nonredundant with those encoded during other exposures. At the neural level, this hypothesis might predict that the less similar the distributed cortical pattern is across an item's encoding exposures, the higher the likelihood the item will be later remembered (e.g., Wagner et al. 2000). In apparent contradiction to this prediction, Xue and colleagues observed that later-remembered stimuli were associated with more similar distributed activity patterns across study encounters than were later-forgotten stimuli. This positive relationship between neural pattern similarity and subsequent memory was observed in many brain regions, including areas of the prefrontal, parietal, occipitotemporal, and MTL cortices. These findings raise the possibility that when common attributes are attended across successive encounters with an item, the mnemonic representation of the item is strengthened. This conclusion would appear to stand in conflict with leading computational theories of memory, which demonstrate that, at least with respect to context, greater encoding variability gives rise to superior subsequent remembering (e.g., Howard & Kahana 2002, Raaijmakers & Shiffrin 1992).

Given the centrality of encoding variability in models of memory, including its role in explaining empirically robust behavioral phenomena, such as the spacing effect, it seems likely that Xue et al.'s (2010) findings will motivate follow-up studies that more fully examine the circumstances in which increased neural variability may help or hinder memory performance (Kuhl et al. 2012). As such, this study is the latest to illustrate how analyses of distributed activity patterns are affording leverage on increasingly more precise mechanistic hypotheses, leading to novel theoretical advances. We expect the coming years will bring considerable progress in delineating how encoding computations relate to later memory performance, with much of this progress stemming from the use of distributed pattern analyses to quantify the similarity between cortical representations of encoded events as well as between cortical representations of retrieval cues and of encoded stimuli.

CONCLUSIONS AND FUTURE DIRECTIONS

As we have sought to highlight, functional neuroimaging research over the past decade has been revolutionized by use of machine learning techniques to extract the representational content of distributed brain activity patterns. While traditional univariate statistical analysis approaches have informed, and will continue to inform, our understanding of the functional contributions of specific brain regions, MVPA approaches have opened new avenues for experimentation and have begun to offer fresh insights into the psychological and neural underpinnings of human cognition. Our goal in this review has been to discuss and critically evaluate some of the ways that researchers have applied MVPA methods to investigate the mechanisms of human memory. Although use of these methods to gain leverage on the workings of memory is at a relatively early stage, we believe their promise is clear, as evidenced by the many insights derived from their application over the past decade. Below we summarize some of these key insights, and we conclude by highlighting open questions that can be profitably addressed through future applications of distributed pattern analyses.

SUMMARY POINTS

1. MVPA techniques offer a powerful means for characterizing and quantifying the strength of information representation in the brain.

2. Cortical representations of stimuli are often highly distributed. By identifying the "neural signatures" of particular stimuli or classes of stimuli, MVPA can evaluate how the brain carves up the sensory world, how frontoparietal mechanisms subserve the representation and implementation of attentional priorities, as well as how moment-to-moment fluctuations of attention affect stimulus processing and memory.

3. The transient maintenance of information in working memory involves recruitment of the same cortical ensembles that mediate the perceptual representation of the information.

4. Activity patterns within subregions of the medial temporal lobe carry information about attributes of an observer's environment, allowing neural decoding of the observer's spatial location and the category of viewed stimuli.

5. Recalling a past event often involves the reinstatement of cortical activity patterns that were elicited during the initial encoding of the event. Through measuring cortical reinstatement, MVPA methods are beginning to shed new light on the psychological and neural processes underlying free recall, source monitoring, the subjective experience of recollection and familiarity, and competition-laden retrieval.

6. Retrieval goals substantially influence the pattern of cortical activity elicited by a retrieval cue. Retrieval oriented toward recollection of particular attributes of past experience fosters cortical reinstatement of those event details; cortical patterns that differentiate old and new stimuli vary depending upon whether memory is probed explicitly or implicitly.

7. Encoding-related distributed activity patterns in neocortex and the medial temporal lobe are informative predictors of subsequent memory performance. The similarity of distributed neural patterns across events influences later retrieval success.

8. Extant studies highlight how MVPA techniques can test mechanistic models of memory as well as how these methods can elucidate factors promoting remembering, or alternatively, increasing the likelihood of forgetting.

FUTURE ISSUES

1. Generative classification approaches offer an exciting avenue for future research into the neural mechanisms of working memory and episodic retrieval. The utilization of a latent feature space circumvents the need to train a classifier on a predefined set of stimuli or contexts, allowing for the interrogation of a far greater range of internally represented mnemonic content (and potentially even facilitating a rudimentary reconstruction of individual memories).

2. Because MVPA techniques can provide a neural metric of interstimulus similarity, they offer a means of drawing on neural data to test computational models of memory (e.g., how experience drives representational differentiation in semantic memory, how item-item similarity gives rise to memory errors, and how subregions of the hippocampus support pattern separation).

3. The utility of memory often rests in its ability to guide subsequent thought and behavior. By quantifying the strength of mnemonic evidence elicited by a retrieval cue, distributed pattern analyses pave the way for researchers to examine how such evidence is monitored and accumulated in the service of decision-making and action. Such an approach may also reveal the presence of nonconscious mnemonic evidence that unknowingly shapes our interpretations of the world.

4. Progress in understanding future thinking (simulating possible future events and actions; Schacter et al. 2007) and prospective memory (remembering to initiate a planned behavior at some point in time; McDaniels & Einstein 2007) may come from efforts to decode the contents of simulated events and intended actions (e.g., Haynes 2011).

5. A complex interplay between midbrain, striatal, and medial temporal lobe structures is thought to support the enhanced encoding of motivationally salient events (Lisman & Grace 2005, Shohamy & Adcock 2010). Future research can exploit the ability of MVPA to decode neural representations of reward value (Kahnt et al. 2010) and of experienced or perceived affective states (Peelen et al. 2010, Rolls et al. 2009) to relate trial-to-trial variance in these dimensions of stimulus salience to neuromodulation and memory outcomes.

6. MVPA could potentially provide an assay of memory replay during sleep (O'Neill et al. 2010). By relating the replay of specific representational content within the hippocampus and neocortex to subsequent memory outcomes, distributed pattern analyses may provide a unique window onto consolidation processes.

7. It is possible to decode aspects of an individual's mental state using a classifier trained exclusively on the data from other individuals (Clithero et al. 2011; Davatzikos et al. 2005; Just et al. 2010; Poldrack et al. 2009; Rissman et al. 2010; Shinkareva et al. 2008, 2011). Such observations raise the possibility that classifiers can be used to identify individuals who deviate from the group in some fundamental way—e.g., processing strategy, stage of neural development, or neurological health.

DISCLOSURE STATEMENT

The authors are not aware of any affiliations, memberships, funding, or financial holdings that might be perceived as affecting the objectivity of this review.

ACKNOWLEDGMENTS

Supported by the National Institute of Mental Health (5R01-MH080309, 5R01-MH076932) and the MacArthur Foundation's Law and Neuroscience Project.

LITERATURE CITED

Aguirre GK, Zarahn E, D'Esposito M. 1998. An area within human ventral cortex sensitive to "building" stimuli: evidence and implications. *Neuron* 21:373–83

Awh E, Jonides J. 2001. Overlapping mechanisms of attention and spatial working memory. *Trends Cogn. Sci.* 5:119–26

Baddeley A. 1992. Working memory. *Science* 255:556–59

Badre D, Wagner AD. 2007. Left ventrolateral prefrontal cortex and the cognitive control of memory. *Neuropsychologia* 45:2883–901

Bar M. 2009. The proactive brain: memory for predictions. *Philos. Trans. R. Soc. Lond. B Biol. Sci.* 364:1235–43

Bar M, Aminoff E, Schacter DL. 2008. Scenes unseen: the parahippocampal cortex intrinsically subserves contextual associations, not scenes or places per se. *J. Neurosci.* 28:8539–44

Barsalou LW. 2008. Grounded cognition. *Annu. Rev. Psychol.* 59:617–45

Binder JR, Desai RH, Graves WW, Conant LL. 2009. Where is the semantic system? A critical review and meta-analysis of 120 functional neuroimaging studies. *Cereb. Cortex* 19:2767–96

Bisley JW, Goldberg ME. 2010. Attention, intention, and priority in the parietal lobe. *Annu. Rev. Neurosci.* 33:1–21

Bode S, Haynes J-D. 2009. Decoding sequential stages of task preparation in the human brain. *NeuroImage* 45:606–13

Bonnici HM, Kumaran D, Chadwick MJ, Weiskopf N, Hassabis D, Maguire EA. 2011. Decoding representations of scenes in the medial temporal lobes. *Hippocampus*. In press

Bower G. 1972. Stimulus-sampling theory of encoding variability. In *Coding Processes in Human Memory*, ed. AW Melton, E Martin, pp. 85–124. Washington, DC: Winston

Brouwer GJ, Heeger DJ. 2009. Decoding and reconstructing color from responses in human visual cortex. *J. Neurosci.* 29:13992–4003

Brown MW, Aggleton JP. 2001. Recognition memory: What are the roles of the perirhinal cortex and hippocampus? *Nat. Rev. Neurosci.* 2:51–61

Burgess N, Maguire EA, O'Keefe J. 2002. The human hippocampus and spatial and episodic memory. *Neuron* 35:625–41

Bussey TJ, Saksida LM. 2007. Memory, perception, and the ventral visual-perirhinal-hippocampal stream: thinking outside of the boxes. *Hippocampus* 17:898–908

Carlson TA, Schrater P, He S. 2003. Patterns of activity in the categorical representations of objects. *J. Cogn. Neurosci.* 15:704–17

Carr VA, Rissman J, Wagner AD. 2010. Imaging the human medial temporal lobe with high-resolution fMRI. *Neuron* 65:298–308

Chadwick MJ, Hassabis D, Weiskopf N, Maguire EA. 2010. Decoding individual episodic memory traces in the human hippocampus. *Curr. Biol.* 20:544–47

Chang K-MK, Mitchell T, Just MA. 2011. Quantitative modeling of the neural representation of objects: how semantic feature norms can account for fMRI activation. *NeuroImage* 56:716–27

Chiu Y-C, Esterman M, Han Y, Rosen H, Yantis S. 2011. Decoding task-based attentional modulation during face categorization. *J. Cogn. Neurosci.* 23:1198–204

Chun MM, Turk-Browne NB. 2007. Interactions between attention and memory. *Curr. Opin. Neurobiol.* 17:177–84

Cichy RM, Chen Y, Haynes J-D. 2011a. Encoding the identity and location of objects in human LOC. *NeuroImage* 54:2297–307

Cichy RM, Heinzle J, Haynes J-D. 2011b. Imagery and perception share cortical representations of content and location. *Cerebral. Cortex.* In press

Clithero JA, Smith DV, Carter RM, Huettel SA. 2011. Within- and cross-participant classifiers reveal different neural coding of information. *NeuroImage* 56:699–708

Corbetta M, Shulman GL. 2002. Control of goal-directed and stimulus-driven attention in the brain. *Nat. Rev. Neurosci.* 3:201–15

Cowan N. 1993. Activation, attention, and short-term memory. *Mem. Cognit.* 21:162–7

Cox DD, Savoy RL. 2003. Functional magnetic resonance imaging (fMRI) "brain reading": detecting and classifying distributed patterns of fMRI activity in human visual cortex. *NeuroImage* 19:261–70

Curtis CE, Rao VY, D'Esposito M. 2004. Maintenance of spatial and motor codes during oculomotor delayed response tasks. *J. Neurosci.* 24:3944–52

Danker JF, Anderson JR. 2010. The ghosts of brain states past: Remembering reactivates the brain regions engaged during encoding. *Psychol. Bull.* 136:87–102

Daugman JG. 1985. Uncertainty relation for resolution in space, spatial frequency, and orientation optimized by two-dimensional visual cortical filters. *J. Opt. Soc. Am. A* 2:1160–69

Davachi L. 2006. Item, context and relational episodic encoding in humans. *Curr. Opin. Neurobiol.* 16:693–700

Davachi L, Mitchell JP, Wagner AD. 2003. Multiple routes to memory: distinct medial temporal lobe processes build item and source memories. *Proc. Natl. Acad. Sci. USA* 100:2157–62

Davatzikos C, Ruparel K, Fan Y, Shen DG, Acharyya M, et al. 2005. Classifying spatial patterns of brain activity with machine learning methods: application to lie detection. *NeuroImage* 28:663–68

Desimone R, Duncan J. 1995. Neural mechanisms of selective visual attention. *Annu. Rev. Neurosci.* 18:193–222

D'Esposito M. 2007. From cognitive to neural models of working memory. *Philos. Trans. R. Soc. Lond. B Biol. Sci.* 362:761–72

Diana RA, Yonelinas AP, Ranganath C. 2008. High-resolution multi-voxel pattern analysis of category selectivity in the medial temporal lobes. *Hippocampus* 18:536–41

Dobbins IG, Foley H, Schacter DL, Wagner AD. 2002. Executive control during episodic retrieval: multiple prefrontal processes subserve source memory. *Neuron* 35:989–96

Donaldson DI, Wheeler ME, Petersen SE. 2010. Remember the source: dissociating frontal and parietal contributions to episodic memory. *J. Cogn. Neurosci.* 22:377–91

Dunn JC. 2008. The dimensionality of the remember-know task: a state-trace analysis. *Psychol. Rev.* 115:426–46

Eger E, Ashburner J, Haynes J-D, Dolan RJ, Rees G. 2008. fMRI activity patterns in human LOC carry information about object exemplars within category. *J. Cogn. Neurosci.* 20:356–70

Eichenbaum H, Cohen NJ. 2001. *From Conditioning to Conscious Recollection: Memory Systems of the Brain*. New York: Oxford Univ. Press

Eichenbaum H, Yonelinas AP, Ranganath C. 2007. The medial temporal lobe and recognition memory. *Annu. Rev. Neurosci.* 30:123–52

Ekstrom AD, Kahana MJ, Caplan JB, Fields TA, Isham EA, et al. 2003. Cellular networks underlying human spatial navigation. *Nature* 425:184–88

Epstein R, Kanwisher N. 1998. A cortical representation of the local visual environment. *Nature* 392:598–601

Epstein RA. 2008. Parahippocampal and retrosplenial contributions to human spatial navigation. *Trends Cogn. Sci.* 12:388–96

Ester EF, Serences JT, Awh E. 2009. Spatially global representations in human primary visual cortex during working memory maintenance. *J. Neurosci.* 29:15258–65

Esterman M, Chiu Y-C, Tamber-Rosenau BJ, Yantis S. 2009. Decoding cognitive control in human parietal cortex. *Proc. Natl. Acad. Sci. USA* 106:17974–79

Farah MJ, McClelland JL. 1991. A computational model of semantic memory impairment: modality specificity and emergent category specificity. *J. Exp. Psychol.: Gen.* 120:339–57

Freeman J, Brouwer GJ, Heeger DJ, Merriam EP. 2011. Orientation decoding depends on maps, not columns. *J. Neurosci.* 31:4792–804

Fuster JM. 2009. Cortex and memory: emergence of a new paradigm. *J. Cogn. Neurosci.* 21:2047–72

Fuster JM, Jervey JP. 1981. Inferotemporal neurons distinguish and retain behaviorally relevant features of visual stimuli. *Science* 212:952–55

Gazzaley A, Cooney JW, McEvoy K, Knight RT, D'Esposito M. 2005. Top-down enhancement and suppression of the magnitude and speed of neural activity. *J. Cogn. Neurosci.* 17:507–17

Gazzaley A, Rissman J, D'Esposito M. 2004. Functional connectivity during working memory maintenance. *Cogn. Affect. Behav. Neurosci.* 4:580–99

Gelbard-Sagiv H, Mukamel R, Harel M, Malach R, Fried I. 2008. Internally generated reactivation of single neurons in human hippocampus during free recall. *Science* 322:96–101

Gonsalves BD, Kahn I, Curran T, Norman KA, Wagner AD. 2005. Memory strength and repetition suppression: multimodal imaging of medial temporal cortical contributions to recognition. *Neuron* 47:751–61

Greenberg AS, Esterman M, Wilson D, Serences JT, Yantis S. 2010. Control of spatial and feature-based attention in frontoparietal cortex. *J. Neurosci.* 30:14330–39

Harrison SA, Tong F. 2009. Decoding reveals the contents of visual working memory in early visual areas. *Nature* 458:632–35

Hassabis D, Chu C, Rees G, Weiskopf N, Molyneux PD, Maguire EA. 2009. Decoding neuronal ensembles in the human hippocampus. *Curr. Biol.* 19:546–54

Haushofer J, Livingstone MS, Kanwisher N. 2008. Multivariate patterns in object-selective cortex dissociate perceptual and physical shape similarity. *PLoS Biol.* 6:e187

Haxby JV, Gobbini MI, Furey ML, Ishai A, Schouten JL, Pietrini P. 2001. Distributed and overlapping representations of faces and objects in ventral temporal cortex. *Science* 293:2425–30

Haynes J-D. 2011. Decoding and predicting intentions. *Ann. N. Y. Acad. Sci.* 1224:9–21

Haynes J-D, Rees G. 2005. Predicting the orientation of invisible stimuli from activity in human primary visual cortex. *Nat. Neurosci.* 8:686–91

Haynes J-D, Rees G. 2006. Decoding mental states from brain activity in humans. *Nat. Rev. Neurosci.* 7:523–34

Haynes J-D, Sakai K, Rees G, Gilbert S, Frith C, Passingham RE. 2007. Reading hidden intentions in the human brain. *Curr. Biol.* 17:323–28

Hintzman DL, Curran T, Oppy B. 1992. Effects of similarity and repetition on memory: registration without learning? *J. Exp. Psychol.: Learn. Mem. Cogn.* 18:667–80

Howard MW, Kahana MJ. 2002. A distributed representation of temporal context. *J. Math. Psychol.* 46:269–99

Hsieh P-J, Vul E, Kanwisher N. 2010. Recognition alters the spatial pattern of FMRI activation in early retinotopic cortex. *J. Neurophysiol.* 103:1501–7

Ishai A, Ungerleider LG, Martin A, Haxby JV. 2000. The representation of objects in the human occipital and temporal cortex. *J. Cogn. Neurosci.* 12(Suppl. 2):35–51

Ishai A, Ungerleider LG, Martin A, Schouten JL, Haxby JV. 1999. Distributed representation of objects in the human ventral visual pathway. *Proc. Natl. Acad. Sci. USA* 96:9379–84

Jacoby LL, Shimizu Y, Daniels KA, Rhodes MG. 2005. Modes of cognitive control in recognition and source memory: depth of retrieval. *Psychon. Bull. Rev.* 12:852–57

Jenkins LJ, Ranganath C. 2010. Prefrontal and medial temporal lobe activity at encoding predicts temporal context memory. *J. Neurosci.* 30:15558–65

Johnson JD, McDuff SGR, Rugg MD, Norman KA. 2009. Recollection, familiarity, and cortical reinstatement: a multivoxel pattern analysis. *Neuron* 63:697–708

Johnson MK, Hashtroudi S, Lindsay DS. 1993. Source monitoring. *Psychol. Bull.* 114:3–28

Jonides J, Lewis RL, Nee DE, Lustig CA, Berman MG, Moore KS. 2008. The mind and brain of short-term memory. *Annu. Rev. Psychol.* 59:193–224

Just MA, Cherkassky VL, Aryal S, Mitchell TM. 2010. A neurosemantic theory of concrete noun representation based on the underlying brain codes. *PLoS ONE* 5:e8622

Kahn I, Davachi L, Wagner AD. 2004. Functional-neuroanatomic correlates of recollection: implications for models of recognition memory. *J. Neurosci.* 24:4172–80

Kahnt T, Heinzle J, Park SQ, Haynes J-D. 2010. The neural code of reward anticipation in human orbitofrontal cortex. *Proc. Natl. Acad. Sci. USA* 107:6010–15

Kamitani Y, Tong F. 2005. Decoding the visual and subjective contents of the human brain. *Nat. Neurosci.* 8:679–85

Kamitani Y, Tong F. 2006. Decoding seen and attended motion directions from activity in the human visual cortex. *Curr. Biol.* 16:1096–102

Kanwisher N, McDermott J, Chun MM. 1997. The fusiform face area: a module in human extrastriate cortex specialized for face perception. *J. Neurosci.* 17:4302–11

Kastner S, Pinsk MA. 2004. Visual attention as a multilevel selection process. *Cogn. Affect. Behav. Neurosci.* 4:483–500

Kay KN, Naselaris T, Prenger RJ, Gallant JL. 2008. Identifying natural images from human brain activity. *Nature* 452:352–55

Kim H. 2011. Neural activity that predicts subsequent memory and forgetting: a meta-analysis of 74 fMRI studies. *NeuroImage* 54:2446–61

Kosslyn SM. 2005. Mental images and the brain. *Cogn. Neuropsychol.* 22:333–47

Kriegeskorte N, Cusack R, Bandettini P. 2010. How does an fMRI voxel sample the neuronal activity pattern: compact-kernel or complex spatiotemporal filter? *NeuroImage* 49:1965–76

Kriegeskorte N, Goebel R, Bandettini P. 2006. Information-based functional brain mapping. *Proc. Natl. Acad. Sci. USA* 103:3863–68

Kriegeskorte N, Mur M, Bandettini P. 2008. Representational similarity analysis—connecting the branches of systems neuroscience. *Front. Syst. Neurosci.* 2:4

Kuhl BA, Rissman J, Chun MM, Wagner A. 2011. Fidelity of neural reactivation reveals competition between memories. *Proc. Natl. Acad. Sci. USA* 108:5903–8

Kuhl BA, Rissman J, Wagner AD. 2012. Multi-voxel patterns of visual category representation during episodic encoding are predictive of subsequent memory. *Neuropsychologia*. In press

Kuhl BA, Shah AT, Dubrow S, Wagner AD. 2010. Resistance to forgetting associated with hippocampus-mediated reactivation during new learning. *Nat. Neurosci.* 13:501–6

Lewis-Peacock JA, Postle BR. 2008. Temporary activation of long-term memory supports working memory. *J. Neurosci.* 28:8765–71

Li S, Ostwald D, Giese M, Kourtzi Z. 2007. Flexible coding for categorical decisions in the human brain. *J. Neurosci.* 27:12321–30

Lisman JE, Grace AA. 2005. The hippocampal-VTA loop: controlling the entry of information into long-term memory. *Neuron* 46:703–13

Liu T, Hospadaruk L, Zhu DC, Gardner JL. 2011. Feature-specific attentional priority signals in human cortex. *J. Neurosci.* 31:4484–95

Macevoy SP, Epstein RA. 2009. Decoding the representation of multiple simultaneous objects in human occipitotemporal cortex. *Curr. Biol.* 19:943–47

Malach R, Reppas JB, Benson RR, Kwong KK, Jiang H, et al. 1995. Object-related activity revealed by functional magnetic resonance imaging in human occipital cortex. *Proc. Natl. Acad. Sci. USA* 92:8135–39

Martin A, Chao LL. 2001. Semantic memory and the brain: structure and processes. *Curr. Opin. Neurobiol.* 11:194–201

Mayes A, Montaldi D, Migo E. 2007. Associative memory and the medial temporal lobes. *Trends Cogn. Sci.* 11:126–35

McClelland JL, McNaughton BL, O'Reilly RC. 1995. Why there are complementary learning systems in the hippocampus and neocortex: insights from the successes and failures of connectionist models of learning and memory. *Psychol. Rev.* 102:419–57

McClelland JL, Rogers TT. 2003. The parallel distributed processing approach to semantic cognition. *Nat. Rev. Neurosci.* 4:310–22

McDaniels MA, Einstein GO. 2007. *Prospective Memory: An Overview and Synthesis of an Emerging Field.* Thousand Oaks, CA: Sage

McDuff S, Frankel HC, Norman KA. 2009. Multivoxel pattern analysis reveals increased memory targeting and reduced use of retrieved details during single-agenda source monitoring. *J. Neurosci.* 29:508–16

Mecklinger A. 2010. The control of long-term memory: brain systems and cognitive processes. *Neurosci. Biobehav. Rev.* 34:1055–65

Mitchell TM, Hutchinson R, Niculescu RS, Pereira F, Wang X. 2004. Learning to decode cognitive states from brain images. *Machine Learn.* 57:145–75

Mitchell TM, Shinkareva SV, Carlson A, Chang K-M, Malave VL, et al. 2008. Predicting human brain activity associated with the meanings of nouns. *Science* 320:1191–95

Miyashita Y, Chang HS. 1988. Neuronal correlate of pictorial short-term memory in the primate temporal cortex. *Nature* 331:68–70

Miyawaki Y, Uchida H, Yamashita O, Sato M-a, Morito Y, et al. 2008. Visual image reconstruction from human brain activity using a combination of multiscale local image decoders. *Neuron* 60:915–29

Moser EI, Kropff E, Moser MB. 2008. Place cells, grid cells, and the brain's spatial representation system. *Annu. Rev. Neurosci.* 31:69–89

Naselaris T, Kay KN, Nishimoto S, Gallant JL. 2011. Encoding and decoding in fMRI. *NeuroImage* 56:400–10

Naselaris T, Prenger RJ, Kay KN, Oliver M, Gallant JL. 2009. Bayesian reconstruction of natural images from human brain activity. *Neuron* 63:902–15

Norman KA, O'Reilly RC. 2003. Modeling hippocampal and neocortical contributions to recognition memory: a complementary-learning-systems approach. *Psychol. Rev.* 110:611–46

Norman KA, Polyn SM, Detre GJ, Haxby JV. 2006. Beyond mind-reading: multi-voxel pattern analysis of fMRI data. *Trends Cogn. Sci.* 10:424–30

Nyberg L, Habib R, McIntosh AR, Tulving E. 2000. Reactivation of encoding-related brain activity during memory retrieval. *Proc. Natl. Acad. Sci. USA* 97:11120–24

O'Craven KM, Kanwisher N. 2000. Mental imagery of faces and places activates corresponding stimulus-specific brain regions. *J. Cogn. Neurosci.* 12:1013–23

O'Keefe J, Nadel L. 1978. *The Hippocampus as a Cognitive Map*. Oxford, UK: Oxford Univ. Press

O'Neill J, Pleydell-Bouverie B, Dupret D, Csicsvari J. 2010. Play it again: reactivation of waking experience and memory. *Trends Neurosci.* 33:220–29

Op de Beeck HP. 2010. Against hyperacuity in brain reading: Spatial smoothing does not hurt multivariate fMRI analyses? *NeuroImage* 49:1943–48

O'Reilly RC, McClelland JL. 1994. Hippocampal conjunctive encoding, storage, and recall: avoiding a trade-off. *Hippocampus* 4:661–82

O'Toole AJ, Jiang F, Abdi H, Haxby JV. 2005. Partially distributed representations of objects and faces in ventral temporal cortex. *J. Cogn. Neurosci.* 17:580–90

Peelen MV, Atkinson AP, Vuilleumier P. 2010. Supramodal representations of perceived emotions in the human brain. *J. Neurosci.* 30:10127–34

Poldrack RA, Halchenko YO, Hanson SJ. 2009. Decoding the large-scale structure of brain function by classifying mental states across individuals. *Psychol. Sci.* 20:1364–72

Polyn SM, Natu VS, Cohen JD, Norman KA. 2005. Category-specific cortical activity precedes retrieval during memory search. *Science* 310:1963–66

Polyn SM, Norman KA, Kahana MJ. 2009. A context maintenance and retrieval model of organizational processes in free recall. *Psychol. Rev.* 116:129–56

Postle BR. 2006. Working memory as an emergent property of the mind and brain. *Neuroscience* 139:23–38

Postle BR, Druzgal TJ, D'Esposito M. 2003. Seeking the neural substrates of visual working memory storage. *Cortex* 39:927–46

Preston AR, Bornstein AM, Hutchinson JB, Gaare ME, Glover GH, Wagner AD. 2010. High-resolution fMRI of content-sensitive subsequent memory responses in human medial temporal lobe. *J. Cogn. Neurosci.* 22:156–73

Puce A, Allison T, Gore JC, McCarthy G. 1995. Face-sensitive regions in human extrastriate cortex studied by functional MRI. *J. Neurophysiol.* 74:1192–99

Pulvermüller F, Kherif F, Hauk O, Mohr B, Nimmo-Smith I. 2009. Distributed cell assemblies for general lexical and category-specific semantic processing as revealed by fMRI cluster analysis. *Hum. Brain Mapp.* 30:3837–50

Quamme JR, Weiss DJ, Norman KA. 2010. Listening for recollection: a multi-voxel pattern analysis of recognition memory retrieval strategies. *Front Hum. Neurosci.* 4:61

Raaijmakers JG, Shiffrin RM. 1992. Models for recall and recognition. *Annu. Rev. Psychol.* 43:205–34

Race EA, Kuhl BA, Badre D, Wagner AD. 2009. The dynamic interplay between cognitive control and memory. In *The Cognitive Neurosciences*, ed. MS Gazzaniga, pp. 705–24. Cambridge, MA: MIT Press

Ranganath C. 2006. Working memory for visual objects: complementary roles of inferior temporal, medial temporal, and prefrontal cortex. *Neuroscience* 139:277–89

Reddy L, Kanwisher N. 2006. Coding of visual objects in the ventral stream. *Curr. Opin. Neurobiol.* 16:408–14

Reddy L, Tsuchiya N, Serre T. 2010. Reading the mind's eye: decoding category information during mental imagery. *NeuroImage* 50:818–25

Redish AD, Battaglia FP, Chawla MK, Ekstrom AD, Gerrard JL, et al. 2001. Independence of firing correlates of anatomically proximate hippocampal pyramidal cells. *J. Neurosci.* 21:RC134

Rissman J, Gazzaley A, D'Esposito M. 2004. Measuring functional connectivity during distinct stages of a cognitive task. *NeuroImage* 23:752–63

Rissman J, Gazzaley A, D'Esposito M. 2009. The effect of non-visual working memory load on top-down modulation of visual processing. *Neuropsychologia* 47:1637–46

Rissman J, Greely HT, Wagner AD. 2010. Detecting individual memories through the neural decoding of memory states and past experience. *Proc. Natl. Acad. Sci. USA* 107:9849–54

Rodriguez PF. 2010. Neural decoding of goal locations in spatial navigation in humans with fMRI. *Hum. Brain Mapp.* 31:391–97

Rolls ET, Grabenhorst F, Franco L. 2009. Prediction of subjective affective state from brain activations. *J. Neurophysiol.* 101:1294–308

Rotello CM, Macmillan NA, Reeder JA. 2004. Sum-difference theory of remembering and knowing: a two-dimensional signal-detection model. *Psychol. Rev.* 111:588–616

Ruchkin DS, Grafman J, Cameron K, Berndt RS. 2003. Working memory retention systems: a state of activated long-term memory. *Behav. Brain Sci.* 26:709–28; discussion 728–77

Rugg MD, Johnson JD, Park H, Uncapher MR. 2008. Encoding-retrieval overlap in human episodic memory: a functional neuroimaging perspective. *Prog. Brain Res.* 169:339–52

Rugg MD, Yonelinas A. 2003. Human recognition memory: a cognitive neuroscience perspective. *Trends Cogn. Sci.* 7:313–19

Schacter DL, Addis DR, Buckner RL. 2007. Remembering the past to imagine the future: the prospective brain. *Nat. Rev. Neurosci.* 8:657–61

Schacter DL, Slotnick SD. 2004. The cognitive neuroscience of memory distortion. *Neuron* 44:149–60

Serences JT, Ester EF, Vogel EK, Awh E. 2009. Stimulus-specific delay activity in human primary visual cortex. *Psychol. Sci.* 20:207–14

Shinkareva SV, Malave VL, Mason RA, Mitchell TM, Just MA. 2011. Commonality of neural representations of words and pictures. *NeuroImage* 54:2418–25

Shinkareva SV, Mason RA, Malave VL, Wang W, Mitchell TM, Just MA. 2008. Using FMRI brain activation to identify cognitive states associated with perception of tools and dwellings. *PLoS ONE* 3:e1394

Shohamy D, Adcock RA. 2010. Dopamine and adaptive memory. *Trends Cogn. Sci.* 14:464–72

Shohamy D, Wagner AD. 2008. Integrating memories in the human brain: hippocampal-midbrain encoding of overlapping events. *Neuron* 60:378–89

Simons JS, Spiers HJ. 2003. Prefrontal and medial temporal lobe interactions in long-term memory. *Nat. Rev. Neurosci.* 4:637–48

Spiridon M, Kanwisher N. 2002. How distributed is visual category information in human occipito-temporal cortex? An fMRI study. *Neuron* 35:1157–65

Stokes M, Saraiva A, Rohenkohl G, Nobre AC. 2011. Imagery for shapes activates position-invariant representations in human visual cortex. *NeuroImage* 56:1540–45

Stokes M, Thompson R, Cusack R, Duncan J. 2009. Top-down activation of shape-specific population codes in visual cortex during mental imagery. *J. Neurosci.* 29:1565–72

Swisher JD, Gatenby JC, Gore JC, Wolfe BA, Moon C-H, et al. 2010. Multiscale pattern analysis of orientation-selective activity in the primary visual cortex. *J. Neurosci.* 30:325–30

Tamber-Rosenau BJ, Esterman M, Chiu Y-C, Yantis S. 2011. Cortical mechanisms of cognitive control for shifting attention in vision and working memory. *J. Cogn. Neurosci.* In press

Tanaka K. 1993. Neuronal mechanisms of object recognition. *Science* 262:685–88

Tong F, Pratte MS. 2012. Decoding patterns of human brain activity. *Annu. Rev. Psychol.* 63:In press

Thirion B, Duchesnay E, Hubbard E, Dubois J, Poline J-B, et al. 2006. Inverse retinotopy: inferring the visual content of images from brain activation patterns. *NeuroImage* 33:1104–16

Tulving E, Thompson DM. 1973. Encoding specificity and retrieval processes in episodic memory. *Psychol. Rev.* 80:352–73

Uncapher MR, Wagner AD. 2009. Posterior parietal cortex and episodic encoding: insights from fMRI subsequent memory effects and dual-attention theory. *Neurobiol. Learn. Mem.* 91:139–54

Wagner AD, Maril A, Schacter DL. 2000. Interactions between forms of memory: when priming hinders new episodic learning. *J. Cogn. Neurosci.* 12(Suppl. 2):52–60

Wagner AD, Shannon BJ, Kahn I, Buckner RL. 2005. Parietal lobe contributions to episodic memory retrieval. *Trends Cogn. Sci.* 9:445–53

Walther DB, Caddigan E, Fei-Fei L, Beck DM. 2009. Natural scene categories revealed in distributed patterns of activity in the human brain. *J. Neurosci.* 29:10573–81

Watanabe T, Hirose S, Wada H, Katsura M, Chikazoe J, et al. 2011. Prediction of subsequent recognition performance using brain activity in the medial temporal lobe. *NeuroImage* 54:3085–92

Weber M, Thompson-Schill SL, Osherson D, Haxby J, Parsons L. 2009. Predicting judged similarity of natural categories from their neural representations. *Neuropsychologia* 47:859–68

Wheeler ME, Petersen SE, Buckner RL. 2000. Memory's echo: Vivid remembering reactivates sensory-specific cortex. *Proc. Natl. Acad. Sci. USA* 97:11125–29

Williams MA, Dang S, Kanwisher NG. 2007. Only some spatial patterns of fMRI response are read out in task performance. *Nat. Neurosci.* 10:685–86

Wixted JT, Mickes L. 2010. A continuous dual-process model of remember/know judgments. *Psychol. Rev.* 117:1025–54

Wixted JT, Squire LR. 2011. The medial temporal lobe and the attributes of memory. *Trends Cogn. Sci.* 15:210–17

Woolgar A, Thompson R, Bor D, Duncan J. 2011. Multi-voxel coding of stimuli, rules, and responses in human frontoparietal cortex. *NeuroImage* 56:744–52

Xue G, Dong Q, Chen C, Lu Z, Mumford JA, Poldrack RA. 2010. Greater neural pattern similarity across repetitions is associated with better memory. *Science* 330:97–101

Yonelinas AP, Aly M, Wang W-C, Koen JD. 2010. Recollection and familiarity: examining controversial assumptions and new directions. *Hippocampus* 20:1178–94

Yonelinas AP, Otten LJ, Shaw KN, Rugg MD. 2005. Separating the brain regions involved in recollection and familiarity in recognition memory. *J. Neurosci.* 25:3002–8

Fear Extinction as a Model for Translational Neuroscience: Ten Years of Progress

Mohammed R. Milad[1] and Gregory J. Quirk[2]

[1]Department of Psychiatry, Massachusetts General Hospital, Harvard Medical School, Boston, Massachusetts 02129

[2]Departments of Psychiatry and Anatomy & Neurobiology, University of Puerto Rico School of Medicine, San Juan, Puerto Rico 00936; email: gjquirk@yahoo.com

Annu. Rev. Psychol. 2012. 63:129–51

The *Annual Review of Psychology* is online at psych.annualreviews.org

This article's doi: 10.1146/annurev.psych.121208.131631

Keywords

conditioning, prefrontal, cingulate, amygdala, fMRI, anxiety

Abstract

The psychology of extinction has been studied for decades. Approximately 10 years ago, however, there began a concerted effort to understand the neural circuits of extinction of fear conditioning, in both animals and humans. Progress during this period has been facilitated by a high degree of coordination between rodent and human researchers examining fear extinction. Here we review the major advances and highlight new approaches to understanding and exploiting fear extinction. Research in fear extinction could serve as a model for translational research in other areas of behavioral neuroscience.

Contents

INTRODUCTION

Fear extinction refers to the decrement in conditioned fear responses that occurs with repeated presentation of a conditioned fear stimulus that is unreinforced. **Figure 1** (see color insert) shows the number of research publications using the key words "fear extinction" since 1990. Note that the number of animal and human studies increased sharply after 2000, with animal studies preceding human studies by several years. In this review, we start with a brief overview of fundamental psychological concepts of extinction and then review the key factors prior to 2000 that led to the recent increase in fear extinction studies. We then focus on fear extinction research during this past decade, which was facilitated by a rodent-to-human translational approach. Finally, we discuss directions for fear extinction research in the next decade. A comprehensive review of the psychological and neurobiological basis of fear extinction is not possible in this venue. Numerous reviews on molecular mechanisms of extinction, clinical relevance, and inhibition circuitry within the amygdala have recently been published (Etkin et al. 2011, Graham & Milad 2011, Herry et al. 2010, Myers et al. 2011, Pape & Paré 2010, Sotres-Bayon & Quirk 2010).

OVERVIEW OF FEAR EXTINCTION AND ITS PSYCHOLOGICAL BASIS

Initial attempts to understand fear extinction focused on psychological and behavioral phenomena. In the 1920s, Pavlov observed that extinguished appetitive responses in dogs would spontaneously recover with the passage of time, and he proposed that extinction was a special form of inhibition (Pavlov 1927). Despite early theoretical formulations of extinction-related inhibition (Konorski 1967), the search for inhibitory circuits had been largely unsuccessful (Chan et al. 2001, Kimble & Kimble 1970). Research focusing on the behavioral and psychological aspects of conditioning and extinction provided key data upon which contemporary studies on the neural mechanisms of fear extinction were based. In addition to the passage of time, it was shown that extinguished responding could be renewed with a change in context (Bouton & King 1983) or reinstated with unconditioned stimuli (US; Rescorla & Heth 1975). The phenomena of spontaneous recovery, fear renewal, and reinstatement, as well accelerated reacquisition (Rescorla 2001), have been described in detail over the past decades (reviewed in Bouton & Moody 2004, Rescorla 1988). Together, they constitute strong evidence that extinction does not erase the initial association between the conditioned stimuli (CS) and US but rather forms a new association (CS–No US) that inhibits expression of the conditioned memory.

Context, in particular, is able to gate expression of conditioning versus extinction memory. That is, when an animal is conditioned in one context (context A) and then extinguished in a different context (context B), the extinction memory can be expressed only if the CS is presented in context B. Though "context" is often defined as the physical place, the internal state of the animal can also be considered a context. Also, the passage of time can be viewed as a contextual shift (Bouton et al. 2006).

SETTING THE STAGE FOR FEAR EXTINCTION MECHANISMS

From Avoidance to Fear Conditioning: The Amygdala as a Hub of Fear

Initial animal work on fear extinction in the 1960s to 1980s used active avoidance paradigms. Systemically administered drugs were used to implicate stress hormones, benzodiazepines, and monoamines in extinction (Buresova et al. 1964, Bohus & De Wied 1966, Kokkinidis 1983, Koob et al. 1986). Setting the stage for later molecular work, it was shown that extinction learning required protein synthesis (Flood et al. 1977) and cortical norepinephrine (Mason et al. 1979). Direct manipulations of the brain were few, but lesion and electrical stimulation techniques implicated the septum, prefrontal cortex, striatum, and hippocampus in extinction of avoidance responses (Brennan

& Wisniewski 1982, Gralewicz & Gralewicz 1984, Lovely 1975, Sanberg et al. 1979).

Our knowledge of fear-learning circuits advanced rapidly during the 1980s to 1990s. Studies of avoidance learning gave way to more ethologically relevant classically conditioned responses such as freezing and potentiation of startle responses (Blanchard & Blanchard 1969, Chi 1965, Davis & Astrachan 1978). The amygdala became the centerpiece of the fear-conditioning circuit when it was shown that discrete lesions of the amygdala could block the acquisition and expression of conditioned fear responses (Hitchcock & Davis 1986, LeDoux et al. 1984) and that the lateral amygdala received direct input from sensory areas of the thalamus (LeDoux et al. 1985). Neurobiological evidence began to detail how the association between tone and shock is formed and expressed within different sub-nuclei of the amygdala (Davis 2000, LeDoux 2000, Maren 2005, Sigurdsson et al. 2007).

During the same time, anatomical studies described the connections of the amygdala central nucleus (Ce) with downstream structures implicated in the expression of conditioned fear responses, including the hypothalamus, periaquaductal gray, pons, and other brainstem regions (Applegate et al. 1982, Kapp et al. 1979, LeDoux et al. 1988, Pitkanen et al. 1997, Romanski & LeDoux 1993). Studies during this period also described the inhibitory circuits within the amygdala that were later found to be involved in fear extinction, such as the gamma-aminobutyric acid (GABA)ergic intercalated cells (Nitecka & Ben Ari 1987, Paré & Smith 1993), lateral division of the Ce (Sun & Cassell 1993), and inhibitory cells within the lateral and basolateral nuclei (Mahanty & Sah 1998). Thus, these advances in understanding fear conditioning provided the framework against which to investigate extinction-induced reduction of fear.

Advent of Human Neuroimaging Tools

Concurrent with the advances in rodent fear circuits was the development of functional

Conditioned fear responses: physiological responses exhibited by the organism during conditioning; triggered by the presentation of the conditioned stimulus. Most commonly measured responses include freezing and potentiated startle in rodents and skin conductance and potentiated startle responses in humans

US: unconditioned stimuli

CS: conditioned stimuli

Extinction learning: the start of extinction training, when the organism begins to learn that the CS no longer predicts the US. Also called within-session extinction

Ce: central nucleus of the amygdala

fMRI: functional magnetic resonance imaging

CS+: a conditioned stimulus paired with the aversive unconditioned stimulus

CS-: a conditioned stimulus that is not paired with the aversive unconditioned stimulus

PTSD: posttraumatic stress disorder

Ventromedial prefrontal cortex (vmPFC): specific definitions of this region in humans vary from study to study, but broadly speaking, it is within the medial wall of prefrontal cortex that corresponds to Brodmann area (BA) 10m. Some studies refer to BA25 (the subgenual cortex) and parts of BA32 as parts of the vmPFC

PET: positron emission tomography

NMDA: N-methyl-D-aspartate

BLA: basolateral nucleus of the amygdala (including the lateral and basal nuclei)

neuroimaging in humans, which began in 1991 with the first functional magnetic resonance imaging (fMRI) study (Belliveau et al. 1991). The initial wave of fMRI studies focused on paradigms involving functional activation of the visual and motor cortices (reviewed in Rosen et al. 1998). With respect to emotional learning, early fMRI studies sought to determine the extent to which rodent models of the amygdala were valid in the human brain. Using a simple differential fear-conditioning paradigm in healthy humans (a blue square as the CS and a mild shock as the US), LaBar et al. (1998) and later Büchel et al. (1999) reported increased amygdala activation in response to the CS+ (CS that is paired with the US) as compared to the CS- (CS that is not paired with the shock). Subsequent fMRI studies using fearful faces as stimuli also showed significant amygdala activation in healthy humans (Breiter et al. 1996, Whalen et al. 1998). These observations were critical for two reasons: (*a*) they provided unequivocal evidence that amygdala function was conserved across species, and (*b*) they validated the use of fMRI for studying fear learning in humans.

A Clinical Connection to Fear Extinction

It was first proposed in the late 1980s that fear conditioning may serve as an animal model for anxiety disorders, such as posttraumatic stress disorder (PTSD), and could be useful for understanding the underlying psychopathology of anxiety disorders. Pitman and colleagues proposed that PTSD patients hypercondition, i.e., form strong associations between traumatic events and sensory cues present at the time of the trauma (Pitman 1988). These strong associations later become resistant to extinction. Moreover, neuroimaging data that emerged during the late 1990s implicated the amygdala and the ventromedial prefrontal cortex (vmPFC) in the psychopathology of anxiety disorders, which resembled the clinical profile of perseverative fear and anxiety. Positron emission tomography (PET) studies showed

decreased prefrontal blood flow in PTSD patients (Bremner et al. 1999, Semple et al. 1996). Furthermore, PTSD patients showed reduced activation of vmPFC, as indicated by fMRI, when recalling traumatic events with the help of script-driven imagery (Shin et al. 1999). Thus, knowledge of fear-learning circuits in rodents provided hypotheses that could be tested in anxiety disorder patients, using contemporary neuroimaging tools.

Initial Research on Fear Extinction Mechanisms: In Search of the Inhibitor

In contrast to fear learning, research on the neurobiology of fear extinction was only just beginning in the 1990s. Harris & Westbrook (1998) confirmed that extinction was a form of inhibition by showing that a beta-carboline antagonist of GABA-A receptors could block the development and expression of extinction. A prescient study by Davis and coworkers (Falls et al. 1992) showed that fear extinction required N-methyl-D-aspartate (NMDA) receptors in the basolateral nucleus of the amygdala (BLA), confirming that extinction was an active form of learning similar to conditioning itself. Initial hints of the involvement of the prefrontal cortex in emotion regulation came from earlier studies showing compulsive-like behavior (disinhibition) in dogs with lesions of the subgenual region of the medial prefrontal cortex (Brutkowski & Mempel 1961) and from monkeys with lesions of orbitofrontal cortex (Butter et al. 1963). Inspired by these early studies, LeDoux and coworkers found that lesions of sensory cortices impaired fear extinction (LeDoux et al. 1989, Teich et al. 1989) and reasoned that sensory areas interacted with frontal or hippocampal cortices to mediate extinction (for review, see Sotres-Bayon et al. 2004).

Anatomical studies appearing at about the same time showed direct projections from the ventral medial prefrontal cortex (vmPFC) to the amygdala (Hurley et al. 1991; McDonald 1991, 1998), in particular to inhibitory areas such as the intercalated cells (Vertes 2004).

The first direct evidence for the involvement of the vmPFC in fear extinction came from LeDoux and coworkers (Morgan et al. 1993), who showed that pretraining lesions of the vmPFC had no effect on the acquisition of conditioned fear but impaired fear extinction across days. The authors described the extinction impairment as "emotional perseveration," reminiscent of perseverative conditioned responses in dogs and monkeys with frontal lesions. Davis and coworkers were unable to replicate extinction deficits with lesions of vmPFC or visual cortex (Falls & Davis 1993, Gewirtz et al. 1997), suggesting a possible difference between extinction of freezing versus potentiated startle, or the specific location of the lesions (Sotres-Bayon et al. 2004). Nevertheless, the findings of Morgan et al. (1993) generated interest in prefrontal cortex as an inhibitor in extinction.

THE INHIBITOR FOUND?

Rodent Infralimbic Prefrontal Cortex

In an attempt to resolve the apparent conflict in previous studies assessing vmPFC's role in extinction (Gewirtz et al. 1997, Morgan et al. 1993), Quirk et al. (2000) made lesions of the vmPFC, focusing on the infralimbic (IL) subregion as opposed to the prelimbic (PL) subregion (**Figure 2**, see color insert). IL lesions did not impair the ability of rats to extinguish conditioned freezing responses within an extinction session, indicating that prefrontal circuits were not necessary for the initial learning of extinction. The following day, however, rats with vmPFC lesions were unable to retrieve their extinction memory at the start of the testing session. Therefore, a distinction was made between the acquisition of extinction and its subsequent retrieval, reflecting behavioral studies showing that retrieval of extinction was regulated by contextual and temporal factors (Bouton 1993, Rescorla 2004). Therefore, dissecting extinction into separate phases of acquisition, consolidation, and retrieval, similar to other types of learning, would be necessary for understanding the neurobiology of extinction (Quirk & Mueller 2008).

Because lesion studies are often difficult to interpret, additional approaches were needed to test the vmPFC hypothesis. Accordingly, Milad & Quirk (2002) used single-cell recording to determine the phase of conditioning and/or extinction training that vmPFC might signal. Paralleling lesion findings, cells in IL did not signal tones during conditioning or extinction phases but did signal tones during the retrieval phase. Furthermore, the magnitude of IL tone responses was inversely correlated with freezing at the retrieval test, consistent with a safety signal. Similar findings have been reported with the activity marker cFos (Hefner et al. 2008, Knapska & Maren 2009) and metabolic mapping methods (Barrett et al. 2003). Moving closer to a test of causality, Milad & Quirk (2002) showed that mimicking IL tone responses with brief microstimulation reduced fear and strengthened extinction (see also Milad et al. 2004). Both recording and stimulation findings were specific to IL and were not observed in the adjacent prelimbic cortex. Taken together, these studies advanced our understanding from a general notion of prefrontal involvement to a specific role of IL plasticity in the retrieval of previously learned extinction. Additional support for a role of vmPFC in extinction came from Garcia and colleagues, who showed that extinction potentiated thalamic and hippocampal inputs to vmPFC (Herry & Garcia 2003) and that extinction memory could be facilitated or impaired by administering high-frequency or low-frequency trains of stimulation, respectively, to vmPFC inputs (Deschaux et al. 2011, Garcia et al. 2008, Herry & Garcia 2002).

Subsequent studies have confirmed the role of IL in the retrieval of extinction using lesions, drug infusions, and stimulation approaches (**Figure 3**, see color insert) (Akirav & Maroun 2007, Holmes & Wellman 2009, Quirk & Mueller 2008; for recent reviews, see Herry et al. 2010, Sotres-Bayon & Quirk 2010). For a listing of studies prior to 2008 implicating vmPFC in extinction, see Quirk & Mueller (2008). More recent studies implicating IL in extinction are listed in **Table 1**. Extinction

IL: infralimbic prefrontal cortex

PL: prelimbic prefrontal cortex

Table 1 Effects of infralimbic cortex manipulations on memory for fear extinction

Method	Task	Extinction memory	Reference
Facilitators			
CB1 receptor agonist	Cued fc	Enhanced	Lin et al. (2009)
BDNF	Cued fc	Enhanced	Peters et al. (2010)
M-type K(+) channel blocker	Cued fc	Enhanced	Santini & Porter (2010)
GABAa antagonist picrotoxin	Cued fc	Enhanced	Thompson et al. (2010)
Microstimulation	Cued fc	Enhanced	Kim et al. (2010)
GABAa antagonist picrotoxin	Cued fc	Enhanced	Chang & Maren (2011)
Histone acetyltransferase	Cued fc	Enhanced	Marek et al. (2011)
Inhibitors			
CB1 receptor antagonist	Cued fc	Impaired	Lin et al. (2009)
Inactivation with muscimol	Context fc	Impaired	Laurent & Westbrook (2009)
D2 antagonist raclopride	Cued fc	Impaired	Mueller et al. (2010)
mGluR5 antagonist MPEP	Cued fc	Impaired	Fontanez-Nuin et al. (2011)
Inactivation with muscimol	Cued fc	Impaired	Sierra-Mercado et al. (2011)

Abbreviations: BDNF, brain-derived neurotrophic factor; CB1, cannabinoid 1; fc, fear conditioning; GABA, gamma-aminobutyric acid; MPEP, 2-methyl-6- phenylethynylpyridine.

memory requires IL activation of NMDA receptors (Burgos-Robles et al. 2007, Sotres-Bayon et al. 2007), protein kinase A (Mueller et al. 2008), MAP kinase (Hugues et al. 2004), cannabinoid receptors (Lin et al. 2009), and protein synthesis (Mueller et al. 2008, Santini et al. 2004). Together, these studies suggest that a calcium-mediated cascade in IL triggers protein kinases and protein synthesis necessary for long-term extinction memory. In addition to tone responding, extinction also increased burst-type firing of IL neurons (Burgos-Robles et al. 2007, Chang et al. 2010) and reversed conditioning-induced depression of intrinsic excitability (Santini et al. 2008). This suggests that extinction-induced potentiation of intrinsic and synaptic mechanisms in IL could increase local plasticity and the impact of IL on its targets. In support of this, the degree of IL bursting is correlated with extinction retrieval (Santini et al. 2008), and pharmacologically augmenting IL excitability strengthens extinction memory (Santini & Porter 2010). Thus, IL rodent data confirmed early observations (Konorski 1967, Pavlov 1927) that extinction does not return the brain to its preconditioning

state, but rather potentiates inhibitory circuits. These findings suggest additional ways of augmenting extinction (see Facilitating Extinction in Rodents sidebar).

Translating IL Findings to Humans

Spurred by rodent data, researchers developed numerous ingenious paradigms for assessing fear conditioning and extinction in healthy humans. These included examinations of fear-potentiated startle (Jovanovic et al. 2005, 2006); return of fear phenomena: renewal, reinstatement, and the context dependency of extinction (Hermans et al. 2005, LaBar & Phelps 2005, Milad et al. 2005a, Norrholm et al. 2006, Vansteenwegen et al. 2005, Vervliet et al. 2005); extinction in adolescents (Pine et al. 2001); and the use of virtual reality for generating contextual and cued-conditioned stimuli (Baas et al. 2004, Grillon et al. 2006, Huff et al. 2010). Initial imaging studies focused mostly on within-session extinction learning (e.g., LaBar et al. 1998) and found increased amygdala and orbitofrontal cortex activation during extinction training (Gottfried & Dolan 2004, Knight et al. 2004). However, rodent data distinguishing recall of extinction from its initial learning called for a multiday conditioning/extinction paradigm in humans.

The Homolog of IL in the Human Brain: Ventromedial Prefrontal Cortex

Phelps and colleagues conducted the first fMRI study to identify a functional homolog of IL in the human brain in a two-day protocol capable of assessing extinction recall (Phelps et al. 2004). They showed that vmPFC increased its activation during recall of extinction in healthy humans, a finding that was later replicated (Kalisch et al. 2006). This suggested that vmPFC might constitute a functional homologue of the rodent IL (see **Figure 2**). We developed and validated a human fear conditioning and extinction paradigm that allowed for contextual manipulation of extinction recall. It also allowed us to compare recall of extinction with recall of conditioning (via the use of extinguished versus unextinguished stimuli) in order to extend the translation of the rodent data to the human brain (Milad et al. 2005a, Rauch et al. 2006). Using this paradigm, we observed vmPFC deactivation during conditioning, which converted to significant activation by the end of extinction learning (Milad et al. 2007b). During extinction recall, the magnitude of vmPFC activation to the extinguished stimulus (relative to the unextinguished stimulus) was positively correlated with the magnitude of extinction retention (Milad et al. 2007b). That is, the stronger the activation of the vmPFC, the more the subject was able to inhibit conditioned responding during extinction recall. Analysis of a separate cohort showed that the thickness of the vmPFC was also correlated with extinction recall (Milad et al. 2005b), a finding that was recently replicated (Hartley et al. 2011). Thus, both structure and function of the human vmPFC positively correlated with the magnitude of extinction memory, similar to rodent IL (**Figure 4**, see color insert).

OPPOSING EXTINCTION

Rodent Prelimbic Prefrontal Cortex

Lying just dorsal to the IL in rodents is the prelimbic cortex. The idea that PL may be important for expression of conditioned fear has historic precedents in studies with rabbits (McLaughlin et al. 2002) and rodents, using a trace conditioning paradigm (delay between CS and US) (Runyan et al. 2004). For classical auditory fear conditioning (where the CS and US overlap), inactivation of PL reduces fear expression (Corcoran & Quirk 2007, Laurent & Westbrook 2009, Sierra-Mercado et al. 2011). Paralleling these inactivation findings, single PL neurons showed sustained increases in firing rate in response to conditioned tones (Burgos-Robles et al. 2009). The time course of PL activity mirrored that of freezing (**Figure 5A**, see color insert) and was excessive in rats showing poor retrieval of extinction. Thus, PL receives a transient fear signal from

Extinction recall: when the organism is presented with the extinguished CS long (e.g., 24–48 hours) after extinction training (also called extinction retention or extinction retrieval). Good recall of extinction, as evidenced by low fear responses, depends on contextual factors

Table 2   Effects of prelimbic cortex manipulations on expression of conditioned fear

Method	Task	Fear expression	Reference
Facilitators			
Microstimulation	Cued fc	Enhanced	Vidal-Gonzalez et al. (2006)
CB1 receptor agonist	Cued fc	Enhanced	Lin et al. (2009)
Inhibitors			
Inactivation with tetrodotoxin	Cued fc	Impaired	Corcoran & Quirk (2007)
Inactivation with muscimol	Context fc	Impaired	Laurent & Westbrook (2009)
Cannabidiol	Context fc	Impaired	Lemos et al. (2010)
Cannabinoid antagonist AM-251	Cued fc	Impaired	Tan et al. (2010)
Site-specific BDNF knockout	Cued fc	Impaired	Choi et al. (2010)
Inactivation with muscimol	Cued fc	Impaired	Sierra-Mercado et al. (2011)

the amygdala and converts it into a sustained signal that returns to the amygdala to sustain fear (see **Figure 5B**). Finally, microstimulation of PL increased freezing responses to conditioned tones and impaired extinction (Vidal-Gonzalez et al. 2006). These and other recent studies (see **Table 2**) indicate that PL drives conditioned freezing responses and opposes extinction. Thus, the prefrontal cortex is not simply an inhibitor but is able to exert dual control over fear expression via separate modules, each with access to separate sets of inputs and outputs (Sotres-Bayon & Quirk 2010).

Translating PL Findings to Humans: Dorsal Anterior Cingulate

Spurred by the PL data in rodents, we reexamined our human structural and functional data for evidence of cortical areas involved in fear expression. As with the vmPFC, both cortical thickness and activation of the dorsal anterior cingulate (dACC) were positively correlated with skin conductance response during the conditioning phase (Milad et al. 2007a; but see Hartley et al. 2011) (see **Figure 4**). The increased responsiveness to conditioned stimuli during fear acquisition was recently replicated in a separate cohort of healthy subjects (Linnman et al. 2011a). Activation of dACC had been noted in previous studies of fear conditioning (Buchel et al. 1998, Cheng et al. 2003, Knight et al. 2004, Phelps et al. 2004),

but its significance as a predictor of fear levels was not emphasized. dACC activation has been observed in response to unconditioned stimuli as well as conditioned stimuli. Moreover, dACC was activated by USs consisting of loud noise (Dunsmoor et al. 2008, Knight et al. 2010) and electric shock (Linnman et al. 2011a). Interestingly, omission of an expected shock also activated dACC (Linnman et al. 2011a). These data further support the role of dACC in the expression of conditioned fear in humans, similar to the rodent PL.

PREFRONTAL CONNECTIVITY WITH AMYGDALA AND HIPPOCAMPUS

Rodent Connectivity

PL and IL cortices can modulate fear expression through descending projections to the amygdala. Whereas PL targets the basal nucleus of the amygdala, IL targets inhibitory areas such as the lateral division of the central nucleus (CeL) and intercalated (ITC) neurons (McDonald 1998, Vertes 2004). Physiological studies support excitatory and inhibitory effects for PL and IL, respectively. PL stimulation excites BLA neurons, which tend to fire at short latencies following PL spikes (Likhtik et al. 2005). In contrast, IL stimulation drives ITC neurons (Amir et al. 2011), which then inhibit Ce output neurons (Royer & Paré 2002). This circuit is consistent with the finding that IL stimulation

Dorsal anterior cingulate (dACC): as with vmPFC, definitions of this brain region vary across studies. Many studies refer to a wide area posterior to the genu of the corpus callosum (BA24) as parts of the dACC. Recent attempts have been made to update the nomenclature of this region, and some refer to this region as the anterior mid-cingulate cortex

ITC: intercalated cells (within the amygdala)

reduces the responsiveness of CeL output neurons to BLA or cortical stimulation (Quirk et al. 2003). It is also consistent with resting state functional connectivity in the rat (Liang et al. 2011). Thus, via divergent projections, PL and IL can bidirectionally gate the expression of amygdala-dependent fear memories.

In addition to gating fear expression, recent evidence suggests that IL contributes to extinction-induced plasticity within the amygdala. ITC cells are essential for fear extinction (Jungling et al. 2008, Likhtik et al. 2008) and show extinction-induced potentiation of BLA inputs (Amano et al. 2010). IL activity is essential for the development of this extinction-induced plasticity in ITC (Amano et al. 2010). The cooperativity between IL and inhibitory circuits within the amygdala suggests that successful extinction requires correlated activity between these areas. Pharmacological inactivation of either IL or BLA (including ITCs) prevents the development of stable extinction memory (Laurent et al. 2008, Sierra-Mercado et al. 2011). Indeed, unit recording data suggest that BLA neurons process extinction via reciprocal connectivity with prefrontal and hippocampal areas (Herry et al. 2008, 2010). BLA input is responsible for conditioned fear signaling in PL (Laviolette et al. 2005, Sotres-Bayon et al. 2010), suggesting that neural activity of these two regions may be correlated during conditioned fear expression (see **Figure 5B**).

The hippocampus plays an essential role in contextual gating of extinction to an explicit CS (Bouton et al. 2006, Ji & Maren 2007) as well as conditioning and extinction of context conditioning (Radulovic & Tronson 2010). The ventral hippocampus (vHPC) projects directly to PL/IL and the BLA and therefore is in a position to modulate fear responses (Hugues & Garcia 2007). Although it is tempting to ask if hippocampal output excites or inhibits fear, there is evidence that the hippocampus may have either effect, depending on the experimental condition examined. Hippocampal inactivation reduces the expression of conditioned fear (Sierra-Mercado et al. 2011) and prevents the

renewal of fear after extinction (Hobin et al. 2006, Ji & Maren 2005), both suggesting a role in fear excitation. However, hippocampal inactivation during extinction training leads to poor recall of extinction (Corcoran et al. 2005, Sierra-Mercado et al. 2011), and low-frequency stimulation of vHPC disrupts extinction memory (Hugues & Garcia 2007), suggesting that plasticity in the hippocampal system normally serves to inhibit fear. The necessity of both IL and hippocampus activity for extinction memory suggests that the two structures may work together during recall of extinction.

Human Connectivity

Given the striking homology between rodent IL/PL and human vmPFC/dACC, one might also predict cross-species parallels in connectivity. In humans, however, it is more challenging to study subregional connectivity. Limits in the spatial resolution of fMRI make it difficult to accurately subdivide a small structure like the amygdala. Furthermore, the extent to which blood oxygen level–dependent (BOLD) signals represent excitatory versus inhibitory inputs, spiking activity, or local processing is only beginning to be explored (Angenstein et al. 2009). Thus, the understanding of the complex nature of the neural circuits within the amygdala in the human brain is very limited. For the hippocampus, its classical role in contextual conditioning and extinction is studied in animals with multimodal shifts and context changes. Such manipulations are technically challenging within an fMRI scanner. Indeed, an initial study did not report hippocampal activation to manipulations of visual contexts during auditory conditioning (Armony & Dolan 2001). More recent studies using visual contextual manipulations were able to observe hippocampal activations during extinction recall (Kalisch et al. 2006, Lang et al. 2009, Milad et al. 2007b).

Despite these challenges, emerging data show that the hippocampus and amygdala work together in the context of fear extinction (Kalisch et al. 2006, Lang et al. 2009, Milad et al. 2007b). Importantly, the hippocampus is

BOLD: blood oxygen level–dependent

activated together with the vmPFC during recall of extinction and is sensitive to changes in visual context (Milad et al. 2007b). In addition to the conventional method of analyzing activations and deactivations, various analytic tools are being used in fMRI to examine the functional connectivity between different brain regions. One such tool is resting-state functional connectivity (fcMRI), which examines the temporal oscillations in spontaneous BOLD signals between a selected seed region and the rest of the brain (Buckner & Vincent 2007, Greicius et al. 2003). This analysis is conducted while subjects are not performing any tasks in the fMRI scanner. Although a positive correlation between a seed region and a given structure does not directly indicate anatomical connectivity, some recent studies indicate that results from fcMRI studies are fairly constrained by anatomical connections (Greicius et al. 2009, Van Dijk et al. 2010). Using this tool, recent reports have shown that applying specific seeds to the approximate location of the central (Ce) and basal (BL) nuclei of the amygdala allows for an estimation of connectivity with that region. Accordingly, BL shows greater resting connectivity with vmPFC than with dACC, and Ce shows greater connectivity with dACC than with vmPFC (Etkin et al. 2009, Roy et al. 2009). Consistent with a role in reducing fear, the hippocampus shows greater connectivity with the BL than with Ce (Roy et al. 2009).

Another important fMRI tool for examining interactions between different brain regions is known as psychophysiological interaction (PPI), which is an analysis conducted on task-driven BOLD activations (Friston et al. 1997). This method examines how a behavioral component of the task can modulate interregional coupling during the same task in response to one condition relative to another. Using this tool, we recently showed that there was decreased coupling between the amygdala and the vmPFC, and increased coupling between the amygdala and dACC, when the subjects were shown the extinguished stimulus during extinction recall (Linnman et al. 2011c)

(see **Figure 5C**). These findings support the interstructural relationships observed in rodent studies and demonstrate the need for PPI analysis of extinction circuits throughout different phases of extinction training.

In addition to functional connectivity, studies are beginning to employ diffusion tensor imaging (DTI) as a tool to examine the integrity of the structural connectivity between the amygdala and different subregions of the medial prefrontal cortex. This tool examines white matter fiber tracts based on the diffusion of water molecules along the tracts. The use of DTI to assess the integrity of prefrontal-amygdala connections during fear extinction has yet to be examined. Nonetheless, DTI, as well as fcMRI and PPI, are already being used in emotion-regulation paradigms (i.e., instructing the participants to suppress their emotions in response to a given stimulus). These studies revealed very similar findings to those observed in fear extinction research, namely, the success of emotion regulation appears to be associated with reduced amygdala activation together with increased activation of various prefrontal regions, including the vmPFC (for reviews, see Hartley & Phelps 2010, Kim et al. 2011b).

TESTING THE CIRCUIT IN AN ANXIETY DISORDER

Human neuroimaging findings predicted that fear extinction recall and its associated network would be impaired in PTSD patients (Milad et al. 2006). This hypothesis was recently tested (Milad et al. 2008, 2009b). Consistent with vmPFC dysfunction, PTSD patients showed normal conditioning and within-session extinction but were unable to recall extinction memory the following day (**Figure 6**, see color insert). Furthermore, this deficit in extinction recall was associated with hypoactivation in the vmPFC and hyperactivation in the dACC in PTSD subjects (Milad et al. 2009b), providing direct support for the prefrontal-amygdala extinction model. Moreover, we recently reported hypoactive vmPFC during the presentation of

fcMRI: resting-state functional connectivity magnetic resonance imaging

PPI: psychophysiological interaction

DTI: diffusion tensor imaging

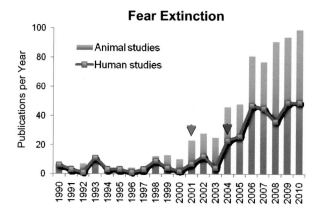

Figure 1

Fear extinction studies have increased exponentially within the past decade. **Figure 1** illustrates the number of peer-reviewed studies identified with the key terms "fear" and "extinction" in PubMed in the past 20 years. Note that the increase in animal studies (*blue bars, blue arrow*) began several years prior to the increase in human studies (*orange line, orange arrow*).

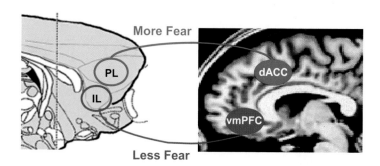

Figure 2

Homologous prefrontal structures in rodent and human brain that modulate fear expression. The rodent prelimbic (PL) cortex and human dorsal anterior cingulate (dACC) cortex increase fear expression and oppose extinction, whereas the rodent infralimbic (IL) cortex and human ventromedial prefrontal cortex (vmPFC) inhibit fear expression and promote extinction.

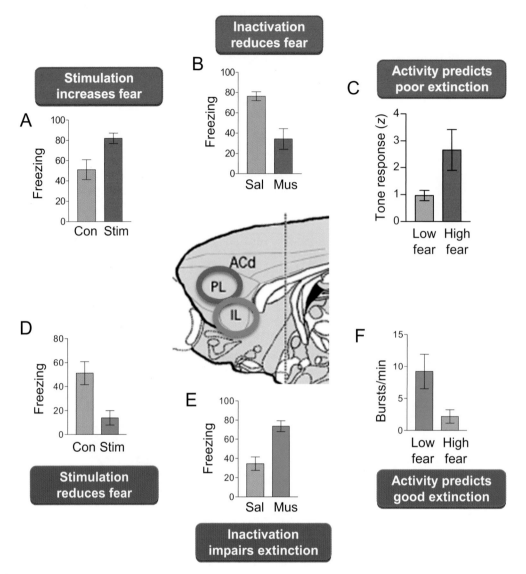

Figure 3

Summary of rodent findings for PL and IL prefrontal cortex. (*A, B, C*) Divergent findings suggest that PL activity increases fear expression. (*D, E, F*) Parallel data suggest that IL inhibits fear expression and strengthens extinction recall. Data adapted from previously published studies: (*A, D*) Vidal-Gonzalez et al. (2006), see also Kim et al. (2010); (*B, E*) Sierra-Mercado et al. (2011), see also Laurent & Westbrook (2009); (*C*) Burgos-Robles et al. (2009); (*F*) Burgos-Robles et al. (2007), see also Chang et al. (2010).

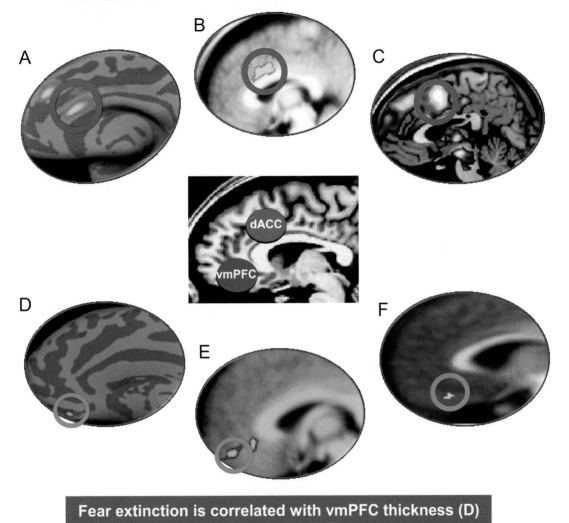

Figure 4

Summary of neuroimaging research demonstrating that the dACC (*A, B, C*) regulates fear acquisition, and vmPFC (*D, E, F*) regulates fear extinction, in healthy humans. From (*A, B*) Milad et al. (2007a); (*C*) Linnman et al. (2011b); (*D*) Milad et al. (2005b); (*E*) Milad et al. (2007b); (*F*) Kalisch et al. 2006.

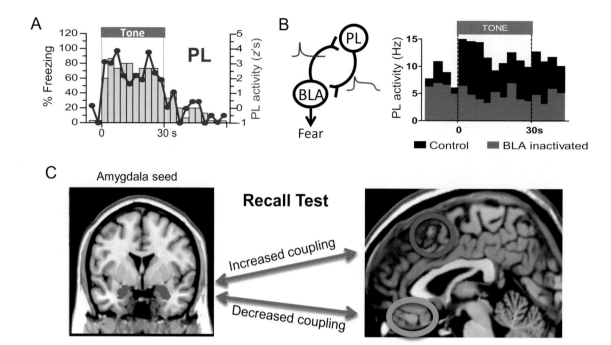

Figure 5

Prefrontal-amygdala interaction in rodents and humans. (*A*) The tone response of a single PL neuron (*blue line*, *z*-score) superimposed upon the rat's freezing to the tone (*gray bars*) (adapted from Burgos-Robles et al. 2009). Note the high correlation between time courses of PL activity and freezing (bin: 3 sec). (*B, left*) Schematic illustrating reciprocal connections between PL and the BLA. Transient tone response (*blue line*) emanating from BLA trigger sustained tone responses in PL that feedback to BLA and drive fear. (*B, right*) Perievent time histogram showing a conditioned tone response of a PL neuron under control conditions (*black bars*) and after inactivation of BLA with infusion of muscimol (*red bars*). Fear signals in PL are driven by BLA. (*C*) Psychophysiological interaction analysis during a recall test in healthy humans. One day after extinction training, increased coupling was observed between amygdala activity (*seed*) and the dACC (*red circle*), and reduced coupling was observed between the amgydala (*seed*) and vmPFC (*green circle*) (adapted from Linnman et al. 2011c).

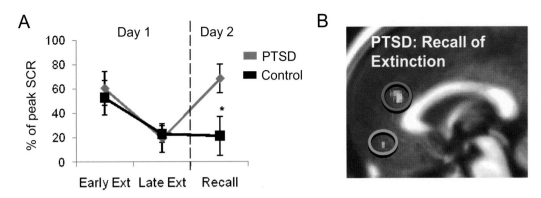

Figure 6

In posttraumatic stress disorder (PTSD), reduced extinction recall is associated with failure to activate ventromedial prefrontal cortex (vmPFC) and increased activation of dorsal anterior cingulate (dACC). (*A*) Skin conductance responses (SCRs) normalized to peak acquisition levels show intact fear learning [indexed in early extinction (early ext)], intact extinction learning (late ext), but impaired extinction recall (day 2) relative to controls. (*B*) Functional magnetic resonance imaging data using a contrast of extinguished versus unextinguished conditioned stimuli during extinction recall, showing hypoactivation of the vmPFC (*green circle*) and a trend toward hyperactivation of dACC (*red circle*) in individuals with PTSD relative to controls. Adapted from Milad et al. (2009b).

the safe (extinction) context during extinction recall in PTSD (Rougemont-Bucking et al. 2011), suggesting that the processing of extinguished cues and extinguished contexts may be impaired in PTSD. Similar observations have been made for schizophrenic subjects (Holt et al. 2009), which suggests that dysfunction in fear extinction circuits might cut across disorders (Graham & Milad 2011, Insel et al. 2010). The model may even be used as a biological marker to predict fear learning and/or fear extinction. It was recently shown that dACC resting metabolism was able to predict fear conditioning and its subsequent extinction (Linnman et al. 2011b,c), and perigenual prefrontal activity was able to predict clinical response to extinction-based therapy for PTSD (Bryant et al. 2008). The ultimate goal, of course, is to facilitate extinction-based therapies (see Impact of Fear Extinction in the Clinic sidebar).

THE NEXT TEN YEARS: WHERE DO WE GO FROM HERE?

The past decade witnessed an expansive growth in the field of fear extinction, with hundreds of publications providing a rich understanding of the neural mechanisms of fear extinction in both rodents and humans. Nonetheless, there is still much to be learned, and new lines of research are extending fear extinction further into psychological and clinical domains.

Extinction Across the Lifespan

Like other forms of learning, the capacity to extinguish varies across the lifespan, and age-related changes in extinction reflect developmental changes in prefrontal-amygdala circuitry. Following early investigations with development of avoidance learning (Myslivecek & Hassmannova 1979), much has been recently learned with auditory fear conditioning. Richardson and colleagues have shown that extinction in preweaning rats violates the "rules" of extinction: It is not context dependent, does not require NMDA receptors, and does not

IMPACT OF FEAR EXTINCTION IN THE CLINIC

Research on fear extinction is beginning to show some potential clinical applications. It is now well established that the NMDA receptor partial agonist d-cycloserine, which facilitates extinction in rodents (Davis et al. 2006), augments the clinical response to cognitive behavioral therapy (CBT) for a number of anxiety disorders (for review, see Ganasen et al. 2010). We may soon see additional classes of CBT adjuncts, such as cannabinoids, noradrenergic drugs, and neurotrophic factors, based on promising results from rodent studies (see **Table 1**). Nonpharmacological approaches to facilitating extinction could come from transcranial magnetic stimulation (Boggio et al. 2010) or from simply modifying the timing of extinction sessions. Extinction performed shortly after reactivation of fear memory results in a stronger extinction memory that resists return of fear manipulations in both rats and humans (Monfils et al. 2009, Schiller et al. 2009). Assessment of fear extinction or activity in extinction structures may identify people at risk for anxiety disorders, such as firefighters (Guthrie & Bryant 2006), or those likely to respond to CBT (Bryant et al. 2008, Lonsdorf et al. 2010).

require the prefrontal cortex (reviewed in Kim & Richardson 2010). Instead of potentiating inhibitory systems, early life extinction appears to erase fear memories from the amygdala (Gogolla et al. 2009, Kim & Richardson 2008). During adolescence, extinction again becomes compromised (Esmoris-Arranz et al. 2008), as twice as many training trials are needed to learn extinction and activate the IL (Kim et al. 2011a). Finally, aged rats show impaired extinction coupled with a shift of excitability from IL to PL (Kaczorowski et al. 2011). Developmental aspects of fear extinction have not yet been studied in humans, but it is known that older individuals show decreased awareness of CS-US contingencies that support conditioned fear responses (LaBar et al. 2004). These findings highlight the existance of windows of vulnerability with respect to extinction, but also windows of opportunity for therapeutic intervention if early extinction can erase fear memories before they become a clinical problem.

BDNF: brain-derived
neurotrophic factor

Sex Differences in Fear Extinction: From Basic Mechanisms to Clinical Relevance

Sexual dimorphism in the vmPFC, amygdala, hippocampus, and dACC is well documented (Goldstein et al. 2001). Sex hormones such as estradiol and progesterone are known modulators of synaptic plasticity, long-term potentiation, and NMDA receptor function (for review, see Gillies & McArthur 2010). Sex hormones also modulate dendritic spine density within the prefrontal cortex (Hao et al. 2006) and modulate how stress influences the function of the vmPFC and the hippocampus (Maeng et al. 2010, Shansky et al. 2010). From a clinical perspective, women are twice as likely as men to develop anxiety and mood disorders (Breslau et al. 1998, Pigott 2003). In addition, damage to human vmPFC differentially affects men and women: Unilateral right damage produces severe emotional defects in men, whereas unilateral left damage produces severe defects in women (Tranel et al. 2005). Despite these findings, the majority of human studies combined data from male and female subjects, and the majority of animal studies used males. Few studies have directly examined the influence of sex differences and the role of sex hormones on fear extinction.

There is growing evidence to suggest that fear extinction may differ between the sexes and that extinction consolidation may be modulated by sex hormones. Indeed, sex differences in emotional memories have consistently been documented in rodents and humans (reviewed in Andreano & Cahill 2009). Recent evidence from rodents and naturally cycling women suggests that fluctuations in the menstrual cycle alter extinction retention (Milad et al. 2009a, 2010; Zeidan et al. 2011). Moreover, exogenous estradiol administration facilitates extinction (Chang et al. 2009, Milad et al. 2009a, Zeidan et al. 2011). Future research in this domain could be informative in describing the mechanistic differences between "his and her" brains in processing fear extinction. Such research could potentially explain the increased

prevalence of PTSD in women and lead to sex-specific treatments for mood and anxiety disorders.

Individual Variability in Fear Extinction: Biomarkers

Traditionally, behavioral neuroscience has emphasized average behavior; however, research on individual variability in fear extinction could potentially explain why some individuals are prone to develop anxiety disorders (Bush et al. 2007). Failure to recall extinction in rats is correlated with decreased excitability in IL neurons (Burgos-Robles et al. 2007, Santini et al. 2008) and decreased brain-derived neurotrophic factor (BDNF) in the hippocampus (Heldt et al. 2007, Peters et al. 2010). Consistent with animal models, humans expressing a single-nucleotide polymorphism correlated with decreased BDNF release (Val66Met) show impaired fear extinction (Soliman et al. 2010) and increased response to social stressors (Shalev et al. 2009). The serotonin transporter short allele is also associated with increased risk for anxiety as well as decreased vmPFC-amygdala connectivity (Hariri et al. 2006, Pezawas et al. 2005). In both of these cases, a reverse translation approach was used to develop mouse models of the human polymorphism (Soliman et al. 2010, Wellman et al. 2007). Both BDNF and serotonin transporter–deficient mice exhibited impaired fear extinction as well as alterations in prefrontal cortex. Such a combined rodent-human approach will be particularly useful in investigating the newest genetic biomarkers of PTSD: the stress-related gene FKBP5 (Binder et al. 2008) and the estrogen-sensitive pituitary adenylate cyclase-activating polypeptide (Ressler et al. 2011).

Another emerging approach is to compare extinction across existing strains of inbred mice or rats. Fear extinction deficits in one particular mouse (129S1) can be reversed with a dietary manipulation that restores the balance of activity in IL versus PL (Hefner et al. 2008, Whittle et al. 2010). A subset of Lewis rats shows impaired fear extinction, but only after exposure to a predator (Goswami et al. 2010), providing an animal model of how traumatic experiences can reveal underlying susceptibilities to extinction failure. Gene knockout techniques have been used to discover new molecules involved in fear extinction, including zinc transporter (Martel et al. 2010), protease nexin-1 (Meins et al. 2010), and metabotropic glutamate receptors (Goddyn et al. 2008, Xu et al. 2009). Thus, the function of candidate genes derived from patients, inbred rodents strains, or knockout studies can be assessed within the prefrontal-amygdala circuits that control fear extinction. Of particular interest will be the extent to which genetic factors contribute to dACC resting metabolism, which has been shown to predict extinction recall (Linnman et al. 2011c).

CONCLUSION

We have shown how translational research in the past 10 years has moved fear extinction from a psychological concept to the activity of a specific circuit that appears to be conserved across species. Human neuroimaging is sometimes criticized as being too descriptive and lacking mechanistic explanations. Animal models, although mechanistic, are often viewed as too simplistic for modeling psychiatric disorders and therefore not relevant. Although both of these criticisms are valid to some extent, we have shown how combining both approaches in a translational research program mitigates the limitations of each approach alone. Perhaps more than other areas of psychology, conditioned fear provides for specific hypotheses in both rodents and humans, which can be tested with new techniques to correlate behavior with neural structure and function. The animal studies allowed us to identify the circuits of fear extinction, characterize molecular machinery, and test ways to manipulate the circuit. The neuroimaging approach allowed for translation of those findings to the human brain, testing specific hypotheses about extinction and its role in anxiety disorders. Continuing parallel lines of fear extinction research in rodents and humans could lead to novel therapeutic approaches for strengthening extinction and help us learn how our brains overcome our fears.

SUMMARY POINTS

1. Rodent research on fear extinction in the past 10 years has made great progress in generating specific hypotheses about neural circuits, which are being tested in humans with neuroimaging.

2. The rodent infralimbic cortex is important for fear extinction recall and is homologous to the human ventromedial prefrontal cortex. The rodent prelimbic cortex is important for fear expression and is homologous to the human dorsal anterior cingulate cortex.

3. IL/vmPFC connects to inhibitory centers within the amygdala, whereas PL/dACC connects to excitatory areas within the amygdala.

4. Activity in PL (rodents) or dACC (humans) can predict the extent of subsequent extinction learning.

5. Failure to properly activate the vmPFC and dACC in humans results in inappropriate fear expression and is observed in anxiety disorders.

DISCLOSURE STATEMENT

M.R.M. has received consulting fees from MicroTransponder Inc. The authors are not aware of any other affiliations, memberships, funding, or financial holdings that might be perceived as affecting the objectivity of this review. M.R.M. is supported by NIH grants K01-MH08036 and R01-MH081975, and DoD grant W81XWH-11-2-0079. G.J.Q. is supported by R01-MH058883, R01-MH081975, and P50-MH086400.

LITERATURE CITED

Akirav I, Maroun M. 2007. The role of the medial prefrontal cortex-amygdala circuit in stress effects on the extinction of fear. *Neural Plast.* 2007:30873

Amano T, Unal CT, Paré D. 2010. Synaptic correlates of fear extinction in the amygdala. *Nat. Neurosci.* 13:489–94

Amir A, Amano T, Paré D. 2011. Physiological identification and infralimbic responsiveness of rat intercalated amygdala neurons. *J. Neurophysiol.* 105:3054–66

Andero R, Heldt SA, Ye K, Liu X, Armario A, Ressler KJ. 2011. Effect of 7,8-dihydroxyflavone, a small-molecule TrkB agonist, on emotional learning. *Am. J. Psychiatry* 168:163–72

Andreano JM, Cahill L. 2009. Sex influences on the neurobiology of learning and memory. *Learn. Mem.* 16:248–66

Angenstein F, Kammerer E, Scheich H. 2009. The BOLD response in the rat hippocampus depends rather on local processing of signals than on the input or output activity. A combined functional MRI and electrophysiological study. *J. Neurosci.* 29:2428–39

Applegate CD, Frysinger RC, Kapp BS, Gallagher M. 1982. Multiple unit activity recorded from amygdala central nucleus during Pavlovian heart rate conditioning in rabbit. *Brain Res.* 238:457–62

Armony JL, Dolan RJ. 2001. Modulation of auditory neural responses by a visual context in human fear conditioning. *NeuroReport* 12:3407–11

Baas JM, Nugent M, Lissek S, Pine DS, Grillon C. 2004. Fear conditioning in virtual reality contexts: a new tool for the study of anxiety. *Biol. Psychiatry* 55:1056–60

Barrett D, Shumake J, Jones D, Gonzalez-Lima F. 2003. Metabolic mapping of mouse brain activity after extinction of a conditioned emotional response. *J. Neurosci.* 23:5740–49

Belliveau JW, Kennedy DN Jr, McKinstry RC, Buchbinder BR, Weisskoff RM, et al. 1991. Functional mapping of the human visual cortex by magnetic resonance imaging. *Science* 254:716–19

Binder EB, Bradley RG, Liu W, Epstein MP, Deveau TC, et al. 2008. Association of FKBP5 polymorphisms and childhood abuse with risk of posttraumatic stress disorder symptoms in adults. *JAMA* 299:1291–305

Blanchard RJ, Blanchard DC. 1969. Crouching as an index of fear. *J. Comp. Physiol. Psychol.* 67:370–75

Boggio PS, Rocha M, Oliveira MO, Fecteau S, Cohen RB, et al. 2010. Noninvasive brain stimulation with high-frequency and low-intensity repetitive transcranial magnetic stimulation treatment for posttraumatic stress disorder. *J. Clin. Psychiatry* 71:992–99

Bohus B, De Wied D. 1966. Inhibitory and facilitatory effect of two related peptides on extinction of avoidance behavior. *Science* 153:318–20

Bonini JS, Da Silva WC, Da Silveira CK, Kohler CA, Izquierdo I, Cammarota M. 2011. Histamine facilitates consolidation of fear extinction. *Int. J. Neuropsychopharmacol.* Jan. 7:1–9

Bouton ME. 1993. Context, time, and memory retrieval in the interference paradigms of Pavlovian learning. *Psychol. Bull.* 114:80–99

Bouton ME, King DA. 1983. Contextual control of the extinction of conditioned fear: tests for the associative value of the context. *J. Exp. Psychol.: Anim. Behav. Process.* 9:248–65

Bouton ME, Moody EW. 2004. Memory processes in classical conditioning. *Neurosci. Biobehav. Rev.* 28:663–74

Bouton ME, Westbrook RF, Corcoran KA, Maren S. 2006. Contextual and temporal modulation of extinction: behavioral and biological mechanisms. *Biol. Psychiatry* 60:352–60

Breiter HC, Etcoff NL, Whalen PJ, Kennedy WA, Rauch SL, et al. 1996. Response and habituation of the human amygdala during visual processing of facial expression. *Neuron* 17:875–87

Bremner JD, Staib LH, Kaloupek D, Southwick SM, Soufer R, Charney DS. 1999. Neural correlates of exposure to traumatic pictures and sound in Vietnam combat veterans with and without posttraumatic stress disorder: a positron emission tomography study. *Biol. Psychiatry* 45:806–16

Brennan JF, Wisniewski C. 1982. The efficacy of response prevention on avoidance behavior in young and adult rats with prefrontal cortical injury. *Behav. Brain Res.* 4:117–31

Breslau N, Kessler RC, Chilcoat HD, Schultz LR, Davis GC, Andreski P. 1998. Trauma and posttraumatic stress disorder in the community: the 1996 Detroit Area Survey of Trauma. *Arch. Gen. Psychiatry* 55:626–32

Brutkowski S, Mempel E. 1961. Disinhibition of inhibitory conditioned responses following selective brain lesions in dogs. *Science* 134:2040–41

Bryant RA, Felmingham K, Whitford TJ, Kemp A, Hughes G, et al. 2008. Rostral anterior cingulate volume predicts treatment response to cognitive-behavioural therapy for posttraumatic stress disorder. *J. Psychiatry Neurosci.* 33:142–46

Buchel C, Dolan RJ, Armony JL, Friston KJ. 1999. Amygdala-hippocampal involvement in human aversive trace conditioning revealed through event-related functional magnetic resonance imaging. *J. Neurosci.* 19:10869–76

Buchel C, Morris J, Dolan RJ, Friston KJ. 1998. Brain systems mediating aversive conditioning: an event-related fMRI study. *Neuron* 20:947–57

Buckner RL, Vincent JL. 2007. Unrest at rest: default activity and spontaneous network correlations. *NeuroImage* 37:1091–96

Buresova O, Bures J, Bohdanecky Z, Weiss T. 1964. Effect of atropine on learning, extinction, retention, and retrieval in rats. *Psychopharmacologia* 5:255–63

Burgos-Robles A, Vidal-Gonzalez I, Quirk GJ. 2009. Sustained conditioned responses in prelimbic prefrontal neurons are correlated with fear expression and extinction failure. *J. Neurosci.* 29:8474–82

Burgos-Robles A, Vidal-Gonzalez I, Santini E, Quirk GJ. 2007. Consolidation of fear extinction requires NMDA receptor-dependent bursting in the ventromedial prefrontal cortex. *Neuron* 53:871–80

Bush DE, Sotres-Bayon F, LeDoux JE. 2007. Individual differences in fear: isolating fear reactivity and fear recovery phenotypes. *J. Trauma. Stress* 20:413–22

Butter CM, Mishkin M, Rosvold HE. 1963. Conditioning and extinction of a food-rewarded response after selective ablation of frontal cortex in rhesus monkeys. *Exp. Neurol.* 7:65–75

Chan KH, Morell JR, Jarrard LE, Davidson TL. 2001. Reconsideration of the role of the hippocampus in learned inhibition. *Behav. Brain Res.* 119:111–30

Chang CH, Berke JD, Maren S. 2010. Single-unit activity in the medial prefrontal cortex during immediate and delayed extinction of fear in rats. *PLoS One* 5:e11971

Chang CH, Maren S. 2011. Medial prefrontal cortex activation facilitates re-extinction of fear in rats. *Learn. Mem.* 18:221–25

Chang YJ, Yang CH, Liang YC, Yeh CM, Huang CC, Hsu KS. 2009. Estrogen modulates sexually dimorphic contextual fear extinction in rats through estrogen receptor beta. *Hippocampus* 19:1142–50

Cheng DT, Knight DC, Smith CN, Stein EA, Helmstetter FJ. 2003. Functional MRI of human amygdala activity during Pavlovian fear conditioning: stimulus processing versus response expression. *Behav. Neurosci.* 117:3–10

Chi CC. 1965. The effect of amobarbital sodium on conditioned fear as measured by the potentiated startle response in rats. *Psychopharmacologia* 7:115–22

Choi DC, Maguschak KA, Ye K, Jang SW, Myers KM, Ressler KJ. 2010. Prelimbic cortical BDNF is required for memory of learned fear but not extinction or innate fear. *Proc. Natl. Acad. Sci. USA* 107:2675–80

Ciocchi S, Herry C, Grenier F, Wolff SB, Letzkus JJ, et al. 2010. Encoding of conditioned fear in central amygdala inhibitory circuits. *Nature* 468:277–82

Corcoran KA, Desmond TJ, Frey KA, Maren S. 2005. Hippocampal inactivation disrupts the acquisition and contextual encoding of fear extinction. *J. Neurosci.* 25:8978–87

Corcoran KA, Quirk GJ. 2007. Activity in prelimbic cortex is necessary for the expression of learned, but not innate, fears. *J. Neurosci.* 27:840–44

Davis M. 2000. The role of the amygdala in conditioned and unconditioned fear and anxiety. In *The Amygdala*, ed. JP Aggleton, pp. 213–88. Oxford, UK: Oxford Univ. Press

Davis M, Astrachan DI. 1978. Conditioned fear and startle magnitude: effects of different footshock or backshock intensities used in training. *J. Exp. Psychol.: Anim. Behav. Process.* 4:95–103

Davis M, Ressler K, Rothbaum BO, Richardson R. 2006. Effects of D-cycloserine on extinction: translation from preclinical to clinical work. *Biol. Psychiatry* 60:369–75

Dunsmoor JE, Bandettini PA, Knight DC. 2008. Neural correlates of unconditioned response diminution during Pavlovian conditioning. *NeuroImage* 40:811–17

Deschaux O, Thevenet A, Spennato G, Arnaud C, Moreau JL, Garcia R. 2010. Low-frequency stimulation of the hippocampus following fear extinction impairs both restoration of rapid eye movement sleep and retrieval of extinction memory. *Neuroscience* 170:92–98

Esmoris-Arranz FJ, Mendez C, Spear NE. 2008. Contextual fear conditioning differs for infant, adolescent, and adult rats. *Behav. Process.* 78:340–50

Etkin A, Egner T, Kalisch R. 2011. Emotional processing in anterior cingulate and medial prefrontal cortex. *Trends Cogn. Sci.* 15:85–93

Etkin A, Prater KE, Schatzberg AF, Menon V, Greicius MD. 2009. Disrupted amygdalar subregion functional connectivity and evidence of a compensatory network in generalized anxiety disorder. *Arch. Gen. Psychiatry* 66:1361–72

Falls WA, Davis M. 1993. Visual cortex ablations do not prevent extinction of fear-potentiated startle using a visual conditioned stimulus. *Behav. Neural Biol.* 60:259–70

Falls WA, Miserendino MJ, Davis M. 1992. Extinction of fear-potentiated startle: blockade by infusion of an NMDA antagonist into the amygdala. *J. Neurosci.* 12:854–63

Flood JF, Jarvik ME, Bennett EL, Orme AE, Rosenzweig MR. 1977. Protein synthesis inhibition and memory for pole jump active avoidance and extinction. *Pharmacol. Biochem. Behav.* 7:71–77

Fontanez-Nuin DE, Santini E, Quirk GJ, Porter JT. 2011. Memory for fear extinction requires mGluR5-mediated activation of infralimbic neurons. *Cereb. Cortex* 21:727–35

Friston KJ, Buechel C, Fink GR, Morris J, Rolls E, Dolan RJ. 1997. Psychophysiological and modulatory interactions in neuroimaging. *NeuroImage* 6:218–29

Ganasen KA, Ipser JC, Stein DJ. 2010. Augmentation of cognitive behavioral therapy with pharmacotherapy. *Psychiatr. Clin. North Am.* 33:687–99

Garcia R, Spennato G, Nilsson-Todd L, Moreau JL, Deschaux O. 2008. Hippocampal low-frequency stimulation and chronic mild stress similarly disrupt fear extinction memory in rats. *Learn. Mem.* 89:560–66

Gewirtz JC, Falls WA, Davis M. 1997. Normal conditioned inhibition and extinction of freezing and fear-potentiated startle following electrolytic lesions of medial prefrontal cortex in rats. *Behav. Neurosci.* 111:712–26

Gillies GE, McArthur S. 2010. Estrogen actions in the brain and the basis for differential action in men and women: a case for sex-specific medicines. *Pharmacol. Rev.* 62:155–98

Goddyn H, Callaerts-Vegh Z, Stroobants S, Dirikx T, Vansteenwegen D, et al. 2008. Deficits in acquisition and extinction of conditioned responses in mGluR7 knockout mice. *Neurobiol. Learn. Mem.* 90:103–11

Gogolla N, Caroni P, Luthi A, Herry C. 2009. Perineuronal nets protect fear memories from erasure. *Science* 325:1258–61

Goldstein JM, Seidman LJ, Horton NJ, Makris N, Kennedy DN, et al. 2001. Normal sexual dimorphism of the adult human brain assessed by in vivo magnetic resonance imaging. *Cereb. Cortex* 11:490–97

Goswami S, Cascardi M, Rodriguez-Sierra OE, Duvarci S, Paré D. 2010. Impact of predatory threat on fear extinction in Lewis rats. *Learn. Mem.* 17:494–501

Gottfried JA, Dolan RJ. 2004. Human orbitofrontal cortex mediates extinction learning while accessing conditioned representations of value. *Nat. Neurosci.* 7:1144–52

Gourley SL, Kedves AT, Olausson P, Taylor JR. 2009. A history of corticosterone exposure regulates fear extinction and cortical NR2B, GluR2/3, and BDNF. *Neuropsychopharmacology* 34:707–16

Graham BM, Milad MR. 2011. Translational research in the neuroscience of fear extinction: implications for anxiety disorders. *Am. J. Psychiatry.* In press

Graham BM, Richardson R. 2011. Memory of fearful events: the role of fibroblast growth factor-2 in fear acquisition and extinction. *Neuroscience* 189:156–69

Gralewicz K, Gralewicz S. 1984. Effects of hippocampal stimulation on retention and extinction of one-way active avoidance response in cats. *Acta Neurobiol. Exp. (Wars.)* 44:61–72

Greenberg BD, Gabriels LA, Malone DA Jr, Rezai AR, Friehs GM, et al. 2008. Deep brain stimulation of the ventral internal capsule/ventral striatum for obsessive-compulsive disorder: worldwide experience. *Mol. Psychiatry* 15:64–79

Greicius MD, Krasnow B, Reiss AL, Menon V. 2003. Functional connectivity in the resting brain: a network analysis of the default mode hypothesis. *Proc. Natl. Acad. Sci. USA* 100:253–58

Greicius MD, Supekar K, Menon V, Dougherty RF. 2009. Resting-state functional connectivity reflects structural connectivity in the default mode network. *Cereb. Cortex* 19:72–78

Grillon C, Baas JM, Cornwell B, Johnson L. 2006. Context conditioning and behavioral avoidance in a virtual reality environment: effect of predictability. *Biol. Psychiatry* 60:752–59

Guthrie RM, Bryant RA. 2006. Extinction learning before trauma and subsequent posttraumatic stress. *Psychosom. Med.* 68:307–11

Hao J, Rapp PR, Leffler AE, Leffler SR, Janssen WG, et al. 2006. Estrogen alters spine number and morphology in prefrontal cortex of aged female rhesus monkeys. *J. Neurosci.* 26:2571–78

Hariri AR, Drabant EM, Weinberger DR. 2006. Imaging genetics: perspectives from studies of genetically driven variation in serotonin function and corticolimbic affective processing. *Biol. Psychiatry* 59:888–97

Harris JA, Westbrook RF. 1998. Evidence that GABA transmission mediates context-specific extinction of learned fear. *Psychopharmacology (Berl.)* 140:105–15

Hartley CA, Fischl B, Phelps EA. 2011. Brain structure correlates of individual differences in the acquisition and inhibition of conditioned fear. *Cereb. Cortex.* 21:1954–62

Hartley CA, Phelps EA. 2010. Changing fear: the neurocircuitry of emotion regulation. *Neuropsychopharmacology* 35:136–46

Hefner K, Whittle N, Juhasz J, Norcross M, Karlsson RM, et al. 2008. Impaired fear extinction learning and cortico-amygdala circuit abnormalities in a common genetic mouse strain. *J. Neurosci.* 28:8074–85

Heldt SA, Stanek L, Chhatwal JP, Ressler KJ. 2007. Hippocampus-specific deletion of BDNF in adult mice impairs spatial memory and extinction of aversive memories. *Mol. Psychiatry* 12:656–70

Hermans D, Dirikx T, Vansteenwegen D, Baeyens F, Van den BO, Eelen P. 2005. Reinstatement of fear responses in human aversive conditioning. *Behav. Res. Ther.* 43:533–51

Herry C, Ciocchi S, Senn V, Demmou L, Muller C, Luthi A. 2008. Switching on and off fear by distinct neuronal circuits. *Nature* 454:600–6

Herry C, Ferraguti F, Singewald N, Letzkus JJ, Ehrlich I, Luthi A. 2010. Neuronal circuits of fear extinction. *Eur. J. Neurosci.* 31:599–612

Herry C, Garcia R. 2002. Prefrontal cortex long-term potentiation, but not long-term depression, is associated with the maintenance of extinction of learned fear in mice. *J. Neurosci.* 22:577–83

Herry C, Garcia R. 2003. Behavioral and paired-pulse facilitation analyses of long-lasting depression at excitatory synapses in the medial prefrontal cortex in mice. *Behav. Brain Res.* 146:89–96

Hitchcock J, Davis M. 1986. Lesions of the amygdala, but not of the cerebellum or red nucleus, block conditioned fear as measured with the potentiated startle paradigm. *Behav. Neurosci.* 100:11–22

Hobin JA, Ji J, Maren S. 2006. Ventral hippocampal muscimol disrupts context-specific fear memory retrieval after extinction in rats. *Hippocampus* 16:174–82

Holmes A, Wellman CL. 2009. Stress-induced prefrontal reorganization and executive dysfunction in rodents. *Neurosci. Biobehav. Rev.* 33:773–83

Holt DJ, Lebron-Milad K, Milad MR, Rauch SL, Pitman RK, et al. 2009. Extinction memory is impaired in schizophrenia. *Biol. Psychiatry* 65:455–63

Huff NC, Zeilinski DJ, Fecteau ME, Brady R, LaBar KS. 2010. Human fear conditioning conducted in full immersion 3-dimensional virtual reality. *J. Vis. Exp.* doi: 10.3791/1993

Hugues S, Deschaux O, Garcia R. 2004. Postextinction infusion of a mitogen-activated protein kinase inhibitor into the medial prefrontal cortex impairs memory of the extinction of conditioned fear. *Learn. Mem.* 11:540–43

Hugues S, Garcia R. 2007. Reorganization of learning-associated prefrontal synaptic plasticity between the recall of recent and remote fear extinction memory. *Learn. Mem.* 14:520–24

Hurley KM, Herbert H, Moga MM, Saper CB. 1991. Efferent projections of the infralimbic cortex of the rat. *J. Comp. Neurol.* 308:249–76

Insel T, Cuthbert B, Garvey M, Heinssen R, Pine DS, et al. 2010. Research domain criteria (RDoC): toward a new classification framework for research on mental disorders. *Am. J. Psychiatry* 167:748–51

Ji J, Maren S. 2005. Electrolytic lesions of the dorsal hippocampus disrupt renewal of conditional fear after extinction. *Learn. Mem.* 12:270–76

Ji J, Maren S. 2007. Hippocampal involvement in contextual modulation of fear extinction. *Hippocampus* 17:749–58

Jovanovic T, Keyes M, Fiallos A, Myers KM, Davis M, Duncan EJ. 2005. Fear potentiation and fear inhibition in a human fear-potentiated startle paradigm. *Biol. Psychiatry* 57:1559–64

Jovanovic T, Norrholm SD, Keyes M, Fiallos A, Jovanovic S, et al. 2006. Contingency awareness and fear inhibition in a human fear-potentiated startle paradigm. *Behav. Neurosci.* 120:995–1004

Jungling K, Seidenbecher T, Sosulina L, Lesting J, Sangha S, et al. 2008. Neuropeptide S-mediated control of fear expression and extinction: role of intercalated GABAergic neurons in the amygdala. *Neuron* 59:298–310

Kaczorowski CC, Davis SJ, Moyer JR Jr. 2011. Aging redistributes medial prefrontal neuronal excitability and impedes extinction of trace fear conditioning. *Neurobiol. Aging.* In press

Kalisch R, Korenfeld E, Stephan KE, Weiskopf N, Seymour B, Dolan RJ. 2006. Context-dependent human extinction memory is mediated by a ventromedial prefrontal and hippocampal network. *J. Neurosci.* 26:9503–11

Kapp BS, Frysinger RC, Gallagher M, Haselton JR. 1979. Amygdala central nucleus lesions: effect on heart rate conditioning in the rabbit. *Physiol. Behav.* 23:1109–17

Kim JH, Li S, Richardson R. 2011a. Immunohistochemical analyses of long-term extinction of conditioned fear in adolescent rats. *Cereb. Cortex* 21:530–38

Kim JH, Richardson R. 2008. The effect of temporary amygdala inactivation on extinction and reextinction of fear in the developing rat: unlearning as a potential mechanism for extinction early in development. *J. Neurosci.* 28:1282–90

Kim JH, Richardson R. 2010. New findings on extinction of conditioned fear early in development: theoretical and clinical implications. *Biol. Psychiatry* 67:297–303

Kim MJ, Loucks RA, Palmer AL, Brown AC, Solomon KM, et al. 2011b. The structural and functional connectivity of the amygdala: from normal emotion to pathological anxiety. *Behav. Brain Res.* 223:403–10

Kim SC, Jo YS, Kim IH, Kim H, Choi JS. 2010. Lack of medial prefrontal cortex activation underlies the immediate extinction deficit. *J. Neurosci.* 30:832–37

Kimble DP, Kimble RJ. 1970. The effect of hippocampal lesions on extinction and "hypothesis" behavior in rats. *Physiol. Behav.* 5:735–38

Knapska E, Maren S. 2009. Reciprocal patterns of c-Fos expression in the medial prefrontal cortex and amygdala after extinction and renewal of conditioned fear. *Learn. Mem.* 16:486–93

Knight DC, Smith CN, Cheng DT, Stein EA, Helmstetter FJ. 2004. Amygdala and hippocampal activity during acquisition and extinction of human fear conditioning. *Cogn. Affect. Behav. Neurosci.* 4:317–25

Knight DC, Waters NS, King MK, Bandettini PA. 2010. Learning-related diminution of unconditioned SCR and fMRI signal responses. *NeuroImage* 49:843–48

Kokkinidis L. 1983. The effects of chronic amphetamine administration on the acquisition and extinction of an active and passive avoidance response in mice. *Pharmacol. Biochem. Behav.* 19:593–98

Konorski J. 1967. *Integrative Activity of the Brain*. Chicago: Univ. Chicago Press

Koob GF, Dantzer R, Bluthe RM, Lebrun C, Bloom FE, Le Moal M. 1986. Central injections of arginine vasopressin prolong extinction of active avoidance. *Peptides* 7:213–18

LaBar KS, Cook CA, Torpey DC, Welsh-Bohmer KA. 2004. Impact of healthy aging on awareness and fear conditioning. *Behav. Neurosci.* 118:905–15

LaBar KS, Gatenby JC, Gore JC, LeDoux JE, Phelps EA. 1998. Human amygdala activation during conditioned fear acquisition and extinction: a mixed-trial fMRI study. *Neuron* 20:937–45

LaBar KS, Phelps EA. 2005. Reinstatement of conditioned fear in humans is context dependent and impaired in amnesia. *Behav. Neurosci.* 119:677–86

Lafenetre P, Chaouloff F, Marsicano G. 2007. The endocannabinoid system in the processing of anxiety and fear and how CB1 receptors may modulate fear extinction. *Pharmacol. Res.* 56:367–81

Lang S, Kroll A, Lipinski SJ, Wessa M, Ridder S, et al. 2009. Context conditioning and extinction in humans: differential contribution of the hippocampus, amygdala and prefrontal cortex. *Eur. J. Neurosci.* 29:823–32

Laurent V, Marchand AR, Westbrook RF. 2008. The basolateral amygdala is necessary for learning but not relearning extinction of context conditioned fear. *Learn. Mem.* 15:304–14

Laurent V, Westbrook RF. 2009. Inactivation of the infralimbic but not the prelimbic cortex impairs consolidation and retrieval of fear extinction. *Learn. Mem.* 16:520–29

Laviolette SR, Lipski WJ, Grace AA. 2005. A subpopulation of neurons in the medial prefrontal cortex encodes emotional learning with burst and frequency codes through a dopamine D4 receptor-dependent basolateral amygdala input. *J. Neurosci.* 25:6066–75

LeDoux JE. 2000. Emotion circuits in the brain. *Annu. Rev. Neurosci.* 23:155–84

LeDoux JE, Iwata J, Cicchetti P, Reis DJ. 1988. Different projections of the central amygdaloid nucleus mediate autonomic and behavioral correlates of conditioned fear. *J. Neurosci.* 8:2517–29

LeDoux JE, Ruggiero DA, Reis DJ. 1985. Projections to the subcortical forebrain from anatomically defined regions of the medial geniculate body in the rat. *J. Comp. Neurol.* 242:182–213

LeDoux JE, Sakaguchi A, Reis DJ. 1984. Subcortical efferent projections of the medial geniculate nucleus mediate emotional responses conditioned to acoustic stimuli. *J. Neurosci.* 4:683–98

LeDoux JE, Xagoraris A, Romanski LM. 1989. Indelibility of subcortical emotional memories. *J. Cogn. Neurosci.* 1:238–43

Lemos JI, Resstel LB, Guimaraes FS. 2010. Involvement of the prelimbic prefrontal cortex on cannabidiol-induced attenuation of contextual conditioned fear in rats. *Behav. Brain Res.* 207:105–11

Liang Z, King J, Zhang N. 2011. Anticorrelated resting-state functional connectivity in awake rat brain. *NeuroImage*. In press

Likhtik E, Pelletier JG, Paz R, Paré D. 2005. Prefrontal control of the amygdala. *J. Neurosci.* 25:7429–37

Likhtik E, Popa D, Apergis-Schoute J, Fidacaro GA, Paré D. 2008. Amygdala intercalated neurons are required for expression of fear extinction. *Nature* 454:642–45

Lin HC, Mao SC, Su CL, Gean PW. 2009. The role of prefrontal cortex CB1 receptors in the modulation of fear memory. *Cereb. Cortex* 19:165–75

Linnman C, Rougemont-Bucking A, Beucke JC, Zeffiro TA, Milad MR. 2011a. Unconditioned responses and functional fear networks in human classical conditioning. *Behav. Brain Res.* 221:237–45

Linnman C, Zeidan MA, Pitman RK, Milad MR. 2011b. Cingulate and amygdala resting metabolism correlate with autonomic and functional activation during fear conditioning. *Biol. Psychiatry*. In press

Linnman C, Zeidan MA, Furtak SC, Pitman RK, Quirk GJ, Milad MR. 2011c. Resting amygdala and medial prefrontal metabolism predict functional activation of the fear extinction circuit. *Am. J. Psychiatry*. In press

Lonsdorf TB, Ruck C, Bergstrom J, Andersson G, Ohman A, et al. 2010. The COMTval158met polymorphism is associated with symptom relief during exposure-based cognitive-behavioral treatment in panic disorder. *BMC Psychiatry* 10:99

Lovely RH. 1975. Hormonal dissociation of limbic lesion effects on shuttle box avoidance in rats. *J. Comp. Physiol. Psychol.* 89:224–30

Maeng LY, Waddell J, Shors TJ. 2010. The prefrontal cortex communicates with the amygdala to impair learning after acute stress in females but not in males. *J. Neurosci.* 30:16188–96

Mahanty NK, Sah P. 1998. Calcium-permeable AMPA receptors mediate long-term potentiation in interneurons in the amygdala. *Nature* 394:683–87

Marek R, Coelho CM, Sullivan RK, Baker-Andresen D, Li X, et al. 2011. Paradoxical enhancement of fear extinction memory and synaptic plasticity by inhibition of the histone acetyltransferase p300. *J. Neurosci.* 31:7486–91

Maren S. 2005. Building and burying fear memories in the brain. *Neuroscientist* 11:89–99

Martel G, Hevi C, Friebely O, Baybutt T, Shumyatsky GP. 2010. Zinc transporter 3 is involved in learned fear and extinction, but not in innate fear. *Learn. Mem.* 17:582–90

Mason ST, Roberts DC, Fibiger HC. 1979. Interaction of brain noradrenaline and the pituitary-adrenal axis in learning and extinction. *Pharmacol. Biochem. Behav.* 10:11–16

McDonald AJ. 1991. Organization of amygdaloid projections to the prefrontal cortex and associated striatum in the rat. *Neuroscience* 44:1–14

McDonald AJ. 1998. Cortical pathways to the mammalian amygdala. *Prog. Neurobiol.* 55:257–332

McLaughlin J, Skaggs H, Churchwell J, Powell DA. 2002. Medial prefrontal cortex and Pavlovian conditioning: trace versus delay conditioning. *Behav. Neurosci.* 116:37–47

Meins M, Herry C, Muller C, Ciocchi S, Moreno E, et al. 2010. Impaired fear extinction in mice lacking protease nexin-1. *Eur. J. Neurosci.* 31:2033–42

Milad MR, Igoe SA, Lebron-Milad K, Novales JE. 2009a. Estrous cycle phase and gonadal hormones influence conditioned fear extinction. *Neuroscience* 164:887–95

Milad MR, Orr SP, Lasko NB, Chang Y, Rauch SL, Pitman RK. 2008. Presence and acquired origin of reduced recall for fear extinction in PTSD: results of a twin study. *J. Psychiatr. Res.* 42:515–20

Milad MR, Orr SP, Pitman RK, Rauch SL. 2005a. Context modulation of memory for fear extinction in humans. *Psychophysiology* 42:456–64

Milad MR, Pitman RK, Ellis CB, Gold AL, Shin LM, et al. 2009b. Neurobiological basis of failure to recall extinction memory in posttraumatic stress disorder. *Biol. Psychiatry* 66:1075–82

Milad MR, Quinn BT, Pitman RK, Orr SP, Fischl B, Rauch SL. 2005b. Thickness of ventromedial prefrontal cortex in humans is correlated with extinction memory. *Proc. Natl. Acad. Sci. USA* 102:10706–11

Milad MR, Quirk GJ. 2002. Neurons in medial prefrontal cortex signal memory for fear extinction. *Nature* 420:70–74

Milad MR, Quirk GJ, Pitman RK, Orr SP, Fischl B, Rauch SL. 2007a. A role of the human dorsal anterior cingulate cortex in expression of learned fear. *Biol. Psychiatry* 62:1191–94

Milad MR, Rauch SL, Pitman RK, Quirk GJ. 2006. Fear extinction in rats: implications for human brain imaging and anxiety disorders. *Biol. Psychol.* 73:61–71

Milad MR, Vidal-Gonzalez I, Quirk GJ. 2004. Electrical stimulation of medial prefrontal cortex reduces conditioned fear in a temporally specific manner. *Behav. Neurosci.* 118:389–94

Milad MR, Wright CI, Orr SP, Pitman RK, Quirk GJ, Rauch SL. 2007b. Recall of fear extinction in humans activates the ventromedial prefrontal cortex and hippocampus in concert. *Biol. Psychiatry* 62:446–54

Milad MR, Zeidan MA, Contero A, Pitman RK, Klibanski A, et al. 2010. The influence of gonadal hormones on conditioned fear extinction in healthy humans. *Neuroscience* 168:652–58

Monfils MH, Cowansage KK, Klann E, LeDoux JE. 2009. Extinction-reconsolidation boundaries: key to persistent attenuation of fear memories. *Science* 324:951–55

Morgan MA, Romanski LM, LeDoux JE. 1993. Extinction of emotional learning: contribution of medial prefrontal cortex. *Neurosci. Lett.* 163:109–13

Morris RW, Bouton ME. 2007. The effect of yohimbine on the extinction of conditioned fear: a role for context. *Behav. Neurosci.* 121:501–14

Mueller D, Bravo-Rivera C, Quirk GJ. 2010. Infralimbic D2 receptors are necessary for fear extinction and extinction-related tone responses. *Biol. Psychiatry* 68:1055–60

Mueller D, Porter JT, Quirk GJ. 2008. Noradrenergic signaling in infralimbic cortex increases cell excitability and strengthens memory for fear extinction. *J. Neurosci.* 28:369–75

Myers KM, Carlezon WA Jr, Davis M. 2011. Glutamate receptors in extinction and extinction-based therapies for psychiatric illness. *Neuropsychopharmacology* 36:274–93

Myslivecek J, Hassmannova J. 1979. Ontogeny of active avoidance in the rat: learning and memory. *Dev. Psychobiol.* 12:169–86

Nitecka L, Ben Ari Y. 1987. Distribution of GABA-like immunoreactivity in the rat amygdaloid complex. *J. Comp. Neurol.* 266:45–55

Norrholm SD, Jovanovic T, Vervliet B, Myers KM, Davis M, et al. 2006. Conditioned fear extinction and reinstatement in a human fear-potentiated startle paradigm. *Learn. Mem.* 13:681–85

Pape HC, Paré D. 2010. Plastic synaptic networks of the amygdala for the acquisition, expression, and extinction of conditioned fear. *Physiol. Rev.* 90:419–63

Paré D, Smith Y. 1993. The intercalated cell masses project to the central and medial nuclei of the amygdala in cats. *Neuroscience* 57:1077–90

Pavlov I. 1927. *Conditioned Reflexes*. London: Oxford Univ. Press

Peters J, Dieppa-Perea LM, Melendez LM, Quirk GJ. 2010. Induction of fear extinction with hippocampal-infralimbic BDNF. *Science* 328:1288–90

Pezawas L, Meyer-Lindenberg A, Drabant EM, Verchinski BA, Munoz KE, et al. 2005. 5-HTTLPR polymorphism impacts human cingulate-amygdala interactions: a genetic susceptibility mechanism for depression. *Nat. Neurosci.* 8:828–34

Phelps EA, Delgado MR, Nearing KI, LeDoux JE. 2004. Extinction learning in humans: role of the amygdala and vmPFC. *Neuron* 43:897–905

Pine DS, Fyer A, Grun J, Phelps EA, Szeszko PR, et al. 2001. Methods for developmental studies of fear conditioning circuitry. *Biol. Psychiatry* 50:225–28

Pigott TA. 2003. Anxiety disorders in women. *Psychiatr. Clin. North Am.* 26:621–72

Pitkanen A, Savander V, LeDoux JE. 1997. Organization of intra-amygdaloid circuitries in the rat: an emerging framework for understanding functions of the amygdala. *Trends Neurosci.* 20:517–23

Pitman RK. 1988. Post-traumatic stress disorder, conditioning, and network theory. *Psychiatr. Ann.* 18:182–89

Quirk GJ, Likhtik E, Pelletier JG, Paré D. 2003. Stimulation of medial prefrontal cortex decreases the responsiveness of central amygdala output neurons. *J. Neurosci.* 23:8800–7

Quirk GJ, Mueller D. 2008. Neural mechanisms of extinction learning and retrieval. *Neuropsychopharmacology* 33:56–72

Quirk GJ, Russo GK, Barron JL, Lebron K. 2000. The role of ventromedial prefrontal cortex in the recovery of extinguished fear. *J. Neurosci.* 20:6225–31

Radulovic J, Tronson NC. 2010. Molecular specificity of multiple hippocampal processes governing fear extinction. *Rev. Neurosci.* 21:1–17

Rauch SL, Shin LM, Phelps EA. 2006. Neurocircuitry models of posttraumatic stress disorder and extinction: human neuroimaging research—past, present, and future. *Biol. Psychiatry* 60:376–82

Rescorla RA. 1988. Behavioral studies of Pavlovian conditioning. *Annu. Rev. Neurosci.* 11:329–52

Rescorla RA. 2001. Retraining of extinguished Pavlovian stimuli. *J. Exp. Psychol.: Anim. Behav. Process.* 27:115–24

Rescorla RA. 2004. Spontaneous recovery. *Learn. Mem.* 11:501–9

Rescorla RA, Heth CD. 1975. Reinstatement of fear to an extinguished conditioned stimulus. *J. Exp. Psychol.: Anim. Behav. Process.* 1:88–96

Ressler KJ, Mercer KB, Bradley B, Jovanovic T, Mahan A, et al. 2011. Post-traumatic stress disorder is associated with PACAP and the PAC1 receptor. *Nature* 470:492–97

Rodriguez-Romaguera J, Do Monte FH, Rodriguez-Resto JO, Quirk GJ. 2010. Deep brain stimulation within the nucleus accumbens of rats strengthens memory for fear extinction. *Soc. Neurosci. Abstr.* 809.3

Romanski LM, LeDoux JE. 1993. Information cascade from primary auditory cortex to the amygdala: cortic-ocortical and corticoamygdaloid projections of temporal cortex in the rat. *Cereb. Cortex* 3:515–32

Rosen BR, Buckner RL, Dale AM. 1998. Event-related functional MRI: past, present, and future. *Proc. Natl. Acad. Sci. USA* 95:773–80

Rougemont-Bücking A, Linnman C, Zeffiro TA, Zeidan MA, Lebron-Milad K, et al. 2011. Altered processing of contextual information during fear extinction in PTSD: an fMRI study. *CNS Neurosci. Ther.* 17:227–36

Roy AK, Shehzad Z, Margulies DS, Kelly AM, Uddin LQ, et al. 2009. Functional connectivity of the human amygdala using resting state fMRI. *NeuroImage* 45:614–26

Royer S, Paré D. 2002. Bidirectional synaptic plasticity in intercalated amygdala neurons and the extinction of conditioned fear responses. *Neuroscience* 115:455–62

Runyan JD, Moore AN, Dash PK. 2004. A role for prefrontal cortex in memory storage for trace fear conditioning. *J. Neurosci.* 24:1288–95

Sanberg PR, Pisa M, Fibiger HC. 1979. Avoidance, operant and locomotor behavior in rats with neostriatal injections of kainic acid. *Pharmacol. Biochem. Behav.* 10:137–44

Santini E, Ge H, Ren K, Pena DO, Quirk GJ. 2004. Consolidation of fear extinction requires protein synthesis in the medial prefrontal cortex. *J. Neurosci.* 24:5704–10

Santini E, Porter JT. 2010. M-type potassium channels modulate the intrinsic excitability of infralimbic neurons and regulate fear expression and extinction. *J. Neurosci.* 30:12379–86

Santini E, Quirk GJ, Porter JT. 2008. Fear conditioning and extinction differentially modify the intrinsic excitability of infralimbic neurons. *J. Neurosci.* 28:4028–36

Schiller D, Monfils MH, Raio CM, Johnson DC, LeDoux JE, Phelps EA. 2009. Preventing the return of fear in humans using reconsolidation update mechanisms. *Nature* 463:49–53

Semple WE, Goyer PF, McCormick R, Compton-Toth B, Morris E, et al. 1996. Attention and regional cerebral blood flow in posttraumatic stress disorder patients with substance abuse histories. *Psychiatry Res.* 67:17–28

Shalev I, Lerer E, Israel S, Uzefovsky F, Gritsenko I, et al. 2009. BDNF Val66Met polymorphism is associated with HPA axis reactivity to psychological stress characterized by genotype and gender interactions. *Psychoneuroendocrinology* 34:382–88

Shansky RM, Hamo C, Hof PR, Lou W, McEwen BS, Morrison JH. 2010. Estrogen promotes stress sensitivity in a prefrontal cortex-amygdala pathway. *Cereb. Cortex* 20:2560–67

Shin LM, McNally RJ, Kosslyn SM, Thompson WL, Rauch SL, et al. 1999. Regional cerebral blood flow during script-driven imagery in childhood sexual abuse-related PTSD: a PET investigation. *Am. J. Psychiatry* 156:575–84

Sierra-Mercado D, Padilla-Coreano N, Quirk GJ. 2011. Dissociable roles of prelimbic and infralimbic cortices, ventral hippocampus, and basolateral amygdala in the expression and extinction of conditioned fear. *Neuropsychopharmacology* 36:529–38

Sigurdsson T, Doyere V, Cain CK, LeDoux JE. 2007. Long-term potentiation in the amygdala: a cellular mechanism of fear learning and memory. *Neuropharmacology* 52:215–27

Soliman F, Glatt CE, Bath KG, Levita L, Jones RM, et al. 2010. A genetic variant BDNF polymorphism alters extinction learning in both mouse and human. *Science* 327:863–66

Sotres-Bayon F, Bush DE, LeDoux JE. 2004. Emotional perseveration: an update on prefrontal-amygdala interactions in fear extinction. *Learn. Mem.* 11:525–35

Sotres-Bayon F, Diaz-Mataix L, Bush DE, LeDoux JE. 2007. Consolidation of fear extinction requires NR2B-containing NMDA receptors in the ventromedial prefrontal cortex, but not in the lateral amygdala. *Soc. Neurosci. Abstr.* 307.5

Sotres-Bayon F, Quirk GJ. 2010. Prefrontal control of fear: more than just extinction. *Curr. Opin. Neurobiol.* 20:231–35

Sotres-Bayon F, Sierra-Mercado D, Quirk GJ. 2010. Ventral hippocampus gates fear-related signals in prelimbic cortex. *Soc. Neurosci. Abstr.* 809.15

Sun N, Cassell MD. 1993. Intrinsic GABAergic neurons in the rat central extended amygdala. *J. Comp. Neurol.* 330:381–404

Tan H, Lauzon NM, Bishop SF, Bechard MA, Laviolette SR. 2010. Integrated cannabinoid CB1 receptor transmission within the amygdala-prefrontal cortical pathway modulates neuronal plasticity and emotional memory encoding. *Cereb. Cortex* 20:1486–96

Teich AH, McCabe PM, Gentile CC, Schneiderman LS, Winters RW, et al. 1989. Auditory cortex lesions prevent the extinction of Pavlovian differential heart rate conditioning to tonal stimuli in rabbits. *Brain Res.* 480:210–18

Thompson BM, Baratta MV, Biedenkapp JC, Rudy JW, Watkins LR, Maier SF. 2010. Activation of the infralimbic cortex in a fear context enhances extinction learning. *Learn. Mem.* 17:591–99

Tranel D, Damasio H, Denburg NL, Bechara A. 2005. Does gender play a role in functional asymmetry of ventromedial prefrontal cortex? *Brain* 128:2872–81

Tye KM, Prakash R, Kim SY, Fenno LE, Grosenick L, et al. 2011. Amygdala circuitry mediating reversible and bidirectional control of anxiety. *Nature* 471:358–62

Van Dijk KR, Hedden T, Venkataraman A, Evans KC, Lazar SW, Buckner RL. 2010. Intrinsic functional connectivity as a tool for human connectomics: theory, properties, and optimization. *J. Neurophysiol.* 103:297–321

Vansteenwegen D, Hermans D, Vervliet B, Francken G, Beckers T, et al. 2005. Return of fear in a human differential conditioning paradigm caused by a return to the original acquisition context. *Behav. Res. Ther.* 43:323–36

Vertes RP. 2004. Differential projections of the infralimbic and prelimbic cortex in the rat. *Synapse* 51:32–58

Vervliet B, Vansteenwegen D, Baeyens F, Hermans D, Eelen P. 2005. Return of fear in a human differential conditioning paradigm caused by a stimulus change after extinction. *Behav. Res. Ther.* 43:357–71

Vidal-Gonzalez I, Vidal-Gonzalez B, Rauch SL, Quirk GJ. 2006. Microstimulation reveals opposing influences of prelimbic and infralimbic cortex on the expression of conditioned fear. *Learn. Mem.* 13:728–33

Walker DL, Ressler KJ, Lu KT, Davis M. 2002. Facilitation of conditioned fear extinction by systemic administration or intra-amygdala infusions of D-cycloserine as assessed with fear-potentiated startle in rats. *J. Neurosci.* 22:2343–51

Wellman CL, Izquierdo A, Garrett JE, Martin KP, Carroll J, et al. 2007. Impaired stress-coping and fear extinction and abnormal corticolimbic morphology in serotonin transporter knock-out mice. *J. Neurosci.* 27:684–91

Whalen PJ, Rauch SL, Etcoff NL, McInerney SC, Lee MB, Jenike MA. 1998. Masked presentations of emotional facial expressions modulate amygdala activity without explicit knowledge. *J. Neurosci.* 18:411–18

Whittle N, Hauschild M, Lubec G, Holmes A, Singewald N. 2010. Rescue of impaired fear extinction and normalization of cortico-amygdala circuit dysfunction in a genetic mouse model by dietary zinc restriction. *J. Neurosci.* 30:13586–96

Xu J, Zhu Y, Contractor A, Heinemann SF. 2009. mGluR5 has a critical role in inhibitory learning. *J. Neurosci.* 29:3676–84

Zeidan MA, Igoe SA, Linnman C, Vitalo A, Levine JB, et al. 2011. Estradiol modulates medial prefrontal cortex and amygdala activity during fear extinction in women and female rats. *Biol. Psychiatry.* In press

The Evolutionary Origins of Friendship

Robert M. Seyfarth and Dorothy L. Cheney

Departments of Psychology and Biology, University of Pennsylvania, Philadelphia, Pennsylvania 19104; email: seyfarth@psych.upenn.edu, cheney@sas.upenn.edu

Annu. Rev. Psychol. 2012. 63:153–77

First published online as a Review in Advance on July 5, 2011

The *Annual Review of Psychology* is online at psych.annualreviews.org

This article's doi: 10.1146/annurev-psych-120710-100337

Keywords

animal behavior, social relationships, evolution, nonhuman primates, mammals

Abstract

Convergent evidence from many species reveals the evolutionary origins of human friendship. In horses, elephants, hyenas, dolphins, monkeys, and chimpanzees, some individuals form friendships that last for years. Bonds occur among females, among males, or between males and females. Genetic relatedness affects friendships. In species where males disperse, friendships are more likely among females. If females disperse, friendships are more likely among males. Not all friendships, however, depend on kinship; many are formed between unrelated individuals. Friendships often involve cooperative interactions that are separated in time. They depend, at least in part, on the memory and emotions associated with past interactions. Applying the term "friendship" to animals is not anthropomorphic: Many studies have shown that the animals themselves recognize others' relationships. Friendships are adaptive. Male allies have superior competitive ability and improved reproductive success; females with the strongest, most enduring friendships experience less stress, higher infant survival, and live longer.

Contents

INTRODUCTION

Nature teaches beasts to know their friends.
(Shakespeare, *Coriolanus*)

Humans form close, enduring relationships and benefit from them. Having a strong social network reduces stress, lowers the risk of disease, and increases longevity (Berkman et al. 2004, Holt-Lunstad et al. 2010). Humans also classify relationships, giving them names like sisters, friends, lovers, allies, or rivals. Each name carries assumptions about the thoughts and emotions that underlie a relationship and reveals our expectations about how the individuals involved (including ourselves) will behave in the future, even in novel situations. Like forming relationships, recognizing and classifying the relationships that exist among others is adaptive because it helps us understand and predict peoples' behavior.

There continues to be debate about the extent to which our social relationships are unique, requiring cognitive skills that appear to be limited to humans, such as language, planning, and the ability to anticipate events long into the future. There is growing evidence, however, that at least some aspects of human social relationships find parallels in the behavior and cognition of animals. In many species, individuals not only form close, enduring social bonds but also recognize these bonds in others.

Of course, scientists have known for years that males and females in many species form pair bonds in which partners cooperate in the care and feeding of offspring. The ecological and social factors that favor the evolution of monogamy are now well known (see Alcock 2009 for review). In birds, the behavior of partners is often beautifully synchronized, and bonds may persist for years. In barnacle geese (*Branta leucopsis*), pairs that maintain long-lasting pair bonds have higher lifetime reproductive success than those with shorter pair durations (Black 2001).

But what about the evolution of close, enduring social bonds that are not directly related to mating: bonds among females, for example, or among males? Here we review recent studies of these long-term relationships in animals. For simplicity, we call them "friendships" (Silk 2005). Our goal is to shed light on the evolution and adaptive value of human friendship. We focus primarily on nonhuman primates because of their close evolutionary relationship to humans and because the most abundant data come from monkeys and apes; however, we also discuss intriguing results from studies of hyenas, elephants, dolphins, and lions. We focus primarily on field research because one goal of this review is to consider how stable, enduring friendships might have evolved.

HISTORICAL BACKGROUND

The scientific study of social relationships in animals began in the 1960s and 1970s, with Harlow's research on "the affectional systems" (Harlow & Harlow 1965) and Hinde's study of behavioral development, attachment, and the consequences of temporary separation in mother and infant rhesus monkeys (*Macaca mulatta*). In order to track the mother-infant interaction over time, Hinde developed measures that quantified the relative roles of mother or infant in maintaining their relationship (see Hinde 1979 for review). Several important results emerged.

First, different pairs had measurably different relationships that remained stable from one age period to the next, and these differences had predictive power. For example, the behavioral consequences of a brief separation between mother and infant were best predicted not by individual attributes such as the infant's age, sex, or the mother's experience, but by characteristics of the relationship before separation occurred. Infants who showed the greatest distress were those who had, before separation, been relatively more active than their mothers in maintaining physical contact (Hinde 1979).

Second, events early in life, such as a temporary separation, were correlated with persistent, long-term changes in behavior. Although it had long been accepted that events during human development could have long-term consequences, Hinde's experiments were the first to suggest a similar phenomenon in nonhuman species.

Third, the dynamics of each mother-infant relationship could only be understood in the context of the animals' relationships with others in their group. Somewhat surprisingly, infants removed from their group and kept in isolation exhibited less stress upon reunion than did infants who remained with their group while their mothers were removed. The explanation, however, lay in the mother's need to restore her own social relations with others after separation. Mothers who had been removed from the group—especially some less sociable, low-ranking individuals—were less responsive to their infants upon reunion than were mothers whose infants had been removed but whose own relationships with others had not been disrupted (Hinde 1979).

Based on these and other observations, Hinde (1976) developed a conceptual scheme for the study of social relationships in animals. Scientists should begin, he argued, by collecting data on social interactions. In monkeys, these were behaviors including grooming, aggression, play, the maintenance of proximity, or the formation of coalitions (which occur when two animals join to direct aggression against a third). Different dyads could then be compared according to the content, quality, and temporal patterning of their interactions. These factors defined their relationship.

Strong, enduring social bonds pose problems for causal theories of behavior because the interactions that define them are often separated in time. In chimpanzees, for example, males who groom together most often are also those most likely to share meat, yet the two activities do not always occur together (see below). What causes the correlation between these behaviors? As we attempt to understand the underlying mechanisms, we confront what our colleague David Premack once called "the Russian Novel Problem": Over any period of time, so many events occur in the lives of two individuals—all remembered and potentially related in so many different ways—that it becomes impossible to know what caused what (see also de Waal 2008). If two chimpanzees groom on a Tuesday afternoon, share meat on Thursday morning, form a coalition on Friday, then groom again on Saturday, how do we know what caused Saturday's grooming? Should the most recent event be given the greatest weight? What about the memory of past interactions, or the cumulative effects of successive interactions over time, or the possibility that a single, pivotal event can have long-term consequences (recall Hinde's data on the long-term consequences of separation)?

Long-term bonds pose problems for evolutionary theories of behavior because they often involve interactions such as grooming that are of relatively low cost and apparently have no direct link to reproduction or survival. Granted, many friendships involve kin, but as we shall see they are by no means limited to close genetic relatives. Why has this behavior evolved?

THE DATA

Baboons

Some of the most detailed data on long-term relationships in any animal species come from two studies of baboons (*Papio* spp.), one conducted for over 30 years in Amboseli National Park, Kenya and another conducted for over 16 years in the Moremi Game Reserve, Botswana. The two sites are 1500 miles apart and involve two different subspecies, *Papio hamadryas cynocephalus* in Amboseli and *P. h. ursinus* in Moremi. Given this geographical and phylogenetic separation, the convergence in their results is striking.

Baboons live throughout Africa in multimale, multifemale groups of 50–150 individuals. Males and females have strikingly different life histories. From the moment they are born, infants of both sexes interact at high rates not only with their mothers but also with those individuals who are also attracted to their mother: their maternal siblings, their mother's maternal sisters, and their maternal grandmother if she is alive. Among male offspring, bonds with matrilineal kin decline in strength with age, ending altogether around adolescence or early adulthood (9–10 years of age) when the male leaves his natal group and emigrates to another. Females, by contrast, remain in their natal group throughout their lives, forming strong friendships with matrilineal kin and sometimes other individuals (see below). Female acquire dominance ranks immediately below those of their mothers. As a result, the stable core of a baboon group consists of a hierarchy of matrilines in which all members of, say, matriline B outrank or are outranked by all members of matrilines C and A, respectively. Rank relations are generally stable over time, with few reversals occurring either within or between families. Females can live for up to 30 years in the wild.

To analyze the behavior of adult females in Amboseli, Silk et al. (2003; 2006a,b) developed a composite sociality index (CSI) based on grooming and proximity. Using the CSI, they measured the extent to which each female-female dyad differed from the mean for all dyads. They also calculated for each dyad the distribution of grooming between partners and measured for each individual the stability of social preferences (that is, the identity of her top three partners) over several years. Silk et al. (2010a) used similar methods to analyze adult female behavior in Moremi.

In both Amboseli (N = 1,430 dyads) and Moremi (N = 975), most dyads formed weak, impermanent social bonds. A smaller number formed strong, enduring friendships. Female social relationships were thus highly differentiated. The best predictor of bond strength was matrilineal kinship: Especially mothers and daughters but also sisters had significantly stronger bonds than other categories of dyads. In Moremi, for example, the mean value of the CSI was by definition 1.0. The median value was 0.45, and approximately 10% of all values were greater than 2.0. The mean CSI value for mothers and daughters was three times higher than that for sisters and nearly 15 times higher than that for unrelated dyads (Silk et al. 2010a). In both studies, matrilineal kin—particularly mothers and daughters—had the most equitable grooming relationships. In Moremi, matrilineal kin had higher rates of aggression than unrelated dyads, but aggressive interactions constituted a smaller portion of their total interactions than in unrelated dyads. In both Amboseli and Moremi, coalitions occurred most often among matrilineal kin. Finally, in both studies matrilineal kin—again, particularly mothers and daughters and sisters—formed the most stable, enduring social bonds (Silk et al. 2006a,b; 2010a).

Demographic events such as predation limited the ability of females to maintain enduring social bonds. In Moremi, only 50% of adult female dyads were coresident for at least three years; 18% were coresident for at least five years. Mother-daughter dyads were most likely to maintain a strong bond over all possible years. Sisters, age-mates, and unrelated individuals were less likely to do so, in that order.

Two other factors affected the strength of social bonds, again in both studies. Correcting for kinship, females closer in age formed stronger social bonds than those whose ages were more disparate. Females closer in age also had more equitable grooming relationships and, in Moremi, supported each other in coalitions at higher rates. In both studies, females closer in age had more stable, enduring bonds than did females of disparate age. Second, females in both studies formed stronger bonds with unrelated females of adjacent rank than with those of more disparate rank. The effect of rank distance was independent of the effects of kinship and age. Although by some measures females closer in rank had bonds that were stronger than those involving females of more disparate ranks, the effects of rank-distance were not as consistent and clear as the effects of matrilineal kinship or age (Silk et al. 2006a,b, 2010a).

Finally, baboon males and lactating females also form strong friendships. These bonds are thought to have evolved as a response against the threat of infanticide by recent immigrant males (Palombit et al. 2000). Like sexual consortships without the sex, male-female friendships are characterized by high rates of proximity, grooming, and mutual support (see Nguyen et al. 2009 for review). In many cases the male friend is the infant's father (Moscovice et al. 2010), but in all cases the male is a long-term resident who was present in the group when the infant was conceived. Formation of a friendship appears to mitigate the stress experienced by lactating females when a potentially infanticidal male enters the group (Beehner et al. 2005, Engh et al. 2006) and may increase infant survivorship (Palombit et al. 2000, Weingrill et al. 2000). The friendship ends if the infant dies or the mother resumes sexual cycling.

Chimpanzees

The society of chimpanzees (*Pan troglodytes*) is strikingly different from that of baboons, yet when it comes to friendships the two species are very similar: Some individuals interact rarely while others interact often, forming stable, long-term bonds that can last for ten years or more.

Chimpanzees live in fission-fusion communities that range in size from 20 to 150 animals. Within each community, individuals form temporary parties of 2–50 animals that fluctuate in size and composition throughout the day (Boesch 2009, Newton-Fisher 2002). Males are generally more social than females: Parties usually include more males than females, and solitary individuals are more likely to be female than male (e.g., Boesch 2009).

After reaching sexual maturity at roughly 11 years of age, most females disperse from their natal community and join another. Males, in contrast, remain in their natal community for life, becoming adult at roughly 16 years of age (Boesch 2009, Goodall 1986). In the wild, chimpanzee males can live into their 30s; chimpanzee females into their 40s or even 50s (Hill et al. 2001).

At any one time, the males in a community can be arranged in a linear, transitive dominance hierarchy (Goodall 1986, Newton-Fischer 2004, Wittig & Boesch 2003a). High rank is associated with high rates of aggression, displays, and coalition formation (see Muller & Mitani 2005 for review). Coalitions between individual males can persist for years or be surprisingly changeable over days and weeks, as males opportunistically "shift their investment in different relationships" during periods of instability (Newton-Fisher 2002, p. 135). The male members of a community also join together in territorial boundary patrols that may include violent, coalitionary attacks on the males in neighboring communities. When successful, these attacks appear to increase the community's access to food resources (Mitani et al. 2010). Roughly 25% to 33% of all patrols involve contact with the males of another community; some confrontations are fatal (see Muller & Mitani 2005 for review).

The most detailed data on chimpanzee friendships come from studies of males in the unusually large Ngogo community (150 individuals), where Watts (1998; 2000a,b; 2002) and Mitani (2006, 2009) have followed the behavior of 35 individuals ranging in estimated age from young (16–20 years), prime (21–33 years), to old (>33 years). Their sample has included nine pairs of maternal half-siblings, 22 pairs of paternal half-siblings, and many more unrelated individuals (Langergraber et al. 2007). Bonds among males were measured in a number of ways, including the frequency with which they were members of the same party or maintained proximity to each other, groomed, formed coalitions, shared meat, and accompanied one another on hunts and border patrols (**Figure 1**, see color insert). Bonds varied in length from one to ten years, and 26 of 28 males formed at least one bond lasting five years or longer.

As among baboons, the formation of stable, enduring relationships among male chimpanzees was correlated with genetic relatedness (Langergraber et al. 2007). In Mitani's (2009) study of 28 males observed for at least five years, strong bonds lasting one year or longer were formed in 56% of maternal kin dyads, 68% of paternal kin dyads, 66% of unrelated age-mates, and 48% of unrelated non-age-mates. The distribution of bonds in one year predicted its distribution in the next. Maternal half-brothers had more equally balanced grooming relationships and formed longer-lasting bonds than did unrelated individuals. Males of similar dominance rank had more equitable grooming relations and longer-lasting bonds than males of disparate ranks. There was no effect of age (Mitani 2009).

Kinship, however, was by no means the only or even the most important determinant of long-term bonds among males. Indeed, 22 of 28 males formed their longest, closest bond with an unrelated animal, and the majority of cooperative behavior was observed between unrelated or distantly related individuals

(Mitani 2009). In a test of reciprocal exchanges among 22 males, Mitani (2006) found significant positive pairwise correlations among several measures: grooming given and received, support given and received in coalitions, meat sharing, participation in hunts (Watts & Mitani 2001), and participation in border patrols (Langergraber et al. 2007). In all cases, results remained significant after controlling for rates of association, age, rank differences, and genetic relatedness. In other words, the best predictor of male X's rate of interaction with male Y by any of the seven measures listed above was male Y's rate of interaction with X according to either the same behavioral measure or any other measure chosen from the list. These results replicate data from previous, independent studies at Ngogo that found significant positive correlations between grooming and coalitionary support (Watts 2000a, 2002), meat sharing and coalitionary support, and reciprocal meat sharing (Mitani & Watts 2001).

During Mitani's 10-year study, seven of 28 males maintained a strong social bond with another male during the entire period. One dyad remained strongly bonded for all 10 years; another dyad did so for nine years. With two exceptions, every male maintained at least one bond that lasted well over half of the time that he was observed (Mitani 2009).

In sum, male chimpanzees formed friendships that lasted for many years, sometimes with maternal kin but more often with unrelated individuals.

The data from Ngogo are strongly supported by data from chimpanzee communities elsewhere. In the Kanyawara community, for example, many male-male dyads maintained strong and stable associations for up to 10 years, as measured by spatial proximity, grooming, and alliances (e.g., Gilby & Wrangham 2008, Newton-Fischer 2004, Nishida & Hosaka 1996, Watts 1998). In the Tai Forest, Wittig & Boesch (2003a) assigned adult dyads a relationship benefit index (RBI) according to the frequency with which they shared food (usually meat) and formed coalitions. Nineteen of 105 dyads exchanged these behaviors frequently. Pairs with a high RBI also had high rates of grooming and were more likely than other pairs to exhibit reconciliatory behavior after aggression (Wittig 2010).

Although early reports suggested that female chimpanzees interacted at low rates and were generally asocial (Goodall 1986), more recent data paint a different picture. In a study of 39 females at Ngogo—the largest sample to date—Langergraber et al. (2009) found that, whereas the average index of dyadic party association among males was higher than the average among females, the strongest dyadic associations were found among females, even though these females were rarely close kin (see also Wittig & Boesch 2003b).

Other Species

A growing body of evidence indicates that the friendships found in baboons and chimpanzees are not aberrations: Similar long-lasting bonds can be found throughout the animal kingdom. For example, long-term studies have revealed stable, enduring social bonds among female African elephants (*Loxodonta africana*: Moss et al. 2010), rhesus and Japanese macaques (*M. fuscata*: Kapsalis 2004, Yamada 1963), and capuchin monkeys (*Cebus apella*: O'Brien & Robinson 1993; *C. capuchinus*: Perry et al. 2008). In all of these species, females are the philopatric sex, and the strongest, most enduring social bonds are formed among mother-daughter pairs and sisters. In elephants, bonds between mothers and daughters and between sisters can persist for over 20 years (see Moss et al. 2010 for review).

In rhesus macaques living on Cayo Santiago, an island off the coast of Puerto Rico, females have the opportunity to form close bonds with many matrilineal kin, including grandmothers and great aunts. As among baboons, close maternal kin (mother-daughter and sister pairs) form the closest friendships (Widdig et al. 2001, 2006; see Kapsalis 2004 for review and Watanabe 2001 for similar data on Japanese macaques). Examining behavior within the matrilineal families of Cayo San-

tiago rhesus macaques, Kapsalis & Berman (1996) found that, if degrees of relatedness (r) were less than 0.125 (equivalent to half first cousins), female interactions with matrilineal kin did not differ from their interactions with nonkin. Like baboons, female rhesus macaques were also more likely to groom, approach, and spend time near individuals of similar age and half-sibs to whom they were related through the paternal line (Widdig et al. 2001).

In capuchin monkeys, long alpha male tenure can lead to groups containing full siblings and both maternal and paternal half-siblings (Perry et al. 2008). In Perry et al.'s (2008) study, paternal half-siblings seemed unable to recognize one another, and the strongest, most enduring bonds involved individuals related through the maternal line. Similarity in rank had a small but significant effect, making bonds between these females stronger than those among females of disparate ranks (Perry et al. 2008).

In hyena (*Crocuta crocuta*) society, virtually all males disperse from their natal clan whereas females remain. In this respect hyenas resemble the elephants and monkeys described above. Within a clan, however, individual hyenas do not forage and travel as a group but instead exhibit fission-fusion behavior much like that found in chimpanzees. Clans may contain up to 80 individuals belonging to one or more matrilineal kin groups. The strongest long-term bonds occur among females who are almost certainly close relatives through the maternal line (see Smith et al. 2010 for review).

In feral horses (*Equus caballus*), both males and females disperse from their natal group, later forming stable breeding groups that include one stallion and several unrelated females. In a four-year study, Cameron et al. (2009) found striking differences in the degree of social integration (as measured by grooming and proximity) among mares in different groups. Mares that interacted at higher rates experienced reduced rates of harassment by males, higher foal birth rates, and greater survival when compared with mares that interacted less often.

Long-term studies of dolphins (*Tursiops aduncus*), begun in the 1970s and 1980s, are currently underway in Sarasota Bay, Florida (Wells 2003) and Shark Bay, Western Australia (Mann et al. 2000). At both sites, some males and many females disperse from their natal range as adolescents, while a few individuals of both sexes continue to use their natal range as adults (Connor et al. 2000, Connor & Mann 2006, Wells 2003). Within this range, dolphins live in a fission-fusion society in which individuals associate in small groups that change composition often (Connor et al. 2000, Frere et al. 2010). In the Shark Bay population of 600 individuals, adult males form "first-order" alliances of two or three males who join together to form a sexual consortship with a female. At a second level of alliances, 4 to 14 males from two or more first-order alliances join to defend or take over females from other second- or first-order alliances. In addition to their cooperation in aggression, allied males exhibit high rates of spatial association, "gentle rubbing" (touching or rubbing each other with pectoral fins), and synchronous swimming and surfacing (Connor & Mann 2006). Males in both first- and second-order alliances are more closely related to each other than would be expected by chance (Krützen et al. 2003). The bonds between individual members of a first-order (and therefore second-order) alliance may last for up to 20 years (Connor 2007).

WHO FORMS FRIENDSHIPS?

Clearly, the distribution of friendships within animal groups is not random. Instead, several patterns recur across species, with each pattern relevant to hypotheses about the evolution of long-term relationships and the mechanisms that underlie them.

Often, the behaviors that define a friendship occur close together in time, as for example when one individual grooms another and then receives grooming in return. This observation has led some authors to suggest that all social interactions reflect nothing more than each individual's "current need" (Henzi & Barrett 2007), resulting in a short-term "business partnership" (Barrett & Henzi 2002). According to this view, describing such interactions as a relationship is inappropriately anthropomorphic, for several reasons. We consider this argument below.

For now, we concentrate on the most consistent patterns in the distribution of friendships: individuals' attraction to matrilineal kin, to age-mates who may be paternal siblings, and to animals of similar dominance rank. These distributions allow us to test hypotheses based on either kin selection or the assumption that animals attempt to form relationships that yield the greatest benefit to them.

Attraction to Matrilineal Kin

Kummer (1971) was the first to propose that long-term bonds among adult matrilineal kin arise as an extension of an infant's interaction with its mother. He suggested that, in species such as baboons, vervet monkeys (*Chlorocebus aethiops*), macaques, hyenas, and elephants, where females remain in their natal group and generations overlap, the close bond between mother and infant brings the infant into frequent contact with her siblings, maternal aunts, and sometimes a maternal grandmother. Repeated interactions are mutually reinforcing, and the bonds formed during infancy persist into adulthood (see Silk 2005 for review).

Forty years of field research have proved Kummer correct: Matrilineal kinship is the single most important factor affecting the development of long-term bonds in animals. Even in species such as chimpanzees and dolphins, where most females disperse from their natal range, genetic relatedness through the maternal line remains an important predictor of friendships (Krützen et al. 2003, Mitani 2009). Within the matrilineal kin groups of baboons, rhesus macaques, Japanese macaques, and capuchin monkeys, the likelihood of finding an enduring, long-term bond is greatest among mothers and daughters, then declines with decreasing relatedness through the maternal line (Silk 2005).

Chapais (2005) proposed that long-term relationships among maternal relatives might occur only as a byproduct of animals' common attraction to a central individual. If this were true, bonds among kin should weaken when the central individual dies. Results do not support this hypothesis. Among baboons, females' bonds with sisters became stronger in their mother's absence. Bonds with aunts, on the other hand, became weaker (Silk et al. 2006b). These data suggest that bonds with different categories of kin are interrelated, but not in exactly the way Chapais suggested. Females seem strongly motivated to form bonds with close matrilineal kin such as mothers and sisters. As a result, when a female loses her mother, this bond is readily "replaced" by strengthened bonds with the female's own daughter or one or more of her sisters. By contrast, females seem less strongly motivated to form bonds with more distant kin such as aunts, nieces, or cousins, perhaps because, as Chapais suggested, these relationships develop only indirectly through a female's close bonds with her mother, sisters, and offspring. As a result, when a female's mother dies, these bonds become weaker.

The crucial role of matrilineal kinship in the formation of friendships should not distract us from another, equally striking result. Even if they had no close kin present in the group, female baboons and male chimpanzees consistently formed at least one enduring friendship with another individual (Mitani 2009, Silk et al. 2010a). This suggests that, for all its importance, attraction among matrilineal kin is not the only factor leading to the formation of long-term bonds. Instead, friendships may be generally beneficial for all individuals, and selection may have favored the motivation to form such bonds even when close kin are not available.

Attraction to Age-Mates Who May Be Patrilineal Siblings

In most group-living mammals, the highest-ranking male accounts for the great majority of matings (Alberts et al. 2006). As a result, infants born close together in time are likely to be paternal sibs, particularly if breeding is seasonal or a male has a long tenure in the alpha position (Altmann 1979). Alpha male tenure averages seven months in baboons (Alberts et al. 2003) but may extend for years in chimpanzees and capuchin monkeys (Perry et al. 2008, Watts 1998).

Scientists long believed that in the absence of paternal care or any special relationship between male and female mates there would be no way for individuals to recognize paternal kin and hence no mechanism by which natural selection could favor cooperation among these individuals through kin selection. Several recent studies suggest, however, that individuals may be able to recognize and cooperate selectively with paternal kin. Such recognition might occur because males remember the females with whom they have mated and selectively defend or cooperate with their infants (Buchan et al. 2003, Moscovice et al. 2010) or because infants and juveniles are selectively attracted to age-mates who are often paternal kin. In Moremi, for example, several lactating females will often form a friendship with the same male, with the result that their offspring (who may be paternal siblings) interact at high rates from infancy. Finally, individuals may be able to recognize their close paternal relatives through some type of "phenotypic matching" that is not yet well understood (Hauber & Sherman 2001).

In two studies of baboons and rhesus macaques where at least some paternal relatedness was known, females had stronger bonds with paternal kin and with unrelated age-mates than with unrelated individuals who were not age-mates. Bonds with paternal kin and/or age-mates were weaker than bonds with maternal kin but stronger than bonds with unrelated individuals. Among baboons, the strength of friendships with age-mates declined steadily as the age difference between females increased (Silk et al. 2006b, 2010a). Among rhesus macaques, paternal kin discrimination was more pronounced among animals of a similar age (Widdig et al. 2001).

By contrast, in a group of capuchin monkeys where male tenure in the alpha position was unusually long, full sisters, maternal half-sisters, and mother-daughter dyads associated at equally high rates, and all associated significantly more than paternal half-sisters (Perry et al. 2008). In a sample of 35 male chimpanzees that included 9 maternal half-sibs and 22 paternal half-sibs, there was no evidence that age or paternal relatedness affected the likelihood that two individuals would form a long-term bond (Langergraber et al. 2007, Mitani 2009). The authors speculate that paternal kin "probably cannot be reliably recognized" (Langergraber et al. 2007, p. 7786).

Attraction to Individuals of Similar Dominance Rank

If the formation of friendships is adaptive, females should be strongly motivated to form bonds with those individuals with whom a friendship would be most beneficial. Seyfarth (1977) proposed that, in addition to their attraction to matrilineal kin, females in groups of baboons and macaques would prefer to interact with high-ranking individuals because these individuals can potentially provide the most useful support in coalitions, tolerance at food sites, reduced aggression, and other benefits. Access to high-ranking partners would be constrained, however, by either competition or competitive exclusion (C cannot groom A or B when they are grooming with each other). High-ranking animals would be least constrained and interact with others of high rank, middle-ranking individuals would compromise by interacting with others of middle rank, and low-ranking animals would be left to interact with each other. In sum, animals would interact with others of similar rank.

This model made a variety of predictions concerning the formation of long-term relationships. Some have been supported, others have not (see Schino & Aureli 2009 for review). In two large meta-analyses, Schino (2001) found a strong preference for grooming high-ranking individuals over others and a significant correlation between grooming and the formation of coalitions (Schino 2007). In

the Amboseli baboon study, females closer in rank had stronger, more equitable, and more enduring bonds independent of kinship and age than did females of more disparate ranks. By contrast, female capuchin monkeys were strongly attracted to those of similar rank when group size was small and matrilineal kin few in number, but this effect of rank distance decreased as group size increased and matrilineal kin became more numerous (Perry et al. 2008). Mitani (2009) found no effect of rank distance in the long-term bonds of male chimpanzees.

Because attraction to kin and attraction to rank are assumed to reinforce one another in high-ranking families but counteract one another in low-ranking families, the model predicts that bonds within high-ranking families should be stronger than bonds within low-ranking families. This prediction is supported by several monkey studies (Berman 1980, Fairbanks 1993, Yamada 1963). The same result, however, can also be explained by the "similarity principle" (de Waal & Luttrell 1986), which proposes that animals establish bonds with those they most resemble, with "resemblance" being based on genetic and social background, age, or hierarchical position.

IS "RELATIONSHIP" AN INAPPROPRIATE, ANTHROPOMORPHIC TERM?

Henzi & Barrett (2007) argued that female baboons in their study had unstable patterns of grooming and proximity over a four-year period (Barrett & Henzi 2002; but see the re-analysis in Silk et al. 2010a). Grooming, however, was often reciprocal within a bout and often occurred when one female was attempting to touch or handle another's infant. Because females seemed to be "trading" grooming given for grooming received or access to a female's infant, Henzi & Barrett (2007) concluded that, "female 'relationships'... need not, and probably do not, take the long-term, temporally consistent form that has been attributed to them...." (p. 73). Instead, they argue for a view, based on "biological markets" (Noë &

Figure 1

Male chimpanzees in Ngogo, Uganda (*a*) engage in grooming, (*b*) share meat after killing a monkey, and (*c*) embark on a border patrol against males of a neighboring community. Among individual males, there is a significant positive correlation among all three behaviors, even though they do not necessarily occur together in time. Photos by John Mitani.

Hammerstein 1994), in which "each of the behaviors linked to theories of female coexistence...can be seen as an independent, contingent response to current need rather than as interlocking components of an overall female strategy to cultivate and enhance relationships in the long-term" (Henzi & Barrett 2007, p. 46). Much of their criticism is based on what they believe is an overly anthropomorphic conception of nonhuman primate relationships in the minds of those who study them. Current use of the term, they argue, is based on the assumptions that "monkeys can anticipate their future social needs" (p. 52), that "the function of relationships is to ensure unstinting mutual support...at unknown, unpredictable future dates" (p. 64) and that the individuals concerned "possess a declarative, explicit knowledge" (p. 64) or an "overt, cognitive understanding" (p. 46) of their relationships with others. This critique is misplaced, for several reasons.

Memory of the Past, Not Projection into the Future

Although "relationship" (and here "friendship") is widely used as a descriptive term, none of those whose research is cited above has ever claimed that monkeys, apes, or any other species can anticipate their future social needs. To the contrary, when scientists have speculated about the mechanisms underlying long-term relationships they have typically assumed that current behavior is affected, wholly or in part, by the individuals' memory of past interactions (Aureli & Schaffner 2002; Cheney & Seyfarth 1990, 2007; Schino & Aureli 2009). Or, as Hinde (1987, pp. 23–24) put it, "When two individuals interact, each will bring preconceptions about the likely behavior of the other, or about the behavior appropriate to the situation. In addition, if two individuals have a series of interactions over time, the course of each interaction may be influenced by experience in the preceding ones. We then speak of them as having a relationship...." Although the ability of animals to plan for the future is controversial, there is no doubt about their ability to learn from experience.

Implicit Knowledge

Nor has anyone claimed that animals' knowledge of their own and each other's relationships is explicit and declarative—indeed, quite the opposite is true. To cite just one example: "when we say that baboons have social theories we do not mean that they have fully conscious, well-worked-out theories that they can describe explicitly.... Instead, baboons appear to have implicit expectations about how individuals will interact with one another. Through processes we do not yet understand, they observe the associations among other group members and generate expectations" about how these individuals will behave under different circumstances (Cheney & Seyfarth 2007, p. 118). Implicit knowledge is widely documented in studies of children and animals. Four-month-old human infants have an implicit knowledge about the behavior of objects in space but they cannot describe what they know (Kellman & Spelke 1983); children of 17 months can readily understand the meaning of sentences, yet no one claims that their behavior is based on an explicit, declarative knowledge of grammar (see Hirsh-Pasek & Golinkoff 1996 for review). Nutcrackers (*Nucifraga columbiana*) remember the locations of thousands of previously hidden seeds (Balda & Kamil 1992), and piñon jays (*Gymnorhinus cyanocephalus*) and fish behave in ways that are difficult to explain without assuming that they have some representation of a transitive rank order (Grosenick et al. 2007, Paz-y-Miño et al. 2004). Yet knowledge in these and other cases is clearly implicit; it influences the animals' behavior but is not accessible to them. They cannot describe what they know. Animals' knowledge of social relationships is no different.

The Recognition of Other Animals' Relationships

There is also now an extensive literature indicating that animals recognize other individuals' relationships. Territorial birds recognize the relations that exist among their neighbors (e.g., Peake et al. 2002), while fish, hyenas, lions, horses, dolphins, and several species of primates recognize other individuals' dominance ranks. When joining a coalition, for example, individual hyenas and monkeys selectively support the higher ranking of two combatants regardless of who is winning at the time (Engh et al. 2005; see Seyfarth & Cheney 2011a for review). When recruiting a coalition partner, male macaques selectively solicit those who rank higher than both their opponent and themselves (Silk 1999); capuchin monkeys selectively solicit allies who rank higher than their opponents and have a social relationship with the solicitor that is closer (as measured by the ratio of past affiliative to aggressive interactions) than their relationship with the opponent. The preferential solicitation of more closely bonded individuals can be explained only by assuming that solicitors somehow compare the bond between the ally and themselves with the bond between the ally and their opponent (Perry et al. 2004). In playback experiments, a sequence of calls that mimics a higher-ranking opponent threatening a lower-ranking animal elicits little response from listeners, but if the individuals' roles are reversed the response is significantly stronger—presumably because the rank-reversal sequence violates the listener's expectations (Bergman et al. 2003; for reviews, see Cheney & Seyfarth 2011a, Schino 2001, Schino et al. 2007).

Animals also recognize the close bonds that exist among others. In playback experiments conducted on vervet monkeys and baboons, females who heard a juvenile's scream were likely to look at the juvenile's mother (Cheney & Seyfarth 1990, 2007). Low-ranking male baboons monitor the sexual consortships of males and females in an apparent attempt to take advantage of "sneaky matings" (Crockford et al. 2007). In vervets and many macaque species, an individual who has just been involved in an aggressive interaction with another will redirect aggression by attacking a third, previously uninvolved individual. Judge (1982) was the first to note that redirected aggression does not occur at random. He found that pigtail macaques do not simply threaten the nearest

lower-ranking individual; instead, they target a close matrilineal relative of their opponent (see Seyfarth & Cheney 2011a for review).

If a baboon receives aggression from another and then, minutes later, hears a grunt from a previously uninvolved animal, the listener's response to the grunt depends on the relationship between the calling animal and the listener's opponent. If the caller is a close matrilineal relative of the opponent, the listener is subsequently more likely to approach her recent opponent and tolerate her opponent's approach than if she hears the grunt of an animal unrelated to her opponent or no grunt at all. In other words, she treats the call as a reconciliatory signal that functions as a proxy for reconciliation with the opponent herself (Wittig et al. 2007). A similar phenomenon occurs among chimpanzees, where the behavior of bystanders and victims following aggression depends on both their own relationships with the combatants and their perception of the relationship between the other animals involved (Wittig & Boesch 2010).

To cite another example, chimpanzees often scream when involved in aggressive disputes. Slocombe & Zuberbuhler (2005) found that victims produce acoustically different screams according to the severity of aggression they are receiving. In playback experiments, listeners responded differently to the different scream types (Slocombe et al. 2009). In cases of severe aggression, victims' screams sometimes seemed to exaggerate the severity of the attack, but victims only gave exaggerated screams if their foraging party included at least one listener whose dominance rank was equal to or higher than that of their aggressor (Slocombe & Zuberbuhler 2007). Victims seemed to alter their screams depending upon their perception of the relationship between their opponent and their potential allies.

In sum, the recognition of other animals' relationships by the animals themselves has been widely documented in many species using many different techniques (for review, see Shettleworth 2010, chapter 12). The representations that underlie such recognition undoubtedly differ from one species to the next and certainly differ from humans' more explicit social knowledge, but there is no doubt that animals acquire and remember information about other animals' relationships and that this knowledge affects their behavior. No special skill is required, nor should we be surprised at these abilities: Animals live in a world where there are predictable, statistical regularities in other individuals' behavior. All they need to do is watch and remember.

Many Behaviors Are Not Contingent Responses to Current Need

Supporting the "current needs" hypothesis, many behaviors that characterize friendships do occur close together in time. In perhaps the paradigmatic example, female primates are strongly attracted to newborn infants and invest many minutes grooming a mother in the apparent hope of being able to touch her infant (Silk et al. 2003). Henzi & Barrett (2002) found that female baboons groomed mothers for longer before handling their infants when there were fewer infants present in the group. Infants, they argued, were a "commodity" whose value depended on the current supply.

Similar data emerged from an experiment in which first one and then a second female vervet monkey was uniquely granted access to a supply of food (Fruteau et al. 2009). When only one female had access to the food, she received significantly more grooming from others. When a second female gained access to the food, the grooming received by the first declined, as predicted by a current benefits, biological market hypothesis.

The best data indicating that one beneficial act is contingent upon another—with or without a short delay—come from experiments in which a single prior event differs from one condition to another and this difference affects behavior (de Waal 1997a, Hemelrijk 1994, Seyfarth & Cheney 1984). In one such test, a baboon who heard another individual's recruitment call responded positively—that is, moved in the direction of the loudspeaker and

approached the individual—if she had recently groomed with that individual and the individual had an infant, but showed no such behavior if she had recently behaved aggressively toward the individual. If the subject had groomed with the individual but not heard a recruitment call, she also showed no tendency to approach. Subjects' responses were therefore dependent upon certain prior and current conditions, suggesting that at least some cooperative interactions depend on a specific, recent, prior interaction (Cheney et al. 2010).

Despite these data, several observations argue against the current needs hypothesis as a complete explanation of the mechanisms underlying friendships. First, it has proved difficult to demonstrate contingent, one-for-one exchanges of cooperative behavior in laboratory settings. This may arise because the settings are too unnatural (but see de Waal 1997b, 2000) or because animals do not keep precise track of favors given and received (see Schino & Aureli 2009, Silk 2007 for review). Brosnan et al. (2009) note that laboratory tests depend primarily on the exchange of goods, particularly food, whereas "exchanges" in the wild are primarily concerned with services, such as grooming and support, which may be more suited to economic exchanges. The argument is intriguing, but it cannot account for the striking difference between chimpanzees' food-sharing behavior in the wild and the lack of it in captivity.

But the strongest argument against the current needs hypothesis comes from the distribution of cooperative behaviors in time and their distribution among individuals. Highly correlated behaviors that are separated in time create an asymmetry whenever the current needs hypothesis is compared with one based on the memory of previous interactions. If two behaviors are closely linked in time, results are consistent with current needs, but one cannot rule out the possibility that behavior has also been caused by the individuals' memories of past interactions. Experiments in captivity get around this problem by testing for cooperation between animals who have never interacted before, but this hardly solves the problem. After all, one goal of such experiments is to explore the conditions under which selection might have favored the evolution of cooperative, long-term bonds under natural conditions—which brings us back to the same problem.

By contrast, if two correlated behaviors are widely separated in time, results can decisively rule out an explanation based on current needs or, at the very least, require that we expand the current needs hypothesis to include behaviors that are widely separated in time and linked by the individuals' memories of past interactions—which brings us back to long-term relationships.

In many monkeys, the pairs of females who groom most often are also those most likely to support each other in coalitions, yet grooming and coalition formation are rarely juxtaposed in time (e.g., Kapsalis 2004, Schino 2007). Among pairs of male chimpanzees at Ngogo, those who groom most often also have the highest rates of coalition formation and participation in border patrols, yet these behaviors do not necessarily occur together. The same holds for meat sharing and coalition formation in the Tai Forest, and for grooming given and grooming received (Kapsalis 2004, Schino 2007). In Japanese macaques (Schino et al. 2003, 2007), chimpanzees (Gomes et al. 2009), baboons (Frank & Silk 2009), and capuchin monkeys (Schino et al. 2009), grooming within a bout is often very one-sided, yet grooming between the same two partners is much more evenly balanced when it is summed over weeks or months. All of these results suggest that primates "are tolerant of temporary imbalances in services given and received and are able to keep track of the help given and received over substantial periods of time" (Silk et al. 2010a, pp. 1743–1744).

This tolerance of temporary imbalances may be particularly evident in closely bonded dyads. For example, in experiments with chimpanzees, vervet monkeys, and baboons, prior grooming had a strong effect on individuals' subsequent cooperative behavior in weakly bonded dyads but no noticeable effect on their behavior in strongly bonded dyads (Brosnan et al. 2005,

Cheney et al. 2010, de Waal 1997a, Seyfarth & Cheney 1984).

In sum, although the current needs hypothesis may account for some of the cooperative interactions that characterize friendships, it cannot explain the many cooperative interactions that are widely separated in time—unless, of course, we broaden the temporal scope of the hypothesis so that it includes the memory of past interactions, tolerance of temporary inequities, and allows individuals somehow to "sum" their notion of prior benefits over days, weeks, or months. But in this case the hypothesis would no longer be based on current benefit. The current needs hypothesis also fails as an exclusive explanation of long-term bonds because so many immediately beneficial interactions involve individuals who interact often and whose long history almost certainly affects what they do. Contingent cooperation does occur in animals, but it cannot account for the existence of enduring, long-term friendships. What hypothesis accounts for the existing data?

ANIMALS' KNOWLEDGE OF RELATIONSHIPS AFFECTS THEIR BEHAVIOR

The current needs hypothesis focuses on temporally juxtaposed interactions, and these interactions alone, as the crucial causal elements in a chain of events. By contrast, in Hinde's original studies the response of a rhesus macaque infant to separation from its mother was best predicted not by any single prior interaction but instead by characteristics of the mother-infant relationship during the preceding weeks. This observation led Hinde to propose that, when animals spend long periods of time together and interact often, the causes of their behavior are to be found not in any single prior event but rather in the cumulative memories and emotions created by many previous interactions: what he called the animals' "relationship." Hinde's results, together with the data reviewed above, suggest an alternative to the current needs hypothesis.

We propose that a series of interactions between two individuals leads, over time, to a relationship that is implicitly recognized both by the participants themselves and by others in their group. In this respect we reify the concept of a relationship. We propose that it exists as an implicit organizing concept, or unit of thought, in the mind of an animal, built up from the memories and emotions generated by the animal's own experiences and by her observation of others. Of course, the animal's knowledge of her own and others' relationships is not explicit—she has no name for different individuals or different social bonds—but it is knowledge nonetheless, like a rat's knowledge of which bar to press or a bird's knowledge of the dominance relations among its neighbors.

We agree with de Waal (2000), Aureli & Schino (2004), and Silk (2007) that, however it is encoded in the brain, an animal's knowledge of her relationships must be affected by several factors, including the memory of past events, the emotions associated with them, and the emotions currently experienced: what de Waal (2008) calls "empathy," Silk (2005) calls "friendship," and Schino & Aureli (2009, p. 59) describe as "a system of emotionally based bookkeeping that allows the long-term tracking of reciprocal exchanges with multiple partners without causing an excessive cognitive load." We further suggest that, like any other knowledge that is built up from memory and emotions—a rat's knowledge of schedules of reinforcement, or a jay's knowledge of where it has hidden and recovered food—an animal's knowledge of relationships has causal power: It affects the animal's behavior. How might this work?

We propose that one animal's behavior toward another does not rely solely on his memory of specific past interactions (although these are undoubtedly important), but derives instead, as a kind of cognitive/emotional shortcut, from his emotions when with that individual and the emotions and memories generated by the recall of many past interactions, all summed over time (Aureli & Schaffner 2002, de Waal 2008). Different memories and emotions, continually updated, cause different patterns of behavior. For some pairs of animals,

memories and emotions lead to more affinitive interactions, which in turn generate more positive memories and emotions. These animals' bonds are strong, enduring, and relatively unaffected by aggression or temporary imbalances in grooming. For other pairs, memories and emotions are less positive or derived from fewer interactions. These animals' bonds are less predictable and may depend more on recent events. Supporting this view, recall that sisters and aunt-niece pairs in baboons maintained strong friendships despite higher rates of aggression than other, less closely bonded dyads, and that in both female baboons and male chimpanzees, pairs with the most equitable grooming relations over long periods of time—but not within a bout—had by other measures the strongest friendships (Aureli & Schaffner 2002). Recall, too, the many cases in which cooperation depended on recent interactions in less closely bonded pairs but was independent of recent events in more strongly bonded pairs (Cheney et al. 2010, de Waal 1997a, Schino & Aureli 2009, Seyfarth & Cheney 1984). Close friends cooperate regardless of what happened recently; others are more concerned with "what have you done for me lately?"

For closely bonded individuals, the emotions created by the memories of past interactions constitute a common currency through which behaviors of different sorts can affect one another. Grooming on Tuesday can create an emotional bond that causes meat sharing on Saturday afternoon. Memories and emotions also allow individuals to adopt a "loose accounting mechanism" that can potentially yield great benefits without relying on more precise calculations based on single past events (Schino & Aureli 2009, p. 57).

Armed with the notion of a relationship— call it a "behavioral abstraction" (Povinelli & Vonk 2004), an "intervening variable" (Shettleworth 2010, p. 451), or a "concept" (Seyfarth & Cheney 2011b)—animals classify others according to their relationships and develop expectations about how they will interact. When a juvenile baboon screams, other animals look toward the mother. When a capuchin, a macaque, or a chimpanzee is involved in aggression, its behavior depends on its perception of the rank relations among others. If two baboons fight and a bystander grunts to the victim, the grunt reconciles victim and aggressor (i.e., changes their behavior), but only if the bystander is a close kin of the victim. If two chimpanzees fight and a bystander behaves in a friendly way toward the victim, this behavior reconciles the combatants, but only if the bystander has a close bond with the aggressor (Cheney & Seyfarth 2007, Wittig 2010, Wittig & Boesch 2010). Just as an animal's own behavior toward another is affected by their relationship, so the animal's behavior toward others is affected by his perception of their relationship.

By treating animals' knowledge of their own and other individuals' relationship as an intervening variable with causal power, we can account for many of the data on friendships that cannot be explained by a hypothesis based on current benefits in a biological market: the correlation of behaviors separated in time, the correlation between qualitatively different behaviors, and the relatively greater importance of contingent cooperation in weakly bonded, as opposed to strongly bonded, dyads.

Finally, this explanation of long-term relationships requires no special mechanism or novel cognitive abilities. It assumes that animals recognize others as individuals, remember past interactions, and observe and remember the interactions of others. It further assumes that, from these memories and the emotions they generate, animals form implicit concepts that allow them to distinguish between their own relations with different individuals as well as the different relationships that these individuals have with each other—but this requires nothing more than the same concept-forming ability we see, for example, in the classification of different song types or the recognition of transitive relations by birds.

MECHANISMS

Monogamy is rare in nonhuman primates and mammals generally. It does occur, however,

among some rodents and New World monkeys (Fernandez-Duqué et al. 2009). Recent research is beginning to reveal some of the genetic and hormonal mechanisms that underlie monogamous bonds and that might also underlie the friendships reviewed here.

It is now clear that the peptide hormones oxytocin and arginine vasopressin are involved in the formation of male-female pair bonds in rodents (see Carter et al. 2008 for review). Oxytocin is associated with prosocial behaviors in female mammals, and the gene coding for its receptor, *OXTR*, is heavily expressed in the brains of female rodents (see Carter et al. 2008 for review). By contrast, the arginine vasopression pathway, including the V1a receptor gene, is involved in the expression of partner preference in male mammals (see Turner et al. 2010 for review). In monogamously mated pairs, different levels of oxytocin may be associated with variation in bond strength. In a study of monogamously bonded tamarins (*Saguinus oedipus*), for example, Snowdon et al. (2010) found that both males and females exhibited a tenfold variation in levels of oxytocin. Within pairs, however, male and female levels were highly correlated, and the pairs that were most strongly bonded exhibited the highest ocytocin levels. Different behavioral variables were correlated with levels of oxytocin in each sex: For females, affiliation duration and affiliation frequency were the best predictors of oxytocin levels; for males, the best predictor was sexual behavior. The variation in mean oxytocin levels across pairs, however, was best explained by a model that included male sexual behavior, male huddle initiation, and female solicitation (Snowdon et al. 2010). In other words, as with Hinde's study of responses to separation, the mean oxytocin level in a pair was best predicted not by any single property of either individual but rather by properties of the pair's relationship.

In both human and nonhuman species, the stress response [as measured by levels of circulating glucocorticoids (GCs)] can be mitigated by social contact and affiliation (for review, see Carter et al. 2008, Cheney & Seyfarth 2009). Increasing GC levels prompt the release of oxytocin, which increases motivation for social bonding and physical contact (Uvnas-Moberg 1997). Oxytocin both inhibits the further release of GCs and promotes affiliative behavior, including the tendency to associate with other females. From a functional perspective, such behavior may be adaptive because it allows females to establish new relationships, maintain existing bonds, or restore bonds that have been damaged. Among both baboons and rhesus macaques, females whose grooming networks were focused on a few partners had lower GC levels than did females whose grooming networks were more diverse (Brent et al. 2011, Crockford et al. 2008).

Consistent with this view, data from several species suggest that, when individuals are under stress or their long-term bonds are challenged, they respond in ways that seem designed either to restore and strengthen existing relationships or to form new ones. Such behavior also has the effect of reducing GC levels. In baboons, for example, females who have lost a close companion to predation increase both their rate of grooming and the diversity of their grooming partners. From a functional perspective, this behavior may allow females to form a close bond with a new partner (Engh et al. 2005). If a female's mother dies, her bonds with sisters grow stronger (Silk et al. 2006b). Lactating females whose infants are threatened by infanticide decrease the diversity of their grooming partners, apparently focusing their interactions on a few preferred individuals (Wittig et al. 2008). They also form friendships with adult males (Palombit et al. 2000). In their study of monogamous tamarins (see above), Snowdon & Ziegler (2007) found high rates of nonconceptive sex not only throughout the ovarian cycle but also during pregnancy. Rates of nonconceptive sex and female solicitation increased after minor disruptions of a pair's relationship, for example by brief separations or olfactory stimulation from novel females. The authors suggest that nonconceptive sex may function to restore or maintain a relationship that is under challenge. A variety of data suggest that "reconciliation" (that is, friendly behavior immediately following aggression) may play a similar role in restoring a relationship that has been temporarily disrupted (see Arnold et al. 2010 for review).

Evidence that animals strive to restore and maintain social bonds when challenged finds parallels in studies of humans, where the loss of a close companion is a potent stressor, and individuals show an increased tendency to associate with others when under stress (e.g., Kendler et al. 2005). The number of "core" individuals on whom people rely for support during times of crisis (3–5 individuals) tends to be significantly smaller than their circle of mutual friends (12–20) or regular acquaintances (30–50) (Zhou et al. 2005). In the elderly, strong social networks enhance survival (Giles et al. 2005), and when humans perceive future social opportunities to be limited or at risk—either as they age or when they become ill—they tend to contract their social networks and become more selective in their social relationships (Carstensen 1995).

EVOLUTION

Whatever the underlying mechanisms, individuals in many species seem strongly motivated to form at least one enduring social bond, even though they may be constrained by demography from doing so with a "preferred" partner. Among female baboons, macaques, hyenas, and elephants, where females remain with their matrilineal kin throughout their lives, individuals preferentially form long-term bonds with close relatives such as mothers, daughters, and sisters (Kapsalis 2004, Moss et al. 2010, Silk et al. 2010a, Smith et al. 2010). In most cases these individuals are readily available, and long-term bonds develop naturally from the close bond established at birth between a mother and her daughter. If close kin are not available, however, individuals form long-term bonds with more distant relatives, with age-mates who may be patrilineal siblings, or with unrelated individuals. Regardless of demography, most individuals form at least one enduring social bond (Mitani 2009, Silk et al. 2010a).

In dolphins and horses (where both sexes disperse from their natal group), chimpanzees (where females disperse but male kin remain with their brothers), and lions (*Panthera leo*) and Assamese macaques (*M. assamensis*) (where only males disperse), long-term alliances among males sometimes involve kin. More often, however, they are formed by unrelated individuals (dolphins: Kopps et al. 2010; horses: Cameron et al. 2009; chimpanzees: Mitani 2009; lions: Packer et al. 1991; Assamese macaques: Schulke et al. 2010). In Mitani's study, for example, despite the presence of many maternal and paternal kin pairs, 22 of 28 male chimpanzees formed their most enduring bond with an unrelated individual.

Natural selection therefore appears to have favored individuals who are motivated to form long-term bonds per se, not just bonds with kin. This suggests that long-term bonds (and the motivation to form them) have not evolved simply as an incidental consequence of the close mother-infant relations in species with overlapping generations. Nor can they be explained simply as the result of selection favoring cooperation between any individuals who are close genetic relatives. Instead, long-term bonds have evolved both through inclusive fitness (in species where bonds are formed with kin) and/or through direct fitness (in species where bonds are formed with unrelated individuals). The exact balance between these two selective pathways is likely to be complex. In lions, for example, individuals in small groups of males are more likely to form enduring bonds with unrelated individuals, probably because without such partners they cannot take over a pride of females. As the number of males increases, however, long-term bonds are more likely to be found exclusively among genetic relatives (Packer et al. 1991; see Smith et al. 2010 for review).

Finally, we now have direct evidence that enduring social bonds can increase individuals' reproductive success. Among female baboons, individuals with the most stable, enduring relationships experience higher infant survival (Silk et al. 2003, 2009) and live longer (Silk et al. 2010b) than individuals without such relationships. Among horses, more closely bonded females exhibit higher birth rates and higher infant survivorship (Cameron et al. 2009); a similar phenomenon appears to exist among female dolphins (Frere et al. 2010). Among male dolphins, the formation of a long-term alliance increases a male's reproductive success over what it would have been had no such alliance been formed (Connor et al. 2000). Allied males compete for access to females, and males within a successful alliance appear to share paternity relatively equally (Kopps et al. 2010). Among chimpanzees and Assamese macaques, a male's reproductive success is directly related to his rank, which in turn is directly related to the coalitionary support he receives from others (chimpanzees: Boesch 2009, Constable et al. 2001, Nishida & Hosaka 1996; macaques: Schulke et al. 2010).

These data from the field are consistent with those from the laboratory. In one study, female rats that lived with their sisters differed in the quality of their relationships, and these differences remained stable for months at a time. Sisters that showed the most reciprocal affiliation when young (as measured by approaching, touching, or inspecting) were less vulnerable to stress and less likely to develop tumors at older ages (Yee et al. 2008). As with much of the data reviewed above, the best predictors of an animal's resistance to stress, susceptibility to tumors, morbidity, and mortality were not properties of the individual herself but rather were "structural features of her relationship" with her sister (p. 1057; see also Weidt et al. 2008).

The data also complement those from clinical studies of humans, where social integration has important effects on the cardiovascular, endocrine, and immune systems, effects that appear to be independent of the personality traits of the individuals involved (Uchino et al. 1996). Social integration is also an important predictor of longevity (Eriksson et al. 1999) and mortality (Berkman et al. 2004; see Holt-Lunstad et al. 2010 for review).

SUMMARY

We can see in many group-living mammals the evolutionary origins of human friendship. In horses, elephants, hyenas, dolphins, monkeys, and chimpanzees, evolution has favored the motivation to form close, enduring social bonds either among females, among males, or between males and females. Genetic relatedness affects the formation of friendships. In species such as baboons, macaques, and elephants, where males disperse and females remain in their natal group throughout their lives, friendships are more likely among females, who form enduring bonds with the most obvious category of partners: close matrilineal kin who are brought together from the moment a female is born. By contrast, in species such as chimpanzees and dolphins, where female dispersal is common and males remain together, long-term bonds are more likely among males.

Not all friendships, however, can be traced to kinship. If a female baboon has no mother or daughter present, she forms her strongest bond with a sister or an unrelated animal, often an age-mate. Many male chimpanzees form their strongest bond with an unrelated male. Mares in a herd of horses form stable, enduring bonds despite being unrelated. Natural selection appears to have favored the motivation to form friendships generally, not just friendships with kin.

Friendships are striking because they often involve cooperative interactions that are widely separated in time. One male chimpanzee supports another in a coalition, three days later his partner offers him meat, and over many months the two behaviors are highly correlated. Enduring friendships are thus built, at least in part, on the memory of past interactions and the emotions associated with them.

Applying the term "friendship" to animals is not anthropomorphic. To the contrary, many observations and experiments have shown that animals recognize the close social bonds that exist among others. Results suggest that friendship is an implicit organizing concept, or unit of thought, in the minds of some animals. Naturally, this concept is neither as rich nor explicit as our own, but it is a concept nonetheless, no different from many concepts already documented in studies of animal learning (Seyfarth & Cheney 2011b).

Friendships are adaptive in different ways for males and females. Among males, allies have superior competitive ability, higher dominance rank, and improved reproductive success. Among females, individuals with the strongest, most enduring social bonds experience less stress, higher infant survival, and live longer.

SUMMARY POINTS

1. Close, enduring relationships (or friendships) occur throughout the animal kingdom, particularly among long-lived mammals such as primates, dolphins, and elephants.

2. These bonds are adaptive for the individuals involved. Among males, they increase the individuals' reproductive success; among females, they reduce stress, increase infant survival, and increase longevity.

3. We can therefore see the evolutionary origins of human friendships in the social bonds formed among nonhuman primates.

FUTURE ISSUES

Unresolved questions include:

1. What are the proximate mechanisms that underlie the formation of close, enduring social bonds? Reduced stress? Decreased vulnerability to predation as a result of becoming less peripheral? In males, greater access to mates?

2. What are the evolutionary benefits? In female primates at least, they appear not to include greater defense against predators, greater access to food, or increased rank. They may include better infant survival and increased longevity. How do these benefits arise?

3. What behavioral traits are most closely correlated with the formation of long-term bonds?

4. Finally, scientists have traditionally believed that sociality evolved either to defend resources (usually food) or to defend against predators. Perhaps we should now revise these assumptions, since female (and in some cases male) sociality appears to be adaptive in its own right, independent of food and predators—so important that even in species where females disperse, such as horses and chimpanzees, they strive to establish bonds with other females. Group formation may have evolved not just because it reduces an individual's risk from predation or increases her ability to find food, but also because it provides her with opportunities to form a long-term bond with another individual.

DISCLOSURE STATEMENT

The authors are unaware of any affiliation, funding, or financial holdings that might be perceived as affecting the objectivity of this review.

ACKNOWLEDGMENTS

We thank Filippo Aureli, Catherine Crockford, John Mitani, Gabriele Schino, Joan Silk, and Roman Wittig for comments on earlier drafts.

LITERATURE CITED

Alberts SC, Buchan JC, Altmann J. 2006. Sexual selection in wild baboons: from mating opportunities to paternity success. *Anim. Behav.* 72:1177–96

Alberts SC, Watts HE, Altmann J. 2003. Queuing and queue-jumping: long-term patterns of reproductive skew among male savanna baboons. *Anim. Behav.* 65:821–40

Alcock J. 2009. *Animal Behavior.* Sunderland, MA: Sinauer. 9th ed.

Altmann J. 1979. Age cohorts as paternal sibships. *Behav. Ecol. Sociobiol.* 6:161–64

Arnold K, Fraser ON, Aureli F. 2010. Postconflict reconciliation. In *Primates in Perspective*, ed. CJ Campbell, A Fuentes, KC MacKinnon, SK Bearder, R Stumpf, pp. 608–25. London: Oxford Univ. Press. 2nd ed.

Aureli F, Schaffner CM. 2002. Relationship assessment through emotional mediation. *Behaviour* 139:393–420

Aureli F, Schino G. 2004. The role of emotions in social relationships. In *Macaque Societies: A Model for the Study of Social Organizations*, ed. B Thierry, W Sinsh, W Kaumanns, pp. 38–55. London: Cambridge Univ. Press

Balda RP, Kamil AC. 1992. Long-term spatial memory in Clark's nutcracker, *Nucifraga columbiana*. *Anim. Behav.* 44:761–69

Barrett L, Henzi PS. 2002. Constraints on relationship formation among female primates. *Behaviour* 139:263–89

Beehner JC, Bergman T, Cheney DL, Seyfarth RM, Whitten P. 2005. The effect of new alpha males on female stress in wild chacma baboons. *Anim. Behav.* 69:1211–21

Bergman T, Beehner JC, Cheney DL, Seyfarth RM. 2003. Hierarchical classification by rank and kinship in baboons. *Science* 302:1234–36

Berkman LF, Melchior M, Chastang JF, Niedhammer I, Leclerc A, Goldberg M. 2004. Social integration and mortality: a prospective study of French employees of Electricity of France-Gas of France: the GAZEL cohort. *Am. J. Epidemiol.* 159:167–74

Berman CM. 1980. Early agonistic experience and rank acquisition among free-ranging infant rhesus monkeys. *Int. J. Primatol.* 1:153–70

Black JM. 2001. Fitness consequences of long-term pair bonds in barnacle geese: monogamy in the extreme. *Behav. Ecol.* 12:640–45

Boesch C. 2009. *The Real Chimpanzee: Sex Strategies in the Forest.* London: Cambridge Univ. Press

Brent LJN, Semple S, Dubuc C, Heistermann M, MacLarnon A. 2011. Social capital and physiological stress levels in free-ranging adult female rhesus macaques. *Physiol. Behav.* 102:76–83

Brosnan SF, Schiff HC, de Waal FBM. 2005. Tolerance for inequity may increase with social closeness in chimpanzees. *Proc. Biol. Sci.* 272:253–58

Brosnan SF, Silk JB, Henrich J, Mareno MC, Lambeth SP, Schapiro SJ. 2009. Chimpanzees (*Pan troglodytes*) do not develop contingent reciprocity in an experimental task. *Anim. Cogn.* 12:587–97

Buchan J, Alberts S, Silk JB, Altmann J. 2003. True paternal care in a multi-male primate society. *Nature* 425:179–81

Cameron EZ, Setsaas TH, Linklater WL. 2009. Social bonds between unrelated females increase reproductive success in feral horses. *Proc. Natl. Acad. Sci. USA* 106:13850–53

Carstensen LL. 1995. Evidence for a lifespan theory of socioemotional selectivity. *Curr. Dir. Psychol. Sci.* 4:151–56

Carter CS, Grippo AJ, Pournajafi-Nazarloo H, Ruscio MG, Porges SW. 2008. Oxytocin, vasopressin, and sociality. *Prog. Brain Res.* 170:331–36

Chapais B. 2005. Kinship, competence, and cooperation in primates. In *Cooperation in Primates and Humans: Mechanisms and Evolution*, ed. PM Kappeler, C van Schaik, pp. 47–64. London: Cambridge Univ. Press

Cheney DL, Moscovice L, Heesen M, Mundry R, Seyfarth RM. 2010. Contingent cooperation in wild female baboons. *Proc. Natl. Acad. Sci. USA* 107:9562–67

Cheney DL, Seyfarth RM. 1990. *How Monkeys See the World.* Chicago: Univ. Chicago Press

Cheney DL, Seyfarth RM. 2007. *Baboon Metaphysics.* Chicago: Univ. Chicago Press

Cheney DL, Seyfarth RM. 2009. Stress and coping mechanisms in female primates. *Adv. Stud. Behav.* 39:1–44

Cheney DL, Seyfarth RM. 2011. The evolution of a cooperative social mind. In *Oxford Handbook of Comparative Evolutionary Psychology*, ed. J Vonk, T Shackelford. London: Oxford Univ. Press. In press

Connor RC. 2007. Complex alliance relationships in bottlenose dolphins and a consideration of selective environments for extreme brain size evolution in mammals. *Philos. Trans. R. Soc. Lond. B Biol. Sci.* 362:587–602

Connor RC, Mann J. 2006. Social cognition in the wild: Macchiavellian dolphins? In *Rational Animals?*, ed. S Hurley, M Nudds, pp. 329–70. London: Oxford Univ. Press

Connor RC, Wells RS, Mann J, Read AJ. 2000. The bottlenose dolphin: social relationships in a fission-fusion society. In *Cetacean Societies*, ed. J Mann, RC Connor, PL Tyack, H Whitehead, pp. 91–126. Chicago: Univ. Chicago Press

Constable J, Ashley M, Goodall J, Pusey AE. 2001. Noninvasive paternity assignment in Gombe chimpanzees. *Mol. Ecol.* 10:1279–300

Crockford C, Wittig RM, Seyfarth RM, Cheney DL. 2007. Baboons eavesdrop to deduce mating opportunities. *Anim. Behav.* 73:885–90

Crockford C, Wittig RM, Whitten P, Seyfarth RM, Cheney DL. 2008. Social stressors and coping mechanisms in wild female baboons (*Papio hamadryas ursinus*). *Horm. Behav.* 53:254–65

de Waal FBM. 1997a. The chimpanzee's service economy: food for grooming. *Evol. Hum. Behav.* 18:375–89

de Waal FBM. 1997b. Food transfers through mesh in brown capuchins. *J. Comp. Psychol.* 111:370–78

de Waal FBM. 2000. Attitudinal reciprocity in food sharing among brown capuchin monkeys. *Anim. Behav.* 60:253–61

de Waal FBM. 2008. Putting the altruism back into altruism: the evolution of empathy. *Annu. Rev. Psychol.* 59:279–300

de Waal FBM, Luttrell LM. 1986. The similarity principle underlying social bonding among female rhesus monkeys. *Folia Primatol.* 46:215–34

Engh AL, Beehner JC, Bergman T, Whitten P, Seyfarth RM, Cheney DL. 2006. Behavioural and hormonal responses to predation in female chacma baboons (*Papio hamadryas ursinus*). *Proc. Biol. Sci.* 273:707–12

A very useful review of tests for contingent reciprocity using captive animals.

Demonstrates the reproductive benefits of long-term bonds in dolphins.

Makes a clear argument for the role of emotions in mediating social bonds.

Engh AL, Siebert AR, Greenberg DA, Holekamp K. 2005. Patterns of alliance formation and postconflict aggression indicate spotted hyenas recognize third party relationships. *Anim. Behav.* 69:209–17

Eriksson BG, Hessler RM, Sundh V, Steen B. 1999. Cross-cultural analysis of longevity among Swedish and American elders: the role of social networks in the Gothenburg and Missouri longitudinal studies compared. *Arch. Gerontol. Geriatr.* 28:131–48

Fairbanks LA. 1993. Juvenile vervet monkeys: establishing relationships and practicing skills for the future. In *Juvenile Primates*, ed. ME Pereira, LA Fairbanks, pp. 211–27. London: Oxford Univ. Press

Fernandez-Duqué E, Valeggia C, Mendoza SP. 2009. The biology of paternal care in human and nonhuman primates. *Annu. Rev. Anthropol.* 38:115–30

Frank RE, Silk JB. 2009. Impatient traders or contingent reciprocators? Evidence for the extended time course of grooming exchanges in baboons. *Behaviour* 146:1123–35

Frere CH, Krützen M, Mann J, Connor RC, Bejder L, Sherwin WB. 2010. Social and genetic interactions drive fitness variation in a free-living dolphin population. *Proc. Natl. Acad. Sci. USA* 107:19949–54

Fruteau C, Voelkl B, van Damme E, Noë R. 2009. Supply and demand determine the market value of food providers in wild vervet monkeys. *Proc. Natl. Acad. Sci. USA* 106:12007–12

Gilby C, Wrangham RW. 2008. Association patterns among wild chimpanzees (*Pan troglodytes schweinfurthii*) reflect sex differences in cooperation. *Behav. Ecol. Sociobiol.* 11:1831–42

Giles LC, Glonek GFV, Luszcz MA, Andrews GR. 2005. Effects of social networks on ten year survival in very old Australians: the Australian Longitudinal Study of Ageing. *J. Epidemiol. Community Health* 59:574–79

Gomes CM, Mundry R, Boesch C. 2009. Long-term reciprocation of grooming in wild West African chimpanzees. *Proc. Biol. Sci.* 276:699–706

Goodall J. 1986. *The Chimpanzees of Gombe*. Cambridge, MA: Harvard Univ. Press

Grosenick L, Clement TS, Fernald R. 2007. Fish can infer social rank by observation alone. *Nature* 446:102–4

Harlow HF, Harlow MK. 1965. The affectional systems. In *The Behavior of Nonhuman Primates*, vol. 2, ed. AM Schrier, HF Harlow, F Stollnitz, pp. 287–334. New York: Academic

Hauber ME, Sherman PW. 2001. Self-referent phenotype matching: theoretical considerations and empirical evidence. *Trends Neurosci.* 24:609–16

Hemelrijk C. 1994. Support for being groomed in long-tailed macaques, *Macaca fascicularis*. *Anim. Behav.* 48:479–81

Henzi SP, Barrett L. 2002. Infants as a commodity in a baboon market. *Anim. Behav.* 63:915–21

Henzi SP, Barrett L. 2007. Coexistence in female-bonded primate groups. *Adv. Stud. Behav.* 37:43–81

Hill K, Boesch C, Goodall J, Pusey AE, Williams J, Wrangham R. 2001. Mortality rates among wild chimpanzees. *J. Hum. Evol.* 40:437–50

Hinde RA. 1976. Interactions, relationships, and social structure. *Man* 11:1–17

Hinde RA. 1979. *Towards Understanding Relationships*. London: Academic

Hinde RA. 1987. *Individuals, Relationships, and Culture*. London: Cambridge Univ. Press

Hirsh-Pasek K, Golinkoff R. 1996. *The Origins of Grammar: Evidence from Early Language Comprehension*. Cambridge, MA: MIT Press

Holt-Lunstad J, Smith TB, Layton JB. 2010. Social relationships and mortality risk: a meta-analytic review. *PLoS Med.* 7:e1000316

Judge P. 1982. Redirection of aggression based on kinship in a captive group of pigtail macaques. *Int. J. Primatol.* 3:301

Kapsalis E. 2004. Matrilineal kinship and primate behavior. In *Kinship and Behavior in Primates*, ed. B Chapais, C. Berman, pp. 153–76. London: Oxford Univ. Press

Kapsalis E, Berman CM. 1996. Models of affiliative relationships among female rhesus monkeys (*Macaca mulatta*). I. Criteria for kinship. *Behaviour* 133:1209–34

Kellman PJ, Spelke ES. 1983. Perception of partially occluded objects in infancy. *Cogn. Psychol.* 15:483–524

Kendler KS, Myers J, Prescott CA. 2005. Sex differences in the relationship between social support and risk for major depression: a longitudinal study of opposite sex twin pairs. *Am. J. Psychol.* 162:250–56

Kopps AM, Connor RC, Sherwin WB, Krützen M. 2010. *Direct and indirect fitness benefits of alliance formation in male bottlenose dolphins*. Poster presented at Annu. Meet. Intl. Soc. Behav. Ecol., Perth, Australia

Krützen M, Sherwin WB, Connor RC, Barré LM, Van de Casteele T, et al. 2003. Contrasting relatedness patterns in bottlenose dolphins (*Tursiops* spp.) with different alliance strategies. *Proc. R. Soc. Lond. B* 270:497–502

Kummer H. 1971. *Primate Societies*. Chicago: Aldine

Langergraber K, Mitani JC, Vigilant L. 2007. The limited impact of kinship on cooperation in wild chimpanzees. *Proc. Natl. Acad. Sci. USA* 104:7786–90

Langergraber K, Mitani JC, Vigilant L. 2009. Kinship and social bonds in female chimpanzees (*Pan troglodytes*). *Am. J. Primatol.* 71:840–51

Mann J, Connor RC, Barre JM, Heithaus MR. 2000. Female reproductive success in bottlenose dolphins (*Tursiops* spp.): life history, habitat, provisioning, and group size effects. *Behav. Ecol.* 11:210–19

Mitani JC. 2006. Reciprocal exchanges in chimpanzees and other primates. In *Cooperation in Primates and Humans*, ed. PM Kappeler, C van Schaik, pp. 107–19. Berlin: Springer-Verlag

Mitani JC. 2009. Male chimpanzees form enduring and equitable social bonds. *Anim. Behav.* 77:633–40

Mitani JC, Watts DP, Amsler SJ. 2010. Lethal intergroup aggression leads to territorial expansion in wild chimpanzees. *Curr. Biol.* 20:R507–8

Moscovice L, DiFiore A, Crockford C, Kitchen DM, Wittig RM, et al. 2010. Hedging their bets? Male and female chacma baboons form friendships based on likelihood of paternity. *Anim. Behav.* 79:1007–15

Moss CJ, Croze H, Lee PC, eds. 2010. *The Amboseli Elephants: A Long-Term Perspective on a Long-Lived Mammal*. Chicago: Univ. Chicago Press

Muller M, Mitani JC. 2005. Conflict and cooperation in wild chimpanzees. *Adv. Stud. Behav.* 35:275–331

Newton-Fisher N. 2002. Relationships of male chimpanzees in the Budongo Forest, Uganda. In *Behavioral Diversity in Chimpanzees and Bonobos*, ed. C Boesch, G Hohmann, L Marchant, pp. 125–37. London: Cambridge Univ. Press

Newton-Fisher N. 2004. Hierarchy and social status in Budongo chimpanzees. *Primates* 45:81–87

Nguyen N, Van Horn RC, Alberts SC, Altmann J. 2009. "Friendships" between new mothers and adult males: adaptive benefits and determinants in wild baboons (*Papio cynocephalus*). *Behav. Ecol. Sociobiol.* 63:1331–34

Nishida T, Hosaka K. 1996. Coalition strategies among adult male chimpanzees of the Mahale Mountains, Tanzania. In *Great Ape Societies*, ed. WC McGrew, L Marchant, T Nishida, pp. 114–34. London: Cambridge Univ. Press

Noë R, Hammerstein P. 1994. Biological markets: Supply and demand determine the effect of partner choice in cooperation, mutualism, and mating. *Behav. Ecol. Sociobiol.* 35:1–11

O'Brien TG, Robinson J. 1993. Stability of social relationships in female wedge-capped capuchin monkeys. In *Juvenile Primates*, ed. ME Pereira, LA Fairbanks, pp. 197–210. London: Oxford Univ. Press

Packer CA, Gilbert DA, Pusey AE, O'Brien SJ. 1991. A molecular genetic analysis of kinship and cooperation in African lions. *Nature* 351:562–65

Palombit RA, Cheney DL, Seyfarth RM, Rendall D, Silk JB, et al. 2000. Male infanticide and defense of infants in chacma baboons. In *Male Infanticide and Its Implications*, ed. CP van Schaik, C Janson, pp. 123–51. London: Cambridge Univ. Press

Paz-y-Miño G, Bond AB, Mail AC, Balda RP. 2004. Pinyon jays use transitive inference to predict social dominance. *Nature* 430:778–82

Peake AM, Terry AMR, McGregor PK, Dabelsteen T. 2002. Do great tits assess rivals by combining direct experience with information gathered by eavesdropping? *Proc. R. Soc. Lond. B* 269:1925–29

Perry S, Barrett C, Manson J. 2004. White-faced capuchin monkeys show triadic awareness in their choice of allies. *Anim. Behav.* 67:165–70

Perry S, Manson J, Muniz L, Gros-Louis J, Vigilant L. 2008. Kin-biased social behaviour in wild adult female white-faced capuchins, *Cebus capuchinus. Anim. Behav.* 76:187–99

Povinelli DJ, Vonk J. 2004. We don't need a microscope to explore the chimpanzee's mind. *Mind Lang.* 19:1–28

Schino G. 2001. Grooming, competition, and social rank among female primates: a meta-analysis. *Anim. Behav.* 62:265–71

An excellent empirical study of long-term bonds in wild chimpanzees.

Schino G. 2007. Grooming and agonistic support: a meta-analysis of primate reciprocal altruism. *Behav. Ecol.* 18:115–20

Schino G, Aureli F. 2009. Reciprocal altruism in primates: partner choice, cognition, and emotions. *Adv. Stud. Behav.* 39:45–69

Schino G, diGiuseppe F, Visalberghi E. 2009. Grooming, rank, and agonistic support in tufted capuchin monkeys. *Am. J. Primatol.* 71:101–5

Schino G, Polizzi di Sorrentino E, Tiddi B. 2007. Grooming and coalitions in Japanese macaques (*Macaca fuscata*): partner choice and the time frame of reciprocation. *J. Comp. Psychol.* 121:181–88

Schino G, Ventura R, Troisi A. 2003. Grooming among female Japanese macaques: distinguishing between reciprocation and exchange. *Behav. Ecol.* 14:887–91

Schülke O, Bhagavatula J, Vigilant L, Ostner J. 2010. Social bonds enhance reproductive success in male macaques. *Curr. Biol.* 20:1–4

Seyfarth RM. 1977. A model of social grooming among adult female monkeys. *J. Theor. Biol.* 65:671–98

Seyfarth RM, Cheney DL. 1984. Grooming, alliances, and reciprocal altruism in vervet monkeys. *Nature* 308:541–43

Seyfarth RM, Cheney DL. 2011a. Knowledge of social relations. In *The Evolution of Primate Societies*, ed. J Mitani, J Call, P Kappeler, R Palombit, J Silk. Chicago: Univ. Chicago Press. In press

Seyfarth RM, Cheney DL. 2011b. The evolution of concepts about agents. In *The Development of Social Cognition*, ed. M Banaji, S Gelman. London: Oxford Univ. Press

Shettleworth SJ. 2010. *Cognition, Evolution and Behaviour*. London: Oxford Univ. Press. 2nd ed.

Silk JB. 1999. Male bonnet macaques use information about third party rank relationships to recruit allies. *Anim. Behav.* 58:45–51

Silk JB. 2005. Practicing Hamilton's rule: kin selection in primate groups. In *Cooperation in Primates and Humans: Mechanisms and Evolution*, ed. PM Kappeler, C van Schaik, pp. 25–46. Cambridge: Cambridge Univ. Press

Silk JB. 2007. The strategic dynamics of cooperation in primate groups. *Adv. Stud. Behav.* 37:1–41

Silk JB, Alberts S, Altmann J. 2003. Social bonds of female baboons enhance infant survival. *Science* 302:1331–34

Silk JB, Alberts S, Altmann J. 2006a. Social relationships among adult female baboons (*Papio cynocephalus*). II. Variation in the quality and stability of social bonds. *Behav. Ecol. Sociobiol.* 61:197–204

Silk JB, Altmann J, Alberts S. 2006b. Social relationships among adult female baboons (*Papio cynocephalus*). I. Variation in the strength of social bonds. *Behav. Ecol. Sociobiol.* 61:183–95

Silk JB, Beehner JC, Bergman T, Crockford C, Engh AL, et al. 2009. The benefits of social capital: Close bonds among female baboons enhance offspring survival. *Proc. R. Soc. Lond. B* 276:3099–104

Silk JB, Beehner JC, Bergman T, Crockford C, Engh AL, et al. 2010a. Female chacma baboons form strong, equitable, and enduring social bonds. *Behav. Ecol. Sociobiol.* 64:1733–47

Silk JB, Beehner JC, Bergman T, Crockford C, Engh AL, et al. 2010b. Strong and consistent social bonds enhance the longevity of female baboons. *Curr. Biol.* 20:1359–61

Slocombe KE, Townsend SW, Zuberbuhler K. 2009. Wild chimpanzees (*Pan troglodytes schweinfurthii*) distinguish between different scream types: evidence from a playback study. *Anim. Cog.* 12:441–49

Slocombe KE, Zuberbuhler K. 2005. Agonistic screams in wild chimpanzees (*Pan troglodytes schweinfurthii*) vary as a function of social role. *J. Comp. Psychol.* 119:67–77

Slocombe KE, Zuberbuhler K. 2007. Chimpanzees modify recruitment screams as a function of audience composition. *Proc. Natl. Acad. Sci. USA* 104:17228–33

Smith JE, Van Horn RC, Powning KS, Cole AR, Graham KE, et al. 2010. Evolutionary forces favoring intragroup coalitions among spotted hyenas and other animals. *Behav. Ecol.* 21:284–303

Snowdon CT, Pieper BA, Boe CY, Cronin KA, Kurian AV, Ziegler TE. 2010. Variation in oxytocin is related to variation in affiliative behavior in monogamous, pairbonded tamarins. *Horm. Behav.* 58:614–18

Snowdon CT, Ziegler TE. 2007. Growing up cooperatively: family processes and infant development in marmosets and tamarins. *J. Dev. Proc.* 2:40–66

Turner LM, Young AR, Römpler H, Schöneberg T, Phelps SM, Hoekstra HE. 2010. Monogamy evolves through multiple mechanisms: evidence from V1aR in deer mice. *Mol. Biol. Evol.* 27:1269–78

Makes a clear argument for the role of emotions in mediating social bonds.

Demonstrates the reproductive benefits of long-term bonds in baboons.

Demonstrates the reproductive benefits of long-term bonds in baboons.

Demonstrates the reproductive benefits of long-term bonds in baboons.

Uchino BN, Cacioppo JT, Kiecolt-Glaser JK. 1996. The relationship between social support and physiological processes: a review with emphasis on underlying mechanisms and implications for health. *Psychol. Bull.* 119:488–531

Uvnas-Moberg K. 1997. Physiological and endocrine effects of social contact. In *The Integrative Neurobiology of Affiliation*, ed. CS Carter, I Lederhendler, B Kirkpatrick, pp. 245–62. Cambridge, MA: MIT Press

Watanabe K. 2001. A review of 50 years of research on the Japanese monkeys of Koshima: status and dominance. In *Primate Origins of Human Cognition and Behavior*, ed. T Matsuzawa, pp. 405–17. Berlin: Springer-Verlag

Watts D. 1998. Coalitionary mate-guarding by male chimpanzees at Ngogo, Kibale National Park, Uganda. *Behav. Ecol. Sociobiol.* 44:43–55

Watts D. 2000a. Grooming between male chimpanzees at Ngogo, Kibale National Park. I. Partner number and grooming and reciprocity. *Int. J. Primatol.* 21:189–210

Watts D. 2000b. Grooming between male chimpanzees at Ngogo, Kibale National Park. II. Male rank and priority of access to partners. *Int. J. Primatol.* 21:211–38

Watts DP. 2002. Reciprocity and interchange in the social relationships of wild male chimpanzees. *Behaviour* 139:343–70

Watts DP, Mitani JC. 2001. Boundary patrols and intergroup encounters in wild chimpanzees. *Behaviour* 138:299–327

Weidt A, Hofmann SE, Konig B. 2008. Not only mate choice matters: fitness consequences of social partner choice in female house mice. *Anim. Behav.* 75:801–8

Weingrill T, Lycett JC, Henzi SP. 2000. Consortship and mating success in chacma baboons (*Papio cynocephalus ursinus*). *Ethology* 106:1033–44

Wells R. 2003. Dolphin social complexity: lessons from long-term study and life history. In *Animal Social Complexity*, ed. FBM de Waal, P Tyack, pp. 32–56. Cambridge, MA: Harvard Univ. Press

Widdig A, Nurnberg P, Krawczak M, Streich WJ, Bercovitch F. 2001. Paternal relatedness and age proximity regulate social relationships among adult female rhesus macaques. *Proc. Natl. Acad. Sci. USA* 98:13768–73

Widdig A, Streich WJ, Nürnberg P, Croucher PJP, Bercovitch F, Krawczak M. 2006. Paternal kin bias in the agonistic interventions of adult female rhesus macaques (*Macaca mulatta*). *Behav. Ecol. Sociobiol.* 61:205–14

Wittig RM. 2010. The function and cognitive underpinnings of post-conflict affiliation in wild chimpanzees. In *The Mind of the Chimpanzee*, ed. EV Lonsdorf, SR Ross, T Matsuzawa, pp. 208–19. Chicago: Univ. Chicago Press

Wittig RM, Boesch C. 2003a. The choice of post-conflict interactions in wild chimpanzees (*Pan troglodytes*). *Behaviour* 140:1527–59

Wittig RM, Boesch C. 2003b. Food competition and linear dominance hierarchy among female chimpanzees of the Tai National Park. *Int. J. Primatol.* 24:847–67

Wittig RM, Boesch C. 2010. Receiving post-conflict affiliation from the enemy's friend reconciles former opponents. *PLoS One* 5:e13995

Wittig RM, Crockford C, Lehmann J, Whitten PL, Seyfarth RM, Cheney DL. 2008. Focused grooming networks and stress alleviation in wild female baboons. *Horm. Behav.* 54:170–77

Wittig RM, Crockford C, Wikberg E, Seyfarth RM, Cheney DL. 2007. Kin-mediated reconciliation substitutes for direct reconciliation in female baboons. *Proc. R. Soc. Lond. B* 274:1109–15

Yamada M. 1963. A study of blood relationship in the natural society of the Japanese macaque: an analysis of co-feeding, grooming, and playmate relationships in Minoo-B troop. *Primates* 4:43–65

Yee JR, Cavigelli SA, Delgado B, McClintock M. 2008. Reciprocal affiliation among adolescent rats during a mild group stressor predicts mammary tumors and lifespan. *Psychosom. Med.* 70:1050–59

Zhou WX, Sornette D, Hill RA, Dunbar RIM. 2005. Discrete hierarchical organization of social group size. *Proc. R. Soc. Lond. B* 272:439–44

Religion, Morality, Evolution

Paul Bloom

Department of Psychology, Yale University, New Haven, Connecticut 06520;
email: paul.bloom@yale.edu

Annu. Rev. Psychol. 2012. 63:179–99

First published online as a Review in Advance on
September 21, 2011

The *Annual Review of Psychology* is online at
psych.annualreviews.org

This article's doi:
10.1146/annurev-psych-120710-100334

Keywords

altruism, atheism, faith, kindness, prejudice, religiosity, supernatural
belief

Abstract

How did religion evolve? What effect does religion have on our moral
beliefs and moral actions? These questions are related, as some scholars
propose that religion has evolved to enhance altruistic behavior toward
members of one's group. I review here data from survey studies (both
within and across countries), priming experiments, and correlational
studies of the effects of religion on racial prejudice. I conclude that
religion has powerfully good moral effects and powerfully bad moral
effects, but these are due to aspects of religion that are shared by other
human practices. There is surprisingly little evidence for a moral effect
of specifically religious beliefs.

Contents

INTRODUCTION

Psychologists typically ignore religion. It is barely mentioned in introductory textbooks, and the best journals rarely publish papers on the topic. Religion is seen as an exotic specialty area, like sexual fetishes or the detection of random number sequences.

This neglect isn't limited to psychology proper. McCauley & Whitehouse (2005, p. 3) note: "... as with so many contemporary intellectuals, cognitive scientists, until quite recently, have mostly found topics like religion to be an embarrassment." They add: "No topic—not even sex, death, taxes, or terrorism—can elicit any more quirky, unpredictable responses from intellectuals than religion." Religion is like sex to a Victorian or dreams to a behaviorist—an awkward and embarrassing phenomenon best not talked about. Many would go further and insist that religion isn't a fit topic for science at all. To study it as a psychologist is to commit the sins of "scientism" and "reductionism" (see Wieseltier 2006 for such an attack).

Since this article explores religious belief and practice, it's worth addressing this concern at the outset. One way to do so is to insist on a distinction made by David Hume. In 1757, Hume began *The Natural History of Religion* with this: "As every enquiry which regards religion is of the utmost importance, there are two questions in particular which challenge our attention, to wit, that concerning its foundation in reason, and that concerning its origin in human nature" (p. 21).

There is a lot to be said about Hume's first question and whether it is the proper focus of empirical inquiry. Some scholars believe that religion's "foundation in reason" falls within the realm of science, while others disagree. But the second question—religion's "origin in human nature"—is bread-and-butter psychology. How could psychology *not* address such an important domain of belief, motivation, and action? Critically, the psychology of religion can be studied independently of one's belief about the truth of religious claims. Regardless of whether God exists, for instance, the question remains as to why so many people believe he does (see Bloom 2009).

Why should psychologists be interested in the topic? One consideration is the universality of religious belief. Most people characterize themselves as belonging to a religion—typically Christianity and Islam; about half of the 6.9 billion people on Earth see themselves as falling into one of these two faiths. Most people engage in various religious practices, such as circumcision and church going and obeying dietary restrictions, and most people hold religious beliefs, such as believing in God or in life after death.

Religion is ubiquitous in the United States, where well over 90% of the population claims to believe in God, and about 40% believe that Jesus Christ will return to Earth in the next half century (Appiah 2006). America is admittedly unusual compared to the countries of Western Europe, where the citizens are less likely to affiliate themselves with a religion and where they often claim not to believe in God. But looking at the world as a whole, it is Western Europe that is the exception. American religiosity sits well with the countries of Asia and Africa and the rest of the Americas—that is, most of the rest of the planet.

Within the United States, there are political and social divides, and these correspond to religiosity in the expected ways, with conservatives being more religious than liberals. But religion is not limited to a conservative subgroup. Most people who identify themselves as Democrats pray daily or more often, and the vast majority believe in life after death (Waldman 2004). Even most American academics, who are among the more secular and liberal members of our species, are religious. A recent study of 40,000 faculty members at 421 colleges (Lindholm et al. 2006) found that almost two thirds said that they considered themselves religious either "to some extent" (29%) or "to a great extent" (35%).

In 1916, a large selection of scientists were asked whether they believe in God, and the question was framed in a fairly strict manner, referring to a God who one could pray to and actually get an answer from. Even with this high bar, about 40% of scientists said yes—the same percentage found in a similar poll in 1996 (Larson & Witham 1997). Only when we look at the most elite scientists—members of the National Academy of Sciences—do we find a strong majority of atheists and agnostics (Larson & Witham 1998).

Finally, religion is highly relevant to many people's lives (Shermer 2003). Religious activities are a major source of everyday pleasure (Bloom 2010). And many important contemporary social and political debates—over gay marriage, abortion, capital punishment, stem cell research, the teaching of evolution in schools, and so on—are affected by people's religious views. It is impossible to make sense of most of human existence, including law, morality, war, and culture, without some appreciation of religion and how it works.

TWO PUZZLES

Religion and Morality

The main focus of this review is the effect of religious belief and religious affiliation on our moral lives. To put it crudely, does religion make people good, does it make them bad, or does it have no effect at all?

Many people think they know the answer. In a 2007 Gallup poll, most Americans said that they would not vote for an otherwise qualified atheist to be president—they were more willing to vote for a Mormon, a Jew, or a homosexual. Another study found that people ranked atheists lower than Muslims, recent immigrants, and homosexuals in "sharing their vision of American society" and were least willing to allow their children to marry them (Edgell et al. 2006). When asked why there were so set against atheists, the answers had to do with morality:

> Some people view atheists as problematic because they associate them with illegality, such as drug use and prostitution—that is, with immoral people who threaten respectable community from the lower end of the status hierarchy. Others saw atheists as rampant materialists and cultural elitists that threaten common values from above—the ostentatiously wealthy who make a lifestyle out of consumption or the cultural elites who think they know better than everyone else. Both of these themes rest on a view of atheists as self-interested individualists who are not concerned with the common good (pp. 225, 227).

This distrust of atheists is shared by many scholars, including those who are otherwise seen as champions of the Enlightenment. John Locke, for instance, did not believe that atheists should be allowed to hold office. He wrote (1689, p. 51): "Promises, covenants, and oaths, which are the bonds of human society, can have no hold upon an atheist" (quoted by Haidt & Kesebir 2010).

There are other scholars who hold the opposite view, arguing that religion makes people worse. Most would agree, after all, that religious fanaticism and extremism can sometimes drive people to do terrible things, and many would agree as well that certain everyday religious practices and beliefs can have a dark side. Examples might include the persecution of homosexuals, the murdering of heretics, and incitements to holy war. As Blaise Pascal pointed out, "Men never do evil so completely and cheerfully as when they do it from a religious conviction." Even Pope Benedict XVI conceded this, noting: "There exist pathologies in religion that are extremely dangerous" (cited by Myers 2008).

Some would take this further, arguing that religion in general has a corrosive effect of our moral lives. Hitchens (2007, p. 56), for instance, argues that religion is "violent, irrational, intolerant, allied to racism and tribalism and bigotry, invested in ignorance and hostile to free inquiry, contemptuous of women and coercive toward children" (see Myers 2008 for discussion). Batson (1976, p. 30) argued that religion is "a double agent": "Espousing the highest good, seeking to make all men brothers, religion has produced the Crusades, the Inquisition and an unending series of witch hunts. Virtually every organized religion has been the excuse, if not the cause, for violent, inhumane, and antisocial acts."

To some extent, the question of the effects of religion falls outside the domain of psychology. Debates about the moral effects of religion are often framed with reference to data from history and sociology and anthropology: Participants in these debates tally up all of the good and all of the bad done by the religious and the nonreligious, and argue about who comes off better in the end. (As I put it in an earlier article, "I see your Crusades and raise you Stalin!") From this standpoint, this question of the moral effects of religion is similar to arguments over the merits of parliamentary democracy, free trade, or the legalization of drugs. These are empirical questions, at least in part, but they are best

addressed through the study of societies, not through psychological research into the minds of individuals.

Still, as we have seen, many believe that religion does have an effect on individuals within a society, and they argue, plausibly enough, that policy implications follow from this. Brooks (2006), for instance, argues that religion makes individuals both happier and kinder, and concludes that organizations such as the American Civil Liberties Union, which seek to staunch displays of religiosity, are harming society. On the other side, the so-called New Atheists, a group that includes Christopher Hitchens, Daniel Dennett, Sam Harris, and Richard Dawkins, argue that religious belief is not just factually mistaken, but makes us worse people. If so, then rational and moral individuals should work toward its demise.

To put the importance of the issue in perspective, consider that psychologists spend great energy exploring whether violent video games have a negative effect on children. Could anyone doubt that the question of the moral effects of Islam and Christianity—practices far more widespread than *Grand Theft Auto*—is at least as interesting?

Evolution of Religion

A second question about religion that I address here is why it exists in the first place. Religion poses certain difficult and intriguing puzzles for anyone interested in the evolution of the human mind.

Consider first the problem of religious beliefs. Nonreligious beliefs that people hold include:

- Unsupported things fall to the ground.
- The sun rises in the morning.
- One plus one equals two.

Such beliefs make Darwinian sense because they are true of the world in which we live. This makes it plausible that they could either arise directly through natural selection (because it is usually adaptive for animals to know true things), or they could arise indirectly through natural selection (because we have evolved fairly accurate mechanisms of perception and learning and can use these mechanisms to learn true things).

Consider now religious beliefs such as:

- God created the universe.
- When people die, they go to heaven or to hell.
- Christ was born from a virgin.

These beliefs illustrate, as H.L. Mencken put it, humanity's "stupendous capacity for believing the incredible." Mencken was an atheist, but even a theist would agree that these beliefs really are incredible in the sense that they don't arise in any clear way from our usual systems for apprehending the world. We can see dogs and trees; we cannot (in any literal sense) see God. The propensity to form such beliefs could be innate, but this raises the question of how such a propensity could have evolved.

Religious activities pose an even more difficult puzzle. Just as with beliefs, many of the nonreligious activities that people choose to do are related in some sense to the dictates of natural selection—eating, drinking, fornicating, caring for children, establishing social relationships, and so on. The psychological mechanisms underlying these behaviors can be seen as adaptations. There are also many activities that don't have obvious selectionist explanations, such as music and art; these can often be understood as by-products of adaptations (see Bloom 2010).

But religious activities fall into a third rather mysterious category. It is not merely that they don't have obvious survival value; it is that they seem maladaptive from a Darwinian standpoint. Religious practices include mutilating one's body, sacrificing valuable goods, choosing celibacy, and so on. One might have expected any desire to engage in such activities to be weeded out by the unforgiving sieve of natural selection. Why this hasn't happened is another of the mysteries that any theory of the evolution of religion has to address.

The study of the origin of religion connects in interesting ways to issues of morality. One increasingly popular theory sees religion as an evolved solution to the problem of bringing together communities of people; religious belief and practice exist to instill cooperation and group feelings, to motivate kindness and compassion to other members of one's tribe. This review critically evaluates this proposal.

In the course of this exploration, I discuss a range of research programs. As noted above, there isn't as much research on the topic as one would hope. Furthermore, the research that does exist is carried out by intellectual communities that don't tend to read one another's work. There is a tradition in social psychology, for instance, that focuses on the relationship between religion and prejudice, and there is another tradition that explores the effect of religious primes on generosity and altruism—and they don't tend to cite one another. The parable of the blind men and the elephant is overused, but here it seems apt. One goal of this article, then, is simply to review and synthesize research. More ambitious goals are to show that these findings can be integrated in a satisfying way and to make some substantive claims about religion, morality, and evolution.

SENSES OF RELIGION

What do we mean when we talk about religion? We can consider three main senses.

One sense of "religion" corresponds to a certain type of transcendent or mystical experience. This was the topic of William James's (1902) classic *The Varieties of Religious Experience*. James was interested in "the feelings, acts, and experiences of individual men in their solitude, so far as they apprehend themselves to stand in relation to whatever they may consider the divine" (p. 31). The contemporary scholars who continue this tradition include those who explore the emotion of awe (e.g., Keltner 2009) and those who study the neuropsychology of religious visions (e.g., Persinger 2001).

A second sense has to do with supernatural beliefs. In 1871, the anthropologist Edward Tylor argued that the "minimum definition of religion" is a belief in spiritual beings, in the supernatural. Much of the work in the psychology and cognitive science of religion concerns the question of why we have such beliefs—why we believe in Gods, spirits, and so on (e.g., Bloom 2004).

A third conception of religion is as a certain sort of social activity, what one does with other people. As we will see, this is the conception that most connects with claims about the evolution of religion and its relationship to morality.

One can be "religious" in these three distinct ways, then, and each of the three senses of religion can exist in the absence of the others. One can experience transcendent experience without any specific beliefs and affiliation; this is what is often meant when people describe themselves as "spiritual." Even some ardent atheists discuss and seek out such transcendent experiences, as in meditative practice. Or one might hold supernatural beliefs without affiliating with a religion or having any transcendent experiences—these individuals are what David Hume called "superstitious atheists." Indeed, most who insist that they have no religious affiliation still believe that they will survive the death of their bodies (Putnam & Campbell 2010). Finally, one can belong to a community that is a religion in every sense except that its adherents don't engage in transcendent experience or believe in supernatural beings. Zuckerman (2008) notes that this is the case for many Christians in Scandinavian countries.

As an exercise, one could continue to mix and match, describing all eight permutations of the above three features. I won't do this here. Note that although these notions of religion are separable, they do tend to fall together. That is, most of those who characterize themselves as adhering to Christianity, Islam, Judaism, Hinduism, and other religions are religious in the sense that they have certain experiences and that they hold certain beliefs and that they engage in certain practices.

RELIGION AND MORALITY: POSSIBLE CONNECTIONS

How might religion, characterized in any of the above ways, affect morality? How can it influence one's views about right and wrong, the extent of one's altruism or selfishness, and so on?

One possibility emphasizes the fact that religions make explicit moral claims that their followers accept. Through holy texts and the proclamations of authority figures, religions make moral claims about abortion, homosexuality, duties to the poor, charity, masturbation, just war, and so on. People believe these claims because, implicitly or explicitly, they trust the sources. They accept them on faith.

This sort of deference is common; many of our moral and political and scientific beliefs have this sort of deferential nature, where we hold a belief because it is associated with our community or with people that we trust. Upon hearing about a welfare plan proposed by a political party, for instance, people are more likely to agree with the plan if it has been proposed by their own political party—although, interestingly, they are not conscious that this is occurring; they mistakenly believe that their judgment is based on the objective merit of the program (Cohen 2003). Most people who claim to believe in natural selection do so not because they are persuaded by the data—indeed, most have no real understanding of what natural selection is—but rather because they trust the scientists (see Bloom & Weisberg 2007).

A second way in which religion can have an effect is by emphasizing certain aspects of morality. As one case of this, Cohen & Rozin (2001) note that Christianity codifies the principle that thoughts are to some extent equivalent to actions. This is expressed in Christ's dictum: "You have heard that it was said 'you shall not commit adultery'; but I say to you, that everyone who looks at a woman with lust for her has already committed adultery with her in her heart." Judaism, in contrast, focuses less on intentions and more on actions. Cohen and Rozin find that this difference has an effect on the intuitions that individual Christians and Jews have about specific situations. For instance, Christians and Jews have different moral evaluations of a person who doesn't like his parents but chooses to take good care of them nonetheless. For the Christians, the person's attitude matters more than it does for the Jews—the Christians judge him more negatively because of his mental states.

More generally, religions tend to emphasize certain aspects of morality that are less important to an atheist. These include what Shweder et al. (1997, p. 138) describe as an "ethics of divinity": a cluster of ethical notions that rely on concepts such as "sacred order, natural order, tradition, sanctity, sin, and pollution. . . [an ethics that] aims to protect the soul, the spirit, the spiritual aspects of the human agent and 'nature' from degradation." There is an especially tight connection between religion and the moralization of purity, particularly in the domains of food and sex (see Graham & Haidt 2010).

Finally, it might be that religion has a more general effect. Religion might turn the dials of compassion. Religious belief and practice might increase one's empathy and caring and love. It might also increase one's prejudice and intolerance, particularly toward those who are seen as outside of the community. Such effects might be triggered by the messages that religions convey or might somehow emerge from the very nature of religious practice and activity. Much of the discussion that follows focuses on this proposal.

MORALITY AND THE EVOLUTIONARY ORIGIN OF RELIGION

One popular view among psychologists who write about the evolution of religion is that religion is an accident. Under this view, religion is a by-product of other evolved systems or traits, what is sometimes described as a "spandrel" (see Gould & Lewontin 1979). It is not the case, under this view, that humans are religious because our more religious ancestors

outlived and outproduced our less religious ancestors. Rather, religion emerges out of capacities, traits, and inclinations that have evolved for other purposes. It is an evolutionary accident.

More specifically, the notion is that certain universal religious beliefs—such as belief in supernatural beings, creationism, miracles, and body-soul dualism—emerge as by-products of certain cognitive systems that have evolved for understanding the physical and social world (for different versions of this proposal, see Atran 2004; Barrett 2004; Bloom 2004, 2007, 2009; Boyer 2001; Evans 2000, 2001; Guthrie 1993; Kelemen 2004; Pinker 1997; Pyysiäinen 2003; see Bloom 2009 for review).

One of the best-known examples of this approach is the theory that humans are highly sensitive to cues to animacy and intention; we are constantly on the lookout for other humans and nonhuman animals, for clear adaptive reasons. This leads us to sometimes assume the existence of entities that don't really exist and hence provides the foundation for animism and deism (Guthrie 1993; see also Barrett's 2004 proposal of a Hyperactive Agency Detection Device). As another example, I have argued that the cognitive systems that underlie "theory of body" and "theory of mind" are functionally and neurologically distinct. As a consequence of this, we think about bodies and minds as distinct sorts of things, which may explain why we are natural-born dualists, why we so naturally believe in immaterial souls, in spirits, and in ghosts and reincarnation (Bloom 2004).

When it comes to explaining religious beliefs, such theories have the virtue of simplicity because they posit no special cognitive capacities beyond what we already have. They also have some empirical support. For instance, if belief in God and other deities is caused by an overextension of social cognition, then adults who fall on the autism spectrum disorder, who have diminished social cognition, should be less prone to believe in a feeling God, and there is some evidence that this is the case (Bering 2002). Women are arguably more sensitive to the mental states of others (see Baron-Cohen

2003), which is nicely consistent with the well-known finding that women tend to be more religious than men. Further, the development of religious and supernatural beliefs in children seems to track the emergence of more general theory-of-mind capacities (e.g., Bloom 2004, Lane et al. 2010).

One problem with this accident view, however, is its narrowness. At best, it explains religious belief. But it says nothing about transcendent experience, religious rituals, or the social nature of religion.

Over the past decade or so, an alternative perspective on religion has emerged that might fill some of these gaps. Religion, under this view, is a constellation of behaviors and thoughts that have evolved to benefit groups, and, in particular, to help solve the problem of free-riders. A community works best if everyone cooperates on certain tasks, such as group hunting, care of children, and warfare. But individual members of the community might benefit from defecting, from accepting the benefits of this cooperative behavior without paying the cost. Religion is arguably a solution to the problem of defection. As Haidt (2007) nicely put it, "Religions, generally speaking, work to suppress our inner chimp and bring out our inner bee" (see also Haidt 2012 for an extended discussion).

This might be one function of rituals (see Alcorta & Sosis 2005, Atran & Norenzayan 2004, Bulbulia 2004, Irons 2004; see Finkel et al. 2010 for review). Consider again the sorts of activities that people do when they are members of a religion: cutting away part of one's genitals (or one's child's genitals), spending a potentially productive day doing nothing, refusing to eat tasty and nutritious foods, enduring agonizing initiation rites, and so on. The painful, difficult, and time-consuming aspects of these rituals seem entirely mysterious until you consider that these negative aspects may be the very point behind their existence. From a costly signaling perspective, these serve as hurdles that weed out the uncommitted: "If fulfilling these obligations is more costly for nonbelievers than believers, then cooperation

can emerge and stabilize" (Finkel et al. 2010, p. 290).[1]

Other religious activities create bonds between members of a group. This might also help with the free-rider problems—to the extent that you feel emotionally close to another, you are less likely to betray him or her. Some ritual activities generate what Durkheim (1912) called "collective effervescence." Dancing and chanting are the best cases of this. Most of us are familiar with the emotional rush of linking arms and dancing at a Jewish wedding, or being at a rave, or dancing in a pub with drunken friends. Laboratory studies find this synchrony has prosocial effects, leading people to sacrifice more money to others in economic games (Wiltermuth & Heath 2009). Indeed, even simple mimicry can increase empathy (Chartrand & Bargh 1999). The reason why this works is unclear; one possibility is that it is due to a glitch in the system. If I dance with others, and they move with me, their bodies moving as I intend my own body to move, it confuses me into expanding the boundaries of my self to include them (Bloom 2010). Regardless of its cause, religions might exploit this fact about our minds in order to increase ingroup solidarity.

To show that this evolutionary theory is correct, however, it's not enough to demonstrate that such activities bring people together as a cohesive and cooperative group. One also has to present evidence that this is why these activities have evolved in the first place; it's what they are *for*. Such evidence is hard to find, but not impossible. One prediction that the evolutionary account does make, for instance, is that the extent to which religious rituals are practiced by a

---

[1] One different interpretation of these rituals builds on the classic cognitive dissonance finding that if you sacrifice to belong to a group, you'll be more committed to that group (e.g., Festinger 1957). Someone who gives up time to work for a political party, say, will be more committed to the party than someone who gets a salary; a patient who pays for therapy will value it more than someone who gets it for free. This is why fraternities and other communities have painful and humiliating hazing rituals. From this perspective, participation in unpleasant religious rituals can be seen as a form of hazing, evolved to increase fidelity to a group.

group should relate to the success of that group. Consistent with this, religious groups that have many costly rituals tend to outlast those that have fewer (Sosis & Bressler 2003).

I have been framing this proposal so far in terms of what's good for the group, as this is the approach that many of its proponents take. A propensity for religious ritual is in our genes, then, not because of the advantages it gives to individuals, but because of the advantages that it gives to the groups that the individuals belong to (e.g., Wilson 2002, 2007). Such an appeal to group selection is controversial, to say the least (Williams 1966; see Sober & Wilson 2011 for discussion). And many would argue that it's unnecessary here and that one can explain the evolution of social traits that suppress free-riders using a more standard Darwinian approach (e.g., Cosmides 1989). This is an interesting debate, though unfortunately one that falls outside the scope of this review.

A quite different approach is sometimes known as "cultural group selection," (Boyd & Richerson 2002, Norenzayan & Shariff 2008). Religion, including religious rituals, might emerge through cultural evolution: Societies that have religion would outlast those that do not. This process can occur without genetic change, and hence, unlike the biological approach, this cultural theory does not predict that our psychologies would be naturally oriented to the creation and practice of religion. Note, however, that biological evolution and cultural evolution are compatible. It might be, for instance, that some aspects of religion initially evolved through natural selection and then cultural evolution kicked in to enhance and transform them (see Norenzayan & Gervais 2012 for discussion).

In both its biological and cultural forms, this free-rider theory focuses on rituals and on community. What about supernatural beliefs? It's possible that these too can be seen as existing for a social function. One specific proposal is that a belief in an omniscient supernatural entity might make people nicer to those with whom they are in constant contact (Bering 2006, 2011; Norenzayan & Shariff 2008). After all, we cheat less and give more when we think someone else is watching. And so belief in an omniscient God might be a clever mechanism—emerging in biological evolution or cultural evolution—that exploits this fact about human nature. Similarly, it is not hard to see how belief in heaven and hell can play a similar role (Johnson 2005, Johnson & Bering 2006). Just like rituals then, religious beliefs might evolve to serve a prosocial function.

MORALITY WITHOUT RELIGION?

How can we tell if religion has an effect on morality?

It is difficult. The standard way to look at the effect of X on human behavior (where X might be exposure to violent video games, testosterone, spanking, psychoanalysis. . . or religion) is to compare people who have been exposed to X to those who haven't. This can be done through correlational studies (do children who have been spanked turn out differently from those who haven't?) or, better, through controlled experiments (what happens if you give a randomly selected subset of patients a certain form of therapy?).

But what if X is everywhere? What if everyone is exposed to X? The dilemma we face is that religion seems to be inescapable. As de Waal (2010) puts it, "It is impossible to know what morality would look like without religion. It would require a visit to a human culture that is not now and never was religious." There are of course relatively atheistic communities and individuals, but many of the customs and morals that they adhere to have emerged long before they became atheistic. One might argue then that the kindness (or cruelty) of such individuals and societies exists only because they ride the coattails of religion.

Still, we do have some access to populations without religion. Indeed, de Waal himself, in the same article, goes on at length about altruism, empathy, and even rudimentary notions of fairness and justice in chimpanzees, bonobos, and monkeys (see also de Waal 1996, 2010).

Consider also the demonstrations of moral, or at least proto-moral, behavior in babies and toddlers, including empathetic responses to the pain of others (e.g., Hoffman 2000), spontaneous altruistic behavior (e.g., Warneken & Tomasello 2006), and some capacity to judge individuals on the basis of their behavior to others (e.g., Hamlin et al. 2007).

We can be confident, then, that at least some good behavior exists prior to religion. This refutes the strong claim that morality requires religion. Then again, an advocate of the importance of religion to morality will respond by pointing out that there are all sorts of moral capacities that chimps and babies don't have, and it is at least possible that the reason they aren't fully moral beings is that they don't have religion.

What about studies with adult humans? Since researchers who study this population aren't able to contrast X from non-X, they do the next best thing and compare more X with less X. And so the studies that explore the effect of religion on our moral lives do so by comparing individuals within cultures that used to be religious but now are not entirely so (such as Danes) versus cultures that are more heartily religious (such as Americans). Within a culture they compare religious people with less religious people; in priming studies they explore the effects of getting people to think about religious notions more than they would normally do. This is the research that is described below.

RELIGION AND GOODNESS, WITHIN AND ACROSS COUNTRIES

One specific question concerns the effect of religion on a person's kindness to strangers. Are the religious more generous and more likely to volunteer to help others?

In his influential book *Who Really Cares?*, Brooks (2006) draws upon existing datasets and concludes that, controlling for education, age, gender, income, and politics, religious people care more. They donate more money to charities, including nonreligious charities; they are

more likely to volunteer, to donate blood, and to give to the homeless. And they are happier. In a 2004 study, the secular are twice as likely to say that they feel like failures, whereas the religious are twice as likely to say that they are very happy with their lives.

These conclusions were recently supplemented by a large set of analyses reported by Putnam & Campbell (2010). They find that giving to religious charities is correlated with giving to nonreligious charities and that frequent churchgoers are particularly likely to give to the needy, the elderly, and the young. And again, this holds even when one rules out other factors, such that the American religious are more likely than average to be older, female, Southern, and African American. These data suggest that there is a moral boost to being religious and that it's not restricted to one's ingroup, but rather it applies more generally.[2]

In a critical discussion of Brooks (2006), Norenzayan & Shariff (2008) note that these data are based on self-report. This raises the concern that religion might not lead to an actual increase in altruism, but rather to an increase in how much people believe they are altruistic or how prone they are to say that they are altruistic. This point applies to Putnam & Campbell (2010) as well. In support of their concern, Norenzayan & Shariff (2008) note that the research of Batson and his colleagues (e.g., Batson et al. 1989, 1993) finds that although religious people report being more altruistic, they are no nicer in laboratory conditions.

This is a serious concern. On the other hand, there are some objective data for the connection

---

[2] As an aside, the major conclusion of Brooks (2006) wasn't about religion; it was about political orientation. His answer to the question "Who really cares?" was: political conservatives (at the top of the cover of the paperback version is, *The Surprising Truth About Compassionate Conservatism*). But Putnam & Campbell (2010) point out that in their own datasets, and in the datasets that Brooks himself used, the moral advantage of political conservatives exists only because of the correlation with religiosity: "Holding religiosity constant, ideology has little significant effect on total giving or total volunteering but liberals assuredly give and volunteer more for *nonreligious* causes than conservatives do" (p. 458; emphasis added).

between religion and altruism: Data from the Internal Revenue Service (IRS) indicate that the more religious states give more to charity than do the less religious states (Brooks 2006). Since the IRS requires receipts for charitable giving, their data suggest that there is a real difference.

Also, there is real-world evidence that religion is a force for charitable giving. It is not unusual for hospitals and other charitable organizations to be religiously based, with the Salvation Army being a prominent example. And some degree of charity is proscribed in all the major religious faiths, as in the parables of Christ, the Jewish notion of *tzedaka*, and the Islamic pillar of *Zakat*.

Other analyses provide a different perspective, however. Paul (2005) presents an analysis of 18 democracies and finds that the more atheist societies are better off with regard to several objective measures of societal health, such as murder and suicide rates, extent of sexually transmitted diseases, abortion, and teen pregnancy. This conclusion has been criticized; among other concerns, it is based on a highly selective sample of countries (Jensen 2006). Still, it does show that religion isn't essential for a moral community. Along the same lines, Zuckerman (2008) provides an extensive case study of the Danes and the Swedes. These are among the least religious of contemporary humans. They tend not to go to church or pray in the privacy of their own homes; they tend not to believe in God or heaven or hell. But, by any reasonable standard, they are nice to one another. Even without belief in a God looming over them, they murder and rape one another significantly less frequently than the much more religious Americans do.

Although it is possible that these correlations exist because religion has a negative effect on a society, it is more plausible, as Paul (2005) suggests, that some drop in religious belief is caused by the prosperity and social health of a community—perhaps rich and stable Western democracies are likely to abandon or reject religious ideals. Paul (2010, p. 642) takes this further: "Prosperous modernity is proving to be the nemesis of religion."

RELIGION AND GOODNESS, LABORATORY MANIPULATIONS

We can now move from the rather messy correlational data and turn to laboratory research. There is a long tradition of experimental studies that explore the role of religion on good actions. Many of these studies work by eliciting religious thoughts and exploring their effects.

The best-known study is famous for its cleverness—and for its null effect. Darley & Batson (1973) tested male seminary students, telling them that they had to make a short presentation, either about the jobs available for seminary students or about the parable of the Good Samaritan, in which Jesus tells about a traveler lying unconscious on the road, attacked by thieves, and the good man who stops to help him. The students were then told to go to another location, and some were told to hurry, that they were already late. On the way, all groups of students passed someone slumped in a doorway, a confederate playing a part of the victim.

The main finding was that students who were told to hurry were more likely to pass the victim by—that aspect of the situation influenced their behavior. But whether or not they were told the story of the Good Samaritan (which, of course, was directly relevant to the situation they were in) had no effect. The authors note that, "on several occasions, a seminary student going to give his talk on the parable of the Good Samaritan literally stepped over the victim as he hurried on his way!" (p. 107).

In a reanalysis, however, Greenwald (1975) noted that the sample size was small, and he reanalyzed the data using different methods. Although being told to hurry clearly did have an effect, Greenwald concluded that it was premature to dismiss the possibility that reading the parable actually did increase the odds of helping. Darley and Batson might well have been the first psychologists to successfully use religion to prime moral behavior.

Several have done so since then. Mazar et al. (2008) asked subjects to either write down ten books they read in high school or write down the Ten Commandments. When later put in a situation where they could cheat, those in the Ten Commandments condition were less likely to do so. Bering et al. (2005) confronted children and adults with supposed supernatural beings. When adults are told that there is a ghost in the laboratory, they are less likely to cheat on a computer task. And when children, ages 5–6 and 8–9, are told that they are in the presence of an invisible agent ("Princess Alice"), they are slower to cheat than are those not given this information. Indeed, when the skeptical children—who did not believe in Princess Alice—were removed from the analysis, the effect of the presence of this invisible figure was the same as the presence of an actual adult (Piazza et al. 2011).

Using a scrambled sentence task, Shariff & Norenzayan (2007) found that getting subjects to unscramble sentences that included religious words—spirit, divine, God, sacred, and prophet—made them more generous in a "dictator game" in which they were free to give an anonymous stranger as much money as they wanted. Randolph-Seng & Nielsen (2007) found that subliminal priming of religious words—flashing them on a screen for 80 milliseconds—made subjects less likely to cheat on a subsequent task. Pichon et al. (2007) found that when primed with religious words, people were later more interested in helping to distribute charity-related information.

Why do these primes cause these effects? One possibility is that they make people think about an invisible and omnipresent God. Subjects believe, perhaps unconsciously, that they are being watched, which leads to better behavior. This meshes well with findings that even subtle cues to the presence of others—such as photographs of eyes or even dot patterns that resemble eyes—affect moral behavior. People are more generous, for instance, in a computer task when they are exposed to eye spots on the screen (Haley & Fessler 2005). And they are less likely to take coffee without paying (Bateson et al. 2006) or to litter (Ernest-Jones et al. 2010) when in the presence of posters with eyes on them.

There is reason to doubt, however, that the felt presence of a supernatural watcher is solely responsible for the priming effects. Other studies find that one can get the same effect with secular moral primes. Shariff & Norenzayan (2007) replicated their finding in a second study when subjects scrambled sentences with the primes: civic, jury, court, police, and contract. Mazar et al. (2008) found that getting subjects to sign a brief statement acknowledging their commitment to the local university honor code (even if their university didn't in fact have an honor code) caused a similar drop in cheating.

RELIGION, INGROUPS, AND OUTGROUPS

The work so far suggests that religion causes a general boost in moral behaviors, such as altruism and reluctance to cheat. But the evolutionary theories described above make a prediction about the limits of religiously triggered niceness. If religion is an adaptation that binds groups together, it shouldn't lead to indiscriminate kindness. Rather, it should drive one to favor the ingroup.

One doesn't have to be steeped in evolutionary theory to make this prediction. Critics of religion have long emphasized its power to divide people, to motivate hatred toward heretics and apostates, and to fuel violence and genocide and war. After all, religious moral teachings are often explicitly parochial. As Graham & Haidt (2010) summarize:

> Many of the religious commandments to treat others compassionately and fairly are limited to the treatment of other individuals within the religious community; for instance, the Hebrew Bible's "love your neighbor as yourself" (Leviticus 19:18) was intended to apply only to other Israelites... The Qur'an commands, "Do not take the Jews and Christians as allies: they are allies only to each other. Anyone who takes them as an ally becomes one of them—God does not guide such wrongdoers" (5:51; see also 29:68–69).

One might ask how religiosity affects one's attitudes toward others who don't belong to the same faith. Does being very Catholic make one more prone to despise Jews, or vice versa? But the focus of most research in social psychology concerns the effects of religiosity on racial prejudice (see also Batson & Stocks 2005 for review), and it is this line of work that I review here.

This topic was first explored in detail in Gordon Allport's classic book, *The Nature of Prejudice* (Allport 1954). In his original studies in the 1940s and 1950s, people's responses to the question "To what degree has religion been an influence in your upbringing?" correlated with prejudicial attitudes toward other groups (see also Allport & Kramer 1946). Subsequent research found that this was true as well in the 1970s: Relative to those whites who claimed to have no religious affiliation, white Protestants were more likely to disapprove of interracial marriage, and white Protestants and Catholics were more likely to agree that "most blacks have less in-born ability to learn" (Putnam & Campbell 2010). And a recent meta-analysis (Hall et al. 2010) looked at 55 studies between 1964 and 2008 and found that a small but statistically significant relationship exists between certain forms of religiosity and racial prejudice.

Some caveats are needed, however. In the Hall et al. meta-analysis, not all form of religiosity had this effect on prejudice: It was found for "extrinsic religiosity," defined as "an instrumental approach to religion that is motivated by external factors such as desires for social status, security, and acceptance from others" (Allport & Ross 1967, p. 127) and for "religious fundamentalism," defined as "an unquestioning, unwavering certainty in basic religious truths" (Altemeyer & Hunsberger 1992, p. 127). But greater "intrinsic religiosity"—being "committed to religion as an end in itself" (p. 128)—was negatively associated with prejudice, as was "Quest," a notion introduced by Batson (1976, p. 128), which corresponds to a "readiness to face existential questions, acknowledge religious doubts, and accept change" (see Sedikides & Gebauer 2010 for review and discussion).

Moreover, in most analyses, the relationship between religion and prejudice has declined since 1964.

One wonders also about the extent that these studies are finding negative effects of religion per se as opposed to other factors that are correlated with religiosity. Unlike the recent studies reported by Brooks (2006) and Putnam & Campbell (2010) discussed above, there is rarely any attempt in these earlier studies to factor out considerations such as age, race, political orientation, and so on. It might well be, for instance, that those with no religious affiliation have more cosmopolitan attitudes and experiences than those who are religious, and it is this that leads them to be less prejudiced, not their lack of religiosity per se. More generally, there is a clear correlation between religiosity (and particularly religious fundamentalism) and political conservatism and authoritarian attitudes, both of which correlate with negative attitudes toward racial minorities (see Jost et al. 2008, Napier & Jost 2008).

Still, there is priming data suggesting that religion in itself can evoke prejudice. In what is, to my knowledge, the only study of this sort, Johnson et al. (2010) found that flashing religious words (such as church, gospel, prayer) on a screen for 35 milliseconds increases prejudice by whites toward African Americans on a range of overt and implicit measures.

Also, a provocative series of studies by Ginges et al. (2009) found strong correlations between religiosity and support for suicide bombings. Interestingly, though, only certain measures of religiosity had an effect. Ginges et al. found that for Palestinian Muslim adults, frequency of mosque attendance predicted support for suicide attacks but frequency of prayer did not. (They also found that students who attended mosque more than once a day were over three times more likely than those who didn't to believe that Islam requires suicide attacks.) Ginges et al. also tested Israeli Jews living in the West Bank and Gaza, asking about their support for the 1994 suicide attack by Baruch Goldstein, who killed 29 Muslims in the Cave of the Patriarchs in the West Bank.

When primed with thoughts about synagogue attendance, they were more likely to describe the act as "heroic" than when primed with thoughts about prayer.

Finally, Ginges et al. (2009) used survey data from Indonesian Muslims, Mexican Catholics, British Protestants, Russian Orthodox in Russia, Israeli Jews, and Indian Hindus to explore the relationship between prayer frequency and frequency of religious attendance on negative feelings toward other groups, as measured by their responses to the questions "I would be willing to die for my God/beliefs" and "I blame people of other religions for much of the trouble in this world." Once again, religious attendance was a positive predictor while regular prayer was not.

EXPLAINING THE COMPLEX EFFECTS OF RELIGION

The available research tells us two things about the moral effects of religion.

First, religion makes people nicer. There is evidence from studies of charitable giving that religious people within the United States devote more time and resources to helping others than the nonreligious. Such studies rely on self-report, but they are backed by laboratory demonstrations that religious primes increase moral behaviors such as generosity to strangers and reduce immoral behaviors such as cheating. All of this makes sense in light of the universalist and enlightened moral notions encoded in all of the major religions (Waldron 2010, Wright 2009).

Second, religion doesn't make people nicer. In laboratory studies, secular primes work just as well to improve behavior as religious primes. Countries filled with the devout, such as the United States, are in many objective regards morally worse than more atheistic countries, such as Sweden. There is evidence that certain sorts of religiosity are associated with increased prejudice toward others. And attendance in religious ceremonies is correlated with an endorsement of suicide bombings. All of this makes sense in light of the parochial

nature of religious beliefs and practices and the explicit religious ideologies that privilege themselves over others (Hall et al. 2010, Harris 2004).

How can we explain these seemingly contradictory effects?

A close look at the data suggests a reasonably coherent account, largely along the lines proposed by Graham & Haidt (2010). Religion exerts many of its effects, good and bad, through its force as a social glue: To belong to a religion is to belong to a social group whose members are close to one another, who share rituals and meet regularly, and hence are more likely to be generous toward each other and less likely to cheat one another—and, under some circumstances, are more likely to be nasty toward others.

From this perspective, it is the community associated with religion that mainly drives its effects, not the belief system. As support for this, Putnam & Campbell (2010) collected extensive data on theological views and practices, asking people about their beliefs in life after death, heaven, and hell; in the importance of religion, evolution, and special creation; and in the importance of God to morality. It turns out that none of these beliefs correlate with behaviors having to do with volunteering and charitable giving. Community is everything: "Once we know how observant a person is in terms of church attendance, nothing that we can discover about the content of her religious faith adds anything to our understanding or prediction of her good neighborliness" (Putnam & Campbell 2010, p. 467). They later add, "In fact, the statistics suggest that even an atheist who happened to become involved in the social life of the congregation (perhaps through a spouse) is much more likely to volunteer in a soup kitchen than the most fervent believer who prays alone. It is religious belongingness that matters for neighborliness, not religious believing" (p. 473).

The same point holds for the data reviewed by Brooks (2006) that find that the religious are happier and more generous than the secular. These surveys do not define "religious" and "secular" in terms of belief. They define it in terms of religious attendance.

This emphasis of community can provide a different perspective on why American atheists are less generous. It's not that they have no sense of right and wrong or are cold-blooded self-maximizers. It is that they have been left out of the dominant modes of American togetherness. And, as P.Z. Myers (2007) puts it, "[S]cattered individuals who are excluded from communities do not receive the benefits of community, nor do they feel willing to contribute to the communities that exclude them."

If this view is correct, then the specifically religious aspects of religion—supernatural beliefs and sacred texts and transcendent experiences—might play little role in its moral force. Indeed, Putnam and his colleagues (Putnam 2000, Putnam & Campbell 2010) use data from survey studies to argue that any form of voluntary association with other people is integral to a fulfilled and productive existence. This makes us "smarter, healthier, safer, richer, and better able to govern a just and stable democracy" (Putnam 2000, p. 290). Putnam argues, for instance, that membership in a bowling league—secular, but social—is just as much of a boost to charitable giving as is affiliation with a religious community.

The importance of sociality—and the relative unimportance of religious belief—is also reflected in the data from the Scandinavian countries. These data were framed above as showing that religion isn't needed for a society to be civil, nonviolent, and, by most standards, morally good. But we can now think about it in a more nuanced way as having to do with the type of religion that is relevant. Zuckerman (2008) points out that most Danes and Swedes have their babies baptized, give some of their income to the church, and feel attached to their religious community—they are Christian, they just don't believe in God. (He suggests that Scandinavian Christians are a lot like American Jews, who are also relatively secularized in belief and practice, have strong communal feelings, and tend to be well behaved.) The Scandinavians might be atheists, then, but they

are also religious—in precisely the sense that matters for morality.

Community can also explain the uglier side of religion. Recall the Ginges et al. (2009) findings discussed above. Religious devotion, as measured by frequency of prayer, had no effect on support for suicide bombing, but religious participation did. Contrary to the claims of Dawkins (2006), Harris (2004), and others, Ginges et al. (2009) conclude, "the relationship between religion and support for suicide attacks is real, but is orthogonal to devotion to particular religious belief" (p. 230). It is commitment to the social group that matters, as reflected by participation in group activities and religious rituals. This commitment might also motivate milder forms of denigration of outgroups, as reflected in the attitudes toward American atheists.

This last point raises a question: If religion is such an insular force, why isn't there a greater effect of religion on prejudice in the studies of Americans? As noted above, such an effect exists, but it is small, restricted to certain sorts of religious orientations, and perhaps a by-product of the fact that religiosity is correlated with other traits, such as certain political attitudes.

One explanation has to do with the sort of prejudice that these studies explore. The research reviewed above was done with white Christians, exploring their attributes and behaviors toward blacks. Even if religion naturally reduces one's compassion toward other groups, then it might not have a negative effect in this case because these blacks are seen as in fact belonging to their group—they are also, for the most part, Christian.[3] Religion can establish boundaries then, but it can also dissolve them. As Allport (1954, p. 444) famously put it, "The role of religion is paradoxical. It makes prejudice and it unmakes prejudice."

_____

[3] This predicts that one would find more antiblack prejudice in the United States by Jews and Hindus, because these individuals don't tend to share the same religion as American blacks.

Much of this is consistent with the evolutionary theory reviewed above, where religion is a solution to the problem of free-riders, a mechanism to bring people together. To put it differently, if it turned out that religion has no positive ingroup moral effects—or no negative outgroup effects—this evolutionary account would be effectively refuted. The finding that social aspects of religion are so linked to their moral effects supports the hypothesis that this is their evolved function, though of course it does not prove it.

What about the claim that supernatural beliefs—belief in gods, afterlife, spirits, miracles, and so on—have also evolved to motivate moral behavior? This hypothesis fares less well. The increased generosity that one finds when people are exposed to religious primes is sometimes attributed to the notion of a supernatural watcher—the primes make one think of the presence of God, one's behavior is no longer anonymous, and so people act nicer. But the problem with this account is that secular moral primes—relating to the legal system, say, or to honor codes—have the same effect as religious primes. It doesn't seem, then, that a belief in a supernatural being plays any distinctive role here.

Note also that the idea of omniscient moral God is a relatively recent invention—the gods of hunter-gatherers were far less impressive (Wright 2009). Moreover, many current humans do not believe in an omnipotent God; they instead hold animistic or polytheistic beliefs. For these reasons, a propensity to believe in a moralizing God is unlikely to be the product of natural selection.

DEBATING THE MORAL RELEVANCE OF BELIEFS

The most controversial claim made above is that religious beliefs play little substantive role in religion's moral effects. I want to conclude by considering, and responding to, counter-arguments.

The importance of religious beliefs might seem obvious to some. It seems perverse to deny, after all, that some religious beliefs motivate how people think and act. Consider suicide attacks. Ginges et al. (2009) found that levels of devotion to religious belief are unrelated to support for suicide attacks, but as Liddle et al. (2010) point out in response, this doesn't entail that religious belief itself is irrelevant. It is likely, after all, that someone who believes that God wants them to kill infidels is going to be a lot more sympathetic toward killing infidels than someone who doesn't believe in God. Dawkins (2006, p. 348) might be right then when he concludes: "Suicide bombers do what they do because they really believe what they were taught in their religious schools: that duty to God exceeds all other priorities, and that martyrdom in his service will be rewarded in the gardens of Paradise."

Consider as an analogy that one might engage in a demonstration or counter-demonstration at an abortion clinic for all sorts of reasons. But surely one relevant consideration is what one thinks about abortion. It might well be that the intensity of one's abortion-related beliefs doesn't correlate well with the likelihood that a demonstrator will show up or turn violent, in the same way that the intensity of religious devotion doesn't correlate with support for suicide bombings. But it would be a mistake to conclude from this that the belief itself is irrelevant.

Some would take this further and argue that the moral effects of religious beliefs are particularly potent, and pernicious, because they are unmoored from the everyday world. Religion, after all, traffics in notions such as life after death, the desires of invisible deities, and the demands of thousand-year-old texts. The argument of Timothy Dwight, the President of Yale from 1795 to 1817, against the morality of the smallpox vaccine ("If God had decreed from all eternity that a certain person should die of smallpox, it would be a frightful sin to avoid and annul that decree by the trick of vaccination") seems like a specifically religious argument (see Hitchens 2007). As the physicist Steven Weinberg (1999) put it, "With or without religion, you would have good people doing good things and evil people doing evil things. But for good people to do evil things, that takes religion."

The defense of the relevance of religious belief has so far been framed in terms of its negative effects. But it is also defended by scholars who think that religious belief has had a uniquely positive effect on our lives. Legal scholar Jeremy Waldron (2010, p. 10) provides an articulate defense of this view:

Challenging the limited altruism of comfortable community has been one of the great achievements of the Western religions. I know the Jewish and Christian traditions best, and what I have in mind are the prescriptions of the Torah, the uncompromising preaching of the Prophets and the poetry of the Psalmist aimed specifically to discomfit those whose prosperity is founded on grinding the faces of the poor, on neglecting the stranger, and on driving away the outcast. I have in mind too the teaching and example of Jesus Christ in associating with those who were marginal and despised, and in making one's willingness to feed the hungry, clothe the naked, take in the stranger, and visit those who are in prison a condition of one's recognition of Him. And it's not just scripture: it is the whole edifice of (say) Catholic natural law reasoning about need, and church doctrine on the perils of complacent and exclusive community.

Waldron concedes that religious conviction is no guarantee of a universalist mentality and can fuel hatred and division. But he suggests that, for most people, religion is the only route available for the sort of broad-spectrum morality that many would aspire to, one that rejects traditional and seemingly natural social and economic boundaries. The notion that religion can ground a cosmopolitan worldview is defended by Appiah (2006) as well, who notes that Christianity in particular has had a universalist ethos. He quotes Saint Paul: "There is neither Jew nor Greek, there is neither bond nor free, there is neither male nor female, for ye all one in Christ Jesus." One might sympathize

with physicist Freeman Dyson's (2006) addition to the Weinberg quote above, "And for bad people to do good things—that takes religion."

It turns out then that scholars who disagree radically about the valence of the moral effects of religion would nonetheless agree that religion has its effects, at least in part, through the substantive claims that it makes about what is right and what is wrong. If the relevance of religious belief doesn't show up in the studies and surveys of empirical researchers, it is because the researchers are asking the wrong questions—for instance, by confusing intensity of belief with the presence of belief.

Alternatively, though, we might be overestimating the power of belief. Nobody could doubt that some actions—good and bad—are motivated by specific religious beliefs. But our intuitions about specific cases cannot be trusted here. Indeed, one of psychology's contributions to the theory of human nature, starting with Freud and continuing through contemporary social psychology, is that we are often wrong about the reasons for our own actions—and we tend to err in the direction of assuming that we do things because of rational justifications (see Haidt 2001). To return to an example given previously, people might believe that they prefer a welfare plan based on its objective merits and be unaware of how much they are influenced by their knowledge that it is proposed by the political party that they belong to (Cohen 2003). Similarly, people might sincerely believe that their disapproval toward homosexuals is rooted in the teachings of Biblical texts. But they might just be mistaken—they might have some animus toward homosexuals for other reasons and then justify this animus by reference to religious faith.

More generally, Wright (2009) argues that although people frequently try to explain their actions through appeals to the Bible or the Koran or other religious texts, the actual causal force is more situational. If individuals are in a zero-sum relationship, they find scriptural motivation for hatred and war; when their fates are intertwined in a positive way, they find tolerance and love. For Wright, it is not that people get their moral views from religious texts and authorities; rather, their moral views are determined by the "the facts on the ground"; people shop around for justifications after the fact.

This is consistent with the data reviewed in this article. In the lab and in the world, moral actions such as suicide bombings, racial prejudice, honest behavior, and generosity to strangers are related to religion—but not to religious belief. Although it is often claimed that the moral ideas encoded in the world's religions have an important effect on our moral lives, there is little evidence for this popular view.

DISCLOSURE STATEMENT

The author is unaware of any affiliation, funding, or financial holdings that might be perceived as affecting the objectivity of this review.

ACKNOWLEDGMENTS

Thanks to Konika Banerjee, Susan Fiske, Jonathan Haidt, Ara Norenzayan, Mark Sheskin, and Christina Starmans for helpful comments on an earlier draft.

LITERATURE CITED

Alcorta C, Sosis R. 2005. Ritual, emotion, and sacred symbols: the evolution of religion as an adaptive complex. *Hum. Nat.* 16:323–59

Allport GW. 1954. *The Nature of Prejudice*. Reading, MA: Addison-Wesley

Allport GW, Kramer BM. 1946. Some roots of prejudice. *J. Psychol.* 22:9–39

Allport GW, Ross JM. 1967. Personal religious orientation and prejudice. *J. Personal. Soc. Psychol.* 5:432–43

Altemeyer B, Hunsberger B. 1992. Authoritarianism, religious fundamentalism, quest, and prejudice. *Int. J. Psychol. Religion* 2:113–33

Appiah K 2006. *Cosmopolitanism: Ethics in a World of Strangers*. New York: Norton

Atran S. 2004. *In Gods We Trust: The Evolutionary Landscape of Religion*. New York: Oxford Univ. Press

Atran S, Norenzayan A. 2004. Religion's evolutionary landscape: counterintuition, commitment, compassion, communion. *Behav. Brain Sci.* 27:713–30

Baron-Cohen S. 2003. *The Essential Difference: The Truth About the Male and Female Brain*. New York: Basic Books

Barrett JL. 2004. *Why Would Anyone Believe in God?* Walnut Creek, CA: AltaMira

Bateson M, Nettle D, Roberts G. 2006. Cues of being watched enhance cooperation in a real-world setting. *Biol. Lett.* 3:412–14

Batson CD. 1976. Religion as prosocial: agent or double agent? *J. Sci. Study Religion* 15:29–45

Batson CD, Oleson KC, Weeks JL, Healy SP, Reeves PJ, et al. 1989. Religious prosocial motivation: Is it altruistic or egoistic? *J. Personal. Soc. Psychol.* 57:873–84

Batson CD, Stocks EL. 2005. Religion and prejudice. In *On the Nature of Prejudice: Fifty Years After Allport*, ed. JF Dovidio, PS Glick, L Rudman, pp. 413–27. Oxford, UK: Blackwell

Batson CD, Schoenrade P, Ventis WL. 1993. *Religion and the Individual: A Social-Psychological Perspective*. New York: Oxford Univ. Press

Bering JM. 2002. The existential theory of mind. *Rev. Gen. Psychol.* 6:3–24

Bering JM. 2006. The folk psychology of souls. *Behav. Brain Sci.* 29:453–98

Bering JM. 2011. *The Belief Instinct: The Psychology of Souls, Destiny, and the Meaning of Life*. New York: Norton

Bering JM, McLeod K, Shackelford TK. 2005. Reasoning about dead agents reveals possible adaptive trends. *Hum. Nat.* 16:360–81

Bloom P. 2007. Religion is natural. *Dev. Sci.* 10:147–51

Bloom P. 2004. *Descartes' Baby: How the Science of Child Development Explains What Makes Us Human*. New York: Basic Books

Bloom P. 2009. Religion belief as an evolutionary accident. In *The Believing Primate*, ed. MJ Murray, J Schloss, pp. 118–27. New York: Oxford Univ. Press

Bloom P. 2010. *How Pleasure Works: The New Science of Why We Like What We Like*. New York: Norton

Bloom P, Weisberg DS. 2007. Childhood origins of adult resistance to science. *Science* 316:996–97

Boyd R, Richerson PJ. 2002. Group beneficial norms spread rapidly in a structured population. *J. Theor. Biol.* 215:287–96

Boyer P. 2001. *Religion Explained*. New York: Basic Books

Brooks AC. 2006. *Who Really Cares: The Surprising Truth About Compassionate Conservatism*. New York: Basic Books

Bulbulia J. 2004. The cognitive and evolutionary psychology of religion. *Biol. Philos.* 19:655–86

Chartrand TL, Bargh JA. 1999. The chameleon effect: the perception-behavior link and social interaction. *J. Personal. Soc. Psychol.* 76:893–910

Cohen AB, Rozin P. 2001. Religion and the morality of mentality. *J. Personal. Soc. Psychol.* 81:697–710

Cohen GL. 2003. Party over policy: the dominating impact of group influence on political beliefs. *J. Personal. Soc. Psychol.* 85:808–22

Cosmides L. 1989. The logic of social exchange: Has natural selection shaped how humans reason? Studies with the Wason selection task. *Cognition* 31:187–276

Darley J, Batson CD. 1973. From Jerusalem to Jericho: a study of situational and dispositional variables in helping behaviour. *J. Personal. Soc. Psychol.* 27:100–8

Dawkins R. 2006. *The God Delusion*. New York: Bantam

de Waal F. 1996. *Good Natured: The Origins of Right and Wrong in Humans and Other Animals*. Cambridge, MA: Harvard Univ. Press

de Waal F. 2010. Morals without God? *N.Y. Times*, Oct. 17

Durkheim E. 1912/1995. *The Elementary Forms of Religious Life*. New York: Free Press

Dyson F. 2006. Religion from the outside. *N.Y. Rev. Books*, June 22

Edgell P, Gerteis J, Hartmann D. 2006. Atheists as "other:" moral boundaries and cultural membership in American society. *Am. Sociol. Rev.* 71:211–34

Ernest-Jones M, Nettle D, Bateson M. 2011. Effects of eye images on everyday cooperative behavior: a field experiment. *Evol. Hum. Behav.* 32:172–78

Evans EM. 2000. Beyond Scopes: why creationism is here to stay. In *Imagining the Impossible: Magical, Scientific and Religious Thinking in Children*, ed. K Rosengren, C Johnson, P Harris, pp. 305–31. Cambridge, UK: Cambridge Univ. Press

Evans EM. 2001. Cognitive and contextual factors in the emergence of diverse belief systems: creation versus evolution. *Cogn. Psychol.* 42:217–66

Festinger L. 1957. *A Theory of Cognitive Dissonance*. Evanston, IL: Row, Peterson

Finkel D, Swartwout P, Sosis R. 2010. The socio-religious brain: a developmental model. In *Proceedings of the British Academy*, ed. R Dunbar, C Gamble, J Gowlett, 158:287–312

Ginges J, Hansen I, Norenzayan A. 2009. Religion and support for suicide attacks. *Psychol. Sci.* 20:224–30

Gould SJ, Lewontin RC. 1979. The spandrels of San Marco and the Panglossian paradigm: a critique of the adaptationist programme. *Proc. R. Soc. Lond. B Biol. Sci.* 205(1161):581–98

Graham J, Haidt J. 2010. Beyond beliefs: religion binds individuals into moral communities. *Personal. Soc. Psychol. Rev.* 14:140–50

Greenwald A. 1975. Does the Good Samaritan parable increase helping? A comment on Darley and Batson's no-effect conclusion. *J. Personal. Soc. Psychol.* 32:578–83

Guthrie S. 1993. *Faces in the Clouds: A New Theory of Religion*. New York: Oxford Univ. Press

Haidt J. 2001. The emotional dog and its rational tail: a social intuitionist approach to moral judgment. *Psychol. Rev.* 108:814–34

Haidt J. 2007. Moral psychology and the misunderstanding of religion. **http://www.edge.org/3rd_culture/haidt07/haidt07_index.html**

Haidt J. 2012. *The Righteous Mind: Why Good People Are Divided by Politics and Religion*. New York: Pantheon

Haidt J, Kesebir S. 2010. Morality. In *Handbook of Social Psychology*, ed. S Fiske, D Gilbert, pp. 797–832. New York: McGraw Hill. 5th ed.

Haley KJ, Fessler DMT. 2005. Nobody's watching? Subtle cues affect generosity in an anonymous economic game. *Evol. Hum. Behav.* 26:245–56

Hall DL, Matz DC, Wood W. 2010. Why don't we practice what we preach? A meta-analytic review of religious racism. *Personal. Soc. Psychol. Rev.* 14:126–39

Hamlin JK, Wynn K, Bloom P. 2007. Social evaluation by preverbal infants. *Nature* 450:557–59

Harris S. 2004. *The End of Faith: Religion, Terror, and the Future of Reason.* New York: Norton

Hitchens C. 2007. *God Is Not Great: How Religion Poisons Everything.* New York: Twelve Books

Hoffman M. 2000. *Empathy and Moral Development.* Cambridge, UK: Cambridge Univ. Press

Hume D. 1956 [1757]. *The Natural History of Religion.* London: Black

Irons W. 2004. An evolutionary critique of the created co-creator concept. *Zygon: J. Religion Sci.* 39:773–90

James W. 1960 [1902]. *The Varieties of Religious Experience.* London: Fontana

Jensen GF. 2006. Religious cosmologies and homicide rates among nations: a closer look. *J. Religion Soc.* 8:1–14

Johnson DDP. 2005. God's punishment and public goods: a test of the supernatural punishment hypothesis in 186 world cultures. *Hum. Nat.* 16:410–46

Johnson DDP, Bering JM. 2006. Hand of God, mind of man: punishment and cognition in the evolution of cooperation. *Evol. Psychol.* 4:219–33

Johnson MK, Rowatt WC, LaBouff JP. 2010. Priming Christian religious concepts increases racial prejudice. *Soc. Psychol. Personal. Sci.* 1:119–26

Jost JT, Nosek BA, Gosling SD. 2008. Ideology: its resurgence in social, personality, and political psychology. *Perspect. Psychol. Sci.* 3:126–36

Kelemen D. 2004. Are children "intuitive theists"? *Psychol. Sci.* 15:295–301

Keltner D. 2009. *Born to Be Good: The Science of a Meaningful Life.* New York: Norton

Lane JD, Wellman HM, Evans ME. 2010. Children's understanding of ordinary and extraordinary minds. *Child Dev.* 81:1475–89

Larson EJ, Witham L. 1997. Scientists are still keeping the faith. *Nature* 389:435–36

Larson EJ, Witham L. 1998. Leading scientists still reject God. *Nature* 394:313

Liddle JR, Machluf K, Shackelford TK. 2010. Understanding suicide terrorism: premature dismissal of the religious-belief hypothesis. *Evol. Psychol.* 10:343–45

Lindholm JA, Astin HS, Astin AW. 2006. *Spirituality and the Professoriate.* Los Angeles, CA: UCLA Higher Educ. Res. Inst.

Locke J. 1983/1689. *A Letter Concerning Toleration.* Indianapolis, IN: Hackett

Mazar N, Amir O, Ariely D. 2008. The dishonesty of honest people: a theory of self-concept maintenance. *J. Mark. Res.* 45:633–44

McCauley RN, Whitehouse H. 2005. Introduction: new frontiers in the cognitive science of religion. *J. Cogn. Cult.* 5:1–13

Myers DG. 2008. *A Friendly Letter to Skeptics and Atheists: Musings on Why God Is Good and Faith Isn't Evil.* San Francisco, CA: Jossey-Bass/Wiley

Myers PZ. 2007. Commentary on "Moral psychology and the misunderstanding of religion," by Jonathan Haidt. **http://www.edge.org/discourse/moral_religion.html#myers**

Napier JL, Jost JT. 2008. The "antidemocratic personality" revisited: a cross-national investigation of working-class authoritarianism. *J. Soc. Issues* 64:595–617

Norenzayan A, Gervais W. 2012. The cultural evolution of religion. In *Creating Consilience: Integrating Science and the Humanities,* ed. E Slingerland, M Collard. Oxford, UK: Oxford Univ. Press. In press

Norenzayan A, Shariff AF. 2008. The origin and evolution of religious prosociality. *Science* 322(5898):58–62

Paul GS. 2005. Cross-national correlations of quantifiable societal health with popular religiosity and secularism in the prosperous democracies. *J. Religion Soc.* 7:1–17

Paul GS. 2010. Religiosity tied to socioeconomic status. *Science* 327(5966):642

Persinger MA. 2001. The neuropsychiatry of paranormal experiences. *J. Neuropsychiatry Clin. Neurosci.* 13:515–24

Piazza J, Bering JM, Ingram G. 2011. "Princess Alice is watching you": children's belief in an invisible person inhibits cheating. *J. Exp. Child Psychol.* 109:311–20

Pichon I, Boccato G, Saroglou V. 2007. Nonconscious influences of religion on prosociality: a priming study. *Eur. J. Soc. Psychol.* 37:1032–45

Pinker S. 1997. *How the Mind Works*. New York: Norton

Putnam R. 2000. *Bowling Alone: The Collapse and Revival of American Community*. New York: Simon & Schuster

Putnam R, Campbell D. 2010. *American Grace: How Religion Divides and Unites Us*. New York: Simon & Schuster

Pyysiäinen I. 2003. *How Religion Works: Towards a New Cognitive Science of Religion*. Leiden: Brill

Randolph-Seng B, Nielsen ME. 2007. Honesty: one effect of primed religious representations. *Int. J. Psychol. Religion* 17:303–15

Sedikides C, Gebauer JE. 2010. Religiosity as self-enhancement: a meta-analysis of the relation between socially desirable responding and religiosity. *Personal. Soc. Psychol. Rev.* 14:17–36

Shariff AF, Norenzayan A. 2007. God is watching you: Priming God concepts increases prosocial behavior in an anonymous economic game. *Psychol. Sci.* 18:803–9

Shermer M. 2003. *How We Believe: The Search for God in an Age of Science*. New York: Freeman

Shweder RA, Much NC, Mahapatra M, Park L. 1997. The "big three" of morality (autonomy, community, divinity), and the "big three" explanations of suffering. In *Morality and Health*, ed. P Rozin, A Brandt, pp. 119–69. New York: Routledge

Sober E, Wilson DS. 2011. Adaptation and natural selection revisited. *J. Evol. Biol.* 24:462–68

Sosis R, Bressler ER. 2003. Cooperation and commune longevity: a test of the costly signaling theory of religion. *Cross-Cult. Res.* 37:211–39

Tylor EB. 1871. *Primitive Culture, Volume 2.* London: John Murray

Waldman S. 2004. Pilgrim's progress. June 29. **http://www.slate.com/id/2103017/**

Waldron J. 2010. Secularism and the limits of community. *NYU School Law, Public Law* Res. Pap. No. 10-88. **http://ssrn.com/abstract = 1722780**

Warneken F, Tomasello M. 2006. Altruistic helping in human infants and young chimpanzees. *Science* 311:1301–3

Weinberg S. 1999. A designer universe? (Did the universe have a cosmic designer?). *N.Y. Rev. Books* 46:46–48

Wieseltier L. 2006. The God genome. *N.Y. Times*, Feb. 19, Sec. 7, p. 11

Williams GC. 1966. *Adaptation and Natural Selection*. Princeton, NJ: Princeton Univ. Press

Wilson DS. 2002. *Darwin's Cathedral: Evolution, Religion and the Nature of Society*. Chicago: Univ. Chicago Press

Wilson DS. 2007. *Evolution for Everyone: How Darwin's Theory Can Change the Way We Think About Our Lives*. New York: Delacorte

Wiltermuth SS, Heath C. 2009. Synchrony and cooperation. *Psychol. Sci.* 20:1–5

Wright R. 2009. *Evolution of God*. New York: Little Brown

Zuckerman P. 2008. *Society Without God: What the Least Religious Nations Can Tell Us About Contentment*. New York: NYU Press

Consequences of Age-Related Cognitive Declines

Timothy Salthouse

Department of Psychology, University of Virginia, Charlottesville, Virginia 22904-4400;
email: salthouse@virginia.edu

Annu. Rev. Psychol. 2012. 63:201–26

First published online as a Review in Advance on
July 5, 2011

The *Annual Review of Psychology* is online at
psych.annualreviews.org

This article's doi:
10.1146/annurev-psych-120710-100328

Keywords

cognitive aging, cognitive functioning, job performance,
accommodations, typical versus maximal performance

Abstract

Adult age differences in a variety of cognitive abilities are well documented, and many of those abilities have been found to be related to success in the workplace and in everyday life. However, increased age is seldom associated with lower levels of real-world functioning, and the reasons for this lab-life discrepancy are not well understood. This article briefly reviews research concerned with relations of age to cognition, relations of cognition to successful functioning outside the laboratory, and relations of age to measures of work performance and achievement. The final section discusses several possible explanations for why there are often little or no consequences of age-related cognitive declines in everyday functioning.

Contents

INTRODUCTION

An intriguing discrepancy exists between the competencies of older adults, assumed on the basis of everyday observations, on the one hand, and their competencies inferred from laboratory results, on the other hand. The laboratory results tend to portray older adults as distinctly inferior to young adults on a number of presumably basic cognitive abilities, and yet we are all aware of competent, and even remarkable, accomplishments of people well into their 60s, 70s, and beyond. One is thus faced with the question of how to account for this apparent discrepancy between the rather pessimistic results of the laboratory and the more encouraging observations of daily life. (Salthouse 1987, p. 142)

The quotation above describes a question that has concerned researchers in the field of cognitive aging for decades. The discrepancy of interest is illustrated with a figure (**Figure 1**) portraying the proportion of people at each age

WAIS-IV: Wechsler Adult Intelligence Scale-Fourth Edition; one of the most widely used tests of adult intelligence

CEO: chief executive officer responsible for overall management of an organization

between 20 and 75 (*a*) in the U.S. population; (*b*) in the top 25% of the distribution of scores in a composite measure of reasoning ability from one of the most popular cognitive ability tests, the Wechsler Adult Intelligence Scale-Fourth Edition (WAIS-IV); and (*c*) who are chief executive officers (CEOs) of Fortune 500 companies in late 2009. The function with U.S. population information provides a baseline of what might be expected if a random sample were drawn from the population. The reasoning function reflects the age distribution that might be expected if selection were based exclusively on this measure of reasoning. Finally, the CEO function indicates the actual distribution of ages of the primary decision makers in major corporations. Note that the reasoning function has a peak before age 30, whereas the peak age for the CEO function is close to 60. The different trends in **Figure 1** have at least two implications: (*a*) reasoning ability as it is assessed with cognitive tests is apparently not the major basis for selection into important decision-making positions in society, and (*b*) age-related declines can presumably occur in important cognitive abilities without major consequences for functioning in society.[1] The primary question in the current article is how this second implication might be explained.

The article is organized into four sections, with assessment of cognition covered in the first section and a discussion of the importance of cognition in life outside the laboratory in the second section. The third section consists of a brief review of research on the relation of age to cognition, and the final section examines consequences of age-related cognitive declines for real-life functioning.

Reviews on topics related to the current one have focused on lifespan development (Baltes et al. 1999), development in midlife (Lachman 2004), and the aging brain (Park & Reuter-Lorenz 2009). However, because

---

[1]One reason for the later age peaks for CEOs is that achieving a leadership position requires not only cognitive abilities, but also a network of acquaintances and relevant leadership experience (cf. Posner 1995, p. 162–163).

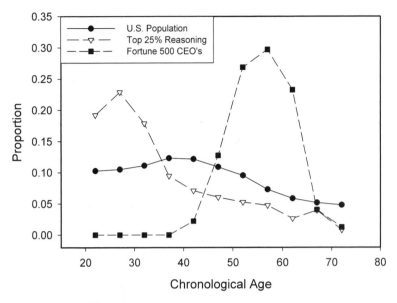

Figure 1

Distributions at each age between 20 and 75 from the U.S. population (2000 Census), the top 25% of the scores on the reasoning composite from the Wechsler Adult Intelligence Scale-Fourth Edition, and CEOs of Fortune 500 companies as of December 2009.

prior reviews have not contained systematic discussions of the consequences of age-related cognitive declines, the current review includes historical background as well as discussion of recent research.

ASSESSING COGNITION

The topic of individual differences in cognition is somewhat controversial in contemporary society because cognitive ability is one of the most valued human characteristics, and consequently there is considerable reluctance to discuss individual or group differences in this characteristic. Because some of the controversy could be attributable to a misunderstanding of the meaning of cognition as the term is used by researchers, it may be helpful to begin by describing some of the types of tests used to assess cognition within the psychometric tradition. Most tests are somewhat abstract because they are deliberately designed to minimize the role of differential experience that would complicate comparisons across people. The tests often involve simple materials but novel

manipulations, such as arranging blocks to match specified patterns, repeating a sequence of elements in a different specified order, identifying the pattern relating a set of elements, or transforming parts into a new configuration.

Major Types of Cognition

Two major categories of cognitive tests have been distinguished. Those used to evaluate proficiency in reasoning, memory, and speed are designed to assess efficiency or effectiveness of processing at the time of assessment. Other tests are designed to assess the cumulative products of processing carried out in the past, typically in the form of evaluations of acquired knowledge with tests of general information or vocabulary. The latter are sometimes designated as measures of crystallized ability, with tests of reasoning and novel problem solving considered to provide measures of fluid ability.

There is some debate whether the results of interactions of one's ability with environmental opportunities should be considered an ability as opposed to an achievement. To

SAT: Scholastic
Aptitude Test used as
a college entrance
selection exam

ACT: American
College Testing
program test used as a
college entrance
selection exam

illustrate, one position is that "Abilities are not the bodies of knowledge that people amass but their aptness in amassing them" (Gottfredson 2003, p. 3). However, the distinction between ability and achievement is somewhat blurred. For example, despite claims that tests used for college selection, such as the Scholastic Aptitude Test (SAT) and American College Testing (ACT) exam, measure achievement more than aptitude, they have been found to have strong correlations with measures of general cognitive ability (e.g., Frey & Detterman 2004, Koenig et al. 2008). Nevertheless, because measures of knowledge and measures of novel problem solving or processing efficiency have different relations with age, and possibly also with everyday functioning, they are kept distinct in the current discussion.

Organization of Cognitive Variables

Cognitive variables can be postulated to have an organizational structure based on the patterns of correlations among the variables. Nearly all of the correlations among different types of cognitive variables are positive, but they vary in strength such that an organization can be specified, with variables having higher correlations located closer to one another in the hypothesized structure. There is currently a consensus for a hierarchical structure of cognitive abilities, with many first-order abilities, a single general factor at the highest level, and different numbers at intermediate levels. Although this type of structure is widely accepted among researchers within the psychometrics field (e.g., Carroll 1993, Deary et al. 2010, Gottfredson 1998, Gustafsson 1988, Jensen 1998, Neisser et al. 1996), the idea of a general factor is sometimes vehemently challenged. A primary concern is that it may be a misleading oversimplification to reduce human variation in such an important characteristic to a single dimension. Although in the studies discussed below several variables are often combined to obtain a broad index of cognitive ability, which some researchers would consider equivalent to the general factor, the theoretical debate about

the existence or meaning of a general factor is not directly relevant in the current context and is ignored.

Many proposals for a broader conceptualization of cognitive ability than that represented by existing psychometric tests have been offered, but few of the suggestions have been accepted by mainstream psychometric researchers either because of methodological concerns (e.g., little information about reliability or validity) or substantive concerns (e.g., should variations in any domain be considered to reflect a dimension of intelligence, or should the term be reserved for particular types of cognitive domains?). A relatively narrow definition of cognition from the psychometric abilities perspectives adopted here, but it is recognized that many other characteristics need to be considered as possible determinants of functioning outside the laboratory, including practical intelligence, social intelligence, emotional intelligence, dispositions to think in a certain way, creativity, empathy, and aspects of personality. In other words, the current perspective does not deny the potential importance of these other factors but instead questions whether there is any advantage of categorizing them as aspects of cognitive ability.

In the remainder of this article, the practice in the field of industrial-organizational psychology is followed in which use of the term intelligence is avoided because it has a connotation in society of a fixed genetically determined potential (e.g., Hunter 1986). Instead, the term general cognitive ability, or often simply cognition, is used to refer to the overall level of performance across several different types of cognitive tests.

IMPORTANCE OF COGNITION

Cognition would be of little interest if it were not associated with differential functioning outside the laboratory or assessment setting, and therefore this section summarizes some of the research on the association between cognitive ability and real-life functioning. A very large number of studies have reported relations of cognitive test scores to miscellaneous life outcomes. For example, cognitive ability has been related to aspects of decision making (e.g., Demaree et al. 2010, Mata et al. 2007, Pachur et al. 2009, Peters et al. 2006, Shamosh & Gray 2008), to performance in simulations of complex systems (e.g., Ackerman & Cianciolo 2002, Gonzalez et al. 2005, Kroner et al. 2005, Wittmann & Hattrup 2004), and to specific outcomes such as the likelihood of staying on a job with a financial penalty for an early exit (e.g., Burks et al. 2009). (See Kuncel et al. 2010 for a review of much of the recent literature.)

Rather than attempting to compile a list of studies reporting relations of cognitive ability to many different types of outcomes, this section briefly summarizes research on work performance, research on indicators of competence for independent living among older adults, and research on life outcomes such as health and mortality studied within the rubric of cognitive epidemiology. The coverage is by no means exhaustive, but these areas are illustrative of the range and magnitude of the relations of cognition with functioning outside the laboratory.

Work Performance

A large literature has accumulated since the 1920s on predictors of occupational level and success. However, until recently interpretation of the results was complicated because many of the early studies were based on relatively small samples, different types of jobs, different types of cognitive measures, and different measures of work performance. To illustrate, work performance has been assessed in terms of occupational level achieved, measures of productivity, evaluations of work samples, supervisor ratings, and indicators of success in training.

Several reviews of the relation of cognitive ability to occupational level have documented that higher average cognitive ability is associated with higher occupational level or income (e.g., Gottfredson 1998; 2004a,b; Nyborg & Jensen 2001; Schmidt & Hunter 2004; von Stumm et al. 2010; Zagorsky 2007). Relations of cognitive ability to occupational level have also

been found in longitudinal studies (see Strenze 2007 for a meta-analysis). For example, Judge et al. (1999) reported that cognitive ability at age 12 had a correlation of 0.51 with occupational level between 41 and 50 years of age, and Wilk & Sackett (1996) found greater upward mobility among individuals with higher levels of cognitive ability. Furthermore, Judge et al. (2010) recently reported that higher cognitive ability was not only associated with a higher initial level of income and occupational prestige, but also with greater increases in these characteristics over time.

Relations of cognitive ability to work performance are frequently examined as validity coefficients, which represent the relation between the cognitive measure and some measure of work performance in the form of a correlation coefficient. For many years, general cognitive ability was assumed to have a relatively modest validity for job performance measures. For example, Ghiselli (1973) reported an average validity coefficient of 0.24 for cognitive ability across a wide variety of jobs. However, beginning in the 1980s, Hunter, Schmidt, and others reported a series of meta-analyses that led to different interpretations. The small sample sizes in many of the studies resulted in considerable variation in the correlations; thus, meta-analyses were particularly helpful because the aggregation across many studies allowed the "signal" corresponding to the relation to be extracted from the variability or "noise." The newer analyses also included adjustments for unreliability of the cognitive measures and of the work measures when examining relations between the two sets of variables, which led to better estimates of the true relations by minimizing influences of measurement error.

The new procedures resulted in validities for general cognitive ability in the 0.4 to 0.6 range across many types of jobs (e.g., Hunter 1986; Hunter & Hunter 1984; Hunter & Schmidt 1996, 1998; Schmidt et al. 1986, 1988; Schmidt & Hunter 2004). Furthermore, the major validity results regarding cognitive ability have been replicated in other data sets with somewhat different analytical methods (e.g., Higgins et al.

Cognitive epidemiology: new subdiscipline concerned with cognitive functioning as a predictor of outcomes such as morbidity and mortality

IADL: instrumental activities of daily living presumed to be essential for living independently

2007, Kuncel et al. 2004, Ng & Feldman 2008, Ree et al. 1994, Ree & Earles 1991), in different countries (e.g., Hulsheger et al. 2007, Salgado & Anderson 2002, Salgado et al. 2003), and with other outcomes, such as leadership (e.g., Judge et al. 2004) and salary (e.g., Judge et al. 2009, Ng & Feldman 2008).

In part because the cognitive ability relations have been found to be higher for more complex jobs (e.g., Hunter 1986, Hunter & Schmidt 1996, Schmidt & Hunter 2004), they have been hypothesized to be largely mediated through job knowledge (e.g., Hunter & Schmidt 1996, Schmidt et al. 1986). That is, one proposed mechanism is that cognitive ability is related to efficient learning, and thus in addition to greater adaptability to new situations and better ability to prioritize, individuals with higher cognitive ability have been hypothesized to have greater and faster acquisition of knowledge relevant to the job (e.g., Hunter 1986, Schmidt & Hunter 2004).

In summary, it is now well established that cognitive ability has moderate positive relations with a variety of measures of work functioning, including success in training, different measures of performance in the job, and level of occupation achieved. The mechanisms responsible for the relations are still largely speculative, but the research is consistent in documenting that level of cognitive ability is one of the strongest predictors of work success currently available.

Independent Living Among Older Adults

Although the primary interest in the current review is the period between about 20 and 75 years of age, many relations of cognition have been investigated among older adults because their declining levels of cognition make them particularly vulnerable to consequences of low cognitive functioning. Most of the relevant research has been on domains related to instrumental activities of daily living (IADL) such as shopping, arranging transportation, handling finances, and comprehending medication instructions

because these activities are assumed to be necessary to maintain independent functioning.

A number of early studies reported relations of general cognitive ability, often assessed with the Mini-Mental Status Exam (Folstein et al. 1975) used to screen for dementia, and self-reported IADL problems (see reviews in Burton et al. 2006, Willis 1991, Willis et al. 1992). The correlations have ranged from 0.3 to 0.8, but interpretation of the results is complicated by the inclusion of individuals with dementia in the samples, a measure of cognition that is not very sensitive for most healthy adults, and reliance on self-reports to assess difficulties in performing IADLs.

More recent research has examined relations of basic cognitive abilities with a variety of tests designed to assess everyday functioning. For example, the Everyday Cognition Battery consists of tests constructed to involve real-world stimuli related to medication use, financial planning, and food preparation (e.g., Allaire & Marsiske 1999, Weatherbee & Allaire 2008). Correlations of factors from this battery with established psychometric cognitive abilities have ranged between 0.42 and 0.86. Allaire & Marsiske (2002) also found that much of the variance in a composite measure of self-rated everyday functioning was accounted for by a combination of basic cognitive abilities and measures from this Everyday Cognition Battery.

The Educational Testing Service (ETS) Basic Skills Test was intended to assess cognitive skills presumed to be essential for functioning in society. The items were created to assess understanding labels on household articles, reading a street map, understanding charts and schedules, comprehending paragraphs, filling out forms, reading newspaper and phone directory ads, understanding technical documents, and comprehending newspaper text. Schaie & Willis (1986) and Willis & Schaie (1986) reported that scores in the Basic Skills Test were strongly correlated with fluid or reasoning ability (0.58) and correlated to a lesser extent with crystallized measures of knowledge (0.29). Willis et al. (1992) also reported that

Basic Skills performance at a second occasion was significantly correlated with fluid reasoning performance seven years earlier. Another paper-and-pencil test, the Everyday Problems Test, contains items designed to assess the IADL domains, including food preparation, medication use and health behaviors, financial management, and transportation. Scores on this test have been found to be correlated 0.87 with the overall score on the ETS Basic Skills Test (Willis 1996) and have also been found to have moderate correlations with a variety of cognitive variables (Burton et al. 2006).

One of the limitations of paper-and-pencil tests of everyday functioning is that they involve the same method of assessment as most cognitive tests, and thus the correlations may reflect a common method of assessment rather than the existence of a common construct. Partially in response to this concern, the Observed Tasks of Daily Living Test was developed in which the examiner observes performance of 31 tasks in the examinee's home with real-life materials (Diehl et al. 1995, 2005). Among the tasks are calculating days of pill supply and activating a call-forwarding mechanism. This test was found to have a correlation of 0.67 with the Everyday Problems Test, which suggests that the two tests may measure some of the same common factors. Of greatest interest in the current context were the moderate relations between cognitive ability factors and Observed Tasks of Daily Living factors, with standardized path analysis coefficients of 0.48 for fluid reasoning and 0.22 for crystallized knowledge.

In summary, several different approaches have been used to assess the competence of older adults to live independently. All of the methods are approximations because there are currently no direct measures of the capability of living independently. However, results from each of the assessment methods have been found to be significantly related to psychometric measures of cognitive abilities, and somewhat surprisingly, the strongest relations have been found with novel problem-solving (or fluid) rather than with knowledge (or crystallized) measures of cognition.

Life Outcomes

A considerable amount of research has examined relations between cognitive ability and different types of life outcomes. Because research with social outcomes is often difficult to interpret due to a confounding of cognitive ability with social class and opportunity, the focus here is on recent research within the emerging subdiscipline of cognitive epidemiology that is concerned with the impact of cognitive ability on health outcomes. This specialty within epidemiology differs from other epidemiological fields in that cognition is viewed as an antecedent, or predictor variable, instead of a consequence, or outcome variable.

A relatively large literature has been concerned with the terminal decline phenomenon in which level of cognitive functioning is often lower several years prior to death (e.g., Backman & MacDonald 2006, Bosworth & Siegler 2002, Lavery et al. 2009, Small et al. 2003, Wilson et al. 2009). However, when the assessment of cognition occurs in old age, it is difficult to rule out reverse causality in which health problems contribute to low levels of cognition. In contrast, interpretations are less ambiguous when cognition is assessed at young ages and mortality occurs decades later; those are the studies of primary interest here.

Perhaps the earliest study in this field was a report by O'Toole & Stankov (1992) of Australian men who were administered a cognitive aptitude test at about age 18 and whose survival was monitored up until age 40. The major finding was that higher cognitive ability assessed prior to age 22 was associated with a lower risk of death, and particularly motor vehicle death, between 22 and 40 years of age.

Another early study was by Whalley & Deary (2001), who capitalized on the availability of cognitive ability scores originally acquired in 1932 from a large number of 11-year-old Scottish children. A search of the death records from 1932 to 1997 yielded mortality information that could be related to childhood cognitive ability. Even after controlling for father's occupation, lower cognitive ability at age 11 was

SES: socioeconomic status

found to be associated with greater risk of mortality up to age 76.

Several reviews of the relations between cognition and mortality have recently been published (e.g., Batty & Deary 2004, Batty et al. 2007, Deary 2005, Gottfredson & Deary 2004). As an example, Batty et al. (2007) described nine studies in which relations between early-life cognitive ability and later mortality risk were examined. All nine studies reported that higher levels of cognitive ability were associated with decreased risk of mortality.

Some of the most impressive findings on cognition-mortality relations were based on analyses of data from nearly one million Swedish men whose cognitive ability was assessed at age 18 and for whom mortality was monitored up to about age 45 (e.g., Batty et al. 2009a,b). Because of the very large sample size, it was possible to examine the relations by type of mortality and also adjust for factors such as blood pressure, body mass index, and socioeconomic status (SES). The researchers were also able to identify a dose-response relation, with higher rates of mortality at successively lower levels of cognitive ability.

A few studies have also reported relations of cognitive ability to health status and not merely with mortality. For example, Der et al. (2009) found that higher cognitive test scores were associated with lower depression scores, better general health, and significantly lower odds of having 6 of 9 diagnosed conditions and 15 of 33 health problems. Walker et al. (2002) also reported that higher cognitive test scores at age 11 were associated with less psychiatric contact up to age 77.

Several hypotheses for the cognition-mortality relations have been discussed by Deary and colleagues (e.g., Batty & Deary 2004, Deary 2005, Whalley & Deary 2001). Among these were that (*a*) both cognition and mortality are a consequence of insults such as birth complications, (*b*) cognition predicts advantageous social circumstances that are the primary factor affecting mortality rates, (*c*) cognition is a proxy for stress management skills, and (*d*) cognition is associated with the acquisition and maintenance of health-conducive behaviors. Some support for this latter hypothesis was provided by Deary et al. (2009), who found that higher verbal ability was associated with greater persistence in taking medications over a two-year period. Stilley and colleagues (Stilley et al. 2004, 2010) also reported that higher levels of cognitive ability were associated with better medication adherence as measured by electronic bottle cap monitors. In addition, Sabia et al. (2010) found that controlling health variables such as smoking, alcoholic consumption, fruit and vegetable consumption, and hours of physical exercise reduced the relation between cognitive ability and mortality, which is consistent with the role of healthy lifestyle as a mediator of the relations.

The interpretation of the cognition-mortality relationship favored by Deary (e.g., Deary 2005, Deary et al. 2009; also see Gottfredson & Deary 2004) is that health self-care is analogous to a complex job in that it requires a variety of cognitive abilities such as knowledge, problem solving, planning, and decision making. A similar view emphasizing cognitive ability, in the form of numeracy, in the context of medical decision making was expressed by Reyna et al. (2009): "Low numeracy distorts perceptions of risks and benefits of screening, reduces medical compliance, impedes access to treatments, impairs risk communication (limiting prevention efforts among the most vulnerable), and . . . appears to adversely affect medical outcomes" (p. 943).

Because many of the cognition relations might be attributable to amount of education or to SES, the role of education and SES on cognition-mortality relations was explicitly discussed by Deary (2008). He noted that although there were some cases in which the cognition-mortality relation was reduced when these factors were controlled, this was not always the case. For example, significant cognition relations were found after controlling for father's occupation (Whalley & Deary 2001), after controlling for father's social class at birth (e.g., Leon et al. 2009), and after controlling for a measure of SES (e.g., Batty et al. 2009a, Jokela et al. 2009, Shipley et al. 2005). Deary (2009) also cautioned that statistical control results can be ambiguous because there is still uncertainty about the causal direction between education (and SES) and cognitive ability, and therefore it is possible that they all reflect cognitive ability.

In summary, many relations have been documented between cognitive ability and important life outcomes, and at least some of these relations do not appear to be attributable to social class or educational level. In a commentary on some of this research, Lubinski (2009) noted, "There is an old saying in applied psychology: for a difference to be a difference it must make a difference. Cognitive differences make real differences in life" (p. 627). The reasons for these linkages are not fully understood, but Gottfredson (2004a,b) noted that many aspects of contemporary life require cognitive abilities, such as filling out job applications or government forms, figuring out a bus or train schedule, and interpreting maps, and that although no single aspect is critical, they can accumulate over one's life to have large consequences.

AGE TRENDS IN COGNITION

Some researchers, including several industrial-organizational psychologists interested in job performance, have assumed that there are little or no age relations on cognition until age 65 or older. For example, Murphy (1989) stated: "Although ability levels may gradually change over one's lifetime, it is reasonable to treat a worker's level of general cognitive ability, over the period of that worker's job tenure, as a constant" (p. 185). However, an extensive research literature has documented sizable relations between age and level of cognitive functioning prior to age 65.

For the current purposes, results based on contrasts of cross-sectional data are referred to as declines even though it is not known if there is decline at the level of individuals because the relevant data are not longitudinal. Nevertheless, the terminology of decline is less cumbersome than is awkward reference to negative age differences.

Because there are many different types of cognitive variables in which performance is expressed in different units, the original scores in cognitive tests are frequently converted to z-score units to facilitate comparisons across variables. This conversion is carried out in **Figure 2**, which illustrates the age trends in composite measures of novel processing (or fluid cognition) and knowledge (or crystallized cognition) from studies by Salthouse and colleagues and from the nationally representative sample used to provide norms for the WAIS-IV (also see Salthouse 2009a). These data clearly indicate that there are two distinct patterns of age trends for the two major types of cognition, with a monotonic decrease for measures of reasoning and other process abilities, and stability followed by decline for measures of acquired knowledge.

Hunt (1995, p. 119) estimated the declines to be about −0.04 standard deviations per year beginning at about age 30 for fluid cognition, with an increase from age 20 to age 65 of 0.03 standard deviations per year for crystallized cognition. However, recent research suggests that both sets of relations are more modest, as the estimates from over 3,000 adults between 20 and 70 years of age in the Salthouse studies are −0.02 for fluid ability and 0.02 for crystallized ability, and estimates of the age relations from the 1,577 adults in the normative WAIS-IV sample are −0.02 for fluid ability and 0.003 for crystallized ability.

Evidence indicates that the cross-sectional age-cognition relations are not only well documented but also quite robust. For example, although the absolute levels of cognitive performance have increased over historical time, the relative age trends have been similar for several generations. That is, parallel age trends are evident over a span of about 50 years in data from Schaie's Seattle Longitudinal Study (e.g., figure 4.5 in Schaie 2005) and over a period of nearly 70 years in the Wechsler tests (e.g., figure 2.6 in Salthouse 2010).

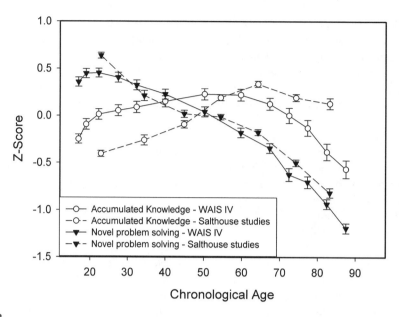

Figure 2

Means (and standard errors) for composite measures of accumulated knowledge and novel problem solving in the Wechsler Adult Intelligence Scale-Fourth Edition (WAIS-IV) standardization sample and in studies by Salthouse and colleagues.

Moreover, the age relations are not restricted to a certain segment of the population because they are evident across different percentiles of the score distribution at each age, with nearly constant standard deviations at different ages (Salthouse 2010). There is also little change in the age relations after controlling for variables such as amount of education, self-rated health, depression, and anxiety (e.g., Salthouse 2009b), and parallel age trends have been reported at different levels of SES (Fozard & Nuttall 1971) and among workers at different levels of job complexity (Avolio & Waldman 1990). Finally, similar trends have been found when examinees were highly motivated because the tests were taken for vocational guidance (Schroeder & Salthouse 2004) or for job selection (Avolio & Waldman 1990, Droege et al. 1963, Fozard & Nuttall 1971, Hartigan & Wigdor 1989, Stein 1962).

Cross-sectional age-cognition relations are sometimes dismissed on the grounds that they reflect many factors other than age. Although the assertion that age is not the only determinant of the cross-sectional trends is certainly true, cross-sectional patterns are arguably the most relevant type of comparison if one is interested in relative level of functioning at a particular point in time. That is, the primary question in the current context concerns the interrelations of age, cognitive functioning, and real-world functioning, and the reasons why people of different ages vary in their level of cognitive functioning is of secondary importance for this particular question.

In summary, nearly monotonic age-related declines in many cognitive variables have been reported between 20 and 75 years of age, with the correlations between age and reasoning or fluid ability often ranging from −0.3 to −0.5. To illustrate, Verhaeghen & Salthouse (1997) reported a meta-analysis of 38 correlations with a total sample size of over 9,000 adults, and their estimate of the age-reasoning correlation was −0.40, which is very close to the correlations of −0.39 in the Salthouse data set and −0.43 in the WAIS-IV normative data. However, different age trends are apparent in measures of acquired knowledge, as the functions typically increase until about age 60 and then gradually decline.

WHAT ARE THE CONSEQUENCES OF AGE-RELATED COGNITIVE DECLINES?

Two major sets of results are described in the preceding sections: a positive relation between cognitive ability and life outcomes (with a correlation in the domain of work of about 0.5) and a negative relation between age and cognitive ability (with a correlation of about −0.4 for measures of novel problem solving). If these two relations are combined in a path analysis model, they lead to an expected correlation of about −0.2 between age and effectiveness of functioning outside the laboratory. In other words, given that increased age is associated with lower levels of performance on certain cognitive tests, and that performance in those tests is positively associated with various measures of real-world functioning, increased age might be expected to be associated with lower levels of functioning outside the laboratory. The current section reviews the evidence

relevant to this predicted age relation and considers possible explanations for why it is seldom found.

Age and Achievement

One area in which the results seem consistent with expectations of negative age relations is research on achievement. Interest in the topic of relations between age and achievement dates at least to Quetelet (1835/1842), with the first inverted-U age-achievement figure published by Beard in 1881. **Figure 3** illustrates the typical shape of age-achievement functions with data from Lehman (1962, 1966). Age is represented along the horizontal axis, and the vertical axis is some measure of achievement or productivity, with Lehman usually converting the raw achievement measures to percentages of the maximum across all ages. This inverted-U function is now well established, with most of the 170 figures in Lehman's (1953) book portraying similar functions across different disciplines and historical periods, and numerous replications have been published in different fields and with alternative measures of achievement (e.g., see Simonton 1988).

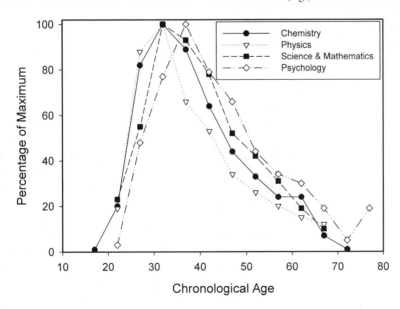

Figure 3

Measures of achievement as a function of age from studies by Lehman (1962, 1966).

The basic phenomenon of a steep increase, a relatively early peak, and a gradual decline has not only proven robust across many different disciplines and historical periods, but also across many types of achievement measures. For example, measures of achievement have ranged from simple counts of products (such as the number of published articles, paintings, inventions, or musical recordings) to consideration of particularly high-quality products (such as highly cited articles or discoveries recognized as the basis for a Nobel Prize). Furthermore, similar functions have been obtained in within-individual comparisons, after control of differences in lifespan to ensure that everyone has potential to contribute at all ages and after control of the size of the competition at different ages to avoid a bias against older contributors when the number of potential contributors is increasing over time (e.g., Lehman 1953, Simonton 1988).

Early interpretations of the age-achievement functions linked them to age-related cognitive declines, and indeed, the functions were originally used to infer age trends in mental faculties. For example, Quetelet (1835/1842) described his rationale for analyses of age and achievement as follows: "We can only appreciate faculties by their effects; in other words, by the actions or works which they produce . . . [and] . . . by bearing in mind the ages at which the authors have produced their works, we possess the necessary elements to follow the development of the mind, or its productive power" (pp. 74–75). Beard (1874) noted, ". . . we have no recognized mental dynamometer by which to measure the comparative cerebral force of the living and the dead. The true and only way by which the subject can be approached is by studying the history of human achievement and comparing the age at which has been done the best work of the world" (p. 4).

However, more recent scholars in the age-achievement field have disagreed with Quetelet and Beard and have generally not assumed that the age-achievement functions were attributable to cognitive declines. For example,

Lehman (1953) suggested that multiple causes were operating in producing the functions, and he provided a list of 16 possible causes in the final chapter of his book. The first possibility on his list was decline ". . . in physical vigor, energy, and resistance to fatigue . . . [which he suggested was] . . . probably far more important than such normal age changes as may occur in adult intelligence" (p. 328).

One aspect of age-achievement functions that does appear consistent with a role of cognitive factors is differences across disciplines in the age of the peak and the steepness of the decline (e.g., Lehman 1953, Simonton 1988). Specifically, fields such as lyric poetry, pure mathematics, and theoretical physics, which may place a premium on novel problem solving, tend to have earlier peaks and more rapid declines than do fields with more reliance on accumulated knowledge (e.g., novel writing, history, philosophy). To illustrate, Simonton (1997) noted that the peak age was 26.5 for mathematicians, but 38.5 for historians. Although these differences are intriguing, they refer to differences across disciplines and are not necessarily relevant to the nature of the trajectory within individuals. That is, the key question in the current context is the role of age-related cognitive decline on the declining segment of the functions, regardless of the field in which the function is observed.

A critical issue in evaluating the cognitive decline interpretation of the age-achievement functions is the distinction between quantity and quality because age-related declines in cognitive functioning might be expected to have a greater role in decreases in quality than in decreases in quantity. Simonton (e.g., 1997) has been a strong advocate of what he terms the "constant probability of success" principle, which refers to the idea that although there may be a decrease with age in productivity, each contribution for a particular individual has a nearly equal chance of success regardless of one's age. His argument is based on empirical analyses of the quality and quantity of achievements, and particularly what he termed the quality ratio, which is the number of major works divided by number of total works over a given period. Analyses in several different disciplines revealed that the quality ratio remained approximately constant across most of adulthood (Simonton 1997).

Direct support for the constant probability of success principle was reported by Oster & Hamermesh (1998) in a study of publications of economists. These researchers examined submission rates and the probability of acceptance in a major journal for authors of different ages. As in other studies, there was an inverted-U relation between age and number of manuscripts submitted, but the acceptance probability was nearly constant at all ages. The lower productivity of older economists was therefore not because they had higher rejection rates when submitting their articles (which might serve as an indication of quality), but rather was attributable to a lower rate of submission (which can be viewed as a reflection of quantity).

To the extent that increased age is associated with a reduction in how much is done, but not in the quality of what is done, it implies a need to explain why there is a decrease in quantity with increasing age when attempting to account for age-achievement functions. One frequently mentioned possibility is that productivity decreases with age because of shifting responsibilities and motivations as people advance in their careers and take on more supervisory, mentoring, or collaborative work, which all introduce competing demands for their time (Stephan & Levin 1993). In fact, there is some evidence of more rapid declines of the age-achievement functions for scholars who take on administrative responsibilities (Goodwin & Sauer 1995). Although the mere existence of shifting responsibilities could not explain why some fields have very shallow declines, it is possible that disciplinary differences are attributable to slower information obsolescence in certain fields. Indeed, McDowell (1982) suggested that the relevant knowledge base changes more slowly in fields such as history and philosophy than in fields such as chemistry and physics, and thus scholars in those fields may experience less disruption in their productivity associated with periods away from their primary work.

Although there are similarities in the age trends in novel problem solving and in various measures of achievement in a variety of domains, a limitation of research on achievement is that a very large number of factors influence the outcome variable, which makes it difficult to identify the role of any single factor such as cognitive ability. It is therefore possible that less ambiguous conclusions about the influence of cognitive ability might be reached by studying age trends in a narrower aspect of behavior with fewer, or more controllable, confounds.

One intriguing example of this more focused approach is a recent study of financial decisions by a group of economists (Agarwal et al. 2008). This project involved analyses of an extensive database containing details of borrowing information and characteristics of individual borrowers, including age. The major finding was that borrowing with the fewest fees in several different contexts, including mortgages, home equity loans, auto loans, and credit card interest rates, occurred for middle-aged adults. Moreover, the relationships were evident even after controlling for many variables that might affect loan pricing, such as credit risk, home value, and income. Additional analyses revealed that the age relations in home equity loans were largely attributable to errors in estimating the value of one's home, which led to an increased borrowing rate. That is, the propensity to make a rate-changing mistake had a U-shaped relation with age, but the borrowing rates for consumers who did not make a rate-changing mistake was independent of age. The authors speculated that this peak for favorable financial decisions at about age 53 might have occurred because this may be the age where there is an optimal balance between high reasoning ability, which declines with age, and relevant experience, which increases at least until middle age. By limiting the focus to a specific type of behavior, these researchers had greater control over a variety of potential confounding factors than is possible with cruder achievement outcomes. Nevertheless, the results still cannot be considered

General Aptitude Test Battery: cognitive test battery developed by the U.S. Department of Labor to assist in employee selection and guidance

ATC: air traffic controller

definitive evidence for a role of cognitive ability because no direct measures of cognitive ability were available from the individuals, and thus the linkage of borrowing rates to cognitive ability remains somewhat speculative.

Age and Job Performance

Because job performance is the domain with the most extensive linkages to cognitive abilities, strong age-performance relations might be expected in measures of job performance. Indeed, Fozard & Nuttall (1971) noted that there were pronounced age relations on summary scores from the General Aptitude Test Battery, which was developed by the Department of Labor to guide employment selection, and that when these age relations were aligned with the minimum levels proposed for different occupations, the results implied that fewer than 50% of 60-year-olds would qualify for many of the jobs. However, with few exceptions, these pessimistic expectations have seldom been confirmed with empirical research.

One occupation in which negative age-performance relations have been well documented is the field of air traffic controllers (ATCs). Age relations in ATC performance are considered to be so pronounced that in the United States there is a mandatory retirement age of 56 for controllers who manage air traffic, and a maximum age of 30 for entry into ATC school. The sizable age relations among ATCs likely occur because of the unique characteristics of that job. That is, ATCs must monitor and direct movement of aircraft within an assigned air space and on the ground under continuously changing conditions, and these activities require numerous cognitive abilities that have been found to be negatively related to age, such as speed and flexibility of closure, inductive and deductive reasoning, and selective and divided attention.

Age-performance relations in ATC activities have been found even in samples of adults with a very restricted age range. That is, because the maximum age of active controllers is typically in the 50s, most are under 50 years of age. Nevertheless, poorer performance with increased age has clearly been documented in ATC training. To illustrate, Trites & Cobb (1963) reported seven times more failures in ATC training among trainees 39 years of age and older compared to younger trainees, and Trites & Cobb (1964) reported a success rate of 50% for trainees under age 33 but only 20% for trainees over age 33. There have also been numerous reports of poorer performance with increased age in aptitude tests related to ATC activities (e.g., Becker & Milke 1998, Cobb et al. 1971, Heil 1999) and poorer supervisor ratings with increased age among active controllers (e.g., Cobb 1968, Cobb et al. 1971, Heil 1999).

Exceptions to the strong age-performance relations among ATCs have been reported in two recent studies, but each has characteristics suggesting that the conclusions may need qualifications. In the first study, Broach & Schroeder (2006) found no differences in the rate of operational errors for controllers under and over 56 years of age. However, the incidence of operational errors was very low, and the power to detect age differences in them may have been weak. Furthermore, because the mandatory retirement age is 56, with a special exemption typically based on exceptional performance needed to continue to age 61, the older controllers in this project may not have been representative of their age cohort. In the second study, Nunes & Kramer (2009) compared Canadian controllers in two age groups (age 20 to 27 and age 53 to 64) on simulated ATC tasks. (Because Canada does not have mandatory retirement of ATCs at age 56, it was possible to obtain a sample of older controllers in this study.) The major finding was that there was little age difference in performance of the simulated air traffic control tasks for controllers, but a large age difference existed for noncontrollers. However, the young controllers in this project had very limited experience (i.e., a mean of 1.6 years), and factors other than controller experience were likely operating in the simulated tasks because the young noncontrollers performed at a level similar to the two controller groups.

Although age-related declines are apparent in jobs such as ATCs and among elite or professional athletes (e.g., Baker et al. 2007, Schulz & Curnow 1988, Schulz et al. 1994), meta-analyses typically reveal little or no systematic relation of age with measures of job performance (e.g., Davies & Sparrow 1988, Hunter & Hunter 1984, Hunter & Schmidt 1998, McEvoy & Cascio 1989, Rhodes 1983, Sturman 2003, Waldman & Avolio 1986). As an example, in their meta-analysis, McEvoy & Cascio (1989) found the correlations between age and performance ranged from -0.44 to $+0.66$, with a meta-analytic estimate of 0.06 and a 95% confidence interval from -0.18 to $+0.30$. The wide range of correlations led to the investigation of possible moderators of the age-performance relations, but there was little evidence of moderation either by type of performance measure (i.e., rating or productivity measure) or by type of job (e.g., blue collar or white collar), and other meta-analyses have also failed to identify strong moderators of the relations between age and job performance.

Many of the studies examining relations of age and work performance can be criticized (e.g., Salthouse 1990, 1994; Salthouse & Maurer 1996) because of selective attrition (in that older workers may not be as representative of their age peers as are younger workers because of advancement of the most competent or dismissal of the least competent) and restricted age range (with few studies containing workers over about 50 years of age). Another frequently mentioned limitation of job performance studies is poor outcome or criterion variables because it is difficult to assess quality of performance in complex jobs, supervisor ratings can be biased, and few objective indicators of performance are available in professional or managerial jobs. Nevertheless, it is important to recognize that some of the same studies that did not find significant relations with age did find significant relations with cognitive ability (e.g., Hunter & Hunter 1984, Hunter & Schmidt 1998), and therefore job performance outcome variables are not completely lacking in reliability or sensitivity.

Why Are There Not Greater Consequences?

The preceding review indicates that with only a few exceptions, there is little evidence of a negative relation of age (at least within the range of 20 to 75 years of age) and indices of overall level of functioning in society. Assuming that the age-cognition and cognition-functioning relations reviewed above are valid estimates of the true population relations, the positive cognition-functioning relation and negative age-cognition relation lead to expectations of negative relations between age and functioning that are rarely observed. The remainder of this section considers four categories of possible explanations for why there are not greater consequences of age-related cognitive declines.

(A) Seldom need to perform at one's maximum. One possible explanation of the discrepancy between the expectation of negative consequences of cognitive declines and the general absence of confirming evidence is related to a distinction between assessments of typical and maximal functioning. The distinction between typical and maximal assessment was apparently first introduced by Cronbach (1949), was later elaborated by Fiske & Butler (1963), Ackerman (1994), Goff & Ackerman (1992), and Dennis et al. (2000), and was discussed from a somewhat different perspective by Posner (1995). The basic idea is that what we do in daily life reflects our typical level of functioning, whereas cognitive tests attempt to assess our maximal level of functioning. To the extent that many outcome criteria reflect typical behavior, whereas the predictions from cognitive tests are based on maximal behavior, it is possible that at least some of the discrepancy between predicted and observed age differences in real-world functioning is attributable to the use of different types of assessments in the predictions and in the observations of everyday functioning.

It is almost certainly true that we do not need to function at our maximum level often; if we did, everyday life would be too stressful. It also seems plausible that relations of cognitive

Fluid intelligence (Gf): term introduced by Raymond Cattell referring to undifferentiated abilities that can "flow" into different domains

Crystallized intelligence (Gc): term introduced by Raymond Cattell to refer to the crystallized products of interactions of fluid abilities with environmental exposure

ability or other factors might only be detectable at the highest levels of functioning, when other factors might be relatively less important. Note that this perspective does not deny the possibility of age-related declines that could impact real-world functioning, but instead suggests that they are not detected because people seldom need to function at the level at which deficits might be manifested.

(B) Shift with age from novel processing to reliance on accumulated knowledge. Many cognitive tests can be considered analogous to exercises in mental gymnastics, in that as with physical gymnastics, they are designed to assess agility or flexibility but do not necessarily have direct counterparts in the everyday world. In a similar vein, it has been noted that "... abilities assessed by these types of tests ... [can be] ... characterized as determining the level of performance that can be achieved when one doesn't know what to do and has no relevant experience" (Salthouse 2006, p. 279). In contrast to this emphasis on novelty, it is possible that much of what we do in our daily life is only slightly different from what we have done in the past. That is, novel problem solving ability may become less important to an individual as more of his or her life problems are solved, and consequently higher proportions of one's daily functioning can occur by retrieval of the prior solutions.

This idea that an advantage of greater knowledge overcomes any disadvantage of less effective novel processing has a long history. In 1933, Jones & Conrad suggested that "... much of the effective power of the adult ... is evidently derived from accumulated stocks of information" (p. 254). Among the recent expressions of the idea that knowledge becomes more important with increased age are the following quotations:

> The concerned reader, who might be over 26 years of age, when fluid intelligence first begins to decline, should note the effects are rather gradual. In any event, the improvement witnessed in the individual's crystallized

intelligence tends to be nature's compensation. (Matthews et al. 2002, p. 108)

> Because job experience and age are often inextricably intertwined, the midlife worker will be more skilled than the younger worker ... thus any loss of Gf abilities will be compensated for by higher levels of job knowledge (Gc). (Kanfer & Ackerman 2004, p. 450)

A very simple empirical example of the potential importance of age-related increases in knowledge is evident in a contrast of the age trends in measures of analytical reasoning with the age trends in a measure of crossword puzzle performance (cf. Salthouse 2010). These two activities are similar in that in both cases the solution requires simultaneous satisfaction of multiple constraints. That is, analytical reasoning problems often specify a number of conditions that must not be violated in order to reach a solution, and solutions in crossword puzzles must simultaneously fit the clue, the number of letters in the target word, and the positions of any letters that have already been identified. As can be seen in **Figure 4**, age trends in the analytical reasoning task closely resemble the monotonic declines evident in novel problem-solving tasks. However, when knowledge is relevant to the task, as in crossword puzzles, the age trends among people with frequent crossword puzzle–solving experiences are actually reversed, with better performance at older ages! These opposite trends in the same individuals are consistent with the view that little or no consequence of cognitive declines may be evident when one can draw upon relevant knowledge.

Closely related to the idea of benefits of accumulated knowledge is the distinction between functioning in new or unfamiliar situations versus functioning in situations in which one has considerable experience. As Droege noted, "Maintenance of ability once acquired is not the same as acquisition of a new ability" (1967, p. 181). This view has been endorsed by a number of researchers, and some have suggested that the distinction might account for the lack of negative age relations in real-world situations (e.g., Hunt 1995). For example,

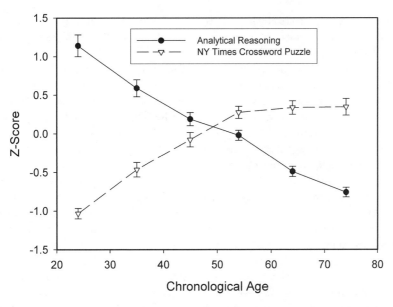

Figure 4

Means (and standard errors) of performance on an analytical reasoning test and on a crossword puzzle test from studies by Salthouse and colleagues.

citing research by Fleischman and Ackerman of reduced correlations between cognitive ability and task performance with increased practice, Murphy (1989) suggested that cognitive ability is primarily important in periods of transition in which new information must be acquired rather than relying on past experience.

However, other researchers, such as Gottfredson (2004b) and Schmidt & Hunter (2004), have argued that many tasks in moderately complex jobs cannot be automated, and hence cognitive ability continues to be important because of the constant need for adaptation and improvisation. The key assumption that there is a dramatic decrease in the need for novel problem solving with increased age can also be questioned. Although it is true that a great deal of novel problem solving may be required when one is first starting a career, considerable problem solving may also be needed in many activities associated with middle age and late adulthood, such as when selecting among investment and retirement plans, making health care decisions, and adhering to medication regimens. The research on tasks

designed to predict independent living in older adults is also relevant in this context because the results suggest that novel problem solving is a stronger predictor of measures related to independent living than measures of accumulated knowledge. The relative importance of novel problem solving versus accumulated knowledge almost certainly varies as a function of many factors, including type of activity and amount of experience, but there may be very few situations at any age in which there is no advantage of high levels of novel problem-solving ability.

(C) Cognition is not the only determinant of success in life. Several researchers have noted in the context of the relation between cognition and job performance that even a correlation of 0.5 leaves about 75% of the variance unexplained (e.g., Higgins et al. 2007, Matthews et al. 2002, Sternberg & Hedlund 2002). Numerous speculations have consequently been offered about what is responsible for the remaining variance in job performance not predicted by cognitive ability. For example, Moss & Tilly (2001) noted that job

KSAO: knowledge, skills, abilities, and others, presumed to be major dimensions of competency of an individual

performance is not only affected by hard skills, which is their term for cognitive and technical skills, but also by soft skills, by which they mean personality and attitude. Posner (1995) mentioned the possibility that psychometric tests do not measure occupationally relevant aspects of application, focus, flexibility, and effort. Furthermore, Gottfredson (2002) suggested that there were three major determinants of job success, which she characterized as "can do" (ability), "will do" (motivation), and "have done" (experience), with only the first typically represented in most assessments.

The existence of factors beyond cognitive ability has been explicitly acknowledged in the field of industrial organizational psychology, in which determinants of job performance are frequently referred to as KSAOs, where K refers to general knowledge, S to task-specific skills, A to physical and cognitive ability, and O to miscellaneous Other factors. Because task-specific skills can be expected to be acquired with experience, it is possible that some relevant skills are greater at older ages and represent a form of experience-based compensation. One example of a positive relation of age on a task-specific skill is available in the domain of transcription typing. Salthouse (1984, 1987) examined various typing-related tasks in samples of adults selected such that there was no relation between age and net typing speed. Although increased age was associated with slower reaction time to individual letters, older typists were found to have larger eye-hand spans, or greater preview of forthcoming keystrokes, than younger typists had, and it is possible that this typing-related skill functioned to compensate for their slower perceptual motor speed. The typing research is only one example in which experienced older individuals perform at higher levels than one would expect based on their levels of basic abilities, but it is likely that many other situations exist in which increased age is associated with the acquisition of task-specific skills that contribute to high proficiency on the job.

Among the many candidates for Other factors in the KSAO framework are aspects of personality (Roberts et al. 2007, Schmidt & Hunter 2004), emotional intelligence (Matthews et al. 2002), practical intelligence (Sternberg & Hedlund 2002, Wagner & Sternberg 1985), decision-making competence or rationality (De Bruin et al. 2007, Parker & Fischoff 2005, Stanovich 2009, Stanovich & West 2008), process analytic ability (Zysberg 2009), and even chance (Gladwell 2008). Evidence for the contribution of other factors is most convincing when they are examined simultaneously with cognitive ability to determine whether the factors are associated with incremental prediction of the relevant criterion. For example, Schmidt & Hunter (1998, 2004; also see Judge et al. 2010) found that conscientiousness had incremental prediction of job performance and success in job training beyond general cognitive ability. Wagner & Sternberg (1990; also see Sternberg et al. 1995) have also reported incremental prediction from tacit knowledge over conventional measures of cognitive ability of performance in managerial simulations.

However, in addition to evidence of incremental prediction, in order to account for the discrepancy between the expected and observed patterns of real-world functioning with increased age there should also be evidence of an interaction, with greater incremental prediction of the relevant outcomes from other factors at older ages than at young ages. That is, if other factors are responsible for the discrepancy between the predicted and observed age-outcome relations, then the other factors either must have higher values at older ages, a stronger relation with the criterion at older ages, or a combination of higher values and stronger relations. In other words, it is not sufficient to demonstrate that factors other than cognitive ability are involved in the outcomes because it also needs to be established that these other factors are related to age and that they have different relations to the criterion as a function of age.

Consider the case of conscientiousness as a candidate for the Other factor. In order for it to be responsible for maintained real-world functioning despite age-related declines in cognitive functioning, not only should it be positively related to age, but there should also be evidence of greater incremental prediction of relevant outcomes at older ages. There is evidence that values of conscientiousness are somewhat higher with increased age (e.g., Roberts & Mroczek 2008, Srivastava et al. 2003, Terracciano et al. 2005), but at the present time there is apparently no research establishing that the incremental contribution of conscientiousness in the prediction of job performance or other important outcomes is greater at older ages.

Cognitive ability is clearly not the only determinant of successful functioning in life, and it is certainly possible that some determinants increase with age and offset any age-related declines in cognitive ability. Although plausible, empirical evidence documenting the compensatory nature of these other determinants is currently quite limited.

(D) Accommodations. A fourth possible interpretation of why there are not greater consequences of age-related cognitive declines is that there might be real consequences of the declines, but they are not apparent because of accommodations of the individual. For example, accommodations could occur if people minimize the consequences of declines by restricting their exposure to deficit-revealing situations. Driving may be an example of this type of restricted exposure as, likely in part due to recognition of their declining levels of sensory and cognitive abilities, many older adults avoid driving in rush hour, at night, and on unfamiliar routes. There is also evidence that workers tend to shift jobs as they experience difficulty in the original job (e.g., Warr & Pennington 1994), which is apparent in different age distributions for different jobs (e.g., Hunt 1995, Kanfer & Ackerman 2004, Warr 1994, Welford 1958). Other possible types of accommodation include a reduction in the range of domains in which one maintains a high level of expertise ("selective optimization"; see Baltes & Baltes 1990) and greater reliance on others, including

delegation of responsibility to junior associates, paid assistants, and children (e.g., Birren 1969).

Still another form of accommodation could occur at the societal level and involve adaptations of the environment in which the individual lives. That is, the nature of many jobs has changed over time as automation and technology have reduced cognitive demands. To illustrate, Hunt (1995) described the case of a cashier who now merely scans bar codes with little or no need to rely on memory and arithmetic. In the past, performance in a job such as this may have had strong relations to cognitive abilities, but that is no longer the case because of the altered requirements of the job.

Although empirical evidence on effects of environmental adaptations in people of different ages is currently limited, it seems likely that there could be differential impact of future technological innovations as a function of the worker's age. For example, if novel problem-solving requirements are reduced by new technology, older individuals will likely have the greatest benefit because they tend to have lower levels of novel problem-solving ability than young adults. In contrast, if technology leads to extraction of relevant knowledge that can be embodied in expert systems, young individuals may experience the greatest benefit because they have not yet acquired the relevant knowledge. (See Posner 1995, p. 69, for a similar argument.) Because at the current time it may be more feasible to build a knowledge base (and it may already exist in the form of Google and its competitors) than to automate novel problem solving, benefits of technology in the reduction of cognitive demands may currently be greater for young adults than for older adults.

Relatively little is known about how people adapt, either consciously or unconsciously, to diminishing cognitive abilities. Nevertheless, it seems likely that many people will tend to alter what they do, or how they do it, to try to maintain a high level of functioning in the face of declines in relevant abilities, and this may contribute to the often minimal consequences of declining abilities.

CONCLUSIONS

Cognitive ability is important in daily life, and there is currently little evidence that its importance declines with increasing age. In fact, there are some reasons to expect that the role of cognitive ability in late adulthood is even more important now than in the past because individuals of all ages are being asked to take more responsibility for financial (Banks & Oldfield 2007, McArdle et al. 2009) and medical (Reyna et al. 2009) decisions.

Negative relations of age to cognition are among the strongest individual difference relations in psychology, and thus it is reasonable to expect consequences of those declines in life outside the laboratory. Very robust inverted-U relations between age and different measures of achievement have been reported in many different domains. Although these trends are superficially consistent with the existence of age-related cognitive declines, the relation is weak because the declines may reflect quantity more than quality, there are many other possible determinants of the functions besides cognitive ability, and there are no direct linkages of cognitive ability and achievement in the same individuals.

At the current time, evidence of negative consequences of age-related decreases in cognitive ability is limited until the level of cognitive ability reaches pathological limits. Reasons for the lack of consequences are still not fully understood, but they probably reflect a combination of several factors, including few life situations in which one needs to perform at his or her maximum, greater reliance with increased age on acquired knowledge or on noncognitive factors that do not decline with age instead of novel problem solving, or because of a variety of different types of accommodations that minimize impact of the declines.

Despite the lack of definitive answers at the current time, it will ultimately be valuable to discover why the consequences of age-related cognitive declines are so small because the reasons may have implications in other areas. For example, understanding why there are few consequences may suggest possibilities for remediation of cognitive disabilities or for the design of interventions to prevent decline.

DISCLOSURE STATEMENT

The author is not aware of any affiliations, memberships, funding, or financial holdings that might be perceived as affecting the objectivity of this review.

ACKNOWLEDGMENTS

Preparation of this manuscript was supported by the Russell Sage Foundation, where the author was a Visiting Scholar for the 2009–2010 academic year. I would like to thank Earl Hunt and Susan Fiske for valuable comments on an earlier draft of this manuscript.

LITERATURE CITED

Ackerman PL. 1994. Intelligence, attention and learning: maximal and typical performance. In *Current Topics in Human Intelligence*, ed. DK Detterman, pp. 1–27. Norwood, NJ: Ablex

Ackerman PL, Cianciolo AT. 2002. Ability and task constraint determinants of complex task performance. *J. Exp. Psychol. Appl.* 8:194–208

Agarwal S, Driscoll J, Gabaix X, Laibson D. 2008. The age of reason: financial decisions over the lifecycle. *Am. Law Econ. Assoc. Annu. Meet.* 97:1–5

Allaire JC, Marsiske M. 1999. Everyday cognition: age and intellectual ability correlates. *Psychol. Aging* 14:627–44

Allaire JC, Marsiske M. 2002. Well- and ill-defined measures of everyday cognition: relationship to older adults' intellectual ability and functional status. *Psychol. Aging* 17:101–15

An intriguing study examining relations of age to actual borrowing decisions in large samples of loan or credit applicants.

Avolio BJ, Waldman DA. 1990. An examination of age and cognitive test performance across job complexity and occupational types. *J. Appl. Psychol.* 75:43–50

Backman L, MacDonald SWS. 2006. Death and cognition: synthesis and outlook. *Eur. Psychol.* 11:224–35

Baker J, Deakin J, Horton S, Pearce GW. 2007. Maintenance of skilled performance with age: a descriptive examination of professional golfers. *J. Aging Phys. Act.* 15:300–17

Baltes PB, Baltes MM, eds. 1990. *Successful Aging: Perspectives from the Behavioral Sciences.* New York: Cambridge Univ. Press

Baltes PB, Staudinger UM, Lindenberger U. 1999. Lifespan psychology: theory and application to intellectual functioning. *Annu. Rev. Psychol.* 50:471–507

Banks J, Oldfield Z. 2007. Understanding pensions: cognitive function, numerical ability and retirement saving. *Fisc. Stud.* 28:143–70

Batty GD, Deary IJ. 2004. Early life intelligence and adult health. *Br. Med. J.* 329:585–86

Batty GD, Deary IJ, Gottfredson LS. 2007. Premorbid (early life) IQ and later mortality risk: systematic review. *Ann. Epidemiol.* 17:278–88

Batty GD, Gale CR, Tynelius P, Deary IJ, Rasmussen F. 2009a. IQ in early adulthood, socioeconomic position, and unintentional injury mortality by middle age: a cohort study of more than 1 million Swedish men. *Am. J. Epidemiol.* 169:606–15

Batty GD, Wennerstad KM, Smith GD, Gunnell D, Deary IJ, et al. 2009b. IQ in early adulthood and mortality by middle age: cohort study of 1 million Swedish men. *Epidemiology* 20:100–9

Beard GM. 1874. *Legal Responsibility in Old Age.* New York: Russells

Beard GM. 1881. *American Nervousness: Its Causes and Consequences. A Supplement to Nervous Exhaustion (Neurasthenia).* New York: Putnam

Becker JT, Milke RM. 1998. Cognition and aging in a complex work environment. *Aviat. Space Environ. Med.* 69:944–51

Birren JA. 1969. Age and decision strategies. In *Interdisciplinary Topics in Gerontology*, vol. 4, ed. AT Welford, JA Birren, pp. 23–36. New York: Karger

Bosworth HB, Siegler IC. 2002. Terminal change in cognitive function: an updated review of longitudinal studies. *Exp. Aging Res.* 28:299–315

Broach D, Schroeder DJ. 2006. Air traffic control specialist age and en route operational errors. *Int. J. Aviat. Psychol.* 16:363–73

Burks SV, Carpenter JP, Goette L, Rustichini A. 2009. Cognitive skills affect economic preferences, strategic behavior, and job attachment. *Proc. Natl. Acad. Sci. USA* 106:7745–50

Burton CL, Strauss E, Hultsch DF, Hunter MA. 2006. Cognitive functioning and everyday problem solving in older adults. *Clin. Neuropsychol.* 20:432–52

Carroll JB. 1993. *Human Cognitive Abilities: A Survey of Factor-Analytic Studies.* New York: Cambridge Univ. Press

Cobb BB. 1968. Relationships among chronological age, length of experience, and job performance ratings of air traffic control specialists. *Aerosp. Med.* 39:119–24

Cobb BB, Lay CD, Bourdet NM. 1971. The relationship between chronological age and aptitude test measures of advanced level air traffic control trainees. *Fed. Aviat. Rep.* Oklahoma City, OK: FAA Civil Aeromed. Inst.

Cronbach LJ. 1949. *Essentials of Psychological Testing.* New York: Harper

Davies DR, Sparrow PR. 1988. Effects of age, tenure, training, and job complexity on job performance. *Psychol. Aging* 3:307–14

Deary IJ. 2005. Intelligence, health and death. *Psychologist* 18:610–13

Deary IJ. 2008. Why do intelligent people live longer? *Nature* 456:175–76

Deary IJ. 2009. Introduction to the special edition on cognitive epidemiology. *Intelligence* 37:517–19

Deary IJ, Gale CR, Stewart MCW, Fowkes FGR, Murray GD, et al. 2009. Intelligence and persisting with medication for two years: analysis in a randomized control trial. *Intelligence* 37:607–12

Deary IJ, Penke L, Johnson W. 2010. The neuroscience of human intelligence differences. *Nat. Rev. Neurosci.* 11:201–11

de Bruin WB, Parker AM, Fischhoff B. 2007. Individual differences in adult decision-making competence. *J. Personal. Soc. Psychol.* 92:938–56

Demaree HA, Burns KJ, DeDonno MA. 2010. Intelligence, but not emotional intelligence, predicts Iowa Gambling Task performance. *Intelligence* 38:249–54

Dennis MJ, Sternberg RJ, Beatty P. 2000. The construction of "user-friendly" tests of cognitive functioning: a synthesis of maximal- and typical-performance measurement philosophies. *Intelligence* 28:193–211

Der G, Batty GD, Deary IJ. 2009. The association between IQ in adolescence and a range of health outcomes at 40 in the 1979 US National Longitudinal Study of Youth. *Intelligence* 37:573–80

Diehl M, Marsiske M, Horgas A, Rosenberg A, Saczynski JS, Willis SL. 2005. The revised observed tasks of daily living: a performance-based assessment of everyday problem solving in older adults. *J. Appl. Gerontol.* 24:211–30

Diehl M, Willis SL, Shaie KW. 1995. Everyday problem solving in older adults: observational assessment and cognitive correlates. *Psychol. Aging* 10:478–91

Droege RC. 1967. Effects of aptitude score adjustments by age curves on prediction of job performance. *J. Appl. Psychol.* 51:181–86

Droege RC, Crambert AC, Henkin JB. 1963. Relationship between G.A.T.B. aptitude scores and age for adults. *Pers. Guid. J.* 41:502–8

Fiske DW, Butler JM. 1963. Experimental conditions for measuring individual differences. *Educ. Psychol. Meas.* 23:249–66

Folstein MF, Folstein SE, McHugh PR. 1975. "Mini-mental state." A practical method for grading the cognitive state of patients for the clinician. *J. Psychiatr. Res.* 12:189–98

Fozard JL, Nuttall RL. 1971. General aptitude test battery scores for men differing in age and socioeconomic status. *J. Appl. Psychol.* 55:372–79

Frey MC, Detterman DK. 2004. Scholastic assessment or *g*? The relationship between the Scholastic Achievement Test and general cognitive ability. *Psychol. Sci.* 15:373–78

Ghiselli EE. 1973. The validity of aptitude tests in personnel selection. *Pers. Psychol.* 26:461–77

Gladwell M. 2008. *Outliers: The Story of Success*. New York: Little Brown

Goff M, Ackerman PL. 1992. Personality-intelligence relations: assessment of typical intellectual engagement. *J. Educ. Psychol.* 84:537–52

Gonzalez C, Thomas RP, Vanyukov P. 2005. The relationships between cognitive ability and dynamic decision making. *Intelligence* 33:169–86

Goodwin TH, Sauer RD. 1995. Life-cycle productivity in academic research: evidence from cumulative publication histories of academic economists. *South. Econ. J.* 61:728–43

Gottfredson LS. 1998. The general intelligence factor. *Sci. Am. Presents* 9:24–30

Gottfredson LS. 2002. Where and why *g* matters: not a mystery. *Hum. Perform.* 15:25–46

Gottfredson LS. 2003. The challenge and promise of cognitive career assessment. *J. Career Assess.* 20:1–21

Gottfredson LS. 2004a. Intelligence: Is it the epidemiologists' elusive "fundamental cause" of social class inequalities in health? *J. Personal. Soc. Psychol.* 86:174–99

Gottfredson LS. 2004b. Life, death and intelligence. *J. Cogn. Educ. Psychol.* 4:23–46

Gottfredson LS, Deary IJ. 2004. Intelligence predicts health and longevity, but why? *Curr. Dir. Psychol. Sci.* 13:1–4

Gustafsson JE. 1988. Hierarchical models of individual differences in cognitive abilities. In *Advances in the Psychology of Human Intelligence*, ed. RJ Sternberg, vol. 4, pp. 35–71. Hillsdale, NJ: Erlbaum

Hartigan J, Wigdor A. 1989. *Fairness in Employment Testing*. Washington, DC: Natl. Acad. Sci. Press

Heil MC. 1999. Air traffic control specialist age and cognitive test performance. *Fed. Aviat. Rep. 99–23*. Oklahoma City, OK: FAA Civil Aeromed. Inst.

Higgins DM, Peterson JM, Pihl RO, Lee AGM. 2007. Prefrontal cognitive ability, intelligence, Big Five personality, and the prediction of advanced academic ability and workplace performance. *J. Personal. Soc. Psychol.* 93:298–319

Hulsheger UR, Maier GW, Stumpp T. 2007. Validity of general mental ability for the prediction of job performance and training success in Germany: a meta-analysis. *Int. J. Sel. Assess.* 15:3–18

Hunt E. 1995. *Will We Be Smart Enough?* New York: Sage Found.

Hunter J. 1986. Cognitive ability, cognitive attitudes, job knowledge, and job performance. *J. Vocat. Behav.* 29:340–62

An early study examining implications of age differences in cognitive abilities in occupational selection.

A monograph examining the implications of cognitive ability, and age differences in cognitive ability, in the current and future workforce.

Hunter J, Hunter R. 1984. Validity and utility of alternate predictors of job performance. *Psychol. Bull.* 96:72–98

Hunter J, Schmidt FL. 1996. Intelligence and job performance: economic and social implications. *Psychol. Public Policy Law* 2:447–72

Hunter J, Schmidt FL. 1998. The validity and utility of selection methods in personnel psychology: practical and theoretical implications of 85 years of research findings. *Psychol. Bull.* 124:262–74

Jensen AR. 1998. *The g Factor: The Science of Mental Ability*. Westport, CT: Praeger

Jokela M, Batty GD, Gale CR, Kivimaki M. 2009. Low childhood IQ and early adult mortality: the role of explanatory factors in the 1958 British birth cohort. *Pediatrics* 124:e380–88

Jones HE, Conrad HS. 1933. The growth and decline of intelligence: a study of a homogenous group between the ages of ten and sixty. *Genet. Psychol. Monogr.* 13:223–98

Judge TA, Colbert AE, Ilies R. 2004. Intelligence and leadership: a quantitative review and test of theoretical propositions. *J. Appl. Psychol.* 89:542–52

Judge TA, Higgins CA, Thoresen CJ, Barrick MR. 1999. The big five personality traits, general mental ability, and career success across the life span. *Pers. Psychol.* 52:621–52

Judge TA, Hurst C, Simon LS. 2009. Does it pay to be smart, attractive, or confident (or all three)? Relationships among general mental ability, physical attractiveness, core self-evaluations, and income. *J. Appl. Psychol.* 94:742–55

Judge TA, Klinger RL, Simon LS. 2010. Time is on my side: time, general mental ability, human capital, and extrinsic career success. *J. Appl. Psychol.* 95:92–107

Kanfer R, Ackerman PL. 2004. Aging, adult development, and work motivation. *Acad. Manag. Rev.* 29:440–58

Koenig KA, Frey MC, Detterman DK. 2008. ACT and general cognitive ability. *Intelligence* 36:153–60

Kroner S, Plass JL, Leutner D. 2005. Intelligence assessment with computer simulations. *Intelligence* 33:347–68

Kuncel NR, Hezlett SA, Ones DS. 2004. Academic performance, career potential, creativity and job performance: Can one construct predict them all? *J. Personal. Soc. Psychol.* 86:148–61

Kuncel NR, Ones DS, Sackett PR. 2010. Individual differences as predictors of work, educational, and broad life outcomes. *Personal. Individ. Differ.* 49:331–36

Lachman ME. 2004. Development in midlife. *Annu. Rev. Psychol.* 55:305–31

Lavery LL, Dodge HH, Snitz B, Ganguli M. 2009. Cognitive decline and mortality in a community-based cohort: the Monongahela Valley Independent Elders Survey. *J. Am. Geriatr. Soc.* 57:94–100

Lehman HC. 1953. *Age and Achievement*. Princeton, NJ: Princeton Univ. Press

Lehman HC. 1962. More about age and achievement. *Gerontologist* 2:141–48

Lehman HC. 1966. Psychologist's most creative years. *Am. Psychol.* 21:363–69

Leon DA, Lawlor DA, Clark H, Batty GD, Macintyre S. 2009. The association of childhood intelligence with mortality risk from adolescence to middle age: findings from the Aberdeen Children of the 1950s cohort study. *Intelligence* 37:520–28

Lubinski D. 2009. Cognitive epidemiology: with emphasis on untangling cognitive ability and socioeconomic status. *Intelligence* 37:625–33

Mata R, Schooler LJ, Rieskamp J. 2007. The aging decision maker: cognitive aging and the adaptive selection of decision strategies. *Psychol. Aging* 22:796–810

Matthews G, Zeidner M, Roberts RD. 2002. *Emotional Intelligence: Science and Myth*. Cambridge, MA: MIT Press

McArdle JJ, Smith JP, Willis R. 2009. *Cognition and economic outcomes in the health and retirement survey*. NBER Work. Pap. Ser., w15266. Cambridge, MA: Natl. Bur. Econ.

McDowell JM. 1982. Obsolescence of knowledge and career publication profiles: Some evidence of differences among fields in costs of interrupted careers. *Am. Econ. Rev.* 72:752–68

McEvoy GM, Cascio WF. 1989. Cumulative evidence of the relationship between employee age and job performance. *J. Appl. Psychol.* 74:11–17

Moss PI, Tilly C. 2001. *Stories Employers Tell: Race, Skill and Hiring in America*. New York: Russell Sage Found.

Murphy KR. 1989. Is the relationship between cognitive ability and job performance stable over time? *Hum. Perform.* 2:183–200

Neisser U, Boodoo G, Bouchard TJ Jr, Boykin AW, Brody N, et al. 1996. Intelligence: knowns and unknowns. *Am. Psychol.* 51:77–101

Classic study of the inverted-U functions relating age to achievement in many different domains.

Ng TWH, Feldman DC. 2008. The relationship of age to ten dimensions of job performance. *J. Appl. Psychol.* 93:392–423

Nunes A, Kramer AF. 2009. Experience-based mitigation of age-related performance declines: evidence from air traffic control. *J. Exp. Psychol. Appl.* 15:12–24

Nyborg H, Jensen AR. 2001. Occupation and income related to psychometric *g*. *Intelligence* 29:45–55

Oster SM, Hamermesh DS. 1998. Aging and productivity among economists. *Rev. Econ. Stat.* 80:154–56

O'Toole BI, Stankov L. 1992. Ultimate validity of psychological tests. *Personal. Individ. Differ.* 13:699–716

Pachur T, Mata R, Schooler LJ. 2009. Cognitive aging and the adaptive use of recognition in decision making. *Psychol. Aging* 24:901–15

Park DC, Reuter-Lorenz P. 2009. The adaptive brain: aging and neurocognitive scaffolding. *Annu. Rev. Psychol.* 60:173–96

Parker AM, Fischoff B. 2005. Decision-making competence: external validation through an individual-differences approach. *J. Behav. Decis. Mak.* 18:1–27

Peters E, Vastfjall D, Slovic P, Mertz CK, Mazzocco K, Dickert S. 2006. Numeracy and decision making. *Psychol. Sci.* 17:407–13

Posner RA. 1995. *Aging and Old Age*. Chicago, IL: Univ. Chicago Press

Quetelet A. 1935/1842. *Facts, Laws and Phenomena of Natural Philosophy: Summary of a Course of General Physics*. Glasgow, UK: Sinclair

Ree MJ, Earles JA. 1991. Predicting training success: not much more than *g*. *Pers. Psychol.* 44:321–32

Ree MJ, Earles JA, Teachout MS. 1994. Predicting job performance: not much more than *g*. *J. Appl. Psychol.* 79:518–24

Reyna VF, Nelson WL, Han PK, Dieckmann NF. 2009. How numeracy influences risk comprehension and medical decision making. *Psychol. Bull.* 135:943–73

Rhodes SR. 1983. Age-related differences in work attitudes and behavior: a review and conceptual analysis. *Psychol. Bull.* 93:328–67

Roberts BW, Kuncel NR, Shiner R, Caspi A, Goldberg LR. 2007. The power of personality: the comparative validity of personality traits, socioeconomic status, and cognitive ability for predicting life outcomes. *Perspect. Psychol. Sci.* 2:313–45

Roberts BW, Mroczek D. 2008. Personality trait change in adulthood. *Curr. Dir. Psychol. Sci.* 17:31–35

Sabia S, Gueguen A, Marmot MG, Shipley MJ, Ankri J, Singh-Manoux A. 2010. Does cognition predict mortality in midlife? Results from the Whitehall II cohort study. *Neurobiol. Aging* 31:688–95

Salgado JF, Anderson N. 2002. Cognitive and GMA testing in the European Community: issues and evidence. *Hum. Perform.* 15:75–96

Salgado JF, Anderson N, Moscoso S, Bertua C, de Fruyt F. 2003. International validity generalization of GMA and cognitive abilities: a European Community meta-analysis. *Pers. Psychol.* 56:573–605

Salthouse TA. 1984. Effects of age and skill in typing. *J. Exp. Psychol. Gen.* 113:345–71

Salthouse TA. 1987. Age, experience, and compensation. In *Cognitive Functioning and Social Structures over the Life Course*, ed. C Schooler, KW Schaie, pp. 142–57. Norwood, NJ: Ablex

Salthouse TA. 1990. Cognitive competence and expertise in aging. In *Handbook of the Psychology of Aging*, ed. JE Birren, KW Schaie, pp. 310–19. Orlando, FL: Academic. 3rd ed.

Salthouse TA. 1994. Age-related differences in basic cognitive processes: implications for work. *Exp. Aging Res.* 20:249–55

Salthouse TA. 2006. Mental exercise and mental aging: evaluating the validity of the "use it or lose it" hypothesis. *Perspect. Psychol. Sci.* 1:68–87

Salthouse TA. 2009a. Decomposing age correlations on neuropsychological and cognitive variables. *J. Int. Neuropsychol. Soc.* 15:650–61

Salthouse TA. 2009b. When does age-related cognitive decline begin? *Neurobiol. Aging* 30:507–14

Salthouse TA. 2010. *Major Issues in Cognitive Aging*. New York: Oxford Univ. Press

Salthouse TA, Maurer. 1996. Aging, job performance and career development. In *Handbook of the Psychology of Aging*, ed. JE Birren, KW Schaie, pp. 353–64. San Francisco, CA: Academic

Schaie KW. 2005. *Developmental Influences on Adult Intelligence: The Seattle Longitudinal Study*. New York: Oxford Univ. Press

Recent monograph summarizing some of the most replicated results concerned with aging and cognition.

Schaie KW, Willis S. 1986. Practical intelligence in later adulthood. In *Practical Intelligence*, ed. RJ Sternberg, RK Wagner, pp. 236–68. New York: Cambridge Univ. Press

Schmidt FL, Hunter J. 1998. The validity and utility of selection methods in personnel psychology: practical and theoretical implications of 85 years of research findings. *Psychol. Bull.* 124:262–74

Schmidt FL, Hunter J. 2004. General mental ability in the world of work: occupational attainment and job performance. *J. Personal. Soc. Psychol.* 86:162–73

Schmidt FL, Hunter JE, Outerbridge AN. 1986. Impact of job experience and ability on job knowledge, work sample performance, and supervisory ratings of job performance. *J. Appl. Psychol.* 71:432–39

Schmidt FL, Hunter JE, Outerbridge AN, Goff S. 1988. Joint relation of experience and ability with job performance: test of three hypotheses. *J. Appl. Psychol.* 73:46–57

Schroeder DH, Salthouse TA. 2004. Age-related effects on cognition between 20 and 50 years of age. *Personal. Individ. Differ.* 36:393–404

Schulz R, Curnow C. 1988. Peak performance and age among superathletes: track and field, swimming, baseball, tennis, and golf. *J. Gerontol.* 43:113–20

Schulz R, Musaa D, Staszewski J, Siegler RS. 1994. The relationship between age and major league baseball performance: implications for development. *Psychol. Aging* 9:274–86

Shamosh NA, Gray JR. 2008. Delay discounting and intelligence: a meta-analysis. *Intelligence* 36:289–305

Shipley BA, Der G, Taylor MD, Deary IJ. 2005. Cognition and all-cause mortality across the entire adult age range: Health and Lifestyle Survey. *Psychosom. Med.* 68:17–24

Simonton DK. 1988. Presidential style: personality, biography, and performance. *J. Personal. Soc. Psychol.* 55:928–36

Simonton DK. 1997. Creative productivity: a predictive and explanatory model of career trajectories and landmarks. *Psychol. Rev.* 104:66–89

Small BJ, Fratiglioni L, von Strauss E, Backman L. 2003. Terminal decline and cognitive performance in very old age: Does cause of death matter? *Psychol. Aging* 18:193–202

Srivastava S, John OP, Gosling SD, Potter J. 2003. Development of personality in early and middle adulthood: set like plaster or persistent change? *J. Personal. Soc. Psychol.* 84:1041–53

Stanovich KE. 2009. *What Intelligence Tests Miss: The Psychology of Rational Thought.* New Haven, CT: Yale Univ. Press

Stanovich KE, West RF. 2008. On the relative independence of thinking biases and cognitive ability. *J. Personal. Soc. Psychol.* 94:672–95

Stein CI. 1962. The G.A.T.B.: the effect of age on intersample variations. *Pers. Guid. J.* 60:779–85

Stephan PE, Levin SG. 1993. Age and the Nobel Prize revisited. *Scientometrics* 28:387–99

Sternberg RJ, Wagner RK, Williams WM, Horvath JA. 1995. Testing common sense. *Am. Psychol.* 50:912–27

Sternberg RJ, Hedlund J. 2002. Practical intelligence, *g*, and work psychology. *Hum. Perform.* 15:143–60

Stilley CS, Bender CM, Dunbar-Jacob J, Sereika S, Ryan CM. 2010. The impact of cognitive function on medication management: three studies. *Health Psychol.* 29:50–55

Stilley CS, Sereika S, Muldoon MF, Ryan CM, Dunbar-Jacob J. 2004. Psychological and cognitive function: predictors of adherence with cholesterol lowering treatment. *Ann. Behav. Med.* 27:117–24

Strenze T. 2007. Intelligence and economic success: a meta-analytic review of longitudinal research. *Intelligence* 35:401–26

Sturman MC. 2003. Searching for the inverted U-shaped relationship between time and performance: meta-analyses of the experience/performance, tenure/performance, and age/performance relationships. *J. Manage.* 29:609–40

Terracciano A, McCrae RR, Brant LJ, Costa PT. 2005. Hierarchical linear modeling analyses of the NEO-PI-R scales in the Baltimore Longitudinal Study of Aging. *Psychol. Aging* 20:493–506

Trites DK, Cobb BB. 1963. Problems in air traffic management IV: comparison of pre-employment, job-related experience, with aptitude tests as predictors of training and job performance as air traffic control specialists. *Fed. Aviat. Rep. 63-31.* Oklahoma City, OK: FAA Civil Aeromed. Inst.

Trites DK, Cobb BB. 1964. CARI research on air traffic control specialists: age, aptitude and experience as predictors of performance. *Fed. Aviat. Rep.* Oklahoma City, OK: FAA Civil Aeromed. Inst.

Verhaeghen P, Salthouse TA. 1997. Meta-analyses of age-cognition relations in adulthood: estimates of linear and nonlinear age effects and structural models. *Psychol. Bull.* 122:231–49

Theoretical analysis of age-achievement functions and discussion of the "constant probability of success" proposal.

Von Stumm S, Macintrye S, Batty DG, Clark H, Deary IJ. 2010. Intelligence, social class of origin, childhood behavior disturbance and education as predictors of status attainment in midlife in men: the Aberdeen Children of the 1950s study. *Intelligence* 38:202–11

Wagner RK, Sternberg RJ. 1985. Practical intelligence in real-world pursuits: the role of tacit knowledge. *J. Personal. Soc. Psychol.* 49:436–58

Wagner RK, Sternberg RJ. 1990. Street smarts: In *Measures of Leadership*, ed. KE Clark, MB Clark, pp. 493–504. West Orange, NJ: Leadership Library Am.

Waldman DA, Avolio BJ. 1986. A meta-analysis of age differences in job performance. *J. Appl. Psychol.* 71:33–38

Walker NP, McConville PM, Hunter D, Deary IJ, Whalley LJ. 2002. Childhood mental ability and lifetime psychiatric contact: a 66-year follow-up study of the Scottish Mental Ability Survey. *Intelligence* 30:233–45

Warr P. 1994. Age and employment. In *Handbook of Industrial and Organizational Psychology*, vol. 4, ed. HC Triandis, MD Dunnette, LM Hough, pp. 485–550. Palo Alto, Consult. Psychol. Press

Warr P, Pennington J. 1994. Occupational age grading: jobs for older and younger non-managerial employees. *J. Vocat. Behav.* 45:328–46

Weatherbee SR, Allaire JC. 2008. Everyday cognition and mortality: performance differences and predictive utility of the everyday cognition battery. *Psychol. Aging* 23:216–21

Welford AT. 1958. *Aging and Human Skill*. London: Oxford Univ. Press

Whalley LJ, Deary IJ. 2001. Longitudinal cohort study of childhood IQ and survival up to age 76. *Br. Med. J.* 322:1–5

Wilk SL, Sackett PR. 1996. Longitudinal analysis of ability-job complexity fit and job change. *Pers. Psychol.* 49:937–67

Willis SL. 1991. Cognition and everyday competence. In *Annual Review of Gerontology and Geriatrics*, vol. 11, ed. KW Schaie, MP Lawton, pp. 80–109. New York: Springer

Willis SL. 1996. Everyday cognitive competence issues in elderly persons: conceptual issues and empirical findings. *Gerontologist* 36:595–601

Willis SL, Jay GM, Diehl M, Marsiske M. 1992. Longitudinal change and prediction of everyday task competence in the elderly. *Res. Aging* 14:68–91

Willis SL, Schaie KW. 1986. Practical intelligence in later adulthood. In *Practical Intelligence*, ed. RJ Sternberg, RK Wagner, pp. 236–68. New York: Cambridge Univ. Press

Wilson RS, Barnes LL, Mendes de Leon CF, Evans DA. 2009. Cognition and survival in a biracial urban population of old people. *Intelligence* 37:545–50

Wittmann WW, Hattrup K. 2004. The relationship between performance in dynamic systems and intelligence. *Syst. Res. Behav. Sci.* 21:393–409

Zagorsky JL. 2007. Do you have to be smart to be rich? The impact of IQ on wealth, income and financial distress. *Intelligence* 35:489–501

Zysberg L. 2009. An emerging new component of cognitive abilities in human resources selection: preliminary evidence to the existence of a "process-analytic" factor in selection batteries. *Int. J. Sel. Assess.* 17:69–75

Child Development in the Context of Disaster, War, and Terrorism: Pathways of Risk and Resilience

Ann S. Masten and Angela J. Narayan

Institute of Child Development, University of Minnesota, Minneapolis, Minnesota 55455;
email: amasten@umn.edu

Annu. Rev. Psychol. 2012. 63:227–57

First published online as a Review in Advance on September 19, 2011

The *Annual Review of Psychology* is online at psych.annualreviews.org

This article's doi:
10.1146/annurev-psych-120710-100356

Keywords

mass trauma, dose gradient, biological embedding

Abstract

This review highlights progress over the past decade in research on the effects of mass trauma experiences on children and youth, focusing on natural disasters, war, and terrorism. Conceptual advances are reviewed in terms of prevailing risk and resilience frameworks that guide basic and translational research. Recent evidence on common components of these models is evaluated, including dose effects, mediators and moderators, and the individual or contextual differences that predict risk or resilience. New research horizons with profound implications for health and well-being are discussed, particularly in relation to plausible models for biological embedding of extreme stress. Strong consistencies are noted in this literature, suggesting guidelines for disaster preparedness and response. At the same time, there is a notable shortage of evidence on effective interventions for child and youth victims. Practical and theory-informative research on strategies to protect children and youth victims and promote their resilience is a global priority.

Contents

INTRODUCTION

Millions of children worldwide are exposed to disasters, war, and terrorism each year, both directly and indirectly through effects on family, community, or society; lost opportunities; and media [Am. Psychol. Assoc. (APA) 2010, Becker-Blease et al. 2010, Furr et al. 2010]. Over the past decade since the World Trade Center attack on September 11, 2001, there has been an alarming series of devastating and highly publicized conflicts and disasters around the world, including terrorism, wars and political violence, earthquakes, tsunamis and hurricanes, industrial accidents, and large fires. As a result, many stakeholders are concerned with the impact of such extreme adversities on children and youth and what might be done to prevent or reduce exposures and consequences for young people, both in advance of catastrophic events and in the aftermath.

The goal of this review is to take stock of current research on the effects of disasters, war, and terrorism on children and youth in regard to conceptual perspectives, robust findings, gaps, and the utility of current evidence for applications. Recent situations are emphasized, particularly those occurring over the decade since 9/11. Excellent reviews and compilations of the research predating 9/11 have been published (e.g., La Greca et al. 2002; Norris et al. 2002a,b). This review is focused on extreme adversities and conditions that affect large groups of children or adolescents and their families at the same time, such as disasters and war (i.e., "mass trauma" experiences), and not on traumatic experiences that arise or happen to individual children and families, such as child abuse, assaults, car accidents, dog bites, and other life-threatening exposures. There are parallels in the concepts and findings in the literature on mass trauma and individual or family traumas, which are noted below, but it was necessary to limit the scope of this review.

The conceptual approach of the review, in keeping with the prevailing conceptual perspectives guiding much of the contemporary research, reflects a risk and resilience framework informed by developmental systems theory and the related core principles of contemporary developmental psychopathology (Betancourt & Khan 2008; Bonanno et al. 2010; Cicchetti 2006, 2010; Masten 2006, 2012;

Masten & Osofsky 2010). Following a brief section on historical perspectives, the salient features of this integrated conceptual perspective are highlighted. The subsequent literature review is organized around key components of risk/resilience models of disaster effects and responses: exposure dose, determinants, and mediators; variability in exposure effects on individuals, including correlates and moderators; and intervention, including exemplary experimental research and consensus guidelines. In the conclusion, we discuss the remarkable consistencies and conspicuous gaps in the literature reviewed and comment on the growing edges of interdisciplinary research on this topic.

Research Challenges

Although the quality of research has improved markedly since early scholars studied the effects of war and disasters on children, research on extreme adversities continues to pose great challenges (Bonanno et al. 2010, Masten & Osofsky 2010). Many ethical issues arise for research in the aftermath of disaster, when there is great concern about harming already traumatized victims and exposing researchers to traumatizing situations. Disasters often occur in remote or economically undeveloped locations with limited research infrastructure and measures available, or the disaster itself destroys or damages the existing infrastructure. Assessment tools suitable to the culture and situation may not be available, and physical or political conditions may be too chaotic or hazardous for research to be implemented. Pre-disaster baseline data is rarely available, and longitudinal follow-ups are challenging due to migration or chaos. Relevant comparison groups may be unavailable or difficult to engage. Finally, funding for such research may be hard to find, inadequate, or too slow in coming. These challenges make all the more impressive what has been accomplished by the investigators who have confronted the daunting issues of field research in the midst or aftermath of mass trauma exposure.

Historical Perspectives

World War II gave rise to a literature on children and war, heralded by Freud & Burlingham's (1943) volume *War and Children*, summarizing their observations, cases studies, and clinical experiences. They observed that there were few signs of "traumatic shock" among children exposed to bombing and other horrors of war when they were in the care of mothers or mother substitutes, but that it was quite a different matter when exposure occurred in a context of absent or lost parents. Accounts of child response to evacuations during the London blitz noted the traumatizing effects of separating children from their parents; many did so poorly they were returned home despite the dangers posed by the bombing (Garmezy 1983). The buffering effect of proximity to parents and other attachment figures for children in the midst of terrifying experiences is one of the most enduring findings in the literature on war and other life-threatening disasters.

After the liberation of the Terezin concentration camp, Anna Freud was in charge of six young orphaned children sent to England for treatment. Freud & Dann (1951) described many behavioral and emotional problems initially observed in these children, but also the strong bonds among them. Many of these and other children liberated from Terezin showed dramatic improvements over time; however, signs of "sensitization" or psychological "scarring" were noted among a substantial number of them. This mixed picture of resilience and lingering vulnerability or harm from extreme and prolonged trauma has continued to characterize the findings on children who survive the horrors of war, including recent cases of rescued child soldiers (Betancourt et al. 2010, Cortes & Buchanan 2007, Klasen et al. 2010).

Other than war, the best-documented observations of child responses to mass trauma or disaster have been reports on particular disasters, such as the Buffalo Creek dam disaster and an Australian bushfire. In 1972, a poorly constructed dam above the mining community of Buffalo Creek in West Virginia burst and flooded the hollow and town below, killing 125 people, injuring many others and devastating this small community (Erikson 1976, Gleser et al. 1981, Korol et al. 2002). Although most of the observations on the child survivors were documented in the course of litigation, with concomitant issues of bias, the accounts have been influential because of their comprehensiveness. In addition, there was a long-term follow-up 17 years post disaster, which was the first of its kind (Green et al. 1994, Korol et al. 2002).

The findings from Buffalo Creek research have been widely replicated. Short-term findings (Gleser et al. 1981) indicated dose effects, with greater exposure to death of family and friends related to more symptoms. Many symptoms in the anxiety-trauma spectrum were observed, and anxiety symptoms predicted more lasting effects. Adjustment problems of children and adolescents were related to adjustment of parents as well as general family atmosphere (indexed by violence, irritability, gloomy mood, and less supportiveness). Girls were rated higher on anxiety symptoms whereas boys were rated higher on "belligerence." Older age at the time of exposure was related to more overall symptoms, particularly anxiety, depression, and belligerence. Adults had more symptoms than adolescents, who had more symptoms than young children, except that younger children had more specific fears and age-specific problems such as toilet-training lapses.

The 17-year follow-up indicated substantial recovery for most survivors, although they had higher current and lifetime rates of posttraumatic stress disorder (PTSD) than a comparison sample, with rates of 7% and 32%, respectively, as compared to 4% and 6% (Green et al. 1994). After nearly two decades, dose effects had largely dissipated; exposure was not strongly related to current function, although specific experiences, such as loss of family and relatives, had lingering effects. Thus, even after an event of this scope and severity, resilience and recovery were normative over the long term.

A second historically significant example is provided by one of the largest and best-studied disasters in the literature, the Australian bushfire of 1983 (MacFarlane 1987, MacFarlane et al. 1987, MacFarlane & Van Hooff 2009). MacFarlane reported initial findings through two years following the disaster and recently reported on results of a 20-year follow-up study. In early reports, MacFarlane observed more symptoms in the fire-exposed children (over 800 children attending primary schools in the devastated fire zone) than a comparison group of children recruited in 1985 (725 children) from a neighboring region not directly affected by the fire. MacFarlane (1987) also reported that child symptoms were more strongly related to separation from the mother or maternal symptoms than they were to dose or direct exposure, highlighting again the salience of parents and their function as a protective or vulnerability factor. The 20-year follow-up in 2009 showed lingering effects related to fire exposure, including anxiety, although differences were described as "relatively small" (p. 146). Bushfire victims reported comparatively high rates of PTSD symptoms of intrusion and hyperarousal related to the fire. Of the exposed children, those who reported another (usually subsequent) event as their "worst" lifetime experience had higher PTSD prevalence and severity, consistent with the possibility of cumulative effects from multiple trauma exposures and with models of "sensitization" or "kindling" that link prior and subsequent trauma exposures, discussed in more detail below.

Conclusions from early reviews of the literature on the extreme stressors of childhood drew conclusions that have held up well over the subsequent decades (Garmezy 1983, Garmezy & Rutter 1985, Rutter 1983). These reviewers concluded, for example, that trauma exposure could have lasting effects on children, though often the effects were short term; that loss and injury to loved ones had greater effects than material losses; and that parent availability, function, and support played significant roles in the responses of children.

CONCEPTUAL ADVANCES

Prevailing conceptual frameworks for understanding and intervening to improve the adaptation of children and youth in the context of disasters, terrorism, and war reflect the emergence over the past four decades of developmental psychopathology and related resilience frameworks for research and practice (Cicchetti 2010, Masten 2011, Masten & Obradović 2008, Pine et al. 2005). The pervasive influence of developmental systems theory (Gottlieb 2007, Thelen & Smith 1998) and Bronfenbrenner's ecological model (1979; Bronfenbrenner & Morris 2006) is evident in contemporary efforts to delineate the processes across multiple levels that lead to diverse phenotypic development in individuals and the different pathways observed in the aftermath of traumatic exposures (Cicchetti 2010; Masten 2006, 2011, 2012). In this perspective, adaptation to mass trauma experiences is conceptualized as a dynamic process involving multiple interacting systems within the individual organism and many interactions of the individual with complex and changing contexts, including relationships with other people and many interrelated systems of the natural and built environment. Individual adaptation will be influenced by the prior development of the individual as manifested in current function, adaptive capacity and strengths (assets; promotive and protective factors available to the organism), and vulnerabilities, as well as the nature of the current challenges impinging on the organism. The latter are often delineated in terms of risks, stressors, or exposure dose. Garmezy and Rutter pioneered this approach to disaster and its consequences for children, as noted above, and this perspective is now well established, as evident in recent reports on children in disaster [Natl. Commiss. Children in Disasters (NCCD) 2010] and war (APA 2010), special journal issues (Betancourt 2011, Masten & Cicchetti 2010), and reviews (Bonanno et al. 2010).

Over the past decade, there has been growing attention in developmental psychopathology and resilience science to multiple levels of analysis and the roles of gene-by-experience interactions and epigenetic processes in development and adaptation, particularly in the context of traumatic experiences (Cicchetti 2010, Sapienza & Masten 2011). As a result, models of adaptation to trauma have expanded to consider genetic and neural mediators and moderators of dose exposure and response. There is a rapidly emerging literature on the role of individual differences in genes, neural plasticity, and brain development in the processes of adaptation before, during, and following traumatic experiences. This new phase of research in trauma fields is transforming conceptual models of causes and effects of extreme adversity, as well as models of intervention. Selective examples are highlighted below.

Resilience in Dynamic Systems

Models have shifted dramatically in recent decades toward a resilience perspective, while at the same time acknowledging the salient role of traumatic exposures or "dose" as an influence on response (APA 2010, Betancourt & Khan 2008, Bonanno et al. 2010, Cicchetti 2010, Masten 2011, Masten & Obradović 2008, Masten & Osofsky 2010, Pine et al. 2005). Resilience can be defined as the capacity of a dynamic system to withstand or recover from significant challenges that threaten its stability, viability, or development (Masten 2011, 2012). Resilience is a dynamic concept that can be applied to many systems across scales, including systems within a person (e.g., stress-response system, immune system, cardiovascular system), the whole person as a system, a family system, a community or communication system, or an ecosystem (Masten 2011, 2012). A resilience framework holds particular appeal for research on child effects of extreme adversities because it highlights the shared goals of many stakeholders (individuals, families, communities, and societies) to mitigate risk and support resilience among children facing grave dangers.

Studies of risk and resilience in diverse populations of children exposed to significant adversities, including war, terrorism, and disaster, indicate a very common set of factors associated with better neurobiological and psychosocial outcomes, often termed promotive factors (predictors of better outcomes under high- as well as low-risk conditions) and protective factors (especially important under high-risk conditions) (Cicchetti 2010; Luthar 2006; Masten 2001, 2007). These widely reported promotive and protective factors, such as self-control and problem-solving skills, close relationships with competent caregivers, or good schools and safe neighborhoods, suggest that adaptive capacity for resilience in the context of significant threats to adaptation and development depends to a large extent on fundamental human adaptive systems embedded in individuals, relationships, families, friends, communities, and cultures (Masten 2001, 2007). These adaptive systems can be harmed by severe adversities (e.g., a parent is killed; a community is destroyed) but often are hypothesized to protect children and promote recovery in the aftermath of war and disaster. In subsequent sections, we review recent evidence on promotive and protective factors for children facing extreme adversity, including research on their roles as naturally occurring compensatory factors or risk moderators and as potential targets for preventive interventions (Masten 2011, Masten & Obradović 2008).

Vulnerability and Sensitivity to Context

There also is great interest in moderators that potentiate the effects of adversities on children, including the sensitizing effects of earlier traumatic experiences, genetic moderators, disabilities, and personality differences (e.g., negative emotionality or ruminative tendencies), often termed vulnerability factors. There is rapid growth in research on genetic moderators (gene polymorphisms or epigenetic status) that appear to potentiate risk in the context of threatening environments (Cicchetti 2010, Kim-Cohen & Gold 2009, Nugent et al. 2011, Pratchett & Yehuda 2011). Although most of

the evidence to date has focused on child maltreatment, the implicated processes are likely to apply to many other forms of adversity characterized by extreme danger and violence. Growing evidence links variations in the serotonin transporter gene, 5-HTT, to susceptibility for anxiety and depression among children exposed to severe trauma. Variations in genes that regulate function of the hypothalamic-pituitary-adrenal (HPA) axis, which plays a key role in stress response, also have been implicated as potential moderators of trauma response in gene-by-environment (G x E) studies, including research on the corticotropin-releasing hormone type 1 receptor and glucocorticoid receptor genes (Cicchetti 2010, Nugent et al. 2011, Pratchett & Yehuda 2011). Additionally, recent advances in neuroimaging of children exposed to trauma indicate decreased brain volume and frontal cortex abnormalities in children with PTSD symptomatology, suggesting neurodevelopmental pathways of trauma effects that also could be related to genetic changes in children exposed to disasters (Carrion et al. 2010).

Recent theory and evidence also suggest that in some cases the purported vulnerability factors may actually be indicators of sensitivity or plasticity in response to experience, which could be bad in an adverse environment but good in a favorable one (Belsky et al. 2007, Belsky & Pluess 2009, Boyce & Ellis 2005, Ellis et al. 2011, Obradović & Boyce 2009). This raises the interesting possibility that some of the children who respond poorly to traumatic experiences may also respond well to positive changes in context provided by interventions.

In regard to the role of previous exposures to extreme adversity, one of the ongoing debates in the dose literature on trauma concerns the question of "inoculation" versus "sensitizing" effects (Bonanno et al. 2010, Silverman & La Greca 2002, Yehuda & Bierer 2009). Prior experience with trauma has been linked in adults and young people both with better response to subsequent traumatic experiences (congruent with an inoculation model) and with worse response, suggesting vulnerability-inducing effects ("kindling" or sensitization model). However, as Bonanno et al. (2010) pointed out, there is limited prospective evidence to date for resolving this issue, and retrospective data is subject to many kinds of confounding effects when subjects simultaneously report on current symptoms and past trauma experiences. A stronger case can be made for inoculation effects when experimental designs are implemented; however, this is not feasible for testing kindling effects. We discuss an example of a recent stress-inoculation training experiment (Wolmer et al. 2011) in the Intervention section below.

Pathways of Adaptation in the Context of Extreme Adversity

The confluence of developmental change, promotive/protective influences, and vulnerabilities/sensitivities is presumed to result in multiple pathways of adaptation in the context of acute or chronic traumatic experiences. Describing different pathways has been a keen interest of investigators studying the impact of adversity or trauma on individuals and their developmental course (see Bonanno 2004; Bonanno et al. 2010; Masten 2011, 2012; Masten & Obradović 2008; Masten & Reed 2002; Silverman & La Greca 2002). Pathway patterns described in the literature, often inspired by case reports as well as empirical observations, show remarkable similarity to each other as well as to pathway models of resilience in other fields, particularly ecology (Tugel et al. 2005), suggesting the potential for a broad theory of adaptation, resistance, and resilience to disturbances in complex, dynamic systems (Masten 2011). **Figures 1a** and **1b** illustrate commonly described pathway patterns of adaptation in response to (a) a disaster with acute-onset and gradually improving conditions and (b) more chronic-onset extreme situations such as war or severe neglect/abuse that subsequently remit or improve. Some of these patterns remain speculative for children and youth. For example, there is considerable interest in the possibility of posttraumatic growth effects, where adaptation improves in the

context of adversity (Bonanno et al. 2010, Masten & Osofsky 2010), reflecting a kind of challenge model; however, pertinent data are extremely scarce to date for children (Kilmer & Gil-Rivas 2010).

Cascading Consequences

Dynamic, developmental system models also suggest that the effects of traumatic experiences can spread over time, from one domain to another, from one level to another, from one person to another, and from one generation to the next, through a multitude of mediating processes. These effects have been called progressive effects, transactional effects, snowball effects, chain reactions, contagion effects, and developmental cascades (Masten & Cicchetti 2010, Pine et al. 2005). Within an individual's life, for example, stress can alter gene expression leading to alterations in brain development (Hochberg et al. 2011, Meaney 2010). These changes can be passed on to the next generation, through biological, behavioral, or socioeconomic processes, including gene methylation, disrupted parenting, or educational attainment. The disruption of adaptive behavior in one area of function can spread to affect other domains of behavior. Posttraumatic symptoms, for example, can disrupt function in school or work (Masten & Cicchetti 2010). In situations of terrorism and torture, perpetrators have the explicit objective of propagating psychological fear and terror across large groups of people (Pine et al. 2005), which can have lasting effects for subsequent generations of offspring (Yehuda et al. 2007).

On the other hand, positive adaptation, protective effects, and resilience also have the potential to spread within individual lives and across generations or populations (Masten & Cicchetti 2010). This possibility has inspired considerable interest in strategies of prevention and intervention that are targeted and timed to initiate cascades, aiming to prepare and protect individuals and communities, not only in the short term, but with expanding effects over time and domains (Fisher et al. 2006, Patterson et al. 2010).

Subsequent sections of this review address the components and processes implicated by these concepts and models of adaptation with respect to the status of research on the effects of exposure to war and disaster in childhood. We focus on the nature and perception of threats impinging on individuals; the developmental and functional status of the individual before and during the period of exposure and response; resources and capacities available to respond to the disturbances set in motion by threat processes, including those embedded in social relationships; and numerous other moderating influences that confer vulnerability or protection in the course of adaptation to extreme adversity.

EXPOSURE: DOSE AND DETERMINANTS

It has long been observed that problems and symptoms tend to rise as the number, intensity, or severity of hazards pile up in a person's life, while at the same time striking individual

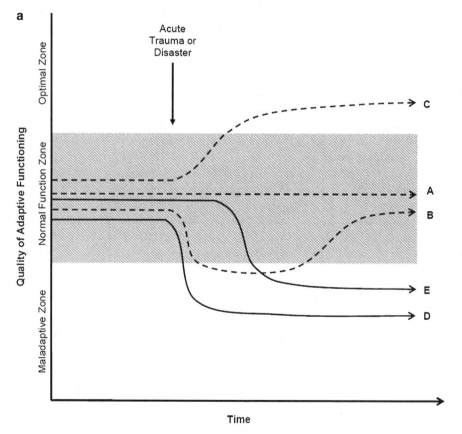

Figure 1

(*a*) Illustrative pathways of adaptive function before and after an acute-onset traumatic experience, such as a disaster or terrorism attack. Dashed paths illustrate forms of resilience, and solid lines indicate maladaptive pathways. Path A illustrates stress resistance. Path B illustrates disturbance with recovery. Path C illustrates posttraumatic growth. Path D illustrates breakdown without recovery (yet), and path E illustrates delayed breakdown without recovery (yet). (*b*) Illustrative pathways of adaptive function before and after exposure to prolonged and severe adversity. Dashed paths illustrate forms of resilience, and the solid line indicates a maladaptive pathway. Paths F and G illustrate decline in the context of chronic adversity and recovery after good conditions are established or restored. Path H illustrates decline with no sign of recovery (yet), despite more favorable conditions.

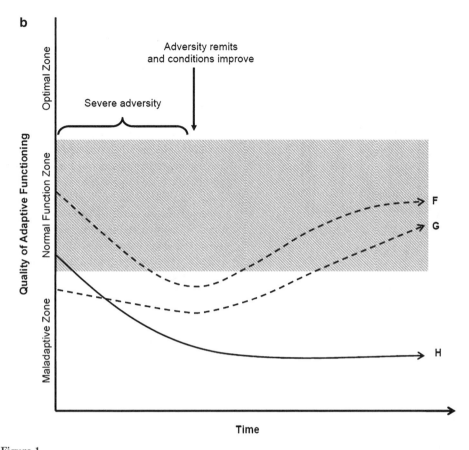

b

Quality of Adaptive Functioning

Optimal Zone

Normal Function Zone

Maladaptive Zone

Adversity remits
and conditions improve

Severe adversity

F

G

H

Time

Figure 1

(*Continued*)

differences were noted among individuals sharing similar levels of risk or adversity (Masten & Obradović 2006). Evidence continues to support the general expectation that exposure to trauma or adversity of greater severity results in a higher average impact on the adaptation of individual children and youth as well as adults. However, there is growing interest in disaggregating dose to identify toxic experiences, understanding nonlinear effects, and delineating the processes that mediate observed dose effects.

Risk and Dose-Response Gradients

Theoretical risk gradients, such as the one shown in **Figure 2**, portray the idea of rising levels of problems as risk level rises. In studies

of trauma or disaster, these models are often described as dose-response figures. On average, for example, traumatic stress symptoms are expected to be higher as the frequency, number, or intensity of exposure rises. But the average level of symptoms may obscure wide variation among individuals at the same level of risk. Thus individuals may appear to be "off the gradient" in the sense that they are doing much better (implying protection or resilience, represented by white dots in the figure) or worse (suggesting vulnerability, represented by black dots in the figure) than one would expect in the population at this level of risk. A linear relation of risk/dose to adaptation is shown in **Figure 2**, but there are numerous other possibilities, including nonlinear threshold

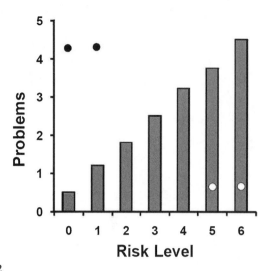

Figure 2

Risk gradient illustrating a rise in average level of problems as a function of higher risk level or exposure to trauma or adversities. White dots represent individuals who are doing much better than average for a given level of risk (suggesting resilience), and black dots represent individuals who are doing much worse than average for a given level of risk (suggesting vulnerability).

models, asymptotic patterns, and inverted-U and challenge models (see Luthar et al. 2000, Masten 2012, Masten et al. 1988).

Dose-response gradients were observed by early reviewers of the literature on extreme adversity (Garmezy 1983, Garmezy & Rutter 1985), and they continue to be corroborated in diverse reviews on children in extreme situations (Furr et al. 2010; Masten & Osofsky 2010; Norris et al. 2002a,b; Pine et al. 2005; Qouta et al. 2008). "Dose" has multiple meanings, and children generally show greater signs of disturbance in response to more severe events characterized in terms of multiple severity indicators, including degree of severity of a single exposure, accumulation or piling up of multiple traumas or severe adversities, trauma occurring in the context of ongoing adversity, and experiences that strike at the heart of the attachment relationship (when there is loss of connection to caregivers or violence that threatens the core attachment relationship, such as when a parent is the victim or perpetrator of violence). Similar dose gradients have been observed in the broader literature on sociodemographic risk and negative life events in the lives of

children, including child maltreatment (Masten & Wright 1998, Obradović et al. 2012, Sameroff 2006, Shonkoff et al. 2009).

In a recent meta-analysis of the empirical literature linking disaster to posttraumatic stress (PTS) symptoms, Furr and colleagues (2010) found a small to medium effect of disaster exposure to PTS in children and youth across all studies meeting inclusion criteria through 2009, with greater effects observed for disasters characterized by greater loss of life and for closer physical proximity to children, greater perceived threat, and loss of a loved one or friend. Assessment timing and informant effects also were found in regard to dose: Studies conducted within one year of the disaster showed greater dose effects than those after one year, and child reports showed greater dose-response linkages than parent reports.

Studies published subsequent to this meta-analysis show similar dose-related effects (see Masten & Osofsky 2010). In terms of timing, for example, Gershoff et al. (2010) found that 15 months after 9/11, only small effects related to dose were observed for mental health function among adolescents, consistent with the possibility that recovery may have already occurred in many cases, even given initial dose effects. In regard to worse effects when disaster occurs in the midst of ongoing turmoil, Catani et al. (2010) observed worse function in children from Sri Lanka who experienced the 2004 tsunami in the context of ongoing war or in conjunction with family violence, as well as worse adaptation among children with greater direct exposure to the tsunami itself. It is clearly important to consider the context in which "new" traumatic experiences occur, both in terms of conditions prior to onset and post-offset, as well as the nature of war- or disaster-related trauma. The question of how prior exposure to trauma may moderate individual susceptibility to future trauma, depending on the nature and developmental timing of exposure, is considered elsewhere in this review, in relation to issues of inoculation, sensitization or desensitization effects, and biological alterations in adaptive response systems.

The possibility of nonlinear or threshold effects in dose-response linkages is a topic of growing interest. Recent research on child soldiers exposed to extreme atrocities raises the possibility of exposures so high that nearly everyone would have passed a threshold expected to overwhelm normal adaptive capacity; therefore, beyond this threshold, additional trauma does not predict response, a kind of asymptote effect. In a recently published study of child soldiers in Uganda with extraordinarily severe and prolonged exposure to life-threatening atrocities and rape, Klasen et al. (2010) found that severity of exposure during captivity did not relate to function after these children returned. Instead, qualities of their recovery context, including exposures to violence and perceived spiritual support, were related to post-return function.

Other nonlinear effects are conceivable. Theoretically, it is possible that only when traumatic experiences pile up do young people show signs of disturbance. This kind of threshold could reflect the inherent limits in the capacity for adaptation: Individuals do fairly well until this capacity is exceeded, and then symptoms emerge, a kind of depletion model. On the other hand, higher levels of adversity could have a mobilizing effect. In their overview of research on Palestinian children in Gaza, Qouta and colleagues (2008) describe curvilinear effects where adaptive behavior declines as adversity exposure rises and then at extreme levels begins to rise again. They suggest that youth engaged in national political struggles were inspired to respond to extreme political violence with greater engagement, strength, or heroism.

There is considerable interest in knowing whether and how specific kinds of exposures cause more or specific kinds of problems in traumatized children and youth, particularly because this could be helpful for intervention design and planning. Layne and colleagues (2010) recently published a study of Bosnian adolescents exposed to war and political conflict that makes a compelling case for unpacking risk in order to illuminate dose-response processes and inform interventions to ameliorate these risks. Exposure to life-threatening and traumatic bereavement experiences appeared to be "traumatogenic," which is consistent with other literature on events that pose high risk for posttraumatic symptoms or disorder among youth and adults, especially those including direct exposure to life-threatening violence (Kessler et al. 1995, La Greca & Silverman 2009). In their study of child soldiers from Sierra Leone, Betancourt and colleagues (2010) described the traumatic exposures to rape and killing others (tragically common among these young people) as "toxic experiences" with apparently long-lasting and distinctive effects. Youth with the experience of killing others showed increasing hostility in this longitudinal study of former child soldiers; the experience of rape was associated with anxiety and hostility and differential gender-related consequences discussed further below.

The Role of Media in Exposure

Interest in the role of media-based exposure during and after major disasters and war has expanded sharply as mass media and personalized media access have expanded. The potential for media exposure varies by the extensiveness of media availability and use in a given region of the world as well as by social class. Media exposure also potentially can be monitored and moderated by societies, media producers and broadcasters, parents, teachers, and oneself to a greater degree than direct exposures can be controlled.

Exposure through media can be extensive during and after a crisis (Comer & Kendall 2007). Although there is some research on the effects of media exposure to disaster on children and youth, primarily related to television viewing, there is little or no research yet available on the role of emerging social network exposures or personalized media exposure. Media exposure effects were reported after the Challenger explosion (Terr et al. 1999), Oklahoma City bombing (Pfefferbaum et al. 2001, 2003), and 9/11 attack (Lengua et al. 2005, Otto et al. 2007, Phillips et al. 2004, Saylor et al. 2003,

Schuster et al. 2001). Findings are consistent with dose effects, but interpretations are complicated by variations in age of viewers, media access and use, developmental understanding of the material, parental monitoring, and assessment strategies. Younger children may experience distress because they do not fully comprehend what they are watching, are sensitive to parental reactions, or do not know that the same incident is being replayed (Franks 2011). After 9/11, a study of Boston families (Otto et al. 2007) found an association of media exposure with PTSD symptoms in the younger children (age 10 or younger). On the other hand, older children are more likely to have greater access to media and might perceive greater threat because they understand the full scope of the situation (Comer & Kendall 2007, Comer et al. 2008).

Additional research on media dose effects (and moderators) is clearly needed. Meanwhile, developmental and child clinical experts who address this issue typically recommend that exposure for younger and more sensitive (e.g., anxious) children be carefully monitored due to the evidence of media dose effects (Bonanno et al. 2010, Comer & Kendall 2007, Lengua et al. 2005, Masten & Obradović 2008, Pine et al. 2005).

Determinants of Exposure

Some exposures to danger and disaster are random while others are not. There are communities, families, and geographical and geopolitical locations where the likelihood of traumatic exposures to natural and human-made disasters is greater, including earthquake-prone and war-prone regions. Exposures of many kinds are related to socioeconomic status (SES), and it is not surprising that SES-health gradients resemble dose-response gradients.

Often, age is found to relate to exposure in studies of disaster and war, with older children experiencing greater adversity (Masten & Osofsky 2010). Higher dose of exposure among older youth can be attributed to greater awareness of what is happening (related to

cognitive development), greater mobility, higher direct exposure to community effects and media exposure, more expansive social networks, and higher likelihood for older children and adolescents of being kidnapped as child soldiers, raped, or recruited into wars or unfolding disaster response efforts. In a rare national survey of exposure to disaster, Becker-Blease et al. (2010) and colleagues analyzed data from a Developmental Victimization Survey of 1,000 adolescents ages 10 to 17 and 1,030 caregivers of children ages 2 to 9 about exposures (both maltreatment and disasters, including terroristic attacks and natural disasters). Age was associated with higher exposure to disasters, both overall and within the two groups (adolescents by self-report and younger children by parent report).

Gender also is related to exposure, but in more complex ways. Males and females may experience different events, interpret and report them differently, and face different kinds of stigma or discrimination based on those experiences, which could also influence reporting (APA 2010, Masten & Osofsky 2010). In their overview of findings from studies of Palestinians living in Gaza, Qouta and colleagues (2008) suggested that parents in extreme threat situations tended to protect and restrict girls whereas they tolerated or encouraged boys to actively participate in the conflict, which would result in very different exposure risks as a function of gender. In her studies of child soldiers, Betancourt et al. (2010) found that female former soldiers reported more rape experiences than males and that sexual violence held greater stigma for females. Generally, greater risk is reported for young females to be victims of sexual trauma and sexual enslavement in political conflicts or war, whereas males have greater risk for exposure to nonsexual violence in armed conflict (APA 2010).

Mediating Processes of Exposure

There are many processes by which disasters and other extremely traumatic experiences could affect children and youth, including direct and indirect pathways at multiple levels. Mediating processes include stress and its many consequences on the body and brain, neural function, and behavior. Direct pathways for children include the physical dangers posed by injury, starvation, contaminated water, toxins, radiation poisoning, or torture, as well as losses or degradation of physical caregiving. Indirect paths include the effects of extreme adversities on caregivers and, consequently, the quality of care or protection the caregiver can provide to dependent infants and young children. Psychological dangers to children include threats posed to loved ones, observing terrifying events, media portrayals of terrifying events, threats of torture, and self-blame. Moreover, from a very early age, children "read" the fear and concerns of their parents to gauge danger, a phenomenon called social referencing. Terrified parents are terrifying to their children (Masten et al. 1990). Thus, the effects of adversities can be mediated in many direct and indirect ways.

Stress processes and the immune system play a central role in the hazards posed by disasters and trauma of many kinds that children and youth experience, both prenatally and after birth (McEwen & Gianaros 2010, Shonkoff et al. 2009). Currently, there is keen interest in the biological embedding or embodiment of stress experiences in childhood and the possible long-term effects of trauma and disaster on development, health, well-being, and the stress reactivity of future generations. There is growing evidence in animal and human models that maternal stress may have "programming" effects on gene expression and the organization of the stress and immune response systems in fetal and postnatal development. Moreover, epigenetic processes now being delineated by numerous scientists provide plausible models of the processes by which such long-term effects could occur (Hackman et al. 2010, Hochberg et al. 2011, Meaney 2010, Miller et al. 2009). This rapidly expanding body of theory and evidence suggests that the timing of extreme adversities in human development may have long-term and even transgenerational consequences. As a result, there is compelling reason to study the effects of traumatic experiences on the children of pregnant mothers and children exposed to intense trauma at different points in development, discussed further below.

Disasters and war also can disrupt many other aspects of life, including function and opportunities at the level of peer groups, schools, neighborhoods, communication systems, the economy, and international relations (Masten & Obradović 2008, Norris et al. 2008). These disruptions can cascade throughout regions and communities to impose many other adversities on children, youth, and families. Disasters may have enormous economic consequences, for example, that cause great stress to parents and young people.

INDIVIDUAL DIFFERENCES IN RESPONSE

Over the years, many clinicians and researchers have noted the marked variation in observed effects of disasters or war on individual children or youth, even for those who appear to be exposed to the "same" situation (Garmezy 1983, Masten 2011, Masten & Osofsky 2010, Rutter 1983). There has been considerable effort to identify correlates of the differential effects of disasters as a first step toward understanding the processes that might account for these differences, both in the individual and the context. The goal of informing prevention, planning, and intervention efforts provided a strong rationale for this body of research, with the expectation that eventually experiments to promote resilience by targeting these processes would serve to test causal models of risk and resilience (Masten 2011).

One of the challenges of research in the context of disaster is that often it is unclear whether observed or reported differences following a traumatic experience are related to exposure, or even whether they postdate the exposure. Predisaster data are rarely available, and there are few studies with low-exposure comparison groups. Also, it is often uncertain whether any differences observed among groups or individuals reflect differences in exposure, response, perceptions, or response bias. Nonetheless, consistently observed differences do afford important clues to hot spots for further investigation (Masten 2007).

Gender

Gender is often studied as a correlate or moderator of risk and resilience in studies of disaster and war. However, as noted above, gender differences in adaptive outcomes are difficult to interpret because of gender-related differences in exposure, how males and females self-report on experiences and symptoms, and the meaning of exposure or behavior in gender-cultural context (stigma or how the self and others interpret the same behavior in males versus females) (APA 2010, Bonanno et al. 2010, Masten & Osofsky 2010). In addition, there are normative differences in the levels of internalizing and externalizing problems reported by and about males (more externalizing) and females (more internalizing), particularly in adolescence and beyond (Crick & Zahn-Waxler 2003), so it is difficult to determine whether a postdisaster difference reflects a change from predisaster functioning when there is no comparison group or pre- to post-disaster comparison data.

The most widely reported gender differences are greater distress and PTS symptoms observed in or reported by females, as noted by Furr et al. (2010) in their meta-analysis and in other reviews of disasters (Bonanno et al. 2010, Masten & Osofsky 2010), terrorism, or war (APA 2010, Comer & Kendall 2007). For example, nine months after a major industrial accident in Toulouse, France, that occurred shortly after 9/11 in 2001, investigators found that both younger adolescent girls (ages 11 to 13) and older adolescent girls (15 to 17) were more likely to display posttraumatic symptoms than either age group of boys (Godeau et al. 2005). Two years after the 2005 Hurricane Katrina, females in school-based assessments of young people ages 9 to 18 reported more symptoms of depression and PTS symptoms than males (Kronenberg et al. 2010). In one of the few studies after Katrina that included a comparison group from similar socio-demographic backgrounds, Vigil et al. (2010) also found relatively high levels of depression among the exposed females compared to other groups.

There have been some reports of greater belligerence, hostility, or externalizing symptoms among males in this literature over the years, but the evidence is mixed (Masten et al. 1990). In their study after Katrina, Vigil et al. (2010) also found a significant interaction of exposure by gender for aggression, indicating that hurricane-exposed adolescent males in their study reported lower levels of aggression compared to males from similar socio-demographic background who were not exposed and females in the study.

More nuanced examinations of gender differences suggest an even more complex picture. For example, after terrorist attacks in Israel, girls reported more symptoms of PTSD and fear, but boys' symptoms were much more severe (Laufer & Solomon 2009). After a wildfire disaster in another study, girls reported more perceived threat than males but not higher rates of PTSD (McDermott et al. 2005). Recent reports also indicate that stress responses indexed by cortisol show different patterns by gender (Delahanty & Nugent 2006, Vigil et al. 2010).

To summarize, gender likely plays complex roles in the context of extreme adversity. Gaining clarity on these roles is going to require better methodology, including norm-referenced assessments, repeated measures, predisaster baseline data, and better comparison groups.

Age, Developmental Timing Effects, and Sensitive Periods

Developmental timing plays a key role in developmental theories of psychopathology and resilience, including many of the conceptual models applied to disaster and its effect on children (APA 2010, Franks 2011, Masten et al. 1990, Masten & Osofsky 2010). Developmental perspectives demand attention to the influences of both past and anticipated developmental changes in individuals over the course of development, including changes in their cognition and interpretation of experiences, emotion and emotional understanding, self-regulation skills, knowledge, social connections and relationships, physical size and strength, beliefs and faith, and many other aspects of function that could influence their interaction with experience, including traumatic experiences. In addition, there are sensitive periods in development when a particular experience may have greater impact on development, either because the organism is especially vulnerable/responsive at that time or because a key experience-dependent adaptive system is organizing and it becomes "programmed" in response to an unusually traumatic situation that does not prepare the organism well for the subsequent environment. It has long been observed that physical traumas, such as brain injuries, have widely varying effects on subsequent development depending on the timing of the insult, time since the insult, and timing of assessment (Taylor & Alden 1997). Similarly, it is widely recognized that psychological trauma and physiological stress have differential effects related to developmental timing (Fox et al. 2010, Masten & Obradović 2008, Meaney 2010).

Recent advances in understanding the processes by which long-term effects of experience can become biologically embedded in a developing organism, and most specifically the processes of epigenetic change and experience-based programming of neural and neurobiological systems, have profound implications for research on the effects of extreme experiences on the developing individual (Cicchetti 2010, Gunnar & Quevedo 2007, Hochberg et al. 2011, Meaney 2010, Miller et al. 2009, Shonkoff et al. 2009, Yehuda & Bierer 2009). Animal studies and a growing human evidence base strongly suggest that the developmental timing of trauma and stress has different consequences for adaptation and development at multiple levels in the organism. Bad timing (discussed further below) can disrupt development, with long-lasting implications for adaptive capacity, health, and vulnerability to later trauma experiences.

Understanding the role of age differences or developmental timing of exposure on impact is complicated by differences in assessment methods as well as differences in exposure related to cognitive awareness and understanding, objective experiences, media access, and differences in adaptive capacities for survival and self-care. From a developmental perspective, young children would be expected to exhibit more acute symptoms of distress in response to separation from caregivers and disrupted routines. On the other hand, young children are actively monitored and protected by caregivers, and there is considerable plasticity in many aspects of early development, including brain development. Lack of awareness due to cognitive immaturity may be protective in some ways (the child is oblivious to some war atrocities and their implications for the future) and problematic in others (a young child separated from a parent may not understand that the parent is returning, or a young child watching television may not understand that video material is being aired repeatedly). Cognitive maturity is associated with great awareness of betrayals, lost futures, stigma associated with rape, and the scope of devastation but also with greater skills for problem-solving, planning, seeking help, and spiritual comfort. The consequences of the same event, such as loss of a parent, may be very different for a younger and older child. The younger child is more dependent on caregiving and thus highly vulnerable but may also elicit more care from surrogate parents than an older child.

Therefore, age and development would be expected to moderate exposure, functional capacities, and adaptive responses in many different ways, making the task of characterizing "age effects" quite difficult and complex, even though the evidence is generally consistent with developmental expectations (APA 2010, Franks 2011, Garbarino & Kostelny 1996, Masten et al. 1990, Pine et al. 2005). Younger children exhibit acute symptoms of distress or trauma, especially when they are separated from parents, when their parents have intense reactions, or when they are exposed to intense media reports (Hoven et al. 2005, McDermott et al. 2005, Otto et al. 2007, Yelland et al. 2010). The developmentally differentiated response of others to traumatized victims of war and terror can be observed as well. In a study of returning child soldiers, those who were younger when they returned home were met with more acceptance than were older youth (Betancourt et al. 2010). To date, there are very limited data on the long-term consequences of differential timing of exposure by age for disasters.

One of the most provocative timing questions in the current literature concerns the impact of prenatal and infant exposures to extreme maternal stress resulting from terror and disaster that may have programming effects on the stress-response systems during sensitive windows of development (Yehuda & Bierer 2009). Yehuda and colleagues (2005) have reported that infants of 9/11-exposed pregnant mothers who developed PTSD had lower salivary cortisol levels than infants of mothers who did not develop PTSD. Moreover, infants' cortisol levels were lower with more severe maternal 9/11 exposure and were particularly low if mothers were in their third trimester. Yehuda and colleagues (2007, 2008) also have studied children of Holocaust survivors, finding that children of survivors with PTSD had lower cortisol levels compared to children of survivors without PTSD and parents not exposed to the Holocaust. Further, maternal (but not paternal) PTSD specifically was related to PTSD risk in the children. As noted above, recent models of alteration in gene expression related to glucocorticoid programming provide a biological model by which maternal stress could influence long-term stress regulation (and health) in offspring during prenatal exposure to stress or postnatal exposure to maternal care or both (Hochberg et al. 2011, McEwen & Gianaros 2010, Yehuda & Bierer 2009). The possibility that extreme stress experienced by mothers could alter the epigenetic status of their children has important implications for the pathways by which trauma could be transmitted to the next generation. Epigenetic processes also provide pathways of neurobiological change by which previous trauma exposure could alter future trauma vulnerability.

Previous Exposure to Trauma: Inoculation or Sensitization?

There has been considerable interest in the possibility that a history of some stress exposure (and adaptation) produces either protective effects (inoculation) or vulnerability effects (sensitization) with respect to future adaptation in the event of extreme adversity. These two possibilities can be integrated in nonlinear models, where moderate degrees of challenge met successfully have beneficial effects, preparing an organism for future challenges better than either no exposure or too much exposure (Rutter 2006, Seery et al. 2010). Stress inoculation training (see Meichenbaum 2007) methods, discussed in the subsequent section on intervention, are designed to prepare individuals or communities in advance to cope better with severe adversity. Presumably it is through processes involved in an adaptive response (analogous to the process of making antibodies after a vaccination) that an organism gains future protective effects for adapting to mild or moderate exposures. If so, then interventions designed to build capacity for resilience would need to scaffold or in other ways ensure an adaptive response in order to avoid risk of breakdown or depletion of resilience capacity.

Conversely, exposure to overwhelming or capacity-depleting levels of adversity might be unlikely to build immunity, but rather could be expected to induce vulnerability to subsequent exposure. Evidence on the effects of cumulative stress and trauma discussed above is congruent with such sensitization or cumulative effects. Recent work on biological programming of early stress and trauma in childhood, as well as functional changes in cortisol levels that adapt and stabilize under chronic stress, have important implications for children's reactions to subsequent stress or trauma. For example, one function of cortisol elevations in response to stress is to regulate adrenergic and catecholamine activity associated with exposure to trauma and to consolidate trauma-related memories (Delahanty & Nugent 2006); however, exposure to trauma or chronic stress can lead to hypoactivation of the HPA axis (which may function to protect the developing brain from excessive cortisol) and depletions in available cortisol over time (Gunnar & Quevedo 2007). Dysregulation of these stress processes can lead to failure to mobilize an adaptive response in the face of subsequent trauma, increasing the risk for PTSD and intrusive or unintegrated memories of traumatic events (Delahanty & Nugent 2006, Yehuda & Harvey 1997, Yehuda et al. 1998).

In sum, exposure to trauma may have sensitizing effects on children that could lead to HPA axis dysfunction; however, findings on the exact nature of HPA disruption are still mixed. A variety of other factors, such as timing, dose, and length of exposure, genetic underpinnings, and availability of social support, likely also play a role in biological responsiveness following disasters (Pratchett & Yehuda 2011). However, the possibility that the stress regulatory system can be chronically altered from exposure to trauma and its developmental timing suggests that children exposed to trauma at an early age might become more vulnerable to subsequent stress or that children exposed to chronic life stress might be particularly vulnerable to the effects of subsequent trauma, as reported for adults by Yehuda and colleagues (2010). It is also conceivable that atypically low levels of cortisol in older children or adults after a traumatic event might be observed among individuals who have a history of previous trauma exposure (Pervanidou 2008). Recent developments in research on biological processes related to trauma represent an important and intriguing future direction for investigation.

Promotive and Protective Factors in Children, Families, and Relationships

Over the years, a consistent set of factors have been implicated as important for adaptation in the context of disasters, war, and many other extreme adversities faced by children and youth (APA 2010, Betancourt & Khan 2008, Cicchetti 2010, Garmezy 1983, Garmezy & Rutter 1985, Luthar 2006, Masten et al. 1990, Masten & Obradović 2008, Masten & Osofsky 2010). These factors, including intelligence, self-regulation skills, hope and beliefs that life has meaning, self-efficacy, close and supportive relationships, religious beliefs and practices, and community supports, likely reflect powerful adaptive systems resulting from biological and cultural evolution (Masten 2001, 2012). Many studies, until very recently, have focused on psychosocial factors. Now, with advances in assessment of genes, biomarkers, and brain function, there is a surge of research on neurobiological processes in adaptation to severe threats, including disasters and war, as well as child maltreatment and family violence (Cicchetti 2010, Sapienza & Masten 2011).

Attachment relationships. Beginning with early studies and continuing to date, researchers have noted the importance of attachment relationships and the functional capabilities of the caregiver for children exposed to disasters and other severe adversities. As noted above, the negative effects of separation from or loss of caregivers during crises was identified long ago as a crucial factor for children, and the functional status of parents—before, during, and after disasters—was recognized as a key influence on child response. Recent research corroborates these observations across diverse calamities. Symptoms in parents could affect children either by undermining parenting behavior or alarming children more directly (even young children perceive emotional distress in parents) or both. Parents who had more mental health symptoms after 9/11 had preschool children who were not doing as well as their peers, according to their teachers (Chemtob et al. 2010). Other studies focus explicitly on parenting, parent-child interaction quality, and perceived family acceptance. Qouta et al. (2008) reported that strong family relationships predicted resilience among children exposed to political violence in Palestine. The quality of parent-child relationships moderated the association of tsunami exposure on adolescent symptoms of PTSD and depression (Wickrama & Kaspar 2007). Family acceptance was associated with all of the outcome indicators of adaptive recovery in child soldiers studied by Betancourt et al. (2010).

Although considerable evidence has linked effective parenting to resilience in disasters and war, it is important to consider whether parents could undermine resilience through overprotectiveness. Bokszczanin (2008) found that high parental involvement after a flood in Poland was associated with higher risk for PTSD in adolescents. Adolescents may interpret high involvement as an indication of parental judgments that they are not capable, in effect undermining their self-confidence or perceived efficacy and agency. Bonanno et al. (2010) have raised this question more broadly in the disaster response field by noting that too much early intervention by outsiders may have the unintended effect of undermining adaptive processes in families and communities.

Cognitive skills and self-regulation. Cognitive skills (general intelligence and cognitive flexibility) and self-regulation skills are widely implicated as protective factors for children in a variety of hazardous circumstances, including disaster (Masten 2007, Masten & Obradović 2008). In a rare study with predisaster assessments, in this case prior to political conflict in Kenya, Kithakye et al. (2010) found that self-regulation skills in preschoolers predicted better postconflict outcomes (less aggression and better prosocial function), controlling for preconflict behavior. Self-control also moderated the effects of exposure severity on prosocial behavior. Similarly, Terranova et al. (2009) reported that effortful control abilities (shifting, planning, and inhibiting unwanted behaviors) buffered sixth-grade childrens' PTSD symptoms after Katrina, consistent with a protective effect. Studies of youth in Palestine also have suggested that cognitive capabilities are protective (Qouta et al. 2008).

Cognitive skills may be a mixed blessing, however. As noted above, more cognitively advanced children may better comprehend the scope of a disaster. Sprung (2008) found that 5- to 8-year-old children who had more developed theory-of-mind skills had more intrusive thoughts after Katrina but were also more receptive to learning strategies to cope with them.

Agency and self-efficacy. Perceived agency and self-efficacy are also associated with resilience in numerous studies (Luthar 2006, Masten 2007, Masten & Obradović 2008). In their longitudinal study of child soldiers, Betancourt et al. (2010) found that youth who survived rape had greater confidence, which they speculate may have resulted from enduring prolonged hardships during the years of captivity. Barber (2008) has found positive effects of activism during the Intifada on postconflict social and civic behavior among Palestinian youth. A sense of competence has also been identified to have protective/promotive effects. Greater competency beliefs promoted more posttraumatic growth in children ages 6 to 15 who were exposed to Hurricane Floyd (Cryder et al. 2006), and higher self-esteem protected against PTS in children ages 9 to 13 who experienced 9/11 (Lengua et al. 2005).

Personality. Personality differences that could influence stress reactivity also have been studied for decades, with particular interest in negative emotionality (the tendency to respond with negative emotion and get upset easily). Though not commonly studied, recent studies continue to verify the importance of individual differences in negative emotionality. In a small study of adolescents exposed to Katrina with prehurricane assessment of this personality trait, negative emotionality predicted postdisaster symptoms of anxiety, depression, and PTSD (Weems et al. 2007). The tendency of individuals to ruminate also holds interest, because rumination is associated with risk for depression among adolescents and adults (Nolen-Hoeksema et al. 2001). After Katrina, however, children's ruminative thoughts, both negative and positive, predicted posttraumatic growth in one study (Kilmer &

Gil-Rivas 2010). The investigators speculated that this finding might signify that rumination facilitates more processing of, meaning making about, and integrating of the experience into memory and identity.

Acculturation skills. For those young people who flee to new cultures and countries as a result of conflict or disaster, acculturation and language skills have been linked to better adaptation over time (APA 2010, Wright et al. 2012). A study of Somali and Oroma refugees (ages 18 to 25 at the time of assessment but typically in their teens at the time of emigration) found that language fluency was associated with fewer PTSD symptoms (Halcón et al. 2004). Language skills similarly were associated with more academic and social success in a study of highly traumatized Cambodian child survivors of Pol Pot who eventually immigrated to the United States (Hubbard 1997). In the same group of young people, positive American or bicultural identity also was associated with competence (Northwood 1996). These factors (language skills in the host nation and bicultural identity) appear to be broadly protective for immigrant youth who have experienced less trauma and are moving into culturally and linguistically different host countries (Masten et al. 2012, Suárez-Orozco et al. 2006).

Meaning and hope. Faith, hope, and spiritual beliefs or religious practices have been implicated in the broad resilience literature and also in a specific subset of disaster or war studies (Crawford et al. 2006). Faith and religion would be expected to have greater significance for older children and adolescents than young children. Among Ugandan former child soldiers, young people who showed posttraumatic resilience (better mental health) also reported more perceived spiritual support (Klasen et al. 2010). The widely reported role of spirituality and religion after devastating disasters or war in older youth and adults may reflect the broad significance of belief systems that give coherence and a meaning to life for resilience in devastating circumstances (Wright et al. 2012).

Neurobiological protections. Individual differences assessed at a neural or biological level remain extremely rare in the disaster literature. In one of these rare efforts, Vigil et al. (2010) assessed two biological systems in exposed and unexposed adolescents post-Katrina, the HPA axis (measuring salivary cortisol) and the sympathetic nervous system (measuring salivary alpha-amylase). The combination of high response in both systems appeared to be associated with resilience. Other studies of cortisol have suggested that low levels immediately following traumatic exposures may be a biomarker of risk for subsequent PTSD (Pervanidou 2008, Yehuda & Harvey 1997, Yehuda et al. 1998).

Broader Recovery Context: Promotive and Protective Factors in the Community

Beyond the family, research indicates that community context and community resilience are important for children and families (Betancourt & Khan 2008, Masten & Obradović 2008, Norris et al. 2008). In extremely devastating disasters or war, communities may be destroyed, and people must resettle temporarily or permanently. The supports and functional capacities of these contexts appear to make a profound difference for children and their families.

School and other child-nurturing institutions. Among the most widely reported protective factors for children offered by communities in the aftermath of disaster, exclusive of survival needs, are functional schools, child-care facilities, and other safe environments for children to play and to learn (APA 2010, Betancourt & Khan 2008, Masten & Obradović 2008, Masten & Osofsky 2010, Osofsky et al. 2007). These institutions serve to reestablish routines in a child's life, may provide respite for parents, and also afford opportunities for peer interaction, constructive activities, connections to competent adults, leadership and agency experiences, etc. Prompt resumption of schooling was one of the most highly endorsed postdisaster practices in a Delphi consensus study based on surveying leading humanitarian agencies that intervene in many crises worldwide (Ager et al. 2010). Staying in school was associated with improved prosocial attitudes and behaviors in the study of former child soldiers from Sierra Leone (Betancourt et al. 2010). Other aspects of the community context have been studied, though research remains very limited. Community acceptance was a key factor associated with better adjustment in former child soldiers from Sierra Leone (Betancourt et al. 2010) and Columbia (Cortes & Buchanan 2007).

INTERVENTION

Research on disaster effects and promotive or protective factors has many implications for intervention designs to protect children and youth and promote resilience. Intervention research, however, remains limited. Perhaps this is not surprising given that research on the effectiveness of interventions intended to help children and youth weather or recover from catastrophic adversities is notoriously challenging to implement. The scarcity of strong research on interventions to mitigate disaster effects has been noted by numerous reviewers and reports (e.g., APA 2010, Bonanno et al. 2010, Hobfoll et al. 2007, Jordans et al. 2009, Tol et al. 2010). The shortage of quality intervention evidence is particularly disappointing given the extensiveness of exposure among young people to devastating disasters and conflicts and also the extensiveness of humanitarian efforts to intervene and help. Peltonen & Punamäki (2010) recently found only four studies that met criteria for their meta-analysis of intervention studies in situations of terrorism or armed conflict.

Nevertheless, disasters continue to unfold, and stakeholders must take action to prepare and respond to disaster, informed by the best evidence and corresponding theory to date. Whether one is preparing for specific kinds of disaster or terrorism in high-risk-for-exposure zones or responding to an unexpected calamity, preparations and responses cannot wait for complete scientific knowledge to accrue. For those who must act, there is a reassuringly strong consensus on broad guidelines for intervention. At the same time, it is clear that greater investment is needed in research infrastructure, methods, and collaborations in order to build a better evidence base going forward. In this section, we highlight examples of the best evidence on intervention for children or youth, describe the broad guidelines that reflect the current consensus, and comment on the importance of better data for future intervention efforts.

Exemplary Studies of Preventive Interventions and Treatments

Among the few studies meeting the gold-standard design feature of randomized assignment to intervention versus comparison or control groups (randomized controlled trial; RCT), several have been done in the former Yugoslavian countries in the aftermath of political violence and war in the region. One of the earliest of these studies, reported by Dybdahl (2001), conducted in the year following the end of the war, focused on mothers of young children ages 5 or 6 in Bosnian families who were exposed to severe war atrocities. Families were randomized to the intervention, which focused on warm and supportive interactions of mothers with children during a five-month group program, with treated families receiving medical care plus the intervention compared to a control group receiving only medical care. Intervention effects on mothers were reflected in better mental health outcomes in mothers and children as well as greater weight gain in children. Layne and colleagues (2008) also conducted an RCT in Bosnia, which focused on war-exposed adolescents with persistent symptoms and significant impairment several years following the cessation of hostilities. Students were randomly assigned to a classroom with psychoeducational and skill-focused intervention (only) or a classroom that also received a school-based trauma and grief-focused group treatment (manualized, 17-session therapy group). Both groups improved over time, although the latter, more intensive treatment group showed greater reduction in maladaptive traumatic grief.

In one of the few studies in the literature testing a theory of change (mediators of treatment effects), Tol and colleagues (2010) examined the mediating role of hope, coping, and peer/emotional/play social support on treatment effects in an RCT study of children ages 8 to 13 in Indonesia who were exposed to political violence. The treatment, based on an ecological theory of resilience, was designed to foster creative expression of experiences with violence by utilizing cognitive-behavioral strategies in a classroom setting. Only peer social support was found to mediate the treatment effects of this manualized classroom intervention.

Efforts to prepare children for terrorism attacks or armed conflict (Ayalon 1983, Wolmer et al. 2011) or disasters (e.g., tornado drills) often combine simulations of the threat and training in adaptive responses. To date, evidence on natural or planned (attenuated) exposures to disaster as a vaccination-like preventive intervention is limited and primarily retrospective (Bonanno et al. 2010). A rare exception can be found in a recent report on stress inoculation training (SIT) in Israel, where a school-based SIT intervention was added to the school curriculum in multiple schools in a high-risk area for armed conflict. Three months following a three-week conflict ("Operation Cast Lead") with rocket attacks and high trauma exposure, children in six schools who received the intervention were compared with children in six schools who had not received it, matched for exposure levels (Wolmer et al. 2011). Results suggested that SIT had preventive effects on PTS and other symptoms of distress. Such results offer intriguing evidence that this kind of approach holds promise for future prevention experiments in areas with predictable high risk for severe adversity, either natural or related to chronic political conflict.

Consensus Guidelines

There are two kinds of consensus in the literature regarding interventions for young people in the context of disaster: systematic efforts to reach consensus guidelines (e.g., Ager et al. 2010, Hobfoll et al. 2007) and recommendations based on reviews of the literature that suggest strong agreement in the field (e.g., APA 2010; Bonanno et al. 2010; Jordans et al. 2009; La Greca & Silverman 2009; Masten & Obradović 2008; Masten & Osofsky 2010; Norris et al. 2002a,b, 2008; Peltonen & Punamäki 2010; Pine et al. 2005). Recommendations from both kinds of consensus are quite consistent and also highly congruent with a risk-and-resilience perspective. These recommendations tend to be broad and oriented to universal/community-level approaches, in part because the evidence base on which to make specific recommendations is so thin.

Consensus guidelines often focus on different phases of disaster, including predisaster preparation, immediate aftermath or crisis phase, and longer-term recovery periods. Bonanno et al. (2010) have recently questioned the value of immediate intervention, beyond the provision of basic tangible necessities (such as water, food, shelter, medicine, or money), information, and support to keep natural social units together or reunite them. There is little or no evidence that prophylactic efforts in the field immediately after disasters have positive effects, and such intrusions may disrupt naturally occurring recovery processes or undermine self-efficacy or community efficacy. For example, two of the best-known crisis interventions, critical incident stress debriefing and grief counseling, do not show positive effects and may have negative effects on traumatized populations (Bonanno et al. 2010, La Greca & Silverman 2009).

Psychological first aid (Ruzek et al. 2007), a much less intrusive form of crisis intervention, currently lacks strong evidence of effectiveness (Bonanno et al. 2010). However, psychological first aid is much more aligned with the broad recommendations of experts on the risk and resilience literature pertaining to disasters, war, and terrorism (cited throughout this review) and experts in related practice or humanitarian fields (e.g., Ager et al. 2010, Hobfoll et al. 2007).

Five broad intervention principles have been proposed for mass trauma based on the literature by Hobfoll et al. (2007): promote a sense of safety, promote calming, promote a sense of self- and collective efficacy, promote connectedness, and promote hope. These recommendations align well with the broad implications of the resilience literature in regard to protecting, supporting, or restoring the most fundamental adaptive systems believed to generate the capacity for resilience (Masten 2001, 2011).

After some time is allowed for natural recovery with broad supports to families and communities in disaster-affected areas, there is considerable support for evaluations to determine if additional help is indicated at the individual, family, or community level (Bonanno et al. 2010, Norris et al. 2008). Numerous investigators recommend screening for treatable problems when symptoms persist or develop among survivors, although it is unclear what the best timing and strategies are for screening or intervention.

There also is strong consensus that disaster or conflict readiness is important to protect children, youth, and families in the event of calamity (Masten & Obradović 2008, Masten & Osofsky 2010, NCCD 2010, Norris et al. 2008, Wolmer et al. 2011). Recommendations for preparedness include training first responders on the needs of children, recognizing that parents, childcare providers, and teachers also are first responders for children, having plans for reuniting children with families, and considering in advance the importance of protecting and restoring the natural protective systems for children as well as their normal routines of school and play.

Cautionary Note on Intervention

There is some consensus as well on cautions to consider in the design and implementation of interventions in the context of disaster, war, and terrorism (Bonanno et al. 2010, La Greca & Silverman 2009). As noted above, there are concerns about intervening at the wrong time, too intrusively, and with strategies that have little basis in research or are even contraindicated by evidence. Moreover, it is important to consider the possibility that intervention may disrupt or undermine naturally occurring resilience and recovery processes. Additional concerns stem from the widely acknowledged risks of imposing culturally or developmentally inappropriate interventions.

CONCLUSIONS AND FUTURE DIRECTIONS

There are striking consistencies and gaps in the literature reviewed here on children and youth exposed to disasters and political violence. Much of the theory and research in the area is guided by a developmental resilience framework, pioneered more than four decades ago, that continues to advance in new directions. There is strong consensus on what matters in terms of both exposure factors and protective factors. Broad guidelines for preventive intervention and policies have emerged, yet there continues to be a marked shortage of intervention research on what works, for whom, and when in relation to meeting the needs of children and youth exposed to disasters and other mass exposures to extreme adversities.

A resilience framework, broadly defined, appears to work well for conceptualizing and summarizing the findings and their implications for intervention. The effects of disasters and mass violence on individual development can be described in relation to exposure dose or cumulative risks that pose significant threats or disturbances to individuals, families, or communities; resources or promotive factors required to counterbalance these threats or adversities; and moderators that exacerbate or ameliorate the consequences of the risks, often described as vulnerability and protective processes. The capacity for resilience in a given child will depend on a confluence of myriad factors, including the developmental status and capabilities of the child (developmental stage and human capital), capacities embedded in the child's relationships and community connections (social capital), and many other potential adaptive systems. The complex processes of adaptation in the aftermath of disaster will depend on many interactions at multiple levels of function, such as biological, psychosocial, and epigenetic influences on development and risk.

There appear to be fundamental adaptive systems that afford much of the capacity for resilience in young individuals faced with disastrous situations. At the behavioral level of analysis, these core protections include supportive and effective caregiving (preferably by established attachment figures in a child's life), problem-solving systems, self-regulation and social-regulation systems, motivational/reward systems underlying self-efficacy, and hope and belief systems that convey a sense of meaning. These systems appear to promote a sense of safety and connectedness, perceived control and agency, regulation of arousal and behavior, and optimistic thinking required in diverse situations for adaptive responses to threats and disturbances in life. Adults in many capacities (parents, mentors, friends, neighbors, first responders, etc.) play crucial roles in the risks and resilience of children in disasters.

Major findings from rather disparate studies of children and youth in disasters and war align very well with resilience theory and the consensus recommendations from field experts. The implications of this body of work suggest that intervention efforts focus on protecting and restoring core human capacity for resilience in addition to mitigating risk and symptoms. A very limited body of empirical intervention research is consistent with the broad principles of intervention that have emerged from theory and basic research.

There is a stunning lack of evidence on intervention, given the scope of worldwide exposure of children and youth to disasters, terrorism, and war, and the likelihood of future exposures. The overall lack of research on interventions and their effectiveness has been noted in every relevant article included in this review. Addressing this profoundly important hole in the evidence base is the most important task for the future.

Informative research on what works to protect children and youth and to promote their resilience in the aftermath of mass disaster and trauma is challenging to execute, for all the reasons noted elsewhere in this review and in numerous other reviews. Yet it is also the case that there is a strong base of evidence and theory to inform intervention models of change. Masten (2011) has argued recently for a synthesis of basic and applied resilience frameworks, what she terms "translational synergy," to guide the needed research that aims to promote resilience in children threatened by extreme adversity. In this integrated model, intervention research is designed collaboratively by field and research experts working together, with the joint goal of fostering resilience in threatened individuals (intervention goals) while simultaneously testing theories of change (science goals).

Given that there are high-risk areas for exposure to natural disasters or political violence, there also is potential to test universal prevention and preparedness efforts. The controlled study by Wolmer et al. (2011) of a universal, teacher-based preventive intervention in Israeli schools provides a recent example. Recent research on military families and large-scale efforts to promote their resilience may also inform efforts to prepare civilian families living in high-risk zones for exposure to war (Saltzman et al. 2012). Studies that fully meet gold-standard design criteria of random assignment may be feasible as well.

It may be time for governmental agencies charged with disaster preparedness recovery to mobilize teams of experts to plan universal preventive experiments. Similar teams are needed to plan (design and secure advance funding) for postdisaster intervention studies that are low risk, ethical, and can be fielded quickly. Capitalizing on research already done or underway in disaster- or war-impacted areas by facilitating postdisaster research is also important (Furr et al. 2010, Masten & Osofsky 2010). In regions at risk for hurricanes, it may be a good investment to routinely survey normative development, behavior, symptoms, and stress levels in schools, which could then serve as baseline, predisaster, or comparison data in the eventuality of disasters.

It is also clear that additional research is needed on methods and measures that work across diverse situations and cultures, in addition to measures suitable to specific situations (Furr et al. 2010, Masten & Osofsky 2010, Peltonen & Punamäki 2010). Measures are often invented or adapted "ad hoc" for disaster research because there are so few validated tools. Evidence can be difficult to aggregate in the absence of systematic and comparable assessments.

Finally, as noted by many scholars in this field, we need to pay more attention to developmental issues and most particularly to developmental timing and the longitudinal course of change following exposures. Development interacts with biological underpinnings of risk and a child's accumulated experience, and there are likely to be sensitive periods for trauma exposure as well as differentially effective interventions related to developmental status and intervention timing after exposure. There is very little information in the literature on long-term outcomes of disaster exposure, or what types of interventions might be most effective for whom and when, in terms of developmental timing or timing following exposure.

New Horizons

Although there are major gaps in the extant literature, most notably on intervention effectiveness, there also are exciting new directions in this research domain. Advances in neuroscience, genetics, and the analysis of complex systems at multiple levels are revolutionizing the study of risk and resilience (Cicchetti 2010, Feder et al. 2009, Sapienza & Masten 2011). There is rapid growth in the biology and neuroscience of resilience and, concomitantly, in the multiple-level study of disaster effects on development, in the short- and long-term and even across generations. There also is growing interest in more comprehensive studies of disaster that integrate models and knowledge across disciplines (Folke et al. 2010, Longstaff 2009, Masten & Obradović 2008). Mass-scale natural disasters and wars represent major disturbances of multiple, interdependent systems across scales from the molecular to the global and also across traditional science boundaries (ecology, psychology, emergency medicine, economics, etc.). Preparing for these extreme and complex situations and promoting recovery in their aftermath requires integrated sciences and strategies. Human development reflects the interplay of many systems across many levels, and eventually the science of human response to disaster must embrace this complex reality.

SUMMARY POINTS

1. Although research in the context of large-scale disasters poses major ethical and methodological challenges, there is notable progress in the quantity and quality of the evidence base over the past decade.

2. Risk and resilience frameworks continue to guide basic and translational research on the effects of extreme adversities in young people and their families.

3. Developmental timing of extreme adversity experiences has important implications for the nature of exposure, mediating and moderating processes, protective factors, future adaptive capacity, and design of interventions. The role of age in exposure and response is complex: Younger children are relatively protected in some ways and vulnerable in others in comparison to older youth.

4. There is growing interest and evidence related to the biological embedding of extreme stress in human development and increasingly plausible explanations of mediating processes that could explain its long-lasting effects on health and well-being, even across generations.

5. Research is needed to understand inoculation versus sensitization effects in response to repeated trauma exposure.

6. Given the striking shortage of data on intervention effectiveness despite pressing international need, research on pre- and postdisaster interventions to promote resilience in young people and families in mass trauma situations is a top priority.

7. Despite limitations in the evidence base, there is a strong consensus on broad guidelines for child-sensitive preparedness and response to disasters and political conflicts, based on theory, basic and applied research, and field experience. These guidelines include training of all disaster-response personnel on special needs and issues of children; recognition of parents, teachers, and care providers as first responders who also need training; avoiding separation of children from caregivers and reuniting separated families; careful monitoring of media exposure in children; and rapid restoration of routines, schools, and opportunities to play or socialize with peers.

8. Understanding and addressing the complexities of risk and resilience in human development under conditions of mass trauma require collaboration and greater integration of knowledge and methods across multiple systems and levels of analysis.

DISCLOSURE STATEMENT

The authors are not aware of any affiliations, memberships, funding, or financial holdings that might be perceived as affecting the objectivity of this review.

ACKNOWLEDGMENTS

Work on this review was supported in part by the National Institute of Mental Health (NIMH) through the Center on Personalized Prevention at the University of Minnesota (PI August, NIMH P20 MH085987) and a predoctoral fellowship to the second author (NIMH 5T32MH015755), and also by a grant to the first author from the National Science Foundation (NSF 0745643). Any opinions, conclusions, or recommendations expressed in this review are those of the authors and do not necessarily reflect the views of NIMH or NSF.

LITERATURE CITED

Ager A, Stark L, Akesson B, Boothby N. 2010. Defining best practice in care and protection of children in crisis-affected settings: a Delphi study. *Child Dev.* 81(4):1271–86

Am. Psychol. Assoc. (APA). 2010. *Resilience and Recovery After War: Refugee Children and Families in the United States.* Washington, DC: Am. Psychol. Assoc.

Ayalon O. 1983. Coping with terrorism: the Israeli case. In *Stress Reduction and Prevention*, ed. D Meichenbaum, M Jaremko, pp. 293–340. New York: Plenum

Barber BK. 2008. Contrasting portraits of war: youths' varied experiences with political violence in Bosnia and Palestine. *Int. J. Behav. Dev.* 32(4):298–309

Becker-Blease KA, Turner HA, Finkelhor D. 2010. Disasters, victimization and children's mental health. *Child Dev.* 81(4):1040–52

Belsky J, Bakermans-Kranenburg JM, van IJzendoorn MH. 2007. For better or for worse: differential susceptibility to environmental influences. *Curr. Direct. Psychol. Sci.* 16(6):300–4

Belsky J, Pluess M. 2009. Beyond diathesis stress: differential susceptibility to environmental influences. *Psychol. Bull.* 135(6):885–908

Betancourt TS. 2011. Attending to the mental health of war-affected children: the need for longitudinal and developmental research perspectives. *J. Am. Acad. Child Adolesc. Psychiatry* 50(4):323–25

Betancourt TS, Borisova II, Williams TP, Brennan RT, Whitfield TH, et al. 2010. Sierra Leone's former child soldiers: a follow-up study of psychosocial adjustment and community reintegration. *Child Dev.* 81(4):1076–94

Betancourt TS, Khan KT. 2008. The mental health of children affected by armed conflict: protective processes and pathways to resilience. *Int. Rev. Psychiatry* 20(3):317–28

Bokszczanin A. 2008. Parental support, family conflict, and overprotectiveness: predicting PTSD symptom levels of adolescents 28 months after a natural disaster. *Anxiety Stress Coping* 21(4):325–35

Bonanno GA. 2004. Loss, trauma, and human resilience: Have we underestimated the human capacity to thrive after extremely aversive events? *Am. Psychol.* 59(1):20–28

Bonanno GA, Brewin CR, Kaniasty K, La Greca AM. 2010. Weighing the costs of disaster: consequences, risks, and resilience in individuals, families and communities. *Psychol. Sci. Public Interest* 11(1):1–49

Boyce WT, Ellis BJ. 2005. Biological sensitivity to context: I. An evolutionary-developmental theory of the origins and functions of stress reactivity. *Dev. Psychopathol.* 17(2):271–301

Bronfenbrenner U. 1979. *The Ecology of Human Development: Experiments by Nature and Design.* Cambridge, MA: Harvard Univ. Press

Bronfenbrenner U, Morris PA. 2006. The bioecological model of human development. In *The Handbook of Child Psychology, Vol. 1: Theoretical Models of Human Development*, ed. RM Lerner, W Damon, pp. 793–828. Hoboken, NJ: Wiley. 6th ed.

Carrion VG, Weems CF, Bradley T. 2010. Natural disasters and the neurodevelopmental response to trauma in childhood: a brief overview and call to action. *Future Neurol.* 5(5):667–74

Catani C, Gewirtz AH, Wieling E, Schauer E, Elbert T, Neuner F. 2010. Tsunami, war, and cumulative risk in the lives of Sri Lankan school children. *Child Dev.* 81(4):1175–90

Chemtob CM, Nomura Y, Rajendran K, Yehuda R, Schwartz D, Abramovitz R. 2010. Impact of maternal posttraumatic stress disorder and depression following exposure to the September 11 attacks on preschool children's behavior. *Child Dev.* 81(4):1128–40

Cicchetti D. 2006. Development and psychopathology. In *Developmental Psychopathology, Vol. 1: Theory and Method*, ed. D Cicchetti, D Cohen, pp. 1–23. Hoboken, NJ: Wiley. 2nd ed.

Cicchetti D. 2010. Resilience under conditions of extreme stress: a multilevel perspective. *World Psychiatry* 9(3):145–54

Comer JS, Furr JM, Beidas RS, Weiner CL, Kendall PC. 2008. Children and terrorism-related news: training parents in coping and media literacy. *J. Consult. Clin. Psychol.* 76(4):568–78

Comer JS, Kendall PC. 2007. Terrorism: the psychological impact on youth. *Clin. Psychol. Sci. Pract.* 14(3):182–212

Cortes L, Buchanan MJ. 2007. The experience of Columbian child soldiers from a resilience perspective. *Int. J. Adv. Couns.* 29:43–55

Crawford E, Wright MO, Masten AS. 2006. Resilience and spirituality in youth. In *The Handbook of Spiritual Development in Childhood and Adolescence*, ed. EC Roehlkepartain, PE King, L Wagener, PL Benson, pp. 355–70. Thousand Oaks, CA: Sage

Crick NR, Zahn-Waxler C. 2003. The development of psychopathology in females and males: current progress and future challenges. *Dev. Psychopathol.* 15(3):719–42

Cryder CH, Kilmer RP, Tedeschi RG, Calhoun LG. 2006. An exploratory study of posttraumatic growth in children following a natural disaster. *Am. J. Orthopsychiatry* 76(1):65–69

Delahanty DL, Nugent NR. 2006. Predicting PTSD prospectively based on prior trauma history and immediate biological responses. *Ann. N.Y. Acad. Sci.* 1071:27–40

Dybdahl R. 2001. Children and mothers in war: an outcome study of a psychosocial intervention program. *Child Dev.* 72(4):1214–30

Ellis BJ, Boyce WT, Belsky J, Bakermans-Kranenburg MJ, van IJzendoorn MH. 2011. Differential susceptibility to the environment: an evolutionary-neurodevelopmental theory. *Dev. Psychopathol.* 23:7–28

Erikson KT. 1976. *Everything in Its Path: Destruction of Community in the Buffalo Creek Flood.* New York: Simon & Schuster

Feder A, Nestler EJ, Charney DS. 2009. Psychobiology and molecular genetics of resilience. *Nat. Rev. Neurosci.* 10:446–57

Fisher PA, Gunnar MR, Dozier M, Bruce J, Pears C. 2006. Effects of therapeutic interventions for foster children on behavioral problems, caregiver attachment, and stress regulatory neural systems. *Ann. N.Y. Acad. Sci.* 1094:215–25

Folke C, Carpenter SR, Walker B, Scheffer M, Chappin T, Rockström J. 2010. Resilience thinking: integrating resilience, adaptability, and transformability. *Ecol. Soc.* 15(4):20–28

Fox SE, Levitt P, Nelson CA. 2010. How the timing and quality of early experiences influence the development of brain architecture. *Child Dev.* 81(1):28–40

Franks BA. 2011. Moving targets: a developmental framework for understanding children's changes following disasters. *J. Appl. Dev. Psychol.* 32(2):58–69

Freud A, Burlingham DT. 1943. *War and Children.* New York: Medical War Books

Freud A, Dann S. 1951. An experiment in group upbringing. *Psychoanal. Study Child.* 6:127–68

Furr JM, Comer JS, Edmunds JM, Kendall PC. 2010. Disasters and youth: a meta-analytic examination of posttraumatic stress. *J. Consult. Clin. Psychol.* 78(6):765–80

Garbarino J, Kostelny K. 1996. The effects of political violence on Palestinian children's behavior problems: a risk accumulation model. *Child Dev.* 67(1):33–45

Garmezy N. 1983. Stressors of childhood. In *Stress, Coping, and Development*, ed. N Garmezy, M Rutter, pp. 43–84. New York: McGraw-Hill

Garmezy N, Rutter M. 1985. Acute reactions to stress. In *Child and Adolescent Psychiatry: Modern Approaches*, ed. M Rutter, L Hersov, pp. 152–76. Oxford, UK: Blackwell Sci. 2nd ed.

Gershoff E, Aber JL, Ware A, Kotler J. 2010. Exposure to 9/11 among youth and their mothers in New York City: enduring associations with mental health and sociopolitical attitudes. *Child Dev.* 81(4):1141–59

Gleser G, Green B, Winget C. 1981. *Prolonged Psychological Effects of Disaster: A Study of Buffalo Creek.* New York: Academic

Godeau E, Vignes C, Navarro F, Iachan R, Ross J, et al. 2005. Effects of a large-scale industrial disaster on rates of symptoms consistent with posttraumatic stress disorders among schoolchildren in Toulouse. *Arch. Pediatr. Adolesc. Med.* 159(6):579–84

Gottlieb G. 2007. Probabilistic epigenesis. *Dev. Sci.* 10(1):1–11

Green BL, Grace MC, Vary MG, Kramer TL, Gleser GC, Leonard AC. 1994. Children of disaster in the second decade: a 17-year follow-up of Buffalo Creek survivors. *J. Am. Acad. Child Adolesc. Psychiatry* 33(1):71–79

Gunnar M, Quevedo K. 2007. The neurobiology of stress and development. *Annu. Rev. Psychol.* 58:145–73

Hackman D, Farah M, Meaney M. 2010. Socioeconomic status and the brain: mechanistic insights from human and animal research. *Nat. Rev. Neurosci.* 11(9):651–59

Halcón LL, Robertson CL, Savik K, Johnson DR, Spring MA, et al. 2004. Trauma and coping in Somali and Oromo youth. *J. Adolesc. Health* 35(1):17–25

Hobfoll SE, Watson P, Bell CC, Bryant RA, Brymer MJ, et al. 2007. Five essential elements of immediate and mid-term mass trauma intervention: empirical evidence. *Psychiatry* 70(4):283–315

Hochberg Z, Feil R, Constancia M, Fraga M, Junien C, et al. 2011. Child health, developmental plasticity, and epigenetic programming. *Endocr. Rev.* 32(2):159–224

Hoven CW, Duarte CS, Lucas CP, Wu P, Mandell DJ, et al. 2005. Psychopathology among New York City public school children 6 months after September 11. *Arch. Gen. Psychiatry* 62:545–52

Hubbard J. 1997. *Adaptive functioning and post-traumatic symptoms in adolescent survivors of massive childhood trauma.* Unpubl. doctoral dissert., Univ. Minn.

Jordans MJD, Tol WA, Komproe IH, de Jong JVTM. 2009. Systematic review of evidence and treatment approaches: psychosocial and mental health care for children in war. *Child Adolesc. Mental Health* 14(1):2–14

Kessler RC, Sonnega A, Bromet E, Hughes M, Nelson CB. 1995. Posttraumatic stress disorder in the National Comorbidity Survey. *Arch. Gen. Psychiatry* 52(12):1048–60

Kilmer R, Gil-Rivas V. 2010. Exploring posttraumatic growth in children impacted by Hurricane Katrina: correlates of the phenomenon and developmental considerations. *Child Dev.* 81(4):1210–26

Kim-Cohen J, Gold AL. 2009. Measured gene-environment interactions and mechanisms promoting resilient development. *Curr. Dir. Psychol. Sci.* 18(3):138–42

Kithakye M, Morris AS, Terranova AM, Myers SS. 2010. The Kenyan political conflict and children's adjustment. *Child Dev.* 81(4):1113–27

Klasen F, Oettingen G, Daniels J, Post M, Hoyer C, Adam H. 2010. Posttraumatic resilience in former Ugandan child soldiers. *Child Dev.* 81(4):1095–112

Korol M, Kramer TL, Grace MC, Green BL. 2002. Dam break: long-term follow-up of children exposed to the Buffalo Creek disaster. See La Greca et al. 2002, pp. 241–57

Kronenberg ME, Hansel TC, Brennan AM, Lawrason B, Osofsky HJ, Osofsky JD. 2010. Children of Katrina: lessons learned about post-disaster symptoms and recovery patterns. *Child Dev.* 81(4):1240–58

La Greca AM, Silverman WK. 2009. Treatment and prevention of posttraumatic stress reactions in children and adolescents exposed to disasters and terrorism: What is the evidence? *Child Dev. Perspect.* 3(1):4–10

La Greca AM, Silverman WK, Vernberg EM, Roberts MC, eds. 2002. *Helping Children Cope with Disasters and Terrorism*. Washington, DC: Am. Psychol. Assoc.

Laufer A, Solomon Z. 2009. Gender differences in PTSD in Israeli youth exposed to terror attacks. *J. Interpers. Violence* 24(6):959–76

Layne CM, Olsen JA, Baker A, Legerski J-P, Isakson B, et al. 2010. Unpacking trauma exposure risk factors and differential pathways of influence: predicting post-war mental distress in Bosnian adolescents. *Child Dev.* 81(4):1053–75

Layne CM, Saltzman WR, Poppleton L, Burlingame GM, Pasalic A, et al. 2008. Effectiveness of a school-based group psychotherapy program for war-exposed adolescents: a randomized controlled trial. *J. Am. Acad. Child Adolesc. Psychiatry* 47(9):1048–62

Lengua LJ, Long AC, Smith KI, Meltzoff AN. 2005. Pre-attack symptomatology and temperament as predictors of children's responses to the September 11 terrorist attacks. *J. Child Psychol. Psychiatry* 46(6):631–45

Longstaff PH. 2009. Managing surprises in complex systems. Multidisciplinary perspectives on resilience. *Ecol. Soc.* 14(1):49–50

Luthar SS. 2006. Resilience in development: a synthesis of research across five decades. In *Developmental Psychopathology, Vol. 3: Risk, Disorder, and Adaptation*, ed. D Cicchetti, DJ Cohen, pp. 739–95. Hoboken, NJ: Wiley. 2nd ed.

Luthar SS, Cicchetti D, Becker B. 2000. The construct of resilience: a critical evaluation and guidelines for future work. *Child Dev.* 71(3):543–62

MacFarlane AC. 1987. Posttraumatic phenomenon in a longitudinal study of children following natural disaster. *J. Am. Acad. Child Adolesc. Psychiatry* 26(5):764–69

MacFarlane AC, Policansky SK, Irwin CI. 1987. A longitudinal study of the psychological morbidity in children due to natural disaster. *Psychol. Med.* 17(3):727–38

MacFarlane AC, Van Hooff M. 2009. Impact of child exposure to disaster on adult mental health: 20-year longitudinal follow-up study. *Br. J. Psychiatry* 195:142–48

Masten AS. 2001. Ordinary magic: resilience processes in development. *Am. Psychol.* 56(3):227–38

Masten AS. 2006. Developmental psychopathology: pathways to the future. *Int. J. Behav. Dev.* 30(1):47–54

Masten AS. 2007. Resilience in developing systems: progress and promise as the fourth wave rises. *Dev. Psychopathol.* 19(3):921–30

Masten AS. 2011. Resilience in children threatened by extreme adversity: frameworks for research, practice, and translational synergy. *Dev. Psychopathol.* 23(2):141–54

Masten AS. 2012. Risk and resilience in development. In *Oxford Handbook of Developmental Psychology*, ed. PD Zelazo. New York: Oxford Univ. Press. In press

Masten AS, Best KM, Garmezy N. 1990. Resilience and development: contributions from the study of children who overcome adversity. *Dev. Psychopathol.* 2(4):425–44

Masten AS, Cicchetti D. 2010. Editorial. Developmental cascades: part 1. *Dev. Psychopathol.* 22(Spec. Issue 3):491–95

Masten AS, Garmezy N, Tellegen A, Pellegrini DS, Larkin K, Larsen A. 1988. Competence and stress in school children: the moderating effects of individual and family qualities. *J. Child Psychol. Psychiatry* 29(6):745–64

Masten AS, Liebkind K, Hernandez DJ, eds. 2012. *Realization the Potential of Immigrant Youth*. New York: Cambridge Univ. Press. In press

Masten AS, Obradović J. 2006. Competence and resilience in development. *Ann. N.Y. Acad. Sci.* 1094:13–27

Masten AS, Obradović J. 2008. Disaster preparation and recovery: lessons from research on resilience in human development. *Ecol. Soc.* 13(1):9–24

Masten AS, Osofsky JD. 2010. Disasters and their impact on child development: introduction to the special section. *Child Dev.* 81(4):1029–39

Masten AS, Reed M-G. 2002. Resilience in development. In *The Handbook of Positive Psychology*, ed. CR Snyder, SJ Lopez, pp. 74–88. New York: Oxford Univ. Press

Masten AS, Wright MO. 1998. Cumulative risk and protection models of child maltreatment. *J. Aggress. Maltreat. Trauma* 2(1):7–30

McDermott BM, Lee EM, Judd M, Gibbon P. 2005. Posttraumatic stress disorder and general psychopathology in children and adolescents following a wildfire disaster. *Can. J. Psychiatry* 50(3):137–43

McEwen BS, Gianaros PJ. 2010. Stress- and allostatic-induced brain plasticity. *Annu. Rev. Med.* 62:431–45

Meaney MJ. 2010. Epigenetics and the biological definition of gene x environment interactions. *Child Dev.* 81(1):41–79

Meichenbaum D. 2007. Stress inoculation training: a preventative and treatment approach. In *Principles of Stress Management*, ed. PM Lehrer, RL Woolfolk, WS Sime, pp. 497–518. New York: Guilford. 3rd ed.

Miller G, Chen E, Cole SW. 2009. Health psychology: developing biologically plausible models linking the social world and physical health. *Annu. Rev. Psychol.* 60(1):501–24

Natl. Commiss. Children in Disasters (NCCD). 2010. *2010 Report to the President and Congress*. Rockville, MD: Agency Healthcare Res. Qual.

Nolen-Hoeksema S, Wisco BE, Lyubomirsky S. 2001. Rethinking rumination. *Perspect. Psychol. Sci.* 3(5):400–24

Norris FH, Friedman MJ, Watson PJ, Byrne CM, Diaz E, Kaniasty K. 2002a. 60,000 disaster victims speak: part I. An empirical review of the empirical literature, 1981–2001. *Psychiatry* 65(3):207–39

Norris FH, Friedman MJ, Watson PJ. 2002b. 60,000 disaster victims speak: part II. Summary and implications of the disaster mental health research. *Psychiatry* 65(3):240–60

Norris FH, Steven SP, Pfefferbaum B, Wyche KF, Pfefferbaum RL. 2008. Community resilience as a metaphor, theory, set of capacities, and strategy for disaster readiness. *Am. J. Community Psychol.* 41:127–50

Northwood A. 1996. *Trauma exposure, posttraumatic symptoms and identity in adolescent survivors of massive childhood trauma*. Unpubl. doctoral dissert., Univ. Minn.

Nugent NR, Tyrka AR, Carpenter LL, Price LH. 2011. Gene-environment interactions: early life stress and risk for depressive and anxiety disorders. *Psychopharmacology* 214:175–96

Obradović J, Boyce WT. 2009. Individual differences in behavioral, physiological, and genetic sensitivities to context: implications for development and adaptation. *Dev. Neurosci.* 31:300–8

Obradović J, Shaffer A, Masten AS. 2012. Risk in developmental psychopathology: progress and future directions. In *The Environment of Human Development: A Handbook of Theory and Measurement*, ed. LC Mayes, M Lewis. New York: Cambridge Univ. Press. In press

Osofsky JD, Osofsky HJ, Harris WW. 2007. Katrina's children: social policy considerations for children in disasters. *Soc. Policy Rep.* 21:3–18

Otto MW, Henin A, Hirshfeld-Becker DR, Pollack MH, Biederman J, Rosenbaum J. 2007. Posttraumatic stress disorder symptoms following media exposure to tragic events: impact of 9/11 on children at risk for anxiety disorders. *J. Anxiety Disord.* 21(7):888–902

Patterson GR, Forgatch MS, DeGarmo DS. 2010. Cascading effects following intervention. *Dev. Psychopathol.* 22(4):941–70

Peltonen K, Punamäki R-L. 2010. Preventative interventions among children exposed to trauma of armed conflict: a literature review. *Aggress. Behav.* 36:95–116

Pervanidou P. 2008. Biology of post-traumatic stress disorder in childhood and adolescence. *J. Neuroendocr.* 20:632–38

Pfefferbaum B, Nixon SJ, Tivis RD, Doughty DE, Pynoos RS, et al. 2001. Television exposure in children after a terrorist incident. *Psychiatry* 64(3):202–11

Pfefferbaum B, Seale TW, Brandt EN, Pfefferbaum RL, Doughty DE, Rainwater RM. 2003. Media exposure in children one hundred miles from a terrorist bombing. *Ann. Clin. Psychiatry* 15(1):1–8

Phillips D, Prince S, Schiebelhut L. 2004. Elementary school children's responses 3 months after the September 11 terrorist attacks: a study in Washington, DC. *Am. J. Orthopsychiatry* 74(4):509–28

Pine DS, Costello J, Masten AS. 2005. Trauma, proximity, and developmental psychopathology: the effects of war and terrorism on children. *Neuropsychopharmacology* 30(10):1781–92

Pratchett LC, Yehuda R. 2011. Foundations of posttraumatic stress disorder: Does early life stress lead to adult posttraumatic stress disorder? *Dev. Psychopathol.* 23(2):477–91

Qouta S, Punamaki R-L, El Sarraj E. 2008. Child development and family mental health in war and military violence: the Palestinian experience. *Int. J. Behav. Dev.* 32(4):310–21

Rutter M. 1983. Stress, coping and development: some issues and some questions. In *Stress, Coping and Development in Children*, ed. N Garmezy, M Rutter, pp. 1–41. New York: McGraw-Hill

Rutter M. 2006. Implications of resilience concepts for scientific understanding. *Ann. N.Y. Acad Sci.* 1094:1–12

Ruzek JI, Brymer MJ, Jacobs AK, Layne CM, Vernberg EM, Watson PJ. 2007. Psychological first aid. *J. Ment. Health Couns.* 29(1):17–49

Saltzman WR, Lester P, Beardslee WR, Layne CM, Woodward K, Nash WP. 2012. Mechanisms of risk and resilience in military families: theoretical and empirical basis of a family-focused resilience enhancement program. *Clin. Child Fam. Psychol. Rev.* In press

Sameroff A. 2006. Identifying risk and protective factors for healthy child development. In *Families Count: Effects on Child and Adolescent Development*, ed. A Clark-Stewart, J Dunn, pp. 53–76. Cambridge, UK: Cambridge Univ. Press

Sapienza JK, Masten AS. 2011. Understanding and promoting resilience in children and youth. *Curr. Opin. Psychiatry* 24:267–73

Saylor CF, Cowart BL, Lipovsky JA, Jackson C, Finch AJ. 2003. Media exposure to September 11. Elementary school students' experiences and posttraumatic symptoms. *Am. Behav. Sci.* 46(12):1622–42

Schuster MA, Stein BD, Jaycox LH, Collins RL, Marshall GN, Elliott MN. 2001. A national survey of stress reactions after the September 11, 2001 terrorist attacks. *N. Engl. J. Med.* 345(20):1507–13

Seery MD, Holman EA, Silver RC. 2010. Whatever does not kill us: cumulative lifetime adversity, vulnerability, and resilience. *J. Personal. Soc. Psychol.* 99(6):1025–41

Shonkoff JP, Boyce WT, McEwen BS. 2009. Neuroscience, molecular biology, and the childhood roots of health disparities. *J. Am. Med. Assoc.* 301(21):2252–59

Silverman WK, La Greca AM. 2002. Children experiencing disasters: definitions, reactions, and predictors of outcomes. See La Greca et al. 2002, pp. 11–33

Sprung M. 2008. Unwanted intrusive thoughts and cognitive functioning in kindergarten and young elementary school-age children following Hurricane Katrina. *J. Child Clin. Adolesc. Psychol.* 37:575–87

Suárez-Orozco C, Suárez-Orozco M, Todorova I. 2006. *Moving Stories: Educational Pathways of Immigrant Youth*. Cambridge, MA: Harvard Univ. Press

Taylor GH, Alden J. 1997. Age-related differences in outcomes following childhood brain insults: an introduction and overview. *Neuropsychol. Soc.* 3(6):555–67

Terr LC, Bloch DA, Michel BA, Shi H, Reinhardt JA, Metayer S. 1999. Children's symptoms on the wake of Challenger: a field study of distant-traumatic effects and an outline of related conditions. *Am. J. Psychiatry* 156(10):1536–44

Terranova AM, Boxer P, Morris AS. 2009. Factors influencing the course of posttraumatic stress following a natural disaster: children's reactions to Hurricane Katrina. *J. Appl. Dev. Psychol.* 30(3):344–55

Thelen E, Smith L. 1998. Dynamic systems theories. In *Handbook of Child Psychology. Vol. 1: Theoretical Models of Human Development*, ed. RM Lerner, pp. 563–634. New York: Wiley. 5th ed.

Tol WA, Komproe IH, Jordans MJD, Gross AL, Susanty D, et al. 2010. Mediators and moderators of a psychosocial intervention for children affected by political violence. *J. Consult. Clin. Psychol.* 78(6):818–28

Tugel AJ, Herrick JE, Brown JR, Mausbach MJ, Puckett W, Hipple K. 2005. Soil change, soil survey, and natural resources decision making: a blueprint for action. *Soil Sci. Soc. Am. J.* 69(3):738–47

Vigil JM, Geary DC, Granger DA, Flinn MV. 2010. Sex differences in salivary cortisol, alpha-amylase, and psychological functioning following Hurricane Katrina. *Child Dev.* 81(4):1227–39

Weems CF, Pina AA, Costa NM, Watts SE, Taylor LK, Cannon MF. 2007. Predisaster trait anxiety and negative affect predict posttraumatic stress in youths after Hurricane Katrina. *J. Consult. Clin. Psychol.* 75(1):154–59

Wickrama KAS, Kaspar V. 2007. Family context of mental health risk in Tsunami-exposed adolescents: findings from a pilot study in Sri Lanka. *Soc. Sci. Med.* 64(3):713–23

Wolmer L, Hamiel D, Laor N. 2011. Preventing children's posttraumatic stress after disaster with teacher-based intervention: a controlled study. *J. Am. Acad. Child Adolesc. Psychiatry* 50(4):340–48

Wright MO, Masten AS, Narayan AJ. 2012. Resilience processes in development: Four waves of research on positive adaptation in the context of adversity. In *Handbook of Resilience in Children*, ed. S Goldstein, RB Brooks. New York: Kluwer/Academic Plenum. 2nd ed. In press

Yehuda R, Bell A, Bierer LM, Schmiedler J. 2008. Maternal, not paternal, PTSD related to increased risk for PTSD in offspring of Holocaust survivors. *J. Psychiatr. Res.* 42(13):1104–11

Yehuda R, Bierer LM. 2009. The relevance of epigenetics to PTSD: implications for the DSM-V. *J. Trauma. Stress* 22(5):427–34

Yehuda R, Engel SM, Brand SR, Seckl J, Marcus SM, Berkowitz GS. 2005. Transgenerational effects of posttraumatic stress disorder in babies of mothers exposed to the World Trade Center attacks during pregnancy. *J. Clin. Endocr. Metab.* 90(7):4115–18

Yehuda R, Flory JD, Pratchett LR, Buxbaum J, Ising M, Holsboer F. 2010. Putative biological mechanism for the association between early life adversity and the subsequent development of PTSD. *Psychopharmacology* 212:405–17

Yehuda R, Harvey P. 1997. Relevance of neuroendocrine alterations in PTSD to memory-related impairments of trauma survivors. In *Recollections of Trauma*, ed. DJ Read, SD Lindsay, pp. 221–52. New York: Plenum

Yehuda R, McFarlane AC, Shalev AY. 1998. Predicting the development of posttraumatic stress disorder from the acute response to a traumatic event. *Biol. Psychiatry* 44(12):1305–13

Yehuda R, Teicher MH, Seckl J, Grossman RA, Morris A, Bierer LM. 2007. Parental posttraumatic stress disorder as a vulnerability factor for low cortisol trait in offspring of Holocaust survivors. *Arch. Gen. Psychiatry* 64(9):1040–48

Yelland C, Robinson P, Lock C, La Greca AM, Kokegei B, et al. 2010. Bushfire impact on youth. *J. Trauma. Stress* 23(2):274–77

Social Functionality of Human Emotion

Paula M. Niedenthal and Markus Brauer

Centre National de la Recherche Scientifique, Paris, France, and Department of Psychology, University of Wisconsin-Madison, Madison, Wisconsin 53706; email: niedenthal@wisc.edu

Annu. Rev. Psychol. 2012. 63:259–85

First published online as a Review in Advance on October 10, 2011

The *Annual Review of Psychology* is online at psych.annualreviews.org

This article's doi:
10.1146/annurev.psych.121208.131605

Keywords

facial expression, vicarious emotion, group emotion, group-based emotion, embodied simulation

Abstract

Answers to the question "What are human emotions for?" have stimulated highly productive programs of research on emotional phenomena in psychology and neuroscience in the past decade. Although a variety of functions have been proposed and examined at different levels of abstraction, what is undeniable is that when emotional processing is compromised, most things social go awry. In this review we survey the research findings documenting the functions of emotion and link these to new discoveries about how emotion is accurately processed and transmitted. We focus specifically on emotion processing in dyads and groups, which reflects the current scientific trend. Within dyads, emotional expressions and learning and understanding through vicarious emotion are the phenomena of interest. Behavioral and brain mechanisms supporting their successful occurrence are evaluated. At the group level, group emotions and group-based emotions, two very different phenomena, are discussed, and mechanistic accounts are reviewed.

Contents

INTRODUCTION

Can scientists study emotion? And if so, should they? And if they should, to what end? For centuries the dominant view of emotions within philosophy and later within psychology was that Passions endanger the lofty processes of Reason (Solomon 1976, 1993). For Plato and for the Stoics such as Zeno de Citium, Epictetus, and Marcus Aurelius, and yet again in the Enlightenment period of eighteenth-century Europe, emotions were defined as animalistic impulses that threaten to disrupt the attainment of higher levels of existence. This opposition between Passion and Reason has finally been abandoned and replaced by more optimistic programs of research, given significant early boosts from neuropsychological (e.g., Damasio 1989) and economic (e.g., Frank 1988) analyses and from an emerging social psychological consensus (e.g., Frijda 1986, Oatley 1992, Scherer 1984). The study of the psychological experience of emotion and of the neural basis of emotion and its relation to other mental processes is a solid scientific enterprise (Barrett et al. 2007, Phelps 2006) and its importance in complex social institutions undeniable (Brief & Weiss 2002).

Still, answers to the question "What are emotions for?" strongly guide the application of scientific tools to the exploration of emotional phenomena. Modern writings on the function of emotion within psychology address the question "What roles do emotions play in the solution of problems that humans confront in living and surviving with others?" (e.g., Buck 1999, Cosmides & Tooby 2000, Frijda 1986, Frijda & Mesquita 1994, Keltner & Gross 1999, Johnson-Laird & Oatley 1992, Keltner & Haidt 1999, Oatley & Jenkins 1992, Scherer 1994); most of these roles derive from the dual needs to cooperate and compete. The scientific strategy that has emerged to empirically address this question involves linking specific emotions to distinct motivations, problems, outcomes, or effects (e.g., Barlett & DeSteno 2009, Fischer & Roseman 2007, Hooge et al. 2010, Tracy & Robins 2008, Williams & DeSteno 2008). For example, recent research found that when participants posed facial expressions of fear, they had subjectively larger visual fields, made more efficient eye movements when localizing targets, and showed increased nasal volume and air velocity during inspiration. Furthermore, the expression of disgust was associated with an opposite pattern of effects (Susskind et al. 2008). These findings are consistent with the claim that facial expressions aid in producing the bodily responses required to perform the actions taken to respond successfully to emotional challenges (Darwin 1872). Ethologists have also pointed out that smiles (Méhu & Dunbar 2008) and facial expressions of aggression

(Griskevicius et al. 2009) play roles that relate to the fundamental social tasks of relationship establishment and maintenance, hierarchy, and group management. General relations such as these can be subjected further to a consideration of the influences of culture on how the problems are construed and the ways in which emotions facilitate their solutions within a cultural context (e.g., Mesquita & Ellsworth 2001, Rodriguez Mosquera et al. 2008).

A survey of the current literature suggests that it is now possible to evaluate functionality from a different angle. The present article reviews research programs and significant findings that begin from the conclusion drawn from extensive recent research on emotional processing gone awry: What happens when an individual does not express his or her emotions to others (Butler et al. 2003, Gross & John 2003, Srivastava et al. 2009) or share them with others (Rimé 2007, Rimé et al. 2004)? And what happens when a person cannot understand the (typical) emotions expressed by other individuals, as may be caused by the incursion of specific brain lesions (e.g., Adolphs 2002, Adolphs et al. 2005), the development of diseases such as Parkinson's (Wieser et al. 2006), autism (e.g., Clark et al. 2008, McIntosh 2006), or early maltreatment (Pollak 2008)? The conclusion is that, as a rule, what happens is not good. Disruptions in emotion processes—the abilities to understand, express, and experience emotion—lead to the loss of social support, disintegration of groups, and failure of economic viability.

Such a conclusion can also be drawn from research on emotional intelligence (e.g., Mayer et al. 2004, Salovey et al. 2003, Salovey & Mayer 1990). Indeed, the premise of the concept of emotional intelligence is that it is possible to define the processing of emotion in self and other as more or less precise, consensual, and useful. Therefore, our analysis of functionality entails a critical review of recent research that provides insights about the mechanisms through which emotions are accurately transmitted (expressed and experienced) in social units as a means of effectively pursuing dyadic- and group-level goals. The

decision to survey research on the function of emotion in social context reflects a clear trend toward going beyond the individual level of analysis, which, starting with Darwin, has been more intensively studied (Oatley & Jenkins 1992, Parrott 2001). We begin the review by examining the function of emotion when the emotion is exchanged between two interacting individuals. In particular, the functional role of facial expression and vicarious emotion take a central role in emotion processing within the dyad. We then review recent research and theory that illuminate the mechanisms by which emotion is transmitted in the dyad. Next we examine new research on the function of emotions in and for the group. The central phenomena here are group emotions (emotions that occur in collectives) and group-based emotions (or emotions on behalf of a group). The mechanisms by which emotion is transmitted within the group is the final consideration. Our analysis of function and mechanism for transmission will not be equally complete across all levels of analysis. This is inevitable and indeed deliberate. In highlighting the gaps in research, we hope to define, and motivate, programs of research for the future.

FUNCTIONAL EMOTION PHENOMENA IN THE DYAD

Dyads for this analysis are immediately interacting partners who have either an established or emergent interdependency. Emotion processes are required in dyads for the successful pre- and nonverbal communication of emotion and for the learning of adaptive behavioral responses. Two specific emotional phenomena are important to examine at this level. One is facial expression of emotion. Through their communication of emotion and social motives, facial expressions of emotion efficiently summarize information about what the partners in the dyad are doing and why, who they are to each other, and how the present situation will or should unfold over time (Buck 1983, Buck et al. 1992, Horstmann 2003, Keltner & Kring 1998).

A second important phenomenon is vicarious emotion. In the treatment of vicarious emotion in this section, we are concerned with the experience of an emotion with, and ultimately for, another person. Although early in development vicarious emotion may necessitate that the observed person is feeling an emotion, which is reproduced in the self, over development the ability to feel vicariously for another individual does not necessitate that the observed individual is actually feeling an emotion. For example, a mother can feel vicarious shame for a child without the child yet knowing that this situation should indeed provoke shame in the particular culture or value system.

Facial Expression of Emotion: Behavior Regulators

One of the first types of dyadic emotion transmission occurs between infants and their caretakers through the facial expression of emotion (Campos et al. 2003). Although there may be hardwired emotional responses to particular challenges and opportunities in the environment (Mineka & Cook 1993), caretakers must also teach infants, within their cultural context, to have specific emotional reactions to (initially) ambiguous objects and events in order to generate in them appropriate and effective behavior. Objects that conduct electricity are an example of an ambiguous stimulus in the sense that they are such a recent technological development that there is no reason to believe that humans would be hardwired to be fearful of them in their current appearance (i.e., distinct from lightning, for instance). By expressing explicit and acute fear when a toddler approaches an electrical outlet or an exposed wire, a caretaker can elicit fear in him or her, which in typically developing children usually results in the appropriate avoidance behavior of transmitters of electricity in the future (Askew & Field 2007, Hertenstein & Campos 2004). It is in this sense that Campos and colleagues (2003) aptly call facial expressions of emotion "behavior regulators": Facial expressions function as rewards (Matthews & Wells 1999) and

punishments (Blair 1995) that serve to increase and decrease behaviors, as in operant conditioning (for review, see Blair 2003, Gerull & Rappee 2002, Mumme & Fernald 1996). Infants who cannot learn through emotional transmission of this type are at significant risk (Field 1982), and maltreated infants may develop strategies that compromise accurate encoding of facial expression (Pollak et al. 2000).

Over development, emotional expressions communicate more nuanced information about the nature of, or the potential of, any dyadic relationship (Frijda & Mesquita 1994; Keltner & Haidt 1999, 2003). Recent research findings demonstrate that emotional facial expression, as well as posture and prosody, do an efficient job of conveying information about the dimensions of personality (Ames & Johar 2009, Harker & Keltner 2001) and the likelihood of the occurrence of social behavior, such as cooperative or prosocial action (Anderson & Thompson 2004, Brown et al. 2003). Consistent with the latter idea, Scharlemann and colleagues (2001) showed that in extensive-form bargaining games, individuals who expressed smiles were trusted more than nonsmiling individuals. Facial expressions of emotion can determine the meaning of verbal communication (Krull et al. 2008) and may provide critical information in the absence of verbal communication (Bonnano et al. 2002).

Consequently, when perceived accurately, facial expressions generate appropriate social intentions in the perceiver. For example, Marsh and colleagues (2007) tested whether the accuracy of fear recognition predicts prosocial behaviors. In a first study, participants were asked to help (with contributions of money or time) a young woman in a difficult situation. Then their accuracy of recognition of facial expressions of anger, fear, happiness, and sadness was measured. Results showed that fear recognition accuracy was the best predictor of their donations. In a second study, participants completed an emotion-recognition task and then rated the facial attractiveness of photographs of target individuals. In the "prosocial" condition, the targets were ostensibly other participants who would later be told how attractive they had been judged to be. In a control condition, the aim of the task was to validate a set of stimuli. As before, participants who could most accurately identify fear responded the most prosocially, and this was moderated by condition such that the effect was observed only in the prosocial condition. The third study replicated the prosocial condition of the second study and included a question that assessed the participant's desire to behave prosocially in this context. Compared to measures of empathy and mood, and even gender, fear recognition accuracy was the best predictor of prosocial behavior. Moreover, the willingness to be kind mediated the relationship between fear recognition and prosocial behavior.

These and similar findings suggest that the accurate recognition of fearful expressions produces prosocial responses in appropriate contexts (Marsh & Ambady 2007). And they complement the finding that selective impairments in identifying facial expressions of fear are observed in populations marked by antisocial behavior and a lack of empathy (e.g., Blair et al. 2001, Kropp & Haynes 1987). Furthermore, the conclusion is conceptually consistent with other findings showing that individuals who are dispositionally high in need to belong are better than others at identifying facial expressions and vocal tones of all sorts (Pickett et al. 2004).

In sum, recent research on the processing of facial expression of emotion not only supports the idea that facial expression is a primary regulator of social development and social interaction, but also that accuracy in facial expression processing facilitates the efficient operation of these social processes.

Vicarious Emotion: Learning Affective Associations

Emotions also occur in dyads when one individual feels an emotion because he or she observes another person experiencing an emotion, or observes the other person in an emotionally evocative situation, even if the situation is not immediately relevant (i.e., threatening or beneficial) to the observer (Iglesias 1996). For instance, people wince in pain when they see someone else get hurt (Bavelas et al. 1986), and they cringe with embarrassment for someone else even when their own personal identity is not threatened (Miller 1987).

Early in development, vicarious emotions seem to play a fundamental role in learning, which complements the role of learning supported specifically by facial expressive cues. As noted, facial expressions can serve to increase and decrease behaviors, as in operant conditioning (Blair 2003). In a complementary way, vicarious emotion is the supportive mechanism of more general observational learning (Olsson & Phelps 2004). Humans and nonhuman primates are able to learn about the emotional implications of objects and events vicariously, through observing the emotional reactions of a conspecific (Ohman & Mineka 2001). Vicarious or observational learning are thus social means of adaptive response acquisition that do not require direct experience with the object or event about which something must be learned. Vaughan & Lanzetta (1980) illustrated this in a study in which participants saw videotaped facial expressions of pain while they worked on a paired associate learning task. The pain expressions followed a target word of the same word category (flower or tree names) and elicited vicarious emotional responses in the observer that became associated with the word category. Furthermore, Vaughan & Lanzetta (1981) showed that the vicarious emotional responses elicited by observing emotions in others can be modified by the extent to which the emotion is simulated in the self. Their instructions to participants to suppress or amplify facial expressions during observation of the emotions moderated the vicarious learning effect.

The social analogue to laboratory instructions to enhance or suppress components of a vicarious emotion is intimacy of the interacting individuals. That is, familiarity and interdependence also affect vicarious emotional responding (Lickel et al. 2005). This finding suggests that vicarious emotion is something distinct from having an emotional reaction to an emotional stimulus (e.g., the sight of an individual in pain or distress; Fultz & Nielsen 1993). The dyadic relationship matters in this process.

Later in development, vicarious emotion does not necessitate the expression or experience of emotion in the target of observation; vicarious emotion may occur when the observer knows that the target could or should feel the particular emotion, according to a social or cultural rule (Kagan 2007, Tangney & Fischer 1995). In other words, the mature observer has learned to associate quite complex social situations with particular emotions and can now feel a given emotion for a target in a situation evocative of a specific emotion regardless of what the target actually feels. For instance, even if a child is feeling discomfort rather than pride when receiving a reward or successfully performing in public, the parents are likely to feel pride on behalf of the child (perhaps in addition to the recognition and empathic experience of discomfort) because in their culture, their appraisal of the situation is one that is appropriately associated with pride. These feelings will then motivate appropriate behaviors toward the target.

In a recent experiment by Stocks and colleagues (2011), participants listened to an individual describe an embarrassing situation. Participants were invited to adopt one of three perspective-taking sets: to remain objective, to imagine themselves in the same situation, or to imagine how the target felt. Dependent variables included measures of vicarious embarrassment, empathic concern, and desires to approach or avoid the target, given the opportunity. Results revealed that, compared with those who took an objective stance, participants who imagined themselves in the target's situation experienced heightened vicarious embarrassment, but not heightened empathic concern, and a greater desire to avoid the target. In contrast, participants who took the target's perspective felt empathic concern, but not vicarious embarrassment, and a desire to approach the target. These results distinguish vicarious emotion and its associated

motivations, perhaps as an associative learning process, from the experience of empathy and empathic concern. The distinction is not new (see, e.g., Batson et al. 1987), but it further highlights the fact that vicarious emotions, as well as the motivations and action tendencies that they produce, are distinct from the cognitive components of empathy.

MECHANISMS SUPPORTING EMOTION PHENOMENA IN DYADS

How do facial expressions get interpreted and emotions get experienced vicariously by perceivers in such a way that they can be useful in supporting regulation, communication, and learning? The reproduction of perceived facial and bodily emotional gestures in the self has long been thought to be important in both processes (Lanzetta & Englis 1989, McIntosh et al. 1994, Vaughan & Lanzetta 1980; for discussion, see Levenson 1996), but the details of such a claim are only beginning to be worked out. Within social psychology, this idea is inspired by an integration of facial feedback theory and affect-as-information theory. According to the facial feedback theory, the mimicry of a target's facial expression provides the perceiver with afferent feedback that can provide cues to infer the internal state of the target (McIntosh 1996, Zajonc et al. 1989). And according to the affect-as-information theory, when perceivers believe that their affective state has been caused by the target of perception, they rely on that state to make judgments of the target, such as how the target is feeling (Clore & Storbeck 2006). In neuroscience, the reproduction of perceived emotional gestures and states has been interpreted in terms of mirror neurons and mirror systems and in terms of the idea that brains can resonate with the states of perceived objects, especially those that are biologically similar (e.g., Gallese 2007, Keysers & Gazzola 2007).

These theories and mechanisms come together to inspire an embodied- or simulated-emotion approach to the processing of emotion in social context (e.g., Atkinson 2007; Decety

& Chaminade 2003, 2005; Gallese 2003, 2005; Goldman & Sripada 2005; Keysers & Gazzola 2007; Niedenthal 2007; Niedenthal et al. 2005; Wilson-Mendenhall et al. 2011; Winkielman et al. 2009). Emotion simulation refers to the idea that in order to understand emotions in others, individuals use their own body and brain representational capacities to simulate themselves making the same gestures in the same context. They can then use this simulation to infer what the other person is feeling and how they should or would respond in this situation. An embodied-emotion approach has been used to account for both the processing of facial expression of emotion and the experience of vicarious emotion.

Simulating Facial Expression

Recently, the behavioral and neural mechanisms implicated in the accurate encoding of facial expression of emotion have received intense empirical scrutiny (Niedenthal et al. 2010). A fundamental mechanism proposed by embodied-emotion accounts is bodily and facial mimicry. We focus here on the mimicry of facial expression of emotion and how it serves to support access to the meaning of the facial expression (see Heberlein & Atkinson 2009 for a review of research on perceiving emotions from moving bodies).

Facial mimicry is the visible or nonvisible use of facial musculature by an observer to match the facial gestures in another person's facial expression (Hess 2009, Niedenthal et al. 2010). Perceivers of expressions often automatically mimic them. Recordings of the electrical activity of skeletal facial muscles, for instance, reveal that when individuals view a smile, their zygomaticus major muscle contracts, usually within 500 milliseconds after the onset of the stimulus (Dimberg & Thunberg 1998). Mojzisch et al. (2006) demonstrated that observers automatically mimicked facial expressions displayed by virtual characters in dynamic animations (see also a review in Hess et al. 1999). Automatically mimicking one expression of emotion also interferes with the concurrent production of an incongruent facial expression, such as anger (Lee et al. 2007).

Facial mimicry exerts a number of effects that together support the idea that it is an important mechanism in the receiving end of emotion transmission. First, mimicry seems to be related to generating a corresponding emotional state in the perceiver. In one demonstration of this, experimenters injected botulinum toxin (Botox) in the forehead muscles of experimental participants (Hennenlotter et al. 2005). Then, the experimental participants and controls who had not received Botox were invited to mimic angry and sad facial expressions while their brains were scanned. When participants were exposed to the photographs of the angry expressions, functional magnetic resonance imaging (fMRI) revealed that Botox-injected participants had significantly less activation in their brain's limbic system compared to the control participants. This same effect was not observed when participants were exposed to sad expressions. Still, the finding for the anger expressions supports a causal link between mimicry and emotional responding because it indicates that inhibiting mimicry decreases activation of the brain's emotion centers. A similar finding was reported by Lee and colleagues (2006), who showed that the more that individuals mimicked facial expressions of happiness (smiles), the greater the activation in the reward centers of their brain (see also Schilbach et al. 2006). In addition to playing a role in generating the emotion corresponding to the perceived emotional expression, mimicry may also be important in defining what the motor movements that constitute the expression "feel like" when the emotion is produced (Niedenthal et al. 2010).

The possibility that the production of the corresponding state and the feeling of the facial expression grounds interpretation of the meaning of a facial expression is suggested in some studies, although the claim is by no means clearly supported. Recent research suggests a link between the mimicry of facial expression and performance on tasks that measure recognition and interpretation (Adolphs 2002,

Heberlein & Atkinson 2009, McIntosh 2006). For example, Stel & van Knippenberg (2008) showed that inhibiting facial mimicry decreased the speed, although not the accuracy, of evaluating facial displays as expressing positive or negative emotion. In a more recent study, Maringer and colleagues (2011) presented participants with dynamic displays of smiles determined in pretests to be "genuine" or "not genuine." Participants were assigned to either a control condition in which they were free to mimic the smiles (presumably as the pretest participants had done) or to an experimental condition in which facial mimicry was inhibited. All participants rated the extent to which the smiles were "genuine." Results revealed an effect of condition such that the control participants distinguished between the genuine and nongenuine smiles, whereas the experimental participants, who could not mimic the smiles, did not distinguish the genuine from the nongenuine smiles to the same degree. The important role of mimicry in the deep processing of facial expression is also suggested by the observation that individuals who mimic facial expressions automatically also show higher levels of empathy (Sonnby-Borgstrom 2002, Zajonc et al. 1987).

Recent experiments by Neal & Chartrand (2011) are consistent with the specific role of afferent feedback in the interpretation of facial expression of emotion. In the first experiment, individuals who had received Botox injections to the face and members of a control group who had received a treatment to the face that does not reduce afferent feedback (a dermal filler called Restylane) performed a task that assesses the encoding of facial emotion. The task was the revised Reading the Mind in the Eyes Test (RMET; Baron-Cohen et al. 2001). The findings supported a causal role for afferent facial feedback in helping people accurately perceive others' facial expressions. When afferent signals were dampened by Botox injections, emotion perception was impaired significantly compared to the performance of the matched control sample that had received Restylane injections. The impairment was observed for both positive and negative facial expressions. In the second experiment, facial afference was amplified or facilitated in the experimental condition. This manipulation increased performance on the RMET compared to the performance of a control group.

Such research is complemented by brain-imaging and brain lesion research, which provides insights about the role of somatosensory cortices in processing facial expression of emotion. In a pioneering study in this area, Adolphs and colleagues showed that right-hemisphere cortices play an important role in simulating emotional expressions (e.g., Adolphs et al. 1996). Adolphs et al. (2000) assessed 108 subjects with focal brain lesions and found that the right somatosensory cortex was central for recognizing the facial expressions associated with the six basic emotions. Such findings suggest that the right somatosensory cortex produces an "image" of the felt state, that is, a representation of the afferent feedback, which is used to produce inferences about how the perceived person feels (e.g., Adolphs 2002, Atkinson 2007).

This interpretation is further supported by recent research using transcranial magnetic stimulation to inhibit processing in brain areas responsible for perceptual processing of the face versus inhibition of the right somatosensory cortex. For instance, Pourtois and colleagues selectively interfered with right somatosensory cortex activation while participants performed a matching task and found significant impairment in the discrimination of different facial expressions (Pourtois et al. 2004). Selective interference with right somatosensory cortex activation also disrupted performance on a similar task in a study by Pitcher and colleagues (2008). Specifically, accuracy on same-different discrimination dropped when pulses were delivered to the right occipital face area, which is responsible for visual processing of the face, at 60–100 ms after the onset of the target stimulus and when they were delivered to the right somatosensory cortex at 100–140 and 130–170 ms after onset. Such impairments provide evidence in favor of both embodied accounts of expression recognition and hierarchical models of face processing, or the idea that both visual and nonvisual cortices are involved at very early stages of facial expression processing.

Despite the importance mimicry may have in processing facial expression of emotion, we end this section by noting that recognition of facial expression can also be accomplished by at least two other processes, namely perceptual analysis and the application of preexisting stereotypes and beliefs. The latter are especially useful when the facial expressions are prototypical in nature. As Niedenthal and colleagues (2010) have outlined in a discussion of smiles in particular, recognition of prototypic facial expressions can be accomplished by perceptual analysis alone (e.g., Adolphs 2002). For example, high-functioning autistic individuals, who do not spontaneously mimic others' facial expressions (e.g., McIntosh et al. 2006), do classify facial expressions of emotion as well as typically developed controls do (e.g., Spezio et al. 2007a). In addition, facial paralysis seems not to disrupt performance on such tasks (e.g., Calder et al. 2000a,b; Keillor et al. 2002).

Still, it is undeniable that inappropriate or deficient mimicry is related to behavioral and attachment disorders (de Wied et al. 2006, Sonnby-Borgstrom & Jonsson 2004) as well as the autism spectrum disorders (Beall et al. 2008, Hepburn & Stone 2006, Moody & McIntosh 2006). Future research will be required to outline the precise effects and contributions of mimicry and corresponding brain input into the process of understanding facial expression of emotion.

Simulating Others' Emotions

A related theoretical account may explain vicarious emotion and even empathy. The inspiration for this analysis from within neuroscience was the discovery of mirror neurons and the subsequent demonstrations that seeing or hearing actions of others could activate specific neurons in monkeys' premotor and posterior parietal cortices, which also fire when those actions are performed by the monkey itself (e.g., Gallese et al. 1996).

In consideration of vicarious emotion, the immediate potential application of the general concept of mirror neurons or mirror systems was for the perception of pain. An early study reported that specific pain-related neurons fire when a painful stimulus is applied to an individual's own hand and also when he or she watches the painful stimulus applied to an another individual's hand (Hutchison et al. 1999). This finding motivated subsequent fMRI studies, which documented pain-related brain regions (i.e., a "pain matrix"), especially the dorsal anterior cingulated cortex, middle to anterior insula, and the cerebellum, which were activated during the personal experience of pain and during the perception of the same type of pain incurred by one's partner (e.g., Singer et al. 2004). These areas code specifically for the affective-motivational rather than sensory aspects of pain (e.g., Lamm et al. 2007). Such studies also suggested that the extent of activation in overlapping sites was related to the participants' level of empathy, suggesting that there is moderation of the effect by motivation to stimulate. Similarly, other fMRI studies documented increases in the activation of pain-related regions during observation of a confederate receiving a painful stimulus, but only if the confederate had played fairly in a previous economic game (Singer et al. 2006).

Vicarious experience of pain, as we suggested above, should be distinct from the broader notion of empathy because we can empathize with dissimilar others and can respond in ways that indicate empathy without dysfunction or distress. How we might do so requires consideration of the cognitive components of empathy, which may be said to be unique to humans and other primates (Decety & Lamm 2006, de Waal 2008). The cognitive components of empathy include the ability to distinguish between self and other and the operation of executive functions, including controlled attention to currently relevant ideas as well as inhibiting irrelevant ones. The brain's support of these processes has been documented in recent fMRI studies. In one study by Cheng and colleagues (2007), physicians who practice acupuncture and control participants were shown body parts being pricked by needles. Activation of the pain matrix was observed in controls but not in the physicians. In the latter, activation of dorsolateral and medial prefrontal cortex, subserving self–other distinction, occurred. In a related study, the perception of stimuli that are normally painful for the self but clearly not painful for a target (e.g., because the inflicted body part was anesthetized) was associated with activation in areas again involved in self–other distinction, as well as prefrontal cortical areas that subserve processes of appraisal (Lamm et al. 2007). It seems thus that vicarious emotion and empathy are quite distinct in both behavioral and in neural ways.

In addition to establishing the neural basis of vicarious pain, research has shown that similar circuits support vicarious emotions of other types. It would be very useful to avoid ingesting substances that are toxic, and so vicarious disgust is an important emotion to analyze from this perspective. Wicker and colleagues (2003) compared the brain systems involved in (first-person) experiences of disgust to those involved in the perception of someone else's (third-person) experience of disgust. To this end, they scanned the participants' brains either while they smelled noxious odors or while they watched a video of another person smell and respond with disgust to the same odors. Similar brain areas, including the anterior insula, and to lesser extent the anterior cingulate cortex, were activated when individuals felt disgust and when they perceived it in someone else. The anterior insula receives connections from olfactory and gustatory brain structures as well as from anterior sectors of the ventral part of the superior temporal sulcus. Cells in the latter structures of monkey brains have been found to respond to the sight of faces (Bruce et al. 1986, Perrett et al. 1982). This suggests that the anterior insula links gustatory, olfactory, and visual input with visceral sensations and the related autonomic and visceromotor responses.

Recent research also documents the role of the amygdala in vicarious fear learning. Olsson et al. (2007) tested the hypothesis that observational fear-learning recruits neural mechanisms, including bilateral amygdala activation, which is similar to the mechanisms underlying fear conditioning. In other words, they expected to find significant overlap in first-person and third-person circuitry responsible for processing first- and second-person experiences of fear. Indeed, their study showed that bilateral amygdala activation occurred both when their participants observed another person enduring an aversive event, knowing that the same treatment awaited themselves, and when they were placed in an analog situation.

As with processing facial expression, a final important neural mechanism for simulating others' emotions is the somatosensory cortices. Whereas the parts of the insular and cingulated cortex just mentioned are considered to be part of the somatosensory "system" and support the affective-motivational responses to seeing someone having an emotion, the somatosensory cortices are used to process tactile, proprioceptive, and nociceptive information. These cortices can support processing the more localized, somatic sensation of pain or the cause of another emotion (for review, see Keysers et al. 2010). Taken together, however, the somatosensory system seems to be able to represent, for an individual, what it is like to feel a stimulus, produce a facial expression, and generate an integrated bodily state, and in this way provide extensive emotional information about the state of a perceived individual in a particular emotional situation (Heberlein & Atkinson 2009).

Whether or not a shared circuits approach can provide a full account of constructs as complex as empathy is not clear (e.g., Decety & Lamb 2006), and the relations between these brain areas and their precise involvement in the production of vicarious emotion and associated behavior responses will require more research (e.g., Niedenthal et al. 2010). Nevertheless, it is clear that deficits in the mechanisms known to be involved in vicarious emotion are associated with dysfunction in social relations and social information processing (Blair 2007, Dapretto et al. 2006, Iacoboni & Dapretto

2006). Furthermore, it may not be surprising from an emotion-simulation perspective that vicarious or observational learning largely relies on the same emotion-processing centers of the brain as instructed learning (Olsson & Phelps 2004). This suggests that many types of learning within dyads rely on emotion simulation. For instance, eating a spoiled fruit, seeing someone eat spoiled fruit, and hearing from someone that fruit is spoiled seem to involve reproduction of the experience of disgust within the self (Barthomeuf et al. 2009). The capability of the human mind and body to reproduce an emotion in the self and use it in dyadic interaction is clearly extraordinary, and this notion, although quite old, should be a leading one in future research.

FUNCTIONAL EMOTION PHENOMENA IN GROUPS

The dynamics of group processes differ from the dynamics of dyadic interaction, and emotions play a role in the unfolding of group-level phenomena as well. Whether assessed within small groups or much larger societal-based groups, the functionality of emotions at this level of analysis can be abstracted from the dyadic level just considered. For the group, emotion processes seem necessary for the creation and maintenance of group viability and for long-term commitment to actions that achieve the goals of the group (Chekroun & Brauer 2002, 2004; Frijda & Mesquita 1994; Haidt 2003; Keltner & Haidt 1999). An account of group viability and sustained collective action requires recourse to two emotion phenomena: group emotions (or collective emotions) and group-based emotions (or group-level emotions).

The first construct, group emotion, refers to emotions that occur in and are shared within a collective of interacting individuals at a moment in time, as when a small group becomes energized with excitement and joy (Barsade 2002, Bartel & Saavedra 2000, Kelly & Barsade 2001) or a crowd becomes gripped by fear or galvanized with anger (Hatfield

et al. 1994, Le Bon 1895). The question of whether group emotions are different from emotions within the individual has been a subject of debate (Niedenthal et al. 2006), and the analysis can be extended to societal groups as well (Bar-Tal et al. 2007). It should be noted immediately that all emotions that arise because of cultural prescription are group emotions, but we do not review the cultural approaches to emotions here. The interested reader should refer to Mesquita et al. (2011).

The second construct, group-based emotion, involves an individual having an emotion on behalf of a group of which he or she is a member and due to his or her identification with this group (Iyer et al. 2004, Leach & Tiedens 2004, van Zomeren et al. 2008). Individuals can have emotions on behalf of their group even when they are alone and are not in a situation that is the elicitor of the emotion or the topic of the emotion. For example, although they had not been involved in any acts against Indigenous Australians themselves, Australian participants in a study by McGarty et al. (2005) reported feeling guilt on behalf of the country, their group of identification. Moreover, as discussed below, these reports of guilt predicted the level of their support for a formal apology to these Indigenous Australians by the Australian government.

Thus, group emotions are the emotions that arise as a function of being in a collective such as a work team or a crowd; they occur in groups. Group-based emotions are emotions that are elicited in an individual because of his or her identification with a group and knowledge that the group has caused or been the target of an emotion-inducing event. In the next sections, we review research documenting these phenomena and their effects.

Group Emotions: Creation and Maintenance of Group Viability

A funeral service is a good place to observe the generation of group emotion. Collective grief in this setting emerges as verbal and nonverbal messages provide evidence for the justified experience of sadness. A potent story or a gasp of unbearable sadness will cause ripples of sobs and tears. Group emotion is difficult to define and study, but its validity is never in question. In an early illustrative study, Totterdell et al. (1998) asked community nurses working in teams to fill out daily measures of mood, work hassles, team commitment, and team climate over a period of three weeks. Analyses of these measures showed that a nurse's mood on one day was significantly predicted by the mood of teammates on the same day. Furthermore, the relationship was significant even when the effect of work hassles was controlled, which shows that the concordance in mood was not completely explained by shared problems and experiences. In a similar way, Totterdell (2000) found that the mood of professional cricket players during a match varied as a function of the mood of their teammates, independent of the objective features of the match itself.

In summarizing the writings of Le Bon (1895/1963), McDougall (1923), and Freud (1922/1959), Barsade & Gibson (1998) describe group emotion as follows: "The diverse emotional tendencies of individuals, then, are submerged into a group emotion... The emotional character thus produced tends to be more extreme than the tendencies of individual members" (p. 84). So people grieving in a group setting will cry more, and more overtly, than they would if they were alone. To what end? As we have already suggested, the literature indicates that group emotions function, first, to create groups. That is, the experience of group emotion can be a basis for the formation of social units per se (Barsade et al. 2000), even if the emotions are negative (Gump & Kulik 1997, Schachter 1959). Recent research on small groups within organizations has provided evidence for this idea, with a focus on positive emotion (Spoor & Kelly 2004, Walter & Bruch 2008). Group experiences of ecstasy and awe can also provide members of groups with a heightened sense of group identity (Heise & O'Brien 1993). Taken together, such research suggests that the collective experience of grief described above can temporarily create in individuals the feeling that the entire set of people gathered together constitutes an emergent group that could work together, for instance, to care for the family of the deceased. Notice that this group process, with emotion serving to mobilize solidarity through perceptions of enhanced similarity, is the opposite of the process of diffusion of responsibility in the areas of helping (e.g., Forsyth et al. 2002, Latané & Nida 1981) and social control (e.g., Brauer & Chekroun 2005, Chekroun & Brauer 2002).

If group emotions serve to create groups by increasing perceived similarity, they maintain established groups' viability through a process of reinforcing group boundaries in intergroup contexts (e.g., Wohl et al. 2010). This effect has been known for a long time with regard to the joy that is propagated among fans and members of the winning team at a sporting event. In such an intergroup setting, group emotion appears to cause particularly strong feelings of cohesiveness among the fans (compared to the opposing team's fans), who then display explicit signs of group identification in the form of team clothing and other insignias (Cialdini et al. 1976). Similar group dynamics are also observed when groups experience collective anxiety (Wohl et al. 2010). In a series of studies, Wilder & Shapiro (1989) induced high (or low) levels of anxiety in four-person groups by having them compete (or cooperate) with another group. After working together on a task, the members of the group watched another four-person group give them feedback on their own performance through a TV monitor. Although the "real" group of participants did not know it, the second group was composed of confederates of the experimenter. Three of the four members of the ostensible other group gave negative feedback, whereas one gave positive feedback and was in this sense an atypical group member. Later, the real participants judged the members of the ostensible evaluating group. Group anxiety caused the judgments of the atypical member to be assimilated toward those of the other three group members, such that the high-anxiety participants rated that person significantly more negatively than did low-anxiety participants. Such findings have been replicated with other manipulations of anxiety as well, and together they suggest that group emotions in intergroup settings make the demarcations between in-group and out-group more defined and salient. Similar effects have been observed in individual emotions in intergroup settings as well (van Zomeren et al. 2007).

Group emotions can be negative or positive, and claims can be made about whether negative or positive emotions are in general more functional in the sense of inhibiting or facilitating characteristics of group behavior. For instance, Barsade (2002) showed that positive emotions were related to greater cooperativeness and less conflict in small groups. And Duffy & Shaw (2000) found that intragroup envy was related to greater social loafing, less cohesiveness, and thus lower productivity. However, consistent with our analysis of emotions in dyads, our point is that collective emotional processing per se is necessary for the creation and maintenance of the group as a social unit (Brief & Weiss 2002).

Group-Based Emotions: Sustaining Collective Action

Intergroup Emotion Theory (Mackie et al. 2000) holds that when people identify themselves as a member of a group, they can experience emotions on behalf of, or from the standpoint of, this group (e.g., Branscombe & Doosje 2004). This emotion can of course be experienced when the individual is alone, but the important difference from other emotion phenomena is that the individual experiences the emotion for the group instead of for himself or herself. Thus, when individuals think of themselves in terms of group membership, their reported emotions differ from their reported individual emotions, and this difference is stronger to the degree that they identify with the group (Bizman et al. 2001, Doosje et al. 1995, Gordijn et al. 2006, Magee & Tiedens 2006, Miller et al. 2004). The types of groups that provide the context for group-based emotions can be social as well as political (Iyer et al. 2003, 2004; Leach et al. 2006),

and most recently, research has focused on opinion-based groups in this regard (McGarty et al. 2009, Musgrove & McGarthy 2008).

Smith and colleagues (2007) established that group emotions are distinct from individual-level emotions and that indeed group emotions depend on the person's degree of group identification. Their work showed further that group emotions contribute to regulating intragroup and intergroup attitudes and behavior. To examine this latter idea, the authors measured intergroup attitudes on thermometer scales and action tendencies (i.e., ingroup support, ingroup solidarity, outgroup confrontation, and outgroup avoidance). They found that intergroup attitudes and action tendencies were predicted by group emotions ("When you think about yourself as an American, to what extent do you feel...") but not by individual emotions ("When you think about yourself as an individual, to what extent do you feel..."). The results further showed that anger at the outgroup and positive group emotions were the most powerful predictors across all categories of action tendencies.

The important role of group-based emotions in sustaining collective action has now been demonstrated in a number of domains. Some analyses of group-based guilt, for instance, suggest that this group-level emotion is related to a commitment to the call for apologies and reparations on the part of governments and institutions (e.g., Berndsen & McGarthy 2010, Branscombe et al. 2002, Doosje et al. 1998, McGarty et al. 2005, Wohl & Branscombe 2005). Other analyses have linked feelings of moral outrage and of anger to a commitment to collective action aimed at righting social inequalities, including discrimination and prejudice (e.g., Crisp et al. 2007, Leach et al. 2006, Thomas 2005, Wakslak et al. 2007, van Zomeren et al. 2004; see Stürmer & Simon 2009 for further interpretation and discussion). Importantly, group-based emotions such as these have been shown in meta-analyses to be better predictors of collective actions against social injustice than are perceptions of the injustice itself (e.g., van Zomeren et al. 2008).

As an example, in a recent study Iyer et al. (2007) assessed the appraisals (i.e., legitimacy, responsibility, and threat), emotions (i.e., guilt, shame, and anger), and political action intentions (i.e., compensation to Iraq, confrontation with those responsible, and withdrawal from Iraq) of American and British university students in the context of the occupation of Iraq. They also experimentally manipulated perceived threat to group image by having participants read a newspaper article in which the wrongdoings of the Americans/British were described as either unintentional (low image threat) or as due to their corrupt, arrogant mentality (high image threat). Image threat and appraisals had predictable effects on emotions. Of interest was the result that emotions were differentially related to preferred strategies for collective action. Anger predicted all three political action intentions. Shame predicted the intention to support policies advocating withdrawal. Guilt was associated with no particular response and was characterized by these authors as a "passive" emotion. The complexity of the possible functions of guilt and associated behavioral responses has been the subject of discussion of research and theory in the context of individual emotion (e.g., de Hooge et al. 2011).

The notion of collective emotional climate (Bar-Tal et al. 2007) should also be mentioned here. Although in theory emotional climate is related to the concept of group emotion, given that it is assumed to involve emotions shared by a group rather than on behalf of one, research tends to use the individual self-report methods of research on group-based emotions. The idea of emotional climate is that an accumulation of repeated group emotional responses to societal events or sociopolitical conditions can produce a general and lasting emotional tone of the nation or society as well as the likely emotional responses to events. For instance, de Rivera et al. (2007) have characterized the emotional climate of countries in terms of the degree to which individuals feel social trust as well as social anger and fear. Interestingly, such climates are independent of the degree to which the country endorses a culture of peace.

Recent research has documented acute emotional climates surrounding terrorist attacks in Spain (e.g., Conejero & Etxebarria 2007) and genocide in Rwanda (Kanyangara et al. 2007). According to Bar-Tal and colleagues (2007), collective emotions play a "pivotal role both in shaping the individual and societal responses to conflicting events (i.e., collective and group-based emotions) and in contributing to the evolution of a social context that maintains the collective emotions that have developed" (p. 442). Emotional climate thus seems to play an important role in signaling the need for and motivating collective action as well as gauging its success.

MECHANISMS SUPPORTING EMOTION PHENOMENA IN GROUPS

The mechanisms for the successful and accurate transmission of group emotion and group-based emotions require the consideration of quite different processes, with those responsible for the former more similar to processes discussed in earlier sections on facial expression and vicarious emotion, and the latter relying on basic group dynamics principles.

Contagion of Emotion Within the Group

Emotional contagion has been offered as a mechanism for the generation of group emotions (e.g., Barsade & Gibson 1998, Sullins 1991). It is defined as the tendency for group members to come to experience and express highly similar emotions (Hatfield et al. 1992, 1993). Similar to the basic components of embodied facial expression, the idea is that individuals unintentionally mimic the public displays of emotion of others. Then, afferent feedback from facial, postural, and vocal mimicry serves to produce a similar emotional state, with its corresponding action tendencies (e.g., Duclos et al. 1989, Neumann & Strack 2000, Strack et al. 1988). Contagion of this type occurs in group conversation, for instance, when members mutually and reciprocally influence each others' affect such that all participants take on a similar emotional intensity and tone (e.g., Quinn & Dutton 2005). However, controlled research on emotion contagion within groups is actually quite sparse.

In one careful study of this phenomenon, Barsade (2002) composed groups of two to four naïve experimental participants and one confederate. Groups were randomly assigned to one of four conditions that resulted from two crossed factors: Pleasantness (pleasant versus unpleasant) and Energy Level (low versus high). The two factors referred to the confederate's nonverbal emotional behavior during the group task. Specifically, groups engaged in a leaderless group discussion that involved making a group decision concerning the way to distribute a limited sum of bonus money to employees from different departments. Participants rated their own emotional state before and after the group discussion. They also evaluated the performance and the contribution of themselves and of other group members. Groups were also filmed during the group discussion. Findings showed a main effect of confederate pleasantness on group members' emotional states: Participants who were exposed to a pleasant confederate were in a more positive state than participants who were exposed to an unpleasant confederate, as indicated by self-ratings and by judges of naïve coders of the video recordings of behavior. Positive state was associated with greater cooperativeness and less group conflict. In the context of group decision-making, Parkinson & Simmons (2009) recently documented emotional contagion as well.

So, emotions can spread among group members, but where does the emotion come from? Whose emotion causes a group emotion in interacting groups? As early as 1942, Redl proposed that group leaders largely determine the emotion that becomes contagious in groups. Cherulnik et al. (2001) note that observers mimic the smiles of especially charismatic leaders, who are particularly potent in expression and eliciting emotions (Friedman & Riggio 1981). And in a series of studies, Bono & Ilies (2006) showed that particularly effective and charismatic leaders tend to use positive words and expressions and express positive emotions in facial expressions. Their studies also documented emotional contagion such that individuals who were exposed to the charismatic leader felt more positive than did individuals exposed to a more neutral-emotion leader.

Fredrickson (2003) further argues that leaders have this effect because of their position in the power hierarchy, and due probably to their motivation to maintain power, leaders express emotion. Indeed, Anderson et al. (2003) specifically showed that the convergence in the similarity of the emotions experienced by individuals in a long-term relationship is most strongly determined by the person in the position of power. This effect was demonstrated for groups in a study by Sy et al. (2005), who manipulated leaders' mood (using videotapes) and then had participants engage in a group task (erecting a tent while subordinates are blindfolded). Results showed that subordinates were in a better mood when their leader was in a positive mood, and this effect was interpreted in terms of emotional contagion.

In summary, we know something about the transmission of emotion within an interacting group. Group leaders, and those perceived as leaders, are usually the focus of attention, the determinant of situational appraisal, and thus the managers of group emotion (e.g., Pescosolido 2002). Descriptions of emotion contagion seem to best depict the appearance of group emotion, and this process probably involves mimicry and the synchronization of bodies and voices that is grounded in the brain centers described in the sections above on vicarious emotion. On the other hand, if group emotion is indeed more intense or involves more loss of self than an individual emotion, researchers still have to account for how and why this is so. Too little research examines the propagation of emotion in interacting groups, no doubt due to the difficulty of producing this phenomenon in the laboratory. On the other hand, the development of virtual environments and their use in experimental research should provide a platform for much-needed research on this topic (Blascovich & Bailenson 2011).

Self-Stereotyping and Emotion Norms

The generation of group-based emotion requires that a convergence in emotional state and readiness occur across individuals who identify themselves as group members, and this convergence has been understood recently in terms of the cognitive processes of self-stereotyping (as members of the group) and in terms of the development of emotion norms within the group.

Smith and colleagues (2007) proposed self-stereotyping as an important mechanism in group-based emotion, akin to the role of self-stereotyping of attitudes, norms, and traits in producing the internalization and incorporation of group characteristics as part of the self. The idea is that self-stereotyping causes group members to experience the emotions they perceive as currently characteristic of their group. Moons et al. (2009) tested this claim in studies that documented a pretest-posttest shift in participants' ratings of the extent to which they felt a given group-based emotion after being told that their fellow in-group members reported high or low levels of that emotion. That is, when they categorized themselves as "Americans" (the category under study), participants converged toward the emotion stereotype in the group-based, but not individual, emotions that they reported to be feeling. Further work on self-stereotyping of emotion by Leonard et al. (2011) showed that knowledge of the anger of women as a group affected female participants' anger (showing self-stereotyping), and this in turn predicted their action tendencies to hypothetical situations of discrimination against women.

The process of self-stereotyping of emotion is not unrelated to the second mechanism, the transmission of injunctive group norms for emotion. Emotion norms are considered as one of three important norms categories in Thomas and colleagues' Normative Alignment Model of Collective Action (Thomas et al. 2009). These authors propose that group commitment to action relies on a process of "crafting a social identity that has a relevant, congruent pattern of norms for action, emotion, and efficacy" (p. 195). Adoption of emotion norms, then, is one criterion for being a "good" group member (Reysen & Branscombe 2008). The way in which the norms for emotion are established is an importantly distinct emotion process that relies on common ways of appraising situations that are relevant to the group's goals (Fischer et al. 2003). So, for instance, a group emotion norm that provides the basis of a group-based emotion of anger would be based on a collective appraisal of the situation (e.g., an injustice) as being illegitimate, negative, and controllable by the group.

Recent research on emotion norms and collective action has demonstrated that group empathy norms can motivate positive changes in attitudes toward outgroups (e.g., Tarrant et al. 2009). Other researchers have studied the production of an outrage norm within the group as an important basis for commitment to action. Thomas & McGarty (2009) constructed opinion-based novel groups of interacting individuals (and noninteracting controls) in the laboratory. The topic under consideration was the Water for Life campaign introduced by the United Nations, which strives to reduce the incidence of waterborne diseases in developing countries by providing clean water and sanitation. Introduced into the groups, of interest for the present treatment, was either a norm of outrage (i.e., toward the existing conditions) or no particular emotion norm. In comparison with noninteracting individuals and groups for which no emotion norm was primed, groups with an outrage norm were more outraged at the end of the discussion and were more committed to the group and its intended action to facilitate the Water for Life aims. This study nicely illustrates the adoption of a group norm for outrage and its relation to collective action.

Self-stereotyping in terms of emotions and self-reports of adherence to group-based emotion norms are clearly associated with commitment to a cause and the likelihood of committing to collective action in the service of that cause. In other words, taking on the emotions of the group as part of the collective self has a motivating function. Future work will need to explore the different emotion mechanisms by which the transmission of group-based emotions, other than claims and social appraisals, actually occurs, and the extent to which group-based emotions are emotional processes or attitudinal ones. The component processes of emotion other than cognitive-appraisal ones, such as facial expression and physiological and central states of the organism, may be most likely to be involved when groups are actually formed and interacting and not when individuals receive consensual information about the state or the norms of the group. In other words, future research in this area will need to focus on the emotional processes in addition to self-report of emotional state.

Moreover, comparing online self-reports of emotion with retrospective or summary reports is a method that would be very productive in this domain. In a now classic study, Barrett and colleagues had participants provide global, retrospective ratings of their emotions (Barrett et al. 1998). Then, over a week-long period these same individuals provided momentary ratings of their emotions and the contexts in which the emotions were experienced. Results revealed gender differences in global descriptions of emotions but not in the averaged momentary ratings of emotion. This and similar findings suggest that when individuals produce global or retrospective self-ratings of emotion, they are more likely to rely on stereotypes and expectations than when they produce online emotion ratings. Showing that group emotion norms and online reports converge when participants are in groups would be a fascinating demonstration of the discrete effect of emotion norms in group processes.

CONCLUSIONS

There will never be an integrative theory of emotion, and no current theory can account for all emotional phenomena. Indeed, the manner in which emotions are defined, labeled, and grouped together as similar and/or different is based on the aims of a given program of research. When the biological basis of certain emotions is considered, categories of primary and secondary emotions may be employed (Damasio 1994, Leyens et al. 2007). When researchers focus on the developmental grounding and cognitive achievements that are necessary for the experience of particular emotions, then basic emotions are contrasted with cognition-dependent emotions (Ackerman & Izard 2004), and labels such as "self-conscious" and "self-evaluative" emotions are proposed (Tracy et al. 2007). When links between emotions and specific behavioral outcomes are under study, categories such as "moral" (Haidt 2003, Tangney et al. 2007) and "prosocial" (Stürmer et al. 2005) emotions are common. When relevant to structural features of interpersonal relationships, words like "powerful" and "powerless" emotions are used (Timmers et al. 2003). And when examining culture, researchers may derive categories from cultural models or values and characterize emotions as "socially engaged" and "socially disengaged" (Kitayama et al. 2006). In sum, emotions can be reasonably defined in terms of neural, peripheral, expressive, cognitive, linguistic, social, literary, historical, cultural, and societal processes and behavior; emotions occur in individuals and can have individual-level definitions, and emotions occur in groups of different sizes and have collective definitions.

In the present review we have surveyed recent literature related to the social functionality of emotion. We propose that facial expression regulates behavior and social perception in dyads in a dense and efficient way. The ability to process facial expression of emotion accurately is thus a social necessity. Vicarious emotion plays a similar though more complex role in learning and social understanding. The brain bases of these two phenomena are slowly becoming clearer as theory in social and emotions psychology is put to the test by techniques and methods in neuroscience. New accounts, such as theories of embodied or simulated emotion, provide an important impetus for such research.

Group emotions and group-based emotions seem to serve more abstract goals of group cohesion and collective action. Although group emotion may rely on many of the same mechanisms as vicarious emotion, group emotion will certainly never be reduced to independent vicarious emotions of a set of interacting individuals. The fact that group emotions can be triggered by powerful people and generated in increasing intensity over time suggests that accounts of this phenomenon are still in their infancy. Group-based emotions are also an emerging topic of study: Their clearly important role in inspiring and maintaining collective action in the service of evolving societies and even smaller groups is now clear. A fuller account of the emotional components of group-based emotions should be part of the research agenda in the coming years.

In summary, emotion processing is a requirement of successful social living. We feel that its utility in dyadic and group dynamics has been established in these pages. We hope to have inspired researchers to pursue full accounts of the mechanisms in the accurate transmission of emotion in these social units.

DISCLOSURE STATEMENT

The authors are unaware of any affiliation, funding, or financial holdings that might be perceived as affecting the objectivity of this review.

ACKNOWLEDGMENTS

The authors acknowledge helpful discussions with Gerrod Parrott, extensive feedback from Keith Oatley, and superb technical help from Mary K. Lokken. The effort of the first author was supported by a grant (FaceExpress–Blanc CSD9 2006) from L'Agence Nationale de la Recherche (ANR), France.

LITERATURE CITED

Ackerman B, Izard C. 2004. Emotion cognition in children and adolescents: introduction to the special issue. *J. Exp. Child Psychol.* 89:271–75

Adolphs R. 2002. Recognizing emotion from facial expressions: psychological and neurological mechanisms. *Behav. Cogn. Neurosci. Rev.* 1:21–62

Adolphs R, Damasio H, Tranel D, Cooper G, Damasio AR. 2000. A role for somatosensory cortices in the visual recognition of emotion as revealed by 3-D lesion mapping. *J. Neurosci.* 20:2683–90

Adolphs R, Damasio H, Tranel D, Damasio AR. 1996. Cortical systems for the recognition of emotion in facial expressions. *J. Neurosci.* 16:7678–87

Adolphs R, Gosselin F, Buchanan T, Tranel D, Schyns P, Damasio A. 2005. A mechanism for impaired fear recognition in amygdala damage. *Nature* 433:68–72

Ames DR, Johar GV. 2009. I'll know what you're like when I see how you feel. *Psychol. Sci.* 20:586–93

Anderson C, Keltner D, John O. 2003. Emotional convergence between people over time. *J. Personal. Soc. Psychol.* 84:1054–68

Anderson C, Thompson LL. 2004. Affect from the top down: how powerful individuals' positive affect shapes negotiations. *Organ. Behav. Hum. Decis. Process.* 95:125–39

Askew C, Field AP. 2007. Vicarious learning and the development of fears in childhood. *Behav. Res. Ther.* 45:2616–27

Atkinson A. 2007. Face processing and empathy. In *Empathy in Mental Illness*, ed. TFD Farrow, PWR Woodruff, pp. 360–85. New York: Cambridge Univ. Press

Barlett MY, DeSteno D. 2009. Gratitude and prosocial behavior: helping when it costs you. *Psychol. Sci.* 1:320–25

Baron-Cohen S, Wheelwright S, Hill J, Raste Y, Plumb I. 2001. The "Reading the Mind in the Eyes" Test revised version: a study with normal adults, and adults with Asperger syndrome or high-functioning autism. *J. Child Psychol. Psychiatry* 42:241–51

Barrett LF, Mesquita B, Ochsner KN, Gross JJ. 2007. The experience of emotion. *Annu. Rev. Psychol.* 58:373–403

Barrett LF, Robin L, Pietromonaco PR, Eyssell KM. 1998. Are women the "more emotional sex?" Evidence from emotional experiences in social context. *Cogn. Emot.* 12:555–78

Barsade SG. 2002. The ripple effect: emotional contagion and its influence on group behavior. *Admin. Sci. Q.* 47:644–75

Barsade SG, Gibson DE. 1998. Group emotion: a view from top and bottom. In *Research on Managing Groups and Teams*, ed. D Gruenfeld, E Mannix, M Neale, pp. 81–102. Stamford, CT: JAI

Barsade SG, Ward AJ, Turner JDF, Sonnenfeld JA. 2000. To your heart's content: the influence of affective diversity in top management teams. *Admin. Sci. Q.* 45:802–36

Bar-Tal D, Halperin E, de Rivera J. 2007. Collective emotions in conflict situations: societal implications. *J. Soc. Issues* 63:441–60

Bartel CA, Saavedra R. 2000. The collective construction of work group mood. *Admin. Sci. Q.* 45:197–231

Barthomeuf L, Droit-Volet S, Rousset S. 2009. Obesity and emotions: differentiation in emotions felt towards food in obese, overweight and normal-weight adolescents. *Food Qual. Pref.* 20:62–68

Batson DC, Fultz J, Schoenrade PA. 1987. Distinct vicarious emotions with different motivational consequences. *J. Personal.* 55:19–39

Bavelas JB, Black A, Lemery CR, Mullett J. 1986. "I show how you feel": motor mimicry as a communicative act. *J. Personal. Soc. Psychol.* 50:322–29

Beall PM, Moody EJ, McIntosh DN, Hepburn SL, Reed CL. 2008. Rapid facial reactions to emotional facial expressions in typically developing children and children with autism spectrum disorder. *J. Exp. Child Psychol.* 101(3):206–23

Berndsen M, McGarty C. 2010. The impact of magnitude of harm and perceived difficulty of making reparations on group-based guilt and reparation towards victims of historical harm. *Eur. J. Soc. Psychol.* 40:500–13

Bizman A, Yinon Y, Krotman S. 2001. Group-based emotional distress: an extension of self-discrepancy theory. *Personal. Soc. Psychol. Bull.* 27:1291–300

Blair RJR. 1995. A cognitive developmental approach to morality: investigating the psychopath. *Cognition* 57:1–29

Blair RJR. 2003. Facial expressions, their communicatory functions and neuro-cognitive substrates. *Philos. Trans. R. Soc. Lond. B Biol. Sci.* 358:561–72

Blair RJR. 2007. The amygdala and ventromedial prefrontal cortex in morality and psychopathy. *Trends Cogn. Sci.* 11:387–91

Blair RJR, Colledge E, Murray L, Mitchell DGV. 2001. A selective impairment in the processing of sad and fearful expressions in children with psychopathic tendencies. *J. Abnorm. Child Psychol.* 29:491–98

Blascovich J, Bailenson J. 2011. *Infinite Reality: Avatars, Eternal Life, New Words, and the Dawn of the Virtual Revolution*. New York: Morrow

Bonnano GA, Keltner D, Noll JG, Putnam FW, Trickett PK, et al. 2002. When the face reveals what words do not: facial expressions of emotion, smiling, and the willingness to disclose childhood sexual abuse. *J. Personal. Soc. Psychol.* 83:94–110

Bono JE, Ilies R. 2006. Charisma, positive emotions and mood contagion. *Leadersh. Q.* 17:317–34

Branscombe NR, Doosje B, eds. 2004. *Collective Guilt: International Perspectives*. London: Cambridge Univ. Press

Branscombe NR, Doosje B, McGarty C. 2002. Antecedents and consequences of collective guilt. In *From Prejudice to Intergroup Emotions: Differentiated Reactions to Social Groups*, ed. DM Mackie, ER Smith, pp. 49–66. Philadelphia, PA: Psychol. Press

Brauer M, Chekroun P. 2005. The relationship between perceived violation of social norms and social control: situational factors influencing the reaction to deviance. *J. Appl. Soc. Psychol.* 35:1519–39

Brief AP, Weiss HM. 2002. Organizational behavior: affect in the workplace. *Annu. Rev. Psychol.* 53:279–307

Brown WM, Palameta B, Moore C. 2003. Are there nonverbal cues to commitment? An exploratory study using the zero-acquaintance video presentation paradigm. *Evol. Psychol.* 1:42–69

Bruce C, Desimone R, Gross C. 1986. Both striate cortex and superior colliculus contribute to visual properties of neurons in superior temporal polysensory area of macaque monkey. *J. Neurophysiol.* 55(5):1057–75

Buck R. 1983. Emotional development and emotional education. In *Emotion in Early Development*, ed. R Plutchik, H Kellerman, pp. 259–92. New York: Academic

Buck R. 1999. The biological affects: a typology. *Psychol. Rev.* 106:301–36

Buck R, Loslow J, Murphy M, Costanzo P. 1992. Social factors in facial display and communication. *J. Personal. Soc. Psychol.* 63:962–68

Butler EA, Egloff B, Wilhelm FW, Smith NC, Erickson EA, Gross JJ. 2003. The social consequences of expressive suppression. *Emotion* 3:48–67

Calder AJ, Keane J, Cole J, Campbell R, Young AW. 2000a. Facial expression recognition by people with Mobius syndrome. *Cogn. Neuropsychol.* 17:73–87

Calder AJ, Keane J, Manes F, Antoun N, Young AW. 2000b. Impaired recognition and experience of disgust following brain injury. *Nat. Neurosci.* 3:1077–78

Campos JJ, Thein S, Owen D. 2003. A Darwinian legacy to understanding human infancy: emotional expressions as behavior regulators. *Ann. N. Y. Acad. Sci.* 1000:110–34

Chekroun P, Brauer M. 2002. The bystander effect and social control behavior: the effect of the presence of others on people's reactions to norm violations. *Eur. J. Soc. Psychol.* 32:853–67

Chekroun P, Brauer M. 2004. Contrôle social et effet spectateur: l'impact de l'implication personnelle [Social control and the spectator effect: the impact of personal implication]. *Ann. Psychol.* 104:83–102

Cheng Y, Lin CP, Liu HL, Hsu YY, Lim KE, et al. 2007. Expertise modulates the perception of pain in others. *Curr. Biol.* 17:1708–13

Cherulnik PD, Donley KA, Wiewel TSR, Miller SR. 2001. Charisma is contagious: the effect of leaders' charisma on observers' affect. *J. Appl. Soc. Psychol.* 31:2149–59

Cialdini RB, Borden RJ, Thorne A, Walker M, Freeman S, Sloan L. 1976. Basking in reflected glory: three (football) field studies. *J. Personal. Soc. Psychol.* 34:366–75

Clark TF, Winkielman P, McIntosh DN. 2008. Autism and the extraction of emotion from briefly presented facial expressions: stumbling at the first step of empathy. *Emotion* 8:803–9

Clore GL, Storbeck J. 2006. Affect as information in social judgments and behaviors. In *Hearts and Minds: Affective Influences on Social Thinking and Behavior*, ed. JP Forgas. Philadelphia, PA: Psychol. Press

Conejero S, Etxebarria I. 2007. The impact of the Madrid bombings on personal emotions, emotional atmosphere and emotional climate. *J. Soc. Issues* 63:273–87

Cosmides L, Tooby J. 2000. Evolutionary psychology and the emotions. In *Handbook of Emotions*, ed. M Lewis, JM Haviland-Jones, pp. 91–115. New York: Guilford. 2nd ed.

Crisp RJ, Heuston S, Farr MJ, Turner RN. 2007. Seeing red or feeling blue: differentiated intergroup emotions and ingroup identification in soccer fans. *Group Process. Intergroup Relat.* 10:9–26

Damasio AR. 1989. Time-locked multiregional retroactivation: a systems-level proposal for the neural substrates of recall and recognition. *Cognition* 33:25–62

Damasio AR. 1994. The brain binds entities and events by multiregional activation from convergence zones. In *Biology and Computation: A Physicist's Choice*, ed. H Gutfreund, G Toulouse, pp. 749–58. River Edge, NJ: World Sci. Publ.

Dapretto M, et al. 2006. Understanding emotions in others: mirror neuron dysfunction in children with autism spectrum disorders. *Nat. Neurosci.* 9:28–30

Darwin C. 1872/1998. *The Expression of the Emotions in Man and Animals*. New York/London: Oxford Univ. Press

Decety J, Chaminade T. 2003. Neural correlates of feeling sympathy. *Neuropsychologia* 41:127–38

Decety J, Chaminade T. 2005. The neurophysiology of imitation and intersubjectivity. *Perspectives on Imitation: From Neuroscience to Social Science: Vol. 1. Mechanisms of Imitation and Imitation in Animals*, ed. S Hurley, N Chater, pp. 119–40. Cambridge, MA: MIT Press

Decety J, Lamm C. 2006. Human empathy through the lens of social neuroscience. *Sci. World J.* 6:1146–63

de Hooge IE, Nelissen RMA, Breugelmans SM, Zeelenberg M. 2011. What is moral about guilt? Acting "prosocially" at the disadvantage of others. *J. Personal. Soc. Psychol.* 100:462–73

de Hooge IE, Zeelenberg M, Breugelmans SM. 2010. Restore and protect motivations following shame. *Cogn. Emot.* 24(1):111–27

de Rivera J, Kurrien R, Olsen N. 2007. The emotional climate of nations and their culture of peace. *J. Soc. Issues* 63(2):255–71

de Waal FBM. 2008. Putting the altruism back into altruism: the evolution of empathy. *Annu. Rev. Psychol.* 59:279–300

de Wied, van Boxtel A, Zaalberg R, Goudena PP, Matthys W. 2006. Facial EMG responses to dynamic emotional facial expressions in boys with disruptive behavior disorders. *J. Psychiatr. Res.* 40(2):112–21

Dimberg U, Thunberg M. 1998. Rapid facial reactions to emotional facial expressions. *Scand. J. Psychol.* 39(1):39–45

Doosje B, Branscombe NR, Spears R, Manstead ASR. 1998. Guilty by association: when one's group has a negative history. *J. Personal. Soc. Psychol.* 75:872–86

Doosje B, Ellemers N, Spears R. 1995. Perceived intragroup variability as a function of group status and identification. *J. Exp. Soc. Psychol.* 31:410–36

Duclos SE, Laird JD, Schneider E, Sexter M, Stern L, Van Lighten O. 1989. Emotion-specific effects of facial expressions and postures on emotional experience. *J. Personal. Soc. Psychol.* 57:100–8

Duffy MK, Shaw JD. 2000. The Salieri syndrome: consequences of envy in groups. *Small Group Res.* 31:3–23

Field T. 1982. Individual differences in the expressivity of neonates and young infants. In *Development of Nonverbal Behavior in Children*, ed. R Feldman, pp. 279–98. New York: Springer-Verlag

Fischer AH, Manstead ASR, Zaalberg R. 2003. Social influences on the emotion process. *Eur. Rev. Soc. Psychol.* 14:171–201

Fischer AH, Roseman IJ. 2007. Beat them or ban them: the characteristics and social functions of anger and contempt. *J. Personal. Soc. Psychol.* 93:103–15

Forsyth DR, Zyzniewski LE, Giammanco CA. 2002. Responsibility diffusion in cooporative collectives. *Personal. Soc. Psychol. Bull.* 28:54–65

Frank R. 1988. *Passions Within Reason: The Strategic Role of Emotions*. New York: Norton

Fredrickson BL. 2003. Positive emotions and upward spirals in organizations. In *Positive Organizational Scholarship. Foundations of a New Discipline*, ed. KS Cameron, JE Dutton, RE Quinn, pp. 163–75. San Francisco, CA: Berrett-Koehler

Freud S. 1922/1959. *Group Psychology and the Analysis of the Ego*. Transl. James Strachey. New York: Norton

Friedman HS, Riggio R. 1981. The effect of individual differences in nonverbal expressiveness on transmission of emotion. *J. Nonverb. Behav.* 6:96–104

Frijda NH. 1986. *The Emotions*. London: Cambridge Univ. Press

Frijda NH, Mesquita B. 1994. The social roles and functions of emotions. In *Emotion and Culture: Empirical Studies of Mutual Influence*, ed. S Kitayama, HR Markus, pp. 51–87. Washington, DC: Am. Psychol. Assoc.

Fultz J, Nielsen ME. 1993. Anticipated vicarious affect and willingness to be exposed to another's suffering. *Basic Appl. Soc. Psychol.* 14:273–83

Gallese V. 2003. The roots of empathy: the shared manifold hypothesis and the neural basis of intersubjectivity. *Psychopathology* 36:171–80

Gallese V. 2005. Being like me: self-other identity, mirror neurons, and empathy. In *Perspectives on Imitation: From Neuroscience to Social Science. Vol. 1: Mechanisms of Imitation and Imitation in Animals*, ed. S Hurley, H Chater, pp. 101–18. Cambridge, MA: MIT Press

Gallese V. 2007. Before and below "theory of mind": embodied simulation and the neural correlates of social cognition. *Philos. Trans. R. Soc. Lond. B Biol. Sci.* 362:659–69

Gallese V, Fadiga L, Fogassi L, Rizzolatti G. 1996. Action recognition in the premotor cortex. *Brain* 119:593–609

Gerull FC, Rappee RM. 2002. Mother knows best: effects of maternal modeling on the acquisition of fear and avoidance behaviour in toddlers. *Behav. Res. Ther.* 40:279–87

Goldman A, Sripada C. 2005. Simulationist models of face-based emotion recognition. *Cognition* 94:193–213

Gordijn E, Yzerbyt VY, Wigboldus D, Dumont M. 2006. Emotional reactions to harmful intergroup behavior: the impact of being associated with the victims or the perpetrators. *Eur. J. Soc. Psychol.* 36:15–30

Griskevicius V, Tybur JM, Gangestad SW, Perea EF, Shapiro JR, Kenrick DT. 2009. Aggress to impress: hostility as an evolved context-dependent strategy. *J. Personal. Soc. Psychol.* 96:980–94

Gross JJ, John OP. 2003. Individual differences in two emotion regulation processes: implications for affect, relationships, and well-being. *J. Personal. Soc. Psychol.* 85:348–62

Gump B, Kulik JA. 1997. Stress, affiliation, and emotional contagion. *J. Personal. Soc. Psychol.* 72:305–19

Haidt J. 2003. The moral emotions. In *Handbook of Affective Sciences*, ed. RJ Davidson, KR Scherer, HH Goldsmith, pp. 852–70. London: Oxford Univ. Press

Harker L, Keltner D. 2001. Expressions of positive emotion in women's college yearbook pictures and their relationship to personality and life outcomes across adulthood. *J. Personal. Soc. Psychol.* 80:112–24

Hatfield E, Cacioppo JT, Rapson RL. 1992. Primitive emotional contagion. In *Emotion and Social Behavior. Review of Personality and Social Psychology*, ed. MS Clark, Vol. 14, pp. 151–77. Thousand Oaks, CA: Sage

Hatfield E, Cacioppo JT, Rapson RL. 1993. Emotional contagion. *Curr. Dir. Psychol. Sci.* 3:96–99

Hatfield E, Cacioppo JT, Rapson RL. 1994. *Emotional Contagion*. New York: Cambridge Univ. Press

Heberlein AS, Atkinson AP. 2009. Neuroscientific evidence for simulation and shared substrates in emotion recognition: beyond faces. *Emot. Rev.* 1(2):162–77

Heise DR, O'Brien J. 1993. Emotion expression in groups. In *Handbook of Emotions*, ed. M Lewis, JM Haviland, pp. 489–98. New York: Guilford

Hennenlotter A, Schroeder U, Erhard P, Catrop F, Haslinger B, et al. 2005. A common neural basis for receptive and expressive communication of pleasant facial affect. *NeuroImage* 26:581–91

Hepburn S, Stone WL. 2006. Longitudinal research on motor imitation in autism. In *Imitation and the Social Mind: Autism and Typical Development*, ed. S Rogers, J Williams. New York: Guilford

Hertenstein MJ, Campos JJ. 2004. The retention effects of an adult's emotional displays on infant behavior. *Child Dev.* 75:595–613

Hess U. 2009. Mimicry. In *Oxford Companion to Affective Sciences*, ed. D Sander, KS Scherer, pp. 253–54. London: Oxford Univ. Press

Hess U, Blairy S, Philippot P. 1999. Facial mimicry. In *The Social Context of Nonverbal Behavior*, ed. P Philippot, R Feldman, E Coats, pp. 213–41. Cambridge: Cambridge Univ. Press

Horstmann G. 2003. What do facial expressions convey: feeling states, behavioral intentions, or action requests? *Emotion* 3(2):150–66

Hutchison WD, Davis KD, Lozano AM, Tasker RR, Dostrovsky JO. 1999. Pain-related neurons in the human cingulate cortex. *Nat. Neurosci.* 2:403–5

Iacoboni M, Dapretto M. 2006. The mirror neuron system and the consequences of its dysfunction. *Nat. Rev. Neurosci.* 7:942–51

Iglesias I. 1996. Vergüenza ajena. In *The Emotions: Social, Cultural and Biological Dimensions*, ed. R Harre, WG Parrott, pp. 122–31. London: Sage

Iyer A, Leach CW, Crosby FJ. 2003. White guilt and racial compensation: the benefits and limits of self-focus. *Personal. Soc. Psychol. Bull.* 29:117–29

Iyer A, Leach CW, Pedersen A. 2004. Racial wrongs and restitutions: the role of guilt and other group-based emotions. In *Collective Guilt: International Perspectives*, ed. N Branscombe, B Doosje, pp. 262–83. Cambridge: Cambridge Univ. Press

Iyer A, Schmader T, Lickel B. 2007. Why individuals protest the perceived transgressions of their country: the role of anger, shame and guilt. *Personal. Soc. Psychol. Bull.* 33:572–87

Johnson-Laird PN, Oatley K. 1992. Basic emotions, rationality, and folk theory. *Cogn. Emot.* 6:201–23

Kagan J. 2007. *What Is an Emotion? History, Measures, and Meanings*. New Haven, CT: Yale Univ. Press

Kanyangara P, Rimé B, Philippot P, Yzerbyt V. 2007. Collective rituals, intergroup perception and emotional climate: participation in "Gacaca" tribunas and assimilation of the Rwandan genocide. *J. Soc. Issues* 63:387–403

Keillor JM, Barrett AM, Crucian GP, Kortenkamp S, Heilman KM. 2002. Emotional experience and perception in the absence of facial feedback. *J. Int. Neuropsychol. Soc.* 8(1):130–35

Kelly JR, Barsade SG. 2001. Mood and emotions in small groups and work teams. *Organ. Behav. Hum. Decis. Process.* 86:99–130

Keltner D, Gross JJ. 1999. Functional accounts of emotions. *Cogn. Emot.* 13:467–80

Keltner D, Haidt J. 1999. Social function of emotions at four levels of analysis. *Cogn. Emot.* 13:505–21

Keltner D, Haidt J. 2003. Approaching awe, a moral, spiritual, and aesthetic emotion. *Cogn. Emot.* 17:297–314

Keltner D, Kring AM. 1998. Emotion, social function, and psychopathology. *Rev. Gen. Psychol.* 2:320–42

Keysers C, Gazzola V. 2007. Integrating simulation and theory of mind: from self to social cognition. *Trends Cogn. Sci.* 11:194–96

Keysers C, Kaas JH, Gazzola V. 2010. Somatosensation in social perception. *Nat. Rev. Neurosci.* 11:417–28

Kitayama S, Mesquita B, Karasawa M. 2006. Cultural affordances and emotional experience: socially engaging and disengaging emotions in Japan and the United States. *J. Personal. Soc. Psychol.* 91(5):890–903

Kropp JO, Haynes OM. 1987. Abusive and nonabusive mothers' ability to identify general and specific emotion signals of infants. *Child Dev.* 58:187–90

Krull DS, Seger CR, Silvera DH. 2008. Smile when you say that: effects of willingness on dispositional inferences. *J. Exp. Soc. Psychol.* 44:735–42

Lamm C, Batson CD, Decety J. 2007. The neural substrate of human empathy: effects of perspective-taking and cognitive appraisal. *J. Cogn. Neurosci.* 19:42–58

Lanzetta JT, Englis BG. 1989. Expectations of cooperation and competition and their effects on observers' vicarious emotional responses. *J. Personal. Soc. Psychol.* 56:543–54

Latané B, Nida S. 1981. Ten years of research on group size and helping. *Psychol. Bull.* 89:308–24

Leach CW, Iyer A, Pedersen A. 2006. Anger and guilt about in-group advantage explain the willingness for political action. *Personal. Soc. Psychol. Bull.* 32:1232–45

Leach CW, Tiedens LZ. 2004. A world of emotion. In *The Social Life of Emotions*, ed. LZ Tiedens, CW Leach, pp. 1–18. Cambridge: Cambridge Univ. Press

Le Bon G. 1895/1963. *Psychologie des Foules*. Paris: Presses Univ. de France

Lee T-W, Dolan RJ, Critchley HD. 2007. Controlling emotional expression: behavioral and neural correlates of nonimitative emotional responses. *Cereb. Cortex* 18(1):104–13

Lee T-W, Josephs O, Dolan RJ, Critchley HD. 2006. Imitating expressions: emotion-specific neural substrates in facial mimicry. *Soc. Cogn. Affect. Neurosci.* 1(2):122–35

Leonard DJ, Moons WG, Mackie DM, Smith ER. 2011. We're mad as hell and we're not going to take it anymore: anger, self-stereotyping and collective action. *Group Process. Intergroup Relat.* 14:99–111

Leyens JP, Demoulin S, Vaes J, Gaunt R, Paladino MP. 2007. Infra-humanization: the wall of group differences. *Soc. Issues Policy Rev.* 1:139–72

Lickel B, Schmader T, Curtis M, Scarnier M, Ames DR. 2005. Vicarious shame and guilt. *Group Process. Intergroup Relat.* 8:145–47

Mackie DM, Devos T, Smith ER. 2000. Intergroup emotions: explaining offensive action tendencies in an intergroup context. *J. Personal. Soc. Psychol.* 79:602–16

Magee JC, Tiedens LZ. 2006. Emotional ties that bind: the roles of valence and consistency of group emotion in inferences of cohesiveness and common fate. *Personal. Soc. Psychol. Bull.* 32:1703–15

Maringer M, Krumhuber E, Fischer A, Niedenthal PM. 2011. Beyond smile dynamics: mimicry and beliefs in judgments of smiles. *Emotion* 11:181–87

Marsh AA, Ambady N. 2007. The influence of the fear facial expression on prosocial responding. *Cogn. Emot.* 21(2):225–47

Marsh AA, Kozak MN, Ambady N. 2007. Accurate identification of fear expressions predicts prosocial behavior. *Emotion* 7:239–51

Matthews G, Wells A. 1999. The cognitive science of attention and emotion. In *Handbook of Cognition and Emotion*, ed. T Dalgleish, MJ Power, pp. 171–92. Chichester, UK: Wiley

Mayer JD, Salovey P, Caruso DR. 2004. Emotional intelligence: theory, findings, and implications. *Psychol. Inq.* 60:197–215

McDougall W. 1923. *Outline of Psychology*. New York: Scribner

McGarty C, Bliuc A-M, Thomas EF, Bongiorno R. 2009. Collective action as the material expression of opinion-based group membership. *J. Soc. Issues* 65:839–57

McGarty C, Pedersen A, Leach CW, Mansell T, Waller J, Bliuc A-M. 2005. Group-based guilt as a predictor of commitment to apology. *Br. J. Soc. Psychol.* 44:659–80

McIntosh DN. 1996. Facial feedback hypotheses: evidence, implications, and directions. *Motiv. Emot.* 20:121–47

McIntosh DN. 2006. Spontaneous facial mimicry, liking and emotional contagion. *Polish Psychol. Bull.* 37:31–42

McIntosh DN, Druckman D, Zajonc RB. 1994. Socially induced affect. In *Learning, Remembering, Believing: Enhancing Human Performance*, ed. D Druckman, RA Bjork, pp. 251–76, 364–71. Washington, DC: Natl. Acad. Press

McIntosh DN, Reichmann-Decker A, Winkielman P, Wilbarger JL. 2006. When the social mirror breaks: deficits in automatic, but not voluntary, mimicry of emotional facial expressions in autism. *Dev. Sci.* 9:295–302

Méhu M, Dunbar RIM. 2008. Relationship between smiling and laughter in humans (*Homo sapiens*): testing the power asymmetry hypothesis. *Folia Primatol.* 79:269–80

Mesquita B, Ellsworth P. 2001. The role of culture in appraisal. In *Appraisal Processes in Emotion: Theory, Methods, Research*, ed. K Scherer, A Schorr, T Johnstone, pp. 233–48. New York: Oxford Univ. Press

Mesquita B, Marinetti C, Delvaux E. 2011. The social psychology of emotions. In *Handbook of Social Cognition*, ed. S Fiske, N Macrae. New York: Sage. In press

Miller DA, Smith ER, Mackie DM. 2004. Effects of intergroup contact and political predispositions on prejudice: role of intergroup emotions. *Group Process. Intergroup Relat.* 7:221–37

Miller RS. 1987. Empathic embarrassment: situational and personal determinants of reactions to the embarrassment of another. *J. Personal. Soc. Psychol.* 53:1061–69

Mineka S, Cook M. 1993. Mechanisms involved in the observational conditioning of fear. *J. Exp. Psychol.: Gen.* 122:23–38

Mojzisch A, Schilbach L, Helmert J, Pannasch S, Velichkovsky B, Vogeley K. 2006. The effects of self-involvement on attention, arousal, and facial expression during social interaction with virtual others: a psychophysiological study. *Soc. Neurosci.* 1:184–95

Moody E, McIntosh DN. 2006. Mimicry and autism: bases and consequences of rapid, automatic matching behavior. In *Imitation and the Social Mind: Autism and Typical Development*, ed. S Rogers, J Williams, pp. 71–95. New York: Guilford

Moons WG, Leonard DJ, Mackie DM, Smith ER. 2009. I feel our pain: antecedents and consequences of emotional self-stereotyping. *J. Exp. Soc. Psychol.* 45:760–69

Mumme DL, Fernald A. 1996. Infants' responses to facial and vocal emotional signals in a social referencing paradigm. *Child Dev.* 67:3219–37

Musgrove L, McGarty CA. 2008. Opinion-based group membership as a predictor of collective emotional responses and support for pro- and anti-war action. *Soc. Psychol.* 39:37–47

Neumann R, Strack F. 2000. "Mood contagion": the automatic transfer of mood between persons. *J. Personal. Soc. Psychol.* 79:211–23

Niedenthal PM. 2007. Embodying emotion. *Science* 316:1002–5

Niedenthal PM, Barsalou LW, Winkielman P, Krauth-Gruber S, Ric F. 2005. Embodiment in attitudes, social perception, and emotion. *Personal. Soc. Psychol. Rev.* 9:184–211

Niedenthal PM, Kruth-Gruber S, Ric F. 2006. *The Psychology of Emotion: Interpersonal Experiential, and Cognitive Approaches. Principles of Social Psychology Series.* New York: Psychol. Press

Niedenthal PM, Mermillod M, Maringer M, Hess U. 2010. The Simulation of Smiles (SIMS) model: embodied simulation and the meaning of facial expression. *Behav. Brain Sci.* 33:417–80

Oatley K, Jenkins JM. 1992. Human emotions: function and dysfunction. *Annu. Rev. Psychol.* 43:55–85

Ohman A, Mineka S. 2001. Fears, phobias, and preparedness: toward an evolved module of fear and fear learning. *Psychol. Rev.* 108:483–522

Olsson A, Nearing KI, Phelps EA. 2007. Learning fears by observing others: the neural systems of social fear transmission. *Soc. Cogn. Affect. Neurosci.* 2:3–11

Olsson A, Phelps EA. 2004. Learned fear of "unseen" faces after Pavlovian, observational and instructed fear. *Psychol. Sci.* 15:822–28

Parkinson B, Simons G. 2009. Affecting others: social appraisal and emotion contagion in everyday decision making. *Personal. Soc. Psychol. Bull.* 35:1071–84

Parrott WG. 2001. Implications of dysfunctional emotions for understanding how emotions function. *Rev. Gen. Psychol.* 5:180–86

Perrett DI, Rolls ET, Caan W. 1982. Visual neurons responsive to faces in the monkey temporal cortex. *Exp. Brain Res.* 47:329–42

Pescosolido AT. 2002. Emergent leaders as managers of group emotion. *Leadersh. Q.* 13:583–99

Phelps EA. 2006. Emotion and cognition: insights from studies of the human amygdala. *Annu. Rev. Psychol.* 57:27–53

Pickett CL, Gardner WL, Knowles M. 2004. Getting a cue: the need to belong and enhanced sensitivity to social cues. *Personal. Soc. Psychol. Bull.* 30:1095–107

Pitcher D, Garrido L, Walsh V, Duchaine B. 2008. TMS disrupts the perception and embodiment of facial expressions. *J. Neurosci.* 28(36):8929–33

Pollak SD. 2008. Mechanisms linking early experience and the emergence of emotions: illustrations from the study of maltreated children. *Curr. Dir. Psychol. Sci.* 17:370–75

Pollak SD, Cicchetti D, Hornung K, Reed A. 2000. Recognizing emotion in faces: development effects of child abuse and neglect. *Dev. Psychol.* 36:679–88

Pourtois G, Grandjean D, Sander D, Vuilleumier P. 2004. Electrophysiological correlates of rapid spatial orienting towards fearful faces. *Cereb. Cortex* 14:619–33

Quinn RA, Dutton JE. 2005. Coordination as energy-in-conversation. *Acad. Manage. Rev.* 30:36–57

Redl F. 1942. Group emotions and leadership. *Psychiatry* 5:573–96

Reysen S, Branscombe NR. 2008. Belief in collective emotions as conforming to the group. *Soc. Influence* 3:171–88

Rimé B. 2007. Interpersonal emotion regulation. In *Handbook of Emotion Regulation*, ed. JJ Gross, pp. 466–85. New York: Guilford

Rimé B, Herbette G, Corsini S. 2004. The social sharing of emotion: illusory and real benefits of talking about emotional experiences. In *Emotional Expression and Health. Advances in Theory, Assessment and Clinical Applications*, ed. I Nyklicek, LR Temoshok, A Vingerhoets, pp. 29–42. Hove, UK/New York: Brunner-Routledge

Rodriguez Mosquera PM, Fischer AH, Manstead ASR, Zaalberg R. 2008. Attack, disapproval, or withdrawal? The role of honour in anger and shame responses to being insulted. *Cogn. Emot.* 22(8):1471–98

Salovey P, Kokkonen M, Lopes PN, Mayer JD. 2003. Emotional intelligence: What do we know? In *Feelings and Emotions: The Amsterdam Symposium*, ed. ASR Manstead, NH Frijda, AH Fischer, pp. 321–40. London: Cambridge Univ. Press

Salovey P, Mayer JM. 1990. Emotional intelligence. *Imagination Cogn. Personal.* 9:185–211

Schachter S. 1959. *The Psychology of Affiliation.* Stanford, CA: Stanford Univ. Press

Scharlemann JPW, Eckel CC, Kacelnik A, Wilson RK. 2001. The value of a smile: game theory with a human face. *J. Econ. Psychol.* 22:617–40

Scherer KR. 1984. On the nature and function of emotion: a component process approach. In *Approaches to Emotion*, ed. KR Scherer, P Ekman, pp. 293–317. Hillsdale, NJ: Erlbaum

Scherer KR. 1994. An emotion's occurrence depends on the relevance of an event to the organism's goal/need hierarchy. In *The Nature of Emotion: Fundamental Questions*, ed. P Ekman, RJ Davidson, pp. 227–31. New York/Oxford: Oxford Univ. Press

Schilbach L, Wohlschlaeger A, Kraemer N, Newen A, Shah NJ, Fink G. 2006. Being with virtual others: neural correlates of social interaction. *Neuropsychologia* 44:718–30

Singer T, Seymour B, O'Doherty J, Kaube H, Dolan RJ, Frith CD. 2004. Empathy for pain involves the affective but not sensory components of pain. *Science* 303:1157–62

Singer T, Seymour B, O'Doherty JP, Stephan KE, Dolan RJ, Frith CD. 2006. Empathic neural responses are modulated by the perceived fairness of others. *Nature* 439:466–69

Smith ER, Seger CR, Mackie DM. 2007. Can emotions be truly group level? Evidence regarding four conceptual criteria. *J. Personal. Soc. Psychol.* 93:431–46

Solomon RC. 1976. *The Passions: The Myth and Nature of Human Emotions.* Notre Dame, IN: Univ. Notre Dame Press

Solomon RC. 1993. The philosophy of emotions. In *Handbook of Emotions*, ed. M Lewis, JM Haviland, pp. 3–15. New York: Guilford

Sonnby-Borgström M. 2002. Automatic mimicry reactions as related to differences in emotional empathy. *Scand. J. Psychol.* 43:433–43

Sonnby-Borgström M, Jönsson P. 2004. Dissmissing-avoidant pattern of attachment and mimicry reactions at different levels of information processing. *Scand. J. Psychol.* 45:103–13

Spezio ML, Huang P-YS, Castelli F, Adolphs R. 2007. Amygdala damage impairs eye contact during conversations with real people. *J. Neurosci.* 27:3994–97

Spoor JR, Kelly JR. 2004. The evolutionary significance of affect in groups: communication and group bonding. *Group Process. Intergroup Relat.* 7:398–412

Srivastava S, Tamir M, McGonigal KM, John OP, Gross JJ. 2009. The social costs of emotional suppression: a prospective study of the transition to college. *J. Personal. Soc. Psychol.* 96:883–97

Stel M, van Knippenberg A. 2008. The role of facial mimicry in the recognition of affect. *Psychol. Sci.* 19:984–85

Stocks EL, Lishner DA, Waits BL, Downum EM. 2011. I'm embarrassed for you: the effect of valuing and perspective taking on empathic embarrassment and empathic concern. *J. Appl. Soc. Psychol.* 41:1–26

Strack F, Martin LL, Stepper S. 1988. Inhibiting and facilitating conditions of the human smile: a nonobtrusive test of the facial feedback hypothesis. *J. Personal. Soc. Psychol.* 54:768–76

Stürmer S, Simon B. 2009. Pathways to collective protest: calculation, identification, or emotion? A critical analysis of the role of group-based anger in social movement participation. *J. Soc. Issues* 65(No. 4):681–70

Stürmer S, Snyder M, Omoto AM. 2005. Prosocial emotions and helping: the moderating role of group membership. *J. Personal. Soc. Psychol.* 88:532–46

Sullins E. 1991. Emotional contagion revisited: effects of social comparison and expressive style on mood convergence. *Personal. Soc. Psychol. Bull.* 17:166–74

Susskind JM, Lee DH, Cusi A, Feiman R, Grabski W, Anderson AK. 2008. Expressing fear enhances sensory acquisition. *Nat. Neurosci.* 11:843–50

Sy T, Côté S, Saavedra R. 2005. The contagious leader: impact of the leader's mood on the mood of the group members, group affective tone, and group processes. *J. Appl. Psychol.* 90:295–305

Tangney JP, Fischer KW, eds. 1995. *Self-Conscious Emotions: Shame, Guilt, Embarrassment, and Pride.* New York: Guilford

Tangney JP, Stuewig J, Mashek DJ. 2007. Moral emotions and moral behavior. *Annu. Rev. Psychol.* 58:345–72

Tarrant M, Dazeley S, Cottom T. 2009. Social categorization and empathy for outgroup members. *Br. J. Soc. Psychol.* 48:427–46

Thomas EF. 2005. The role of social identity in creating positive beliefs and emotions to motivate volunteerism. *Aust. J. Volunteerism* 10:45–52

Thomas EF, McGarty C. 2009. The role of efficacy and moral outrage norms in creating the potential for international development activism through group-based interaction. *Br. J. Soc. Psychol.* 48:115–34

Thomas EF, McGarty C, Mavor I. 2009. Aligning identities, emotions, and beliefs to create commitment to sustainable social and political action. *Personal. Soc. Psychol. Rev.* 13:194–217

Timmers M, Fischer AH, Manstead ASR. 2003. Ability versus vulnerability: beliefs about men's and women's emotional behavior. *Cogn. Emot.* 17:41–63

Totterdell P. 2000. Catching moods and hitting runs: mood linkage and subjective performance in professional sport teams. *J. Appl. Psychol.* 85:848–59

Totterdell P, Kellett S, Teuchmann K, Briner RB. 1998. Evidence of mood linkage in work group. *J. Personal. Soc. Psychol.* 74:1504–15

Tracy JL, Robins RW. 2008. The nonverbal expression of pride: evidence for cross-cultural recognition. *J. Personal. Soc. Psychol.* 94:516–30

Tracy JL, Robins RW, Tangney JP. 2007. *The Self-Conscious Emotions: Theory and Research.* New York: Guilford

van Zomeren M, Fischer AH, Spears R. 2007. Testing the limits of tolerance: how intergroup anxiety amplifies negative and offensive responses to out-group-initiated contact. *Personal. Soc. Psychol. Bull.* 33:1686–99

van Zomeren M, Spears R, Fisher AH, Leach CW. 2004. Put your money where your mouth is! Explaining collective action tendencies through group-based anger and group efficacy. *J. Personal. Soc. Psychol.* 87:649–64

van Zomeren M, Spears R, Leach CW. 2008. Exploring psychological mechanisms of collective action: Does relevance of group identity influence how people cope with disadvantage? *Br. J. Soc. Psychol.* 47:353–72

Vaughan K, Lanzetta J. 1980. Vicarious instigation and conditioning of facial expressive and autonomic responses to a model's expressive display of pain. *J. Personal. Soc. Psychol.* 38:909–23

Vaughan K, Lanzetta J. 1981. The effect of modification of expressive display on vicarious emotional arousal. *J. Exp. Soc. Psychol.* 17:16–30

Wakslak CJ, Jost JT, Tyler TR, Chen ES. 2007. Moral outrage mediates the dampening effect of system justification on support for redistributive social policies. *Psychol. Sci.* 18:267–74

Walter F, Bruch H. 2008. The positive group affect spiral: a dynamic model of the emergence of positive affective similarity in work groups. *J. Org. Behav.* 29:239–61

Wicker B, Keysers C, Plailly J, Royet JP, Gallese V, Rizzolatti G. 2003. Both of us disgusted in *my* insula: the common neural basis of seeing and feeling disgust. *Neuron* 40:655–64

Wieser MJ, Mühlberger A, Ampers GW, Macht M, Ellgring H, Pauli P. 2006. Emotion processing in Parkinson's disease: dissociation between early neuronal processing and explicit ratings. *Clin. Neurophysiol.* 117:94–102

Wilder DA, Shapiro PN. 1989. Role of competition-induced anxiety in limiting the beneficial impact of positive behavior by an out-group member. *J. Personal. Soc. Psychol.* 56:60–69

Williams LA, DeSteno D. 2008. Pride and perseverance: the motivational role of pride. *J. Personal. Soc. Psychol.* 94:1007–17

Wilson-Mendenhall CD, Barrett LF, Simmons WK, Barsalou LW. 2011. Grounding emotion in situated conceptualization. *Neurologica* 49:1105–27

Winkielman P, McIntosh DN, Oberman L. 2009. Embodied and disembodied emotion processing: learning from and about typical and autistic individuals. *Emot. Rev.* 2:178–90

Wohl MJA, Branscombe NR. 2005. Forgiveness and collective guilt assignment to historical perpetrator groups depends on level of social category inclusiveness. *J. Personal. Soc. Psychol.* 88:288–303

Wohl MJA, Giguère B, Branscombe NR, McVicar DN. 2010. One day we might be no more: collective angst and protective action from potential distinctiveness loss. *Eur. J. Soc. Psychol.* 41:289–300

Zajonc RB, Adelmann PK, Murphy ST, Niedenthal PM. 1987. Convergence in the physical appearance of spouses: an implication of the vascular theory of emotional efference. *Motiv. Emot.* 11:335–46

Zajonc RB, Murphy ST, Inglehart M. 1989. Feeling and facial efference: implications of the vascular theory of emotion. *Psychol. Rev.* 96:395–416

RELATED RESOURCES

Feldman Barrett L, Niedenthal PM, Winkielman P, eds. 2005. *Emotion: Conscious and Unconscious.* New York: Guilford

Fredrickson B. 2009. *Positivity: Groundbreaking Research Reveals How to Embrace the Hidden Strengh of Positive Emotions, Overcome Negativity, and Thrive.* New York: Crown. **http://www. positivityratio.com/**

Gutman R, on TED. 2011. The hidden power of smiling. **http://www.ted.com/talks/lang/eng/ ron_gutman_the_hidden_power_of_smiling.html**

Hanson D, on TED. 2009. Robots that "show emotion." **http://www.ted.com/talks/lang/ eng/david_hanson_robots_that_relate_to_you.html**

Niedenthal PM, Krauth-Gruber S, Ric F. 2006. *The Psychology of Emotion: Interpersonal, Experiential, and Cognitive Approaches. Principles of Social Psychology Series.* New York: Psychol. Press

Sander D, Scherer K, eds. 2009. *Oxford Companion to the Affective Sciences.* London: Oxford Univ. Press

Vohs KD, Baumeister RF, Loewenstein G. 2007. *Do Emotions Help or Hurt Decision Making? A Hedgefoxian Perspective.* New York: Russell Sage Found. Press

Geneva Emotion Research Group. **http://www.unige.ch/cisa/gerg.html**

Laboratory for Affective Neuroscience, University of Wisconsin-Madison. **http://psyphz.psych. wisc.edu/**

Software for recognizing facial expression for emotion: **http://www.sciencedaily.com/releases/ 2008/02/080223125318.htm; http://mplab.ucsd.edu/~marni/Projects/CERT.htm**

Mechanisms of Social Cognition

Chris D. Frith[1,3] and Uta Frith[2,3]

[1]Wellcome Trust Center for Neuroimaging and [2]Institute of Cognitive Neuroscience, University College London, WCIN 3AR United Kingdom, and [3]Center of Functionally Integrative Neuroscience, Aarhus University, 8000 Aarhus, Denmark; email: c.frith@ucl.ac.uk, u.frith@ucl.ac.uk

Annu. Rev. Psychol. 2012. 63:287–313

First published online as a Review in Advance on August 11, 2011

The *Annual Review of Psychology* is online at psych.annualreviews.org

This article's doi: 10.1146/annurev-psych-120710-100449

0066-4308/12/0110-0287$20.00

Keywords

observational learning, imitation, reputation, teaching, mentalizing, meta-cognition

Abstract

Social animals including humans share a range of social mechanisms that are automatic and implicit and enable learning by observation. Learning from others includes imitation of actions and mirroring of emotions. Learning about others, such as their group membership and reputation, is crucial for social interactions that depend on trust. For accurate prediction of others' changeable dispositions, mentalizing is required, i.e., tracking of intentions, desires, and beliefs. Implicit mentalizing is present in infants less than one year old as well as in some nonhuman species. Explicit mentalizing is a meta-cognitive process and enhances the ability to learn about the world through self-monitoring and reflection, and may be uniquely human. Meta-cognitive processes can also exert control over automatic behavior, for instance, when short-term gains oppose long-term aims or when selfish and prosocial interests collide. We suggest that they also underlie the ability to explicitly share experiences with other agents, as in reflective discussion and teaching. These are key in increasing the accuracy of the models of the world that we construct.

Contents

INTRODUCTION

What Is Social About Social Cognition?

Consider the red-footed tortoise. These are not social animals. They live lives of almost complete isolation, apart from the brief interactions necessary for reproduction. And yet they can learn to perform a difficult detour task simply by observing an experienced conspecific (Wilkinson et al. 2010). Imagine a hive of bees. Bees are undeniably social animals.

Remarkably, their social behavior is governed by rules that allow them to share knowledge and make group decisions (Visscher 2007). Like the tortoise, human beings can learn a lot from simply observing others even when this behavior has no deliberate communicative intent and when social information is being used just like any other publicly available information in the environment (Danchin et al. 2004). But also, like bees, human beings cooperate and can make group decisions that are better than those made by individuals (Couzin 2009).

Gaining benefit by watching and interacting with conspecifics—and even other species—is widespread among animals, including humans (Galef & Laland 2005, Leadbeater & Chittka 2007). We review work that shows that by following others and by observing their choices it is possible to learn not only about places, but also about actions, objects, and other agents. This is very useful because by observing what happens to others, we can learn without experiencing potentially disastrous errors. We also discuss cognitive processes that enable deliberate communication, teaching, and cooperation but are beyond the capacities of tortoises and bees. These are processes that enable individuals to understand one another with a high degree of precision. They are often referred to as mentalizing or having a theory of mind. A largely implicit form of mentalizing is likely to be involved in perspective taking and tracking the intentional states of others, and this has been claimed for a variety of social animals as well as humans (e.g., Clayton et al. 2007). It is only the explicit form of mentalizing that appears to be unique to humans (see Apperly & Butterfill 2009 for a discussion of the two forms of mentalizing). We point out that explicit mentalizing is closely linked to meta-cognition: the ability to reflect on one's action and to think about one's own thoughts. This ability, we argue, confers significant benefits to human social cognition over and above the contribution from the many powerful implicit processes that we share with other social species. However, these abilities also have

emerged as the end result of a long evolutionary process.

The Importance of Comparative Studies

Neural mechanisms, which have evolved to allow social interaction, need to be studied systematically across species, and most of this work still remains to be done. In this review we do not go into details of such mechanisms when pertinent reviews already exist. This is the case in particular for general learning mechanisms, which are also fundamental to social learning. These involve conditioning and associative and instrumental learning (see, e.g., Schultz 2008). This comparative approach to social cognition can identify processes in common across species. It can also help identify the nature of those processes that are dramatically more highly developed in humans.

We passionately believe that social cognitive neuroscience needs to break away from a restrictive phrenology that links circumscribed brain regions to underspecified social processes. Although we build on such links, as shown in **Table 1**, we are committed to the idea that it is necessary to develop a mechanistic account of these processes. In this review we provide some pointers toward such accounts.

The Importance of Implicit Processes

One of the proudest achievements of human beings is the ability to reflect on themselves and their past, present, and future. This tends to obscure the fact that most of our cognition occurs automatically and without awareness. It comes as a surprise that even such sophisticated social processes as group decision and mentalizing can occur automatically and can happen without a deliberate attempt to achieve that decision, individually or collectively. Here we follow the tradition of cognitive psychologists who make a fundamental distinction between implicit (automatic, unconscious) processes and processes that generate explicit, conscious products (e.g.,

Mentalizing: implicit or explicit attribution of mental states to others and self (desires, beliefs) in order to explain and predict what they will do

Meta-cognition: reflection on mental states, including own mental states (introspection); others' mental states (popular psychologizing); mental states in general (philosophy of mind)

Table 1 Neural mechanisms underpinning processes relevant to social cognition*

	Mechanism	Relevant brain regions	Social processes
1. Reward learning	Updating estimated value of reward through prediction error signals, whether about primary reinforcers or money (e.g., Peters & Buchel 2010)	Ventral striatum	*Social rewards*
		Ventromedial PFC/ medial OFC	Smiling face (Lin et al. 2011)
			Gaining status (Zink et al. 2008)
			Gaining reputation (Izuma et al. 2010a)
			Agreement of others (Campbell-Meiklejohn et al. 2010)
			Being imitated (Schilbach et al. 2010)
			Observing mimicry (Kühn et al. 2010)
			Experiencing fairness & cooperation (Tabibnia & Lieberman 2007)
			Sight of cooperative person (Singer et al. 2004a)
			Reward for similar other (Mobbs et al. 2009)
			Social modulation of reward value
			Object value affected by others (Campbell-Meiklejohn et al. 2010)
			Value of cooperation modified by knowledge of intentions (Cooper et al. 2010)
2. Imitation			
Who to imitate	Orienting to agents and faces (Klein et al. 2009)	Posterior STS FFA and posterior STS	Perception of biological motion (Puce & Perrett 2003)
			Facial identity & eye gaze (Hoffman & Haxby 2000)
How to imitate	Linking observed to executed behavior via associative learning (e.g., Heyes 2011)	IFG and IPL ACC and anterior insula Lateral interparietal area	Mirroring action (Rizzolatti & Craighero 2004)
			Mirroring emotion (Singer et al. 2004b)
			Gaze following (Shepherd et al. 2009)
When to imitate	Representing the value of social information	LIP	Signaling value of gaze following (Klein et al. 2008)
3. Tracking intentions	Predictive coding: updating estimated intention through prediction, error signals relating expected to observed behavior (e.g., Kilner et al. 2007)	pSTS/TPJ (and mPFC)	*Implicit mentalizing*
			Monitoring own actions (Miele et al. 2011)
			Monitoring others' actions (Pelphrey et al. 2004, Saxe et al. 2004)
			Monitoring others' trustworthiness (Behrens et al. 2008)
			Monitoring others' generosity (Cooper et al. 2010)
			Monitoring influence on others (Hampton et al. 2008)
4. Supervisory system	Top-down biasing of competition between low-level processes (Beck & Kastner 2009)	dlPFC	Overcoming race prejudice (Cunningham et al. 2004)
			Overcoming response to unfairness (Kirk et al. 2011)
			Overriding trial-and-error learning of reputation by instructed knowledge (Li et al. 2011)
		dlPFC and ACC	Managing conflicting information about emotional states (Zaki et al. 2010)

(Continued)

Table 1 *(Continued)*

	Mechanism	Relevant brain regions	Social processes
5. Meta-cognition	Reflection on our knowledge about the mental states of self and others (Perner & Lang 1999)	mPFC	Explicit mentalizing or theory of mind (Van Overwalle 2009)
			Intentional stance (Gallagher et al. 2002)
			Mentalizing stance (Hampton et al. 2008)
			Impression formation (Mitchell et al. 2006)
			Monitoring own reputation (what others think of us) (Bengtsson et al. 2009, Izuma et al. 2010b)
	Reflection on communication		Communicative signaling (Kampe et al. 2003)
			Communicative pointing (Cleret de Langavant et al. 2011)
	Estimation of the reliability of our knowledge (Lau 2007)	Anterior PFC (BA10)	Judgment of perception (Fleming et al. 2010)
			Judgment of agency (Miele et al. 2011)
		mPFC	Judgment of strategy of others (Coricelli & Nagel 2009)
			Uncertainty about partner's strategy (Yoshida et al. 2010)

*This table is organized in terms of mechanisms and processes rather than brain regions. We have restricted our list to five mechanisms for which there is some evidence of the specific neural processes involved. We attempt to specify the mechanisms through connected brain systems rather than circumscribed brain regions. However, at this stage our knowledge is so limited that we still end up with list of brain regions. Note that since we are emphasizing mechanisms rather than localized functions, the same brain region is sometimes linked with more than one mechanism. The social processes that are enabled by the five selected mechanisms are listed in the right hand column.

Abbreviations: ACC, anterior cingulate cortex; dlPFC, dorsolateral prefrontal cortex; FFA, fusiform face area; IPL, inferior parietal lobe; mPFC, medial prefrontal cortex; OFC, orbital frontal cortex; pSTS, posterior part of the superior temporal sulcus; TPJ, temporo-parietal junction; vmPFC, ventromedial prefrontal cortex; vSTR, ventral striatum.

Kahneman & Frederick 2002). Many recent reviews of social cognition have emphasized the same distinction (Adolphs 2009), although it is by no means straightforward to categorize behavior in this way (Heyes 2011).

Explicit processes can be recognized through their interference with currently ongoing activity. Implicit processes can be recognized when people cannot report the stimulus that elicits their behavior or are unaware of the behavior that is elicited. However, many cognitive abilities that seem so evidently "explicit" actually work just as well without awareness, as shown, for instance, in Dijksterhuis's (2006) study of complex decision making. Furthermore, the study of explicit processes in nonhumans is extremely difficult (see the thoughtful discussion of this problem in relation to the study of declarative memory by Murray & Wise (2010). We certainly cannot assume that explicit cognition is unique to humans.

LEARNING THROUGH OBSERVING OTHERS

Learning About Places

Fish are among the many animals that learn about the location of food by observing the behavior of others. Here is an example. An individual, isolated nine-spined stickleback learns that food can be found on the left side of a tank (private information) and will therefore swim to the left when given the choice. But, after a delay of seven days, if he can observe other fish feeding on the right side of the tank (public information), he will swim to the right (van Bergen et al. 2004). This is presumably because the private information the fish has about food being on the left is now too old and unreliable. Examples of social influence on foraging behavior can be observed in many other animals (Galef & Giraldeau 2001), including humans.

A related process is gaze following, through which we automatically look at the place toward which someone else is looking. This example of social influence has been demonstrated in ravens, goats, dogs, and primates (reviewed in Zuberbühler 2008). Gaze following is reliably used by human infants to learn about objects and events from around one year of age (Flom & Johnson 2011). In adult humans, gaze following seems to be automatic, in the sense that people follow the gaze of another person even when this behavior runs counter to their intentions. Bayliss & Tipper (2006) used a target-detection task to show that individuals would follow the gaze of another person even when that person persistently looked in the wrong direction. Intriguingly, although participants were unable to stop themselves in their gaze following and were unaware of the contingency, they did register a socially relevant fact: They rated the person who looked in the wrong direction as less trustworthy.

Learning About Objects

Animals need to distinguish between nice objects that should be approached and dangerous objects that should be avoided. Here again, learning commonly occurs through observation. For example, in a series of experiments, Mineka and colleagues have demonstrated that rhesus monkeys acquire a fear of snakes very quickly by observing another monkey showing fear toward a snake (see, e.g., Mineka & Ohman 2002). Fear conditioning through observation has also been demonstrated in humans (Olsson et al. 2007). But learning about objects is not just restricted to fear conditioning. For example, objects looked at by other people are preferred more than objects that do not receive attention (Bayliss et al. 2006).

Learning About Actions

Many animals learn which actions to perform by observing others (Huber et al. 2009). For example, chimpanzees will imitate a demonstrated sequence of actions to gain access to food in a puzzle box (see Whiten et al. 2009). Wild mongoose pups learned, by observing an adult, to open plastic containers of food (modified Kinder eggs) by either smashing them on the ground or biting them (Müller & Cant 2010). Both actions are equally effective at getting access to the food inside the container. However, the action chosen by the pups was determined by what they saw the adult do. Such imitative learning can also be seen in human infants from around the age of one year (e.g., Carpenter et al. 1998). By this age infants will imitate both instrumental and arbitrary actions when they see an adult interacting with a novel object. For example, they quickly learn that they can press buttons on remote controls and phones with remarkable ease.

Learning About Agents

How do animals distinguish agents from objects? Agents move of their own intention and have motion patterns that are different from moving physical objects. Specific brain structures in the temporal lobe are involved in detecting this difference. Thus, in humans, perception of biological motion is subserved by a circumscribed brain region, the posterior part of the superior temporal sulcus (pSTS; Puce & Perrett 2003; see **Table 1**), and the ability to distinguish this motion from other kinds of motion is exquisitely tuned.

Over and above detecting animacy, animals need the ability to detect agents who might be friend or foe. This is critical for survival even immediately after birth. One would therefore expect to see specially adapted neural mechanisms that require little if any learning. Indeed, newly hatched chicks exhibit a spontaneous preference for biological motion patterns, and this mechanism facilitates imprinting (Vallortigara et al. 2005).

Agents also typically have faces, and their eyes give cues to what they are interested in. A posterior region of STS is specialized for analysis of facial movements, while invariant aspects of faces are analyzed in the fusiform gyrus [fusiform face area (FFA)] (Haxby et al. 2000; see **Table 1**).

Another important cue to agency is contingent responding. Human infants and adults alike are likely to treat a shapeless object as being animate if the object moves or makes noises that are contingent on their own actions (Johnson 2003). Learning about other individuals and how to interact with them is vital for all social animals. This is most particularly relevant for mate choice. Naïve female fruit flies will choose as partners male flies they have seen mating with experienced females (Mery et al. 2009). Effects of observation on mate choice are also seen in guppies and quail (White 2004).

Well-disposed agents need to be distinguished from those who are not. Pre-verbal human infants (aged 6 to 10 months), after observing agents interacting with each other, prefer those who help others to those who hinder others (e.g., Jacob & Dupoux 2008). Learning about the status of conspecifics is also important for knowing whom to approach and whom to avoid. Many animals can infer social rank by observation alone. For instance, fish learn whom not to pick a fight with through observation (Grosenick et al. 2007).

NEURAL MECHANISMS OF LEARNING THROUGH OBSERVATION

Association Learning

It seems plausible that learning through observation (see **Table 1**) could be built from the basic mechanisms of association learning (Catmur et al. 2010). Mineka & Cook (1993) report that the model monkey's behavior on seeing a snake elicits fear in the observer monkey. For the observer monkey, the fear response of the model monkey acts as an unconditioned stimulus (through emotional contagion) and elicits the fear response. Through classical conditioning the snake becomes associated with the fear response in the observer monkey. Note, however, that classical conditioning has strict limitations

forged by evolution (Breland & Breland 1961). Thus, a potentially dangerous thing like a snake readily triggers conditioning of the fear response in the observer monkey but an innocuous flower does not (Cook & Mineka 1989).

Fear conditioning through observation in humans presumably uses the same mechanism (Olsson & Phelps 2004). It can occur even when the conditioned stimulus is presented subliminally, which suggests that the learning depends on an implicit process. Indeed, we suspect that most, if not all, of the learning processes we have discussed so far are examples of implicit processes.

Reward Learning

Conditioning mechanisms can be applied to other kinds of social learning through observation. We know that places and objects acquire value through being associated with reward. We go to the places and approach the objects with the highest value. A simple extension of this mechanism would entail that places and objects should gain value if they are approached by others and lose value if they are avoided by others. Evidence for such a simple model comes from the finding that in many species including fish and rodents, the probability that an observer will adopt a particular behavior increases monotonically with the proportion of potential models exhibiting that behavior (Pike & Laland 2010).

Social learning seems to involve the same neural systems as nonsocial reward-based learning. Lin and colleagues (2011) have shown that learning for social rewards involves the same neural system as learning for money, with values being represented in ventromedial prefrontal cortex (vmPFC) and reward prediction errors being represented in the ventral striatum (vSTR). Furthermore, this same reward-learning system is activated when we see others choosing the objects we like. Neural signals in this system that reflect how much we value an object increase when we know that others also value this object (Campbell-Meiklejohn et al. 2010; see **Table 1**).

vmPFC: ventromedial prefrontal cortex

vSTR: ventral striatum

Gaze Following

Investigations of the neural basis of gaze following indicate something of the complexity of the mechanisms involved when we imitate actions (Klein et al. 2009). At least three highly automatic components are necessary. The observer must first recognize an agent and orient toward the face and eyes. This is probably mediated by a long-established subcortical route. The observer must then work out the target of the gaze from the position of the agent's eyes. It is not sufficient simply to imitate the eye movement since the observer and the agent have different viewpoints. The lateral interparietal area (LIP), a brain region previously linked to attention and saccade planning, is likely to have a role in this computation. Mirror neurons have been located here, which fire when a monkey looks in the preferred direction of the neuron and also when observed monkeys look in this direction (Shepherd et al. 2009). In addition, the observer must believe that gaze following is likely to lead to a valuable outcome. Here again LIP neurons seem relevant because they signal the value of social (and nonsocial) information, but only when this information is relevant to decisions about orienting (Klein et al. 2008).

Mirroring

The aspect of learning through observation that has been most extensively investigated at the neural level relates to action. When we learn about actions from observing others, we are effectively learning to copy them. Forms of copying are often referred to as imitation, mimicry, and emulation, each emphasizing different aspects of copying a model. The process underlying these forms of copying has recently been reinterpreted as a direct result of a specifically social neural mechanism associated with mirror neurons. Rizzolatti & Craighero (2004) were the first to identify such neurons in the ventral premotor cortex (F5) of the rhesus monkey. Although there is still some controversy about the role of this mechanism as a facilitator or a product of imitation (Heyes 2001), the

discovery of mirror neurons has had a major impact on our understanding of the nature and role of imitation. The tendency to imitate the actions of others is likely to be automatic. This is shown by the finding that a high working-memory load facilitates rather than hinders behavioral imitation (van Leeuwen et al. 2009). Nevertheless, imitation can be controlled in a top-down fashion, and we do not imitate the actions of everyone we observe (Spengler et al. 2010).

Perceiving an emotional response of another person elicits the same emotional response in ourselves. This is also called emotional contagion and allows us to share the emotion of the person we are observing (de Vignemont & Singer 2006), a prerequisite of empathy. Emotional contagion supplies a basic conditioning mechanism through which we can learn from others on the basis of their emotional expressions.

COSTS AND BENEFITS OF OBSERVATIONAL LEARNING

Self-Interest and Copying

How important is observational learning in comparison with nonsocial alternatives such as trial-and-error learning? Laland and colleagues (Rendell et al. 2010) assessed this question by means of a computer tournament in which participants proposed strategies for combining learning by observation (copying) with learning by direct experience (trial and error) in order to acquire adaptive behavior in a complex environment. The most successful strategy relied almost exclusively on copying. Why was copying so successful in this context? First, the observer avoids having to make errors that are an essential part of trial-and-error learning. In addition, demonstrators selectively perform the actions that they have found to be most beneficial for themselves. Therefore, they effectively and inadvertently act as a filter to provide the information that is most useful for an observer. Copying is a highly adaptive means of gaining knowledge (Rendell et al. 2010).

Imitation: used in automatic learning by observation, including repeating the actions (mimicry) and aiming for the goals of another agent (emulation)

Prosocial Effects of Copying

While learning from observation can serve purely short-term self-interest, contagion and copying can also bias us toward the long-term interests of our group (which also serves self-interest). This effect is seen in experiments that reveal subtle effects of copying. If we are covertly mimicked, we tend to like that person. Furthermore, we become more helpful to people in general (van Baaren et al. 2004). Similar effects have been demonstrated in monkeys, who are more likely to approach and share food with an imitator (Paukner et al. 2009). These effects are likely to be unconscious. In contrast, when people are aware that they are being imitated (see Bailenson et al. 2008), they experience high levels of discomfort and thus the prosocial effects do not occur. At the neural level there is evidence that mimicry is rewarding. When we observe someone else being imitated, activity increases in reward-related regions such as vmPFC (Kühn et al. 2010). When others choose the same song that we have just chosen ourselves, because we liked it, a reward area of our brain is activated. Furthermore it is exactly the same area in the vSTR that is activated when we actually receive the desired song (Campbell-Meiklejohn et al. 2010). Thus, there is reward in being endorsed by others, and this may result in reinforcing group-oriented behavior and conformity.

When is it a good idea to stop learning by observation and learn instead by trial and error? This will depend upon an implicit cost-benefit analysis. As long as our own knowledge is sufficient for achieving success (e.g., knowing the location of a food source), we will continue to exploit that knowledge. Once that knowledge becomes unreliable (e.g., the food source at that location is depleted), we switch to learning by observing others. Finally, when the knowledge acquired by observation becomes unreliable, we start to explore innovative choices on our own (Laland 2004). This is an extension into the social world of the exploit/explore dichotomy developed in models of reinforcement learning (Sutton

& Barto 1998). In observational learning, this may become a trichotomy of exploit own knowledge–exploit others' knowledge–explore.

Alignment

A necessary consequence of learning by observation is the formation of behavioral similarity across a population. This is most obviously the case when learning about actions. When we interact with others, we often automatically imitate their behavior (Chartrand & Bargh 1999). In the case of verbal interactions this alignment can occur at many levels. During a productive discourse, speakers will automatically tend to align their posture, their speech rate, their choice of words, and their syntactic forms (Garrod & Pickering 2009). This alignment enhances communication (e.g., Adank et al. 2010). But language does not always have to be involved. Alignment has a similar advantage for any joint action, where two players need to coordinate their behavior (Sebanz et al. 2006). Alignment in synchronized tapping can be manifest in mutual adjustments occurring at the level of 1 or 2 ms (Konvalinka et al. 2010).

Group Decisions

Social insects, such as ants and bees, make successful group decisions by collating information from several individuals (Couzin 2009). One way in which such group decisions can be achieved relies on learning through observation, e.g., the process through which a swarm of honeybees uses information from scouts to locate a new nesting site (Visscher 2007).

The mechanism by which a group decision can be made in the absence of any central coordination is an example of the more general principle of herding, through which complex group behavior can emerge from simple local interactions, which can occur automatically and without awareness (Raafat et al. 2009). In humans, Dyer and colleagues (2008) have shown how a few informed individuals, the equivalent of scouts in the case of bees, can guide a group to a target without verbal communication or any obvious signaling.

Group Identity

There is a value to learning about people as types as opposed to people as individuals. It provides prior knowledge to guide our behavior when confronted with someone we have never met before. Inevitably, this prior knowledge feeds into stereotypes and prejudices, and these play a major role in in-group cohesion and, conversely, in out-group hostility.

A child might observe her mother being gracious when approached by a member of an in-group and ungracious when approached by a member of an out-group. Thus, through emotional contagion, human infants can learn to favor members of the in-group. The use of stereotypes is already present by age three (Hirschfeld 1996). At the neural level, prejudice and stereotyping are likely to be underpinned by brain areas associated with evaluative processing (vmPFC and amygdala; Quadflieg et al. 2009). As mentioned already, conformity itself is rewarding and thus may provide a basis for both producing and confirming stereotypic behavior (Richerson & Boyd 2001).

Of great relevance for the study of group conformity is "overimitation." Children and chimpanzees have been studied when they learn, by observation, how to open a puzzle box to get a reward. The model in these studies performs additional actions that are irrelevant for getting to the reward. Nevertheless, children of three to five years persist in imitating the irrelevant actions, even in situations when there are countervailing task demands and even in the face of direct warnings (Lyons et al. 2011). Adults perform the task with even more emphasis on conformity with the irrelevant actions (McGuigan et al. 2011). Chimpanzees, on the other hand, are much less likely to imitate the irrelevant components of the action and go to the reward as quickly as possible (Horner & Whiten 2005). The faithful copying of actions, which overrides getting a primary reward

by other means, is a striking feature of human culture and provides a means for creating distinct group identities, emphasizing not so much what we do but rather the way we do it.

LEARNING ABOUT OTHER MINDS

Taking Account of Other Individuals

Arguably the most important and valuable aspect of social cognition is learning about other agents not just as types but also as individuals. Stereotypes often result in inaccurate predictions and do not take account of changeable predispositions. The relevant cognitive processes in dyadic interactions have been extensively investigated by social psychologists, and an account of their likely neural basis can be found in a review by Liebermann and colleagues (2002). Here we consider changeable attributes of others, such as their current status and their beliefs, knowledge, and intentions, all attributes that need to be continually updated.

How is it possible to keep track of the status of several individuals at the same time? The term "keeping track of" is a spatial metaphor. However, it may actually reflect the evolutionary origins of the mechanism involved. Many animal species, including, for example, monkeys and dolphins, emit sounds as they move about in groups, foraging for food (see Boinski & Garber 2000 for many examples). It is important for their survival that everyone in the group keeps in close contact, but they cannot necessarily see each other. The problem can be solved if all the group members emit frequent calls. If these calls are sufficiently individualistic, then each member of the group knows roughly where the other individuals are. The implication of this idea is that each individual has an internal map of the relative locations of the other members of the group that is continually updated.

A similar principle can be applied to aspects of individuals in the group other than their positions in space. For example, the relative status of the individuals in a group can be represented spatially by distances along a line. For humans at least, status does seem to be represented this way. Differences in both numerical magnitude and social status scale with activity in the inferior parietal cortex (Chiao et al. 2009). Knowledge of status also helps us to keep track of who is currently allied with whom (Fiske 2010). We also need to keep track of who has the most relevant knowledge. Young children at first are mainly concerned with learning by observing their parents, whom they trust implicitly. However, from about age eight, they switch to copying the local expert instead (Henrich & Broesch 2011).

Tracking Past Behavior to Predict Future Actions

The human face provides many clues as to how a person will behave. First there is the emotional expression that is reflected in the continually changing configuration of a face. From this information we can tell whether a person is fearful or happy even if we have never met that person before. Many studies have now demonstrated that this can happen in the absence of any awareness of the expression (e.g., Dimberg et al. 2000). Another kind of information can also be inferred from the faces of unfamiliar people through fixed configurations of the face, such as the width of the jaw. This information relates to dispositions such as dominance and trustworthiness (Oosterhof & Todorov 2008).

The third kind of information relates to the faces of people we know. When we recognize that this is the face of Fred, we know from past experience with this individual how he is likely to behave. Through our interactions we continually update this knowledge, and it is our knowledge of the person that is more important than his facial appearance (Todorov et al. 2007).

There is some validity to the beliefs we have about the personality of our friends. There is much greater agreement between close acquaintances about the personality traits of an individual (and with the individual's self-ratings) than between strangers who have interacted

with the individual only once (Funder & Colvin 1988). This ability may depend on association learning mechanisms through which we locate everyone we know in a "personality space," with these locations being continually updated (Todorov 2011).

We also implicitly learn from subtle cues in social interactions. Imagine playing the game of stone-paper-scissors. In some cases, the behavior of your opponent enables you to predict what his response would be. For example, a very brief eyebrow movement might consistently precede the choice of stone. Participants can learn to use such a cue because it makes them more likely to win on these trials (Heerey & Velani 2010). This effect was observed even when participants had no idea which cue had been predictive, as revealed in a debriefing session after the game.

Learning about people can certainly occur without awareness (see also Todorov & Uleman 2003). Such learning is likely to be procedural and semantic (i.e., association learning) rather than episodic. This is suggested by the observation that patients with amnesia associated with hippocampal damage can still acquire person knowledge, but only if the damage does not extend into the amygdala and the temporal pole (Todorov & Olson 2008).

There is also some evidence that person knowledge is accessed automatically whenever we see a familiar face (Todorov et al. 2007). If a particular kind of behavior has been associated with a particular face, then the mere presentation of that face elicits stronger brain activity compared with a novel face. Such activity was observed in anterior paracingulate cortex and the STS regardless of the nature of the specific behavior associated with the face. We speculate that this reflects taking an intentional stance toward people we know (see **Table 1**). As yet, however, we lack models of how person representations are rapidly updated in the brain.

Reputation and Audience Effect

Species whose interactions are characterized by indirect reciprocity benefit from keeping track of reputation. They are more likely to cooperate with a partner who has a reputation for cooperativeness. For example, clients of the reef cleaner fish, *labroides dimidiatus*, eavesdrop on cleaning sessions and spend more time next to cleaners known to be cooperative. Furthermore, the cleaners behave more cooperatively when they are being observed (Bshary & Grutter 2006).

The audience effect means that we behave differently when we believe ourselves to be observed. For example, to ensure that others will continue to cooperate with us we need to maintain our own reputation for being cooperative (Tennie et al. 2010). Cooperative behavior rapidly declines in trust games where the players are anonymous (Milinski et al. 2002). Under conditions of anonymity, there is no longer any need to guard one's reputation. On the other hand, a watching pair of eyes, even in the form of a photograph, is sufficient to increase prosocial behavior (Bateson et al. 2006). This is presumably an automatic effect because people would be well aware that a photograph cannot record their behavior or damage their reputation.

The evidence for audience effects in cleaner fish suggests that these effects need not depend upon complex cognitive processes. However, such high-level processes are likely to have an additional role in humans (Bshary & Bergmuller 2008). Social psychologists have long studied the processes by which the presence of an audience improves performance (Zajonc 1965). This may in part be due to an increase in arousal when others are present, but there is also evidence that the presence of others increases reflective self-focus and attention to ideal behavioral standards (Carver & Scheier 1981).

How do humans keep track of the trustworthiness of others? This question has been investigated using economic games, such as iterated prisoner's dilemma or trust games. These studies show that the brain's reward system [vSTR and medial orbitofrontal cortex (mOFC)] (see **Table 1**) is activated by reciprocated cooperation (Rilling et al. 2004) and also by fair behavior (Tabibnia et al. 2008). Participants in

the study of Phan and colleagues (2010) rapidly learned about the cooperativeness and fairness of the people they were playing with during a trust game involving iterative exchanges. Positive reciprocity robustly activated vSTR and mOFC. In an earlier study by Singer and colleagues (2004a) using a similar paradigm, the mere presentation of the face of a cooperative partner elicited activity in reward areas. Izuma and colleagues (2010b) scanned participants while they made self-disclosures. Activity in medial prefrontal cortex (mPFC) during self-disclosure was greatly enhanced by the presence of an audience, as was activity in vSTR.

It seems plausible from these observations that we keep track of others' reputation for cooperativeness on the basis of the same fundamental learning mechanisms that we use to learn about objects. Behrens and colleagues (2008) specifically investigated the mechanism by which we update this knowledge. This was a learning study, where a human advisor provided information about where a reward was likely to be found. However, the reliability of the advice was continually varied. The results suggest that the same computational mechanism was engaged for tracking the location of the reward as for tracking the reliability of the advisor: associative learning updated through prediction errors. However, whereas prediction errors associated with reward learning were associated with activity in the vSTR, those relating to social learning were associated with activity in mPFC and temporo-parietal junction (TPJ), regions previously associated with mentalizing (i.e., the ability to attribute mental states to others) (Van Overwalle 2009; see **Table 1**).

Tracking Mental States

Although experience of their past behavior can help us to predict what people are likely to do next in various situations, we can do better. It is extremely useful to know something about their current intentions, desires, knowledge, and beliefs. Because these mental states are variable, keeping track of them enhances the accuracy of our predictions. For example, people will not reach for something they cannot see, and their actions will be determined more by what they know, i.e., believe to be the case rather than what is actually the case. Thus, for successful interactions, it pays to keep track of people's continually changing inner states relating to their goals and their knowledge. There is increasing evidence that keeping track of these mental states also occurs automatically and without the need for awareness.

Tracking Other Points of View

Samson, Apperly, and their colleagues (2010) have shown that observers were slowed down when they had to report the number of dots visible to them in the presence of another agent who could not see all of these dots. In fact, the other agent was an avatar placed in a schematic room with variable numbers of dots on its walls. This result suggests that we automatically take note of the fact that others may have knowledge that differs from our own knowledge due to their different point of view. The idea that this process is automatic was confirmed by a subsequent experiment looking at the effects of cognitive load (Qureshi et al. 2010). Here, the addition of a cognitive load did not stop participants from automatically taking note of the avatar's perspective. However, cognitive load did impair participants' capacity to switch between their own and the avatar's perspective when they were explicitly required to do so. Remarkably, while we automatically keep track of the knowledge of others, it requires cognitive effort to deliberately take their perspective. Awareness into this deliberate process dawns between the ages of two and four years (Flavell 1992).

Tracking False Beliefs

There is evidence that it is possible not only to automatically keep track of what other people see but also what they (invisible to the eye) believe. The critical insight here is the recognition that people's behavior is determined by their beliefs rather than by physical reality,

even if this belief happens to be false. This insight is a result of mentalizing or having a theory of mind. Although the latter label suggests a conscious process, it is important to bear in mind that there is both an implicit and an explicit version of theory of mind, and this is why we prefer the term mentalizing. Why is it useful to track other people's beliefs about the state of the world? This knowledge allows you to predict what they are going to do much better than if you used your own belief about the world. Children from around the age of four to six years are aware that own beliefs and others' beliefs of the same state of affairs can be interestingly different (Wellman et al. 2001). They can also work out implications. With greater experience, adolescents and adults are increasingly able to manipulate other people's beliefs, for instance through persuasion or deception.

There is now evidence that already in the first and second year of life infants have an implicit recognition of false belief (Kovács et al. 2010). These results suggest that infants (and adults) automatically note when someone has a different belief from themselves. There is also increasing evidence for the ability to keep track of the knowledge of others in nonhuman animals including birds (e.g., Bugnyar 2011), although there is still controversy to what extent this is the case for chimpanzees (Call & Tomasello 2008).

As yet we know very little about the physiological underpinnings of the implicit processes by which we keep track of the mental states of others. There is a large literature on mentalizing tasks implicating mPFC and TPJ/pSTS (e.g., Van Overwalle 2009), but all of these studies involve explicit processes. There are also several studies on visual perspective taking. Many of these also implicate TPJ (see Spengler et al. 2010 for a useful review of links between perspective taking and mentalizing) but, here again, only for explicit processes.

The mechanisms underlying mentalizing are likely to involve the same predictive coding principles as are involved in vision (Kilner et al. 2007). On the basis of an estimated intention, the behavior of the agent is predicted. The estimated intention can then be updated on the basis of prediction errors. Activity in pSTS reflects such prediction errors (e.g., Behrens et al. 2008). Mechanisms that support explicit forms of mentalizing probably differ from those involved in implicit forms, but systematic distinctions between these forms have yet to be delineated (Apperly & Butterfill 2009).

COSTS AND BENEFITS OF LEARNING ABOUT OTHER MINDS

The Dark Side of Mentalizing

Corvids, who show implicit mentalizing, use this ability in selfish and antisocial ways: Its main purpose seems to be to avoid sharing food with other corvids (Clayton et al. 2007). There are many parallels in human societies. Getting the better of others through scheming and lying is typical for human societies, and Machiavellianism has been used to describe the main outcome of mentalizing (Byrne & Whiten 1988). However, at the same time, mentalizing abilities, both implicit and explicit, are used in the service of reciprocal communication and cooperation.

Helping Behavior

Helping is extremely widespread among social animals and does not depend on keeping track of others' mental states. However, human infants show evidence of a more refined and flexible helping behavior. For example, infants of 18 months spontaneously helped an adult by opening a cupboard door when the adult's hands were full (Warneken & Tomasello 2006). Chimpanzees also showed some evidence of this kind of helping behavior, but in a much reduced form. In another study, Liszkowski et al. (2007) showed that infants age 12 months would point more often to an object whose location an adult did not know than to an object whose location was known. Again, such helpful actions depend upon infants keeping track of what others know.

Mutual Trust

One of the main socially beneficial effects of keeping track of other minds is enhanced and flexible cooperation. As predicted by formal evolutionary theory (Axelrod & Hamilton 1981), we seem to expect, at least to start with, that our partner in a game will be cooperative (Andreoni & Miller 1993). Furthermore, if trust can be established, then players will do better. The mechanism underlying trust building through tracking of partners' intentions to cooperate has been studied using the model of Rousseau's stag and rabbit hunt game (Skyrms 2003). In this game a small reward is gained by catching a rabbit, and this can be obtained regardless of what the other person does. A much bigger reward can be obtained by catching a stag, and this reward is obtained only if both partners choose to cooperate. But there is always the risk that one partner will not cooperate. Successful cooperation in this game depends upon players making inferences about the beliefs of their partner and also making inferences about what their partner believes about them, e.g., they believe that their partner will cooperate when their partner believes that they will cooperate. This is an example of the recursive process that seems to lie at the heart of many human social interactions.

According to a recently developed computational model of this game, players need to estimate the depth of inference being made by their partner in order to optimize success (i.e., achieve cooperation; Yoshida et al. 2008). This suggests that the model is also relevant to reciprocal communication. We have referred to this as "closing the loop" (Frith 2007). Reciprocal communication plays an important role in teaching, as both teacher and learner need to keep track of the differences in their state of knowledge. However, whether these processes are implicit or explicit remains to be determined. A scanning study (Yoshida et al. 2010) found that activity in mPFC was related to participants' uncertainty about their partner's depth of inference. We believe that the approach offered by computational functional magnetic resonance imaging using models such as the one applied to the stag hunt game could lead to a much more precise formulation of the role of the brain regions involved in mentalizing.

EXPLICIT PROCESSES IN SOCIAL COGNITION AND THEIR MECHANISMS

Clearly, many processes associated with social cognition occur automatically and without awareness. We have shown that these are typically present in many species including humans and are also present in very young human infants. What is there left to do for explicit processes? We suggest a particular role for explicit processes in fostering social interactions, which may be unique to humans. These processes are characterized not simply by awareness but also by reflective awareness. By this we mean the meta-cognitive ability to think about our thinking. We argue that it is through reflective awareness that humans manage to outstrip the performance of other social species.

Top-Down Modulation of Competing Implicit Processes

It is a truism that our senses are bombarded by many signals, from which just a few must be selected for controlling our actions. This selection can be achieved bottom-up by direct competition between the many different signals. However, it can also be achieved top-down by prior biases that are applied to some signals and not to others. This is the biased competition model, whose neural basis has been analyzed in some detail (see Beck & Kastner 2009). The same principles as apply to physical information about the world also apply to social information.

Executive Control of Social Cognition

There is continual competition between the various implicit processes relevant to social interactions, such as self-interest versus group interest or short-term gain versus long-term gain. This competition can also be biased by top-down, executive processes.

One important role for these executive processes is to overcome biases such as race prejudice. We all tend to have an implicit fear of out-group members (Phelps et al. 2000) and fail to show empathy for people in the out-group (e.g., Avenanti et al. 2010). For example, if white observers are shown the faces of unknown black people for 30 ms, activity is typically elicited in the amygdala. That this result occurs with such a short presentation time suggests that the processing of the face occurs without awareness. Furthermore, the amygdala activity is correlated with measures of the strength of the observer's implicit race prejudice. However, if the faces are shown for 525 ms, then activity is elicited in dorsolateral prefrontal cortex (dlPFC), and the amygdala response is reduced (Cunningham et al. 2004). This result suggests that explicit executive processes, instantiated in frontal cortex, can modulate the automatic evaluation of people.

More direct evidence for a role for executive processes in resolving conflicts between different social processes comes from a study by Zaki and colleagues (2010). Participants were scanned while making inferences about the emotional states of agents. Relevant information was available from two sources: silent video clips of people depicting positive or negative autobiographical events and written sentences describing such events. The idea was that the video clips would activate the brain's mirror system while the sentences would engage the brain's mentalizing system. The pattern of brain activity associated with these different cues confirmed this expectation. In the incongruent condition, activity was elicited in areas associated with executive control [dlPFC and anterior cingulate cortex (ACC)], and there was also evidence that this control was associated with biasing toward a participant's preferred source of information. These results demonstrate that social processes are subject to top-down executive control using the same mechanisms as nonsocial processes (see **Table 1**).

dlPFC: dorsolateral prefrontal cortex

ACC: anterior cingulate cortex

Verbal Instruction

Ostensive gestures: deliberately signaling the intention to communicate; signals can be verbal (call, prosody) and nonverbal (look, touch)

Just as we can learn by observing others, we can also learn from what others tell us. Work from Milinski's group shows that reputation, conveyed through word of mouth, can have a strong effect on group behavior. In a trust game an effect was found even when participants could access the same information by direct observation (Sommerfeld et al. 2007). The same effect can be observed at the neural level. Delgado and colleagues (2005) found that participants would make more risky investment choices with partners when they had been told that the partners had a good reputation. In addition, in this case the activation in the caudate nucleus that normally reflects whether the partner cooperates or defects on a trial-by-trial basis was significantly reduced. The indirect spreading of information about others is known as gossip and is an important part of human communication (Spacks 1982). It seems that gossip reduces our reliance on the feedback mechanisms underlying trial-and-error learning, as is typical of a top-down mechanism (Li et al. 2011).

Verbal instruction can also affect how we respond to objects, not just people. The instruction "When you see the blue square, you will receive at least one shock" is sufficient to induce fear of the blue square. But, in this case, the feared object does not elicit a response when presented subliminally (Olsson & Phelps 2007). It seems that learning through verbal instruction depends upon explicit top-down brain processes. These do not establish an automatic response to objects that we believe to be threatening but of which we have no direct experience.

Teaching

Most human learning arguably occurs through deliberate teaching rather than mere observation and is greatly dependent on the use of language. However, the human advantage of learning from a teacher extends even to situations in which language is not involved.

Teaching, in a broad sense understood as actively helping a learner to benefit from the teacher's experience, has been observed in a variety of animals including ants and bees (Hoppitt et al. 2008). Meerkats provide a vivid example (Thornton & Clutton-Brock 2011). To kill and eat a scorpion without being stung requires considerable skill. So the mother prepares this food in line with her pups' gradually increasing abilities. At first, mothers find and kill scorpions, then bring them to the pups. As the young meerkats grow up, their mothers disable the scorpions rather than killing them. They remove their deadly sting and then present the live scorpion. Through such teaching, the young meerkats eventually learn to kill a scorpion. This kind of instruction does not depend on keeping track of constantly changing mental states. Instead it is finely attuned to the physical states of the pups, which are signaled by the pitch of their vocalization. It is this vocalization that triggers the adult's food preparation behavior.

We would argue that in humans the continuous tracking of mental states enables a more flexible type of instruction (referred to as natural pedagogy; Csibra & Gergely 2006). In adult-child interactions in particular, deliberate and explicit teaching occurs, with both adult and child knowing when teaching is intended. This usually involves ostensive gestures, such as eye contact or the high-pitched speech mode of "motherese" (Senju & Csibra 2008). In such interactions the child is not simply learning by observation. A shared intention has been formed between the adult, the child, and—importantly—also the object of their intention. Intriguingly, we all expect, infants included, that we are taught something important about the object, not about a fleeting and precise moment of interpersonal interaction. In this way we are continuously teaching each other and learning from each other about the world.

Teaching here is a cooperative activity of which social games would also be examples. In a study by Warneken and colleagues (2006), 18- to 24-month-old children engaged in cooperative games with adults. At one point in these games the adult partner stopped participating. All of the children made at least one communicative attempt to re-engage the adult. Here it is the child rather than the adult who is using an ostensive gesture to restart the interaction. In contrast to human children, the chimpanzees in this study never made any communicative attempt to re-engage their partner.

We are aware of only two explorations of the neural basis of ostensive, communicative gestures. In our group, Kampe et al. (2003) found that both eye contact with a participant and calling the participant's name elicited activity in anterior rostral medial prefrontal cortex and in the temporal poles, both regions associated with mentalizing. Another study investigated brain activity elicited when individuals communicated through pointing at an object compared with just pointing at an object without the intention to communicate (Cleret de Langavant et al. 2011). In this study, when pointing was communicative, the pointers subtly altered their behavior to take account of the point of view of the observer. The brain regions specifically activated by communicative pointing were right pSTS and right mPFC.

As we have seen, activity in mMPFC seems to be elicited in many different situations when we need to think about mental states. In a study by Mitchell and colleagues (2006), participants were presented with a series of sentences describing a person. Some of these sentences were informative as to the personality of the person ("he turned down three parties to study for organic chemistry") whereas others were not ("he photocopied the article"). When the task was to form an impression of the person, both kinds of sentence elicited activity in MPFC. However, when the task was simply to remember the order of the people, only the sentences relevant to personality activated MPFC. We speculate that the instruction to form an impression was a form of ostensive signal, indicating that the sentences that followed would be relevant to this task. The activity in the MPFC reflects the adoption by participants of a mentalizing stance toward all subsequent information. In the absence of such an instruction, only the sentences about personality elicited this stance. This is consistent with the idea that MPFC has a high-level role in top-down biasing toward treating information as socially relevant. This speculation is also consistent with the various studies in which greater activity was elicited in MPFC when subjects were told that they were interacting with a person rather than a computer (e.g., Gallagher et al. 2002).

An even more specific role for this brain region, consistent with its activation by ostensive gestures and by the presence of an audience, might be in linking mental states of the self and the partner during communicative interactions (Amodio & Frith 2006). In line with these observations, Saxe (2006) has suggested that cognitive processes supported by mPFC may be a uniquely human form of social cognition (see **Table 1**).

SHARING EXPERIENCES: THE IMPORTANCE OF META-COGNITION

Reflective Discussion

We have suggested that there is an important distinction between learning through observation of others, which can occur without explicit awareness, and learning through explicit communication with others. We have discussed gossip, through which we learn about the reputation of others, and instruction, through which we are taught about objects in the world. In this final section we discuss another major topic of explicit communicative interactions. We refer to it as reflective discussion. We frequently talk to each other about our mental states, describing our sensory experiences and justifying our decisions. Such interactions would be impossible without a special high-level ability, meta-cognition, which may well be uniquely human (Metcalfe 2008). Meta-cognition is the ability to reflect upon our mental states and describe these states to others. This self-reflection requires taking a step away from the representations of the world and of other people, and this step appears to be a mental "decoupling" (Leslie 1987). We are normally unaware of our representations of the world. Instead, we take for granted that the world is an open book

Reflective discussion: mutual communication of meta-cognitive knowledge; comparison of confidence in own perception increases joint performance

directly accessible to our experience (Frith 2007). Meta-cognition allows reflection and can give us a rare glimpse into the fragility of our mental world. This makes it possible for us to recognize representations as just that, representations (Perner 1991). From this it follows that other minds may have different representations, and even more startling, that our representations of the world might be illusory or false. Since we all are able to have these insights, we can discuss them. Thus, reflective discussions enable us to compare our views of the world and to create improved shared views of the world. In this way meta-cognition has a vital role in the generation of cultural values and institutions.

Reflective Discussion of Action Changes Behavior

A major feature of our mental life involves the vivid experience of being in control of our actions and choosing one option rather than another. Yet, this experience seems to be largely post hoc and has little to do with actual control. We believe that the value of this experience arises because we can discuss the sources of our actions with others (Frith 2010). People readily explain and justify their decisions, even though these explanations and justifications may be inaccurate and self-serving. Johansson and colleagues (2005) have shown how readily people will justify a choice even when, unbeknown to them, it was not the choice they actually made. The importance of such discussions with other people is that they enable us to understand better the factors that determine our own decisions and can change the way we make decisions in the future (e.g., Vohs & Schooler 2008).

Reflective Discussion of Sensations Creates a More Accurate Model of the World

In humans the explicit meta-cognitive process of sharing sensory experience enables pairs of participants to enhance their perception of basic sensory signals, even beyond the abilities of the better member of the pair. In our group,

Bahrami and colleagues (2010) studied pairs of participants collaborating in the performance of a signal detection task. If the pair disagreed as to when the signal was presented, then they had to come up with a joint decision through discussion. As long as the members of the dyad had relatively similar perceptual abilities, the group performance was significantly better than the better member of the pair. Furthermore, this group advantage critically depended upon the occurrence of the discussion. We believe that this advantage depends on one or all of the following components. First, the partners need to reflect on their performance; second, they need to be able to convey to each other their confidence in what they have observed, and third, they have to be able to compare their reflections.

The Neural Basis of Meta-Cognition

The exploration of the neural basis of our meta-cognitive abilities (see **Table 1**) has barely begun. However, the frontal cortex is clearly implicated. In relation to perception, the bilateral application of TMS to DLPFC has a specific effect on confidence in perception without affecting discrimination (Rounis et al. 2010). This suggests that TMS can cause a reduction in meta-cognitive sensitivity, presumably by increasing neural noise in PFC. Lesions of prefrontal cortex are also associated with greater effects on subjective report than on objective performance (Del Cul 2009). Individuals can differ considerably in their meta-cognitive sensitivity even when they do not differ in perceptual sensitivity. People with greater meta-cognitive sensitivity in a perceptual task have a greater density of gray matter in anterior prefrontal cortex (BA10) (Fleming et al. 2010).

In relation to action and the experience of agency, Lau and colleagues (2004) found that the requirement to make reports about the intention to act was associated with activity in presupplementary motor area (preSMA). A more recent paper (Miele et al. 2011) has taken the study of action considerably further, revealing brain regions relating to a hierarchy of cognitive processes underlying meta-cognition. In this study, right TPJ activity was associated with the detection of discrepancies between expected and observed states, whereas activity in preSMA and rostral ACC was associated with being in control of one's actions (i.e., few violations of expectations). However, judgments of control (i.e., meta-cognitive reflections upon control) were associated with activity in anterior prefrontal cortex (BA10), a location close to that identified as relevant to perceptual meta-cognition in the study of Fleming and colleagues (2010).

It remains to be explored whether there is an intimate relationship between meta-cognition and the executive processes associated with prefrontal cortex through which competing automatic social processes are modulated. One possibility is that the biasing of competition exerted by top-down control requires explicit representations of the processes that are competing for the control of behavior.

CONCLUSIONS

In this review we have emphasized the importance of comparisons of different species and the use of an evolutionary framework for understanding social interaction. Much of human social behavior derives from the same range of cognitive processes that can be seen in other social animals. We distinguished mechanisms from processes and suggested that it is largely general mechanisms that enable specifically social processes. That is, many of the underlying mechanisms can also be used to solve problems without social content or social aims. There are many different social processes, from observational learning and copying to mentalizing and reflective discussion. We found that we share some, but not all, with other species and that many of the processes are implicit and automatic. For instance, the mere presence of others biases us toward group-oriented behavior, and our behavior is automatically influenced in the presence of others with a different perspective. We also share with other social species the ability automatically to keep track of the agents we are interacting with,

as well as their status and predispositions. There are hints that this ability may derive from spatial tracking ability. We suggest that mentalizing, that is, tracking the intentions, knowledge, and beliefs of others, may depend on predictive coding mechanisms. In the case of other species, tracking others' mental states appears to be limited to certain domains of interest, for instance, food caching in corvids. In the case of humans, we are continually updating our representations of other people's constantly changing dispositions, emotions, intentions, point of view, knowledge, and beliefs. Though complex, much of this updating also appears to be automatic and implicit.

What then in social cognition is specific to human beings? First, through language, humans have the means of creating processes that are explicit. Second, humans, in comparison with other species, have a much greater ability to exert top-down control over automatic processes. This is particularly important when there is competition between different components of social cognition. Third, humans have the extraordinary ability to reflect upon their own mental states. This is a prime example of meta-cognition, which may well lie at the heart of conscious awareness.

Finally, how do the explicit, controllable, and meta-cognitive abilities that human beings can put to use in the service of social cognition benefit social interaction? We believe that our specific communicative abilities, both verbal and nonverbal, greatly enhance the value of our social interactions. Unlike other animals, humans teach and learn in a deliberately interactive manner and can share intentions and experiences very effectively. Learning by instruction can often be even more efficient than learning by observation. The ability to discuss and share mental states is perhaps the most valuable of the social processes we discussed. This ability to share experiences can enhance the accuracy of the models of the world that we construct and thus our potential to make better decisions. It is this uniquely human kind of social cognition that makes possible joint endeavors, such as cultural institutions, arts, and science.

SUMMARY POINTS

1. Social cognition needs to explain the use of social cues for selfish interest and for group-directed altruistic behavior. Even altruistic behavior serves self-interest in the long term. The automatic effect of social cues (presence of others, being imitated by others) usually increases prosocial tendencies. The action of social cues is seen in the audience and the chameleon effects.

2. Learning by observation is largely automatic; it is widespread and has many advantages over trial-and-error learning. It has benefits for the individual who can avoid making errors and can make use of others' experience. It is also of benefit for the group by making individuals more similar. However, for exploration of novelty, trial-and-error learning may be necessary.

3. Gossip is an important means to gauge the reliability of potential partners, and it feeds into reputation management. There is pressure for reputation management to facilitate trust and cooperation as well as to punish those who break trust. This is usually an automatic process and is seen in social animals that use the mechanism of indirect reciprocity to balance selfish and group interests. In the framework of neuroeconomics, there is a never-ending arms race between investors and free riders.

4. Mentalizing is likely to be based on predictive coding. This mechanism is carried by a network of frontal and temporo-parietal regions of the brain. An implicit form of mentalizing is observed in infants under 12 months, and homologous forms have been observed in other species, e.g., corvids. The explicit form of mentalizing is linked to the development of meta-cognition and language and is unique to humans, being universally present beginning at about age 4 to 6 years. Classic false-belief tasks test explicit mentalizing; looking behavior is used to test implicit mentalizing.

5. An implicit form of teaching young infants is signaled by ostension. Deliberate instruction, in which both pupil and teacher are aware of the intention to teach, is abundant in human societies from the time that children reach age 4 to 6 years. Many networks of the social brain (mentalizing, meta-cognition, mirroring, language) are involved.

6. Meta-cognition plays a crucial role in human social interactions and provides a basis for human consciousness. Consciously applied top-down processes can control automatic processes. Prefrontal regions of the human brain and their connections to other cortical regions are thought to be crucial in this control.

FUTURE ISSUES

1. Find a principled distinction between implicit and explicit processes at the cognitive and the experimental level.

2. Find a principled distinction between accidental signals that are broadcast publicly and deliberate signals of communication.

3. Use computational models of mentalizing combined with neuroimaging to lead to a better understanding of the mechanisms involved.

4. Elucidate the relationship between meta-cognition and executive function.

5. Elucidate the role of meta-cognition in social interaction.

6. Comparisons of group decision making in social insects and humans will be important for revealing underlying mechanisms.

7. Study how conflicts are resolved between the use of social signals for an individual's own selfish benefit and for group-oriented behavior.

DISCLOSURE STATEMENT

The authors are not aware of any affiliations, memberships, funding, or financial holdings that might be perceived as affecting the objectivity of this review.

ACKNOWLEDGMENTS

We are very grateful to the following colleagues who gave very constructive comments on a first draft of this paper: Ralph Adolphs, Ian Apperly, Sarah-Jayne Blakemore, Cecilia Heyes, William Hoppitt, Kevin Laland, Matthew Liebermann, Rosalind Ridley, and Matthew Rushworth. Where we have failed to take their advice this is due to our own obduracy and space limitations. We are also grateful to Susan Fiske for her encouragement. Our work is supported by the Danish National Research Foundation through the Interacting Minds project.

LITERATURE CITED

Adank P, Hagoort P, Bekkering H. 2010. Imitation improves language comprehension. *Psychol. Sci.* 21:1903–9

Adolphs R. 2009. The social brain: neural basis of social knowledge. *Annu. Rev. Psychol.* 60:693–716

Amodio DM, Frith CD. 2006. Meeting of minds: the medial frontal cortex and social cognition. *Nat. Rev. Neurosci.* 7:268–77

Andreoni J, Miller JH. 1993. Rational cooperation in the finitely repeated prisoner's dilemma. *Econ. J.* 103:570–85

Apperly IA, Butterfill SA. 2009. Do humans have two systems to track beliefs and belief-like states? *Psychol. Rev.* 116:953–70

Avenanti A, Sirigu A, Aglioti SM. 2010. Racial bias reduces empathic sensorimotor resonance with other-race pain. *Curr. Biol.* 20:1018–22

Axelrod R, Hamilton WD. 1981. The evolution of cooperation. *Science* 211:1390–96

Bahrami B, Olsen K, Latham PE, Roepstorff A, Rees G, Frith CD. 2010. Optimally interacting minds. *Science* 329:1081–85

Bailenson JN, Yee N, Patel K, Beall AC. 2008. Detecting digital chameleons. *Comput. Hum. Behav.* 24:66–87

Bateson M, Nettle D, Roberts G. 2006. Cues of being watched enhance cooperation in a real-world setting. *Biol. Lett.* 2:412–14

Bayliss AP, Paul MA, Cannon PR, Tipper SP. 2006. Gaze cuing and affective judgments of objects: I like what you look at. *Psychon. Bull. Rev.* 13:1061–66

Bayliss AP, Tipper SP. 2006. Predictive gaze cues and personality judgments: Should eye trust you? *Psychol. Sci.* 17:514–20

Beck DM, Kastner S. 2009. Top-down and bottom-up mechanisms in biasing competition in the human brain. *Vision Res.* 49:1154–65

Behrens TE, Hunt LT, Woolrich MW, Rushworth MF. 2008. Associative learning of social value. *Nature* 456:245–49

Bengtsson SL, Lau HC, Passingham RE. 2009. Motivation to do well enhances responses to errors and self-monitoring. *Cereb. Cortex* 19:797–804

Demonstrates a common mechanism for tracking reward and social information instantiated in different brain regions.

Boinski S, Garber PA, eds. 2000. *On the Move: How and Why Animals Travel in Groups*. Chicago, IL: Univ. Chicago Press. 822 pp.

Breland K, Breland M. 1961. The misbehavior of organisms. *Am. Psychol.* 16:681–84

Bshary R, Bergmuller R. 2008. Distinguishing four fundamental approaches to the evolution of helping. *J. Evol. Biol.* 21:405–20

Bshary R, Grutter AS. 2006. Image scoring and cooperation in a cleaner fish mutualism. *Nature* 441:975–78

Bugnyar T. 2011. Knower-guesser differentiation in ravens: Others' viewpoints matter. *Proc. Biol. Sci.* 278:634–40

Byrne R, Whiten A, eds. 1988. *Machiavellian Intelligence*. Oxford, UK: Oxford Univ. Press

Call J, Tomasello M. 2008. Does the chimpanzee have a theory of mind? 30 years later. *Trends Cogn. Sci.* 12:187–92

Campbell-Meiklejohn DK, Bach DR, Roepstorff A, Dolan RJ, Frith CD. 2010. How the opinion of others affects our valuation of objects. *Curr. Biol.* 20:1165–70

Carpenter M, Nagell K, Tomasello M. 1998. Social cognition, joint attention, and communicative competence from 9 to 15 months of age. *Monogr. Soc. Res. Child Dev.* 63:i–vi, 1–143

Carver CS, Scheier MF. 1981. The self-attention-induced feedback loop and social facilitation. *J. Exp. Soc. Psychol.* 17:545–68

Catmur C, Mars RB, Rushworth MF, Heyes C. 2011. Making mirrors: Premotor cortex stimulation enhances mirror and counter-mirror motor facilitation. *J. Cogn. Neurosci.* 23:2352–62

Chartrand TL, Bargh JA. 1999. The chameleon effect: the perception-behavior link and social interaction. *J. Personal. Soc. Psychol.* 76:893–910

Chiao JY, Harada T, Oby ER, Li Z, Parrish T, Bridge DJ. 2009. Neural representations of social status hierarchy in human inferior parietal cortex. *Neuropsychologia* 47:354–63

Clayton NS, Dally JM, Emery NJ. 2007. Social cognition by food-caching corvids. The western scrub-jay as a natural psychologist. *Philos. Trans. R. Soc. Lond. B Biol. Sci.* 362:507–22

Cleret de Langavant L, Remy P, Trinkler I, McIntyre J, Dupoux E, et al. 2011. Behavioral and neural correlates of communication via pointing. *PLoS ONE* 6:e17719

Cook M, Mineka S. 1989. Observational conditioning of fear to fear-relevant versus fear-irrelevant stimuli in rhesus monkeys. *J. Abnorm. Psychol.* 98:448–59

Cooper JC, Kreps TA, Wiebe T, Pirkl T, Knutson B. 2010. When giving is good: ventromedial prefrontal cortex activation for others' intentions. *Neuron* 67:511–21

Coricelli G, Nagel R. 2009. Neural correlates of depth of strategic reasoning in medial prefrontal cortex. *Proc. Natl. Acad. Sci. USA* 106:9163–68

Couzin ID. 2009. Collective cognition in animal groups. *Trends Cogn. Sci.* 13:36–43

Csibra G, Gergely G. 2006. Social learning and social cognition: the case for pedagogy. In *Processes of Change in Brain and Cognitive Development. Attention and Performance XXI*, ed. Y Munakata, MH Johnson, pp. 249–74. Oxford, UK: Oxford Univ. Press

Cunningham WA, Johnson MK, Raye CL, Chris Gatenby J, Gore JC, Banaji MR. 2004. Separable neural components in the processing of black and white faces. *Psychol. Sci.* 15:806–13

Danchin E, Giraldeau LA, Valone TJ, Wagner RH. 2004. Public information: from nosy neighbors to cultural evolution. *Science* 305:487–91

Del Cul A, Dehaene S, Reyes P, Bravo E, Slachevsky A. 2009. Causal role of prefrontal cortex in the threshold for access to consciousness. *Brain* 132:2531–40

Delgado MR, Frank RH, Phelps EA. 2005. Perceptions of moral character modulate the neural systems of reward during the trust game. *Nat. Neurosci.* 8:1611–18

de Vignemont F, Singer T. 2006. The empathic brain: how, when and why? *Trends Cogn. Sci.* 10:435–41

Dijksterhuis A, Bos MW, Nordgren LF, van Baaren RB. 2006. On making the right choice: the deliberation-without-attention effect. *Science* 311:1005–7

Dimberg U, Thunberg M, Elmehed K. 2000. Unconscious facial reactions to emotional facial expressions. *Psychol. Sci.* 11:86–89

Dyer JRG, Ioannou CC, Morrell LJ, Croft DP, Couzin ID, et al. 2008. Consensus decision making in human crowds. *Anim. Behav.* 75:461–70

Identifies pedagogy as a crucial process in human social cognition.

Fiske ST. 2010. Interpersonal stratification: status, power, and subordination. In *Handbook of Social Psychology*, ed. ST Fiske, DT Gilbert, G Lindzey, pp. 941–82. Hoboken, NJ: Wiley

Flavell JH. 1992. Perspectives on perspective-taking. In *Piaget's Theory: Prospects and Possibilities*, ed. H Beilin, PB Pufall, pp. 107–39. Hillsdale, NJ: Erlbaum

Fleming SM, Weil RS, Nagy Z, Dolan RJ, Rees G. 2010. Relating introspective accuracy to individual differences in brain structure. *Science* 329:1541–43

Flom R, Johnson S. 2011. The effects of adults' affective expression and direction of visual gaze on 12-month-olds' visual preferences for an object following a 5-minute, 1-day, or 1-month delay. *Br. J. Dev. Psychol.* 29:64–85

Frith CD. 2007. *Making Up the Mind: How the Brain Creates Our Mental World*. Oxford, UK: Blackwell. 232 pp.

Frith CD. 2010. What is consciousness for? *Pragmat. Cogn.* 18:497–551

Funder DC, Colvin CR. 1988. Friends and strangers: acquaintanceship, agreement, and the accuracy of personality judgment. *J. Personal. Soc. Psychol.* 55:149–58

Galef BG Jr, Giraldeau LA. 2001. Social influences on foraging in vertebrates: causal mechanisms and adaptive functions. *Anim. Behav.* 61:3–15

Galef BG Jr, Laland KN. 2005. Social learning in animals: empirical studies and theoretical models. *Bioscience* 55:489–99

Gallagher HL, Jack AI, Roepstorff A, Frith CD. 2002. Imaging the intentional stance in a competitive game. *Neuroimage* 16:814–21

Garrod S, Pickering MJ. 2009. Joint action, interactive alignment, and dialog. *Topics Cogn. Sci.* 1:292–304

Grosenick L, Clement TS, Fernald RD. 2007. Fish can infer social rank by observation alone. *Nature* 445:429–32

Hampton AN, Bossaerts P, O'Doherty JP. 2008. Neural correlates of mentalizing-related computations during strategic interactions in humans. *Proc. Natl. Acad. Sci. USA* 105:6741–46

Haxby JV, Hoffman EA, Gobbini MI. 2000. The distributed human neural system for face perception. *Trends Cogn. Sci.* 4:223–33

Heerey EA, Velani H. 2010. Implicit learning of social predictions. *J. Exp. Soc. Psychol.* 46:577–81

Henrich J, Broesch J. 2011. On the nature of cultural transmission networks: evidence from Fijian villages for adaptive learning biases. *Philos. Trans. R. Soc. Lond. B Biol. Sci.* 366:1139–48

Heyes C. 2001. Causes and consequences of imitation. *Trends Cogn. Sci.* 5:253–61

Heyes C. 2011. Automatic imitation. *Psychol. Bull.* 137:463–83

Hirschfeld L. 1996. *Race in the Making*. Cambridge, MA: MIT Press

Hoffman EA, Haxby JV. 2000. Distinct representations of eye gaze and identity in the distributed human neural system for face perception. *Nat. Neurosci.* 3:80–84

Hoppitt WJ, Brown GR, Kendal R, Rendell L, Thornton A, et al. 2008. Lessons from animal teaching. *Trends Ecol. Evol.* 23:486–93

Horner V, Whiten A. 2005. Causal knowledge and imitation/emulation switching in chimpanzees (*Pan troglodytes*) and children (*Homo sapiens*). *Anim. Cogn.* 8:164–81

Huber L, Range F, Voelkl B, Szucsich A, Viranyi Z, Miklosi A. 2009. The evolution of imitation: What do the capacities of non-human animals tell us about the mechanisms of imitation? *Philos. Trans. R. Soc. Lond. B Biol. Sci.* 364:2299–309

Izuma K, Saito DN, Sadato N. 2010a. Processing of the incentive for social approval in the ventral striatum during charitable donation. *J. Cogn. Neurosci.* 22:621–31

Izuma K, Saito DN, Sadato N. 2010b. The roles of the medial prefrontal cortex and striatum in reputation processing. *Soc. Neurosci.* 5:133–47

Jacob P, Dupoux E. 2008. Developmental psychology: a precursor of moral judgment in human infants? *Curr. Biol.* 18:R216–18

Johansson P, Hall L, Sikstrom S, Olsson A. 2005. Failure to detect mismatches between intention and outcome in a simple decision task. *Science* 310:116–19

Johnson SC. 2003. Detecting agents. *Philos. Trans. R. Soc. Lond. B Biol. Sci.* 358:549–59

Kahneman D, Frederick S. 2002. Representativeness revisited: attribute substitution in intuitive judgment. In *Heuristics and Biases*, ed. T Gilovich, D Griffin, D Kahneman, pp. 49–81. New York: Cambridge Univ. Press

Kampe KK, Frith CD, Frith U. 2003. "Hey John": Signals conveying communicative intention toward the self activate brain regions associated with "mentalizing," regardless of modality. *J. Neurosci.* 23:5258–63

Kilner JM, Friston KJ, Frith CD. 2007. Predictive coding: an account of the mirror neuron system. *Cogn. Process.* 8:159–66

Kirk U, Downar J, Montague PR. 2011. Interoception drives increased rational decision-making in meditators playing the Ultimatum Game. *Frontiers Neurosci.* 5:49

Klein JT, Deaner RO, Platt ML. 2008. Neural correlates of social target value in macaque parietal cortex. *Curr. Biol.* 18:419–24

Klein JT, Shepherd SV, Platt ML. 2009. Social attention and the brain. *Curr. Biol.* 19:R958–62

Konvalinka I, Vuust P, Roepstorff A, Frith CD. 2010. Follow you, follow me: continuous mutual prediction and adaptation in joint tapping. *Q. J. Exp. Psychol. (Colchester)* 63:2220–30

Kovács AM, Téglás E, Endress AD. 2010. The social sense: susceptibility to others' beliefs in human infants and adults. *Science* 330:1830–34

Kühn S, Müller BC, van Baaren RB, Wietzker A, Dijksterhuis A, Brass M. 2010. Why do I like you when you behave like me? Neural mechanisms mediating positive consequences of observing someone being imitated. *Soc. Neurosci.* 5:384–92

Laland KN. 2004. Social learning strategies. *Learn. Behav.* 32:4–14

Lau HC. 2007. A higher order Bayesian decision theory of consciousness. In *Progress in Brain Research*, ed. B Rahul, KC Bikas, pp. 35–48. Oxford, UK: Elsevier

Lau HC, Rogers RD, Haggard P, Passingham RE. 2004. Attention to intention. *Science* 303:1208–10

Leadbeater E, Chittka L. 2007. Social learning in insects—from miniature brains to consensus building. *Curr. Biol.* 17:R703–13

Leslie AM. 1987. Pretense and representation: the origins of "theory of mind." *Psychol. Rev.* 94:412–26

Li J, Delgado MR, Phelps EA. 2011. How instructed knowledge modulates the neural systems of reward learning. *Proc. Natl. Acad. Sci. USA* 108:55–60

Lieberman MD, Gaunt R, Gilbert DT, Trope Y. 2002. Reflexion and reflection: a social cognitive neuroscience approach to attributional inference. *Adv. Exp. Soc. Psychol.* 34:199–249

Lin A, Adolphs R, Rangel A. 2011. Social and monetary reward learning engage overlapping neural substrates. *Soc. Cogn. Affect. Neurosci.* DOI: 10.1093/scan/nsr006. In press

Liszkowski U, Carpenter M, Tomasello M. 2007. Pointing out new news, old news, and absent referents at 12 months of age. *Dev. Sci.* 10:F1–7

Lyons DE, Damrosch DH, Lin JK, Macris DM, Keil FC. 2011. The scope and limits of overimitation in the transmission of artefact culture. *Philos. Trans. R. Soc. Lond. B Biol. Sci.* 366:1158–67

McGuigan N, Makinson J, Whiten A. 2011. From over-imitation to super-copying: Adults imitate causally irrelevant aspects of tool use with higher fidelity than young children. *Br. J. Psychol.* 102:1–18

Mery F, Varela SA, Danchin E, Blanchet S, Parejo D, et al. 2009. Public versus personal information for mate copying in an invertebrate. *Curr. Biol.* 19:730–34

Metcalfe J. 2008. Evolution of metacognition. In *Handbook of Metamemory and Memory*, ed. J Dunlosky, R Bjork, pp. 29–46. New York: Psychol. Press

Miele DB, Wager TD, Mitchell JP, Metcalfe J. 2011. Dissociating neural correlates of action monitoring and metacognition of agency. *J. Cogn. Neurosci* 23:3620–36

Milinski M, Semmann D, Krambeck HJ. 2002. Reputation helps solve the "tragedy of the commons." *Nature* 415:424–26

Mineka S, Cook M. 1993. Mechanisms involved in the observational conditioning of fear. *J. Exp. Psychol.: Gen.* 122:23–38

Mineka S, Ohman A. 2002. Phobias and preparedness: the selective, automatic, and encapsulated nature of fear. *Biol. Psychiatry* 52:927–37

Mitchell JP, Cloutier J, Banaji MR, Macrae CN. 2006. Medial prefrontal dissociations during processing of trait diagnostic and nondiagnostic person information. *Soc. Cogn. Affect. Neurosci.* 1:49–55

Outlines the neurophysiology of social attention.

Demonstrates automatic effects of an agent's false belief on looking behavior in infants and adults.

Reviews the role of overimitation in the development of human culture.

Reveals the neural basis of the meta-cognition of agency.

Demonstrates the importance of reputation for the emergence of cooperation.

Mobbs D, Yu R, Meyer M, Passamonti L, Seymour B, et al. 2009. A key role for similarity in vicarious reward. *Science* 324:900

Müller CA, Cant MA. 2010. Imitation and traditions in wild banded mongooses. *Curr. Biol.* 20:1171–75

Murray EA, Wise SP. 2010. What, if anything, can monkeys tell us about human amnesia when they can't say anything at all? *Neuropsychologia* 48:2385–405

Olsson A, Nearing KI, Phelps EA. 2007. Learning fears by observing others: the neural systems of social fear transmission. *Soc. Cogn. Affect. Neurosci.* 2:3–11

Olsson A, Phelps EA. 2004. Learned fear of "unseen" faces after Pavlovian, observational, and instructed fear. *Psychol. Sci.* 15:822–28

Olsson A, Phelps EA. 2007. Social learning of fear. *Nat. Neurosci.* 10:1095–102

Oosterhof NN, Todorov A. 2008. The functional basis of face evaluation. *Proc. Natl. Acad. Sci. USA* 105:11087–92

Paukner A, Suomi SJ, Visalberghi E, Ferrari PF. 2009. Capuchin monkeys display affiliation toward humans who imitate them. *Science* 325:880–83

Pelphrey KA, Morris JP, McCarthy G. 2004. Grasping the intentions of others: The perceived intentionality of an action influences activity in the superior temporal sulcus during social perception. *J. Cogn. Neurosci.* 16:1706–16

Perner J. 1991. *Understanding the Representational Mind*. Cambridge, MA: MIT Press. 348 pp.

Perner J, Lang B. 1999. Development of theory of mind and executive control. *Trends Cogn. Sci.* 3:337–44

Peters J, Buchel C. 2010. Neural representations of subjective reward value. *Behav. Brain Res.* 213:135–41

Phan KL, Sripada CS, Angstadt M, McCabe K. 2010. Reputation for reciprocity engages the brain reward center. *Proc. Natl. Acad. Sci. USA* 107:13099–104

Phelps EA, O'Connor KJ, Cunningham WA, Funayama ES, Gatenby JC, et al. 2000. Performance on indirect measures of race evaluation predicts amygdala activation. *J. Cogn. Neurosci.* 12:729–38

Pike TW, Laland KN. 2010. Conformist learning in nine-spined sticklebacks' foraging decisions. *Biol. Lett.* 6:466–68

Puce A, Perrett D. 2003. Electrophysiology and brain imaging of biological motion. *Philos. Trans. R. Soc. Lond. B Biol. Sci.* 358:435–45

Quadflieg S, Turk DJ, Waiter GD, Mitchell JP, Jenkins AC, Macrae CN. 2009. Exploring the neural correlates of social stereotyping. *J. Cogn. Neurosci.* 21:1560–70

Qureshi AW, Apperly IA, Samson D. 2010. Executive function is necessary for perspective selection, not level-1 visual perspective calculation: evidence from a dual-task study of adults. *Cognition* 117:230–36

Raafat RM, Chater N, Frith C. 2009. Herding in humans. *Trends Cogn. Sci.* 13:420–28

Rendell L, Boyd R, Cownden D, Enquist M, Eriksson K, et al. 2010. Why copy others? Insights from the social learning strategies tournament. *Science* 328:208–13

Richerson PJ, Boyd R. 2001. The evolution of subjective commitment to groups: a tribal instincts hypothesis. In *Evolution and the Capacity for Commitment*, ed. RM Nesse, pp. 186–202. New York: Russell Sage Found.

Rilling J, Sanfey A, Aronson J, Nystrom L, Cohen J. 2004. Opposing BOLD responses to reciprocated and unreciprocated altruism in putative reward pathways. *Neuroreport* 15:2539–43

Rizzolatti G, Craighero L. 2004. The mirror-neuron system. *Annu. Rev. Neurosci.* 27:169–92

Rounis E, Maniscalco B, Rothwell JC, Passingham RE, Lau H. 2010. Theta-burst transcranial magnetic stimulation to the prefrontal cortex impairs metacognitive visual awareness. *Cogn. Neurosci.* 1:165–75

Samson D, Apperly IA, Braithwaite JJ, Andrews BJ, Bodley Scott SE. 2010. Seeing it their way: evidence for rapid and involuntary computation of what other people see. *J. Exp. Psychol.: Hum. Percept. Perform.* 36:1255–66

Saxe R. 2006. Uniquely human social cognition. *Curr. Opin. Neurobiol.* 16:235–39

Saxe R, Xiao DK, Kovacs G, Perrett DI, Kanwisher N. 2004. A region of right posterior superior temporal sulcus responds to observed intentional actions. *Neuropsychologia* 42:1435–46

Schilbach L, Wilms M, Eickhoff SB, Romanzetti S, Tepest R, et al. 2010. Minds made for sharing: Initiating joint attention recruits reward-related neurocircuitry. *J. Cogn. Neurosci.* 22:2702–15

Schultz W. 2008. Introduction. Neuroeconomics: the promise and the profit. *Philos. Trans. R. Soc. Lond. B Biol. Sci.* 363:3767–69

Uses a computer tournament to demonstrate the advantages of copying others over trial-and-error learning.

Demonstrates the automatic effects on response times due to tracking the viewpoint of another agent.

Sebanz N, Bekkering H, Knoblich G. 2006. Joint action: bodies and minds moving together. *Trends Cogn. Sci.* 10:70–76

Senju A, Csibra G. 2008. Gaze following in human infants depends on communicative signals. *Curr. Biol.* 18:668–71

Shepherd SV, Klein JT, Deaner RO, Platt ML. 2009. Mirroring of attention by neurons in macaque parietal cortex. *Proc. Natl. Acad. Sci. USA* 106:9489–94

Singer T, Kiebel SJ, Winston JS, Dolan RJ, Frith CD. 2004a. Brain responses to the acquired moral status of faces. *Neuron* 41:653–62

Singer T, Seymour B, O'Doherty J, Kaube H, Dolan RJ, Frith CD. 2004b. Empathy for pain involves the affective but not sensory components of pain. *Science* 303:1157–62

Skyrms B. 2003. *The Stag Hunt and the Evolution and Social Structure.* London: Cambridge Univ. Press

Sommerfeld RD, Krambeck HJ, Semmann D, Milinski M. 2007. Gossip as an alternative for direct observation in games of indirect reciprocity. *Proc. Natl. Acad. Sci. USA* 104:17435–40

Spacks PM. 1982. In praise of gossip. *The Hudson Rev.* 35:19–38

Spengler S, von Cramon DY, Brass M. 2010. Resisting motor mimicry: Control of imitation involves processes central to social cognition in patients with frontal and temporo-parietal lesions. *Soc. Neurosci.* 5:401–16

Sutton RS, Barto AG. 1998. *Reinforcement Learning: An Introduction.* Cambridge, MA: MIT Press

Tabibnia G, Lieberman MD. 2007. Fairness and cooperation are rewarding: evidence from social cognitive neuroscience. *Ann. N. Y. Acad. Sci.* 1118:90–101

Tabibnia G, Satpute AB, Lieberman MD. 2008. The sunny side of fairness: preference for fairness activates reward circuitry (and disregarding unfairness activates self-control circuitry). *Psychol. Sci.* 19:339–47

Tennie C, Frith U, Frith CD. 2010. Reputation management in the age of the world-wide web. *Trends Cogn. Sci.* 14:482–88

Thornton A, Clutton-Brock T. 2011. Social learning and the development of individual and group behaviour in mammal societies. *Philos. Trans. R. Soc. Lond. B Biol. Sci.* 366:978–87

Todorov A. 2011. Evaluating faces on social dimensions. In *Social Neuroscience: Toward Understanding the Underpinnings of the Social Mind*, ed. A Todorov, ST Fiske, D Prentice. Oxford, UK: Oxford Univ. Press. In press

Todorov A, Gobbini MI, Evans KK, Haxby JV. 2007. Spontaneous retrieval of affective person knowledge in face perception. *Neuropsychologia* 45:163–73

Todorov A, Olson IR. 2008. Robust learning of affective trait associations with faces when the hippocampus is damaged, but not when the amygdala and temporal pole are damaged. *Soc. Cogn. Affect. Neurosci.* 3:195–203

Todorov A, Uleman JS. 2003. The efficiency of binding spontaneous trait inferences to actors' faces. *J. Exp. Soc. Psychol.* 39:549–62

Vallortigara G, Regolin L, Marconato F. 2005. Visually inexperienced chicks exhibit spontaneous preference for biological motion patterns. *PLoS Biol.* 3:e208

van Baaren RB, Holland RW, Kawakami K, van Knippenberg A. 2004. Mimicry and prosocial behavior. *Psychol. Sci.* 15:71–74

van Bergen Y, Coolen I, Laland KN. 2004. Nine-spined sticklebacks exploit the most reliable source when public and private information conflict. *Proc. Biol. Sci.* 271:957–62

van Leeuwen ML, van Baaren RB, Martin D, Dijksterhuis A, Bekkering H. 2009. Executive functioning and imitation: Increasing working memory load facilitates behavioural imitation. *Neuropsychologia* 47:3265–70

Van Overwalle F. 2009. Social cognition and the brain: a meta-analysis. *Hum. Brain Mapp.* 30:829–58

Visscher PK. 2007. Group decision making in nest-site selection among social insects. *Annu. Rev. Entomol.* 52:255–75

Vohs KD, Schooler JW. 2008. The value of believing in free will: encouraging a belief in determinism increases cheating. *Psychol. Sci.* 19:49–54

Warneken F, Chen F, Tomasello M. 2006. Cooperative activities in young children and chimpanzees. *Child Dev.* 77:640–63

Warneken F, Tomasello M. 2006. Altruistic helping in human infants and young chimpanzees. *Science* 311:1301–3

Wellman HM, Cross D, Watson J. 2001. Meta-analysis of theory-of-mind development: the truth about false belief. *Child Dev.* 72:655–84

White DJ. 2004. Influences of social learning on mate-choice decisions. *Learn. Behav.* 32:105–13

Whiten A, McGuigan N, Marshall-Pescini S, Hopper LM. 2009. Emulation, imitation, over-imitation and the scope of culture for child and chimpanzee. *Philos. Trans. R. Soc. Lond. B Biol. Sci.* 364:2417–28

Wilkinson A, Kuenstner K, Mueller J, Huber L. 2010. Social learning in a non-social reptile (*Geochelone carbonaria*). *Biol. Lett.* 6:614–16

Yoshida W, Dolan RJ, Friston KJ. 2008. Game theory of mind. *PLoS Comput. Biol.* 4:e1000254

Yoshida W, Seymour B, Friston KJ, Dolan RJ. 2010. Neural mechanisms of belief inference during cooperative games. *J. Neurosci.* 30:10744–51

Zajonc RB. 1965. Social facilitation. *Science* 149:269–74

Zaki J, Hennigan K, Weber J, Ochsner KN. 2010. Social cognitive conflict resolution: contributions of domain-general and domain-specific neural systems. *J. Neurosci.* 30:8481–88

Zink CF, Tong Y, Chen Q, Bassett DS, Stein JL, Meyer-Lindenberg A. 2008. Know your place: neural processing of social hierarchy in humans. *Neuron* 58:273–83

Zuberbühler K. 2008. Gaze following. *Curr. Biol.* 18:R453–55

Uses a computational model of cooperation to elucidate the neural basis of mentalizing.

Personality Processes: Mechanisms by Which Personality Traits "Get Outside the Skin"

Sarah E. Hampson

Oregon Research Institute, Eugene, Oregon 97403; email: sarah@ori.org

Annu. Rev. Psychol. 2012. 63:315–39

First published online as a Review in Advance on July 5, 2011

The *Annual Review of Psychology* is online at psych.annualreviews.org

This article's doi: 10.1146/annurev-psych-120710-100419

Keywords

negative emotionality, positive emotionality, constraint, mediation, moderation, social cognition

Abstract

It is time to better understand why personality traits predict consequential outcomes, which calls for a closer look at personality processes. Personality processes are mechanisms that unfold over time to produce the effects of personality traits. They include reactive and instrumental processes that moderate or mediate the association between traits and outcomes. These mechanisms are illustrated here by a selection of studies of traits representing the three broad domains of personality and temperament: negative emotionality, positive emotionality, and constraint. Personality processes are studied over the short term, as in event-sampling studies, and over the long term, as in lifespan research. Implications of findings from the study of processes are considered for resolving issues in models of personality structure, improving and extending methods of personality assessment, and identifying targets for personality interventions.

Contents

INTRODUCTION

The study of personality processes examines how personality is manifested in people's thoughts, feelings, and behaviors to result in consequential outcomes. Whereas psychologists more commonly investigate how external, environmental influences affect internal processes within the individual, that is, how these factors get "under the skin," in this review I reverse the direction of the metaphor. What are the processes that produce the effects of personality traits? In other words, how do traits get outside the skin?

Reviews of studies documenting associations between traits and important life outcomes amply confirm the predictive power of personality (Ozer & Benet-Martínez 2006, Roberts et al. 2007). Personality traits predict consequential outcomes for individuals (e.g., happiness, longevity), couples (e.g., relationship quality), groups, and society (e.g., volunteerism, criminality). These reviews provide an extensive catalogue of *what* personality predicts but do not examine *how* personality gives rise to these associations. With such a strong foundation of empirical evidence in place, research can now focus on the processes underlying these observed associations between personality traits and outcomes. A greater understanding of personality processes may inform personality theory and measurement and foster beneficial personality development and change.

My focus in this article is on personality trait processes. Trait theories assume that people differ reliably from one another in their stable patterns of cross-situational behavior, and personality traits describe these individual differences in terms of characteristic thoughts, feelings, and behaviors (Funder 2001). Most of those who study trait structure agree that individual differences in personality are captured by the dimensions of the five-factor model or Big Five taxonomy, comprising the broad trait dimensions of extraversion, agreeableness, conscientiousness, emotional stability, and openness to experience/intellect, and their more specific facets (Digman 1990; Goldberg 1990; John et al. 2008; McCrae & Costa 2003, 2008; Saucier & Goldberg 2001). An alternative six-factor structure, which includes a dimension of honesty-humility (Ashton & Lee 2007, Lee & Ashton 2008), has proved useful in cross-language studies (Saucier 2009).

However, the study of the structure of personality traits is primarily descriptive. It is the "what" of personality, rather than the "how" or the "why" (Revelle 1995). Even McCrae and Costa's well-elaborated five-factor theory of personality (McCrae & Costa 1996, 2008), which places traits in the context of biology, biography, external influences, self concept, and characteristic adaptations, leaves the dynamic processes linking these various elements largely unspecified. Understanding personality processes goes beyond describing individual differences by explaining the expression of individual differences. The study of personality processes asks why personality traits have their consequential effects on important life outcomes. Why do extraverted people tend to be happier than introverted people? Why do less conscientious and more neurotic people tend to live shorter lives than more conscientious or more emotional stable people?

As we try to answer these kinds of questions, it is helpful to keep in mind a simple definition of a "process." An unsystematic survey of online dictionary definitions reveals that most boil down to this: "A process is a series of actions that take place over time to produce a result." For example, the process of natural selection results in the evolution of species, the burning of fossil fuels contributes to global warming, and evaporation produces potable water from the ocean. Similarly, personality processes may be defined as actions or reactions over time that produce the outcomes associated with personality constructs. Two theoretical approaches to personality have proved useful for the study of personality processes: temperament models and social-cognitive models.

Temperament and Personality

To begin to answer "why" questions, it is necessary to view personality traits in a broader theoretical context that goes beyond descriptive or taxonomic issues. Categories for personality description do not help us to understand why a neurotic person erupts in anger to a mild provocation, or when an

Table 1 Correspondence between the five broad personality traits and the five broad temperament constructs

Personality traits	Temperament constructs
Extraversion	Positive affect
Agreeableness	Affiliativeness
Conscientiousness	Effortful control
Neuroticism	Negative affect
Intellect/openness	Orienting sensitivity

impulsive adolescent will, surprisingly, use a condom. In searching for such explanations, the relation between temperament and personality becomes important. Biologically based individual differences in temperament include the broad dimensions of negative emotionality, positive emotionality, constraint (effortful control), and their more specific components (Rothbart 2011). Temperament is studied primarily in infants and young children but, over the course of development, temperament forms the basis for many aspects of personality, and the distinction between temperament and personality becomes less meaningful. By adulthood, temperaments map quite well onto the Big Five traits. As summarized in **Table 1**, negative emotionality is most highly correlated with neuroticism; positive emotionality with extraversion; constraint with conscientiousness; affiliativeness with agreeableness; and orienting sensitivity with openness to experience (Evans & Rothbart 2007).

The biological bases of temperament address processes going on under the skin but also provide insight into personality processes outside the skin. Theories of temperament include psychobiological and developmental mechanisms to explain why people behave as they do. For example, in temperament theory, biologically based approach and avoidance systems have been proposed that produce individual differences in sensitivity to reward and punishment (Gray 1987). These biological systems give rise to differences in approach and avoidance behaviors that temperament researchers call "positive emotionality" and "negative emotionality" and personality trait

Instrumental personality processes: the tendency to create opportunities that promote certain thoughts, feelings, behaviors, and outcomes

CAPS: cognitive and affective processing system

KAPA: knowledge-and-appraisal personality architecture

"If...then" profiles: characteristic patterns of within-person variability in behaviors across situations

researchers label with trait terms such as "extraversion" and "neuroticism." Caspi and colleagues viewed the development of personality as a gradual merger of temperament and the five-factor model and, in so doing, addressed both trait structure and processes (Caspi et al. 2005). They identified several mechanisms that maintain stability or create change in personality traits over the life course, one of which in particular, niche building or situation selection, has proved useful for thinking about personality processes more generally. That is, people create, seek out, or otherwise gravitate to environments that are compatible with their traits. This tendency is comparable to instrumental processes described by McCrae & Costa (1991). In contrast to temperamental processes, which refer to trait-consistent reactions people have to their environments, instrumental personality processes refer to the active alteration of environments to attain trait-consistent outcomes.

As we shall see, integrating biological and taxonomic approaches to traits generates hypotheses about trait processes and, in so doing, extends the utility of trait theories. Social-cognitive approaches to personality provide another perspective that has been influential in the study of processes. In contrast to trait approaches, social-cognitive models propose a more unified view of the structures and processes characterizing individuals.

Social-Cognitive Perspectives on Personality Processes

Kelly's personal construct theory is an early example of a unified approach to personality structure and processes, and it remains relevant today with its echoes in contemporary social-cognitive models of personality (Walker & Winter 2007). In Kelly's theory, personal constructs were postulated to be unique cognitive schemas that individuals develop to categorize their social world and shape their behavior (Kelly 1955/1991). The cognitive and affective processing system (CAPS; Mischel 2004; Mischel & Shoda 1998, 2008) and the

knowledge-and-appraisal personality architecture (KAPA; Cervone 2004, 2005) are more recent social-cognitive models with roots in construct theory.

According to CAPS, personality consists of five kinds of cognitive and affective subsystems that process information from the social world and generate behavior. These "mediating units" are (a) encodings (categories for construing the world); (b) expectancies and beliefs about the world (e.g., self-efficacy); (c) affects, goals, and values; (d) competencies; and (e) self-regulatory plans. Individuals are uniquely characterized by the content of these systems, by the particular way they are interconnected, and by their accessibility. The centerpiece of CAPS is the proposition that, as a result of the unique workings of the interrelated system of mediating units, individuals' behavior can be described in terms of stable "if...then" profiles or behavioral signatures. These are characteristic patterns of within-person variability in behaviors across situations (e.g., Shoda et al. 1994, Wright & Mischel 1987). The social-cognitive perspective is intended to improve upon the trait approach for behavioral prediction because it provides a way to take situational factors, as uniquely processed by the individual, into account.

Patterns of behavior in existing observational datasets have been described with if...then behavioral signatures, but CAPS has not been widely applied to predict behavior. If...then profiles are complex ways of describing individuals that cannot be reduced to a smaller number of explanatory principles, which limits their utility. Moreover, the CAPS model does not integrate the now widely accepted five-factor trait structure with its processing dynamics. Similar limitations apply to KAPA. Although KAPA has been applied successfully to predict behavior (Cervone 2004, Cervone et al. 2008), the detailed assessments required to do so reduce the appeal of this approach, particularly in applied settings. More recently, as discussed later in this review, others have drawn on CAPS in their studies of personality trait processes, uniting elements of trait and social-cognitive approaches to the benefit of both.

At this point, we might wonder what exactly is to be gained by studying trait processes. The renaissance in trait psychology, triggered ironically by Mischel's (1968) critique of trait constructs, has emphasized personality structure and measurement to the neglect of personality processes (John & Srivistava 1999). The study of personality traits has made significant advances in the prediction of behavior without studying personality processes. However, to actually use our newfound knowledge about the role of traits in shaping people's lives for good or for ill, the next leap forward for personality psychology is to increase our understanding of trait processes.

Trait Processes: Moderating and Mediating Mechanisms

Two mechanisms that are commonly invoked in the study of processes are moderation and mediation (Rusting 1998). Moderation and mediation are distinct theoretical concepts that help us hypothesize about how traits affect outcomes (Hampson 2008, Rothbart & Bates 2006), and they are associated with different statistical methods (Baron & Kenny 1986, MacKinnon et al. 2007). **Figures 1–4** depict, respectively, a direct association between a trait and an outcome, a trait as a moderator, a moderated trait effect, and a mediated trait effect. **Figure 1** shows an association between a trait and an outcome without specifying any intervening processes, for example, the association between extraversion and happiness, conscientiousness and longevity, or neuroticism and interpersonal difficulties. **Figure 2** illustrates a moderating process in which a trait affects the association between a nontrait predictor and an outcome. For example, the association between socializing and feeling happy may depend on a person's level of extraversion: as a result of socializing, those who are more extraverted may feel happier than those who are less extraverted. Another kind of moderating process, shown in **Figure 3**, is one in which the association

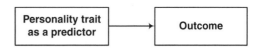

Figure 1

Direct association between a personality trait and an outcome.

between a trait predictor and an outcome is moderated by another individual difference. To illustrate, the association between neuroticism and interpersonal difficulties may be moderated by problem-solving skills: For those with better problem-solving skills, neuroticism may have less of an effect on interpersonal difficulties. **Figure 4** shows mediation, in which a trait influences an outcome through an intervening variable. For example, conscientiousness may result in longevity because people who are more conscientious are more likely to engage in health-enhancing behaviors.

Broadly speaking, mediation corresponds to instrumental or self-regulative trait processes, whereas moderation is typically a reactive process (McCrae & Costa 1991, Rothbart & Derryberry 1981). Reactive personality processes influence outcomes indirectly by having moderating effects (see **Figure 2**). That is, an association between a predictor and an outcome (e.g., aversive events are associated with depression) may be even stronger for those with higher levels of a relevant trait (e.g., neuroticism). Instrumental or self-regulatory processes imply a mediating mechanism (see **Figure 4**) through which proactive trait-related actions bring about changes in outcomes (e.g., more conscientious people adhere to treatment regimens and have better health outcomes). There are exceptions to the general principle that mediation

Moderation: the association between a predictor and an outcome differs depending upon the level of a third (moderator) variable

Mediation: the influence of a predictor on an outcome occurs through an intervening (mediating) variable

Reactive personality processes: the tendency to experience certain thoughts, feelings, behaviors, and outcomes

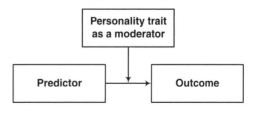

Figure 2

Moderation of the association between a predictor and an outcome by a personality trait.

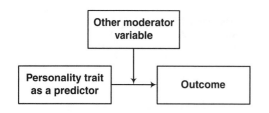

Figure 3

Moderation of the association between a personality trait and an outcome by another variable.

processes are instrumental and moderation processes are reactive. As we shall see later, instrumental processes involving constraint can also involve moderating mechanisms, for example, when constraint is applied to reduce the impact of a predictor on an outcome (e.g., resisting peer pressure to experiment with drugs).

Above, I defined personality processes as a series of actions or reactions over time. Mediation clearly fits this view because, in the ideal test of mediation, the assessment of the predictor, hypothesized mediator, and outcome is performed in sequence across time (MacKinnon et al. 2007). It is less obvious that moderation processes unfold over time, but they also take place in sequence. Take the case of trait reactivity, which is commonly studied in terms of moderation. For example, it is hypothesized that more neurotic people react more strongly (e.g., with greater anxiety) to threatening situations. The implicit timeline is that higher neuroticism is a pre-existing condition that people bring to the threatening situation, which results in greater anxiety. Therefore, the ideal design to test this hypothesis would be to assess neuroticism prior to exposing participants to threat and to assess anxiety shortly after: That is, the moderation process involves a sequence over time. In reality, both mediation and moderation are often tested cross-sectionally, limiting inferences about causality.

Longitudinal studies permit more confident inferences about the likely causal sequence of events involved in both kinds of personality process.

Moderation is tested by the interaction between the trait and the predictor variable on the outcome. Mediation is tested by evaluating the paths between the trait predictor, hypothesized mediator, and the outcome. Both processes can be tested using traditional regression techniques and more complex structural equation models (Kline 2010) and latent growth models (Duncan et al. 2006). The two processes are not mutually exclusive, nor are they the only possible trait mechanisms (Gross et al. 1998). For example, there are also more complex processes, such as moderated mediation and mediated moderation, but fortunately for the comprehensibility of this article, these have not yet been widely applied to personality processes (Muller et al. 2005).

Overview

In what follows, I examine a selection of studies investigating personality processes organized by domains common to models of both personality and temperament: negative emotionality (neuroticism and anger), positive emotionality (extraversion), and constraint (conscientiousness and effortful control). The starting point for this selection was a review of articles appearing in major personality journals from 2008 through 2010 identifying studies that investigated trait processes as I have chosen to define them. Some of these articles led down a winding trail to other journals and even other subdisciplines of psychology. The result is a selective and illustrative review, not a systematic one. For each personality/temperament domain, one or more traits are described, some of their more striking direct effects

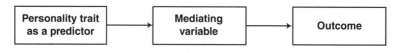

Figure 4

Mediated (indirect) effect of a personality trait on an outcome.

on consequential outcomes are noted, and examples of studies of personality processes are presented. The implications for trait theory and measurement are discussed, and the review concludes by suggesting directions for future research on personality trait processes.

NEGATIVE EMOTIONALITY

A selection of studies of neuroticism and anger illustrates trait processes for negative emotionality. Neuroticism and anger are closely aligned with the temperament of negative emotionality (Clark & Watson 2008, John et al. 2008, Rothbart 2011) and with the neurological behavioral inhibition system (BIS; Gray 1987, Gray & McNaughton 2000). The central feature of negative emotionality is a greater sensitivity to negative events leading to orientation of behavior and attention to negative stimuli (Canli 2006, Eysenck & Eysenck 1985, Gray & McNaughton 2000). From this perspective, negative emotionality includes both internalized emotions such as fear and externalized emotions such as anger and frustration. Hence Elliot & Thrash's (2010) labeling of negative emotionality as "avoidance" temperament is somewhat misleading. Negative emotionality does not preclude traits that may be more conventionally thought of as "approach," or proactive, such as aggression. Indeed, Costa & McCrae (1992) include angry hostility as one of the six facets of neuroticism.

However, in the Big Five taxonomic approach to personality (Goldberg 1993, John & Srivistava 1999), and also in the interpersonal circumplex (Wiggins 1991), the broad dimension of agreeableness contrasts traits describing positive versus negative interpersonal thoughts, feelings, and behaviors, including hostility (e.g., warm, kind, helpful, cooperative versus cold, cruel, hostile, thoughtless). Although compelling from a descriptive point of view, this solution is not consistent with current biological theory. Here is an instance where the language for describing individual differences apparently does not map neatly onto the underlying biological systems that give rise to them. For example, the neurotransmitter serotonin is associated with quarrelsome behavior (Moskowitz 2010) and is believed to be involved in the BIS, which would relate quarrelsomeness more closely to neuroticism than disagreeableness in models of trait structure (Smillie 2008).

Neuroticism

The trait of neuroticism is the chronic tendency for some individuals to experience more negative thoughts and feelings than others, to be emotionally unstable, and to be insecure. In contrast to those who are emotionally stable, more neurotic individuals are prone to being worried, anxious, moody, irritable, and depressed (Costa & McCrae 1992, John & Srivistava 1999). Neuroticism predicts a wide range of negative outcomes, including psychopathology (Clark & Watson 2008). People who are more neurotic have lower self-esteem and subjective well-being (Ozer & Benet-Martínez 2006). Higher levels of neuroticism are associated with undesirable interpersonal consequences such as less satisfying relationships and divorce (Roberts et al. 2007) and more aggressive behavior (Wilkowski & Robinson 2008). Neuroticism predicts negative health outcomes, such as reporting more somatic symptoms (Costa & McCrae 1987, Watson & Pennebaker 1989).

The overlap between the indicators of neuroticism and measures of self-reported health suggests that neuroticism may predict subjective distress but not more objective measures of disease. However, there is an impressive body of evidence showing prospective associations between negative emotionality and physical disease, particularly cardiovascular disease (Friedman & Booth-Kewley 1987, Suls & Bunde 2005) as well as physical distress (Charles et al. 2008). Mortality is incontrovertibly an objective outcome, and a number of studies have associated higher levels of neuroticism with reduced longevity (Roberts et al. 2007, Shipley et al. 2007, Terracciano et al. 2008, Wilson et al. 2003). Mroczek & Spiro (2007) related neuroticism assessed over a 12-year period in

BIS: behavioral inhibition system

old age to mortality, looking at both the level of neuroticism and the rate of increase. Men with a combination of high and more rapidly increasing neuroticism had the highest mortality risk. This is a landmark study because it established the importance of trait level and trait change over time as predictors of a consequential outcome. Of course, the association between level of neuroticism and mortality could be due to some unknown third variable, but the predictive power of the rate of change of neuroticism suggests a trait process is at work and strengthens the argument that neuroticism may be causally related to mortality. Nevertheless, neuroticism is not uniformly and consistently found to be related to mortality or poor health outcomes (Friedman et al. 2010). The heightened attention and sensitivity to negative stimuli that characterizes negative emotionality may also have protective effects for health (Kern & Friedman 2011).

Neuroticism and Moderation Processes

Neuroticism as a moderator of predictor-outcome relations. The conceptualization of neuroticism as heightened sensitivity to negative stimuli implies that, compared to more emotionally stable people, those who are more neurotic will have stronger emotional responses to the same adverse experiences. Many studies support this temperamental or reactivity hypothesis (e.g., Canli 2006, Gross et al. 1998, Suls & Martin 2005). Recent research confirms the greater emotional reactivity of more neurotic individuals across a variety of everyday settings. Tong (2010) related the experiencing of anger, sadness, fear, and guilt in response to events recorded over the course of two days. Participants also rated their appraisals of these events on dimensions such as fairness. Higher neuroticism was associated with stronger appraisal-emotion associations, confirming that, for example, a more neurotic person reacts to unfair events with more anger than does a less neurotic person. In a similar vein, Denissen & Penke (2008) found that the

relation between poor relationship quality and low self-esteem was stronger for people high on neuroticism. Wasylkiw and colleagues investigated whether neuroticism moderated the effect on depression of ideal self-discrepancy, an aversive state in which one is failing to live up to one's aspirations (Wasylkiw et al. 2010). In a questionnaire study, and in an experimental study where the saliency of the ideal self-discrepancy was manipulated, the amount of discrepancy between actual and ideal selves was a stronger predictor of depression for those with higher levels of neuroticism.

In contrast, Taga and colleagues observed a beneficial modifying effect of neuroticism in the Terman Lifecycle study (Taga et al. 2009). Surprisingly, bereavement in this sample was associated with decreased risk of mortality. Moreover, for bereaved men, higher neuroticism at age 30 was associated with even lower mortality risk, demonstrating that neuroticism can be associated with more positive health outcomes. This finding may be unique to this particular cohort. However, as a longitudinal study of personality processes unfolding over time, it suggests that the moderating effect of neuroticism (and perhaps other traits) may differ over the short term versus the long term. Neuroticism may increase the immediate experience of negative emotions, but this stronger emotional response may also lead to longer-term adaptive behaviors such as increased vigilance with regard to health or more concerted efforts to find a new partner. The contrast between moderation effects of neuroticism observed in short-term experience sampling studies such as Tong's (2010) versus long-term lifespan studies such as Taga and colleagues' (Taga et al. 2009) highlights the value of using both methodologies in studying personality processes (Mroczeck et al. 2003).

Neuroticism-outcome effects moderated by other variables. We can all probably recall a regrettable incident when we gave way to a strong emotional reaction. To avoid minor embarrassments and much more serious consequences of emotional reactivity, it would be helpful to find ways to reduce the association between neuroticism and emotional reactivity. Feltman and colleagues investigated whether mindfulness could moderate the effects of neuroticism on anger and depressive symptoms: A mindful state directs attention and awareness to the present (Feltman et al. 2009). They demonstrated that the association between neuroticism and anger, and neuroticism and depression, was stronger for those at lower levels of mindfulness. In a longitudinal study of couples in the community, Hellmuth & McNulty (2008) found that neuroticism was associated with subsequent intimate partner violence. However, neuroticism resulted in less violence for individuals who had less stress and who had more effective problem-solving skills.

These two studies demonstrate the importance of the context provided by the individual's other traits and abilities for predicting the impact of neuroticism on emotional outcomes. In so doing, these studies provide promise for interventions to reduce undesirable trait effects, not necessarily by attempting to change the trait itself, but instead by changing other aspects of the context, including the intrapersonal context, in which the trait operates. However, interventions to reduce the undesirable effects of negative emotionality may not be entirely beneficial for people high in neuroticism. For example, increasing their positive emotions could detract from the benefits to cognitive functioning they experience from the effects of trait-consistent negative mood (Tamir & Robinson 2004). Moreover, neuroticism's effects may be difficult or impossible to modify by increasing the experience of positive events. In a diary study, Longua and colleagues observed that the experience of daytime positive events buffered the effects of negative daytime events on negative affect and nighttime stress, but only for those low on neuroticism (Longua et al. 2009). Such findings are consistent with the view that neuroticism is associated with heightened sensitivity to negative events, and consequently increases in positive events may have no impact on subsequent negative emotions for those high on neuroticism.

In an experimental study, Moeller and colleagues examined both self-reported trait neuroticism and an implicit measure of aggressive responding as predictors of aggressive tendencies (Moeller et al. 2010). The implicit measure assessed the extent to which individuals differed in the strength of their associations between stress primes and aggressive thoughts. Moeller and colleagues likened the implicit association to if…then behavioral signatures in CAPS (i.e., "if" primed with a stress word, "then" this person is more likely to make an aggressive word association). They examined whether this implicit measure interacted with neuroticism to predict aggressive behavioral tendencies. They found a tendency for physical aggression to be highest for those with the combination of high neuroticism and high implicit stress-aggression associations (i.e., moderation by neuroticism).

Neuroticism and Mediation Processes

Investigations of potential mediators of neuroticism appear to be less common, perhaps because personality processes associated with neuroticism are generally considered to be temperamental (i.e., reactive) rather than instrumental (McCrae & Costa 1991). An instrumental process that could apply to neuroticism is mediation via health behaviors. Neurotic individuals, prone to experience intense negative emotions, may use health-damaging behaviors such as substance use to reduce their negative affect. Mroczek and colleagues examined whether the association between neuroticism and mortality observed in the Normative Aging Study could be explained by such a health-behavior model (Mroczek et al. 2009). They found that cigarette smoking partially mediated the effects of neuroticism on mortality, whereas drinking alcohol did not. These findings provide only modest support for the health-behavior model.

In another form of mediated instrumental process, niche building or situational selection (Caspi et al. 2005), people may experience more negative life events as a consequence of their higher neuroticism, which in turn may

ICM: integrated
cognitive model

result in more adverse outcomes. In a diary
study of married couples, Bolger & Schilling
(1991) investigated both situation selection
and reactivity processes. They found that those
higher in neuroticism did experience more
stressful events (situation selection). However,
this greater exposure to stressful events was
only half as powerful at explaining distress as
neurotics' greater reactivity to these events, indicating that reactivity was the more important
process. Research continues to amass showing
that neurotics are generally more reactive to
stress than are nonneurotics (Suls & Martin
2005). However, the assessment of stress,
independent of neurotics' greater reactivity
to their stress, is challenging. Studies using
more objective measures of stress, such as the
Life Events and Difficulties Schedule, in which
self-reported life events are objectively coded
for their level of stress by independent raters,
would be helpful in this context (Monroe 2008).

Anger

Trait anger is the tendency to experience anger
on a chronic, ongoing basis, whereas state anger
is a transitory negative emotion. Anger and hostility are associated with cardiovascular disease
and early mortality (Suls & Bunde 2005), as
well as harmful behavioral outcomes such as
domestic violence, child abuse, violence in the
workplace, and substance use (Wilkowski &
Robinson 2008). Processes involved in trait
anger and hostility are important for developing
interventions to reduce the negative outcomes
associated with these aspects of negative emotionality and may help resolve the conundrum
of where these traits should be placed in structural models of personality.

Anger and Moderation Processes

What personality processes result in someone high in trait anger actually expressing
that anger? Aggressive behavior is not well explained by either situational or dispositional
factors alone, making it an ideal candidate for
a combined social-cognitive and dispositional
approach. In their integrated cognitive model

(ICM), Wilkowski & Robinson (2010) draw on
three cognitive processes: interpretation, rumination, and effortful control. Consistent with
a reactive view, they proposed that those with
high trait anger are automatically more likely
to interpret situational input as hostile. However, ruminating on this hostile interpretation
will amplify the anger response to the situation,
whereas exerting effortful control will suppress
the anger response. They propose a moderating process in which those low in trait anger
are more likely than those high in trait anger
to use effortful control to down-regulate their
angry responses when hostile thoughts are activated. Support for their model comes from
both self-report and implicit evidence for these
different cognitive processes. For example, individuals low on trait anger showed less effect of
hostile priming than those high on trait anger,
but only if the experimental design permitted
them to use temperamental effortful control
(Wilkowski & Robinson 2007). Consistent with
CAPS (Mischel & Shoda 1998), in the ICM
trait anger is conceptualized as an integration
of several processes. A person predisposed to
angry acts is more likely to respond with anger
in a situation that is interpreted as hostile and
ruminated upon and in which he or she fails to
exert effortful control.

Summary and Implications for
Personality Theory and Measurement

The illustrative studies of moderation processes
for neuroticism and anger show that people
with higher levels of these traits are more
emotionally reactive, which usually has adverse
consequences for them. Other factors can
moderate this reactivity, which is promising for
intervention purposes. Traits of negative emotionality also influence outcomes by mediation
processes, such as through health behaviors and
niche selection. These studies also illustrate the
role that other personality traits play in trait
processes. Consequences of higher emotional
reactivity, associated with traits such as neuroticism and anger, can be reduced or amplified
by the modifying effects of effortful control.

Does this research help resolve the location of anger and hostility in structural models of personality? Viewed as different forms of negative affect, they work well subsumed together under the broad temperamental dimension of negative emotionality, and the identification of various moderating effects also suggests that anger and hostility are temperament based. Yet, trait disagreeableness involves interpersonally directed negative affect (externalizing behavior), and hence hostility is found as a facet of agreeableness-disagreeableness in the Big Five taxonomy. Although the broad trait dimension of agreeableness has not typically been viewed as a temperament-based trait, it is interesting that, in line with the findings from process studies, more recent conceptualizations of temperament include affiliativeness, which aligns with agreeableness (Zentner & Shiner 2011). The ultimate resolution of these kinds of inconsistencies should come about when we better understand the underlying biological bases of temperaments and traits.

Where traits of negative emotionality are placed in a structural framework affects how they are measured (e.g., as facets of neuroticism or disagreeableness). Another factor to consider when measuring these traits is their social undesirability. As a result, they are prone to inaccuracies in descriptions of the self and others. The implicit measure used by Moeller and colleagues to assess the strength of aggressive associations offers an approach that may reduce the impact of social-desirability bias (Moeller et al. 2010). The combination of both explicit (questionnaire) and implicit measures provides a more complete assessment of negative emotionality as well as a new approach to the study of reactive processes.

POSITIVE EMOTIONALITY

In contemporary theories of the neurobiological bases of personality, sensitivity to reward is central to positive emotionality (e.g., Canli 2006, Cloninger 1987, Corr 2006, Depue 2006, Gray 1987, Gray & McNaughton 2000, Smillie et al. 2006, Zuckerman 1994).

For example, the neurological behavioral approach system (BAS; Gray & McNaughton 2000), in which dopamine is believed to play a major role, is triggered by rewards, and BAS activity is assumed to underlie positive affect and approach motivation (Smillie 2008). Elliot & Thrash (2010) argue that approach temperament, which orients behavior and attention toward positive stimuli, is the common underlying core of the temperament of positive emotionality and of the trait of extraversion.

BAS: behavioral approach system

Extraversion

Extraversion is closely aligned with the temperament of positive emotionality or positive affect (Clark & Watson 2008, John et al. 2008, Rothbart 2011) and emerges as a broad dimension in all descriptions of personality structure. Extraversion-introversion contrasts people who are described as sociable, energetic, and assertive with ones who are reserved, withdrawn, and submissive (Eysenck & Eysenck 1985, John & Srivastava 1999).

People who are more extraverted experience greater happiness, subjective and existential well-being, than those inclined to introversion. Consistent with an underlying approach temperament, extraverts are more likely to use coping strategies that involve engaging with a challenge, such as problem-solving, than strategies of disengagement or avoidance (Carver & Connor-Smith 2010). They are more likely to be popular, have higher status, get satisfaction from their work, and be accepted by their peers (Ozer & Benet-Martínez 2006). However, extraversion has only rarely been found to be directly related to some of the other widely studied consequential outcomes such as longevity, marital stability, and occupational success (Roberts et al. 2007).

Extraversion: Mediation and Moderation Processes

Extraversion processes illustrated here are drawn from studies of happiness. Although extraversion is manifested in other forms of direct effects, many of these contribute to greater happiness (e.g., being successful, being popular). On average, people who are more extraverted are happier than those who are less extraverted, regardless of their circumstances. This is testimony to the power of personality. Happiness is enormously valued, yet it evades many people, so a better understanding of the personality processes by which extraverts experience happiness would be widely appreciated. In pursuing this quest, personality researchers have examined both mediation and moderation mechanisms.

From an instrumental perspective, extraverts are happier because they are more likely to actively create situations for themselves that make them happy. In particular, extraverts describe themselves as enjoying socializing with other people. Hence, compared to introverts, extraverts should spend more time with other people, and consequently they should be happier. This is a mediation hypothesis because extraversion's effect on happiness is postulated to be the result of greater social participation. From a temperamental, reactive, perspective, when extraverts and introverts are exposed to the same situation such as a social event, extraverts should experience greater happiness. According to the reward-sensitivity account, extraverts' greater happiness is explained by their capacity to attend and orient to positive, rewarding aspects of their environments. This biological account of extraversion implies a moderating mechanism whereby extraverts should consistently derive greater happiness than introverts from the same situations.

As an account of extraverts' higher levels of happiness, mediation through social participation has received only modest empirical support. Doing things with other people does make us happy, but whether extraverts spend more time socializing than introverts and, in doing so, increase their happiness has not been well established. Experience sampling methodologies yield the kind of fine-grained data necessary to identify small but important differences in sources of daily happiness necessary to study these personality processes.

For example, Srivastava and colleagues studied individuals' social interactions and their associated emotions over the course of a day (Srivastava et al. 2008). Higher extraversion was associated with experiencing more positive affect, but extraversion was also associated with only somewhat more social participation, which only partially mediated the relation between extraversion and positive affect.

Lucas and colleagues studied extraverts' greater happiness assessed at random intervals throughout the day as well as by daily diaries (Lucas et al. 2008). Across these two methods, extraverts were happier than introverts, and they did spend more time socializing. However, after controlling for their greater social activity, extraverts were still happier than introverts, so again the mediation hypothesis was not fully supported. Interestingly, those who were more extraverted did not get much more of a boost in happiness from social situations than those who were less extraverted. That is, extraverts were consistently happier than introverts, but this was not because they obtained substantially greater pleasure from socializing. This finding is contrary to what would be expected if extraversion was a strong moderator of the relation between socializing and happiness. Overall, in this study the majority of participants' happiness was a direct effect of their extraversion, regardless of social activity, suggesting that there may be other as yet untested processes involved. The process of "acting extraverted" could be such a mechanism.

In our daily lives, we behave in more or less extraverted ways, and Fleeson and colleagues hypothesized that individuals would feel happier when they were being more extraverted (Fleeson et al. 2002). The within-person association between behaving in an extraverted way and feeling happy may also be stronger among more extraverted people. This is a moderation process: Extraversion should moderate the association between behaving in an extraverted way and feeling happy. Using three different methodologies (experience sampling several times a day, a diary study conducted over a week, and a laboratory study), participants reported being happier when their behavior was more extraverted. This association was not consistently stronger for more extraverted people, contrary to a moderating process.

Summary and Implications for Personality Theory and Assessment

The association between happiness and extraversion can be explained to a modest degree by mediating mechanisms involving social participation and by moderating effects of extraversion on the link between social activity and happiness. However, much work remains to be done to understand the trait process involved in experiencing happiness and the moment-by-moment variability in happiness levels that we all experience in our daily lives. Social activity is just one of many influences on subjective well-being, so there may be other mediators to explore in addition to socializing (e.g., physical activity) to better understand extraversion processes and happiness.

If being briefly more extraverted makes a person happier for that moment, perhaps repeated experience of extraverted states could result in more lasting happiness by, in effect, making a person more extraverted. This is a promising idea for clinical intervention and has the wider implication that personality traits are amenable to change. This idea is, in fact, present in current personality theorizing (Roberts et al. 2008). For example, the proposition that repeated experiences of states could change traits is part of sociogenomic personality psychology advocated by Roberts & Jackson (2008) to explain personality development and change. They draw on sociogenomic biology to demonstrate that even genetic effects, once thought immutable, are in fact subject to alteration and triggering by environmental factors (Krueger & Johnson 2008). In their model, states play a key mediating role: Repeated experience of states eventually will result in changes in traits.

Findings on extraversion processes also have implications for trait measurement. Questionnaire scales to measure extraversion typically include many items assessing social participation. However, although extraverts may not consistently derive more pleasure than introverts from social events, their capacity to extract greater happiness from life seems incontrovertible. To align questionnaire measures more closely with theory and findings on extraversion processes, there should be less emphasis on social activity and more items that tap into other potentially rewarding situations.

Sociogenomic biology: gene expression is influenced by the environment, and consequently the relation between genes and phenotypes is transactional

CONSTRAINT

In addition to positive and negative emotionality, constraint is a third well-established area of temperament and personality (Carver 2005, Rothbart 2011). Unalloyed approach and avoidance tendencies cannot have been adaptive during human evolution and certainly cause problems in today's world. The underlying biological basis of constraint is believed to be located in attentional networks in the brain, although these have yet to be fully charted (Nigg 2000, Rothbart 2007, Rothbart & Rueda 2005). Accordingly, the deployment of effortful control depends on there being sufficient mental capacity, such as working memory, available to regulate the other systems (Rothbart 2007). Such capacity is viewed by some investigators as a relatively fixed attribute of the person, whereas others hypothesize that it fluctuates. For example, the strength model of ego depletion postulates that effortful control fluctuates because it diminishes with use but can be replenished (Baumeister et al. 2007, Hagger et al. 2010). Others have suggested that in addition to intentional, goal-based inhibition there is reactive, automatic inhibition (Eisenberg et al. 2004, Nigg 2000, Rothbart & Ahadi 1994).

Another perspective on constraint is provided by Strack & Deutsch's (2004) reflective impulsive model, in which the impulsive system activates automatic approach or avoidance behavior, whereas the reflective system governs reasoned action and can regulate the impulsive system. Together, according to the model, these systems result in social behavior. Moreover, the impulsive and reflective systems are not limited to conscientiousness but are implicated in all the broad personality dimensions. Similarly, in Rothbart's model of temperament, effortful control moderates negative and positive emotional reactivity (Rothbart 2011). The burgeoning of these various models demonstrates that impulsivity and constraint are coming under increasing scrutiny, with implications for the study of the personality processes related to conscientiousness and perhaps other traits.

Conscientiousness

Studies of trait conscientiousness illustrate processes for constraint. In temperament models, constraint is presumed to be the precursor to later trait conscientiousness (Carver 2005, Clark & Watson 2008, Elliot & Thrash 2010, Rothbart 2011). The trait of conscientiousness describes individual differences in adhering to socially prescribed rules and norms for impulse control, in being task- and goal-directed, and in being able to delay gratification (John & Srivastava 1999). At the extremes, the conscientiousness dimension distinguishes people who are orderly, industrious, and planful from those who are undisciplined, lazy, and unreliable. These qualities reflect impulse control and restraint versus a lack thereof.

The two most striking associations between conscientiousness and consequential outcomes are with health and job performance (Ozer & Benet-Martínez 2006). Friedman and colleagues (Friedman et al. 1995) first demonstrated that lower levels of childhood conscientiousness are associated with earlier mortality, and this finding has subsequently been replicated in other longitudinal studies (Kern & Friedman 2008). Barrick & Mount's (1991) meta-analysis established that higher levels of conscientiousness are associated with better job performance, a finding that holds up across different measures of conscientiousness and widely differing occupations. Many studies demonstrate that lack of conscientiousness is associated with health-damaging behaviors (Bogg & Roberts 2004), and lack of self-control and constraint is associated with a range of significant behavioral problems including conduct disorder and substance abuse (Wills & Dishion 2004).

Conscientiousness and Moderation Processes

The direct association between conscientiousness and health behaviors is well established, and both moderating and mediating processes involved in this relation have been examined. Risky sex is of particular significance as a health behavior. HIV/AIDS infection is primarily transmitted via sexual contact, so understanding the factors that determine whether or not people engage in safe sex is necessary for the development of appropriate interventions. Low conscientiousness has been consistently associated with unsafe sex. Nevertheless, the association is comparatively modest, indicating that many other factors are involved and that interactions among these factors should be examined.

Cooper (2010) investigated the effects of personality traits and situational factors on risky sex in a longitudinal study of adolescents and emerging adults. Multilevel models of a large corpus of reported occurrences of sexual intercourse were collected over time, which enabled the evaluation of between- and within-person variability. Although there was evidence of modest levels of stable between- and within-person effects of personality traits on risky sex (e.g., sex without a condom) and modest stable situational effects (e.g., first-time partner versus long-term relationship), the interactions between traits and situations generated the major findings from this study (i.e., moderated effects). The preponderance of the between-person effects showed that personality traits were most likely to predict risky sex with first-time or casual sex partners. Within-person effects showed that adolescents with traits that put them at most risk (e.g., low conscientiousness) showed the greatest variability across situations and the riskiest behavior. Moreover, interaction patterns were not consistent across the different measures of risky sex (e.g., alcohol involved, condom use), adding another level of complexity to the findings. Importantly, in some situations, impulsive (low conscientious) individuals displayed no risky behaviors at all. This study demonstrates the significance of examining moderation and within-person variability for a more complete understanding of when dispositions are translated into highly consequential behaviors.

Studies such as Cooper's (2010), in which multilevel event sampling methods have been applied to the study of conscientiousness processes, are still relatively rare. These findings, however, indicate that this approach uncovers effects that may remain hidden in studies limited to between-person data. For example, in a diary study of a community sample, the relations between daily hassles and health behaviors such as snacking, alcohol consumption, and smoking were moderated by certain facets of conscientiousness (O'Connor et al. 2009). Those with lower self-efficacy ate fewer vegetables on days when they experienced hassles, and those with higher levels of order were more likely to exercise on days when they experienced hassles. Surprisingly, those with higher levels of self-discipline smoked more and drank more caffeine on days when they experienced hassles, perhaps as a consequence of their high motivation for task completion in the face of these hassles.

Other studies illustrate how personality processes may be investigated in the context of cognitive social-psychological theories such as the Theory of Planned Behavior (Ajzen 1985, 1991) using more conventional prospective, between-person designs. Such studies have shown beneficial moderating effects of higher levels of conscientiousness on the relation between intentions and the performance of health behaviors, including exercise behaviors (Rhodes et al. 2002, 2005) and smoking initiation (Conner et al. 2009). In a similar vein, drawing on the prototype-willingness model, Wills and colleagues demonstrated moderating effects of good self-control on the association between risk factors such as deviant peers and media exposure on substance use (Wills et al. 2010). Although derived from a different theoretical tradition, the cognitive constructs in these theories (e.g., self-efficacy, subjective normative beliefs, prototypes) overlap with or are comparable to constructs in Mischel & Shoda's (1998) CAPS model for personality. These studies demonstrate that the addition of personality traits increases the explanatory power of processes involving social-cognitive constructs.

Conscientiousness and Mediation Processes

Mediation has also been invoked as a mechanism underlying the effects of conscientiousness, perhaps more commonly than moderation. When studying those aspects of conscientiousness that involve the exertion of effortful control, such as being planful and delaying gratification, instrumental processes, whereby conscientious people influence their environments, are more likely to be identified than reactive processes. Inspired by the now well-established finding that conscientiousness predicts longevity, a major research effort is under way to identify the pathways by which the influences of early conscientiousness on later health outcomes are mediated. Conscientious people are more likely to engage in health-protective behaviors and to avoid health-damaging behaviors (Bogg & Roberts 2004), but what remains to be demonstrated convincingly is that these health-behavior pathways result in longer, healthier lives for more conscientious people.

Health is not easily reduced to a single variable, being composed of objective and medical factors, psychosocial factors, and subjective perceptions. However, vital status is the ultimate objective measure of health. Friedman et al. (1995) found that the association between childhood conscientiousness at age 11 and longevity among members of the Terman Lifecycle study was partially mediated by lifetime patterns of cigarette use and other health behaviors. More recently, analyzing additional follow-up data, Martin and colleagues found that both child and adult conscientiousness predicted longevity, and the effects of adult conscientiousness were mediated by health behaviors, particularly smoking (Martin et al. 2007). Participants in the Terman Lifecycle study were children with IQs of 135 recruited in 1921–1922. Using a very different longitudinal sample, my colleagues and I investigated subjective health status at midlife (Hampson et al. 2007). Our participants were drawn from entire classrooms of elementary school children aged 6–12 years who were assessed between 1959 and 1967 in Hawaii. In this 40-year follow-up study, the relation between childhood conscientiousness assessed in elementary school and self-rated health at middle age was partially mediated by smoking and other health behaviors. It is interesting that both studies indicate only partial mediation by health behaviors, leaving other mechanisms to be discovered. Furthermore, in both studies, despite the sample differences, some of the effects of conscientiousness were mediated by educational level, a key determinant of socioeconomic status and hence of numerous life outcomes, suggesting another important mediating mechanism for this trait (Chapman et al. 2010, Nabi et al. 2008).

Mediating mechanisms have also been identified for conscientiousness in studies testing cognitive social-psychological models of health behaviors. In a study predicting fruit consumption from a combination of personality traits and concepts from the Theory of Planned Behavior, individuals who were more conscientious reported eating more fruit, and this relation was mediated by two of the theory's concepts: attitude toward and perceived behavioral control over the outcome (de Bruijn et al. 2009). Drawing on the transtheoretical model of behavior change (Prochaska & DiClemente 1984), Bogg (2008) showed that the effects of the industriousness facet of conscientiousness on stage of change for exercise behavior were mediated by processes associated with the stages of change. Those with higher levels of industriousness reported greater use of processes such as re-evaluation and overcoming resistance, and these processes fully mediated the effects of industriousness in predicting stage of change.

Summary and Implications for Personality Theory and Measurement

Processes by which traits of constraint such as conscientiousness and self-control influence outcomes include both moderation and mediation, reflecting both reactive and instrumental mechanisms. Much of the illustrative research is drawn from health psychology. Studies of moderation show that conscientiousness can reduce or amplify associations between some predictors and health outcomes. Unlike the moderation processes discussed for negative and positive emotionality, moderation by effortful control involves the deliberate moderation of a response, such as resisting the urge to snack in response to stress. Automatic inhibition represents a more reactive form of constraint that has not been nearly as extensively studied. Other studies show that conscientiousness exerts an indirect influence on health outcomes through the instrumental processes of mediation by intervening variables such as health behaviors.

Current theorizing in personality psychology is addressing the relation of trait conscientiousness to other constraint constructs and the temperament of effortful control. One view is that a broad latent construct of disinhibition resulting from inadequate executive functioning encompasses all constructs tapping impulsivity versus constraint. For example, behavioral disinhibition modeled as a latent construct indicated by impulsive sensation seeking (i.e., low conscientiousness), antisociality, and externalizing problem behaviors was negatively correlated with IQ and the capacity of working and short-term memory (Bogg & Finn 2010).

Inhibition is an important aspect of executive functioning; however, the inhibition construct (or metaphor) is itself multifaceted (Nigg 2000). There are numerous forms of cognitive inhibition (e.g., interference control, suppression of ideation, suppression of cued responses), and the tasks used to measure them do not necessarily correlate. Edmonds and colleagues related several laboratory measures of impulsivity and self-report questionnaire measures to self-reported health behaviors (Edmonds et al.

2009). The laboratory and questionnaire measures were mostly unrelated, and they contributed independently to the prediction of health behaviors. The different laboratory measures of impulsivity were also not highly intercorrelated, which raises the question of whether it is appropriate to regard these kinds of tasks as indicators of the same underlying construct. Straightforward relations between measures of executive functioning and personality traits are unlikely. Despite this, researchers, particularly in the field of health behavior, see promise in measuring individual differences in cognitive competencies to understand behaviors that require the ability to override an automatic response (Suchy 2009, Williams & Thayer 2009).

Effortful control, viewed as trait conscientiousness, is conceptualized as a stable, cross-situationally consistent disposition. However, from a temperament perspective, deriving in part from cognitive neuroscience, it is a capacity that is demonstrated in response to situational cues (Robinson & Wilkowski 2010). These two views may not, in fact, be that discrepant. Studies of within-person variability such as Cooper's (2010) discussed above demonstrate that even those who are highly impulsive only behave impulsively under specific conditions. The study of personality processes addresses exactly these kinds of issues—that is, the conditions under which dispositions are manifested in behavior. The recent interest in executive functioning and conscientiousness processes has implications for personality measurement. Although people can describe their tendencies to respond impulsively, to the extent that cognitive inhibitory processes occur outside of awareness, the assessment of constraint may be enhanced by the addition of implicit techniques.

CONCLUSIONS AND FUTURE DIRECTIONS

At the beginning of this review, distinguishing personality processes ("how" and "why") from personality structure ("what") proved useful. However, personality processes need to be united with personality structure, measurement, and theory. To study trait processes, it is

necessary to have at least a rudimentary theory about how an internal disposition is manifested in behavior. As we have seen, these theories typically draw on moderating or mediating mechanisms. What determines whether trait processes are best conceptualized as mediation or moderation? As the studies reviewed here illustrate, reactive processes are commonly examined with moderation and instrumental processes with mediation. However, this is not a hard-and-fast rule. Nor should it be concluded that reactive processes necessarily occur automatically whereas instrumental processes involve deliberation and conscious choice. Examples of moderation and mediation were identified for negative emotionality, positive emotionality, and constraint, indicating no simple relation between trait domain and type of process. It appears that approach and avoidance tendencies, and their regulation by constraint, operate through multiple mechanisms involving moderation and mediation and probably many other processes. For an investigator planning a trait-process study, the bewildering choice among these mechanisms must be guided by a theoretical position regarding the nature of the trait and the factors hypothesized to influence its expression.

Theoretical frameworks based on temperament or reactivity that generate hypotheses about moderation, such as BIS and BAS, are discussed above. Another promising direction for the study of trait processes is the combination of constructs from social-cognitive theories with personality traits. We have seen examples of combining traits with elements of CAPS (e.g., Moeller et al. 2010, Moskowitz 2010) and with elements from theories such as the theory of planned behavior and the transtheoretical model (e.g., Bogg 2008, Conner et al. 2009). The neo-socioanalytic theory of Roberts & Wood (2006) provides a framework to help guide these kinds of integration of constructs at various levels of breadth drawn from different theoretical models.

Neo-socioanalytic theory identifies four kinds of individual differences (traits, motives/values, abilities, and narratives), each

Neo-socioanalytic theory: an approach to integrating individual differences across different hierarchically structured domains (e.g., traits and motives)

of which is organized hierarchically. The broadest level in each hierarchy is decontextualized (e.g., conscientiousness, general intelligence), whereas the lower levels become increasingly specified. Within a hierarchy, the effects of higher-level constructs on specific behavioral outcomes may be mediated by lower-level constructs. Associations among constructs will be stronger within one type of individual-difference hierarchy (e.g., traits) than between different hierarchies (e.g., traits and motives/values). However, associations that cut across the type of individual difference will be stronger to the extent that they share features (i.e., are psychologically proximal). Applying the principles of neo-socioanalytic theory should be particularly useful when selecting potential mediators of trait effects, either within the trait hierarchy or from another hierarchy (Bogg et al. 2008).

For the most part, the trait processes described here have been studied for effects of personality at the level of the individual, yet traits also have consequential interpersonal outcomes for dyadic relationships and for larger social groups. When personality processes are studied in social contexts, effects of individual differences on responses to factors such as social exclusion (DeWall et al. 2011), sexual motivation (Cooper et al. 2011), and impression management (Leary & Batts Allen 2011) are observed. There is much scope for further research and theoretical development on personality processes that account for trait influences at the interpersonal and group levels.

The study of trait processes has introduced the field of personality to some new methodologies. In particular, more fine-grained studies of behaviors in context have used various methods for recording activities and situations at random intervals throughout the day or by diaries kept on a once-daily basis (Furr 2009). These methodologies are particularly suited to studying situational influences on behavior over relatively short periods of time. They generate multiple events for each participant, which can then be aggregated in different ways to examine the patterning of behavior across different situations (Moskowitz & Zuroff 2004). Technological advances in programmable portable devices (e.g., cell phones, personal digital assistants, audio recorders) make increasing use of these kinds of data likely in the study of personality processes.

Neuroscience theories of personality are rapidly developing as more powerful technologies for studying brain activity are becoming available to personality psychologists (Canli 2006). Neuroimaging offers a window on personality processes that occur under the skin (in this case, under the skull). As such, these processes are not the focus of this review. However, one important consequence of neuroscience theories of personality is that they have generated new measurement approaches. Guided by neuroscience theories of traits, functional magnetic resonance imaging is being used to map areas of the brain related to personality processes, and rapid advances in this field are likely (Harris et al. 2007).

The study of processes that occur outside of awareness is advanced by using techniques such as implicit associations. For example, Back and colleagues showed that implicit measures of extraversion and neuroticism provided incremental predictive value to questionnaires (explicit measures) in the prediction of behavior related to those traits, whereas implicit measures of conscientiousness did not (Back et al. 2009). They concluded that the underlying approach and avoidance tendencies of extraversion and neuroticism involve automatic processes best captured by implicit measures, whereas conscientiousness involves more conscious control of impulses, best assessed by self-reflective measures such as questionnaires. Whether automatic and reflective processes map so neatly onto the trait domains remains to be seen, but the addition of implicit measures to more traditional questionnaires should be valuable if they can assess aspects of dispositional tendencies that operate outside awareness.

One implication of the study of personality processes is that broader contextual factors, which can be important determinants of when traits are actually manifested in behaviors, should also be assessed. A system for categorizing situations that is useful for personality psychology has remained elusive (Saucier et al. 2007). Denissen & Penke's (2008) integration of the five-factor trait structure with motivation represents a new approach to this longstanding problem: They used the existing five-factor model as a way to categorize situations. They proposed that traits reflect individual differences in people's motivational reactions to environmental stimuli and developed a version of a five-factor questionnaire in which the items for each trait dimension describe typical cognitive or affective reactions to specified situations. Their measure is an attempt to combine trait measurement with a motivational theory of trait processes.

Another methodological development with implications for the study of trait processes is the increasing use of longitudinal data and techniques for describing trait change over time, such as growth curve modeling (Duncan et al. 2006). With these techniques, we can now evaluate trait development in terms of level and rate of change and relate both these parameters to outcomes such as mortality (Mroczek & Spiro 2007, Mroczek et al. 2009) or substance use (Hampson et al. 2010). Measuring trait change over time may stimulate the discovery of new trait processes involving rate of change. Trait processes unfold over time, during which traits themselves are also changing, adding a layer of complexity to mechanisms studied longitudinally.

Longitudinal studies provide opportunities for studying personality processes over extended periods of time. The study of these processes represents the opposite extreme of the fine-grained analyses of personality processes occurring over the course of a day revealed by event-sampling studies. Studies of personality processes across the lifespan are beginning to identify explanatory pathways to account for associations between traits and outcomes such as mortality (Friedman 2000). A challenge for this work is that few longitudinal studies have been conducted over substantial portions of the lifespan or have repeatedly assessed all the necessary variables to study personality processes over time. Moreover, findings from any single longitudinal study may be unique to that cohort. One solution to this challenge is to combine data across different studies. Recent developments in integrative data analysis techniques have great potential for the study of lifespan personality processes (Hofer & Piccinin 2009).

Discovering the processes by which traits have their effects will identify opportunities for intervention. As evidence has mounted for the important role played by personality traits in consequential life outcomes, there is increasing interest in the possibility of using this knowledge to bring about beneficial personality change (Moffitt et al. 2011). Interventions may be directed at changing the level or rate of growth of traits, or they may be directed at the processes through which traits are manifested in behavior. For example, the idea that effortful control can be trained and that this can have a lasting impact on the brain offers exciting possibilities for the development of interventions to modify trait conscientiousness (Posner & Rothbart 2007).

The study of trait processes offers an important direction for the future for personality psychology. A focus on personality processes will ground our understanding of personality in its biological roots in temperament and highlight personality change, both developmental change that occurs across the lifespan and deliberate change brought about by interventions. A better understanding of trait processes will inform trait structure and measurement that in turn can be used to further advance the study of trait processes. The study of trait processes necessitates an integrative perspective, requiring researchers to cross traditional boundaries such as social-cognitive versus trait theory, biological versus social explanations, or experimental versus correlational methods. Examples of such research have been reviewed here. Understanding trait processes that explain why personality traits have consequential effects on life outcomes has already become an exciting research agenda for personality psychology.

DISCLOSURE STATEMENT

The author is not aware of any affiliations, memberships, funding, or financial holdings that might be perceived as affecting the objectivity of this review.

ACKNOWLEDGMENTS

I am indebted to Grant E. Edmonds, Lewis R. Goldberg, Daniel K. Mroczek, and Mary K. Rothbart for their helpful comments on earlier drafts. This work was supported in part by NIH grants AG20048 and DA10767 and by the Oregon Research Institute.

LITERATURE CITED

Ajzen I. 1985. From intentions to actions: a theory of planned behavior. In *Action-Control: From Cognition to Behavior*, ed. J Kuh, J Beckman, pp. 11–39. Heidelberg, Germany: Springer

Ajzen I. 1991. The theory of planned behavior. *Organ. Behav. Hum. Dec.* 50:179–211

Ashton MC, Lee K. 2007. Empirical, theoretical, and practical advantages of the HEXACO model of personality structure. *Personal. Soc. Psychol. Rev.* 11:150–66

Back MD, Schmukle SC, Egloff B. 2009. Predicting actual behavior from the explicit and implicit self-concept of personality. *J. Personal. Soc. Psychol.* 97:533–48

Baron RM, Kenny DA. 1986. The moderator-mediator variable distinction in social psychological research: conceptual, strategic and statistical considerations. *J. Personal. Soc. Psychol.* 51:1173–82

Barrick MR, Mount MK. 1991. The Big Five personality dimensions and job performance: a meta-analysis. *Pers. Psychol.* 44:1–26

Baumeister RF, Vohs KD, Tice DM. 2007. The strength model of self-control. *Curr. Dir. Psychol. Sci.* 16:396–403

Bogg T. 2008. Conscientiousness, the transtheoretical model of change, and exercise: a neo-socioanalytic integration of trait and social-cognitive frameworks in the prediction of behavior. *J. Personal.* 76:775–802

Bogg T, Finn PR. 2010. A self-regulatory model of behavioral disinhibition in late adolescence: integrating personality traits, externalizing psychopathology, and cognitive capacity. *J. Personal.* 78:441–70

Bogg T, Roberts BW. 2004. Conscientiousness and health-related behaviors: a meta-analysis of the leading behavioral contributors to mortality. *Psychol. Bull.* 130:887–919

Bogg T, Voss MW, Wood D, Roberts BW. 2008. A hierarchical investigation of personality and behavior: examining neo-socioanalytic models of health-related outcomes. *J. Res. Personal.* 42:183–207

Bolger N, Schilling EA. 1991. Personality and the problems of everyday life: the role of neuroticism in exposure and reactivity to daily stressors. *J. Personal.* 59:355–86

Canli T. 2006. Genomic imaging of extraversion. In *Biology of Personality and Individual Differences*, ed. T Canli, pp. 93–115. New York: Guilford

Carver CS. 2005. Impulse and constraint: perspectives from personality psychology, convergence with theory in other areas, and potential for integration. *Personal. Soc. Psychol. Rev.* 9:312–33

Carver CS, Connor-Smith J. 2010. Personality and coping. *Annu. Rev. Psychol.* 61:679–704

Caspi A, Roberts BW, Shiner R. 2005. Personality development. *Annu. Rev. Psychol.* 56:453–84

Cervone D. 2004. The architecture of personality. *Psychol. Rev.* 111:183–204

Cervone D. 2005. Personality architecture: within-person structures and processes. *Annu. Rev. Psychol.* 56:423–52

Cervone D, Caldwell TL, Fiori M, Orom H, Shadel WG, et al. 2008. What underlies appraisals? Experimentally testing a knowledge-and-appraisal model of personality architecture among smokers contemplating high-risk situations. *J. Personal.* 76:929–67

Chapman BP, Fiscella K, Kawachi I, Duberstein PR. 2010. Personality, socioeconomic status, and all-cause mortality in the United States. *Am. J. Epidemiol.* 171:83–92

Charles ST, Gatz M, Kato K, Pedersen NL. 2008. Physical health twenty-five years later: the predictive ability of neuroticism. *Health Psychol.* 27:369–78

Clark LA, Watson D. 2008. Temperament: an organizing paradigm for trait psychology. See John et al. 2008, pp. 265–86

Cloninger CR. 1987. A systematic method for clinical description and classification of personality variants. *Arch. Gen. Psychiatry* 44:573–88

Conner MT, Grogan S, Fry G, Gough B, Higgins AR. 2009. Direct, mediated and moderated impacts of personality variables on smoking initiation in adolescents. *Psychol. Health* 24:1085–104

Cooper ML. 2010. Toward a person X situation model of sexual risk-taking behaviors: illuminating the conditional effects of traits across sexual situations and relationship contexts. *J. Personal. Soc. Psychol.* 98:319–41

Cooper ML, Barber LL, Zhaoyang R, Talley AE. 2011. Motivational pursuits in the context of human sexual relationships. *J. Personal.* In press

Corr PJ. 2006. *Understanding Biological Psychology*. Oxford, UK: Blackwell

Costa PT, McCrae RR. 1987. Neuroticism, somatic complaints, and disease: Is the bark worse than the bite? *J. Personal.* 55:299–316

Costa PT, McCrae RR. 1992. *Revised NEO Personality Inventory (NEO-PI-R) and NEO Five-Factor Inventory (NEO-FFI) Professional Manual*. Odessa, FL: Psychol. Assess. Resourc.

de Bruijn G-J, Brug J, Van Lenthe FJ. 2009. Neuroticism, conscientiousness and fruit consumption: exploring mediator and moderator effects in the theory of planned behavior. *Psychol. Health* 24:1051–69

Denissen JJA, Penke L. 2008. Neuroticism predicts reactions to cues of social inclusion. *Eur. J. Personal.* 22:497–517

Depue RA. 2006. Interpersonal behavior and the structure of personality. In *Biology of Personality and Individual Differences*, ed. T Canli, pp. 60–92. New York: Guilford

DeWall CN, Deckman T, Pond RS, Bonser I. 2011. Belongingness as a core personality trait: how social exclusion influences social functioning and personality expression. *J. Personal.* In press

Digman JM. 1990. Personality structure: emergence of the five-factor model. *Annu. Rev. Psychol.* 41:417–40

Duncan TE, Duncan SC, Strycker LA. 2006. *An Introduction to Latent Variable Growth Curve Modeling Concepts, Issues, and Applications*. Mahwah, NJ: Erlbaum

Edmonds GE, Bogg T, Roberts BW. 2009. Are personality and behavioral measures of impulse control convergent or distinct predictors of health behaviors? *J. Res. Personal.* 43:806–14

Eisenberg N, Spinrad TL, Fabes RA, Reiser M, Cumberland A, et al. 2004. The relations of effortful control and impulsivity to children's resiliency and adjustment. *Child Dev.* 75:25–46

Elliot AJ, Thrash TM. 2010. Approach and avoidance temperament as basic dimensions of personality. *J. Personal.* 78:865–906

Evans DE, Rothbart MK. 2007. Development of a model for adult temperament. *J. Res. Personal.* 41:868–88

Eysenck HJ, Eysenck MW. 1985. *Personality and Individual Differences: A Natural Science Approach*. New York: Plenum

Feltman R, Robinson MD, Ode S. 2009. Mindfulness as a moderator of neuroticism-outcome relations: a self-regulation perspective. *J. Res. Personal.* 43:953–61

Fleeson W, Malanos A, Achille N. 2002. An intra-individual, process approach to the relationship between extraversion and positive affect: Is acting extraverted as "good" as being extraverted? *J. Personal. Soc. Psychol.* 83:1409–22

Friedman HS. 2000. Long-term relations of personality and health: dynamisms, mechanisms, tropisms. *J. Personal.* 68:1089–108

Friedman HS, Booth-Kewley S. 1987. The "disease-prone personality": a meta-analytic view of the construct. *Am. Psychol.* 42:539–55

Friedman HS, Kern ML, Reynolds CA. 2010. Personality and health, subjective well being, and longevity. *J. Personal.* 78:179–215

Friedman HS, Tucker J, Schwartz JE, Martin LR, Tomlinson-Keasey C, et al. 1995. Childhood conscientiousness and longevity: health behaviors and cause of death. *J. Personal. Soc. Psychol.* 68:696–703

Funder DC. 2001. Personality. *Annu. Rev. Psychol.* 52:197–221

Furr RM. 2009. Personality psychology as a truly behavioral science. *Eur. J. Personal.* 23:369–401

Goldberg LR. 1990. An alternative "description of personality": the Big-Five factor structure. *J. Personal. Soc. Psychol.* 59:1216–29

Goldberg LR. 1993. The structure of phenotypic personality traits. *Am. Psychol.* 48:26–34

Gray JA. 1987. *The Psychology of Fear and Stress*. Cambridge: Cambridge Univ. Press

Gray JA, McNaughton N. 2000. *The Neuropsychology of Anxiety: An Enquiry into the Functions of the Septo-Hippocampal System*. New York: Oxford Univ. Press. 2nd ed.

Gross JJ, Sutton SK, Ketelaar T. 1998. Relations between affect and personality: support for the affect-level and affective-reactivity views. *Personal. Soc. Psychol. Bull.* 24:279–88

Hagger MS, Wood C, Stiff C, Chatzisarantis NLD. 2010. Ego-depletion and the strength model of self-control: a meta-analysis. *Psychol. Bull.* 136:495–525

Hampson SE. 2008. Mechanisms by which childhood personality traits influence adult well-being. *Curr. Dir. Psychol. Sci.* 17:264–68

Hampson SE, Goldberg LR, Vogt TM, Dubanoski JP. 2007. Mechanisms by which childhood personality traits influence adult health status: educational attainment and healthy behaviors. *Health Psychol.* 26:121–25

Hampson SE, Tildesley E, Andrews JA, Luyckx K, Mroczek DK. 2010. The relation of change in hostility and sociability during childhood to substance use in mid adolescence. *J. Res. Personal.* 44:103–14

Harris LT, McClure SM, Van Den Boss W, Cohen JD, Fiske ST. 2007. Regions of the MPFC differentially tuned to social and nonsocial affective evaluation. *Cogn. Affect. Behav. Neurosci.* 7:309–16

Hellmuth JC, McNulty JK. 2008. Neuroticism, marital violence, and the moderating role of stress and behavioral skills. *J. Personal. Soc. Psychol.* 95:166–80

Hofer SM, Piccinin AM. 2009. Integrative data analysis through coordination of measurement and analysis protocol across independent longitudinal studies. *Psychol. Methods* 14:150–64

John OP, Naumann LP, Soto CJ. 2008. Paradigm shift to the integrative Big-Five trait taxonomy: history, measurement, and conceptual issues. See John et al. 2008, pp. 114–58

John OP, Robins RW, Pervin LA, eds. 2008. *Handbook of Personality: Theory and Research*. New York: Guilford. 3rd ed.

John OP, Srivastava S. 1999. The Big Five Trait taxonomy: history, measurement, and theoretical perspectives. In *Handbook of Personality: Theory and Research*, ed. LA Pervin, OP John, pp. 102–38. New York: Guilford. 2nd ed.

Kelly GA. 1955/1991. *The Psychology of Personal Constructs*. New York: Norton/London: Routledge

Kern ML, Friedman HS. 2011. Personality and pathways of influence on physical health. *Soc. Personal. Psychol. Compass.* 5:76–87

Kern ML, Friedman HS. 2008. Do conscientious individuals live longer? A quantitative review. *Health Psychol.* 27:505–12

Kline RB. 2010. *Principles and Practice of Structural Equation Modeling*. New York: Guilford. 3rd ed.

Krueger RF, Johnson W. 2008. Behavioral genetics and personality: a new look at the integration of nature and nurture. See John et al. 2008, pp. 287–310

Leary MR, Batts Allen A. 2011. Personality and persona: personality processes in self-presentation. *J. Personal.* In press

Lee K, Ashton MC. 2008. The HEXACO personality factors in the indigenous personality lexicons of English and 11 other languages. *J. Personal.* 76:1001–53

Longua J, DeHart T, Tennen H, Armeli S. 2009. Personality moderates the interaction between positive and negative daily events predicting negative affect and stress. *J. Res. Personal.* 43:547–55

Lucas RE, Le K, Dyrenforth PE. 2008. Explaining the extraversion/positive affect relation: Sociability cannot account for extraverts' greater happiness. *J. Personal.* 76:385–414

MacKinnon DP, Fairchild AJ, Fritz MS. 2007. Mediation analysis. *Annu. Rev. Psychol.* 58:593–614

Martin LR, Friedman HS, Schwartz JE. 2007. Personality and mortality risk across the lifespan: the importance of conscientiousness as a biopsychosocial attribute. *Health Psychol.* 26:428–36

McCrae RR, Costa PT Jr. 1991. Adding *liebe und arbeit:* the full five-factor model and well-being. *Personal. Soc. Psychol. Bull.* 17:227–32

McCrae RR, Costa PT Jr. 1996. Toward a new generation of personality theories: theoretical contexts for the five-factor model. In *The Five-Factor Model of Personality*, ed. JS Wiggins, pp. 51–87. New York: Guilford

McCrae RR, Costa PT Jr. 2003. *Personality in Adulthood. A Five-Factor Theory*. New York: Guilford. 2nd ed.

McCrae RR, Costa PT Jr. 2008. The five-factor theory of personality. See John et al. 2008, pp. 159–81

Mischel W. 1968. *Personality and Assessment*. New York: Wiley

Mischel W. 2004. Toward an integrative science of the person. *Annu. Rev. Psychol.* 55:1–22

Mischel W, Shoda Y. 1998. Reconciling processing dynamics and personality dispositions. *Annu. Rev. Psychol.* 49:229–58

Mischel W, Shoda Y. 2008. Toward a unified theory of personality: integrating dispositions and processing dynamics within the cognitive-affective processing system (CAPS). See John et al. 2008, pp. 208–41

Moeller SK, Robinson MD, Bresin K. 2010. Integrating trait and social-cognitive views of personality: neuroticism, implicit stress priming, and neuroticism-outcome relationships. *Personal. Soc. Psychol. Bull.* 36:677–89

Moffitt TE, Arseneault L, Belsky D, Dickson N, Hancox RJ, et al. 2011. A gradient of childhood self-control predicts health, wealth, and public safety. *Proc. Natl. Acad. Sci. USA* 108:2693–98

Monroe SM. 2008. Modern approaches to conceptualizing and measuring human life stress. *Annu. Rev. Clin. Psychol.* 4:33–52

Moskowitz DS. 2010. Quarrelsomeness in daily life. *J. Personal.* 78:39–66

Moskowitz DS, Zuroff DC. 2004. Flux, pulse, and spin: dynamic additions to the personality lexicon. *J. Personal. Soc. Psychol.* 86:880–93

Mroczek DK, Spiro A. 2007. Personality change influences mortality in older men. *Psychol. Sci.* 18:371–76

Mroczek DK, Spiro A, Almeida DM. 2003. Between- and within-person variation in affect and personality over days and years: how basic and applied approaches can inform one another. *Ageing Int.* 28:260–78

Mroczek DK, Spiro A, Turiano NA. 2009. Do health behaviors explain the effect of neuroticism on mortality? Longitudinal findings from the VA Normative Aging Study. *J. Res. Personal.* 43:653–59

Muller D, Judd CM, Yzerbyt VY. 2005. When moderation is mediated and mediation is moderated. *J. Personal. Soc. Psychol.* 89:852–63

Nabi H, Kivimäki M, Marmot MG, Ferrie J, Zins M, et al. 2008. Does personality explain social inequalities in mortality? The French GAZEL cohort study. *Int. J. Epidemiol.* 37:591–602

Nigg JT. 2000. On inhibition/disinhibition in developmental psychopathology: views from cognitive and personality psychology as a working inhibition taxonomy. *Psychol. Bull.* 126:220–46

O'Connor DB, Conner MT, Jones FA, McMillan BRW, Ferguson E. 2009. Exploring the benefits of conscientiousness: an investigation of the role of daily stressors and health behaviors. *Ann. Behav. Med.* 37:184–96

Ozer DJ, Benet-Martínez V. 2006. Personality and the prediction of consequential outcomes. *Annu. Rev. Psychol.* 57:401–21

Posner M, Rothbart M. 2007. *Educating the Human Brain*. Washington, DC: Am. Psychol. Soc.

Prochaska JO, DiClemente CC. 1984. *The Transtheoretical Approach: Crossing Traditional Boundaries of Change*. Homewood, IL: Dorsey Press

Revelle W. 1995. Personality processes. *Annu. Rev. Psychol.* 46:295–328

Rhodes RE, Courneya KS, Hayduk LA. 2002. Does personality moderate the theory of planned behavior in the exercise domain? *J. Sport Exerc. Psychol.* 24:120–32

Rhodes RE, Courneya KS, Jones LW. 2005. The theory of planned behavior and lower order personality traits: interaction effects in the exercise domain. *Personal. Individ. Differ.* 38:251–65

Roberts BW, Jackson JJ. 2008. Sociogenomic personality psychology. *J. Personal.* 76:1523–44

Roberts BW, Kuncel N, Shiner RN, Caspi A, Goldberg LR. 2007. The power of personality: the comparative validity of personality traits, socio-economic status, and cognitive ability for predicting important life outcomes. *Perspect. Psychol. Sci.* 2:313–45

Roberts BW, Wood D. 2006. Personality development in the context of the neo-socioanalytic model of personality. In *Handbook of Personality Development*, ed. D Mroczek, T Little, pp. 11–39. Mahwah, NJ: Erlbaum

Roberts BW, Wood D, Caspi A. 2008. The development of personality traits in adulthood. See John et al. 2008, pp. 375–98

Robinson MD, Wilkowski BM. 2010. Personality processes in anger and reactive aggression: an introduction. *J. Personal.* 78:1–8

Rothbart MK. 2007. Temperament, development, and personality. *Curr. Dir. Psychol. Sci.* 16:207–12

Rothbart MK. 2011. *Becoming Who We Are: Temperament and Personality in Development.* New York: Guilford

Rothbart MK, Ahadi SA. 1994. Temperament and the development of personality. *J. Abnorm. Psychol.* 103:55–66

Rothbart MK, Bates JE. 2006. Temperament. In *Handbook of Child Psychology, Sixth Edition: Social, Emotional, and Personality Development*, vol. 3, ed. W Damon, R Lerner, N Eisenberg, pp. 99–106. New York: Wiley

Rothbart MK, Derryberry D. 1981. Development of individual differences in temperament. In *Advances in Developmental Psychology*, vol. 1, ed. ME Lamb, AL Brown, pp. 37–86. Hillsdale, NJ: Erlbaum

Rothbart MK, Rueda MR. 2005. The development of effortful control. In *Developing Individuality in the Human Brain: A Tribute to Michael I. Posner*, ed. U Mayr, E Awh, SW Keele, pp. 167–88. Washington, DC: Am. Psychol. Assoc.

Rusting CL. 1998. Personality, mood, and cognitive processing of emotional information: three conceptual frameworks. *Psychol. Bull.* 124:165–96

Saucier G. 2009. Recurrent personality dimensions in inclusive lexical studies: indications for a big six structure. *J. Personal.* 77:1577–614

Saucier G, Bel-Bahar T, Fernandez C. 2007. What modifies the expression of personality tendencies? Defining basic domains of situation variables. *J. Personal.* 75:479–504

Saucier G, Goldberg LR. 2001. Lexical studies of indigenous personality factors: premises, products, and prospects. *J. Personal.* 69:847–79

Shipley BA, Weiss A, Der G, Taylor MD, Deary IJ. 2007. Neuroticism, extraversion, and mortality in the UK Health and Lifestyle Survey: a 21-year prospective cohort study. *Psychosom. Med.* 69:923–31

Shoda Y, Mischel W, Wright JC. 1994. Intra-individual stability in the organization and patterning of behavior: incorporating psychological situations into the idiographic analysis of personality. *J. Personal. Soc. Psychol.* 67:674–87

Smillie LD. 2008. What is reinforcement sensitivity? Neuroscience paradigms for approach-avoidance process theories of personality. *Eur. J. Personal.* 22:359–84

Smillie LD, Pickering AD, Jackson CJ. 2006. The new Reinforcement Sensitivity Theory: implications for psychometric measurement. *Personal. Soc. Psychol. Rev.* 10:320–35

Srivastava S, Angelo KM, Vallereux SR. 2008. Extraversion and positive affect: a day reconstruction study of person-environment transactions. *J. Res. Personal.* 42:1613–18

Strack F, Deutsch R. 2004. Reflective and impulsive determinants of social behavior. *Personal. Soc. Psychol. Rev.* 8:220–47

Suchy Y. 2009. Executive functioning: overview, assessment, and research issues for non-neuropsychologists. *Ann. Behav. Med.* 37:106–16

Suls J, Bunde J. 2005. Anger, anxiety, and depression as risk factors for cardiovascular disease: the problems and implications of overlapping affective dispositions. *Psychol. Bull.* 131:260–300

Suls J, Martin R. 2005. The daily life of the garden-variety neurotic: reactivity, stress exposure, mood spillover, and maladaptive coping. *J. Personal.* 73:1–25

Taga KA, Friedman HS, Martin LR. 2009. Early personality traits as predictors of mortality risk following conjugal bereavement. *J. Personal.* 77:669–90

Tamir M, Robinson MD. 2004. Knowing good from bad: the paradox of neuroticism, negative affect, and evaluative processing. *J. Personal. Soc. Psychol.* 87:913–25

Terracciano A, Lockenhoff CE, Zonderman AB, Ferrucci L, Costa PT Jr. 2008. Personality predictors of longevity: activity, emotional stability, and conscientiousness. *Psychosom. Med.* 70:621–27

Tong EMW. 2010. Personality influences in appraisal-emotion relationships: the role of neuroticism. *J. Personal.* 78:393–417

Walker BM, Winter DA. 2007. The elaboration of personal construct psychology. *Annu. Rev. Psychol.* 58:453–77

Wasylkiw L, Fabrigar LR, Rainboth S, Reid A, Steen C. 2010. Neuroticism and the architecture of the self: exploring neuroticism as a moderator of the impact of ideal self-discrepancies on emotion. *J. Personal.* 78:471–92

Watson D, Pennebaker JW. 1989. Health complaints, stress, and distress: exploring the central role of negative affectivity. *Psychol. Rev.* 96:234–54

Wiggins JS. 1991. Agency and communion as conceptual coordinates for the understanding and measurement of interpersonal behavior. In *Thinking Clearly About Psychology, Vol. 2: Personality and Psychopathology*, ed. WM Grove, D Cicchetti, pp. 89–113. Minneapolis: Univ. Minn. Press

Wilkowski BM, Robinson MD. 2007. Keeping one's cool: trait anger, hostile thoughts, and the recruitment of limited capacity control. *Personal. Soc. Psychol. Bull.* 33:1201–13

Wilkowski BM, Robinson MD. 2008. The cognitive basis of trait anger and reactive aggression: an integrative analysis. *Personal. Soc. Psychol. Rev.* 12:3–28

Wilkowski BM, Robinson MD. 2010. The anatomy of anger: an integrative cognitive model of trait anger and reactive aggression. *J. Personal.* 78:9–38

Williams PG, Thayer JF. 2009. Executive functioning and health: introduction to the special series. *Ann. Behav. Med.* 37:101–5

Wills TA, Dishion TJ. 2004. Temperament and adolescent substance use: a transactional analysis of emerging self-control. *J. Clin. Child Adolesc.* 33:69–81

Wills TA, Gibbons FX, Sargent JD, Gerrard M, Lee HR, Dal Cin S. 2010. Good self-control moderates the effect of mass media on adolescent tobacco and alcohol use: tests with studies of children and adolescents. *Health Psychol.* 29:539–49

Wilson RS, Bienias JL, Mendes de Leon CF, Evans DA, Bennett DA. 2003. Negative affect and mortality in older persons. *Am. J. Epidemiol.* 158:827–35

Wright JC, Mischel W. 1987. A conditional approach to dispositional constructs: the local predictability of social behavior. *J. Personal. Soc. Psychol.* 55:454–69

Zentner M, Shiner R, eds. 2011. *Handbook of Temperament*. New York: Guilford. 2nd ed. In press

Zuckerman M. 1994. *Behavioural Expressions and Biosocial Bases of Sensation Seeking*. Cambridge: Cambridge Univ. Press

Job Attitudes

Timothy A. Judge[1] and John D. Kammeyer-Mueller[2]

[1]Mendoza College of Business, University of Notre Dame, Notre Dame, Indiana 46556;
email: tjudge@nd.edu

[2]Department of Management, University of Florida, Gainesville, Florida 32611;
email: kammeyjd@ufl.edu

Annu. Rev. Psychol. 2012. 63:341–67

The *Annual Review of Psychology* is online at
psych.annualreviews.org

This article's doi:
10.1146/annurev-psych-120710-100511

Keywords

job attitudes, job satisfaction, mood, emotions, personality,
performance

Abstract

Job attitudes research is arguably the most venerable and popular topic
in organizational psychology. This article surveys the field as it has
been constituted in the past several years. Definitional issues are addressed first, in an attempt to clarify the nature, scope, and structure
of job attitudes. The distinction between cognitive and affective bases
of job attitudes has been an issue of debate, and recent research using
within-persons designs has done much to inform this discussion. Recent
research has also begun to reformulate the question of dispositional or
situational influences on employee attitudes by addressing how these
factors might work together to influence attitudes. Finally, there has
also been a continual growth in research investigating how employee
attitudes are related to a variety of behaviors at both the individual and
aggregated level of analysis.

Contents

INTRODUCTION

Job attitudes are one of the oldest, most popular, and most influential areas of inquiry in all of organizational psychology. As of this writing, the PsycINFO database reveals 33,348 records pertaining to "job attitudes," "work attitudes," "job satisfaction," or "organizational commitment." Of these entries, one of those terms appears in the title of 6,397 entries, and the trend appears to be accelerating. We are therefore pleased—and a bit daunted—to provide the first review of this literature for the *Annual Review of Psychology*. Previous reviewers (e.g., Brief & Weiss 2002, Miner & Dachler 1973, O'Reilly 1991, Staw 1984) have made reference to job attitudes research. These reviews tended to treat the job attitudes literature in brief, or in service of another topic. In this review, we focus exclusively on job attitudes.

Despite this exclusive focus on job attitudes, given the breadth and depth of job attitudes research, we must place several bounds on this review. As is the tradition of the *Annual Review of Psychology*, we purposely orient our review with a recency bias in that we consider newer and current topics to a greater degree than older ones. Similarly, most of our citations are relatively recent works (articles published in the past 10 years). However, our focus on the current status of the job attitudes literature does not mean that we ignore the traditional contributions of job attitudes research. Finally, our bibliography is selective rather than exhaustive.

In organizing this review, we first discuss the nature of and define job attitudes in the context of the larger social attitudes literature. We devote a substantial amount of space to discussions of discrete job attitudes, including job satisfaction, organizational commitment, and other attitudes. We then discuss states and traits in job attitudes research, including emotions and dispositional influences. We examine situational antecedents, including a discussion of how job and organizational characteristics and the social environment affect job attitudes. We conclude by reviewing research linking job attitudes to prominent work behaviors and outcomes.

WHAT ARE JOB ATTITUDES?

Link Between Job Attitudes and Social Attitudes

The substantive nature of job attitudes flows from the broader literature on social attitudes, so we begin our review by discussing how these literatures are related. A job attitude, of course, is a type of attitude, and therefore it is important to place job attitudes research in the broader context of social attitudes research. As noted by Olson & Zanna (1993, p. 119), "Despite the long history of research on attitudes, there is no universally agreed-upon definition." Perhaps the most widely accepted definition of an attitude, however, was provided by Eagly & Chaiken (1993, p. 1): "A psychological tendency that is expressed by evaluating a particular entity with some degree of favor or disfavor." Thus, the concept of evaluation is a unifying theme in attitudes research. One problem for attitudes research is that individuals may form an evaluation of (and thus hold an attitude about) a nearly limitless number of entities. Some of these attitudes may border on the trivial, at least in a general psychological sense (we may have an attitude about a famous actor, about oak wood, or about the color green), or may be

sufficiently segmented that they are only of specialized interest (e.g., an attitude about private enterprise, about expressionist art, etc.). Given this multiplicity of attitude objects, why is it justified to consider job attitudes as an important and central aspect of social attitudes?

There are three ways to answer this question. First, though it is reasonable, perhaps even necessary, to view job attitudes as social attitudes, there are important differences between these research traditions; the differences may tell us as much about social attitudes as they do about job attitudes. Though the attitudes literature has revealed many important and interesting insights, on the whole, the literature is limited in the range of populations, settings, and content or targets of the attitudes. As Judge et al. (2011) have noted, the limitations are in the form of what (e.g., overwhelmingly, political or cultural attitudes or identities as opposed to contextual attitudes about one's job, one's life, one's family, etc.), with whom (e.g., heavy reliance on college undergraduates, which may limit the scope and nature of the investigations), and how (e.g., behavior is often not studied or is studied in a sterile, though well-controlled, experimental context) attitudes are studied. That the job attitudes literature provides different contexts, populations, and methods for studies suggests that social attitudes researchers would benefit as much from reading the job attitudes literature as the converse.

Second, job attitudes are important insofar as jobs are important entities. Even in times of economic duress, the vast majority of the adult population age 25–75 is employed in some capacity (most adults have a job). Although the time people spend working obviously varies greatly by the person, the average person spends more time working than in any other waking activity. But the meaning of work to individuals goes far beyond time allocation. As Hulin (2002) noted, people's identities often hinge on their work, as evidenced by how the typical person responds to the question, "What do you do?" or "What are you?" Job attitudes are also closely related to more global measures of life satisfaction (Judge & Watanabe 1993).

Job satisfaction: an evaluative state that expresses contentment with and positive feelings about one's job

Organizational commitment: an individual's psychological bond with the organization, as represented by an affective attachment to the organization, a feeling of loyalty toward it, and an intention to remain as part of it

Job attitudes: evaluations of one's job that express one's feelings toward, beliefs about, and attachment to one's job

Attitude: a psychological tendency that is expressed by evaluating a particular entity with some degree of favor or disfavor (of which job attitudes are examples)

Job attitudes matter because jobs matter—to people's identities, to their health, and to their evaluations of their lives.

Third and finally, like any attitude (Olson & Zanna 1993), job attitudes matter to the extent they predict important behavior. This has been the dominant assumption in job attitudes research to such an extent that it is relatively rare to find an article in the top organizational journals that does not link job attitudes to behaviors. Although it certainly is not our argument that job attitudes are irrelevant to behavior—as we note, the evidence is clear that they are relevant—we also think job attitude research would benefit from some nuances in the attitude-behavior relationship that have been noted in social attitudes research. First, behavior may shape attitudes. This has been a prominent area of investigation in the attitudes literature generally, but curiously relatively little effort has been made on this front in job attitudes research (Judge et al. 2011). Second, as some have argued in the attitudes literature (e.g., Fazio & Olson 2003), the tripartite nature of attitudes—affect, cognition, and behavior—although an important heuristic representation, has its problems. Most significantly, research suggests that attitudes can form as a result of any one of these three factors in isolation, and that an affectively based attitude, for example, functions quite differently from a cognitively based attitude. Another problem is the assumption that all three components must be consistent with one another, which also is not supported by reviews of the literature that show even strongly held attitudes may not be manifested in behavior. Affect and cognitive components of attitudes can be at odds with one another and, as we note below, are quite difficult to separate in practice.

While keeping these concerns in mind, we address the departure of the study of job attitudes from the original tripartite definitions of social attitudes that emphasize cognitive, affective, and behavioral elements of attitude space but try to separate these aspects from one another as appropriate. Past studies on job satisfaction have focused on judgment-based,

cognitive evaluations of jobs on characteristics or features of jobs and generally ignored affective antecedents of evaluations of jobs as well as the episodic events that happen on jobs. Accordingly, we devote considerable space in this review to the affective nature of job satisfaction and how consideration of job affect necessitates revision in how we conceptualize and measure job attitudes, how we relate the concept to other variables, and how we study job attitudes and affect. Other topics—such as job attitudes at the between-unit level of analysis and the contrast between job attitudes and related phenomena like descriptions of a situation and motivation for behavior—are also discussed.

Definition of Job Attitudes

We define job attitudes as follows: Job attitudes are evaluations of one's job that express one's feelings toward, beliefs about, and attachment to one's job. This definition encompasses both the cognitive and affective components of these evaluations while recognizing that these cognitive and affective aspects need not be in exact correspondence with one another (Schleicher et al. 2004). Although this definition is relatively simple, there are nuances and complexities that underlie it.

In this definition, we consider "job" a broad term that encompasses one's current position (obvious), one's work or one's occupation (less obvious), and one's employer (less obvious still). One's attitudes toward one's work need not be isomorphic with one's attitudes toward one's employer, and indeed these often diverge. Moreover, within each of these targets there are more specific targets whose boundaries are necessarily fuzzy. For example, is an attitude toward one's advancement opportunities an evaluation of one's job, one's occupation, or one's employer? To be sure, job attitudes have some hierarchical structure with global attitudes as a composite of lower-order, more specific attitudes (Harrison et al. 2006, Parsons & Hulin 1982). Yet delineating this structure across very different types of work, careers, and employers is difficult. It is possible that the structure of job attitudes for an associate professor of medieval history at a prestigious university, a drive-up window worker at Burger King, and a stonemason are the same, but we are agnostic.

Multifaceted Nature of Job Attitudes

Job attitudes are multifaceted in their composition, in their structure, and in their temporal nature. Employees, of course, do not have only one job attitude. The composition of attitudes employees have about their job and their work vary along many dimensions, most notably their target (e.g., their pay versus their supervision), their specificity (e.g., their most recent pay raise versus their job as a whole), and their nature (e.g., evaluative assessments versus behavioral propensities). Structurally, job attitudes are hierarchically organized, with perhaps an overall job attitude being the most general factor, followed by still relatively general job attitudes such as overall job satisfaction, organizational commitment, and perhaps others, followed by more specific attitudes such as job satisfaction facets, specific dimensions of organizational commitment, and so on.

Are job attitudes latent variables—top-down constructs that are indicated by their more specific attitudes—or manifest variables—bottom-up constructs composed of their lower-order terms? Although clarity in thinking about concepts is often recommended in this literature (Bollen 2002), considerable confusion can be created by drawing false dichotomies. Specifically, we think job attitudes may be either manifest or latent, depending on how the researcher wishes to treat them (see also Ironson et al. 1989). Clearly, when considering the facets of job satisfaction, it is a manifest variable in that overall job satisfaction is composed of more specific satisfactions in different domains. Just as clearly, though, broad job attitudes can be latent variables in the sense that individuals' general attitudes about their job cause specific attitudes to be positively correlated. Thus, although it is important for researchers to consider the issue and to be clear about their treatment of attitudes, we do not think that conceptualizations or measures of job attitudes are advanced by forcing false dichotomies into the literature. One researcher may treat overall job satisfaction as a latent construct and another may treat it as manifest. Although this is not a problem, the purposes of the research, and the modeling of the data, will of course be different under each approach.

Recent Emphasis on Affect

In our definition of job attitudes, we have purposely included both cognition (beliefs) and affect (feelings). We have learned, however, that affect and cognition are not easily separable. Neuropsychology has shown us that the thinking and feeling parts of the brain, although separable in architecture, are inextricably linked in operation (Adolphs & Damasio 2001). Higher-level cognition relies on evaluative input in the form of emotion; cognition and emotion are interwoven in our psychological functioning. Evidence indicates that when individuals perform specific mental operations, a reciprocal relationship exists between cerebral areas specialized for processing emotions and those specialized for processing cognitions (Drevets & Raichle 1998). Even measures of affect are substantially cognitive in nature (e.g., Ashby et al. 1999). As applied to job attitudes, when we think about our jobs, we have feelings about what we think. When we have feelings while at work, we think about these feelings. Cognition and affect are thus intimately related, and this connection is not easy to separate for psychology in general and job attitudes in particular. Although an evaluation of the nature of one's job may seem affect free in theory, it is practically impossible for one to evaluate one's pay as poor in an affect-free manner. New methodologies assist in this separation, but we do not believe this is a methodological issue. Rather, to a nontrivial degree, cognition and affect are inseparable, a statement that, if true, applies equally well to social and to job attitudes.

The difficulty of separating cognition and affect notwithstanding, historically, it is fair to say that organizational psychology theory and measures have implicitly emphasized the cognitive nature of job attitudes (and, for reasons noted above, their behavioral consequences) to the neglect of their affective nature (Judge et al. 2011). In recent years, however, the pendulum has swung in the other direction, and there has been more progress on the affective components of job satisfaction, especially as they vary over time, with less attention to the importance of cognitive aspects of satisfaction. The assertion that researchers have variously emphasized cognition or affect may seem at odds with the previous one: If affect and cognition are inseparable, how can organizational psychologists have emphasized one over the other? To some degree, this apparent contradiction is answered by "what" (What role do discrete emotional states play in job attitudes?) and "how" (If job attitudes are affective in nature, does this necessarily alter the way in which they are studied?). We reserve discussion of the "what" question for later (see section titled State and Traits in Job Attitudes Research). We now turn to the "how" question.

Multilevel, Experience-Sampling Designs

If affect is central to a definition of job attitudes, a problem for job attitudes researchers is that affective reactions are likely to be fleeting and episodic. Lest researchers become enmeshed in a methodological stalemate—where the attempt to study propositions of newly developed theories is hamstrung by methods and analyses appropriate only to the needs of an older generation of theoretical models—the conceptualization and measurement of job attitudes are altered by the central role of affect. Put another way, if job attitudes are, at least in part, affective reactions, then job attitudes need to be measured in ways that are consistent with the necessarily ephemeral nature of affect.

Increasingly, job attitudes researchers have responded to this problem through the use of experience-sampling methodology (ESM), where job attitudes are measured once a day over a period of a week or two, or even several times a day (e.g., Ilies & Judge 2002, Miner et al. 2005, Weiss et al. 1999). One great advantage of ESM designs is that they permit multilevel modeling of job attitudes, which allows for both within-individual (state) and between-individual (trait) effects. This research has shown that when job attitudes are measured on an experience-sampled basis, roughly one-third to one-half of the variation in job satisfaction is within-individual variation. Thus, typical "one-shot" between-person research designs miss a considerable portion of the variance in job satisfaction by treating within-individual variation as a transient error. We have more to say on this issue in the section titled States and Traits in Job Attitude Research.

DISCRETE JOB ATTITUDES

Defining the Construct Space

Having covered definitional material related to attitudes in general, we now turn our attention to discrete job attitudes. Research in organizational behavior has been largely conducted through the use of Likert scale measures of a variety of attitudes, perceptions, intentions, and motivations. Although on the surface many of these scales are similar in format and are closely correlated with one another, a large proportion of these scales do not measure attitudes and thus fall outside the scope of this review. We consider how measures of perceptions, intentions, and motivations are different from attitudes below, with special attention to where these constructs might fit in a causal sequence.

First, it is important to differentiate attitudes from perceptions and descriptions. Many variables are like attitudes, in that they involve cognitive judgments, and may lead to behavioral responses. However, these constructs are not attitudes if they do not include an explicit appraisal or evaluation of the object in question as it relates to personal values. For example, although role clarity scales (e.g., Rizzo et al. 1970) ask respondents to describe the extent to which their organization has clearly defined policies and procedures, routines, and expectations for behavior, role clarity scales do not ask respondents to evaluate whether they find the policies, procedures, routines, and expectations good or bad, or excessive or insufficient. Thus, the evaluative component central to our definition of attitudes is missing. Similarly, most measures of organizational justice (e.g., Colquitt 2001) require respondents to describe how their organization treats them but do not require respondents to evaluate whether they like the treatment they receive. These perception-based scales are typically conceptualized as antecedents to attitudes (e.g., role clarity and justice lead to satisfaction) rather than as attitudes themselves. It is true that the Job Descriptive Index (JDI) (Smith et al. 1969), as its name implies, asks employees to describe their jobs. However, it is important to remember that many if not most of these descriptions are heavily evaluative in nature (e.g., pay is "BAD," work is "PLEASANT," etc.). Most measures of job attitudes are even more evaluative.

Second, general attitudes should be differentiated from attitudes toward behavior and intentions to engage in behaviors. There is a clear link between attitudes and intentions at a conceptual and empirical level. However, the theories of reasoned action and planned behavior (Ajzen 1991), which are the justification for much of the research on attitudes and intentions, clearly describe attitudes toward an object, attitudes toward a behavior, and intentions to perform a behavior as three distinct constructs occupying distinct places in a causal chain. Unlike attitudes toward a behavior, intentions are shaped by both opportunities to perform an action as well as social norms of others toward the behavior in question. Consistent with this differentiation of attitudes from intentions and action, a growing body of research we consider in a later section has shown that situational variables moderate the relationship between attitudes and behavior.

Third, motivational constructs such as effort expended toward a task and job engagement should also be differentiated from job attitudes. Most research agrees that engagement reflects

investment or involvement of one's physical, cognitive, and emotional energy in work performance (Rich et al. 2010). However, one's evaluations of these investments is not assessed—only the existence or nonexistence of these investments. Thus, engagement reflects how one directs one's energies, rather than an attitude toward the behavior, job, or organization. Motivational energies are likely to be influenced by, and to influence, attitudes, but the actual energy to achieve ends and one's attitudes toward the sources and objects of these energies are distinct constructs.

In sum, researchers should carefully differentiate attitude measures from descriptions of the work environment, intentions to act on the work environment, and motivations. These variables are conceptually closely related to one another and are likely to covary, but considerable definitional and theoretical work has been devoted to the differentiation of these constructs from one another, and researchers would be well advised to consider their models in light of what theory proposes they should measure and how these measures will relate to other constructs of interest.

With these thoughts in mind, we define job satisfaction as follows: Job satisfaction is an evaluative state that expresses contentment with, and positive feelings about, one's job. As is apparent in this definition, we include both cognition (contentment) and affect (positive feelings) in our definition. Our definition also implies that overall or global job satisfaction results from a process of evaluation—typically, that consists of evaluation of one's job facets or characteristics. This leads to the next section of our review—the interplay between global or overall job satisfaction and job satisfaction facets.

Global Job Attitudes

Another issue that pertains to job attitudes research is the level of specificity at which attitudes are measured. There are studies that measure global attitudes toward one's job, the organization, and the social environment as a whole, which can be contrasted with more

Job Descriptive Index (JDI): perhaps the most validated measure of job satisfaction. In addition to a Job-In-General scale, the JDI includes the satisfaction facets: work, supervision, coworkers, pay, and promotion

Job performance:
employee behaviors that are consistent with role expectations and that contribute to organizational effectiveness; composed of task performance, citizenship behavior, withdrawal/counterproductivity, and creative performance

narrowly defined scales that measure specific facets of job attitudes. Conceptually, the bandwidth of measures should show fidelity to the variables expected to correlate with them (Fishbein & Ajzen 1974). If one wants to understand broad phenomena like overall total working conditions or job performance, broad attitudes such as overall job satisfaction should be examined. Conversely, if one is interested in more specific phenomena, such as the effect of compensation practices on employee attitudes or the impact of attitudes on helping behavior, more specific attitudes such as satisfaction with pay or coworkers should be examined. The most relevant level of attitudinal specificity will depend on the bandwidth of the antecedents and consequences under consideration.

Overall job satisfaction is probably the most researched attitude in organizational behavior. This global approach is exemplified by scales such as the affect-centric "faces" scale (Kunin 1955), Likert scales asking respondents to directly describe their level of satisfaction with work (Brayfield & Rothe 1951), or the more cognitive "job in general" scale (e.g., Ironson et al. 1989). These global measures attempt to capture an overarching level of satisfaction with the job across a variety of attributes. These global scales either ask respondents to indicate their overall reaction to the job as a whole or ask them for their summary judgment of all aspects of the job including work, pay, supervision, coworkers, and promotion opportunities. The principle of fidelity suggests that such global scales are likely to be best predicted by broad measures of the respondent, such as affective disposition or aggregate measures of job characteristics, and to be predictive of broad criteria such as job performance or work withdrawal.

Facets of Job Satisfaction

From an alternative perspective, researchers are often interested in the relative importance of specific facets of satisfaction. Much of the research on facet-level satisfaction has used the JDI (Smith et al. 1969). The five facets of job satisfaction examined in the JDI are satisfaction with work, supervision, coworkers, pay, and promotions. These five facets are related to one another, but they show discriminant validity as well, with meta-analytic correlations among dimensions of satisfaction averaging about $r = 0.2$ to $r = 0.3$ (Kinicki et al. 2002), though our experiences with these facets suggest somewhat higher intercorrelations. The Minnesota Satisfaction Questionnaire (MSQ) and the Index of Organizational Reactions (IOR) also measure satisfaction with the same or similar dimensions (e.g., the MSQ has a dimension of advancement) and include other subdimensions as well (e.g., the MSQ has dimensions on job security and social status, among others). There are substantial correlations between these disparate measures' scores for each dimension (Kinicki et al. 2002), though not so high as to suggest that there is no meaningful unique variance attributable to each dimension. Because of the importance of the JDI facets to job satisfaction research, we now consider these five satisfaction facets in turn.

Evidence from several lines of inquiry suggests that the facet of job satisfaction that is most closely related to global measures is satisfaction with the work itself. Of the facets, satisfaction with the work itself also has the strongest correlations with global measures of satisfaction (Ironson et al. 1989, Rentsch & Steel 1992). The antecedents of work satisfaction have been the subject of much research. The model of job characteristics described by Hackman & Oldham (1976) has received a great deal of support. This model proposes that skill variety, task identity, task significance, autonomy, and feedback all contribute to employee satisfaction with their work. Consistent with this model at a higher level of analysis, recent research has confirmed that employee empowerment climate in groups is associated with higher levels of individual job satisfaction (Seibert et al. 2004). There is also evidence that individuals who are higher in other orientation have weaker relationships between work attributes and job satisfaction, which suggests that those who are less likely to pursue their self-interest in a systematic way are less prone to form satisfaction judgments based on the rational, calculating model proposed by job characteristics theory (Meglino & Korsgaard 2007).

There are also numerous studies that have focused specifically on employee satisfaction with organizational practices such as compensation and promotion policies. The dimensionality of pay satisfaction questionnaires has been examined, and research suggests that the four main dimensions of pay satisfaction include pay level, benefits, pay raise, and structure/administration (e.g., Judge & Welbourne 1994). Theoretical models of overall pay satisfaction suggest that satisfaction with compensation is based on a small discrepancy between the amount of pay that is received and the amount of pay the worker believes he or she should receive (Williams et al. 2006). Meta-analysis shows that comparisons of one's own pay to others have very strong correlations with pay satisfaction, whether the target of comparisons is internal to the organization ($r = 0.56$, $r_c = 0.94$) or external to the organization ($r = 0.57$, $r_c = 1.00$) (Williams et al. 2006).

The social context for work is emphasized by researchers exploring satisfaction with supervisors and coworkers. Perhaps mirroring a general lack of attention to the social aspects of the working environment in organizational behavior in general, relatively little research has focused on coworker satisfaction. In contrast to the nuanced dimensions of pay satisfaction, research has not explored the dimensionality of relationships with coworkers or supervisors. Instead, most researchers are content to measure a unidimensional satisfaction with coworkers. However, more theoretically developed measures of relationship attitudes developed in social psychology and relationship science literature suggest that such unidimensional measures fail to address the complexity of relationships sufficiently. For example, the Positive and Negative Quality in Marriage Scale examines a two-dimensional space akin to positive and negative affectivity, demonstrating that it is possible for a relationship to be high on positive relationship qualities, high on negative relationship qualities, high on both positive and negative relationship qualities, or high on neither (e.g., Mattson et al. 2007).

Organizational Commitment

Besides examining satisfaction with one's job, other research has examined commitment toward the organization. Consistent with Solinger et al. (2008), we define organizational commitment as an individual's psychological bond with the organization, as represented by an affective attachment to the organization, internalization of its values and goals, and a behavioral desire to put forth effort to support it. As an attitude, organizational commitment reflects a psychological state linking an individual to the organization based on identification with the organization's values and goals (e.g., Allen & Meyer 1990, O'Reilly & Chatman 1986). Commitment scales also have multiple dimensions, but unlike satisfaction, most have examined the nature of commitment rather than the focus of commitment (but see Meyer et al. 2004 for an exception). Thus, research has primarily examined affective, normative, and continuance commitment, with an especially large body of research focused on affective commitment. Affective commitment scales require respondents to describe the extent to which they value the organization, feel attached to and included in the organization, and see the organization's goals as similar to their own. Continuance commitment scales require respondents to evaluate whether or not they are able to leave the organization in the near future, or if leaving the job would incur too many financial costs. Finally, normative commitment asks respondents to describe their evaluation of whether or not quitting a job is a negative behavior. It appears that affective commitment generally has the highest validity in predicting organizational behaviors such as job performance (Dunham et al. 1994).

Affective Events
Theory (AET): an
integrative model
emphasizing the links
between job events
and job affect and
hypothesizing links
between job affect and
job behaviors that are
unique to affect and
affective events

A meta-analysis of this literature found that data do not strongly line up with the theoretical three-component model of commitment (Meyer et al. 2002). The tripartite typology of commitment has come under criticism by those who note that affective commitment is best understood as an attitude regarding the employing organization, whereas normative and continuance commitment are attitudes regarding the specific behaviors of staying or leaving (Solinger et al. 2008). The distinction between attitudes toward the organization and a behavior may explain why convergent validity for scales of commitment is so comparatively low. Thus, researchers have been encouraged to refine their thinking about organizational commitment by replacing the three-component model of commitment with the tripartite attitudes model from social attitudes research that focuses on affect toward the organization, cognition about the organization in terms of identification and internalization, and action readiness for generalized behaviors to support the organization.

Attitudes Toward Behaviors

Besides measures of the job and organization, there has also been a tradition of research on attitudes toward specific behaviors and goals. There is evidence for a structural model that positions attitudes toward a behavior as an antecedent to intentions, which in turn serve as an antecedent for action. For example, one study found that positive attitudes toward voluntary training and development activities generate intentions to engage in such activities and that these intentions are related to participation rates (Hurtz & Williams 2009). A similar relationship between attitudes toward job search and intentions to engage in job search was found in a longitudinal study with unemployed individuals (Wanberg et al. 2005). Consistent with the bandwidth-fidelity principle mentioned previously, it is expected that attitudes toward behaviors will be more strongly related to those behaviors than will generalized attitudes.

STATES AND TRAITS IN JOB ATTITUDES RESEARCH

Affective Events Theory

Research in organizational psychology has, in recent years, considered aspects of stable trait-like attitudes about work and their relationship with more ephemeral state attitudes. In an attempt to address organizational psychology's neglect of affect, Weiss & Cropanzano (1996) proposed a theory of job attitudes that emphasizes affect in the study of job attitudes (and the attitude-behavior relationship). This theory, termed Affective Events Theory (AET), emphasizes links between job events and job affect and hypothesizes links between job affect and job behaviors that are unique to affect and affective events. Specifically, AET emphasizes links between job affect and short-term or statelike behaviors, such as work withdrawal and organizational citizenship behaviors (non-task behaviors that contribute to the social and psychological environment of the workplace, such as helping and supporting others) rather than the more reasoned long-term behaviors (such as turnover) that have been related to job satisfaction.

As noted by Judge et al. (2011), AET is differentiated from other current approaches by (a) the distinctions between job structure or features and job events, although job features (e.g., organizational policies, which we review later) are likely to influence distributions of job events; (b) an emphasis on affect as an important feature of job attitudes; and (c) the hypothesized independent links between job affect and affect-driven behaviors, on the one hand, and between more evaluation-focused cognitions and judgment-driven behaviors, on the other. Dispositions are hypothesized to moderate the link between events and affect.

The promise of AET is clear. Analyses of affective events, affect, and the on-the-job consequences of affect may answer some questions about job attitudes and behaviors on the job that are unanswered by the traditional studies of relations between cognitive evaluations and job performance (see, for example, Beal et al. 2005). Indeed, nearly every study published investigating moods or emotions at work or within-individual variation in job attitudes prominently features AET as a general framework.

Recent Research on Within-Individual Variation in Job Attitudes

As we have noted, job attitudes have both stable (between-individual variation) and dynamic (within-individual variation over time) qualities. We should therefore expect significant between-person and within-person variation in job attitudes. We also expect significant covariation between job attitudes and cofluctuations in affect and similarly time-variant states (exogenous events, moods or emotions) that should predict it. Similarly, within-individual variation in job attitudes should be reflected in within-individual variation in job behaviors. This dynamic nature of job affects and job behaviors is illustrated by Organ & Ryan (1995), who note that predictions of organizational citizenship behaviors (OCBs) from affective states "... will somehow have to reckon with the problem of *detecting discrete episodes of OCB* (rather than subjective reactions that presumably reflect aggregations or trends of OCB over time) *and the psychological states antecedent to or concurrent with those episodes*" (p. 781, emphasis added). As we noted above, this problem has been addressed by ESM designs, which provide ecological momentary assessments of job attitudes and job behaviors. It is striking that most of these studies show nearly as much within-person variability in job attitudes as in moods and emotions. This certainly suggests support for the importance of affect to job attitudes. As noted by Judge et al. (2011), "It is not premature to conclude that ESM has become an expected element of the research."

It is not the case that one expects between-individual and within-individual relationships to operate in opposite directions or even to operate in the same direction but with dramatically different magnitudes. Rather,

our argument is that no inferences about the within-person level should be made solely on the basis of data collected at the between-person level. Chen et al. (2005) maintain that, because researchers know so little about how constructs operate at levels of analysis other than the one at which they are typically studied, assessments of the similarity of relationships between analogous constructs across levels "can and should play an integral role in the validation of multilevel constructs and theories" (p. 376).

The recent literature on within-person variation in job attitudes can be grouped into three overlapping categories. Studies that link moods or discrete emotional states to job attitudes comprise the first category. Within this category of studies, two further differentiations must be made. First is the issue of whether moods/emotions are antecedents (e.g., Bono et al. 2007, Ilies & Judge 2004, Judge et al. 2006, Weiss et al. 1999) or consequences (e.g., Judge & Ilies 2004) of job attitudes, with the former greatly outnumbering the latter. Of course there are reasons why either direction of influence might occur. Demonstrating causal directions in such studies is difficult, though some studies are noteworthy for their use of lagged designs, whereby job attitudes on Time 1 are used to predict affect on Time 2 (e.g., Judge & Ilies 2004) or affect at Time 1 is used to predict job attitudes at Time 2 (Ilies & Judge 2002). Another differentiation is the issue of whether broad mood factors (generally as represented by positive and negative affect) or discrete emotions are studied. Emotion researchers have struggled in vain to delineate an accepted taxonomy of "core" emotions (see Power 2006). Another challenge is that discrete emotions, although theoretically separable, are empirically less so. This is especially true with respect to positive emotions (Watson 2000). On the other hand, broad mood factors have controversies of their own, such as disagreements over the structure of mood: either the positive affect/negative affect rotation or the hedonic tone/arousal rotation.

The second category of studies investigates within-person variability in job attitudes

Moods and emotions: affective states that are important to job satisfaction and that may be distinguished from one another in terms of generality, duration, and event specificity without including moods or emotions. Such studies have typically examined antecedents of job satisfaction. For example, one study found that daily interpersonal and informational justice were related to daily levels of job satisfaction (Loi et al. 2009). Another repeated measures study found that dispositional affect influenced employees' typical levels of satisfaction and moderated how sensitive employee job attitudes were to workplace events (Bowling et al. 2005).

The third category of studies links within-individual variation in job attitudes to within-individual variation in work behaviors. Although there is a growing body of within-person research showing how affect is related to job performance (e.g., Miner & Glomb 2010, Trougakos et al. 2011, Tsai et al. 2007), comparatively less research has investigated how variability in job attitudes is related to performance. Studies have shown that variations in job attitudes are related to higher levels of organizational citizenship (Ilies et al. 2006). Other research has found a relationship between variations in job attitudes and workplace deviance (Judge et al. 2006). However, it is unclear whether these findings are primarily the results of affect or if other components of attitudes such as appraisals, beliefs, or attitudes toward behaviors will also play a complementary role. This is clearly an area where more research is needed.

Before ending this section, we note another important distinction. Previously we mentioned multilevel models of job attitudes. Here we define multilevel models as models where multiple observations of job attitudes are nested within individuals, to predict or be predicted by other within-individual states, and wherein these within-individual relationships are predicted by between-individual differences. Although all ESM studies and multilevel models are often treated as synonymous in job attitude research, that is not necessarily a valid commingling. It is true that most ESM studies are multilevel in that both within- and between-person effects are modeled. However, that is not inherently the case. More importantly,

some multilevel models of job attitudes are not based on, or tested with, ESM designs. For example, if within-individual variation in job attitudes is studied over a very long period of time (say, yearly measurements over 10 years), both within- and between-individual variation would likely to be modeled, but it is unlikely data were collected using an ESM design.

DISPOSITIONAL ANTECEDENTS OF JOB ATTITUDES

Early Influences

The importance of personality to job satisfaction was explicitly recognized in the earliest writings on job attitudes (e.g., Hoppock 1935). These early findings, however, appeared to quickly fall out of favor, coinciding with the nadir of personality research in the 1970s and 1980s. This state of affairs changed with the publication of two seminal studies by Staw and colleagues, a study by Arvey and colleagues, and an integrative piece by Adler & Weiss (1988). Staw & Ross (1985) found that measures of job satisfaction were reasonably stable over time, even when individuals changed employers or occupations. Critics of the study noted that it is difficult to establish a dispositional basis of job satisfaction unless one actually measures dispositions, and that other, nondispositional factors might explain job attitude stability. Staw et al. (1986) corrected this deficiency: Using a unique longitudinal data set and childhood ratings of personality, Staw et al. reported results showing that affective disposition assessed at ages 12–14 correlated 0.34 (p < 0.05) with overall job satisfaction assessed at ages 54–62. In a similarly provocative study, Arvey et al. (1989) found significant consistency in job satisfaction levels between 34 pairs of monozygotic twins reared apart from early childhood. Judged from the vantage point of today, these studies may seem less revolutionary than they were at the time. It is not much of an overstatement to argue that in the late 1980s, dispositional explanations were eschewed or, more likely, ignored entirely in the literature.

Specific Dispositions

Although much early research on the importance of dispositions was able to describe whether there was a dispositional aspect to job satisfaction, this research did not specify which theoretically derived personality dispositions would be most likely related to consistencies in job attitudes. Subsequent research has attempted to clarify this omission. One study found that the dispositional taxonomy of positive and negative affectivity was related to job satisfaction over a period of several months, even after accounting for job changes and occupational quality variables (Watson & Slack 1993). Subsequent meta-analytic research demonstrated that the five-factor model of personality could also explain variations in job satisfaction, with neuroticism ($r_c = -0.29$), extraversion ($r_c = 0.25$), and conscientiousness ($r_c = 0.26$) showing especially strong relationships with job satisfaction (Judge et al. 2002).

Core Self-Evaluations

In a different approach to dispositional influences on job attitudes, Judge et al. (1997) focus on core self-evaluations (CSEs), fundamental beliefs individuals hold about themselves, their functioning, and the world. CSEs are hierarchical, with specific traits comprising a broad, general trait. Judge et al. (1997) identified four specific traits as indicators of CSEs based on these evaluative criteria: (*a*) self-esteem, (*b*) generalized self-efficacy, (*c*) neuroticism, and (*d*) locus of control. Increasingly, research has utilized direct measures of CSEs. Though CSE research has expanded well beyond job satisfaction research, there have been more than 50 studies of the link between CSEs and job satisfaction. Judge & Bono (2001) completed a meta-analysis of 169 independent correlations between each of the four core traits and job satisfaction. When the four meta-analyses are combined into a single composite measure, the overall core trait correlates $r_c = 0.37$ with job satisfaction.

Given the various ways of considering affective disposition noted in this review, one might ask what either taxonomy adds beyond PA/NA (Watson 2000), the affective predisposition scale (Judge & Hulin 1993), or the Big Five personality model. This is a particularly relevant question given that CSEs are not uncorrelated with traits from these taxonomies. Judge et al. (2008) found that of the three taxonomic structures (five-factor model, PA/NA, and CSEs), CSEs were the most useful predictor of job satisfaction. Altogether, the three frameworks explained 36% of the variance in self-reported job satisfaction and 18% of the variance when using reports by significant others. Judge et al. (2008) further showed that these frameworks could be reduced to three sets of factors for the purposes of predicting job satisfaction: (*a*) CSEs/neuroticism (all four core traits, plus NA), (*b*) extraversion (including PA), and (*c*) conscientiousness. Their results showed that when these three factors were related to job satisfaction, however, only the first factor—CSE—consistently influenced job satisfaction across studies.

Best et al. (2005) presented further evidence for the influence of CSE on job satisfaction via appraisals of the work environment. The authors found that CSE was negatively related to perceptions of organizational obstacles to goal fulfillment (perceived organizational constraint). Perceived organizational constraint mediated between CSE and burnout, which negatively predicted job satisfaction. These results suggest that employees high in CSE are less likely to view their job tasks and organizational environment as stressful, shielding them from burnout and its deleterious effects on job satisfaction.

Studies that focus only on perceptual measures of job characteristics make it impossible to distinguish whether high-CSE individuals simply hold a rosier picture of objective attributes or whether they actually select into jobs with better attributes. To address this issue, Judge et al. (2000) examined the mediating role of objective job complexity, ascertained by coding job titles, as well as subjective job characteristics. They found that both subjective and objective indicators of job complexity were partial mediators of the relationship between CSE—measured in childhood and early adulthood—and later job satisfaction for individuals between the ages of 41 and 50. These results suggest that CSEs influence not only how favorably people view their jobs, but also the actual level of complexity of the jobs they obtain.

In addition to selecting into more challenging jobs, people with a high CSE may find their work more satisfying because they choose personally meaningful goals. Self-concordance theory posits that goals pursued for fun or on the basis of personally relevant values increase subjective well-being and goal attainment. Judge et al. (2005) proposed that individuals with positive self-concept should be less vulnerable to external pressures and therefore more likely to set self-concordant goals. Self-concordant goals partially mediated between CSEs and life satisfaction and between CSEs and goal attainment. It appears that CSEs do lead to the pursuit of self-concordant goals, which increases life satisfaction and goal attainment. The authors concluded that CSEs "may serve more like a trigger than an anchor. People with positive CSEs strive for 'the right reasons,' and therefore 'get the right results'" (p. 266).

Integration of State and Trait Perspectives

The foregoing description of research on job attitudes as temporary states of being does not necessarily mean that research investigating job attitudes as more traitlike (i.e., influenced by stable individual dispositions and unchanging job characteristics) is no longer relevant. An interactionist perspective on job attitudes suggests that dispositions have their effects on behavior through the interaction of individuals and the work environment (Magnusson 1999). People respond to their dispositionally influenced perceptions of the environment, so it is still possible for personality to affect attitudes even when situations are found to be important (Mischel & Shoda 1998). Thus, the question of whether attitudes can be attributed to states or traits is poorly posed; rather, the question

involves how situations contribute to the expression of traits and how traits contribute to the reactions to situations.

SITUATIONAL ANTECEDENTS OF JOB ATTITUDES

Job Characteristics

As the preceding section notes, there is strong evidence that perceptions of jobs are influenced by dispositions of the individual worker. However, there is also evidence that situations influence attitudes. One tradition of situational antecedents of job attitudes that has already been mentioned is the job characteristics model. Most research has examined how subjective perceptions of work characteristics are related to employee attitudes, convincingly demonstrating that employee self-reports of the five core characteristics (skill variety, task identity, task significance, autonomy, and feedback) identified by Hackman & Oldham (1976) are related to higher levels of job satisfaction. However, data measured from self-reports cannot be readily distinguished from the influence of dispositions, since evidence already discussed shows that personality traits are related to perceptions of job characteristics. When self-report and job analyst–based job characteristics are studied in tandem, the self-reported, more subjective perceptions of job characteristics are more closely related to job satisfaction than are analyst-based, more objective estimates of job characteristics (Judge et al. 2000). Organizational interventions to increase these sources of satisfaction via job enlargement have been shown to be effective at improving job satisfaction in the past (e.g., Neuman et al. 1989), which does bolster the argument that objective job characteristics influence job attitudes, although recent research on this topic is lacking.

Social Environment Characteristics

Although the features of the work itself have clearly been linked to higher levels of job satisfaction and engagement, such models omit the importance of the social environment.

Surprisingly, it is only in recent years that researchers have systematically demonstrated that social environment variables, such as relationships with coworkers and supervisors, can be as closely related to overall job satisfaction as job conditions are related to satisfaction. A comprehensive investigation of the relationships between job characteristics and work attitudes found that perceived social support predicted satisfaction levels above and beyond characteristics of the work itself (Morgeson & Humphrey 2006). Meta-analysis shows that there is a consistent positive relationship between coworker support behaviors and job satisfaction, job involvement, and organizational commitment (Chiaburu & Harrison 2008). This meta-analysis also found that the relationship between coworker support and the attitudes of satisfaction and commitment was stronger than the relationship between coworker antagonism and these attitudinal constructs.

Another method for examining the relationship between social characteristics of the work environment and job attitudes is to examine social network ties. Evidence from one study of network ties found that job-related affect scores tended to be similar among individuals who interacted with one another frequently (Totterdell et al. 2004). These results reinforce the notion that attitudes toward work are significantly related to the social relationships one has.

The demographic makeup of one's workgroup has also been a concern for researchers. Theory suggests that individuals who are demographically dissimilar from their coworkers may feel less accepted and therefore experience more negative job attitudes. Some research has shown that ethnic dissimilarity is negatively related to organizational commitment, but it is not related to job satisfaction (Liao et al. 2004). On the other hand, this same study found that differences from coworkers in extraversion and openness to experience are negatively related to satisfaction with coworkers. Other research found that perceived age similarity to one's coworkers is associated with higher levels of engagement among older workers if they were also satisfied with their older coworkers (Avery et al. 2007). One study found that when supervisors were higher in control orientation than subordinates, subordinates were more satisfied with their supervisor compared with situations in which the supervisor and subordinate had similar levels of control orientation (Glomb & Welsh 2005). This is a rather unique example, showing that personality dissimilarity can sometimes have beneficial effects on job attitudes.

Leadership

In organizational context, leadership styles and behaviors can have a particularly powerful effect on employee job attitudes. Leader consideration has a meta-analytic correlation of $r_c = 0.78$ with subordinate satisfaction (Judge et al. 2004). The strength of this relationship suggests that leader consideration behaviors such as showing concern and respect for followers, looking out for their welfare, and expressing appreciation and support are nearly synonymous with the extent to which followers are satisfied with their leaders. Initiating structure has a somewhat weaker but still positive correlation of $r_c = 0.33$ with subordinate satisfaction with the leader.

Having established strong meta-analytic main-effect relationships between leadership and follower attitudes, researchers have turned their attention toward moderating relationships. The aforementioned relationship between leader-member exchange and employee attitudes is stronger when employees identify their supervisor with the organization (Eisenberger et al. 2010). Transformational leadership has been linked to more positive employee emotions during the course of the workday, and transformational leadership can buffer the relationship between emotion regulation and job dissatisfaction (Bono et al. 2007). Longitudinal research also shows that declines in supervisor support during the period of organizational entry were associated with declines in job satisfaction (Jokisaari & Nurmi 2009).

Conversely, negative leader behaviors, such as abusive supervision (Tepper 2000), are also associated with negative employee attitudes.

Organizational Practices

There is a substantial body of research within organizational psychology examining the nature of organizational practices and their influence on employee job attitudes. The largest body of research under this area concerns the relationship between organizational justice and employee attitudes. Much of the research on justice and pay practices has been grounded in discrepancy theory, which proposes that dissatisfaction is the result of a discrepancy between the pay that one thinks one should receive and the amount of pay one actually receives. Such discrepancies are strongly, negatively related to pay level satisfaction ($r_c = -0.54$) in meta-analytic research (Williams et al. 2006). Meta-analysis shows that distributive justice correlates at $r_c = 0.79$ with pay level satisfaction, suggesting that perceptions of distributive justice are nearly identical to attitudes toward organizational pay practices (Williams et al. 2006). Procedural justice of compensation also has a substantial but slightly smaller ($r_c = 0.42$) relationship with pay satisfaction.

Surprisingly, meta-analytic evidence suggests that the relationship between merit pay raises and pay-level satisfaction is quite small ($r_c = 0.08$) (Williams et al. 2006). One study demonstrated that pay satisfaction following a merit raise was much greater for those who received a high merit raise and who also had high pay-raise expectations (Schaubroeck et al. 2008). The authors noted that this result suggests that only individuals who believe that pay decisions are connected to performance will be more satisfied when merit raises are disbursed. Another study showed that pay satisfaction is often based on whom one compares oneself to—those who compare their pay to those who make much more than themselves are less satisfied than those who compare their pay to those who make only slightly more than themselves (Harris et al. 2008).

Besides the main effect of organizational practices related to compensation, research utilizing a polynomial regression approach to assess congruence suggests that the correspondence between employee values and organizational values is associated with more positive job attitudes (Edwards & Cable 2009). High levels of interpersonal justice are also significantly related to both organizational commitment and satisfaction with one's supervisor (Liao & Rupp 2005).

Although many studies have correlated individual reports of organizational characteristics as predictors of individual attitudes, concerns about common method variance have prompted many researchers to examine these phenomena using multiple reports of practices. For example, one study found that the favorableness of organizational changes, the extent of the change, and the individual relevance of the change combined to predict employee commitment (Fedor et al. 2006). One other study showed that establishment-level reports of high-performance human resources practices were associated with higher levels of employee job satisfaction and organizational commitment (Takeuchi et al. 2009). A study involving cross-level mediation found that the relationship between individual perceptions of organizational justice with job attitudes and job satisfaction was moderated by group-level justice climate (Mayer et al. 2007). These studies, taken together, suggest that collective perceptions of situations are predictive of individual attitudes and that there are indeed relationships between organizational characteristics and job attitudes.

Time and Job Attitudes

Some researchers have begun to examine the role of time itself as a situational shaper of employee attitudes. Researchers in this domain examine how employee attitudes tend to change over time from the point of hire to some subsequent point in time, typically using latent growth modeling or hierarchical linear modeling. One program of research has examined the pattern of "honeymoons and hangovers" in employee attitudes from the point of hire to several months later (e.g., Boswell et al. 2005, 2009). These studies show that early in the employment relationship, most individuals have a period of highly positive job attitudes, followed soon after by a deterioration in their appraisal of their new jobs.

Other research has investigated the trajectory of organizational commitment over time. Most research suggests that like job satisfaction, organizational commitment tends to decline over time among organizational newcomers (Bentein et al. 2005). There is also evidence that individuals who perceive that there is a psychological contract breach in their organization will have a negative trajectory of organizational commitment as well (Ng et al. 2010).

As we have noted, job attitudes often vary over time. Affective events theory specifically argues for the idea that emotion-laden events in the workplace can explain the variability in job satisfaction people experience on a day-to-day basis. One cross-sectional study involving 2,091 call center representatives found that work emotions can be explained by work features and that the relationship between these work features and job satisfaction was mediated by emotions (Wegge et al. 2006). An experience-sampling study of 41 employees found that negative events had a strong positive relationship with negative moods at work, whereas positive events had a positive relationship with positive moods at work (Miner et al. 2005). Another diary study found that interpersonal conflicts with customers acted as an environmental trigger that produced more negative attitudes (Grandey et al. 2002). Collectively, these studies demonstrate again that job attitudes will differ depending upon when they are measured.

OUTCOMES OF JOB ATTITUDES

Overview

The final consideration in models of attitudes is their relationship with behavior. Because organizational behavior research is concerned primarily with the outcomes of employee attitudes in organizations, the behavioral consequences of attitudes are clearly important. As we have noted previously, the dominant model linking attitudes to behaviors is the theory of planned behavior (Ajzen 1991), which proposes that general attitudes give rise to specific attitudes, which in turn can give rise to intentions to perform the behavior in question. A theory-building article also described how commitment can lead to behavior as a result of a translation of attitudes toward the organization, supervisor, and team to the development of specific commitments to goals, which in turn facilitates motivation to engage in specific actions (Meyer et al. 2004). Other studies propose a more emotion-centric view of the relationship between attitudes and behavior. For example, one study suggested that employees' affect toward the job and organization will lead them to behave in ways that support the organization, as affect gives cues about the state of the environment and therefore suggests appropriate responses (Foo et al. 2009).

Consistent with prior theory, we emphasize the relationship between job attitudes and theoretical constructs rather than the relationship between job attitudes and specific behaviors. This decision is consistent with the prior discussion of the bandwidth-fidelity principle as well as research showing that broad attitudes are poor predictors of specific behaviors but are good predictors of broad classes of related behaviors (e.g., Fishbein & Ajzen 1974). As this principle of using broad attitudes to predict broad outcomes would suggest, one structural meta-analysis found that overall job attitude (a combination of satisfaction and commitment) was highly correlated with a broad measure of several aspects of contribution to the work role (Harrison et al. 2006).

We define job performance as employee behaviors that are consistent with role expectations and that contribute to organizational effectiveness. Consistent with an accumulated body of research, we consider job performance as a multidimensional construct, composed of task performance (duties and behaviors that are formally required to perform one's job), organizational citizenship behavior (behaviors that go beyond formal role expectations and are generally contextual or interpersonal in nature), and withdrawal/counterproductivity (behaviors that are responses to dissatisfaction and that often go against organizational interests or norms). We also consider creative performance, as it is not clear that it fits well within the aforementioned categories of behaviors.

Task Performance

The link between job satisfaction and job performance has long been of interest to organizational psychologists. Meta-analysis suggests that there is indeed a substantial relationship between job satisfaction and job performance (Judge et al. 2001). Because this evidence comes primarily from cross-sectional studies, it is not possible to assess whether it is the case that job satisfaction causes job performance or if performance leads to satisfaction. To help answer this question, Riketta (2008) meta-analyzed the relationship between performance and satisfaction in longitudinal research and found that the evidence was stronger for a satisfaction-to-performance link than for a performance-to-satisfaction link.

Although broad measures of satisfaction generally do correlate with job performance, other studies have examined the importance of facets of satisfaction as predictors of performance. Different facets of job satisfaction show different relationships with outcomes of interest. Of the JDI dimensions, satisfaction with work has the strongest relationship with motivation, but all dimensions have similar relationships with job performance, with corrected meta-analytic correlations ranging from $r_c = 0.15$ to $r_c = 0.23$ (Kinicki et al. 2002). Other research examining multiple dimensions of pay satisfaction at the school district level of analysis has shown that aggregated pay satisfaction is related to student academic competency (Currall et al. 2005).

Given the evidence for a substantive relationship between satisfaction and performance, researchers have begun to explore moderators.

One study explored the relationship between affective satisfaction (as measured by an overall index of positive and negative emotions about the job) and cognitive satisfaction (as measured by a cognitive appraisal of the characteristics of a job) as a potential moderated relationship (Schleicher et al. 2004). Their research showed that when affective attitudes toward a job and cognitive appraisal of a job were consistent with one another, there was a stronger relationship between performance and satisfaction than when affective and cognitive attitudes were less related to one another.

The relationship between organizational commitment and job performance has been established in a number of studies, although the relationship is not particularly strong (Wright & Bonett 2002). However, not all studies find only main effects. Meta-analytic research demonstrated that the positive relationship between commitment and performance declined significantly with increasing employee tenure, suggesting that less-tenured employees have a stronger attitude-behavior link (Wright & Bonett 2002). Another study that examined different clusters of affective and continuance commitment found that moderate levels of continuance commitment and low levels of affective commitment were particularly related to poorer supervisor ratings of performance (Sinclair et al. 2005). In another study, employees who were low in affective commitment had a negative relationship between stress and performance, whereas employees who were high in affective commitment had a positive relationship between stress and performance (Hunter & Thatcher 2007). This last study demonstrates that attitudes can moderate the relationship between other work-related constructs and behaviors.

Creative Performance

The relationship between employee attitudes and creative performance has been the topic of vigorous debate. Although much research demonstrates that positive mood states associated with job satisfaction encourage more flexible and open thought processes (e.g., Lyubomirsky et al. 2005), others have contended that negative moods can generate active attention and critical thinking required for creativity (George & Zhou 2002). Some integrative recent work suggests that looking at positive or negative moods may be putting emphasis on the wrong portion of the affect circumplex, insofar as all activated moods, positive or negative, are associated with higher levels of creativity (De Dreu et al. 2008). Less research has looked at how these affective states pertain to the job attitudes–creativity link, although some work has been done in this area. One study showed that dissatisfied employees were more creative when they had high levels of continuance commitment and had support from the organization and coworkers (Zhou & George 2001). However, another study found that aggregate job satisfaction was positively related to measures of organizational innovation two years later (Shipton et al. 2006). As such, the form of the relationship between satisfaction and performance remains somewhat uncertain and may differ at the individual and group levels.

Citizenship Behavior

Although there is a conceptual reason to expect a moderate relationship between job attitudes and task performance, theory is even more strongly supportive of a relationship between citizenship behaviors and job attitudes (Organ & Ryan 1995). Meta-analysis demonstrates that overall satisfaction is related to citizenship behavior and that this relationship mediates the relationship between the personality traits of agreeableness and conscientiousness with citizenship (Ilies et al. 2009). Turning to facets of satisfaction, the relationship between citizenship behaviors and the JDI dimensions of pay, coworkers, and work are roughly equal in magnitude ($r_c = 0.16$ to $r_c = 0.23$), with an especially strong relationship between supervisor satisfaction and citizenship behaviors with $r_c = 0.45$ (Kinicki et al. 2002). Research in a union context using cross-lagged regression found that early union commitment was associated with voluntary informal participation in

the union ten years later (Fullagar et al. 2004). A meta-analytic path analysis study showed that job satisfaction and perceived fairness independently were related to higher levels of organizational citizenship behaviors, whereas a model suggesting that satisfaction mediates the relationship between fairness and citizenship behaviors was less well supported (Fassina et al. 2008). In sum, research does indeed show that job attitudes are related to citizenship.

Withdrawal/Counterproductivity

If positive job attitudes are expected to relate to positive behavioral decisions at work in the form of citizenship behavior, then negative attitudes are expected to relate to a broad class of negative behaviors at work in the form of withdrawal and counterproductivity. The negative behaviors constituting withdrawal include psychological withdrawal, absenteeism, turnover decisions, and decisions to retire.

Of the dimensions of the JDI, satisfaction with the work itself has the strongest relationship with both withdrawal cognitions and turnover intentions (Kammeyer-Mueller et al. 2005, Kinicki et al. 2002). Relationships between dimensions of performance and absenteeism are comparatively weaker for all other dimensions (Kinicki et al. 2002).

Most empirical tests suggest that job satisfaction is not directly related to turnover, but rather that job satisfaction leads to thoughts about quitting and comparison of one's job to alternatives, which in turn will eventually lead to turnover (e.g., Hom & Kinicki 2001). Research has also shown that job satisfaction is more likely to lead to turnover for individuals who are higher in cognitive ability, education, and occupation-specific training (Trevor 2001). In other words, job satisfaction is more likely to lead to withdrawal behavior in the form of turnover when there are opportunities for the attitude to express itself in the form of concrete behavior. Similar conclusions about the role of opportunity in the satisfaction-turnover relationship can be drawn from other research in this area (Lee et al. 2008). Evidence suggests that the relationship between satisfaction and unit-level absence is also stronger when the unemployment rate is low (Hausknecht et al. 2008). This might occur because employees are less worried about being fired from their jobs when there are ample alternatives in the labor market.

There is also ample evidence that organizational commitment is related to deviance and work withdrawal. Most research has focused on the relationship between affective commitment and turnover. Multivariate research also consistently shows that attitudes toward the job and attitudes toward the organization have independent and complementary effects on turnover behavior (Kammeyer-Mueller et al. 2005). Evidence suggests that steeper declines in organizational commitment over time are related to increased intention to quit and actually quitting (Bentein et al. 2005). Research also suggests that when a group's mean satisfaction and dispersion of satisfaction scores are low, attendance is likely to be particularly low (Dineen et al. 2007).

There are also possible interactions between commitment and satisfaction in predicting work withdrawal. Theory suggests that committed employees who have low levels of satisfaction will be less likely to engage in work withdrawal since they have some level of organizational loyalty, whereas employees with low levels of commitment will tend to have lower attendance across the board. For example, one study demonstrated that when organizational commitment was low, group-level absenteeism was high regardless of job satisfaction, but when organizational commitment was high, absence was especially low among those who were most satisfied (Hausknecht et al. 2008).

Organizational Performance

Although there are many reasons to be interested in the relationship between individual-level job attitudes and individual work behavior, organizational leaders are especially interested in the degree to which employee attitudes are related to overall organizational performance. Most organizational interventions to improve employee attitudes toward their work are designed to generate higher profits for the organization as a whole. Do these investments pay off? Meta-analysis suggests that there are indeed substantial, generalizable relationships between unit-level employee satisfaction and engagement with customer satisfaction, productivity, profit, turnover, and accidents (Harter et al. 2002). These results also were found in cross-lagged regression analyses in a diverse sample of individuals from 35 companies (Schneider et al. 2003), suggesting that employee job attitudes are related to subsequent organizational performance. Another study found that manager satisfaction levels were associated with customer satisfaction and store performance (Netemeyer et al. 2010). Moreover, this same study found an interaction that showed that when manager performance and manager satisfaction were high, employee and store performance were higher.

CONCLUSION

Although research on job attitudes has been at the core of the field of organizational psychology since its inception, new methods for conceptualizing and investigating job attitudes continue to enliven the field. In particular, the increased focus on within-persons studies has helped to significantly clarify the questions of states and traits in job attitudes research and to highlight the role of emotions and affective events as influences on job attitudes. A sizeable body of research has demonstrated that job attitudes are related to a variety of organizationally relevant behaviors including task performance, citizenship, creative performance, and organizational profitability.

As this review has also shown, new models of job attitudes involving within-person variability and team/organizational levels of analyses continue to enrich our understanding of core job attitudes. New models that demonstrate how situational perceptions mediate the relationship between dispositions and behavior, and models that demonstrate how dispositions moderate the relationship between situations and behavior, would be welcome.

SUMMARY POINTS

1. A job attitude is a social attitude; it may be one of the more central social attitudes because most individuals spend a majority of their waking hours at work, work is central to individuals' identities, and job attitudes have important consequences.

2. Affect and cognition are both important to job attitudes; at various times, each has occupied a more central place in research.

3. Job attitudes are multilevel concepts that show both traitlike (stable individual differences) and statelike (within-individual variation) properties.

4. A major thrust of recent research has used experience-sampling methodologies to study job satisfaction. This research has suggested that job satisfaction varies significantly on a day-to-day basis, and this variation is not merely transient error (it predicts and can be predicted by other meaningful concepts).

5. Of the major job satisfaction facets, work satisfaction appears to be the most important in predicting overall job satisfaction.

6. Personality is important to job attitudes; recent multilevel research suggests that personality affects individual differences in job satisfaction and within-individual relationships involving job satisfaction and other within-individual variables.

7. Recent research has shown that the social environment is important to job satisfaction, including coworker support, social networks, effective leadership, and demographic similarity between employee and coworkers.

8. Job attitudes predict many organizational behaviors; to achieve optimal prediction, correspondence needs to be maintained between the attitude and the behavior being predicted.

FUTURE ISSUES

1. Given that job attitudes are social attitudes, how do emerging research topics in social attitudes inform job attitudes research? Given that job attitudes research has some conceptual and methodological advantages, how might accumulated knowledge about job attitudes inform social attitudes research?

2. Recent evidence clearly indicates that job attitudes and moods/emotions covary. What is the causal direction: Do workplace attitudes cause moods/emotions, do moods/emotions cause job attitudes, or both?

3. How can state and trait perspectives on job attitudes—each of which has received considerable support but for which there is little integrative work—be further integrated?

4. Increasingly, researchers are conceptualizing job attitudes in a temporal context. Some of these temporal studies examine job attitudes over a relatively short period of time (daily variation over a week) whereas others examine temporal fluctuations over a very long time period (as long as 20 years). How does the time frame affect our understanding of temporal variations in job attitudes?

DISCLOSURE STATEMENT

The authors are not aware of any affiliations, memberships, funding, or financial holdings that might be perceived as affecting the objectivity of this review.

LITERATURE CITED

Adler S, Weiss HM. 1988. Recent developments in the study of personality and organizational behavior. In *International Review of Industrial and Organizational Psychology*, ed. CL Cooper, IT Robertson, pp. 307–30. Chichester, UK: Wiley

Adolphs R, Damasio AR. 2001. The interaction of affect and cognition: a neurobiological perspective. In *Handbook of Affect and Social Cognition*, ed. JP Forgas, pp. 27–49. Mahwah, NJ: Erlbaum

Ajzen I. 1991. The theory of planned behavior. *Organ. Behav. Hum. Decis. Process.* 50:179–211

Allen NJ, Meyer JP. 1990. The measurement and antecedents of affective, continuance, and normative commitment to the organization. *J. Occup. Psychol.* 63:1–18

Arvey RD, Bouchard TJ, Segal NL, Abraham LM. 1989. Job satisfaction: environmental and genetic components. *J. Appl. Psychol.* 74:187–92

Ashby FG, Isen AM, Turken AU. 1999. A neuro-psychological theory of positive affect and its influence on cognition. *Psychol. Rev.* 106:529–50

Avery DR, McKay PF, Wilson DC. 2007. Engaging the aging workforce: the relationship between perceived age similarity, satisfaction with coworkers, and employee engagement. *J. Appl. Psychol.* 92:1542–56

Beal DJ, Weiss HM, Barros E, MacDermid SM. 2005. An episodic process model of affective influences on performance. *J. Appl. Psychol.* 90:1054–68

Bentein K, Vandenberghe C, Vandenberg R, Stinglhamber F. 2005. The role of change in the relationship between commitment and turnover: a latent growth modeling approach. *J. Appl. Psychol.* 90:468–82

Best RG, Stapleton LM, Downey RG. 2005. Core self-evaluations and job burnout: the test of alternative models. *J. Occup. Health Psychol.* 10:441–51

Bollen KA. 2002. Latent variables in psychology and the social sciences. *Annu. Rev. Psychol.* 53:605–34

Bono JE, Foldes HJ, Vinson G, Muros JP. 2007. Workplace emotions: the role of supervision and leadership. *J. Appl. Psychol.* 92:1357–67

Boswell WR, Boudreau JW, Tichy J. 2005. The relationship between employee job change and job satisfaction: the honeymoon-hangover effect. *J. Appl. Psychol.* 90:882–92

Boswell WR, Shipp AJ, Payne SC, Culbertson SS. 2009. Changes in newcomer job satisfaction over time: examining the pattern of honeymoons and hangovers. *J. Appl. Psychol.* 94:844–58

Bowling NA, Beehr TA, Wagner SH, Libkuman TM. 2005. Adaptation-level theory, opponent process theory, and dispositions: an integrated approach to the stability of job satisfaction. *J. Appl. Psychol.* 90:1044–53

Brayfield AH, Rothe HF. 1951. An index of job satisfaction. *J. Appl. Psychol.* 35:307–11

Brief AP, Weiss HM. 2002. Organizational behavior: affect in the workplace. *Annu. Rev. Psychol.* 53:279–307

Chen G, Bliese PD, Mathieu JE. 2005. Conceptual framework and statistical procedures for delineating and testing multilevel theories of homology. *Organ. Res. Methods* 8:375–409

Chiaburu DS, Harrison DA. 2008. Do peers make the place? Conceptual synthesis and meta-analysis of coworker effects on perceptions, attitudes, OCBs, and performance. *J. Appl. Psychol.* 93:1082–103

Colquitt JA. 2001. On the dimensionality of organizational justice: a construct validation of a measure. *J. Appl. Psychol.* 86:386–400

Currall SC, Towler AJ, Judge TA, Kohn L. 2005. Pay satisfaction and organizational outcomes. *Pers. Psychol.* 58:613–40

De Dreu CKW, Baas M, Nijstad BA. 2008. Hedonic tone and activation level in the mood-creativity link: toward a dual pathway to creativity model. *J. Personal. Soc. Psychol.* 94:739–56

Dineen BR, Noe RA, Shaw JD, Duffy MK, Wiethoff C. 2007. Level and dispersion of satisfaction in teams: using foci and social context to explain the satisfaction-absenteeism relationship. *Acad. Manage. J.* 50:623–43

Drevets WC, Raichle ME. 1998. Reciprocal suppression of regional cerebral blood flow during emotional versus higher cognitive processes: implications for interactions between emotion and cognition. *Cogn. Emot.* 12:353–85

Dunham RB, Grube JA, Castaneda MB. 1994. Organizational commitment: the utility of an integrative definition. *J. Appl. Psychol.* 79:370–80

Eagly AH, Chaiken S. 1993. *The Psychology of Attitudes*. Belmont, CA: Wadsworth

Edwards JR, Cable DM. 2009. The value of value congruence. *J. Appl. Psychol.* 94:654–77

Eisenberger R, Karagonlar G, Stinglhamber F, Neves P, Becker TE, et al. 2010. Leader-member exchange and affective organizational commitment: the contribution of supervisor's organizational embodiment. *J. Appl. Psychol.* 95:1085–103

Fassina NE, Jones DA, Uggerslev KL. 2008. Relationship clean-up time: using meta-analysis and path analysis to clarify relationships among job satisfaction, perceived fairness, and citizenship behaviors. *J. Manage.* 34:161–88

Fazio RH, Olson MA. 2003. Attitudes: foundations, functions, and consequences. In *The Handbook of Social Psychology*, ed. MA Hogg, J Cooper, pp. 139–60. London: Sage

Fedor DB, Caldwell S, Herold DM. 2006. The effects of organizational changes on employee commitment: a multilevel investigation. *Pers. Psychol.* 59:1–29

Fishbein M, Ajzen I. 1974. Attitudes towards objects as predictors of single and multiple behavioral criteria. *Psychol. Rev.* 81:59–74

Foo MD, Uy MA, Baron RA. 2009. How do feelings influence effort? An empirical study of entrepreneurs' affect and venture effort. *J. Appl. Psychol.* 94:1086–94

Fullagar CJ, Gallagher DG, Clark PF, Carroll AE. 2004. Union commitment and participation: a 10-year longitudinal study. *J. Appl. Psychol.* 89:730–37

George JM, Zhou J. 2002. Understanding when bad moods foster creativity and good ones don't: the role of context and clarity of feelings. *J. Appl. Psychol.* 87:687–97

Glomb TM, Welsh ET. 2005. Can opposites attract? Personality heterogeneity in supervisor-subordinate dyads as a predictor of subordinate outcomes. *J. Appl. Psychol.* 90:749–57

Grandey AA, Tam AP, Brauburger AL. 2002. Affective states and traits in the workplace: diary and survey data from young workers. *Motiv. Emot.* 26:31–55

Hackman JR, Oldham GR. 1976. Motivation through the design of work: test of a theory. *Organ. Behav. Hum. Perf.* 16:250–79

Harris MM, Anseel F, Lievens F. 2008. Keeping up with the Joneses: a field study of the relationships among upward, lateral, and downward comparisons and pay level satisfaction. *J. Appl. Psychol.* 93:665–73

Harrison DA, Newman DA, Roth PL. 2006. How important are job attitudes? Meta-analytic comparisons of integrative behavioral outcomes and time sequences. *Acad. Manage. J.* 49:305–25

An important review of, and a call for more research on, moods and emotions in organizational research.

A meta-analysis showing the importance of coworkers to job attitudes.

Tests relative validity of three organizational commitment dimensions based on meta-analytic data.

Provides support for an overall job attitude factor and tests models of its relationship to withdrawal.

Harter JK, Schmidt FL, Hayes TL. 2002. Business-unit-level relationship between employee satisfaction, employee engagement, and business outcomes: a meta-analysis. *J. Appl. Psychol.* 87:268–79

Hausknecht JP, Hiller NJ, Vance RJ. 2008. Work-unit absenteeism: effects of satisfaction, commitment, labor market conditions, and time. *Acad. Manage. J.* 51:1223–45

Hom PW, Kinicki AJ. 2001. Toward a greater understanding of how dissatisfaction drives employee turnover. *Acad. Manage. J.* 44:975–87

Hoppock R. 1935. *Job Satisfaction*. New York: Harper

Hulin CL. 2002. Lessons from industrial and organizational psychology. In *The Psychology of Work: Theoretically Based Empirical Research*, ed. JM Brett, F Drasgow, pp. 3–22. Mahwah, NJ: Erlbaum

Hunter LW, Thatcher SMB. 2007. Feeling the heat: effects of stress, commitment, and job experience on job performance. *Acad. Manage. J.* 50:953–68

Hurtz GM, Williams KJ. 2009. Attitudinal and motivational antecedents of participation in voluntary employee development activities. *J. Appl. Psychol.* 94:635–53

Ilies R, Fulmer IS, Spitzmuller M, Johnson MD. 2009. Personality and citizenship behavior: the mediating role of job satisfaction. *J. Appl. Psychol.* 94:945–59

Ilies R, Judge TA. 2002. Understanding the dynamic relationships among personality, mood, and job satisfaction: a field experience sampling study. *Organ. Behav. Hum. Dec. Process.* 89:1119–39

Ilies R, Judge TA. 2004. An experience-sampling measure of job satisfaction and its relationships with affectivity, mood at work, job beliefs, and general job satisfaction. *Eur. J. Work Organ. Psychol.* 13:367–89

Ilies R, Scott BA, Judge TA. 2006. The interactive effects of personal traits and experienced states on intraindividual patterns of citizenship behavior. *Acad. Manage. J.* 49:561–75

Ironson GH, Smith PC, Brannick MT, Gibson WM, Paul KB. 1989. Construction of a Job in General scale: a comparison of global, composite, and specific measures. *J. Appl. Psychol.* 74:193–200

Jokisaari M, Nurmi J. 2009. Change in newcomers' supervisor support and socialization outcomes after organizational entry. *Acad. Manage. J.* 52:527–44

Judge TA, Bono JE. 2001. Relationship of core self-evaluations traits—self-esteem, generalized self-efficacy, locus of control, and emotional stability—with job satisfaction and job performance: a meta-analysis. *J. Appl. Psychol.* 86:80–92

Judge TA, Bono JE, Erez A, Locke EA. 2005. Core self-evaluations and job and life satisfaction: the role of self-concordance and goal attainment. *J. Appl. Psychol.* 90:257–68

Judge TA, Bono JE, Locke EA. 2000. Personality and job satisfaction: the mediating role of job characteristics. *J. Appl. Psychol.* 85:237–49

Judge TA, Heller D, Klinger R. 2008. The dispositional sources of job satisfaction: a comparative test. *Appl. Psychol. Int. Rev.* 57:361–72

Judge TA, Heller D, Mount MK. 2002. Five-factor model of personality and job satisfaction: a meta-analysis. *J. Appl. Psychol.* 87:530–41

Judge TA, Hulin CL. 1993. Job satisfaction as a reflection of disposition: a multiple source casual analysis. *Organ. Behav. Hum. Decis. Process.* 56:388–421

Judge TA, Hulin CL, Dalal RS. 2011. Job satisfaction and job affect. In *The Oxford Handbook of Industrial and Organizational Psychology*, ed. SWJ Kozlowski. New York: Oxford Univ. Press

Judge TA, Ilies R. 2004. Affect and job satisfaction: a study of their relationship at work and at home. *J. Appl. Psychol.* 89:661–73

Judge TA, Locke EA, Durham CC. 1997. The dispositional causes of job satisfaction: a core evaluations approach. *Res. Organ. Behav.* 19:151–88

Judge TA, Piccolo RF, Ilies R. 2004. The forgotten ones? The validity of consideration and initiating structure in leadership research. *J. Appl. Psychol.* 89:36–51

Judge TA, Scott BA, Ilies R. 2006. Hostility, job attitudes, and workplace deviance: test of a multilevel model. *J. Appl. Psychol.* 91:126–38

Judge TA, Thoresen CJ, Bono JE, Patton GK. 2001. The job satisfaction–job performance relationship: a qualitative and quantitative review. *Psychol. Bull.* 127:376–407

Judge TA, Watanabe S. 1993. Another look at the job satisfaction–life satisfaction relationship. *J. Appl. Psychol.* 78:939–48

Provides comprehensive quantitative review of the job satisfaction–job performance relationship.

Judge TA, Welbourne TM. 1994. A confirmatory investigation of the dimensionality of the Pay Satisfaction Questionnaire. *J. Appl. Psychol.* 79:461–66

Kammeyer-Mueller JD, Wanberg CR, Glomb TM, Ahlburg D. 2005. The role of temporal shifts in turnover processes: It's about time. *J. Appl. Psychol.* 90:644–58

Kinicki AJ, McKee-Ryan FM, Schriesheim CA, Carson KP. 2002. Assessing the construct validity of the Job Descriptive Index: a review and meta-analysis. *J. Appl. Psychol.* 87:14–32

Kunin T. 1955. The construction of a new type of attitude measure. *Pers. Psychol.* 8:65–77

Lee TH, Gerhart B, Weller I, Trevor CO. 2008. Understanding voluntary turnover: path-specific job satisfaction effects and the importance of unsolicited job offers. *Acad. Manage. J.* 51:651–71

Liao H, Joshi A, Chuang A. 2004. Sticking out like a sore thumb: employee dissimilarity and deviance at work. *Pers. Psychol.* 57:969–1000

Liao H, Rupp DE. 2005. The impact of justice climate and justice orientation on work outcomes: a cross-level multifoci framework. *J. Appl. Psychol.* 90:242–56

Loi R, Yang J, Diefendorff JM. 2009. Four-factor justice and daily job satisfaction: a multilevel investigation. *J. Appl. Psychol.* 94:770–81

Lyubomirsky S, King L, Diener E. 2005. The benefits of frequent positive affect: Does happiness lead to success? *Psychol. Bull.* 131:803–55

Magnusson D. 1999. Holistic interactionism: a perspective for research on personality development. In *Handbook of Personality: Theory and Research*, ed. LA Pervin, OP John, pp. 219–47. New York: Guilford. 2nd ed.

Mattson RE, Paldino D, Johnson MD. 2007. The increased construct validity and clinical utility of assessing relationship quality using separate positive and negative dimensions. *Psychol. Assess.* 19:146–51

Mayer D, Nishii L, Schneider B, Goldstein H. 2007. The precursors and products of justice climates: group leader antecedents and employee attitudinal consequences. *Pers. Psychol.* 60:929–63

Meglino BM, Korsgaard MA. 2007. The role of other orientation in reactions to job characteristics. *J. Manage.* 33:57–83

Meyer JP, Becker TE, Vandenberghe C. 2004. Employee commitment and motivation: a conceptual analysis and integrative model. *J. Appl. Psychol.* 89:991–1007

Meyer JP, Stanley DJ, Herscovitch L, Topolnytsksy L. 2002. Affective, continuance, and normative commitment to the organization: a meta-analysis of antecedents, correlates, and consequences. *J. Vocat. Behav.* 61:20–52

Miner AG, Glomb TM. 2010. State mood, task performance, and behavior at work: a within-persons approach. *Organ. Behav. Hum. Decis. Process.* 112:43–57

Miner AG, Glomb TM, Hulin C. 2005. Experience sampling mood and its correlates at work. *J. Occup. Organ. Psychol.* 78:171–93

Miner JB, Dachler HP. 1973. Personnel attitudes and motivation. *Annu. Rev. Psychol.* 24:379–402

Mischel W, Shoda Y. 1998. Reconciling processing dynamics and personality dispositions. *Annu. Rev. Psychol.* 49:229–58

Morgeson FP, Humphrey SE. 2006. The Work Design Questionnaire (WDQ): developing and validating a comprehensive measure for assessing job design and the nature of work. *J. Appl. Psychol.* 91:1321–39

Netemeyer RG, Maxham JG, Lichtenstein DR. 2010. Store manager performance and satisfaction: effects on store employee performance and satisfaction, store customer satisfaction, and store customer spending growth. *J. Appl. Psychol.* 95:530–45

Neuman GA, Edwards JE, Raju NS. 1989. Organizational development interventions: a meta-analysis of their effects on satisfaction and other attitudes. *Pers. Psychol.* 42:461–89

Ng TWH, Feldman DC, Lam SSK. 2010. Psychological contract breaches, organizational commitment, and innovation-related behaviors: a latent growth modeling approach. *J. Appl. Psychol.* 95:744–51

Olson JM, Zanna MP. 1993. Attitudes and attitude change. *Annu. Rev. Psychol.* 44:117–54

O'Reilly CA. 1991. Organizational behavior: where we've been, where we're going. *Annu. Rev. Psychol.* 42:427–58

O'Reilly CA, Chatman J. 1986. Organizational commitment and psychological attachment: the effects of compliance, identification, and internalization of prosocial behavior. *J. Appl. Psychol.* 71:492–99

Organ DW, Ryan K. 1995. A meta-analytic review of attitudinal and dispositional predictors of organizational citizenship behavior. *Pers. Psychol.* 48:775–802

Parsons CK, Hulin CL. 1982. An empirical comparison of item response theory and hierarchical factor analysis in applications to the measurement of job satisfaction. *J. Appl. Psychol.* 67:826–34

Power MJ. 2006. The structure of emotion: an empirical comparison of six models. *Cogn. Emot.* 20:694–713

Rentsch JR, Steel RP. 1992. Construct and concurrent validation of the Andrews and Withey job satisfaction questionnaire. *Educ. Psychol. Meas.* 52:357–67

Rich BL, Lepine JA, Crawford ER. 2010. Job engagement: antecedents and effects on job performance. *Acad. Manage. J.* 53:617–35

Tests underlying causal directions of the relationship between job attitudes and performance.

Riketta M. 2008. The causal relation between job attitudes and performance: a meta-analysis of panel studies. *J. Appl. Psychol.* 93:472–81

Rizzo JR, House RJ, Lirtzman SI. 1970. Role conflict and ambiguity in complex organizations. *Admin. Sci. Q.* 15:150–63

Schaubroeck J, Shaw JD, Duffy MK, Mitra A. 2008. An under-met and over-met expectations model of employee reactions to merit raises. *J. Appl. Psychol.* 93:424–34

Schleicher DJ, Watt JD, Greguras GJ. 2004. Reexamining the job satisfaction-performance relationship: the complexity of attitudes. *J. Appl. Psychol.* 89:165–77

Schneider B, Hanges PJ, Smith DB, Salvaggio AN. 2003. Which comes first: employee attitudes or organizational financial and market performance? *J. Appl. Psychol.* 88:836–51

A study that illustrates the insights produced by multilevel conceptualizations of job attitudes.

Seibert SE, Silver SR, Randolph WA. 2004. Taking empowerment to the next level: a multiple-level model of empowerment, performance, and satisfaction. *Acad. Manage. J.* 47:332–49

Shipton HJ, West MA, Parkes CL, Dawson JF, Patterson MG. 2006. When promoting positive feelings pays: aggregate job satisfaction, work design features, and innovation in manufacturing organizations. *Eur. J. Work Organ. Psychol.* 15:404–30

Sinclair RR, Tucker JS, Cullen JC, Wright C. 2005. Performance differences among four organizational commitment profiles. *J. Appl. Psychol.* 90:1280–87

Smith PC, Kendall L, Hulin CL. 1969. *The Measurement of Satisfaction in Work and Retirement: A Strategy for the Study of Attitudes*. Chicago: Rand McNally

Reviews theoretical bases for attitudes research, with a special focus on bringing commitment research more in line with general attitudes research.

Solinger ON, van Olffen W, Roe RA. 2008. Beyond the three-component model of organizational commitment. *J. Appl. Psychol.* 93:70–83

Staw BM. 1984. Organizational behavior: a review and reformulation of the field's outcome variables. *Annu. Rev. Psychol.* 35:627–66

Staw BM, Bell NE, Clausen JA. 1986. The dispositional approach to job attitudes: a lifetime longitudinal test. *Admin. Sci. Q.* 31:437–53

Staw BM, Ross J. 1985. Stability in the midst of change: a dispositional approach to job attitudes. *J. Appl. Psychol.* 70:469–80

An early and important paper suggesting the importance of personality to job attitudes.

Takeuchi R, Chen G, Lepak DP. 2009. Through the looking glass of a social system: cross-level effects of high-performance work systems on employees' attitudes. *Pers. Psychol.* 62:1–29

Tepper BJ. 2000. Consequences of abusive supervision. *Acad. Manage. J.* 43:178–90

Totterdell P, Wall T, Holman D, Diamond H, Epitropaki O. 2004. Affect networks: a structural analysis of the relationship between work ties and job-related affect. *J. Appl. Psychol.* 89:854–67

Trevor CO. 2001. Interactions among actual ease-of-movement determinants and job satisfaction in the prediction of voluntary turnover. *Acad. Manage. J.* 44:621–38

Trougakos JP, Jackson CL, Beal DJ. 2011. Service without a smile: comparing the consequences of neutral and positive display rules. *J. Appl. Psychol.* 96:350–62

Tsai W, Chen C, Liu H. 2007. Test of a model linking employee positive moods and task performance. *J. Appl. Psychol.* 92:1570–83

Wanberg CR, Glomb TM, Song Z, Sorenson S. 2005. Job-search persistence during unemployment: a 10-wave longitudinal study. *J. Appl. Psychol.* 90:411–30

Watson D. 2000. *Mood and Temperament*. New York: Guilford

Watson D, Slack AK. 1993. General factors of affective temperament and their relation to job satisfaction over time. *Organ. Behav. Hum. Decis. Process.* 54:181–202

Wegge J, van Dick R, Fisher GK, West MA, Dawson JF. 2006. A test of basic assumptions of Affective Events Theory (AET) in call centre work. *Br. J. Manage.* 17:237–54

Weiss HM, Cropanzano R. 1996. Affective events theory: a theoretical discussion of the structure, causes and consequences of affective experiences at work. *Res. Organ. Behav.* 19:1–74

Weiss HM, Nicholas JP, Daus CS. 1999. An examination of the joint effects of affective experiences and job beliefs on job satisfaction and variations in affective experiences over time. *Organ. Behav. Hum. Decis. Process.* 78:1–24

Williams ML, McDaniel MA, Nguyen NT. 2006. A meta-analysis of the antecedents and consequences of pay level satisfaction. *J. Appl. Psychol.* 91:392–413

Wright TA, Bonett DG. 2002. The moderating effects of employee tenure on the relation between organizational commitment and job performance: a meta-analysis. *J. Appl. Psychol.* 87:1183–90

Zhou J, George JM. 2001. When job dissatisfaction leads to creativity: encouraging the expression of voice. *Acad. Manage. J.* 44:682–96

A seminal article providing a framework for the study of moods and emotions in job attitudes research.

The Individual Experience of Unemployment

Connie R. Wanberg

Carlson School of Management, University of Minnesota, Minneapolis, Minnesota 55455;
email: wanbe001@umn.edu

Annu. Rev. Psychol. 2012. 63:369–96

First published online as a Review in Advance on July 1, 2011

The *Annual Review of Psychology* is online at psych.annualreviews.org

This article's doi:
10.1146/annurev-psych-120710-100500

Keywords

job loss, job search, job seeker, layoff, reemployment, mental health

Abstract

This review describes advances over the past decade in what is known about the individual experience of unemployment, predictors of reemployment, and interventions to speed employment. Research on the impact of unemployment has increased in sophistication, strengthening the causal conclusion that unemployment leads to declines in psychological and physical health and an increased incidence of suicide. This work has elucidated the risk factors and mechanisms associated with experiencing poor psychological health during unemployment; less so for physical health and suicide. Psychologists have begun to contribute to the study of factors associated with reemployment speed and quality. The past decade has especially illuminated the role of social networks and job search intensity in facilitating reemployment. Evidence suggests some individuals, especially members of minority groups, may face discrimination during their job search. Although more work in this arena is needed, several intervention-based programs have been shown to help individuals get back to work sooner.

Contents

INTRODUCTION

A financial crisis beginning in 2007 produced the worst unemployment situation the world has encountered since the Great Depression. An estimated 210 million people worldwide were registered as out of work in the third quarter of 2010, a 30 million increase from the beginning of the crisis (Int. Monetary Fund, Int. Labor Organ. 2010). Increases in unemployment levels have been most severe in the United States, New Zealand, Spain, and Taiwan. In the United States, the unemployment rate as of December 2010 was 9.4%, with even higher levels among youth aged 16 to 24, among some minority groups, and in certain states such as Nevada (Bur. Labor Stat. 2011). In Spain, unemployment rates are even higher, at a startling 20.6% (Newsweek 2011). In a press release preceding a global conference to discuss the outlook for employment, the director general at the International Labor Organization stated, "We are now seeing signs of a fragile recovery, but for millions of people and

Unemployment: individuals are considered to be unemployed if they meet a country-specified minimum working age, do not currently hold a job, and are actively seeking and available for work (Hussmanns 2007)

enterprises around the world the [economic] crisis is far from over" (Int. Labor Organ. 2010).

Empirical research on unemployment has been approached from both macro (encompassing topics such as job creation and unemployment insurance policies) and micro (emphasizing the individual experience of unemployment) perspectives. The current review covers individual-focused research on unemployment, research that has examined the experience of unemployment from the unemployed individual's perspective. Several narrative reviews have summarized this research (e.g., Catalano 1991, DeFrank & Ivancevich 1986, Dooley et al. 1996, Eisenberg & Lazarsfeld 1938, Fryer & Payne 1986, Hanisch 1999, Kasl et al. 1998, Leana & Feldman 1988, Winefield 1995). This review builds upon these past summaries by focusing on research on unemployment from the 2000–2010 decade. The review does not focus on unemployment in special groups such as individuals with mental illness, chronic health issues, or disabilities.

Advances in knowledge in the past ten years in three primary areas are explored. First, how does unemployment affect individual well-being (including psychological health, physical health, and suicide)? Second, what do we know about the job search process and other key variables associated with faster (and higher-quality) reemployment? Finally, what interventions have been proposed to speed reemployment, and how effective are they? Emphasizing psychological research but integrating work from other disciplines such as economics and sociology, the review delineates how our understanding of these three areas has progressed in the past decade.

IMPACT OF UNEMPLOYMENT

A substantial amount of research, dating back to the Great Depression, has focused on the impact of unemployment on individual well-being. This research suggests that being unemployed may result in a range of stress-related consequences for the individual including depression, anxiety, physical ailments such as stomachaches and headaches, and even suicide. The negative effects of unemployment on psychological well-being have been explained through a variety of theories (see Creed & Bartrum 2006 for a review). Perhaps the most influential theory has been Jahoda's (1982, 1987) latent deprivation model. Jahoda proposed that employment provides both manifest (e.g., income) and latent (e.g., time structure, social contact, sharing of common goals, status, and activity) benefits to the individual. While unemployed, individuals are deprived of these benefits and thus experience lower psychological health. Several pathways through which unemployment is thought to affect physical health and suicide have also been suggested (Korpi 2001). For example, the stress involved with being unemployed may directly translate into physical symptoms or suicide. In addition, physical health may be diminished by an inability to afford healthy food and other necessities, and if an individual is not able to afford health care, certain health conditions can go untreated. Individuals having problems coping psychologically may also be unable to afford psychological help.

A frequent focus of recent research on unemployment and well-being has been on issues of causality. Specifically, researchers have attempted, through a myriad of methods, to examine whether the lower well-being of unemployed individuals is a causal outcome of unemployment or whether it is instead due to a tendency of individuals with poor psychological and physical health to lose their jobs (i.e., a selection effect). Appearing on a more limited basis in the extant literature, but not described here, is research that examines the impact of unemployment on the family unit (e.g., Kalil 2009) and health-related behaviors such as smoking and drinking (e.g., Falba et al. 2005).

Unemployment and Psychological Health

Psychological health refers to an individual's emotional and mental well-being, ability to function in society, and capacity to meet the demands of day-to-day life. A significant advancement in the past decade relevant to the understanding of unemployment and psychological health came from two meta-analytic summaries of the many studies that have been conducted across time on this topic (McKee-Ryan et al. 2005, Paul & Moser 2009). These meta-analyses provide insight into the effect size of the relationship between unemployment and reduced psychological health (i.e., how strong is the association?) as well as a differentiation of results from studies with stronger versus weaker methodological designs.

In the most recent meta-analysis, Paul & Moser (2009) first summarized the results of 237 cross-sectional studies (involving a total of 458,820 participants) that had compared the psychological health of unemployed individuals with the psychological health of an employed comparison group. Consistent with the results of the earlier meta-analysis (McKee-Ryan et al. 2005), this analysis showed unemployed individuals had significantly lower levels of psychological health than employed individuals (Paul & Moser 2009). The standardized mean difference in psychological health between the two groups, assessed through Cohen's d, was 0.54. Cohen's effect sizes can be roughly categorized as small, medium, or large; 0.54 is a medium-sized effect, likely to be "visible to the naked eye of a careful observer" (Cohen 1992, p. 156). The proportion of individuals that could be deemed as clinically distressed was twice as high in the unemployed sample as in the employed sample. The differences in mental health between the unemployed and employed were highest in studies with more men, blue-collar workers, long-term unemployed, and countries with weak unemployment protection systems. The authors also examined whether the year of data collection was a moderator of study findings. Given the changing context of work and the normalization of unemployment due to recurrent layoffs, the question of whether unemployment is as harmful to well-being now as it was in earlier periods has been raised in the popular press (e.g., Brady 2010). Paul & Moser (2009) found

Meta-analysis: a statistical aggregation of results across studies

r_c: the average sample weighted correlation across studies

k: the number of studies

N: the total sample across studies

no evidence suggesting that the association between unemployment and lower psychological health was stronger in earlier decades.

Cross-sectional studies do not allow strong causal conclusions about the link between unemployment and psychological health. Specifically, cross-sectional findings that unemployed groups have lower psychological health may be due to a selection effect—i.e., individuals with poor psychological health may be more apt to lose their jobs. To address this concern, Paul & Moser (2009) identified a subset of the cross-sectional studies (n = 27) that had assessed the psychological health of individuals who had been part of a factory closure (a situation where it is highly unlikely that job loss was produced by poor psychological health). In these studies, unemployed individuals again had higher levels of distress than employed individuals, strengthening the conclusion that it is the unemployment situation that is responsible for heightened distress.

Paul & Moser (2009) also summarized the results of 64 longitudinal studies: 19 studies that followed individuals from employment into unemployment and 45 studies that followed individuals from unemployment into employment. Longitudinal research, although not without limitations, is a more robust design since it follows the same individuals over time as they have changes in their employment status. The meta-analytic findings suggested that across studies, there was a significant increase in distress (d = 0.19) as individuals moved into unemployment and a significant decrease in distress as individuals moved into employment (d = −0.35). These effect sizes, although considered small by Cohen (1992), are still meaningful changes. Once again, these findings are consistent with those reported by the McKee-Ryan et al. (2005) meta-analysis.

Some evidence for selection effects was shown in the meta-analysis, although not enough to overpower the findings that unemployment is uniquely associated with lower psychological health (Paul & Moser 2009). For example, employed individuals who later lost their jobs had slightly higher distress levels than individuals who did not lose their jobs. In addition, students who were unemployed after high school had slightly higher distress levels while at school than did their peers who found jobs. In balance, the selection effects are small. The cumulative data, triangulated with different research methods, strongly suggest that lower psychological health levels among unemployed individuals occur beyond those explained through selection effects.

These meta-analytic results describe the average impact of unemployment, aggregated across individuals. There is considerable variability in how individuals appraise and react to job loss. In the past decade, there has been an improved understanding of risk factors and the processes associated with experiencing diminished psychological health during unemployment. McKee-Ryan et al. (2005) quantitatively summarized the results of available studies from 2002 and earlier that had examined predictors of psychological health during unemployment. The authors identified five variable categories that have been studied in relation to psychological health during unemployment: work role centrality (how important work is to the individual); coping resources (the individual's personality, social support, financial resources, and ability to structure one's time during unemployment); cognitive appraisal (how individuals interpret the job loss); coping strategies (the cognitive and behavioral strategies individuals use to manage the demands associated with unemployment); and demographics. The five strongest correlates of psychological health identified by the meta-analysis included core self-evaluations ($r_c = 0.55$, $k = 26$, $N = 5,186$), financial strain ($r_c = −0.45$, $k = 17$, $N = 5,257$), stress appraisal ($r_c = −0.38$, $k = 4$, $N = 881$), social undermining from significant others ($r_c = −0.36$, $k = 2$, $N = 1,700$), and work role centrality ($r_c = −0.34$, $k = 19$, $N = 4,398$). These results indicate that individuals are likely to fare better during unemployment if they have a higher sense of self-worth, perceived control, and optimism, less financial strain, a less negative appraisal of being unemployed, are not strongly identified with work, and if they do not have a spouse or significant other who nags and berates them.

Although not one of the strongest correlates, job search effort was negatively correlated with psychological health ($r_c = -0.11, k = 20, N = 8,214$), indicating that individuals who spend more time and effort looking for a job have lower levels of psychological health. A subsequent study examined the directionality of this relationship (Song et al. 2009). This study, using a repeated measures design over a 14-day period, suggests the relationship is reciprocal. Specifically, job search seems to increase psychological distress and psychological distress seems to increase job search effort (perhaps individuals are motivated to end the pain of unemployment). The authors also assessed whether a third variable, financial hardship, might be responsible for producing a spurious relationship between job search and mental health. Examination of this third variable hypothesis was not supported.

Other research has proposed detailed process models to describe mechanisms through which variables important to psychological health during unemployment play their roles. For example, Price et al. (2002a) highlight financial strain as the key stressor during unemployment. Their data suggest unemployment produces a "chain of adversity." Severe financial strain impacts levels of depression, which in turn increases feelings of helplessness and erodes feelings that one can exert control over life outcomes. Decreasing personal control contributes further to poor health and lower emotional functioning.

Additional stressors of unemployment, including pension applications, updating one's resume, job search, interviews, job rejections, financial adversity, relationship problems, and boredom are portrayed in the COPES (Coping, Psychological, and Employment Status) model (Waters 2000). The effect of these stressors on psychological health is mediated by cognitive appraisal (how the individual evaluates the stressor) and choice of coping strategies. Individuals may choose several ways to cope with the stressors of unemployment including problem-focused strategies such as job search activity or retraining and emotion-focused strategies such as seeking support from others. Negative appraisals along with ineffective coping strategies produce lower well-being during unemployment.

Finally, unemployment was portrayed as a process that requires extensive self-regulation of both effort and emotion by Wanberg et al. (2011). Self-regulation of effort is needed to sustain one's job search over time, despite continued rejections and the monotony of the process. Self-regulation of emotion is needed when individuals feel discouraged, angry, worried, or frustrated about the multiple stressors involved with job search and being unemployed. Their findings suggest that individual differences with respect to how individuals approach goals predict vacillations in self-defeating cognition (negative or dysfunctional self-talk) as well as motivational control (goal setting or other strategies to stay on course with one's job search) from week to week over the unemployment experience. Over the 20-week duration of the study, the mental health of participants was lower when unemployed participants engaged in self-defeating cognition. In weeks where unemployed participants engaged in more motivational control, their mental health and job search intensity was higher.

Unemployment and Suicide

At the extreme, unemployment may be distressing enough to some individuals to lead to suicide. The last comprehensive review of the relationship between unemployment and suicide was conducted by Platt & Hawton in 2000. These authors summarized the results of 165 empirical studies on this topic from the period 1984–1999. Some studies examining suicide have used the same techniques as described in the previous section, such as comparing suicide levels of unemployed and employed groups. However, aggregate studies are also used. Aggregate studies examine the relationship between macro indices such as unemployment and suicide rates in given regions. The amassed literature on unemployment and suicide has been difficult to summarize because of inconsistent findings, a large array of designs and methodologies, and differences in study quality. However, Platt & Hawton (2000) conclude, on the basis of their review, that unemployment is associated with an increased risk of both suicide and parasuicide (self-injurious behavior). They were unable, on the basis of the studies available, to make a strong statement about causality (e.g., to what extent these results represent self-selection of suicidal individuals into unemployment versus a stress-produced outcome of the experience of unemployment).

In the past decade, researchers have continued to study the relationship between unemployment and suicide. Of 18 post-2000 articles identified for the current review, 15 reported findings that unemployment and suicide are related (Åhs & Westerling 2006, Blakely 2003, Chen et al. 2010, Chung 2009, Classen & Dunn 2011, Koo & Cox 2008, Kposowa 2001, Lin 2006, Noh 2009, Rehkopf & Buka 2006, Stack & Wasserman 2007, Taylor 2003, Voss et al. 2004, Wu & Cheng 2010, Yamasaki et al. 2005). Chen et al. (2010), using longitudinal aggregate data from Taiwan from the years 1978 to 2006, found that a 1% increase in the unemployment rate corresponded to a 4.9% increase in the suicide rate. U.S. data analyzed by Classen & Dunn (2011) depicted one additional death by suicide for every 4,200 males who lose their job during a mass layoff, with a lower rate for females (one out of 7,100). The Classen & Dunn study is unique because it focused on the relationship between suicide rates and numbers of individuals losing their jobs through mass layoffs or establishment closings, where many individuals lose their jobs at the same time. This methodology substantially reduces arguments that linkages between suicide and unemployment can be explained by selection effects, such as a tendency of suicidal individuals being more likely to lose their jobs.

A review of 86 peer-reviewed publications examining the relationship between aggregate measures of socioeconomic status and incidence of suicide suggests that the size of the area aggregated is important (Rehkopf & Buka 2006). Specifically, studies that focus on smaller geographical units are more likely to report increased suicide in areas of low socioeconomic position. When studies report the relationship between indices such as unemployment rate and suicide at large levels of aggregation (e.g., at a state or country level), there is large heterogeneity within these units that can confound results (Rehkopf & Buka 2006). Other reasons for result heterogeneity include the geographical area or sample that is the focus of the study. For example, of the three post-2000 studies that did not show unemployment and suicide to be related, one was focused on European countries where there are substantial safety nets (Andrés 2005), one was focused on Latvia, during a period when there were several social and economic changes taking place (Rancans et al. 2001), and the last was focused specifically on suicide rates for individuals over the age of 65 (Shah 2008).

A different approach to examining the relationship between unemployment and suicide, using qualitative methods, was used by Stack & Wasserman (2007). These authors examined suicide files from a county medical examiner's office from 1997 to 2000. Nearly half of the 62 suicides reviewed mentioned unemployment in the description of the cause, such as a 61-year-old man who killed himself after losing his job at a lawn service. The study found that 43 of the 62 suicides were marked by multiple strains, such as being unemployed combined with losing one's home or being unemployed combined with being in a poor relationship.

Unemployment and Physical Health

Post-2000, researchers have used increasingly sophisticated methods to examine the premise that unemployment may not only affect psychological health, but also physical health. Similar to the research on psychological health and suicide, this research has aimed to differentiate between selection effects of poor health into unemployment and the extent to which unemployment reduces physical health. In this work, physical health has been operationalized in a variety of ways, including via self-reports of health, health symptom checklists, mortality (not specific to suicide), and biochemical indices such as cortisol levels.

Findings suggest that individuals do lose their jobs as a consequence of poor health. Using a large nationally representative data set from the U.S. Panel Study of Income Dynamics, Strully (2009) found a significant relationship between previous poor health and being subsequently fired or leaving a job voluntarily. Yet, this same study showed unemployment is linked to declines in physical health beyond that explainable through selection effects. For example, compared to a stably employed reference group, individuals who lost their jobs due to an establishment closure had a 54% increase in the odds of reporting only fair or poor health and an 83% increase in the odds of reporting a new health condition such as hypertension, arthritis, or diabetes. Because the analysis focused on individuals who had lost their jobs due to an establishment closure (i.e., a mass layoff), arguments that the results are due to selection issues are very weak. This finding held even after controlling for several variables such as previous health status, gender, ethnicity, education, occupation, marital status, family income, and having experienced a recent move or change in marital status. Having been fired or laid off raised the odds of a new health problem by 43%.

Similar results were reported by Korpi (2001). This author used data from the 1981 and 1991 Swedish Level of Living Survey, a survey that includes both physical health data and employment status data over time. The physical health data were represented by a total symptom index, composed of responses about experiencing several illnesses or ailments including aches or pains in the chest, bronchitis, stomach pains, and backache. Although the results suggest that ill health increases the risk of job loss and the risk of remaining unemployed, they also portray a worsening of health status (especially among individuals with multiple or long spells of unemployment) that does not seem to be attributable to selection.

Another recent study showed that males who lost their jobs in the early and mid 1980s in Pennsylvania had significantly higher mortality rates than individuals in a nondisplaced comparison group (Sullivan & von Wachter 2009). The data for this study involved matching worker employment and wage data from 1974 to 1991 to death records from 1974 to 2006. Because the data did not indicate whether job displacements were voluntary or involuntary, the authors counted individuals as displaced if they had been working in a firm whose employment was 30% or more below its peak. Other individuals leaving their firms, along with stably employed individuals, were included in the comparison group. In the immediate period after experiencing a job loss (i.e., between 1987 and 1993), displaced individuals had a 40% higher likelihood of dying than nondisplaced individuals (5.15 per 1,000 versus 3.67 per 1,000). The effect was reduced yet sustained over time; 20 years later mortality rates were approximately 15% higher for the displaced individuals in the sample. To help control for selection effects, the authors controlled for industry and earnings for several years prior to job loss, and included only individuals with several years of stable employment prior to job loss in the displaced worker sample. The authors also found that job displacement was associated with a 15% to 20% decline in long-term earnings. The employment situation in Pennsylvania during the 1980s was particularly dire, which possibly reduced the generalizability of the findings.

These findings are not inconsistent with studies (e.g., Gerdtham & Ruhm 2006) that show in the aggregate, times of higher unemployment tend to be associated with a slight decline in overall mortality rates (perhaps because there is less commuting, fewer work accidents, and more leisure time). Sullivan & von Wachter (2009) argue that it is possible for mortality to be elevated among involuntarily displaced individuals and for this trend to be masked in aggregate analyses of mortality levels across the whole population. They also argue that mortality consequences of job loss are not contemporaneous with the time of job loss and may take much longer to show up.

The past decade showed new methodologies to examine the impact of unemployment on biomedical measures. Maier et al. (2006) examined changes in both general physical capacity and cortisol levels among 71 unemployed individuals at three time points during their first year of unemployment. Physical capacity was measured by having individuals engage in an ergonomic test on a bicycle. Cortisol levels, which have been linked to several health-related problems, were examined via blood samples drawn after fasting overnight. The 23 unemployed individuals showed a decrease in physical working capacity of 16.3% throughout the duration of the study. Cortisol levels for males increased throughout the study duration, signaling a stress response; cortisol levels for women increased for the first six months and then declined. The authors suggest, but do not have evidence to support this possibility, that the decline in cortisol levels for women may be due to women adopting the role as housewife rather than continuing their job search.

Results of another study showed having previous spells of unemployment was associated with higher levels of c-reactive protein (CRP) five to eight years later, even after controlling for age, education, body mass index, initial CRP levels, and household income (Janicki-Deverts et al. 2008). CRP is a marker of inflammation that has been linked to elevated stress and an increased risk for diabetes, hypertension, and cardiovascular disease. Part, but not all, of the observed relationship between unemployment and CRP levels was explained by participant levels of tobacco and alcohol use, physical activity, and depression. The authors examined for selection issues by assessing whether there was a relationship between early assessments of CRP and change in employment status; the authors found no evidence that elevated CRP influenced incidence of unemployment in the following three years.

Findings inconsistent with the conclusion that unemployment has an impact on physical health were reported by Bockerman & Ilmakunnas (2009), based on a large nationally representative sample in Finland over the period 1996–2001. Their results show that lower levels of self-reported physical health predict later episodes of unemployment. Unemployment, however, was not associated with a decline in physical health. Sullivan & von Wachter (2009) argue that these results are not necessarily inconsistent with the conclusion that unemployment impacts physical health. Specifically, they note that the Finnish system provides more generous unemployment and health benefits than, for example, is the case in the United States. This may mean that unemployment is less likely to affect physical health in certain countries.

Summary

Despite some inconsistent findings, the studies illustrate that unemployment can impact not only psychological health, but also physical health, suicide, and mortality. Selection effects of poor well-being into unemployment occur, but the research provides evidence (through a mixture of diverse methodologies) that poor health effects are not solely due to selection. Significant individual differences in the experience of unemployment occur, however, and the portrayal of unemployment as a damaging experience does not apply to everyone. The past decade of research has delineated the most important risk factors for psychological health during unemployment and has begun to examine in more detail the process and mechanisms involved. Less research has examined the process or mechanisms involved in the linkages between unemployment and suicide or reduced physical health.

JOB SEARCH AND REEMPLOYMENT

What, then, do we know about the job search process and other factors associated with successfully finding work? Pre-2000, psychological research examining the job search and especially reemployment outcomes was relatively sparse in comparison to the substantial attention paid to the impact of unemployment. Although even more research is needed, extensive progress has been made in advancing understanding of the job search process and factors predictive of reemployment in the past decade. Some research has broadly focused on delineating the myriad of factors related to reemployment success. Yet, the bulk of micro-level research has focused on specific topics relevant to reemployment success, especially the sources of information used to learn about jobs, other aspects of the job search, and discrimination in hiring.

General Factors Related to Reemployment Success

A large number of factors are relevant to reemployment success, variously defined as finding work quickly and/or finding a good job (i.e., with satisfactory wages, benefits, and commute time, fit with the individual's interests or skills, etc.). To help organize these factors, a comprehensive model of the variable groups associated with reemployment success was proposed by Wanberg et al. (2002). According to this model, a job seeker's reemployment success depends on the labor market's need for employees (nationally, regionally, and by occupation and industry of the displaced individual) and the job seeker's human capital (i.e., his or her job-related knowledge, skills, and abilities and other individual differences). Also important are characteristics of the individual's job search (including job search intensity and quality) and his or her level of social capital (i.e., having a large and ideally high-status social network of friends, relatives, previous coworkers, and other acquaintances). Finally, situational constraints (e.g., having a disability or illness), self-imposed constraints (e.g., setting a high level of desired pay), discrimination on the part of employers, and an individual's financial need to work are also relevant. These variable groups, with the exception of job search quality and employer discrimination, were operationalized by the authors and studied as predictors of reemploy-

ment success. The variables explained only a small percentage of the variance in an array of reemployment success outcomes, suggesting that additional variables, interactions of variables, and better ways to measure relevant variables are all needed to better explain reemployment outcomes.

Another conceptualization of factors necessary to experience reemployment success was put forth by Fugate et al. (2004). These authors argue an individual's employability requires high levels of career identity, personal adaptability, and social and human capital. Career identity involves having a clear grasp of one's work-related experiences and aspirations (i.e., who am I, and who do I want to be?). Personal adaptability entails a willingness and ability to adjust to changing situations and requires optimism, openness to learn, flexibility, agency, and self-efficacy. Social capital allows individuals greater access to information and access to career opportunities. Human capital denotes a myriad of factors including age, education, work experience, skills, occupational knowledge, emotional intelligence, and cognitive ability.

A meta-analysis conducted by Kanfer et al. (2001) helps to summarize the relationships between various antecedents and the duration of unemployment. Although based on very few studies, several personality and other individual difference variables were related to shorter unemployment duration, including extroversion ($r_c = -0.10$, k = 2), openness to experience ($r_c = -0.08$, k = 2), agreeableness ($r_c = -0.09$, k = 2), conscientiousness ($r_c = -12$, k = 4), self-esteem ($r_c = -0.24$, k = 5), and job search self-efficacy ($r_c = -0.12$, k = 4). Higher financial need is also associated with faster reemployment (r_c with duration $= -0.07$, k = 5). The mean sample weighted correlation (r_c) between job search intensity (encompassing greater effort and time put into job search) and unemployment duration was -0.14 (k = 9). Small relationships were found between educational levels and ethnicity and unemployment duration, suggesting that individuals become reemployed faster if they have higher education and are white. Quality of employment was not examined as an outcome variable in this meta-analysis due to insufficient numbers of studies measuring quality of employment outcomes.

Additional research suggests that individuals who receive more generous unemployment insurance benefits may become reemployed less quickly (Krueger & Meyer 2002). Several studies have noted a "spike" of reemployment that occurs when unemployment benefits lapse. However, these findings may be overstated because many studies do not account for individuals who simply stop receiving benefits (e.g., drop out of the system) rather than actually finding jobs (Card et al. 2007).

The relationship between psychological health and reemployment success has been examined in a few studies. For example, does lower psychological health reduce speed of reemployment (i.e., by impairing search efforts and signaling negative characteristics to an employer) or increase speed of reemployment (i.e., motivating individuals to find work faster)? Studies tend to find that lower psychological health slightly impairs reemployment speed (Paul & Moser 2009, Vinokur & Schul 2002) or that there is no relationship at all between psychological health and reemployment success (Ginexi et al. 2000, Wanberg et al. 2010b). One exception was reported by Crossley & Stanton (2005), who found higher combined levels of depression, anxiety, and stress to be positively related to job search success. It is likely that this result is due to multicolinearity produced by inclusion of both negative affectivity and distress in a multivariate model. Yet, further examination of the psychological health/reemployment success may be in order, with careful attention to types of measures (i.e., depression may reduce job search effort whereas anxiety may stimulate effort) as well as curvilinear effects (i.e., anxiety up to a certain level may amplify employment success, but if it surpasses that level it may diminish employment success).

Predictors of reemployment quality have been studied less often than predictors of reemployment speed. Available research highlights two sets of variables that are predictive of postunemployment job quality: demographics and career planning. First, the prevalence of underemployment (i.e., working in a job that requires less education than one has, or working part-time when wishing to work full-time) is highest among younger (18–24) and older (55–64) age groups. Women, minorities (especially American Indians, Hispanics, and African Americans) and individuals in extractive industries such as farming, forestry, mining, or fishing are also at higher risk for underemployment (Jensen & Slack 2003). Second, research has shown that individuals who engage in a careful and deliberate job search, employ career planning and decision making, and are confident about their job search tend to be more satisfied with their postunemployment jobs (Crossley & Highhouse 2005, Koen et al. 2010, Saks 2006, Saks & Ashforth 2002, Wanberg et al. 2002, Zikic & Klehe 2006). Some research, however, has indicated that career planning has both its upsides and downsides. Specifically, "maximizers" (individuals who have a trait-based tendency to seek out the very best choice following an exhaustive examination of many possibilities) tend to find jobs with higher wages than "satisficers" (individuals who seek a good choice without looking for perfection). Yet, maximizers are more likely than satisficers to experience anxiety during the search and be less satisfied with the search outcome (Iyengar et al. 2006). Career planning may also be less beneficial for individuals with low financial resources. If individuals do not have the financial means to hold out for the right job, they may be forced to take the first job that comes along (Wanberg et al. 2002).

As reviewed in the next section, a few studies suggest that there may be a link between the job information source used to find one's job and some aspects of job quality. Finding work through social connections may facilitate a better match between the worker and the job due to the depth of information the job seeker is able to secure about the job before taking it. Finding work through public employment offices usually yields lower wages than private employment offices, but this is likely due to selection effects with regard to the type of individuals who use these job information sources.

Job Information Sources

In order to obtain employment, most individuals have to acquire information about job openings. The literature has typically differentiated between formal (e.g., print and electronic advertisements, employment agencies) and informal (e.g., friends, relatives, acquaintances) sources of job information or search methods. In the past decade, several studies have focused on examining the use and effectiveness of these various search sources.

Research dating back to the 1960s has highlighted the particular importance of informal networks in finding a job (e.g., see Granovetter 1995). Work in the past decade has continued to show that a substantial proportion of job seekers secure jobs through social networks, not only in the United States, but around the world. For example, on the basis of a survey of individuals in 28 countries, Franzen & Hangartner (2006) found that the proportion of job seekers finding jobs through contacts was highest in Brazil, Chile, Cyprus, and the Philippines (ranging from 67% to 83%) and lowest in Finland, Austria, Denmark, and Norway (ranging from 26% to 28%). In the U.S. portion of the sample, 44% of job seekers found their last job through a social contact. A member of one's social network may help by offering information about available jobs, alerting the organization that the job seeker is available or interested, exerting actual influence over the decision to hire the job seeker, or standing behind the job seeker as a good hire (Lin 2001).

Arguing that chance can play a role in job finding, McDonald (2010) introduced serendipity as an underdiscussed concept in finding work through social connections. Specifically, many individuals find jobs by fortuitously running into someone rather than through a planned or formal inquiry made to a friend or acquaintance. Even an unplanned conversation between a job seeker's mother and a neighbor may produce a job (McDonald 2010). A survey of nearly 3,000 adults indicated that socially advantaged individuals are the most likely to experience "serendipitous" job leads (McDonald 2010). Social investment before a job search, even investment that is noninstrumental in nature, may lead to a later job. Time spent networking during the job search, however, still seems to make a difference. Two studies that have explicitly examined time spent in networking suggest that individuals who put more time and effort into networking in their job search are more likely to find jobs (Wanberg et al. 2000) and attain more offers (Van Hoye et al. 2009).

In aggregate, it seems that finding a job through a social contact does not result in higher wages. However, several studies have found that finding a job through a higher-quality connection (e.g., higher status) is associated with the receipt of higher wages (for a review, see Mouw 2003). These findings may be confounded, however, because job seekers with better qualifications may be the ones with higher-quality connections (Mouw 2003). Because informal connections may be a good source of information about potential jobs, research has linked finding work through social connections to nonpecuniary benefits. For example, jobs found through informal, rather than formal, search methods were more likely to fit individuals' level of education and long-term career needs (Franzen & Hangartner 2006). In a study in China, getting a job through a social tie (*guanxi*) was related to higher job satisfaction than getting a job through other methods such as authority assignment (Cheung & Gui 2006).

The possibility that social networks may be used differently or yield fewer benefits for ethnic minorities and women (e.g., because of their reduced power status in the workforce) was explored in several studies. In a four-city study using data collected from 1992 to 1994, white men and Hispanics were more likely to find jobs through social connections than were white women and blacks (Smith 2000).

Some evidence suggests that women who have a greater proportion of men in their networks receive more offers (Belliveau 2005), and that men and women who find jobs through male contacts receive higher wages than those who find jobs through female contacts (Loury 2006). Women tend to disseminate information to other women about lower-paying and female-dominated, rather than male-dominated, jobs (Huffman & Torres 2002, Mencken & Winfield 2000). Inner-city blacks may tend to rely on close ties within their neighborhood to find work, meaning they will rely on a network that is socially isolated, homogenous, and higher in poverty (Mouw 2002). These networks should not necessarily be avoided, however, because turning to formal postings may not yield better jobs. Individuals without college degrees, for example, may need to rely more on social networks to find work than do individuals with college degrees (Zang 2003).

Another study found that individuals in rural areas need to rely more on informal networks than do individuals in urban areas (Matthews et al. 2009). In a Canadian study using stratified random samples from both rural (n = 2,881) and big-city urban (n = 2,230) areas, only 20% of individuals from urban areas reported finding their current job through an informal channel. In contrast, 53% of the rural sample reported finding their current job through an informal channel. The importance of informal networks in rural communities makes it especially difficult for newcomers to those communities; if newcomers want to find a job, they need to first establish their reputation (Matthews et al. 2009). Jobs in rural communities are also less likely to be posted; information about openings is circulated by word of mouth (Lindsay et al. 2005).

Not everyone is comfortable using informal search methods or networking. Many individuals have weak networks, are uncomfortable with a systematized networking process, and don't know how to go about contacting friends, family, and acquaintances during their job search. Recent research characterizes the type of job seeker likely to spend less time networking

during a job search. Individuals with lower extraversion, conscientiousness, and proactivity and those with smaller networks will be most likely to avoid networking during their job search (Lambert et al. 2006, Tziner et al. 2004, Van Hoye et al. 2009, Wanberg et al. 2000).

Although most of the research on job information sources has focused on the use of social networks, a few post-2000 studies were focused on the effectiveness of public employment offices. Public employment offices provide employer listings and aim to help job seekers find work within (or outside of) these listings. Research has linked the use of public employment offices to lower earnings and shorter tenure in the new job (Addison & Portugal 2002, Weber & Mahringer 2008). However, this lack of effectiveness may reflect the types of jobs advertised through public employment offices as well as the lower qualifications of individuals using these services. For example, data from the Norwegian Graduate Surveys (1995–2000) suggest that new market entrants who used the public employment service were from fields with higher unemployment rates and had lower grade point averages in school (Try 2005). Furthermore, a study in Austria showed that a job found through the public employment service paid 16% less than jobs found through other methods. Yet, individuals who found work through the service also had lower pay before securing a job through the service. In comparison, the use of private employment services tends to be associated with higher wage levels and faster reemployment; these agencies tend to work with individuals with higher levels of qualifications (Bortnick & Ports 1992, Huffman & Torres 2001, Weber & Mahringer 2008).

A major change in search methods in the past decade has been the increasing sophistication, availability, and use of the Internet as a source of job postings. Available research portrays no advantage with regard to reemployment speed to individuals who use the Internet to look for jobs (Kuhn & Skuterud 2004), perhaps because most job seekers now use this tool (Fountain 2005). Despite this finding, the Internet is a central job search tool, and the number of jobs that individuals can find on the Internet greatly exceeds what can be found in print outlets (Van Rooy et al. 2003). Social networking sites such as LinkedIn, Facebook, and Twitter also have utility with respect to finding information about open positions (Challenger, Gray, & Christmas Inc. 2009).

Overall, although job search methods differ with respect to their effectiveness, jobs are found through many means, including newspaper and online advertisements, direct contact with employers, networking, private and public employment offices, and unsolicited offers. As such, it is recommended that job seekers use an array of search methods in their job search (Mau & Kopischke 2001, Van Rooy et al. 2003, Wanberg et al. 2000).

Other Aspects of the Job Search

Beyond the sources that individuals use to identify job openings, other dimensions of job search behavior that are important to reemployment success include intensity-effort (the amount of time and effort an individual puts into looking for work), temporal-persistence (whether an individual persists in his or her efforts and how the job search is changed over time), and other aspects of the content and direction of the search (such as the quality of search behaviors) (Kanfer et al. 2001). Of these dimensions, the intensity or effort individuals put into their job search has received the greatest amount of research attention.

In studies focusing on this construct, job search intensity is typically operationalized as the frequency of engagement in various job search activities, such as how many times in the previous two weeks an individual has viewed job openings online or in a newspaper. Measures of job search effort typically ask about the number of hours or amount of energy an individual is putting into one's job search. Meta-analytic data show that higher levels of both job search intensity and effort are related to receiving more job offers and shorter unemployment duration (Kanfer et al. 2001).

Some authors have also distinguished between preparatory and active search intensity following some research that originated with employed job seekers (Blau 1993, 1994). Preparatory search involves gathering information, considering a search, and getting everything in order to search (e.g., revising one's resume or reading a book about job search). Active job search has been conceptualized as expressing one's availability for work (e.g., listing oneself as a job applicant) and actually applying for open positions. The distinction between preparatory and active behaviors from a measurement standpoint can be murky for unemployed job seekers. Specifically, some search behaviors that are scored as active (e.g., contacting an employment agency) may actually be preparatory (the job seeker may attend a job search workshop at the agency). Likewise, some behaviors typically counted as preparatory (e.g., speaking with a previous employer to get job leads) indicate availability for work and may involve an actual employment request. Furthermore, preparatory behaviors are thought to come in advance of active behaviors (Blau 1993, 1994). This may be suitable for employed or college student job seekers preparing for graduation (Saks 2006). However, unemployed individuals may engage in preparatory behaviors such as revising one's resume on a continual basis while also engaging in active search. Research including measures of both preparatory and active job search intensity suggests active search intensity has stronger relationships with reemployment outcomes (Saks 2006, Saks & Ashforth 2000).

Estimates suggest unemployed individuals spend an average of 41 minutes to 3.5 hours a day on their job search in the United States (Krueger & Mueller 2010; Wanberg et al. 2010b, 2011). This level of job search effort is substantially higher than that reported in European countries (Krueger & Mueller 2010). More time is spent in job search within countries and U.S. states that provide lower unemployment benefits. Furthermore, time spent in job search increases as the time of benefit exhaustion approaches (Krueger &

Mueller 2010). Time spent in search differs considerably across individuals. For example, in a U.S. sample of individuals self-reporting they were actively pursuing jobs, 5.2% reported an average of 0–1 hours of search a day across a three-week period. In contrast, 1.3% reported 8–9 hours a day (Wanberg et al. 2010b).

A motivational, self-regulatory conceptualization of job search was proposed by Kanfer et al. (2001) to explain individual differences in time spent in job search. Self-regulation theories suggest that individuals differ in their abilities to successfully modulate their emotions, attention, effort, and performance during goal-directed activity (see, for example, Bandura 1986, Kuhl 1985). The ability to self-regulate emotions and effort is important in the job search context. Specifically, looking for work is a highly autonomous activity, requiring individuals to self-organize and manage their search. Discouragement, frustration, distraction, uncertainty, and many other factors may make it difficult for some individuals to expend effort on their job search. Kanfer et al. (2001) suggest that individual differences in personality, expectancies, self-evaluation, and motives are relevant to effective functioning in such a context. Meta-analytic data provided by these authors suggest that job seekers who put more time and effort into their job searches have higher levels of extraversion, openness to experience, agreeableness, emotional stability, and conscientiousness, as well as higher perceived control over life events, self-esteem, and self-efficacy. Job search intensity is also positively correlated with financial need, employment commitment, and social support. Demographics have very small relationships with search intensity. For example, men tend to report higher levels of job search than women, but the sample weighted correlation between gender and job search intensity was only 0.05.

Following the Kanfer et al. (2001) meta-analysis, a number of studies in the past decade have used self-regulatory frameworks to further elucidate the job search process. Several individual differences relevant to how individuals tend to approach goal-based situations (i.e., autonomous and controlled motivation, action and state orientation, and goal orientation) have been shown to be related to the time and effort individuals devote to their job search. Collectively, these studies show that job search effort and intensity are higher among individuals who (a) initiate and commit to action and (b) engage in goal striving volitionally, for the purpose of personal growth or because they find it interesting (Creed et al. 2009, Song et al. 2006, Vansteenkiste et al. 2004, Wanberg et al. 2011).

Self-regulatory theories have also been used to help understand the mechanisms involved in job search—e.g., how self-regulation occurs and through which processes individual differences exert their influence. For example, proactive personality (having a tendency to take initiative) may help an individual get more interviews and offers through increasing one's employment confidence and job search intensity (Brown et al. 2006). Extraversion, conscientiousness, and leadership experience may facilitate interview self-efficacy, which in turn improves chances of interview success (Tay et al. 2006). Meta-cognitive activities (setting goals, developing plans, and monitoring progress) and emotional control (managing one's emotions during unemployment) mediate the relationship between more stable personality traits and job search intensity (Creed et al. 2009, Turban et al. 2009, Wanberg et al. 2011). Non-self-determined motivation, defined as performing job search activities because one is pressured to do so rather than because one wants to do so, predicts procrastination in job search activities; procrastination is related to increased hopelessness (Senecal & Guay 2000). In another study, procrastination did not help to explain the extent to which intentions to search translate into actual search behavior (van Hooft et al. 2005).

Some additional studies aimed to deepen the understanding of factors and mechanisms important to the job search by using other, non-self-regulatory perspectives. Data from Cote et al. (2006) suggest that job search clarity (having clear job search objectives as well as clarity about the job search process) is higher among individuals with higher conscientiousness and positive affectivity. Job search clarity mediated the relationship between positive affectivity and job search intensity. Because the Dutch culture is highly individualistic, Van Hooft et al. (2006a,b) expected to find that Dutch job seekers would be more likely to apply for jobs endorsed by their significant others than would job seekers from more collectivist minority groups in the Netherlands. Contrary to these expectations, the views of significant others were predictive of inclination to apply for a position for both groups.

The majority of studies in the literature examine job search at only one point in time, disregarding the possibility that job search intensity (or an individual's search approach) may change over time. The past decade yielded a few studies aiming to understand the dynamic processes involved in job search. Graduating college seniors, surveyed in their final term and four months later, showed an increase in preparatory and active search intensity and formal and informal source usage from the first survey to the second (Saks & Ashforth 2000). Another study assessed job search intensity every two weeks over 20 weeks and found that individuals with a higher positive self-concept and efficacy with dealing with life's challenges (i.e., core self-evaluation) reported higher persistence in their job search over time (Wanberg et al. 2005). This study also assessed whether cumulative, average job search intensity (measured across several weeks) would be more predictive of reemployment probability and speed than a Time 1, initial assessment of job search intensity. Although both Time 1 and average levels of job search were associated with reemployment success, aggregated levels of job search intensity did not improve the prediction of the reemployment outcomes.

Daily and weekly changes occurring over the duration of the job search were reported by Wanberg et al. (2010b, 2011). For example, Wanberg et al. (2010b) surveyed job seekers every weekday for three weeks. On days that job seekers perceived progress had been made in their job search, their mood and

feelings of confidence about finding work were elevated, especially among individuals with lower levels of financial hardship. Perceived progress, even without an actual offer in hand, was related to lower levels of search in the next day. This finding is consistent with control theory, which suggests that when individuals make progress toward achieving a goal, they may "coast" or take time off to devote to other activities (Carver 2006). In another study, job seekers experienced insights over time from learning the job search process, seeking guidance from others, and through self-reflection (Wang et al. 2007).

Especially when the unemployment rate is high, putting substantial time and effort into one's job search is a necessary condition for reemployment to occur (Prussia et al. 2001). Yet, job search intensity only accounts for a relatively small part of the variance in reemployment success outcomes (Kanfer et al. 2001). Authors during the past decade have begun to call for research that extends beyond looking at job search intensity (and sources) to other aspects of the job search, such as quality of individuals' search and presentation to employers as well as employers' decision-making practices (Kanfer et al. 2001, Sverko et al. 2008, Vinokur & Schul 2002).

Two recent studies provide insight into how a job seeker's search strategy and application materials can be improved. The efficacy of three job search strategies was examined by Crossley & Highhouse (2005). Individuals vary in the extent that they engage in a focused search (having a clearly defined employment objective and searching specifically for jobs that meet one's specified criteria), an exploratory search (gathering information about various employment options and being open to examining different opportunities), and a haphazard search (viewing and applying for opportunities without a plan or collection of information). A focused search was related to higher satisfaction in the postsearch job. An exploratory search was not related to job satisfaction but was related to getting more offers. Finally, a haphazard approach was negatively related to number of offers and job satisfaction in the postsearch job. Another study found that adding competency statements to a resume or cover letter to describe the job seeker's knowledge, skill, or abilities in relation to the job posting resulted in higher interest on the part of hiring managers (Bright & Hutton 2000).

A few other studies elucidate issues relevant to performance in the job interview. Various dimensions that comprise interview anxiety were delineated by McCarthy & Goffin (2004). According to these authors, during an interview individuals may experience communication anxiety (e.g., becoming so uneasy they may not be able to express their thoughts clearly), appearance anxiety (e.g., worrying about if they are dressed appropriately), social anxiety (e.g., apprehension about the impression one is making), performance anxiety (e.g., worrying about what will happen if they don't get the job), and/or behavioral anxiety (e.g., shaking hands, fast heartbeat, fidgeting, dry mouth). A scale was developed to assess these dimensions. Higher levels of interview anxiety were negatively related to interview performance as rated by an interviewer ($r = -0.34$). Consistent with this finding, individuals with high self-efficacy about the search process are more likely to have their interviews translate into job offers than individuals with low self-efficacy (Moynihan et al. 2003).

A recent meta-analysis addressed the relationship between self-presentation tactics and interview performance (Barrick et al. 2009). Results show candidate appearance is important: Across multiple studies, individuals evaluated to have a more professional appearance ($k = 8$, $r_c = 0.48$) and physical attractiveness ($k = 17$, $r_c = 0.54$) were given higher interview scores and deemed more suitable for hire. Impression management behaviors during the interview, including self-promotion (revealing positive information about oneself; $k = 18$, $r_c = 0.32$) and other-enhancement (e.g., agreeing with the interviewer or making ingratiating remarks; $k = 15$, $r_c = 0.26$) were also positively correlated with interviewer ratings. Finally, control over verbal (e.g., not talking too fast) and nonverbal behavior (e.g., smiling) in the interview was related to more positive interviewer ratings ($k = 7$ and 20 and $r_c = 0.24$ and 0.40, respectively).

Discrimination

The extent to which racial, ethnic, gender, age, or other types of discrimination may limit the employment success of individuals was the focus of several studies. These studies tended to be conducted by selection or workplace equity researchers, rather than unemployment researchers, suggesting there is potential for unemployment researchers to be more actively involved in this stream of research. Issues related to discrimination are difficult to study because discrimination is often very subtle and difficult to prove given the millions of one-on-one employer/job applicant interactions that take place each year. Many studies have consequently taken place in university laboratory settings, using undergraduates posing as employers to evaluate artificial resumes. Although these methods have been heavily criticized, triangulation of laboratory studies with other creative methodologies suggests that discrimination of various sorts occurs in the hiring process as well as within other work-related decisions (Leslie et al. 2008).

In the United States, the 2010 unemployment rate was 7.3% higher among black or African Americans in comparison with whites (Bur. Labor Stat. 2010). Similar inequities in joblessness occur between majorities and minorities in other countries. Differences in unemployment rates across racial and ethnic groups may occur for several reasons, including differential skills, location of residence, and discrimination on the part of employers. One recent study aimed to examine possible racial bias in hiring using creative means to remove variance in hiring that might be attributable to differential skills. In this study, white, black, and Hispanic individuals were recruited to pose as job seekers applying for a total of 240 entry-level positions in New York City over a nine-month period in 2004 (Pager et al. 2009). The individuals were clean-cut and matched with respect to social skills, interview and test performance, and physical attractiveness. The extent of the effort that went into this matching process is apparent—the researchers began with a field of 300 potential confederates and chose 10 that were matched on these criteria. The confederates applied for open positions with resumes that were constructed to be as similar as possible (without being identical) with respect to type and level of experience and education. A number of precautions and robustness checks were used to reduce alternative explanation issues such as the black applicants performing poorly in the interviews due to the expectation of being discriminated against. Results showed a significantly higher callback rate (i.e., second interview or job offer) for whites (31%) compared to Latinos (25.2%) and blacks (15.2%). Multiple examples of discrimination were documented through the process, such as when one employer told three of the confederates (one of each race) she was not going to interview them. As they all walked away, she asked the Hispanic and white individual to come back for a moment. She then told the two of them to return later that day to begin work.

Another U.S.-based study examined race discrimination by sending fictitious resumes with either common African American names (e.g., Lakisha Washington) or common white names (e.g., Emily Walsh). Resumes with African American names had a 3.2% lower chance of receiving a callback than resumes with white names (Bertrand & Mullainathan 2004). Comparable results have been shown in other countries with other minority groups. For example, in Greece, Albanians were 21.4% less likely to receive an interview than Greeks (Drydakis & Vlassis 2010). In the Netherlands and the United States, resumes with common Arabic names were rated lower on job suitability than resumes with common white names, although this effect depended on job characteristics and the rater's implicit prejudice (Derous et al. 2009). In India, there was evidence of discrimination against Other Backwards Caste and Scheduled Caste applicants for jobs involving soft skills, but not for software jobs (Banerjee et al. 2009).

Other research addressed gender and sexual orientation as factors affecting hiring. In a study in Britain, gender discrimination occurred when women applied to male-dominated jobs and when men applied to female-dominated jobs (Riach & Rich 2006). In another study, male applicants were evaluated more harshly than female applicants for experiencing employment gaps (Smith et al. 2005). Pregnant job applicants and women who indicate they are parents may receive lower hiring recommendation ratings (Correll et al. 2007, Cunningham & Macan 2007). One study had individuals posing as job applicants alternatively wear (or not wear) a pregnancy prosthesis (Hebl et al. 2007). Audiotaped interactions indicated the pregnant applicant was treated with greater hostility than the nonpregnant applicant. Findings with respect to whether sexual orientation affects hirability ratings have been mixed (Horvath & Ryan 2003, Van Hoye & Lievens 2003).

A significant area of concern to job seekers is the possibility of age discrimination. Some job seekers even take radical steps such as plastic surgery to appear younger (Rubin 2011). A recent review of the research on age discrimination in hiring suggests that although several laboratory studies (often using undergraduate raters of resumes) reveal age discrimination, evidence for age bias is less consequential in field studies (Morgeson et al. 2008).

Many job applicants, especially women, report they have been discriminated against because of their weight (Roehling et al. 2007). This perception is supported by a recent meta-analysis that reported that overweight individuals receive lower recommendations for hire than nonoverweight individuals (d $= -0.70$, k $= 31$; Rudolph et al. 2009). As with studies on age discrimination, most of these studies are laboratory studies and vary in their level of sophistication. In one of the more innovative studies, a computer program allowed for weight to be added or subtracted from a photo of a job applicant. Undergraduates rated the applicant with weight added to have more negative work attributes, but hiring decisions were not affected (Polinko & Popovich 2001). In a less realistic experimental manipulation, 30 men were shown full-page images of women with varying levels of body fat (from emaciated to obese) with their heads obscured to avoid bias induced by judgments of facial attractiveness. With the simple information that all of these women had equal qualifications, the men were asked how likely they were to hire individuals with each body type. Individuals with emaciated and obese body types were less likely to be hired than individuals with normal body types (Swami et al. 2008).

Summary

Several factors are pertinent to reemployment success. Beyond the labor market situation, other factors of importance include the job seekers' level of human and social capital, job search methods and sources of job information, job search intensity and quality, situational and self-imposed constraints, level of financial need, and demographic and personal characteristics including factors such as weight. Most available micro research in this area has focused on understanding the roles of job search and discrimination in hiring practices. The research on job search shows that many individuals find jobs through social networks and that the increasing use of the Internet as a source of job postings has not seemed to produce a faster match between employer and applicant. Individuals vary in the amount of time they devote to their job search, and several studies, many using a self-regulatory framework, have identified individual differences and mechanisms involved in the job search process. The research on discrimination reflects the difficulties of studying biases of employers. Available research suggests that various types of discrimination occur in the hiring process and may slow the speed of reemployment for some individuals. Researchers used especially varied methodologies in the studies devoted to ethnic/racial discrimination, bolstering the conclusion that biases in hiring from a racial/ethnic perspective occur.

INTERVENTIONS

Prevention or assistance-focused research aimed at helping individuals find work faster has attracted less attention than topics related to describing the difficulties of being unemployed (Hammarström & Janlert 2005). From 1994 through 1998, only four different interventions were described in the unemployment literature (Hanisch 1999). These interventions were focused on stress management, expressive writing, a job club, and the JOBS program, with multiple studies focusing on the JOBS program. Post-2000, the JOBS program commanded continued attention, building additional evidence for its efficacy and cross-cultural generalizability. In addition, several new intervention-based studies were published.

The JOBS program, developed by researchers at the University of Michigan, has two primary objectives: (a) enhancement of job search skills and self-confidence and (b) helping the job seeker prepare for the rejections and demoralization involved in the job search process (Price et al. 2002b). During the intervention, unemployed individuals identify their marketable skills, learn how to locate job opportunities, and practice responding to interview questions. Contributing to pre-2000 studies showing strong short-term outcomes, a two-year follow-up of the JOBS program found that participants continued to have higher levels of employment, higher monthly income, and lower levels of depression than did individuals in a randomly assigned control group (Vinokur et al. 2000).

Although initial examinations of the JOBS program were in the United States (for a review, see Caplan et al. 1997), more recently the benefits of the JOBS program were examined in Finland, where individuals have more substantial unemployment benefits following job loss (Vuori et al. 2002). A six-month follow-up showed the Finnish intervention participants to have higher stable employment and lower psychological distress than individuals in a control group, but there were no differences between the two groups on other indices such as wage rate or job satisfaction. Passive job seekers and those unemployed for only a moderate amount of time (rather than recently unemployed or unemployed long-term) benefitted most from the intervention. Two years later, participants continued to be more engaged in the labor market (e.g., through employment or vocational training) than nonparticipants were (Vuori & Silvonen 2005).

Additional interventions not involving the JOBS program were examined in the past decade. An intervention involving verbal self-guidance training was developed by Yanar et al. (2009) to help Turkish women job seekers. The labor force participation level for women in Turkey is low (26.9% compared to 73.1% for men). Most women are expected to attend to household and childcare duties rather than to a career. Built upon Bandura's (1986) social cognitive theory, the intervention involved coaching the trainees to reverse negative self-statements that pertained to their employability. Individuals were coached to revise thoughts such as "I can't find a job no matter how hard I try" into positive statements such as "I know what I am capable of doing and I am very determined to get what I want" (p. 592). Following the training, participants reported higher job search self-efficacy, higher levels of job search behavior, and faster reemployment than individuals in a control group reported. Interventions to enhance perceptions of competence and self-efficacy among job seekers were also developed by Creed et al. (2001), Harris et al. (2002), Jackson et al. (2009), Joseph & Greenberg (2001), and Latham & Budworth (2006).

Although many job search interventions have been based on social cognitive theories, two researchers tested an alternative approach based on the concept of goal orientation (van Hooft & Noordzij 2009). Unemployed job seekers in the Netherlands were randomly assigned into one of three conditions (learning goal orientation, performance goal orientation, or a control group). The learning orientation group was trained to view their job search as a chance to learn from mistakes, to improve

their job search skill, and to set goals for learning. The performance orientation group was encouraged to focus on competing with others and performing well in the job search. Consistent with theory, which suggests that individuals who view goals from a learning perspective are better suited to cope with obstacles and challenges, individuals in the learning orientation group were more likely to be reemployed eight months after the workshop than were individuals in the two other groups.

The post-2000 literature also described several government interventions aimed at speeding reemployment. Several countries with extensive unemployment benefit structures (such as Denmark, Australia, and Switzerland) have experimented with requiring individuals to participate in programs meant to keep them active in their job searches (Borland & Tseng 2007, Graversen & van Ours 2008, Lalive et al. 2008). In Australia, where eligible individuals receive unemployment benefits for as long as they are unemployed, an intervention known as the Jobseeker Diary program was tested as a means of speeding reemployment (Borland & Tseng 2007). This intervention requires job seekers to apply for a specified number of jobs and record details about each application in a diary. Most individuals were required to apply for eight jobs in each 14-day period, but this varied by region. The program was highly successful, especially in regions with more favorable labor market conditions. Participants in the program were reemployed faster than individuals in a control group, and cost-benefit calculations suggest the program results in a net monetary gain for the government (Borland & Tseng 2007). A few programs involving job training (skill upgrading) and retraining (e.g., training in new areas) were also examined (Daniels et al. 2000, Fitzenberger & Speckesser 2007, Lechner et al. 2007). To be effective, it is especially important that retraining programs accurately gauge future job needs. For example, in Germany in the early 1990s, several unemployed individuals were retrained in the area of construction, right before construction experienced a serious decline (Lechner et al. 2007).

One issue that practitioners find challenging is matching available services to the individuals who need those services. To help with this issue, a needs assessment inventory for job seekers was developed by Wanberg et al. (2010a). This inventory, currently in use in the state of Minnesota, asks job seekers to indicate their status on several items related to reemployment success, such as how much time is being spent in the search, what search methods are being used, confidence about tasks such as writing a good resume, and levels of stress and worry. The inventory is used to identify areas job seekers may need to work on to improve their chances of successful reemployment.

In summary, peer-reviewed research on interventions to enhance reemployment speed and quality is relatively sparse. Challenging the current foci of academic work on unemployment, Hammarström & Janlert (2005) argue that more intervention- and prevention-focused work in the area of unemployment is needed. Extending current work that tends to focus on the individual, the authors suggest more work should be done at organizational, community, and national levels. For example, research could examine the incentive structure of different institutions to decrease unemployment levels. Complementing research that attends to secondary prevention (reducing the duration of unemployment) and tertiary prevention (helping individuals cope with unemployment), the authors suggest more attention should be paid to primary prevention (reducing incidence of unemployment). Finally, the authors note that intervention research must stay abreast with niche unemployment problems, such as underemployment and migrant unemployment.

PROGRESS AND NEXT DIRECTIONS

In the past 10 years, unemployment research has shown significant progress. Research on the impact of unemployment has grown in its sophistication, strengthening the conclusion that unemployment reduces psychological and physical health for individuals. Several studies have used creative approaches (e.g., considering issues of selection) to improve the extent to which causal statements can be made about the relationship between unemployment and health-related outcomes. In addition, new methods involving biomedical measures have been introduced to investigate the physical health impact of being without work. Because the literature on the physical health impacts of unemployment is less developed than that on psychological health, additional research on unemployment and physical health and health behaviors would be valuable. For example, investigators have speculated, but have not empirically tested the proposition, that declines in physical health following job loss may stem in part from individuals bypassing necessary health care due to lack of health insurance.

Given the many studies that have explored the relationship between unemployment and psychological well-being, simple descriptive studies showing that unemployment is stressful are no longer of value. However, work that extends theory and empirical understanding about the mechanisms and process by which unemployment has its negative effects is important. A deeper understanding of how job loss affects an individual's life, including short- and long-term career outcomes (a topic that has not received much attention), is also needed. Given that research has only just begun to parse to what extent poor well-being during unemployment can be causally attributed to being without work, more work designed to carefully attend to selection issues will also be valuable.

The past decade showed an increase in psychological research focused on the job search and the prediction of reemployment speed and quality. A myriad of variables are associated with reemployment success. We need additional models that depict and examine the relative importance of these variables (as well as interactions among these variables) to reemployment success outcomes. Most of the work examining job search–related predictors of reemployment has focused on sources of job information and job search intensity. More work on other aspects of job search is necessary, including a deeper understanding of what happens day-to-day in the job search process, challenges individuals face as they look for work, and what a high-quality job search looks like. More work investigating individual differences in job search strategies as well as how the job search changes over time as an individual remains unemployed is also important. Finally, a deeper level of precision regarding how social networks help individuals find work and for whom they are the most helpful is needed. For example, we know that individuals who spend more time networking during their unemployment find jobs sooner, but is this true even for individuals with weak networks?

Available research suggests that discrimination of various sorts occurs in the hiring process. Although the research on ethnic/racial discrimination used a variety of methodologies and approaches, the literature examining other types of discrimination has continued to rely heavily on laboratory studies. The protocol of using undergraduates posing as employers evaluating artificial candidates for artificial jobs is especially overused. In order to bolster the strength of conclusions that bias occurs in hiring, triangulation of results using a variety of methods should continue to be a goal in this line of research (Leslie et al. 2008). A far deeper understanding of the extent to which this occurs and which job seeker characteristics are most vulnerable to discrimination is required. Furthermore, it is necessary to identify characteristics of the employers, interviewers, and regions most apt to discriminate against job seekers. The troubling trends in this area suggest employers must continue to use structured interviews as well as interviewer training to avoid potential biases.

Finally, several intervention-focused studies were conducted in the past decade. However, echoing the sentiments of Hammarström & Janlert (2005), additional work focused on niche unemployment problems, such as efforts to reduce discrimination on the part of interviewers, or on helping minority job seekers, would be valuable. Intervention studies should include cost-benefit discussions delineating financial estimates involved with large-scale adoptions of a given program as well as predicted benefits. These studies should include considerations of how to choose individuals who should be included in the intervention. Interventions perfectly suited to all unemployed individuals are difficult to develop. Who benefits most from a given intervention, and how would agencies identify these individuals and get them into such a program?

Recommendations given to job seekers should integrate the rich findings available across studies. For example, recommendations meant to help individuals reduce their anxiety or depressive affect during unemployment might focus too extensively on taking time off or taking breaks. Such advice should be paired with attempts to increase search intensity (at least for individuals who put in only a small amount of search time each week), given that higher search intensity is related to faster reemployment. Recommendations to increase search intensity must likewise be paired with making sure the job seeker is engaging in quality search behaviors (e.g., using a diversity of sources of job information, engaging in a focused rather than a haphazard search). It would be useful, too, for researchers to conduct investigations that will allow more refined and specific practice-based recommendations, such as how many hours of job search per week are optimal for what types of job seekers (rather than simply more is better) and how to avoid common mistakes of job seekers.

In conclusion, it is exciting to see the progress this literature has made in the past 10 years. Yet, it is critical to further advance our understanding of the three key areas (the impact of unemployment, variables associated with faster and better reemployment, and interventions to help individuals find work) that are emphasized in this review.

DISCLOSURE STATEMENT

The author is unaware of any affiliation, funding, or financial holdings that might be perceived as affecting the objectivity of this review.

ACKNOWLEDGMENTS

A special thank you to Yongjun Choi and Tiffany Trzebiatowski for completing the detailed literature search necessary for this project.

LITERATURE CITED

Addison JT, Portugal P. 2002. Job search methods and outcomes. *Oxf. Econ. Pap.* 54:505–33

Ãhs A, Westerling R. 2006. Mortality in relation to employment status during different levels of unemployment. *Scand. J. Public Health* 34:159–67

Andrés AR. 2005. Income inequality, unemployment, and suicide: a panel data analysis of 15 European countries. *Appl. Econ.* 37:439–51

Bandura A. 1986. *Social Foundations of Thought and Action: A Social Cognitive Theory.* Englewood Cliffs, NJ: Prentice Hall

Banerjee A, Bertrand M, Datta S, Mullainathan S. 2009. Labor market discrimination in Delhi: evidence from a field experiment. *J. Compar. Econ.* 37:14–27

Barrick MR, Shaffer JA, DeGrassi SW. 2009. What you see may not be what you get: relationships among self-presentation tactics and ratings of interview and job performance. *J. Appl. Psychol.* 94:1394–411

Belliveau MA. 2005. Blind ambition? The effects of social networks and institutional sex composition on the job search outcomes of elite coeducational and women's college graduates. *Organ. Sci.* 16:134–50

Bertrand M, Mullainathan S. 2004. Are Emily and Greg more employable than Lakisha and Jamal? A field experiment on labor market discrimination. *Am. Econ. Rev.* 94:991–1013

Blakely TA. 2003. Unemployment and suicide. Evidence for a causal association? *J. Epidemiol. Community Health* 57:594–600

Blau G. 1993. Further exploring the relationship between job search and voluntary individual turnover. *Pers. Psychol.* 46:313–30

Blau G. 1994. Testing a two-dimensional measure of job search behavior. *Organ. Behav. Hum. Decis. Process.* 59:288–312

Bockerman P, Ilmakunnas P. 2009. Unemployment and self-assessed health: evidence from panel data. *Health Econ.* 18:161–79

Borland J, Tseng Y-P. 2007. Does a minimum job search requirement reduce time on unemployment payments? Evidence from the jobseeker diary in Australia. *Ind. Labor Relat. Rev.* 60:357–78

Bortnick SM, Ports MH. 1992. Job search methods and results: tracking the unemployed, 1991. *Mon. Labor Rev.* 115:29–35

Brady D. 2010. Out of work, not out of oomph. *Bloomberg Businessweek*, Sep. 13. **http://www.businessweek. com/managing/content/sep2010/ca2010098_547992.htm**

Bright JEH, Hutton S. 2000. The impact of competency statements on resumes for short-listing decisions. *Int. J. Sel. Assess.* 8:41–53

Brown DJ, Cober RT, Kane K, Levy PE, Shalhoop J. 2006. Proactive personality and the successful job search: a field investigation with college graduates. *J. Appl. Psychol.* 91:717–26

Bur. Labor Stat. 2010. *Labor force statistics from the current population survey: household data annual averages—3. Employment status of the civilian noninstitutional population by sex, age, and race.* Washington, DC: Bur. Labor Stat. **http://www.bls.gov/cps/cpsaat5.pdf**

Bur. Labor Stat. 2011. *Regional and state employment and unemployment.* Washington, DC: Bur. Labor Stat. News release, USDL-11–0083, Jan. 25. **http://www.bls.gov/news.release/pdf/laus.pdf**

Caplan RD, Vinokur AD, Price RH. 1997. From job loss to reemployment: field experiments in prevention-focused coping. In *Primary Prevention Works*, ed. GW Albee, T Gullotta, pp. 341–79. Thousand Oaks, CA: Sage

Card D, Chetty R, Weber A. 2007. The spike at benefit exhaustion: leaving the unemployment system or starting a new job? *Am. Econ. Rev.* 97:113–18

Carver CS. 2006. Approach, avoidance, and the self-regulation of affect and action. *Motiv. Emot.* 30:105–10

Catalano R. 1991. The health effects of economic insecurity. *Am. J. Public Health* 81:1148–52

Challenger, Gray, & Christmas Inc. 2009. *Job fairs, newspaper help wanted ads rank as least effective.* **http://www.itworld.com/career/74764/job-fairs-newspaper-help-wanted-ads-rank-least-effective**

Chen VC, Chou J, Lai T, Lee CT. 2010. Suicide and unemployment rate in Taiwan, a population-based study, 1978–2006. *Soc. Psychiatr. Psychiatry Epidemiol.* 45:447–52

Cheung CK, Gui Y. 2006. Job referral in China: the advantages of strong ties. *Hum. Relat.* 59:847–72

Chung A. 2009. Gender difference in suicide, household production and unemployment. *Appl. Econ.* 41:2495–504

Classen TJ, Dunn RA. 2011. The effect of job loss and unemployment duration on suicide risk in the United States: a new look using mass-layoffs and unemployment insurance claims. *Health Econ.* In press

Cohen J. 1992. A power primer. *Psychol. Bull.* 112:155–59

Correll SJ, Benard S, Paik I. 2007. Getting a job: Is there a motherhood penalty? *Am. J. Sociol.* 112:1297–338

Cote S, Saks AM, Zikic J. 2006. Trait affect and job search outcomes. *J. Vocat. Behav.* 68:233–52

Creed PA, Bartrum D. 2006. Explanations for deteriorating wellbeing in unemployed people: specific unemployment theories and beyond. In *Unemployment and Health International and Interdisciplinary Perspectives*, ed. T Kieselbach, AH Winefield, C Boyd, S Anderson, pp. 1–20. Bowen Hills, Australia: Australian Acad.

Creed PA, Bloxsome TD, Johnston K. 2001. Self-esteem and self-efficacy outcomes for unemployed individuals attending occupational skills training programs. *Community Work Fam.* 4:285–303

Creed PA, King V, Hood M, McKenzie R. 2009. Goal orientation, self-regulation strategies, and job-seeking intensity in unemployed adults. *J. Appl. Psychol.* 94:806–13

Crossley CD, Highhouse S. 2005. Relation of job search and choice process with subsequent satisfaction. *J. Econ. Psychol.* 26:255–68

Crossley CD, Stanton JM. 2005. Negative affect and job search: further examination of the reverse causation hypothesis. *J. Vocat. Behav.* 66:549–60

Cunningham J, Macan T. 2007. Effects of applicant pregnancy on hiring decisions and interview ratings. *Sex Roles* 57:497–508

Daniels SE, Gobeli CL, Findley AJ. 2000. Reemployment programs for dislocated timber workers: lessons from Oregon. *Soc. Nat. Resour.* 13:135–50

DeFrank RS, Ivancevich JM. 1986. Job loss: an individual level review and model. *J. Vocat. Behav.* 28:1–20

Derous E, Nguyen H, Ryan AM. 2009. Hiring discrimination against Arab minorities: interactions between prejudice and job characteristics. *Hum. Perform.* 22:297–320

Dooley D, Fielding J, Levi L. 1996. Health and unemployment. *Annu. Rev. Public Health* 17:449–65

Drydakis N, Vlassis M. 2010. Ethnic discrimination in the Greek labor market: occupational access, insurance coverage and wage offers. *Manch. Sch.* 78:201–18

Eisenberg P, Lazarsfeld PF. 1938. The psychological effects of unemployment. *Psychol. Bull.* 35:358–90

Falba T, Teng HM, Sindelar JL, Gallo WT. 2005. The effect of involuntary job loss on smoking intensity and relapse. *Addiction* 100:1330–39

Fitzenberger B, Speckesser S. 2007. Employment effects of the provision of specific professional skills and techniques in Germany. *Empir. Econ.* 32:529–73

Fountain C. 2005. Finding a job in the internet age. *Soc. Forces* 83:1235–62

Franzen A, Hangartner D. 2006. Social networks and labor market outcomes: the non-monetary benefits of social capital. *Eur. Sociol. Rev.* 22:353–68

Fryer D, Payne R. 1986. Being unemployed: a review of the literature on the psychological experience of unemployment. In *International Review of Industrial and Organizational Psychology*, vol. 1, ed. CL Cooper, IT Robertson, pp. 235–78. Chichester, UK: Wiley

Fugate M, Kinicki AJ, Ashforth BE. 2004. Employability: a psycho-social construct, its dimensions, and applications. *J. Vocat. Behav.* 65:14–38

Gerdtham UG, Ruhm CJ. 2006. Deaths rise in good economic times: evidence from the OECD. *Econ. Hum. Biol.* 4:298–316

Ginexi EM, Howe GW, Caplan RD. 2000. Depression and control beliefs in relation to reemployment: What are the directions of the effect? *J. Occup. Health Psychol.* 5:323–36

Granovetter M. 1995. *Getting a Job: A Study of Contacts and Careers.* Chicago, IL: Univ. Chicago Press. 2nd ed.

Graversen BK, van Ours JC. 2008. How to help unemployed find jobs quickly: experimental evidence from a mandatory activation program. *J. Public Econ.* 92:2020–35

Hammarström A, Janlert U. 2005. An agenda for unemployment research: a challenge for public health. *Int. J. Health Serv.* 35:765–77

Hanisch KA. 1999. Job loss and unemployment research from 1994 to 1998: a review and recommendations for research and intervention. *J. Vocat. Behav.* 55:188–220

Harris E, Lum J, Rose V, Morrow M, Comino E, Harris M. 2002. Are CBT interventions effective with disadvantaged job-seekers who are long-term unemployed? *Psychol. Health Med.* 7:401–10

Hebl MR, King EB, Glick P, Singletary SL, Kazama S. 2007. Hostile and benevolent reactions toward pregnant women: complementary interpersonal punishments and rewards that maintain traditional roles. *J. Appl. Psychol.* 92:1499–511

Horvath M, Ryan AM. 2003. Antecedents and potential moderators of the relationship between attitudes and hiring discrimination on the basis of sexual orientation. *Sex Roles* 48:115–30

Huffman ML, Torres L. 2001. Job search methods: consequences for gender-based earnings inequality. *J. Vocat. Behav.* 58:127–41

Huffman ML, Torres L. 2002. It's not only "who you know" that matters: gender, personal contacts, and job lead quality. *Gend. Soc.* 16:793–813

Hussmanns R. 2007. Measurement of employment, unemployment and underemployment—current international standards and issues in their application. *Bull. Labor Stat.* 1:1–23

Int. Labor Organ. 2010. *IMF and ILO launch background paper on the "Challenges of growth, employment and social cohesion" for high-level conference on September 13 in Oslo.* Genève, Switzerland: Int. Labor Organ. Press release, Sep. 2. **http://www.ilo.org/global/about-the-ilo/press-and-media-centre/press-releases/WCMS_144399/lang–en/index.htm**

Int. Monetary Fund, Int. Labor Organ. 2010. The challenges of growth, employment and social cohesion. *Proc. Jt. Int. Labor Organ. Int. Monetary Fund Conf.*, Oslo, Norway, Sep. 13, Discussion document. **http://www.osloconference2010.org/discussionpaper.pdf**

Iyengar SS, Wells RE, Schwartz B. 2006. Doing better but feeling worse: Looking for the "best" job undermines satisfaction. *Psychol. Sci.* 17:143–50

Jackson SE, Hall NC, Rowe PM, Daniels LM. 2009. Getting the job: attributional retraining and the employment interview. *J. Appl. Soc. Psychol.* 39:973–98

Jahoda M. 1987. Unemployed men at work. In *Unemployed People: Social and Psychological Perspectives*, ed. D Fryer, P Ullah, pp. 1–73. Milton Keynes, UK: Open Univ. Press

Jahoda M. 1982. *Employment and Unemployment: A Social-Psychological Analysis.* London: Cambridge Univ. Press

Janicki-Deverts D, Cohen S, Matthews KA, Cullen MR. 2008. History of unemployment predicts future elevations in C-reactive protein among male participants in the coronary artery risk development in young adults (CARDIA) study. *Ann. Behav. Med.* 36:176–85

Jensen L, Slack T. 2003. Underemployment in America: measurement and evidence. *Am. J. Community Psychol.* 32:21–31

Joseph LM, Greenberg MA. 2001. The effects of a career transition program on reemployment success in laid-off professionals. *Consult. Psychol. J.* 53:169–81

Kalil A. 2009. Joblessness, family relations and children's development. *Fam. Matters* 83:15–22

Kanfer R, Wanberg CR, Kantrowitz TM. 2001. Job search and employment: a personality-motivational analysis and meta-analytic review. *J. Appl. Psychol.* 86:837–55

Kasl SV, Rodriguez E, Lasch KE. 1998. The impact of unemployment on health and well-being. In *Adversity, Stress, and Psychopathology*, ed. BP Dohrenwend, pp. 111–31. New York: Oxford Univ. Press

Koen J, Klehe UC, Van Vianen AEM, Zikic J, Nauta A. 2010. Job-search strategies and reemployment quality—the impact of career adaptability. *J. Vocat. Behav.* 77:126–39

Koo J, Cox WM. 2008. An economic interpretation of suicide cycles in Japan. *Contemp. Econ. Policy* 26:162–74

Korpi T. 2001. Accumulating disadvantage: longitudinal analyses of unemployment and physical health in representative samples of the Swedish population. *Eur. Sociol. Rev.* 17:255–73

Kposowa AJ. 2001. Unemployment and suicide: a cohort analysis of social factors predicting suicide in the US National Longitudinal Mortality Study. *Psychol. Med.* 31:127–38

Krueger A, Meyer BD. 2002. Labor supply effects of social insurance. In *Handbook of Public Economics*, vol. 4, ed. AJ Auerbach, M Feldstein, pp. 2327–92. Amsterdam: North Holland

Krueger AB, Mueller A. 2010. Job search and unemployment insurance: new evidence from time use data. *J. Public Econ.* 94:298–307

Kuhl J. 1985. Volitional mediators of cognitive-behavioral consistency: self-regulatory processes and action versus state orientation. In *Action Control: From Cognition to Behavior*, ed. J Kuhl, J Beckmann, pp. 101–28. New York: Springer-Verlag

Kuhn P, Skuterud M. 2004. Internet job search and unemployment durations. *Am. Econ. Rev.* 94:218–32

Lalive R, van Ours JC, Zweimüller J. 2008. The impact of active labor market programmes on the duration of unemployment in Switzerland. *Econ. J.* 118:235–57

Lambert TA, Eby LT, Reeves MP. 2006. Predictors of networking intensity and network quality among white-collar job seekers. *J. Career Dev.* 32:351–65

Latham GP, Budworth M. 2006. The effect of training in verbal self-guidance on the self-efficacy and performance of Native North Americans in the selection interview. *J. Vocat. Behav.* 68:516–23

Leana CR, Feldman DC. 1988. Individual responses to job loss: perceptions, reactions, and coping behaviors. *J. Manag.* 14:375–89

Lechner M, Miquel R, Wunsch C. 2007. The curse and blessing of training the unemployed in a changing economy: the case of East Germany after unification. *Ger. Econ. Rev.* 8:468–509

Leslie LM, King EB, Bradley JC, Hebl MR. 2008. Triangulation across methodologies: all signs point to persistent stereotyping and discrimination in organizations. *J. Ind. Organ. Psychol.* 1:399–404

Lin N. 2001. Building a network theory of social capital. In *Social Capital: Theory and Research*, ed. N Lin, K Cook, RS Burt, pp. 3–29. Hawthorne, NY: Aldine de Gruyter

Lin S. 2006. Unemployment and suicide: panel data analyses. *Soc. Sci. J.* 43:727–32

Lindsay C, Greig M, McQuaid RW. 2005. Alternative job search strategies in remote rural and peri-urban labor markets: the role of social networks. *Sociol. Ruralis* 45:53–70

Loury LD. 2006. Some contacts are more equal than others: informal networks, job tenure, and wages. *J. Labor Econ.* 24:299–318

Maier R, Egger A, Barth A, Winker R, Osterode W, et al. 2006. Effects of short- and long-term unemployment on physical work capacity and on serum cortisol. *Int. Arch. Occup. Environ. Health* 79:193–98

Matthews R, Pendakur R, Young N. 2009. Social capital, labor markets, and job-finding in urban and rural regions: comparing paths to employment in prosperous cities and stressed rural communities in Canada. *Sociol. Rev.* 57:306–30

Mau WC, Kopischke A. 2001. Job search methods, job search outcomes, and job satisfaction of college graduates: a comparison of race and sex. *J. Employ. Couns.* 38:141–49

McCarthy J, Goffin R. 2004. Measuring job interview anxiety: beyond weak knees and sweaty palms. *Pers. Psychol.* 57:607–37

McDonald S. 2010. Right place, right time: serendipity and informal job matching. *Socio-Econ. Rev.* 8:307–31

McKee-Ryan F, Song Z, Wanberg CR, Kinicki AJ. 2005. Psychological and physical well-being during unemployment: a meta-analytic study. *J. Appl. Psychol.* 90:53–76

Mencken FC, Winfield I. 2000. Job search and sex segregation: does sex of social contact matter? *Sex Roles* 42:847–64

Morgeson F, Reider M, Campion M, Bull R. 2008. Review of research on age discrimination in the employment interview. *J. Bus. Psychol.* 22:223–32

Mouw T. 2002. Racial differences in the effects of job contacts: conflicting evidence from cross-sectional and longitudinal data. *Soc. Sci. Res.* 31:511–38

Mouw T. 2003. Social capital and finding a job: Do contacts matter? *Am. Sociol. Rev.* 68:868–98

Moynihan LM, Roehling MV, LePine MA, Boswell WR. 2003. A longitudinal study of the relationships among job search self-efficacy, job interviews, and employment outcomes. *J. Bus. Psychol.* 18:207–33

Newsweek. 2011. What recovery? *Newsweek*, Jan. 25, p. 8

Noh Y. 2009. Does unemployment increase suicide rates? The OECD panel evidence. *J. Econ. Psychol.* 30:575–82

Pager D, Bonikowski B, Western B. 2009. Discrimination in a low-wage labor market: a field experiment. *Am. Sociol. Rev.* 74:777–99

Paul KI, Moser K. 2009. Unemployment impairs mental health: meta-analyses. *J. Vocat. Behav.* 74:264–82

Platt S, Hawton K. 2000. Suicidal behaviour and the labor market. In *The International Handbook of Suicide and Attempted Suicide*, ed. K Hawton, K van Heeringen, pp. 309–84. West Sussex, UK: Wiley

Polinko NK, Popovich PM. 2001. Evil thoughts but angelic actions: responses to overweight job applicants. *J. Appl. Soc. Psychol.* 31:905–24

Price RH, Choi JN, Vinokur AD. 2002a. Links in the chain of adversity following job loss: how financial strain and loss of personal control lead to depression, impaired functioning, and poor health. *J. Occup. Health Psychol.* 7:302–12

Price RH, Vinokur AD, Friedland DS. 2002b. The job seeker role as resource: achieving reemployment and enhancing mental health. In *Socioeconomic Conditions, Stress and Mental Health Disorders: Toward a New Synthesis of Research and Public Policy*, ed. A Maney, J Ramos. Washington, DC: NIMH. **http://www.mhsip.org/nimhdoc/socioeconmh_home.htm**

Prussia GE, Fugate M, Kinicki AJ. 2001. Explication of the coping goal construct: implications for coping and reemployment. *J. Appl. Psychol.* 86:1179–90

Rancans E, Salander Renberg E, Jacobsson L. 2001. Major demographic, social and economic factors associated to suicide rates in Latvia 1980–98. *Acta Psychiatr. Scand.* 103:275–81

Rehkopf DH, Buka SL. 2006. The association between suicide and the socio-economic characteristics of geographical areas: a systematic review. *Psychol. Med.* 36:145–57

Riach PA, Rich J. 2006. An experimental investigation of sexual discrimination in hiring in the English labor market. *B. E. J. Econ. Anal. Policy* 6(2):Article 1

Roehling MV, Roehling PV, Pichler S. 2007. The relationship between body weight and perceived weight-related employment discrimination: the role of sex and race. *J. Vocat. Behav.* 71:300–18

Rubin BM. 2011. Looks are the latest wrinkle for aging unemployed: Seeking to stay competitive, older workers are turning to cosmetic enhancements. *Star Tribune*, Jan. 9. **http://www.startribune.com/lifestyle/health/113105179.html?elr=KArksLckD8EQDUoaEyqyP4O:DW3ckUiD3aPc:_Yyc:aUvDEhiaE3miUsZ**

Rudolph CW, Wells CL, Weller MD, Baltes BB. 2009. A meta-analysis of empirical studies of weight-based bias in the workplace. *J. Vocat. Behav.* 74:1–10

Saks AM. 2006. Multiple predictors and criteria of job search success. *J. Vocat. Behav.* 68:400–15

Saks AM, Ashforth BE. 2002. Is job search related to employment quality? It all depends on the fit. *J. Appl. Psychol.* 87:646–54

Saks AM, Ashforth BE. 2000. Change in job search behaviors and employment outcomes. *J. Vocat. Behav.* 56:277–87

Senecal C, Guay F. 2000. Procrastination in job-seeking: an analysis of motivational processes and feelings of hopelessness. *J. Sociol. Behav. Personal.* 15:267–82

Shah A. 2008. Possible relationship of elderly suicide rates with unemployment in society: a cross-national study. *Psychol. Rep.* 102:398–400

Smith FI, Tabak F, Showail S, Parks JM, Kleist JS. 2005. The name game: employability evaluations of prototypical applicants with stereotypical feminine and masculine first names. *Sex Roles* 52:63–82

Smith SS. 2000. Mobilizing social resources: race, ethnic, and gender differences in social capital and persisting wage inequalities. *Sociol. Q.* 41:509–37

Song ZL, Uy MA, Zhang SH, Shi K. 2009. Daily job search and psychological distress: evidence from China. *Hum. Relat.* 62:1171–97

Song ZL, Wanberg CR, Niu XY, Xie YZ. 2006. Action-state orientation and the theory of planned behavior: a study of job search in China. *J. Vocat. Behav.* 68:490–503

Stack S, Wasserman I. 2007. Economic strain and suicide risk: a qualitative analysis. *Suicide Life Threat. Behav.* 37:103–12

Strully KW. 2009. Job loss and health in the U.S. labor market. *Demography* 46:221–46

Sullivan D, von Wachter T. 2009. Job displacement and mortality: an analysis using administrative data. *Q. J. Econ.* 124:1265–306

Sverko B, Galic Z, Sersic DM, Galesic M. 2008. Unemployed people in search of a job: reconsidering the role of search behavior. *J. Vocat. Behav.* 72:415–28

Swami V, Chan F, Wong V, Furnham A, Tovée MJ. 2008. Weight-based discrimination in occupational hiring and helping behavior. *J. Appl. Soc. Psychol.* 38:968–81

Tay C, Ang S, Van Dyne L. 2006. Personality, biographical characteristics, and job interview success: a longitudinal study of the mediating effects of interviewing self-efficacy and the moderating effects of internal locus of causality. *J. Appl. Psychol.* 91:446–54

Taylor P. 2003. Age, labor market conditions and male suicide rates in selected countries. *Ageing Soc.* 23:25–40

Try S. 2005. The use of job search strategies among university graduates. *J. Socio-Econ.* 34:223–43

Turban DB, Stevens CK, Lee FK. 2009. Effects of conscientiousness and extraversion on new labor market entrants' job search: the mediating role of metacognitive activities and positive emotions. *Pers. Psychol.* 62:553–73

Tziner A, Vered E, Ophir L. 2004. Predictors of job search intensity among college graduates. *J. Career Assess.* 12:332–44

van Hooft EAJ, Born MP, Taris TW, Van Der Flier H. 2006a. The cross-cultural generalizability of the theory of planned behavior—a study on job seeking in the Netherlands. *J. Cross-Cult. Psychol.* 37:127–35

van Hooft EAJ, Born MP, Taris TW, Van Der Flier H. 2006b. Ethnic and gender differences in applicants' decision-making processes: an application of the theory of reasoned action. *Int. J. Select. Assess.* 14:156–66

van Hooft EAJ, Born MP, Taris TW, Van Der Flier H, Blonk RWB. 2005. Bridging the gap between intentions and behavior: implementation intentions, action control, and procrastination. *J. Vocat. Behav.* 66:238–56

van Hooft EAJ, Noordzij G. 2009. The effects of goal orientation on job search and reemployment: a field experiment among unemployed job seekers. *J. Appl. Psychol.* 94:1581–90

Van Hoye G, Lievens F. 2003. The effects of sexual orientation on hirability ratings: an experimental study. *J. Bus. Psychol.* 18:15–30

Van Hoye G, van Hooft EAJ, Lievens F. 2009. Networking as a job search behaviour: a social network perspective. *J. Occup. Organ. Psychol.* 82:661–82

Van Rooy DL, Alonso A, Fairchild Z. 2003. In with the new, out with the old: Has the technological revolution eliminated the traditional job search process? *Int. J. Select. Assess.* 11:170–74

Vansteenkiste M, Lens W, De Witte S, De Witte H, Deci EL. 2004. The "why" and "why not" of job search behaviour: their relation to searching, unemployment experience, and well-being. *Eur. J. Soc. Psychol.* 34:345–63

Vinokur AD, Schul Y. 2002. The web of coping resources and pathways to reemployment following a job loss. *J. Occup. Health Psychol.* 7:68–83

Vinokur AD, Schul Y, Vuori J, Price RH. 2000. Two years after a job loss: long-term impact of the JOBS program on reemployment and mental health. *J. Occup. Health Psychol.* 5:32–47

Voss M, Nylen L, Floderus B, Diderichsen F, Terry PD. 2004. Unemployment and early cause-specific mortality: a study based on the Swedish twin registry. *Am. J. Public Health* 94:2155–61

Vuori J, Silvonen J. 2005. The benefits of a preventive job search program on re-employment and mental health at 2-year follow-up. *J. Occup. Organ. Psychol.* 78:43–52

Vuori J, Silvonen J, Vinokur AD, Price RH. 2002. The Työhön job search program in Finland: benefits for the unemployed with risk of depression or discouragement. *J. Occup. Health Psychol.* 7:5–19

Wanberg CR, Glomb TM, Song ZL, Sorenson S. 2005. Job-search persistence during unemployment: a 10-wave longitudinal study. *J. Appl. Psychol.* 90:411–30

Wanberg CR, Hough LM, Song Z. 2002. Predictive validity of a multidisciplinary model of reemployment success. *J. Appl. Psychol.* 87:1100–20

Wanberg CR, Kanfer R, Banas JT. 2000. Predictors and outcomes of networking intensity among unemployed job seekers. *J. Appl. Psychol.* 85:491–503

Wanberg CR, Zhang Z, Diehn EW. 2010a. Development of the "getting ready for your next job" inventory for unemployed individuals. *Pers. Psychol.* 63:439–78

Wanberg CR, Zhu J, Kanfer R, Zhang Z. 2011. After the pink slip: applying dynamic motivation frameworks to the job search experience. *Acad. Manag. J.* In press

Wanberg CR, Zhu J, Van Hooft EAJ. 2010b. The job search grind: perceived progress, self-reactions, and self-regulation of search effort. *Acad. Manag. J.* 53:788–807

Wang C, Lo YY, Xu YY, Wang Y, Porfeli E. 2007. Constructing the search for a job in academia from the perspectives of self-regulated learning strategies and social cognitive career theory. *J. Vocat. Behav.* 70:574–89

Waters LE. 2000. Coping with unemployment: a literature review and presentation of a new model. *Int. J. Manag. Rev.* 2:169–82

Weber A, Mahringer H. 2008. Choice and success of job search methods. *Empir. Econ.* 35:153–78

Winefield AH. 1995. Unemployment: its psychological costs. In *International Review of Industrial and Organizational Psychology*, vol. 10, ed. CL Cooper, IT Robertson, pp. 169–212. Chichester, UK: Wiley

Wu W, Cheng H. 2010. Symmetric mortality and asymmetric suicide cycles. *Soc. Sci. Med.* 70:1974–81

Yamasaki A, Sakai R, Shirakawa T. 2005. Low income, unemployment, and suicide mortality rates for middle-age persons in Japan. *Psychol. Rep.* 96:337–48

Yanar B, Budworth MH, Latham GP. 2009. The effect of verbal self-guidance training for overcoming employment barriers: a study of Turkish women. *Appl. Psychol. Int. Rev.* 58:586–601

Zang XW. 2003. Network resources and job search in urban China. *J. Sociol.* 39:115–29

Zikic J, Klehe U. 2006. Job loss as a blessing in disguise: the role of career exploration and career planning in predicting reemployment quality. *J. Vocat. Behav.* 69:391–409

The Rise and Fall of Job Analysis and the Future of Work Analysis

Juan I. Sanchez[1] and Edward L. Levine[2]

[1]Department of Management and International Business, Florida International University, Miami, Florida 33199; email: sanchezj@fiu.edu

[2]Psychology Department, University of South Florida, Tampa, Florida 33620; email: elevine@mail.usf.edu

Annu. Rev. Psychol. 2012. 63:397–425

First published online as a Review in Advance on September 28, 2011

The *Annual Review of Psychology* is online at psych.annualreviews.org

This article's doi: 10.1146/annurev-psych-120710-100401

Keywords

occupations, job profile, selection, validity, KSAO, competencies

Abstract

This review begins by contrasting the importance ascribed to the study of occupational requirements observed in the early twentieth-century beginnings of industrial-organizational psychology with the diminishing numbers of job analysis articles appearing in top journals in recent times. To highlight the many pending questions associated with the job-analytic needs of today's organizations that demand further inquiry, research on the three primary types of job analysis data, namely work activities, worker attributes, and work context, is reviewed. Research on competencies is also reviewed along with the goals of a potential research agenda for the emerging trend of competency modeling. The cross-fertilization of job analysis research with research from other domains such as the meaning of work, job design, job crafting, strategic change, and interactional psychology is proposed as a means of responding to the demands of today's organizations through new forms of work analysis.

Contents

INTRODUCTION

Job analysis constitutes the preceding step of every application of psychology to human resources (HR) management including, but not limited to, the development of selection, training, performance evaluation, job design, deployment, and compensation systems (Brannick et al. 2007, Gael et al. 1988, Harvey 1991, Levine 1983). Because it serves as a foundation of so many applications, one would assume that job analysis research, much like research on other areas of applied psychology such as selection that has had a long history of coverage in the *Annual Reviews* (e.g., from Taylor & Naviz 1961 to Sackett & Lievens 2008), would have been the object of periodic *Annual Review of Psychology* articles. Ours is, however, the very first *Annual Reviews* chapter ever dedicated to job-analytic research, notwithstanding the brief coverage of selected developments in job-analytic research included in prior syntheses of the selection literature (e.g., Borman et al. 1997, p. 301; Hough &

Oswald 2000, p. 632; Landy et al. 1994, p. 266; Sackett & Lievens 2008, p. 429).

This relatively sparse coverage of job analysis research is startling in light of the principle of person-environment fit (P-E fit), which underlies most HR management applications of psychology since early pioneers began to wonder how to best fit individuals to occupations and vice versa (Münsterberg 1913, Parsons 1909). One would argue that a successful P-E match depends on the quality of the study of both sides of this equation, the E side and the interaction between P and E being core elements in job analysis. However, the purpose of our review is not to fill this void by providing an exhaustive account of job analysis research to date, because such monographs are already available elsewhere (Brannick et al. 2007; Harvey 1991; Morgeson & Dierdorff 2011; Pearlman & Sanchez 2010; Sanchez & Levine 1999, 2001), as well as accounts of the history of job analysis (Mitchell & Driskill 1996, Primoff & Fine 1988, Wilson 2007). Instead, we were inspired by calls to adapt job analysis practice and research to the changing nature of work (Sanchez 1994, 2000; Sanchez & Levine 1999; Schneider & Konz 1989; Siddique 2004; Singh 2008), as well as by recent observations that job analysis research is not keeping up with the staffing practices demanded by today's dynamic and diverse workplaces (Morgeson & Dierdorff 2011, Sackett & Laczo 2003). The inability of traditional job analysis to answer the demands of today's organizations is illustrated by the warm reception of the proposal to rename the field "work analysis" (Sanchez 1994; Sanchez & Levine 1999, 2001), a label that best reflects the boundaryless nature of the evolving roles that individuals play within organizations (Ilgen & Hollenbeck 1991, Morgeson & Dierdorff 2011). As a result, we aim to identify not only the trends in the evolution of job analysis research that account for current thinking in the domain, but also those that represent promising avenues by which the job analysis domain may catch up with the needs of today's organizations. With this purpose in mind, we not only culled

Job analysis: the process through which one gains an understanding of the activities, goals, and requirements demanded by a work assignment

HR: human resources

P-E fit: person-environment fit

the job analysis literature, but also borrowed insights from research in a number of related domains (e.g., the experience of work, work stress) that, through cross-fertilization, may stimulate the kind of innovative job analysis research demanded by today's world of work. In fact, an overarching conclusion of our review is that we must thoroughly revise the core assumptions that have dominated the job analysis domain in the face of the magnitude of the transformations that have taken place in the world of work over recent decades.

The review is organized as follows. First, we contrast our view that job analysis research has lost ground in recent times with the central role that job analysis was accorded in the beginnings of the field of industrial and organizational psychology. Next, we review the debate concerning what the appropriate object of study should be in job analysis in the context of the various types of job-analytic data, namely work activities, worker attributes, and work context. We then proceed to review research concerning these major types of data, emphasizing the latest research trends such as research on competencies. Because job-analytic research has largely focused on the quality of job-analytic data, we also group research around the primary criteria by which data have been evaluated. Specifically, we distinguish among evaluations that have focused on the reliability, the validity, and the consequences (i.e., the inferences drawn from job-analytic data and the rules employed to draw them). Finally, we offer a set of conclusions and suggestions regarding the repositioning of job analysis research.

An important caveat about the scope of our literature review is in order. The wide variety of job analysis applications has led to clearly separated streams of literature such as research on human factors and engineering psychology (e.g., cognitive task analysis; Schraagen et al. 2000). This line of research has been covered in prior *Annual Reviews* articles (e.g., Carroll 1997, Proctor & Vu 2010). Related applications of job analysis in the study of training needs analysis and in the determination of job worth have also been covered in former *Annual Reviews*

articles (e.g., Aguinis & Kraiger 2009 and England & Dunn 1988, respectively). Thus, our review does not delve into these domain-specific applications, even though the research reviewed here has obvious implications for them.

Moreover, instead of dedicating a separate section to the Occupational Information Network (O*NET), which was developed by the U.S. Department of Labor (Peterson et al. 1999), we interspersed O*NET-related research within those sections where we felt it fit best throughout our review.

THE RISE AND FALL OF JOB ANALYSIS

The reduced space dedicated to job analysis in recent reviews of the selection literature mentioned earlier is justifiable in light of Morgeson & Dierdorff's (2011) compilation of job analysis journal articles published since 1960. They found that, even though the volume of job-analytic research has not decreased in the past two decades, the proportion of job analysis articles published in the top journals in industrial and organizational psychology and HR management has decreased considerably from an all-time high in the 1960–1979 period, when approximately 77% of the total of job analysis articles published appeared in a list of seven top outlets, to just 27% of the total of job analysis articles published since 2000. This decline is dramatically illustrated by the counts of articles published in the *Journal of Applied Psychology* (*JAP*) and in *Personnel Psychology* (*PP*) provided by Cascio & Aguinis (2008), from an all-time peak of 22 articles dedicated to job analysis in the 1978–1982 period to just four in the 2003–2007 period. The declining rate of job analysis publications contrasts sharply with the steady flow of articles concerned with predictors of performance published in *JAP* and *PP* (Cascio & Aguinis 2008).

Accounts of early research in personnel selection in the first part of the twentieth century, however, suggest a better balance between the spread of relative interest in the two sides of the P-E equation than that observed in recent times

O*NET:
Occupational Information Network

(Salgado et al. 2010). For instance, the German psychologist Stern (1911) developed "psychography" to compare an individual profile to the profile of the attributes presumably demanded by an occupation (Lamiell 2000, Stern 1934). A partial English translation of the very first structured job analysis questionnaire created by his German colleague Otto Lipmann was published in the *Monthly Review* of the U.S. Bureau of Census Statistics (1918, pp. 131–133). A similarly balanced P-E emphasis seemed to have dominated pre-WWII occupational research in the United States, where Viteles (1923) was an early adopter of Stern's psychographic methods. Even the U.S. Department of Labor's Division of Standards and Research was organized in two sections dedicated to worker and job analysis, respectively (Otis 2009, Primoff & Fine 1988, Shartle 1959).

The reduced status of job analysis research in recent times, however, is not due to a lack of important, pending research developments that respond to the emerging HR trends (e.g., personality-oriented work analysis, team and cognitive task analysis, and strategic competency modeling), which have been advocated elsewhere (Morgeson & Dierdorff 2011; Sackett & Laczo 2003; Sanchez 1994; Sanchez & Levine 1999, 2009; Schneider & Konz 1989; Siddique 2004; Singh 2008). In sections to follow, we not only identify gaps but also uncover insights from related domains to stimulate research of the high caliber sought by top outlets, hopefully taking a step toward remediating the absence of job-analytic research that answers the most pressing HR management questions while advancing scientific knowledge across domains in which job analysis plays a role.

THE OBJECT OF STUDY IN JOB ANALYSIS

Harvey (1991, p. 73) and Harvey & Wilson (2000) took the stance that job analysis should be concerned solely with "objective" or "verifiable" aspects of jobs, such as job behaviors and working conditions, and should exclude inferences concerning job specifications or human attributes required for performance. By contrast, Sanchez & Levine (2001) argued that deriving the worker characteristics required for job performance is an intrinsic component of job analysis (e.g., Primoff 1975), opining that the formulation of worker attributes is what makes job analysis a truly psychological endeavor. An examination of selection texts suggests that the derivation of worker attributes or job specifications tends to be included under the rubric of job analysis (Gatewood et al. 2008, Guion & Highhouse 2006, Heneman & Judge 2009, Ployhart et al. 2006). Therefore, we review research on not only observables such as work behavior, but also construals such as human attributes thought to be required for successful performance.

The distinction between two broadly defined kinds of job-analytic data, namely tasks and the characteristics or attributes of people performing such tasks, is widely accepted (Sackett & Laczo 2003; Sanchez & Levine 1999, p. 56). We also review a third but equally important type of job analysis data concerning the environment or context in which work activities are performed, including the situational opportunities and constraints that influence behavior (Meyer et al. 2010). These three major objects of job-analytic study (i.e., work behavior, worker attributes, and context) resemble the building blocks of successful job analysis proposed by Fine & Cronshaw (1999, p. 21). In the next three sections, research on each one of these building blocks is grouped according to the criteria along which the job-analytic data were evaluated, beginning with reliability and validity. These psychometric properties are important because they influence the inferences that such data are meant to inform (Dierdorff & Wilson 2003, McCormick 1976, Morgeson & Campion 1997). However, we also include a third class of studies concerned with the type of consequence-oriented criteria, such as the inferences derived from job-analytic data and the rules governing the making of such inferences, that Sanchez & Levine (2000) advocated for the evaluation of job analysis.

We believe that the focus on inferences and on the rules by which they are made is critical to propel job analysis research beyond its current stalemate. Partly, this stalemate might have been fueled by the support obtained for the validity of general mental ability (GMA) tests for most jobs in most settings (see Le et al. 2007 for a summary of these findings), which has fed the conclusion that a detailed job analysis may constitute an unnecessary expense when the purpose is to ascertain the generalizability of GMA tests (Pearlman et al. 1980, p. 376; Schmidt et al. 1981). An unwarranted generalization drawn from this stream of research is that there is not much return on investment in a detailed job analysis because job-analytic information is not helpful to identify the conditions under which a test may or may not work. This conclusion is predicated on the false premises that (*a*) validity generalization findings regarding GMA tests can be extended to other predictors such as personality and psychomotor tests and employment interviews and, perhaps most importantly, (*b*) current job-analytic practices already provide the best information the field has to offer in regard to potential occupational moderators of validity. The evidence to be reviewed here suggests otherwise. For instance, O*NET-based determinations of specific ability requirements rely on single-item scales of limited discriminant validity (Harvey & Wilson 2010, Sanchez & Autor 2010). Similarly, inasmuch as meta-analyses suggest that personality measures can predict job performance (e.g., Barrick & Mount 1991, Hough 1992, Salgado 1997, Tett et al. 1991), evidence concerning the specific occupational conditions under which such tests work best is only beginning to emerge (Meyer et al. 2010, Raymark et al. 1997, Tett & Burnett 2003).

We purposefully avoided using the term "descriptor" when referring to any kind of job-analytic information because we disagree with the implicit assumption that the primary purpose of job analysis is to describe jobs. Instead, job analysis should aim to understand the successful experience of work, and therefore many of the pieces of data produced in job analysis research are unobservable construals meant to explain rather than describe the worker's behavior.

RESEARCH ON WORK ACTIVITY INFORMATION

Although terms such as job, duty, function, responsibility, and task are often employed to refer to work activities, most researchers agree that these terms reflect work activities ranging from the very specific or molecular level (i.e., task), to a medium level (i.e., functions, duties, or responsibilities), to the general or molar level (i.e., groupings of activities that comprise a job) (Gael 1983, p. 7). A majority of research has been conducted using task inventories prepared in the tradition of Allen's (1919) "trade analysis." These inventories depict long lists of prestandardized tasks, which are rated on scales such as frequency, time spent, and difficulty (Christal & Weissmuller 1988). Research has also emerged on the 42 generalized work activities (GWAs) included in O*NET, which were derived through a literature review of various taxonomies of work activity data (Cunningham & Ballentine 1982, McCormick et al. 1972) to form a common metric for all occupations (Cunningham 1996).

Reliability Studies

Studies of the reliability of work activity inventories have employed two basic approaches: intrarater (i.e., test-retest or repeated items within the same administration) and interrater reliability (Gael 1983, p. 23). However, disagreement among incumbents of the same job title may reflect legitimate variation, such as differences in positions classified under the same job title (Harvey 1991, Lindell et al. 1998, Sanchez et al. 1998, Stutzman 1983, Wilson 1997). Sanchez & Levine (2000) warned that interrater disagreement may also reflect idiosyncratic approaches to the manner in which two or more incumbents interpret and carry out the same job. Harvey & Wilson (2000) noted their disagreement with Sanchez

GMA: general mental ability

GWAs: generalized work activities

& Levine's stance, indicating that interrater reliability is an appropriate means to gauge reliability when the object of study is what in their view constitutes verifiable job information (e.g., work behaviors). Nevertheless, the research on reliability of job analysis data yields a complex and not altogether consistent picture.

Dierdorff & Wilson's (2003) meta-analysis revealed that task data produced higher estimates of interrater reliability than statements of broader GWAs (weighted $r = 0.77$ versus 0.60). Dierdorff & Morgeson (2009) reported similar differences in the interrater reliability estimates of GWAs and tasks (i.e., 0.65 versus 0.80). In contrast, in a different meta-analysis Voskuijl & van Sliedgregt (2002) reported the exact opposite finding, namely that task statements were less reliable than broader behaviors (0.29 versus 0.62). Findings from research on the merits of decomposed (or task-based) versus holistic (job-based) ratings have been equally mixed, with a majority of studies indicating the superior interrater reliability of molecular estimates (Butler & Harvey 1988, Gibson et al. 2004, Harvey et al. 1994, Sanchez & Levine 1994), whereas some suggested no differences (Cornelius & Lyness 1980). One of the reasons offered for these somewhat mixed findings is that the presumably challenging demands of holistic judgments, which require a great deal of information integration (Cornelius & Lyness 1980), are sometimes exceeded by the demands involved in rating a very large number of molecular (task) units. Still another explanation, which is consistent with Dierdorff & Wilson's finding that molecular-molar reliability differences are largely confined to interrater reliability estimates, is that incumbents are more likely to endorse idiosyncratic views of the role expectations associated with their job than of the specific activities involved in discharging such roles. Whether these idiosyncratic opinions regarding their role represent unreliability is questionable because they may capture real differences in how the job is interpreted and even performed (Dierdorff & Morgeson 2007, Dierdorff et al. 2010, Sanchez & Levine 2000).

Jeanneret et al. (1999) reported GWA intraclass correlations obtained in a pilot study of 35 occupations with 4 to 88 incumbents. For the level scale, they reported correlations of at least 0.90 for 35 of the 42 GWAs. Slightly lower reliabilities were reported for the importance and frequency scales (the frequency scale was later eliminated in the final version of O*NET). Their results did not significantly change when GWAs rated as "not relevant" were eliminated, in spite of the potentially inflating effects of "does not apply" items on interrater reliability (Friedman & Harvey 1986, Smith & Hakel 1979). Dierdorff & Morgeson (2009) reported a lower mean interrater reliability of 0.65 for O*NET GWAs using a large sample of incumbents (N = 47,137) spanning over 300 different occupations whose ratings had been collected by the U.S. Department of Labor to populate O*NET.

Dierdorff & Wilson (2003) observed that the pattern of reliabilities differed between their interrater and intrarater estimates. These differences were most notable for ratings produced by technical experts ($r = 0.81$ versus 0.47 for intra- and interrater, respectively). Whereas descriptive scales dealing with perceptions of relative value (i.e., importance) showed higher interrater reliabilities than those of scales involving temporal judgments (i.e., frequency), importance and frequency had similarly acceptable intrarater reliabilities. Intrarater ratings of difficulty were lower than interrater ones. Again, it could be that incumbents' ratings of constructs that are most closely associated with the process of learning one's job, such as task difficulty, legitimately change over time, even though perceptions of the relative value of tasks (e.g., task importance) do not.

Taken together, these findings appear to question the assumption that the reliability of work activity ratings can be equivalently measured through either interrater or intrarater designs. Specifically, interrater reliability estimates do not distinguish between variance due to random factors and variance due to legitimate differences in the manner in which each incumbent approaches his/her job.

Similarly, although intrarater designs concerned with the stability of ratings over time are not affected by between-rater differences in idiosyncratic views of the job, they are still likely to reflect true variations in the longitudinal evolution of the incumbent's approach to the job. Longitudinal studies that track incumbent ratings of, for instance, time spent and difficulty may illuminate the learning sequence through which incumbents acquire job mastery.

Note that our recommendation to separately examine the estimates provided by each type of reliability design does not deny the importance of the psychometric properties of job-analytic data. In fact, our recommendation is predicated on one of classical reliability's primary tenets, specifically, the distinction between systematic and random variance. We are simply arguing that some of the variance that is sometimes deemed "random" in work activity ratings may indeed reflect systematic differences in the way some incumbents interpret and, most importantly, perform their job. Sanchez & Levine (2009) argued that the "objectified" (see also Cronshaw 1998) understanding of a job as an object or entity that displays minimal variation across each of the incumbents holding the same job was a reasonable assumption to make when work was organized around the principles of Taylorism such as task standardization and division of labor. However, such an assumption holds less well in today's world of work, where electronic equipment has taken over many standardized activities and where the emphasis often is on empowering employees to perform tasks according to their own discretion, all of which is likely to exacerbate the amount of legitimate, between-position variance within the same job title.

Prior research has indeed suggested that interrater differences may reflect not just perceptual differences of dubious theoretical or practical value, but also tangible correlates in the manner in which incumbents perform their job. For instance, Borman et al. (1992) found that time spent amounts declared for some tasks by high performers differed from those reported by low performers. Dierdorff et al. (2010) and

Morrison (1994) provided further evidence that employees' views of certain work activities were associated with the extent to which they engaged in citizenship behavior. Further evidence that variability in within-job title ratings is not always random was provided by Sanchez et al. (1998), who found that the job-analytic rating profile of branch managers working for a temporary personnel agency moderated sales performance, with high performers endorsing a more sales-oriented conception of the job and low performers endorsing a more administrative view. In a separate study reported in the same article, Sanchez et al. (1998) also revealed that prior professional experience shaped the tasks that assistant public defenders emphasized in their ratings, such that those with prior trial experience declared themselves more likely to litigate rather than settle cases than those without such experience. Prien et al. (2003) reported that social workers with longer professional tenure tended to perform their job quite differently from those with shorter professional tenure. Befort & Hattrup (2003) found that the importance that managers assigned to task and contextual performance varied as a function of their experience, with more experienced managers placing a higher value on contextual behaviors such as compliance and extra effort.

It appears that the premise that jobs are stable objects with fixed properties, which has prevailed in job analysis research until recently (Cronshaw 1998, Sanchez & Levine 2009), has resulted in a rather passive view of incumbents, who are conceived as merely the recipients of a job assignment rather than the actors who shape it according to their own initiative. Other streams of research, however, have endorsed a more agentic view, thereby recognizing that job incumbents are active agents who perform their jobs according to their role identity, past experience, motivation, and personal and professional goals. Wrzesniewski & Dutton (2001) termed this process job crafting, which they defined as "the physical and cognitive changes individuals make in the task or relational boundaries of their work" (p. 179). Other theories, including role theory (Biddle 1986), share this view of incumbents as the main architects of their job rather than the mere executers of a predetermined work assignment (Dierdorff et al. 2009, Grant 2007, Roberts et al. 2005). This notion applies perhaps even more to self-directed work teams (Mathieu et al. 2008).

Within-job title variability, however, may not exist uniformly across all individuals and all jobs. For instance, job incumbents have been shown to differ in their motivation to craft their job in unique ways, and antecedents of this motivation, such as self-image, perceived control, readiness to change (e.g., Lyons 2008), role orientation (Parker 2007), and the desire to make a prosocial difference (Grant 2007), have been uncovered. However, certain jobs are more likely to provide situational opportunity to engage in job crafting than others (Wrzesniewski & Dutton 2001). Research should attempt to gain a better understanding of the sources of interrater variation (Sanchez & Levine 2000), which should largely coincide with the factors promoting or inhibiting the situational opportunity to shape one's role as explained by job crafting and role theories.

A number of studies have begun to pursue this research goal. First, Sanchez et al. (1998) hypothesized that job complexity would make idiosyncratic interpretations of the job more likely. Using a sample of incumbents and job analysts for 19 jobs, they found that agreement between incumbents and nonincumbents was indeed moderated by job data-oriented occupational complexity, such that agreement was highest for the less complex jobs. Using individual-level O*NET ratings from 20,000 incumbents across 98 occupations collected by the U.S. Department of Labor, Dierdorff & Morgeson (2007) found support for a series of role theory-based predictions arguing that the context wherein employees work promotes or restricts within-title variance. These authors found that some elements of the occupational context (i.e., interdependence and routinization) increased the level of agreement in O*NET ratings, presumably because they suppressed individuation in role enactment. They also found that autonomy reduced

rating consensus, presumably because it promotes exploring new tasks. Lievens et al. (2010) found that certain kinds of work activities, such as the extent to which occupations involved equipment-related and direct contact activities, increased consensus on competency ratings, whereas managerial activities decreased it.

As a whole, these findings enhance our understanding of the conditions that foster job individuation, thereby strengthening job crafting theory, which has recognized the existence of situational antecedents of job crafting but focused instead on its individual difference antecedents (e.g., Grant 2007). In addition, because the presence of interrater disagreement among incumbents of the same job title understandably hurts the face validity of the job analysis data (Jones et al. 2001, Sanchez & Levine 2000), a better understanding of the nonrandom sources of disagreement should increase practitioners' ability to explain to end users the pros of further exploring the sources of within-job title variation (e.g., uncovering different approaches to carrying out work activities in the same job that may impact outcomes such as employee performance; Borman et al. 1992, Sanchez et al. 1998). This is a particularly pressing concern given the calls for greater discretion for workers in loosely organized units such as self-directed work teams.

Carelessness Studies

A stream of research has developed around ways to detect rater indifference or purposeful obstruction in work activity ratings. One approach taken has relied upon repeating some of the same items to see if respondents answer them consistently. However, the presence of repeated items in the same inventory may puzzle respondents (Wilson et al. 1990), who may choose to answer them inconsistently for a variety of reasons.

A different route to assess the trustworthiness of the data gathered involves the computation of veracity and carelessness indices, which typically include work activities that are known to be performed by all incumbents or bogus items that are known not to be part of the job at all, respectively (Pine 1995). Green & Veres (1990) found that indices relying on the frequency with which bogus items were endorsed correlated significantly with the elevation of respondents' task ratings. Green & Stutzman (1986), however, reported that different indices of carelessness led to discarding different incumbents' data. These procedures warrant continued research because it is not inconceivable that the inclusion of bogus items may, as occurs with repeated items, induce the respondents to answer these items in unsuspected ways. In addition, Dierdorff & Rubin (2007) found that these items might not always capture carelessness or biases, but rather legitimate variations in incumbents' interpretation (and possible enactment) of their job, such as differences in incumbents' perceived role ambiguity. Further research is needed to uncover the constructs and response sets that arise when these types of items are employed. From a practical standpoint, discarding those respondents' data whose answers suggest carelessness according to these indices may, as it did in the case of those responding inconsistently to repeated items (Wilson et al. 1990), result in significant reductions in reliability and sample size. A more potentially fruitful research avenue involves reducing the time and the cognitive demands imposed on subject matter experts (SMEs) through cognitive-oriented redesign of lengthy inventories (Willis 2005).

Validity Studies

Assessments of the validity of work activity information span a number of different approaches that vary in the manner and in the degree to which they assess validity. One of the most straightforward approaches involves asking SMEs how well the inventory covers the scope of activities that comprise the job, usually in the form of a percentage judgment. Wilson (1997) conducted a field experiment revealing that both incumbents and supervisors provided unrealistically high judgments of inventory completeness, even when presented

with inventories where two-thirds of the tasks had been removed. Wilson recommended a serious re-examination of this approach to estimate the quality of work inventories, which may be vulnerable to experimenter demands and other forms of biases. A potentially fruitful research avenue involves conducting interviews and other forms of qualitative research on the types of work behaviors that are missing in these inventories. For instance, well-rounded incumbents may be most likely to detect the absence of other-oriented and extrarole activities, which are work requirements of critical importance in today's organizations (Borman & Motowidlo 1993).

Early research by McCormick and his associates revealed that asking SMEs to make precise estimates of time spent (e.g., allocating a percentage of time to each work activity) was problematic (McCormick 1960), as SMEs lacked the ability to judge time spent with such precision. As a result, later research adopted primarily "relative scales," which were supposed to represent a less demanding judgment because they simply asked SMEs to compare tasks to each other (e.g., "compared to all other tasks on the job, how much time do you spend on this one?"). Harvey (1991) challenged the use of relative scales, arguing that relative scales require ipsative judgments that preclude cross-job comparisons, plus they do not meet the statistical assumptions needed for many types of data analysis. These limitations, however, appear to be more conceptual than empirical, as Manson et al. (2000) found that relative and absolute scales of the same and different constructs had generally satisfactory patterns of convergent and discriminant validity and provided virtually equivalent rank-orderings of tasks within the same job. Absolute judgments, however, are sometimes necessary to quantify, for instance, the frequency and time spent on physically challenging tasks such as lifting objects of different weights. This type of research on job analysis for physically arduous jobs is sorely needed, given an aging population, the postponement of retirement age, and the larger number of workers seeking partial

SMEs: subject matter experts

or total disability certification (Fleishman et al. 1986). In the United States, the Social Security Administration (SSA) decided that O*NET was not a suitable replacement of the *Dictionary of Occupational Titles* (DOT) for purposes of disability determination, so the SSA is now embarked on a project to develop an occupational information system capable of evaluating the physical and mental demands of work (Occup. Inform. Advis. Panel 2009).

Research on the construct validity of work activity scales such as criticality or importance has been bolstered by the job-relatedness provisions of the Uniform Guidelines (Equal Employ. Opport. Comm. 1978), which call for selection procedures that are demonstrably linked to job behaviors identified to be critical or important. Prior research suggested that work activity scales load on one of two major factors: a time-oriented factor represented by time spent, frequency, and duration scales, and an importance/complexity factor involving scales of criticality, overall importance, difficulty, and difficulty of learning (Friedman 1990, 1991; Manson et al. 2000; Sanchez & Fraser 1992; Sanchez & Levine 1989). It is thus not surprising that O*NET scales of importance and level, which are employed for GWAs and other types of items, are largely redundant (their intercorrelation is $r = 0.95$ according to analyses performed using pilot O*NET data by Hubbard et al. 2000). Subsequent analyses using the aggregated ratings included in the 14.0 O*NET database by Sanchez & Autor (2010) revealed similarly high importance by level correlations for GWAs ($r = 0.92$), with type of scale (i.e., importance versus level) accounting for only 0.50% of the variance in GWA ratings.

Still another indirect but fairly widespread approach to assessing the validity of work activity data involves examining the presence and the magnitude of presumptively extraneous sources of variance in work activity ratings. The logic underlying these studies is that third variables such as job experience, sex, and other demographic variables are job unrelated; therefore, their detection would signal the presence of some kind of bias in job-analytic

data, thus casting doubt on their validity. Work experience seems to be the most widely studied extraneous influence. Evidence of experience effects, however, has been elusive. Whereas some studies have failed to detect experience effects (Schmitt & Cohen 1989, Silverman et al. 1984), a majority of them have uncovered some form of experience effect (Borman et al. 1992, Ford et al. 1991, Landy & Vasey 1991, Tross & Maurer 2000). As we argued in the section dedicated to reliability, we believe that just searching for effects of experience and of other demographic variables is not likely to advance the theory and practice of job analysis beyond what we currently know. First, as illustrated earlier, many substantive variables are confounded with demographic variables such as work experience (e.g., Lindell et al. 1998, Prien et al. 2003, Sanchez et al. 1998); therefore, interrater differences associated with work experience may reflect true differences in how incumbents not only interpret but also perform the job. For instance, the differences between less- and more-experienced branch managers and stockbrokers uncovered by Borman et al. (1992) and Sanchez et al. (1998), respectively, in regard to sales-oriented tasks had tangible correlates such as higher sales among those who emphasize sales-oriented tasks.

The occasionally null correlations between work activity ratings and performance (Aamodt et al. 1982, Conley & Sackett 1987, Wexley & Silverman 1978) are not surprising in light of studies suggesting that job crafting is unlikely to surface when the job context does not provide a great deal of discretion to incumbents (Dierdorff & Morgeson 2007, Lievens et al. 2010, Lindell et al. 1998). Also, different approaches to carrying out work activities may impact performance criteria that have not been measured in a given setting. However, even if differences in work activity ratings associated with experience were merely perceptual and did not affect the manner in which incumbents performed the job, such differences could not easily be attributed to erroneous or biasing factors. Consider, for example, the case of an arguably "objective" property of the job such as task importance. When judging task importance, it appears that experienced job incumbents focus on time spent, as suggested by the relationship between these two variables, whereas inexperienced ones focus on difficulty of learning the task (Ford et al. 1991, Sanchez 1990). That is, the conceptual definition of their job differs across incumbents because new employees rely on their still fresh memory of how hard it is to learn certain tasks when they evaluate their importance. This memory has probably faded among experienced incumbents, whose judgments of time spent on each task may provide a more logical standard of what tasks are truly important. Affirming that some incumbents are correct whereas others are mistaken overlooks that incumbents employ a different frame of reference when judging the importance of their job demands.

We argue that future research should follow the path already initiated by others (Prien et al. 2003, Sanchez et al. 1998) and focus on understanding the substantive roots of why work experience and other demographic characteristics influence work activity ratings rather than on whether such effects are present. Morgeson & Dierdorff (2011) suggested that Tesluk & Jacobs' (1998) model of work experience, which distinguishes among indices of work experience (i.e., amount, time, density, timing, and type) and levels of analysis (i.e., task, job, work group, organization, and career/occupation), provides a useful framework along which theoretical and empirical inquiry may proceed. Indeed, we agree that continued "fishing" for differences observed among incumbents as a function of demographic breakdowns of dubious theoretical value (e.g., incumbents' race or sex) will simply replicate what we already know, namely that statistically significant differences among such groupings of incumbents are erratic, their effect sizes small, and their practical significance questionable (Arvey et al. 1977, 1982; Hazel et al. 1964; Landy & Vasey 1991; Meyer 1959; Schmitt & Cohen 1989). More substantive variables, such as the manner in which incumbents define their professional and social identity, may better explain differences in how they view their jobs, including which tasks they deem most important. This information might be useful in, for example, framing training programs according to the level of career maturity of prospective trainees. Again, our recommendation is that instead of trying to hide or eliminate disagreement, job analysis research should embrace it by looking more deeply into its causes. Legitimate disagreement represents unique ways in which incumbents experience their job, and a better understanding of their ideographic representations might increase our grasp on the various forms in which jobs can be crafted along with their requirements and consequences. It is this broader purpose of understanding the experience of work that in our opinion holds the key to the future of work analysis (Rosso et al. 2010) because of its potential to better explain worker outcomes such as performance.

Competencies

Many organizations have incorporated competency modeling (CM) as opposed to job analyses in their HR applications (Lucia & Lepsinger 1999, Schippmann 1999). The difference between job analysis and CM, however, seems still blurry, as the two are often lumped together. A group of experts surveyed regarding the main differences between job analysis and CM opined that, unlike job analysis, CM is linked to strategic goals, but also that it is less rigorous than job analysis in regard to data collection, level of detail, assessment of reliability, and documentation of the research process (Schippmann et al. 2000). A more definitive answer to the difference between CM and job analysis probably awaits clarity in the definition of "competency," which has been vaguely defined as "any individual characteristic that can be measured or counted reliably and that can be shown to differentiate significantly between superior and average performers" (Spencer et al. 1994, p. 4). Some have recently suggested that competencies refer to knowledge, skill, ability, and other

CM: competency modeling

characteristics (KSAOs) that are needed for effective performance in the jobs in question (Campion et al. 2011). However, some degree of consensus is beginning to emerge around the view of competencies as broadly defined elements of the job performance space (Tett et al. 2000), which led us to include them in this section dedicated to work activities. In the words of Bartram (2005), competencies are "sets of behaviors that are instrumental in the delivery of desired results or outcomes" (p. 1187). Sanchez & Levine (2009) also noted that most lists of competencies resemble loosely coupled patterns of behavior or "behavioral themes" that are considered to be critical success factors or strategic performance drivers (see also Becker et al. 2001). Lievens et al. (2010) also took the position that competencies are best classified as part of the performance space.

The definition of competencies as sets of behaviors or behavioral themes that are instrumental in the delivery of strategic results is seemingly consistent with the primary purpose of CM. In this respect, Sanchez & Levine (2009) suggested that whereas the purpose of job analysis is to better understand and measure work assignments, the primary purpose of CM is to influence the manner in which such assignments are performed so that presumably strategic, behavioral themes are emphasized when performing every job. They drew a parallel with the notions of "trait relevance" and "situation strength," which correspond to the notions of "channel" and "volume" in signal detection theory (Tett & Burnett 2003). In other words, whereas job analysis is concerned with determining attribute or trait relevance or the appropriate channels that are called for by the nature of the work assignment, CM attempts to raise the volume of those channels that signal the importance of certain behavioral themes aligned with the organization's strategy—i.e., situation strength. These "loud" signals are intended to create a shared climate or collective understanding of the behavioral themes that are expected and rewarded (Bowen & Ostroff 2004, Chatman & Cha 2003, O'Reily & Chatman 1996, Werbel & DeMarie

2005). Thus, according to Sanchez & Levine (2009), job analysis and CM belong in different domains: Job analysis is best positioned in the domain of applied measurement, whereas CM is closest to a mechanism of informal control.

The relatively scarce CM research to date has largely mirrored the research questions that are often pursued in job analysis research, thus focusing on the accuracy, interrater agreement, and discriminant validity of competency ratings. Not surprisingly, the results of such exercises are frequently disappointing because ratings of broadly defined competencies often have trouble meeting the levels of interrater agreement found for job analysis data, such as job tasks (Lievens et al. 2004, Lievens & Sanchez 2007, Morgeson et al. 2004). Instead, Sanchez & Levine (2009) suggested that CM research should focus on the main dependent variable of CM, that is, the extent to which CM influences employees' day-to-day behavior along strategic lines, including the development of competency language that is accessible to end users, the development of behavioral examples that are demonstrative of each competency for different jobs, and the cross-fertilization of job analysis and CM to develop measurement models for each competency, so that the underlying traits of the relatively complex behavioral syndromes dubbed competencies are better understood.

RESEARCH ON WORKER ATTRIBUTE INFORMATION

Reliability Studies

Generalizability analysis has been employed to evaluate the proportion of variance in job analysis ratings that is attributable to idiosyncratic sources as compared to the facets of the job that are purportedly being evaluated (Dierdorff & Morgeson 2007, Lievens et al. 2010, Sanchez et al. 1998). This approach is based on the premise that variance due to raters prevents the reliable aggregation of ratings across raters. Van Iddekinge et al. (2005) used this approach to analyze KSAO ratings produced by 381 raters across five organizations. They partitioned the variance due to raters, rater-by-KSAO, and error, and found considerable idiosyncratic variance as represented by the rater-by-KSAO component. Subsequent analyses found that variance components due to rater-by-KSAO and to error were not explained by the organization, position level, and demographic characteristics of the raters, hence casting doubt on the sources of variance underlying these ratings.

In regard to personality attributes, which are termed work styles in the O*NET model, Borman et al. (1999) reported a median intraclass reliability of 0.66 for the level scale using a pilot O*NET study of 35 occupations with 4 to 88 incumbents. The attribute Dependability had the lowest reliability at 0.15, and personality attributes had a similar range of reliabilities when evaluated on the importance scale. Using ratings collected by the U.S. Department of Labor to populate O*NET from 47,137 incumbents spanning more than 300 occupations, Dierdorff & Morgeson (2009) found that variance due to raters was more pervasive among ratings of personality traits (up to 35%) than among responsibility ratings (16%). Similarly, sample-size weighted estimates of reliability were 0.45 and 0.80 for personality traits and tasks, respectively.

Turning now to the domain of abilities, research by Fleishman and his colleagues resulted in the development of a set of single-item scales to gauge job requirements along 52 abilities (Fleishman & Quaintance 1984, Fleishman & Reilly 1992). This set of scales has been incorporated into O*NET in a functionally equivalent form as compared to the original developed by Fleishman, even though the critical incidents (Flanagan 1954) or behavioral anchors included in the scales, which represent various levels of the abilities, were apparently rescaled for O*NET (Peterson et al. 1999, p. 185). Fleishman et al. (1999) employed the same O*NET pilot study of 35 occupations with 4 to 88 incumbents mentioned earlier to assess the reliability of the 52 ability scales. They reported that most of the

intraclass correlation reliabilities were above 0.80. The O*NET project developed similar, behaviorally anchored scales for other types of worker attribute data such as personality requirements (termed work styles) and skills.

Unlike those in other O*NET domains, questionnaires relating to the ability and skill domains are completed by occupational analysts, not incumbents. Apparently, the decision to have analysts rate abilities and skills was based on theoretical and practical considerations, including the assumption that trained analysts are more likely to understand the ability and skill constructs than incumbents are. Whether O*NET work styles, which capture similarly psychological constructs but in the personality arena, should continue to be rated by incumbents warrants further research. Nevertheless, a study conducted by the O*NET Center found that incumbents provided higher ratings than analysts and that analysts' ratings were more reliable than incumbents' ratings were, even though these differences were deemed minimal (Tsacoumis & Van Iddekinge 2006). A series of reliability studies conducted on the analyst ratings associated with each wave of O*NET data collection reported median intraclass correlation reliabilities of 0.95 (Tsacoumis 2009a). These reliability studies used a maximum of 31 unique analysts, who apparently are responsible for all of the ability and skill ratings produced in the various cycles of O*NET data collection to date, with some occupations having been rated by a minimum of eight analysts (Tsacoumis & Van Iddekinge 2006). Whether these intraclass correlations overestimate the reliability of O*NET ratings, however, has been the object of debate (Harvey 2009, Tsacoumis 2009b).

Other research has shown that analysts may produce more reliable activity-attribute linkages, i.e., the presumptive extent to which an attribute is called for in carrying out an activity, than incumbents would (Baranowski & Anderson 2005). However, a potentially more important aspect than whether analysts or incumbents are employed to make ratings is the information or stimulus on which such ratings are based. For example, in O*NET, since analysts neither interview nor observe incumbents, the rating materials are the sole information on which analyst ratings are based. The O*NET rating materials provided to analysts are prepared to rid the rating stimulus materials of items (i.e., knowledge, skills, education and training, and work styles) thought to be unimportant for ability ratings (Donsbach et al. 2003). The materials are further simplified by selecting GWAs and work context items that were judged to be relevant to the focal ability, regardless of the occupation, by a panel of eight industrial and organizational psychologists. These GWA and work context items were further screened by selecting those that had achieved a certain cut-off among incumbent ratings. Although it can be argued that these streamlined materials (they occupy about one page of information for each ability rating, according to appendix E of the Donsbach et al. 2003 report) eliminate unnecessary information and therefore result in more reliable ratings, future research should investigate whether or not such reliability gains are made at the expense of eliminating potentially relevant job information, including information that could be gained firsthand by interviewing or observing incumbents rather than by studying a paper description of the job. In this respect, Voskuijl & Sliedregt's (2002) meta-analysis suggests that occupational analysts produce more reliable ratings when such ratings are based on actual contact with job incumbents rather than a job description ($r = 0.87$ versus 0.71). Prior research also suggests that increasing (rather than reducing) the amount of job information can indeed have a positive effect on job-analytic ratings of both work activity and worker attributes (Harvey & Lozada-Larsen 1988, Lievens et al. 2004).

Hubbard et al. (2000) reported that the behavioral anchors used in the O*NET ability rating scales were potentially confusing. They speculated that these anchors may be confusing because they were drawn from occupations with which most job incumbents are unfamiliar and, therefore, the level of difficulty of the requirements is confounded with the degree of familiarity with the occupation. For instance, the anchor "reading a scientific article describing surgical procedures," which appears at the high end of the reading comprehension scale, may in fact gauge a relatively low level of reading comprehension for trained surgeons. Further research on how to anchor attribute scales for validity, user acceptability, and ease of usage is warranted, but as it has also occurred in the performance appraisal domain (Tziner et al. 2000), the employment of critical incidents as behavioral anchors may not be the answer.

Still a more substantive argument advanced to explain the typically lower reliabilities obtained for worker attributes is that they represent unobservable construals that require a larger "inferential leap" than ratings of more observable aspects of the job such as work activities (Dierdorff & Morgeson 2009). Whether reliable ratings of ostensibly complex, unobservable construals such as the "flexibility of closure" ability can be reliably formulated using the type of single-item scales employed in O*NET has also been questioned (Harvey 2009, Harvey & Wilson 2010). Further research comparing single- to multiple-item scales of these constructs is warranted.

Validity Studies

A stream of research that has indirectly examined the validity of worker attributes is concerned with the extent to which ratings are influenced or biased by cognitive processes. This research stems from the recognition that job analysis places a great burden on the information-processing capabilities of SMEs (Arvey et al. 1982), and it draws from the literature on the shortcomings of human judgment (Hogarth 1981).

The use of rater training has been explored to eliminate or reduce the potential biases thought to influence raters. Sanchez & Levine (1994) found that a rater training program intended to reduce the presumptively biasing effect of Tversky & Kahneman's (1974) representativeness and availability heuristics increased interrater agreement as long as the number of ratings was low to moderate. Using the frame of reference (FOR) rater training paradigm, which attempts to standardize the FOR employed by raters, Lievens & Sanchez (2007) found that rater training increased interrater agreement and discriminant validity of competency ratings. Aguinis et al. (2009) used FOR training to reduce the correlation between SMEs' self-reported personality and job-analytic ratings of personality requirements (rater training also lowered job-analytic ratings). Although rater training interventions might indeed suppress idiosyncratic variance, whether this suppression of idiosyncratic views comes at the expense of significant information losses in the manner in which incumbents experience the demands of their job merits further research.

Morgeson & Campion (1997) identified 16 distinct potential social and cognitive sources of biases in job analysis ratings. Social sources are thought to represent normative pressures from the social environment in which individuals are embedded (e.g., conformity, group polarization, impression management), whereas the cognitive sources capture limitations in raters' information-processing capabilities (e.g., information overload, heuristics). Morgeson et al. (2004) began to test some of these biasing factors. Specifically they hypothesized that self-presentation biases would result in higher ratings and more frequent endorsements of ability statements than of task statements. Their findings supported their prediction, because ability statements that were identical to task statements but were preceded by the phrase "ability to" drew higher ratings than their corresponding tasks.

Overall, a potential concern with studies examining social or cognitive biases lies in the absence of a true score that would allow an objective estimation of bias. For instance, the elevated ratings assigned to certain items by certain individuals may simply reflect these individuals' unique but legitimate approach to performing the job. In addition, differences in rating elevation between scales of different constructs do not necessarily signal the presence of biases. For instance, abilities may be legitimately scaled quite differently from tasks, as a higher level of ability may indeed be required by an only moderately important or infrequent task. As others have noted (Hogarth 1981, Kruglanski 1989), many of the so-called biases or inaccuracies observed in laboratory tasks reflect simplifying judgment strategies that indeed have functional value when judging complex environments such as one's job. In our opinion, experimental and quasi-experimental studies that attempt to detect or reduce biases or "inaccuracy" in job-analytic judgments should make sure that the differences that are thought to demonstrate such biases do not reflect substantive variance that may increase our understanding of how people truly approach and experience their jobs. A less-than-desirable course of action for job analysis research would be to repeat the same mistakes made in the performance appraisal literature, whose findings regarding performance rating biases and inaccuracy have been qualified on the account of their limited utility (Bretz et al. 1992).

Turning now to the discriminant validity of worker attributes, the factorial structure of O*NET ability ratings has been explored (e.g., Fleishman et al. 1999). It appears that the single ratings employed to gauge each one of the 52 abilities included in the model can understandably be reduced to a smaller set of higher-order factors (e.g., a broad psychomotor/perceptual factor grouping abilities such as depth perception and dynamic strength), which are capable of explaining the majority of the variance in these ratings. The seemingly high colinearity among the single ratings representing each ability is not altogether surprising because ability estimates based on limited job information may understandably produce items showing less discriminant validity than those resulting from assessment scores of individuals on those same abilities. This redundancy is likely to increase when average ratings across SMEs are factor analyzed, as illustrated by Sanchez & Autor's (2010) finding that a single factor accounts for 43% of the variance in the aggregated ability ratings included in the 14.0 version

FOR: frame of reference

of the O*NET database—aggregated ratings are the only O*NET ratings publicly available to O*NET users or to researchers outside of the O*NET development team. Harvey & Wilson (2010) also provided evidence suggesting that ratings of O*NET abilities can be more parsimoniously explained by a reduced set of higher-order factors. Whether information on ability requirements and on other worker attributes is too redundant should be determined in future investigations. The criteria for such determination should include practical significance and cost-effectiveness of data collection (e.g., gathering data on fewer abilities may not impact many of the typically coarse human resource usages of O*NET data uncovered in a recent survey of O*NET users; Natl. Res. Counc. 2010, pp. 140–148).

In addition to potential redundancy among worker attributes, there seems to be redundancy in the two scales employed to rate attributes in O*NET, namely importance and level. Sanchez & Autor (2010) reported level by importance Pearson correlations among the aggregated ratings of 832 occupations included in the O*NET 14.0 database of 0.97, 0.95, and 0.97 for abilities, skills, and knowledge, respectively. Similarly, the type of scale (i.e., importance or level) accounted for just 3%, 1.54%, and 1.31% of the variance in ability, skill, and knowledge ratings, respectively. These findings suggest the information provided by these two scales in the O*NET database is largely redundant. Overall, more research is needed on the discriminant and convergent validity of worker attribute scales, which is certainly more scarce than research on the scales employed to characterize work activities such as time spent and criticality (Friedman 1990, 1991; Sanchez & Fraser 1992; Sanchez & Levine 1989).

One of the worker attribute scales in need of additional research attention is trainability or the extent to which worker attributes are appropriately learned after significant exposure on the job or in a training program versus possessed by applicants at the point of hire or easily acquired soon afterward. This determination is mandated by the Uniform Guidelines on Employee Selection Procedures (Equal Employ. Opportun. Commiss. 1978), which advises against the use of easy-to-learn or already mastered KSAOs in selection procedures. A study by Van Iddekinge et al. (2011) correlated ratings of the extent to which KSAOs were needed at entry with an external criterion of perceived KSAO trainability formulated by a panel of 31 organizational psychologists. Their findings indicated less validity evidence for ratings of the more abstract "AO" attributes than for those of more concrete "KS" attributes. Whereas job experts rated certain attributes as needed-at-entry, psychologists identified them as ones that could be developed on the job.

More uncommon are studies that have attempted to validate attribute ratings against consequence-oriented criteria of the type proposed by Sanchez & Levine (2000) and Levine & Sanchez (2007), such as the inferences made using job-analytic ratings. Jones et al. (2001) found that job analysts made better predictions of worker attribute trainability than incumbents and students when trainability ratings were compared with actual changes in student learning. Although the results of Jones et al. (2001) suggest that the validity of worker attribute ratings may vary depending on the source of the ratings, we recommend that, in keeping with themes we have developed earlier, the psychological factors that account for these differences should be the focus. In this respect, the work of Jones et al. highlights the idea that ratings of presumably more malleable KSs require different expertise from those of more fixed abilities and other characteristics AOs, a point that has also been raised by others (e.g., Harvey 1991, Morgeson & Campion 1997).

Still another example of consequence-oriented evaluation was provided by Levine et al. (1980), who showed that different depictions of jobs analyzed by different methods led HR professionals to develop very similar examination plans in the selection context. Yet there were small rated differences in the quality of assessment and screening approaches, suggesting for instance that the critical incidents method resulted in higher-quality examination plans than those derived from other methods. Manson (2004), on the other hand, found that the amount and specificity of information had an effect on the cognitive challenge and the quality of the selection plans prepared on the basis of job-analytic information, thereby supporting the collection of at least moderately specific information such as the ten most important tasks and ten most important KSAOs. However, the question of whether detailed job analysis has consequences that are equivalent to those of cursory job analysis is moot unless one considers the goals that the job analysis serves. For instance, even though different job-analytic methodologies varying in the degree of detail have been found to produce similar job classifications (Sackett et al. 1981), whether detailed job analyses make a difference in potentially more complex decisions, such as developing a testing plan, warrants further research.

Another approach that is ripe for an examination of its consequential validity is the mechanical estimation of worker attributes through job component validation (Arvey et al. 1992, Cunningham 1964, Goiffin & Woycheshin 2006, McCormick et al. 1972, Sanchez & Fraser 1994). Job component validation, which may be classified as a case of synthetic validity, involves statistically capturing the form in which worker attributes are predictable from scores on more specific job components. For example, LaPolice et al. (2008) used a job component validation approach that relied on O*NET data to identify adult literacy requirements across occupations. They found multiple correlation coefficients ranging from 0.79 to 0.81 (corrected for shrinkage) when predicting literacy scores from O*NET items. Jeanneret & Strong (2003) followed a similar procedure to predict general aptitude test scores using GWA data from O*NET and found lower multiple correlations ranging from 0.35 to 0.89. An issue with job component validation research is how good the statistical predictions or multiple Rs need to be in order to consider the mechanically estimated scores to be equivalent to actual ratings of SMEs (Harvey 2011,

Walmsley et al. 2011). However, whether scores determined through job component validation are statistically different from those directly produced by SMEs may not be as important as determining if, when, and through what rules they lead to practically different inferences and decisions regarding, for instance, an assessment strategy.

Indeed, future evaluations of the consequences of job-analytic data should consider the rules governing the manner in which data are employed to support inferences. For instance, the exact same data on work activities and worker attributes may produce rather different selection plans when the elaborate procedures for establishing linkages between work activities and underlying worker attributes outlined by several authors (Baranowski & Anderson 2005, Goldstein et al. 1993, Landy 1988) are applied than when the selection plan is determined solely on the grounds of loosely defined professional judgment. Similarly, the very specific rules provided by Fine & Cronshaw (1999, pp. 133–136) regarding the use of a task bank to develop behavioral questions in an employment interview may result in more valid interviewing than simply letting interviewers formulate their own questions after studying the job analysis. More research on the impact of the rules through which job-analytic data are transformed into inferences, including inferences regarding appropriate assessment tools, is needed, because the failure to demonstrate that detailed information matters may feed continued skepticism about the need to invest in detailed job analyses. Such research should serve to inform evidence-based standards of job analysis practice for HR programs.

The conclusion that a molar job analysis suffices in most applications has been formulated in the context of discussing the validity of GMA tests, which has proven robust in spite of relatively large task differences among jobs (Le et al. 2007). Unfortunately, this argument against detailed job analysis probably found fertile grounds in many business settings, where job analysis is accused of being a legalistic obstacle to flexibility and innovation (Drucker 1987,

Olian & Rynes 1991). As Sanchez & Levine (1999) lamented, the job-relatedness provisions embodied in the Uniform Guidelines on Employee Selection Procedures (Equal Employ. Opportun. Commiss. 1978) and in the Americans with Disabilities Act (U.S. Dept. Justice 1991) were not meant to boost the role of job analysis as a risk-management device to be used in litigation. Instead, these provisions were meant to promote the development of selection procedures that were tied to business results and, as a result, would be more effective at identifying top performers. Nevertheless, one of the unintended consequences of this legislation has been promoting the perception of job analysis as a necessary evil whose sole purpose is to mitigate the risk associated with potential legal challenges to selection procedures (Olian & Rynes 1991). Research demonstrating that job analysis, and specifically, detailed job analysis, can be consequential in terms of facilitating better inferences is needed to overcome prejudice against job analysis (Sanchez & Levine 2000).

An impediment to the acceptability of worker attributes as the language of choice when discussing work lies in the development of suitable job-analytic terminology. Industrial and organizational psychologists have long aspired to a "common metric" in the language of work through which work requirements could be compared across jobs. This aspiration led to the development of the DOT (U.S. Dept. Labor 1965a,b). In fact, one of the motivations behind the DOT's replacement, namely O*NET, was the DOT's reliance on occupation-specific tasks that interfered with cross-occupational comparisons. A review of current usages of O*NET (Natl. Res. Counc. 2010, pp. 139–155), however, suggested that many of the psychologically worded items employed in O*NET, especially those intended to capture abilities like "flexibility of closure" in the abilities domain, are understandably eschewed in favor of more user-friendly labels in applications like career planning.

The popularity of competency models that translate these types of worker attribute terms into more accessible ones for end users suggests that traditional taxonomies of worker attributes that employ rather arcane terminology are unlikely to become the language of choice when discussing the content of work, at least among end users (Sanchez & Levine 2009). Understandability is a key determinant of the extent to which such terminology is likely to be adopted in HRM systems (Bowen & Ostroff 2004), and therefore traditional job analytic terminology may have to be revised to rid it of unnecessary jargon. Our recommendation is not to water down job analysis research by replacing traditional terms with pop-psychology ones, but simply to recognize that the acceptability of job analysis by its end users is key in any job analysis application and that such acceptability is better served by user-friendly terminology accessible to those in charge of performing the jobs (Sanchez & Levine 2009).

RESEARCH ON WORK CONTEXT INFORMATION

Interactional psychology has recognized that the situation or context moderates the relationship between dispositions or traits and behavior (Frederiksen 1972, Hattrup & Jackson 1996, Johns 2006, Mischel 1977). Situational strength refers to the characteristics of situations that do or do not restrict the expression of individual differences, particularly those in nonability domains such as personality traits (Meyer et al. 2010, Mullins & Cummings 1999, Weiss & Adler 1984). Although situational strength has been operationalized in ways that recognize the importance of situational constraints (LaFrance et al. 2003), it has not been operationalized in job-analytic terms until recently. Meyer et al. (2009) constructed an O*NET-based measure of situational strength using 14 items from the GWAs and work context domains. They distinguished between two aspects of situational strength: constraints and consequences. Although their meta-analysis of validity coefficients of personality measures showed stronger validity coefficients for occupations that were deemed weak from a situational strength viewpoint, the differences were small.

Meyer et al. (2010) provided a more in-depth analysis of the various occupational elements that may contribute to situational strength and which should be incorporated in future studies.

One of the obstacles to the infusion of an interactional view of context in job analysis is that the traditional view of contextual factors such as physical working conditions, environmental hazards, and the machines, tools, and equipment employed on the job has typically considered them to be a "main effect" type of job demand. That is, context, just like work activities, has been considered a source that calls for certain worker attributes, such as harsh working conditions calling for physical resilience. Drawing an analogy with signal detection theory (Tett & Burnett 2003), job analysis has traditionally viewed context as job demands that, like work activities, determine the "channels" or worker attributes required for job performance. This view of context is not an interactive one at all because it ignores that context is an interactional variable that alters the functional relationships between job demands and behavior (Johns 2006). In the terminology of signal detection theory, an interactional approach suggests that context raises or lowers the "volume" of certain channels; for example, performing certain work activities may call for increased levels of social sensitivity if performed in a certain social context.

Tett & Burnett (2003) propose that context provides trait-relevant cues through three sources (organizational, social, and task) that moderate the relationship between traits and work behavior. They further speculate that job demands, which are presumably derived from the job responsibilities or work activities to be carried out on the job, activate certain traits, but that such activation interacts with context or situation features that distract, constrain, release, or facilitate the expression of those traits or worker attributes. For instance, agreeableness may be activated by job demands involving helping customers, but it may be distracted by groupthink conditions in one's work unit and constrained by a mechanistic atmosphere in the organization (Tett & Burnett 2003). This approach goes beyond the more simplistic worker activity × worker attribute matrix that has been proposed elsewhere (Baranowski & Anderson 2005) because it suggests that such activity-attribute relationships are altered by contextual variables.

Further understanding of these contingencies requires a departure from the manner in which SMEs are usually approached in job analysis research. Indeed, SMEs are typically employed as "observers" of an allegedly external reality dubbed the job, while their subjective experience of such a reality has been largely ignored in a manner that is consistent with the rejection of subjectivity as a valid object of psychological study that has prevailed in industrial and organizational psychology (Weiss & Rupp 2011). A person-centric approach to the analysis of work is needed to better understand how the demands of work as job incumbents experience and interpret them are affected by contextual aspects that may augment or constrain them. In other words, job analysis should delve more deeply into the study of the psychology of the workers' experience and, more specifically, into the contextual aspects that are perceived to modify the extent to which job demands call for certain responses. Qualitative job analysis methods such as the critical incidents technique (Flanagan 1954) may be used to identify these types of contingencies by exploring the relationships between the three basic elements of a critical incident: the situation, the behavior to which it is perceived to have led, and the consequences of such behavior.

Note that when we advocate delving deeper into the manner in which incumbents experience their work, we are not promoting a purely phenomenological approach to job analysis that denies or ignores the objective reality in which job incumbents are embedded; neither do we advocate solipsism or the belief that reality (work experiences in our case) is the creation of one's mind (Connell & Nord 1996). Instead, we are simply arguing for the study of how incumbents perceive and interpret the objective reality of their work because such study does, in our opinion, hold the key to a better understanding of work requirements.

Research from other domains may also provide useful conceptual models to frame these contextual influences. For instance, work stress research has noted that reactions to aspects of the work environment are moderated by secondary appraisals or the extent to which employees perceive to have an adequate repertoire of coping responses (Lazarus & Folkman 1984). In this respect, certain job demands accompanied by contextual factors that are perceived to make them insurmountable would exacerbate the need for certain worker attributes. This approach probably requires new types of job-analytic inquiries from SMEs, such as the extent to which they feel capable of coping with certain job demands under varying sets of contextual conditions. Other examples of interactional models that could be fruitfully borrowed by job analysis researchers exist in the assessment center literature, where trait activation theories have been employed to explain behavioral inconsistencies as a function of situational cues (e.g., Lievens et al. 2006).

One more area that relates to context concerns the research topic of person–work environment fit. That stream of research attempts to assess work environments and their components such as teams, jobs, supervisors, vocations, or organization culture on the one hand and parallel personal attributes on the other (Edwards et al. 2006, Kristof-Brown et al. 2005). The extent of match or mismatch is then related to presumptive outcomes such as job satisfaction or job performance. Although a modicum of success at predicting these outcomes has been demonstrated using measures of match (Kristof-Brown et al. 2005), the methods employed to assess environments and their components and the degree of fit fall outside the realm of conventional job analysis approaches. Indeed, often the most successful predictions are found when respondents report their perceptions of the degree to which they fit with their environment, a method termed molar fit by Edwards et al. (2006). Although this research stream on P-E fit is not considered part

of job analysis, it highlights the need to broaden the notion of work context, which should also incorporate multilevel variables such as shared team cognition, shared climate, and other team and organization-level variables. A better understanding of these cross-level interactions should illuminate mechanisms by which contextual cues modify the demands on workers to employ types and levels of worker attributes (Ployhart & Moliterno 2011).

Conventionally, job analysis assumes that there will be a linear relationship between the attributes and job outcomes—a more-is-better notion. However, an emerging stream of research suggests that contextual factors interact with worker attributes such that there is a nonlinear relationship between certain personality attributes such as openness to experience and certain contextual conditions such as support for creativity (Baer & Oldham 2006, Burke & Witt 2002, George & Zhou 2001, Shalley et al. 2004). Further research is needed on whether these nonlinear relationships may apply to cognitive attributes. For example, the widely used Wonderlic Personnel Test provides min-max normative test scores for a host of jobs such that people scoring above and below the ideal range are predicted to be less successful once hired (e.g., Levine 1997). The potential determination of these types of nonlinear relationships depends to a large extent on future improvements in the measurement of work context at multiple levels of analysis so that the contextual conditions that act as moderators of worker attributes can be reliably pinpointed. Clearly, more research is needed to refine extant taxonomies of work context influences. For instance, in spite of the generally acceptable reliabilities reported in pilot O*NET studies, whether there is conceptual and empirical overlap between the task, physical, and social context variables adopted in O*NET deserves further examination (Strong et al. 1999).

Future research should also acknowledge that work context is a dynamic phenomenon, and therefore there are wide variations in work context within the same job title. Dierdorff & Morgeson (2007) and Dierdorff et al. (2009)

have reported research suggesting that work context induces variations in the manner in which incumbents of the same job experience job demands, especially incumbents of managerial and other loosely defined jobs. This conception is consistent with interactional models of behavior such as the cognitive-affective personality system model proposed by Mischel & Shoda (1995, 1998), in which within-person variability is explained by situation-response contingencies such as, "if this situation, then that response." Mischel & Shoda (1995, 1998) summarized empirical evidence suggesting that individual variability in behavior across situations can be explained by within-job variations in context, which are likely to trigger different job demands throughout the course of discharging one's job responsibilities. Future research may incorporate experience-sampling methodology, which is increasingly being employed to study dynamic organizational phenomena such as momentary performance (Fisher & Noble 2004) and organizational citizenship behavior (Ilies et al. 2006).

CONCLUSIONS AND FUTURE TRENDS

Recent reviews of the job-analytic literature have largely been organized around decisions related to the procedure through which job information should be gathered, thereby emphasizing the various choices among the sources, methods, and level of detail of the data to be gathered (Pearlman & Sanchez 2010; Sackett & Laczo 2003; Sanchez & Levine 1999, 2001). The view of job analysis as an information-gathering process whose sole purpose is to serve as the antecedent of other applications has possibly fed the notion of job analysis as essentially nothing more than a set of methods. As Pearlman & Sanchez (2010) put it, job analysis is "...seldom an end in itself but is almost always a tool in service of some application, a means to an end." The notion of job analysis as an information-gathering tool might have unintentionally created the impression that its sole purpose is to do the dirty work needed for subsequent, truly scientific endeavors such as

selection. Several authors have expressed their discontent with this prevailing perception of job analysis within the discipline of industrial and organizational psychology (Cunningham 1989, Mitchell & Driskill 1996, Morgeson & Dierdorff 2011), which Harvey (1991) synthesized as the "image problem" of job analysis.

The view of job analysis as a support or subservient activity might have deterred interest in cutting-edge research on the job analysis domain. This view might be unintentionally fueled by the stance that jobs consist of solely objective or verifiable behaviors and working conditions and that their analysis is therefore a somewhat cut-and-dry actuarial task. This emphasis on observables implicitly assumes that jobs are epistemologically self-sustaining objects, and it resembles the approach taken in the physical and biological sciences, where an object is studied externally through primarily unobtrusive observation and measurement (Cronshaw 1998). Primoff & Fine (1988) perceptively noted that this objectified approach to job analysis is shortsighted, because job analysts should not forget that unlike (to use the words of Primoff & Fine) flowers and rocks, jobs do not exist separately from the individuals who perform them. In fact, Primoff & Fine observed that the sole process of analyzing the job often changes it, as incumbents are led to reflect on their approach to fulfill their job duties, and this reflection frequently alters the manner in which the job is performed afterward. We maintain that it is the insight into work demands as experienced by incumbents that turns job analysis into a truly psychological endeavor (Sanchez & Levine 1999, p. 72) whose primary goal is precisely to gain an understanding of the psychological requirements of jobs. Fortunately, our review of job analysis research suggests that the job analysis domain has already turned that corner, and accordingly, the scope of job analysis research is being expanded toward a better understanding of work demands as experienced by job incumbents, both individually and collectively through shared perceptions. As such, our hope is that this review will be the first of many to cover job and work analysis in the *Annual Review of Psychology* over time, thereby documenting meaningful advances that may enable optimization of the outcomes produced and enjoyed by people in one of the most critical domains of human activity—their work.

DISCLOSURE STATEMENT

The authors are unaware of any affiliation, funding, or financial holdings that might be perceived as affecting the objectivity of this review.

LITERATURE CITED

Aamodt MG, Kimbrough WW, Keller RJ, Crawford KJ. 1982. Relationship between sex, race, and job performance level and the generation of critical incidents. *Educ. Psychol. Res.* 2:227–34

Aguinis H, Kraiger K. 2009. Benefits of training and development for individuals and teams, organizations, and society. *Annu. Rev. Psychol.* 60:451–74

Aguinis H, Mazurkiewicz MD, Heggestad ED. 2009. Using web-based frame-of-reference training to decrease biases in personality-based job analysis: an experimental field study. *Pers. Psychol.* 62:405–38

Allen CR. 1919. *The Instructor, the Man and the Job.* Philadelphia, PA: Lippincott

Arvey RD, Davis GA, McGowen SL, Dipboye RL. 1982. Potential sources of bias on job analytic processes. *Acad. Manag. J.* 25:618–29

Arvey RD, Passino EM, Lounsbury JW. 1977. Job analysis results as influenced by sex of incumbent and sex of analyst. *J. Appl. Psychol.* 62:411–16

Arvey RD, Salas E, Gialluca KA. 1992. Using task inventories to forecast skills and abilities. *Hum. Perform.* 5:171–90

Baer M, Oldham GR. 2006. The curvilinear relation between experienced creative time pressure and creativity: moderating effects of openness to experience and support for creativity. *J. Appl. Psychol.* 91:963–70

Baranowski LE, Anderson LE. 2005. Examining rating source variation in work behavior to KSA linkages. *Pers. Psychol.* 58:1041–54

Barrick MR, Mount MK. 1991. The Big Five personality dimensions and job performance: a meta-analysis. *Pers. Psychol.* 44:1–26

Bartram D. 2005. The great eight competencies: a criterion-centric approach to validation. *J. Appl. Psychol.* 90:1185–203

Becker BE, Huselid MA, Ulrich D. 2001. *The HR Scorecard: Linking People, Strategy, and Performance.* Boston, MA: Harvard Bus. School Press

Befort N, Hattrup K. 2003. Valuing task and contextual performance: experience, job roles, and ratings of the importance of job behaviors. *Appl. Hum. Resour. Manag. Res.* 8(1):17–32

Biddle BJ. 1986. Recent developments in role theory. *Annu. Rev. Sociol.* 12:67–92

Borman WC, Dorsey D, Ackerman L. 1992. Time-spent responses as time allocation strategies: relations with sales performance in a stockbroker sample. *Pers. Psychol.* 45:763–77

Borman WC, Hanson MA, Hedge JW. 1997. Personnel selection. *Annu. Rev. Psychol.* 48:299–337

Borman WC, Kubisiak UC, Schneider RJ. 1999. Work styles. In *An Occupational Information System for the 21st Century: The Development of O*NET*, ed. NG Peterson, MD Mumford, WC Borman, PR Jeanneret, EA Fleishman, pp. 213–26. Washington, DC: Am. Psychol. Assoc.

Borman WC, Motowidlo SJ. 1993. Expanding the criterion domain to included elements of contextual performance. In *Personnel Selection in Organizations*, ed. N Schmitt, WC Borman, pp. 71–98. San Francisco, CA: Jossey-Bass

Bowen DE, Ostroff C. 2004. Understanding HRM-firm performance linkages: the role of the "strength" of the HRM system. *Acad. Manag. Rev.* 29:203–21

Brannick MT, Levine EL, Morgeson FP. 2007. *Job Analysis: Methods, Research, and Applications for Human Resource Management.* Thousand Oaks, CA: Sage. 2nd ed.

Bretz RD, Milkovich GT, Read W. 1992. Current state of performance appraisal research and practice: concerns, directions, and implications. *J. Manag.* 18:321–52

Burke LA, Witt LA. 2002. Moderators of the openness to experience-performance relationship. *J. Manag. Psychol.* 17:712–21

Butler SK, Harvey RJ. 1988. A comparison of holistic versus decomposed rating of Position Analysis Questionnaire work dimensions. *Pers. Psychol.* 41:761–71

Campion MA, Fink AA, Ruggeberg BJ, Carr L, Phillips GM, Odman RB. 2011. Doing competencies well: best practices in competency modeling. *Pers. Psychol.* 64:225–62

Carroll JM. 1997. Human-computer interaction. Psychology as a science of design. *Annu. Rev. Psychol.* 48:61–83

Cascio WF, Aguinis H. 2008. Research in industrial and organizational psychology from 1963 to 2007. *J. Appl. Psychol.* 93:1062–81

Chatman JA, Cha SE. 2003. Leading by leveraging culture. *Calif. Manag. Rev.* 45:20–34

Christal RE, Weissmuller JJ. 1988. Job-task inventory analysis. In *The Job Analysis Handbook for Business, Industry, and Government*, Vol. II, ed. S Gael, pp. 1036–50. New York: Wiley

Conley PR, Sackett PR. 1987. Effects of using high- versus low-performing job incumbents as sources of job-analysis information. *J. Appl. Psychol.* 72:434–37

Connell AF, Nord WR. 1996. The bloodless coup: the infiltration of organization science by uncertainty and values. *J. Appl. Behav. Sci.* 32:407–27

Cornelius ET, DeNisi AS, Blencoe AG. 1984a. Expert and naïve raters using the PAQ: Does it matter? *Pers. Psychol.* 37:453–64

Cornelius ET, Lyness KS. 1980. A comparison of holistic and decomposed judgment strategies in job analysis by job incumbents. *J. Appl. Psychol.* 65:155–63

Cornelius ET, Schmidt FL, Carron TJ. 1984b. Job classification approaches and the implementation of validity generalization results. *Pers. Psychol.* 37:247–60

Cronshaw SF. 1998. Job analysis: changing nature of work. *Can. Psychol.* 39(1):5–13

Cunningham JW. 1964. *Worker-oriented job variables: their factor structure and use in determining job requirements.* Unpublished doctoral dissertation, Purdue Univ., West Lafayette, IN

Cunningham JW. 1989. Discussion. In *Applied measurement issues in job analysis*, ed. RJ Harvey (Chair). Symposium presented at annu. meet. Am. Psychol. Assoc., New Orleans, LA

Cunningham JW. 1996. Generic job descriptors: a likely direction in occupational analysis. *Mil. Psychol.* 8(3):247–62

Cunningham JW, Ballentine RD. 1982. *The General Work Inventory.* Raleigh, NC: Authors

Dierdorff EC, Morgeson FP. 2007. Consensus in work role requirements: the influence of discrete occupational context on role expectations. *J. Appl. Psychol.* 92:1228–41

Dierdorff EC, Morgeson FP. 2009. Effects of descriptor specificity and observability on incumbent work analysis ratings. *Pers. Psychol.* 62:601–28

Dierdorff EC, Rubin RS. 2007. Carelessness and discriminability in work role requirement judgments: influences of role ambiguity and cognitive complexity. *Pers. Psychol.* 60:597–625

Dierdorff EC, Rubin RS, Bachrach DG. 2010. Role expectations as antecedents of citizenship and the moderating effect of work context. *J. Manag.* doi: 10.1177/0149206309359199. In press

Dierdorff EC, Rubin RS, Morgeson FP. 2009. The milieu of managerial work: an integrative framework linking work context to role requirements. *J. Appl. Psychol.* 94:972–88

Dierdorff EC, Wilson MA. 2003. A meta-analysis of job analysis reliability. *J. Appl. Psychol.* 88:635–46

Donsbach J, Tsacoumis S, Sager C, Updegraff J. 2003. *O*NET Analyst Occupational Abilities Ratings: Procedures.* Raleigh, NC: Natl. Cent. O*NET Dev. **http://www.onetcenter.org/reports/AnalystProc.html**

Drucker PF. 1987. Workers' hands bound by tradition. *Wall Street J.* Aug. 2, p. 18

Edwards J, Cable D, Williamson I, Lambert L, Shipp A. 2006. The phenomenology of fit: linking the person and environment to the subjective experience of person-environment fit. *J. Appl. Psychol.* 91:802–27

England P, Dunn D. 1988. Evaluating work and comparable worth. *Annu. Rev. Sociol.* 14:227–48

Equal Employ. Opportun. Commiss., Civil Serv. Commiss., Dep. Labor, Dep. Justice. 1978. Uniform Guidelines on Employee Selection Procedures. *Fed. Regist.* 43(166):38295–309

Fine SA, Cronshaw SF. 1999. *Functional Job Analysis. A Foundation for Human Resource Management.* Mahwah, NJ: Erlbaum

Fisher CD, Noble CS. 2004. A within-person examination of correlates of performance and emotions while working. *Hum. Perform.* 17:145–68

Flanagan JC. 1954. The critical incident technique. *Psychol. Bull.* 51:327–58

Fleishman EA, Costanza DP, Marshall-Mies J. 1999. Abilities. In *An Occupational Information System for the 21st Century: The Development of O*NET*, ed. NG Peterson, MD Mumford, WC Borman, PR Jeanneret, EA Fleishman. Washington, DC: Am. Psychol. Assoc.

Fleishman EA, Gebhardt DL, Hogan JC. 1986. The perception of physical effort in job tasks. In *The Perception of Exertion in Physical Work*, ed. G Borg, D Ottoson, pp. 225–42. Stockholm, Sweden: Macmillan

Fleishman EA, Quaintance MK. 1984. *Taxonomies of Human Performance*. Orlando, FL: Academic

Fleishman EA, Reilly ME. 1992. *Handbook of Human Abilities. Definitions, Measurements, and Job Task Requirements*. Palo Alto, CA: Consult. Psychol. Press

Ford JK, Smith EM, Sego DJ, Quinones MA. 1991. Impact of task experience and individual factors on training-emphasis ratings. *J. Appl. Psychol.* 78:583–90

Frederiksen N. 1972. Toward a taxonomy of situations. *Am. Psychol.* 27:114–23

Friedman L. 1990. Degree of redundancy between time, importance, and frequency task ratings. *J. Appl. Psychol.* 75:748–52

Friedman L. 1991. Correction to Friedman 1990. *J. Appl. Psychol.* 76:366

Friedman L, Harvey RJ. 1986. Can raters with reduced job descriptive information provide accurate position analysis questionnaire (PAQ) ratings? *Pers. Psychol.* 39:779–89

Gael S. 1983. *Job Analysis: A Guide to Assessing Work Activities*. San Francisco, CA: Jossey-Bass

Gael S, Cornelius ET III, Levine EL, Salvendy G, eds. 1988. *The Job Analysis Handbook for Business, Industry, and Government*. New York: Wiley

Gatewood RD, Field HS, Barrick M. 2008. *Human Resource Selection*. Mason, OH: Thomson/South-Western. 6th ed.

George JM, Zhou J. 2001. When openness to experience and conscientiousness are related to creative behavior: an interactional approach. *J. Appl. Psychol.* 86:513–24

Gibson SG, Harvey RJ, Quintela Y. 2004. *Holistic versus decomposed ratings of general dimensions of work activity*. Presented at Annu. Conf. Soc. Ind. Organ. Psychol., Chicago, IL

Goiffin RD, Woycheshin DE. 2006. An empirical method of determining employee competencies/KSAOs from task-based job analysis. *Mil. Psychol.* 18:121–30

Goldstein IL, Zedeck S, Schneider B. 1993. An exploration of the job analysis-content validity process. In *Personnel Selection in Organizations*, ed. N Schmitt, WC Borman, pp. 3–34. San Francisco, CA: Jossey-Bass

Grant AM. 2007. Relational job design and the motivation to make a prosocial difference. *Acad. Manag. Rev.* 32:393–417

Green SB, Stutzman T. 1986. An evaluation of methods to select respondents to structured job-analysis questionnaires. *Pers. Psychol.* 39:543–64

Green SB, Veres JG. 1990. Evaluation of an index to detect inaccurate respondents to a task analysis inventory. *J. Bus. Psychol.* 5:47–61

Guion RM, Highhouse S. 2006. *Essentials of Personnel Assessment and Selection*. Mahwah, NJ: Erlbaum

Harvey RJ. 1991. Job analysis. In *Handbook of Industrial and Organizational Psychology*, ed. MD Dunnette, LM Hough, vol. 2, pp. 71–163. Palo Alto, CA: Consult. Psychol. Press. 2nd ed.

Harvey RJ. 2009. *The O*NET: Do too-abstract titles +unverifiable holistic ratings + questionable raters + low agreement +inadequate sampling + aggregation bias = (a) validity, (b) reliability, (c) utility, or (d) none of the above?* Paper provided to Panel to Rev. Occupat. Inform. Netw. (O*NET). **http://www7.nationalacademies. org/cfe/O_NET_RJHarvey_Paper1.pdf**

Harvey RJ. 2011. *Deriving Synthetic Validity Models: Is R = 0.80 Large Enough?* Presented at Annu. Conf. Soc. Ind. Organ. Psychol., Chicago, IL

Harvey RJ, Lozada-Larsen SR. 1988. Influence of amount of job descriptive information on job analysis rating accuracy. *J. Appl. Psychol.* 73:457–61

Harvey RJ, Wilson MA. 2000. Yes Virginia, there *is* an objective reality in job analysis. *J. Organ. Behav.* 21:829–54

Harvey RJ, Wilson MA. 2010. *Discriminant validity concerns with the O*NET holistic rating scales*. Presented at Annu. Conv. Soc. Ind. Org. Psychol., Atlanta

Harvey RJ, Wilson MA, Blunt JH. 1994. *A comparison of rational/holistic versus empirical/decomposed methods of identifying and rating general work behaviors*. Presented at Ann. Conf. Soc. Ind. Org. Psychol., Nashville

Hattrup K, Jackson SE. 1996. Learning about individual differences by taking situations seriously. In *Individual Differences and Behavior in Organizations*, ed. KR Murphy, pp. 507–47. San Francisco, CA: Jossey-Bass

Hazel JT, Madden JM, Christal EE. 1964. Agreement between worker-supervisor descriptions of the worker's job. *J. Ind. Psychol.* 2:71–79

Heneman HG, Judge TA. 2009. *Staffing Organizations*. Boston, MA: Irwin/McGraw Hill. 6th ed.

Hogarth RM. 1981. Beyond discrete biases: functional and dysfunctional aspects of judgmental heuristics. *Psychol. Bull.* 90:197–217

Hough LM, Oswald FL. 2000. Personnel selection: looking toward the future—remembering the past. *Annu. Rev. Psychol.* 51:631–64

Hubbard M, McCloy R, Campbell J, Nottingham J, Lewis P, et al. 2000. *Revision of O*NET Data Collection Procedures*. Raleigh, NC: Natl. Cent. O*NET Dev. **http://www.onetcenter.org/reports/Data_appnd.html**

Hough LM. 1992. The "Big Five" personality variables—construct confusion: description versus prediction. *Hum. Perform.* 5:139–55

Ilgen DR, Hollenbeck JR. 1991. The structure of work: job design and roles. In *Handbook of Industrial and Organizational Psychology*, ed. MD Dunnette, LM Hough, vol. 2, pp. 165–207. Palo Alto, CA: Consult. Psychol. Press. 2nd ed.

Ilies R, Scott BA, Judge TA. 2006. A multilevel analysis of the effects of positive personal traits, positive experienced states and their interactions on intraindividual patterns of citizenship behavior at work. *Acad. Manag. J.* 49:561–75

Jeanneret PR, Borman WC, Kubisiak UC, Hanson MA. 1999. Generalized work activities. In *An Occupational Information System for the 21st Century: The Development of O*NET*, ed. NG Peterson, MD Mumford, WC Borman, PR Jeanneret, EA Fleishman, pp. 105–25. Washington, DC: Am. Psychol. Assoc.

Jeanneret PR, Strong MH. 2003. Linking O*NET job analysis information to job require predictors: an O*NET application. *Pers. Psychol.* 56:465–92

Johns G. 2006. The essential impact of context on organizational behavior. *Acad. Manag. Rev.* 31:386–408

Jones RG, Sanchez JI, Parameswaran G, Phelps J, Shoptaugh C, et al. 2001. Selection or training? A two-fold test of the validity of job-analytic ratings of trainability. *J. Bus. Psychol.* 15:363–89

Kristof-Brown A, Zimmerman R, Johnson E. 2005. Consequences of individuals' fit at work: a meta-analysis of person-job, person-organization, person-group, and person-supervisor fit. *Pers. Psychol.* 58:281–342

Kruglanski AW. 1989. The psychology of being "right": the problem of accuracy in social perception and cognition. *Psychol. Bull.* 106:395–409

LaFrance M, Hecht MA, Paluck EL. 2003. The contingent smile: a meta-analysis of sex differences in smiling. *Psychol. Bull.* 129:305–34

Lamiell JT. 2000. A periodic table of personality elements? The "Big Five" and trait "psychology" in critical perspective. *J. Theor. Philos. Psychol.* 20:1–24

Landy FJ. 1988. Selection procedure development and usage. In *The Job Analysis Handbook for Business, Industry, and Government*, vol. I, ed. S Gael, pp. 271–87. New York: Wiley

Landy FJ, Shankster LJ, Kohler SS. 1994. Personnel selection and placement. *Annu. Rev. Psychol.* 45:261–92

Landy FJ, Vasey J. 1991. Job analysis: the composition of SME samples. *Pers. Psychol.* 44:27–50

LaPolice CC, Carter GW, Johnson JJ. 2008. Linking O*NET descriptors to occupational literacy requirements using job component validation. *Pers. Psychol.* 61:405–41

Lazarus RS, Folkman S. 1984. *Stress, Appraisal, and Coping*. New York: Springer

Le H, Oh I, Shaffer J, Schmidt F. 2007. Implications of methodological advances for the practice of personnel selection: how practitioners benefit from meta-analysis. *Acad. Manag. Perspect.* 21:6–15

Levine EL. 1983. *Everything You Always Wanted to Know About Job Analysis*. Tampa, FL: Mariner

Levine EL. 1997. Review of the Wonderlic Personnel Test (WPT). *Secur. J.* 8:179–81

Levine EL, Ash RA, Bennett N. 1980. Exploratory comparative study of four job analysis methods. *J. Appl. Psychol.* 65:524–35

Levine EL, Sanchez JI. 2007. Evaluating work analysis in the 21st century. *Ergometrika* 4:1–11

Lievens F, Chasteen CS, Day EA, Christiansen ND. 2006. Large-scale investigation of the role of trait activation theory for understanding assessment center convergent and discriminant validity. *J. Appl. Psychol.* 91:247–58

Lievens F, Sanchez JI. 2007. Can training improve the quality of inferences made by raters in competency modeling? A quasi-experiment. *J. Appl. Psychol.* 92:812–19

Lievens F, Sanchez JI, Bartram D, Brown A. 2010. Lack of consensus among competency ratings of the same occupation: noise or substance? *J. Appl. Psychol.* 95:562–71

Lievens F, Sanchez JI, De Corte W. 2004. Easing the inferential leap in competency modeling: the effects of task-related information and subject matter expertise. *Pers. Psychol.* 57:881–904

Lindell MK, Clause CS, Brandt CJ, Landis RS. 1998. Relationship between organizational context and job analysis task ratings. *J. Appl. Psychol.* 83:769–76

Lucia A, Lepsinger R. 1999. *The Art and Science of Competency Models: Pinpointing Critical Success Factors in Organizations.* San Francisco, CA: Jossey-Bass

Lyons P. 2008. The crafting of jobs and individual differences. *J. Bus. Psychol.* 23:25–36

Manson TM. 2004. *Cursory Versus Comprehensive Job Analysis for Personnel Selection: A Consequential Validity Analysis.* Unpublished doctoral dissertation, Univ. S. Florida, Tampa

Manson TM, Levine EL, Brannick MT. 2000. The construct validity of task inventory ratings: a multitrait-multimethod analysis. *Hum. Perform.* 13:1–22

Mathieu J, Maynard MT, Rapp T, Gilson L. 2008. Team effectiveness 1997–2007: a review of recent advancements and a glimpse into the future. *J. Manag.* 34:410–76

McCormick EJ. 1960. Effect of amount of job information required on reliability of incumbents' check-list reports. *USAF Wright Air Dev. Div. Tech. Note* 60–142

McCormick EJ. 1976. Job and task analysis. In *Handbook of Industrial and Organizational Psychology*, ed. MD Dunnette, pp. 651–96. Chicago, IL: Rand McNally

McCormick EJ, Jeanneret PR, Mecham RC. 1972. A study of job characteristics and job dimensions as based on the position analysis questionnaire (PAQ). *J. Appl. Psychol.* 56:347–68

Meyer HH. 1959. A comparison of foreman and general foreman conceptions of the foreman's job responsibilities. *Pers. Psychol.* 12:445–52

Meyer RD, Dalal RS, Bonaccio S. 2009. A meta-analytic investigation into the moderating effects of situational strength on the conscientiousness-performance relationship. *J. Organ. Behav.* 30:1077–102

Meyer RD, Dalal RS, Hermida R. 2010. A review and synthesis of situational strength in the organizational sciences. *J. Manag.* 36:121–40

Mischel W. 1977. The interaction of person and situation. In *Personality at the Crossroads: Current Issues in Interactional Psychology*, ed. D Magnusson, NS Endler, pp. 333–52. Hillsdale, NJ: Erlbaum

Mischel W, Shoda Y. 1995. A cognitive–affective system theory of personality: reconceptualizing situations, dispositions, dynamics, and invariance in personality structure. *Psychol. Rev.* 102:246–68

Mischel W, Shoda Y. 1998. Reconciling processing dynamics and personality dispositions. *Annu. Rev. Psychol.* 49:229–58

Mitchell JL, Driskill WE. 1996. Military job analysis: a historical perspective. *Mil. Psychol.* 8:119–42

Morgeson FP, Campion MA. 1997. Social and cognitive sources of potential inaccuracy in job analysis. *J. Appl. Psychol.* 82:627–55

Morgeson FP, Delaney-Klinger K, Mayfield MS, Ferrara P, Campion MA. 2004. Self-presentation processes in job analysis: a field experiment investigating inflation in abilities, tasks, and competencies. *J. Appl. Psychol.* 89:674–86

Morgeson FP, Dierdorff EC. 2011. Work analysis: from technique to theory. In *APA Handbook of Industrial and Organizational Psychology*, ed. S Zedeck, vol. 2, pp. 3–41. Washington, DC: Am. Psychol. Assoc.

Morrison EW. 1994. Role definitions and organizational citizenship behavior: the importance of the employee's perspective. *Acad. Manag. J.* 37:1543–67

Mullins JM, Cummings LL. 1999. Situational strength: a framework for understanding the role of individuals in initiating proactive strategic change. *J. Organ. Change Manag.* 12:462–79

Münsterberg H. 1913. *Psychology and Industrial Efficiency.* Boston, MA: Houghton Mifflin

Natl. Res. Counc. 2010. A database for a changing economy: review of the Occupational Information Network (O*NET). Panel to Review the Occupational Information Network (O*NET). In *Committee on National Statistics, Division of Behavioral and Social Sciences and Education*, ed. NT Tippins, ML Hilton. Washington, DC: Natl. Acad. Press

Occup. Inform. Advis. Panel. 2009. *Content Model and Classification Recommendations for the Social Security Administration Occupational Information System.* **http://www.ssa.gov/oidap/Documents/FinalReportRecommendations.pdf**

Olian JD, Rynes SL. 1991. Making total quality work: aligning organizational processes, performance measures, and stakeholders. *Hum. Resour. Manag.* 30:303–33

O'Reily C, Chatman J. 1996. Cultures as social control: corporations, cults, and commitment. In *Research in Organizational Behavior*, vol. 18, ed. L Cummings, B Staw, pp. 157–200. Greenwich, CT: JAI

Otis J. 2009. *Bits and Pieces of My Life.* Bowling Green, OH: Soc. Industr. Organ. Psychol. **http://www.siop.org/presidents/otis.aspx**

Parker SK. 2007. "That is my job": How employees' role orientation affects their job performance. *Hum. Relat.* 60:403–34

Parsons F. 1909. *Choosing a Vocation.* Boston, MA: Houghton Mifflin.

Pearlman K, Sanchez JI. 2010. Work analysis. In *Handbook of Employee Selection*, ed. JL Farr, NT Tippins, pp. 73–98. New York: Routledge

Pearlman K, Schmidt FL, Hunter JE. 1980. Validity generalization results for tests used to predict job proficiency and training success in clerical occupations. *J. Appl. Psychol.* 65:373–406

Peterson NG, Mumford MD, Borman WC, Jeanneret PR, Fleishman EA. 1999. *An Occupational Information System for the 21st Century: The Development of O*NET.* Washington, DC: Am. Psychol. Assoc.

Pine DE. 1995. Assessing the validity of job ratings: an empirical study of false reporting in task inventories. *Public Pers. Manag.* 24:451–59

Ployhart RE, Moliterno TP. 2011. Emergence of the human capital resource: a multilevel model. *Acad. Manag. Rev.* 36:127–50

Ployhart RE, Schneider B, Schmitt N. 2006. *Staffing Organizations: Contemporary Theory and Practice.* Mahwah, NJ: Erlbaum

Prien KO, Prien EP, Wooten W. 2003. Interrater reliability in job analysis: differences in strategy and perspective. *Public Pers. Manag.* 32:125–41

Primoff ES. 1975. How to prepare and conduct job-element examinations. *U.S. Civil Serv. Commiss. Tech. Study 75-1.* Washington, DC: U.S. Gov. Printing Off.

Primoff ES, Fine SA. 1988. A history of job analysis. In *The Job Analysis Handbook for Business, Industry, and Government*, vol. I, ed. S Gael, pp. 14–29. New York: Wiley

Proctor RW, Vu KL. 2010. Cumulative knowledge and progress in human factors. *Annu. Rev. Psychol.* 61:623–51

Raymark PH, Schmit MJ, Guion RM. 1997. Identifying potentially useful personality constructs for employee selection. *Pers. Psychol.* 50:723–36

Roberts LM, Dutton JE, Spreitzer GM, Heaphy ED, Quinn RE. 2005. Composing the reflected best-self portrait: building pathways for becoming extraordinary in work organizations. *Acad. Manag. Rev.* 30:712–36

Rosso BD, Dekas KH, Wrzesniewski A. 2010. On the meaning of work: a theoretical integration and review. *Res. Organ. Behav.* 30:91–127

Sackett PR, Cornelius ET, Carron ET. 1981. A comparison of global judgment versus task-oriented approaches to job classification. *Pers. Psychol.* 34:791–804

Sackett PR, Laczo RM. 2003. Job and work analysis. In *Comprehensive Handbook of Psychology: Industrial and Organizational Psychology*, vol. 12, ed. WC Borman, DR Ilgen, RJ Klimoski, pp. 21–37. New York: Wiley

Sackett PR, Lievens F. 2008. Personnel selection. *Annu. Rev. Psychol.* 59:419–50

Salgado JF. 1997. The five-factor model of personality and job performance in the European Community. *J. Appl. Psychol.* 82:30–43

Salgado JF, Anderson NR, Hülsheger UR. 2010. Employee selection in Europe: psychotechnics and the forgotten history of modern scientific employee selection. In *Handbook of Employee Selection*, ed. JL Farr, NT Tippins, pp. 921–42. New York: Routledge

Sanchez JI. 1990. *The effects of job experience on judgments of task importance.* Presented at Annu. Conf. Soc. Ind. Organ. Psychol., Miami, FL

Sanchez JI. 1994. From documentation to innovation: reshaping job analysis to meet emerging business needs. *Hum. Resour. Manag. Rev.* 4:51–74

Sanchez JI. 2000. Adapting work analysis to a fast-paced and electronic business world. *Int. J. Sel. Assess.* 8:204–12

Sanchez JI, Autor DH. 2010. Dissent. In *A Database for a Changing Economy: Review of the Occupational Information Network (O*NET)*, ed. NT Tippins, ML Hilton, pp. 195–97. Washington, DC: Natl. Acad. Press

Sanchez JI, Fraser SL. 1992. On the choice of scales for task analysis. *J. Appl. Psychol.* 77:545–53

Sanchez JI, Fraser SL. 1994. An empirical procedure to identify job duty-skill linkages in managerial jobs: a case example. *J. Bus. Psychol.* 8:309–26

Sanchez JI, Levine EL. 1989. Determining important tasks within jobs: a policy-capturing approach. *J. Appl. Psychol.* 74:336–42

Sanchez JI, Levine EL. 1994. The impact of raters' cognition on judgment accuracy: an extension to the job analysis domain. *J. Bus. Psychol.* 9:47–58

Sanchez JI, Levine EL. 1999. Is job analysis dead, misunderstood, or both? New forms of work analysis and design. In *Evolving Practices in Human Resource Management*, ed. A Kraut, A Korman, pp. 43–68. San Francisco, CA: Jossey-Bass

Sanchez JI, Prager I, Wilson A, Viswesvaran C. 1998. Understanding within-job title variance in job-analytic ratings. *J. Bus. Psychol.* 12:407–20

Sanchez JI, Levine EL. 2000. Accuracy or consequential validity: Which is the better standard for job analysis data? *J. Organ. Behav.* 21:809–18

Sanchez JI, Levine EL. 2001. The analysis of work in the 20th and 21st centuries. In *Handbook of Industrial, Work and Organizational Psychology*, ed. N Anderson, DS Ones, HK Sinangil, C Viswesvaran, vol. 1, pp. 71–89. Thousand Oaks, CA: Sage

Sanchez JI, Levine EL. 2009. What is (or should be) the difference between competency modeling and traditional job analysis? *Hum. Resour. Manag. Rev.* 19:53–63

Schippmann JS. 1999. *Strategic Job Modeling: Working at the Core of Integrated Human Resources*. Mahwah, NJ: Erlbaum

Schippmann JS, Ash RA, Battista M, Carr L, Eyde LD, et al. 2000. The practice of competency modeling. *Pers. Psychol.* 53:703–40

Schmidt FL, Hunter JE, Pearlman K. 1981. Task differences as moderators of aptitude test validity in selection: a red herring. *J. Appl. Psychol.* 66:166–85

Schmitt N, Cohen SA. 1989. Internal analyses of task ratings by job incumbents. *J. Appl. Psychol.* 74:96–104

Schneider B, Konz AM. 1989. Strategic job analysis. *Hum. Resour. Manag.* 28:51–63

Schraagen JM, Chipman SF, Shalin VL, eds. 2000. *Cognitive Task Analysis*. Mahwah, NJ: Erlbaum

Shalley CE, Zhou J, Oldham GR. 2004. The effects of personal and contextual characteristics on creativity: Where should we go from here? *J. Manag.* 30:933–58

Shartle C. 1959. *Occupational Information: Its Developments and Application*. Englewood Cliffs, NJ: Prentice-Hall

Siddique CM. 2004. Job analysis: a strategic human resource management practice. *Int. J. Hum. Resour. Manag.* 15:219–44

Silverman SB, Wexley KN, Johnson JC. 1984. The effects of age and job experience on employee responses to a structured job analysis questionnaire. *Public Pers. Manag.* 13:355–59

Singh P. 2008. Job analysis for a changing workplace. *Hum. Resour. Manag. Rev.* 18:87–99

Smith J, Hakel MD. 1979. Convergence among data sources, response bias, and reliability and validity of a structured job analysis questionnaire. *Pers. Psychol.* 32:677–92

Spencer LM, McLelland DC, Spencer S. 1994. *Competency Assessment Methods: History and State of the Art*. Boston, MA: Hay-McBer

Stern W. 1911. *Die Differentielle Psychologie in ihren methodischen Grundlagen*. Leipzig: Barth

Stern W. 1934. Otto Lipmann: 1880–1933. *Am. J. Psychol.* 46:152–54

Strong MH, Jeanneret PR, McPhail SM, Blakley BR, D'Egidio EL. 1999. Work context: taxonomy and measurement of the work environment. In *An Occupational Information System for the 21st Century: The Development of O*NET*, ed. NG Peterson, MD Mumford, WC Borman, PR Jeanneret, EA Fleishman, pp. 127–45. Washington, DC: Am. Psychol. Assoc.

Stutzman TM. 1983. Within classification job differences. *Pers. Psychol.* 36:503–16

Taylor EK, Nevis EC. 1961. Personnel selection. *Annu. Rev. Psychol.* 12:389–412

Tesluk PE, Jacobs RR. 1998. Toward an integrated model of work experience. *Pers. Psychol.* 51:321–55

Tett RP, Burnett DD. 2003. A personality trait-based interactionist model of job performance. *J. Appl. Psychol.* 88:500–17

Tett RP, Guterman HA, Bleier A, Murphy PJ. 2000. Development and content validation of a "hyperdimensional" taxonomy of managerial competence. *Hum. Perform.* 13:205–51

Tett RP, Jackson DN, Rothstein M. 1991. Personality measures as predictors of job performance: a meta-analytic review. *Pers. Psychol.* 44:703–42

Tross SA, Maurer TJ. 2000. The relationship between SME job experience and job analysis ratings: findings with and without statistical control. *J. Bus. Psychol.* 15:97–110

Tsacoumis S. 2009a. *O*NET analyst ratings.* Presented to NRC Panel to Rev. Occup. Inform. Netw. **http://www7.nationalacademies.org/cfe/O_NET_Suzanne_Tsacoumis_Presentation.pdf**

Tsacoumis S. 2009b. *Responses to Harvey's criticisms of HumRRO's analysis of the O*NET analysts' ratings.* Paper provided to Panel to Rev. Occup. Inform. Netw (O*NET). **http://www7.nationalacademies.org/cfe/Response%20to%2oRJ%20Harvey%20Criticism.pdf**

Tsacoumis S, Van Iddekinge C. 2006. *A Comparison of Incumbent and Analyst Ratings of O*NET Skills.* **http://www.onetcenter.org/reports/SkillsComp.html**

Tversky A, Kahneman D. 1974. Judgment under uncertainty: heuristics and biases. *Science* 185:1124–31

Tziner A, Joanis C, Murphy KR. 2000. A comparison of three methods of performance appraisal with regard to goal properties, goal perception, and ratee satisfaction. *Group Organ. Manag.* 25:175–90

U.S. Bur. Census Stat. 1918. Monthly review of the U.S. Bureau Census Statistics. 6(4):131–33

U.S. Dep. Justice. 1991. *The Americans with Disabilities Act. Questions and Answers.* Washington, DC: U.S. Dep. Justice, Civil Rights Div.

U.S. Dep. Labor. 1965a. *Dictionary of Occupational Titles, Volume 1.* Washington, DC: U.S. Gov. Print. Off. 3rd ed.

U.S. Dep. Labor. 1965b. *Dictionary of Occupational Titles, Volume 2.* Washington, DC: U.S. Gov. Print. Off. 3rd ed.

Van Iddekinge CH, Putka DJ, Raymark PH, Eidson CE. 2005. Modeling error variance in job specification ratings: the influence of rater, job, and organization-level factors. *J. Appl. Psychol.* 90:323–34

Van Iddekinge CH, Raymark PH, Edison CE. 2011. An examination of the validity and incremental value of needed-at-entry ratings for a customer service job. *Appl. Psychol. Int. Rev.* 60:24–45

Viteles MS. 1923. Psychology in business—in England, France, and Germany. *Ann. Am. Acad. Pol. Soc. Sci.* 110:207–20

Voskuijl OF, van Sliedregt T. 2002. Determinants of interrater reliability of job analysis: a meta-analysis. *Eur. J. Psychol. Assess.* 18:52–62

Walmsley P, Natali M, Campbell JP. 2011. *Only incumbent ratings in O*NET? Yes! Oh no!* Presented at Annu. Conf. Soc. Ind. Organ. Psychol., Chicago, IL

Weiss HM, Adler S. 1984. Personality and organizational behavior. *Res. Organ. Behav.* 6:1–50

Weiss HM, Rupp DE. 2011. Experiencing work: an essay on a person-centric work psychology. *Ind. Organ. Psychol. Perspect. Sci. Pract.* 4:83–97

Werbel JD, DeMarie SM. 2005. Aligning strategic human resource management and person–environment fit. *Hum. Resour. Manag. Rev.* 15:247–62

Wexley KN, Silverman SB. 1978. An examination of differences between managerial effectiveness and response patterns on a structured job analysis questionnaire. *J. Appl. Psychol.* 63:646–49

Willis G. 2005. *Cognitive Interviewing: A Tool for Improving Questionnaire Design.* Newbury Park, CA: Sage

Wilson MA. 1997. The validity of task coverage ratings by incumbents and supervisors. *J. Bus. Psychol.* 12:85–95

Wilson MA. 2007. A history of job analysis. In *Historical Perspectives in Industrial and Organizational Psychology,* ed. L Koppes, pp. 219–41. Mahwah, NJ: Erlbaum

Wilson MA, Harvey RJ, Macy BA. 1990. Repeating items to estimate the test-retest reliability of task inventory ratings. *J. Appl. Psychol.* 75:158–63

Wrzesniewski A, Dutton JE. 2001. Crafting a job: revisioning employees as active crafters of their work. *Acad. Manag. Rev.* 26:179–201

Rapid Automatized Naming (RAN) and Reading Fluency: Implications for Understanding and Treatment of Reading Disabilities

Elizabeth S. Norton and Maryanne Wolf

Center for Reading and Language Research, Eliot-Pearson Department of Child Development, Tufts University, Medford, Massachusetts 02155;
email: elizabeth.norton@tufts.edu, maryanne.wolf@tufts.edu

Annu. Rev. Psychol. 2012. 63:427–52

First published online as a Review in Advance on August 11, 2011

The *Annual Review of Psychology* is online at psych.annualreviews.org

This article's doi: 10.1146/annurev-psych-120710-100431

Keywords

dyslexia, neuroimaging, multicomponent view of reading

Abstract

Fluent reading depends on a complex set of cognitive processes that must work together in perfect concert. Rapid automatized naming (RAN) tasks provide insight into this system, acting as a microcosm of the processes involved in reading. In this review, we examine both RAN and reading fluency and how each has shaped our understanding of reading disabilities. We explore the research that led to our current understanding of the relationships between RAN and reading and what makes RAN unique as a cognitive measure. We explore how the automaticity that supports RAN affects reading across development, reading abilities, and languages, and the biological bases of these processes. Finally, we bring these converging areas of knowledge together by examining what the collective studies of RAN and reading fluency contribute to our goals of creating optimal assessments and interventions that help every child become a fluent, comprehending reader.

Contents

INTRODUCTION AND OVERVIEW

Reading has been compared to rocket science and to conducting a symphony, yet we expect children to have mastered this deeply sophisticated set of skills by the age of seven. Literacy has become so deep-rooted in our culture that we often take for granted the complex cognitive abilities that are required to read effortlessly in so many contexts, from sharing a Dr. Seuss story with a child to enjoying a favorite novel via an e-reader on a busy train. Perhaps the most remarkable thing about reading is that children develop reading skills seemingly in spite of nature. Reading began so recently in the evolutionary history of our species that we have no innate biological processes devoted specifically to reading.

Rather, children are born with a rich neural architecture in place to support the acquisition of oral language, which provides the pre-eminent platform for written language. Certain brain areas are activated in response to the sounds and structure of language from infancy (Minagawa-Kawai et al. 2011, Peña et al. 2003). In sharp contrast, each child must develop reading skills using brain areas that have evolved for other purposes, such as language, vision, and attention (see Dehaene 2009). Psychologist Steven Pinker (1997) famously noted that children are born "wired" for language, "but print is an optional accessory that must be painstakingly bolted on." Indeed, to be a successful reader, one must rapidly integrate a vast circuit of brain areas with both great accuracy and remarkable speed. This "reading circuit" is composed of neural systems that support every level of language—phonology, morphology, syntax, and semantics—as well as visual and orthographic processes, working memory, attention, motor movements, and higher-level comprehension and cognition. As our reading abilities develop, each of these components works smoothly with both accuracy and speed; the reader develops what is called automaticity. As a cognitive process becomes automatic, it demands less conscious effort. Although at first the child experiences a laborious and slow process to decode a simple word or sentence, most adult readers can't help but instantaneously, effortlessly read almost any word they perceive. The development of automaticity at all the lower levels of reading represents the great apex of development that provides us with the bridge to true reading with its capacity to direct cognitive resources to the deepest levels of thought and comprehension.

When a child begins learning to read, many assume that to accurately decode each word of a simple story aloud represents reading. In reality, simply to translate printed words into a stream of speech is but the beginning step, however necessary, of reading. Indeed, even the initial comprehension that comes next is but a second necessary step. Essentially, one must be able to comprehend the meaning of a text in order to go beyond what is on the page: making connections to existing knowledge, analyzing the writer's argument, and predicting the next twist in the story. It is here that the way we define successful reading is important. The

term "fluency" has been used to describe the speed and quality of oral reading, often emphasizing prosody, yet this definition does not encompass all the goals of reading or reflect the fact that most of our reading is done silently rather than aloud. We conceptualize fluency in a more comprehensive way. In this review, we examine reading fluency in the sense of what has been called "fluent comprehension": a manner of reading in which all sublexical units, words, and connected text and all the perceptual, linguistic, and cognitive processes involved in each level are processed accurately and automatically so that sufficient time and resources can be allocated to comprehension and deeper thought (Wolf & Katzir-Cohen 2001).

This is a figure-ground shift from conceptualizing fluency based largely on rapid word identification. How did we arrive at this more encompassing conceptualization of fluency, and why is it important that educators and researchers view reading in this way? This multicomponential view of reading is based largely on our understanding of the reading circuit in the brain. Additional research from many sources, including longitudinal, intervention, and cross-linguistic studies, supports this multicomponential model of reading. However, many current approaches to reading instruction, as well as methods for identifying children who are having reading difficulties or for providing intervention struggling readers, do not reflect this more comprehensive view. If our goal is to have children develop fluent comprehension, then our instruction, assessment, and intervention must reflect these ideas.

A closely related aspect of our study that has contributed greatly, albeit unexpectedly, to our understanding of reading fluency involves what is called rapid automatized naming, or RAN (Denckla & Rudel 1976b). The seemingly simple task of naming a series of familiar items as quickly as possible appears to invoke a microcosm of the later developing, more elaborated reading circuit. Our ability to understand the multicomponential structure of RAN, therefore, has helped us to reconceptualize the later development of reading fluency, not as the simple consequence of accurate word recognition processes, but as an equally complex circuitry of multiple components, all of which contribute to the overall reading fluency and comprehension of text.

To be sure, the precise relationship between RAN and reading continues to elude researchers, many of whom have sought to study and single out individual components of RAN, such as visual or phonological processes. We have taken a different view, in which RAN is conceptualized as a microcosm or mini-circuit of the later-developing reading circuitry. There is an extensive body of research (described in this review) that leads us and other researchers to consider RAN tasks as one of the best, perhaps universal, predictors of reading fluency across all known orthographies (Georgiou et al. 2008b, Tan et al. 2005). Within this view, RAN tasks and reading are seen to require many of the same processes, from eye saccades to working memory to the connecting of orthographic and phonological representations. Equally importantly, RAN tasks depend on automaticity within and across each individual component in the naming circuit. It is within this context that Eden, Perfetti, and their colleagues refer to RAN as one of the universal processes that predict the young child's later ability to connect and automatize whole sequences of letters and words with their linguistic information, regardless of writing system (Tan et al. 2005). We consider the ability to automate both the individual linguistic and perceptual components and the connections among them in visually presented serial tasks the major reason why RAN consistently predicts later reading.

The advancement of our knowledge of both RAN and reading fluency has led us to a point where we have the capacity to make great improvements in our ability to identify children with reading difficulties early on and to provide appropriate, effective intervention. Many children develop accurate decoding with basic instruction and then achieve automaticity with time and practice. However, approximately 10% of children in the United States have developmental dyslexia, defined as unexpected difficulty learning to read despite adequate instruction, intelligence, and effort (Lyon et al. 2003). There is no single test and no absolute criteria for diagnosing dyslexia. This is in part due to the fact that there are so many processes in reading that can break down to cause reading failure. Inaccuracy at any level of language or processing or a lack of automaticity in connecting any of these circuits can lead to poor reading. More than 100 years of research into developmental reading difficulties has yet to reveal anything resembling one single explanation for all the symptoms of dyslexia, yet such pursuits continue unabated today.

Given the multicomponential nature of reading, we begin with the premise that dyslexia is not a simple thing. Taking the view that dyslexia is a heterogeneous disorder reflecting difficulty with reading due to any number of sources is essential for successfully identifying and remediating reading disabilities in children. For too many years, schools have waited for children to "grow up a bit" so that the reading troubles will disappear with time, or intervention has been provided that was insensitive to the individual child's profile of strengths and weaknesses. These two mindsets can be deeply detrimental because the consequences of having unremediated reading difficulties can be severe and life-long. Children with dyslexia not only show poorer academic performance, but also socioemotional and behavioral effects such as lower self-esteem and higher rates of entry in to the juvenile justice system (Grigorenko 2006, Humphrey & Mullins 2002, Svensson et al. 2001).

Our potential to ameliorate these outcomes, on the other hand, is significant. Research shows that accurate early identification and appropriate targeted intervention improve reading ability as well as the other potential negative effects associated with dyslexia (Foorman et al. 1997, Vellutino et al. 1998). Thus, it has become crucial to identify dyslexia early and to characterize the precise strengths and vulnerabilities of each child individually so that targeted intervention can be provided to develop accuracy and then automaticity of each aspect of the reading system. If risk for reading difficulties can be determined very early, the chances to improve reading skills are greater. RAN tasks have proven of great potential because children can perform RAN tasks, naming familiar objects or colors, well before they are able to read and because RAN is correlated with reading ability in kindergarten and beyond. Indeed, research on longitudinal predictors of reading has repeatedly shown that RAN is one of the strongest predictors of later reading ability, and particularly for reading fluency.

A BRIEF HISTORY OF RESEARCH ON READING DISABILITIES, RAN, AND FLUENCY

Early Research on Reading Difficulties

Reading difficulties can be classified into two main types: developmental and acquired. Developmental dyslexia affects a person beginning in childhood and makes learning to read and developing reading skills difficult. On the other hand, acquired reading difficulties, usually called alexia, often result from a brain trauma such as an injury or stroke. Although today we recognize these as unique disorders that have different causes, symptoms, and optimal treatments, this was not always the case.

The first medical reports of people with unexpected and specific difficulties with reading were published in Europe in the late 1800s (for a review of this history, see Hallahan & Mercer 2002). Physicians including Jules Dejerine and Adolf Kussmaul described patients who suffered brain injury with subsequent difficulty with reading despite intact language and vision: thus the first term for the condition— "word-blindness." John Hinshelwood and W. Pringle Morgan were among the first to describe "congenital word blindness," that is, difficulty reading beginning in childhood and not due to injury (Hallahan & Mercer 2002).

Subsequent significant work on developmental dyslexia was undertaken by Samuel Orton, a neurologist in the United States. After studying many children with reading difficulties, Orton developed a theory in which inappropriate cerebral dominance accounted for the reversed letters and words sometimes seen in children with reading difficulties (Orton 1925). Orton made several important observations that influence our understanding and treatment of dyslexia today: he noted that many of the struggling readers he saw had average or above-average intellectual abilities; that perhaps as many as 10% of children might suffer from reading difficulties; and that reading difficulties were not likely due to a single brain abnormality. The latter conclusion was based on the premise that the very complexity of reading would require the integration of several brain areas (Orton 1925, 1939). The next major advances in our understanding of reading disabilities would come from two separate theories of the core deficit(s) in dyslexia: rapid automatized naming ability and phonological awareness.

Development of RAN Tasks

In the 1960s, neurologist Norman Geschwind studied various cases of individuals with alexia to determine both what kind of brain damage led to their reading difficulties and exactly what aspects of reading were affected. Based in part on the foundation of Dejerine's earlier findings as well as Wernicke's notions of connections among cerebral areas, Geschwind's (1965) paper "Disconnexion Syndromes in Animals and Man" conceptualized the core deficit in alexia as a disconnection between the visual and verbal processes in the brain. In so doing, like Wernicke before him, Geschwind emphasized the importance of connectivity among brain regions, particularly "association areas," such as the angular gyrus, which act as a switchboard or relay station for different brain regions.

Geschwind also reported the case of a patient with alexia who also experienced great difficulty with naming colors despite the ability to perceive colors accurately (Geschwind & Fusillo 1966). Geschwind was interested in the slow and effortful processing required for this individual to come up with the names of colors, and he devised a timed test of color naming.

This measure was based on an array of 50 colored squares arranged in a grid with five rows, where each of five familiar colors was repeated in random order. Geschwind suggested that the deficit in color naming displayed by this patient might also be due to loss of visual-auditory connections. He further speculated that "congenital dyslexia," what we now call developmental dyslexia, might be due to an impairment in the visual-auditory pathways of the brain, especially in the angular gyrus. Geschwind also suggested that "it is conceivable that even the age of attainment of color naming might be a significant clue to the age at which reading can be acquired" (1965, p. 283). Unlike many of the other theories of developmental dyslexia, which focused on the surface level, this idea suggested that there might be a deeper, more abstract ability that supported reading. Geschwind didn't believe that color naming was an aspect of reading, but rather that the neural processes supporting rapid serial color naming might be similar to those involved in reading.

Neurologist Martha Denckla then explored the idea of a relationship between naming and reading, testing boys with reading difficulties on a speeded naming task. As her mentor Geschwind had done with patients, Denckla used an array of 50 colored squares arranged in five rows. Though color-naming ability wasn't considered to be generally impaired in children with dyslexia, in studying color naming in a large group of kindergarteners, Denckla (1972) discovered five boys who had dyslexia and were particularly slow and inconsistent in serial color naming for their age, despite typical intelligence and color vision.

Together with Rita Rudel, Denckla created three other versions of the speeded serial naming test, using objects, letters, and numbers as stimuli. They coined the term "rapid automatized naming" to describe these tasks that were designed to measure the speed of naming familiar items (1976b). They found that RAN latencies were not related to how early certain stimuli were learned, but instead how "automatized" the naming process was; object names were learned much earlier in

development, but elementary school children were faster to name letters and numbers, which were learned later but enjoyed a greater degree of automaticity. They were thoughtful in the design of these tasks, for example, including both the letters "p" and "d," which if not fully automatized were easy to confuse with their mirror-reversed counterparts. They also kept the design and procedure of naming left-to-right across rows, which parallels the motoric and visual processes in reading. These early studies showed that performance on RAN tasks differentiated children with reading difficulties from typical readers of the same age and from children with other, nonlanguage-based learning disabilities (Denckla & Rudel 1976a). In a separate line of research investigating a possible speech-motor encoding deficit in boys with dyslexia, Spring & Capps (1974) had also found similar group differences in serial object, color, and digit naming.

Toward a Multicomponential View of Reading and Reading Disability

Also in the early 1970s, notions of reading fluency were developing in parallel. LaBerge & Samuels (1974) proposed a model of reading that was one of the first to emphasize what we now know as "fluency": the idea that successful reading depends on not only accuracy but automaticity of multiple cognitive and linguistic processes, requiring minimal conscious effort. Similar ideas were presented by Perfetti (1986) in his verbal efficiency theory of reading, where he noted that reading comprehension was associated with accuracy as well as speed of single-word identification.

Another more widely known line of research was unfolding regarding another possible core deficit in dyslexia: difficulty with phonological awareness (PA), which involves the explicit ability to identify and manipulate the sound units that comprise words. Isabelle Liberman promoted the idea that reading development depends on an explicit awareness of the sounds of language and that perhaps the greatest challenge facing young readers is learning to match the phonemes of speech with the graphemes that represent them in print (Liberman 1971). This work was extended to show that children with reading difficulties had trouble with phonological awareness (e.g., Bradley & Bryant 1978, Wagner & Torgesen 1987).

The field generally now agrees that PA is a crucial precursor to reading acquisition in alphabetic languages and that many, if not most, children with dyslexia have PA deficits (Morris et al. 1998, Natl. Inst. Child Health Human Dev. 2000). Though the exact nature of the deficit continues to be specified with some debate about differences across writing systems with more regular orthographies, the fact that phonological deficits can cause reading difficulty has been extensively researched and well accepted. Indeed, many of the most studied and successful reading instruction and intervention programs are centered around this approach.

The fact that a deficit in phonological awareness can cause dyslexia does not mean, however, that a phonological deficit is the single and universal cause of dyslexia, a view espoused by many researchers and clinicians. Many children have difficulty reading despite intact PA and decoding skills. As a result, those children with a reading difficulty not due to phonological awareness and decoding are less likely to be identified as having a reading disability on traditional single-word decoding tests. Further and more importantly, they will be less likely to benefit from standard instruction or intervention that focuses only on phonological deficits. Beginning with research from Orton to Geschwind, and continuing with the increasingly expanding research from neuroimaging, we know that the reading circuit is intrinsically complex and that a lack of accuracy or automaticity at one of any number of levels can cause reading difficulties. Any single-deficit view, however important individually, is at odds with a multicomponential conceptualization of reading.

An understanding of the complexity of the reading circuit and its multiple processes undergirds the efforts by Wolf & Bowers (1999) to move beyond a unidimensional conceptualization of reading disabilities. By studying large samples of children with reading disabilities in the United States and Canada, they found that phonological awareness and RAN contributed separately to reading ability. In an attempt to show the importance of both sets of processes, Wolf & Bowers (1999) proposed the double deficit hypothesis (DDH) as a way to show how children can be characterized in various subgroups according to their performances on each set of processes. According to this hypothesis, a deficit in either phonological awareness or naming speed (as measured by RAN tasks) can cause reading difficulties, with RAN deficits indicating weakness in one or more of the underlying fluency-related processes, not simply a naming speed deficit. In addition, these deficits can co-occur, and children with a double deficit in PA and RAN characterize the most severely impaired readers. Wolf and Bowers developed the DDH as a first step toward a multidimensional understanding of reading difficulties, intending it to promote further research and discussion on the variety of impairments that can cause developmental dyslexia. Researchers around the world have taken up this challenge; both the DDH and the relationship between rapid naming and reading have been studied extensively over the past decade. These studies have suggested that 60% to 75% of individuals with reading or learning disabilities exhibit RAN deficits (Katzir et al. 2008, Waber et al. 2004, Wolf et al. 2002).

DEFINING THE RAN TASKS

Basic Structure of RAN Tasks

Most RAN tasks appear very similar to the original tasks developed nearly 40 years ago by Denckla and Rudel. These tasks have been described in the literature using slightly different terms, such as rapid serial naming, serial visual naming, continuous rapid naming, rapid naming, and naming speed. In this review, we use "RAN" to mean generally any rapid automatized naming task or process. Essentially, a task falls into the broader category of a RAN task if it involves timed naming of familiar stimuli presented repeatedly in random order, in left-to-right serial fashion. In some uses of the RAN task, self-corrections and errors are noted for the purposes of qualitative observations, but the key dependent variable is the total time taken to name the items. It is crucial that the items to be named, whether objects, colors, letters, or numbers, are sufficiently familiar to the examinee. For this reason, as in Denckla and Rudel's original studies, most rapid naming tests begin with practice or pretest trials asking examinees to name each of the stimulus items individually to ensure that they are named accurately in isolation.

Published Standardized Measures of RAN

The two most widely used standardized tests of RAN in the United States are the Rapid Automatized Naming-Rapid Alternating Stimulus (RAN-RAS) Tests developed by Denckla and expanded by Wolf & Denckla (2005; published by Pro-Ed), and the rapid naming subtests of the Comprehensive Test of Phonological Processing (CTOPP), by Wagner and colleagues (1999; published by Pro-Ed). The CTOPP uses a briefer format that is considered by its authors to measure phonological retrieval. Both of these measures are standardized and normed on large, nationally representative samples in the United States and have been used in many research studies. A child's raw score on these tests can be used to derive a

standard score and percentile rank, which provides information about how the child performed relative to others of the same age or grade level. Self-corrections and errors can be noted for qualitative interpretation but do not factor into the scores. This is not to say that these do not affect the score at all, as errors and corrections are often related to a lack of fluency and, as a result, increase the time it takes to complete the task.

RAN-RAS Tests. The published RAN-RAS Tests include the four classic subtests used in Denckla and Rudel's original RAN measures: objects, colors, numbers, and letters, as well as two RAS subtests. Each of the RAN-RAS subtests has 50 items arranged in 5 rows of 10 items each. The five different token items for each subtest are pseudorandomized, with no item appearing consecutively on the same line (**Figure 1**). Age- or grade level–based standard scores and percentiles are calculated based on the total naming time (latency) for each subtest. Norms are available for individuals age 5 through 18.

The RAN-RAS tests are unique in their inclusion of rapid alternating stimulus, or RAS subtests. The RAS was first developed in the 1980s by Wolf as a way to incorporate processes involved in switching and disengaging attention to rapid-naming tests (Wolf 1986). The RAS is structured analogously to the RAN, with two or three types of items repeated alternately throughout the card, reflecting the demands of shifting attention and processing between sets of different stimuli. The RAN-RAS Tests include a two-set RAS composed of alternating letters and numbers and a three-set RAS with alternating letters, numbers, and colors.

CTOPP rapid-naming subtests. The authors of the CTOPP conceptualize rapid naming as one of three subcomponents of phonological processing, along with phonological awareness and phonological memory (Wagner et al. 1999). (This view differs from the theoretical viewpoint of the authors of the RAN-RAS Tests and our viewpoint in this review.) The

d	s	a	p	o	s	p	d	a	o
s	a	o	d	p	a	d	o	p	s
d	a	p	o	a	s	p	s	o	d
a	p	s	d	o	d	s	a	p	o
p	s	o	p	d	o	a	d	s	a

Figure 1

Rapid automatized naming (RAN) letters stimulus card, in the same format used by Denckla & Rudel (1976b) and Wolf & Denckla (2005).

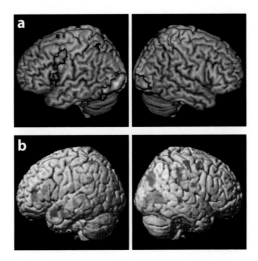

Figure 2

fMRI brain activations for a RAN letters task from Christodoulou et al. (2011). (*a*) Whole-brain activations for RAN letters >visual fixation. N = 18 typical adults. Activations significant at height threshold of $p < 0.05$, FWE (family-wise error) corrected, k > 10 voxels. (*b*) Whole brain differences for RAN letters >visual fixation in typical adult readers (N = 9) versus adults with dyslexia (N = 9). Activations significant at height threshold of $p < 0.05$, FDR (false discovery rate) corrected, k > 10 voxels.

CTOPP rapid naming subtests measure rapid object, color, digit, and letter naming. The test is normed for individuals ages 5 through 24. For each subtest, there are six token items, and the task is divided into two parts, with the items arranged in two arrays on separate pages. Each of the two arrays includes 4 rows of 9 items, for a total of 72 items. The examiner determines a score by adding the total number of seconds to complete both arrays, and this raw score can be used to determine age- and grade level–based percentiles and standard scores. The CTOPP raw scores can also be used to derive composite scores based on multiple subtests.

Differences. Though the RAN-RAS Tests and CTOPP rapid naming subtests share many similarities, the two measures differ slightly in their format, reflecting different theoretical viewpoints in the field about the relationship of rapid naming to other cognitive processes. The RAN-RAS tests treat rapid naming as a cognitive ability that includes phonology but also other linguistic and visual processes; furthermore, the collective processes underlying RAN are conceptualized as contributing independent variance to the prediction of reading skills, particularly reading fluency. In contrast, the CTOPP was designed on the basis of a model of overall phonological processing that includes phonological awareness, phonological memory, and rapid naming as related subcomponents. These theoretical differences and evidence for a model where naming speed is separate from phonological processes are discussed below.

Other criterion-based measures of naming speed. Several other psychoeducational assessment tests include RAN subtests, such as the Kaufman Test of Educational Achievement-II, Clinical Evaluation of Language Fundamentals-4, and Process Assessment of the Learner; however, in most cases, the RAN measures are not fully normed, and only criterion scores are given (e.g., performance is categorized only as normal versus nonnormal). The Dynamic Indicators of Basic Literacy Skills (DIBELS) contains several "fluency" subtests, including letter-naming fluency, but this test uses all the upper and lowercase letters in one array and scores the number of letters correctly identified in one minute, a procedure that differs significantly from classic RAN tasks.

Subcomponents of the RAN Task

Like reading, performing a RAN task requires a synchronization and integration across a wide range of processes. Wolf and colleagues (Wolf & Bowers 1999, Wolf & Denckla 2005) enumerated seven related processes that are involved in rapid naming:

> (a) attentional processes to the stimulus; (b) bihemispheric visual processes responsible for initial feature detection, visual discrimination, and pattern identification; (c) integration of visual features and pattern information with stored orthographic representations; (d) integration of visual and orthographic information with stored phonological representations; (e) access and retrieval of phonological labels; (f) activation and integration of semantic and conceptual information with all other input; and (g) motoric activation leading to articulation. (Wolf & Denckla 2005, p. 2)

Several factors, such as the exact items to be named and the precise number of rows and columns, have varied between the many experiments that have investigated RAN. Even with deviations from the traditional RAN, the strong relationship with reading seems to be preserved as long as the factors that underlie the theoretical link between RAN and reading are intact, including naming in a serial, left-to-right fashion, and sufficient familiarity of items to be named. For example, an "alternate" version of the RAN used in the Colorado Learning Disabilities Research Project contained 13 rows of 5 items each, with some consecutively repeated items, and in which examinees are instructed to name as many items as possible in 15 seconds. This RAN task showed relationships to reading ability similar to those of a traditional RAN task and actually predicted more of the variance in reading ability than did traditional RAN in slower namers and children whose naming ability was influenced by attention issues (Compton et al. 2002).

In order to investigate which aspects of rapid naming might drive the relationship with reading, researchers have broken down the RAN task into component parts. At the surface level, one can consider the amount of time taken to articulate each item's name versus the amount of time taken for processing between items (often called pause time). Several studies have found that articulation time itself is not strongly associated with reading in the same manner as are overall RAN scores (Clarke et al. 2005, Cutting & Denckla 2001, Georgiou et al. 2006, Neuhaus et al. 2001, Obregon 1994). Instead, it seems that the interitem processing or pause time may reflect the components of RAN that drive their close association with reading. In considering pause and articulation times, Neuhaus and colleagues (2001) found that the two were not strongly related to each other and that pause time, especially on the RAN letters task, predicted both single-word reading and reading comprehension in first- and second-graders. Georgiou and colleagues (2006) found that pause times at the end of kindergarten were significantly correlated with reading accuracy and fluency in first grade. In contrast, Clarke and colleagues (2005) found that pause time was not correlated with reading single words or nonwords, though their sample was small (n = 30), and their RAN measure included many more different token items (10 digits and 25 different letters) than are typically used. Although these findings give us some insight as to how the component parts of RAN relate to reading, the overall RAN time is much easier to measure than pause time and shows similar patterns of correlation with reading outcomes (Georgiou et al. 2006).

Another dimension of the RAN that has been considered in research is the differences between each row of stimuli. Berninger and colleagues (Amtmann et al. 2007) examined changes in time to name each row of stimuli on a standard 50-item RAN task (as in Denckla & Rudel 1976b and the published RAN-RAS tests, Wolf & Denckla 2005). This allowed them to examine various factors related to initiating the task (e.g., retrieval of item names) versus continuously operating processes (such as executive functioning or sustaining item names in working memory). They found that individuals who were slower namers overall tended to take longer to name subsequent rows, whereas row time was more stable in faster namers. The time for the first row was also slower in the overall slower namers. Children with dyslexia were slower to name the first row of stimuli than were slightly younger typically developing readers, suggesting that the slow naming times seen in dyslexia might be related to automaticity of retrieval or a difficulty sustaining processes needed for retrieval.

RAN Differentiated from Similar Tasks

Single-item naming. It has been thought that timed single-item naming and serial naming would be closely related. However, the added demands of serial naming in RAN render it quite different from single-item naming. Across several studies, single-item and serial naming have been found to be only moderately correlated, with correlation coefficients of about 0.5 (see Logan et al. 2009). The added demands associated with the continuous, serial nature of RAN make it a better predictor of reading than is single-item naming (Bowers & Swanson 1991, Meyer et al. 1998). Logan and colleagues showed that single-item naming does explain any variance in reading beyond that of PA and RAN and may even be a suppressor of serial naming (Logan et al. 2009). Further, in their longitudinal analysis from kindergarten through second grade, single-item naming and serial naming speed grew at different rates as children got older, supporting the notion that RAN is not a simple permutation of single-item naming, nor are both governed by an underlying system (as considered in the global processing speed model of explaining RAN, below).

Stroop tasks. Some characteristics of RAN tasks bear resemblance to the classic Stroop color-word interference task developed in the 1930s, in which participants name the color of the ink rather than the name of a printed color word. The Stroop task is designed to take advantage of the relatively greater automaticity for word reading than color naming, requiring the examinee to inhibit reading the word and instead attend to naming the color. Studies of the Stroop task in relation to reading show several patterns of association similar to the RAN and reading (MacLeod 1991). The RAN has been studied more extensively in relation to reading, however, because it removes the extra executive function demands of the Stroop task.

General processing speed. Researchers including Kail & Hall (1994) have argued that RAN should be considered one facet of general or global processing speed. Global processing speed deficits have been associated with other developmental difficulties, including general learning disabilities and attention deficit hyperactivity disorder (Willcutt et al. 2005). The majority of studies using alphanumeric RAN (that is, rapid naming of letters or numbers) find that processing speed does not account for the RAN–reading relationship (though see Catts et al. 2002, who found that nonalphanumeric RAN did not account for variance in reading beyond the contribution of general processing speed). In a large study using structural equation modeling, Powell et al. (2007) found that although children with slower RAN had slightly slower global processing speed than did matched peers, RAN made a significant contribution to reading after processing speed was controlled for. Similarly, Cutting & Denckla (2001) found that in a path analysis, RAN and other reading-related skills contributed to the understanding of word reading after general processing speed was controlled for. Although general processing speed certainly affects both RAN and reading (especially in terms of speed and fluency), these results underscore the ideas of Wolf & Bowers (1999) that RAN builds on the existing architecture for more general speeded processing. The slow naming speed observed in many individuals with dyslexia might occur at a level higher than simple processing speed; for example, it may occur in the connections between visual and speech circuits in the brain.

Independence of RAN and Phonological Awareness

A crucial question for our understanding of reading is the relationship between RAN and phonological awareness. These two constructs have been perhaps the most widely studied and consistently implicated in predicting reading ability. Some controversy has existed in the field regarding whether rapid naming should be considered a subskill related to phonological processing or whether RAN is a separate process and should be so considered. A major argument that has been made for including RAN as a part of a larger phonological construct is that rapid naming tasks depend on the retrieval of phonological codes (e.g., Torgesen et al. 1997). To subsume rapid naming tasks under phonological processing for this reason alone would, however, be inaccurate. Consider tests of vocabulary, where an examinee is asked to name or provide information about a word. These responses require retrieval of phonological information just as rapid naming does, yet a vocabulary task would never be considered a subcomponent of phonology.

At least three areas of research provide evidence against considering RAN as a subset of phonology. These notions are each reviewed in an earlier paper (Wolf et al. 2000), so we summarize previous findings focusing on more recent data that add to these discussions. First, RAN and phonological processing are not strongly correlated. A comprehensive meta-analysis of the relationship of PA and RAN confirms that these two abilities are only moderately correlated, with an overall correlation coefficient of $r = 0.38$ (Swanson et al.

2003), and that these load on separate factors in an exploratory factor analysis. Based on data from the norming of the Comprehensive Test of Phonological Processing (Wagner et al. 1999), the rapid naming components of the test were moderately correlated with phonological awareness and phonological memory, $r = 0.46$ and 0.45, respectively, for children ages 5–6; $r = 0.38$ and 0.38 for ages 7–24. By comparison, the other aspects of phonological processing, PA and phonological memory, were strongly correlated at $r = 0.88$ for ages 5–6 and $r = 0.85$ for ages 7–24.

Second, regression and structural equation models consistently report that RAN and PA account for unique variance in reading ability (e.g., Cutting & Denckla 2001, Katzir et al. 2006). Models that treated RAN as a separate latent variable from phonological awareness and memory provided a better fit to the data, and confirmatory factor analysis studies suggest that different underlying factors support RAN and PA (Powell et al. 2007). These relationships may change somewhat with age; Wagner and colleagues (1997) found that RAN contributed to the variance in reading skill after PA was controlled for only until third grade (although measures in subsequent grades in their longitudinal study controlled for earlier reading ability, which depends on RAN). Furthermore, RAN varies independently from several potential sources of covariance with phonology. In a recent review, Kirby and colleagues (2010) point out that RAN retains its relationship with reading even after a host of possible explanatory factors have been accounted for. These include verbal and nonverbal IQ, prior reading ability, attention deficit disorder, socioeconomic status, articulation rate, speed of processing, phonological short-term memory, morphological awareness, and orthographic processing (see Kirby et al. 2010 for references).

Third, genetic and neuroimaging studies find different biological bases for RAN and PA abilities. In the past decade, substantial advancements have occurred in this area, allowing us to identify the genetic and neural underpinnings of these abilities. Though research has yet to directly compare RAN with phonological tasks, functional brain imaging studies of the two tasks show some shared regions, as would be expected with their similar task demands, yet also separate areas of processing. These studies are discussed further in the section titled Contributions of Neuroscience and Genetics to Understanding RAN and Fluency.

CHARACTERISTICS AND PREDICTIVE VALUE OF RAN ACROSS DEVELOPMENT

RAN and phonological processing tasks are valuable tools because both are excellent predictors of reading ability that can be assessed before children learn to read and thus can be used as early indicators of risk for reading difficulties. Published measures of RAN are normed to provide standard scores and percentile ranks for children beginning at age 5 years. Importantly, most 5-year-old children in the United States are very familiar with the common objects and colors presented on rapid naming tests, yet many are still learning the numbers and alphabet. As a result, 5- and 6-year-olds often name the color and object stimuli more quickly than letters and numbers. With more practice and exposure to letters and numbers, the alphanumeric stimuli become much more automatic. At this point, alphanumeric stimuli are named faster and alphanumeric RAN becomes more strongly associated with reading ability (Meyer et al. 1998, Wolf et al. 1986). These differences underscore the importance of considering alphanumeric RAN separately from nonalphanumeric RAN stimuli. It is also important to consider the predictive ability of RAN across groups, as research suggests that its predictive value may be different for poor than for typical readers. The study design and type of reading outcome may affect these findings, as research studies have found that RAN–reading relationships are stronger in poor than in typical readers (Frijters et al. 2011, Meyer et al. 1998, Scarborough 1998).

Prediction in Kindergarteners and Prereaders

Several longitudinal studies have examined early predictors of later reading abilities. Understanding these factors is extremely important because our ability to understand which measures predict later reading scores directly informs our ability to identify reading difficulties as early as possible. The overarching goal is to use this information to inform what would be the most effective intervention for a particular profile. To date, our ability to correctly identify which children will go on to have dyslexia based on kindergarten data has been insufficient, lacking both sensitivity and specificity.

Although different studies have used different assessments, the measures that most consistently predict future reading difficulty in English are phonological processing/awareness, letter-name knowledge, and RAN (Pennington & Lefly 2001, Scarborough 1998, Schatschneider et al. 2004). In perhaps the largest study of kindergarten prediction of later reading abilities, Schatschneider and colleagues (2004) assessed typically developing children at four points throughout kindergarten and followed them through second grade. Measures of RAN objects and PA in the fall of kindergarten showed similar correlations with second-grade outcomes on untimed passage comprehension (both $r = 0.36$). However, as seen in earlier work (Bowers & Swanson 1991), RAN was more highly correlated ($r = 0.55$) than PA ($r = 0.35$) to timed measures of single-word and nonword reading in second grade. The authors also performed dominance analysis to see which variables contributed more substantially to explaining variance in the outcomes. Here, RAN letters scores in the fall and spring of kindergarten was a more dominant predictor than was PA of word reading efficiency at the end of first grade and second grade. This suggests that RAN may have a stronger impact on timed reading measures; unfortunately, no timed measures of comprehension or text fluency were included. Despite the importance of RAN and PA in predicting reading

outcomes, a more meta-view is important here: Even by putting together these best predictors of reading at kindergarten, the best statistical models only accounted for about half of the variance of second-grade reading ability.

There is additional evidence that RAN may be an important factor in determining risk for dyslexia in young children. In a longitudinal study in Finland, children who were identified as having dyslexia at the end of second grade were slower for an object RAN task in previous testing at age 3.5 (Torppa et al. 2010). In addition, RAN appears to differentiate between English children with and without a history of dyslexia (Raschle et al. 2011). Again, a meta-view of these comparative performances is important. Scores on a number of other variables, including expressive and receptive language and phonological variables, did not differ significantly between the groups, whereas RAN did. Overall, these studies suggest that RAN is one of the best predictors of later reading abilities, yet we are still far from being able to predict reading from our current behavioral assessments.

Prediction of Reading from RAN Through Primary School and Beyond

Given these close relationships between RAN and reading early in the school years, does RAN continue to predict reading scores as children become older and more proficient readers? This issue has been much debated in the literature (e.g., Torgesen et al. 1997).

This relationship can vary depending on the ability of the readers being studied. Scarborough (1998) found that second-grade RAN scores significantly predicted eighth-grade reading and spelling scores, and the predictive value of RAN was much stronger in poor readers than in typical readers. Meyer and colleagues (1998) found that the relationships between RAN and reading were strong and lasting, but only in poor readers. Among poor readers, RAN scores in third grade significantly predicted untimed single word-reading in fifth grade and eighth grade, accounting for as much as 18% of variance in eighth-grade word reading after SES and IQ were controlled for, and 14% when third-grade reading ability was controlled for. Phonological awareness and nonword reading, on the other hand, were not significant predictors. Looking at the broadest lens, RAN was strongly related to decoding, but it did not predict untimed reading comprehension measures in the later grades in typical or disabled readers. Unfortunately, the outcome measures in these studies did not include any timed reading or fluency tasks, which have been shown to be more closely related to RAN by most researchers.

How does RAN change into adolescence and beyond? Published tests of RAN contain norms for people through the late teens to early twenties (age 18 for the RAN-RAS and age 22 for the CTOPP, described previously). Differences in RAN ability persist between young adults with and without dyslexia through age 25 (Vukovic et al. 2004). Van den Bos and his Dutch colleagues (2002) studied how RAN changes with age and its relationship with reading. Their cross-sectional study included groups of Dutch children ages 8, 10, 12, and 16, and a group of adults ages 36 to 65. They found that the developmental trajectory of alphanumeric RAN reached an asymptote after age 16 but that RAN latencies for colors and objects continued to decrease through adolescence and adulthood. The correlations between alphanumeric RAN and reading are also significant through adulthood, at $r = 0.53$ in adults. The adults were considered a single group; it is unclear whether there are slight differences in RAN or its relationship with reading associated with aging.

CROSS-LINGUISTIC STUDIES OF RAN AND FLUENCY

RAN and its relationship to reading have now been studied in many of the world's languages. This growing list includes, to our knowledge, Arabic, Chinese, Dutch, Finnish, French, German, Greek, Hebrew, Hungarian, Italian, Korean, Japanese, Norwegian, Persian, Polish, Portuguese, Spanish, and Swedish. Research findings in these languages follow the general patterns of what we know about RAN in English: that RAN predicts reading, both concurrently and longitudinally, in typically developing and reading-impaired populations (e.g., Georgiou et al. 2008a,b; Ramus et al. 2011; Tan et al. 2005; Vaessen et al. 2010; Ziegler et al. 2003). Studying the subcomponents of reading across languages helps us to understand what factors are universal and which are language- or orthography-specific factors in the reading system. We know from imaging studies that the reading circuit shifts accordingly to accommodate different emphases in different orthographies. That said, we should be better able to understand dyslexia when we know what types of deficits account for reading failure across various languages.

Shallow Orthographies

Much of the research regarding reading is conducted in English, although English is substantially different from many other languages. Alphabetic languages can be considered as falling along a continuum based on the complexity of the mapping between sounds and letters, or phonology and orthography. The orthography of English is considered very deep or opaque because the correspondences from phonemes to graphemes are not consistent. On the other hand, many other alphabetic languages such as German, Spanish, and Greek have what is called a shallow or transparent orthography, where grapheme-phoneme correspondences are highly predictable. As a result, learning sound-to-letter correspondences and decoding is more straightforward in these orthographically shallow languages. Because there are fewer rules to learn, children who speak these languages usually master accurate decoding by the end of first grade (Seymour et al. 2003), whereas children learning deep orthographies take longer at a proportion based on the opacity of the language.

Several recent studies have compared the effects of orthographic depth on reading processes (Vaessen et al. 2010, Ziegler et al. 2003). Overall, it appears that PA is important early in reading acquisition but that as children essentially reach ceiling in their ability to decode words accurately, a shift occurs in which the relationship between RAN and reading becomes much stronger. The orthographic depth of the language dictates when this shift from reliance on phonology to fluency-related skills occurs; children reading more transparent languages shift away from phonology earlier in schooling (Vaessen et al. 2010).

A current project that has exciting potential to answer more questions in this area is the NeuroDys consortium project in Europe. This group is studying the longitudinal course of reading and dyslexia across six languages in eight countries, using a large sample of about 2,000 children with and without dyslexia. The first set of results from their research suggest that orthographic complexity affects the relationship of PA and reading ability but that the relationship of RAN and reading is essentially consistent across languages (Ramus et al. 2011). The measures that are used to define reading ability are also important. Across languages, PA was a stronger predictor than RAN for untimed word-reading measures, but RAN was stronger than PA for timed reading. A study by Georgiou and colleagues (2008b) corroborates these findings. They studied typically developing children who spoke English, Greek, and Chinese and found that the relationships between RAN and reading fluency were similar across languages. Similar to now extensive findings in the field, they reported that the correlation of RAN with fluency measures was stronger than its correlation with reading accuracy measures.

Patterns of fluency and naming speed are also similar in poor readers across languages. Overall, children who are poor readers in shallow orthographies do exhibit lower phonological awareness scores than those of both age-matched and younger reading-matched peers (Landerl et al. 1997, Ziegler et al. 2003). However, there is also evidence that, as in English, multiple deficits can cause dyslexia and that difficulties with PA versus RAN will affect readers differently depending on the orthography of their language. Cross-linguistic research suggests that similar proportions of RAN, PA, and double-deficits exist in other European languages (Ramus et al. under review) and in Hebrew (Shany & Share 2011), which is consistent with the double-deficit hypothesis. Again, these findings underscore that a variety of deficits can cause reading difficulties but that these factors interact depending on language.

Nonalphabetic Orthographies

Whereas English is considered a rather deep orthography, nonalphabetic languages, such as Chinese and Japanese orthographies, are composed of thousands of characters that are essentially unrelated or much less related to phonemes. At the syllable level, Chinese words share many similar syllables, with each syllable represented by many different characters (Tan et al. 2005). Phonological decoding plays a much more minor role in reading standard Chinese and Japanese, although somewhat more phonologically based systems (e.g., Chinese Pin-yin, Japanese Kana) do exist for introducing children to reading in these languages. As one would expect, phonological awareness is a weaker predictor of timed reading in Chinese; in a regression model, PA did not account for significant variance in timed single-word reading when RAN was controlled for (Tan et al. 2005). One might imagine that orthographic knowledge accounts for much of the variance in Chinese reading ability because of the many characters that must be learned and recognized. However, RAN is strongly correlated with reading in Chinese and accounts for additional variance after writing (orthographic) ability is controlled for. In several cases, correlations reported between RAN and reading in Chinese and Japanese are even greater than those reported in Swanson and colleagues' (2003) meta-analysis of English (Georgiou et al. 2008a, Kobayashi et al. 2005, Tan et al. 2005). This may reflect the powerful contribution of visual processes also measured within RAN to reading the logosyllabaries of China and Japan.

Underscoring the fact that some factors may be language specific and others may be more general, McBride-Chang and colleagues (2011) studied Chinese-English bilinguals who had reading difficulties in one language or in both. Individuals who had difficulty reading both Chinese and English were significantly slower namers than were peers who struggled in just one of their languages or who were typical readers. Furthermore, this effect was stable in children who were followed longitudinally from ages 5 through 9. Overall, the differences in RAN across languages and orthographies are small in comparison with the many similarities. We have seen no evidence of a language in which RAN has not been shown to be important for reading.

CONTRIBUTIONS OF NEUROSCIENCE AND GENETICS TO UNDERSTANDING RAN AND FLUENCY

Perhaps the greatest advances in our understanding of reading disabilities over the past decade have come from neuroimaging studies. Developments in magnetic resonance imaging (MRI) technology have progressed such that it can be used easily with children to address questions about the brain structures and associated functions involved in reading. In addition, recent genetic and twin studies have produced results that give first-time insights to the biological mechanisms that underlie brain and behavioral differences in dyslexia.

Functional Brain Networks in Reading and Dyslexia

Brain activation for reading-related tasks has been consistently found in three main areas of the left hemisphere: the inferior frontal gyrus (IFG), temporoparietal area, and occipitotemporal area (see meta-analyses by Maisog et al. 2008, Richlan et al. 2009). The IFG has been implicated in a wide variety of reading and language-related functions, from semantic search to working memory. The temporoparietal aspect of the reading circuit includes areas of posterior temporal cortex as well as the angular gyrus and supramarginal gyrus. These regions are classic "association areas" as described by Geschwind, responsible for the integration of information across visual and auditory modalities. The occipitotemporal region includes the fusiform gyrus and inferior temporal gyrus and is most often implicated in orthographic processing.

In people with dyslexia relative to controls, the most consistent finding is an underrecruitment (hypoactivation) of left temporoparietal and left occipitotemporal areas (Maisog et al. 2008, Richlan et al. 2009). Functional brain differences in both of these areas are thought to be related to the etiology of dyslexia, rather than absolute level of reading ability, because younger children matched for ability to dyslexic readers do not show hypoactivation of these areas (Hoeft et al. 2007). In addition to these areas of the reading circuit that show reduced activation in dyslexia, many individual studies have identified areas of the right frontal and temporal lobes that show greater activation in people with dyslexia relative to controls. These are thought to represent compensatory mechanisms or effortful processing, as they are sometimes engaged in younger relative to older typically developing readers (Hoeft et al. 2007). Several studies have reported cerebellar differences associated with dyslexia, but these have varied widely and were not significant in meta-analyses of imaging studies (Maisog et al. 2008, Richlan et al. 2009).

The tasks used in nearly all brain imaging studies to date have focused on accuracy rather than fluency. One recent study to focus on fluency had typical adult readers read sentences presented at rates slower than, equal to, and faster than their normal reading speed (Benjamin & Gaab 2011). As compared to a letter-reading baseline task, the posterior middle temporal gyrus was engaged at all reading speeds, whereas areas of the left IFG and occipitotemporal region were more active at both slow and fast, but not normal, speeds. These findings suggest that when the automaticity of normal reading is disrupted, activation in reading-related regions changes, consistent with a multicomponent view of fluency.

Several important questions remain to be answered, including whether readers with different subtypes of dyslexia use different areas of the brain in reading and how activation for timed reading might differ from untimed accuracy measures. However, we are starting to gain some insight into the brain processes that support RAN. There is some evidence that phonological and RAN or fluency abilities may have separate neural substrates. Eden and colleagues (Turkeltaub et al. 2003) examined correlations between activation for an fMRI implicit reading task and behavioral measures of RAN, phonological awareness, and working memory. They found that patterns of correlations with brain activation were spatially distinct for each task, suggesting that each of these processes may tap separate aspects of the reading network.

To our knowledge, the brain basis of RAN tasks has been examined in only two studies. Misra and colleagues (2004) and Christodoulou and colleagues (2011, Lymberis et al. 2009) had adults name stimuli, as in a traditional RAN task (5 × 10 matrix), on a screen during fMRI scanning. Both studies found that for letter naming contrasted with fixation, the RAN task engaged the left inferior frontal gyrus, left posterior middle frontal gyrus, and bilateral inferior occipital areas (**Figure 2a**, see color insert). Misra et al. (2004) found additional activation in left parietal and right frontal areas, although their statistical thresholds were much more liberal. These areas are consistent with areas involved in the reading network as well as for tasks that require eye saccades.

Christodoulou and colleagues (2011, Lymberis et al. 2009) also compared in-scanner RAN performances of typical adult readers and adults with dyslexia who were matched on age and IQ. The adults with dyslexia had lower standardized RAN scores and lower in-scanner performance. The typical controls engaged several posterior areas in the occipital and parietal regions bilaterally more than did the group with dyslexia (shown in red, **Figure 2b**), whereas the adults with dyslexia (shown in blue) showed greater activity than did controls in a variety of bilateral temporal, motor, and left supramarginal gyrus (part of the temporoparietal area). These results suggest that readers with dyslexia are employing a more distributed network that may represent compensatory mechanisms for performing RAN tasks.

Timing of Brain Processes in Reading and Dyslexia

Functional MRI studies have provided us with a clearer picture of what happens in the brain while we read, but what do we know at this juncture about the timing aspect of reading that is so important for fluency? Electroencephalography (EEG) allows us to examine the precise timing of neural processes, which can complement information obtained about the location of processes determined by fMRI. EEG records the electrical activity of the brain from the scalp, so researchers can present stimuli and analyze the response, called an event-related potential (ERP), to each type of stimulus. From EEG research we know that different aspects of words are processed along a timeline. For example, initial visual processing occurs within the first 50 milliseconds after a word is presented. Word-specific orthographic processing begins around 150 msec and executive and attention processes at about 200 msec, with phonological processes between 150 and 300 msec, followed by semantic and comprehension processes (Wolf 2007). Ongoing debate, however, concerns whether phonological processing occurs well before other linguistic processes, perhaps in an interactive mode with orthographic processes. As we have noted, a lack of automaticity in any one of these areas can cause a delay that leads to less time available for comprehension. Indeed, research finds that individuals with dyslexia show later peak responses for several of these different components during word reading (see Shaul 2008 for a review). Not surprisingly, the peak of each of the ERP components involved in rapid naming was delayed in adults with dyslexia relative to controls (Breznitz 2005).

Because EEG systems are relatively inexpensive and portable as compared to MRI, EEG research regarding early indicators of reading disability is especially promising. In particular, the mismatch negativity (MMN) ERP component, which is a preattentive response to a difference within a series of auditory stimuli, has been studied as a possible correlate of automatic language processing. The MMN response is a significant predictor of reading outcomes, even better than a combination of behavioral assessments in children (Maurer et al. 2009), and differs among infants with and without a family history of reading disability (Leppänen et al. 2002). Recently, we found that the MMN response in children was significantly correlated with RAN, timed single-word reading, and timed connected text reading, but not with PA or untimed reading (Norton et al. 2011), suggesting that it might reflect processes important for the rapid processing of stimuli necessary for fluent reading. Further research in this area has great potential to help us understand the relationship between automaticity of language processing and reading fluency.

Brain Structure and Connectivity Differences in Dyslexia

Researchers have also used structural MRI to look for an anatomical basis of reading and language disorders. In a series of studies, Leonard, Eckert, Berninger, and colleagues (e.g., Eckert et al. 2003, Leonard et al. 2006) have examined the brain structure differences associated with RAN, single-word reading, and reading comprehension. Children with dyslexia showed smaller volumes of the pars triangularis area of the IFG bilaterally as well as an area of the right cerebellum. On the basis of these anatomical markers, more than 80% of the subjects could be correctly classified as dyslexic or typical readers. These anatomical measurements were also significantly correlated with RAN

scores. On the other hand, a separate set of anatomical predictors related to the size and symmetry of the planum temporale (part of the temporoparietal area implicated in successful reading) has been related to word reading and comprehension. However, conflicting results as to the lateralization of the asymmetry have arisen from postmortem anatomy studies and in vivo MRI studies (Leonard et al. 2006). It may be the case that extreme asymmetries of the planum temporale in either direction may induce risk for dyslexia. Pernet and colleagues (2009) also found that structural volumes either much larger or smaller than those of controls were associated with atypical reading. In their sample, 100% of adults could be accurately classified as typical or dyslexic on the basis of the volumes of the right cerebellar declive and left lentiform nucleus (part of the basal ganglia). Their findings also suggested that the concept of a U-shaped curve, in which extreme values on either the high or low end can cause a disorder, could also help explain the conflicting findings of asymmetry noted above. In particular, smaller volumes of the cerebellar declive were associated with more severe phonological deficits. Although the precise role of the cerebellum relating to PA is not entirely clear, notable research has implicated the lentiform nucleus in the automaticity for automatic, serial processing of language, such as is required for rapid naming (Smits-Bandstra & De Nil 2007). Although anatomical differences relating to RAN have been less studied, a few differences have been reported, including greater rightward asymmetry of pars triangularis of left IFG and right cerebellum associated with lower RAN scores (Eckert et al. 2003).

Because RAN and fluency depend on the speed and integration of multiple processes throughout the brain, the extent and quality of white matter pathways may play a substantial role in helping us to understand the biological basis of fluency-related processes. A newer type of MRI scan, called diffusion tensor imaging (DTI), has allowed researchers to look at white matter pathways of the brain. Studies suggest that white matter differences exist between typical and dyslexic readers in reading-related regions including IFG, temporoparietal, and occipitotemporal areas (Rimrodt et al. 2010); white matter characteristics in these areas were also correlated with speeded word-reading ability.

Furthermore, one of the first and most striking insights into the fluency circuits in the brain came from research on a rare genetic brain malformation known as periventricular nodular heterotopia (PNH), in which neurons migrate into the ventricles of the brain to form nodules in various areas both posterior and anterior. Subjects with PNH all demonstrate specific deficits in reading fluency despite intact IQ and single-word reading ability and despite great diversity in where the nodules formed across individuals (Chang et al. 2007). In people with PNH, RAN letters and numbers were strongly correlated ($r = 0.78$ and 0.91, respectively) with a DTI measure of white matter quality called fractional anisotropy (FA). DTI scans also revealed that white matter tracts were disorganized around areas where nodules occurred in each individual. This unique disorder provides further evidence that reading can be disrupted at the fluency level only and that the connectivity of various regions in the brain may play a strong part in determining fluency.

Genetics of RAN and Fluency

Although researchers have long recognized that dyslexia is heritable, the leap from genes to behavior in a process that is not genetically dictated (like vision or language) is likely to be extraordinarily complex. Our relatively recent ability to compare genetic samples from twins or groups of different reading abilities and to scan the genome for markers associated with behavioral variables allows us another window into the processes of the reading circuit and underlying causes of dyslexia.

Heritability estimates for dyslexia range widely, from 0.3 to 0.7 (a trait that was 100% determined by genetics would measure 1.0). The precise level of heritability is difficult to ascertain because of the different reading measures, diagnostic criteria, and methods used, but the concordance of dyslexia is consistently reported to be higher in monozygotic than in dizygotic twins (Scerri & Schulte-Körne 2010). Several studies have examined the relationship between RAN and PA and whether they are based on shared or unique genetic factors. Several researchers have reported that there is a set of common genetic influences that affect PA, RAN, and reading (that is, they are all affected by some common genes) but that there are also separate genetic influences on PA and RAN (Byrne et al. 2005, Compton et al. 2001, Petrill et al. 2006).

At least nine major candidate genes for susceptibility to dyslexia have been identified, located on eight different chromosomes (Scerri & Schulte-Körne 2010). Most of these are related to neuronal migration and axon growth in utero (Galaburda et al. 2006). Indeed, the importance of neuronal migration for dyslexia is echoed in findings of PNH as well as in Galaburda's and Geschwind's earlier studies of postmortem brains that showed abnormal migration, especially between cortical layers. It will be essential in future research to link findings from structural and functional MRI, DTI, EEG, and genetics, to learn how biology and behavior interact to affect reading ability. Researchers including Hoeft, Gaab, and Gabrieli have begun work in this area.

IMPLICATIONS OF RAN AND FLUENCY FOR IDENTIFYING READING DIFFICULTIES, INSTRUCTION, AND INTERVENTION

Identification and Assessment

Although the relationships between rapid naming ability and reading abilities have been studied extensively, there remains insufficient understanding of its clinical uses among some practitioners. It is our assessment that RAN tasks can be best used by educators and psychologists as part of a clinical assessment to identify risk for reading and learning difficulties and as a measure of the development and efficiency of processes related to word retrieval and reading fluency (Wolf & Denckla 2005).

RAN tasks take only a few minutes to administer and require only modest training to administer and score. It is essential that RAN and other fluency measures be included in psychoeducational assessment batteries. For early screening for potential reading difficulties, we presented evidence from multiple longitudinal studies that show that RAN is one of the most robust early indicators of potential reading difficulties, along with phonological skills and letter name and sound knowledge. Using published normed measures, examiners can determine how a child's RAN ability compares with what is typical for a given age or grade. A second important reason for assessing RAN and other fluency issues is that speed and automaticity are essential components of what it means to be a good reader, yet we tend to measure reading too often only in terms of accuracy. Myriad studies have shown that one can be an accurate reader without being a fluent reader (see Breznitz 2006). Often, children who have an "invisible" speed deficit are not identified until later in school, and they may start to suffer the negative effects of having a reading difficulty, such as poorer academic performance in other subjects. For this reason, fluency measures that take into account speed and comprehension should be included in reading assessments.

Interventions for Fluency

A question that naturally follows from these findings is, can we train children to improve their RAN ability and thus impact their reading skills? Children with phonological weaknesses who receive high-quality phonological interventions tend to improve both their PA skills and decoding ability (Torgesen 2004). A host of well-designed, structured, multisensory phonology programs exist, and they are indeed effective in remediating phonological deficits. However, the question of how to improve reading fluency, and whether one can improve RAN ability, is much more difficult. First, the RAN task itself is a surface indicator of the efficiency of the underlying processes shared by naming and reading. There have been no large-scale, well-controlled studies that have tried to explicitly train naming speed. Here, a gap in the literature is not a bad thing—most researchers would agree that training students on a RAN task would not be the optimal way to improve their reading fluency. RAN seems to be related to individual developmental processes; RAN times improve with age, but individuals seem to be relatively consistent in their overall naming ability across time, relative to peers. In terms of assessment, we would expect to see raw scores for RAN change as children develop and become more automatic, but an individual's standard score based on age would be more consistent. Our own studies have shown that although our best interventions can improve most reading and language variables, the RAN changes little from pre- to posttreatment, indicating that RAN taps a more basic index of processing.

How, then, do we promote reading fluency and provide intervention for students who struggle with this skill? How do we train this system that seems inherently untrainable? One technique that has been widely used as a purported way to improve fluency is repeated reading. In this technique, a student reads a passage multiple times, with increasing speed. After repeated reading, students show some generalizible increases in speed and accuracy of decoding (see Meyer & Felton 1999 for a review). However, these results and the entire approach of repeated reading measures yield changes in speed that may not be related to improvements in our sine qua non of reading, fluent comprehension. Whereas we know that fluent comprehension depends on accuracy and automaticity at every level of language, few intervention programs reflect this. There are numerous programs designed to address phonological decoding skills, but few programs explicitly address multiple components of language, such as orthography, morphology, syntax, and semantics, with the goal of improving fluent comprehension.

Few random-assignment treatment-control studies examine the effects of different reading intervention programs. One such study, led by Lovett, Morris, and Wolf, examined the impact of intervention on 279 students with reading difficulties (Morris et al. 2011). Students were randomly assigned to one of four different intervention programs designed to contrast different types of instruction: (*a*) study skills and math instruction (no reading instruction), (*b*) PHAB + study skills, a phonological program plus study skills instruction, (*c*) PHAST, a multicomponential word-identification strategy and phonological program, or (*d*) PHAB+RAVE-O, a multicomponential program designed to address each level of reading (Wolf et al. 2009) and a phonology program. Students were matched for IQ, race, and socioeconomic status among groups, and each group received 70 hours of small-group instruction.

Results showed that children who received multicomponential interventions (PHAST or PHAB+RAVE-O) had significantly greater growth than did other intervention groups on timed and untimed word and nonword reading and passage comprehension. The multicomponential groups also maintained these levels of growth at follow-up one year after intervention. In terms of fluency, which is notoriously difficult to improve, children in the multicomponential groups again outperformed the other interventions, with only the RAVE-O group gaining more than six standard score points on the Gray Oral Reading Quotient (Morris et al. 2011). In sum, the two multicomponential interventions significantly improved children's reading accuracy and fluent comprehension relative to closely matched programs that included phonology-only or general academic instruction, and RAVE-O, which targeted the most components, had the best results for fluent comprehension

and also on vocabulary measures, both post-treatment and at one-year follow-up. These results highlight the importance of explicitly addressing the multiple levels of language and multiple cognitive processes involved in reading.

The present review of the fluency research highlights the need for multicomponential interventions, such as PHAST, RAVE-O, and Language!, especially for students with RAN or double deficits whose weaknesses are not adequately addressed by a phonological decoding program. As we better understand each child's ability, we can better tailor instruction to benefit each child. Children whose teachers were trained in individualizing literacy instruction (including more emphasis at the subword and word levels versus connected text comprehension) during first grade had better literacy outcomes than those of matched classrooms without individualized instruction (Connor et al. 2009). Ultimately, our goal should be to understand the abilities of all children and to provide the types of instruction that best addresses their needs.

CONCLUSION

The field of reading research has come a long way toward understanding the complex set of skills that allow fluent comprehension of text. Research across the globe studying individuals' brains and whole classrooms' development has shown that RAN is deeply linked with reading processes. Slowly but surely, the field is moving from narrow, polarized views on the best ways to teach reading and conceptualize dyslexia to multicomponential frameworks for assessment and intervention. Even the long-held ideal that fluency is mostly reflected in the quality of prosody in oral reading is changing (Kuhn et al. 2010), so that fluency is understood as the crux of when many processes at multiple levels integrate seamlessly to promote the comprehension of text.

SUMMARY POINTS

1. Rapid automatized naming (RAN) measures act as a microcosm of the reading system, providing an index of one's abilities to integrate multiple neural processes.

2. RAN and phonological awareness are both robust early predictors of reading ability, and one or both are often impaired in people with dyslexia. Longitudinal, cross-linguistic, genetic, and neuroimaging studies suggest that these two crucial reading-related processes should be considered distinct constructs rather than subcomponents of a single construct.

3. It is advantageous to conceptualize fluent reading as a complex ability that depends on automaticity across all levels of cognitive and linguistic processing that are involved in reading, allowing time and thought to be devoted to comprehension.

4. Successful intervention for reading disabilities depends on accurate assessment of a child's profile in terms of both accuracy and speed across all levels of reading, from the subword to connected text. Multicomponential intervention programs that target phonology as well as multiple levels of language show the greatest promise in improving reading fluency.

FUTURE ISSUES

1. To better understand RAN and fluency as behavioral predictors and outcome measures, based on longitudinal studies incorporating brain imaging and/or genetics (such work is underway among the Neurodys consortium in Europe and by our colleagues Nadine Gaab and John Gabrieli in Boston).

2. To determine the most appropriate instruction and intervention techniques for certain profiles of readers or subtypes of dyslexia, especially those with fluency and naming deficits who may not benefit from traditional phonologically based interventions.

3. To research how reading in new and electronic media (e.g., on the Internet or from an e-reader) affects automaticity and fluent comprehension.

DISCLOSURE STATEMENT

The authors are unaware of any affiliation, funding, or financial holdings that might be perceived as affecting the objectivity of this review.

LITERATURE CITED

Amtmann D, Abbott RD, Berninger V. 2007. Mixture growth models of RAN and RAS row by row: insight into the reading system at work over time. *Read. Writ.* 20:785–813

Benjamin C, Gaab N. 2011. What's the story? The tale of reading fluency told at speed. *Hum. Brain Mapp.* In press

Bowers PG, Swanson LB. 1991. Naming speed deficits in reading disability: multiple measures of a singular process. *J. Exp. Child Psychol.* 51:195–219

Bradley L, Bryant PE. 1978. Difficulties in auditory organisation as a possible cause of reading backwardness. *Nature* 217:746–47

Breznitz Z. 2005. Brain activity during performance of naming tasks: comparison between dyslexic and regular readers. *Sci. Stud. Read.* 9:17–42

Breznitz Z. 2006. *Reading Fluency: Synchronization of Processes*. Mahwah, NJ: Erlbaum

Byrne B, Wadsworth S, Corley R, Samuelsson S, Quain P, et al. 2005. Longitudinal twin study of early literacy development: preschool and kindergarten phases. *Sci. Stud. Read.* 9:219–35

Catts HW, Gillispie M, Leonard LB, Kail RV, Miller CA. 2002. The role of speed of processing, rapid naming, and phonological awareness in reading achievement. *J. Learn. Disabil.* 35:510–25

Chang B, Katzir T, Liu T, Corriveau K, Barzillai M, et al. 2007. A structural basis for reading fluency: white matter defects in a genetic brain malformation. *Neurology* 69:2146–54

Christodoulou JA, Del Tufo S, Lymberis J, Saxler PK, Triantafyllou C, et al. 2011. Neural correlates of rapid automatized naming in skilled and struggling readers. Manuscript under review

Clarke P, Hulme C, Snowling M. 2005. Individual differences in RAN and reading: a response timing analysis. *J. Res. Read.* 28:73–86

Compton DL, Davis CJ, DeFries JC, Gayan J, Olson RK. 2001. Genetic and environmental influences on reading and RAN: an overview of results from the Colorado twin study. In *Time, Fluency, and Developmental Dyslexia*, ed. M Wolf, pp. 277–303. Baltimore, MD: York Press

Compton DL, Olson RK, DeFries JC, Pennington BF. 2002. Comparing the relationships among two different versions of alphanumeric rapid automatized naming and word level reading skills. *Sci. Stud. Read.* 6:343–68

Connor CM, Piasta SB, Fishman B, Glasney S, Schatschneider C, et al. 2009. Individualizing student instruction precisely: effects of child × instruction interactions on first graders' literacy development. *Child Dev.* 80:77–100

Cutting LE, Denckla MB. 2001. The relationship of rapid serial naming and word reading in normally developing readers: an exploratory model. *Read. Writ.* 14:673–705

Dehaene S. 2009. *Reading in the Brain: The Science and Evolution of a Human Invention*. New York: Viking

Denckla MB. 1972. Color naming deficits in dyslexic boys. *Cortex* 8:164–76

Denckla MB, Rudel RG. 1976a. Naming of objects by dyslexic and other learning disabled children. *Brain Lang.* 3:1–15

Denckla MB, Rudel RG. 1976b. Rapid automatized naming (R.A.N): dyslexia differentiated from other learning disabilities. *Neuropsychologia* 14:471–79

Eckert MA, Leonard CM, Richards TL, Aylward EH, Thomson J, Berninger VW. 2003. Anatomical correlates of dyslexia: frontal and cerebellar findings. *Brain* 126:482–94

Foorman BR, Francis DJ, Shaywitz SE, Shaywitz BA, Fletcher JM. 1997. The case for early reading intervention. In *Foundations of Reading Acquisition and Dyslexia: Implications for Early Intervention*, ed. B Blachman, pp. 243–64: London: Psychol. Press

Frijters JC, Lovett MW, Steinbach KA, Wolf M, Sevcik RA, Morris RD. 2011. Neurocognitive predictors of reading outcomes for children with reading disabilities. *J. Learn. Disabil.* 44:150–66

Galaburda AM, LoTurco J, Ramus F, Fitch RH, Rosen GD. 2006. From genes to behavior in developmental dyslexia. *Nat. Neurosci.* 9:1213–17

Georgiou GK, Parrila R, Kirby J. 2006. Rapid naming speed components and early reading acquisition. *Sci. Stud. Read.* 10:199–220

Georgiou GK, Parrila R, Kirby JR, Stephenson K. 2008a. Rapid naming components and their relationship with phonological awareness, orthographic knowledge, speed of processing, and different reading outcomes. *Sci. Stud. Read.* 12:325–50

Georgiou GK, Parrila R, Liao CH. 2008b. Rapid naming speed and reading across languages that vary in orthographic consistency. *Read. Writ.* 21:885–903

Geschwind N. 1965. Disconnexion syndromes in animals and man. *Brain* 27:237–94

Geschwind N, Fusillo M. 1966. Color-naming defects in association with alexia. *Arch. Neurol.* 15:137–46

Grigorenko EL. 2006. Learning disabilities in juvenile offenders. *Child Adolesc. Psychiatr. Clin. N. Am.* 15:353–71

Hallahan DP, Mercer CD. 2002. Learning disabilities: historical perspectives. In *Identification of Learning Disabilities: Research to Practice*, ed. R Bradley, LC Danielson, DP Hallahan, pp. 1–67. Mahwah, NJ: Erlbaum

Hoeft F, Meyler A, Hernandez A, Juel C, Taylor-Hill H, et al. 2007. Functional and morphometric brain dissociation between dyslexia and reading ability. *Proc. Natl. Acad. Sci. USA* 104:4234–9

Humphrey N, Mullins PM. 2002. Self-concept and self-esteem in developmental dyslexia. *J. Res. Spec. Educ. Needs* 2:1–13

Kail R, Hall LK. 1994. Processing speed, naming speed, and reading. *Dev. Psychol.* 30:949–54

Katzir T, Kim Y, Wolf M, Morris R, Lovett MW. 2008. Comparing subtypes of children with dyslexia at letter, word, and connected text levels of reading. *J. Learn. Disabil.* 41:47–66

Katzir T, Kim Y, Wolf M, O'Brien B, Kennedy B, et al. 2006. Reading fluency: the whole is more than the parts. *Ann. Dyslexia* 56:51–82

Kirby JR, Georgiou GK, Martinussen R, Parrila R, Bowers P, Landerl K. 2010. Naming speed and reading: from prediction to instruction. *Read. Res. Q.* 45:341–62

Kobayashi MS, Haynes CW, Macaruso P, Hook PE, Kato J. 2005. Effects of mora deletion, nonword repetition, rapid naming, and visual search performance on beginning reading in Japanese. *Ann. Dyslexia* 55:105–28

Kuhn M, Schwanenflugel P, Meisinger E. 2010. Aligning theory and assessment of reading fluency: automaticity, prosody, and definitions of fluency. *Read. Res. Q.* 45:230–51

LaBerge D, Samuels SJ. 1974. Toward a theory of automatic information processing in reading. *Cogn. Psychol.* 6:293–323

Landerl K, Wimmer H, Frith U. 1997. The impact of orthographic consistency on dyslexia: a German-English comparison. *Cognition* 63:315–34

Leonard C, Eckert M, Given B, Virginia B, Eden G. 2006. Individual differences in anatomy predict reading and oral language impairments in children. *Brain* 129:3329–42

Leppänen PH, Richardson U, Pihko E, Eklund KM, Guttorm TK, et al. 2002. Brain responses to changes in speech sound durations differ between infants with and without familial risk for dyslexia. *Dev. Neuropsychol.* 22:407–22

Liberman IY. 1971. Basic research in speech and lateralization of language: some implications for reading disability. *Ann. Dyslexia* 21:71–87

Logan JAR, Schatschneider C, Wagner RK. 2009. Rapid serial naming and reading ability: the role of lexical access. *Read. Writ.* 24:1–25

Lymberis J, Christodoulou JA, O'Loughlin P, Del Tufo S, Gabrieli JDE. 2009. *Neural correlates of rapid automatized naming.* Presented at Soc. Neurosci. Annu. Meet., 38th, Chicago, IL

Lyon GR, Shaywitz SE, Shaywitz BA. 2003. A definition of dyslexia. *Ann. Dyslexia* 53:1–14

MacLeod CM. 1991. Half a century of research on the Stroop effect: an integrative review. *Psychol. Bull.* 109:163–203

Maisog JM, Einbinder ER, Flowers DL, Turkeltaub PE, Eden GF. 2008. A meta-analysis of functional neuroimaging studies of dyslexia. *Ann. N. Y. Acad. Sci.* 1145:237–59

Maurer U, Bucher K, Brem S, Benz R, Kranz F, et al. 2009. Neurophysiology in preschool improves behavioral prediction of reading ability throughout primary school. *Biol. Psychiatry* 66:341–48

McBride-Chang C, Liu PD, Wong T, Wong A, Shu H. 2011. Specific reading difficulties in Chinese, English, or both: longitudinal markers of phonological awareness, morphological awareness, and RAN in Hong Kong Chinese children. *J. Learn. Disabil.* DOI: 10.1177/0022219411400748. In press

Meyer MS, Felton RH. 1999. Repeated reading to enhance fluency: old approaches and new directions. *Ann. Dyslexia* 1:283–306

Meyer MS, Wood FB, Hart LA, Felton RH. 1998. Selective predictive value of rapid automatized naming in poor readers. *J. Learn. Disabil.* 31:106–17

Minagawa-Kawai Y, van der Lely H, Ramus F, Sato Y, Mazuka R, Dupoux E. 2011. Optical brain imaging reveals general auditory and language-specific processing in early infant development. *Cereb. Cortex* 21:254–61

Misra M, Katzir T, Wolf M, Poldrack RA. 2004. Neural systems for rapid automatized naming in skilled readers: unraveling the RAN-reading relationship. *Sci. Stud. Read.* 8:241–56

Morris RD, Lovett MW, Wolf M, Sevcik RA, Steinbach KA, et al. 2011. Multiple-component remediation for developmental reading disabilities: IQ, socioeconomic status, and race as factors in remedial outcome. *J. Learn. Disabil.* DOI: 10.1177/0022219409355472. In press

Morris RD, Stuebing KK, Fletcher JM, Shaywitz SE, Lyon GR, et al. 1998. Subtypes of reading disability: variability around a phonological core. *J. Educ. Psychol.* 90:347–73

Natl. Inst. Child Health Human Dev. 2000. Report of the National Reading Panel. Teaching children to read: an evidence-based assessment of the scientific research literature on reading and its implications for reading instruction: reports of the subgroups. *NIH Publ. No. 00-4754.* Washington, DC: US Gov. Print. Off.

Neuhaus G, Foorman BR, Francis DJ, Carlson CD. 2001. Measures of information processing in rapid automatized naming (RAN) and their relation to reading. *J. Exp. Child Psychol.* 78:359–73

Norton ES, Eddy MD, Perrachione T, Cyr AB, Wolf M, et al. 2011. *Mismatch negativity predicts reading fluency in young children.* Presented at Cogn. Neuro. Soc. Annu. Meet. 18th, San Francisco, CA

Obregon M. 1994. *Exploring Naming Timing Patterns by Dyslexic and Normal Readers on the Serial RAN Task.* Medford, MA: Tufts Univ. Press

Orton ST. 1925. "Word-blindness" in school children. *Arch. Neurol. Psychiatry* 14:581–615

Orton ST. 1939. A neurological explanation of the reading disability. *Educ. Rec.* 20:58–68

Peña M, Maki A, Kovacić D, Dehaene-Lambertz G, Koizumi H, et al. 2003. Sounds and silence: an optical topography study of language recognition at birth. *Proc. Natl. Acad. Sci. USA* 100:11702–5

Pennington BF, Lefly DL. 2001. Early reading development in children at family risk for dyslexia. *Child Dev.* 72:816–33

Perfetti CA. 1986. Continuities in reading acquisition, reading skill, and reading disability. *Rem. Spec. Educ.* 7:11–21

Pernet CR, Poline JB, Demonet JF, Rousselet GA. 2009. Brain classification reveals the right cerebellum as the best biomarker of dyslexia. *BMC Neurosci.* 10:67–86

Petrill SA, Deater-Deckard K, Thompson LA, DeThorne LS, Schatschneider C. 2006. Genetic and environmental effects of serial naming and phonological awareness on early reading outcomes. *J. Educ. Psychol.* 98:112–21

Pinker S. 1997. Foreword. In *Why Our Children Can't Read and What We Can Do About It: A Scientific Revolution in Reading*, ed. D McGuinness, pp. ix–x. New York: Free Press

Powell D, Stainthorp R, Stuart M, Garwood H, Quinlan P. 2007. An experimental comparison between rival theories of rapid automatized naming performance and its relationship to reading. *J. Exp. Child Psychol.* 98:46–68

Ramus F, Landerl K, Moll K, Lyytinen H, Leppanen PHT, et al. 2011. Predictors of literacy skills and developmental dyslexia in six European orthographies. Manuscript under review

Raschle NM, Chang M, Gaab N. 2011. Structural brain alterations associated with dyslexia predate reading onset. *NeuroImage* 57:742–49

Richlan F, Kronbichler M, Wimmer H. 2009. Functional abnormalities in the dyslexic brain: a quantitative meta-analysis of neuroimaging studies. *Hum. Brain Mapp.* 30:3299–308

Rimrodt SL, Peterson DJ, Denckla MB, Kaufmann WE, Cutting LE. 2010. White matter microstructural differences linked to left perisylvian language network in children with dyslexia. *Cortex* 46:739–49

Scarborough H. 1998. Predicting the future achievement of second graders with reading disabilities: contributions of phonemic awareness, verbal memory, rapid naming, and IQ. *Ann. Dyslexia* 48:115–36

Scerri TS, Schulte-Korne G. 2010. Genetics of developmental dyslexia. *Eur. Child Adolesc. Psychiatry* 19:179–97

Schatschneider C, Fletcher JM, Francis DJ, Carlson CD, Foorman BR. 2004. Kindergarten prediction of reading skills: a longitudinal comparative analysis. *J. Educ. Psychol.* 96:265–82

Seymour PHK, Aro M, Erskine JM. 2003. Foundation literacy acquisition in European orthographies. *Br. J. Psychol.* 94:143–74

Shany M, Share DL. 2011. Subtypes of reading disability in a shallow orthography: a double dissociation between accuracy-disabled and rate-disabled readers of Hebrew. *Ann. Dyslexia* 61:64–84

Shaul S. 2008. Event-related potentials (ERPs) in the study of dyslexia. In *Brain Research in Language*, ed. Z Breznitz, pp. 51–92. New York: Springer

Smits-Bandstra S, De Nil LF. 2007. Sequence skill learning in persons who stutter: implications for cortico-striato-thalamo-cortical dysfunction. *J. Fluency Disord.* 32:251–78

Spring C, Capps C. 1974. Encoding speed, rehearsal, and probed recall of dyslexic boys. *J. Educ. Psychol.* 66:780–86

Svensson I, Lundberg I, Jacobson C. 2001. The prevalence of reading and spelling difficulties among inmates of institutions for compulsory care of juvenile delinquents. *Dyslexia* 7:62–76

Swanson HL, Trainin G, Necoechea DM, Hammill DD. 2003. Rapid naming, phonological awareness, and reading: a meta-analysis of the correlation evidence. *Rev. Educ. Res.* 73:407–40

Tan LH, Spinks JA, Eden GF, Perfetti CA, Siok WT. 2005. Reading depends on writing, in Chinese. *Proc. Natl. Acad. Sci. USA* 102:8781–85

Torgesen JK. 2004. Avoiding the devastating downward spiral: the evidence that early intervention prevents reading failure. *Am. Educator* 28:6–19

Torgesen JK, Wagner RK, Rashotte CA, Burgess S, Hecht S. 1997. Contributions of phonological awareness and rapid naming ability to the growth of word reading skills in second-to-fifth-grade children. *Sci. Stud. Read.* 1:161–85

Torppa M, Lyytinen P, Erskine J, Eklund K, Lyytinen H. 2010. Language development, literacy skills, and predictive connections to reading in Finnish children with and without familial risk for dyslexia. *J. Learn. Disabil.* 43:308–21

Turkeltaub PE, Gareau L, Flowers DL, Zeffiro TA, Eden GF. 2003. Development of neural mechanisms for reading. *Nat. Neurosci.* 6:767–73

Vaessen A, Bertrand D, Tóth D, Csépe V, Faísca L, et al. 2010. Cognitive development of fluent word reading does not qualitatively differ between transparent and opaque orthographies. *J. Educ. Psychol.* 102:827–42

van den Bos KP, Zijlstra BJH, Spelberg HC. 2002. Life-span data on continuous-naming speeds of numbers, letters, colors, and pictured objects, and word-reading speed. *Sci. Stud. Read.* 6:25–49

Vellutino FR, Scanlon DM, Tanzman MS. 1998. The case for early intervention in diagnosing specific reading disability. *J. School Psychol.* 36:367–97

Vukovic RK, Wilson AM, Nash KK. 2004. Naming speed deficits in adults with reading disabilities. *J. Learn. Disabil.* 37:440–50

Waber DP, Forbes PW, Wolff PH, Weiler MD. 2004. Neurodevelopmental characteristics of children with learning impairments classified according to the double-deficit hypothesis. *J. Learn. Disabil.* 37:451–61

Wagner RK, Torgesen JK. 1987. The nature of phonological processing and its causal role in the acquisition of reading skills. *Psychol. Bull.* 101:192–212

Wagner RK, Torgesen JK, Rashotte CA. 1999. *Comprehensive Test of Phonological Processing (CTOPP)*. Austin, TX: Pro-Ed

Wagner RK, Torgesen JK, Rashotte CA, Hecht SA, Barker TA, et al. 1997. Changing relations between phonological processing abilities and word-level reading as children develop from beginning to skilled readers: a 5-year longitudinal study. *Dev. Psychol.* 33:468–79

Willcutt EG, Pennington BF, Olson RK, Chhabildas N, Hulslander J. 2005. Neuropsychological analyses of comorbidity between reading disability and attention deficit hyperactivity disorder: in search of the common deficit. *Dev. Neuropsychol.* 27:35–78

Wolf M. 1986. Rapid alternating stimulus naming in the developmental dyslexias. *Brain Lang.* 27:360–79

Wolf M. 2007. *Proust and the Squid: The Story and Science of the Reading Brain*. New York: HarperCollins

Wolf M, Bally H, Morris R. 1986. Automaticity, retrieval processes, and reading: a longitudinal study in average and impaired readers. *Child Dev.* 57:988–1000

Wolf M, Barzillai M, Gottwald S, Miller L, Norton E, et al. 2009. The RAVE-O intervention: connecting neuroscience to the classroom. *Mind Brain Educ.* 3:84–93

Wolf M, Bowers PG. 1999. The double-deficit hypothesis for the developmental dyslexias. *J. Educ. Psychol.* 91:415–38

Wolf M, Bowers PG, Biddle K. 2000. Naming-speed processes, timing, and reading. *J. Learn. Disabil.* 33:387–407

Wolf M, Denckla MB. 2005. *RAN/RAS: Rapid Automatized Naming and Rapid Alternating Stimulus Tests*. Austin, TX: Pro-Ed

Wolf M, Goldberg O'Rourke A, Gidney C, Lovett M, Cirino P, Morris R. 2002. The second deficit: an investigation of the independence of phonological and naming-speed deficits in developmental dyslexia. *Read. Writ.* 15:43–72

Wolf M, Katzir-Cohen T. 2001. Reading fluency and its intervention. *Sci. Stud. Read.* 5:211–39

Ziegler JC, Perry C, Ma-Wyatt A, Ladner D, Schulte-Korne G. 2003. Developmental dyslexia in different languages: language-specific or universal? *J. Exp. Child Psychol.* 86:169–93

Intelligence

Ian J. Deary

Centre for Cognitive Ageing and Cognitive Epidemiology, Department of Psychology, University of Edinburgh, Edinburgh EH8 9JZ, United Kingdom; email: i.deary@ed.ac.uk

Annu. Rev. Psychol. 2012. 63:453–82

First published online as a Review in Advance on September 19, 2011

The *Annual Review of Psychology* is online at psych.annualreviews.org

This article's doi:
10.1146/annurev-psych-120710-100353

Keywords

IQ, cognitive ability, psychometrics, behavior genetics, cognitive epidemiology, twins, education, health

Abstract

Individual differences in human intelligence are of interest to a wide range of psychologists and to many people outside the discipline. This overview of contributions to intelligence research covers the first decade of the twenty-first century. There is a survey of some of the major books that appeared since 2000, at different levels of expertise and from different points of view. Contributions to the phenotype of intelligence differences are discussed, as well as some contributions to causes and consequences of intelligence differences. The major causal issues covered concern the environment and genetics, and how intelligence differences are being mapped to brain differences. The major outcomes discussed are health, education, and socioeconomic status. Aging and intelligence are discussed, as are sex differences in intelligence and whether twins and singletons differ in intelligence. More generally, the degree to which intelligence has become a part of broader research in neuroscience, health, and social science is discussed.

Contents

INTRODUCTION

Some people are cleverer than others. The ways in which this occurs, and the causes and consequences of these individual differences, are the topics of this review.

It is some time since the *Annual Review of Psychology* contained an article that dealt substantially with human intelligence differences. Therefore, the period that is covered is broadly the past ten years: the first decade of the twenty-first century. Historically, this is neat, because the foundations of the scientific study of human intelligence differences were laid in the first decade of the twentieth century. Then, there were the statistical developments, empirical discoveries, and conceptual innovations of Spearman (1904) and the intelligence testing technology begun by Binet (1905). Some key questions that Spearman and Binet addressed are still lively topics of research: Along which dimensions of mental abilities do people differ? Do these differences matter? And what are the causes of these differences? These and other questions—such as the effect of aging on intelligence—are included in the present review.

One should be explicit about the difficulties that accompany the topic of human intelligence differences (which will normally, here, be shortened to just intelligence). The study of individual differences has never been in the mainstream of psychology. With respect to psychology's two cultures—experimental and differential (Cronbach 1957)—differential is the small minority. Not only that, but the statistical procedures used by differential psychologists are relatively abstruse to those outside the field. These factors—and the fact that intelligence-type tests have been used so widely in practical settings and have been the subject of controversies—contribute to the range of attitudes that intelligence research attracts from lay and professional outsiders. These attitudes include interest (research reports on intelligence often attract much media interest), indifference (much of mainstream psychology and wider social science ignores individual differences in intelligence), and hostility (the emotional heat generated by some aspects of intelligence research is matched by few other topics in psychology). However, this review also describes how researchers from a number of other disciplines—e.g., neuroscience and epidemiology—are newly and keenly including intelligence as a topic in their research. Intelligence is rarely discussed for long before the word "controversial" appears; this is another difficulty. Because there is controversy attached to some research topics in intelligence, it is important that there are clear and even-handed accounts of what is known and what is unknown about it. The present piece attempts to be both, with examples of influential studies and pointers to areas of disagreement.

RECENT BOOKS ON INTELLIGENCE

The Remarkable 1990s

Books in the past 10 years followed a remarkable decade, because the 1990s witnessed several important publishing events in intelligence. Carroll's (1993) *Human Cognitive Abilities* was his decades-in-preparation analysis of over 400 intelligence data sets that synthesized human cognitive differences in a three-level psychometric hierarchy. Jensen's (1998) *The g Factor* was a massive review of the construct of general intelligence (*g*). Brand's (1996) book of the same name—*The g Factor*—was withdrawn by Wiley after some of the author's remarks in the press about group differences. The book was given a postmortem review in *Nature* (Mackintosh 1996), which commented that, "This seems a singularly cack-handed attempt at censorship... How is it that they found out about the repellant nature of Brand's views only *after* they had printed and distributed copies of the book" (p. 33). Of these books, Carroll's is singled out here for its usefulness in cementing a psychometric structure for intelligence that brought "harmony where there had been discord," although similar models had been available for decades. However, the intelligence publishing event of the 1990s was Herrnstein & Murray's (1994) *The Bell Curve*, which spawned an industry of mainly hostile reaction that continues into the twenty-first century. The book is an unusual mixture of overview, empirical analyses, statistical tutorials, policy reflections, and appendixes and notes (approximately 300 pages of the latter). For example, Part II of the book was almost 150 pages of analyses of the white people in the National Longitudinal Survey of Youth 1979. The authors ran regression models that enquired about the relative importance of measured intelligence and parental socioeconomic status for important social outcomes such as poverty, education, employment, injury, marriage, divorce, childbearing, welfare dependency, parenting, crime, and citizenship.

Intelligence Books from the Past Decade

Because of space limitations, it is possible only to select some books about intelligence from the previous decade. Inevitably, someone's favorite book on intelligence will be missing. However, the following have been chosen because they provide interesting and still-useful accounts of different aspects of intelligence.

With regard to general books on intelligence, there are two books for the lay person or beginning student: Deary's (2000) *Intelligence: A Very Short Introduction* and Cianciolo & Sternberg's (2004) *Intelligence: A Brief History* are both elementary introductions to the science of the area, and they also cover some of the controversies in intelligence research. Bartholomew's (2004) *Measuring Intelligence* is a useful view of intelligence research from the perspective of a statistician, making it more objective than most accounts. Probably the best book on human intelligence differences to appear for many years, Hunt's (2011) *Human Intelligence* is superb. It is written by someone almost equally at home in experimental and differential psychology, with an engaging wit, comprehensive knowledge, and clear writing style. Most of all, it is written with great even-handedness; even for the controversial areas of intelligence it is strongly recommended as an excellent account of the science of intelligence research to date. It also has the merit of not avoiding the technicalities involved in intelligence research, and it explains them well.

The previous decade saw some interesting books on the history of intelligence. Carson's (2007) *The Measure of Merit* is a detailed look at the origins of the idea of merit and mental testing, especially in France and the United States, and begins, historically, well prior to current intelligence testing technology. It is light on the psychometric aspects and arguments of intelligence, but very careful and painstaking in, for example, describing how the military were won over to mental testing in World War I. Wright Gillham's (2001) *A Life of Sir Francis Galton: From African Exploration to the Birth of*

Eugenics is probably the best biography of the Victorian genius to date and includes his seminal work on intelligence. Remarkably, this pioneer of intelligence research and statistics was a significant contributor to many other scientific areas; so much so that, despite the importance of Galton's contribution to intelligence and cognate topics, these take up a small section of the book. White's (2006) *Intelligence, Destiny and Education* is an intriguing examination of the originators of intelligence testing. His thesis is that these researchers were largely characterized by a nonconformist religious background, which in turn led them to emphasize gifted and "feeble-minded" individuals (and less so the middle of the continuum), heredity, and the usefulness of examinations. Although intriguing, the thesis is not convincing.

In addition to history books there have also been several of what might be characterized as broadly anti-IQ-type books. These include Murdoch's (2007) *IQ: A Smart History of a Failed Idea*, Nisbett's (2009) *Intelligence and How to Get It*, Shenk's (2010) *The Genius In All of Us: Why Everything You've Been Told About Genetics, Talent and Intelligence is Wrong*, and Stanovich's (2009) *What Intelligence Tests Miss: The Psychology of Rational Thought*. All are readable, often highly so. Murdoch reviews the history and major areas of controversy in intelligence research, with clear antagonism toward IQ testing and a preference for theories that emphasize multiple mental abilities. Stanovich, in particular, emphasizes aspects of reasoning that are poorly correlated with intelligence and often lacking in people who are intelligent. Shenk emphasizes gene-environment interactions in human life, downplays main effects of intelligence, and argues that the attainment of excellence may be found more in effort. Of these three books, Stanovich's and Shenk's stand out as having the better empirical bases. However, the empirical surveys take them where they will. Stanovich could easily have emphasized the value of rational thought without the negative reference to intelligence tests in the title. None of the four authors is a researcher on intelligence, and it is interesting to reflect on how many other areas of psychological research attract such attention from journalists and psychologists from outside their fields.

There have been several books on the causes of intelligence differences. Deary's (2000) *Looking Down On Human Intelligence: From Psychometrics to the Brain* was a relatively pessimistic survey of what had been contributed by studying cognitive components of intelligence and also the relatively limited findings that had come from biological approaches to intelligence during the twentieth century. Geary's (2005) *The Origin of Mind: Evolution of Brain, Cognition, and General Intelligence* took a more evolutionary approach and tried to fit intelligence differences within broader ideas in the development of brain and mind. Garlick's (2010) *Intelligence and the Brain: Solving the Mystery of Why People Differ in IQ and How a Child Can Be a Genius* had a particular thesis concerning white matter and processing speed and how they produce intelligence, but it was probably at too general a level and with too little empirical information to validate the interesting ideas fully. Duncan's (2010) *How Intelligence Happens* is a welcome account of intelligence from an experimental psychologist who acknowledges the existence and omnipresence of Spearman's g, with biological leanings. Flynn's (2007) *What Is Intelligence?* was an interesting culmination of his work since he had demonstrated the Flynn effect of rising intelligence. I have largely avoided edited books in this survey. However, Wilhelm & Engle's (2005) *Handbook of Understanding and Measuring Intelligence* and Sternberg & Grigorenko's (2002) *The General Factor of Intelligence: How General Is It?* both remain useful edited compilations of different viewpoints on the causes of intelligence differences.

Books on intelligence that concern individual, long-term cohort studies appeared in the past decade. The latest monograph from Schaie (2005)—*Developmental Influences on Adult Intelligence: The Seattle Longitudinal Study*—was an update on the Seattle longitudinal aging study. This cross-sequential study started in the 1950s, and this is an indispensable book about cognitive aging. Deary et al.'s (2009c) *A Lifetime of Intelligence: Follow-up Studies of the Scottish Mental Surveys of 1932 and 1947* was a summary of 10 years of work on follow-up studies of the population-wide intelligence tests that took place in Scotland. Because these two cover aspects of aging and intelligence, it should be noted that Salthouse's (2010) *Major Issues in Cognitive Aging* appeared recently and is a highly recommended source of information and toolkit for those concerned with aging aspects of intelligence.

Lynn & Vanhanen's (2002) *IQ and the Wealth of Nations* attempted to analyze prosperity at the national level and IQ. This type of global, country-level epidemiology has many critics. Lynn followed this up with three other books on international aspects of intelligence and productivity. At the personal level of success, Saunders's (2010) *Social Mobility Myths* summarized his and others' research, with a conclusion that social mobility is far greater and more meritocratic in U.K. society than most people—especially politicians and sociologists—think, and that mobility substantially depends on intelligence and effort.

THE PSYCHOMETRIC STRUCTURE OF INTELLIGENCE

Following Carroll's (1993) synthetic account of the psychometric structure of intelligence, there has been a broad consensus that meaningful variance among people exists at three levels: third-level general cognitive ability (g), second-level broad domains of cognitive functioning (group factors), and first-level test-specific variation. To explain these levels simply, consider the answer to the following question: Why are some people good at explaining the meanings of words in their first language? The answers are that people who are good at one mental task tend to be good at other types of mental task (third level; g); people who are good within one domain (e.g., verbal ability) tend to be good at other tasks in that domain; and people have strengths in specific, narrow mental skills. Thus, when a diverse battery of mental

tests is applied to a sample of the population, some of the between-subject variation is shared by all tests, some is shared by tests that have family resemblances within a cognitive domain, and some is specific to the individual test. g often accounts for nearly half the variance when a broad battery of cognitive tests is applied to a representative sample of the adult population. Relatively little of the variance lies at the domain level. Researchers do not always agree on the nature of the domains—they can vary in number, name and content between samples depending on the battery applied—and there have long been worries about whether the nature of g might vary between cognitive batteries.

The latter worry was addressed directly using over 400 subjects from the Minnesota Study of Twins Reared Apart (Johnson et al. 2004). The subjects had taken three large cognitive test batteries, originating from different theoretical orientations: the Hakstian and Cattell Comprehensive Ability Battery (14 tests); the Hawaii Battery, with Raven's Matrices added (17 tests); and the Wechsler Adult Intelligence Scale (11 tests). Each battery had a strong g factor, and the correlations among the three g factors—from a hierarchical confirmatory factor analysis—were 0.99, 0.99, and 1.00. That is, the individual differences in g were identical from the three different batteries, leading the authors to title the paper "Just one g." The result was replicated in a sample of over 500 Dutch seamen who had been tested on five different cognitive batteries (Johnson et al. 2008c). These two papers are important contributions to the psychometric structure of intelligence. As the authors stated, "our results provide the most substantive evidence of which we are aware that most psychological assessments of mental ability of any breadth are consistently identifying a common underlying component of general intelligence. These results provide evidence both for the existence of a general intelligence factor and for the consistency and accuracy of its measurement" (Johnson et al. 2008c, p. 91).

The subjects' mental test data from the Minnesota Study of Twins Reared Apart were also used to tweak Carroll's (1993) proposed three-level hierarchy of intelligence differences (Johnson & Bouchard 2005a). The authors inquired whether there might usefully be proposed some more general—but not as general as g—latent traits between the several second-level factors (group factors, or cognitive domains) and g, thus giving a four-level hierarchy. Carroll's results had suggested no. The second-level factors were called crystallized (12 tests), fluency (4), fluid (12), memory (6), perceptual speed (11), and visualization (14). Johnson and Bouchard's proposed candidates for new, third-level general factors were the Cattell-Horn fluid and crystallized factors and Vernon's verbal-educational (v:ed) and perceptual (k:m; spatial:mechanical) factors. Vernon's factors arose because, contra Spearman, he thought that, "It may be concluded that *no* test measures nothing but g and a specific factor, since the type of test material employed always introduces some additional common element" (Vernon 1956, p. 144). Therefore, according to Vernon, the v:ed domain influenced all tests involving verbal material and those that required the manipulation of words. The k:m domain influenced tests that required the mental manipulation of shapes, spatial imagination, and mechanical knowledge. However, better fitting than any of these three models was one that included three factors at the third level: verbal, perceptual, and image rotation. All three loaded very highly on g. The authors called this the VPR model of intelligence. The verbal and perceptual, and perceptual and image rotation, factors correlated very highly, and verbal and image rotation less so. The same four-level model was tested versus the other three using Thurstone's data on 60 mental tests from 1941 and again was found to fit best (Johnson & Bouchard 2005b).

Whereas the hierarchical structure of intelligence differences does allow researchers and interested others to focus on the variance accounted for in cognitive abilities at different levels of generality, there is still some impetus from those looking for an alternative formulation of intelligence or for additions to individual general intelligence. There was an attempt to operationalize Gardner's (1983, 1993) multiple intelligences as tests and to examine their intercorrelations and correlations with a standard psychometric intelligence test (Wonderlic Personnel Test) (Visser et al. 2006). There were clear results. As operationalized by these authors, most of the Gardner mental skills were correlated substantially with psychometric intelligence; formed a substantial g factor; and musical and body-kinesthetic intelligence were more separate and intrapersonal intelligence harder to measure. One group of investigators claimed to have found a "group intelligence" that can explain how well a group performs on tasks but is not just the mean or maximum of the individual general intelligence of the members of the group (Woolley et al. 2010). Group intelligence was higher in groups where turn-taking in speaking was relatively evenly distributed among members and in groups whose members had higher mean social sensitivity. Their practical suggestions were that it might be easier to boost the intelligence of a group than of an individual and that it might be useful to introduce group intelligence testing for teams of workers. Replication of this finding is necessary. The study has possible limitations in that the individual intelligence test was a single test, versus a range of tests for group intelligence, which, therefore, would have more general variation and be more likely to be correlated with a criterion measure. Furthermore, there was more overlap in content between the group intelligence test and the criterion tasks than looked likely with the individual intelligence measure.

It is often stated that the major historical challenge to Spearman's conception of intelligence differences as being largely based on g was from Thurstone and his Primary Mental Abilities (PMAs). This is only partly correct. It was clear from the late 1930s and certainly by the 1940s that the PMAs were not independent and that Thurstone's own data contained a statistical g factor. Probably the strongest psychometric challenge to Spearman's account of intelligence differences was from Godfrey Thomson (Bartholomew et al. 2009). Thomson never denied Spearman's positive manifold of correlations among mental tests, but he suggested a radically different reason for its occurring. Instead of *g*—perhaps, according to Spearman, the result of people having generally more or less of mental energy or power—Thomson found that the universally positive correlations among tests could also arise from each test's sampling a subset of numerous, independent mental bonds; thus his "bonds" or "sampling" theory of intelligence. The Spearman-Thomson debates lasted from the First World War until almost the end of World War II. A fresh look at Thomson's ideas concluded that his model of intelligence was not inferior to Spearman's, either on statistical or biological grounds, though that was partly because both were vague biologically (Bartholomew et al. 2009). A related development is the mutual interaction model of intelligence, which also posits the emergence of a general factor without a general cause (van der Maas et al. 2006). The basic idea is that a statistical *g* emerges through the mutual interaction, over the course of their development, of several cognitive processes.

COGNITIVE CORRELATES OF INTELLIGENCE

Those taking a reductionist view of intelligence have not always gone straight down to biology. Three levels of reduction have been visited that stop short of, say, genetics or brain imaging: other psychometric measures; measures from experimental psychology, especially reaction times; and measures from psychophysics, including inspection time. With the increased accessibility of brain imaging, studies that use these sorts of tasks and their related constructs along with intelligence are probably declining from a peak between the 1970s and 2000 (Deary 2000). Much interest has focused, in the broadly psychometric-experimental levels, on processing speed and working memory as potential explanatory variables for intelligence. However, there are new findings to report from each of these areas, some of which are being incorporated within brain imaging and genetic studies of intelligence. That is, a study may be potentially more informative if it includes intelligence phenotypes, a biological marker, and an additional, potentially explanatory psychological construct.

Odd as it is to report, and in spite of there being a hundred years of research in these areas, an indication of the true correlation between intelligence and sensory discrimination and reaction time appeared only in the past decade. Spearman (1904) proposed what he termed a functional correspondence between general intelligence and sensory discrimination. Ninety-seven years after this, it was reported, in a large sample (N = 899) of healthy adults in the United States, that general intelligence (from a battery of 13 tests) correlated 0.21 with pitch discrimination and 0.31 with color discrimination (Acton & Schroeder 2001). These bivariate correlations between general intelligence and sensory discrimination do not actually test what Spearman (1904) hypothesized; namely, that whatever was common to discrimination measures was almost perfectly correlated with whatever is common to cognitive test measures. Acton & Schroeder's sample was reanalyzed using structural equation modeling, and the correlation between general intelligence and general sensory ability latent traits was 0.68; in a separate Scottish sample of children, it was 0.92 (Deary et al. 2004a). Spearman was substantially correct, although we still do not know what causes the correlation between these two latent traits.

With regard to reaction time, the first large (N = 900) population-representative study of its correlation with intelligence found, in a very narrow age cohort about 56 years old, as follows: four-choice reaction time mean = −0.49; four-choice reaction time intraindividual variability = −0.26; simple reaction time mean = −0.31; and simple reaction time intraindividual variability = −0.26 (Deary et al. 2001). A series of empirical reviews—but not formally conducted or presented meta-analyses—of processing speed and intelligence correlations gathered findings from 172 studies containing over 50,000 subjects in total (Sheppard

2008). The correlation was slightly lower than that of Deary et al. (2001) but included convenience samples; that is, samples of participants where no attempt is made to match to population characteristics and that often involve students or other relatively cognitively homogeneous groups. Much of Sheppard's account concerns cognitive components—such as the reaction time for processing in short-term memory or speed of retrieval from long-term memory—but I consider these to be a distraction when the correlation with straightforward choice reaction time is so high. The cognitive components claimed to be isolable from reaction time models tend to be unreliable and not, in any case, to improve the correlation with intelligence (Deary 2000, chapter 6). This was emphasized by Lohman (1994) in his overview of such attempts: "attempts to isolate component scores that decompose individual differences on homogeneous tasks into process measures cannot succeed, and so our efforts should be directed elsewhere" (p. 9). The mean correlation between general intelligence and visual inspection time—a psychophysical task that does not involve reaction speed but, instead, records correct discriminations based on a simple stimulus that is presented for different durations—was −0.36 (Sheppard 2008); people with higher intelligence test scores were more efficient in accumulating accurate information from briefly presented stimuli. The equivalent correlation with auditory inspection time was −0.31.

Therefore, the current situation is that apparently lower-level mental tasks—such as sensory discrimination, visual processing and reaction time—have fairly well-established significant and far-from-trivial correlations with intelligence. Less is known about why these correlations occur, and that is largely because of lack of understanding of the causes of individual differences in these so-called elementary cognitive tasks. Although reaction time tasks are quite widely applied in mental testing, current research is in a state whereby there is less interest in these sorts of tasks to explore the origins of intelligence differences. On the one hand, this might reflect a correct judgment that explanations have not been and will not be forthcoming from that research route. On the other hand, it might be that researchers in intelligence have prematurely left this field to explore other routes that promise more by way of a reductionistic account of intelligence differences; for example, in brain imaging and molecular genetics.

THE BIOLOGY OF INTELLIGENCE

Around 2000, there were two overviews of the biological correlates of human intelligence differences (Deary 2000, Jensen 1998). They dealt with the same assortment of biological tools: genetics (behavioral and molecular studies), brain imaging (structural and functional), the brain's electrical responses (analyses of the electroencephalograph [EEG] and evoked responses), nerve conduction velocity, and an assortment of less-studied approaches. Little was certain at that time. Two things seemed relatively firm: People with higher measured intelligence tended to have larger brains, and intelligence differences had a substantial heritability. An emerging finding was that older people with the e4 allele of the gene for apolipoprotein E (*APOE*) tended to have lower cognitive ability. Apart from these findings, most approaches suffered from lack of replicability. There were many, mostly modestly sized, studies reporting correlations between a biological variable and intelligence, but typically these were either not replicated or attempted replications tended to be too different to be characterized as such (Deary 2000, Jensen 1998). EEG and brain-evoked response studies suffered particularly in that regard. In looking forward to the research after 2000, my opinion was that, "it is tempting to say that the hope lies mainly in the less-put-to-the-test approaches of functional brain scanning and molecular genetics" (Deary 2000, p. 312). This prognostication, made a decade ago, is both correct and wrong. Probably it is correct to have identified brain imaging and genetics as the two techniques that would be most applied to human intelligence research and would deliver the most solid findings. However, it backed the wrong horse in both cases. Behavioral genetics and structural brain imaging have added more than their respective molecular and functional counterparts in our search for the causes of human intelligence. A recent review of the biological foundations of intelligence—from the point of view of neuroscience—covers behavioral and molecular genetic studies and structural and functional brain imaging, and it provides more detail than space allows in the present account (Deary et al. 2010a).

Genetics

This overview of advances in the genetic contributions to human intelligence differences divides the research into behavioral and molecular approaches. Behavioral studies use twin-, adoption-, and family-based designs to obtain estimates of the proportion of the population variance in intelligence caused by genetic (mostly additive) differences and by the shared and nonshared aspects of the environment. Molecular genetic studies use candidate gene or genomewide association techniques. Candidate gene studies are hypothesis driven. On the basis of prior findings or on the known function of a gene's protein, a gene that is polymorphic (has multiple alleles and might thereby express different phenotypes) is selected and a test is made to discover whether people with different alleles tend to differ on intelligence generally or on specific cognitive domains. Genomewide association studies (widely referred to using the acronym GWAS) are hypothesis free: One tests the association between a phenotype (e.g., an intelligence test score or g factor) and a large number of genetic variants spread across the human genome. Then one tries to find out which of the many nominally significant associations are replicable and then what they might mean mechanistically (if they replicate). There have been at least five reviews of the genetic studies of human intelligence in the past few years (Deary et al. 2006, 2009b; Lee et al. 2010; Payton 2009; Plomin & Spinath 2004).

The broad conclusions are that the heritability of intelligence is now well established, with some important moderation by age and other factors; that multivariate behavior genetic studies have been informative about the causes of correlations between intelligence and some other variables with which intelligence correlates; and that molecular genetic studies—with the exception of variation in *APOE*—have yet to identify variations in specific genes that are firmly associated with intelligence differences.

Behavior genetics. Individual studies from the past decade may be used to exemplify important advances or consolidations in the understanding of the environmental and genetic contributions to intelligence differences.

Much of the additive genetic effect on intelligence is attributable to the general cognitive ability (g) factor, as is much of the genetic influence on specific cognitive tests. A Dutch study administered the 11 subtests of the Wechsler Adult Intelligence Scale and Raven's Matrices (a test of nonverbal reasoning) to 194 twin pairs in their later teens (Rijsdijk et al. 2002). The variation in full-scale IQ (almost equivalent to g) attributable to additive genetic factors was 82%. The additive genetic contributions to individual tests were examined according to the psychometric three-level hierarchy, as described by Carroll (1993). Additive genetic contributions to the g factor, which capture the variance shared by all 12 tests, accounted for a mean of 31% (range = 8 to 53) of the variation in individual test scores. Additive genetic contributions to cognitive domains—verbal comprehension, freedom from distraction, perceptual organization—accounted for a mean of 12% (range = 1 to 30). Additive genetic contributions to test-specific variation accounted for a mean of 14% (range = 0 to 38). Therefore, these diverse mental tests correlate phenotypically largely due to genetic causes of g. In the VPR model of intelligence, based on data from the Minnesota Study of Twins Reared Apart, the additive genetic contributions were calculated for general intelligence (*g*) and for cognitive domains at different levels of generality-specificity (Johnson et al. 2007). For *g*, at the fourth stratum in their hierarchical model, which contained the variance shared by all tests, additive genetic causes accounted for 77% of the variance. The third stratum, one step below *g*, had factors that accounted for variance shared by tests drawing on broad verbal, perceptual, and image rotation abilities, and the additive genetic contribution to these was 78%, 77%, and 76%, respectively. The second stratum had still-more-specific factors accounting for variance shared by tests drawing on the following abilities, with the percentages of variation accounted for by additive genetic causes given in parentheses: narrow verbal (79%), scholastic (69%), fluency (79%), number (72%), content memory (33%), perceptual speed (67%), spatial (76%), and rotation (75%). There are two remarkable points here. The first is the consistently high genetic contribution to variance at the second to fourth strata. Of course, it must be emphasized that much of the genetic influence on the second and third strata derives from the genetic influence on *g*, because factors at these levels load highly on it. The second is the relatively high environmental contribution to content memory.

The heritability of intelligence is not the same at different ages. A Dutch study with 209 pairs of twins examined intelligence at ages 5, 7, and 10 years (RAKIT battery) and again at 12 years (Wechsler Intelligence Scale for Children-Revised) (Bartels et al. 2002). Across these four ages, from 5 to 12, the percentages of variation in intelligence accounted for were as follows: additive genetic effects = 26, 39, 54, 64; shared environment effects = 50, 30, 25, 21 (the latter three values were nonsignificant); and unique environment effects (includes error) = 24, 31, 21, 15. Similarly, the Twins Early Development Study in the United Kingdom found that, for general intelligence, the heritability was 23% in early childhood (with shared environment accounting for 74% of the variance) and that this increased to 62% by middle childhood (with shared environment only 33% by this stage) (Davis et al. 2009).

When extended to adult samples, Dutch twin family studies demonstrate that the percentages of variance accounted for by additive genetic effects rise to over 80% for verbal IQ and almost 70% for performance IQ (Posthuma et al. 2001). Lower estimates, however, were indicated from the results of the Vietnam Era Twin Registry, which estimated that genetic factors cause 49% of variation in the Armed Forces Qualification Test in young adulthood and 57% in late middle age, with the genetic effects also explaining almost all of the 0.74 correlation between the two administrations of the test in this longitudinal study (Lyons et al. 2009). Results from repeated cognitive testing of participants in the Swedish Adoption Twin Study of Aging indicate that genetic influences remain substantial into old age, with a lowering of the contribution (though it is still the majority) at about 80 years (Reynolds et al. 2005). A review of twins studies with older people estimated the heritability of *g* to be about 80% at 65 years and about 60% at age 82 (Lee et al. 2010).

In old age, the genetic contribution is almost entirely to the level (intercept) of intelligence rather than its change (slope) (Lee et al. 2010). Latent growth curve models of the Swedish Adoption Twin Study of Aging showed that genetic effects were largely to the intercepts and not the slopes. Any small genetic effect on the slope tended to be on the smaller quadratic rather than the much larger linear effect (Reynolds et al. 2005). Among the cognitive domains, the genetic effects on memory increased with age, but those on processing speed and fluid ability decreased somewhat.

The heritability of intelligence might be moderated by environmental factors. This idea was tested in 229 pairs of seven-year-old twins from the National Collaborative Perinatal Project, in which over half the sample was black and there was a high proportion of poor families (Turkheimer et al. 2003). To give just one interesting result, when socioeconomic status was split into high and low, the percentage of variance in intelligence accounted for by genetic factors was 71% and 10%, respectively. The shared environment effects were 15% and

58%, respectively. Life events have also been found to moderate genetic and environmental contributions to general intelligence variation in adults (Vinkhuyzen et al. 2011).

Multivariate genetic-environmental studies have been useful in exploring the causes of the associations between intelligence and some of its correlates. To explain, behavior genetic methods may be used to describe the proportions of environmental and genetic influences on single phenotypes, and they can also be used to describe the proportions of environmental and genetic influences on the correlations between two or more phenotypes. For example, an adolescent twin sample of over 500 twin pairs examined the correlations between psychometric intelligence and processing speed measures including choice reaction time and inspection time (Luciano et al. 2004a). A general genetic factor influenced intelligence and processing speed tests. More specific genetic factors accounted for some test covariance and test-specific variance. Environmental effects were mostly nonshared and test specific. A bivariate environmental-genetic study using Australian and Dutch participants in a twin family design explored causal hypotheses concerning the correlation between inspection time and intelligence; in the literature there were competing suggestions about which caused the other (Luciano et al. 2005). The best model was one of pleiotropy; that is, a common set of genes influences both intelligence and inspection time, but neither of these variables mediated the genetic influence on the other. For processing speed and other cognitive models of intelligence this is instructive: It suggests that these so-called elementary cognitive tasks are aspects of *g* rather than causes of it. Strong genetic correlations exist between IQ scores from the Wechsler battery and the heavily genetically influenced general executive function and the updating specific aspect of executive function (Friedman et al. 2008). There is mixed evidence about whether the small but consistent correlation between intelligence and birth weight (in the normal range; Shenkin et al. 2004) is caused by shared genetic factors (Luciano et al. 2004b). Brain volume is highly heritable (Thompson et al. 2001), and it correlates modestly with intelligence (McDaniel 2005). A bivariate genetic-environmental study of this correlation showed that the correlations between intelligence and the total volumes of gray matter and white matter were caused by genetic factors (Posthuma et al. 2002).

Molecular genetics. With almost-equal justification, this section of the overview could be very long or very short: very long, because dozens of candidate genes have been reported as being associated with intelligence; very short, because almost none of them has been replicated. As a compromise, this section attempts to steer a course between the two extremes of giving a list of type 1 statistical errors and bleakly stating that we, as yet, know nothing about the genes that influence intelligence differences.

Candidate gene studies of intelligence differences have been disappointing. A review surveyed a period of about 14 years in which there were more than 200 studies on approximately 50 genes with polymorphisms that might be related to intelligence (Payton 2009). It was concluded that, as yet, no individual genetic variants are conclusively related to intelligence or its change with age in healthy individuals. An exception is the gene for apolipoprotein E (*APOE*), which is involved in cholesterol transport and neuronal repair. Possession of the e4 allele for this gene was the subject of a meta-analysis of 77 studies with nearly 41,000 healthy individuals (Wisdom et al. 2011). People with the e4 allele have, on average, lower general cognitive function, with an effect size (d) of about −0.05. The effect is found in late-middle and old age, and the effect appears to strengthen with age. There may also be a very small effect of a polymorphism in the gene for catechol-O-methyl transferase (Barnett et al. 2008). A meta-analysis of polymorphisms in the gene for dystrobrevin-binding protein 1, which is associated with risk of schizophrenia, showed effect sizes for two single-nucleotide polymorphisms around the 0.1 value (Zhang et al. 2010). It is also worth mentioning the Val66Met polymorphism of the gene for brain-derived neurotrophic factor, which might have a small effect on intelligence, although there are uncertainties about the direction of association (Payton 2009).

A fascinating molecular genetic contribution was an interaction between variants in the gene for fatty acid desaturase 2 and the effect of breastfeeding on children's intelligence (Caspi et al. 2007). Though this was shown in two cohorts, another large cohort has not replicated the direction of association (Steer et al. 2010). And, though maternal intelligence did not appear to explain the effects in the original study, a meta-analysis of breastfeeding effects on children's intelligence did show that maternal intelligence accounted for much of the apparent protective effect of breastfeeding, leaving it nonsignificant overall (Der et al. 2006).

With regard to GWAS, the past decade has seen a remarkable maturing of genetic studies of intelligence. The first genomewide scans for intelligence used a few to many hundreds of microsatellite markers and hundreds of sibling pairs or families in linkage analyses (e.g., Luciano et al. 2006, Posthuma et al. 2005). Linkage refers to the fact that genetic loci that are relatively close to each other on the same chromosome tend to be inherited together. Fundamentally, then, linkage analyses explore whether, among related individuals, certain genetic marker loci tend to co-occur with phenotypic characteristics. These types of analyses, for example, indicated the possible importance of variants in the chromosome 6p region. Linkage designs have, for the present, been pushed to the periphery of genetic research on intelligence with the coming of so many GWAS that test unrelated subjects. However, linkage designs might well reappear in the search for rare variants that influence intelligence. The first genome-wide studies of intelligence to use hundreds of thousands of single-nucleotide polymorphisms have appeared. Even with this density of genotyping, a few hundreds or thousands of subjects, and attempts at replication, it is becoming clear that the effects of individual genetic variants will be very small, and for

replicable discoveries to be made, the scale of this research will have to be far larger (Cirulli et al. 2010, Davis et al. 2010).

Through the use of a novel statistical technique applied to genomewide data, the first purely biological evidence for the substantial heritability of fluid and crystallized general intelligence has appeared (Davies et al. 2011). The study analyzed more than 500,000 single-nucleotide polymorphisms in over 3,500 older people from Scotland and England. The authors used a new technique that employs information from all of the half-million-plus genetic variants to calculate "relatedness" in these unrelated individuals. The method afforded an estimate of the narrow-sense heritability of intelligence based purely on these biological data. The heritability estimate was 40% for crystallized intelligence and 51% for fluid general intelligence. This means that unknown causal genetic variants in linkage disequilibrium with the assessed single-nucleotide polymorphisms account for much of the genetic variation in intelligence. The results point to the possibility of many genes of small effect contributing to human intelligence variation. Moreover, the authors were also able to use the purely biological information from the Scottish and English samples significantly to predict about 1% of the variance in intelligence scores in an independent Norwegian sample.

The best genetically oriented research on intelligence now appreciates that individual gene effects are likely to be small or very small; examines hundreds of thousands of single-nucleotide polymorphisms on every participant (and, indeed, uses the fact that single-nucleotide polymorphisms that occur quite close together show linkage disequilibrium—that is, there is a greater than zero chance of certain variants being inherited together—to impute these effectively to provide a few million); gathers in consortia that can bring together several or even many thousands of participants; often involves researchers with a primary interest in medical or other social variables but who happened to have collected intelligence data on their participants; and has rigorous approaches to significance and replication. This has arisen after finding that no studies to date at the smaller scale—either candidate gene or genomewide—have found large or medium effects. The same maturing of studies has occurred with other quantitative traits, such as height. A consortium of studies on height, which reported results on over 180,000 individuals, found significant effects at more than 180 genetic loci, which together explained 10% of the phenotypic variation (Lango Allen et al. 2010). At present, at least three international consortia of studies are conducting genomewide association analyses of intelligence-related phenotypes. All have participant numbers well into five figures; none has reported findings to date.

If it is the case that genomewide searches for intelligence do not throw up any large or medium effects—or even a collection of smaller effects that seem to account for most of the additive genetic effect that is apparent from behavioral genetic studies—then the genetic contributions lie elsewhere. One option is in a very large number of very small effects, as suggested by Davies et al. (2011). A second is in rare variants (Penke et al. 2007), where the idea is that the accumulation of these across generations causes differences in intelligence. Another is in what are called copy number variations: deletions and duplications of stretches of DNA. Although based on very few subjects and requiring replication, one study examined this possibility and found that people with more rare deletions had lower Wechsler Adult Intelligence Scale scores (Yeo et al. 2011).

Brain Imaging

In the early years of brain imaging and intelligence—the 1980s and 1990s—there were studies using positron and single-photon emission tomography. Both techniques were expensive and involved the administration of radioactive substances to subjects. These techniques have been eclipsed by magnetic resonance imaging (MRI) in its various structural and functional forms. Although it is still not inexpensive to scan each subject's brain, its

safety and relatively low cost have meant that almost all the brain imaging studies of intelligence have used MRI. Below, some studies exemplifying key empirical advances in the association between brain structure and functions are described. First, though, attention is directed toward an adventurous and helpful synthesis of brain imaging–intelligence work. The parieto-frontal integration theory of intelligence (P-FIT) brought together 37 studies that had employed neuroimaging techniques to investigate differences in intelligence and reasoning (Jung & Haier 2007). They included structural and functional MRI, diffusion tensor MRI, magnetic resonance spectroscopy, and positron emission tomography studies, all of which they thought could be used to sketch a coherent account of what it means to have a brighter brain. Congruent brain imaging–intelligence associations overlapped on how the association cortices were linked by key white matter pathways (particularly the arcuate fasciculus and superior longitudinal fasciculus). In the P-FIT account, abstraction and elaboration of incoming sensory information are conducted in the parietal cortex; the parietal interacts with the frontal cortex, which tests hypotheses concerning a problem; following a best solution, the anterior cingulate constrains the selection of responses and inhibits competing ones; and the whole process depends for its efficiency on intact white matter connections between the regions. In addition to the P-FIT paper—and its associated discussion—readers are directed to a recent special issue of the journal *Intelligence* that was devoted to brain imaging, as introduced by Haier (2009).

Structural brain imaging. Only in the past decade has there been enough evidence to conclude with confidence something that had been mooted, debated, and, at times, ridiculed for over a century: People with larger brains do tend to have higher intelligence test scores. In a meta-analysis of 37 samples examining whole-brain volume in healthy subjects (total N = 1,530), the raw correlation was 0.29 (0.33 after correction for range restriction; McDaniel

2005). A more recent review reckoned the correlation between whole-brain size and general intelligence is about 0.4 and that the correlation between external head size and intelligence (based on 59 samples with a total N = 63,405) is 0.20 (Rushton & Ankney 2009).

That being established, there has been interest in whether certain brain regions and the pathways between them are associated with intelligence differences—see the P-FIT theory above (Jung & Haier 2007)—and more generally the extent to which intelligence is localized or distributed through the brain. One issue has been whether intelligence is more strongly associated—and where in the brain—with gray or white matter. Certainly, gray matter volume seems to be correlated significantly with intelligence. In 216 children and adolescents, there were positive correlations between general intelligence (from a short Wechsler battery) and brain cortical thickness distributed through frontal, parietal, temporal, and occipital brain regions (Karama et al. 2009). These were in agreement with, if partly more extensive than, the regions identified in the P-FIT theory. Data from 65 men and women showed that cortical thickness (gray matter) was associated with intelligence, particularly in the prefrontal and posterior temporal areas (Narr et al. 2007). The study had also found an intelligence–overall brain volume correlation of 0.36 (0.37 for overall gray matter; 0.26 for intracranial white matter volume). This correlation between overall brain volume and intelligence is almost identical to McDaniel's (2005) estimate and that from a study of over 200 young adults, in which the correlation was 0.35 (Choi et al. 2008). Intelligence scores and voxel-based morphometry analyses of brain MRI data from twins provided evidence for an intelligence differences–associated network of frontal-occipital-parahippocampal gray matter and connecting white matter of the superior occipito-frontal fasciculus and corpus callosum (Hulshoff Pol et al. 2006). Investigators using voxel-based morphometry analysis of MRIs of 48 adult human brains to separate gray and white matter identified positive correlations between g from the Wechsler Adult Intelligence Scale and gray matter volumes in the frontal, temporal, occipital, and some sublobar (lentiform nucleus, thalamus, etc.) brain regions (Colom et al. 2006). More sophisticated than these cross-sectional studies, a study of 307 children aged 7 to 19—who had been imaged between one and three times with a two-year interval—investigated the association between general intelligence and the developmental trajectory of brain cortical thickness (Shaw et al. 2006). An examination of their findings—where, for illustration, intelligence was divided into superior, high, and average groups—revealed that the superior intelligence group had a distinct trajectory whereby their cortical thickness was the lowest of the three groups at age 7, highest at about age 12, and average again at age 19.

The above studies were performed on healthy individuals. Validation of the principal P-FIT ideas was found from an innovative study of 241 patients with brain lesions who underwent brain imaging (with voxel-based lesion-symptom mapping) and were tested on the Wechsler Adult Intelligence Scale battery (Gläscher et al. 2010). Conceptually, this is what they did: They divided the brain into voxels and asked what the association was between having a lesion in a given voxel and the score obtained on the g factor from the Wechsler battery. The significant associations with g were with damage in a frontal-parietal network and the white matter tracts that connected them, with the superior longitudinal/arcuate fasciculus again being prominent.

The P-FIT ideas include both gray and white matter in the brain as contributing intelligence differences. The past decade has seen increasing evidence of correlations between white matter–related brain-imaging variables and intelligence. People with more lesions in the white matter tend to have lower intelligence, although this has been found—with small effect sizes—mainly in older people, in whom these lesions tend to accumulate and can be rated using brain MRI images (Frisoni et al. 2007). Eleven studies show, overall, some evidence of an association between n-acetylaspartate—a brain metabolite measured by magnetic resonance spectroscopy—and cognitive abilities, but the associations do not always go in the same direction (Jung et al. 2009). The development of diffusion tensor MRI has meant that indices of brain white matter integrity can be produced in vivo. Several studies show that people with higher intelligence tend to have greater white matter integrity—typically assessed using a parameter called fractional anisotropy—which accords with a distributed and connectionist view of what it means to be higher in intelligence (Deary et al. 2010a provide an overview). Brain white matter integrity is highly heritable, and the modest phenotypic correlation with intelligence appears to be caused by shared genetic factors (Chiang et al. 2009).

Functional brain imaging. Early in the past decade there were two high-profile articles that made many intelligence researchers sit up and take notice because of their striking titles: "A neural basis for general intelligence" (Duncan et al. 2000) and "Neural mechanisms of general fluid intelligence" (Gray et al. 2003). In the first study, a PET experiment on only 13 subjects devised high- and low-g-demanding versions of three tasks and looked for the brain regions that were consistently associated with greater activation in the high-g task versions. The answer was the lateral frontal cortex, and the authors argued against a diffuse neural recruitment mechanism for g differences, but instead, "g reflects the function of a specific neural system, including as one major part a specific region of the lateral frontal cortex" (Duncan et al. 2000, p. 459). It is clear from the P-FIT theory (Jung & Haier 2007) and lesion-based studies (Gläscher et al. 2010) that Duncan did identify an important brain region for intelligence and that it is just one region in a network. In the second study (Gray et al. 2003), the straightforward result was that neural activity (inferred from the blood oxygen–level dependent signal in functional MRI) in the lateral prefrontal cortex almost completely attenuated the association between intelligence

(Raven's Advanced Progressive Matrices) and the ability, correctly, to ignore "lure" stimuli in a 3-back working memory task. Gray and colleagues (2003) concluded this was "the first direct support for a major hypothesis about the neurobiological basis of gf" (p. 319). An attempt to replicate this result beyond lure detection in an n-back task was not successful (Waiter et al. 2009). Both of these studies had interesting findings based on well-aimed hypotheses. However, their ambitious titles must be read with appropriate skepticism: They appear to offer too broad a conclusion from small studies that are the beginnings rather than the end of a long research effort to explain intelligence differences.

A very valuable integrative review, which included functional brain imaging and EEG techniques, converges on an account of the intelligent brain that is distributed (Neubauer & Fink 2009). It also provides much diverse support for the view that the intelligent brain is more efficient.

Fluctuating Asymmetry

On the basis of the idea that intelligence is an indicator of fitness, there has been considerable activity in examining whether it associated with other aspects of bodily fitness. One aspect is health, and that is covered here under the section on cognitive epidemiology; another is fluctuating asymmetry (Van Valen 1962): the degree to which the same bodily parts on the two sides of the body show an absolute deviation from being identical in size. This is covered here because it is an aspect of research into the biology of intelligence that emerged only in the previous decade or so. Except for the original report of two samples (Furlow et al. 1997)—each with just over 100 participants—in which intelligence correlated just over 0.2 with symmetry, all studies have appeared in the twenty-first century. A meta-analysis of 14 samples (published and unpublished) with a total N of 1,871 estimated that the correlation between intelligence and fluctuating asymmetry was −0.12 to −0.20 (Banks et al. 2010). That is, people with higher intelligence test scores tend to be more symmetrical. To explain these findings, Banks et al. appealed to an account which suggests that both intelligence and symmetry are markers of a general fitness latent trait that is associated with survival and reproductive success (Miller 2000, Keller & Miller 2007). However, a first attempt to examine the genetic correlation between intelligence and symmetry found neither a genetic nor a phenotypic correlation (Johnson et al. 2008b).

PREDICTIVE VALIDITY OF INTELLIGENCE

Intelligence predicts important things in life. The predictive validity of intelligence for education, occupational success, and social mobility was well documented prior to the past decade. That said, there was some new research in these areas. Some progress was also made in assessing the association between intelligence and related personal-social constructs. A useful meta-analysis showed that the correlation between intelligence and ego-development stage is between 0.20 and 0.34, making them related but not identical concepts (Cohn & Westenberg 2004). Long-term follow-up studies of the British cohorts born in 1958 and 1970 showed strong associations between higher childhood intelligence and more socially liberal attitudes at age about 30 years (Deary et al. 2008, Schoon et al. 2010). The most novel contribution of intelligence as a predictor was the emergence and growth of the new research field of cognitive epidemiology; the first years of the twenty-first century established intelligence as a predictor of health, illness, and death.

Education, Occupation, and Social Mobility

Although they have been studied for many years, it is useful to see a meta-analytic approach to the associations of intelligence with some of its well-known correlates in the field of socioeconomic success. Intelligence had average correlations (95% confidence intervals,

total number of studies, total number of subjects) as follows: education = 0.46 (0.36 to 0.75, 59, 84,828); occupation = 0.37 (0.28 to 0.57, 45, 72,290); and income = 0.21 (−0.01 to 0.40, 31, 58,758) (Strenze 2007). With only the objectively defined better studies included, with sample-size weighting, and with correction for unreliability and dichotomization, the effect sizes were estimated as, respectively, 0.56, 0.45, and 0.23. In this meta-analysis, education was assessed using educational level. If objective results are used from national examinations, the correlation between intelligence and education is considerably higher. For example, the prospective correlation between the general intelligence latent trait from the Cognitive Abilities Test at age 11 years and a general educational latent trait (based on English national General Certificate of Secondary Education scores at age 16 years; N = 13,248) was 0.81 (Deary et al. 2007a). By way of balance—albeit in a study with two orders of magnitude fewer subjects—it is noted that self-discipline (as rated by the person or by others) can have stronger associations with educational outcomes than intelligence has (Duckworth & Seligman 2005). There is also evidence for some people's being more motivated than others in certain intelligence testing situations, which could inflate intelligence–life outcomes correlations (Duckworth et al. 2011). In another investigation of real-life outcomes of intelligence, a large study of trainee truckers showed that intelligence was associated with "preferences and choices in ways that favor economic success" (Burks et al. 2009). Those with higher intelligence were more patient, were better at taking calculated risks, were better at predicting how other people would act and how they should act as a result, and persevered longer in a job when there was a financial penalty for leaving.

Much remains to be discovered about social mobility. The United Kingdom, because it has various prospective cohorts that have been studied from youth and are now at various stages of adulthood and old age, has been especially informative, but of course these results do not necessarily generalize to other countries or cultures. However, even using the same cohort's data, different researchers have come to different conclusions. For example, consider some analyses from the past decade on the U.K.'s National Child Development Study (the 1958 British Birth Cohort), which gathered prospective data on all children born in Great Britain in one week in March 1958. Some researchers emphasized that, with respect to social class destinations at age 33, there were still substantial effects of parental social class after adjusting for intelligence and academic effort (Breen & Goldthorpe 2002). With the same data, others emphasized that whereas parental social class accounted for about 25% of people's own social class at age 33, intelligence, motivation, and qualifications accounted for over 60% (Saunders 2002). Others have shown that social mobility from all the social classes is driven about equally by intelligence from childhood (Nettle 2003). General findings—using structural equation modeling—from analyses of various British cohorts (born in 1921, 1936, the 1950s, and 1970) are that education tends to mediate the influence of childhood intelligence on adult socioeconomic status; the effect of intelligence on education is stronger (insofar as they can be compared numerically) than that of parental social class; and that childhood behavioral disturbance is correlated significantly with intelligence and contributes, at most, only small amounts of additional (beyond intelligence and parental social class) variance to education or adult social class (Deary et al. 2005a; Johnson et al. 2010; von Stumm et al. 2009, 2010). Most of these latter analyses were completed in men because of the difficulty in assessing socioeconomic status among women at historical times when women either tended not to be in employment to the extent that they are now or tended to be less likely to attain employment in accordance with their abilities.

Health, Illness, and Death

Prior to the past decade, health was not an outcome that counted intelligence as one of its determinants to any extent. That has changed. Two of the prominent social correlates of intelligence—education and social class (parental and own in adulthood)—were already known to be associated with health inequalities; therefore, it is not surprising to see intelligence added to the list. The first journal report of an intelligence-death association was with Australian male Vietnam veterans; those whose mental test scores were lower on entry to the armed services were more likely to have died (principally from external causes) by midlife (O'Toole & Stankov 1992). Subsequent findings took place in the next decade. A follow-up of over 2,000 subjects of the Scottish Mental Survey of 1932 (of people born in 1921) found that a standard deviation disadvantage in childhood (age 11 years) intelligence was associated with 21% (95% confidence interval 25% to 16%) lower survival up to age 76 (Whalley & Deary 2001). This was a new and healthy development for intelligence research: its being included in large-scale epidemiological health research with population-representative samples. A few years later the term "cognitive epidemiology" was coined (Deary & Der 2005) to describe this field of research. A glossary of the field is available (Deary & Batty 2007), and a special issue of the journal *Intelligence* (2009) appeared, with 13 new empirical studies on the topic.

The association between lower intelligence test scores in childhood or youth and dying earlier has been replicated in many studies, typically involving the follow-up of thousands of subjects for up to several decades. The largest single study to date included about one million men (Batty et al. 2009). This was conducted in Sweden and was possible because almost all Swedish men are conscripted into military or civil service in young adulthood. For decades, young Swedish males have taken the same set of mental tests. Thereafter, the unique code number that is assigned to Swedish citizens was used prospectively to link these cognitive test data with data held in education, health, and other public databases. A systematic review and meta-analysis has identified 16 independent studies of the intelligence-mortality association and found that one standard deviation advantage in intelligence was associated with 24% lower risk of death (95% CI = 23% to 25%) over a follow-up range of 17 to 69 years (Calvin et al. 2011). This paper and an extensive narrative review with discussion (Deary et al. 2010b) debate possible causes of the association and the range of causes of death with which intelligence is significantly associated. The latter include deaths from cardiovascular disease, suicide, homicide, and accidents, but not cancer.

Prospectively, physical and mental health outcomes are both associated with childhood or early adult intelligence, especially cardiovascular disease among the physical illnesses (Deary et al. 2010b). This applies to most categories of psychiatric disorders, and a standard deviation disadvantage in intelligence at about age 20 has been associated with, for example, about 50% greater risk of hospitalization for schizophrenia, mood disorder, and alcohol-related disorders (Gale et al. 2010) and for personality disorders (Moran et al. 2009). Lower childhood intelligence is also associated in early to middle adulthood with more self-reported psychological distress (Gale et al. 2009) and with a greater risk of vascular dementia (McGurn et al. 2008).

Although demonstrating, replicating, and partially refining the association between intelligence and illness and mortality has been a substantial achievement in the past ten years, the major interest now lies in understanding the association. Finding its mechanisms will be important for applying these discoveries in public health. The attempt to understand has seen differential psychologists work more closely with epidemiologists than before and has also seen the two professions challenge each other. One challenge came from what is arguably cognitive epidemiology's most comprehensive theoretical statement, in which it was suggested that the associations between health and education and socioeconomic status might be caused by intelligence (Gottfredson 2004). Direct tests of this idea with large epidemiological samples from the United Kingdom suggest that the hypothesis has some merit but does not fully account for the effects (Batty et al. 2006, Singh-Manoux et al. 2005). A promising route toward understanding has been the finding that childhood intelligence is associated with many health behaviors during the life course: smoking, alcohol intake, physical activity, and dietary choices (Batty et al. 2007, Deary et al. 2010b, Weiser et al. 2009); risk factors for cardiovascular disease, including the metabolic syndrome as well as its elements such as poor glucose regulation, higher blood pressure, high waist-hip ratio, and disadvantageous lipid profile (Batty et al. 2008, Power et al. 2010); and a disadvantageous diurnal cortisol profile in middle age (Power et al. 2008).

There are other suggestions to explain the intelligence-mortality association. For example, it has been suggested that education and adult social class mediate and explain the association, perhaps in association with stress (Sapolsky 2005). Substantial mediation has been found statistically, but it is moot whether these are explanatory factors or partial surrogates for intelligence (Calvin et al. 2011). The idea that intelligence—even in childhood—relates to later health because it is an index of general bodily "system integrity" achieved some validation when it was found that reaction time variance largely accounted for the association (Deary & Der 2005). The idea needs further development: theoretically, to elaborate more fully the notion of system integrity; and empirically, to identify more marker variables of the construct and the testing of their association with each other, intelligence, and mortality, illness, and health.

INTELLIGENCE AND AGING

This is a topic that is growing in importance in intelligence research, and it also has significant public policy relevance (Beddington et al. 2008). People are living longer, the proportion of older people in the population is growing, and losing cognitive ability is an especially feared aspect of growing older. Research includes the following questions: How do aspects of intelligence change with age? Do all domains of cognitive ability decline together? How much stability and variation is there in intelligence across the life course? Is age kinder to the initially more able? Are there discoverable (and ideally modifiable) determinants of individual differences in the aging of intelligence? And can the decline in age-sensitive aspects intelligence be ameliorated? My opinion is that cognitive aging should be an integrated part of broader intelligence research, not a topic on its own: Intelligence as a whole should be seen as a life-course topic, with developmental psychology, individual differences, and aging aspects contributing to a rounded account of how and why intelligence differences develop, are maintained, and decline (e.g., Foresight Mental Capital Wellbeing Project 2008). Here, some advances over the past decade are highlighted.

Aging research on intelligence has been modeled using the hierarchical account of intelligence differences (Carroll 1993). This is the hierarchy that was described at the start of this article, whereby cognitive ability variance may be portioned into variance shared by all tests (g), variance shared by tests assessing the same cognitive domain, and variance specific to each test. A comprehensive example is a combined analysis of 33 cross-sectional studies, involving 16 cognitive tasks, with a total N of about 7,000 (Salthouse 2004). The covariance of the 16 tasks formed a hierarchy with g at the pinnacle and group factors of reasoning, spatial ability, memory, processing speed, and vocabulary. Apart from vocabulary tests—which tended to peak at about age 60—the other types of test showed mean declines from young or middle adulthood. It is notable, too, that Salthouse modeled processing speed as one of the domains of intelligence that ages, alongside others at the second level, instead of its being the cause of other domains' aging effects, as he has done previously. The largest effect of age was on general intelligence, with additional, specific smaller effects on memory and processing speed. In a longitudinal study, Wilson et al. (2002) also found that when one aspect of intelligence declines, the other aspects tend to go also. A

common factor representing people's aging slopes on seven different cognitive domains accounted for 62% of the variance. A study that is congruent with these, and extended their findings, was by Tucker-Drob (2011). He reported analyses on over 1,200 people aged from 18 to 95 years and who had been tested over a period of up to seven years on a dozen mental tests. Again, the analyses employed the three-level hierarchical model of cognitive differences. The domains of function tested were abstract reasoning, spatial visualization, episodic memory, and processing speed. A general factor—common to all the domains—accounted for an average of 39% of the differences in individual variables, 33% was accounted for at the domain level, and a mean of 28% was test specific. It is notable that the general effect on 'aging' was found even in younger and middle-age groups as well as in older people.

The past decade has seen the longest follow-up studies of intelligence differences, with follow-up studies of the Scottish Mental Surveys of 1932 and 1947. When the same intelligence test is administered at age 11 years and again to individuals when they are in their late seventies, the correlations are between 0.6 and 0.7 (Deary et al. 2000, 2004b) and are still above 0.5 when the individuals are in their late eighties (Gow et al. 2011). Obviously, these correlations imply that at least one-quarter to one-half of the variance in intelligence is stable across most of the human life course. The obverse is that there is also considerable change in the rank order of intelligence across the life course, and there is a lively and varied set of research directions seeking the determinants—psychosocial and biomedical—of aging-associated cognitive change. Overviews of this research are provided by Deary et al. (2009c), Foresight Mental Capital and Wellbeing Project (2008), and Plassman et al. (2010). Plassman and colleagues systematically reviewed observational studies and randomized controlled trials and covered genetics, environmental toxins, medical factors, social and behavioral factors, and nutrition. Support for most factors was limited, although it was better for the risk factors of smoking, the

APOE e4 allele, and some medical conditions. Among the determinants of age-related cognitive change, there is still controversy about whether people with relatively high childhood intelligence have more gentle cognitive decline in middle and old age, with some studies suggesting they do (Richards et al. 2004) and some suggesting that there is no such association (Gow et al. 2011).

With regard to ameliorating the aging of intelligence among people without cognitive pathology, there is still discussion about how to separate normal and pathological cognitive aging, though with a suggestion that the former might be a specific target for therapeutics (Shineman et al. 2010). There is still uncertainty, too, about whether retaining engagement in physical, social, and intellectual activity helps to preserve what intelligence we have (Bielak, 2010), although some are positive about this (Hertzog et al. 2009).

CONTROVERSY OR CONSENSUS?

Two long-running controversies in intelligence research attracted much empirical attention in the past decade: whether—and if so, why— there are twin-singleton or male-female differences in intelligence. Both are discussed below. There was also a major re-examination of the issue of race differences in intelligence, and readers are referred to the target article and its subsequent discussion (Rushton & Jensen 2005).

Two analyses of whole-population or population-representative sets of twins found that, for children aged 11 years in Scotland in the 1930s, 1940s, and 1960s, twins had mean IQ scores of about one-third of a standard deviation lower than singletons (Deary et al. 2005b, Ronalds et al. 2005). However, a population-representative study of 11-year-olds tested on the Cognitive Abilities Test in the United Kingdom in 2004 showed no significant difference: Twins were only about 1% of a standard deviation lower than singletons on general intelligence (Calvin et al. 2009). Studies of more recently born Dutch twins also suggest a much lower—or no—cognitive deficit among

twins and that any small deficit probably disappears by adolescence (Webbink et al. 2008). These large, new analyses of recently born children probably override the recent opinion that although there was heterogeneity in studies of singleton–twin intelligence differences, this might not be explained by a date-of-study effect (Voracek & Haubner 2008). This disappearance of the "cognitive cost" of being a twin is fascinating. Some have put this down to better perinatal care, but this has not been demonstrated clearly.

Sex differences in intelligence remains a hot topic, and the past decade saw much debate as well as substantial new analyses. Four issues appear to be important in assessing this question. First is the quality of the samples: Some have much better population representativeness than others. Second is the age of the samples: Some suggest that mean differences appear only after puberty. Third is the type of mental ability: The issue addressed here will be general intelligence rather than abilities such as spatial or verbal that, for whatever causes, tend to be accepted as having more replicable sex differences. Fourth is the research issue at hand: There are questions about whether the mean and/or the variance of intelligence is different between males and females. These will all be kept in mind and referred to as some recent research results on sex differences in intelligence are discussed.

In whole populations of Scottish 11-year-olds from the 1930s and 1940s there was more variance among males in intelligence by comparison with females, but little difference in mean intelligence; proportionately, more males were at both ends of the intelligence distribution and fewer were in the middle (Deary et al. 2003, Johnson et al. 2008b). This pattern was replicated in a population-representative sample of almost one-third of a million boys and girls tested on the Cognitive Abilities Test in the United Kingdom in the early 2000s: There were trivial differences in mean general intelligence and proportionately more boys than girls at the extremes (Strand et al. 2006). This pattern was replicated in the same test in a population-representative sample of 300,000+ students in grades 3 to 11 in the United States, with the authors concluding that, "The results showed an astonishing consistency in sex differences across countries, grades, cohorts, and test forms" (Lohman & Lakin 2009).

Whereas these epidemiological-quality data in children make the state of sex differences clear, the picture is less clear among adults. On the basis of meta-analyses of studies using Raven's Progressive Matrices—a widely used nonverbal intelligence test with items composed using abstract line drawings and demanding inductive reasoning—it was argued that men have a higher mean level of general intelligence than do women (Irwing & Lynn 2005, Lynn & Irwing 2004). It was argued against this that the better-quality studies tended to show no differences and that many of the samples might be biased toward less selectivity among women, which would reduce their mean scores as a group (Blinkhorn 2005). To test this idea, a novel design was applied to data from the U.S. National Longitudinal Survey of Youth 1979 (Deary et al. 2007b). When brother-sister pairs (N = 1,292 pairs) were compared on a general cognitive ability (g) factor derived from the Armed Services Vocational Aptitude Battery and the shorter Armed Forces Qualification Test, the male mean advantage was trivial (less than 7% of a standard deviation), but males once again had substantially greater variance.

A suggestion was made that an apparent male advantage in tests of general intelligence could in part be due to the combination of the following factors: Males have greater variance in intelligence, and recruitment into studies and into subsequent follow-ups of existing studies is restricted by intelligence and sex, with more women and people of higher intelligence tending to take part (Dykiert et al. 2009). The authors argued that the combination of these factors could produce an apparently higher male intelligence mean even when none existed in the population. This was tested in the British Cohort Study 1970 and found to be true: Sex differences in intelligence at age 10 became more

biased toward higher male means when only those subjects who took part in subsequent waves were tested. This was extended further—to include a mathematical model of the recruitment process and to analyses of both the 1958 and 1970 British birth cohorts—and it was again found that sample restriction by these means can bring about apparently higher mean intelligence in males even when none is present in the original samples (Madhyastha et al. 2009).

CONCLUDING REMARKS

A desultory reading of this necessarily selective overview of intelligence research in the first decade of the twentieth century—about one hundred years after the first scientific research on intelligence—will lead some readers to echo Jean-Baptiste Alphonse Karr: "*Plus ça change, plus c'est la même chose.*" They would be wrong, for two reasons.

First, yes, some issues do seem to have continued for a very long time: the psychometric structure of intelligence, sex differences in intelligence, environment and genetic contributions to intelligence, the aging of intelligence, and whether intelligence drives educational attainment and social mobility. In all of these, the basics of what we know now were available empirically decades ago. However, there was often so much opposition to the findings—creating uncertainty—that more, newer, and better research has now far more firmly founded the conclusions that can be offered in these areas. In addition, research in most of these areas has added important details to the basic findings that were available early on. In part, these have come from better samples, better research designs, and more sophisticated and appropriate statistical modeling. On that last point, it remains the case that fully to engage in the discussions about intelligence research it is necessary to be numerate, and to quite an advanced level in specialist areas such as aging and environment-genetics.

Second, there are some genuinely new developments. The importance of intelligence for health, illness, and mortality is new. It adds a great deal to the predictive validity of intelligence. The brain associations of intelligence are new: They might not be large in effect size, but they offer foundational findings for a developing biological account of what it means to have higher levels of intelligence. The molecular genetics knowledge about intelligence—albeit largely knowing what the molecular genetics of intelligence is *not* like—is new. Because longitudinal cohorts—first studied in childhood—are still being studied at older ages, we now have a far better knowledge about how intelligence plays out into social as well as health outcomes in middle and older ages. In health, genetics, biology, and social science we are seeing and will see the incorporation of measured intelligence as a phenotype in better samples, of more epidemiological quality: larger, more population-representative, followed up for longer, and better characterized in terms of other phenotypes and genetic information. The past decade has seen the first studies of the stability and change in intelligence that have lasted more than 70 years, health-related studies of over one million men, brain imaging studies with numbers in three figures (instead of two or one), and the first genetic studies using hundreds of thousands of genetic markers. The forthcoming consortia on the genetics of intelligence will have sample sizes in at least five figures, and large studies that will include intelligence and brain imaging and genetics will increasingly appear. In social matters we shall know more too: As cohorts such as the United Kingdom's 1946, 1958, and 1970 cohorts grow older, we shall know more about the lifelong social mobility of these individuals (and their children) and the part played by intelligence in concert with other factors.

Real progress in the cognitive correlates of intelligence has been made over the past decade: It is clear that there is a sensory discrimination–intelligence correlation; the inspection time–intelligence correlation has been firmed up in larger samples and in adults and children; a much larger reaction time–intelligence correlation has emerged than had been appreciated heretofore; and working memory has large correlations and fresh evidence of apparent causal associations with intelligence. Nevertheless, this area is not as active as it was. A mountaineering analogy might help. For those seeking a causal account of intelligence differences, genetic and brain imaging approaches are far more reachable handholds and footholds than they were a decade ago. Perhaps researchers are wondering whether they can simply bypass the intermediate cognitive construct footholds, some of which might be illusory (based on unvalidated constructs) and some of which might take the researcher laterally rather than vertically (because they end up redescribing intelligence in terms at the same explanatory level).

If reorienting is the correct word—or perhaps it is synthesis or consolidation—then a reorienting of intelligence research is possible because of the research in the past decade or two, in terms of a life-course model. The fairly newly appreciated very long-term stability of intelligence, the influences of birth weight and perinatal growth, and the associations among intelligence, sensation, and health all point toward the need for intelligence researchers to be integrated with a wide range of cognate scientists interested in general health and well-being across the human life course. Intelligence is part of health. Whether it is called intelligence, or cognitive capital, or cognitive reserve, and whether we explain these links with ideas of general bodily system integrity or common cause (or a set of common causes), the development, adult operation, and eventual trajectory of decline in people's intelligence will be a combination of shared influences with the rest of the body and—who knows how much?—influences that are specific to the brain. An attempt at displaying the integrated science that lifelong intelligence research should be is shown in a U.K. government report (Foresight Mental Capital and Wellbeing Project 2008, appendix B, p. 53).

And before one hears the old saws that there is more to life than being clever—sure there is, like being happy, healthy, and free—and that there is more to achieving one's desired position than being clever—that's trivially true, as studies looking at personality traits and effort and motivation, for example, show—we should remember that research on the nature, causes, and consequences of intelligence is about some-thing that people value and that has a big influ-ence on people's lives. This brings with it the responsibility to be broad-minded and intelli-gent in researching intelligence.

SUMMARY POINTS

1. Intelligence differences continue to be a focus for lively research in psychology and also of considerable interest to nonspecialist psychologists, academics in other fields, and the public.

2. The past decade produced many books on intelligence, from introductory accounts to specialist discussions of specific issues. There are also historical accounts and books challenging the measurement and study of intelligence differences.

3. There is new research on the psychometric structure of intelligence. The *g* factor from different test batteries ranks people in the same way. There is still debate about the number of levels at which the variations in intelligence is best described. There is still little empirical support for an account of intelligence differences that does not include *g*.

4. There has been progress in establishing that sensory discrimination, inspection time, and reaction time are all associated with intelligence and achieving estimates of the population effect sizes. However, they now attract less attention as possible ways to understand intelligence differences, although sensory discrimination does attract attention as part of the common cause account of aging and intelligence.

5. The biology of intelligence is the subject of much research. Behavior genetics research continues to refine what we know about environmental and genetic contributions to intelligence, such as moderating effects of age and social circumstances, and the shared genetic influences of intelligence with, for example, brain size, processing speed, and birth weight. Molecular genetic research on intelligence has had a dry time with candidate gene studies and is now poised to take on sufficiently powered genomewide association studies. Brain imaging studies of intelligence are providing more replicated findings that are cohering around an account of a defined but distributed network in the brain that works more efficiently in people with higher intelligence scores.

6. New work on education and social mobility and social position as the outcomes of intelligence differences has plotted people's life courses from impressive longitudinal studies. Health outcomes are a new and burgeoning outcome for intelligence differ-ences, and it is only in the past decade that the new field of cognitive epidemiology has emerged.

7. Aging is another expanding focus for intelligence research, with new findings. Also, this field increasingly takes a life-course view and is becoming more integrated with the study of intelligence differences in younger adulthood and in child development.

8. Controversial issues continue to be studied in intelligence. One such issue is the changing twin–singleton intelligence difference. Also, sex differences in intelligence continue to attract new research, with studies of both mean and variance differences.

DISCLOSURE STATEMENT

The author is not aware of any affiliations, memberships, funding, or financial holdings that might be perceived as affecting the objectivity of this review.

ACKNOWLEDGMENTS

The work was undertaken within the University of Edinburgh Center for Cognitive Ageing and Cognitive Epidemiology, part of the cross-council Lifelong Health and Wellbeing Initiative (G0700704/84698). Funding from the Biotechnology and Biological Sciences Research Council (BBSRC), Engineering and Physical Sciences Research Council (EPSRC), Economic and Social Research Council (ESRC), and Medical Research Council (MRC) is gratefully acknowledged.

LITERATURE CITED

Acton GS, Schroeder DH. 2001. Sensory discrimination as related to general intelligence. *Intelligence* 29:263–71

Banks GC, Batchelor JH, McDaniel MA. 2010. Smarter people are (a bit) more symmetrical: a meta-analysis of the relationship between intelligence and fluctuating asymmetry. *Intelligence* 38:393–401

Barnett JH, Scoriels L, Munafo MR. 2008. Meta-analysis of the cognitive effects of the catechol-O-transferase gene Val158Met polymorphism. *Biol. Psychiatry* 64:137–44

Bartels M, Rietveld MJH, Van Baal GCM, Boomsma DI. 2002. Genetic and environmental influences on the development of intelligence. *Behav. Genet.* 32:237–49

Bartholomew DJ. 2004. *Measuring Intelligence: Facts and Fallacies*. Cambridge, UK: Cambridge Univ. Press

Bartholomew DJ, Deary IJ, Lawn M. 2009. A new lease of life for Thomson's bonds model of intelligence. *Psychol. Rev.* 116:567–79

Batty DJ, Deary IJ, Schoon I, Gale CR. 2007. Mental ability across childhood in relation to risk factors for premature mortality in adult life: the 1970 British Cohort Study. *J. Epidemiol. Comm. Health* 61:997–1003

Batty GD, Der G, Macintyre S, Deary IJ. 2006. Does IQ explain socioeconomic inequalities in health? Evidence from a population based cohort study in the west of Scotland. *Br. Med. J.* 332:580–84

Batty GD, Gale CR, Mortensen LH, Langenberg C, Shipley MJ, et al. 2008. Pre-morbid intelligence, the metabolic syndrome and mortality: the Vietnam Experience Study. *Diabetologia* 51:436–43

Batty GD, Wennerstad KM, Davey Smith G, Gunnell D, Deary IJ, et al. 2009. IQ in late adolescence/early adulthood and mortality by middle age: cohort study of one million Swedish men. *Epidemiology* 20:100–9

Beddington J, Cooper CL, Field J, Goswami U, Huppert FA, et al. 2008. The mental wealth of nations. *Nature* 455:1057–60

Bielak AAM. 2010. How can we not "lose it" if we still don't understand how to "use it"? *Gerontology* 56:507–19

Binet A. 1905. New methods for the diagnosis of the intellectual level of subnormals. *L'Annee Psychol.* 12:191–244. Transl. ES Kite, 1916, in *The Development of Intelligence in Children*. Vineland, NJ: Publ. Training School Vineland

Blinkhorn S. 2005. Intelligence: a gender bender. *Nature* 438:31–32

Brand CR. 1996. *The g Factor*. Chichester, UK: Wiley. (This book was withdrawn by the publisher shortly after publication.)

Breen R, Goldthorpe JH. 2002. Merit, mobility and method: another reply to Saunders. *Br. J. Sociol.* 53:575–82

Burks SV, Carpenter JP, Goette L, Rustichini A. 2009. Cognitive skills affect economic preferences, strategic behavior, and job attachment. *Proc. Natl. Acad. Sci. USA* 106:7745–50

Calvin C, Deary IJ, Fenton C, Roberts BA, Der G, et al. 2011. Intelligence in youth and all-cause mortality: systematic review with meta-analysis. *Int. J. Epidemiol.* In press

Calvin C, Fernandes C, Smith P, Visscher PM, Deary IJ. 2009. Is there still a cognitive cost of being a twin in the UK? *Intelligence* 37:243–48

Carroll JB. 1993. *Human Cognitive Abilities: A Survey of Factor Analytic Studies*. Cambridge, UK: Cambridge Univ. Press

Carson J. 2007. *The Measure of Merit: Talents, Intelligence, and Inequality in the French and American Republics, 1750–1940*. Princeton, NJ: Princeton Univ. Press

Caspi A, Williams B, Kim-Cohen J, Craig IW, Milne BJ, et al. 2007. Moderation of breastfeeding effects on the IQ by genetic variation in fatty acid metabolism. *Proc. Natl. Acad. Sci. USA* 104:18860–65

Chiang M-C, Barysheva M, Shattuck DW, Lee AD, Madsen SK. 2009. Genetics of brain fiber architecture and intellectual performance. *J. Neurosci.* 29:2212–24

Choi YY, Shamosh NA, DeYoung CG, Lee MJ, Lee J-M, et al. 2008. Multiple bases of human intelligence revealed by cortical thickness and neural activation. *J. Neurosci.* 28:10323–29

Cianciolo AT, Sternberg RJ. 2004. *Intelligence: A Brief History*. Malden, MA: Blackwell

Cirulli ET, Kasperaviciute D, Attix DK, Need AC, Ge D, et al. 2010. Common genetic variation and performance on standardized cognitive tests. *Eur. J. Hum. Genet.* 18:815–20

Cohn LD, Westenberg PM. 2004. Intelligence and maturity: meta-analytic evidence for the incremental and discriminant validity of Loevinger's measure of ego development. *J. Personal. Soc. Psychol.* 86:760–72

Colom R, Jung RE, Haier RJ. 2006. Distributed brain sites for the *g*-factor of intelligence. *NeuroImage* 31:1359–65

Cronbach LJ. 1957. The two disciplines of scientific psychology. *Am. Psychol.* 12:671–84

Davies G, Tenesa A, Payton A, Yang J, Harris SE, et al. 2011. Genome-wide association studies establish that human intelligence is highly heritable and polygenic. *Mol. Psychiatry*. doi:10.1038/mp.2011.85. In press

Davis OS, Butcher LM, Docherty SJ, Meaburn EL, Curtis CJ, et al. 2010. A three-stage genome-wide association study of general cognitive ability: hunting the small effects. *Behav. Genet.* 40:759–67

Davis OS, Haworth CM, Plomin R. 2009. Dramatic increase in heritability of cognitive development from early to middle childhood: an 8-year longitudinal study of 8700 pairs of twins. *Psychol. Sci.* 20:1301–8

Deary IJ. 2000. *Looking Down on Human Intelligence: From Psychometrics to the Brain*. Oxford, UK: Oxford Univ. Press

Deary IJ. 2001. *Intelligence: A Very Short Introduction*. Oxford, UK: Oxford Univ. Press

Deary IJ, Batty GD. 2007. Cognitive epidemiology: a glossary. *J. Epidemiol. Comm. Health* 61:378–84

Deary IJ, Batty GD, Gale CR. 2008. Bright children become enlightened adults. *Psychol. Sci.* 19:1–6

Deary IJ, Bell PJ, Bell AJ, Campbell ML, Fazal ND. 2004a. Sensory discrimination and intelligence: testing Spearman's other hypothesis. *Am. J. Psychol.* 117:1–19

Deary IJ, Corley J, Gow AJ, Harris SE, Houlihan LM, et al. 2009a. Age-associated cognitive decline. *Br. Med. Bull.* 92:135–52

Deary IJ, Der G. 2005. Reaction time explains IQ's association with death. *Psychol. Sci.* 16:64–69

Deary IJ, Der G, Ford G. 2001. Reaction times and intelligence differences: a population-based cohort study. *Intelligence* 29:389–99

Deary IJ, Irwing P, Der G, Bates TC. 2007b. Brother-sister differences in the *g* factor in intelligence: analysis of full, opposite-sex siblings from the NLSY1979. *Intelligence* 35:451–56

Deary IJ, Johnson W, Houlihan LM. 2009b. Genetic foundations of human intelligence. *Hum. Genet.* 126:215–32

Deary IJ, Pattie A, Wilson V, Whalley LJ. 2005b. The cognitive cost of being a twin: two whole-population surveys. *Twin Res. Hum. Genet.* 8:376–83

Deary IJ, Penke L, Johnson W. 2010a. The neuroscience of human intelligence differences. *Nat. Rev. Neurosci.* 11:201–11

Deary IJ, Spinath FM, Bates TC. 2006. Genetics of intelligence. *Eur. J. Hum. Genet.* 14:690–700

Deary IJ, Strand S, Smith P, Fernandes C. 2007a. Intelligence and educational achievement. *Intelligence* 35:13–21

Deary IJ, Taylor MD, Hart CL, Wilson V, Davey Smith G, et al. 2005a. Intergenerational social mobility and mid-life status attainment: influences of childhood intelligence, childhood social factors, and education. *Intelligence* 33:455–72

Deary IJ, Thorpe G, Wilson V, Starr JM, Whalley LJ. 2003. Population sex differences in IQ at age 11: the Scottish Mental Survey 1932. *Intelligence* 31:533–42

Deary IJ, Weiss A, Batty GD. 2010b. Intelligence and personality as predictors of illness and death: how researchers in differential psychology and chronic disease epidemiology are collaborating to understand and address health inequalities. *Psychol. Sci. Publ. Interest* 11:53–79

Deary IJ, Whalley LJ, Lemmon H, Crawford JR, Starr JM. 2000. The stability of individual differences in mental ability from childhood to old age: follow-up of the 1932 Scottish Mental Survey. *Intelligence* 28:49–55

Deary IJ, Whalley LJ, Starr JM. 2009c. *A Lifetime of Intelligence: Follow-up Studies of the Scottish Mental Surveys of 1932 and 1947.* Washington, DC: Am. Psychol. Assoc.

Deary IJ, Whiteman MC, Starr JM, Whalley LJ, Fox HC. 2004b. The impact of childhood intelligence in later life: following up the Scottish Mental Surveys of 1932 and 1947. *J. Personal. Soc. Psychol.* 86:130–47

Der G, Batty GD, Deary IJ. 2006. Effect of breast feeding on intelligence in children: prospective study, sibling pairs analysis, and meta-analysis. *Br. Med. J.* 333:945–48

Duckworth AL, Quinn PD, Lynam DR, Loeber R, Stouthamer-Loeber M. 2011. Role of test motivation in intelligence testing. *Proc. Natl. Acad. Sci. USA* 108:7716–20

Duckworth AL, Seligman MEP. 2005. Self-discipline outdoes IQ in predicting academic performance of adolescents. *Psychol. Sci.* 16:939–44

Duncan J. 2010. *How Intelligence Happens.* New Haven, CT: Yale Univ. Press

Duncan J, Seitz RJ, Kolodny J, Bor D, Herzog H, et al. 2000. A neural basis for general intelligence. *Science* 289:457–60

Dykiert D, Gale CR, Deary IJ. 2009. Are apparent sex differences in mean IQ scores created in part by sample restriction and increased male variance? *Intelligence* 37:42–47

Flynn J. 2007. *What Is Intelligence?* Cambridge, UK: Cambridge Univ. Press

Foresight Mental Capital and Wellbeing Project. 2008. *Final Project Report—Executive Summary.* London: Gov. Off. Sci.

Friedman NP, Miyake A, Young SE, DeFries JC, Corley RP, et al. 2008. Individual differences in executive functions are almost entirely genetic in origin. *J. Exp. Psychol.: Gen.* 137:201–25

Frisoni GB, Galluzzi S, Pantoni L, Filippi M. 2007. The effect of white matter lesions on cognition in the elderly: small but detectable. *Nat. Clin. Pract. Neurol.* 3:620–27

Furlow B, Armijo-Prewitt T, Gangestad SW, Thornhill R. 1997. Fluctuating asymmetry and psychometric intelligence. *Proc. R. Soc. Lond. B* 264:823–29

Gale CR, Batty GD, Tynelius P, Deary IJ, Rasmussen F. 2010. Intelligence in early adulthood and subsequent hospitalization for mental disorders. *Epidemiology* 21:70–77

Gale CR, Hatch SL, Batty GD, Deary IJ. 2009. Intelligence in childhood and risk of psychological distress in adulthood: the National Child Development Survey and the 1970 British Cohort Study. *Intelligence* 37:592–99

Gardner H. 1983. *Frames of Mind*. New York: Basic Books

Gardner H. 1993. *Multiple Intelligences*. New York: Basic Books

Garlick D. 2010. *Intelligence and the Brain: Solving the Mystery of Why People Differ in IQ and How a Child Can Be a Genius*. Burbank, CA: Aesop

Geary DC. 2005. *The Origin of Mind: Evolution of Brain, Cognition, and General Intelligence*. Washington, DC: Am. Psychol. Assoc.

Gläscher J, Rudrauf D, Colom R, Paul LK, Tranel D, et al. 2010. Distributed neural system for general intelligence revealed by lesion mapping. *Proc. Natl. Acad. Sci. USA* 107:4705–9

Gottfredson LS. 2004. Intelligence: is it the epidemiologists' elusive "fundamental cause" of social class inequalities in health? *J. Personal. Soc. Psychol.* 86:174–99

Gow AJ, Johnson W, Pattie A, Brett CE, Roberts B, et al. 2011. Stability and change in intelligence from age 11 to ages 70, 79, and 87: the Lothian Birth Cohorts of 1921 and 1936. *Psychol. Aging* 26:232–40

Gray JR, Chabris CF, Braver TS. 2003. Neural mechanisms of general fluid intelligence. *Nat. Neurosci.* 6:316–22

Haier RJ. 2009. Neuro-intelligence, neuro-metrics and the next phase of brain imaging studies. *Intelligence* 37:121–23

Herrnstein RJ, Murray C. 1994. *The Bell Curve: Intelligence and Class Structure in American Life*. New York: Free Press

Hertzog C, Kramer AF, Wilson RS, Lindenberger U. 2009. Enrichment effects on adult cognitive development. *Psychol Sci. Publ. Int.* 9:1–65

Hulshoff Pol H, Schnack HG, Posthuma D, Mandl RCW, Barré WF, et al. 2006. Genetic contributions to human brain morphology and intelligence. *J. Neurosci.* 26:10235–42

Hunt E. 2011. *Human Intelligence*. Cambridge, UK: Cambridge Univ. Press

Intelligence. 2009. Special issue. Intelligence, health and death: the emerging field of cognitive epidemiology. *Intelligence* 37:6(whole issue)

Irwing P, Lynn R. 2005. Sex differences in means and variability on the progressive matrices in university students: a meta-analysis. *Br. J. Psychol.* 96:505–24

Jensen AR. 1998. *The g Factor*. New York: Praeger

Johnson W, Bouchard TJ. 2005a. The structure of human intelligence: It is verbal, perceptual, and image rotation (VPR), not fluid and crystallized. *Intelligence* 33:393–416

Johnson W, Bouchard TJ. 2005b. Constructive replication of the visual [*sic*]-perceptual-image rotation model in Thurstone's (1941) battery of 60 tests of mental ability. *Intelligence* 33:417–30

Johnson W, Bouchard TJ, Krueger RF, McGue M, Gottesman II. 2004. Just one *g*: consistent results from three test batteries. *Intelligence* 32:95–107

Johnson W, Bouchard TJ, McGue M, Segal NL, Tellegen A, et al. 2007. Genetic and environmental influences on the Verbal-Perceptual-Image Rotation (VPR) model of the structure of mental abilities in the Minnesota Study of Twins Reared Apart. *Intelligence* 35:542–62

Johnson W, Carothers A, Deary IJ. 2008a. Sex differences in variability in general intelligence: a new look at the old question. *Perspect. Psychol. Sci.* 3:518–31

Johnson W, Gow AJ, Corley J, Starr JM, Deary IJ. 2010. Location in cognitive and residential space at age 70 reflects a lifelong trait over parental and environmental circumstances: the Lothian Birth Cohort 1936. *Intelligence* 38:402–11

Johnson W, Segal NL, Bouchard TJ. 2008b. Fluctuating asymmetry and general intelligence: no genetic or phenotypic association. *Intelligence* 36:279–88

Johnson W, te Nijenhuis J, Bouchard TJ. 2008c. Still just 1 *g*: consistent results from five test batteries. *Intelligence* 36:81–95

Jung RE, Gasparovic C, Chavez RS, Caprihian A, Barrow R, et al. 2009. Imaging intelligence with magnetic resonance spectroscopy. *Intelligence* 37:192–98

Jung RE, Haier RJ. 2007. The Parieto-Frontal Integration Theory (P-FIT) of intelligence: converging neuroimaging evidence. *Behav. Brain Sci.* 30:135–54, discussion 154–87

Karama S, Ad-Dab'bagh Y, Haier RJ, Deary IJ, Lyttelton OC, et al. 2009. Positive association between cognitive ability and cortical thickness in a representative US sample of healthy 6 to 18 year-olds. *Intelligence* 37:145–55

Keller MC, Miller G. 2007. Resolving the paradox of common, harmful, heritable mental disorders: Which evolutionary genetic models work best? *Behav. Brain Sci.* 29:385–404

Lango Allen H, Estrada K, Lettre G, Berndt SI, Weedon MN, et al. 2010. Hundreds of variants clustered in genomic loci and biological pathways affect human height. *Nature* 467:832–38

Lee T, Henry JD, Trollor JN, Sachdev PS. 2010. Genetic influences on cognitive functions in the elderly: a selective review of twin studies. *Brain Res. Rev.* 64:1–13

Lohman DF. 1994. Component scores as residual variation (or why the intercept correlates best). *Intelligence* 19:1–11

Lohman DF, Lakin JM. 2009. Consistencies in sex differences on the Cognitive Abilities Test across countries, grades, test forms, and cohorts. *Br. J. Educ. Psychol.* 79:389–407

Luciano M, Posthuma D, Wright M, de Geus EJC, Smith GA, et al. 2005. Perceptual speed does not cause intelligence, and intelligence does not cause perceptual speed. *Biol. Psychol.* 70:1–8

Luciano M, Wright MJ, Duffy DL, Wainwright MA, Zhu G, et al. 2006. Genome-wide scan of IQ finds significant linkage to a quantitative trait locus on 2q. *Behav. Genet.* 36:45–55

Luciano M, Wright MJ, Geffen GM, Geffen LB, Smith GA, et al. 2004a. A multivariate genetic analysis of cognitive abilities in an adolescent twin sample. *Aust. J. Psychol.* 56:79–88

Luciano M, Wright M, Martin N. 2004b. Exploring the etiology of the association between birthweight and IQ in an adolescent twin sample. *Twin Res.* 7:62–71

Lynn R, Irwing P. 2004. Sex differences on the progressive matrices: a meta-analysis. *Intelligence* 32:481–98

Lynn R, Vanhanen T. 2002. *IQ and the Wealth of Nations*. Westport, CT: Praeger

Lyons MJ, York TP, Franz CE, Grant MD, Eaves LJ, et al. 2009. Genes determine stability and the environment determines change in cognitive ability during 35 years of adulthood. *Psychol. Sci.* 20:1146–52

Mackintosh NJ. 1996. Science struck dumb. *Nature* 381:33

Madhyastha TM, Hunt E, Deary IJ, Gale CR, Dykiert D. 2009. Recruitment modeling applied to longitudinal studies of group differences in intelligence. *Intelligence* 37:422–27

McDaniel MA. 2005. Big-brained people are smarter: a meta-analysis of the relationship between in vivo brain volume and intelligence. *Intelligence* 33:337–46

McGurn B, Deary IJ, Starr JM. 2008. Childhood cognitive ability and risk of late-onset Alzheimer and vascular dementia. *Neurology* 71:1051–56

Miller GF. 2000. *The Mating Mind*. New York: Doubleday

Moran P, Klinteberg BA, Batty GD, Vagero D. 2009. Childhood intelligence predicts hospitalization with personality disorder in adulthood: evidence from a population-based study in Sweden. *J. Personal. Disord.* 23:535–40

Murdoch S. 2007. *IQ: The Smart History of a Failed Idea*. Hoboken, NJ: Wiley

Narr KL, Woods RP, Thompson PM, Szeszko P, Robinson D, et al. 2007. Relationships between IQ and regional cortical gray matter thickness in healthy adults. *Cereb. Cortex* 17:2163–71

Nettle D. 2003. Intelligence and class mobility in the British population. *Br. J. Psychol.* 94:551–61

Neubauer AC, Fink A. 2009. Intelligence and neural efficiency. *Neurosci. Biobehav. Rev.* 33:1004–23

Nisbett R. 2009. *Intelligence and How to Get It*. New York: Norton

O'Toole BI, Stankov L. 1992. Ultimate validity of psychological tests. *Personal. Individ. Differ.* 13:699–716

Payton A. 2009. The impact of genetic research on our understanding of normal cognitive aging: 1995 to 2009. *Neuropsychol. Rev.* 19:451–77

Penke L, Denissen JJA, Miller GF. 2007. The evolutionary genetics of personality. *Eur. J. Personal.* 21:549–87

Plassman BL, Williams JW, Burke JR, Holsinger T, Benjamin S. 2010. Systematic review: factors associated with risk for and possible prevention of cognitive decline in later life. *Ann. Int. Med.* 153:182–93

Plomin R, Spinath F. 2004. Intelligence: genetics, genes and genomics. *J. Personal. Soc. Psychol.* 86:112–29

Posthuma D, de Geus EJC, Barré WF, Hulshoff Pol HE, Kahn RS, et al. 2002. The association between brain volume and intelligence is of genetic origin. *Nat. Neurosci.* 5:83–84

Posthuma D, de Geus EJC, Boomsma DI. 2001. Perceptual speed and IQ are associated through common genetic factors. *Behav. Genet.* 31:593–602

Posthuma D, Luciano M, de Geus EJC, Wright MJ, Slagboom PE, et al. 2005. A genomewide scan for intelligence identifies quantitative trait loci on 2q and 6p. *Am. J. Hum. Genet.* 77:318–26

Power C, Jefferis BJ, Manor O. 2010. Childhood cognition and risk factors for cardiovascular disease in midadulthood: the 1958 British Birth Cohort Study. *Am. J. Public Health* 100:129–36

Power C, Li L, Hertzman C. 2008. Cognitive development and cortisol patterns in mid-life: findings from a British birth cohort. *Psychoneuroendocrinology* 33:530–39

Reynolds CA, Finkel D, McArdle JJ, Gatz M, Berg S, et al. 2005. Quantitative genetic analysis of latent growth curve models of cognitive abilities in adulthood. *Dev. Psychol.* 41:3–16

Richards M, Shipley B, Fuhrer R, Wadsworth MEJ. 2004. Cognitive ability in childhood and cognitive decline in midlife: longitudinal birth cohort study. *Br. Med. J.* 328:552–56

Rijsdijk FV, Vernon PA, Boomsma DI. 2002. Application of hierarchical genetic models to Raven and WAIS subtests: a Dutch twin study. *Behav. Genet.* 32:199–210

Ronalds GA, De Stavola BL, Leon DA. 2005. The cognitive cost of being a twin: evidence from comparisons within families in the Aberdeen children of the 1950s cohort. *Br. Med. J.* 331:1306

Rushton JP, Ankney CD. 2009. Whole brain size and general mental ability: a review. *Int. J. Neurosci.* 119:691–731

Rushton JP, Jensen AR. 2005. Thirty years of research on race differences in cognitive ability. *Psychol. Publ. Policy Law* 11:235–94

Salthouse TA. 2004. Localizing age-related individual differences in a hierarchical structure. *Intelligence* 32:541–61

Salthouse TA. 2010. *Major Issues in Cognitive Aging.* Oxford, UK: Oxford Univ. Press

Sapolsky RM. 2005. The influence of social hierarchy on primate health. *Science* 308:648–52

Saunders P. 2002. Reflections on the meritocracy debate in Britain: a response to Richard Breen and John Goldthorpe. *Br. J. Sociol.* 53:559–74

Saunders P. 2010. *Social Mobility Myths.* London: Civitas

Schaie KW. 2005. *Developmental Influences on Adult Intelligence: The Seattle Longitudinal Study.* Oxford, UK: Oxford Univ. Press

Schoon I, Cheng H, Gale CR, Batty GD, Deary IJ. 2010. Social status, cognitive ability, and educational attainment as predictors of liberal social attitudes and political trust. *Intelligence* 38:144–50

Shaw P, Greenstein D, Lerch J, Clasen L, Lenroot R, et al. 2006. Intellectual ability and cortical development in children and adolescents. *Nature* 440:676–79

Shenk D. 2010. *The Genius in All of Us: Why Everything You've Been Told About Genetics, Talent and Intelligence is Wrong.* London: Icon

Shenkin SD, Starr JM, Deary IJ. 2004. Birth weight and cognitive ability in childhood: a systematic review. *Psychol. Bull.* 130:989–1013

Sheppard LD. 2008. Intelligence and information processing: a review of 50 years of research. *Personal. Individ. Differ.* 44:533–49

Shineman DW, Salthouse TA, Launer LJ, Hof PR, Bartzokis G, et al. 2010. Therapeutics for cognitive aging. *Ann. N. Y. Acad. Sci.* 1191:E1–10

Singh-Manoux A, Ferrie JE, Lynch JW, Marmot M. 2005. The role of cognitive ability (intelligence) in explaining the association between socioeconomic position and health: evidence from the Whitehall II prospective cohort study. *Am. J. Epidemiol.* 161:831–39

Spearman C. 1904. "General intelligence" objectively determined and measured. *Am. J. Psychol.* 15:201–93

Stanovich KE. 2009. *What Intelligence Tests Miss: The Psychology of Rational Thought.* New Haven, CT: Yale Univ. Press

Steer CD, Davey Smith G, Emmett PM, Hibbeln JR, Golding J. 2010. FADS2 polymorphisms modify the effect of breastfeeding on child IQ. *PLoS One* 5:e11570

Sternberg RJ, Grigorenko EL. 2002. *The General Factor of Intelligence: How General Is It?* Mahwah, NJ: Erlbaum

Strand S, Deary IJ, Smith P. 2006. Sex differences in cognitive abilities test scores: a UK national picture. *Br. J. Educ. Psychol.* 76:463–80

Strenze T. 2007. Intelligence and socioeconomic success: a meta-analytic review of longitudinal research. *Intelligence* 35:401–26

Thompson PM, Cannon TD, Narr KL, van Erp T, Poutanen VP, et al. 2001. Genetic influences on brain structure. *Nat. Neurosci.* 4:1253–58

Tucker-Drob EM. 2011. Global and domain-specific changes in cognition throughout adulthood. *Dev. Psychol.* 47:331–43

Turkheimer E, Haley A, Waldron M, D'Onfrio BM, Gottesman II. 2003. Socioeconomic status modified heritability of IQ in young children. *Psychol. Sci.* 14:623–28

van der Maas HLJ, Dolan CV, Grasman RP, Wicherts JM, Huizenga HM, Raijmakers ME. 2006. A dynamical model of general intelligence: the positive manifold of intelligence by mutualism. *Psychol. Rev.* 13:842–60

Van Valen L. 1962. A study of fluctuating asymmetry. *Evolution* 16:125–42

Vernon PE. 1956. *The Measurement of Abilities*. London: Univ. London Press

Vinkhuyzen AAE, van der Sluis S, Posthuma D. 2011. Life events moderate variation in cognitive ability (*g*) in adults. *Mol. Psychiatry* 16:4–6

Visser BA, Ashton MC, Vernon PA. 2006. Beyond *g*: putting multiple intelligences to the test. *Intelligence* 34:487–502

von Stumm S, Gale CR, Batty GD, Deary IJ. 2009. Childhood intelligence, behaviour, and locus of control as determinants of intergenerational social mobility: the British Cohort Study 1970. *Intelligence* 37:329–40

von Stumm S, Macintyre S, Batty GD, Clark H, Deary IJ. 2010. Intelligence, social class of origin, childhood behavior disturbance and education as predictors of status attainment in midlife in men: the Aberdeen Children of the 1950s study. *Intelligence* 38:202–11

Voracek M, Haubner T. 2008. Twin-singleton differences in intelligence: a meta-analysis. *Psychol. Rep.* 102:951–62

Waiter GD, Deary IJ, Staff RT, Murray AD, Fox HC, et al. 2009. Exploring possible neural mechanisms of intelligence differences using processing speed and working memory tasks: an fMRI study. *Intelligence* 37:199–206

Webbink D, Posthuma D, Boomsma DI, de Geus EJC, Visscher PM. 2008. Do twins have lower cognitive ability than singletons? *Intelligence* 36:539–47

Weiser M, Zarka S, Wrbeloff N, Kravitz E, Lubin G. 2009. Cognitive test scores in male adolescent cigarette smokers compared to non-smokers: a population-based study. *Addiction* 105:358–63

Whalley LJ, Deary IJ. 2001. Longitudinal cohort study of childhood IQ and survival up to age 76. *Br. Med. J.* 322:819–22

White J. 2006. *Intelligence, Destiny and Education: The Ideological Roots of Intelligence Testing*. London: Routledge

Wilhelm O, Engle RW, eds. 2005. *Handbook of Measuring and Understanding Intelligence*. London: Sage

Wilson RS, Beckett LA, Barnes LL, Schneider JA, Bach J, et al. 2002. Individual differences in rates of change in cognitive abilities of older persons. *Psychol. Aging* 17:179–93

Wisdom NM, Callahan JL, Hawkins KA. 2011. The effects of apolipoprotein E on non-impaired cognitive function: a meta-analysis. *Neurobiol. Aging* 32:63–74

Woolley AW, Chabris CF, Pentland A, Hashmi N, Malone TW. 2010. Evidence for a collective intelligence factor in the performance of human groups. *Science* 330:686–88

Wright Gillham N. 2001. *A Life of Sir Francis Galton: From African Exploration to the Birth of Eugenics*. Oxford, UK: Oxford Univ. Press

Yeo RA, Gangestad SW, Liu J, Calhoun VD, Hutchison KE. 2011. Rare copy number deletions predict individual variation in intelligence. *PLoS One* 6:e16339

Zhang J-P, Burdick KE, Lencz T, Malhotra AK. 2010. Meta-analysis of genetic variation in DTNBP1 and general cognitive ability. *Biol. Psychiatry* 68:1126–33

Decoding Patterns of Human Brain Activity

Frank Tong and Michael S. Pratte

Psychology Department and Vanderbilt Vision Research Center, Vanderbilt University,
Nashville, Tennessee 37240; email: frank.tong@vanderbilt.edu

Annu. Rev. Psychol. 2012. 63:483–509

First published online as a Review in Advance on
September 19, 2011

The *Annual Review of Psychology* is online at
psych.annualreviews.org

This article's doi:
10.1146/annurev-psych-120710-100412

Keywords

fMRI, multivoxel pattern analysis, MVPA

Abstract

Considerable information about mental states can be decoded from noninvasive measures of human brain activity. Analyses of brain activity patterns can reveal what a person is seeing, perceiving, attending to, or remembering. Moreover, multidimensional models can be used to investigate how the brain encodes complex visual scenes or abstract semantic information. Such feats of "brain reading" or "mind reading," though impressive, raise important conceptual, methodological, and ethical issues. What does successful decoding reveal about the cognitive functions performed by a brain region? How should brain signals be spatially selected and mathematically combined to ensure that decoding reflects inherent computations of the brain rather than those performed by the decoder? We highlight recent advances and describe how multivoxel pattern analysis can provide a window into mind-brain relationships with unprecedented specificity, when carefully applied. However, as brain-reading technology advances, issues of neuroethics and mental privacy will be important to consider.

Contents

INTRODUCTION

Imagine that it is the future, an unknown year in the twenty-first century. A participant is brought into a neuroimaging lab and asked to lie back comfortably on a padded bed table, which is slowly glided into a brain scanner. The participant watches a brightly colored display as it provides a virtual tour of every painting in the Musée d'Orsay. All the while,

Decoding: neural decoding involves determining what stimuli or mental states are represented by an observed pattern of neural activity

noninvasive measures of that person's brain activity are discretely taken, and the arrays of numbers are quickly transferred to the memory banks of a high-speed digital computer. After hours of brain scanning and computer analysis, the real scientific test begins. A randomly drawn painting is shown again to the observer. The computer analyzes the incoming patterns of brain activity from the participant's visual cortex and makes the following prediction with 99% confidence: She is looking at painting #1023, Cézanne's *Still Life with Apples and Oranges*. The experimenter turns to look at the computer screen, and indeed, the participant is looking at a plateful of pastel-colored red and yellow apples, and ripe oranges stacked in a porcelain bowl, all carefully arranged in the thick folds of a tousled white tablecloth. Another randomly drawn picture is shown, and the computer correctly predicts *Landscape with Green Trees* by Maurice Denis.

What does this remarkable scientific demonstration reveal—successful mind reading? Have the neuroscientists effectively cracked the brain's internal code for vision, such that they now understand how features and objects are represented in the mind's internal eye? We will refer to this as Science Fiction Story #1.

The lab volunteer has kindly offered to participate in a second experiment. This time she is shown two paintings in quick succession (*Bedroom in Arles, The White Horse*) and then is asked to pick one and hold that image in mind for several seconds. She imagines a horse standing in a shallow river, head bent low as if looking at its own reflection in the slowly flowing stream. The computer quickly scans the matrix of numbers streaming in. Although brain activity levels are substantially weaker as she gazes steadily at the blank screen, compared to moments ago, a pattern begins to emerge from her visual cortex. The computer announces, with 85% confidence, that the participant is imagining the second painting, *The White Horse*. Would successful decoding in this case indicate that the neural codes for imagination and internal visual thoughts have been successfully decoded? More generally, what would such a demonstration reveal about the visual and cognitive functions performed by the brain? We will refer to this as Science Fiction Story #2.

In reality, these stories represent more fact than fiction. A simplified version of Science Fiction Story #1 was carried out at the start of the twenty-first century in a pioneering study by Haxby and colleagues (2001). The authors used functional magnetic resonance imaging (fMRI) to measure patterns of blood level oxygen–dependent (BOLD) activity, focusing on object-responsive regions in the ventral temporal cortex. By comparing the similarity of brain activity patterns between the first and second half of the experiment, the authors showed that these high-level object areas could accurately predict whether participants were viewing pictures of faces, houses, chairs, cats, bottles, shoes, scissors, or scrambled stimuli (**Figure 1a**, see color insert). The use of more sophisticated pattern-classification algorithms (**Figure 1b**) greatly improved researchers' ability to predict what object categories people were viewing (Carlson et al. 2003, Cox & Savoy 2003). Subsequently, Kamitani & Tong (2005) discovered that it was possible to decode orientation- and direction-selective responses with surprising accuracy (**Figure 2**, see color insert), even though such feature-selective information is primarily organized at the scale of submillimeter columns in the visual cortex. Thus, fMRI pattern analysis could reveal cortical information that would otherwise fail to be detected. Perhaps the most striking demonstration of Science Fiction Story #1 comes from the work of Kay et al. (2008). They presented more than 1,000 natural images to observers and then characterized the response preferences of each voxel in the visual cortex, specifying their selectivity for retinotopic position, spatial frequency, and orientation. When the observers were shown a new set of 120 pictures, each of a different real-world scene, the authors could accurately predict which new image was being viewed by finding the best match between the observed pattern of activity and the predicted activity of these modeled voxels.

These studies reveal an unprecedented ability to predict the basic visual features, complex objects, or natural scenes that are being viewed by the participant. By combining fMRI with sensitive pattern-analysis methods, accurate predictions about the viewed stimulus can be made. Yet it would be a mistake to consider such feats as examples of mind reading. Why? Because the experimenter does not need a mind-reading device to achieve this performance. The same result could be achieved by simply looking over the participant's shoulder, "Oh, she is looking at painting #1023, Cezanne's *Still Life with Apples and Oranges.*" Put another way, one could perform these same feats by reading out the activity patterns formed on the retina even though conscious processing of the image has yet to take place. Activity patterns on the retina would remain robust even if the person were anesthetized or fell into a deep coma. So instead, Science Fiction Story #1 should be considered an example of brain reading.

Science Fiction Story #2 can be better justified as a demonstration of mind reading. Here, information that is fundamentally private and subjective is being decoded from the person's brain; the only alternative would be to ask the participant directly about what she is thinking and to hope for an honest reply. Ongoing research is just beginning to probe the possibilities and limits of reading out subjective information from the human brain.

In this review, we discuss recent advances in brain reading and mind reading, and we consider important conceptual and methodological issues regarding how to apply these techniques to the study of human cognition. The brain reading approach has revealed how different types of stimulus information are represented in specific brain areas, and some studies provide clues to the functional organization of these representations. Pattern analysis of brain activity can also be adapted to perform feats of mind reading to extract information about a person's subjective mental state or cognitive goal. We consider whether such feats of mind reading should be likened to fancy parlor tricks that require the assistance of a brain scanner or whether these methods can be used to genuinely advance our understanding of brain function. Studies employing this mind-reading approach have revealed how particular representations are activated or called upon during conscious perception, attentional selection, imagery, memory maintenance and retrieval, and decision making. As will be seen, careful consideration of experimental design, analysis, and interpretation of the data is essential when adopting powerful pattern analysis algorithms to probe the functions that might be carried out by a brain area. As these methodologies continue to advance, it will become increasingly important to consider the ethical implications of this technology.

There have been previous reviews on the topic of fMRI decoding (sometimes called multivoxel pattern analysis, or MVPA (Haynes & Rees 2006, Norman et al. 2006), as well as more in-depth reviews on the technical aspects of decoding and encoding (Kriegeskorte 2011, Naselaris et al. 2011, O'Toole et al. 2007, Pereira et al. 2009). In this review, we highlight recent studies and discuss key issues regarding how fMRI pattern analysis can be used to advance understanding of the bases of human cognition.

BRIEF TUTORIAL ON MULTIVOXEL PATTERN ANALYSIS

Traditional methods of fMRI analysis treat each voxel as an independent piece of data, using statistical tests to determine whether that voxel responded more in some experimental conditions than in others. Such analyses are univariate: the analysis of one voxel has no impact on the analysis of any other. By contrast, multivariate pattern analysis extracts the information contained in the patterns of activity among multiple voxels so that the relative differences in activity between voxels can provide relevant information. Whereas univariate statistical analyses are

designed to test whether some voxels respond more to one condition than another, multivariate analyses are designed to test whether two (or more) experimental conditions can be distinguished from one another on the basis of the activity patterns observed in a set of voxels. Critically, multivariate methods might be able to tell apart the activity patterns for two different conditions even if the average level of activity does not differ between conditions.

Figure 1*b* illustrates the simplest example of multivariate pattern analysis involving two experimental conditions (shown in red and green) and just two voxels, with the response amplitude of each voxel shown on separate axes. Each dot corresponds to a single activity pattern or data sample, with its position indicating the strength of the response for voxels 1 and 2. The Gaussian density plots in the margins indicate that either voxel alone does a rather poor job of separating the two experimental conditions. Nevertheless, the two conditions can be well separated by considering the pattern of responses to both voxels, as indicated by the separating boundary line. In this particular example, the responses of voxels 1 and 2 are positively correlated, and the classification boundary helps to remove this correlated "noise" to better separate the two experimental conditions. If there were three voxels, a third dimension would be added; the red dots and greens dots would form two largely separated (but still overlapping) clouds of points, and the classification boundary would consist of a linear plane that best divides those two clouds. Typically, anywhere from a few dozen to several thousand voxels might be used for fMRI pattern analysis, so an activity pattern with N voxels would be represented in an N-dimensional space, and clouds of dots representing the two classes would be separated by a linear hyperplane. (Multiclass classification analysis involves calculating multiple hyperplanes to carve up this multidimensional space among three or more conditions.)

The goal of linear pattern classification algorithms, such as support vector machines (SVM), linear discriminant analysis (LDA), or logistic regression, is to find the linear hyperplane that best separates the two (or more) conditions in this multidimensional voxel space. The accuracy of classification performance is usually assessed using cross-validation, which involves dividing the full set of data samples into separate sets for training and testing the classifier. Typically, an entire fMRI run or perhaps just one sample from each condition is reserved for the test set. The classifier is trained with the remaining data to obtain the classification boundary, which is then used to predict the class of each data sample (e.g., "red" or "green") in the test set. This procedure can be done iteratively so that every sample in the data set is tested and an overall measure of classification accuracy is obtained. Classification accuracy reflects the amount of information available in a set of voxels for discriminating between the experimental conditions tested.

Here, we focus on linear pattern classification, since the performance of nonlinear classifiers applied to a brain region could potentially reflect computations performed by the classifier rather than by brain itself (Kamitani & Tong 2005). For example, if one were to apply sufficiently complex nonlinear classifiers to the patterns of activity observed on the retina, it would be possible to construct the functional equivalent of receptive fields with position-invariant tuning to visual orientation, curved lines, sharp corners, or even a smiley face cartoon of Bart Simpson, despite the lack of any such pattern detectors in the human retina. All brain processes essentially reflect a series of nonlinear computations; therefore, to characterize the information processed by a brain region, we believe it is important to avoid adding additional nonlinear steps.

The reliability of linear classification performance depends on several factors: (*a*) the degree of separation between the two classes of data samples (i.e., pattern separability or signal-to-noise ratio), (*b*) the number of data samples available for analysis, since having more samples will allow for better estimation of the optimal classification hyperplane, (*c*) the choice of classification algorithm and its suit-ability for the data set to be analyzed (Misaki et al. 2010), and (*d*) the voxels used for pattern analysis. Adding more voxels should lead to better classification performance if those voxels contain some relevant information that can be used to better distinguish between the two conditions. However, if these additional voxels are uninformative, they may simply add noise or unwanted variability to the activity patterns and could thereby impair classification performance (Yamashita et al. 2008).

REVIEW OF FUNCTIONAL MAGNETIC RESONANCE IMAGING STUDIES

Decoding Visual Features

In their original study of orientation decoding, Kamitani & Tong (2005) found that activity patterns in early visual areas could predict which of several oriented gratings was being viewed with remarkable accuracy (**Figure 2a**). How was this possible, given that BOLD responses were sampled from the visual cortex using 3mm-wide voxels, whereas orientation columns are organized at submillimeter spatial scales (Obermayer & Blasdel 1993, Yacoub et al. 2008)? The authors performed simulations to show that random local variations in cortical organization could lead to weak orientation biases in individual voxels. By pooling the information available from many independent voxels, a pattern classifier could achieve robust predictions of what orientation was being presented in the visual field. In subsequent work, high-resolution functional imaging studies of the cat and human visual cortices have provided support for this hypothesis (Swisher et al. 2010). These experiments show that orientation information exists at multiple spatial scales, extending from that of submillimeter cortical columns to several millimeters across the cortex (**Figure 2b**). In effect, variability in columnar organization at a submillimeter scale appears to lead to modest feature biases at coarser spatial scales on the order of millimeters. It should be noted that studies find the presence of some global preference for orientations radiating outward from the fovea as well (Freeman et al. 2011, Sasaki et al. 2006), but when such radial biases are controlled for, substantial orientation information can still be extracted from the visual cortex (Harrison & Tong 2009, Mannion et al. 2009).

These orientation-decoding studies suggest that pattern analysis can be used to detect signals of columnar origin by pooling weakly feature-selective signals that can be found at the scale of millimeters, presumably due to variability in the organization of the columns. Thus, fMRI pattern analysis could be used to reveal hidden signals originating from fine-scale cortical columns that would otherwise be difficult or impossible to isolate with noninvasive imaging. Previously, researchers had to rely on fMRI measures of visual adaptation to assess the feature selectivity of responses in the human visual cortex (Boynton & Finney 2003, Engel & Furmanski 2001).

This decoding approach has been used to investigate cortical responses to many basic visual features. Studies have revealed how the human visual system responds selectively to motion direction (Kamitani & Tong 2006), color (Brouwer & Heeger 2009, Goddard et al. 2010, Sumner et al. 2008), eye-of-origin information (Haynes et al. 2005, Shmuel et al. 2010), and binocular disparity (Preston et al. 2008). The reliability of feature decoding depends on the strength of the sensory signal; for example, the orientation of high-contrast gratings can be decoded more readily than low-contrast gratings (Smith et al. 2011). Moreover, the amplitude of the stimulus-driven BOLD response serves as a good predictor of how much feature-selective information can be extracted from the detailed pattern of activity found in a given visual area. Pattern classification has also revealed sensitivity to more complex visual features. For example, sensitivity to orientations defined by motion boundaries and by illusory contours has been found in early visual areas, including the human primary visual cortex (Clifford et al. 2009). It has also been used to show that motion patterns that are more difficult

to see, namely second-order texture-defined motion, lead to direction-selective patterns of activity in the human visual cortex that are similar to basic first-order motion (Hong et al. 2011).

The feature-decoding approach has also been used to test for selectivity to conjunctions of features (Seymour et al. 2009, 2010). For example, Seymour et al. (2009) tested for sensitivity to conjunctions of color and motion by presenting observers with compound displays consisting of red dots moving clockwise and overlapping with green dots moving counterclockwise, or green dots moving clockwise paired with red dots moving counterclockwise. Activity patterns in early visual areas could discriminate between these different combinations of color and motion, implying that these areas contain neurons sensitive to the conjunction of these features. These findings inform current theories of perceptual binding, which have debated whether top-down attentional processes are required to represent conjunctions of features (Treisman 1996).

What are the underlying neural sources of these feature-selective responses in the human visual cortex? In the case of orientation or eye-of-origin signals, these feature-selective responses appear to reflect local biases in columnar organization to a considerable extent (Shmuel et al. 2010, Swisher et al. 2010). In other cases, feature selectivity might reflect random variations in the distribution of feature-selective neurons (Kamitani & Tong 2006) or more global biases such as a preference for radial patterns or radial motions across the retinotopic visual cortex (Clifford et al. 2009, Sasaki et al. 2006). For example, optical imaging has revealed the presence of ocular dominance columns, orientation columns, and color-sensitive blobs in the primary visual cortex (V1) of monkeys, but no evidence of direction-selective columns (Lu et al. 2010). Nonetheless, it is possible to decode strong direction-selective responses from human V1 (Kamitani & Tong 2006). Multiple factors can contribute to the spatial distribution of these feature preferences in the cortex, and these factors could have a strong impact on the efficacy of fMRI pattern analysis. In many cases, future studies using high-resolution fMRI in humans or optical imaging in animals will be required to map the feature-selective properties of the visual cortex.

Decoding Visual Perception

In the study by Kamitani & Tong (2005), a major goal was to extend the pattern-classification approach from the problem of brain reading to that of mind reading, which had not been demonstrated before. They reported the results of a visual mind-reading experiment, showing that it is possible to decode whether an observer is covertly attending to one set of oriented lines or the other when viewing an ambiguous plaid display. Activity patterns in early visual areas (V1–V4) allowed for reliable prediction of the observer's attentional state (~80% accuracy). Moreover, decoding of the attended orientation was successful even in V1 alone, indicating that feature-based attention can bias orientation processing at the earliest possible cortical site.

Encouraged by these findings, several research groups began to pursue fMRI pattern classification methods to investigate the neural underpinnings of subjective perceptual and cognitive states. Haynes & Rees (2005b) showed that fMRI pattern classification can effectively decode which of two stimuli are perceptually dominant during binocular rivalry, with perceptual alternations occurring every several seconds. Similarly, they found that orientation-selective responses were disrupted by backward visual masking, although a small amount of orientation information could still be detected in V1 for unseen visual orientations (Haynes & Rees 2005a). Perhaps most striking, they were able to apply these methods to extract monocular responses in the lateral geniculate nucleus (**Figure 3**, see color insert) and showed that binocular rivalry leads to modulations at this very early site of visual processing (Haynes et al. 2005, see also Wunderlich et al. 2005). This latter study provided novel evidence to in-

form neural models of binocular rivalry (Blake & Logothetis 2002, Tong et al. 2006). Other research groups demonstrated that the perception of ambiguous motion displays could be decoded at greater-than-chance levels from human motion area MT+ and other dorsal visual areas (Brouwer & van Ee 2007, Serences & Boynton 2007b).

An intriguing study by Scolari & Serences (2010) revealed that these feature-selective responses can also be linked to the accuracy of behavioral performance. The researchers first characterized the very modest orientation preference of every voxel in the visual cortex. Next, they tested whether voxel responses to a particular orientation might be boosted on trials in which observers correctly discriminate a small change in visual orientation, as compared to incorrect trials. When observers correctly discriminated a change in orientation centered around, say, 45°, responses in V1 were not enhanced for voxels tuned specifically to 45°; instead, they were enhanced for voxels that preferred neighboring orientations (~10° and 80°). This counterintuitive result is predicted by models of optimal visual coding, which propose that discrimination performance will be most improved by enhancing neighboring off-channel responses.

Decoding Visual Objects

The pioneering work by Haxby et al. (2001) suggested that categorical information about objects is represented in a distributed manner throughout the ventral temporal lobe. Activity patterns in this region could accurately discriminate between multiple object categories, even when the most strongly category-selective voxels were removed from the analysis. In effect, the authors could perform "virtual lesions" on these activity patterns, and they thereby revealed the distributed nature of object information (but see also Spiridon & Kanwisher 2002). Curiously, however, subsequent studies found that activity patterns in low-level visual areas could outperform high-level object areas at telling apart viewed objects (Cox & Savoy 2003). How was this possible, given that low-level visual areas are primarily tuned to the retinotopic position of low-level features? These results indicate that the images in each object category differed in some of their low-level properties and that these low-level confounds can persist even when multiple images are shown in a stimulus block. Although low-level confounds can be reduced by manipulations of object size or 3D vantage point, they might not be eliminated, as indicated by the fact that early visual areas can still classify an object across changes in size and 3D viewpoint (Eger et al. 2008).

These findings reveal a core challenge for fMRI decoding studies. Pattern classifiers are quite powerful and will try to leverage any discriminating information that is present in brain activity patterns. Even if a brain area can distinguish between certain object images, how can one go further to show that a brain area is genuinely sensitive to object properties and not simply the low-level features of those objects?

Work by Kanwisher and colleagues has provided several lines of evidence linking the activity patterns in object-selective areas to object perception. In a study of backward visual masking, they found that activity patterns in object-selective areas were severely disrupted on trials in which the observer failed to recognize a briefly presented target (Williams et al. 2007). By contrast, activity patterns remained stable in early visual areas, despite the participant's impaired performance. Another study manipulated the physical similarity of simple 2D shapes and estimated the perceptual similarity between pairs of stimuli based on the confusion errors that participants made with visually masked stimulus presentations. Multivariate pattern analysis revealed a striking dissociation: Activity patterns in the lateral occipital area reflected the physical similarity of the images, whereas those in the ventral temporal cortex correlated with perceptual similarity (Haushofer et al. 2008). However, other studies have found that activity patterns in the lateral occipital area reflect the perceived 3D shape of "bumps" and "dimples" conveyed by shape-from-shading cues, even when the physical image is greatly altered by changes in the source of illumination (Gerardin et al. 2010).

Activity patterns in the lateral occipital and ventral temporal cortices show strong position-invariant selectivity and remain quite stable for a particular object across changes in retinal position (Schwarzlose et al. 2008). However, these areas show some evidence of position selectivity as well. Face- and body-selective areas can better discriminate between pictures of different body parts if those parts are presented at a familiar location (Chan et al. 2010). For example, a front-view image of a person's right shoulder will lead to more reliable activity patterns if the stimulus appears to the left of fixation, as it would if one were looking at the head or chest, than if it appears to the right of fixation. It is also possible to decode the retinotopic position of an object from activity patterns in high-level object areas. Moreover, perceptual illusions that lead to shifts in apparent position are better predicted by the position information contained in the activity patterns in high-level object areas than those in the early visual areas (Fischer et al. 2011).

When objects are subliminally presented to an observer, activity in object-selective areas is greatly attenuated, but somewhat greater-than-chance-level decoding is still possible, indicating the presence of some unconscious visual information in these areas (Sterzer et al. 2008). Subliminal stimuli also appear to evoke more variable patterns of activity in object-selective areas across repeated presentations, which partly accounts for the poorer decoding of subliminal stimuli (Schurger et al. 2010).

A major challenge in object recognition concerns the ability to distinguish a particular exemplar from other items in the same category. In an ambitious study, Kriegeskorte and colleagues (2008) presented 92 images of different real-world objects and assessed which images tended to evoke more similar patterns of activity. Images of animate and inanimate stimuli led to broadly distinctive patterns of activity in the human ventral temporal cortex, and a similar animate/inanimate distinction was observed when analyzing neuronal activity patterns obtained from single-unit recordings in monkeys (Kiani et al. 2007). This study also found evidence of exemplar-specific activity. Activity patterns in the human inferotemporal cortex were better at discriminating between images of different human faces than between the faces of nonhuman primates, whereas a trend toward the opposite pattern of results was observed in the monkey data.

Attempts to isolate exemplar-specific information from small cortical regions have met with limited success, with decoding performance reaching levels just slightly greater than chance (Kaul et al. 2011, Kriegeskorte et al. 2007). When large portions of the ventral temporal cortex are pooled for analysis, then considerably better decoding of specific faces can be obtained (Kriegeskorte et al. 2008, Natu et al. 2010). However, it remains to be seen whether these large-scale distributed representations are truly important for representing individual faces or whether the diverse shape codes throughout this region simply provide more information for the classifier to capitalize upon when performing these subtle discriminations. Single-unit recordings from isolated face-selective patches in the monkey indicate that a cluster of a few hundred neighboring neurons can provide remarkably detailed information for distinguishing between individual faces (Freiwald et al. 2009, Freiwald & Tsao 2010, Tsao et al. 2006). However, current fMRI technology cannot isolate information at this level of detail.

Identifying and Reconstructing Novel Visual Scenes

Decoding algorithms can classify a person's brain state as belonging to the same category as a previously recorded brain state, but these methods lack the flexibility to identify novel brain states. To address this, Kay and colleagues (2008) devised a visual encoding model to predict how early visual areas should respond to novel pictures of complex real-world scenes. First, they presented 1,750 different images to observers, and from the resulting fMRI data, they were able to characterize the response preferences of each voxel in visual cortex, specifying its preference for particular retinotopic locations, spatial frequencies, and orientations. When the observers were later shown a new set of 120 pictures, the model predicted how these voxels should respond to each new image. By comparing the predicted and actual patterns of activity, the model correctly identified 110 out of 120 test images for one participant. In a follow-up experiment, the observer was tested with 1,000 new images, of which 820 were correctly identified.

This level of identification performance is akin to Science Fiction Story #1, identifying which painting the participant is viewing at the Musée d'Orsay. An even loftier goal would be to reconstruct the painting, using only the brain activity that results from viewing that work of art. An early attempt at fMRI reconstruction met with limited success—only small portions of the simple shapes that were viewed could be reconstructed with some degree of accuracy (Thirion et al. 2006). In a more recent fMRI study, observers were presented with hundreds of different random patterns of flickering checks placed within a 10x10 square grid, and pattern analysis was used to predict whether or not any given tile of the grid was flickering (Miyawaki et al. 2008). Using this model, the authors could effectively reconstruct novel stimuli shown to the participant, including simple shapes and letters (**Figure 4a**, see color insert). Moreover, the authors could reconstruct the viewed stimulus from single brain volumes to show how this information evolved over the time course of the BOLD response (**Figure 4b**). Extending the work of Kay et al. (2008), Naselaris et al. (2009) attempted to reconstruct complex natural scenes using local-feature models and were able to capture regions of high contrast and some of the "blurry" low-spatial-frequency components of the image (**Figure 4c**). By incorporating the category-specific information available in higher-level object areas, they could also select an image (from a set of 6 million possible images) that best matched the visual features and category properties evoked by the original viewed image ("natural image prior" condition).

Decoding Top-Down Attentional Processes

The ability to decode feature-selective responses has helped advance the study of visual attention and, in particular, feature-based attention. Kamitani & Tong (2005) showed that the activity patterns evoked by single orientations can predict which of two overlapping orientations is being attended by an observer. Similar results were obtained in studies of attention to overlapping motion stimuli (Kamitani & Tong 2006). These findings indicate that top-down attention can bias the strength of feature-selective responses in early visual areas, consistent with models of early attentional selection. Serences & Boynton (2007a) demonstrated that attending to one of two overlapping sets of moving dots leads to biased direction-selective responses not only at the site of the attended stimulus, but also in unstimulated portions of the visual field. Such spatial spreading of feature-based attention is consistent with neurophysiological studies in monkeys (Treue & Maunsell 1996). A recent study found that spatial and feature-based attention can lead to distinct effects in the visual cortex (Jehee et al. 2011). When spatial attention was directed to one of two laterally presented gratings, overall BOLD activity was enhanced for the attended stimulus, and yet the orientation-selective component of these responses improved only when observers focused on discriminating the orientation of the stimulus rather than its contrast. This suggests that enhanced processing of a specific visual feature may depend more on feature-based attention than on spatial attention (Jehee et al. 2011, but see also Saproo & Serences 2010).

Recent studies have also investigated the possible top-down sources of these attentional signals. Activity patterns in posterior parietal areas and the frontal eye fields contain reliable information about whether participants are attending to features or spatial locations (Greenberg et al. 2010) and can even discriminate which of two features or locations is being attended (Liu et al. 2011). These parietal and frontal areas could serve as plausible sources of attentional feedback to early visual areas.

Multivariate pattern analysis has also been used to quantify the extent to which spatial attention can bias activity in category-selective object areas, for example, when face and house stimuli are simultaneously presented in different locations (Reddy et al. 2009). When observers view overlapping face-house stimuli, it is possible to decode the focus of object-based attention from activity patterns in high-level object areas as well as in early visual areas, indicating that top-down feedback serves to enhance the local visual features belonging to the attended object (E.H. Cohen & F. Tong, manuscript under review). Interestingly, attending to objects in the periphery leads to pattern-specific bias effects in the foveal representation of early visual areas, perhaps suggesting some type of remapping of visual information or reliance on foveal representations to recognize peripheral stimuli (Williams et al. 2008). Pattern classification has also been used to investigate visual search for objects in complex scenes. Activity patterns in the lateral occipital complex can reveal what object category participants are actively searching for, as well as those occasions when the target object briefly appears at an attended or unattended location (Peelen et al. 2009). Overall, fMRI pattern classification has greatly expanded the possibilities for studies of visual attention by providing an effective tool to measure attention-specific signals in multiple brain areas, including parietal and frontal areas.

Decoding Imagery and Working Memory

In an early fMRI study of mental imagery, O'Craven & Kanwisher (2000) showed that it was possible to predict with 85% accuracy whether a person was imagining a famous face or place by inspecting the strength of activity in the fusiform face area and parahippocampal place area. A more recent study used MVPA and found that activity patterns in the ventral temporal cortex could predict whether participants were imagining famous faces, famous buildings, tools, or food items with reasonable accuracy (Reddy et al. 2010). Similar results have been reported in studies of working memory for faces, places, and common objects (Lewis-Peacock & Postle 2008). It is also possible to decode the imagery of simple shapes such as an X or O from these object-sensitive visual areas (Stokes et al. 2009). In these studies, the activity patterns observed during imagery or working memory were very similar to those observed during perception, consistent with perception-based theories of imagery (Kosslyn et al. 2001). Interestingly, it is also possible to distinguish silent clips of movies that imply distinctive sounds (e.g., howling dog, violin being played) from activity patterns in the auditory cortex, presumably because these visual stimuli elicit spontaneous auditory imagery (Meyer et al. 2010).

Although early visual areas have been implicated in visual imagery (Kosslyn & Thompson 2003), these areas typically show little evidence of sustained BOLD activity during visual working memory tasks (Offen et al. 2008). However, recent fMRI decoding studies have provided novel evidence to suggest that early visual areas are important for retaining precise information about visual features (Harrison & Tong 2009, Serences et al. 2009). Serences and colleagues cued participants in advance to remember either the color or orientation of a grating, and after a 10-second delay, presented a second grating to evaluate working memory for the cued feature. They found that activity patterns in V1 allowed for prediction of the task-relevant feature (~60% accuracy) but not of the task-irrelevant feature; information in extrastriate visual areas proved unreliable. Harrison & Tong (2009) used a postcueing method to isolate memory-specific activity by presenting two near-orthogonal gratings at the beginning of each trial, followed by a cue indicating which orientation to retain in working memory [for a timeline of trial events, refer to **Figure 5a** (see color insert)]. Activity patterns in areas V1–V4 allowed for reliable decoding of the remembered orientation (mean accuracy of 83%), and reliable working memory information was found in each visual area, including V1 (~70% to 75% accuracy). Moreover, they found evidence of a striking dissociation between the overall amplitude of BOLD activity and the decoded information contained at individual fMRI time points. Whereas BOLD activity fell over time (**Figure 5a**), information about the remembered grating was sustained throughout the delay period (**Figure 5b**). In half of their participants, activity in V1 fell to baseline levels, equivalent to viewing a blank screen, yet decoding of the retained orientation proved as effective for these participants as for those who showed significantly elevated activity late in the delay period. These results suggest that visually precise information can be retained in early visual areas with very little overall increase in metabolic activity, due to subtle shifts in the patterns of activity in these areas.

Decoding Episodic Memory

Although long-term memories are stored via modified synaptic connections in the hippocampus and cortex in their inactive state, it is possible to decode these memories when they are actively recalled or reinstated by the participant (for an in-depth review, see Rissman & Wagner 2012). Polyn et al. (2005) had participants study images of famous faces, famous places, and common objects in the MRI scanner and trained pattern classifiers on whole-brain activity to discriminate between these categories. When participants were later asked to freely recall these items, the classifier readily tracked the category that was being recalled from memory (**Figure 5c**). Remarkably, this category-selective activity emerged several seconds before participants switched to reporting items from a new category, suggesting that this categorical information might have served as a reinstated contextual cue to facilitate memory retrieval (Howard & Kahana 1999,

Tulving & Thomson 1973). Evidence of contextual reinstatement has even been observed when participants fail to recall the studied context (Johnson et al. 2009). Whole-brain activity patterns could predict which of three different encoding tasks was performed on an item at study, based on the reinstated patterns of activity that were later observed during a recognition memory test. Task-specific patterns of activity were found for correctly recognized items, and this proved true even for items that were rated as merely familiar, despite participants' reports that they could not recollect any details surrounding the time of studying the target item. These findings argue against proposed dissociations between conscious recollection and feelings of familiarity, and further suggest that cortical reinstatement of the studied context might not be sufficient for experiencing explicit recollection (McDuff et al. 2009). Decoding can also reliably predict whether an item will be judged as old or new. When participants performed a recognition memory task involving faces, multiple brain regions responded more strongly to items judged as old than new, including the lateral and medial prefrontal cortex and posterior parietal cortex (Rissman et al. 2010). The pooled information from these regions could reliably distinguish between correctly recognized or correctly rejected items with 83% mean accuracy but failed to distinguish missed items from correctly rejected items. Explicit performance of these recognition memory judgments was necessary for decoding, as the classifier could no longer distinguish between old and new items when participants instead performed a gender discrimination task. The studies described above reveal how fMRI pattern analysis can provide a powerful tool for investigating item-specific memory processing at the time of study and test and how such data can be used to address prevalent theories of memory function.

Decoding can also be used to isolate content-specific information from fine-scale activity patterns in the human hippocampus. After participants learn the spatial layout of a virtual environment, decoding applied to hippocampal activity can reveal some reliable information about the participant's current location in that learned environment (Morgan et al. 2011, Rodriguez 2010). It has also been shown that activity patterns in the hippocampus can predict which of three short movie clips a participant is engaged in recalling from episodic memory (Chadwick et al. 2010). Although decoding performance for the hippocampus was modest (~60% accuracy), activity patterns in this region were found to perform significantly better than neighboring regions of the entorhinal cortex or the posterior parahippocampal gyrus. The ability to target specific episodic memories in the hippocampus may greatly extend the possibilities for future studies of human long-term memory.

Extracting Semantic Knowledge

Semantic knowledge is fundamentally multidimensional and often multimodal, consisting of both specific sensory-motor associations and more abstracted knowledge. For example, we know that a rose is usually red, has soft petals but sharp thorns, smells sweetly fragrant, and that the flowers of this plant make for an excellent gift on Valentine's Day. Given the multidimensional nature of semantic information, multivariate pattern analysis might be well suited to probe its neural bases.

An early fMRI study demonstrated that it was possible to decode whether participants were viewing words belonging to 1 of 12 possible semantic categories, such as four-legged animals, fish, tools, or dwellings (Mitchell et al. 2003). Subsequent studies have consistently found that animate and inanimate visual objects lead to highly differentiated patterns of activity in the ventral temporal cortex (Kriegeskorte et al. 2008, Naselaris et al. 2009). Remarkably, people who have been blind since birth exhibit a similar animate/inanimate distinction in the ventral temporal cortex when presented with tactile objects (Mahon et al. 2009, Pietrini et al. 2004), leading to the proposal that this semantic differentiation might be innately determined rather than driven by visual experience (Mahon & Caramazza 2011).

How might one characterize the broader semantic organization of the brain or predict how the brain might respond to any item based on its many semantic properties? Mitchell et al. (2008) developed a multidimensional semantic feature model to address this issue. They tried to predict brain responses to novel nouns by first quantifying how strongly these nouns were associated with a basis set of semantic features, consisting of 25 verbs (e.g., see, hear, touch, taste, smell, eat, run). In essence, these semantic features served as intermediate variables to map between novel stimuli and predicted brain activity (cf. Kay et al. 2008). The strength of the semantic association between any noun and these verbs could be estimated on the basis of their frequency of co-occurrence, from analyzing a trillion-word text corpus provided by Google Inc. Using fMRI activity patterns elicited by 60 different nouns, the authors characterized the distinct patterns of activity associated with each verb and could then predict brain responses to novel nouns by assuming that the resulting pattern of activity should reflect a weighted sum of the noun's association to each of the verbs (**Figure 6**, see color insert). Using this method, Mitchell et al. could predict which of two nouns (excluded from the training set) was being viewed with 77% accuracy and could even distinguish between two nouns belonging to the same semantic category with 62% accuracy. The activity patterns for particular verbs often revealed strong sensorimotor associations. For example, "eat" predicted positive activity in frontal regions associated with mouth movements and taste, whereas "run" predicted activity in the superior temporal sulcus associated with the perception of biological motion. These findings are quite consistent with the predictions of neural network models of semantic processing, in which specific items are linked to multiple associated features through learning, and semantically related items are represented by more similar patterns of activated features (McClelland & Rogers 2003).

Decoding has also been applied to other domains of knowledge such as numerical processing. One study found that activity patterns in the parietal cortex reflected not only spatial attention directed to the left or right side of space, but this spatial bias also could be used to predict whether participants were engaged in a subtraction or addition task (Knops et al. 2009). Another study found that activity patterns in the parietal cortex could distinguish between different numbers, whether conveyed by digit symbols or dot patterns (Eger et al. 2009). In general, these studies are consistent with the proposal that number representations are strongly associated with the parietal lobe and may be represented according to an implicit spatial representation of a number line (Hubbard et al. 2005).

Decoding Phonological Representations and Language Processing

Some recent studies have begun to use fMRI decoding methods to investigate the neural underpinnings of phonological and language processing. In one study, participants were presented with audio clips of three different speakers uttering each of three different vowel sounds (Formisano et al. 2008). Activity patterns in the auditory cortex could successfully discriminate which vowel was heard even when the classifier was tested on a voice not included in the training set. Likewise, pattern classifiers could identify the speaker at above-chance levels even when tested with vowels not included in the training set. Another study showed that activity patterns in the auditory cortex can distinguish between normal speech and temporally reordered versions of these stimuli, implying sensitivity to speech-specific content (Abrams et al. 2011).

Another fruitful approach has been to investigate the role of experience in the development of phonological representations. An analysis of activity patterns in the auditory cortex revealed better discrimination of the syllables /ra/ or /la/ in native English speakers than in Japanese participants who often have difficulty distinguishing between these phonemes (Raizada et al. 2010). Moreover, the authors found evidence of a correlation within each group, between an individual's decoding performance and his or her behavioral ability to distinguish between these phonemes, suggesting that fMRI decoding may be sensitive to individual differences in language processing. A recent study of reading ability provides further evidence for this view (Hoeft et al. 2011). The authors instructed children with dyslexia to perform a phonological processing task in the scanner and later assessed whether their reading skills had improved two and a half years later. Although purely behavioral measures taken in the first session failed to predict which children would improve in reading skills over time, a pattern classifier trained on the whole-brain data was able to predict improvement with over 90% accuracy. These results raise the exciting possibility of using fMRI pattern analysis for diagnostic purposes with respect to language processing.

Decoding Decisions in the Brain

Decoding has revealed that it is possible to predict the decisions that people are likely to make, even in advance of their actual choices. For example, activity in the anterior cingulate cortex, medial prefrontal cortex, and the ventral striatum is predictive of the participants' choices in a reward-learning paradigm (Hampton & O'Doherty 2007). Here, one of two stimuli is associated with a higher likelihood of reward and the other with a lower likelihood, but these reward probabilities are reversed at unpredictable times. Activity in these areas is highly predictive of whether participants will switch their choice of stimulus on a given trial, and activity on the trial prior to a switch is also somewhat predictive, indicating an accrual of information over time regarding whether the current regime should be preferred or not. Such valuation responses can also be observed in the insula and medial prefrontal cortex for unattended stimuli, and these decoded responses correspond quite well to the participants' valuation of as item, such as a particular model of car (Tusche et al. 2010). fMRI decoding can even predict participants' choices of real-world products at greater-than-chance levels. In these experiments, participants were offered the opportunity to purchase or decline to purchase a variety of discounted items ranging in value from $8 to $80, with the foreknowledge that two of their purchase choices would be realized at the end of the experiment (Knutson et al. 2007). In studies of arbitrary decisions, such as deciding to press a button with one's left or right hand at an arbitrary time, participants show evidence of preparatory activity in motor and supplementary motor areas a few seconds in advance of their action. Remarkably, however, a small but statistically reliable bias in activity can be observed in the frontopolar cortex up to 10 seconds prior to the participant's response, suggesting some form of preconscious bias in the decision-making process (Soon et al. 2008).

CONCEPTUAL AND METHODOLOGICAL ISSUES

Whenever a new methodology is developed, important conceptual and methodological issues can emerge regarding how the data should be analyzed, interpreted, and understood. Pattern classification algorithms are statistically powerful and quite robust. However, these very strengths can pose a challenge, as the algorithms are designed to leverage whatever information is potentially available in a brain region to make better predictions about a stimulus, experimental condition, mental state, or behavioral response. An example of unwanted leveraging was apparent in one of the reported results of the 2006 Pittsburgh Brain Competition (http://pbc.lrdc.pitt.edu/), an open competition that was designed to challenge research groups to develop state-of-the-art analytic methods for the purposes of brain reading and mind reading. This competition assessed the accuracy of decoding the presence of particular actors, objects, spatial locations, and periods of humor from the time series of fMRI data collected while participants watched episodes of the TV series "Home Improvement." To decode scenes containing humorous events, it turned out that the ventricles proved to be the most informative region of the brain—this high-contrast region in the functional images tended to jiggle whenever the participant felt an urge to laugh. Despite the remarkable accuracy of decoding periods of mirth from this region, it would clearly be wrong to conclude that this brain structure has a functional role in the cognitive processing of humorous information. If the accuracy of decoding is not sufficient for establishing function, then how can one determine precisely what information is processed by a brain region? Below, we consider these and other conceptual and methodological issues.

What Is Being Decoded?

A long-standing problem in fMRI research concerns the potential pitfalls of reverse inference. As an example, it is well established that the human amygdala responds more strongly to fear-related stimuli than to neutral stimuli, but it does not logically follow that if the amygdala is more active in a given situation that the person is necessarily experiencing fear (Adolphs 2010, Phelps 2006). If the amygdala's response varies along other dimensions as well, such as the emotional intensity, ambiguity, or predictive value of a stimulus, then it will be difficult to make strong inferences from the level of amygdala activity alone.

A conceptually related problem emerges in fMRI decoding studies when one identifies a brain region that can reliably discriminate between two particular sensory stimuli or two cognitive tasks. For example, Haxby et al. (2001) showed that activity patterns in the human ventral temporal cortex were reliably different when participants viewed images of different object categories. The authors interpreted this decoding result to suggest that the ventral temporal object areas are sensitive to complex object properties. However, subsequent studies revealed that early visual areas could discriminate between the object categories just as well as or better than the high-level object areas because of the pervasiveness of low-level differences between the object categories (Cox & Savoy 2003). Therefore, successful decoding of a particular property from a brain region, such

as object category, does not necessarily indicate that the region in question is truly selective for that property. The inferences one can make with multivariate pattern analysis still depend on strong experimental design, and in many cases multiple experiments may be needed to rule out potential confounding factors.

One approach for determining the functional relevance of a particular brain area is to test for links between behavioral performance and decoding performance. For example, if one compares correct versus incorrect trials in a fine-grained orientation discrimination task, greater activity in the primary visual cortex is found specifically in those voxels tuned to orientations neighboring the target orientation (Scolari & Serences 2010). Similarly, decoding of object-specific information from the lateral occipital complex is much better on trials with successful than unsuccessful recognition (Williams et al. 2007). Related studies have found that functional activity patterns in the ventral temporal object areas are more reliable and reproducible when a stimulus can be consciously perceived than when it is subliminally presented (Schurger et al. 2010). Interestingly, when participants must study a list of items on multiple occasions, items that evoke more similar activity patterns across repeated presentations are also more likely to be remembered (Xue et al. 2010).

Because of the high-dimensional nature of visual input, it is possible to investigate the similarity of cortical activity patterns across a variety of stimulus conditions to assess the properties they might be attuned to. For example, similar orientations evoke more similar activity patterns in early visual areas (Kamitani & Tong 2005), and similar colors have been found to do so in visual area V4 (Brouwer & Heeger 2009). However, the similarity relationships of responses to objects are quite different in early visual areas and high-level object areas, with the object areas exhibiting a sharp distinction in their activity patterns for animate and inanimate objects (Kriegeskorte et al. 2008, Naselaris et al. 2009). Studies of olfactory perception have revealed comparable findings in the posterior piriform cortex, with more similar odors leading to more similar patterns of fMRI activity (Howard et al. 2009). Thus, if neural activity patterns share the similarity structure of perceptual judgments, this can provide strong evidence to implicate the functional role of a brain area.

One can further investigate the functional tuning properties of a brain area by assessing generalization performance: Do the activity patterns observed in a brain area generalize to very different stimulus conditions or behavioral tasks? In Harrison & Tong's (2009) study of visual working memory, the authors trained a classifier on visual cortical activity patterns elicited by unattended gratings and tested whether these stimulus-driven responses might be able to predict which of two orientations was being maintained in working memory while participants viewed a blank screen. Successful generalization was found despite the differences in both stimulus and task across the experiments, thereby strengthening the inference that orientation-specific information was being maintained in the visual cortex during the working memory task. In a study of auditory perception, classifiers trained using phonemes pronounced by one speaker could successfully generalize to the corresponding phonemes spoken by another speaker, despite changes in the auditory frequency content (Formisano et al. 2008). Perhaps the most rigorous test of generalization performance comes from demonstrations of the ability to predict brain responses to novel stimuli, as has been shown by Kay and Gallant's visual encoding model and Mitchell et al.'s semantic encoding model (Kay et al. 2008, Mitchell et al. 2008). Successful generalization can be an effective tool for ruling out potential low-level stimulus confounds or task-related factors.

In studies of high-level cognition, isolating the specific function of a brain area may be more challenging if the experimental design focuses on discriminating between two cognitive tasks. When participants perform cognitive tasks differing in the stimuli, task demands, and behavioral judgments required, almost the entire

cerebral cortex can show evidence of reliable discriminating activity (Poldrack et al. 2009). Differential activity can result from many factors, including differences in low-level sensory stimulation, working memory load, language demands, or the degree of response inhibition required for the task. Even when two tasks are quite closely matched, such as performing addition or subtraction (Haynes et al. 2007) or directing attention to features or spatial locations (Greenberg et al. 2010), it is important to consider potential confounding factors. If one task is slightly more difficult or requires a bit more processing time for a given participant, then larger or longer fMRI amplitudes could occur on those trials, which could allow decoding to exceed chance-level performance. This potential confound has sometimes been addressed by performing decoding on the average amplitude of activity in a brain region to see if overall activity is predictive or whether more fine-grained information is needed for reliable decoding. Another approach might be to attempt to assess decoding of fast versus slow reaction times using the same brain region and to test whether these activity patterns resemble those that distinguish the two tasks.

Where in the Brain to Decode From?

Many fMRI decoding studies have focused on the human visual system, which contains many well-defined visual areas. In addition, it is common to map the particular region of visual space that will be stimulated in an experiment so that only the corresponding voxels in the retinotopic visual cortex are used for decoding analysis. There are several advantages to applying pattern analysis to well-defined functional areas. First, localization of function is possible, and the information contained in each functional region can be independently assessed and compared to other regions. Second, there is reduced concern that decoding performance might reflect information combined across functionally distinct areas. Finally, decoding performance can be compared to other known functional properties of that brain area to ask whether

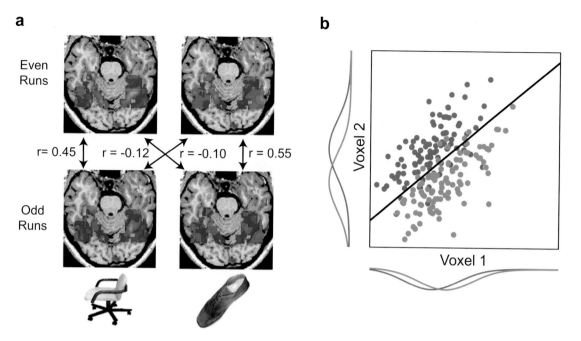

Figure 1

Correlation and classification approaches to decoding brain activity patterns. (*a*) Average activity patterns for chairs and shoes in the ventral temporal cortex, calculated separately for even and odd runs. Correlations between these spatial patterns of activity were calculated between even and odd runs. Pairwise classifications between any two object categories were considered correct if the correlations were higher within an object category than between the two object categories. Adapted with permission from Haxby et al. (2001). (*b*) Hypothetical responses of two voxels to two different experimental conditions, denoted by red and green points. Density plots in the margins indicate the distribution of responses to the two conditions for each voxel considered in isolation. The dividing line between red and green data points shows the classification results from a linear support vector machine applied to these patterns of activity; any points above the line would be classified as red, and those below would be classified as green.

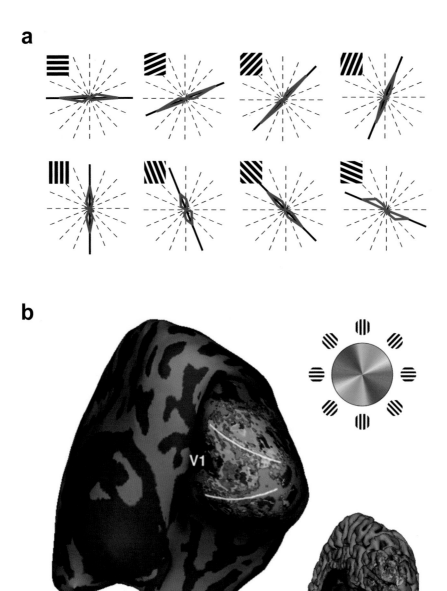

Figure 2

Decoding the orientation of viewed gratings from activity patterns in the visual cortex. (*a*) Blue curves indicate the distribution of predicted orientations shown on polar plots, with thick black lines indicating the true orientations. Note that common values are plotted at symmetrical directions because stimulus orientation repeats every 180°. Reproduced with permission from Kamitani & Tong (2005). (*b*) Spatial distribution of weak orientation preferences in the visual cortex, measured using high-resolution functional magnetic resonance imaging with 1mm isotropic voxels and plotted on an inflated representation of the cortical surface. Reproduced with permission from Swisher et al. (2010).

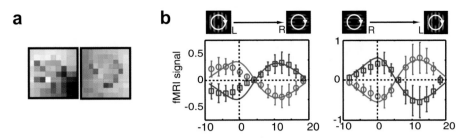

Figure 3

Eye-specific modulation of activity in the lateral geniculate nucleus (LGN) during binocular rivalry.
(*a*) Distribution of weak monocular preferences in the LGN of a representative participant. (*b*) Time course of the decoded eye-specific signal from these LGN activity patterns is correlated with fluctuations in perceptual dominance during rivalry between left-eye and right-eye stimuli. Reproduced with permission from Haynes et al. (2005).

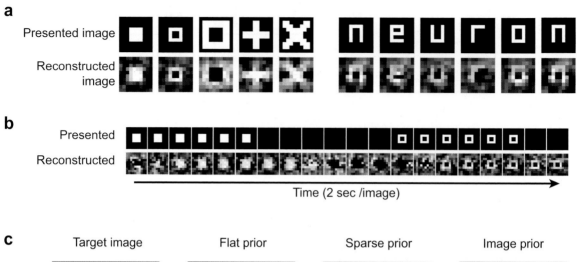

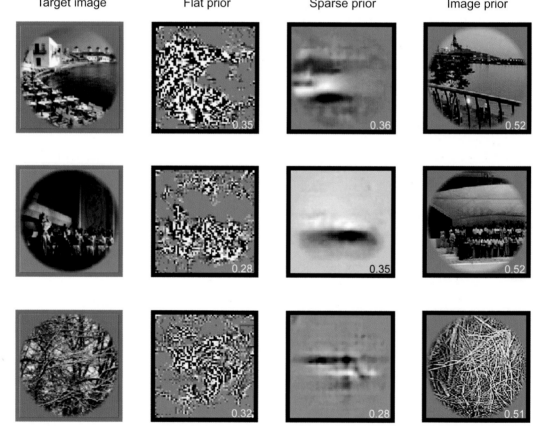

Figure 4

Reconstruction of viewed images from activity patterns in the visual cortex, based on averaged fMRI activity patterns (*a*) and single fMRI volumes acquired every 2 seconds (*b*). Reproduced with permission from Miyawaki et al. (2008). (*c*) Reconstruction of natural scenes from visual cortical activity. Various methods are used to reconstruct the image's high-contrast regions (flat prior) or low-spatial-frequency components (sparse prior), or to select the most visually and semantically similar image to the target from a database of 6 million predefined images (image prior). Reproduced with permission from Naselaris et al. (2009).

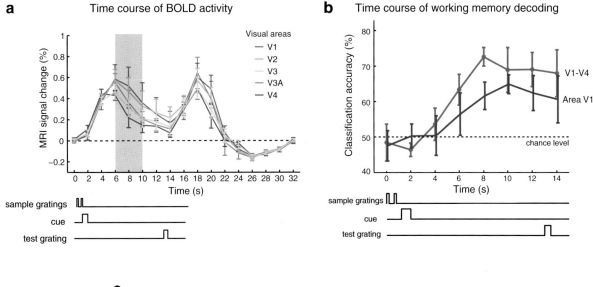

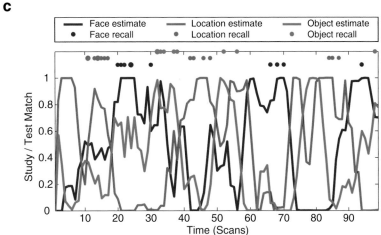

Figure 5

Decoding item-specific information over time during working memory or free recall from long-term memory. (*a*) Average time course of BOLD activity during a visual working memory task in which two oriented gratings were briefly shown, followed by a postcue indicating which orientation to retain until test. Although the mean BOLD signal steadily declined during the memory retention interval, decoding accuracy for the retained orientation remained elevated (*b*) throughout the delay period. Adapted with permission from Harrison & Tong (2009). (*c*) Classification of the reinstated context during a participant's free recall of famous faces, famous places, and common objects. Dots indicate when the participant verbally reported an item from a given category. Curves show estimates of match between fMRI activity patterns at each time point during free recall, using classifiers trained on activity patterns from the prior study period with each of the three categories. Reproduced with permission from Polyn et al. (2005).

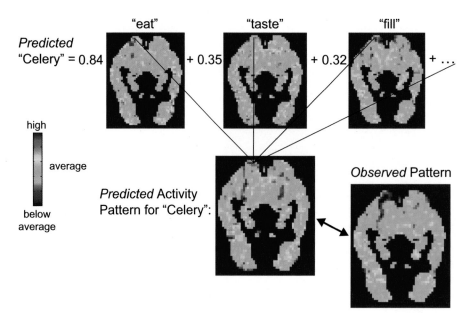

Figure 6

Semantic encoding model used to predict brain activity patterns to novel nouns. Neural responses to viewed objects and their name, such as "celery," were modeled as the sum of weighted activity patterns to intermediate semantic features consisting of 25 different verbs. Examples of activity patterns for three semantic features ("eat," "taste," and "fill") are shown, and the weight of their contribution to the predicted activity pattern reflects their frequency of co-occurrence with the target word. Predicted activity patterns are then compared with the observed activity for celery. Adapted with permission from Mitchell et al. (2008).

the results seem reasonable and readily interpretable. Focused investigations of the human hippocampus have also benefitted from having a targeted anatomical locus (Chadwick et al. 2010, Hassabis et al. 2009).

In studies of higher-level cognition, predefined regions of interest usually are not available, and multiple distributed brain areas might be involved in the cognitive task. Many of these studies rely on decoding of whole-brain activity, sometimes first selecting the most active voxels in the task or applying a method to reduce the dimensionality of the data (e.g., principal components analysis) prior to classification analysis. [When selecting a subset of voxels prior to the decoding analysis, it is important to ensure that the selection process is independent of the property to be decoded so it will not bias decoding performance to be better than it should (Kriegeskorte et al. 2009).] The advantage of the whole-brain approach lies in its ability to reveal a majority of the information available throughout the brain. Moreover, it is possible to inspect the pattern of "weights" in the classifier and to project these onto the cortex to reveal how this information is distributed throughout the brain. For example, Polyn and colleagues (2005) found that that fusiform face area was one of the regions most active during the free recall of famous faces, whereas the parahippocampal place area and retrosplenial cortex were most active during the recall of famous places. Thus, decoding of whole-brain activity can reveal what information is present in the brain and where in the brain such information is most densely concentrated.

However, classification analysis implicitly assumes a "readout mechanism," in which relative differences between the strengths of particular brain signals are calculated and leveraged to compute useful information. It is not clear whether the brain is actually comparing or combining the neural signals that are being analyzed by the classifier, especially when information from distinct brain regions is combined. For example, a semantic model might find that the word "rose" leads to whole-brain activity that is well predicted by the

patterns associated with "smell," "plants," and "seeing" vivid colors such as red. Should each of the respective components of this activity be considered part of a single unified representation or as entirely separate components that are being unified outside of the brain by the classifier (Mahon & Caramazza 2009, Mitchell et al. 2008)? This distinction can be made more vivid with a somewhat different example. Assume it is possible to decode whether something smells "floral" or "citrus" from activity patterns in the olfactory piriform cortex, and it is also possible to decode whether the color "red" or "yellow" is being perceived from the visual cortex. Now, if decoding of whole-brain activity can tell apart a floral-scented red rose from one that smells like lemon or has lemon-colored petals, can it be argued that the brain contains a unified representation of the color and smell of roses? According to a recent fMRI study of perceptual binding (Seymour et al. 2009), establishing evidence of a conjoint representation of color and smell would require demonstrating that brain activity patterns can distinguish between a floral-scented red rose paired with a citrus-scented yellow rose as distinct from a citrus-scented red rose paired with a floral-scented yellow rose. This issue also points to a longstanding debate regarding whether the brain relies on modular or distributed representations for information processing (Haxby et al. 2001, Op de Beeck et al. 2008). Recent fMRI studies indicate that many types of information are distributed quite widely throughout the brain but that there also exist highly stimulus-selective modules that may form a more local, exclusive network (Moeller et al. 2008, Tsao et al. 2006).

An alternative to decoding whole-brain activity is to perform a searchlight analysis, in which decoding is iteratively performed on local activity patterns sampled throughout the cortex (Kriegeskorte et al. 2006). This typically involves using a moveable searchlight to sample a local "sphere" of voxels (say a 5 × 5 × 5 voxel cubic region) from each point in the cortex. This approach reveals the information contained in local activity patterns, which reduces the extent to which information will be combined across distinct functional areas. A potential concern is that brain signals from disparate areas may sometimes be combined across a sulcus, so this approach could be further strengthened by analyzing activity patterns based on a flattened representation of the cortical surface. A disadvantage of this approach is the need to correct for multiple comparisons for each iteration of the search, which reduces statistical power. For these reasons, searchlight analyses are often combined with group-level statistical analyses to evaluate whether reliable information is consistently found in a particular region of the brain across participants.

At What Spatial Scales of Cortical Representation Is Decoding Most Useful?

MVPA may serve different purposes depending on whether the sought-after information resides at fine or coarse spatial scales in the brain. At the finest scale, multivoxel pattern classification may be particularly advantageous at detecting signals arising from variability in the spatial arrangement of cortical columns, which can lead to locally biased signals on the scale of millimeters (Swisher et al. 2010). Pattern analysis of fine-scale signals has proven effective not only in the visual cortex but also in high-resolution fMRI studies of the hippocampus (Hassabis et al. 2009). Such fine-grained information would otherwise be very difficult or impossible to detect using traditional univariate methods of analysis. At a somewhat coarser scale, pattern classifiers are also very effective at extracting category-selective information from the ventral temporal cortex, which reveals a strong functional organization at spatial scales of several millimeters to centimeters (Haxby et al. 2001). These methods can be helpful for pooling distributed information about objects or semantic categories, particularly when there is no single "hotspot" of functional selectivity available in the broad cortical region to be analyzed. Decoding has also been applied to activity patterns of large spatial scale, including

whole-brain activity, even when differentially activated regions can be seen using traditional univariate analyses such as statistical parametric mapping. For example, one can attain much better predictions of an observer's near-threshold perceptual judgments regarding fearful versus nonfearful faces by pooling information across multiple activated regions (Pessoa & Padmala 2007). Beyond the benefits of signal averaging, combining signals from multiple regions of interest can be beneficial if each region contains some unique information. Another example of whole-brain decoding comes from a recognition memory study, which compared participants' behavioral performance at old-new judgments with the discriminating performance of the pattern classifier (Rissman et al. 2010). Although the patterns picked up by the classifier closely resembled the statistical maps, the decoding analysis revealed a compelling relationship between subjective ratings of memory confidence and differential brain responses to old versus new items on individual trials. These examples illustrate how decoding can be useful when applied at large spatial scales. Nevertheless, interpreting the combined results from disparate brain areas can be challenging and may warrant careful consideration of exactly what is being decoded, as we have described above.

ETHICAL AND SOCIETAL CONSIDERATIONS

What are the potential implications of human neuroimaging and brain-reading technologies as this rapidly growing field continues to advance? Over the past decade, there has been steadily growing interest in neuroethics, which focuses on the current and future implications of neuroscience technology on ethics, society, and law (Farah 2005, Roskies 2002). Although some had thought these concerns to be premature, the intersection between law and neuroscience (sometimes called neurolaw) has rapidly evolved in recent years (Jones & Shen 2012).

In October 2009, Dr. Kent Kiehl appeared at a Chicago court hearing to find out whether the fMRI scans he had collected of Brian Dugan's brain might be admissible as evidence in a high-profile death penalty case. Dugan, who had already served more than 20 years in prison for two other murders, had recently confessed to murdering a 10-year-old girl in 1983, following the discovery of DNA evidence linking him to the crime.

On November 5, 2009, the fMRI scans of a defendant's brain were considered as evidence in the sentencing phase of a murder trial, for what appears to be the first time (Hughes 2010). Dr. Kiehl provided expert testimony, describing the results of two psychiatric interviews and the unusually low levels of activity in several regions of Dugan's brain, similar to levels of many other criminal psychopaths when they were shown pictures of violent or morally wrong actions (Harenski et al. 2010). He pointed to these regions on cartoon drawings of the brain, as the judge had decided that the presentation of actual brain pictures might unduly influence the jury (Weisberg et al. 2008). Expert testimony from the prosecution refuted the brain imaging data on two grounds: Dugan's brain might have been very different 26 years ago, and Dr. Kiehl's neuroimaging studies of criminal psychopaths showed average trends in the data and were not designed for individual diagnosis. After less than an hour of deliberation, the jury initially reached a mixed verdict (10 for and 2 against the death penalty), but then asked for more time, switching to a unanimous verdict in favor of the death penalty the next day. Dugan's lawyer noted that although the verdict was unfavorable, Kiehl's testimony "turned it from a slam dunk for the prosecution into a much tougher case."

If courts are primarily concerned that neuroimaging evidence appears unreliable for individual diagnosis, then recent advances in brain classification methods for diagnosing neurological disorders could lead to the increasing prevalence of such evidence in courtrooms. Recent studies have shown that pattern-classification algorithms applied to structural MRI scans or functional MRI scans can distinguish whether an individual is a normal control or is a patient suffering from schizophrenia (Nenadic et al. 2009), depression (Craddock et al. 2009), or psychopathy (Sato et al. 2011), with reported accuracy levels ranging from 80% to 95%. In the context of a court case, these accuracy levels might be high enough to influence a jury's decision. For example, a diagnosis of paranoid schizophrenia might influence decisions regarding whether a defendant was likely to have been psychotic at the time of the crime. Although a diagnosis of psychopathy might be unlikely to affect the determination of whether a defendant should be considered guilty based on his or her actions, such evidence could prove to be an influential mitigating factor during the sentencing phase of the trial. As neuroscience continues to advance our understanding of the neural mechanisms that lead to decisions and actions, neuroscientists and perhaps society more generally may feel motivated to reconsider our traditional definitions of free will and personal responsibility (for discussions of this issue, see Greene & Cohen 2004, Roskies 2006, Sapolsky 2004).

Brain classification methods for individual diagnosis could have strong ethical implications in medical settings as well, especially concerning disorders of consciousness. Some patients who partially recover from coma are diagnosed as being in a vegetative state if they exhibit periods of wakefulness but appear to lack awareness or any purpose in their motor actions. Despite this apparent lack of awareness, it was recently discovered that some vegetative-state patients are capable of voluntarily performing mental imagery tasks (Owen et al. 2006). When asked to imagine either playing tennis or walking around a house, differential patterns of activity can be observed in their brains. Recently, this imagery paradigm has been combined with fMRI decoding to obtain reliable yes/no responses from a patient to questions such as "Is your father's name Alexander?" (Monti et al. 2010). If highly reliable communication can be established with such patients, this could lead to uncharted territories in terms of the ethical and legal considerations regarding, for example, any medical requests made by the patient.

Perhaps the strongest ethical concerns have been raised regarding the potential application of fMRI decoding to detect lies or the presence of guilty knowledge (Bizzi et al. 2009). Much attention has focused on recent studies of lie detection and their claims, as well as the efforts made by private companies to develop and market this nascent technology. In a study by Langleben and colleagues, participants were given two cards in an envelope and asked in advance to lie whenever they were asked if they had one card and to tell the truth about the other card (Davatzikos et al. 2005). Pattern classification applied to whole-brain activity revealed that truths and lies could be distinguished in this task with 88% accuracy on individual trials because of the greater activity observed for lies in multiple areas, including the prefrontal cortex, anterior cingulate, and insula. On the basis of these findings, some rather bold claims were made about the prospects of future fMRI lie detection technology. However, it is critical to note that it is not lying per se that is being decoded from these brain areas but rather the cognitive and emotional processes that are associated with lying (Spence et al. 2004). Thus, lie-detection technology suffers the same problem of reverse inference that we have discussed previously. Although lying typically leads to the activation of a certain set of brain areas, the activation of these brain areas does not necessarily indicate lying. In real world settings, such as when a defendant is strongly suspected of committing a crime or feels guilty for having witnessed the crime, any questions about the crime might elicit strong emotional and cognitive responses akin to those evoked by lying. It is also not clear whether criminals, particularly those with psychopathy, would show the same activity patterns during lying. Other fMRI studies have shown that brain activity patterns differ for prepared lies and spontaneous lies (Ganis et al. 2003) and that fMRI lie-detection technology can be subverted by covertly engaging in a separate cognitive task during brain scanning (Ganis et al. 2011). These major shortcomings bring into serious question whether it will be possible to develop an ecologically valid and reliable fMRI lie detector anytime in the near future.

However, this has not prevented the recent efforts of private companies to market such technology or to prepare for their use in courtrooms. In May 2010, the first Daubert hearing was held in Tennessee to determine whether fMRI lie detection might be considered admissible as scientific evidence (Miller 2010). Dr. Steven Laken, CEO of Cephos, a company that provides fMRI lie-detection services, presented evidence in favor of admitting the brain scans he had performed on the defendant, which according to him, indicated innocence on the charges of fraud. The prosecution invited expert testimony from neuroscientist Marcus Raichle and statistician Peter Imrey to dispute the reliability of the current technology. In the end, the judge determined that fMRI lie-detection technology was supported by peer-reviewed publications but had not gained wide acceptance among scientists. Moreover, its reliability and accuracy had yet to be validated in real-world settings, and a well-standardized protocol for implementing such tests had yet to be established (Shen & Jones 2012).

It remains to be seen whether fMRI lie detection will ever improve enough to meet general scientific acceptance or gain admission into courts. Nevertheless, it would be prudent to consider the potential ethical and societal ramifications of such technology should it improve to the point that detection accuracy is no longer the primary concern. There would be obvious benefits in a legal setting if accuracy were extremely high. However, mental privacy could face enormous new challenges, in both legal settings and beyond, as there has been no precedent for being able to look into the mind of another human being. Although DNA can be obtained as evidence from a suspect on the basis of a court order, brain reading of thoughts might fall under the category of testimony, in which case defendants would be protected by the Fifth Amendment. Even so, if the technology were ever to develop to near-perfect levels of accuracy, a refusal to voluntarily submit to fMRI lie detection might be interpreted as an implicit admission of guilt by some juries even when instructed not to make such an interpretation. In the worlds of business and personal relationships, the availability of such technology could have far-reaching consequences, particularly in situations involving employers and employees, business partners, or even spouses. Just the existence of such technology and the pressure of being asked to undergo testing could lead people to disclose information that they otherwise would have declined to share.

Given the conceptual challenges of developing reliable fMRI lie detection and the fact that people can use countermeasures to alter their patterns of brain activity, we are doubtful that the technology will progress to being truly reliable and ecologically valid. Nonetheless, it is important to consider potential implications in case such progress is ever made.

CONCLUDING REMARKS

In recent years, fMRI pattern classification has led to rapid advances in many areas of cognitive neuroscience, encompassing perception, attention, object processing, memory, semantics, language processing, and decision making. These methods have allowed neuroimaging researchers to isolate feature-selective sensory responses, neural correlates of conscious perception, content-specific activity during attention and memory tasks, and brain activity patterns that are predictive of future decisions.

Furthermore, multivariate analyses can be used to characterize the multidimensional nature of neural representations, such as the functional similarity between object representations, scene representations, or semantic representations, allowing one to predict how the brain should respond to novel stimuli. Looking forward, the enhanced sensitivity and information content provided by these methods should greatly facilitate the investigation of mind-brain relationships by revealing both local and distributed representations of mental content, functional interactions between brain areas, and the underlying relationships between brain activity and cognitive performance.

Despite, or perhaps because of, the statistical power of these analytic tools, careful experimentation and interpretation are required when making inferences about successful decoding of a stimulus, task, or mental state from human brain activity. The extension of these methods into real-world applications could prove very useful for medical diagnoses and neuroprostheses (Hatsopoulos & Donoghue 2009). However, there are major concerns regarding the reliability and ecological validity of current attempts to perform real-world lie detection. Much more research will be needed to determine whether such methods might be valid or not. Strong ethical considerations also revolve around the prospect of developing reliable lie detection technology, and it would be prudent to consider how mental privacy would be protected if such technology were allowed to gain prominent use.

DISCLOSURE STATEMENT

The authors are unaware of any affiliation, funding, or financial holdings that might be perceived as affecting the objectivity of this review.

ACKNOWLEDGMENTS

The authors would like to thank Owen Jones, Yukiyasu Kamitani, Sean Polyn, Elizabeth Counterman, and Jascha Swisher for helpful comments on earlier versions of this manuscript. The authors were supported by grants from the National Eye Institute (R01EY017082), the National Science Foundation (BCS-0642633), and the Defense Advanced Research Projects Agency.

LITERATURE CITED

Abrams DA, Bhatara A, Ryali S, Balaban E, Levitin DJ, Menon V. 2011. Decoding temporal structure in music and speech relies on shared brain resources but elicits different fine-scale spatial patterns. *Cereb. Cortex* 21:1507–18

Adolphs R. 2010. What does the amygdala contribute to social cognition? *Ann. N.Y. Acad. Sci.* 1191:42–61

Bizzi E, Hyman SE, Raichle ME, Kanwisher N, Phelps EA, et al. 2009. *Using Imaging to Identify Deceit: Scientific and Ethical Questions*. Cambridge, MA: Am. Acad. Arts Sci.

Blake R, Logothetis NK. 2002. Visual competition. *Nat. Rev. Neurosci.* 3:13–21

Boynton GM, Finney EM. 2003. Orientation-specific adaptation in human visual cortex. *J. Neurosci.* 23:8781–87

Brouwer GJ, Heeger DJ. 2009. Decoding and reconstructing color from responses in human visual cortex. *J. Neurosci.* 29:13992–4003

Brouwer GJ, van Ee R. 2007. Visual cortex allows prediction of perceptual states during ambiguous structure-from-motion. *J. Neurosci.* 27:1015–23

Carlson TA, Schrater P, He S. 2003. Patterns of activity in the categorical representations of objects. *J. Cogn. Neurosci.* 15:704–17

Chadwick MJ, Hassabis D, Weiskopf N, Maguire EA. 2010. Decoding individual episodic memory traces in the human hippocampus. *Curr. Biol.* 20:544–47

Chan AW, Kravitz DJ, Truong S, Arizpe J, Baker CI. 2010. Cortical representations of bodies and faces are strongest in commonly experienced configurations. *Nat. Neurosci.* 13:417–18

Clifford CW, Mannion DJ, McDonald JS. 2009. Radial biases in the processing of motion and motion-defined contours by human visual cortex. *J. Neurophysiol.* 102:2974–81

Cox DD, Savoy RL. 2003. Functional magnetic resonance imaging (fMRI) "brain reading": detecting and classifying distributed patterns of fMRI activity in human visual cortex. *NeuroImage* 19:261–70

Craddock RC, Holtzheimer PE 3rd, Hu XP, Mayberg HS. 2009. Disease state prediction from resting state functional connectivity. *Magn. Reson. Med.* 62:1619–28

Davatzikos C, Ruparel K, Fan Y, Shen DG, Acharyya M, et al. 2005. Classifying spatial patterns of brain activity with machine learning methods: application to lie detection. *NeuroImage* 28:663–68

Eger E, Ashburner J, Haynes JD, Dolan RJ, Rees G. 2008. fMRI activity patterns in human LOC carry information about object exemplars within category. *J. Cogn. Neurosci.* 20:356–70

Eger E, Michel V, Thirion B, Amadon A, Dehaene S, Kleinschmidt A. 2009. Deciphering cortical number coding from human brain activity patterns. *Curr. Biol.* 19:1608–15

Engel SA, Furmanski CS. 2001. Selective adaptation to color contrast in human primary visual cortex. *J. Neurosci.* 21:3949–54

Farah MJ. 2005. Neuroethics: the practical and the philosophical. *Trends Cogn. Sci.* 9:34–40

Fischer J, Spotswood N, Whitney D. 2011. The emergence of perceived position in the visual system. *J. Cogn. Neurosci.* 23:119–36

Formisano E, De Martino F, Bonte M, Goebel R. 2008. "Who" is saying "what"? Brain-based decoding of human voice and speech. *Science* 322:970–73

Freeman J, Brouwer GJ, Heeger DJ, Merriam EP. 2011. Orientation decoding depends on maps, not columns. *J. Neurosci.* 31:4792–804

Freiwald WA, Tsao DY. 2010. Functional compartmentalization and viewpoint generalization within the macaque face-processing system. *Science* 330:845–51

Freiwald WA, Tsao DY, Livingstone MS. 2009. A face feature space in the macaque temporal lobe. *Nat. Neurosci.* 12:1187–96

Ganis G, Kosslyn SM, Stose S, Thompson WL, Yurgelun-Todd DA. 2003. Neural correlates of different types of deception: an fMRI investigation. *Cereb. Cortex* 13:830–36

Ganis G, Rosenfeld JP, Meixner J, Kievit RA, Schendan HE. 2011. Lying in the scanner: covert countermeasures disrupt deception detection by functional magnetic resonance imaging. *NeuroImage* 55:312–19

Gerardin P, Kourtzi Z, Mamassian P. 2010. Prior knowledge of illumination for 3D perception in the human brain. *Proc. Natl. Acad. Sci. USA* 107:16309–14

Goddard E, Mannion DJ, McDonald JS, Solomon SG, Clifford CW. 2010. Combination of subcortical color channels in human visual cortex. *J. Vis.* 10:25

Greenberg AS, Esterman M, Wilson D, Serences JT, Yantis S. 2010. Control of spatial and feature-based attention in frontoparietal cortex. *J. Neurosci.* 30:14330–39

Greene J, Cohen J. 2004. For the law, neuroscience changes nothing and everything. *Philos. Trans. R. Soc. Lond. B Biol. Sci.* 359:1775–85

Hampton AN, O'Doherty JP. 2007. Decoding the neural substrates of reward-related decision making with functional MRI. *Proc. Natl. Acad. Sci. USA* 104:1377–82

Harenski CL, Harenski KA, Shane MS, Kiehl KA. 2010. Aberrant neural processing of moral violations in criminal psychopaths. *J. Abnorm. Psychol.* 119:863–74

Harrison SA, Tong F. 2009. Decoding reveals the contents of visual working memory in early visual areas. *Nature* 458:632–35

Hassabis D, Chu C, Rees G, Weiskopf N, Molyneux PD, Maguire EA. 2009. Decoding neuronal ensembles in the human hippocampus. *Curr. Biol.* 19:546–54

Hatsopoulos NG, Donoghue JP. 2009. The science of neural interface systems. *Annu. Rev. Neurosci.* 32:249–66

Haushofer J, Livingstone MS, Kanwisher N. 2008. Multivariate patterns in object-selective cortex dissociate perceptual and physical shape similarity. *PLoS Biol.* 6:e187

Haxby JV, Gobbini MI, Furey ML, Ishai A, Schouten JL, Pietrini P. 2001. Distributed and overlapping representations of faces and objects in ventral temporal cortex. *Science* 293:2425–30

Haynes JD, Deichmann R, Rees G. 2005. Eye-specific effects of binocular rivalry in the human lateral geniculate nucleus. *Nature* 438:496–99

Haynes JD, Rees G. 2005a. Predicting the orientation of invisible stimuli from activity in human primary visual cortex. *Nat. Neurosci.* 8:686–91

Haynes JD, Rees G. 2005b. Predicting the stream of consciousness from activity in human visual cortex. *Curr. Biol.* 15:1301–7

Haynes JD, Rees G. 2006. Decoding mental states from brain activity in humans. *Nat. Rev. Neurosci.* 7:523–34

Haynes JD, Sakai K, Rees G, Gilbert S, Frith C, Passingham RE. 2007. Reading hidden intentions in the human brain. *Curr. Biol.* 17:323–28

Hoeft F, McCandliss BD, Black JM, Gantman A, Zakerani N, et al. 2011. Neural systems predicting long-term outcome in dyslexia. *Proc. Natl. Acad. Sci. USA* 108:361–66

Hong SW, Tong F, Seiffert AE. 2011. Direction-selective patterns of activity in human visual cortex reveal common neural substrates for different types of motion. *Neuropsychologia.* In press doi:10.1016/j.neuropsychologia.2011.09.016

Howard JD, Plailly J, Grueschow M, Haynes JD, Gottfried JA. 2009. Odor quality coding and categorization in human posterior piriform cortex. *Nat. Neurosci.* 12:932–38

Howard MW, Kahana MJ. 1999. Contextual variability and serial position effects in free recall. *J. Exp. Psychol.: Learn. Mem. Cogn.* 25:923–41

Hubbard EM, Piazza M, Pinel P, Dehaene S. 2005. Interactions between number and space in parietal cortex. *Nat. Rev. Neurosci.* 6:435–48

Hughes V. 2010. Science in court: head case. *Nature* 464:340–42

Jehee JF, Brady DK, Tong F. 2011. Attention improves encoding of task-relevant features in the human visual cortex. *J. Neurosci.* 31:8210–19

Johnson JD, McDuff SG, Rugg MD, Norman KA. 2009. Recollection, familiarity, and cortical reinstatement: a multivoxel pattern analysis. *Neuron* 63:697–708

Jones OD, Shen FX. 2012. Law and neuroscience in the United States. In *International Neurolaw: A Comparative Analysis*, ed. TM Spranger. New York: Springer. In press

Kamitani Y, Tong F. 2005. Decoding the visual and subjective contents of the human brain. *Nat. Neurosci.* 8:679–85

Kamitani Y, Tong F. 2006. Decoding seen and attended motion directions from activity in the human visual cortex. *Curr. Biol.* 16:1096–102

Kaul C, Rees G, Ishai A. 2011. The gender of face stimuli is represented in multiple regions in the human brain. *Front. Hum. Neurosci.* 4:238

Kay KN, Naselaris T, Prenger RJ, Gallant JL. 2008. Identifying natural images from human brain activity. *Nature* 452:352–55

Kiani R, Esteky H, Mirpour K, Tanaka K. 2007. Object category structure in response patterns of neuronal population in monkey inferior temporal cortex. *J. Neurophysiol.* 97:4296–309

Knops A, Thirion B, Hubbard EM, Michel V, Dehaene S. 2009. Recruitment of an area involved in eye movements during mental arithmetic. *Science* 324:1583–85

Knutson B, Rick S, Wimmer GE, Prelec D, Loewenstein G. 2007. Neural predictors of purchases. *Neuron* 53:147–56

Kosslyn SM, Ganis G, Thompson WL. 2001. Neural foundations of imagery. *Nat. Rev. Neurosci.* 2:635–42

Kosslyn SM, Thompson WL. 2003. When is early visual cortex activated during visual mental imagery? *Psychol. Bull.* 129:723–46

Kriegeskorte N. 2011. Pattern-information analysis: from stimulus decoding to computational-model testing. *NeuroImage* 56:411–21

Kriegeskorte N, Formisano E, Sorger B, Goebel R. 2007. Individual faces elicit distinct response patterns in human anterior temporal cortex. *Proc. Natl. Acad. Sci. USA* 104:20600–5

Kriegeskorte N, Goebel R, Bandettini P. 2006. Information-based functional brain mapping. *Proc. Natl. Acad. Sci. USA* 103:3863–68

Kriegeskorte N, Mur M, Ruff DA, Kiani R, Bodurka J, et al. 2008. Matching categorical object representations in inferior temporal cortex of man and monkey. *Neuron* 60:1126–41

Kriegeskorte N, Simmons WK, Bellgowan PS, Baker CI. 2009. Circular analysis in systems neuroscience: the dangers of double dipping. *Nat. Neurosci.* 12:535–40

Lewis-Peacock JA, Postle BR. 2008. Temporary activation of long-term memory supports working memory. *J. Neurosci.* 28:8765–71

Liu T, Hospadaruk L, Zhu DC, Gardner JL. 2011. Feature-specific attentional priority signals in human cortex. *J. Neurosci.* 31:4484–95

Lu HD, Chen G, Tanigawa H, Roe AW. 2010. A motion direction map in macaque V2. *Neuron* 68:1002–13

Mahon BZ, Anzellotti S, Schwarzbach J, Zampini M, Caramazza A. 2009. Category-specific organization in the human brain does not require visual experience. *Neuron* 63:397–405

Mahon BZ, Caramazza A. 2009. Concepts and categories: a cognitive neuropsychological perspective. *Annu. Rev. Psychol.* 60:27–51

Mahon BZ, Caramazza A. 2011. What drives the organization of object knowledge in the brain? *Trends Cogn. Sci.* 15:97–103

Mannion DJ, McDonald JS, Clifford CW. 2009. Discrimination of the local orientation structure of spiral Glass patterns early in human visual cortex. *NeuroImage* 46:511–15

McClelland JL, Rogers TT. 2003. The parallel distributed processing approach to semantic cognition. *Nat. Rev. Neurosci.* 4:310–22

McDuff SG, Frankel HC, Norman KA. 2009. Multivoxel pattern analysis reveals increased memory targeting and reduced use of retrieved details during single-agenda source monitoring. *J. Neurosci.* 29:508–16

Meyer K, Kaplan JT, Essex R, Webber C, Damasio H, Damasio A. 2010. Predicting visual stimuli on the basis of activity in auditory cortices. *Nat. Neurosci.* 13:667–68

Miller G. 2010. Science and the law. fMRI lie detection fails a legal test. *Science* 328:1336–37

Misaki M, Kim Y, Bandettini PA, Kriegeskorte N. 2010. Comparison of multivariate classifiers and response normalizations for pattern-information fMRI. *NeuroImage* 53:103–18

Mitchell TM, Hutchinson R, Just MA, Niculescu RS, Pereira F, Wang X. 2003. Classifying instantaneous cognitive states from fMRI data. *AMIA Annu. Symp. Proc.* 2003:465–69

Mitchell TM, Shinkareva SV, Carlson A, Chang KM, Malave VL, et al. 2008. Predicting human brain activity associated with the meanings of nouns. *Science* 320:1191–95

Miyawaki Y, Uchida H, Yamashita O, Sato MA, Morito Y, et al. 2008. Visual image reconstruction from human brain activity using a combination of multiscale local image decoders. *Neuron* 60:915–29

Moeller S, Freiwald WA, Tsao DY. 2008. Patches with links: a unified system for processing faces in the macaque temporal lobe. *Science* 320:1355–59

Monti MM, Vanhaudenhuyse A, Coleman MR, Boly M, Pickard JD, et al. 2010. Willful modulation of brain activity in disorders of consciousness. *N. Engl. J. Med.* 362:579–89

Morgan LK, Macevoy SP, Aguirre GK, Epstein RA. 2011. Distances between real-world locations are represented in the human hippocampus. *J. Neurosci.* 31:1238–45

Naselaris T, Kay KN, Nishimoto S, Gallant JL. 2011. Encoding and decoding in fMRI. *NeuroImage* 56:400–10

Naselaris T, Prenger RJ, Kay KN, Oliver M, Gallant JL. 2009. Bayesian reconstruction of natural images from human brain activity. *Neuron* 63:902–15

Natu VS, Jiang F, Narvekar A, Keshvari S, Blanz V, O'Toole AJ. 2010. Dissociable neural patterns of facial identity across changes in viewpoint. *J. Cogn. Neurosci.* 22:1570–82

Nenadic I, Sauer H, Gaser C. 2009. Distinct pattern of brain structural deficits in subsyndromes of schizophrenia delineated by psychopathology. *NeuroImage* 49:1153–60

Norman KA, Polyn SM, Detre GJ, Haxby JV. 2006. Beyond mind-reading: multi-voxel pattern analysis of fMRI data. *Trends Cogn. Sci.* 10:424–30

Obermayer K, Blasdel GG. 1993. Geometry of orientation and ocular dominance columns in monkey striate cortex. *J. Neurosci.* 13:4114–29

O'Craven KM, Kanwisher N. 2000. Mental imagery of faces and places activates corresponding stiimulus-specific brain regions. *J. Cogn. Neurosci.* 12:1013–23

Offen S, Schluppeck D, Heeger DJ. 2008. The role of early visual cortex in visual short-term memory and visual attention. *Vis. Res.* 49:1352–63

Op de Beeck HP, Haushofer J, Kanwisher NG. 2008. Interpreting fMRI data: maps, modules and dimensions. *Nat. Rev. Neurosci.* 9:123–35

O'Toole AJ, Jiang F, Abdi H, Penard N, Dunlop JP, Parent MA. 2007. Theoretical, statistical, and practical perspectives on pattern-based classification approaches to the analysis of functional neuroimaging data. *J. Cogn. Neurosci.* 19:1735–52

Owen AM, Coleman MR, Boly M, Davis MH, Laureys S, Pickard JD. 2006. Detecting awareness in the vegetative state. *Science* 313:1402

Peelen MV, Fei-Fei L, Kastner S. 2009. Neural mechanisms of rapid natural scene categorization in human visual cortex. *Nature* 460:94–97

Pereira F, Mitchell T, Botvinick M. 2009. Machine learning classifiers and fMRI: a tutorial overview. *NeuroImage* 45:S199–209

Pessoa L, Padmala S. 2007. Decoding near-threshold perception of fear from distributed single-trial brain activation. *Cereb. Cortex* 17:691–701

Phelps EA. 2006. Emotion and cognition: insights from studies of the human amygdala. *Annu. Rev. Psychol.* 57:27–53

Pietrini P, Furey ML, Ricciardi E, Gobbini MI, Wu WH, et al. 2004. Beyond sensory images: object-based representation in the human ventral pathway. *Proc. Natl. Acad. Sci. USA* 101:5658–63

Poldrack RA, Halchenko YO, Hanson SJ. 2009. Decoding the large-scale structure of brain function by classifying mental states across individuals. *Psychol. Sci.* 20:1364–72

Polyn SM, Natu VS, Cohen JD, Norman KA. 2005. Category-specific cortical activity precedes retrieval during memory search. *Science* 310:1963–66

Preston TJ, Li S, Kourtzi Z, Welchman AE. 2008. Multivoxel pattern selectivity for perceptually relevant binocular disparities in the human brain. *J. Neurosci.* 28:11315–27

Raizada RD, Tsao FM, Liu HM, Kuhl PK. 2010. Quantifying the adequacy of neural representations for a cross-language phonetic discrimination task: prediction of individual differences. *Cereb. Cortex* 20:1–12

Reddy L, Kanwisher NG, VanRullen R. 2009. Attention and biased competition in multi-voxel object representations. *Proc. Natl. Acad. Sci. USA* 106:21447–52

Reddy L, Tsuchiya N, Serre T. 2010. Reading the mind's eye: decoding category information during mental imagery. *NeuroImage* 50:818–25

Rissman J, Greely HT, Wagner AD. 2010. Detecting individual memories through the neural decoding of memory states and past experience. *Proc. Natl. Acad. Sci. USA* 107:9849–54

Rissman J, Wagner AD. 2012. Distributed representations in memory: insights from functional brain imaging. *Annu. Rev. Psychol.* In press

Rodriguez PF. 2010. Neural decoding of goal locations in spatial navigation in humans with fMRI. *Hum. Brain Mapp.* 31:391–97

Roskies A. 2002. Neuroethics for the new millenium. *Neuron* 35:21–23

Roskies A. 2006. Neuroscientific challenges to free will and responsibility. *Trends Cogn. Sci.* 10:419–23

Sapolsky RM. 2004. The frontal cortex and the criminal justice system. *Philos. Trans. R. Soc. Lond. B Biol. Sci.* 359:1787–96

Saproo S, Serences JT. 2010. Spatial attention improves the quality of population codes in human visual cortex. *J. Neurophysiol.* 104:885–95

Sasaki Y, Rajimehr R, Kim BW, Ekstrom LB, Vanduffel W, Tootell RB. 2006. The radial bias: a different slant on visual orientation sensitivity in human and nonhuman primates. *Neuron* 51:661–70

Sato JR, de Oliveira-Souza R, Thomaz CE, Basilio R, Bramati IE, et al. 2011. Identification of psychopathic individuals using pattern classification of MRI images. *Soc. Neurosci.* May 14:1–13

Schurger A, Pereira F, Treisman A, Cohen JD. 2010. Reproducibility distinguishes conscious from nonconscious neural representations. *Science* 327:97–99

Schwarzlose RF, Swisher JD, Dang S, Kanwisher N. 2008. The distribution of category and location information across object-selective regions in human visual cortex. *Proc. Natl. Acad. Sci. USA* 105:4447–52

Scolari M, Serences JT. 2010. Basing perceptual decisions on the most informative sensory neurons. *J. Neurophysiol.* 104:2266–73

Serences JT, Boynton GM. 2007a. Feature-based attentional modulations in the absence of direct visual stimulation. *Neuron* 55:301–12

Serences JT, Boynton GM. 2007b. The representation of behavioral choice for motion in human visual cortex. *J. Neurosci.* 27:12893–99

Serences JT, Ester EF, Vogel EK, Awh E. 2009. Stimulus-specific delay activity in human primary visual cortex. *Psychol. Sci.* 20:207–14

Seymour K, Clifford CW, Logothetis NK, Bartels A. 2009. The coding of color, motion, and their conjunction in the human visual cortex. *Curr. Biol.* 19:177–83

Seymour K, Clifford CW, Logothetis NK, Bartels A. 2010. Coding and binding of color and form in visual cortex. *Cereb. Cortex* 20:1946–54

Shen FX, Jones OD. 2011. Brain scans as evidence: truths, proofs, lies, and lessons. *Mercer Law Rev.* 62:In press

Shmuel A, Chaimow D, Raddatz G, Ugurbil K, Yacoub E. 2010. Mechanisms underlying decoding at 7 T: ocular dominance columns, broad structures, and macroscopic blood vessels in V1 convey information on the stimulated eye. *NeuroImage* 49:1957–64

Smith AT, Kosillo P, Williams AL. 2011. The confounding effect of response amplitude on MVPA performance measures. *NeuroImage* 56:525–30

Soon CS, Brass M, Heinze HJ, Haynes JD. 2008. Unconscious determinants of free decisions in the human brain. *Nat. Neurosci.* 11:543–45

Spence SA, Hunter MD, Farrow TF, Green RD, Leung DH, et al. 2004. A cognitive neurobiological account of deception: evidence from functional neuroimaging. *Philos. Trans. R. Soc. Lond. B Biol. Sci.* 359:1755–62

Spiridon M, Kanwisher N. 2002. How distributed is visual category information in human occipito-temporal cortex? An fMRI study. *Neuron* 35:1157–65

Sterzer P, Haynes JD, Rees G. 2008. Fine-scale activity patterns in high-level visual areas encode the category of invisible objects. *J. Vis.* 8:101–2

Stokes M, Thompson R, Cusack R, Duncan J. 2009. Top-down activation of shape-specific population codes in visual cortex during mental imagery. *J. Neurosci.* 29:1565–72

Sumner P, Anderson EJ, Sylvester R, Haynes JD, Rees G. 2008. Combined orientation and colour information in human V1 for both L-M and S-cone chromatic axes. *NeuroImage* 39:814–24

Swisher JD, Gatenby JC, Gore JC, Wolfe BA, Moon CH, et al. 2010. Multiscale pattern analysis of orientation-selective activity in the primary visual cortex. *J. Neurosci.* 30:325–30

Thirion B, Duchesnay E, Hubbard E, Dubois J, Poline JB, et al. 2006. Inverse retinotopy: inferring the visual content of images from brain activation patterns. *NeuroImage* 33:1104–16

Tong F, Meng M, Blake R. 2006. Neural bases of binocular rivalry. *Trends Cogn. Sci.* 10:502–11

Treisman A. 1996. The binding problem. *Curr. Opin. Neurobiol.* 6:171–78

Treue S, Maunsell JH. 1996. Attentional modulation of visual motion processing in cortical areas MT and MST. *Nature* 382:539–41

Tsao DY, Freiwald WA, Tootell RB, Livingstone MS. 2006. A cortical region consisting entirely of face-selective cells. *Science* 311:670–74

Tulving E, Thomson DM. 1973. Encoding specificity and retrieval processes in episodic memory. *Psychol. Rev.* 80:352–73

Tusche A, Bode S, Haynes JD. 2010. Neural responses to unattended products predict later consumer choices. *J. Neurosci.* 30:8024–31

Weisberg DS, Keil FC, Goodstein J, Rawson E, Gray JR. 2008. The seductive allure of neuroscience explanations. *J. Cogn. Neurosci.* 20:470–77

Williams MA, Baker CI, Op de Beeck HP, Shim WM, Dang S, et al. 2008. Feedback of visual object information to foveal retinotopic cortex. *Nat. Neurosci.* 11:1439–45

Williams MA, Dang S, Kanwisher NG. 2007. Only some spatial patterns of fMRI response are read out in task performance. *Nat. Neurosci.* 10:685–86

Wunderlich K, Schneider KA, Kastner S. 2005. Neural correlates of binocular rivalry in the human lateral geniculate nucleus. *Nat. Neurosci.* 8:1595–602

Xue G, Dong Q, Chen C, Lu Z, Mumford JA, Poldrack RA. 2010. Greater neural pattern similarity across repetitions is associated with better memory. *Science* 330:97–101

Yacoub E, Harel N, Ugurbil K. 2008. High-field fMRI unveils orientation columns in humans. *Proc. Natl. Acad. Sci. USA* 105:10607–12

Yamashita O, Sato MA, Yoshioka T, Tong F, Kamitani Y. 2008. Sparse estimation automatically selects voxels relevant for the decoding of fMRI activity patterns. *NeuroImage* 42:1414–29

Human Intracranial Recordings and Cognitive Neuroscience

Roy Mukamel[1,2] and Itzhak Fried[1,3,4]

[1]Department of Neurosurgery, David Geffen School of Medicine and Semel Institute for Neuroscience and Human Behavior, University of California, Los Angeles, Los Angeles, California 90095; [2]Department of Psychology, [3]Sackler School of Medicine, Tel Aviv University, Tel Aviv 69978, Israel; [4]Functional Neurosurgery Unit, Tel Aviv Medical Center, Tel Aviv 64239, Israel; email: rmukamel@post.tau.ac.il, ifried@mednet.ucla.edu

Annu. Rev. Psychol. 2012. 63:511–37

First published online as a Review in Advance on September 19, 2011

The *Annual Review of Psychology* is online at psych.annualreviews.org

This article's doi: 10.1146/annurev-psych-120709-145401

Keywords

local field potentials, extra-cellular unit recording, electrocorticography (ECoG), depth electrodes, brain-machine interface, deep brain stimulation

Abstract

The ultimate goal of neuroscience research is to understand the operating mechanism of the human brain and to exploit this understanding to devise methods for repair when it malfunctions. A key feature of this operating mechanism is electrical activity of single brain cells and cell assemblies. For obvious ethical reasons, scientists rely mostly on animal research in the study of such signals. Research in humans is often limited to electrical signals that can be recorded at the scalp or to surrogates of electrical activity, namely magnetic source imaging and measures of regional blood flow and metabolism. Invasive brain recordings performed in patients during various clinical procedures provide a unique opportunity to record high-resolution signals in vivo from the human brain—data that are otherwise unavailable. Of special value are the rare opportunities to record in awake humans the activity of single brain cells and small cellular assemblies. These recordings provide a unique view on aspects of human cognition that are impossible to study in animals, including language, imagery, episodic memory, volition, and even consciousness. In the current review we discuss the unique contribution of invasive recordings from patients to the field of cognitive neuroscience.

Contents

Electroencephalography (EEG): a noninvasive method for recording the brain's electrical activity by placing recording electrodes over the scalp. The measured signal corresponds to ionic current flow from large neural populations (mostly pyramidal cells)

Functional magnetic resonance imaging/ blood oxygen level–dependent (fMRI/BOLD): the most commonly measured signal in functional MRI studies. The BOLD signal measures changes in blood oxygen content that are used as a proxy to estimate the underlying neural activity

INTRODUCTION

In the past, advances in the study of the human brain relied on a number of sources for scientific data. Seminal histological studies by Cajal, Golgi, Brodmann, Vogt, and others using animal brain tissue or human tissue obtained either postmortem or during surgery provided invaluable information about brain structure at the micro- and macroanatomical levels (De Carlos & Borrell 2007, Loukas et al. 2011). Brain function (as opposed to structure) was mainly inferred from clinical cases [such as the works of Wernicke (Thomson et al. 2008) and Broca (Dronkers et al. 2007)] relating damaged brain structures to observed behavioral deficits. Further insight was provided by noninvasive recordings of electric and magnetic signals from the human scalp, namely electroencephalography (EEG) since Berger's seminal discovery (Berger 1929), and later magnetoencephalography (MEG). A unique and important source of information regarding brain function was provided by neurosurgeons such as Penfield and others who recorded electrical activity or electrically stimulated the brains of neurosurgical patients during clinical procedures (Penfield 1950). Over the past few decades, technological advances have supplemented these tools with advanced neuroimaging methods that allow probing the structure and function of the living human brain in patients and healthy subjects in a noninvasive manner. These techniques have opened exciting new research fields that are now addressing the relationship between brain structure, function, and behavior.

Noninvasive tools can be largely classified into two categories on the basis of the type of information they provide—structural or functional. Structural tools such as computerized tomography (CT), magnetic resonance imaging (MRI), and diffusion tensor imaging (DTI) provide images that are static in time. The anatomical information can range from emphasizing, for example, gray matter, white matter, cerebrospinal fluid, blood vessels, or fiber tracks. On the other hand, functional tools such as EEG, MEG, positron emission tomography (PET), and functional MRI (fMRI) provide information about the temporal dynamics of various physiological measures. These dynamics are most relevant because they allow examining the relationship between physiological measures in specific brain regions while the subject is engaged in various tasks and cognitive states that change in time. However, given that the brain communicates and functions by electrical activity of individual neurons at millisecond resolution, all noninvasive techniques suffer from poor spatial and/or temporal resolution.

Certain clinical procedures involve invasive recording of electrophysiological measures in patient populations for clinical purposes. These procedures provide a unique opportunity to probe the human brain at high spatio-temporal resolution, which is otherwise unavailable. Some of the advantages these techniques provide include:

(*a*) Signal source. Invasive techniques allow direct recording of the electrical activity from populations of cells or even individual cells while techniques such as fMRI or PET record surrogate signals (such as blood flow or metabolism rate), which are indirectly linked to the electrical activity of very large neural populations.

(b) Spatial resolution. Targeting and localization of implanted recording electrodes is within ~1–2 mm. Depending on the type of signal recorded (see below), electrodes can measure the spiking activity of individual neurons or the local field potentials from populations of neurons within a diameter of a few millimeters. For comparison, source localization of EEG or MEG signals provides an effective spatial resolution that is an order of magnitude lower (~1 cm).

(c) Temporal resolution. Invasive recordings have millisecond resolution (similar to EEG and MEG), which is compatible with the timescale of neural activity. For comparison, the fMRI signal measures slow hemodynamic fluctuations that are on the timescale of seconds.

(d) Signal-to-noise ratio (SNR). Invasive recordings have higher SNR compared with scalp EEG and MEG. Noninvasive methods are more susceptible to artifacts (due to eye blinks and movement), and the signal is weaker because it has to pass the cranium and scalp before reaching the recording electrodes. The higher SNR provided by direct invasive recordings allows examination of high-frequency bands that are unavailable from scalp recordings.

(e) Spatial distribution. In some invasive procedures (see below), recordings are performed from multiple brain regions simultaneously, providing relatively large coverage of the brain.

(f) Human cognition. By far, the major advantage of invasive recordings in humans over similar recordings in animals is the possibility to address questions that are unique to human cognition and behavior such as language, episodic memory, imagery, volition, and emotion. These aspects of human cognition clearly lack an experimental animal model and are unavailable at high spatio-temporal resolutions using noninvasive techniques.

Although these advantages are pertinent, it is important to note the following limitations of such recordings:

(a) Subject population. The most obvious limitation is the fact that these recordings are only conducted in patients with various pathologies and clear clinical justification for performing these procedures. Therefore, it can be argued that results from such recordings might not always generalize to brain function in healthy population. Nevertheless, as in the case of epileptic patients, recording sites typically include multiple brain regions and not only the region eventually found to be pathologic.

(b) Limited spatial distribution. In many cases sampling is directed to a few targets, and it is never targeted to whole brains.

(c) Study time. Study time for performing the recordings is limited and constrained by the clinical setup, therefore making long experiments impractical. Depending on the type of recording (acute or semichronic; see below), the duration of a typical experimental session can range between 15 and 40 minutes.

(d) Medication. The patients are usually under various medication regimens that might affect the functional properties of recorded tissue. This can be often controlled for by performing the recordings when the patients are tapered off medication or alternatively recording from many patients who are on different medication types and therefore diminishing the effect (if any) of specific medications.

(e) Homogeneity of subjects. Relative to studies on healthy volunteers, patient populations may be more heterogeneous and range in age, cognitive skills, and task performance levels. These factors add variability to the collected data.

In the current article, we provide an overview of the various invasive recording techniques available in humans, the type of signals that can be measured, and the relevant clinical populations in which there is clinical opportunity to perform such recordings. We continue by highlighting unique contributions of such studies to various fields in cognitive neuroscience. We conclude by pointing out fields in cognitive neuroscience in which invasive techniques will undoubtedly prove useful in future research.

RECORDING TECHNIQUES AND SIGNAL TYPES

Invasive procedures allow recording of the extracellular electrical activity from the brain at two levels of resolution—either at the level of action potentials emitted by individual (or very few) cells (single or multi units) or at the level of local field potentials (LFPs), which are the electrical signals resulting from the activity of large populations of cells near the electrode tip. Whereas the action potentials reflect the local processing and output of the cells, the LFP signal most probably reflects both action potentials and synaptic activity localized to the dendrites, thus corresponding better with the input to the cells. Depending on the type of implant, recording sessions can be conducted in the operating room (acute), the hospital ward (semichronic; between several days and two weeks or longer), or in a chronic manner (see Brain-Machine Interface section). Acute recordings are performed during surgery and are therefore typically short (~15 minutes), whereas recordings from electrodes implanted semichronically can be longer (~30 minutes, across multiple sessions) because recordings are performed during the patient's stay at the ward.

Several types of electrodes are commonly used:

(a) Subdural strips/grids. These are one- or two-dimensional arrays (strips or grids, respectively) of platinum-iridium or steel electrodes with a diameter of 2–4 mm and spaced several mm apart, although more dense arrays have been recently developed (Viventi et al. 2010). These electrodes are typically implanted under the dura, over the exposed cortex, and allow recording of the field potentials from the underlying brain tissue. Implantation is usually semichronic, allowing recording over periods of several days/weeks (**Figure 1A**, *top*; see color insert).

(b) Depth electrodes. Unlike subdural electrodes, depth electrodes penetrate the brain parenchyma in order to target deep brain structures. These electrodes allow recording field potentials from contacts along the electrode shaft. Additionally, microwires can be inserted into the core of the shaft to allow recording of single/multi-unit activity from the tip of the electrode (Fried et al. 1999) or along the shaft (**Figure 1B**, *top*). Another type of depth electrode is the hybrid depth electrode (HDE), which has high-impedance contacts for recording action potentials from single/multi units interspersed between low-impedance contacts for recording the electroencephalographic signal (Howard et al. 1996b). Using multiple, closely placed microwire tips (as in the case of stereotrodes or tetrodes) improves the yield and isolation of single from multi units (Gray et al. 1995). Depth electrodes can be used in acute or semichronic fashion depending on the procedure (see Clinical Opportunities section below).

(c) Intracortical electrodes. These are electrodes that penetrate the cortex by a few millimeters and allow recording unit activity and LFP from superficial regions. The Utah array is a matrix of 10×10 electrodes that allows simultaneous recording from up to 100 channels (Nordhausen et al. 1996) (**Figure 1B**). A linear array multielectrode is a thumbtack-shaped array of 20–24 electrodes, separated by 75–200 μm, that are placed on the subdural cortical surface to allow recording of

LFPs and unit activity from distinct cortical layers (Ulbert et al. 2001). Another type of electrode is the neurotrophic electrode, which induces growth of cortical neurites into a recording chamber (Kennedy 1989).

(d) Microdialysis. These are probes that allow measuring neurochemical concentration from brain dialysate samples and can be inserted via the lumen of depth electrodes or along the shaft (Fried et al. 1999). These probes can be used in semichronic implantations for measuring levels of neurotransmitter release at different time points (During et al. 1994, During & Spencer 1993, Fried et al. 2001).

In addition to passive recording, some electrode types also allow electrical stimulation of the underlying tissue. This powerful combination makes it possible to stimulate one region while measuring activity in other regions and thus to examine the functional connectivity between them. In addition, stimulation allows the examination of causal links between neural activity in the stimulated region and overt behavior.

Clinical Opportunities

The opportunities to perform intracranial recordings of neural activity or to electrically stimulate neural tissue can be divided into two categories: acute situations during brain surgery (intraoperative) and chronic or semichronic conditions involving electrodes implanted in the human brain for diagnostic or therapeutic reasons.

Acute recordings and stimulation. Awake brain surgery for brain mapping was pioneered by Wilder Penfield, who kept his patients awake during surgery to be able to map functional properties of brain regions by using electrical stimulation. The lack of pain receptors in the brain allows stimulating brain tissue while patients are awake and examining correlated

behavioral manifests (Penfield & Jasper 1954). This surgery was done mostly in patients with pharmacologically resistant epilepsy and was aimed at the safe resection of epileptogenic brain tissue when a focus for the seizures could be identified. Intraoperative stimulation and recording are carried out in modern neurosurgery in operations on a wide spectrum of patients, mainly those with epilepsy or brain tumors, where surgery is planned in brain regions critical for certain functions such as language, motor, or sensation (Ojemann 2010).

Another set of procedures, known as deep brain stimulation (DBS), is aimed at small functional regions within the brain. Electrodes are stereotactically inserted, and chronic stimulation is then used to ameliorate disabling symptoms in several neurological disorders. DBS for patients with Parkinson's disease and for patients with dystonia or essential tremor is now part of clinical practice in selected cases. DBS is also emerging as a potential therapy for patients with epilepsy and for patients with psychiatric disorders such as major depression and obsessive compulsive disorder. In the operating room, stimulation and extracellular recordings of neural activity are used to optimally identify the desired target for chronic stimulation. This provides the opportunity to examine cognitive and motor functions intraoperatively (Engel et al. 2005).

Acute recordings and stimulation in the operating room have the advantage of studying brain targets in the living brain under direct vision or stereotactic control, with the ability to move the electrodes while obtaining physiological data. However, clinical time constraints and the pressured setting of surgery limit the behavioral paradigms that can be employed.

Chronic or semichronic recordings. In certain neurosurgical conditions, electrodes are inserted inside the cranium for longer periods of time. In DBS procedures, electrode leads that are used for chronic stimulation are sometimes externalized before the pulse generator is inserted. Therefore, for a limited period of time,

Deep brain stimulation (DBS): involves chronic electrical stimulation of specific brain targets for therapeutic purpose, such as in treatment of Parkinson's disease or dystonia. This is typically achieved by a chronically implanted electrode and a pulse generator

usually several days, these externalized leads can be used for recording intracranial EEG (iEEG).

By far, the most common opportunities in contemporary neurosurgery to record neuronal signals from inside the human brain outside the operating room are in patients with intractable epilepsy who are evaluated for potential curative surgery. About 1% of the population suffers from recurrent epileptic seizures. Although in most cases medication helps control these seizures, in about one-third of the cases the seizures are resistant to pharmacological intervention, and surgical resection of the seizure focus may be the only clinical resort. In a small subset of these patients, noninvasive methods are not sufficient to identify a seizure focus. These patients then require placement of intracranial electrodes in order to identify a seizure focus for potential subsequent surgical removal. These electrodes may be subdural arrays of multiple contacts placed on the surface of the brain or depth electrodes placed at suspected targets inside the brain parenchyma. After electrode implantation, the patients are monitored around the clock for the occurrence of spontaneous seizures. Patients remain in the monitoring ward for a period of one to two weeks until sufficient clinical data for localizing the seizure focus are obtained. During this time the patients very often can participate in research studies. The research is done at no added risk to the patients, as the electrodes are already there for clinical reasons. Although in acute recordings electrode position can be adjusted, once the patient is out of the operating room, the electrode position during chronic recordings is fixed and cannot be adjusted to accommodate signal quality.

An obvious limitation in conducting neurophysiological research of cognitive functions in epilepsy patients is that recordings are carried out in brains that have abnormal electrical activity. However, it should be pointed out that recordings are performed in multiple suspected brain regions, and often merely a subset of these are eventually found to be involved in epileptogenic activity. Additionally, recordings are carried out during long periods when no seizures occur. Findings in epileptogenic regions can often be compared with findings in regions that are not involved. Finally, results from studies in these patients should always be interpreted in view of existing knowledge from animal neurophysiology and noninvasive neurophysiology in humans obtained by other methods. In the history of neuroscience, studies in epilepsy patients have provided important windows into normal brain mechanisms, as evidenced by seminal discoveries such as the motor homunculus in humans (Penfield & Boldrey 1937) and the distribution of speech and language areas in human cortex (Ojemann et al. 1989, Penfield & Roberts 1959).

It is expected that the opportunities to record signals from within the human brain will evolve in the near future to include novel developments in DBS and in the emerging field of brain-machine interfaces (BMIs). DBS is emerging as a potential therapy for neuropsychiatric disorders such as major depression and obsessive-compulsive disorders and cognitive enhancement in conditions of cognitive disorders and memory impairment. BMIs may use intracranial signals to modify human motor and cognitive abilities. Therefore, the study of signals recorded from the brain parenchyma relevant to human cognitive function may undergo substantial evolution in the coming years. We now describe various fields of cognitive neuroscience in which invasive clinical recordings have already provided valuable data.

COGNITIVE FUNCTIONS STUDIED BY INTRACRANIAL ELECTRODES

Perception

Throughout the brain, neurons are organized in an orderly fashion along various functional dimensions. A salient organization principle found in auditory cortex of experimental animals is tonotopy. Cells in auditory cortex form an anatomical gradient of sensitivity according to sound frequency. Consistent with animal studies, a tonotopic organization has been demonstrated in humans with high frequencies represented in caudal medial Heschl's gyrus and lower frequencies in anterolateral regions (Howard et al. 1996a). Interestingly, the width of the tuning curves (i.e., the range of tone frequencies a single neuron is sensitive to) was found to be much narrower in humans than is expected based on recordings in most mammals (Bitterman et al. 2008). In visual cortex, iEEG studies demonstrate that receptive field size and response latencies increase from early regions (V1) to more anterior regions (V3/V4). Lateral regions (corresponding to middle temporal/middle superior temporal areas in monkey) have larger receptive fields, although response latencies are similar to those of V1 (Yoshor et al. 2007a).

In ventral visual cortex, a recurring theme is that of categorization. Neighboring cells within a small patch of cortex respond selectively to stimuli with similar attributes. Faces are an important stimulus category, and many studies using various techniques have shown that specific regions of the fusiform gyrus and inferior temporal gyrus respond preferentially to the visual presentation of faces. Invasive EEG studies have demonstrated that the negative component of the evoked response (N200) has higher amplitude during the presentation of human faces compared with many other stimulus categories (such as scrambled images, objects, and animals) (Allison et al. 1999). This selectivity is also invariant to changes in face representation such as color versus black and white, photo image versus line drawing, and size (McCarthy et al. 1999) (see also Seeck et al. 2001). Electrical stimulation of these regions corroborates these results by demonstrating temporary inability to name familiar faces or by evoking face-related hallucinations (Allison et al. 1994, Puce et al. 1999). Although the amplitude of the N200 component measured in iEEG studies is insensitive to degree of attention, noninvasive studies have shown that attention modulates the fMRI signal in face-related regions (for a similar discrepancy in V1, see Yoshor et al. 2007b). A recent iEEG study reconciles this apparent discrepancy in face-selective regions by demonstrating that although the N200 component is indeed invariant to the level of attention, gamma band LFP power modulations (30–100 Hz) are increased when attending a face (Engell & McCarthy 2010). Indeed, the fMRI BOLD signal in human sensory regions has been shown to correspond with modulations in the gamma band LFP power (Mukamel et al. 2005, Nir et al. 2007, Privman et al. 2007). These results demonstrate that different components of the electrophysiological signal show differential sensitivity to task aspects that are not always available to current imaging techniques.

Another stimulus category, letter strings, has also been shown to selectively engage specific regions in the fusiform gyrus (regions distinct from the face-selective regions described above). In one iEEG study, the early positive component of the evoked response (P200) in the posterior fusiform responded equally strongly to word and nonword letter strings, whereas the later positive component (P400) in the anterior fusiform responded preferentially to words (Nobre et al. 1994), suggesting additional processing perhaps through feedback mechanisms from other regions. Another region, in left ventral occipitotemporal cortex, has been suggested by imaging studies to be selective to written words [the visual word form area (VWFA)]. A recent case report in one patient has demonstrated that the evoked iEEG response in this region is indeed larger for words and that subsequent resection of this region resulted in a reading deficit at the behavioral level accompanied by lack of functional selectivity for words in the fMRI signal. These results provide both correlation and causal evidence linking activity in this region with the detection of written words (Gaillard et al. 2006).

Functional selectivity to specific categories (e.g., faces, tools, houses) has also been demonstrated in other studies measuring evoked responses (Privman et al. 2007) and gamma band power modulations in the LFP signal (30–70 Hz) (Fisch et al. 2009). Another category of visual stimuli that has received attention lately is body parts. Pourtois and colleagues compared

N200 or P400: modulations in the ERP signal contain negative and positive peaks at specific time points. N200 and P400 refer to negative (N200) or positive (P400) peaks in the ERP signal 200 or 400 ms poststimulus onset, respectively

Gamma band: the high-frequency range of oscillations in the LFP or EEG signal. The exact definition of this frequency range varies among studies, but it typically refers to frequencies higher than 30 Hz and lower than 130 Hz

Medial temporal lobe (MTL): specific anatomical structures in the MTL include the amygdala, hippocampus, parahippocampal gyrus, and entorhinal cortex

the responses evoked by presentation of pictures of human body parts with those evoked by presentation of faces, tools, and mammals. They report a focal region in right lateral occipital cortex demonstrating larger evoked responses to pictures of body parts compared with other stimulus categories. The location of this region is compatible with the extrastriate body area (EBA) described in noninvasive fMRI studies (Pourtois et al. 2007).

The iEEG studies described above demonstrate that distinct regions of cortex respond in a selective manner to various stimulus categories. This grouping into categories is complemented by a lack of sensitivity to low-level features (stimulus size, color, etc.). Such results could have two alternative underlying sources: (a) distinct but neighboring neural populations that are sensitive to different aspects of the stimulus, but due to low spatial resolution of recording techniques, they give rise to an invariant average population signal or (b) truly invariant cells that are anatomically grouped.

Single-cell recordings of spiking activity (as opposed to the iEEG signal which stems from the pre- and postsynaptic activity of large populations of cells) allow examining this issue at a much finer scale. Indeed, category selectivity has been demonstrated at the spiking level of individual neurons. In the medial temporal lobe (MTL), 14% of cells have been shown to respond preferentially to stimuli belonging to a particular category (faces, natural scenes, houses, famous people, or animals) (Kreiman et al. 2000a). The results in MTL suggest that category selectivity in ventral and lateral occipitotemporal cortex demonstrated at the population level by evoked responses might also hold true at the single-cell level. However, a direct comparison of selectivity between spiking activity and LFP in MTL shows nonoverlapping anatomical distribution of category representation between the two signals (Kraskov et al. 2007). Therefore, category selectivity at the single-cell level in regions outside MTL remains to be demonstrated.

Although visual category represents one level of abstraction, a different type of abstraction for specific images within a category has been demonstrated at the single-cell level. Individual cells—particularly in hippocampus and entorhinal cortex—have been shown to respond to particular images (~1–3 out of a total of ~100 different images presented to the patient), with neighboring cells responding to different stimuli. The selective response of these cells was invariant across stimulus representations such that a cell responding to an image of the Sydney Opera House responded also to many other images of the Sydney Opera House regardless of low-level features such as angle or lighting and did not respond to images of other buildings. Similarly, a cell responding to the picture of a particular famous actress responded regardless of different clothing or hairstyle and did not respond to pictures of other famous actresses (Quiroga et al. 2005). The same cells also responded in an invariant manner across modalities (i.e., for spoken words and text strings representing the same concept) (Quian Quiroga et al. 2009). Thus these neurons respond to a common concept, regardless of representation type (**Figure 2**, see color insert).

Within different MTL regions, there seems to be a hierarchy. Neurons in parahippocampal gyrus respond earliest (~270 ms), in a less selective manner (i.e., respond to more stimuli), and in a similar fashion to repeated stimuli, whereas neurons in entorhinal cortex, hippocampus, and amygdala respond later (~400 ms), more selectively, and with reduced firing rates to repeated stimuli (Mormann et al. 2008, Pedreira et al. 2009). Indeed, electrical stimulation of the parahippocampal gyrus (and also amygdala) is less probable to evoke response in hippocampal formation compared with stimulation in entorhinal cortex and presubiculum (Wilson et al. 1990), supporting a hierarchy in their connections.

Taken together, neural activity in ventral and lateral occipitotemporal regions is anatomically grouped by response preference to specific stimulus categories (such as faces, letter strings, and body parts). As the neural signal propagates from high-order visual areas in occipital and inferior temporal regions to structures in the MTL, there seems to be a hierarchy of processing, with neurons in parahippocampal gyrus responding earlier and in a less selective manner compared with neurons in entorhinal cortex, hippocampus, and amygdala. Neurons in the hippocampus respond to highly abstract concepts and are insensitive to low-level representation features.

Sensory stimulation and conscious perception. A physical stimulus can elicit different percepts across individuals or even different percepts within the same individual across different time points (as in the case of binocular rivalry or bi-stable perception of ambiguous stimuli; Rees et al. 2002). In the lack of a one-to-one correspondence between conscious perception and external objective measures, the experimenter must rely on the subjective report of the subject. Although experimental animals can report their perception, this requires extensive training that can affect the underlying neural system. Furthermore, imagery, which is an internally generated percept, is virtually impossible to study in animals. In what follows, we discuss single-unit and LFP studies examining the correlation between neural activity and conscious perception of visual stimuli in humans.

Flash suppression is a phenomenon in which one stimulus is presented to one eye and is consciously perceived. After a short period, a different stimulus is presented to the other eye (while the first stimulus is still presented to the original eye). Behaviorally, perception switches to the new stimulus. In a study using flash suppression, Kreiman and colleagues (2002) demonstrated that ~70% of neurons in MTL structures (i.e., amygdala, hippocampus, entorhinal cortex, and parahippocampal gyrus) follow perceptual alterations rather than retinal input. In other words, a neuron that responded selectively to one of the two stimuli (assessed during a previous monocular stimulation session) will respond during the binocular period only if the preferred stimulus is the one being consciously perceived. If the same stimulus is presented binocularly but is not consciously perceived, the

neuron does not respond (Kreiman et al. 2002). Similarly, in a backward masking paradigm, Quiroga and colleagues (2008) parametrically changed the duration of picture presentation (from 16 ms to 256 ms) followed by a scrambled image serving as a backward mask. Behaviorally (especially for the short presentation durations), picture recognition was variable across trials, and neural firing rates in MTL correlated with recognition behavior. In other words, when a stimulus is presented for 66 ms, a selective neuron responds only on trials in which the patient recognized the picture, whereas on physically identical trials in which the stimulus is not recognized, the same neuron did not fire (Quiroga et al. 2008) (**Figure 3**). A similar correlation between perception and neural firing has been demonstrated using a change detection task (Reddy et al. 2006). In addition to these studies, the correlation between perception and neural firing is further supported by the fact that neurons in MTL that respond during visual perception of a specific picture respond also when there is no physical stimulus and the patient simply imagines the same picture

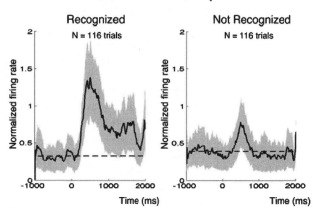

Figure 3

Neural activity and conscious perception. Stimulus perception can be manipulated by using short presentation durations and backward masking. In such conditions, perception varies from trial to trial even when identical stimulation parameters are used. The figure shows the average normalized firing rate of 29 MTL neurons during recognized and not-recognized trials (four trials in each condition). Note how the increase in neural activity corresponds with behavior. Reproduced from Quiroga et al. (2008) with permission.

Event-related potential (ERP): the EEG signal, locked to stimulus onset (or any other temporal event of interest), is averaged across many trials to produce the ERP. Only modulations that are locked to event onset will be evident in the ERP signal

(Kreiman et al. 2000b). Thus, firing patterns in MTL structures correspond to specific percepts whether externally or internally generated.

Although the studies described above focused on spiking activity, other studies have examined the correspondence between perception and LFP power modulations. Using a backward masking paradigm, Fisch and colleagues (2009) presented patients with pictures from various categories including manmade objects, faces, and houses. Pictures were presented for a brief period (16 ms) followed by a mask (250 ms), and perception was manipulated by changing the duration of an intervening blank screen between the two (16–200 ms). Perceived stimuli were characterized by enhanced gamma power (30–70 Hz) relative to nonperceived stimuli. This enhancement was pronounced in high-order visual areas and absent in retinotopic regions. Additionally, successful recognition was characterized by an increase in evoked response amplitude in high-order (and not low-order) visual areas in the temporal lobe (Fisch et al. 2009). In a similar vein, Gaillard and colleagues employed a masking paradigm using printed words. In the first 200 ms, masked and unmasked words elicit a similar evoked response and increase in the high gamma band (50–100 Hz) LFP power, mostly in posterior occipital and visual areas. After ∼200 ms, the event-related potential (ERP) and gamma band signals decay for masked words while successful recognition is characterized by longer-lasting ERPs and sustained increase in the high gamma LFP power that propagates to occipital, parietal, and prefrontal regions (Gaillard et al. 2009).

Finally, electrical stimulation in low-level visual areas has been shown to elicit visual percepts. In V4 color-sensitive regions, electrical stimulation elicits color percepts that correspond with the color evoking the strongest LFP signal (Murphey et al. 2008). In more anterior regions (such as the fusiform face area), evoking face percepts corresponds better with long stimulations (5 seconds; Puce et al. 1999) compared with short stimulations (300 ms; Murphey et al. 2009).

Taken together, findings from invasive studies support the notion that the conscious perception of a stimulus is correlated with neural activity in MTL and the propagation of neural activity (measured by increased high gamma band LFP power) to high-order visual areas and parietal and frontal regions. The mechanisms underlying these neural correlates of consciousness are an important topic of further research.

Memory

In many respects, we are defined by our memories: from what we can do (procedural/skill memory), what we know (semantic memory), who we know (familiarity), and how we met (episodic memory). Deficits in any of these aspects of memory, such as in the case of dementia or amnesia, can have devastating consequences on our notion of self (Eichenbaum & Cohen 2001, Schacter 1996, Squire 2004, Tulving & Schacter 1990). Understanding the mechanisms that underlie successful memory formation—encoding, retention, and recall—has tremendous consequences on learning, cognition, and rehabilitation. Certain types of memories, such as fear conditioning or skill learning, are relatively amenable to manipulation in experimental animals. Other memory types, such as episodic, require self-report and are therefore extremely difficult to probe in animals. In the current section we review recent single-unit and iEEG studies addressing the neural mechanism of human memory. Because many of the epilepsy patients evaluated with invasive electrodes for identifying a focus amenable to surgical removal are implanted with electrodes in the temporal lobe, the opportunity to study declarative and episodic memory is especially pertinent, as it enables direct access to the critical MTL structures. MTL structures and particularly the hippocampus are chiefly responsible for our ability to transform percepts into lasting memories that are available for later conscious access.

The ability to distinguish between novel stimuli and stimuli that one has been exposed to in the past is an important aspect of memory, in which the hippocampus and MTL structures play an important role (Corkin 2002, Squire et al. 2004). Recent studies suggest that both the hippocampus and amygdala contain subsets of neurons that modulate their firing rates to stimuli according to their degree of novelty (novelty versus familiarity detectors). Thus, in the case of familiarity detectors, the first encounter with a stimulus (encoding) does not elicit a significant neural response, whereas a second exposure (retrieval) elicits a robust and significant response. In the case of novelty detectors, a strong neural response during the first stimulus encounter is subsequently suppressed during repeated stimulus presentations. On the basis of the activity of a small pool of neurons in hippocampus and amygdala, the degree of novelty (whether the stimulus was previously seen or not) can be predicted with high accuracy, even if the behavioral response is erroneous. (Fried et al. 1997, 2002; Rutishauser et al. 2006). Interestingly, neuronal activity in entorhinal cortex during retrieval is better correlated with behavioral judgments (Cameron et al. 2001). Recordings from both lateral temporal lobe (superior and middle portions of the middle temporal gyrus) and more medial sections (inferior portion of middle temporal gyrus and collateral sulcus) suggest a functional/anatomical subdivision. Inferior/medial sites are more sensitive to specific stages of explicit memory (encoding, storage, or recall), and lateral regions are more active during recognition of previously seen stimuli (Ojemann et al. 2002).

Although these studies distinguished between "new" and "old" stimuli, a finer distinction is between familiar and recollected stimuli. In the case of familiar stimuli, subjects remember that the stimulus was previously seen, whereas for recollected stimuli they also remember the context (e.g., where on the screen the stimulus was presented) (Diana et al. 2007, Yonelinas et al. 2005). Cells in hippocampus and amygdala show a graded response during retrieval between new, familiar, and recollected stimuli. Thus, higher firing rate of a familiarity detector during retrieval corresponds with higher probability that the stimulus will be also recollected (Rutishauser et al. 2008). The involvement of the hippocampus in encoding is also supported by electrical stimulation studies showing that stimulation of the hippocampus during encoding to memory results in memory deficits (Coleshill et al. 2004, Lacruz et al. 2010). Further studies have shown that during encoding, firing rate as well as the degree of phase locking of spiking activity of hippocampal/amygdala neurons to the theta-band (3–7 Hz) LFP is predictive of subsequent memory recall (Cameron et al. 2001, Rutishauser et al. 2010). For stimuli that will be remembered in the future, spiking activity tends to occur at a specific phase of the theta-band LFP, whereas spiking activity during presentation of stimuli that are later forgotten are less phase locked. (Rutishauser et al. 2010). Phase locking of hippocampal spiking activity to the delta LFP band (1–4 Hz) (Jacobs et al. 2007) and stimulus-related LFP phase resetting (4–20 Hz) (Mormann et al. 2005) have been shown during virtual navigation and word memory paradigms.

As animals cannot readily declare their recollections, recall is a particularly difficult memory function to study in nonhuman primates and other animals. In a different set of studies, it has been found that the same neural network that is active during stimulus encoding is reactivated during successful retrieval (for review, see Danker & Anderson 2010). When presented with various audiovisual clips, individual neurons in hippocampus and entorhinal cortex increase firing rate to certain clips but not to others. When the subject is later asked to describe the various videoclips that were presented (in the absence of any sensory input), the same neuron that responded during encoding increased its firing rate ~1 second prior to the onset of verbal recall of the same specific clip (Gelbard-Sagiv et al. 2008). Indeed electrical stimulation of amygdala, hippocampus, and parahippocampal gyrus has been shown to evoke a sensation of déjà vu or déjà vécu (Gloor 1990, Vignal et al. 2007). In addition, the temporal correlations of spiking activity in hippocampal cells during stimulus presentation (how much the firing rate at time t is predictive of the firing rate at time $t+1$) increase each time an audiovisual stimulus is repeatedly shown. The degree of this temporal correlation is also predictive of subjects' future recall performance, suggesting a mechanism for binding successive events across time (Paz et al. 2010).

The picture emerging from intracranial studies of the ventral pathways in humans is that of visual stimuli eliciting neural signals that propagate through visual areas in occipitotemporal lobes to MTL structures. Along this pathway, the neural representation becomes more and more selective to specific categories or exemplars within a category and invariant to different representations of the same stimulus. Thus, at the level of hippocampus and entorhinal cortex, the top of the visual hierarchy in the ventral stream, the cells exhibit both increased specificity in that they respond to a particular concept, be it a person or a place, yet at the same time they exhibit the highest degree of invariance and abstraction, ignoring low-level features. In MTL, stimulus presentation evokes a phase resetting in the low-frequency bands (1–8 Hz) accompanied by increased firing rates of specific neurons in a selective manner. Increased firing rates in MTL regions correlate with conscious stimulus perception. Successful encoding to memory is associated with spiking activity phase locked to the theta (3–7 Hz) band LFP oscillations. During retrieval, the same selective neural networks are engaged (Gelbard-Sagiv et al. 2008). Thus, the hippocampus and entorhinal cortex seem to be important nodes in transforming sensory input into abstract concepts that can be consciously recollected.

Spatial navigation. An important area of memory research involves the model of spatial navigation in rodents. "Place cells" are a special class of cells originally described in the rodent hippocampus. These cells increase their firing rates every time the animal is in a particular location in the environment, thus forming one node in a "virtual" map of spatial locations (O'Keefe & Dostrovsky 1971). Using a computer-simulated virtual navigation task,

Ekstrom and colleagues demonstrated that cells in the human hippocampus increase their firing rate when the subject is in a particular place within the virtual environment (place cells). These cells are sensitive to position in space regardless of viewing perspective (i.e., if the subject is facing north or south). On the other hand, cells in parahippocampal gyrus were sensitive to viewing perspective (Ekstrom et al. 2003). In a subsequent study, it has been found that cells, mostly in entorhinal cortex, encode both position in space and direction of motion. In other words, some cells increase firing rates while traversing a specific location in space in a clockwise direction but not when traversing the same location in a counterclockwise direction (Jacobs et al. 2010). Another important class of cells described in the rodent entorhinal cortex is "grid cells." These cells fire at repeated spatial locations that are equally separated in distance and form triangular grid-like patterns across the environment (Hafting et al. 2005). Such cells in humans have not yet been directly identified by intracranial recordings, although supportive evidence has been provided by fMRI study (Doeller et al. 2010).

Place cells in the rodent hippocampus constitute high-level abstractions of the spatial environment, with specific cells representing a particular location in space and not another (selectivity), regardless of head position (invariance). In humans, the same principle guidelines characterize neural responses in the MTL. Place cells in human hippocampus are an obvious parallel. Interestingly, in humans, these principles hold not only for spatial locations but also for sensory (or imagined) percepts, raising the possibility that the selective and invariant responses demonstrated in human MTL are an evolutionary expansion of the place cells described in animal physiology and represent a special class of cells, "concept cells" (Fried et al. 1997, Quian Quiroga et al. 2008). Finally, during free recall, the same neurons in human MTL that were active during encoding are reactivated (Gelbard-Sagiv et al. 2008). Animal studies suggest a similar reactivation of traversed paths in rodent place cells during

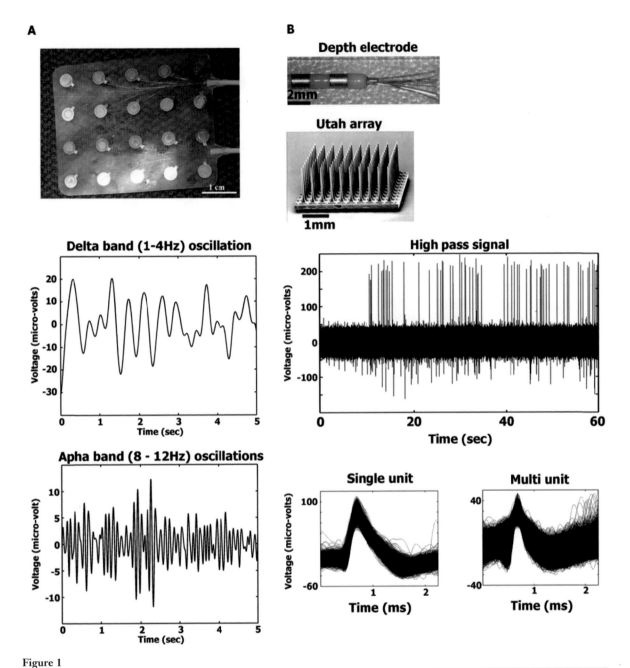

Figure 1

Electrode and signal types. (*A*) A 4 × 5 grid of intracranial electrodes for recording the iEEG signal (*top*). Filtering the recorded signal to different frequency bands (e.g., Delta, *middle panel*; Alpha, *bottom panel*) allows examining power changes across time and cognitive tasks. (*B*) Depth electrodes penetrate the brain parenchyma and allow targeting of deep brain structures. Contacts along the shaft allow recording of the iEEG signal while the microwires at the tip allow recording of high-frequency activity (*middle panel*) of single or very few neurons (*bottom panels*). The Utah array is a 10 × 10 matrix of electrodes that allow recording unit activity from superficial cortical regions (reproduced with permission from Hochberg et al. 2006).

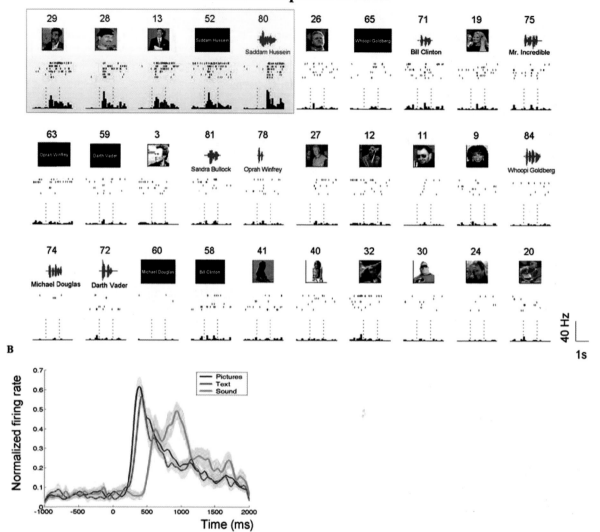

Figure 2

Selectivity and invariance. (*A*) Raster plots and peri-stimulus time histograms of a neuron in entorhinal cortex during visual presentation of pictures, text words, or auditory words. This cell responded selectively to the concept of Saddam Hussein and not to other stimuli. Regardless of low-level representation (different images of Saddam, the printed word of his name, or even the sound of his name), the neuron responded in an invariant manner. (*B*) Mean normalized firing rates of 17 medial temporal lobe neurons exhibiting invariance to low-level cues. Reproduced with permission from Quian Quiroga et al. (2009).

sleep (Wilson & McNaughton 1994), providing another parallel between animal and human physiology.

Emotion

Emotion, pain, disgust, and reward are other functional dimensions that have been explored invasively in humans. In the amygdala and hippocampus, cells have been shown to respond selectively to specific emotional expressions and the conjunction of specific facial expressions and gender during recognition (Fried et al. 1997). Additionally, induced high-gamma-power increases in the amygdala have been shown to be selective to aversive versus neutral or pleasant visual stimuli (Oya et al. 2002) and fearful versus neutral/happy faces (Sato et al. 2010). The ERP signal is also larger for fearful faces versus faces displaying happiness, disgust, or neutral emotion (Krolak-Salmon et al. 2004). In the case of subliminal priming by briefly presented text words, the evoked response in the amygdala displays significant differences ~800 ms after stimulus onset to threatening versus neutral words despite the fact that the subject's recognition is at chance (Naccache et al. 2005). Neural activity in amygdala also correlates (some neurons positively and some negatively) with level of monetary value assigned to items (Jenison et al. 2011). Taken together, these results suggest that the amygdala is sensitive to stimulus valence regardless of conscious awareness.

Another recent iEEG study reports that induced gamma band (50–150 Hz) power changes in the ventral temporal cortex, probably including regions of the amygdala, can be used to decode happy/fearful faces (Tsuchiya et al. 2008). At the neuronal level, cells in the right ventromedial prefrontal cortex have been shown to respond to aversive stimuli (pictures of aversive scenes or fearful versus happy faces) with short-latency (~120 ms) inhibition of spiking activity (Kawasaki et al. 2001).

Although the amygdala and prefrontal cortex respond to fear, evoked responses in the ventral anterior insula are stronger for faces expressing disgust (Krolak-Salmon et al. 2003). Furthermore, electrical stimulation of the posterior insula elicits painful and nonpainful somaesthetic sensations (Ostrowsky et al. 2002). In frontal cortex, neurons in the anterior cingulate cortex (ACC) have been shown to respond to noxious (thermal or mechanical) pain, although electrical stimulation did not elicit these feelings (Hutchison et al. 1999). Neurons in the ACC have also been shown to respond to words with high emotional valence (Davis et al. 2005) and to attention-demanding tasks (Davis et al. 2000). Finally, cells in this region increased firing rate during a motor response following perceived reduced reward, suggesting that this region links reward-related information with a change in motor plan (Williams et al. 2004).

Language

Substantial insight into the distribution of speech and language functions in human cortex was advanced by Penfield and colleague (Penfield & Roberts 1959) and later by Ojemann and colleagues (Ojemann et al. 1989). The latter authors point to substantial variability in language organization in the dominant hemisphere. The "language sites" in the dominant hemisphere, where electrical stimulation alters language and speech function, were also found to have characteristic changes in the event-related potentials to language stimuli (Fried et al. 1981). Ojemann and colleagues, as well as Bechtereva and colleagues, have recorded single-neuron activity acutely from awake epilepsy patients undergoing language mapping during surgery (Bechtereva et al. 1991, Ojemann et al. 1988, Ojemann & Schoenfield-McNeill 1999). Neural activity in anterior temporal lobe (mostly superior temporal gyrus) has been shown to be associated with listening to certain combinations of consonants, word length, or syllable structure (Creutzfeld et al. 1989a), whereas in the middle temporal gyrus, more neurons respond to overt speaking than to listening alone (Creutzfeld et al. 1989b). Despite hemispheric dominance to language (assessed by intracarotid sodium amobarbital procedure or electrical stimulation), laterality in neural activity during language tasks was not found (although neurons in the dominant hemisphere may respond earlier).

More recently, sequential processing of lexical, grammatical, and phonological information has been demonstrated using iEEG recorded from Broca's area (Sahin et al. 2009). In this study, subjects had to either read words out loud or inflect a base word (single/plural or past/present) according to a sentence shown earlier. In some cases (null inflection), the base word was appropriate and did not require further conversion, whereas in other cases (overt inflection), a conversion was needed. Responses in Broca's area were triphasic. The initial response ~200 ms after word onset was sensitive to word frequency, with stronger responses to infrequent words. The subsequent response ~320 ms after word onset was sensitive to task. In the reading condition, the evoked response was weaker, and in the inflection condition, it was stronger (regardless of inflection level null or overt). The final response ~450 ms after word onset was sensitive to the degree of inflection, with the strongest response to overt inflection and a weaker response to null inflection (Sahin et al. 2009). These results demonstrate that different linguistic aspects are processed at different time windows within Broca's area. The anatomical location of responsive electrodes corresponded to fMRI activations from the same patients during the same task (and activation sites obtained from healthy subjects), demonstrating spatial congruency between techniques. However, the temporal resolution of the fMRI does not allow differentiating between the fast temporal components described above.

Self-vocalization has been also examined using iEEG. During speech production, the auditory-evoked response in lateral superior temporal gyrus is suppressed, and induced responses in the high gamma band are restricted to vocalization onset. During playback of the same speech (i.e., in lack of speech production), the evoked response and power modulation in the high gamma band are more pronounced. These results suggest that during speech production, premotor regions send efference copies that modulate neural activity in auditory cortex (Greenlee et al. 2011). For single-unit activity during self-vocalization, see Creutzfeld et al. (1989b).

Listening to speech elicits auditory-evoked potentials and event-related increases in gamma (>70 Hz) band power in postero-medial Heschl's gyrus. When speech is time compressed, spiking activity and LFP power modulations follow stimulus envelope even at high compression rates where speech is unintelligible. Evoked responses, on the other hand, failed to follow stimulus envelope at high compression rates (Mukamel et al. 2010b, Nourski et al. 2009). Taken together, these results suggest that the ability of spiking activity and high gamma LFP power modulations to follow stimulus envelope is not a limiting factor in speech comprehension.

Motor Cortex and Volition

A salient attribute of primary motor and somatosensory cortex is that of an organized representation of body parts (somatotopic organization). In the precentral gyrus, electrical stimulation of neighboring regions elicits movement in adjacent body parts, forming a map in which the entire body is represented, with the feet in the medial and dorsal regions and hand and mouth in the ventral and lateral regions. In humans, such somatotopic maps in primary motor and somatosensory cortex (on the postcentral gyrus) were first described by Penfield & Boldrey (1937), who used electrical stimulation during operations on neurosurgical patients.

In the supplementary motor area (SMA), electrical stimulation evokes movement mostly on the contralateral side, with a progression from feet movement during stimulation in caudal regions and head and neck movement during stimulation of more rostral sites (Fried et al. 1991; see also Lim et al. 1994). Similarly, iEEG recordings have shown a high gamma band power increase in sensorimotor cortex during contralateral movement that is in agreement with a somatotopic organization (Crone et al. 1998a). Somatotopic organization has also been reported when examining alpha (8–13 Hz) and beta (15–25 Hz) band power decreases; however, these are more widespread and bilateral (Crone et al. 1998b). Regions exhibiting power increases in the gamma band and decreases in the low-frequency bands during hand and tongue movement have been also shown to correspond with evoked movement during electrical stimulation (Miller et al. 2007). At the level of single cells, a somatotopic organization has been demonstrated in the subthalamic nucleus (STN) of patients with Parkinson's disease (Abosch et al. 2002, Rodriguez-Oroz et al. 2001, Romanelli et al. 2004) and in sensory thalamus recording in patients with pain following spinal cord transection (Lenz et al. 1994).

Although the existence of a rough mapping of body parts in different motor regions has been demonstrated many times, it is not clear whether the organizing principle behind this is indeed anatomical proximity of body parts or rather action categories, with actions involving similar effectors (i.e., grasping or pulling with the hand) grouped in similar anatomic locations. Further studies are needed to clarify this point.

In addition to somatotopic organization, spiking activity of SMA neurons has been shown to correspond with movement speed and direction. Firing rates show an inverse relationship with speed, with lower firing rates preceding higher speed movements (Tankus et al. 2009). Neurons in SMA (and also in pre-SMA) have been shown to increase firing rate also during a preparatory delay period preceding action execution. Interestingly, SMA neurons also responded during imagery of motor movement (Amador & Fried 2004). At the population level, power increases in high-frequency LFP bands (76–100 Hz) and power decreases in low-frequency bands (8–32 Hz) have been shown during hand and tongue movement. During motor imagery, power changes in the same electrodes (but with lower amplitude) are observed. Electrical stimulation of these electrodes evoked movement in the corresponding body part, suggesting a shared representation for movement whether physically performed or imagined (Miller et al. 2010). This is similar to the overlapping representation of perceived and imagined visual stimuli in MTL structures described previously.

Although electrical stimulation of the SMA can evoke movement, in some cases it can also elicit an "urge" to move, as reported by the patients, even in lack of any overt movement (Fried et al. 1991). Indeed, a recent report demonstrates that spiking activity in SMA proper and pre-SMA not only precedes motor action but can also predict the time point at which the subject reports first feeling the urge to perform the motor act (Fried et al. 2011). Another study reports that stimulation of inferior parietal cortex evokes the feeling of an urge to move and that increasing stimulation intensity even produces the illusion that the movement was performed (even in the absence of any overt movement or EMG signal). In contrast, stimulation of the premotor regions (lateral BA 6 excluding the SMA) produced overt movement that was denied having any volitional aspect by the patients (Desmurget et al. 2009). Stimulation of the anterior part of the SMA (most probably pre-SMA) has been shown to evoke laughter, which is perceived by subjects as voluntary and is accompanied by them providing a context-dependent cognitive explanation for it (Fried et al. 1998). A similar phenomenon has been reported with fusiform and parahippocampal gyrus stimulation (Arroyo et al. 1993). Further invasive recordings will be invaluable in elucidating these fascinating phenomena.

Linking action and perception. Recent findings in macaque monkeys have demonstrated that cortical regions predominantly engaged in motor output, such as the ventral premotor cortex and rostral part of parietal cortex, also respond in lack of overt movement but during perception of similar actions. The activity of such motor neurons "reflects" perceived actions performed by others; thus, they have been termed mirror neurons. In humans, single-cell recordings demonstrate that a subset of neurons in SMA respond during action execution (facial gestures or hand grasps) and also during observation of these acts performed by others. Interestingly, such functional overlap between observation and execution of actions also has been shown in some MTL regions (parahippocampal gyrus, hippocampus, and entorhinal cortex), suggesting that not only motor cortex is sensitive to perceived actions performed by others, but sensory cortex is also sensitive to self-performed actions (Mukamel et al. 2010a). In the anterior cingulate, a similar overlap of neural firing rate during pain reception and observation of someone else receiving a painful stimulus has been shown (Hutchison et al. 1999). At the population level, iEEG studies show that motor and language regions that exhibit reduced alpha power (7.5–12.5 Hz) during finger tapping also show reduced alpha power during observation of finger tapping (Tremblay et al. 2004). Similar reduction in mu rhythm (12–20 Hz) is also seen in motor cortex for action sounds (finger clicks) (Lepage et al. 2010). In the insula, regions exhibiting enhanced ERPs during observation of disgusted facial expressions also elicit a feeling of disgust during electrical stimulation (Krolak-Salmon et al. 2003). Taken together, these studies suggest multiple overlapping neural representations for self and other, providing a link between perceived and executed actions that might facilitate communication across individuals and nonverbal learning.

INTRACRANIAL ELECTROPHYSIOLOGY AND FUNCTIONAL MRI

The use of fMRI as a neuroimaging tool has grown exponentially over the past two decades. This is mainly due to several advantages it offers over other available techniques. First, it is noninvasive and does not involve injecting radioactive tracers (as in PET). Furthermore, the discomfort to subjects during the scan is relatively minor (lying still, albeit in a confined, noisy space). Second, it allows recording signals from the entire brain (unlike EEG or MEG, which do not reach subcortical regions). Third, the spatial resolution is better than that of all other noninvasive techniques. Although these advantages are pertinent, the major drawback of the fMRI method is the indirect, and not fully understood, relationship of the measured signal with underlying neural activity (Logothetis 2008).

The BOLD fMRI signal measures changes in oxygen level that are used as a proxy to estimate underlying neural activity. The degree of coupling between this surrogate signal and different aspects of the electrophysiological signal that triggers it (namely spiking activity or local field potentials) has been a hot topic of research over the past decade. Due to the benefits of fMRI described above and its potential use as a noninvasive clinical tool, it has become increasingly important to resolve this issue of coupling between the fMRI signal and underlying electrophysiology. Invasive studies in humans provide a unique opportunity to compare the two signals in the living human brain.

Several studies have examined the degree of correspondence between the fMRI signal and electrophysiology in sensory, motor, and premotor cortex. Puce and colleagues (1995) have measured the fMRI signal while patients performed a motor task or during tactile stimulation of the hand. The sensory-motor regions of the same patients were also mapped electrophysiologically by cortical stimulation of motor cortex (to elicit hand/finger movement) and by recording evoked responses in somatosensory cortex during tactile stimulation of the hand. fMRI and electrophysiological mapping yielded anatomically congruent results demonstrating that fMRI can provide valid noninvasive localization of the hand representation of sensory and motor cortex (Puce et al. 1995). In another study, Brovelli and colleagues compared changes in gamma band LFP power in premotor cortex from one patient, with the fMRI signal from a group of healthy subjects performing similar tasks contrasting spatial attention with motor instruction/preparation. Gamma band

(60–200 Hz) power increases recorded from the patient colocalized with the fMRI activation sites, with preferential activation in the dorsal aspect of premotor cortex during the spatial attention aspect of the task and preferential activation in cingulate gyrus and SMA during the motor instruction/preparation aspect of the task (Brovelli et al. 2005).

In sensory cortex, Puce and colleagues (1997) have recorded evoked responses and fMRI activation patterns in two patients during presentation of face stimuli. The ERP N200 component and the fMRI activations were compatible and colocalized to the right fusiform gyrus (Puce et al. 1997). Compatibility between fMRI activation patterns and cortical function has also been demonstrated in the posterior temporal lobe. Schlosser and colleagues reported that electrical stimulation of cortical sites involved in language (as assessed by fMRI) produce language deficits (Schlosser et al. 1999). Other studies using a semantic versus visual discrimination task have also demonstrated spatial congruency between fMRI activations and gamma band (40–150 Hz) power increases in superior temporal gyrus and inferior frontal gyrus (Lachaux et al. 2007). Repetition effects, comparing activation to new versus old words, have also demonstrated fMRI signal colocalization with gamma band LFP power (70–190 Hz) in occipitotemporal, inferior parietal, and dorsolateral prefrontal cortex (McDonald et al. 2010). Similar colocalization was found in temporal lobe during a paired-word task (Ojemann et al. 2010).

In another study, Huettel and colleagues (2004) compared intracranially recorded ERPs from patients with the fMRI BOLD signal from healthy subjects during presentation of static checkerboards with variable duration (between 100 and 1,500 ms). In the peri-calcarine cortex, both the fMRI signal and LFP power in the gamma range (20–45 Hz) increased monotonically with stimulus duration. In the fusiform gyrus, on the other hand, the fMRI signal increased with stimulus duration whereas the LFP power did not (although this discrepancy might be due to the lower-frequency range

examined in this study compared with others) (Huettel et al. 2004).

The correlation between electrophysiology and fMRI in visual cortex has also been demonstrated using dynamic stimuli. Privman and colleagues (2007) have shown that during presentation of an audiovisual movie segment, the gamma band (30–70 Hz) LFP power fluctuations along the hierarchy of visual areas correspond with the temporal dynamics of the fMRI signal of healthy subjects in the same regions. In auditory cortex, Mukamel and colleagues (2005) recorded spiking activity and local field potentials from patients and compared them with the fMRI signals recorded from healthy subjects exposed to the same audiovisual segment. The results demonstrate a strong correlation between spiking activity, gamma band (40–130 Hz) LFP power modulation, and BOLD fMRI signal in auditory cortex during natural audiovisual stimulation.

From the studies mentioned above, the emerging picture is that in sensory (visual, auditory, and somatosensory cortex) and motor regions there seems to be anatomical congruency between gamma band LFP power changes and the fMRI BOLD signal. In auditory cortex, there is also strong coupling between the temporal dynamics of spiking activity, gamma band LFP, and the temporal dynamics of the fMRI signal. In the hippocampus, on the other hand, this does not seem to be the case. One study measured the fMRI signal in patients during a virtual navigation task and subsequently measured electrophysiological signals (unit activity and LFPs) from the same patients in a different session. The results of this study demonstrate that the BOLD fMRI signal in the parahippocampal gyrus correlates with theta-band power changes (both increases and decreases), and in the hippocampus it correlates only to increases in theta-band power. In both regions, no correlation between neural firing rate and the fMRI signal was found (Ekstrom et al. 2009).

The differences in the coupling of fMRI signal and electrophysiological signals across different brain structures (sensory versus medial temporal lobe) can be explained by different functional properties. Nir and colleagues (2007) have demonstrated that the coupling between the spiking activity and LFP/fMRI signal fluctuates in time and depends on the degree of spatial correlation among neighboring cells. When correlation between spiking activity of neighboring cells is high, the correlation between spiking activity and gamma band LFP is also high. When correlation between spiking activity of neighboring neurons is low, the correlation between spiking activity of individual neurons and gamma band LFP is also low. In both cases, the correlation between gamma band LFP and fMRI BOLD signal remained high (Nir et al. 2007). In other words, when large populations of neurons fire in a correlated pattern, a sample of the activity of few neurons is representative of the population activity and correlates with the local field and fMRI signals. When individual neurons fire in a decorrelated fashion, a sample of the activity of few neurons is not a good estimate of the population activity, and therefore correlation with the other two measures is low. Thus, the difference in the level of coupling between fMRI signal and electrophysiology in MTL structures compared with sensory regions could be due to differences in the functional (coding) properties of neurons in the two regions. Neighboring neurons in sensory regions tend to fire in a correlated fashion (e.g., columnar organization), whereas neurons in the hippocampus respond selectively to specific stimuli, with neighboring neurons responding to different stimuli, resulting in low spatial correlations and weak coupling to the fMRI signal.

Brain-Machine Interface

Recent advances in technology and science have set the stage for exploring the feasibility of restoring neurological functionality in disabled patients by creating a control interface between neural activity and computer devices. Such interfaces take one of two forms: either hardware devices providing input to the nervous system or the nervous system providing input to hardware devices. Deep-brain stimulators and cochlear implants are examples of devices that provide input to the nervous system by sending electrical impulses. Using neural activity as input for an external hardware device (such as a computer cursor, wheelchair, or robotic arm) is an example of communication in the other direction. The closure of the input-output loop creates a bidirectional interface in which the nervous system modifies the environment, which in turn modifies the nervous system, and so forth. The emerging field of brain-machine interface (BMI) provides not only potential for enhancement of function, but also precious insight into mechanisms of learning and neural plasticity, volition, and conscious control of neural activity.

The first step in designing a successful BMI is discerning the goal and degrees of freedom in the task that needs to be accomplished. For example, if the goal of the BMI is to move a computer cursor on a 2D screen, one needs two degrees of freedom (x and y planes) and to map neural signals into 2D space. On the other hand, controlling a multijoint robotic arm in 3D space involves many more degrees of freedom and requires mapping neural signals into a much higher dimensional space. The task the BMI needs to accomplish and the associated degrees of freedom determine the type of brain signals and spatio-temporal resolution that are required. The technical challenge is then to obtain these signals in a chronic and noncumbersome manner. For example, posthoc decoding of fMRI signals might be relevant for occasional communication with locked-in patients (Shoham et al. 2001) but is impractical for controlling a prosthetic limb on a daily basis. The next challenge is to develop smart algorithms that map the recorded raw signals into one specific state in the multidimensional space defined by the task. By itself, this mapping is not enough. It needs to be fast and efficient if the task requires real-time response. Finally, after mapping the raw signal to the relevant state, the specific goal-directed action associated with that state must be executed by hardware (e.g., move the computer cursor to the right). As if all these challenges were not enough, the ultimate bottleneck is whether or not a person can learn how to exert volition in order to control and switch between the relevant neural states. In other words, if neural state A is associated with action A' and neural state B is associated with action B'– then the patient needs to be able to switch between neural states A and B at will.

Facing these challenges requires a collaborative effort spanning multiple fields including neuroscience, engineering, robotics, and computer science, to name a few. In the current section, we review developments in the field, focusing on single-unit studies for controlling hardware devices. For iEEG studies, see, for example, Felton et al. (2007), Kennedy et al. (2004), Leuthardt et al. (2004), Marquez-Chin et al. (2009), Reddy et al. (2009), and Wilson et al. (2006).

Several studies now have used spiking activity recorded from motor cortex to control an external device such as a computer cursor. In a locked-in patient suffering from amyotrophic lateral sclerosis (ALS), Kennedy and colleagues (Kennedy & Bakay 1998) recorded action potentials from right motor cortex using a neurotrophic electrode (Bartels et al. 2008, Kennedy 1989). The patient was asked to do "whatever mental activity" to increase or decrease neural activity of a group of recorded neurons while visual and aural feedback regarding firing rates was provided. Results demonstrate that the patient could switch between high/low firing rates when instructed to do so, thus proving volitional control of neural activity. In another patient (tetraplegic following a brainstem stroke), volitional increases in firing rates were demonstrated and further decoded into rightward cursor movement on the screen (1D). This controlled cursor movement allowed construction of sentences by moving the cursor to letters or icons on a virtual keyboard even 17 months after implant (Kennedy et al. 2000).

In another study, a tetraplegic patient was implanted with a 96 microelectrodes array in the hand area of primary motor cortex. The patient was asked to imagine different hand movements while spiking activity from small neuronal pools (3–57 cells) were recorded. These spiking patterns were successfully decoded to allow 2D control of a computer cursor on the screen (Hochberg et al. 2006). In addition to cursor movement, the same signal sources could be used to simulate a mouse click (Kim et al. 2007). In a subsequent study, two tetraplegic patients were implanted with electrodes in the arm representation of the left precentral gyrus. Spiking activity was used to control the 2D position of a computer cursor in a center-out task where the subject had to guide a computer cursor from a central position to peripheral positions upon instruction. Reliable decoding was achieved even ~1 year after electrode implantation (Kim et al. 2008; see also Truccolo et al. 2008).

The studies described above demonstrate how neural activity can be used to simulate a computer mouse and control a cursor on a 2D screen. In another study, spiking activity recorded in left precentral gyrus was used to simulate vowel generation. The electrode was implanted in the speech motor region of a locked-in patient following a brainstem stroke, and signals were sent wirelessly to control a speech synthesizer. Speech dimensionality was reduced to three target vowel sounds (OO, A, and IY). Applying online decoding of spiking activity, hit rate reached 75% and movement time reached ~4 sec after 25 training sessions over five months (Guenther et al. 2009).

In contrast to the chronic implantations in motor cortex described above, other studies performed intraoperative recordings in patients during a procedure for DBS implant. In one study, extracellular neural activity from ensembles of neurons in thalamic motor areas or the subthalamic nucleus was recorded. Patients were instructed to vary grip force on a squeeze ball, and feedback was provided visually by cursor position along the x-axis. Offline decoding of spiking activity demonstrated that activity from a small population of cells (3–55 cells) was sufficient to successfully predict the actual grip force that was used during recording (Patil et al.

2004). In another study, recordings from premotor regions (area 6) demonstrated that small neural ensembles contain information about the intention to move as well as the direction of movement (Ojakangas et al. 2006). The results of these intraoperative studies suggest that neural activity in subcortical as well as premotor regions contains parametric information that could be used in future BMIs. Whether patients can learn to exert volition on these signals in order to control an external device is not yet clear.

Motor imagery is known to evoke activity in corresponding cortical motor regions that are active during actual movement execution. Therefore, to date, most studies recording neural activity for the purpose of controlling an external device have focused on decoding signals from motor regions under the premise that it is more intuitive for patients to learn to modulate neural activity in those regions using imagery. In a recent study, Cerf and colleagues (2010) demonstrated volitional control of neural activity in medial temporal lobe. First, the visual selectivity of different MTL neurons was assessed (e.g., cell 1 in amygdala was found to respond to the visual presentation of picture A and not picture B, while cell 2 in entorhinal cortex was found to respond to picture B and not A). These response profiles were later used to successfully "guess" in real time the picture that the patient was thinking about. Interestingly, patients learned to modulate the activity of these neurons even if they were in different regions or hemispheres (Cerf et al. 2010). These results demonstrate that volitional control of neural states is not limited to motor cortex and that neural activity in MTL can also be used for future BMI purposes.

The studies described in this section demonstrate that we have the technology and scientific knowledge to record neural activity in a chronic manner and to decode this activity in real time as long as the dimensionality of the task is low (e.g., 2D movement of a cursor or selecting vowels in a three-vowel space). In motor cortex, it seems that even after years of paralysis, neurons retain a level of functional selectivity that can be used for this purpose. Patients can learn to control neural states in frontal and medial temporal regions. The big challenge remains: reading a high-dimensional neural code and transforming it into sophisticated computer code that will allow the control of assistive external devices with multiple degrees of freedom. In facing this challenge, chronic invasive recordings play an important role, providing insights into the basic mechanisms of learning, plasticity, and the conscious control of neural activity.

CONCLUDING REMARKS AND FUTURE DIRECTIONS

Recording signals from inside the human cranium is a small yet critical part of cognitive neuroscience research. It is positioned between invasive animal neurophysiology and noninvasive human studies using other techniques such as scalp EEG, MEG, fMRI, and clinical case studies. Although conducted in patients with neurological problems and only under strictly guided clinical procedures, these recordings provide a rare opportunity to probe electrical activity of single neurons and neuronal assemblies in the brain with high spatial and temporal resolutions, in conscious human subjects who can report their experience, declare their percepts and memory, and describe their wants and plans. Emerging diagnostic and therapeutic modalities, including implantation of dense microelectrode arrays, deep brain stimulation, and brain-computer interfaces present new opportunities for such recordings. Aside from the obvious benefit to patients, these modalities may provide insights into the mechanisms of neural plasticity, perception, learning and memory, language, imagery, emotion, motor planning, volition, and conscious control of neural activity. Neurosurgeons are in a unique position to probe the living human brain and elucidate the neural mechanisms of human cognition that cannot be directly accessed by animal neurophysiology or noninvasive human physiology (Abbott 2009, Crick et al. 2004).

DISCLOSURE STATEMENT

The authors are unaware of any affiliation, funding, or financial holdings that might be perceived as affecting the objectivity of this review.

ACKNOWLEDGMENTS

The authors thank G. Kreiman for helpful comments on the manuscript and E. Behnke for help with figures. R.M. is supported by a career development award from the International Human Frontier Science Program Organization (HFSPO), and I.F. is supported by grants from the National Institute of Neurological Disorders and Stroke (NINDS), the Dana Foundation, the G. Harold & Leila Y. Mathers Charitable Foundation, and the Israeli Science Foundation.

LITERATURE CITED

Abbott A. 2009. Neuroscience: opening up brain surgery. *Nature* 461:866–68

Abosch A, Hutchison WD, Saint-Cyr JA, Dostrovsky JO, Lozano AM. 2002. Movement-related neurons of the subthalamic nucleus in patients with Parkinson disease. *J. Neurosurg.* 97:1167–72

Allison T, Ginter H, McCarthy G, Nobre AC, Puce A, et al. 1994. Face recognition in human extrastriate cortex. *J. Neurophysiol.* 71:821–25

Allison T, Puce A, Spencer DD, McCarthy G. 1999. Electrophysiological studies of human face perception. I: Potentials generated in occipitotemporal cortex by face and non-face stimuli. *Cereb. Cortex* 9:415–30

Amador N, Fried I. 2004. Single-neuron activity in the human supplementary motor area underlying preparation for action. *J. Neurosurg.* 100:250–59

Arroyo S, Lesser RP, Gordon B, Uematsu S, Hart J, et al. 1993. Mirth, laughter and gelastic seizures. *Brain* 116(Pt. 4):757–80

Bartels J, Andreasen D, Ehirim P, Mao H, Seibert S, et al. 2008. Neurotrophic electrode: method of assembly and implantation into human motor speech cortex. *J. Neurosci. Methods* 174:168–76

Bechtereva NP, Abdullaev YG, Medvedev SV. 1991. Neuronal activity in frontal speech area 44 of the human cerebral cortex during word recognition. *Neurosci. Lett.* 124:61–64

Berger H. 1929. Ueber das Elektroenkephalogramm des Menschen. *Arch. Psychiatr. Nervenkr.* 87:527–70

Bitterman Y, Mukamel R, Malach R, Fried I, Nelken I. 2008. Ultra-fine frequency tuning revealed in single neurons of human auditory cortex. *Nature* 451:197–201

Brovelli A, Lachaux JP, Kahane P, Boussaoud D. 2005. High gamma frequency oscillatory activity dissociates attention from intention in the human premotor cortex. *NeuroImage* 28:154–64

Cameron KA, Yashar S, Wilson CL, Fried I. 2001. Human hippocampal neurons predict how well word pairs will be remembered. *Neuron* 30:289–98

Cerf M, Thiruvengadam N, Mormann F, Kraskov A, Quiroga RQ, et al. 2010. On-line, voluntary control of human temporal lobe neurons. *Nature* 467:1104–8

Coleshill SG, Binnie CD, Morris RG, Alarcon G, van Emde Boas W, et al. 2004. Material-specific recognition memory deficits elicited by unilateral hippocampal electrical stimulation. *J. Neurosci.* 24:1612–16

Corkin S. 2002. What's new with the amnesic patient H.M.? *Nat. Rev. Neurosci.* 3:153–60

Creutzfeld O, Ojemann G, Lettich E. 1989a. Neural activity in the human lateral temporal lobe. I. Responses to speech. *Exp. Brain Res.* 77:451–75

Creutzfeld O, Ojemann G, Lettich E. 1989b. Neuronal activity in the human lateral temporal lobe. II. Responses to the subject's own voice. *Exp. Brain Res.* 77:476–89

Crick F, Koch C, Kreiman G, Fried I. 2004. Consciousness and neurosurgery. *Neurosurgery* 55:273–81; discussion 281–82

Crone NE, Miglioretti DL, Gordon B, Lesser RP. 1998a. Functional mapping of human sensorimotor cortex with electrocorticographic spectral analysis. II. Event-related synchronization in the gamma band. *Brain* 121(Pt. 12):2301–15

In a series of three papers, the authors used iEEG to examine extensively the representation of faces, objects, and letter strings in occipitotemporal cortex.

Crone NE, Miglioretti DL, Gordon B, Sieracki JM, Wilson MT, et al. 1998b. Functional mapping of human sensorimotor cortex with electrocorticographic spectral analysis. I. Alpha and beta event-related desynchronization. *Brain* 121(Pt. 12):2271–99

Danker JF, Anderson JR. 2010. The ghosts of brain states past: Remembering reactivates the brain regions engaged during encoding. *Psychol. Bull.* 136:87–102

Davis KD, Hutchison WD, Lozano AM, Tasker RR, Dostrovsky JO. 2000. Human anterior cingulate cortex neurons modulated by attention-demanding tasks. *J. Neurophysiol.* 83:3575–77

Davis KD, Taylor KS, Hutchison WD, Dostrovsky JO, McAndrews MP, et al. 2005. Human anterior cingulate cortex neurons encode cognitive and emotional demands. *J. Neurosci.* 25:8402–6

De Carlos JA, Borrell J. 2007. A historical reflection of the contributions of Cajal and Golgi to the foundations of neuroscience. *Brain Res. Rev.* 55:8–16

Desmurget M, Reilly KT, Richard N, Szathmari A, Mottolese C, Sirigu A. 2009. Movement intention after parietal cortex stimulation in humans. *Science* 324:811–13

Diana RA, Yonelinas AP, Ranganath C. 2007. Imaging recollection and familiarity in the medial temporal lobe: a three-component model. *Trends Cogn. Sci.* 11:379–86

Doeller CF, Barry C, Burgess N. 2010. Evidence for grid cells in a human memory network. *Nature* 463:657–61

Dronkers NF, Plaisant O, Iba-Zizen MT, Cabanis EA. 2007. Paul Broca's historic cases: high-resolution MR imaging of the brains of Leborgne and Lelong. *Brain* 130:1432–41

During MJ, Fried I, Leone P, Katz A, Spencer DD. 1994. Direct measurement of extracellular lactate in the human hippocampus during spontaneous seizures. *J. Neurochem.* 62:2356–61

During MJ, Spencer DD. 1993. Extracellular hippocampal glutamate and spontaneous seizure in the conscious human brain. *Lancet* 341:1607–10

Eichenbaum H, Cohen NJ. 2001. *From Conditioning to Conscious Recollection: Memory Systems of the Brain.* New York: Oxford Univ. Press

Ekstrom A, Suthana N, Millett D, Fried I, Bookheimer S. 2009. Correlation between BOLD fMRI and theta-band local field potentials in the human hippocampal area. *J. Neurophysiol.* 101:2668–78

Ekstrom AD, Kahana MJ, Caplan JB, Fields TA, Isham EA, et al. 2003. Cellular networks underlying human spatial navigation. *Nature* 425:184–88

Engel AK, Moll CK, Fried I, Ojemann GA. 2005. Invasive recordings from the human brain: clinical insights and beyond. *Nat. Rev. Neurosci.* 6:35–47

Engell AD, McCarthy G. 2010. Selective attention modulates face-specific induced gamma oscillations recorded from ventral occipitotemporal cortex. *J. Neurosci.* 30:8780–86

Felton EA, Wilson JA, Williams JC, Garell PC. 2007. Electrocorticographically controlled brain-computer interfaces using motor and sensory imagery in patients with temporary subdural electrode implants. Report of four cases. *J. Neurosurg.* 106:495–500

Fisch L, Privman E, Ramot M, Harel M, Nir Y, et al. 2009. Neural "ignition": enhanced activation linked to perceptual awareness in human ventral stream visual cortex. *Neuron* 64:562–74

Fried I, Cameron KA, Yashar S, Fong R, Morrow JW. 2002. Inhibitory and excitatory responses of single neurons in the human medial temporal lobe during recognition of faces and objects. *Cereb. Cortex* 12:575–84

Fried I, Katz A, McCarthy G, Sass KJ, Williamson P, et al. 1991. Functional organization of human supplementary motor cortex studied by electrical stimulation. *J. Neurosci.* 11:3656–66

Fried I, MacDonald KA, Wilson CL. 1997. Single neuron activity in human hippocampus and amygdala during recognition of faces and objects. *Neuron* 18:753–65

Fried I, Mukamel R, Kreiman G. 2011. Internally generated preactivation of single neurons in human medial frontal cortex predicts volition. *Neuron* 69:548–62

Fried I, Ojemann G, Fetz E. 1981. Language-related potentials specific to human language cortex. *Science* 212:353–56

Fried I, Wilson CL, MacDonald KA, Behnke EJ. 1998. Electric current stimulates laughter. *Nature* 391:650

Fried I, Wilson CL, Maidment NT, Engel J Jr, Behnke E, et al. 1999. Cerebral microdialysis combined with single-neuron and electroencephalographic recording in neurosurgical patients. Technical note. *J. Neurosurg.* 91:697–705

Fried I, Wilson CL, Morrow JW, Cameron KA, Behnke ED, et al. 2001. Increased dopamine release in the human amygdala during performance of cognitive tasks. *Nat. Neurosci.* 4:201–6

Gaillard R, Dehaene S, Adam C, Clemenceau S, Hasboun D, et al. 2009. Converging intracranial markers of conscious access. *PLoS Biol.* 7:e61

Gaillard R, Naccache L, Pinel P, Clemenceau S, Volle E, et al. 2006. Direct intracranial, FMRI, and lesion evidence for the causal role of left inferotemporal cortex in reading. *Neuron* 50:191–204

Gelbard-Sagiv H, Mukamel R, Harel M, Malach R, Fried I. 2008. Internally generated reactivation of single neurons in human hippocampus during free recall. *Science* 322:96–101

Gloor P. 1990. Experiential phenomena of temporal lobe epilepsy. Facts and hypotheses. *Brain* 113(Pt. 6):1673–94

Gray CM, Maldonado PE, Wilson M, McNaughton B. 1995. Tetrodes markedly improve the reliability and yield of multiple single-unit isolation from multi-unit recordings in cat striate cortex. *J. Neurosci. Methods* 63:43–54

Greenlee JD, Jackson AW, Chen F, Larson CR, Oya H, et al. 2011. Human auditory cortical activation during self-vocalization. *PLoS One* 6:e14744

Guenther FH, Brumberg JS, Wright EJ, Nieto-Castanon A, Tourville JA, et al. 2009. A wireless brain-machine interface for real-time speech synthesis. *PLoS One* 4:e8218

Hafting T, Fyhn M, Molden S, Moser MB, Moser EI. 2005. Microstructure of a spatial map in the entorhinal cortex. *Nature* 436:801–6

Hochberg LR, Serruya MD, Friehs GM, Mukand JA, Saleh M, et al. 2006. Neuronal ensemble control of prosthetic devices by a human with tetraplegia. *Nature* 442:164–71

Howard MA 3rd, Volkov IO, Abbas PJ, Damasio H, Ollendieck MC, Granner MA. 1996a. A chronic micro-electrode investigation of the tonotopic organization of human auditory cortex. *Brain Res.* 724:260–64

Howard MA 3rd, Volkov IO, Granner MA, Damasio HM, Ollendieck MC, Bakken HE. 1996b. A hybrid clinical-research depth electrode for acute and chronic in vivo microelectrode recording of human brain neurons. Technical note. *J. Neurosurg.* 84:129–32

Huettel SA, McKeown MJ, Song AW, Hart S, Spencer DD, et al. 2004. Linking hemodynamic and electro-physiological measures of brain activity: evidence from functional MRI and intracranial field potentials. *Cereb. Cortex* 14:165–73

Hutchison WD, Davis KD, Lozano AM, Tasker RR, Dostrovsky JO. 1999. Pain-related neurons in the human cingulate cortex. *Nat. Neurosci.* 2:403–5

Jacobs J, Kahana MJ, Ekstrom AD, Fried I. 2007. Brain oscillations control timing of single-neuron activity in humans. *J. Neurosci.* 27:3839–44

Jacobs J, Kahana MJ, Ekstrom AD, Mollison MV, Fried I. 2010. A sense of direction in human entorhinal cortex. *Proc. Natl. Acad. Sci. USA* 107:6487–92

Jenison RL, Rangel A, Oya H, Kawasaki H, Howard MA. 2011. Value encoding in single neurons in the human amygdala during decision making. *J. Neurosci.* 31:331–38

Kawasaki H, Kaufman O, Damasio H, Damasio AR, Granner M, et al. 2001. Single-neuron responses to emotional visual stimuli recorded in human ventral prefrontal cortex. *Nat. Neurosci.* 4:15–16

Kennedy PR. 1989. The cone electrode: a long-term electrode that records from neurites grown onto its recording surface. *J. Neurosci. Methods* 29:181–93

Kennedy PR, Bakay RA. 1998. Restoration of neural output from a paralyzed patient by a direct brain con-nection. *Neuroreport* 9:1707–11

Kennedy PR, Bakay RA, Moore MM, Adams K, Goldwaithe J. 2000. Direct control of a computer from the human central nervous system. *IEEE Trans. Rehabil. Eng.* 8:198–202

Kennedy PR, Kirby MT, Moore MM, King B, Mallory A. 2004. Computer control using human intracortical local field potentials. *IEEE Trans. Neural Syst. Rehabil. Eng.* 12:339–44

Kim S-P, Simeral JD, Hochberg LR, Donoghue JP, Friehs GM, Black MJ. 2007. *Proc. 3rd Int. IEEE EMBS Conf. Neural Eng., Kohala Coast, Hawaii*, pp. 486–89

Kim SP, Simeral JD, Hochberg LR, Donoghue JP, Black MJ. 2008. Neural control of computer cursor velocity by decoding motor cortical spiking activity in humans with tetraplegia. *J. Neural. Eng.* 5:455–76

Kraskov A, Quiroga RQ, Reddy L, Fried I, Koch C. 2007. Local field potentials and spikes in the human medial temporal lobe are selective to image category. *J. Cogn. Neurosci.* 19:479–92

This unique case study combined iEEG recordings, electrical stimulation, pre- and post-lesion functional MRI to demonstrate a link between reading ability and neural activity in left inferotemporal cortex.

This study provides first direct evidence at single-cell level that in MTL the same neurons that are active during sensory perception (encoding) are reactivated during memory recall (in the absence of any sensory stimulation).

The first report of a successful chronic brain-machine interface in a tetraplegic patient.

Kreiman G, Fried I, Koch C. 2002. Single-neuron correlates of subjective vision in the human medial temporal lobe. *Proc. Natl. Acad. Sci. USA* 99:8378–83

Kreiman G, Koch C, Fried I. 2000a. Category-specific visual responses of single neurons in the human medial temporal lobe. *Nat. Neurosci.* 3:946–53

Kreiman G, Koch C, Fried I. 2000b. Imagery neurons in the human brain. *Nature* **408:357–61**

Krolak-Salmon P, Henaff MA, Isnard J, Tallon-Baudry C, Guenot M, et al. 2003. An attention modulated response to disgust in human ventral anterior insula. *Ann. Neurol.* 53:446–53

Krolak-Salmon P, Henaff MA, Vighetto A, Bertrand O, Mauguiere F. 2004. Early amygdala reaction to fear spreading in occipital, temporal, and frontal cortex: a depth electrode ERP study in human. *Neuron* 42:665–76

Lachaux JP, Fonlupt P, Kahane P, Minotti L, Hoffmann D, et al. 2007. Relationship between task-related gamma oscillations and BOLD signal: new insights from combined fMRI and intracranial EEG. *Hum. Brain Mapp.* 28:1368–75

Lacruz ME, Valentin A, Seoane JJ, Morris RG, Selway RP, Alarcon G. 2010. Single pulse electrical stimulation of the hippocampus is sufficient to impair human episodic memory. *Neuroscience* 170:623–32

Lenz FA, Kwan HC, Martin R, Tasker R, Richardson RT, Dostrovsky JO. 1994. Characteristics of somatotopic organization and spontaneous neuronal activity in the region of the thalamic principal sensory nucleus in patients with spinal cord transection. *J. Neurophysiol.* 72:1570–87

Lepage JF, Tremblay S, Nguyen DK, Champoux F, Lassonde M, Theoret H. 2010. Action related sounds induce early and late modulations of motor cortex activity. *Neuroreport* 21:250–53

Leuthardt EC, Schalk G, Wolpaw JR, Ojemann JG, Moran DW. 2004. A brain-computer interface using electrocorticographic signals in humans. *J. Neural. Eng.* 1:63–71

Lim SH, Dinner DS, Pillay PK, Luders H, Morris HH, et al. 1994. Functional anatomy of the human supplementary sensorimotor area: results of extraoperative electrical stimulation. *Electroencephalogr. Clin. Neurophysiol.* 91:179–93

Logothetis N. 2008. What we can do and what we cannot do with fMRI. *Nature* 453:869–78

Loukas M, Pennell C, Tubbs RS, Cohen-Gadol AA. 2011. Korbinian Brodmann (1868–1918) and his contribution to mapping the cerebral cortex. *Neurosurgery* 68:6–11

Marquez-Chin C, Popovic MR, Cameron T, Lozano AM, Chen R. 2009. Control of a neuroprosthesis for grasping using off-line classification of electrocorticographic signals: case study. *Spinal Cord* 47:802–8

McCarthy G, Puce A, Belger A, Allison T. 1999. Electrophysiological studies of human face perception. II: Response properties of face-specific potentials generated in occipitotemporal cortex. *Cereb. Cortex* 9:431–44

McDonald CR, Thesen T, Carlson C, Blumberg M, Girard HM, et al. 2010. Multimodal imaging of repetition priming: using fMRI, MEG, and intracranial EEG to reveal spatiotemporal profiles of word processing. *NeuroImage* 53:707–17

Miller KJ, Leuthardt EC, Schalk G, Rao RP, Anderson NR, et al. 2007. Spectral changes in cortical surface potentials during motor movement. *J. Neurosci.* 27:2424–32

Miller KJ, Schalk G, Fetz EE, den Nijs M, Ojemann JG, Rao RP. 2010. Cortical activity during motor execution, motor imagery, and imagery-based online feedback. *Proc. Natl. Acad. Sci. USA* 107:4430–35

Mormann F, Fell J, Axmacher N, Weber B, Lehnertz K, et al. 2005. Phase/amplitude reset and theta-gamma interaction in the human medial temporal lobe during a continuous word recognition memory task. *Hippocampus* 15:890–900

Mormann F, Kornblith S, Quiroga RQ, Kraskov A, Cerf M, et al. 2008. Latency and selectivity of single neurons indicate hierarchical processing in the human medial temporal lobe. *J. Neurosci.* 28:8865–72

Mukamel R, Ekstrom A, Kaplan J, Iacoboni M, Fried I. 2010a. Single-neuron responses in humans during execution and observation of actions. *Curr. Biol.* 20:1–7

Mukamel R, Gelbard H, Arieli A, Hasson U, Fried I, Malach R. 2005. Coupling between neuronal firing, field potentials, and FMRI in human auditory cortex. *Science* **309:951–54**

Mukamel R, Nir Y, Harel M, Arieli A, Malach R, Fried I. 2010b. Invariance of firing rate and field potential dynamics to increased stimulus speed in human auditory cortex. *Hum. Brain Mapp.* 32:1181–93

Murphey DK, Maunsell JH, Beauchamp MS, Yoshor D. 2009. Perceiving electrical stimulation of identified human visual areas. *Proc. Natl. Acad. Sci. USA* 106:5389–93

Demonstrates that individual cells in MTL that respond during visual presentation of a specific image respond also when subjects close their eyes and imagine that particular image.

Demonstrates that in auditory cortex of awake humans, the fMRI BOLD activity correlates with spiking activity and gamma-band LFP.

Murphey DK, Yoshor D, Beauchamp MS. 2008. Perception matches selectivity in the human anterior color center. *Curr. Biol.* 18:216–20

Naccache L, Gaillard R, Adam C, Hasboun D, Clemenceau S, et al. 2005. A direct intracranial record of emotions evoked by subliminal words. *Proc. Natl. Acad. Sci. USA* 102:7713–17

Nir Y, Fisch L, Mukamel R, Gelbard-Sagiv H, Arieli A, et al. 2007. Coupling between neuronal firing rate, gamma LFP, and BOLD fMRI is related to interneuronal correlations. *Curr. Biol.* 17:1275–85

Nobre AC, Allison T, McCarthy G. 1994. Word recognition in the human inferior temporal lobe. *Nature* 372:260–63

Nordhausen CT, Maynard EM, Normann RA. 1996. Single unit recording capabilities of a 100 microelectrode array. *Brain Res.* 726:129–40

Nourski KV, Reale RA, Oya H, Kawasaki H, Kovach CK, et al. 2009. Temporal envelope of time-compressed speech represented in the human auditory cortex. *J. Neurosci.* 29:15564–74

Ojakangas CL, Shaikhouni A, Friehs GM, Caplan AH, Serruya MD, et al. 2006. Decoding movement intent from human premotor cortex neurons for neural prosthetic applications. *J. Clin. Neurophysiol.* 23:577–84

Ojemann G. 2010. Cognitive mapping through electrophysiology. *Epilepsia* 51(Suppl. 1):72–75

Ojemann G, Ojemann J, Lettich E, Berger M. 1989. Cortical language localization in left, dominant hemisphere: an electrical stimulation mapping investigation in 117 patients. *J. Neurosurg.* 71:316–26

Ojemann GA, Corina DP, Corrigan N, Schoenfield-McNeill J, Poliakov A, et al. 2010. Neuronal correlates of functional magnetic resonance imaging in human temporal cortex. *Brain* 133:46–59

Ojemann GA, Creutzfeldt O, Lettich E, Haglund MM. 1988. Neuronal activity in human lateral temporal cortex related to short-term verbal memory, naming and reading. *Brain* 111(Pt. 6):1383–403

Ojemann GA, Schoenfield-McNeill J. 1999. Activity of neurons in human temporal cortex during identification and memory for names and words. *J. Neurosci.* 19:5674–82

Ojemann GA, Schoenfield-McNeill J, Corina DP. 2002. Anatomic subdivisions in human temporal cortical neuronal activity related to recent verbal memory. *Nat. Neurosci.* 5:64–71

O'Keefe J, Dostrovsky J. 1971. The hippocampus as a spatial map. Preliminary evidence from unit activity in the freely-moving rat. *Brain Res.* 34:171–75

Ostrowsky K, Magnin M, Ryvlin P, Isnard J, Guenot M, Mauguiere F. 2002. Representation of pain and somatic sensation in the human insula: a study of responses to direct electrical cortical stimulation. *Cereb. Cortex* 12:376–85

Oya H, Kawasaki H, Howard MA 3rd, Adolphs R. 2002. Electrophysiological responses in the human amygdala discriminate emotion categories of complex visual stimuli. *J. Neurosci.* 22:9502–12

Patil PG, Carmena JM, Nicolelis MA, Turner DA. 2004. Ensemble recordings of human subcortical neurons as a source of motor control signals for a brain-machine interface. *Neurosurgery* 55:27–35; discussion 35–38

Paz R, Gelbard-Sagiv H, Mukamel R, Harel M, Malach R, Fried I. 2010. A neural substrate in the human hippocampus for linking successive events. *Proc. Natl. Acad. Sci. USA* 107:6046–51

Pedreira C, Mormann F, Kraskov A, Cerf M, Fried I, et al. 2009. Responses of human medial temporal lobe neurons are modulated by stimulus repetition. *J. Neurophysiol.* 103:97–107

Penfield W. 1950. *The Cerebral Cortex of Man: A Clinical Study of Localization of Function.* New York: Macmillan

Penfield W, Boldrey E. 1937. Somatic motor and sensory representation in the cerebral cortex of man as studied by electrical stimulation. *Brain* 60:389–443

Penfield W, Jasper HH. 1954. *Epilepsy and the Functional Anatomy of the Human Brain.* Boston: Little Brown

Penfield W, Roberts L. 1959. *Speech and Brain Mechanisms.* Princeton, NJ: Princeton Univ. Press. 300 pp.

Pourtois G, Peelen MV, Spinelli L, Seeck M, Vuilleumier P. 2007. Direct intracranial recording of body-selective responses in human extrastriate visual cortex. *Neuropsychologia* 45:2621–25

Privman E, Nir Y, Kramer U, Kipervasser S, Andelman F, et al. 2007. Enhanced category tuning revealed by intracranial electroencephalograms in high-order human visual areas. *J. Neurosci.* 27:6234–42

Puce A, Allison T, McCarthy G. 1999. Electrophysiological studies of human face perception. III: Effects of top-down processing on face-specific potentials. *Cereb. Cortex* 9:445–58

Puce A, Allison T, Spencer SS, Spencer DD, McCarthy G. 1997. Comparison of cortical activation evoked by faces measured by intracranial field potentials and functional MRI: two case studies. *Hum. Brain Mapp.* 5:298–305

Puce A, Constable RT, Luby ML, McCarthy G, Nobre AC, et al. 1995. Functional magnetic resonance imaging of sensory and motor cortex: comparison with electrophysiological localization. *J. Neurosurg.* 83:262–70

Quian Quiroga R, Kraskov A, Koch C, Fried I. 2009. Explicit encoding of multimodal percepts by single neurons in the human brain. *Curr. Biol.* 19:1308–13

Quian Quiroga R, Kreiman G, Koch C, Fried I. 2008. Sparse but not "grandmother-cell" coding in the medial temporal lobe. *Trends Cogn. Sci.* 12:87–91

Quiroga RQ, Mukamel R, Isham EA, Malach R, Fried I. 2008. Human single-neuron responses at the threshold of conscious recognition. *Proc. Natl. Acad. Sci. USA* 105:3599–604

Quiroga RQ, Reddy L, Kreiman G, Koch C, Fried I. 2005. Invariant visual representation by single neurons in the human brain. *Nature* 435:1102–7

Reddy CG, Reddy GG, Kawasaki H, Oya H, Miller LE, Howard MA 3rd. 2009. Decoding movement-related cortical potentials from electrocorticography. *Neurosurg. Focus* 27:E11

Reddy L, Quiroga RQ, Wilken P, Koch C, Fried I. 2006. A single-neuron correlate of change detection and change blindness in the human medial temporal lobe. *Curr. Biol.* 16:2066–72

Rees G, Kreiman G, Koch C. 2002. Neural correlates of consciousness in humans. *Nat. Rev. Neurosci.* 3:261–70

Rodriguez-Oroz MC, Rodriguez M, Guridi J, Mewes K, Chockkman V, et al. 2001. The subthalamic nucleus in Parkinson's disease: somatotopic organization and physiological characteristics. *Brain* 124:1777–90

Romanelli P, Heit G, Hill BC, Kraus A, Hastie T, Bronte-Stewart HM. 2004. Microelectrode recording revealing a somatotopic body map in the subthalamic nucleus in humans with Parkinson disease. *J. Neurosurg.* 100:611–18

Rutishauser U, Mamelak AN, Schuman EM. 2006. Single-trial learning of novel stimuli by individual neurons of the human hippocampus-amygdala complex. *Neuron* 49:805–13

Rutishauser U, Ross IB, Mamelak AN, Schuman EM. 2010. Human memory strength is predicted by theta-frequency phase-locking of single neurons. *Nature* 464:903–7

Rutishauser U, Schuman EM, Mamelak AN. 2008. Activity of human hippocampal and amygdala neurons during retrieval of declarative memories. *Proc. Natl. Acad. Sci. USA* 105:329–34

Sahin NT, Pinker S, Cash SS, Schomer D, Halgren E. 2009. Sequential processing of lexical, grammatical, and phonological information within Broca's area. *Science* 326:445–49

Sato W, Kochiyama T, Uono S, Matsuda K, Usui K, et al. 2010. Rapid amygdala gamma oscillations in response to fearful facial expressions. *Neuropsychologia* 49:612–17

Schacter DL. 1996. *Searching for Memory: The Brain, the Mind, and the Past.* New York: Basic Books

Schlosser MJ, Luby M, Spencer DD, Awad IA, McCarthy G. 1999. Comparative localization of auditory comprehension by using functional magnetic resonance imaging and cortical stimulation. *J. Neurosurg.* 91:626–35

Seeck M, Michel CM, Blanke O, Thut G, Landis T, Schomer DL. 2001. Intracranial neurophysiological correlates related to the processing of faces. *Epilepsy Behav.* 2:545–57

Shoham S, Halgren E, Maynard EM, Normann RA. 2001. Motor-cortical activity in tetraplegics. *Nature* 413:793

Squire LR. 2004. Memory systems of the brain: a brief history and current perspective. *Neurobiol. Learn. Mem.* 82:171–77

Squire LR, Stark CE, Clark RE. 2004. The medial temporal lobe. *Annu. Rev. Neurosci.* 27:279–306

Tankus A, Yeshurun Y, Flash T, Fried I. 2009. Encoding of speed and direction of movement in the human supplementary motor area. *J. Neurosurg.* 110:1304–16

Thomson AD, Cook CC, Guerrini I, Sheedy D, Harper C, Marshall EJ. 2008. Wernicke's encephalopathy revisited. Translation of the case history section of the original manuscript by Carl Wernicke "Lehrbuch der Gehirnkrankheiten fur Aerzte und Studirende" (1881) with a commentary. *Alcohol Alcohol.* 43:174–79

Tremblay C, Robert M, Pascual-Leone A, Lepore F, Nguyen DK, et al. 2004. Action observation and execution: intracranial recordings in a human subject. *Neurology* 63:937–38

Truccolo W, Friehs GM, Donoghue JP, Hochberg LR. 2008. Primary motor cortex tuning to intended movement kinematics in humans with tetraplegia. *J. Neurosci.* 28:1163–78

Tsuchiya N, Kawasaki H, Oya H, Howard MA 3rd, Adolphs R. 2008. Decoding face information in time, frequency and space from direct intracranial recordings of the human brain. *PLoS One* 3:e3892

Demonstrates the high level of abstraction of MTL neurons. Cells in these regions (mostly hippocampus) responded to specific concepts (a person or a landmark) regardless of low-level features.

This study demonstrates that the degree of phase locking between spiking activity in hippocampus and amygdala and slow oscillations (3–8 Hz) in the LFP signal are a marker of subsequent memory performance.

Tulving E, Schacter DL. 1990. Priming and human memory systems. *Science* 247:301–6

Ulbert I, Halgren E, Heit G, Karmos G. 2001. Multiple microelectrode-recording system for human intracortical applications. *J. Neurosci. Methods* 106:69–79

Vignal JP, Maillard L, McGonigal A, Chauvel P. 2007. The dreamy state: hallucinations of autobiographic memory evoked by temporal lobe stimulations and seizures. *Brain* 130:88–99

Viventi J, Blanco J, Litt B. 2010. *32nd Annu. Int. Conf. IEEE EMBS, Buenos Aires, Argentina*, pp. 3825–26

Williams ZM, Bush G, Rauch SL, Cosgrove GR, Eskandar EN. 2004. Human anterior cingulate neurons and the integration of monetary reward with motor responses. *Nat. Neurosci.* 7:1370–75

Wilson CL, Isokawa M, Babb TL, Crandall PH. 1990. Functional connections in the human temporal lobe. I. Analysis of limbic system pathways using neuronal responses evoked by electrical stimulation. *Exp. Brain Res.* 82:279–92

Wilson JA, Felton EA, Garell PC, Schalk G, Williams JC. 2006. ECoG factors underlying multimodal control of a brain-computer interface. *IEEE Trans. Neural Syst. Rehabil. Eng.* 14:246–50

Wilson MA, McNaughton BL. 1994. Reactivation of hippocampal ensemble memories during sleep. *Science* 265:676–79

Yonelinas AP, Otten LJ, Shaw KN, Rugg MD. 2005. Separating the brain regions involved in recollection and familiarity in recognition memory. *J. Neurosci.* 25:3002–8

Yoshor D, Bosking WH, Ghose GM, Maunsell JH. 2007a. Receptive fields in human visual cortex mapped with surface electrodes. *Cereb. Cortex* 17:2293–302

Yoshor D, Ghose GM, Bosking WH, Sun P, Maunsell JH. 2007b. Spatial attention does not strongly modulate neuronal responses in early human visual cortex. *J. Neurosci.* 27:13205–9

Sources of Method Bias in Social Science Research and Recommendations on How to Control It

Philip M. Podsakoff,[1] Scott B. MacKenzie,[2] and Nathan P. Podsakoff[3]

[1] Department of Management, Kelley School of Business, Indiana University, Bloomington, Indiana 47405; email: podsakof@indiana.edu

[2] Department of Marketing, Kelley School of Business, Indiana University, Bloomington, Indiana 47405; email: mackenz@indiana.edu

[3] Department of Management and Organizations, Eller College of Management, University of Arizona, Tucson, Arizona 85721; email: podsakof@email.arizona.edu

Annu. Rev. Psychol. 2012. 63:539–69

First published online as a Review in Advance on August 11, 2011

The *Annual Review of Psychology* is online at psych.annualreviews.org

This article's doi: 10.1146/annurev-psych-120710-100452

Keywords

common method variance, response style biases, marker variable technique, instrumental variable technique, unmeasured latent variable technique

Abstract

Despite the concern that has been expressed about potential method biases, and the pervasiveness of research settings with the potential to produce them, there is disagreement about whether they really are a problem for researchers in the behavioral sciences. Therefore, the purpose of this review is to explore the current state of knowledge about method biases. First, we explore the meaning of the terms "method" and "method bias" and then we examine whether method biases influence all measures equally. Next, we review the evidence of the effects that method biases have on individual measures and on the covariation between different constructs. Following this, we evaluate the procedural and statistical remedies that have been used to control method biases and provide recommendations for minimizing method bias.

Contents

INTRODUCTION

Over 50 years ago, Campbell & Fiske (1959) voiced their concerns about the biasing effects that methods of measurement may have on the validity of measures:

> In any given psychological measuring device, there are certain features or stimuli introduced specifically to represent the trait (construct) that it is intended to measure. There are other features which are characteristic of the method being employed, features which could also be present in efforts to measure quite different

traits (constructs). The test, or rating scale, or other device, almost inevitably elicits systematic variance due to both groups of features. To the extent that irrelevant method variance contributes to the scores obtained, these scores are invalid. (Campbell & Fiske 1959, p. 84; words in parentheses added by present authors)

In the years since, a number of researchers have discussed a related problem—the biasing effects that measuring two or more constructs with the same method may have on estimates of the relationships between them. The major concern with measuring different constructs with the same method is the danger that at least some of the observed covariation between them may be due to the fact that they share the same method of measurement.

This concern with method bias is potentially important because the situations in which it is likely to be a problem are quite common. For example, Bodner (2006) reviewed the literature in six areas of psychology and found that most studies (76%) involved only a single measurement method, and of the studies that involved human subjects and adequately explained the measurement procedures, 33% involved self-report questionnaires as the sole measurement method. Similarly, Woszczynski & Whitman (2004) reviewed the studies reported in the top management information systems journals from 1996 to 2000 and found that 27% of the 428 articles published in this literature during this time period used a survey with self-reports as the predominant method of data gathering.

Unfortunately, despite the concern that has been expressed about method bias, and the pervasiveness of research settings with the potential to produce it, there is little agreement about whether it really is a problem for researchers. For example, although many authors believe that method bias is an important problem that needs to be controlled (e.g., Campbell & Fiske 1959; Cote & Buckley 1987, 1988; Doty & Glick 1998; Podsakoff et al. 2003; Podsakoff & Organ 1986; Sharma et al. 2009; Williams & Anderson 1994; Williams et al. 1989, 2010), some claim that it is a myth or urban legend (e.g., Chen & Spector 1991; Spector 1987, 2006; Spector & Brannick 2009).

Within the context of the above discussion, the purpose of this review is to explore the current state of knowledge about method biases. The first issue we explore is the question of what is method bias. It is obvious from reading the literature that scholars have different interpretations of what is meant by this term (e.g., Campbell & Fiske 1959, Edwards 2008, Lance et al. 2009, Messick 1991). In addition, there is a difference of opinion about what constitutes a bias (Cote & Buckley 1987, Spector & Brannick 2009, Williams et al. 1989). Is it the effect of method factors on the validity and reliability of individual measures, the covariation between measures of different constructs, or both? Finally, scholars also disagree about whether method bias affects all measures equally or some measures more than others (Lindell & Whitney 2001, Williams et al. 2010). Differences in these assumptions about the nature of method bias influence the way in which researchers try to control for it and the conclusions they reach regarding its effects.

The second issue we address is what the empirical evidence indicates about the extent to which method bias is a problem in behavioral research. For the purposes of this analysis, we examine the evidence of the effects of method factors on the reliability and validity of individual measures and the effects of method factors on the covariation between measures of different constructs.

The third issue we discuss is how researchers can control method biases. We start by reviewing the literature on the procedural and statistical remedies that researchers commonly use to control method biases, and we then discuss the strengths and limitations of each of these remedies for dealing with specific types of method biases.

In the final section, we address two related issues: (*a*) when method biases are likely to be a major problem in a study and (*b*) what researchers can do to mitigate their effects. We then conclude with a brief summary of the state

of our knowledge about method biases in the behavioral sciences.

WHAT IS METHOD BIAS AND WHY IS IT A PROBLEM?

What Is a Method?

It is obvious from reading the literature that there are differences in how scholars define the term method. The term has traditionally been defined broadly to include several key aspects of the measurement process (Campbell & Fiske 1959, Fiske 1982). For example, according to Fiske (1982, p. 82),

> the term *method* encompasses potential influences at several levels of abstraction. Taking a paper-and-pencil instrument as an example, these influences include the content of the items, the response format, the general instructions and other features of the test-task as a whole, the characteristics of the examiner, other features of the total setting, and the reason why the subject is taking the test. Two units that have any one of these elements in common can show convergence due to that source, so the relationship obtained between them cannot safely be interpreted as associated with the traits or constructs in those units. For any single investigation, the only certain protection against this threat to validity is units using completely independent methods.

This is consistent with the views of most researchers (Bagozzi 1984, Baumgartner & Steenkamp 2001, Johnson et al. 2011, Messick 1991, Podsakoff et al. 2003, Siemsen et al. 2010, Weijters et al. 2010c), including Edwards (2008, p. 476), who argues that method biases arise from "response tendencies that raters apply across measures, similarities in item structure or wording that induce similar responses, the proximity of items in an instrument, and similarities in the medium, timing, or location in which measures are collected."

However, others have argued for a narrower definition (e.g., Lance et al. 2009, Sechrest et al. 2000). For example, Lance et al. (2009, p. 351) argue that the term method should be restricted to those measurement facets that represent "alternative approaches to assigning numbers to observations to represent [an individual's] standing on latent constructs." Based on this definition, Lance et al. (2009, 2010) include similarities in item content, structure, or format that induce similar responses and explicitly exclude effects due to response tendencies that raters apply across measures, occasions of measurement, and different situations in which measurement may occur. In addition, based on this definition we presume this also excludes item proximity and item order effects because these are not "alternative approaches to assigning numbers to observations."

For our part, we prefer the broader definition of method because regardless of whether one considers various rater response styles, item characteristics, and aspects of the measurement context to be "method" factors, they are all sources of systematic measurement error that threaten the validity of a study's findings. Indeed, if they are ignored they can threaten construct validity, distort the dimensional structure of psychological domains, and obscure relationships between constructs/traits (Messick 1991). Therefore, in the remainder of this review we adopt this broader conceptualization of the term method. In so doing we acknowledge Campbell & Fiske's (1959, p. 85) observation that, "The distinction between trait and method is of course relative to the test constructor's intent. What is an unwanted response set for one tester may be a trait for another who wishes to measure acquiescence, willingness to take an extreme stand, or tendency to attribute socially desirable attributes to oneself."

What Is Method Bias?

There is also disagreement about what constitutes a bias. Two detrimental effects produced by method factors have been recognized in the literature (e.g., Cote & Buckley 1987, 1988; Doty & Glick 1998; Podsakoff et al. 2003; Williams et al. 2010). The first detrimental effect is that method factors can bias estimates of construct reliability and validity (e.g., Bagozzi 1984, Baumgartner & Steenkamp 2001, Cote & Buckley 1987, Williams et al. 2010). A latent construct captures systematic variance among its measures. If systematic method variance is not controlled, this variance will be lumped together with systematic trait variance in the construct. This is a problem because it can lead to erroneous perceptions about the adequacy of a scale's reliability and convergent validity (Baumgartner & Steenkamp 2001, Lance in Brannick et al. 2010, Williams et al. 2010), and it can lead to underestimates of corrected correlations in meta-analyses because the reliability estimates will be artificially inflated due to method variance (Le et al. 2009).

In addition, Bollen (1989) demonstrated that in multiple regression models, uncontrolled systematic or random measurement error in a predictor can also bias estimates of the effects of other error-free predictors on a criterion variable even if this systematic measurement error is not shared with the criterion variable or with any of the other predictors. The direction of the bias will depend on the magnitude and sign of the relationships (a) between the imperfect predictor and the criterion variable and (b) between the imperfect predictor and the other predictors. Thus, although it is true that systematic measurement error in a predictor that is not shared with a criterion variable will tend to attenuate estimates of the effect of the predictor on the criterion variable (Spector & Brannick 2009), it can also bias estimates of the effects of other correlated predictors on the criterion variable.

The second important detrimental effect of uncontrolled method factors is that it can bias parameter estimates of the relationship between two different constructs. Several researchers (e.g., Baumgartner & Steenkamp 2001, Cote & Buckley 1988, Podsakoff et al. 2003, Siemsen et al. 2010) have demonstrated that method bias can inflate, deflate, or have no effect on estimates of the relationship between two constructs. Depending upon whether the method bias inflates or deflates the relationship, this is a serious problem because it can (*a*) affect hypothesis tests and lead to type I or type II errors, (*b*) lead to incorrect perceptions about how much variance is accounted for in a criterion construct, and (*c*) enhance or diminish the nomological or discriminant validity of a scale. Note, however, that Siemsen et al. (2010) and Evans (1985) have shown that although interaction and quadratic effects can be severely deflated by method bias, they cannot be artifacts of it.

It is for these reasons that, even though Spector & Brannick (2009, p. 348) argue that the effects of method factors on item validity and reliability are unimportant because they "do not speak to the issue of CMV and how it might inflate correlations," the overwhelming consensus among researchers is that both forms of bias are important and should be controlled whenever possible (Bagozzi & Yi 1990, Baumgartner & Steenkamp 2001, Cote & Buckley 1987, Doty & Glick 1998, Podsakoff et al. 2003, Siemsen et al. 2010, Williams et al. 2010).

Does Method Bias Affect All Measures Equally?

Finally, there is also some disagreement about how method bias affects the measures in a given study. Some researchers assume that if a method factor has any effect, it affects all measures equally. For example, researchers who use the correlational marker variable technique for controlling method bias (see table 1 in Williams et al. 2010) implicitly assume that a method factor has an equal effect on all measures because this technique is based on the assumption that, "the observed variables are contaminated by a single unmeasured factor that has an equal effect on all of them" (Lindell & Whitney 2001, p. 114). However, other researchers argue that method factors may have unequal effects on different measures. This is important because if equal effects are wrongly assumed when attempting to statistically control (or test) for method bias, the result will be the overestimation of the effect of method factors in some

cases and the underestimation of them in others. Empirical tests of whether method factor loadings are equal or unequal have generally found support for the assumption of unequal effects of method bias (Rafferty & Griffin 2004, 2006; Williams et al. 2010). Similarly, Baumgartner & Steenkamp (2001) found that the proportion of variance in measures of different types of constructs that is attributable to specific response styles ranged from 0% to 29%. Finally, Cote & Buckley's (1987) meta-analytic estimates of the proportion of method variance in measures of different types of constructs ranged from 22% to 41%. Thus, the weight of the evidence suggests that method factors are likely to have unequal effects on different measures—whether they are different measures of the same construct (as in Rafferty & Griffin 2004, 2006; Williams et al. 2010) or measures of different constructs (as in Baumgartner & Steenkamp 2001, Cote & Buckley 1987).

EMPIRICAL EVIDENCE OF THE EFFECTS OF METHOD BIASES

Effects of General Method Bias on Item Reliability or Validity

Evidence of the impact of method biases on item validity and reliability comes from a number of meta-analyses of the results of confirmatory factor analyses of multi-trait multi-method (MTMM) matrices (e.g., Buckley et al. 1990, Cote & Buckley 1987, Doty & Glick 1998, Lance et al. 2010, Williams et al. 1989). These studies used previously published MTMM matrices to estimate confirmatory factor models with multiple trait and method factors. Typically, the correlations among the trait factors and among the method factors, but not between the trait and method factors, were estimated. A summary of these studies is provided in **Table 1**. Taken together, they indicate that 18% to 32% of the total variance in the items used in these studies was due to method factors.

Scherpenzeel & Saris (1997) went one step further by (*a*) estimating confirmatory factor models for 50 MTMM matrices involving

Table 1 Summary of studies using multi-trait multi-method matrices to partition trait and method variance in empirical relationships

Study	Sample	Variance attributable to trait factors	Variance attributable to method factors	Variance attributable to error
Cote & Buckley (1987)	70 matrices examining a wide variety of constructs	42%	26%	32%
Williams et al. (1989)[a]	11 matrices involving perceptions of jobs and work environments	48%	25%	21%
Buckley et al. (1990)	61 matrices examining a variety of constructs	42%	22%	36%
Doty & Glick (1998)	28 matrices	46%	32%	22%
Lance et al. (2010)	18 matrices	40%	18%	42%

[a]Values reported for variance estimates represent medians.

601 measures, (b) calculating the validity and reliability for each item, and then (c) examining the effect of 15 specific method factors on these item validities. Among the most important predictors of the item validities and reliabilities were the type of construct being measured, form and length of the response scale, social desirability of the item, mode of data collection, position of item in a battery of questions with the same instructions and response scale, and type of information requested (judgment, frequency, agree-disagree). Another study that examined the effect of specific types of method factors on item validity and reliability is that of Baumgartner & Steenkamp (2001). Across 60 measures of 11 constructs, they found that an average of 8% (ranging from 0% to 29%) of the variance in an item was due to five specific response sets/styles.

However, there are some potential criticisms of this MTMM-based evidence of method bias. One is that the estimates of the proportion of item variance due to method provided by these studies are not completely independent because the MTMM matrices they analyze overlap to some extent. However, the overlap is relatively small (about 13%). Another criticism is that trait and method variance becomes confounded as the correlations among traits and among methods increase. Specifically, Bagozzi (1993, p. 66) noted that when the correlations among the traits and

among the methods are high, "the correlations among the method factors may represent the convergence of [a] general trait factor across methods, rather than true relationships among the methods." Whether the average method correlation of 0.47 found in the studies cited is large enough to support this interpretation is a matter of judgment. A third criticism is that serious problems resulting in nonconvergence and/or improper estimates can arise when attempting to fit a confirmatory factor model to MTMM data (Brannick & Spector 1990). However, the results of the studies reported in **Table 1** were based only on solutions that converged and had proper estimates. Thus, although these criticisms are important, we believe the MTMM-based evidence supports the general conclusion that method biases have an impact on individual item validities and reliabilities.

Effects of General Method Bias on the Covariation Between Constructs

Estimates based on MTMM meta-analytic studies. The results of MTMM studies can also be used to obtain estimates of the average effects of method biases on the correlation between different traits (or constructs). Assuming that trait, method, and random error interactions do not exist, Cote & Buckley (1988) show that the observed correlation between two variables x and y (R_{xy}) is equal to

$$R_{x,y} = (\text{true}R_{ti,tj}\sqrt{t_x}\sqrt{t_y})$$
$$+ (\text{true}R_{mk,ml}\sqrt{m_x}\sqrt{m_y}) \quad (1)$$

where true $R_{ti,tj}$ = average correlation between trait i and trait j; t_x = percent of trait variance in measure x; t_y = percent of trait variance in measure y; true $R_{mk,ml}$ = average correlation between method k and method l; m_x = percent of method variance in measure x; and m_y = percent of method variance in measure y.

More importantly, they demonstrate how Equation 1 and the variance estimates from MTMM meta-analytic studies can be used to decompose the average observed correlation between measures of two different traits that share the same method into the proportion due to (*a*) the correlation between the traits they represent and (*b*) the common method they share. For example, Cote & Buckley's (1987) meta-analysis reports that the average true correlation between traits across 70 MTMM samples was 0.674, the average percentage of trait variance in each measure was 0.417, the average true correlation between methods was 0.484, and the average percentage of method variance in each measure was 0.263. Therefore, using Equation 1, the average observed correlation can be decomposed into the proportion due to (*a*) the correlation between the traits they represent [$0.674*\sqrt{0.417}*\sqrt{0.417} = 0.281$] and (*b*) the common method they share [$0.484*\sqrt{0.263}*\sqrt{0.263} = 0.127$]. This suggests that the correlation between the traits was inflated approximately 45% (0.127/0.281) by method bias. Similar estimates of the percent of inflation due to method bias obtained from other meta-analyses of MTMM studies are 38% in Buckley et al. (1990), 92% in Doty & Glick (1998), and 60% in Lance et al. (2009).

Several points regarding these estimates are worth noting. First, these estimates are conservative because they are based on MTMM studies that used two or more less-than-perfectly correlated methods, and in many cases the biggest concern regarding method bias is in studies that use only a single method (which

implies a true $R_{mk,ml}$ of 1.00). Indeed, if a single method had been used to calculate these estimates, they would have ranged from 94% to 270%. Second, the MTMM studies included in these meta-analyses overlap to some extent, so the estimates of inflation are not independent. Third, there is quite a bit of variance in the estimates—ranging from 38% to 92%. Nevertheless, regardless of which estimate is used, the bottom line is that the amount of method bias is substantial.

Estimates based on method-method pair meta-analytic technique. Another way to use meta-analytic data to estimate the impact of method biases has been proposed by Sharma et al. (2009). Their technique involves categorizing the meta-analytic correlations from previous studies on the basis of the susceptibility to method biases of the pair of methods used to measure the predictor and criterion. Their argument is that some method-method (M-M) pairs are more susceptible to method biases than others and that organizing the meta-analytic data on the basis of these pairings allows researchers to obtain an estimate of the effects that method biases have on the relationships of interest. To illustrate how this method can be applied, Sharma et al. (2009) conducted a meta-analysis of 75 samples of data reported in 48 studies examining the technology acceptance model. The results indicated that (*a*) the mean correlation between the focal constructs was about 0.16 when the susceptibility of the M-M pairs to method biases was low and about 0.59 when the susceptibility of the M-M pairs to method biases was high, and (*b*) about 56% of the between-studies variance in this literature was attributable to method biases. They concluded that method bias "presents a major potential validity threat to the findings of IS research" (Sharma et al. 2009, p. 474).

Estimates of Specific Types of Method Bias on the Covariation Between Constructs

The effects of same versus different sources. In addition to using meta-analytic techniques to assess the impact of method

Table 2 Summary of meta-analytic studies comparing same-source versus different-source relationships

Relationship	Estimates from same source				Estimates from different source				% inflation
	k	N	r	ρ	k	N	r	ρ	
Leader behaviors → outcome variables	255	2,874	0.414	0.456	255	2,354	0.156	0.191	239%
Personality variables → job performance	123	1,504	0.259	0.312	139	898	0.113	0.147	212%
Job attitudes → OCB	98	6,729	0.270	0.340	155	13,551	0.190	0.230	148%
Participative decision making → work outcomes	91	391	0.343	0.343	140	1,453	0.165	0.165	208%
Organizational commitment → job performance	148	3,745	0.180	0.183	159	1,924	0.138	0.138	133%
Person-organization fit → job performance	12	639	0.230	0.283	21	813	0.073	0.093	304%
OCB → performance evaluations	95	2,808	0.490	0.595	56	2,889	0.260	0.323	184%

Abbreviations: k, sum of number of studies used to calculate the averages across meta-analyses of a specific relationship; N, harmonic mean for the specific relationship using reported sample sizes across meta-analyses; OCB, organizational citizenship behavior; r, unweighted average of raw correlations reported in meta-analyses; ρ, unweighted average of corrected correlations reported in meta-analyses; % inflation was calculated as $(\rho_{\text{same source}} / \rho_{\text{different source}})$.

factors on responses to individual measures (e.g., Cote & Buckley 1987), these techniques have been used to assess the effects that method factors have on the strength of the relationships between two or more constructs. **Table 2** reports a summary of these types of meta-analytic studies. For this table, we searched for meta-analytic studies that had explored the moderating effect of the source of the ratings on the relationships that were examined, and we then combined the data across the different meta-analyses that had examined the same general content areas to get an estimate of the effects that same-source method biases had on the strength of the relationships reported. The results indicate that the average corrected correlation between leader behaviors and outcome variables (employee performance, ratings of leader effectiveness, etc.) when taken from the same source is 0.456, but only 0.191 when obtained from different sources. This means that the average corrected correlation between measures of leader behaviors and outcome variables is 239% (0.456/0.191) larger when these measures are obtained from the same source than when they are obtained from different sources. Similarly, the corrected correlation between measures of personality variables and job performance, job attitudes and organizational

citizenship behaviors (OCBs), participative decision making and work outcomes, organizational commitment and job performance, person-organization fit and job performance, and OCB and performance evaluations are 213%, 147%, 208%, 133%, 304%, and 184% larger, respectively, when these measures are obtained from the same source than when they are obtained from different sources. Thus, it appears that the relationships between many widely studied constructs are strongly influenced by whether their measures are obtained from the same or different sources. However, it is important to recognize that although a large portion of the difference in the magnitudes of these correlations is undoubtedly due to method bias, some portion of it may also be due to the different perspectives of the raters on what constitutes job performance (Lance et al. 2010).

The effects of response styles. Using data from a large representative sample of consumers (N = 10,477) from 11 countries, Baumgartner & Steenkamp (2001) examined the biasing effects of acquiescence, disacquiescence, extreme, midpoint, and noncontingent response styles/sets on the correlations among 14 consumer constructs. Overall, they found that 27% of the variance in the magnitude of the 91 intercorrelations among the 14 constructs was due to the five response styles (64% of the variance was due to the traits). The effect of the response styles on the magnitude of the correlations among the constructs depended upon whether the (a) true correlation between the constructs was positive or negative and (b) response style components affecting the scales were positively or negatively correlated. If the true correlation between the constructs was positive and the correlation between the response styles was positive, they found that the magnitude of the observed correlation was inflated by 54% (the average correlation increased from 0.13 to 0.20). If the true correlation between the constructs was negative and the correlation between the response styles was negative, they found that the magnitude of the observed correlation was inflated by 67% (average correlation increased from −0.09 to −0.15). In contrast, if the true correlation between the constructs was positive and the correlation between the response styles was negative so that the substantive and response style components have opposing effects, they found that the observed correlation was deflated by 55% (average correlation decreased from 0.11 to 0.05); if the true correlation between the constructs was negative and the correlation between the response styles was positive, they found that the average observed correlation decreased from −0.07 to 0.01 and changed signs. They also found evidence that the amount of method bias varied across different types of constructs.

The effects of proximity and reversed items. Weijters et al. (2009) manipulated the proximity and the nature of the conceptual relationship between two items and examined their effects on the strength of the correlation between the items. Next, they specified a regression model that explained the correlation between all possible pairs of 76 items (N = 2,850) as a function of their distance apart on the questionnaire, and their conceptual relationship (nonreversed items measuring the same construct, reversed items measuring the same construct, or items measuring unrelated constructs). They found that, on average, two items measuring unrelated constructs had a correlation of only 0.04 when they were positioned six items apart, but the correlation increased to 0.09 when the items were positioned right next to each other. In other words, the correlation between unrelated items increases by 225% when they are positioned next to each other, as opposed to when they are positioned a few items further apart. For nonreversed item pairs, the average correlation significantly and substantially increases with decreasing interitem distance. When positioned six or more items apart, the average correlation between a pair of nonreversed items was 0.35, but this correlation increased to 0.62 (an increase of 177%) when these items were positioned next to each other. In contrast, when positioned six or more items apart, a reversed item pair had a correlation of −0.26, which decreased in magnitude to −0.06 when these item pairs were placed next to each other. Thus, Weijters et al. (2009, p. 7) concluded that up to a point, "correlations become weaker for nonreversed items and stronger for reversed items the further items are positioned from each other . . ."

The effects of item wording. Harris & Bladen (1994) examined the effect of stress versus comfort item wording on the relationships between role ambiguity, role conflict, role overload, job satisfaction, and job tension. They found that the average correlation among these five constructs was 0.21 when item word bias was controlled but increased to 0.50 when it was not controlled (an increase of 238%). In addition, they found that the effect of method bias also varied depending upon the constructs involved.

The effects of item context. Harrison et al. (1996) manipulated the order of the questions measuring four constructs (voice, options, objectivity, and standards) to create either a positive or negative measurement context for the questions about outcome favorability and fairness perceptions. They found that the correlation between outcome favorability and fairness was only 0.10 in a positive measurement context but increased to 0.50 in a negative measurement context. This difference was significant and found to be due to the effect of the measurement context manipulation on the variance in fairness perceptions. They concluded that "researchers would have come to different substantive conclusions about the existence and strength of influences on fairness, solely because of the position in which proposed antecedents were measured" (Harrison et al. 1996, p. 257).

Taken together, the evidence presented in this section is not consistent with Spector & Brannick's (2009) assertion that "the effects of method have generally been small and rarely pose a threat" and instead supports Johnson et al.'s (2011) conclusion that "CMV is not an urban legend, but rather a specter that has the potential to haunt interpretations of observed relationships." Thus, it is no surprise that editors of major journals in several disciplines (Chang et al. 2010, Kozlowski 2009, Straub 2009, Zinkhan 2006) consider method biases an important problem that needs to be addressed.

WAYS TO CONTROL FOR DIFFERENT SOURCES OF METHOD BIAS

Procedural Remedies

Obtain measures of predictor and criterion variables from different sources. One obvious way to help control for method bias is to obtain the measures from different sources. There are two main ways this can be done: (*a*) obtain the predictor measure(s) from one person and the criterion measure(s) from another; or (*b*) obtain either the predictor or criterion measure(s) from one person and the other measure from secondary data sources (e.g., company records, annual reports). These procedures can diminish or eliminate the effects of consistency motifs, idiosyncratic implicit theories, social desirability tendencies,

dispositional mood states, and tendencies on the part of the rater to acquiesce or respond in a lenient, moderate, or extreme manner because they make it impossible for the mindset of a common rater to bias the predictor-criterion relationship.

Evidence of the effectiveness of obtaining the predictor measure(s) from one person and the criterion measure(s) from another person is summarized in **Table 2**. The data reported in this table indicate that although the average corrected correlation between predictor and criterion variables was 0.359 when they were obtained from the same source, it decreased to 0.184 when they were obtained from different sources (a 49% decrease). Using a variation of this procedure, Ostroff et al. (2002) found that obtaining the predictor and criterion variables from different sources (rather than the same source) decreased the average split-level correlations between several dimensions of work climate and satisfaction by 71%. More specifically, their results indicated that separating the sources decreased the average split-level correlation from 0.07 to 0.02 when the individual was the unit of analysis, and from 0.24 to 0.07 when the department was the unit of analysis. Evidence of the effectiveness of controlling for method bias by obtaining either the predictor or criterion measure(s) from one person and the other measure from secondary data sources comes from two meta-analyses. First, a meta-analysis of research on the relationship between leadership style and effectiveness by Lowe et al. (1996) found that obtaining both the predictor and criterion variables from different sources decreased the correlation between leadership style and effectiveness by 67% (from 0.57 to 0.19) compared to when both measures were obtained from the same source. Second, a meta-analysis by Hulsheger et al. (2009) on the relationship between four team-process variables and team innovation found that obtaining both the predictor and criterion variables from different sources decreased the relationship by about 49% (from 0.45 to 0.23) compared to when both measures came from the same source.

Despite the fact that this approach seems to control for several important sources of method bias, it may not be appropriate to use in all cases. For example, this procedure is not appropriate when both the predictor and criterion variables are capturing an individual's perceptions, beliefs, judgments, or feelings. Beyond this, Chan (in Brannick et al. 2010) noted that this procedure is problematic for self-referential attitude and perception constructs because (a) the individual's perceptions may not translate into observable behaviors, (b) others may not have the opportunity to observe these behaviors, and (c) valid measurement by others requires them to accurately infer the individual's attitudes or perceptions based on the observation of the individual's behavior. Furthermore, this technique may not be feasible to use in all cases. For example, in some situations it may not be possible to obtain archival data that adequately represent one of the constructs of interest. In other situations, this technique may require more time, effort, and/or cost than the researcher can afford. In addition, when the sample size is small and the individual is the unit of analysis, the split-group procedure used by Ostroff et al. (2002) may not be feasible because it requires cutting the sample size in half and can result in too little power to detect the effects hypothesized.

Temporal, proximal, or psychological separation between predictor and criterion. Another way to control for method bias is to introduce a separation between the measures of the predictor and criterion variables (Feldman & Lynch 1988, Podsakoff et al. 2003). This separation may be (a) temporal (i.e., a time delay between measures is introduced), (b) proximal (i.e., the physical distance between measures is increased), or (c) psychological (i.e., a cover story is used to reduce the salience of the linkage between the predictor and criterion variables). Podsakoff et al. (2003) noted that these types of separation should reduce the respondent's ability and/or motivation to use previous answers to fill in gaps in what is recalled, infer missing details, or answer subsequent questions. A temporal separation does this by allowing previously recalled information to leave short-term memory, whereas a proximal separation does this by eliminating common retrieval cues, and a psychological separation does this by reducing the perceived relevance of the previously recalled information in short-term memory.

Evidence of the effectiveness of introducing a temporal separation between the measurement of the predictor and criterion variables comes from several studies. First, Ostroff et al. (2002) compared predictor-criterion variable correlations for concurrent ratings of both variables to ratings obtained after a one-hour or one-month delay. Although they found no significant differences in the average correlations between the concurrent and one-hour delay conditions, they reported that the average correlations were 32% lower after a one-month delay than they were in the concurrent condition. Second, Johnson et al. (2011, study 2) examined the effects of a three-week delay on the correlation between a latent predictor construct and a latent criterion construct. Their results indicated that the correlation between the constructs was 43% smaller after a three-week delay than it was when both were measured at the same time (although the design makes it unclear how much of this difference was due to the time delay rather than sample differences). Finally, in a firm-level analysis, Rindfleisch et al. (2008, table 5) found few significant differences in the correlations between several predictor and criterion variables after either no delay or a 30- to 36-month delay.

Although the weight of the evidence suggests that introducing a temporal separation is an effective means of controlling for some method biases, there are several disadvantages of this approach. First, introducing a temporal separation will obviously increase the complexity of the research design and potentially its cost. Second, when a temporal separation is introduced, it may allow other nonmethodological factors to influence the level of the outcome variable. Third, the longer the temporal delay, the greater the chance of respondent attrition. Fourth, it is difficult to determine what the appropriate delay should be for any given relationship, and it is likely that the appropriate delay varies across types of relationships. If the delay is too short, the temporal separation may be ineffective; and if the delay is too long, intervening factors are likely to affect the criterion variable. Fifth, and most importantly, the temporal separation procedure is based on the assumption that the true relationship between the constructs is relatively stable over the time period of the delay and that method bias will dissipate over time. If it is suspected that either of these assumptions is inaccurate, this method of control should not be used. Indeed, recent empirical research (Alessandri et al. 2010, Weijters et al. 2010a) suggests that the assumption that the method bias dissipates over time may be questionable.

Indirect evidence of the effectiveness of introducing a proximal separation between the measures of the predictor and criterion variables comes from studies demonstrating that separation attenuates method biases due to context effects (Tourangeau et al. 2000) and question order effects (Tourangeau et al. 2003). However, the most direct evidence comes from the study by Weijters et al. (2009) that found that proximal separation prevents the correlation between nonreversed (reversed) items from being artificially inflated (deflated). Based on their analysis, they concluded that researchers should try to position measures of the same-construct at least six items apart, separated by measures of other constructs using the same or different formats, or by means of dedicated buffer items.

Although there is some evidence that proximal separation is an effective means of controlling for some method biases, there are some disadvantages of this approach. First, it can increase the length of the questionnaire and that may cause fatigue, decrease response rates, or increase costs. Second, if the filler items are conceptually related to the measures of interest, they could create context effects that increase method bias.

Empirical evidence of the effectiveness of psychological separation as a means of reducing method bias is not readily available. However, there is no shortage of studies that recommend this procedure. For example, Aronson et al. (1998) note that one way to psychologically separate the predictor and criterion variables is to use a "multiple study" cover story, in which participants are told that for reasons of convenience or efficiency several unrelated studies are being conducted at the same time. This ruse is frequently employed in priming experiments (e.g., Higgins et al. 1977) and attitudinal research (e.g., Rosenberg 1965). Other ways to psychologically separate the predictor and criterion measures might be to (a) camouflage interest in the criterion or predictor variable by embedding it in the context of other questions so that it is less psychologically prominent (i.e., diminishing the salience of the measure) or (b) disguise the reasons for obtaining the predictor or criterion measure by leading respondents to believe that it is tangential to the main purpose of the study (i.e., making respondents think it is unimportant).

The principal disadvantage of this technique is that its effectiveness is dependent upon the credibility of the cover story, but a considerable amount of creativity and ingenuity is required to develop a convincing cover story. Consequently, it is essential to thoroughly pretest the cover story in order to ensure its effectiveness.

Eliminate common scale properties. Several authors (e.g., Campbell & Fiske 1959, Cronbach 1946, Feldman & Lynch 1988, Podsakoff et al. 2003, Tourangeau et al. 2000) have observed that method bias can result from common scale properties (i.e., scale type, number of scale points, anchor labels, polarity, etc.) shared by the items used to measure different constructs. For example, Feldman & Lynch (1988, p. 427) note that method bias "will occur to the extent that the question formats are perceived to be similar by respondents," because the similarity of the response format "enhances the probability that cognitions generated in answering one question will be retrieved to answer subsequent questions." The obvious remedy to this problem is to try to minimize the scale properties shared by the measures of the predictor and criterion variables.

Evidence of the effectiveness of this remedy comes from several studies. Kothandapani (1971) measured three constructs using four different scale formats (Likert, Thurstone, Guttman, and Guilford) and found that the average correlation was 0.45 when the criterion and predictor shared the same scale format and dropped to 0.18 when they did not share this scale property, a decrease of 60%. Arora (1982) measured three constructs using three different scale formats (Likert, semantic differential, and Stapel) and found that the average correlation was 0.34 when the criterion and predictor shared the same scale format and dropped to 0.23 when they did not share this scale property, a decrease of 32%. Flamer (1983) measured three constructs using three different scale formats (Likert, semantic differential, and Thurstone) in two different samples and found that the average correlation was 0.06 in sample A and 0.09 in sample B when the criterion and predictor shared the same scale format and dropped to 0.04 in sample A and 0.08 in sample B when they did not share this scale property, a decrease of 33% in sample A and 11% in sample B. Finally, Weijters et al. (2010c) examined the effect of common scale labeling on the correlation between attitudes and intentions and found that the average correlation was 0.69 when both the predictor and criterion variables had only the extreme end points of the scale labeled, and dropped to 0.60 when the criterion had the extreme end points labeled and the predictor had all points on the scale labeled, a decrease of 15%.

An advantage of this procedure is that it is often easy to translate some types of scale formats (e.g., Likert) into other formats (e.g., semantic differential) without changing the content of the item or other properties of the item (e.g., number of scale points). However, that is not always the case. For example, although it can be done, translating Likert or semantic differential items into Thurstone or Guttman scales is often difficult to do without altering the conceptual meaning of the measures (Nunally & Bernstein 1994). In these instances, it is important to give priority to maintaining the content validity of the items because a lack of content validity poses an even bigger threat to construct validity than does common method bias (MacKenzie et al. 2011). Thus, although minimizing common scale properties is always a good idea, there are practical limits to the extent to which this can be done.

Improving scale items to eliminate ambiguity. Ambiguous items are ones that are difficult to interpret and require people to construct their own idiosyncratic meanings for them. Johnson (2004) identifies several causes of item ambiguity, including the presence of indeterminate words such as "many" and "sometimes," words with multiple meanings, multiple ideas linked together with conjunctions or disjunctions, or complex constructions such as double negatives.

According to several authors (Cronbach 1950, Feldman & Lynch 1988, Podsakoff et al. 2003), the problem with ambiguous items is that they cause respondents to be uncertain about how to respond on the basis of the item's content, which increases the likelihood that their responses will be influenced by their systematic response tendencies (e.g., acquiescent, extreme, or midpoint response styles). The best solution to this problem is to make every effort to: keep questions simple, specific, and concise; define ambiguous or unfamiliar terms; decompose questions relating to more than one possibility into simpler, more focused questions; avoid vague concepts and provide examples when such concepts must be used; avoid double-barreled questions; and avoid complicated syntax (see Tourangeau et al. 2000). In addition, Krosnick (1991) notes that labeling every point on the response scale (rather than only the end points) is also an effective means of reducing item ambiguity. Unfortunately, we were unable to find any empirical evidence that specifically examined the effect of item ambiguity on estimates of the relationships between two different constructs.

Reducing social desirability bias in item wording. There is a great deal of evidence that items differ in perceived social desirability and that this affects responses to the item. For example, Edwards (1970) measured the impact of item social desirability on responses to the Minnesota Multiphasic Personality Inventory. He found that ratings of the social desirability of self-descriptive items made by a sample of judges were correlated 0.87 with endorsements of the items by another sample of subjects. This suggests that item wording can potentially undermine the accuracy of responses by causing subjects to edit their responses for social acceptability. If this editing affects both predictor and criterion measures in a similar manner, it could possibly bias the relationship between them. There are two commonly used procedures for controlling item social desirability (e.g., Kuncel & Tellegen 2009). The first is to obtain an assessment of the perceived social desirability of the items from judges and to revise the wording of the highly rated items to minimize or reduce the perceived level of social desirability. The other is to calculate the correlation between subjects' responses to each item and responses to a recognized social desirability scale (e.g., Paulhus 1984) and to revise the wording of items that correlate highly with this scale to minimize or reduce the perceived level of social desirability.

Although these procedures have been widely used and seem to have few disadvantages, we were unable to find any direct empirical evidence of their ability to prevent item social desirability from biasing the correlations between measures of different constructs. Moreover, implementing these procedures may be more difficult than it appears for two reasons. First, revising the items to eliminate their social desirability without compromising their content validity may be easier said than done. Second, Kuncel & Tellegen (2009, p. 201) have shown that "the relation between degree of endorsement of an item and its judged desirability level is often nonlinear and varies across items such that no general model of item desirability can be adopted that will accurately represent the relations across all items, traits, and trait levels." This would suggest that the linear correlation between responses to an item and responses to a social desirability scale may not always be a valid indication of the tendency of the item to evoke socially desirable responses.

Balancing positive and negative items. A number of authors (Baumgartner & Steenkamp 2001, Billiet & McClendon 2000, Mirowsky & Ross 1991, Weijters et al. 2010b) have noted that scale formats that ask respondents how strongly they agree or disagree with statements may be susceptible to acquiescence or disacquiescence response style biases. Respondents who exhibit acquiescence response styles tend to disproportionately use the positive side of the scale, whereas those that exhibit disacquiescence response styles tend to disproportionately use the negative side of the scale. As noted by Mirowsky & Ross (1991), these response style tendencies are problematic because they inflate the estimates of the reliability of measures, may produce misleading factor analytic solutions, and may inflate or deflate correlation and regression coefficients, depending on the type of questions that are asked. One procedural remedy that has been used to try to reduce this type of bias is "balancing" the positively worded (i.e., agreement with the item indicates a higher score on the underlying construct) and negatively worded (i.e., agreement with the item indicates a lower score on the underlying construct) measures of each construct. According to Baumgartner & Steenkamp (2001, p. 147), "although balanced scales do not eliminate the occurrence of acquiescence per se, they contain a built-in control for contamination of observed scores by yea-saying, because the bias is upward for half of the items and downward for the other half."

The advantage of this technique is that it is a proactive way to control for acquiescence and disacquiescence biases. However, there are several limitations of this technique (Baumgartner & Steenkamp 2001, Mirowsky & Ross 1991, Weijters et al. 2010b). First, many existing scales do not contain an equal number of positively and negatively worded items, and reversing the wording of some items may alter their content. Second, reversed items may be confusing for some respondents. Finally, empirical research suggests that because this technique does not always completely control for these biases, it should be used in conjunction with the statistical methods of control described in the next section.

Statistical Remedies

Although it is possible that the use of the procedural remedies discussed above will minimize the detrimental effects of method biases, researchers may not always be able to implement them beforehand. In these circumstances, they may find it useful to use one of the statistical remedies.

Unmeasured latent method factor technique. This is perhaps the oldest latent variable control technique (Bagozzi 1984, Bagozzi & Phillips 1982, Widaman 1985), and it has been used in approximately 50 studies (see Richardson et al. 2009). This technique involves adding a first-order method factor whose only measures are the indicators of the theoretical constructs of interest that share a common method. This technique has several advantages: (*a*) it does not require the researcher to measure the specific factor responsible for the method effect; (*b*) it models the effect of the method factor at the measurement level, rather than at the latent construct level (Schaubroeck et al. 1992, Williams et al. 1996); and (*c*) it does not require the effects of the method factor on each measure to be equal.

However, this approach has been criticized for several reasons. First, as noted by Podsakoff et al. (2003, p. 894), the unmeasured latent method factor "may reflect not only different types of common method variance but also variance due to relationships between the constructs other than the one hypothesized." This is considered to be a serious flaw (e.g., Richardson et al. 2009), but it could also be considered a virtue, since it is desirable to control for all systematic sources of bias when testing hypotheses about the relations between constructs. Indeed, Phillips & Lord (1986) noted a similar confounding of method and substantive variance when trying to control for halo effects and concluded that there are advantages to controlling for both. Second, if the ratio of the number of indicators to the number of substantive constructs is low, the addition of a method factor can cause identification problems. Finally, this procedure is based on the assumption that the method factor does not interact with the trait factors; an assumption that has been questioned by several researchers (see Bagozzi & Yi 1990, Campbell & O'Connell 1967, Wothke & Browne 1990).

Correlation-based marker variable technique. This approach (Lindell & Whitney 2001) ideally requires researchers to (*a*) identify a "marker variable" that is expected for theoretical reasons to be completely unrelated to the substantive variables of interest, (*b*) use the smallest correlation between the marker variable and the substantive variables as an estimate of the effects of method bias, (*c*) adjust the zero-order correlation between every pair of substantive variables of interest by subtracting this estimate from the zero-order correlation between any pair of substantive variables and dividing by the quantity of 1 minus this estimate, and (*d*) examine whether the resulting partial correlation is significantly different from zero. They argue that if this partial correlation remains significant, the substantive relationships still hold even after controlling for method bias. According to Williams et al. (2010), this technique has been widely used in recent years.

The primary advantage of this technique is that it is easy to implement. The disadvantages are many. First, Lindell & Whitney (2001) do not require the marker variable to share any method characteristics with the substantive variables. Indeed, they suggest that the variable with the smallest correlation with the substantive variables can be arbitrarily selected in an ad hoc manner as a marker variable.

As noted by Williams et al. (2010, p. 507) this is problematic because if the marker variable does not share method characteristics with the substantive variables, "it cannot provide the vehicle for partialling out these biases from estimates of relations among substantive variables so as to obtain a 'truer' estimate of the relation, which is the goal behind the use of marker variables." Second, it assumes that method bias can only inflate and never deflate relationships among the substantive variables. Several researchers have demonstrated that this assumption is incorrect (Baumgartner & Steenkamp 2001, Cote & Buckley 1988, Podsakoff et al. 2003). Third, this technique ignores measurement error that could attenuate the correlations between the marker variable and the substantive variables that are used to obtain an estimate of method bias (Lance et al. 2010, Podsakoff et al. 2003, Williams et al. 2010). Fourth, this approach controls for method bias at the scale level rather than the item level (Williams et al. 2010). Fifth, this method is based on the assumption that the method factor represented by the marker variable does not interact with the substantive variables of interest, which has been disputed by several researchers (Bagozzi & Yi 1990, Campbell & O'Connell 1967, Wothke & Browne 1990). Sixth, it is based on the assumption that the smallest correlation between the marker variable and the substantive variables is a reasonable estimate of the effects of all types of method bias, which is not justified because the marker variable is not required to share any measurement characteristics (e.g., common scale format, anchors) with the substantive variables (cf. Podsakoff et al. 2003, Williams et al. 2010). Finally, this technique assumes that the method factor represented by the marker variable has an identical effect on every substantive variable of interest in the study. However, this assumption has been widely criticized (e.g., Podsakoff et al. 2003, Richardson et al. 2009, Sharma et al. 2009). Indeed, Williams et al. (2010) note that an analytical technique that can incorporate unequal method effect is needed in most organizational research settings because there

is evidence that different types of variables contain differing amounts of method variance.

Regression-based marker variable technique. Siemsen et al. (2010) recently proposed that common method bias can be eliminated when estimating a regression equation subject to method bias by adding a marker variable that (*a*) is uncorrelated with the substantive variables of interest and (*b*) suffers from some type of method bias. In the event that the marker variable is modestly correlated with the substantive variables, their numerical analysis suggests that the addition of 3 to 5 variables is necessary.

Perhaps the greatest advantage of this technique is that it is easy to implement. However, there are several disadvantages. Like the correlational marker variable technique, this technique (*a*) ignores measurement error that could attenuate the correlation between the marker variable(s) and the substantive variables of interest, (*b*) controls for method bias at the scale level rather than the item level, and (*c*) is based on the assumption that the method factor represented by the marker variable(s) does not interact with the substantive variables of interest. In addition, this technique controls for only the net effect of the sources of method bias common to the marker variable(s) and the substantive variables and applies only to single-equation models. Furthermore, it is unclear what is being controlled by the addition of the marker variables. It is assumed to be "method bias" based on the subjective judgment that the marker variables are "theoretically unrelated" to the substantive variables. However, that may not be true. Finally, Siemsen et al. (2010, p. 472) limited their analysis to a single method factor even though they note that, "In practice, observed variables may suffer from multiple different methods factors... Although we expect our insights to hold if these methods factors are uncorrelated with each other, examining multiple correlated methods factors may lead to different results."

Instrumental variable technique. This technique is based on the fact that the presence of a method factor that influences both the predictor and the criterion variable in a model will cause the structural error term for the equation to be correlated with the predictor. In this instance, the supposedly exogenous predictor variable is really an endogenous predictor. This is an important problem because it violates an assumption of many estimation techniques [e.g., ordinary least squares (OLS), maximum likelihood (ML)] and causes the estimate of the effect of the predictor on the criterion variable to be biased (i.e., inconsistent). Antonakis et al. (2010) point out that method bias can be controlled, and an unbiased (i.e., consistent) estimate of the effect of the predictor on the criterion can be obtained, by adding appropriate instrumental variables (IVs) to the model and estimating the effect of the predictor on the criterion variable using two-stage least squares (2SLS). Briefly, in the first stage of the 2SLS estimation process the endogenous predictors are regressed on the IVs (and any other truly exogenous variables included in the model) to obtain predicted values for the endogenous predictors. In the second stage, the criterion variable is regressed on the predicted values of the endogenous predictors obtained in the first stage (and any other truly exogenous variables in the model). An instrumental variable is a truly exogenous variable (i.e., it does not depend on other variables) that is (a) correlated with the endogenous predictor for which it is to serve as an instrument and (b) uncorrelated with the structural error term for the equation. Thus, an IV is indirectly related to the criterion variable through the endogenous predictor but not directly related to the criterion variable. Antonakis et al. (2010) recommend adding at least one more IV than there are endogenous predictors in the model.

In order to be useful, each IV must satisfy two essential requirements (Antonakis et al. 2010, Kennedy 2008). First, the IV must be significantly and strongly related to the predictor it represents. This is required for two reasons. One is that IV estimators (although asymptotically unbiased) are biased in the same direction as OLS in small samples. Even in large samples, Kennedy (2008, p. 145) notes that the magnitude of this bias (a) can be quite large if the IV is not strongly correlated with the endogenous predictor it represents and (b) becomes even worse if several weak IVs are used. Indeed, even a slight correlation between a weak IV and the structural error term for the equation (perhaps caused by method bias) can cause the IV estimate to exhibit more bias (even asymptotically) than an OLS estimate. Another reason why strong IVs are required, according to Kennedy (2008, p. 145), is that "A weak instrument also causes the IV variance to be underestimated in small samples; this causes the true type I error rate to be higher than its chosen level." Thus, weak IVs lead to biased estimates and unreliable inference.

Second, the IV must be completely uncorrelated with the structural error term for the equation. Antonakis et al. (2010) emphasize that "the instruments must first pass a 'theoretical overidentification' test before an empirical one" because "if all the modeled instruments are not truly exogenous the overidentification test will not necessarily catch the misspecification." According to Kennedy (2008), this "theoretical overidentification test" for each IV should involve the use of existing literature and theory to (a) defend the implicit assumption that the IV is not an explanatory variable in the equation being estimated (i.e., that the IV does not have any direct effect on the criterion variable) and (b) explain why the IV could not be influenced by any of the method factors that influence the criterion variable or by any other omitted variables that affect the criterion variable (because if the IV is affected by these factors, it would be correlated with the structural error for the equation). Assuming that the IVs pass these theoretical tests, Antonakis et al. (2010) recommend using a Sargan chi-square test of overidentification to test empirically the assumption that the IVs are uncorrelated with the structural error term. If the IVs are unrelated to the structural error term, the overidentification tests will all be nonsignificant. If they are not, one must find better instruments.

The primary advantage of the instrumental variable technique is that it provides a straightforward solution to the problem of common method bias in situations where its causes cannot be identified or measured directly (Antonakis et al. 2010). However, perhaps the biggest disadvantage of this technique is the difficulty of selecting IVs that are related to the endogenous predictors and completely uncorrelated with the structural error term for the equation. Indeed, if (as is often the case) all of the possible sources of method bias that might affect the endogenous predictors and the criterion variable cannot be identified, then it is unclear how the IVs could pass Antonakis et al.'s theoretical overidentification test and how one could be confident that they were not affected by these unidentified method biases as well. In addition, it may prove to be difficult to identify IVs that are strongly related to the endogenous predictors, and as noted above, weak IVs lead to biased estimates and unreliable inference. Unfortunately, if these two requirements are not met, this technique will produce biased estimates and inflate the type I error rates, and researchers would be better off using another technique to control for method biases. A final disadvantage is that because the results are dependent upon the IVs selected, a test of the robustness of the second-stage estimates should probably be conducted.

CFA marker technique. To address some of the problems with the correlation-based marker variable technique, Williams et al. (2010) recommend using a series of marker variables that share measurement characteristics with the substantive variables of interest as indicators of a latent method factor. They propose a three-phase confirmatory factor analysis (CFA) marker technique to identify and control for method biases. Phase I of this analysis tests for the presence and quality of method effects associated with the latent marker variable. This phase requires specifying five different latent variable models and comparing their relative fit to each other. The first model (the CFA model) estimates loadings for each marker variable on

a latent method factor and estimates all possible correlations among the method factor and the substantive constructs of interest, but it sets the loadings from the method factor to the indicators of the substantive constructs to zero. The second model requires that (*a*) the correlations between the method and substantive latent factors be set to zero, (*b*) the indicator loadings of the latent method factor be fixed at the estimates obtained from the CFA model, and (*c*) the loadings from the latent method factor to the indicators of the substantive constructs be set to zero. This model is called the baseline model because it serves as the baseline against which the method effects are assessed. The third model is called the method-C model (i.e., a constrained model). This model estimates the loadings from the latent method factor to the indicators of the substantive constructs but constrains these loadings to be equal to each other. A comparison of the fit of this model to the fit of the Baseline model provides a test of the assumption that the latent method factor has equal (tau equivalent) effects on the indicators of the substantive constructs of interest. In contrast to this assumption, the fourth model (called the method-U, or unconstrained, model) allows the loadings from the method factor to the indicators of the substantive variables to be freely estimated (i.e., unconstrained). A comparison of the fit of this model to the fit of the method-C model provides a test of the assumption that the method factor has unequal effects on the indicators of the substantive constructs. Finally, the fifth model, which is referred to as the method-R model (to represent restrictions on the parameters) is specified. This model is identical to the method-C and method-U models, with the exception that the correlations among the substantive constructs are constrained to the values estimated in the baseline model. A comparison of the fit of this model to the fit of either the method-C model or the method-U model (depending on which of these models fits the best) provides a test of the bias in the correlations among the substantive constructs that is due to the latent method factor.

Phase II of this analysis is devoted to quantifying how method variance affects the reliability of the substantive constructs. This is important because if method variance is not controlled, it will bias the reliability estimates of the substantive constructs. First, the completely standardized estimates of the factor loadings and error variances for each substantive construct from the baseline model are used to obtain reliability estimates for each construct (Werts et al. 1974). Next, the completely standardized substantive construct factor loadings, method factor loadings, and the error variances (from either the method-C or method-U model, depending upon which was supported) are used to decompose the total reliability calculated in the first step into the proportion due to the substantive construct and the proportion due to the method factor.

Finally, phase III is used to conduct a sensitivity analysis to increase confidence in the findings. Briefly, Williams et al. (2010) argue that since the amount of method variance associated with each indicator of the substantive constructs is represented by the magnitude of their loadings on the method factor, the sensitivity of the estimates of the correlations between the substantive constructs to method bias can be examined by substituting larger alternative values for these method factor loadings. The specific alternative values selected should be based on the confidence intervals of the unstandardized method factor loadings from either the method-C or method-U models (depending on which one was supported). The examination of this model allows researchers to determine the sensitivity of their results to increasing amounts of method variance associated with sampling error in the indicators.

Williams et al. (2010) have identified several advantages of this approach over the partial correlation approach proposed by Lindell & Whitney (2001). First, it models the effects of method biases at the indicator level (rather than construct level). Second, it provides a statistical test of method bias based on model comparisons. Third, it permits a test of whether

method biases affect all measures equally or differentially.

Despite these advantages, there are a few potential problems regarding this approach that should be noted. First, it doesn't identify the nature of the method bias being controlled. Indeed, Williams et al. (2010, p. 507) note that, "without conceptual analysis of the nature of the marker variable, the meaning of its covariation with substantive variables cannot be understood." Related to this, a second problem is that the conceptual meaning of the latent method factor is ambiguous. Empirically, this construct is defined as the common variance among the marker variables. Although this technique requires the marker variables to be theoretically unrelated to the substantive constructs, it places no constraints on their theoretical relationships to each other. This means that potentially the marker variables could all come from a scale for a recognized construct (albeit one that is theoretically unrelated to the substantive constructs of interest). Consequently, it is unknown whether the common variance that empirically defines the marker variable construct is due to method artifacts or to some theoretically meaningful construct that is confounded with it. This would affect the loadings of the marker variables on this latent construct in Williams et al.'s CFA model as well as their baseline model (since it uses these estimates from the CFA model as fixed parameters).

Another problem is that the results are sensitive to the specific variables used as indicators of the latent method factor. This technique will only control for the net effect of the method characteristics that are shared by all of the marker variables and the indicators of the substantive constructs. If there are many relatively important method characteristics shared, this procedure will provide a strong test of method bias, but if there are only a few relatively unimportant method characteristics shared, this procedure will provide only a weak test of method bias.

A final problem is that in phases I and III, this procedure requires fixing parameter estimates in one model at specific values obtained from the estimation of an alternatively specified model. This two-step estimation process may not provide correct standard errors and goodness-of-fit statistics to test the fit of the resulting model (Kennedy 2008, Jöreskög 1998).

Directly measured latent method factor technique. To apply this technique, researchers must be able to anticipate the potential source of method bias and obtain measures of it. If direct measures of this particular source of method bias are available, bias can be controlled by adding to the theoretical model a method factor that has both the direct measures and the measures of the substantive constructs of interest as reflective indicators. This technique has been used in several studies (e.g., Bagozzi 1984, Schaubroeck et al. 1992, Williams & Anderson 1994, Williams et al. 1996). For example, Williams et al. (1996) used this technique to control for the effects of negative affectivity on the relationship between job attitudes and role perceptions. In general, it can be used to control for any contaminating factor for which direct measures are available (e.g., social desirability, positive affectivity).

The advantages of this approach are that (*a*) it unambiguously identifies the source of the method bias, (*b*) it controls for measurement error, (*c*) it models the effects of the biasing factor at the item level rather than at the construct level, and (*d*) it does not constrain the effects of the methods factor on the measures of the substantive construct to be equal. Perhaps the biggest disadvantage of this technique is that it requires researchers to anticipate the most important sources of method biases in their studies and to include measures of these sources. This is a serious problem because it is often difficult to identify the key sources of method bias in a given situation, and valid measures for these sources may not exist. In addition, this technique assumes that the method factor does not interact with the substantive constructs, which has been questioned by several researchers (Bagozzi & Yi 1990, Campbell & O'Connell 1967, Wothke & Browne 1990).

Measured response style technique. Another promising technique is to systematically measure common response styles and partial out their effects on responses. This procedure requires several steps. First, the relevant item population must be defined and a random sample taken of it to produce a representative heterogeneous set of items. As noted by Weijters et al. (2010b, p. 118), "The items should relate to constructs that do not form a meaningful nomological network." In order to develop reliable measures of the response styles, they recommend that a minimum of three sets of five items each should be used. Second, this random sample of heterogeneous items should be inserted as buffer items between the scales of substantive interest using the same scale format as for the other items on the questionnaire. Third, as many researchers have noted (e.g., Baumgartner & Steenkamp 2001; Weijters et al. 2008, 2010a,b), the most common response styles can be measured for each set of items as follows: (*a*) acquiescence response style (ARS)—calculate the extent of agreement with both positively and negatively worded items in each set (before negatively worded items have been reverse-scored), (*b*) disacquiescence response style (DRS)—calculate the extent of disagreement with both positively and negatively worded items in each set (before negatively worded items have been reverse-scored), (*c*) extreme response style (ERS)—calculate the proportion of items in each set on which the respondent endorses the most extreme (positive or negative) scale categories, and (*d*) midpoint response style (MRS)—calculate the proportion of items in each set on which the respondent endorses the middle scale category. Weijters et al. (2008, p. 414) provide an excellent illustration of how these operationalizations can be applied to a 7-point Likert scale (1 = strongly disagree, 7 = strongly agree). For each set of k items, they compute the measures of each response style as follows: ARS = $[f(5) \times 1 + f(6) \times 2 + f(7) \times 3]/k$; DRS = $[f(1) \times 3 + f(2) \times 2 + f(3) \times 1]/k$; ERS = $[f(1) + f(7)]/k$; MRS = $f(4)/k$; where $f(o)$ refers to the frequency of response option o. This results in a measure of each of the four response styles for each of the sets of k items. Fourth, for each of the response styles, the measures obtained from each set of items are used as indicators of a latent construct. This means that, if there are three sets of items, there would be three indicators of each response-style latent construct.[1] Fifth, the latent constructs representing each response style are added to a latent variable model and their effects on the measures of the substantive constructs of interest are added.[2]

A few words of caution are in order. First, in order to ensure that the response-style measures only capture method variance, it is essential for the content of the set of items used to measure the response styles to be independent of the content of the measures of the substantive constructs. De Beuckelaer et al. (2010) found that using ad hoc sets of items is suboptimal at detecting ARS and ERS compared to using random heterogeneous items. Second, it is important to use a complete profile of response styles because it is difficult to decide a priori which response style may cause bias (Weijters et al. 2010a).

With these caveats in mind, if the effects of the response-style constructs on the measures of the substantive constructs are significant, it is evidence of method bias. However, if the estimate of the relationship between the constructs of interest is significant after controlling for these response styles, then one can be confident that the relationship is not solely due to these forms of method bias.

Using multiple indicators to measure response-style constructs has several advantages (Weijters et al. 2010b). First, it facilitates evaluation of the method construct(s) in terms of convergent and discriminant validity. Second, it allows for unique variances in the response-style item sets. Therefore, these unique variances are not confounded with the method construct(s) itself. Third, using multiple indicators of the method construct(s) enhances the stability of the model. Finally, unlike the unmeasured latent variable, marker variable, or CFA-marker variable approaches, it specifies the nature of the method construct (e.g., ARS, ERS) whose effects are being controlled. However, despite these advantages, there are also some limitations of this approach. First, it only controls for the response styles explicitly measured. Second, it requires the researchers to collect additional data to measure the response styles.

RECOMMENDATIONS

In this section, we suggest strategies for (a) identifying when method bias is likely to be a problem and (b) mitigating its effects. However, as Podsakoff et al. (2003, p. 899) emphasize, "The key point to remember is that the procedural and statistical remedies selected should be tailored to fit the specific research question at hand. There is no single best method for handling the problem of common method variance because it depends on what the sources of method variance are in the study and the feasibility of the remedies that are available." The goal is to reduce the plausibility of method biases as a rival explanation for the relationships observed in a study.

When Is Method Bias Likely To Be a Problem?

There is widespread agreement that generating an optimal answer to even a single question can require a great deal of cognitive work, and the effort required to answer a long series of questions on a wide range of topics is substantial (Krosnick 1999, Sudman et al. 1996, Tourangeau et al. 2000). Although we may wish otherwise, not all respondents will be willing and able to exert the cognitive effort required

---

[1] Weijters et al. (2010b) found that the loadings of the response-style indicators on the method factors are essential tau equivalent (complemented with a time-invariant autoregressive effect): "This means that ARS and ERS are largely but not completely consistent over the course of a questionnaire" (p. 105). Note that they did not examine whether the method factor had tau equivalent effects on the measures of any other "substantive" constructs.

[2] When specifying this model, the covariances among the response styles should be estimated, and the indicators that are based on the same sets of items should have correlated error terms across response styles.

to generate accurate answers to the questions on a typical research instrument. What then? Krosnick (1999) argues that when the difficulty of the task of generating an optimal answer is high but a respondent's ability or motivation to expend the required amount of cognitive effort are low, respondents may "satisfice" rather than generate the most accurate answers by simply being less thorough in question comprehension, memory retrieval, judgment, and response selection. In our view, when respondents are satisficing rather than optimizing, they will be more likely to respond stylistically and their responses will be more susceptible to method bias. In other words, we expect that responses will be more strongly influenced by method bias when the respondents can't provide accurate responses (which is a function of their ability and the difficulty of the task) or when they are unwilling to try to provide accurate responses (which is a function of motivation).

Ability factors that may cause biased responding. The first question to consider is whether respondents are able to provide accurate answers, because if they are not, they may respond stylistically or be more susceptible to method bias. For example, Krosnick (1999) summarizes research that shows that respondents who are low in verbal ability or education are more likely to respond in a nondifferentiated manner when asked to rate objects on a single response scale (i.e., by giving all objects the same rating) and that nondifferentiated responding is more prevalent toward the end of a questionnaire due to fatigue. Similarly, there is evidence (e.g., Schwarz et al. 1992) that the amount of experience a respondent has had thinking about the topic of a question decreases his/her tendency to select the most recent of several response alternatives mentioned (regardless of content), presumably because it makes the respondent's knowledge of the topic more accessible.

Beyond this, Baumgartner & Steenkamp (2001) note that the tendency to agree with items regardless of content (i.e., ARS) can result from a respondent's low cognitive ability, poorly differentiated cognitive structure, or uncertainty about how to respond to the question. They also provide an excellent summary of several personality characteristics that are associated with biased responding. They cite research indicating that (*a*) "stimulation-seeking extroverts" may have a tendency to accept statements impulsively and agree with them regardless of content (i.e., ARS or positivity bias), (*b*) "controlled and reflective introverts who try to avoid external stimulation" may have a tendency to disagree with items regardless of content (i.e., DRS or negativity bias), and (*c*) respondents who are rigid, dogmatic, anxious, or intolerant of ambiguity may have a tendency to endorse the most extreme response categories regardless of content (i.e., ERS).

Thus, method biases and stylistic responding may be more likely to the extent that the respondents in a study have these ability limitations or possess these personality characteristics. Consequently, under these circumstances researchers would be wise to implement the appropriate procedural and statistical remedies discussed below.

Motivational factors that may cause biased responding. A second question to consider is whether respondents are motivated to provide accurate answers. Method biases and stylistic responding should be less likely to the extent that respondents are motivated to provide optimal responses to the questions and more likely to the extent that respondents are motivated to expend less effort by satisficing. Krosnick (1999) notes several factors that increase a respondent's motivation to exert the cognitive effort required to provide optimal answers including the need for cognition; the desire for self-expression, intellectual challenge, self-understanding, or emotional catharsis; and the desire to help employers improve working conditions, manufacturers produce better quality products, or governments make better-informed policy decisions. To the extent that respondents possess these needs/desires, they may be more likely to expend the effort required to generate an optimal answer, and the threat of method bias should be lower. In contrast, respondents may be motivated to minimize effort when they feel the questions are unimportant; believe their responses will not have useful consequences; feel compelled to participate in a survey to fulfill a course requirement; become fatigued by a seemingly unending stream of questions; or dislike the interviewer, experimenter, or source of the survey. To the extent that these things are true, respondents may be more likely to minimize their effort and rely on stylistic tendencies or other decision heuristics to arrive at a merely satisfactory answer.

In addition to considering the general factors that might motivate respondents to attempt to minimize effort by satisficing, researchers should also consider aspects of the measurement conditions that might increase the threat of specific types of bias. For example, researchers should consider the magnitude of the social consequences of a respondent's answers and the extent to which the measurement conditions make those consequences salient (see Paulhus 1984, Steenkamp et al. 2010). The more serious the social consequences of a particular response, the stronger a respondent's desire to provide a socially acceptable response is likely to be. Similarly, the more that the measurement conditions threaten a respondent's self-esteem, heighten his/her defensiveness, or increase the benefits (costs) of presenting a good (bad) impression, the more the respondent is likely to be motivated to respond in a socially desirable manner. Baumgartner & Steenkamp (2001) suggest that researchers should also consider whether aspects of the measurement context motivate respondents to conceal their true opinion by using the middle scale category regardless of their true feelings (MRS) or by responding to items carelessly, randomly, or nonpurposefully (NCR). The former may happen because respondents become suspicious about how their data will be used (Schmitt 1994), and the latter may happen because respondents are motivated to leave the testing situation, wish

to rebel against a testing procedure, or are not motivated to invest the cognitive energy required to read and interpret questionnaire items (Jackson 1967). Finally, researchers should also consider whether respondents are likely to believe that two constructs are related by an implicit theory, because if they are, then the respondents may be motivated to provide answers that are consistent with that theory.

Task factors that may cause or facilitate biased responding. A third question that researchers should consider is the impact of the task on respondents. More specifically, researchers should evaluate the extent to which respondents will have difficulty generating accurate answers to the questions and the extent to which the measurement conditions may make it easy for them to minimize their effort by responding in a stylistic manner. For example, Doty & Glick (1998) argue that one reason why Cote & Buckley (1987) found that some types of measures contain more method variance than others is that responding to complex, abstract questions is a more difficult task for respondents than answering simple, concrete questions. In addition, they note that complex, abstract questions are more likely to trigger social psychological processes that increase the "covariation among the systematic error variance components, thereby increasing the bias in the observed relationships between constructs" (Doty & Glick 1998, p. 381).

Another task characteristic that makes it more difficult for respondents to provide accurate responses is item ambiguity. Because ambiguity makes respondents less certain about how to accurately answer a question (e.g., Podsakoff et al. 2003), it increases the likelihood that they will rely on their own stylistic response tendencies to generate a merely satisfactory answer and increases the sensitivity of their answers to context effects (see Tourangeau et al. 2000). Consequently, when evaluating the potential threat of method bias, researchers should consider the extent to which their questions fail to define ambiguous or unfamiliar terms, refer to vague concepts without providing clear examples, have complicated syntax, or are double-barreled. In addition, Krosnick (1991) notes that item ambiguity is greater if only the end points of a response scale are labeled (rather than every point).

In contrast, rather than making the task of providing an accurate response more difficult, other aspects of the measurement context may enhance the threat of method bias by making it easier to provide an alternative, merely satisfactory, response. For example, it is easier for respondents to provide answers that are consistent with each other or with an implicit theory if the answers to previous questions are readily available (physically or in memory) at the time of answering a later question. This is likely to be the case in a self-administered paper and pencil questionnaire and is often (but need not be) the case for online questionnaires. This may also be the case when questions are grouped together in close proximity by construct on the questionnaire. Alternatively, it seems plausible that ERS or MRS response styles would be easier to implement if the measures were grouped together by scale type, with the same number of scale points, with common anchor labels, and without any reversed item wording.

What Can Be Done To Mitigate the Problem?

Procedural remedies. Generally, studies should be designed to maximize respondent motivation and ability and minimize task difficulty so that respondents are more likely to respond accurately. To increase the probability that respondents can provide accurate answers to the questions, it is necessary to implement procedures that ensure that respondents have the ability to answer the questions asked, decrease the difficulty of responding accurately, and increase the difficulty of responding stylistically. To increase the probability that respondents will try to provide accurate answers, it is necessary to implement not only procedures that increase their motivation to provide accurate answers, but also procedures

that decrease their motivation to respond stylistically by increasing the effort required to do so.

The key thing that must be done to make sure that respondents have the ability to answer questions accurately is to match the difficulty of the task of answering the questions with the capabilities of the respondents. One obvious way to do this is to make sure that you don't ask respondents to "tell more than they can know" (Ericsson & Simon 1980, Nisbett & Wilson 1977). This can be avoided by exercising caution when asking respondents about the motives for their behavior, the effects of situational factors on their behavior, or other things pertaining to cognitive processes that they are unlikely to have attended to or stored in short-term memory. Beyond this, researchers can decrease the difficulty of responding accurately by using clear and concise language, avoiding complicated syntax, defining ambiguous or unfamiliar terms, not referring to vague concepts without providing clear examples, avoiding double-barreled items, and labeling all scale points rather than just the end points.

Perhaps the easiest way to increase the probability that respondents will try to provide accurate answers to the questions is by developing a good cover story and instructions (Aronson et al. 1998). For example, the desire for self-expression or emotional catharsis may be enhanced by explaining in the cover story or instructions that "we value your opinion," "we need your feedback," or that we want respondents to "tell us what you think." The tendency to respond in a socially desirable manner, threats to self-esteem, and defensiveness may be diminished through anonymity, telling respondents in the cover story or instructions there are no right or wrong answers, and assuring them that people have different opinions about the issues addressed in the questionnaire. The motivation of respondents to provide accurate answers may also be increased by explaining how the information will be used or how it will benefit them or their organization (e.g., by mentioning that the data will help their employer to improve working conditions or make their job easier). Promising feedback to respondents may motivate them to respond more accurately so that they can gain greater self-understanding. Motivation can also be increased through endorsement of the study by senior management. Finally, motivation to respond accurately can be maintained by keeping the questionnaire short and minimizing redundancies to the extent possible. However, because multiple measures of the same construct are usually essential, the best approach may be to vary the wording of the items rather than just using synonyms.

In addition to increasing the motivation to respond accurately, it is also important to decrease the motivation to respond stylistically by increasing the effort required to do so. This can be done in several ways. The first is by reversing the wording of some of the items to balance the positively and negatively worded items. Of course, this is only a good idea if it can be done without altering the content validity or conceptual meaning of the scale and if the reverse-worded items are not confusing to respondents. A second way is by separating items on the questionnaire to eliminate proximity effects. However, this may not be feasible if the questionnaire is too short. A third way is by varying the scale types and anchor labels to the extent that it is conceptually appropriate.

Of course, the procedures outlined above are not likely to fully control for every type of method bias. For example, it is unlikely that self-deception biases, memory biases (e.g., things that were recently activated are more accessible), or perceptual biases (e.g., Gestalt principles of perception) would be controlled by these efforts. To the extent that these things are a concern, try to obtain the measures of the predictor and criterion constructs from different sources. This is most easily done if there are multiple observers of the phenomenon of interest who have access to the same information and if the phenomenon is not self-referential (Chan in Brannick et al. 2010). Under these circumstances, separating sources should help to diminish the effects of involuntary memory-based and perceptual biases and may help to reduce the biasing effects of stylistic

responding. However, if these conditions are not met, this procedure may also introduce information biases or attribution biases.

If separating the sources is not feasible or desirable, another procedure that should help to diminish method bias is to separate the measurement of the predictor and criterion constructs temporally, methodologically, or psychologically. Temporal separation involves introducing a time lag between measurement of the predictor and criterion variables. This procedure is appropriate if (a) the phenomenon is not ephemeral, short lived, or rapidly changing; (b) the phenomenon is based on long-term (rather than short-term) memory effects; (c) a significant amount of respondent attrition is not likely to occur; and (d) it is financially and logistically feasible. To be effective, it is important for the temporal delay to be long enough to produce forgetting, clear short-term memory, or to disassociate cues in the two measurement occasions.

Methodological separation involves having respondents complete the measurement of the predictor variable under different methodological conditions than the criterion variables. For example, researchers can use different scale properties, response modes, and data collection locations for the predictor and criterion measures, or they can physically separate the predictor and criterion measures on the questionnaire. Methodological separation is appropriate provided that varying the scale properties or response mode does not alter the conceptual meaning of the measures and that the questionnaire is of sufficient length to separate the measures. This can diminish method bias by increasing the difficulty of responding stylistically, eliminating the saliency of any contextually provided retrieval cues, and/or reducing the respondent's ability to use previous answers to fill in gaps in what is recalled or to use prior responses to answer subsequent questions (Podsakoff et al. 2003).

The measures of the predictor and criterion variables can be separated psychologically by using a "multiple study" cover story, camouflaging interest in the criterion or predictor variable (i.e., by embedding it in the context of other questions so that it is less psychologically prominent), or disguising the reasons for obtaining the predictor or criterion measure (i.e., by leading respondents to believe that it is tangential to the main purpose of the study). These procedures diminish method biases by reducing the perceived diagnosticity of responses to the measures of the predictor variable as cues for how to respond to the measures of the criterion variable (cf. Feldman & Lynch 1988). However, psychological separation is unlikely to diminish biases due to the accessibility of responses to the measures of the predictor variable in memory. For this reason, it may be wise to use this procedure in conjunction with a temporal separation long enough to clear short-term memory. Of course, implementing this procedure (i.e., psychological separation) is contingent upon the researcher's ability to create a credible cover story, and it is only useful if the means of producing the psychological separation does not cause a temporal delay that is longer than the phenomenon of interest.

Statistical remedies. In situations where method bias is still an important concern, even after implementing procedural methods of control, we recommend that researchers follow this up with appropriate statistical remedies. More specifically, we recommend that researchers first try to use the directly measured latent factor technique or the measured response style technique because both of these techniques control for measurement error and specify the nature of the method bias. The former would be used if a researcher is concerned about a particular source of bias for which a valid measure of the biasing factor is available or could be developed. The latter would be used if a researcher is concerned with the biasing effects of response styles (e.g., ARS, ERS). In this case, we recommend following the guidelines outlined in Weijters et al. (2008).

If the specific source of the method bias is unknown or valid measures of the source of bias are not available, then we recommend using the CFA marker technique or the common method factor technique because these approaches control for measurement error, even though they do not clearly specify the nature of the method bias. The CFA marker technique requires the researcher to include appropriate marker variables that are theoretically unrelated to any of the measures of the focal constructs of interest in the questionnaire. The common method factor technique does not require the inclusion of any additional measures, but it is problematic because it may capture irrelevant trait variance in addition to systematic method variance.

A final technique that could be used to control statistically for method biases is the instrumental variable technique. Although it provides no insight into the nature of the method bias, if it could be properly implemented it would be effective. However, as we noted earlier, it is extremely difficult to identify instrumental variables that are strongly related to the endogenous predictor variables but completely uncorrelated with the structural error term for the equation. This is a serious barrier to implementing this technique because if these requirements are not met, this technique can produce biased estimates and inflate the type I error rates; even a slight correlation between a weak IV and the structural error term for the equation can cause the IV estimate to exhibit more bias (even asymptotically) than an OLS estimate (Kennedy 2008). Therefore, although the use of this technique to control for method bias is possible in principle, it may be difficult to put into practice.

Additional approaches. Two final approaches that might help rule out method bias as a rival explanation for a study's findings have been identified recently. The first alternative approach is based on the simulation findings of Evans (1985) and a proof by Siemsen et al. (2010), which demonstrate that although method bias can inflate (or deflate) bivariate linear relationships, it cannot inflate (but does deflate) quadratic and interaction effects. Consequently, if a study is designed to test hypotheses about quadratic or interaction effects, rather than main effects, then method bias would not be able to account for any statistically significant effects observed. Although this may not be possible or desirable in many instances, in those cases where it is conceptually appropriate and possible, it may be a reasonable alternative to the procedural and statistical remedies described above. The second alternative approach, recently suggested by Chan (in Brannick et al. 2010), is to (*a*) identify one or more potential sources of method bias, (*b*) manipulate them in the design of the study, and (*c*) test whether the hypothesized estimates of the relationships among the constructs generalize across conditions. Importantly, Chan notes that when used in combination with the statistical techniques described above, this method provides a powerful means of detecting and controlling method bias.

CONCLUSION

The purpose of this article has been to review the current state of knowledge about method biases. Our review indicates that although there is some disagreement about the way "method" and method "biases" are defined, the evidence shows that method biases can significantly influence item validities and reliabilities as well as the covariation between latent constructs. This suggests that researchers must be knowledgeable about the ways to control method biases that might be present in their studies. Consequently, we recommend procedural and statistical remedies that can be used to achieve this control. Although space constraints prevent us from addressing all of the issues regarding this important topic, we hope that we have provided some recommendations that researchers can use to deal with the detrimental effects of method biases in their research.

DISCLOSURE STATEMENT

The authors are unaware of any affiliation, funding, or financial holdings that might be perceived as affecting the objectivity of this review.

LITERATURE CITED

Alessandri G, Vecchione M, Fagnani C, Bentler PM, Barbaranelli C, et al. 2010. Much more than model fitting? Evidence for the heritability of method effect associated with positively worded items of the life orientation test revised. *Struct. Equ. Model.* 17:642–53

Antonakis J, Bendahan S, Jacquart P, Lalive R. 2010. On making causal claims: a review and recommendations. *Leadersh. Q.* 6:1086–20

Aronson E, Wilson TD, Brewer MB. 1998. Experimentation in social psychology. In *The Handbook of Social Psychology*, ed. DT Gilbert, ST Fiske, G Lindzey, Vol. 1, pp. 99–142. Boston, MA: McGraw-Hill. 4th ed.

Arora R. 1982. Validation of an S-O-R model for situation, enduring, and response components of involvement. *J. Mark. Res.* 19:505–16

Bagozzi RP. 1984. A prospectus for theory construction in marketing. *J. Mark.* 48:11–29

Bagozzi RP. 1993. Assessing construct-validity in personality research: applications to measures of self-esteem. *J. Res. Personal.* 27:49–87

Bagozzi RP, Phillips LW. 1982. Representing and testing organizational theories—a holistic construal. *Admin. Sci. Q.* 27:459–89

Bagozzi RP, Yi Y. 1990. Assessing method variance in multitrait-multimethod matrices: the case of self-reported affect and perceptions at work. *J. Appl. Psychol.* 75:547–60

Baumgartner H, Steenkamp JBEM. 2001. Response styles in marketing research: a cross-national investigation. *J. Mark. Res.* 38:143–56

Billiet JB, McClendon MJ. 2000. Modeling acquiescence in measurement models for two balanced sets of items. *Struct. Equ. Model.* 7:608–28

Bodner TE. 2006. Designs, participants, and measurement methods in psychological research. *Can. Psychol.* 47:263–72

Bollen KA. 1989. *Structural Equations with Latent Variables*. New York: Wiley

Brannick MT, Chan D, Conway JM, Lance CE, Spector PE. 2010. What is method variance and how can we cope with it? A panel discussion. *Organ. Res. Methods* 13:407–20

Brannick MT, Spector PE. 1990. Estimation problems in the block-diagonal model of the multitrait-multimethod matrix. *Appl. Psychol. Meas.* 14:325–39

Buckley MR, Cote JA, Comstock SM. 1990. Measurement errors in the behavioral sciences: the case of personality attitude research. *Educ. Psychol. Meas.* 50:447–74

Campbell DT, Fiske D. 1959. Convergent and discriminant validation by the multitrait-multimethod matrix. *Psychol. Bull.* 56:81–105

Campbell DT, O'Connell EJ. 1967. Methods factors in multitrait-multimethod matrices: multiplicative rather than additive? *Multivar. Behav. Res.* 2:409–26

Chang S-J, van Wittleloostuijn A, Eden L. 2010. From the editors: common method variance in international business research. *J. Int. Bus. Stud.* 41:178–84

Chen PY, Spector PE. 1991. Negative affectivity as the underlying cause of correlations between stressors and strains. *J. Appl. Psychol.* 76:398–407

Cote JA, Buckley R. 1987. Estimating trait, method, and error variance: generalizing across 70 construct validation studies. *J. Mark. Res.* 24:315–18

Cote JA, Buckley R. 1988. Measurement error and theory testing in consumer research: an illustration of the importance of construct validation. *J. Consum. Res.* 14:579–82

Cronbach LJ. 1946. Response sets and test validity. *Educ. Psychol. Meas.* 6:475–94

Cronbach LJ. 1950. Further evidence on response sets and test validity. *Educ. Psychol. Meas.* 10:3–31

De Beuckelaer A, Weijters B, Rutten A. 2010. Using ad hoc measures for response styles: a cautionary note. *Qual. Quant.* 44:761–75

Doty DH, Glick WH. 1998. Common methods bias: Does common methods variance really bias results? *Organ. Res. Methods* 1:374–406

Edwards AL. 1970. *The Measurement of Personality Traits by Scales and Inventories*. New York: Holt, Rinehart & Winston

Edwards JR. 2008. To prosper, organizational psychology should... overcome methodological barriers to progress. *J. Organ. Behav.* 29:469–91

Ericsson KA, Simon HA. 1980. Verbal reports as data. *Psychol. Rev.* 87:215–57

Evans MG. 1985. A Monte Carlo study of the effects of correlated method variance in moderated multiple regression analysis. *Organ. Behav. Hum. Decis. Process.* 36:305–23

Feldman JM, Lynch JG. 1988. Self-generated validity and other effects of measurement on belief, attitude, intention, and behavior. *J. Appl. Psychol.* 73:421–35

Fiske DW. 1982. Convergent-discriminant validation in measurements and research strategies. In *Forms of Validity in Research*, ed. D Brinberg, LH Kidder, pp. 77–92. San Francisco, CA: Jossey-Bass

Flamer S. 1983. Assessment of the multitrait-multimethod matrix validity of Likert scales via confirmatory factor analysis. *Multivar. Behav. Res.* 18:275–308

Harris MM, Bladen A. 1994. Wording effects in the measurement of role conflict and role ambiguity: a multitrait-multimethod analysis. *J. Manage.* 20:887–901

Harrison DA, McLaughlin ME, Coalter TM. 1996. Context, cognition, and common method variance: psychometric and verbal protocol evidence. *Organ. Behav. Hum. Decis. Process.* 68:246–61

Higgins ET, Rholes WS, Jones CR. 1977. Category accessibility and impression formation. *J. Exp. Soc. Psychol.* 13:141–54

Hulsheger UR, Anderson N, Salgado JF. 2009. Team-level predictors of innovation at work: a comprehensive meta-analysis spanning three decades of research. *J. Appl. Psychol.* 94:1128–45

Jackson DN. 1967. Acquiescence response styles: problems of identification and control. In *Response Set in Personality Assessment*, ed. IA Berg, pp. 71–114. Chicago: Aldine

Johnson JA. 2004. The impact of item characteristics on item and scale validity. *Multivar. Behav. Res.* 39:273–302

Johnson RE, Rosen CC, Djurdevic E. 2011. Assessing the impact of common method variance on higher-order multidimensional constructs. *J. Appl. Psychol.* 96:744–61

Jöreskög KG. 1998. Interaction and nonlinear modeling: issues and approaches. In *Interaction and Nonlinear Effects in Structural Equation Modeling*, ed. RE Schumacker, GA Marcoulides, pp. 239–50. Mahwah, NJ: Erlbaum

Kennedy P. 2008. *A Guide to Econometrics*. Malden, MA: Blackwell. 6th ed.

Kozlowski S. 2009. Editorial. *J. Appl. Psychol.* 94:1–4

Kothandapani V. 1971. Validation of feeling, belief, and intention to act as three components of attitude and their contribution to prediction of contraceptive behavior. *J. Personal. Soc. Psychol.* 19:321–33

Krosnick JA. 1991. Response strategies for coping with the cognitive demands of attitude measures in surveys. *Appl. Cogn. Psychol.* 5:213–36

Krosnick JA. 1999. Survey research. *Annu. Rev. Psychol.* 50:537–67

Kuncel NR, Tellegen A. 2009. A conceptual and empirical reexamination of the measurement of the social desirability of items: implications for detecting desirable response style and scale development. *Pers. Psychol.* 62:201–228

Lance CE, Baranik LE, Lau AR, Scharlau EA. 2009. If it ain't trait it must be method: (mis)application of the multitrait-multimethod design in organizational research. In *Statistical and Methodological Myths and Urban Legends: Doctrine, Verity, and Fable in the Organizational and Social Sciences*, ed. CE Lance, RL Vandenberg, pp. 337–60. New York: Routledge

Lance CE, Dawson B, Birkelbach D, Hoffman BJ. 2010. Method effects, measurement error, and substantive conclusions. *Organ. Res. Methods* 13:407–20

Le H, Schmidt FL, Putka DJ. 2009. The multifaceted nature of measurement artifacts and its implications for estimating construct-level relationships. *Organ. Res. Methods* 12:165–200

Lindell MK, Whitney DJ. 2001. Accounting for common method variance in cross-sectional designs. *J. Appl. Psychol.* 86:114–21

Lowe KB, Kroeck KG, Sivasubramaniam N. 1996. Effectiveness correlates of transformational and transactional leadership: a meta-analytic review of the MLQ literature. *Leadersh. Q.* 7:385–425

MacKenzie SB, Podsakoff PM, Podsakoff NP. 2011. Construct measurement and validity assessment in behavioral research: integrating new and existing techniques. *MIS Q.* 35: 293–334

Messick S. 1991. Psychology and methodology of response styles. In *Improving the Inquiry in Social Science: A Volume in Honor of Lee J. Cronbach*, ed. RE Snow, DE Wiley, pp. 161–200. Hillsdale, NJ: Erlbaum

Mirowsky J, Ross CE. 1991. Eliminating defense and agreement bias from measures of the sense of control: a 2 × 2 index. *Soc. Psychol. Q.* 54:127–45

Nisbett RE, Wilson TD. 1977. Telling more than we can know: verbal reports on mental processes. *Psychol. Rev.* 84:231–59

Nunally JC, Bernstein IH. 1994. *Psychometric Theory*. New York: McGraw-Hill. 3rd ed.

Ostroff C, Kinicki AJ, Clark MA. 2002. Substantive and operational issues of response bias across levels of analysis: an example of climate-satisfaction relationships. *J. Appl. Psychol.* 87:355–68

Paulhus DL. 1984. Two-component models of socially desirable responding. *J. Personal. Soc. Psychol.* 46:598–609

Phillips JS, Lord RG. 1986. Notes on the theoretical and practical consequences of implicit leadership theories for the future of leadership measurement. *J. Manage.* 12:31–41

Podsakoff PM, MacKenzie SB, Lee J-Y, Podsakoff NP. 2003. Common method biases in behavioral research: a critical review of the literature and recommended remedies. *J. Appl. Psychol.* 88:879–903

Podsakoff PM, Organ DW. 1986. Self-reports in organizational research—problems and prospects. *J. Manage.* 12:531–44

Rafferty AE, Griffin MA. 2004. Dimensions of transformational leadership: conceptual and empirical extensions. *Leadersh. Q.* 15:329–54

Rafferty AE, Griffin MA. 2006. Refining individualized consideration: distinguishing developmental leadership and supportive leadership. *J. Occup. Organ. Psychol.* 79:37–61

Richardson HA, Simmering MJ, Sturman MC. 2009. A tale of three perspectives: examining post hoc statistical techniques for detection and correction of common method variance. *Organ. Res. Methods* 12:762–800

Rindfleisch A, Malter AJ, Ganesan S, Moorman C. 2008. Cross-sectional versus longitudinal research: concepts, findings, and guidelines. *J. Mark. Res.* 45:261–79

Rosenberg MJ. 1965. When dissonance fails: on eliminating evaluation apprehension from attitude measurement. *J. Personal. Soc. Psychol.* 1:28–42

Scherpenzeel A, Saris W. 1997. The validity and reliability of survey questions: a meta-analysis of MTMM studies. *Soc. Methods Res.* 25:341–83

Schaubroeck J, Ganster DC, Fox ML. 1992. Dispositional affect and work-related stress. *J. Appl. Psychol.* 77:322–35

Schmitt N. 1994. Method bias: the importance of theory and measurement. *J. Organ. Behav.* 15:393–98

Schwarz N, Hippler HJ, Noelle-Neumann E. 1992. A cognitive model of response-order effects in survey measurement. In *Context Effects in Social and Psychological Research*, ed. N Schwarz, S Sudman, pp. 187–201. New York: Springer-Verlag

Sechrest L, Davis MF, Stickle TR, McKnight PE. 2000. Understanding method variance. In *Research Design: David Campbell's Legacy*, ed. L Bickman, Vol. 2, pp. 63–88. Thousand Oaks, CA: Sage

Sharma R, Yetton P, Crawford J. 2009. Estimating the effect of common method variance: the method-method pair technique with an illustration from TAM research. *MIS Q.* 33:473–90

Siemsen E, Roth A, Oliveira P. 2010. Common method bias in regression models with linear, quadratic, and interaction effects. *Organ. Res. Methods* 13:456–76

Spector PE. 1987. Method variance as an artifact in self-reported affect and perceptions at work: myth or significant problem. *J. Appl. Psychol.* 72:438–43

Spector PE. 2006. Method variance in organizational research: truth or urban legend? *Organ. Res. Methods* 9:221–32

Spector PE, Brannick MT. 2009. Common method variance or measurement bias? The problem and possible solutions. In *The Sage Handbook of Organizational Research Methods*, ed. DA Buchanan, A Bryman, pp. 346–62. Los Angeles, CA: Sage

Steenkamp JBEM, De Jong MG, Baumgartner H. 2010. Socially desirable response tendencies in survey research. *J. Mark. Res.* 47:199–214

Straub DW. 2009. Creating blue oceans of thought via highly citable articles. *MIS Q.* 33:iii–vii

Sudman S, Bradburn NM, Schwarz N. 1996. *Thinking About Answers: The Application of Cognitive Processes to Survey Methodology.* San Francisco, CA: Jossey-Bass

Tourangeau R, Rips LJ, Rasinski KA. 2000. *The Psychology of Survey Response.* London: Cambridge Univ. Press

Tourangeau R, Singer E, Presser S. 2003. Context effects in attitude surveys—effects on remote items and impact on predictive validity. *Soc. Methods Res.* 31:486–513

Weijters B, Cabooter E, Schillewaert N. 2010c. The effect of rating scale format on response styles: the number of response categories and response category labels. *Int. J. Mark.* 27:236–47

Weijters B, Geuens M, Schillewaert N. 2009. The proximity effect: the role of inter-item distance on reverse-item bias. *Int. J. Res. Market.* 26:2–12

Weijters B, Geuens M, Schillewaert N. 2010a. The stability of individual response styles. *Psychol. Methods* 15:96–110

Weijters B, Geuens M, Schillewaert N. 2010b. The individual consistency of acquiescence and extreme response style in self-report questionnaires. *Appl. Psychol. Meas.* 34:105–21

Weijters B, Schillewaert N, Geuens M. 2008. Assessing response styles across modes of data collection. *J. Acad. Mark. Sci.* 36:409–22

Werts CE, Linn RL, Joreskog KG. 1974. Intraclass reliability estimates—testing structural assumptions. *Educ. Psychol. Meas.* 34:25–33

Widaman KF. 1985. Hierarchically nested covariance structural models for multitrait-multimethod data. *Appl. Psychol. Meas.* 9:1–26

Williams LJ, Anderson SE. 1994. An alternative approach to method effects by using latent-variable models: applications in organizational behavior research. *J. Appl. Psychol.* 79:323–31

Williams LJ, Cote JA, Buckley MR. 1989. Lack of method variance in self-reported affect and perceptions at work: reality or artifact? *J. Appl. Psychol.* 74:462–68

Williams LJ, Gavin MB, Williams ML. 1996. Measurement and nonmeasurement processes with negative affectivity and employee attitudes. *J. Appl. Psychol.* 81:88–101

Williams LJ, Hartman N, Cavazotte F. 2010. Method variance and marker variables: a review and comprehensive CFA marker technique. *Organ. Res. Methods* 13:477–514

Woszczynski AB, Whitman ME. 2004. The problem of common method variance in IS research. In *Handbook of Information Systems Research*, ed. ME Whitman, AB Woszczynski, pp. 66–77. Hershey, PA: Idea Group

Wothke W, Browne MW. 1990. The direct product model for the MTMM matrix parameterized as a second order factor analysis model. *Psychometrika* 55:255–62

Zinkhan GM. 2006. Research traditions and patterns in marketing scholarship. *J. Acad. Mark. Sci.* 34:281–83

Neuroethics: The Ethical, Legal, and Societal Impact of Neuroscience

Martha J. Farah

Center for Neuroscience & Society, University of Pennsylvania, Philadelphia, Pennsylvania 19104; email: mfarah@psych.upenn.edu

Annu. Rev. Psychol. 2012. 63:571–91

The *Annual Review of Psychology* is online at psych.annualreviews.org

This article's doi:
10.1146/annurev.psych.093008.100438

Keywords

brain imaging, enhancement, free will, privacy, soul

Abstract

Advances in cognitive, affective, and social neuroscience raise a host of new questions concerning the ways in which neuroscience can and should be used. These advances also challenge our intuitions about the nature of humans as moral and spiritual beings. Neuroethics is the new field that grapples with these issues. The present article surveys a number of applications of neuroscience to such diverse arenas as marketing, criminal justice, the military, and worker productivity. The ethical, legal, and societal effects of these applications are discussed. Less practical, but perhaps ultimately more consequential, is the impact of neuroscience on our worldview and our understanding of the human person.

Contents

WHY NEUROETHICS, WHY NOW?

The word "neuroethics" entered the vocabulary of academic neuroscientists and bioethicists at the beginning of the twenty-first century. It was coined by William Safire, a scholar of word history and meaning (for 30 years he wrote the *New York Times* column "On Language") who also stayed abreast of developments in neuroscience as chairman of the Dana Foundation. From its first mention in a 2001 Safire column, "neuroethics" has come to refer to a broad range of ethical, legal, and social issues raised by progress in neuroscience. To understand the emergence of neuroethics as a field, meriting a name of its own, we must consider some recent scientific history.

For much of the latter twentieth century, genetics was viewed as the science most likely to challenge our ethical, legal, and social practices and assumptions (e.g., Silver 1997). Findings from twin studies and other behavioral genetics methods demonstrated the substantial role of genes in most aspects of human psychology, and the development of molecular genetics promised to reveal the mechanisms by which personality, intelligence, psychiatric vulnerabilities, and other traits developed, as well as to open the door to targeted interventions (e.g., Parens 2004). By the turn of the century, however, it had become clear that psychological traits bore only the weakest relationships with individual genes and that the genetics of human psychology involve extremely complex patterns of interaction among genes and between genes and environment, limiting the ease with which theories could be constructed and also the effectiveness with which interventions to change behavior could be achieved (e.g., Van Gestel & Van Broeckhoven 2003).

Contemporaneous with the lowering of expectations for genetics, neuroscience was undergoing rapid development into the areas of cognition, emotion, and social processes, thanks in large part to the advent of functional neuroimaging. Like genetics, neuroscience deals with the biological essence of persons,

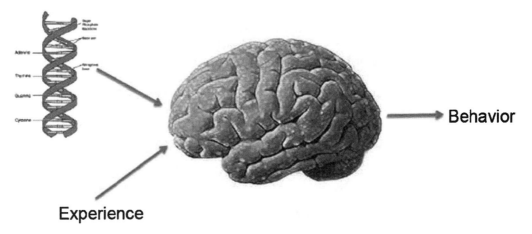

Experience

Behavior

Figure 1

Schematic illustration of the relations between genes, experience, the brain, and behavior.

including their minds and behaviors. However, as represented in **Figure 1**, neuroscience encompasses the totality of genetic influences on behavior combined with environmental influences. Also apparent in **Figure 1**, the brain is one causal step closer to behavior than to genes or features of the environment. These considerations suggest that neuroscience may turn out to be far more successful than genetics in explaining, predicting, and changing human behavior. Indeed, so far neuroscience has been living up to this promise. For example, whereas single genes account, typically, for 2% to 4% of the variance in personality traits (Van Gestel & Van Broeckhoven 2003), brain imaging studies typically capture an order of magnitude more variance (Farah et al. 2009).

As a result of these developments in cognitive, affective, and social neuroscience, neuroscience can now be brought to bear in many different spheres of human life, beyond the traditional application area for biological science, medicine. Any endeavor that depends on being able to understand, assess, predict, control, or improve human behavior is, in principle, a potential application area for neuroscience. This includes diverse sectors of society, for example, education, business, politics, law, entertainment, and warfare. The goal of this article is to review the current and near-term

role of neuroscience in our lives and evaluate its likely impact on individuals and society.

What Can We Do? What Should We Do?

The next two sections of the article address the issues that emerge from neuroscience-based technologies, in other words, relatively pragmatic issues concerning how the fruits of social neuroscience can and should be applied. These include ethical, legal, and social challenges raised by newfound abilities to image the brain and thereby obtain information about mental states and personal traits, as well as by our growing ability to intervene in individuals' brain function to alter these states and traits. These first two sections in effect begin with the question, "What can we do with neuroscience?" and go on to analyze the ethical question that follows, "Should we do it?"

What Do We Know? How Should We View Ourselves?

The final section addresses neuroethical issues that emerge from the impact of social neuroscience on our understanding of human beings. In this section it is the knowledge per se, not its technological applications, that is the focus

MRI: magnetic resonance imaging

Incidental finding: abnormality that is unintentionally discovered in the process of laboratory testing

PET: positron emission tomography

of the review. This section includes the ways in which our evolving understanding of the human person challenges our long-held beliefs about morality and spirituality. The questions of this section are, in effect, "What do we know about the neural bases of the human mind?" and "How does this knowledge change the way we view ourselves, as moral and spiritual beings?"

NEUROETHICS OF BRAIN IMAGING

Ethical Issues, Familiar and New

Developments in brain imaging have engendered a large literature in neuroethics. Some of this literature is concerned with issues for which we can find helpful precedents in clinical bioethics. For example, now that magnetic resonance imaging (MRI) of healthy normal subjects is a widespread research method, we face the issue of what to do when anatomical abnormalities or signs of disease are revealed in the course of scanning. Do researchers have a duty to search scans for such abnormalities? If they are not qualified to screen for abnormalities themselves, must they show them to someone who is? Should subjects be allowed to opt out of being informed of such findings in advance of the scan? There is currently no universally accepted procedure for dealing with incidental findings from research scans (Illes et al. 2004). Of course, the ethical issues raised by incidental findings from brain scans are not fundamentally different from those that would be raised by imaging other organ systems or by genetic testing. Although important work remains to be done on this topic, the issues are not particularly unique to the brain.

Another important neuroethical issue with close analogies in clinical bioethics is predictive and diagnostic imaging for progressive diseases that lack effective treatments, such as Alzheimer's disease (Karlawish 2011). Such scans are intended for research aimed at understanding the pathophysiology of neurodegenerative disease and the development of treatments for use in the presymptomatic phase. However,

these scans could be used for other reasons by the "worried well" of the baby boomer generation or their worried employers or insurers. In such cases, the benefits of foreknowledge, for example the greater opportunity to plan, must be weighed against the psychological burden of this knowledge and its potential impact on employability or insurability. As with the problem of incidental findings, the ethical, legal, and societal dimensions of this problem are largely familiar from clinical bioethics outside of brain imaging, particularly in the area of genetic testing.

In other cases, brain imaging raises new ethical, legal, and social issues that stem directly from the special relationship between brain and mind. The ability of brain imaging to deliver information about our psyches—about who we are and what we might be thinking or feeling while in the scanner—opens up a range of ethical challenges with few, if any, direct precedents. These relatively new neuroethical issues provide the focus for the remainder of this section.

Imaging the Mind

Since Michael Posner and Marcus Raichle first adapted positron emission tomography (PET) scanning to the study of cognitive processes in the 1980s, brain imaging revolutionized the study of psychology and neuroscience and led eventually to the scientific capabilities that today present ethical, legal, and social challenges as well as benefits.

The first phase of this process was the harnessing of functional brain imaging for the study of human psychology, which required the ability to isolate the brain activity associated with specific component mental processes from the totality of brain activity evoked by the numerous processes engaged when people perform psychological tasks. To do this, the pattern of brain activity associated with performing one task was subtracted from the pattern of brain activity associated with another task, hypothesized to require all the same component processes as the first along with one additional process (see, e.g., Posner & Raichle 1994). By the assumptions of the subtraction method, the difference image resulting from the subtraction of two images would depict the brain activity associated with that single additional process. The subtraction method and later elaborations and variations, such as conjunction and disjunction and parametric and habituation methods, allowed imaging to isolate individual psychological processes. Instead of presenting us with the superposition of all processes involved in performing a task, for example solving mental rotation problems, these methods enabled researchers to disentangle the component processes, for example perceiving the 3-D form of the mental rotation stimulus, the process of mentally rotating that stimulus, and the process of responding. These advances enabled the rapid growth of cognitive neuroscience in the 1990s.

Although the methods just described were initially applied to the study of cognition (e.g., language, memory, visual perception), by the mid-1990s researchers had begun to use them for the study of emotion (see, e.g., Phan et al. 2002 for a review of early work in this area). Soon thereafter the field of social neuroscience was born, and the more complex emotions and cognitions involved in interpersonal processes became subjects of study in functional neuroimaging (see, e.g., Lieberman 2007 for a review). During the same period, functional neuroimaging methods developed further to include better statistical solutions to the false-positive activations in whole-brain analyses and methods for studying functional connectivity (Aguirre 2010), both of which helped to realize the potential of functional imaging to illuminate the functioning of the brain as a whole system, and were joined by new methods for studying structure, including voxel-based morphometry and diffusion tensor imaging (Le Bihan 2001, Mechelli et al. 2005).

As a result of continued methodological development of imaging, and especially its growing use for the study of affective and social processes, by the turn of the century neuroimaging had entered the public's awareness.

Pictures showing the brain bases of deeply personal aspects of ourselves—fear, joy, love—made striking news. Brain imaging seemed to show that our highest human virtues and worst human vices were localizable functions of the brain, revealed as colored hot spots on anatomically detailed grayscale images. Even the scientifically sophisticated among us had to admit to the occasional feeling of wonder or awe when viewing such evidence. As is discussed in the final section of this review, by demonstrating the existence of physical correlates of our most important human qualities and experiences, neuroimaging has contributed to a fundamental change in how we think of ourselves and our fellow persons.

Imaging Individual Minds and Mental States

One more type of methodological development was needed in order for brain imaging to become a tool that poses practical ethical, legal, and social challenges. This was the development of methods for disaggregating imaging data by subject and by mental event. In the early decades of functional brain imaging research, inferences were made about groups of subjects with the goal of generalizing about typical normal brains or about brains that are typical of a group of interest (e.g., males or females, depressed or nondepressed people). For such analyses, variation between subjects within the group was treated as a form of measurement error. Similarly, imaging experiments generally involved a small number of conditions, for example a baseline condition and one or two experimental conditions, with many trials per condition. The trials were treated as repeated measures of the condition of interest and not analyzed for the sake of making inferences about the individual events themselves. This changed around the turn of the century, with different groups of researchers focusing on the problem of analyzing the results of single trials and on the study of individual differences in brain activity.

Voxel-based morphometry: MRI method of assessing the size and shape of a brain by comparing it, voxel by voxel, to reference brain

Diffusion tensor imaging: MRI method using degree of anisotropy of water diffusion to assess the integrity of white matter tracts in the brain

Implicit Association Test: a reaction-time test developed in social psychology to assess the degree to which different concepts are associated in someone's mind

fMRI: functional MRI

If cognitive neuroimaging was the achievement of the 1980s and social-affective neuroimaging was the achievement of the 1990s, then the imaging of individual people and individual mental states was the achievements of the next decade, the 2000s. This enabled imaging to deliver information with pragmatic ethical, legal, and societal implications, such as correlates of the social and affective traits of individuals. Examples of research on individual differences include many examples with the potential to be developed as tools for screening or assessment. Such uses could benefit individuals and society or introduce new harms. Consider the following findings, all of which are the results of basic research, not attempts at measurement.

Personality traits such as neuroticism, extraversion, conscientiousness, and empathy, which have been the mainstays of self-report studies of individual differences in personality, have become active topics of brain imaging research (Hamann & Canli 2004). In addition, many traits that fall outside the realm of traditional personality psychology, such as attitudes and propensity to violence, have also been found to have neural correlates measurable by brain imaging. For example, an early and influential study by Phelps and collaborators found that white subjects' amygdala activation correlates with the degree of unconscious negative evaluation of black faces (Phelps et al. 2000). Specifically, the discrepancy between amygdala activation to black and white faces correlated with the magnitude of unconscious bias against blacks measured in the Implicit Association Test (Greenwald et al. 1998). Coccaro et al. (2007) showed subjects with and without a history of impulsive aggression photos of faces displaying different emotions while measuring neural responses to these photos with functional MRI (fMRI). In addition to finding overall differences between aggressive and nonaggressive subjects in their response to the sight of an angry face, including greater activation of the amygdala and less activation of the presumably regulatory orbitofrontal cortex, they also found a correlation between amygdala

activation and aggression. The more aggressive one's behavior, measured over one's lifetime, the higher the activation of the left amygdala to angry faces. Turning to a more desirable trait, altruistic cooperation, Rilling et al. (2002) scanned subjects while they played an iterated Prisoner's Dilemma game and assessed the relationship between the tendency to prolong mutually cooperative play and the activation of reward-related brain areas by such cooperation. They found a correlation between cooperative behavior in the scanner and the activation it evoked in the ventral striatum, an area associated with the enjoyment of rewards from money to chocolate (Delgado 2007). In these studies just cited the correlations are moderate in size, between 0.5 and 0.7, and this accords well with the majority of appropriately analyzed fMRI studies of individual differences in social and affective traits (e.g., Vul et al. 2009).

Nonmedical Applications of Brain Imaging

Given the moderately strong relationships that exist between some psychological traits and imaging measures, could imaging be used as a method for assessing personality or ability? My colleagues and I addressed this issue in secondary analyses of data published prior to 2007, taking into account both the prediction error attributable to the less-than-perfect correlations and the prediction error attributable to the less-than-perfect estimates of the correlations themselves (Farah et al. 2009). We concluded that by scanning a new subject in a typical imaging paradigm from this literature, one could gain a modest degree of information about an individual. For example, if the best prediction from a person's brain activity is to a very high or low value of a psychological trait, one could conclude that the person is in fact unlikely to be low or high, respectively, on that trait. Such minimal predictive power would not be a practical use. However, among the studies we reviewed, some were more predictive. Assuming that imaging protocols with different tasks and different regions of interest provide nonredundant information about traits, more precise prediction may be possible by combining paradigms for the purpose of trait measurement.

Whereas brain imaging is not being used to assess psychological traits for practical purposes, it is being used to assess psychological states. One state that researchers have attempted to read from brain activation is lying. Early studies of deception were aimed at the basic science goal of characterizing the differences in brain activation between lying and truth-telling (e.g., Langleben et al. 2002) and showed that the anterior cingulate cortex as well as regions of prefrontal and parietal cortex were more active during lies (for reviews, see Bles & Haynes 2008, Christ et al. 2009). Some of the more recent research on deception with fMRI has been aimed explicitly at the reverse inference of determining the truthfulness of individual statements on the basis of brain activation. Two companies currently offer fMRI lie detection services: Cephos (**http://www.cephoscorp.com/**) and No Lie MRI (**http://www.noliemri.com/**). Among the purposes for which they advertise their services are vindication "if your word, reputation or freedom is in dispute," reduction of "risk in dating," and as a substitute for drug screening, resume validation and security background checks in employment screening. Both companies have scanned defendants in legal cases, but as of this writing neither has succeeded in having its results admitted as evidence in court. In the 2010 case of *United States v. Semrau*, the Cephos method was the subject of a hearing to determine whether it met the criteria for admissibility set out in *Daubert v. Merrell Dow Pharmaceuticals*. The court determined that it did not satisfy the Daubert requirements because its accuracy outside of artificial laboratory tasks had not been examined. In this connection it is worth noting that an electroencephalography (EEG)-based method for detecting deception has been used for several years in Indian courts (Aggarwal 2009).

Neuromarketing is another example of the use of brain imaging to assess mental states for a practical purpose. The emotions and motivations of consumers are crucial for many marketing decisions, from brand identity to pricing, but consumers are notoriously poor at reporting these aspects of their own psychology. The prospect of directly "reading" consumers' brain states is therefore of great interest to marketers. In addition, brain imaging is relatively well suited to this type of reverse inference. Compared with some psychological states, states of liking and wanting have a relatively straightforward relation to patterns of brain activity. EEG and fMRI have therefore become widely used tools in market research.

Published research in the field of neuromarketing has illuminated the ways in which packaging design, price, brand identity, spokesperson celebrity, and other marketing factors that are separate from the product itself affect neural responses to the product and how accurately those neural responses predict purchasing decisions (for reviews, see Hubert & Kenning 2008, Lee et al. 2007). The success of neuromarketing as a business tool is harder to assess, but the list of companies paying for neuromarketing suggests that many corporate decision makers have faith in it. *Forbes* magazine reported that this list includes Chevron, Disney, eBay, Google, Hyundai, Microsoft, Pepsico, and Yahoo (Burkitt 2009).

The techniques of neuromarketing are not limited to selling products and services. They have also been used to study preferences for health behaviors (Langleben et al. 2009) and political candidates (Westen et al. 2006). The firm FKF Applied Research published advice, based on their fMRI studies, to American presidential candidates for the 2008 election in the Op Ed pages of the *New York Times* (Iacoboni 2007). Their advice received widespread attention in the media and online (Aron et al. 2007, Farah 2007; see also Iacoboni 2008, Poldrack 2008). Less public attempts to understand voters' reactions to candidates on the basis of measures of brain function have reportedly

Reverse inference: inferring a psychological state from brain data rather than starting with a known psychological state and discovering its neural correlate

EEG: electroencephalography

been carried out at the request of specific political campaigns (Lindstrom 2008).

Ethical, Legal, and Societal Issues in Brain Imaging

Concerns about the ethics of brain imaging fall into two general categories, which can roughly be described as the "damned if you do and damned if you don't" categories. To the extent that brain imaging can actually deliver useful information about a person's mental states or traits, the issue of privacy is important. To the extent that it cannot, but people believe that it can, the issue of public misunderstanding is important.

Brain Privacy

A number of writers have commented on the potential threat to privacy posed by functional neuroimaging (e.g., Comm. Sci. Law, Assoc. Bar City N.Y. 2005; Hyman 2004). On the face of things, brain imaging poses a novel challenge to privacy in that it can in principle deliver information about thoughts, attitudes, beliefs, and traits even when someone offers no behavioral responses.

More concretely, and perhaps more importantly, imaging-based psychological investigations lend themselves to stealth uses in ways that more conventional paper-and-pencil or other low-tech methods do not. Both structural and functional brain images can be obtained with consent for one purpose but later analyzed for other purposes. Furthermore, in many studies the stimuli and instructions do not reveal the nature of the psychological information being sought. For example, in two of the studies cited previously, unconscious racial attitudes and impulsive aggression were both correlated with brain activity evoked by simply viewing pictures of faces (Coccaro et al. 2007, Phelps et al. 2000). Hence, in principle it seems possible to obtain information about racial attitudes and aggressive tendencies without subjects' knowledge or consent by misleading them into thinking the study concerns face perception.

Overpersuasiveness of Brain Images

At present, the problem of public misunderstanding of neuroimaging is a more immediate challenge than is the problem of mental privacy. A number of authors have suggested that laypersons may attribute greater objectivity and certainty to brain images than to other types of information about the human mind (Dumit 2004, McCabe & Castel 2007, Racine et al. 2005, Roskies 2008). This may contribute to the premature commercialization of brain imaging for various real-world applications.

Tovino (2007) outlines a range of possible regulatory responses to nonmedical neuroimaging, aimed primarily at protecting consumers and citizens from overhyped and underperforming methods. She is rightly cautious about strict or blanket restrictions. Not all premature or unvalidated applications of neuroimaging pose serious danger, and entrepreneurs should have some motivation to develop new solutions to societal problems using brain imaging. Different application areas call for different levels of regulatory protection. For example, lie detection for vetting potential dates (an advertised application) should not have to meet the same standards of evidence as for national security-related interrogations. It has even been argued that brain-based lie detection need not meet the same standards of accuracy expected of scientific evidence to be appropriate legal evidence (Schauer 2010).

From a global perspective, it seems unlikely that regulation of neuroimaging applications will be uniform. Thus, efforts to discourage imaging-based approaches to problems with potentially significant economic or security relevance have an element of unilateral disarmament. Although the risks of premature adoption of these methods, to individuals and society, are substantial, overly restrictive policies can also be counterproductive. Neither the unrealistic science fiction scenarios of mind reading nor the irresponsible hawking of unvalidated methods are reasons to discourage the development and validation of neuroimaging approaches to lie detection, employment or security screening, business, and education.

NEUROETHICS OF BRAIN ENHANCEMENT

Ethical Issues, Familiar and New

As used in the neuroethics literature, "brain enhancement" refers to interventions that make normal, healthy brains better, in contrast with treatments for unhealthy or dysfunctional brains. People have been chemically enhancing their brains for millennia, far longer than they have been treating brain disorders. Coffee, tea, coca leaves, and alcohol are among the familiar substances used to alter brain chemistry for improved cognition or mood. Yet with the advent of biological psychiatry, drugs developed for the purpose of treating neuropsychiatric disease can now be used by healthy people for enhancement, greatly increasing the variety and potency of methods for adjusting our brain states chemically. In addition, nonpharmacologic means of altering brain function, for example by magnetically stimulating specific brain regions to achieve specific psychological effects, are now poised to make the same transition from clinical to lifestyle use. These developments raise a host of new questions concerning personal improvement in the age of psychopharmaceuticals and neurotechnology.

One important set of issues concerns the tangled relationships connecting the pharmaceutical industry, university research, regulatory oversight, and physician education, especially in the United States (Lo & Field 2009). These problems are not unique to psychopharmacology, although they weigh especially heavily there for at least two reasons. One is the chronic nature of many neuropsychiatric conditions. Drugs that must be taken for decades by each individual patient are subject to especially powerful profit motives. Another is the problematic state of psychiatric nosology and the associated shortcomings of current diagnostic criteria. In the absence of valid diagnostic tests, it is difficult to draw the line between sick and borderline or borderline and well. Treatment of milder cases, like treatment for longer periods, increases sales. Thus the corporate profit motive plays a role in the expanding use of psychopharmacology by the relatively healthy. However, this can be viewed as a special case of a more general trend toward developing and marketing of medications for chronic conditions and for treating less severe forms of those conditions, a trend that is also evident in medical approaches to high blood pressure, high cholesterol, and diabetes.

The safety of brain enhancement is another topic of relevance to neuroethics. Most people find it reasonable to hold enhancements to a higher standard of safety than treatments. In terms of risk:benefit ratio, this is because we assume that treatments have greater benefits than enhancements; the value of returning someone to health is greater than the value of making a healthy person even better off. Yet little is known about the long-term safety of using neuropsychiatric medications or neurotechnology for enhancement. Indeed, relatively little is known about the long-term effects, both efficacy and safety, of many neuropsychiatric treatments, and evidence concerning their effects on normal healthy subjects is generally confined to early, short-term clinical trials (Hackshaw 2009). The safety of enhancement has recently attracted attention in the neuroethics literature, and deservedly so. Of particular concern have been the risks associated with prescription stimulants, including heart attack, psychosis, and addiction (Chatterjee 2009, Volkow & Swanson 2008). Of course, the question of how to weigh safety against potential benefits and methods for assessing safety are essentially the same, whether one is considering cognitive enhancement or cosmetic surgery.

In the remainder of this section we explore the more distinctive neuroethical issues associated with the enhancement of cognitive and social-affective brain functions. By manipulating our intellects, personalities, and moods, are we distorting our own nature? Or are we expressing that very nature, as a species driven to innovate and improve our world and ourselves?

ADHD: attention deficit hyperactivity disorder

SSRI: selective serotonin reuptake inhibitor

Cosmetic psychopharmacology: the use of psychiatric medications to enhance mood or personality

How will the growing trend toward brain enhancement affect us, as individuals and as a society?

Cognitive Enhancement

Amphetamine has a long history of nonmedical use (Rasmussen 2008), and the past decade saw a distinct rise in its use as a study aid on college campuses in the form of Adderall, a mixture of amphetamine salts intended primarily for the treatment of attention deficit hyperactivity disorder (ADHD). The cognitive neuroscience literature is mixed concerning the effectiveness of stimulants as cognitive enhancers for normal healthy subjects, with some studies finding improvements in learning and executive function and some finding null results or even occasionally impairment for subsets of subjects (Smith & Farah 2011). Nevertheless, many college students are at least occasional users. The results of a 2001 survey of more than 10,000 American college and university students showed that 7% had used a prescription stimulant such as Adderall nonmedically, and this figure ranged as high as 20% on some campuses (McCabe et al. 2005). Smaller and less scientific samples have produced estimates as high as 50% in more recent years (DeSantis et al. 2009). A number of studies reviewed by Smith & Farah (2011) indicate that academic performance enhancement was the most common reason students use these drugs, although other "lifestyle" uses such as weight control were occasionally reported.

Anecdotal evidence and informal journalists' surveys suggest that some professionals, as well as students, have added amphetamine and other stimulants to their work routines (Arrington 2008, Madrigal 2008, Maher 2008, Sahakian & Morein-Zamir 2007, Talbot 2009). Among the newer compounds mentioned in such surveys is modafinil. This drug was initially developed to reduce sleepiness in narcoleptic patients, but it also counteracts many of the cognitive symptoms of sleep deprivation in healthy normal users, allowing for more comfortable and productive "all-nighters" (Arrington 2008,

Hart-Davis 2005, Madrigal 2008, Plotz 2003). Some research suggests that modafinil may also enhance aspects of cognition in healthy people who are not sleep deprived (Turner et al. 2003). The ability to control when one gets sleepy, and perhaps even work smarter as well as work longer, has obvious allure.

Looking to the next decade or two, a number of new cognitive enhancers are likely to be available. Several companies are developing drugs to manipulate learning and memory. Spearheaded by scientists such as Eric Kandel, Mark Bear, Gary Lynch, Tim Tully, and other molecular neurobiologists, these companies are developing drugs designed to treat cognitive disorders and also to enhance the memory abilities of normal people (Marshall 2004). If one projects the market for normal memory-enhancing drugs from sales of nutritional supplements sold for this purpose, it is clear that the economic motivation is huge to develop memory-enhancing drugs to help normal people deal with their complex lives. Drugs to suppress unwanted memories are also the object of research and development (Singer 2009).

Social-Affective Enhancement

Neuroscientists have succeeded in manipulating normal levels of mood, personality, empathy, trust, aggression, and so forth, although little of this work has been translated into clinical or enhancement use. The modern age of social-affective enhancement began with the introduction of selective serotonin reuptake inhibitors (SSRIs) such as Prozac in the 1980s. These drugs offered much-needed new treatment options for patients suffering from depression and anxiety disorders and had wider societal effects as well. Peter Kramer (1997) foretold many of the current dilemmas concerning the manipulation of mood, personality, and identity in his book *Listening to Prozac*, coining the term "cosmetic psychopharmacology."

Any discussion of brain enhancement must address the question of where to draw the line between enhancement and treatment. For cognitive enhancement, the question is usually framed in terms of diagnostic boundaries between everyday distractibility and ADHD, or between normal cognitive aging and dementia. In the case of SSRIs for social-emotional enhancement, the question is more complex, partly because there are so many different therapeutic uses of SSRIs—including depression, premenstrual dysphoria, general anxiety, social anxiety, obsessive-compulsive disorder—and partly because the relevant diagnostic boundaries appear to have shifted because of the SSRIs themselves. In the case of depression, antidepressant medications before Prozac had more troublesome side effects and were therefore reserved for patients with major depression. The greater tolerability of SSRIs, combined with the pharmaceutical industry's energetic marketing to patients and doctors, has led to a larger number of less-ill patients using these drugs and to a revision of diagnostic categories (Healy 2004). As the division between pathology and health moves to include more people on the pathological side of the line, uses of medication that would originally have been considered enhancement become therapy.

Antidepressants are now the most widely used class of drugs in the United States, with an estimated 10% of the population having received a prescription for them in the year 2005 (Olfson & Marcus 2009). In light of this, recent findings that SSRIs alter personality take on broad societal significance. A recent study in depressed patients found that the SSRI paroxetine affects personality above and beyond its effect on depression (Tang 2009). The most pronounced effect on personality was on the trait of neuroticism, the tendency to experience negative emotions. Studies that have examined the effects of SSRIs in nondepressed subjects have found that their main effect appears to be the diminution of negative affect or neuroticism (Knutson et al. 1998). For example, Knutson and colleagues (1998) administered paroxetine or placebo for four weeks and assessed the effects of the drug on personality and social behavior. The drug reduced negative affect, particularly hostility, and increased affiliative behaviors. For example, subjects on the drug spoke fewer commands and instead made more suggestions to their partners in a problem-solving exercise. Among the subjects who received the drug, plasma levels correlated with changes in negative affect and social behavior.

In subjects selected for criminal behavior rather than psychiatric diagnosis or lack thereof, SSRIs have demonstrated potential for another socially relevant use: promotion of prosocial and law-abiding behavior. Impulsive violence is associated with abnormalities in seratonergic systems, and SSRIs reliably decrease aggression in individuals prone to violence (Berman et al. 2009, Walsh & Dinan 2001). SSRIs have been found to decrease repeat offending in sex offenders and are used for this purpose, along with hormonal treatments to decrease sex drive (Bourget & Bradford 2008).

Love, romance, and sexuality in healthy normal people constitute another realm for brain enhancements. Drugs that affect these aspects of life through central nervous system mechanisms have not achieved the success of, for example, Viagra, but more limited successes have been reported. The drug known as ecstasy (MDMA) increases feelings of closeness and interpersonal connection and can be used to enhance relationships, although serious risks accompany its use (Sessa 2007). Hormone supplementation has been used by low-testosterone men and postmenopausal women to increase libido. A number of new drugs are being explored for improving sexual function in young women suffering from low libido (Fitzhenry & Sandberg 2005).

In recent years a wealth of new findings has emerged on the role of the hormones oxytocin and vasopressin in trust, altruism, and bonding (Donaldson & Young 2008). Intravenous or inhaled doses of these hormones have been shown to alter the same range of behaviors. Oxytocin has been shown to engender more trusting and generous strategies in economic games (Kosfeld et al. 2005, Zak et al. 2007) and to interfere with normal responses to betrayal in such games (Baumgartner et al. 2008). This research has obvious potential for translation

TMS: transcranial magnetic stimulation

tDCS: transcranial direct current stimulation

rTMS: repetitive TMS

into a number of applied domains. It provides a proof of concept for altering the interpersonal relationships between spouses, parents and children, and business associates. It could also be used in diplomatic, forensic, and security contexts. The practical difficulties of administering oxytocin are being overcome by the development of oral drugs that target oxytocin receptors in the brain (Ring et al. 2010).

Nonpharmacological Enhancement

A very different set of technologies influences brain function with electronics. The two least invasive, and thus most promising for brain enhancement, are transcranial magnetic stimulation (TMS) and transcranial direct current stimulation (tDCS). The physics of these methods is simple, although their physiological effects are another matter. Both methods have transient and more lasting effects, and the latter have been found to include enhanced psychological functions in normal volunteers.

With TMS, a magnetic field penetrates the head and induces current flow that, among its physiological effects, triggers action potentials in targeted neurons. Repetitive TMS (rTMS) involves pulsing the magnetic field, which can increase or decrease cortical excitability, depending on the frequency of stimulation. In contrast, tDCS puts the head in a simple circuit by applying two electrodes, anode and cathodes, to the outside of the head with a weak power source between them. The currents resulting from tDCS are of lower amperage and are thought to modulate the resting membrane potentials of neurons rather than cause action potentials. Cortex near the anode, where current enters the brain, is rendered temporarily more excitable, whereas cathodal stimulation renders the cortex less excitable. At present the development of rTMS and tDCS protocols is based partly on general rules of thumb concerning stimulation parameters (duration, intensity, and location for rTMS frequency and for tDCS polarity) but remains largely trial and error.

Hamilton and colleagues (2011) have reviewed the prospects of noninvasive brain stimulation for psychological enhancement of normal, healthy subjects. They cite research that has demonstrated enhancement of learning and memory, including language learning, complex problem solving, and mood.

Ethical, Legal, and Societal Issues in Brain Enhancement

Individuals, organizations, and societies have a multitude of interests that can be served by influencing people's behavior, for example making people (self or other) smarter, happier, more generous, or more law-abiding. Our growing ability to influence normal healthy brain function is being harnessed for many of these purposes, and this raises an array of ethical, legal, and social issues almost as diverse as the reasons for brain enhancement.

Voluntary Physician-Assisted Enhancement

Let us begin with the ethically simplest situation, voluntary enhancement with medical supervision. Here there is no coercion and health risks are minimized. What is the ethical and legal status of such a scenario, and how might it impact society beyond the individual patient and physician?

Concerning the physician's role, the main ethical issue is whether physicians should promote the well being of their patients beyond healing illness and alleviating suffering. Although other medical specialties now include "lifestyle" services such as cosmetic surgery and cosmetic dermatology, those treating the brain have only begun to grapple with this expansion of their role. Clinicians report widely varying attitudes toward providing their patients with brain enhancement (Banjo et al. 2010). However, at least one professional body has examined the ethical issues and concluded that the practice is not intrinsically problematic. In a report entitled "Responding to requests from adult patients for neuroenhancements," the American Academy of Neurology's Ethics, Law and Humanities Committee recently advised that it is morally and legally permissible for physicians to prescribe brain-enhancing medications to healthy individuals (Larriviere et al. 2009).

What ethical considerations apply to the individual who is choosing to enhance his or her brain? These depend in part on the psychological traits being enhanced. For example, issues of competition, fairness, and freedom arise mainly in connection with cognitive enhancement, as mental ability is a positional good as well as having value in its own right. That is, the benefits of cognitive enhancement come in part from being smarter than the competition, as well as from the inherent desirability of improved cognition. By increasing the competitive advantage of some, cognitive enhancement influences others. In contrast, social-affective enhancements have relatively less-direct effects on people other than the user of the enhancement, so the externalities are relatively weaker. Instead, the value of authenticity and human feeling are the main issues that arise.

Ethical, Legal, and Societal Implications of Cognitive Enhancement

The two main issues that arise with cognitive enhancement are fairness and freedom. Cognitive enhancement has been characterized as unfair in the same way that doping in sports is unfair. Although there are similarities, the analogy is imperfect for at least two reasons. First, there are reasons to enhance cognition that have nothing to do with competition, for example improved understanding and increased productivity, whereas performance enhancement in sports is primarily for the purpose of competition. Individuals who do not engage in competition of any kind could still have reason to enhance their cognition.

Second, even in competitive situations the purpose of the competition is typically different for athletic and cognitive competitions. For athletics, the goal is ostensibly to find out who is the best athlete without performance enhancement because of the value given to athletic talent, training, and effort. For cognitive competitions, in contrast, we are generally interested in predicting future performance. Aptitude tests, such as the Scholastic Assessment Test and the Medical College Admission Test, are designed to assess capacity for success in college or medical school. Licensing exams are intended to discriminate between those who will and will not practice their trade or profession competently. Even quizzes and exams in school are essentially means of assessing how much knowledge and understanding the student is likely to carry forward out of the course.

If someone routinely uses cognitive enhancement and plans to continue doing so, then using cognitive enhancement during a test would provide a representative estimate of his future capabilities. From this perspective, enhanced test taking is not unfair unless the test taker plans not to use cognitive enhancement in the future.

Cognitive enhancement can also be unfair to individuals or groups who do not have access to it. The drugs now used for this purpose are more available to the wealthier members of society, and this seems likely to be true for future drugs as well as devices. Cognitive enhancement therefore has the potential to exacerbate socioeconomic disparities within and between countries.

Finally, although cognitive enhancement can be enabling, it can also limit individual freedom. This could take the form of direct coercion by employers or schools. For example, it is in an employer's interest to have workers with enhanced attention or the ability to work through the night periodically. It is in a school's interest to have students who score well on tests and follow classroom instructions easily. Indeed, in some school districts the proportion of students on pediatrician-prescribed stimulant medication is higher than the prevalence of ADHD, suggesting that enhancement is taking place (Diller 1996). Possibly in response to schools' conflict of interest, the U.S. government has enacted a federal law preventing schools from requiring treatment for ADHD.

Unfortunately, it is more difficult to legislate against indirect coercion, which will naturally emerge as enhancement becomes more common. Once a single employee wows the boss with the productivity made possible by medication-enabled all-nighters, that boss will want to encourage others to do the same. Workers may get the message that those who do not regularly pull high-productivity all-nighters are likely to be replaced with workers who do. As more young learners are able to surpass expectations for classroom behavior and academic performance, schools may raise their expectations, and students with average abilities may find themselves performing below par if they do not engage in enhancement.

The U.S. Air Force is explicit in providing pilots with a choice concerning enhancement that is indirectly coercive: They are told that they may choose whether or not to use stimulant medication on long flights, but if they choose not to, they may be found unfit for duty (Borin 2003). Any profession for which work must be performed under conditions of distraction, sleep deprivation, or stress, especially those for which the safety of others is at stake, could become subject to such a choice.

Ethical, Legal, and Societal Implications of Social-Affective Enhancement

The problems reviewed above in connection with cognitive enhancement concerned relatively pragmatic considerations of market forces, productivity, and the protection of workplace freedoms. Although some of the same issues arise in connection with social-affective enhancement, as cheerful and outgoing individuals may be more successful in some work contexts, they are not the most obvious or pressing ones. Rather, concerns about enhancing our emotional and social lives tend to be more philosophical in nature, focusing on the value of authenticity in our feelings about ourselves, our relationships, and our world.

The enhancement of mood and personality using SSRIs has been criticized for distorting our perspective on ourselves and our lives. Although few experts would discourage a depressed person from using antidepressant medication, some see serious problems with the use of such medications for minor mood disturbances or gloomy temperaments. Fukuyama (2002) has worried that SSRIs inappropriately raise the self-esteem of the user, thus undermining an important source of motivation in our lives. He asks if Caesar and Napoleon would have created their empires had they been able to raise their self-esteem simply by popping a pill (Fukuyama 2002, p. 46). Elliott et al. (e.g., 2004) has raised another danger of chemically induced contentment. Perhaps the angst or alienation we feel about our lives is an important signal that can prompt us to seek a more meaningful life if it is not medicated away with an SSRI.

These critiques rest on psychological assumptions that, although plausible, are not necessarily true. Does low self-esteem motivate people to achieve greatness, or does it more often discourage people from trying to realize their goals? Perhaps there were other leaders and military strategists as visionary as Caesar and Napoleon, or even more so, who never built their empires because they did not have sufficient faith in themselves. More generally, does raised self-esteem lead to more or less self-efficacy? As for the assumptions underlying Elliott's critique, it is plausible that an increased sense of well-being might rob us of the incentive to seek more meaningful activities and relationships or to work toward a better world, yet it might also enable us to imagine better possibilities and to have the energy and optimism to pursue them.

The ethical, legal, and social implications of brain enhancement to alter interpersonal relationships are somewhat hypothetical. On the one hand, basic research shows that oxytocin, as well as related hormones such as vasopressin, can alter our feelings and behavior toward others. On the other hand, the effects of these hormones on human behavior have only begun to be investigated, and their effects in different genders, individuals, and circumstances, in combination with one another and with other hormones, requires more systematic study before they form the basis of useful brain enhancements. In addition, the difficulty of intranasal administration limits current usefulness. This will change if drugs are developed that can cross the blood-brain barrier to target oxytocin receptors.

In the meantime, there may be some special circumstances under which intranasal administration is feasible. Anecdotal evidence suggests that some psychiatrists use oxytocin in couples therapy (L. Young, personal communication). Given the effectiveness of personal rapport and trust in obtaining information during interrogation, intranasal oxytocin could be used in law enforcement and national security contexts (Moreno 2006). In view of this, Dando (2009) has called for inclusion of oxytocin as a chemical weapon in international law concerning war, for example, the Geneva Convention. With better delivery methods or new drugs, surreptitious manipulation of the oxytocin system could be a profitable, if unethical, business strategy. By increasing trust, generosity, and forgiveness in one's opponents, one could influence the outcomes of financial, political, or other negotiations.

The ethical issues raised by relationship enhancement are complex. Whereas drugging an unsuspecting business associate for financial advantage seems clearly wrong, what if we could obtain socially valuable information from an unwilling informant without causing physical or psychological pain? What about encouraging a successful resolution of difficult negotiations by enhancing feelings of bonding and brotherhood in both parties? With both parties' informed consent?

Some commentators emphasize the ethical similarity of relationship enhancement by neurochemical means and by other means (Savulescu & Sandberg 2008). From a purely consequentialist point of view, sufficiently high benefits to society should tip the moral balance in favor of oxytocinizing interrogees or all parties in a political conflict, even without their consent. Yet most of us sense a troubling violation of personhood in these scenarios. It is

not just the assault on autonomy inherent in influencing people without their knowledge; it is the co-opting of our highest moral emotions for instrumental purposes. After all, part of what makes these emotions so precious, to individuals and society, is precisely that they guide us away from selfishness. They shift us from the pursuit of our own selfish ends to consideration for the well being of others. The prospect of someone harnessing these emotions for their own ends is therefore especially repugnant.

Similarly, involuntary enhancement of criminal offenders to improve their personality, mood, and self-control (with SSRIs) or to promote trust and empathy for others (oxytocin) presents us with another set of tradeoffs between potentially desirable outcomes and troubling infringement of personhood. If these treatments can enable offenders to live outside of prison and can protect society against crime, then the "benefit" side of the equation is substantial. However, state-imposed psychopharmacology poses a relatively new kind of limitation on offenders' autonomy and privacy. In contrast to the restrictions on autonomy and privacy imposed by incarceration, which mainly concern physical restrictions, brain interventions would restrict offenders' abilities to think, feel, and react as they normally would.

THE NEUROSCIENCE WORLDVIEW

Neuroscience does not merely give us new tools to be used to the benefit or detriment of humanity; it gives us a new way of thinking about humanity. The idea that human behavior can be understood in terms of physical mechanisms runs counter to deeply ingrained intuitions. Whereas we naturally think in terms of physical causality to understand the behavior of most objects and systems in the world—why a bicycle is easier to pedal uphill in low gear, why a plant grows in the sun or withers in the shade, why a printer jams—when it comes to human behavior we think about people's intentions and reasons. There is evidence that even infants understand human behavior in

Consequentialist: an approach to ethics whereby the rightness or wrongness of an action depends solely on the value of its consequences

terms of intentions and reasons rather than physical causes (Woodward 2009).

Neuroscience provides an alternative perspective, from which human behavior can also be understood as the result of physical causes. Even for people who do not follow the latest trends in science or spend time thinking about the nature of humanity, the applications of neuroscience reviewed in the previous two sections will provide many reminders that our minds are, at root, physical mechanisms. By making people part of the clockwork universe, neuroscience challenges many assumptions about morality and personhood. Three challenges are reviewed here.

Moral Agency and Responsibility

The idea that all of our behavior, moral and immoral, is physically caused by brain processes throws a monkey wrench into our intuitive reasoning about moral responsibility. We think of ourselves as moral agents when we act intentionally, with free will. Thus, I am morally responsible for knocking down the old lady if I pushed her, on purpose, to get her out of my way, but not if I stumbled or was myself pushed and thereby pushed her because of the physics of my body and its interactions with other parts of the scene. Far more could be said about the notion of free will and its relation to responsibility (e.g., see Morse 2005), but for present purposes the important point is that we are intuitively disinclined to hold someone responsible for an action they performed when the action is physically caused.

Of course, many people believe in the abstract that human behavior is physically determined. However, we tend to put aside such abstractions when making moral judgments. We do not say, "But he had no choice—the laws of physics made him do it!" However, as the neuroscience of personality, decision making, and impulse control begins to offer a more detailed and specific account of the physical processes leading to irresponsible or criminal behavior, the deterministic viewpoint will probably gain a stronger hold on our intuitions.

Whereas the laws of physics are a little too abstract to displace the concept of personal responsibility in our minds, our moral judgments might well be moved by a demonstration of subtle damage to prefrontal inhibitory mechanisms wrought by, for example, past drug abuse or childhood neglect. This has already happened, to an extent, with the disease model of drug abuse (Leshner 1997). As a result largely of neuroscience research showing how addictive behavior arises from drug-induced changes in brain function (Rogers & Robbins 2001, Verdejo-García et al. 2004), addiction is now viewed as more of a medical problem than a failure of personal responsibility.

Presumably because specific neuroscience accounts of behavior are more compelling than generalizations about physical determinism, neuroimaging evidence is increasingly presented by the defense during the sentencing phase of criminal trials (Hughes 2010). A study examining the influence of neuroscientific evidence in the guilt phase found that when it is included, judges and juries are more inclined to find defendants not guilty by reason of insanity (Gurley & Marcus 2008). Outside the courtroom, people tend to judge the behavior of others less harshly when it is explained in light of physiological rather than psychological processes (Monterosso et al. 2005). This is as true for serious moral transgressions, such as killing, as for behaviors that are merely socially undesirable, such as overeating. The decreased moral stigma surrounding drug addiction is undoubtedly due in part to our emerging view of addiction as a brain disease.

What about our own actions? Might an awareness of the neural causes of behavior influence our own behavior? Perhaps so, according to a study by Vohs & Schooler (2008). They asked subjects to read a passage on the incompatibility of free will and neuroscience from Francis Crick's (1995) book, *The Astonishing Hypothesis: The Scientific Search for the Soul.* This included the statement, "'You', your joys and your sorrows, your memories and your ambitions, your sense of personal identity and free will, are in fact no more than the behavior of a vast assembly of nerve cells and their associated molecules." The researchers found that these people were then more likely to cheat on a computerized test than those who had read an unrelated passage.

Will neuroscience change our laws, ethics, and mores? The growing use of brain scans in courtrooms, societal precedents such as the destigmatization of addiction, and studies such as those described above seem to say the answer is yes.

Religion and the Nature of Persons

Most religions endorse a two- or three-part view of the person: body and mind or soul, or body, soul, and spirit. This accords well with most people's intuitions, according to which there is some essence of a person that is more than just the matter that we can see and touch. Yet as neuroscience advances, all aspects of a person are increasingly understood to be the functioning of a material system. This first became clear in the realms of perception and motor control, where mechanistic models of these processes have been under development for decades. Of course, such models do not seriously threaten the multipart view of the person: You can still believe in what Arthur Koestler called "the ghost in the machine" and simply conclude that color vision and gait are features of the machine rather than the ghost.

However, as neuroscience begins to reveal the mechanisms of personality, love, morality, and spirituality, the idea of a ghost in the machine becomes strained. Brain imaging indicates that all of these traits have physical correlates in brain function. Furthermore, pharmacologic influences on these traits, as well as the effects of localized stimulation or damage, demonstrate that the brain processes in question are not mere correlates but are the physical bases of these central aspects of our human personhood. If these aspects of the person are all features of the machine, why have a ghost at all?

By raising questions like this, it seems likely that neuroscience will pose a far more fundamental challenge than evolutionary biology to

many religions. After all, the genesis myth of the Old Testament is taken as literal truth by a relatively small number of fundamentalist Christians. In contrast, belief in an immaterial mind or soul is common to most of the world's religions.

Finding Meaning in a Material World

Just as we have traditionally viewed persons as different from other objects because of their capacity for moral agency, we have also viewed them as having a special moral value, as distinct from all other kinds of objects. Persons deserve protection from harm just because they are persons. Whereas we value objects for what they can do—a car because it transports us, a book because it contains information, a painting because it looks beautiful—the value of persons transcends their abilities, knowledge, or attractiveness. Persons have what Kant called "dignity," meaning a special kind of intrinsic value that trumps the value of any use to which they could be put (Kant 1996).

This categorical distinction between persons and other things is difficult to maintain if everything about persons arises from physical mechanisms (Farah & Heberlein 2007). If we are really no more than physical objects, albeit very complex objects containing powerful computational networks, then does it matter what becomes of any of us? Why should the fate of these objects containing human brains matter more than the fate of other natural or man-made objects? The physicist Steven Weinberg (1993) has written, "The more the universe seems comprehensible, the more it seems pointless." This seems an even more acute problem in neuroscience than in physics.

In sum, neuroscience is calling into question our age-old understanding of the human person. Much as the natural sciences became the dominant way of understanding the world around us in the eighteenth century, so neuroscience may be responsible for changing our understanding of ourselves in the twenty-first century. Such a transformation could reduce us to machines in each other's eyes, mere clockwork devoid of moral agency and moral value. Alternatively, it could help bring about a society that is more understanding and humane as people's behavior is seen as part of the larger picture of causal forces surrounding them and acting through them.

SUMMARY POINTS

1. Like genetics, neuroscience concerns the biological essence of who we are; in comparison to genetics, neuroscience has advanced rapidly since the year 2000 and offers an array of feasible methods for predicting and controlling human behavior.

2. The newfound ability of neuroscience to explain and influence human behavior has made it relevant to many new areas of application outside the traditional biomedical realm, including education, business, and criminal justice.

3. Brain imaging has advanced to the point where it can provide reliable information about the mental traits and states of individuals in at least some circumscribed contexts.

4. The ethical, legal, and social challenge posed by progress in brain imaging is to use information from imaging judiciously, protecting privacy while resisting exaggerated claims based on the scientific aura and appeal of brain images.

5. Neurotechnologies including drugs and noninvasive brain stimulation can be used to enhance normal brain function.

6. Brain enhancement raises a host of ethical, legal, and social issues related to safety, freedom, fairness, and personal authenticity.

7. Neuroscience supports a physicalist view of the human person, according to which our thoughts, feelings, and actions all result from physical mechanisms. This view cannot easily be reconciled with traditional notions of moral responsibility, spirituality, and meaning.

DISCLOSURE STATEMENT

The author is unaware of any affiliation, funding, or financial holdings that might be perceived as affecting the objectivity of this review.

LITERATURE CITED

Aggarwal NK. 2009. Neuroimaging, culture, and forensic psychiatry. *J. Am. Acad. Psychiatry Law* 37(2):239–44

Aguirre GK. 2010. Experimental design and data analysis for fMRI. In *BOLD fMRI: A Guide to Functional Imaging for Neuroscientists*, ed. SH Faro, FB Mohamed, pp. 55–69. New York: Springer

Aron A, Badre D, Brett M, Cacioppo J, Chambers C, et al. 2007. Politics and the brain. *N.Y. Times*, Nov. 14

Arrington M. 2008. How many Silicon Valley startup executives are hopped up on Provigil? *TechCrunch*, July 15. **http://techcrunch.com/2008/07/15/how-many-of-our-startup-executives-are-hopped-up-on-provigil/**

Banjo OC, Nadler R, Reiner PB. 2010. Physician attitudes towards pharmacological cognitive enhancement: Safety concerns are paramount. *PLoS One* 5(12):e14322

Baumgartner T, Heinrichs M, Vonlanthen A, Fischbacher U, Fehr E. 2008. Oxytocin shapes the neural circuitry of trust and trust adaptation in humans. *Neuron* 58(4):639–50

Bennett CM, Wolford GL, Miller MB. 2009. The principled control of false positives in neuroimaging. *Soc. Cogn. Affect. Neurosci.* 4:417–22

Berman ME, McCloskey MS, Fanning JR, Schumacher JA, Coccaro EF. 2009. Serotonin augmentation reduces response to attack in aggressive individuals. *Psychol. Sci.* 20:714–20

Bles M, Haynes JD. 2008. Detecting concealed information using brain-imaging technology. *Neurocase* 14:82–92

Borin E. 2003. The U.S. military needs its speed. *Wired*, Feb. 10. **http://www.wired.com/medtech/health/news/2003/02/57434**

Bourget D, Bradford JMW. 2008. *Evidential Basis for the Assessment and Treatment of Sex Offenders.* London: Oxford Univ. Press

Burkitt L. 2009. Neuromarketing: Companies use neuroscience for consumer insights. *Forbes*, Nov. 16

Chatterjee A. 2009. A medical view of potential adverse effects. *Nature* 457:532–33

Christ SE, Van Essen DC, Watson JM, Brubaker LE, McDermott KB. 2009. The contributions of prefrontal cortex and executive control to deception: evidence from activation likelihood estimate meta-analyses. *Cereb. Cortex* 19(7):1557–66

Coccaro EF, McCloskey MS, Fitzgerald DA, Phan KL. 2007. Amygdala and orbitofrontal reactivity to social threat in individuals with impulsive aggression. *Biol. Psychiatry* 62(2):168–78

Comm. Sci. Law, Assoc. Bar City N.Y. 2005. *Are your thoughts your own? Neuroprivacy and the legal implications of brain imaging.* ABCNY Rep., June. **http://www.abcny.org/pdf/report/Neuroprivacy-revisions.pdf**

Crick F. 1995. *The Astonishing Hypothesis: The Scientific Search for the Soul.* New York: Touchstone

Dando M. 2009. Biologists napping while work militarized. *Nature* 460:950–51

Delgado MR. 2007. Reward-related responses in the human striatum. *Ann. N.Y. Acad. Sci.* 1104:70–88

DeSantis AD, Noar SM, Webb EM. 2009. Nonmedical ADHD stimulant use in fraternities. *J. Stud. Alcohol. Drugs* 70:952–54

Diller LH. 1996. The run on Ritalin: attention deficit disorder and stimulants in the 1990s. *Hastings Center Rep.* 25:12–18

Donaldson ZR, Young LJ. 2008. Oxytocin, vasopressin, and the neurogenetics of sociality. *Science* 322:900–4

Dumit J. 2004. *Picturing Personhood: Brain Scans and Biomedical Identity.* Princeton, NJ: Princeton Univ. Press

Elliott R, Ogilvie A, Rubinsztein JS, Calderon G, Dolan RJ, Sahakian BJ. 2004. Abnormal ventral frontal response during performance of an affective go/no go task in patients with mania. *Biol. Psychiatry* 55(12):1163–70

Farah M. 2007. This is your brain on politics? *Neuroethics & Law Blog, Nov. 12.* **http://kolber.typepad.com/ethics_law_blog/2007/11/this-is-your-br.html**

Farah MJ, Heberlein AS. 2007. Personhood and neuroscience: naturalizing or nihilating? *Am. J. Bioeth. Neurosci.* 7:37–48

Farah MJ, Smith ME, Gawuga C, Lindsell D, Foster D. 2009. Brain imaging and brain privacy: a realistic concern? *J. Cogn. Neurosci.* 21(1):119–27

Fitzhenry D, Sandberg L. 2005. Female sexual dysfunction. *Nat. Rev. Drug Discov.* 4:99–100

Fukuyama F. 2002. *Our Posthuman Future.* London: Profile Books

Greenwald AG, McGhee DE, Schwartz JL. 1998. Measuring individual differences in implicit cognition: the implicit association test. *J. Personal. Soc. Psychol.* 1464–80

Gurley JR, Marcus DK. 2008. The effects of neuroimaging and brain injury on insanity defenses. *Behav. Sci. Law* 26:85–97

Hackshaw A. 2009. *A Concise Guide to Clinical Trials.* Oxford, UK: BMJ Books

Hamann S, Canli T. 2004. Individual differences in emotion processing. *Curr. Opin. Neurobiol.* 14(2):233–38

Hamilton R, Messing S, Chatterjee A. 2011. Rethinking the thinking cap: ethics of neural enhancement using noninvasive brain stimulation. *Neurology* 76:187–93

Hart-Davis A. 2005. The Genius Pill: Would you be an idiot to take it? *The Evening Standard*, Nov. 22

Healy D. 2004. *Let Them Eat Prozac.* New York: NYU Press

Hubert M, Kenning P. 2008. A current overview of consumer neuroscience. *J. Consum. Behav.* 7(4-5):272–92

Hughes V. 2010. Science in court: head case. *Nature* 464(7287):340–42

Hyman SE. 2004. Introduction: the brain's special status. *Cerebrum* 6(4):9–12

Iacoboni M. 2007. This is your brain on politics. *N.Y. Times*, Nov. 11

Iacoboni M. 2008. Iacoboni responds to neuropolitics criticism. *Neuroethics & Law Blog, June 3.* **http://kolber. typepad.com/ethics_law_blog/2008/06/iacoboni-respon.html**

Illes J, Kirschen MP, Edwards E, Stanford LR, Bandettini P, et al. 2004. Incidental findings in brain imaging research. *Science* 311:783–84

Kant I. 1996. *Critique of Pure Reason.* Indianapolis, IN: Hackett

Karlawish J. 2011. Addressing the ethical, policy, and social challenges of diagnosing pre-clinical Alzheimer's disease. *Neurology* 77:1487–93

Knutson B, Wolkowitz OM, Cole SW, Chan T, Moore EA, et al. 1998. Selective alteration of personality and social behavior by serotonergic intervention. *Am. J. Psychiatry* 155:373–79

Kosfeld M, Heinrichs M, Zak PJ, Fischbacher U, Fehr E. 2005. Oxytocin increases trust in humans. *Nature* 435(7042):673–76

Kramer PD. 1997. *Listening to Prozac: A Psychiatrist Explores Antidepressant Drugs and the Remaking of the Self—Revised Edition.* New York: Penguin

Langleben DD, Schroeder L, Maldjian JA, Gur RC, McDonald S, et al. 2002. Brain activity during simulated deception: an event-related functional magnetic resonance study. *NeuroImage* 15:727–32

Langleben DD, Loughead JW, Ruparel K, Hakun JG, Busch-Winokur S, et al. 2009. Reduced prefrontal and temporal processing and recall of high "sensation value" ads. *NeuroImage* 46(1):219–25

Larriviere D, Williams MA, Rizzo M, Bonnie RJ, AAN Ethics, Law & Humanit. Comm. 2009. Responding to requests from adult patients for neuroenhancements: guidance of the Ethics, Law and Humanities Committee. *Neurology* 73(17):1406–12

Le Bihan D, Mangin JF, Poupon C, Clark CA, Pappata S, et al. 2001. Diffusion tensor imaging: concepts and applications. *J. Magn. Reson. Imaging* 13:534–46

Lee N, Broderick AJ, Chamberlain L. 2007. What is "neuromarketing"? A discussion and agenda for future research. *Int. J. Psychophysiol.* 63:199–204

Leshner AI. 1997. Addiction is a brain disease, and it matters. *Science* 278:45–47

Lieberman MD. 2007. Social cognitive neuroscience: a review of core processes. *Annu. Rev. Psychol.* 58:259–89

Lindstrom M. 2008. *Buyology: Truth and Lies About Why We Buy.* New York: Random

Lo B, Field MJ. 2009. *Conflict of Interest in Medical Research, Education, and Practice.* Washington, DC: Natl. Acad. Press

Madrigal A. 2008. Wired.com readers' brain-enhancing drug regimens. *Wired,* April 24. **http://www. wired.com/medtech/drugs/news/2008/04/smart_drugs**

Maher B. 2008. Poll results: look who's doping. *Nature* 452:674–75

Marshall E. 2004. A star-studded search for memory-enhancing drugs. *Science* 304:36–38

McCabe DP, Castel AD. 2007. Seeing is believing: the effect of brain images on judgments of scientific reasoning. *Cognition* 107(1):343–52

McCabe SE, Knight JR, Teter CJ, Wechsler H. 2005. Non-medical use of prescription stimulants among US college students: prevalence and correlates from a national survey. *Addiction* 100:96–106

Mechelli A, Price CJ, Friston KJ, Ashburner J. 2005. Voxel-based morphometry of the human brain: methods and applications. *Curr. Med. Imaging Rev.* 1:105–13

Monterosso J, Royzman EB, Schwartz B. 2005. Explaining away responsibility: effects of scientific explanation on perceived culpability. *Ethics Behav.* 15:139–58

Moreno JD. 2006. *Mind Wars: Brain Research and National Defense.* New York: Dana Press

Morse SJ. 2005. Brain overclaim syndrome and criminal responsibility: a diagnostic note. *Ohio State J. Criminal Law* 3:397–412

Olfson M, Marcus SC. 2009. National patterns in antidepressant medication treatment. *Arch. Gen. Psychiatry* 66:848–56

Parens E. 2004. Genetic differences and human identities: on why talking about behavioral genetics is important and difficult. *Hastings Center Rep.* 34:S1–36

Phan KL, Wager T, Taylor SF, Liberzon I. 2002. Functional neuroanatomy of emotion: a meta-analysis of emotion activation studies in PET and fMRI. *NeuroImage* 16(2):331–48

Phelps EA, O'Conner KJ, Cunningham WA, Funayama ES, Gatenby JC, et al. 2000. Performance on indirect measures of race evaluation predicts amygdala activation. *J. Cogn. Neurosci.* 12(5):729–38

Plotz D. 2003. Wake up, Little Susie: Can we sleep less? *Slate*, March 7

Poldrack R. 2008. Poldrack replies to Iacoboni neuropolitics discussion. *Neuroethics & Law Blog, June 3.* **http://kolber.typepad.com/ethics_law_blog/2008/06/poldrack-replie.html**

Posner MI, Raichle ME. 1994. *Images of Mind.* New York: Sci. Am. Books

Racine E, Bar-Ilan O, Illes J. 2005. fMRI in the public eye. *Nat. Rev. Neurosci.* 6(2):159–64

Ramsey JD, Hanson SJ, Hanson C, Halchenko YO, Poldrack RA, Glymour C. 2010. Six problems for causal inference from fMRI. *NeuroImage* 49:1545–58

Rasmussen N. 2008. *On Speed: The Many Lives of Amphetamine.* New York: NYU Press

Rilling J, Gutman D, Zeh T, Pagnoni G, Berns G, Kilts C. 2002. A neural basis for social cooperation. *Neuron* 35(2):395–405

Ring RH, Schechter LE, Leonard SK, Dwyer JM, Platt BJ, et al. 2010. Receptor and behavioral pharmacology of WAY-267464, a non-peptide oxytocin receptor agonist. *Neuropharmacology* 58:69–77

Rogers RD, Robbins TW. 2001. Investigating the neurocognitive deficits associated with chronic drug misuse. *Curr. Opin. Neurobiol.* 11:250–57

Roskies AL. 2008. Neuroimaging and inferential distance. *Neuroethics* 1(1):19–30

Sahakian B, Morein-Zamir S. 2007. Professor's little helper. *Nature* 450:1157–59

Savulescu J, Sandberg A. 2008. Neuroenhancement of love and marriage: the chemicals between us. *Neuroethics* 1:31–44

Schauer F. 2010. Neuroscience, lie-detection, and the law: a contrarian view. *Trends Cogn. Sci.* 14:101–3

Sessa B. 2007. Is there a case for MDMA-assisted psychotherapy in the UK? *J. Psychopharmacol.* 21(2):220–24

Silver LM. 1997. *Remaking Eden: Cloning and Beyond in a Brave New World.* New York: Avon Books

Singer E. 2009. Manipulating memory. *Technol. Rev.* 54. **http://www.technologyreview.com/biomedicine/22451/**

Smith ME, Farah MJ. 2011. Are prescription stimulants "smart pills?" The epidemiology and cognitive neuroscience of prescription stimulant use by normal healthy individuals. *Psychol. Bull.* 137:717–41

Talbot M. 2009. Brain gain. The underground world of "neuroenhancing" drugs. *New Yorker*, April 27. **http://www.newyorker.com/reporting/2009/04/27/090427fa_fact_talbot**

Tang TZ. 2009. Personality change during depression treatment: a placebo-controlled trial. *Arch. Gen. Psychiatry* 66(12):1322–30

Tovino SA. 2007. Imaging body structure and mapping brain function: a historical approach. *Am. J. Law Med.* 33:19

Turner DC, Robbins TW, Clark L, Aron AR, Dowson J, Sahakian BJ. 2003. Cognitive enhancing effects of modafinil in healthy volunteers. *Psychopharmacology (Berl.)* 165:260–69

Van Gestel S, Van Broeckhoven CV. 2003. Genetics of personality: Are we making progress? *Mol. Psychiatry* 8:840–52

Verdejo-Garcia A, Lopez-Torrecillas F, Gimenez CO, Perez-Garcia M. 2004. Clinical implications and methodological challenges in the study of the neuropsychological correlates of cannabis, stimulant, and opioid abuse. *Neuropsychol. Rev.* 14:1–41

Vohs KD, Schooler JW. 2008. The value of believing in free will: Encouraging a belief in determinism increases cheating. *Psychol. Sci.* 19:49–54

Volkow ND, Swanson JM. 2008. The action of enhancers can lead to addiction. *Nature* 451:521

Vul E, Harris C, Winkielman P, Pashler H. 2009. Puzzlingly high correlations in fMRI studies of emotion, personality, and social cognition. *Perspect. Psychol. Sci.* 4:274–90

Walsh MT, Dinan TG. 2001. Selective serotonin reuptake inhibitors and violence: a review of the available evidence. *Acta Psychiatr. Scand.* 104(2):84–91

Weinberg S. 1993. *The First Three Minutes: A Modern View of the Origin of the Universe—Updated.* New York: Basic Books

Westen D, Blagov PS, Harenski K, Kilts C, Hamann S. 2006. Neural bases of motivated reasoning: an FMRI study of emotional constraints on partisan political judgment in the 2004 U.S. Presidential election. *J. Cogn. Neurosci.* 18:1947–58

Woodward AL. 2009. Infants' grasp of others' intentions. *Curr. Dir. Psychol. Sci.* 18:53–57

Zak PJ, Stanton AA, Ahmadi S. 2007. Oxytocin increases generosity in humans. *PLoS One* 2:e1128

Cumulative Indexes

Contributing Authors, Volumes 53–63

Iyer A, 57:585–611
Izard CE, 60:1–25

J

Johnson EJ, 60:53–85
Johnson M, 56:517–43
Joiner TE Jr, 56:287–314
Jonides J, 59:193–224
Jost JT, 60:307–37
Judge TA, 63:341–67
Jundt D, 56:517–43

K

Kagan J, 54:1–23
Kammeyer-Mueller JD, 63:341–67
Kanwisher N, 55:87–124
Karp J, 55:333–63
Kaschak MP, 54:91–114
Kazdin AE, 54:253–76
Keefe FJ, 56:601–30
Keen R, 62:1–21
Keil FC, 57:227–54
Keller H, 54:461–90
Kelley K, 59:537–63
Kelloway EK 60:671–92
Kelman HC, 57:1–26
Kerr NL, 55:623–55
Kersten D, 55:271–304
Kestler L, 55:401–30
Kiecolt-Glaser JK, 53:83–107
Kingdom FAA, 59:143–66
Kitayama S, 62:419–49
Klin A, 56:315–36
Knobe J, 63:81–99
Koob GF, 59:29–53
Kopp CB, 62:165–87
Kraiger K, 60:451–74
Krantz DS, 53:341–69
Kruglanski AW, 58:291–316
Kutas M, 62:621–47

L

Lachman ME, 55:305–31
Lackner JR, 56:115–47
Langdon R, 62:271–98
Latham GP, 56:485–516
Leary MR, 58:317–44

LeBoeuf RA, 53:491–517
Lehman DR, 55:689–714
Le Moal M, 59:29–53
Leonardo ED, 57:117–37
Leuner B, 61:111–40
Leventhal EA, 59:477–505
Leventhal H, 59:477–505
Levine B, 53:401–33
Levine EL, 63:397–425
Lewis RL, 59:193–224
Lieberman MD, 58:259–89
Lievens F, 59:419–50
Lilienfeld SO, 53:519–43
Loewenstein G, 59:647–72
Logan GD, 55:207–34
Loken B, 57:453–85
Lord RG, 61:543–68
Lotto AJ, 55:149–79
Lowenstein AE, 62:483–500
Lucas RE, 54:403–25
Lussier JP, 55:431–61
Lustig CA, 59:193–224

M

MacKenzie SB, 63:539–69
MacKinnon DP, 58:593–614; 62:299–329
Maddox WT, 56:149–78
Maher CP, 61:599–622
Mahon BZ, 60:27–51
Major BN, 56:393–421
Mamassian P, 55:271–304
Mar RA, 62:103–34
Marshall PJ, 56:235–62
Martin A, 58:25–45
Martin C, 61:353–81
Martin RC, 54:55–89
Mashek DJ, 58:345–72
Masicampo EJ, 62:331–61
Masten AS, 63:227–57
Matthews KA, 62:501–30
Maxwell SE, 59:537–63
Mayer JD, 59:507–36
Mayer RE, 55:715–44
Maynard A, 54:461–90
Mays VM, 58:201–25
McAdams DP, 61:517–42
McArdle JJ, 60:577–605
McCeney MK, 53:341–69
McDermott C, 55:519–44
McGuffin P, 54:205–28

McGuire L, 53:83–107
McKay R, 62:271–98
McKenna KYA, 55:572–90
McNally RJ, 54:229–52
Meaney MJ, 61:439–66
Meece JL, 57:487–503
Mehl MR, 54:547–77
Mehler J, 61:191–218
Mermelstein RJ, 60:229–55
Mesquita B, 58:373–403
Metzger A, 57:255–84
Milad MR, 63:129–51
Miller GE, 60:501–24
Mischel W, 55:1–22
Monahan J, 56:631–59
Moore KS, 59:193–224
Morris R, 59:451–75
Morris RG, 61:49–79
Morrison C, 59:55–92
Moskowitz JT, 55:745–74
Mukamel R, 63:511–37
Mulliken GH, 61:169–90

N

Nader K, 61:141–67
Nagayama Hall GC, 60:525–48
Nairne JS, 53:53–81
Napier JL, 60:307–37
Narayan AJ, 63:227–57
Nee DE, 59:193–224
Nesbit JC, 61:653–78
Nezworski MT, 53:519–43
Nichols KE, 56:235–62
Nichols S, 63:81–99
Niedenthal PM, 63:259–85
Niederhoffer KG, 54:547–77
Nitschke JB, 53:545–74
Norton ES, 63:427–52
Norton MI, 60:475–99

O

O'Brien LT, 56:393–421
Ochsner KN, 58:373–403
Ogle CM, 61:325–51
Oishi S, 54:403–25
Olson BD, 61:517–42
Olson EA, 54:277–95
Olson GM, 54:491–516

Olson JS, 54:491–516
Olson MA, 54:297–327
Orehek E, 58:291–316
Ozer DJ, 57:401–21

P

Paloutzian RF, 54:377–402
Paluck EL 60:339–67
Paradise R, 54:175–203
Park DC, 60:173–96
Parke RD, 55:365–99
Parks L, 56:571–600
Peissig JJ, 58:75–96
Penn DC, 58:97–118
Pennebaker JW, 54:547–77
Penner LA, 56:365–92
Pennington BF, 60:283–306
Peplau LA, 58:405–24
Peretz I, 56:89–114
Phelps EA, 57:27–53
Phillips DA, 62:483–500
Phillips LA, 59:477–505
Piliavin JA, 56:365–92
Pinder CC, 56:485–516
Pittman TS, 59:361–85
Pizzagalli D, 53:545–74
Plomin R, 54:205–28
Podsakoff NP, 63:539–69
Podsakoff PM, 63:539–69
Polivy J, 53:187–213
Posner MI, 58:1–23
Poulos AM, 56:207–34
Povinelli DJ, 58:97–118
Pratte MS, 63:483–509
Price DD, 59:565–90
Prislin R, 57:345–74
Proctor RW, 61:623–51
Putnam K, 53:545–74

Q

Quas JA, 61:325–51
Quevedo K, 58:145–73
Quirk GJ, 63:129–51

R

Rafaeli E, 54:579–616
Rausch JR, 59:537–63
Rauschecker AM, 63:31–53

Recanzone GH, 59:119–42
Rensink RA, 53:245–77
Reuter-Lorenz P, 60:173–96
Revenson TA, 58:565–92
Rhodes G, 57:199–226
Rick S, 59:647–72
Rilling JK, 62:23–48
Rissman J, 63:101–28
Robbins P, 63:81–99
Roberts BW, 56:453–84
Roberts RD, 59:507–36
Robinson TE, 54:25–53
Robles TF, 53:83–107
Roediger HL III, 59:225–54
Rogoff B, 54:175–203
Rothbart MK, 58:1–23
Rourke BP, 53:309–39
Rubin KH, 60:141–71
Rubin M, 53:575–604
Ruble DN, 61:353–81
Runco MA, 55:657–87
Rusbult CE, 54:351–75
Russell JA, 54:329–49
Rutter M, 53:463–90
Rynes SL, 56:571–600

S

Sackett PR, 59:419–50
Salmon DP, 60:257–82
Salthouse T, 63:201–26
Samuel AG, 62:49–72
Sanchez JI, 63:397–425
Sandler IN, 62:299–329
Sanfey AG, 62:23–48
Sargis EG, 57:529–55
Saribay SA, 59:329–60
Sarkissian H, 63:81–99
Saxe R, 55:87–124
Schall JD, 55:23–50
Schaller M, 55:689–714
Schippers MC, 58:515–41
Schmidt AC, 61:543–68
Schoenfelder EN, 62:299–329
Schroeder DA, 56:365–92
Schultz W, 57:87–115
Serbin LA, 55:333–63
Seyfarth RM, 54:145–73;
   63:153–77
Shadish WR, 60:607–29
Shafir E, 53:491–517
Shanks DR, 61:273–301

Shaywitz BA, 59:451–75
Shaywitz SE, 59:451–75
Sherry DF, 57:167–97
Shevell SK, 59:143–66
Shiffrar M, 58:47–73
Shiner RL, 56:453–84
Shinn M, 54:427–59
Shors TJ, 57:55–85
Siegel JM, 55:125–48
Silberg J, 53:463–90
Simonton DK, 54:617–40
Sincharoen S, 57:585–611
Skinner EA, 58:119–44
Skitka LJ, 57:529–55
Smetana JG, 57:255–84
Snyder DK, 57:317–44
Sobel N, 61:219–41
Sommers T, 63:81–99
Spears R, 53:161–86
Sporer AK, 60:229–55
Staddon JER, 54:115–44
Stanton AL, 58:565–92
Staudinger UM, 62:215–41
Stewart AJ, 55:519–44
Stewart MO, 57:285–315
Stickgold R, 57:139–66
Strunk D, 57:285–315
Stuewig J, 58:345–72
Stuss DT, 53:401–33
Sue S, 60:525–48
Suh EM, 53:133–60
Sutter ML, 59:119–42

T

Tangney JP, 58:345–72
Tarr MJ, 58:75–96
Tennen H, 58:565–92
Thau S, 60:717–41
Thompson LL, 61:491–515
Thompson RF, 56:1–23
Tindale RS, 55:623–55
Tipsord JM, 62:189–214
Tolan P, 57:557–83
Tong F, 63:483–509
Toohey SM, 54:427–59
Tourangeau R, 55:775–801
Triandis HC, 53:133–60
Trickett EJ, 60:395–419
Tulving E, 53:1–25
Turk-Browne NB, 62:73–101
Tyler TR, 57:375–400

U

Uleman JS, 59:329–60
Uskul AK, 62:419–49

V

van Knippenberg D, 58:515–41
Van Lange PAM, 54:351–75
Vohs KD, 62:331–61
Volkmar F, 56:315–36
Vu KL, 61:623–51

W

Wagner AD, 63:101–28
Walker BM, 58:453–77
Walker E, 55:401–30
Walker MP, 57:139–66
Walumbwa FO, 60:421–49

Wanberg CR, 63:369–96
Wandell BA, 63:31–53
Wang J, 61:491–515
Wang S, 61:49–79
Warriner EM, 53:309–39
Weber EU, 60:53–85
Weber TJ, 60:421–49
Weinman J, 59:477–505
Weiss H, 53:279–307
Weisz JR, 56:337–63
Wells GL, 54:277–95
Welsh DP, 60:631–52
Whisman MA, 57:317–44
Wigfield A, 53:109–32
Williams KD, 58:425–52
Willis H, 53:575–604
Wilson TD, 55:493–518
Wingate LR, 56:287–314
Winne PH, 61:653–78
Winter DA, 58:453–77

Wixted JT, 55:235–69
Wolchik SA, 62:299–329
Wolf M, 63:427–52
Wood J, 61:303–24
Wood JM, 53:519–43

Y

Yeatman JD, 63:31–53
Yeshurun Y, 61:219–41
Yuille A, 55:271–304

Z

Zane N, 60:525–48
Zatorre RJ, 56:89–114
Zhang T, 61:439–66
Zimmer-Gembeck MJ,
    58:119–44

Chapter Titles, Volumes 53–63

Marketing and Consumer Behavior

Organizational Psychology or Organizational Behavior

Cognition in Organizations

Groups and Teams

Leadership

Work Attitudes (Job Satisfaction, Commitment, Identification)

Work Motivation

Psycholinguistics

See COGNITIVE PROCESSES

Psychology and Culture

Psychopathology (See also Clinical and Counseling Psychology)

Sleep

See BIOLOGICAL PSYCHOLOGY

Social Psychology

Altruism and Aggression

Attention, Control, and Automaticity

Attitude Change and Persuasion

Attitude Structure

Attraction and Close Relationships

Bargaining, Negotiation, Conflict, Social Justice

Gender

Vision

See SENSORY PROCESSES